BOATER'S BOWDITCH

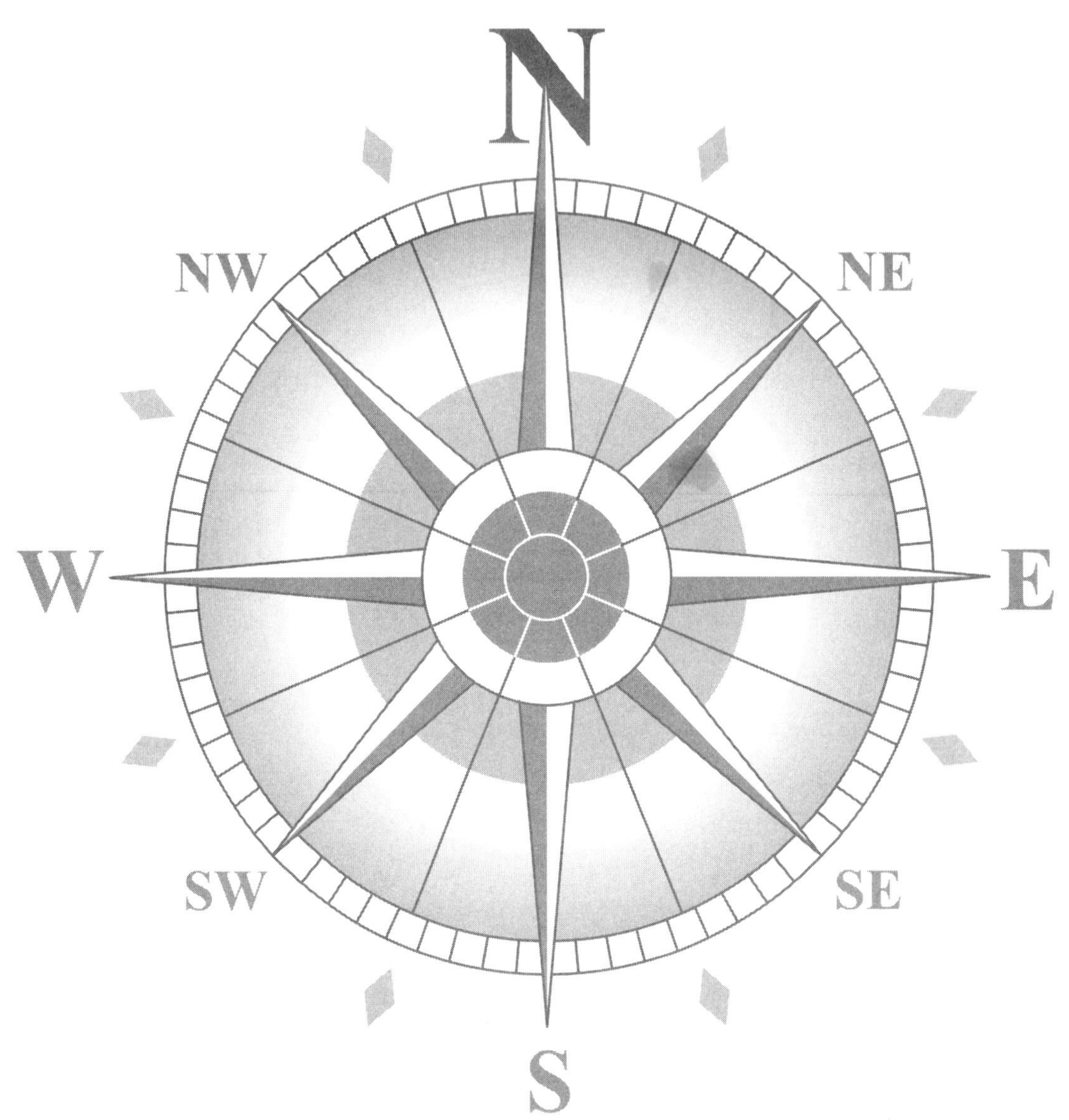
N
NW
NE
W
E
SW
SE
S

BOATER'S BOWDITCH

THE SMALL-CRAFT *AMERICAN PRACTICAL NAVIGATOR*

RICHARD K. HUBBARD

INTERNATIONAL MARINE
CAMDEN, MAINE

International Marine

A Division of The **McGraw-Hill** *Companies*

1 3 5 7 9 10 8 6 4 2

The Library of Congress has catalogued the cloth edition as follows:

Library of Congress Cataloging-in-Publication Data

Hubbard, Richard, 1946–

Boater's Bowditch : the small-craft American practical navigator / Richard Hubbard.

p. cm.

Includes bibliographical references (p.) and index.

ISBN 0-07-030866-7 (alk. paper)

1. Navigation. I. American practical navigator. II. Title.

VK555.H825 1997

623.89—dc21 97-19486

CIP

Paperback ISBN 0-07-136136-7

Questions regarding the content of this book should be addressed to:

International Marine
P.O. Box 220
Camden, ME 04843

Questions regarding the ordering of this book should be addressed to:

The McGraw-Hill Companies
Customer Service Department
P.O. Box 547
Blacklick, OH 43004
Retail customers: 1-800-262-4729
Bookstores: 1-800-722-4726

Boater's Bowditch is printed on acid-free paper.
This book was typeset using the following Adbobe typefaces: Arial, Garamond, Helvetica Condensed, Minion, Bookman, Universal and Caflisch

Printed by Quebecor Printing Co., Fairfield, PA
Design by Rob Johnson
Jacket Design by Eugenie Delaney, adapted for paperback by Shannon Thomas
Cover Photo by Onne Van Der Wal/Stock Newport, Map of World Currents by Kim Downing
Production and Art Coordination by Janet Robbins
Page Layout by Deborah Krampf
Edited by Jonathan Eaton, Jon Cheston, Nancy Hauswald, Tom McCarthy, John Kettlewell
Art Editing and Technical Illustrations by Kim Downing
Color Plates Courtesy Marine Observation Program, National Weather Service, NOAA, and Environment Canada

Contents

Preface vii
Acknowledgments ix
Introduction xi

Part 1: **FUNDAMENTALS OF NAVIGATION**

1. Basic Navigational Concepts 3
2. Buoys, Beacons, and Lights 23
3. The Compass 40
4. Tides 53
5. Dead Reckoning 63
6. Piloting 75

Part 2: **ELECTRONIC NAVIGATION**

7. Radio Waves in Navigation 91
8. Satellite Navigation 99
9. Loran-C Navigation 108
10. Radar Navigation 121
11. Electronic Charts 129

Part 3: **CELESTIAL NAVIGATION**

12. Navigational Astronomy 141
13. The Sextant 157
14. Time 169
15. The Almanacs 176
16. Sight Reduction 185
17. Practical Techniques in Navigation 213

Part 4: **NAVIGATION SAFETY**

18. Navigation Rules and Regulations 229
19. Navigation Safety 236
20. Marine Weather 249
21. Oceanography 301

Tables 322
Glossary 331
Bibliography 394
Index 396

Preface

The winds and the waves are always on the side of the ablest navigators.
—Edward Gibbon

Boater's Bowditch is the result of 11 years in the practice of navigation, 17 years in the study and application of navigation principles both in my shoreside job and at sea, and more than two years of full-time work editing, writing, and compiling the 1995 edition of *The American Practical Navigator,* the Bible of navigation first written by Nathaniel Bowditch in 1802.

Few people realize what an unheralded genius Nathaniel Bowditch was, or the importance of his contribution to American freedom through sea power. We will never know how many ships were *not* lost at sea or arrived safely and quickly at their destinations because of *The American Practical Navigator.*

It was while editing the 1995 edition of this venerable work that I decided to demystify Bowditch for the average boater. I had learned navigation at the U.S. Coast Guard Officer Candidate School in Yorktown, Virginia, and then practiced it as operations officer/navigator aboard a seagoing buoy tender. When I left the Coast Guard three years later, I was asked to navigate an ocean-racing sailboat, a position I enjoyed so much I turned it into a semi-career for several years. I became skipper of several private yachts, including a small square rigger, and did a number of deliveries sailing the Great Lakes, the U.S. East Coast, and the Caribbean. After eight years, I moved ashore and began a career with the U.S. Government writing Notices to Mariners, Sailing Directions, Light Lists, and other publications. I started work on *The American Practical Navigator* early in 1992.

While editing Bowditch, I became convinced of two things. First, the book was too valuable a work to be reserved only for the professional navigator. Second, with my background in small-boat navigation and writing, I could simplify it for the average boater. I hope I have succeeded.

Navigation remains very much an art, despite technological advances that attempt to turn it into more of a science. The fundamental techniques discussed here have been practiced for generations. And since computers and calculators have removed the drudgery of navigational calculations, I encourage you to take advantage of them: If you understand the basic concepts, you can rely on calculators, computers, and navigational instruments to do the small amount of mathematics. It's much safer to use a calculator for navigation than to be scared away by a lot of intricate mathematics and not learn the skill at all. This is especially true in celestial work. Reliance on traditional navigational methods may be enjoyable and a source of pride, but it is not inherently safer than reliance on technology. Technology just makes navigation easier, and thus more enjoyable.

The art of navigation will be with us until we learn to control—not just predict—the weather, the tides, the climate, the ocean currents, and all the other factors that influence our navigational decisions every time we sail. We'll never reach that goal, and we should be thankful. Seafaring would be too dull.

RICHARD K. HUBBARD
Gaithersburg, Maryland
August 1997

Acknowledgments

This book would not have been possible without the work and encouragement of many people. My family supported me wholeheartedly. I apologize for all the times I was using the computer when the kids wanted to play games, and for the activities postponed in favor of this book. I especially thank my wife, who went off to bed so many nights while I continued tapping away at the keyboard.

I deeply appreciate the help of Judy Hubbard, my sister-in-law and an English teacher, for her suggestions on the use of language, style, and grammar. If this text is readable, it is to her credit. I wish I'd had her for high school English in addition to Miss Utz, who along with Mr. Nucholls in journalism class, tried to teach me how to write clearly.

Thanks are due to Karen Kollenberg for her encouragement and wise advice. Her friendship for more than 25 years has been a delight, and her personal accomplishments an inspiration.

Technical review was done with dispatch and absolute professionalism by Mike Carr and Jon Cheston. I appreciate their suggestions and comments. They were right on the mark. I'd sail with them anywhere, and I hope someday I can.

For the color plates, thanks are due to Martin Baron and Vincent Zegowitz of the Marine Observation Program, National Weather Service, NOAA; and Environment Canada.

Many other individuals and organizations had direct and indirect input into this effort, among them, in no particular order:

Better Boating Association
Jim Sexton, Nautical Technologies Ltd.
Ken Gebhart, Celestaire Inc.
Wayne Paugh, U.S. Coast Guard
Office of Coast Guard History
Jack Fuschsel
Steve Debrecht, NIMA
Carl Clauson, NIMA
Carla Wallace, NOAA
Karen Kear, Ritchie Navigation
Laura Seitz of ACR Electronics
Capt. John R. Phillips, USAF
NAVSTAR GPS Joint Program Office
Ralph Steele of Weems and Plath
Joseph Hilsenrath
Steve Tripp of MacNavigator
John Watkins of Celesticomp
Michelle LeBeau of COMSAT
Staff of U.S. Geological Survey

And most important, thanks go to my Mother and Dad, to whom this book is gratefully dedicated.

Introduction

Boater's Bowditch is written for novice to intermediate navigators aboard small craft of all types—yachts (power or sail), small commercial craft, fishing vessels—and for anyone else engaged in the work or pleasure of "messing about in boats" (in the words of the famous rat).

While there are a number of books available from which to learn basic navigation, many of those texts often present a less-than-complete picture of the range of knowledge necessary to be a good navigator. They omit basic scientific data or important aspects of navigation science, such as elements of oceanography and weather forecasting.

At the other end of the spectrum are books intended for the professional navigator or the cadet training to be one. These delve into minute, complex details and scientific theories. However necessary this depth is for the professional ship captain or naval officer, the detail is beyond both the understanding and needs of the average small-craft owner. The professional captain or naval officer, for example, will have a thorough understanding of spherical trigonometry before studying celestial navigation. The novice, on the other hand, needs only to know how to shoot a star, get the time of the sight, and enter the values into a calculator or computer program. As a backup, the novice should understand how to use tables to reduce the sight to a line of position.

Don't be afraid of learning the science behind modern navigational systems. The basic principles behind the most complex navigation systems ever developed can be explained in everyday terms without a lot of complex theoretical discussions, formulas, and technical jargon. The Global Positioning System, for example, can be illustrated with a child's bubbles, and Loran C can be explained by imagining a football or soccer field. *Boater's Bowditch* does that.

Though this work was inspired by *The American Practical Navigator* (or Bowditch, as it is commonly called), and is organized loosely along the same lines, it is an entirely new work. Its organization is based not so much on Bowditch but on the logical presentation of ideas and procedures, each building on the previous ones.

Part 1 offers basic information on the navigator's craft, the sources of information needed to practice it, and the tools used. This includes chapters on nautical charts and publications, visual aids to navigation, compasses, and tides. It further explains the procedures and skills needed in basic navigational work, including dead reckoning and piloting.

Part 2 starts with a discussion of radio waves, explaining how they are generated, how they travel, and what they can and cannot do for the mariner. It continues by explaining the principles of electronic navigation systems: how they work, why they work, and their capabilities and limitations. This includes chapters on satellite navigation systems, Loran C, radar, and electronic charts.

Part 3 explains the basics of celestial navigation. It does not go into great detail about the sophisticated techniques used by the professional world navigator, but it does discuss in simple language a few procedures for finding one's way at sea when all the sytems discussed in Part 2 have failed. In a departure from traditional practice, it also recommends and explains the use of navigational calculators in sight reduction.

Part 4 contains general information and practical tips for making navigation enjoyable and safe. Here you'll find an explanation of weather phenomena and oceanography as it applies to small craft, discussions of rules and regulations navigators must follow, and routines and techniques to ensure a safe voyage.

Boater's Bowditch stresses the need to practice techniques and procedures while you're still in familiar waters. It's best to learn to take fixes when you know exactly where you are, because that is the only time you'll know if you made a mistake without endangering yourself and others. Navigational mistakes tend to be very expensive in terms of both life and property, and though insurance can make one financially whole, no amount of insurance can restore a life. While the sea can be very romantic and peaceful, it can also be disastrous for the unprepared.

Good navigational skills can turn a terrifying ordeal into a merely uncomfortable one. Lack of them can lead to a tragedy.

PART 1

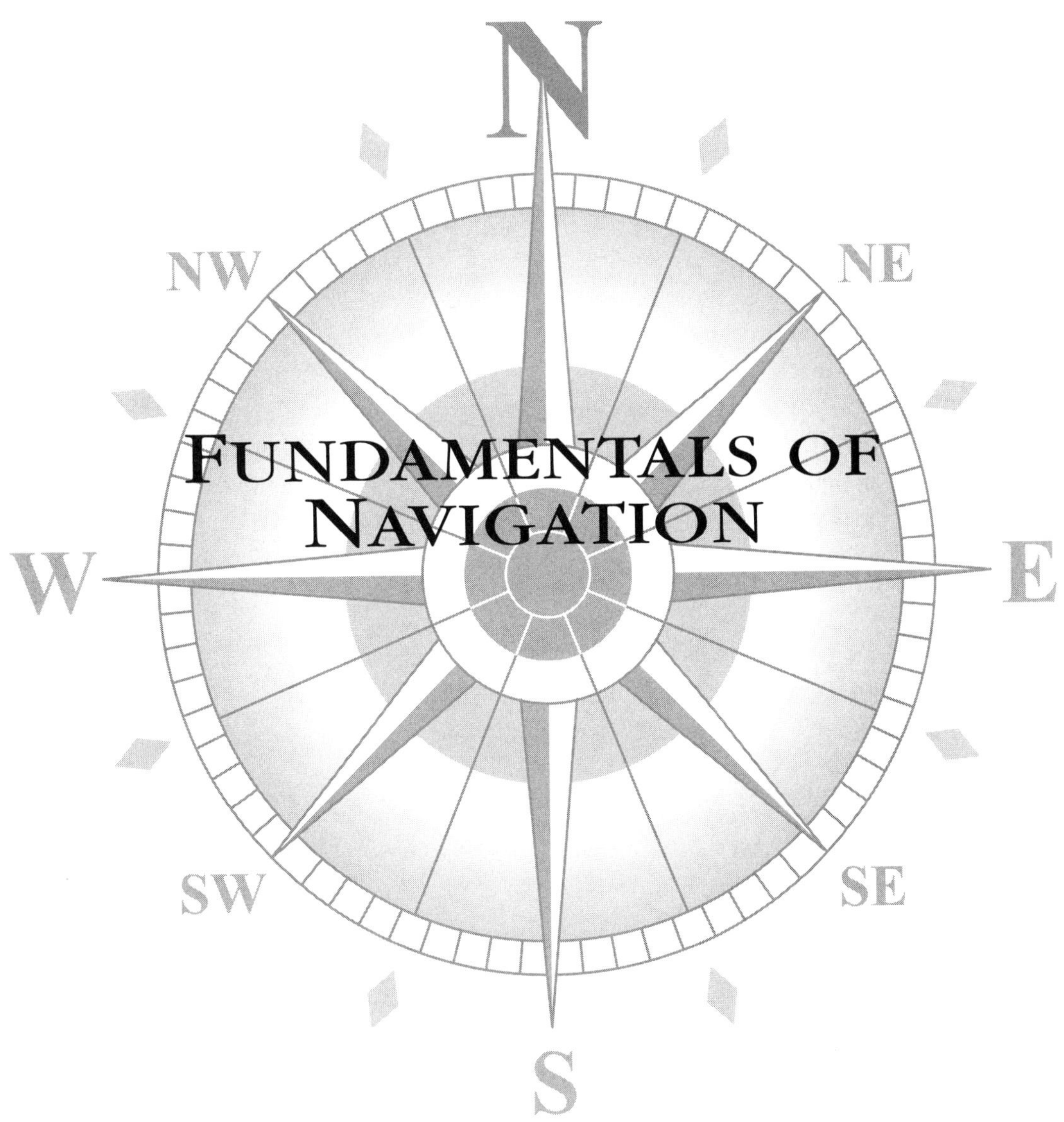

FUNDAMENTALS OF NAVIGATION

Chapter One

Basic Navigational Concepts

The first primitive person who floated on a log used marine navigation. But throughout history, few subjects have been so poorly recorded, so little understood, or so carelessly preserved in artifacts and historical documents as navigation. Much of the navigation we practice today is based on sciences developed by the great thinkers of antiquity. Some we know well today; others have been lost to history entirely.

- Thales *(ca. 640–547 B.C.) was a Greek mathematician and astronomer who learned how to accurately predict eclipses of the sun, providing the scientific basis for today's nautical almanacs.*

- Eratosthenes *(ca. 276–196 B.C.) was another Greek mathematician and astronomer. He became head of the great library of Alexandria and calculated the circumference of the earth, thus enabling accurate measurements on its surface.*

- Meton *(fifth-century B.C.) was an Athenian astronomer who discovered that the moon repeats its cycle on the same dates every 18.6 years, thus establishing the Metonic Cycle, the basis for all tidal calculations.*

- Pythagoras *(ca. 580–500 B.C.) was a Greek mathematician and philosopher who is credited with discovery of the theorem named for him, which states that the square of the hypotenuse of a right triangle is equal to the sum of the squares of the other two sides. Navigation uses triangles extensively.*

- Ptolemy *(second-century A.D.) was a Greek astronomer and mathematician who figured out the system of degrees, minutes, and seconds used to measure circles. He also calculated the value of pi (3.1415 . . .). Unfortunately, he thought the earth was the center of the universe, a belief not seriously challenged until Copernicus.*

- Copernicus *(1473–1543) was a Polish astronomer (they weren't all Greeks) who promoted the radical idea that the sun was the center of the solar system and that the earth was not the center of the universe. His investigations formed the basis of modern astronomy.*

Historical Perspectives

The science of navigation is rooted in the work of men such as Ptolemy, Meton, Pythagoras, Pythias, Thales, Eratosthenes, and Copernicus. Each made a vital contribution—sometimes quite by accident—to the body of knowledge on which navigation today is based. Most of the early scientific discoveries that led to advances in navigation methods were not achieved by research into navigation at all. Rather, these discoveries were born of investigations of basic scientific concepts in such fields as mathematics, astronomy, and physics.

These classic scientific advances were certainly fundamental in shaping modern navigation methods, but they were not all-encompassing. They leave room for art in navigation—and for mystery. Consider, for example, the navigational feats of the Arctic tern, which unerringly finds its way each year from the Arctic Ocean to the Antarctic and back, some 7,000 miles each way. Or the monarch butterfly which, after hatching from a chrysalis anywhere in North America, somehow knows how to find a particular section of rainforest in Mexico where it meets millions of its fellows in a place it has never been; or the Atlantic salmon which, after hatching from a tiny egg, swims downstream to the ocean, feeds and grows there for as many as seven years, and then returns to the same stream in which it hatched.

Development of Nautical Charts

Navigators have used *nautical charts* for centuries, along with written *pilots* or *sailing directions,* which amplify or explain the graphic information on charts with drawings and textual information. Early charts, however, were not well suited for navigation

Our human perceptions of the earth are unique; other animals have an entirely different picture. Recently, a biologist who was analyzing the incredibly loud (180dB) blue whale sounds recorded on Navy sonar tapes asked a naval sonar expert how the whale could use such sounds. The expert replied that the whale might be able to form a mental image of a good part of the western North Atlantic Ocean. Perhaps whales can "see" with sound far better than we can with our eyes. Recent oceanographic research reveals that underwater objects can be discerned by analyzing the changes they make in background sound patterns, much the way we see by discerning changes in patterns of light against different backgrounds.

With our modern perception, we tend to view navigation as a purely mathematical science. But early navigators accomplished amazing feats without mathematics. The Polynesians—at least 1,000 years before Columbus accidentally found America—settled every island group in the South Pacific, including many separated from the nearest continent by thousands of miles. Their voyages spanned an area equal to about one quarter of the earth's surface. Their methods, only minimally documented today, had much more in common with the intuitive navigational techniques of birds, whales, and fish than with modern Western scientific, mathematics-based navigation.

Future generations may one day consider our own "high-tech" systems of navigation, which can locate our position on the earth to within a few millimeters, as primitive as we now view those of Columbus and Magellan. We can keep a proper perspective by recognizing that we still use principles and techniques well known to these, and even earlier, navigators. The formal techniques of dead reckoning and triangulation, and the informal methods of relating wave patterns to location and gauging depth by changes in water color, have not changed for thousands of years.

because they did not portray the earth in ways that met navigators' needs. These charts contained serious errors, usually in longitude because it was impossible to measure accurately using contemporary methods. Because navigation methods were also primitive, these errors were tolerated. Lacking a way to find longitude, navigators sailed north or south to the latitude of their destination, then east or west until they ran into it. This technique is still useful in certain situations.

The Mercator Projection

A *projection* is a way of portraying the spherical earth on flat paper. Several dozen projections are used for various purposes and each is a compromise of various factors. The *Mercator projection* is the best compromise for most marine navigation.

The Mercator projection is a *cylindrical projection* that derives its name from the geo-

Despite technical advances in navigation, the sea continues to humble navigators and exploit their weaknesses. Their best defense is to develop good "sea sense," where the art of navigation can overcome the limitations of the science. Navigators need to bring a "seat of the pants" feeling to bear when things just don't look right, when the instruments don't agree, or when they feel uneasy, even though the instruments show no danger. Sea sense can't be learned in a classroom or from experienced navigators or from copious reading. It can only be learned by experience, coupled with solid basic knowledge.

Ancient navigators used their intuition and informal techniques much more than we do today. Polynesian navigators memorized dozens of well-known star patterns and used ocean swells, waves, winds, currents, birds, clouds, smells, sounds, and other factors to find their way across distances that challenge modern small-craft navigators using the latest sophisticated gear. The best modern navigators also know how to interpret these natural signs; their ability to do so adds great strength to their skill.

The nautical chart as we know it today was developed during the Age of Discovery, between A.D. 1400 to 1700, and was in large measure the product of a Flemish geographer named Gerhard Kramer, known to us by his Latinized name, Gerhardus Mercator.

Mercator was the first to publish a chart of the world designed for marine navigation, in a projection suited for that purpose. We use the same projection today, even for advanced electronic charts. Mercator introduced his chart in 1569 when other cartographers weren't meeting the high demand for accurate charts. With European explorers setting off on voyages all over the world, Mercator enjoyed great commercial success.

Though it is named for him, research indicates that Mercator was not the originator of the so-called Mercator Projection. The formula used to develop the projection was published 30 years after its introduction, not by Mercator, but by Englishman Edward Wright. And, in fact, Mercator's mentor was a mathematician named Gemma Frisius who was an expert in geometry and map projections. We persist in naming the projection after Mercator, however, because he was first in publishing a truly navigator-friendly chart that gained widespread use in worldwide ocean navigation.

Mercator was imprisoned during the Inquisition but was rescued by influential friends and then quickly moved to Germany. There, his family business making charts, maps, and geographical instruments grew and prospered.

metric figure used to develop it. Other projections use other shapes to develop the spherical earth into a flat surface. For example, charts of polar areas are usually *conical projections,* made with the apex of a cone placed over the poles. Because nearly all nautical charts are on the Mercator projection, this type is examined here in some detail.

In a Mercator projection, a cylinder is slipped over the earth, tangent at the equator, and the earth's latitude and longitude lines are "projected" out onto it—as though a light bulb at the earth's center were casting the shadows of the latitude and longitude lines onto the cylinder. The cylinder is then cut vertically and flattened.

A cylinder may be made tangent to the earth at some place other than the equator. In that case, it's an *oblique cylindrical projection.*

In a Mercator projection, all latitude and longitude lines are straight, parallel lines. Latitude lines, those that define distance north or south of the equator, are parallel on the real earth. However, longitude lines on the real earth converge at the poles. A Mercator projection reforms these converging lines into parallel lines. (See Figure 1-1.)

To make them parallel at any given latitude, except the equator, the lines of longitude must be expanded, or separated, by a certain ratio dependent on that latitude—more at higher latitudes, less at lower ones. By that same ratio, the latitude must also be expanded, or else angular relationships of points on the chart will be distorted. The crucial advantage of the Mercator projection is that it maintains correct angular relationships, thus allowing the mariner to sail straight courses from place to place. The relative sizes of features are not true, but this distortion is tolerable to sailors in all but polar regions, where the amount of distortion is extreme. In recognition of this fact, Mercator's first chart includes separate insets of polar regions. Figure 1-1 shows the expansion of latitudes with increasing longitude.

Types of Navigation

Each type of navigation has advantages and disadvantages. Some require electrical power; some don't. Some require precise optical or electronic instruments; some don't. You should be familiar with all the types and use

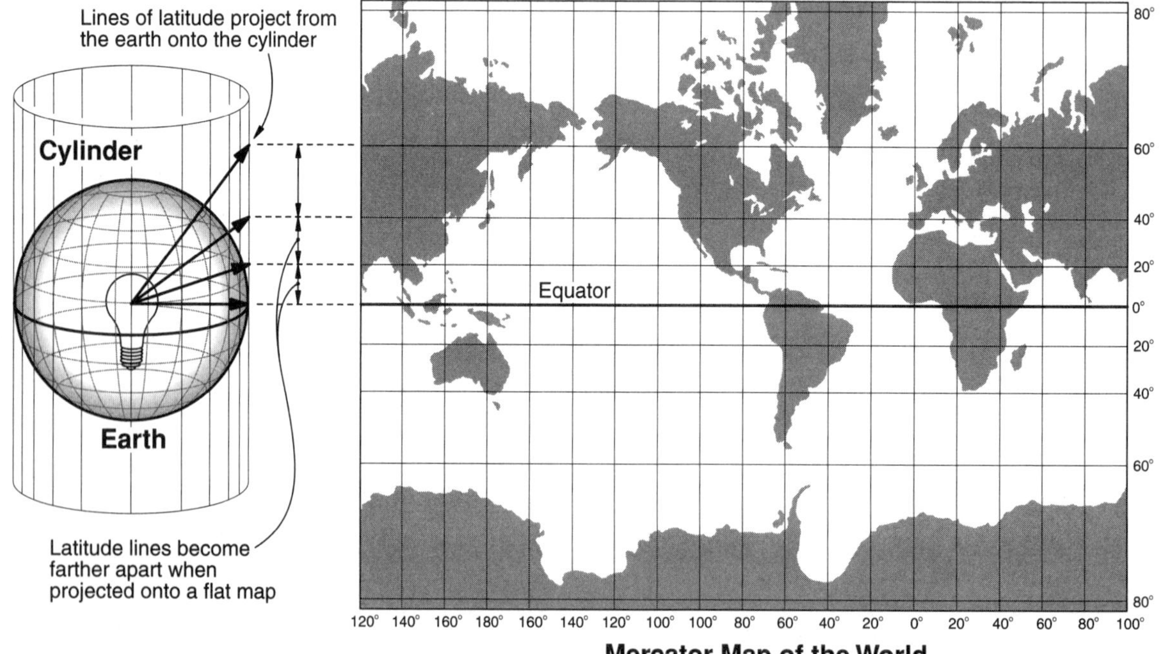

Figure 1-1. *The cylindrical projection is developed from a cylinder slipped over the earth, tangent to it around its entire circumference. The Mercator projection is one of several types of cylindrical projections.*

In this illustration, the spherical earth is "projected" outward onto a flat surface. Notice how the longitude lines become straight parallel lines, and how latitude lines remain parallel, but expand as distance from the equator increases. This increase is directly proportional to the expansion of the longitude lines at that latitude.

them in different combinations according to the situation, making maximum use of the advantages while minimizing the disadvantages. Using one or more of these methods, a navigator determines (and often plots) the vessel's position in relation to surrounding dangers and to the destination. (Boaters operating in familiar waters appropriately do not commonly keep a navigational plot on a chart. Instead, the "plot" is in their head.)

The principal *types of navigation* are:

Dead reckoning—Determining a position by plotting courses and speeds from a previously known position. (The "dead" in dead reckoning is probably an abbreviated form of "deduced" reckoning.)

Piloting—Using visual sightings of fixed objects to determine position.

Celestial—Using the sun, moon, planets, and stars to determine position.

Radio—Using one of several types of radio signals to determine position.

Radar—Using radar to determine position (exclusive of its use in avoiding collisions with other vessels).

Satellite—Using orbiting satellites to determine position.

This list is in order of sophistication and historical development and the order of presentation of each system in this book. It is also the order in which the beginning navigation student should study the subject because mastery of advanced techniques depends to some extent on knowledge of the more fundamental ones.

Phases of Navigation

Navigation can be divided into different phases, based on location. The *phases* are:

Inland waterway—Navigation in narrow canals, channels, or rivers.

Harbor/Harbor approach—Navigation close to land, in harbors, and in the channels leading to docks, wharves, and piers.

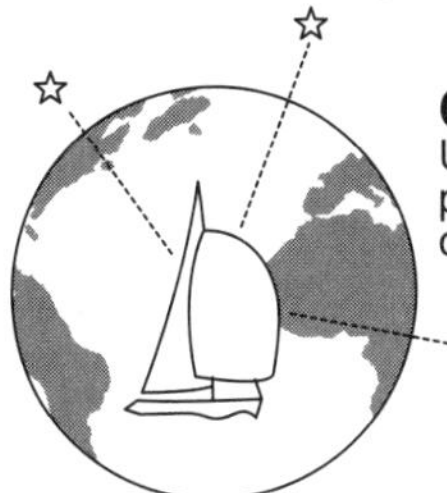

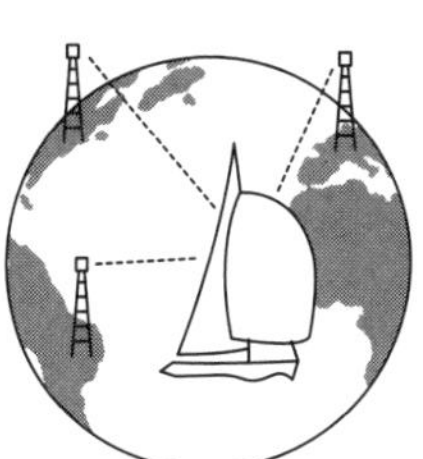

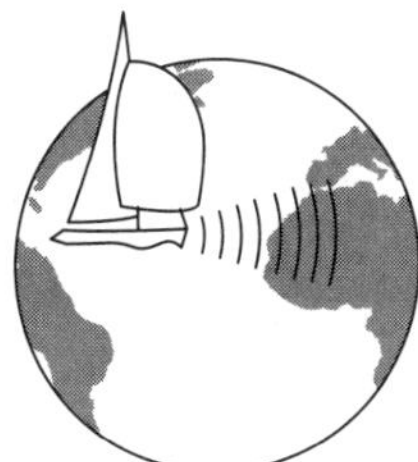

Radar Navigation
Using radar to plot bearings of charted objects, exclusive of its use in avoiding collisions with other vessels.

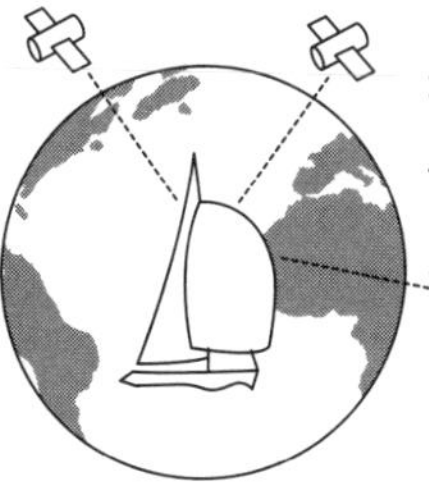

Figure 1-2. *The principal types of navigation, in order of sophistication and historical development. Navigation students should study them in this order because mastery of advanced techniques may depend on knowledge of fundamental ones.*

Coastal—Navigation along a coast, or in large bays, straits, and sounds.

Ocean—Navigation in the open sea out of sight of land.

These divisions are somewhat arbitrary; there is no distinct line between them. The movement of a vessel from one phase to another often involves a gradual transition. These phases are similar to the distinctions among types of nautical charts that we'll examine just ahead. You must choose the types of navigation appropriate for each phase, keeping in mind the advantages and disadvantages of each. You wouldn't, for example, use celestial navigation in a harbor or use radar if no prominent land features were within range (though you still might use it to avoid collisions).

The following table summarizes the uses of types of navigation during the various phases.

Navigation Types and Uses

	Inland	Harbor	Coastal	Ocean
Dead Reckoning	•	•	•	•
Piloting	•	•	•	
Celestial			•	•
Radio	•	•	•	•
Radar	•	•	•	
Satellite	•	•	•	•

Modern Nautical Charts

Navigators use four general types of nautical charts, categorized by location and loosely based on *scale,* which is the ratio of the size of the charted area to the size of the earth (see accompanying sidebar). These types parallel the phases of navigation discussed above. The four types of charts are:

Harbor charts—The largest-scale charts are harbor charts, designed to show in greatest possible detail the navigationally important features of harbors. The scales of these charts range from about 1:5,000 to 1:50,000.

The scale *of a chart is ratio of any unit of any measure on the chart to the same measure on the real earth. In a 1:10,000 scale, one millimeter, one inch, or one foot on the chart represents 10,000 such units in the real world. A scale of 1:10,000 is larger than a scale of 1:100,000 because $^1/_{10,000}$ is a larger fraction than $^1/_{100,000}$. A larger scale shows a smaller area in greater detail; a smaller scale shows a larger area in lesser detail.*

Coastal charts—These range in scale from about 1:50,000 to 1:150,000 and are used for coastal navigation. Many of the details of harbor areas are omitted, especially when harbor charts are available, and only the features needed for coastal navigation are included.

General charts—These are used for route planning and navigating along coastal areas outside of outlying reefs, shoals, and island groups. Scales range from 1:150,000 to about 1:600,000. Features are further generalized and only the major coastal aids to navigation and features are shown.

Sailing charts—These charts show major areas of ocean basins and are used for offshore or ocean navigation. Scales are usually smaller than 1:600,000. Features are further generalized so that only the most prominent and visible are included.

Generalization is the process of selectively including or eliminating features according to scale. On a coastal chart, for example, it is impossible to show all the details included on a harbor chart—they would be too small to see. For this reason, cartographers generalize features as chart scale decreases, removing the least important and simplifying others so that the portrayal is readable.

These designations are not rigid, and there is considerable overlap among them. Some charts include *insets* or *plans* showing areas of interest at a scale larger than the one used on the base chart. It's important for the navigator to assemble all the appropriate charts for each voyage, however short, and, at each stage, to use the largest-scale chart available.

Using a Chart

When shopping for a chart, be sure to purchase the latest edition because new editions render old ones obsolete. New editions are prepared because the supplies of the present edition are running low, because the present edition requires a multitude of corrections, or because there is significant new information about the area. Perhaps a recent hydrographic survey shows new shoal areas, or maybe new harbor dredging and port construction needs to be portrayed. Reputable chart agencies will have the latest editions and will not sell old ones, which they return for credit against their new stock.

Before first using a chart, look at the *title block,* which gives the title and scale. Next, determine the reference points, known as *datums,* for heights of objects, water depths, and tides. Then verify the *projection* on which it is drawn (almost always Mercator) and the latitude/longitude grid. Finally, note the measurement system used for depths and heights (meters, fathoms, or feet). Figure 1-3 shows a typical title block.

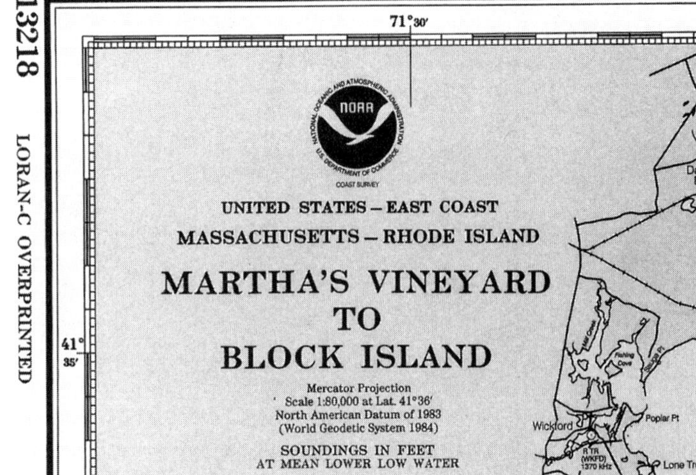

Figure 1-3. *This is a typical chart title block that gives information about the area covered, the scale, projection, geodetic (horizontal) datum, and the datum used for water depths (vertical).*

You should also read any *notes* placed on the chart. They contain general information about the area or about certain features on the chart that may affect navigational decisions. These simple steps are vital, but many navigators overlook them.

It's important to understand the *latitude/longitude grid,* consisting of the lines of latitude and longitude. There are several different formats. The grid, more precisely called a

---

A datum *is a reference point used to measure other points. Charts have both* horizontal datums *and* vertical datums.

The horizontal datum for modern charts is the World Geodetic System 84 (WGS-84), *adopted in 1984. This system defines a particular mathematical shape of the earth (not a true sphere) that allows cartographers to define a distinct mathematical grid on which to draw maps and charts. WGS-84 thus defines the exact dimensions of the latitude/longitude grid for a given area of the earth.*

Vertical datums are used to measure heights of objects and depths. Heights listed on charts are measured from one of several averages of high tides. This gives you a safe estimate of clearance under bridges and power cables. You know that the water level will be at or below the high tide reference point of high tide, so you can be confident in having at least as much clearance under the bridge or cable as is noted on the chart.

Conversely, depths are referenced to some average of low tide, again giving you a conservative assumption. You know that there will be at least as much water as shown, for if the tide is higher, the water will be deeper than the charted depth.

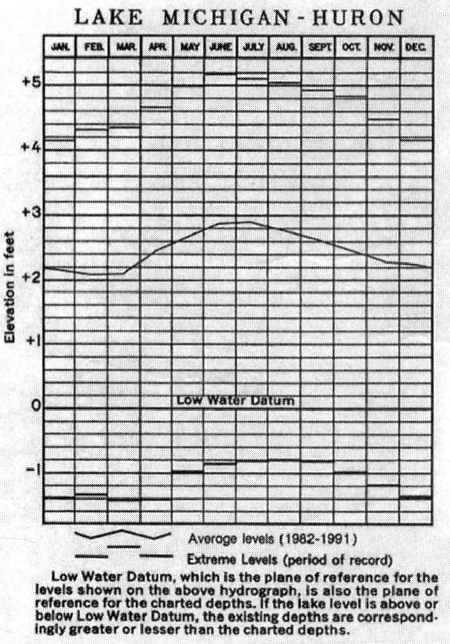

Figure 1-4. *Datum graph from a Great Lakes chart.*

You must often convert fractions of minutes to seconds or vice versa in picking off positions on charts. Most electronic navigation devices read out in degrees, minutes, and tenths. This can be confusing when the chart is graduated in seconds. Just remember that a minute of longitude or latitude equals 60 seconds. For example, to convert 0.25 minutes to seconds, multiply 60 seconds (one minute) by 0.25 to get 15 seconds. To convert 15 seconds to minutes, divide 15 by 60 to get 0.25. Because longitude lines expand to become parallel on Mercator charts, never use them to measure distances; always use latitude lines.

graticule, is chosen by the cartographer to give you a useful presentation without being too "busy."

Lines are drawn at regular intervals, such as every 10, 20, or 30 minutes of latitude and longitude, and *tick marks* are placed on the sides and top and bottom of the chart so you can pick off lat/long positions. Remember that one minute of latitude equals one nautical mile, and note how far one mile (one minute of latitude) is on the side of the chart. Also note whether the individual seconds marks on large-scale charts are shown in intervals of one, five, six or more seconds. This initial orientation is important groundwork for later use of the chart. Figure 1-7 shows various types of border formats.

Notice to Mariners

A chart is on the course to obsolescence as soon as it is published. New harbor construction and hydrographic surveys, as well as changes in the aids to navigation and other charted features are detailed in a publication called *Notice to Mariners.* Two types of *Notices* are published: local and national.

Periodically, each Coast Guard District office publishes a *Local Notice to Mariners* for its own area. It contains detailed information on matters of navigational importance in the district, including changes in aids to navigation, marine events, and general maritime safety information. Figure 1-8 shows a typical chart correction section in a *Local Notice to Mariners.*

TIDAL INFORMATION

Place		Height referred to datum of soundings (MLLW)			
Name	(LAT/LONG)	Mean Higher High Water	Mean High Water	Mean Low Water	Extreme Low Water
		feet	feet	feet	feet
Gay Head, Martha's Vineyard	(41°21'N/70°50'W)	3.2	3.0	0.1	-2.5
Woods Hole, Little Harbor	(41°31'N/70°40'W)	1.6	1.5	0.1	-2.5
New Bedford	(41°38'N/70°55'W)	4.1	3.8	0.1	-2.5
Newport	(41°30'N/71°20'W)	3.9	3.7	0.1	-2.9
Point Judith Harbor	(41°22'N/71°29'W)	3.5	3.2	0.1	-3.0
Old Harbor, Block Island	(41°10'N/71°33'W)	3.2	3.0	0.1	-3.0

(595) latest information available.

Figure 1-5. *A tidal information note from an East Coast chart.*

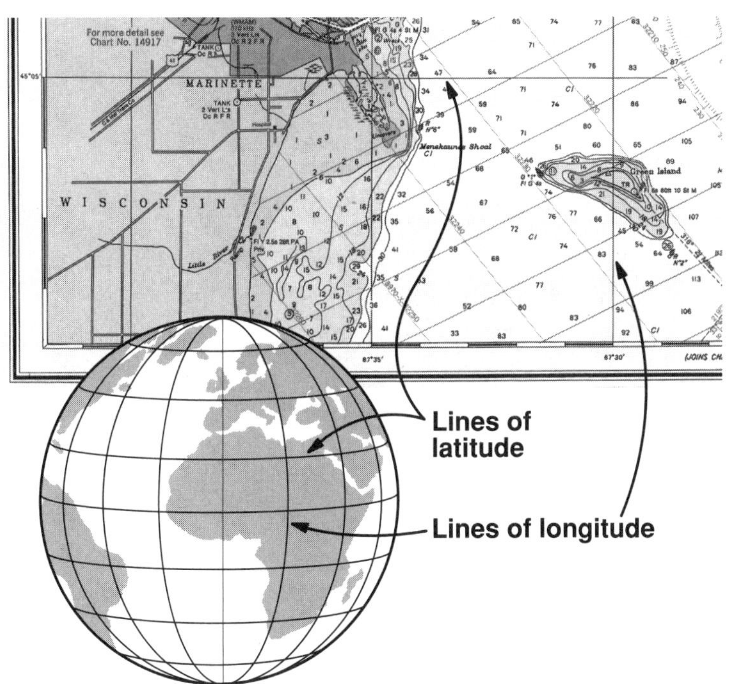

Figure 1-6. *To create a chart, cartographers choose the best grid, consisting of the lines of latitude and longitude, with just enough interval between the lines to be useful without being too "busy" to the eye.*

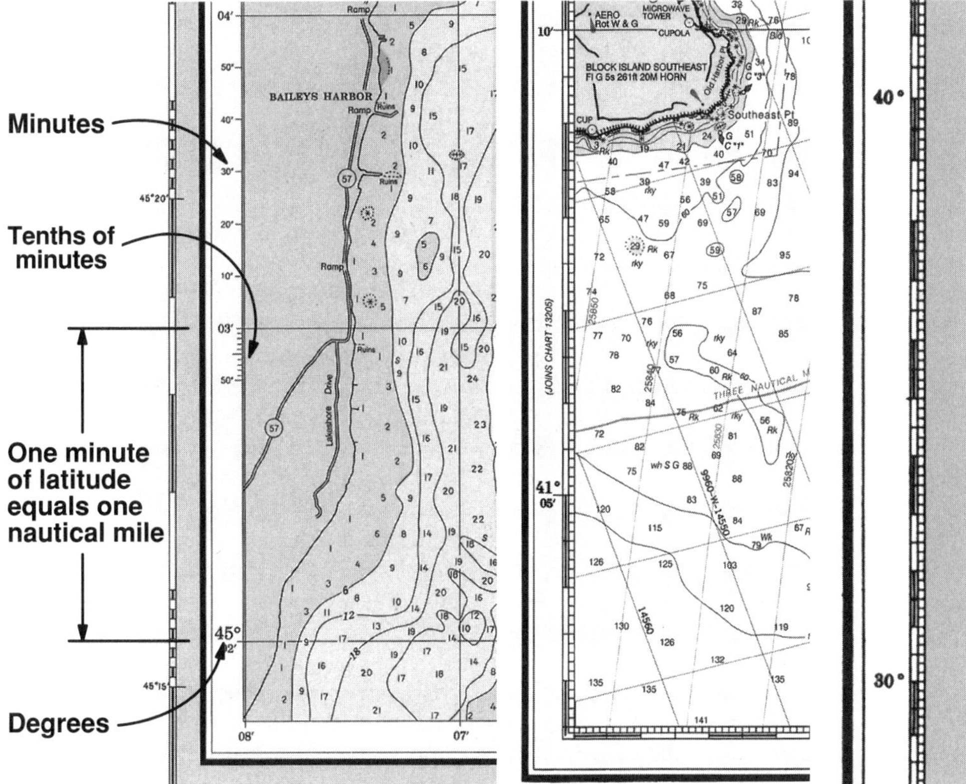

Figure 1-7. *Various formats are used for the borders of charts, graduated in seconds or tenths of minutes. All of them indicate the geographic coordinates for the chart, but in several differing ways depending on the scale of the chart. A chart plan or inset at a different scale usually has a different border format than the main chart.*

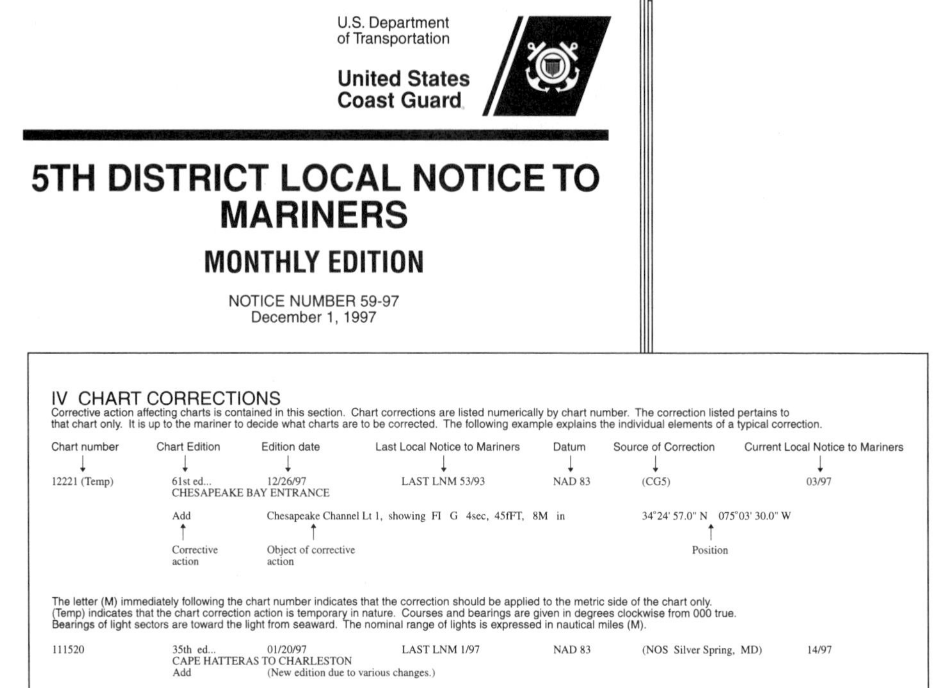

U.S. Department
of Transportation

**United States
Coast Guard**

5TH DISTRICT LOCAL NOTICE TO MARINERS

MONTHLY EDITION

NOTICE NUMBER 59-97
December 1, 1997

IV CHART CORRECTIONS

Corrective action affecting charts is contained in this section. Chart corrections are listed numerically by chart number. The correction listed pertains to that chart only. It is up to the mariner to decide what charts are to be corrected. The following example explains the individual elements of a typical correction.

Chart number	Chart Edition	Edition date	Last Local Notice to Mariners	Datum	Source of Correction	Current Local Notice to Mariners
12221 (Temp)	61st ed...	12/26/97	LAST LNM 53/93	NAD 83	(CG5)	03/97
	CHESAPEAKE BAY ENTRANCE					
	Add	Chesapeake Channel Lt 1, showing Fl G 4sec, 45fFT, 8M in			34°24' 57.0" N 075°03' 30.0" W	
	Corrective action	Object of corrective action			Position	

The letter (M) immediately following the chart number indicates that the correction should be applied to the metric side of the chart only.
(Temp) indicates that the chart correction action is temporary in nature. Courses and bearings are given in degrees clockwise from 000 true.
Bearings of light sectors are toward the light from seaward. The nominal range of lights is expressed in nautical miles (M).

111520	35th ed...	01/20/97	LAST LNM 1/97	NAD 83	(NOS Silver Spring, MD)	14/97
	CAPE HATTERAS TO CHARLESTON					
	Add	(New edition due to various changes.)				
12221	64th ed...	10/28/97	LAST LNM 12/96	NAD 83	(NOS Silver Spring, MD)	14/97
	CHESAPEAKE BAY ENTRANCE					
	Change	York River Channel Lighted Buoy 13 to show: Q G in			37°13' 25.6"N 076°18' 36.8" W	
12237	24th ed...	08/28/97	LAST LNM 05/96	NAD 83	(CG5)	14/97
	RAPPAHANNOCK RIVER - CORROTOMAN RIVER TO FREDRICKSBURG					
	Change	Robinson Creek Daybeacon 1 to Light 1 showing F1 G 4s in			37°39' 06.5"N 076°34' 34.8" W	

Figure 1-8. *The* Local Notice to Mariners *is issued by the district office of the Coast Guard for the local region. It is intended for both small craft and large ships and contains chart corrections and other important navigation safety information for the local area.*

The national notice is issued by the *National Imagery and Mapping Agency (NIMA).* It contains only that information of the *Local Notices* that is relevant to large commercial or military vessels. It would not, for example, include information about a buoy or depth change in a small-boat harbor. It also provides worldwide information, obtained mostly from the notice to mariners published by other countries. Figure 1-9 shows the format of the *NIMA Notice to Mariners* chart correction section.

The *Local Notice to Mariners,* the one appropriate for most small craft, also lists new editions of charts. Obtain new editions at the earliest opportunity rather than simply correct old charts because new charts may contain a lot of information not given in the *Notices to Mariners*. In fact, the availability of extensive new information may be the principal reason the new charts were produced.

It is your responsibility to use the latest editions of charts and to correct them with the *Notice to Mariners*. Failure to do so may cause accidents. More than one ship has been lost for the simple reason that the *Notice to Mariners* was ignored. If failure to update a chart is deemed in legal proceedings to have caused an accident, then the offending mariner generally must assume liability.

The updating job is made easier by the periodic inclusion in the NIMA *Notice* of a summary listing of all charts that have notices written for them, along with the notice number. These are the only notices you need to apply, and only to charts that you'll use. Each *Notice* consists of three parts: action, object, and position. To make the correction, simply do *exactly* as instructed. For example, in Fig-

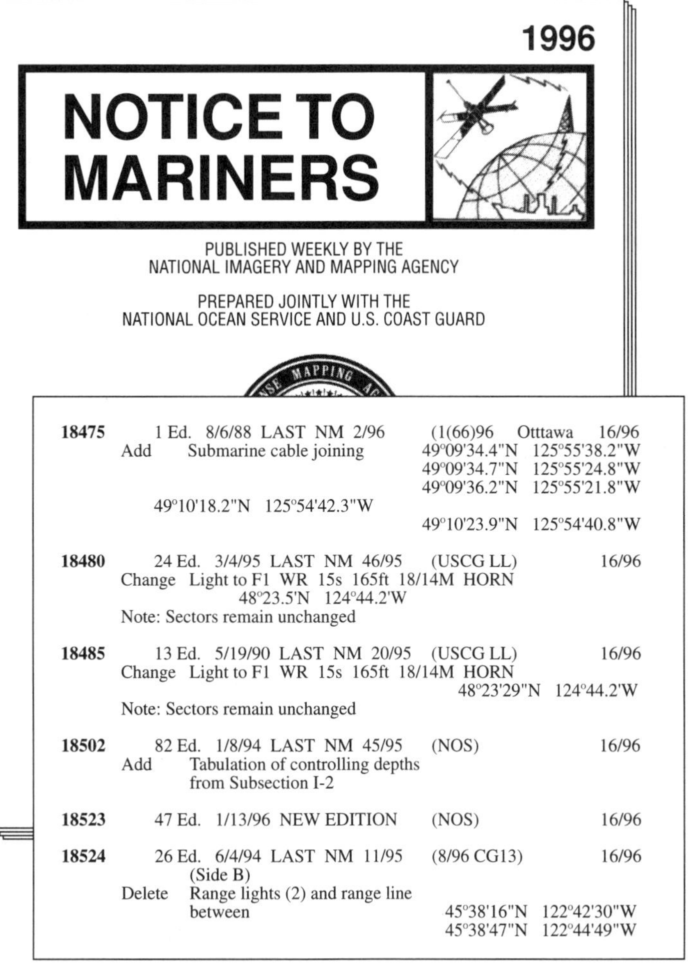

1996

NOTICE TO MARINERS

PUBLISHED WEEKLY BY THE
NATIONAL IMAGERY AND MAPPING AGENCY

PREPARED JOINTLY WITH THE
NATIONAL OCEAN SERVICE AND U.S. COAST GUARD

18475 1 Ed. 8/6/88 LAST NM 2/96 (1(66)96 Otttawa 16/96
Add Submarine cable joining 49°09'34.4"N 125°55'38.2"W
49°09'34.7"N 125°55'24.8"W
49°09'36.2"N 125°55'21.8"W
49°10'18.2"N 125°54'42.3"W
49°10'23.9"N 125°54'40.8"W

18480 24 Ed. 3/4/95 LAST NM 46/95 (USCG LL) 16/96
Change Light to Fl WR 15s 165ft 18/14M HORN
48°23.5'N 124°44.2'W
Note: Sectors remain unchanged

18485 13 Ed. 5/19/90 LAST NM 20/95 (USCG LL) 16/96
Change Light to Fl WR 15s 165ft 18/14M HORN
48°23'29"N 124°44.2'W
Note: Sectors remain unchanged

18502 82 Ed. 1/8/94 LAST NM 45/95 (NOS) 16/96
Add Tabulation of controlling depths from Subsection I-2

18523 47 Ed. 1/13/96 NEW EDITION (NOS) 16/96

18524 26 Ed. 6/4/94 LAST NM 11/95 (8/96 CG13) 16/96
(Side B)
Delete Range lights (2) and range line between 45°38'16"N 122°42'30"W
45°38'47"N 122°44'49"W

Figure 1-9. *The national* Notice to Mariners *is issued by the National Imagery and Mapping Agency and contains chart corrections and other navigational information for all U.S. charts worldwide. Because it does not include information for shallow, inland waters not usually traversed by commercial and military vessels, it's of limited use to small-craft navigators.*

ure 1-8, to correct chart 12221, write on the chart in ink the new characteristic of the light on Buoy "13": quick-flashing green.

Even navigators of commercial and naval ships do not correct all their charts. Instead, they save time by keeping a file of the corrections in summaries and applying them only to charts they're using. (For use with charts that are several years old, there is also a bound *Summary of Corrections* that in several volumes covers all corrections for all charts. You only need the volume for your area.)

Subscriptions to the *Notice* are free and can be obtained from the issuing agency. Chart dealers have the addresses of the agencies and should also have copies of appropriate *Notices* for you to review.

Most small-craft boaters don't bother getting the *Notice to Mariners,* local or national. But the conscientious small-craft navigator realizes its importance and refers to it regularly. For local use, the *Local Notice to Mariners* is best and can be obtained from the nearest Coast Guard District office. (See Figure 1-10.)

In addition, the Coast Guard has a web site at <www.navcen.uscg.mil> with complete information and contacts for many Coast Guard offices and programs.

The *NIMA Notice to Mariners* is available via computer modem through a menu-driven program called the *NAVigation INFOrmation NETwork (NAVINFONET)* that gives access to the NIMA database for all notice corrections

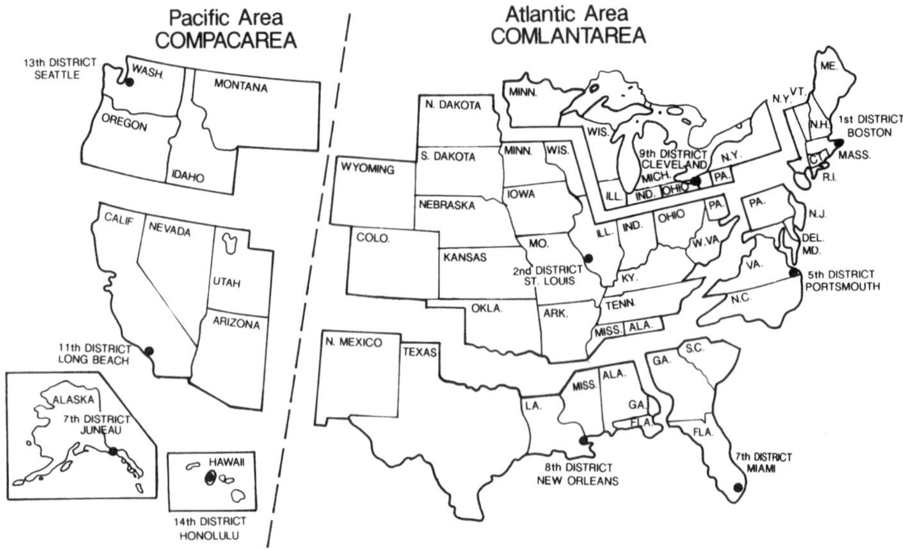

Figure 1-10. *Coast Guard districts issue* Local Notice to Mariners. *Most districts use web sites or fax services to provide instantaneous* Notice to Mariners *information. Call your local Coast Guard office for a web site address.*

for all charts. This also provides access to light lists, electronic navigation system data, and other information. Users first must register by calling (301) 227-3296 and must pay all long-distance charges. This text-based system is accessible via satellite communications, making it possible to get chart corrections at sea.

The Coast Guard provides facsimile *Local Notice to Mariners* from its *Navigation Information Service* in Washington, D.C. These notices are posted monthly and updated by weekly supplements. The fax number is (703) 313-5931 or 5932. A permanent watchstander is on call at (703) 313-5900. In this service, like NIMA's NAVINFONET, the user pays telephone charges, but connect times are quite short and it's a bargain to get so much information so conveniently, especially since it could prevent a maritime disaster.

Chart Features

The nautical chart portrays navigationally significant features using three different types of symbols: point, line, and area. These three types can portray all features on both paper and electronic charts. Being familiar with these types will help you later in understanding how electronic charts work.

Point features, like towers, stacks, buildings, and lighthouses, have position but no horizontal dimension at chart scale. However, a point feature on a small-scale chart may be an area feature at large scale. For example, a building that is shown only as a point on a 1:250,000 scale chart may be shown in its actual dimensions on a 1:10,000-scale harbor chart. Lights and other fixed aids to navigation are always shown as points, even though a large structure on which they are placed may be shown as an area feature.

Line features have one dimension only. Examples are shorelines, depth contours, and maritime limits and boundaries.

Area features have two-dimensional extent and include such features as reefs, islands, mainland, spoil grounds, and anchorage areas.

The symbols used to portray features on charts are summarized in a publication named *Chart No. 1*—which is actually a booklet instead of a chart. It contains sections on hydrography, topography, aids to navigation, services, and other subjects.

A version of *Chart No. 1* is published by every country that produces charts, as a guide to its use of symbols. There is increasing standardization among countries, and the growth of the electronic chart industry is gradually

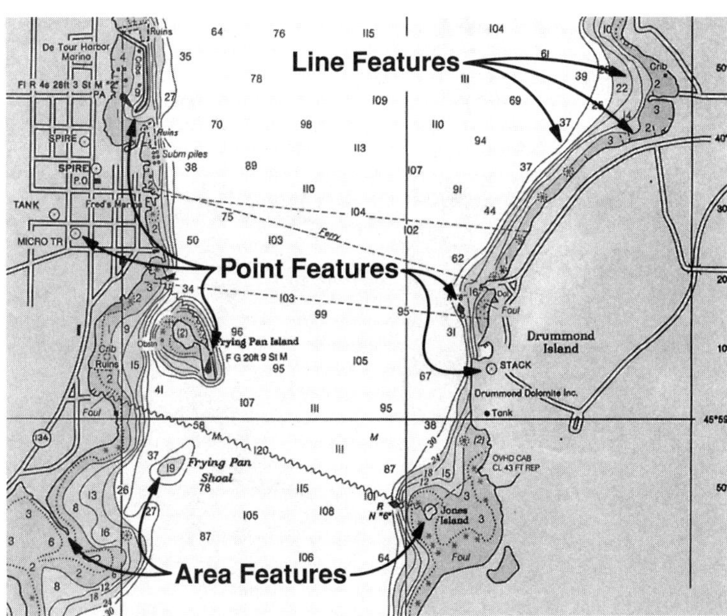

Figure 1-11. *A chart showing significant* point, line, *and* area *features.*

changing the symbols because digital systems have limitations and capabilities far different from paper and ink. Figure 1-12 shows the back cover of the U.S. *Chart No. 1,* which gives the organization of symbols.

The *compass rose* indicates true and magnetic directions on charts. Its name is probably derived from the way it was drawn on ancient charts, with oblong shapes resembling petals of a flower radiating outward from the center, rather than simple plain circles and lines. Figure 1-13 shows a typical compass rose.

Placed on charts in convenient areas mostly free of other features, compass roses enable you to measure and transfer specific bearings from place to place on the chart.

The outside ring of numbers on the rose represents *true directions,* measured from true north clockwise through 360°. The inside ring represents *magnetic directions,* measured from magnetic north. Magnetic north and true north differ by the *magnetic variation* for the area. (See Chapter 3, "The Compass," which deals in detail with true and magnetic directions.)

Some small-scale charts use lines of equal variation called *isogonic lines* instead of compass roses to indicate variation. On those charts, the compass rose contains only true bearings.

U.S. Charts

Charts of United States waters are produced by the *National Ocean Service (NOS),* a part of the *National Oceanographic and Atmospheric Administration (NOAA).* The aforementioned *National Imagery and Mapping Agency (NIMA)* produces charts of non-U.S. waters. Both agencies are located in Washington, D.C., and, although both use different formats and color schemes for their charts, their numbering systems are the same.

The quantity and order of digits in the chart number is significant. Single-digit charts have no scale (such as *Chart No. 1, Nautical Chart Symbols and Abbreviations*). Two-digit charts have scales of 1:9 million and smaller (for example, *Chart 42, Lines of Magnetic Variation*). Three-digit charts have scales of 1:2 million to 1:9 million (ocean-voyage planning charts). Special purpose charts (such as bathymetric charts) have four digits, and charts with scales of 1:2 million and larger (which include all the commonly used navigation charts) have five digits.

The first digit of a chart number identifies the *chart region.* The first and second number together identify the *subregion,* and the last

Figure 1-12. Chart No. 1 *contains a list of symbols used to portray navigational information on charts. The symbols are organized by type and coded with letters for easy identification.*

Chart No.1

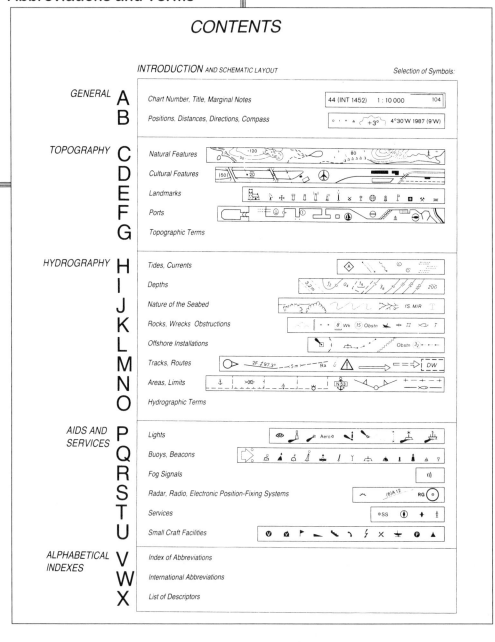

United States of America

Nautical Chart Symbols Abbreviations and Terms

CONTENTS

INTRODUCTION AND SCHEMATIC LAYOUT — *Selection of Symbols:*

GENERAL	A	*Chart Number, Title, Marginal Notes*
	B	*Positions, Distances, Directions, Compass*
TOPOGRAPHY	C	*Natural Features*
	D	*Cultural Features*
	E	*Landmarks*
	F	*Ports*
	G	*Topographic Terms*
HYDROGRAPHY	H	*Tides, Currents*
	I	*Depths*
	J	*Nature of the Seabed*
	K	*Rocks, Wrecks Obstructions*
	L	*Offshore Installations*
	M	*Tracks, Routes*
	N	*Areas, Limits*
	O	*Hydrographic Terms*
AIDS AND SERVICES	P	*Lights*
	Q	*Buoys, Beacons*
	R	*Fog Signals*
	S	*Radar, Radio, Electronic Position-Fixing Systems*
	T	*Services*
	U	*Small Craft Facilities*
ALPHABETICAL INDEXES	V	*Index of Abbreviations*
	W	*International Abbreviations*
	X	*List of Descriptors*

three digits locate an individual chart in geographic sequence within the subregion. (See Figure 1-14.)

In general, charts are numbered counterclockwise around continents and land masses and counterclockwise within each subregion. Charts with scales of 1:200,000 to 1:250,000 are assigned every even twentieth number (except that the first 40 numbers of every 100 are reserved for smaller-scale coverage). Numbers between these are preserved for larger-scale charts. Not every number is used, so chart planners can assign unused numbers to charts that are developed for new areas.

Chart catalogs are maintained in two forms. NIMA issues an edition for military users, and NOS provides a civilian edition that includes NIMA charts of foreign waters and NOS charts of U.S. waters. Most boating stores are chart agents for both NOS and NIMA charts.

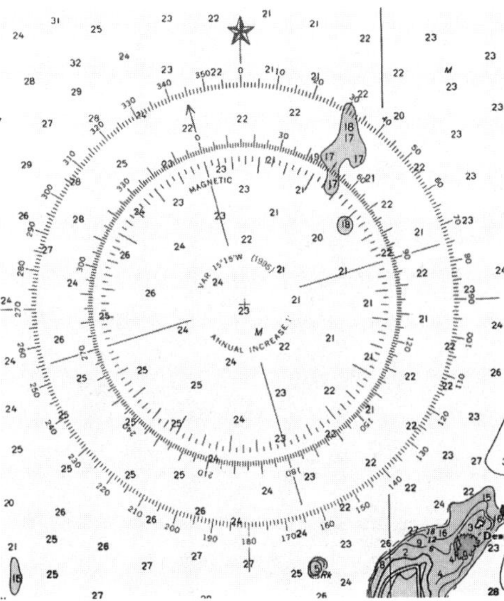

Figure 1-13. *The compass rose, probably named for its resemblance to a flower on early charts, shows the direction of true north and often magnetic north as well. It is placed on charts so that you can measure and draw bearings, courses, and other directions.*

Nautical Publications

The nautical publications discussed here are those used for operational navigation and don't include instruction manuals or textbooks. We have already discussed a couple of them—the *Notice to Mariners* and *Chart No. 1*. The others included here are *Coast Pilots, Sailing Directions, Tide Tables, Light Lists, List of Lights* (not quite the same thing), and almanacs.

Pilots

The history of *pilots,* sometimes known as *sailing directions,* goes back thousands of years. Early navigators wrote descriptions of oceans, coasts, ports, and harbors for use by mariners who would follow them. These descriptions were often assembled in books whose value was extremely high before the printing press eliminated the need to copy the directions by hand. Gradually, information was developed that covered the entire world and mariners shared information, resisting the temptation to hoard it for military or economic reasons. Today, each country still generally shares its updated information with others, so that all mariners can benefit from worldwide experience.

Coast Pilots are issued in nine volumes by NOS for U.S. waters. They are updated continually from field reports of government vessels, contributing mariners, harbor authorities, and others. Each volume covers a specific geographic area and describes the navigation elements of that area in great detail, including coastal features, regulations, currents, weather, communications, and other important operational data. Figure 1-15 shows an example of this format. The *Coast Pilot* is an essential book for all mariners and must,

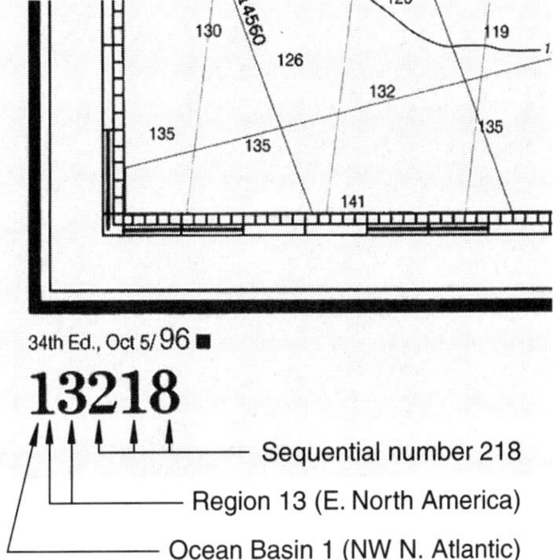

Figure 1-14. *The chart number indicates the region (ocean basin), the subregion, and the sequential number. The same format is used for all U.S. government charts, including both NOS and NIMA charts.*

Figure 1-15. Coast Pilots *are published by the National Ocean Service (NOS) and describe in detail the navigational features of U.S. coastal waters.*

Figure 1-16. Sailing Directions, *issued by the National Imagery and Mapping Agency, describe the navigational details of foreign waters.*

United States Coast Pilot 3

Atlantic Coast: Sandy Hook to Cape Henry

(29) **Charts 12281, 12278.-Baltimore**, one of the major ports of the United States, is at the head of tidewater navigation on Patapsco River. The midharbor point, at the intersection of Fort McHenry and Ferry Bar Channels 0.6 mile southeast of Fort McHenry, is 8 miles from the mouth of the river, 150 miles above the Virginia Capes, and 62 miles from Delaware River.

(30) Principal imports are general cargo, crude petroleum and petroleum products, iron ore, chrome and manganese, gypsum, lumber, motor vehicles, fertilizers, sugar, and bananas: exports are chiefly general cargo, grains, metal products, coal, and chemicals. Coastwise receipts are crude petroleum and petroleum products, fertilizers, sulfur, sugar, and lumber: shipments are mostly petroleum and metal products.

(31) **Channels.**-Federal project channels were discussed at the beginning of the chapter. The branch channels will be covered in the descriptions of the tributaries.

(32) **Anchorages.**- General, dead ship, and small craft anchorages are in Baltimore Harbor. (See **110.1 and 110.158, chapter 2,** for limits and regulations.)

(33) **Tides and Currents.**- The mean range of tide is 1.1 feet at Baltimore: daily predictions are given in the Tide Tables. Prolonged winds of constant direction may cause substantial variation in the tide. Currents in the harbor are 0.8 knot on the flood and ebb. (See the tide Current Tables for daily predictions.) In May 1981, strong currents were reported in the vicinity of Fort Carroll and Brewerton Angle on the change of tides.

(34) **Weather.**- Baltimore is in a region about midway between the rigorous climates of the North and the mild climates of the South and adjacent to the modifying influences of the Chesapeake Bay and Atlantic Ocean to the east and the Appalachian Mountains to the west. the net effect is to produce a more equable climate compared to inland locations of the same latitude.

(35) Rainfall distribution throughout the year is rather uniform: however, the greatest intensities are confined to the summer and fall.

PUB. 145
SAILING DIRECTIONS
(ENROUTE)

NOVA SCOTIA AND THE SAINT LAWRENCE

WEST COAST OF GRAND MANAN ISLAND

1.13 The W coast of Grand Manan Island from **Southwest Head** (44°36'N., 66°55'W.) to the entrance to Dark Harbor, 9 miles NNE, is wooded with steep rocky cliffs from 91 to 10m high and free from dangers. Bradford Cove, a small bight about 2 miles NNE of Southwest Head, affords temporary anchorage with offshore winds in depths of 14.6 to 18.3m. Dark Harbor is a remarkable inlet with depths of 9 to 13m, the mouth of which is almost closed by a single beach. The coast from Dark Harbor to Long Eddy Point continues bold and wooded, with an elevation of about 122m. A ledge extends about 275m NW from Long Eddy Point.

NORTHWEST SIDE OF GRAND MANAN CHANNEL

1.14 **Little River Island** (44°39'N., 67°12'W.), in the middle of the entrance to Little River, is wooded and rocky, and can be easily recognized by the white conical tower on its NE corner. Little River, entered N of Little River Island, is small and easy to access through a channel with a depth of about 8.5m. Is an excellent harbor of refuge, sheltered from all winds, and never obstructed by ice. Two tree-covered islets of Western Head, on the S side of the entrance and as tree-covered islet on the N side of the river entrance, are conspicuous.

From Little River to West Quoddy Head, about 14.5 miles NE, the coast is mostly high, rocky, wooded, and steep-to. The only thing off-lying dangers are an unmarked 3.7m shoal, about 0.2 mile offshore, about 1.8 miles ENE of Little River Island, and Morton Ledge, with a depth of 1.8m and marked by a buoy, about 0.4 mile offshore and about 2.3 miles SW of West Quoddy Head Light.

The coast is broken by a number of unimportant coves. The largest of these, Moose Cove and Baileys Mistake, appear from seaward to be good open anchorages, but neither has good holding ground nor any values as a harbor of refuge. Both have ledges at their entrances and afford shelter from N winds only.

West Quoddy Head (44°49'N., 66°57'W.), the E point of the United States, is bold, high, and wooded. West Quoddy Head Light is shown from a white and red banded tower on the E edge of the headland. The abandoned Coast Guard lookout tower, 70m high, near the summit of the ridge about 0.5 mile W of the light, is the most conspicuous landmark in the approach.

by law, be carried on commercial vessels. It is highly recommended for small-craft operators venturing out of well-known waters.

Sailing Directions are published by NIMA for waters outside the U.S. There are 10 volumes of the *Planning Guide* and 37 volumes of *Enroute Sailing Directions*. The *Planning Guide* is used in planning ocean voyages. Each volume contains general information about a major ocean basin. It discusses countries of the region and their navigation regulations, ocean currents, climate patterns, maritime safety information, weapons firing and other danger areas, traffic separation schemes, and the system of aids to navigation used in the region. Appendices to each volume contain detailed climatological and meteorological charts.

The 37 volumes of *Enroute Sailing Directions* provide the same type of information for other countries that is found in U.S. *Coast Pilots*—descriptions of land features, local currents and weather patterns, harbor information, communications procedures, and other operational data. Figure 1-16 shows an example of the format. *Sailing Directions* are extremely helpful in foreign waters because the text is often compiled directly from relevant foreign pilots. They are available from agents who sell NIMA charts.

Light Lists are issued by the U.S. Coast Guard (published by the U.S. Government

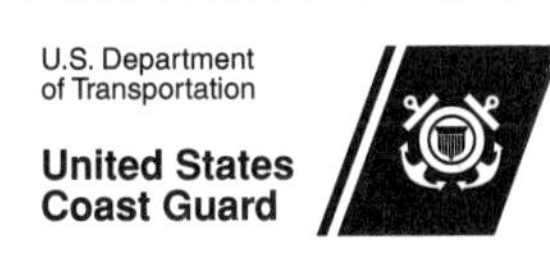

LIGHT LIST
Volume 1
ATLANTIC COAST
St. Croix River, Maine to
Toms River, New Jersey

(1) No.	(2) Name and Location	(3) Position	(4) Characteristic	(5) Height	(6) Range	(7) Structure	(8) Remarks
	MASSACHUSETTS - First District						
		N/W					
	BOSTON INNER HARBOR (Chart 13272)						
	Bird Island Flats						
10720	Buoy 1	42 21.5 71 01.9				Green can.	
10725	Buoy 2					Red can.	
10730	Buoy 3					Red and Green bands; nun.	
10735	Jeffries Point Wreck Buoy WR	42 21.7 71 01.9				Red and Green bands; nun.	
10736	EAST BOSTON DOCK LIGHT SE	42 21.7 71 01.9	F Y			On pile.	Private aid
10736	EAST BOSTON DOCK LIGHT NW		F Y			On pile.	Private aid
	BOSTON HARBOR (Chart 13270)						
	Dorchester Bay						
10755	*Lighted Buoy 5*	42 19.0 71 01.3	Fl G 4s		4	Green.	Replaced by can from Dec. 1 to Mar. 15

Figure 1-17. Light Lists *are issued by the U.S. Coast Guard in several volumes and contain detailed information about aids to navigation, lighted and unlighted, in U.S. waters.*

Printing Office) and list all the major lights, beacons, and buoys in U.S. waters. Each aid is listed in sequence along a coastline and into harbors and bays. Each entry includes a complete description of the aid, a detailed description of the characteristic of any light, its height and range, and its approximate geographic location to help locate it on a chart. Some of this information is too detailed for even the largest-scale chart, so *Light Lists* are an important additional asset to navigation safety. (See Figure 1-17.)

Lists of Lights are issued in seven volumes by the National Imagery and Mapping Agency and contain the same information as the Coast Guard's *Light Lists,* but for foreign waters (see Figure 1-18). Both publications are updated continually by the *Notice to Mariners.* When correcting charts, remember that any change in a major navigation aid should also be noted at the appropriate *Light List* entry, too. See Figure 1-19 for an example of the format.

Other Publications

The U.S. government publishes several other publications of interest to the navigator. Although these are chiefly for commercial ships and serious professional navigators, they also contribute to the education of amateur navi-

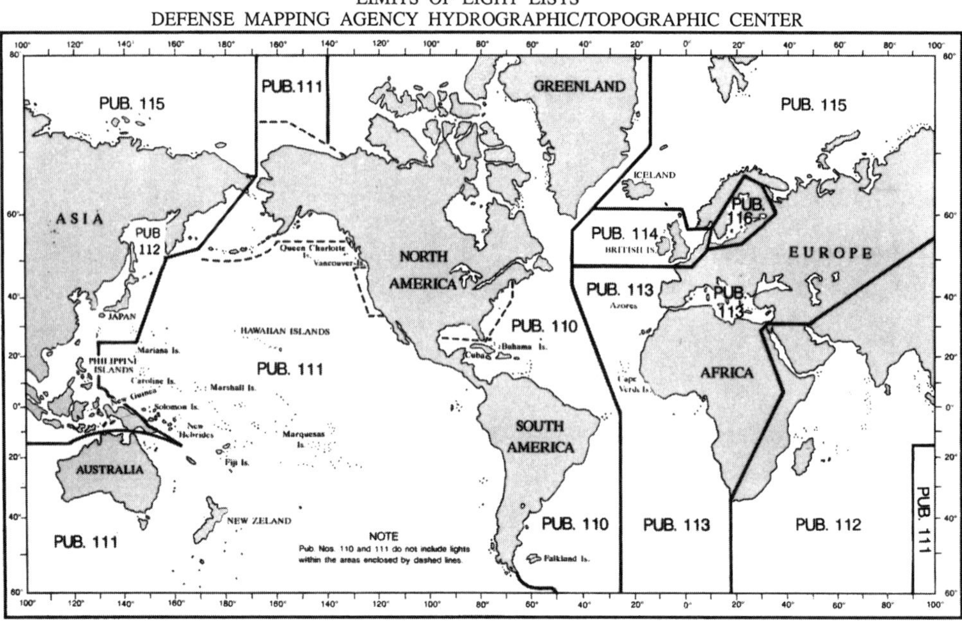

Figure 1-18. *NIMA's* List of Lights *are issued in several volumes for worldwide coverage. This chart shows the areas covered by each volume. Note that U.S. waters are not covered by these volumes, but by the U.S. Coast Guard's* Light List.

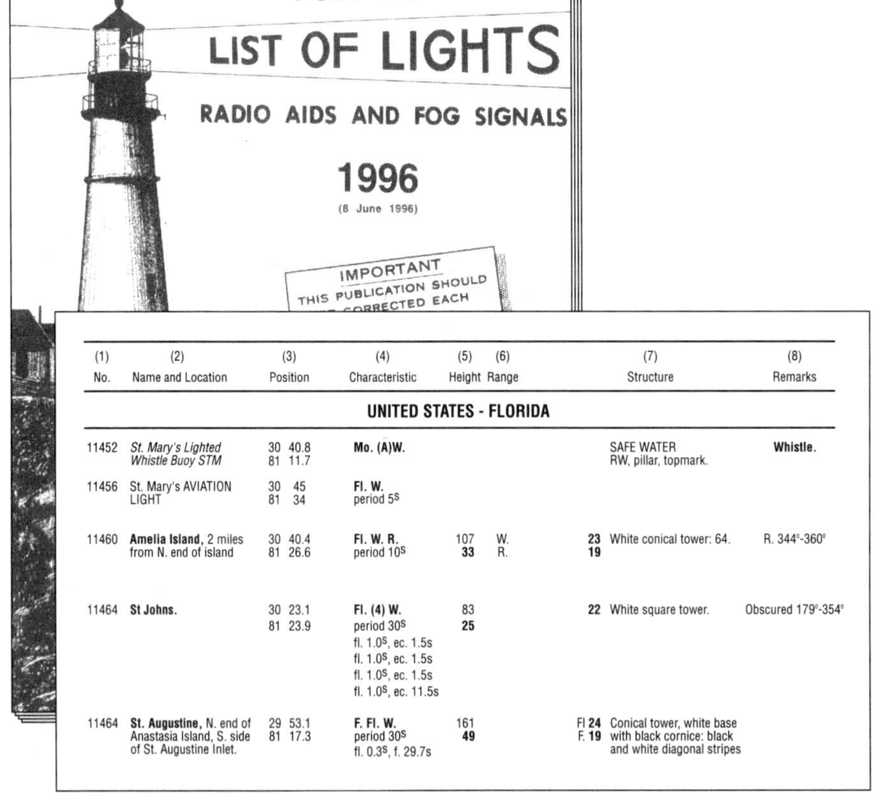

(1) No.	(2) Name and Location	(3) Position	(4) Characteristic	(5) Height	(6) Range	(7) Structure	(8) Remarks
			UNITED STATES - FLORIDA				
11452	*St. Mary's Lighted Whistle Buoy STM*	30 40.8 81 11.7	**Mo. (A)W.**			SAFE WATER RW, pillar, topmark.	**Whistle.**
11456	St. Mary's AVIATION LIGHT	30 45 81 34	**Fl. W.** period 5s				
11460	**Amelia Island,** 2 miles from N. end of island	30 40.4 81 26.6	**Fl. W. R.** period 10s	107 **33**	W. **23** R. **19**	White conical tower: 64.	R. 344°-360°
11464	**St Johns.**	30 23.1 81 23.9	**Fl. (4) W.** period 30s fl. 1.0s, ec. 1.5s fl. 1.0s, ec. 1.5s fl. 1.0s, ec. 1.5s fl. 1.0s, ec. 11.5s	83 **25**	**22**	White square tower.	Obscured 179°-354°
11464	**St. Augustine,** N. end of Anastasia Island, S. side of St. Augustine Inlet.	29 53.1 81 17.3	**F. Fl. W.** period 30s fl. 0.3s, f. 29.7s	161 **49**	Fl **24** F. **19**	Conical tower, white base with black cornice: black and white diagonal stripes	

Figure 1-19. Lists of Lights *are volumes of aids to navigation published by the National Imagery and Mapping Agency for Greenland, the east coasts of North and South America (with the exception of the east coast of Florida, they exclude the continental U.S.), and the West Indies.*

gators who should at least be familiar with their contents and possibly keep some of them aboard.

Radio Navigation Aids (Pub. 117) is a worldwide listing of radio navigation and safety services to the mariner, including information on radio direction-finding stations, broadcast navigation warnings, distress and safety communications, radio navigation systems, and other worldwide operational radio information.

World Port Index (Pub. 150) is a listing of several thousand ports and the services they offer. This publication is largely used by commercial and military ships. Only a world-voyaging sailor needs this book.

Distances Between Ports (Pub. 151) lists the sailing distance, along commonly sailed routes, between many major ports of the world. It also is used mostly by commercial and military navigators.

Tide Tables were published by the National Ocean Service (NOS) until 1994, when budget strictures prompted the government to stop publishing the actual books and instead release the data. Now you can buy tide tables that are published by marine publishing houses, including International Marine, at boating or chart supply stores. Although these tables often contain advertisements, which the former government publications did not, they may also include other useful information in addition to the tide tables. Many local newspapers and regional boating newspapers or magazines also publish tide data. Boating stores and suppliers also sell computer software that predicts tides. The software is often advertised in boating periodicals. More information on tides and the products used to predict them is found in Chapter 4, "Tides."

Almanacs list the precise positions at certain times of celestial bodies commonly used in navigation. Two almanacs are most often used for celestial navigation—the *Nautical Almanac,* designed for marine navigation, and the *Air Almanac,* designed for air navigation but used by many marine navigators. The *Air Almanac* is slightly less accurate than the *Nautical Almanac*. These almanacs are discussed in greater detail in Chapter 15, "The Almanacs."

Privately produced almanacs are also available and, though these contain advertisements, they, too, may contain useful information not found in government publications.

The *Floppy Almanac,* or *Interactive Computer Ephemeris (ICE),* produced by the U.S. Naval Observatory, is a DOS-formatted series of computer programs that not only contains almanac data but also computes twilight times for sights, finds stars, computes great circle and rhumb-line courses, does complete sight reductions of multiple bodies with weighted analysis of the resulting lines of position, and produces plotted results.

Almanacs are available from nautical chart suppliers.

Sight Reduction Tables *come in two types.* Pub. 229, Sight Reduction Tables for Marine Navigation, *consist of a set of six books, each covering 15° of latitude, and give the solutions of spherical triangles. Chapter 16, "Sight Reduction," explains how to use these books.*

You only need the sight reduction tables for the latitudes you sail in. Two volumes will suffice if you don't sail in very high or very low latitudes. (See Figure 1-20.)

The other type of tables, *Pub. 249, Sight Reduction Tables for Air Navigation,* are published in three volumes. Although a little less accurate than *Pub. 229,* they are slightly easier to use.

Other government publications used in navigation are the *Maneuvering Board Manual,* the *Radar Navigation Manual, International Code of Signals,* and chart/publication catalogs. These are primarily used by full-time professional mariners, although the *Navigation Rules* should be carried on every boat and studied by everyone who sails a boat, however small.

PUB. NO. 249
VOLUME 3

SIGHT REDUCTION TABLES
FOR
AIR NAVIGATION
LATITUDES 39°—89°
DECLINATIONS 0°—29°

DEFENSE MAPPING AGENCY
HYDROGRAPHIC/TOPOGRAPHIC CENTER

PUB. NO. 229
VOL. 4

SIGHT REDUCTION TABLES
FOR
MARINE NAVIGATION
LATITUDES 45°-60°, Inclusive

DEFENSE MAPPING AGENCY
HYDROGRAPHIC/TOPOGRAPHIC CENTER

Figure 1-20. *Sight reduction tables are used to solve some celestial navigation problems. There are two types:* Pub. 249 *is intended for air navigation and* Pub. 229 *for marine use, but small-boat navigators often use* Pub. 249 *as well.*

The government's role in providing nautical publications is changing. With increasing frequency, publications are provided in official form only to government vessels and offices. To supply the commercial market, the government has simply released the basic data for use by commercial publishers in publications such as sight reduction tables, tide tables, and pilots. These publications are not constrained by the rules and formats of government publishing and so often contain useful material beyond the basic data. (You do have to put up with some advertising.) You can buy these publications at marine stores and through catalogs.

The Most Important Factor

Navigation must be practiced to be mastered. Instruction can't substitute for experience. All the tools, books, electronic gadgets, and knowledge are useless without practical experience. Practice navigation skills in good weather and familiar areas so you can perform well under adverse conditions. The sea is relentless; it is only a matter of time before your navigation skills will be tested.

Chapter Two

Buoys, Beacons, and Lights

ONE OF THE SEVEN wonders of the ancient world was the lighthouse at Alexandria, Egypt, built in about 270 B.C. More than 400 feet tall and lighted by a fire on a platform at the top, it guided ships into the harbor at Alexandria for some 1,500 years until toppled by an earthquake in the fourteenth century.

Of all the systems of navigational aids, visual aids have always been, and remain today, the most important, especially for the small-craft operator. Indeed, the lighthouse has been so vital for so long to anxious and endangered mariners that it has transcended its practical purpose to become a romantic symbol, a beacon of hope, or a guiding light.

Although not as old as lighthouses, buoys and smaller beacons are just as vital. They are all parts of a system of aids to navigation, each one carefully chosen for its role.

Definitions

The term *aids to navigation* refers to visual aids such as buoys, lights, ranges, and beacons. Officially they are termed *short-range aids to navigation,* a category that also includes certain short-range electronic aids.

Aids to navigation are grouped into two broad categories. One is intended to mark hazardous points, shoals, rocks, and other navigational menaces. This category is known as the *cardinal system* because it makes use of the four major or cardinal points of the compass in indicating the direction of safe water. This system is used primarily in Europe.

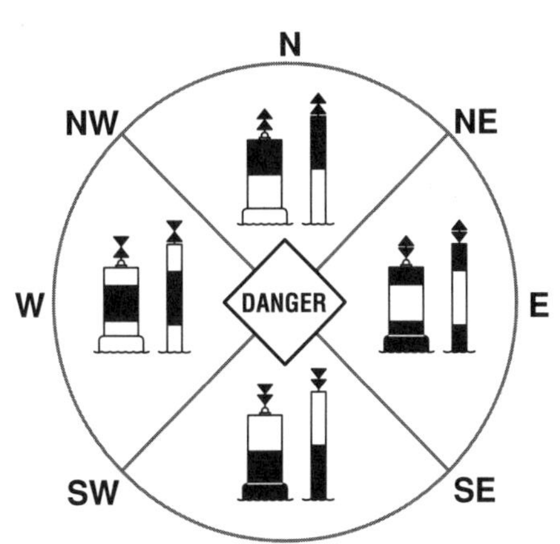

Cardinal Marks
The orientation of Cardinal Marks can be remembered by:

North	2 triangles up
South	2 triangles down
East	triangles form a diamond, and diamonds come from the east.
West	2 triangles form a sideways W

Figure 2-1. *Cardinal marks use the four major, or cardinal, points of the compass to indicate the direction of safe water.*

The other category indicates safe channels by marking deepwater areas where navigation is generally safe. This *lateral system* marks the sides of channels and is generally used in the United States.

Each system is designed to give you needed assistance at an economical cost. Each aid is carefully chosen to fit with those surrounding it as a part of the system. For example, two adjacent lights on a coast should neither be painted the same color pattern nor have the same light characteristic. The same is also true for adjacent channel buoys.

The U.S. Coast Guard is responsible for designing, establishing, and maintaining the U.S. aids to navigation. The many different types of aids are chosen for function, location, and maintainability.

Buoys are floating aids to navigation that are anchored in place. They may be large or small, lighted or not, with or without a sound signal. They may be specially colored or shaped and have numbers or letters. Their individual features distinguish each aid from every other one in the vicinity.

Lights fall into several classes. The brightest are *primary seacoast lights,* with ranges from

The U.S. Coast Guard can't afford to place as many aids to navigation as it might like. Floating aids are particularly expensive to build and maintain; each one is selected on the basis of its utility and cost-effectiveness. Each is part of an overall system that is carefully designed to keep the mariner away from dangers—at the lowest possible cost to the Coast Guard. Aids to navigation engineering is a specialized function of U.S. Coast Guard headquarters in Washington, D.C.

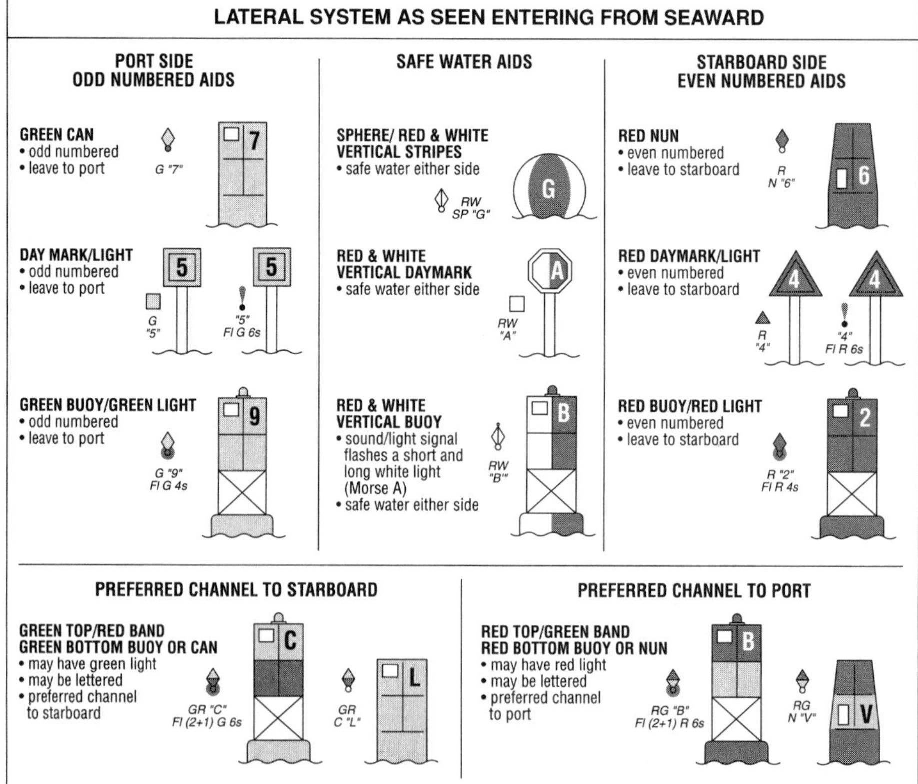

Figure 2-2. *Lateral marks, marking the sides of safe, deepwater channels.*

Figure 2-3. *Aids to navigation are maintained by the U.S. Coast Guard. Here, a 180-foot Coast Guard buoy tender services a buoy in New York Harbor. (Official U.S. Coast Guard photograph)*

Figure 2-4. *Buoys may be large or small. This one, St. Georges Reef buoy "SG" off the California coast, is one of the largest, designed to be moored in the open ocean. Visible are the light lenses (primary and secondary) and a radio antenna for remote monitoring. Nearby is St. Georges Reef Light. (Official U.S. Coast Guard photograph)*

Figure 2-5. *This is a lighted gong buoy typically seen in exposed coastal waters. Note the wave-activated gongs in the lower structure, the light on top, and the angular radar reflecting surfaces just below the light. Inside the hull are batteries that last up to a year or more. (Official U.S. Coast Guard photograph)*

Figure 2-6. *A variety of smaller buoys is used in harbors, bays, and other protected and semi-protected waters. "2A" is the buoy's designation, part of the numbering scheme for the area. The light on top is powered by batteries stored under the round hatches in the hull. (Official U.S. Coast Guard photograph)*

Figure 2-7. *Primary seacoast lights are the brightest, often visible for 20 nautical miles or more. Their height gives them a large geographic range and distinctive color schemes such as this diamond pattern are used to differentiate adjacent lights. (Official U.S. Coast Guard photograph)*

about 15 to 30 or more nautical miles. The primary lights are placed on prominent seacoast points, at the entrances to straits and bays, and other important locations.

Secondary lights are less bright, with ranges of about 8 to 15 nautical miles. They are placed on secondary points of land, at major harbor entrances, and along coastlines between major lights.

Minor lights, the dimmest, with ranges of about 4 to 8 nautical miles, are placed along channels, in inland waters, and inside harbors.

A primary seacoast light may be mounted on a building or in a large skeleton tower, but is most commonly found in a traditional brick or stone lighthouse. Its height and placement ensure that its geographic range (distance to its horizon) is sufficient to give you adequate warning. Thus, lighthouses are generally tall unless they are placed on high bluffs and cliffs.

Most lighthouses turn on automatically at sunset and switch off at sunrise. Remote lights, often the most important, are sometimes monitored by radio or telephonic signals from a local Coast Guard station.

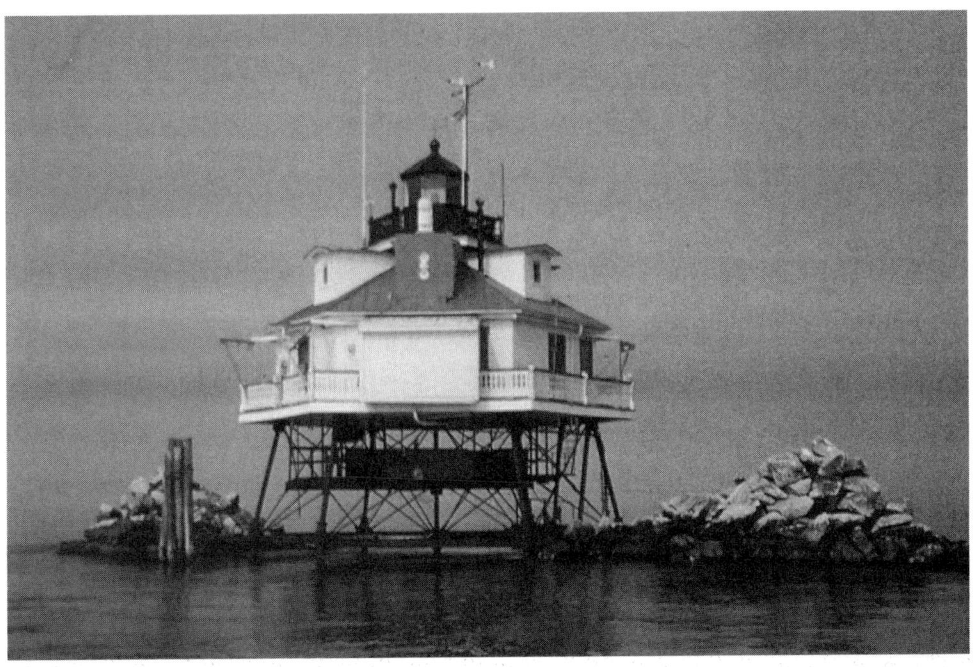

Figure 2-8. *Secondary lights, visible for about 8 to 15 nautical miles, are placed along the coast between primary seacoast lights and in straits, bays, and sounds. Thomas Point Light, shown here, is typical of a type found in Chesapeake Bay, but others may be simple steel skeleton towers. (Official U.S. Coast Guard photograph)*

Figure 2-9. *Minor lights have ranges of 4 to 8 nautical miles. They mark isolated dangers, channel limits, shoals, and other nearby hazards. (Official U.S. Coast Guard photograph)*

Figure 2-10. *A beacon is any fixed aid to navigation, lighted or unlighted. It can be a large lighthouse or, as shown here, a simple colored dayboard on a piling. (Official U.S. Coast Guard photograph)*

A beacon is any stationary aid that is built upon the ground or bottom. A lighthouse is a type of beacon, as is a dayboard on a single piling. A lighted beacon is usually called simply a *light;* an unlighted one is called a *daybeacon*. The daymark portion of a light is distinguished by the color and pattern of its paint, whether it be the barber pole pattern of a picturesque lighthouse or a simple pattern painted on a plywood shape on a piling.

A *buoyant beacon,* a seeming contradiction in terms, is actually a floating aid to navigation, but it acts almost like a beacon because of its design. Once called an "articulated light," it consists of a large pipe that floats vertically in the water because it is moored on a short scope of chain to a heavy sinker.

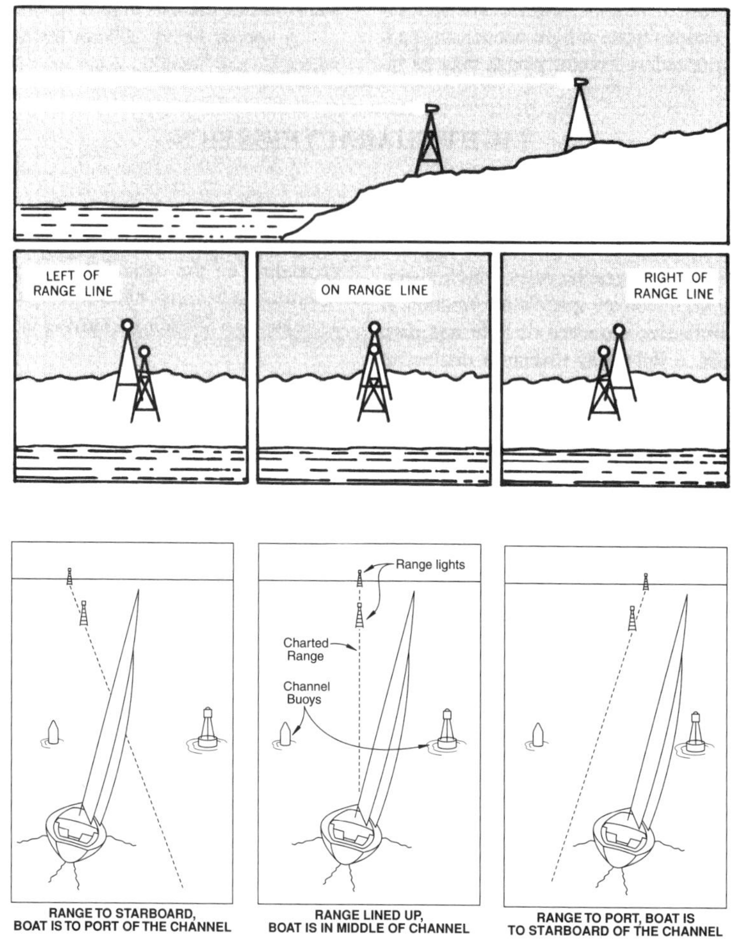

Figure 2-11a. *Range lights locate your position in relation to the center of a channel. If the front range is to the left of the rear range, you are to the right of the centerline, and vice versa. Only when the two are in line are you in the center of the channel.*

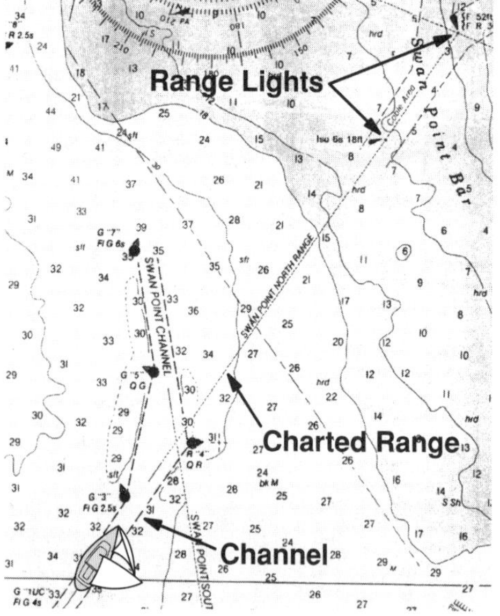

Figure 2-11b. *Swan Point North Range is shown on this section of Chesapeake Bay chart 12278.*

A *range* is a pair of lights or daymarks that mark a narrow channel. A *front range* is placed lower and in front of a *rear range*. When the lights or daymarks are aligned, the vessel is lined up directly on the preferred path. Some ranges are lighted 24 hours a day. They indicate with precision whether you're in the channel's center.

In an experimental range light known as the *light pipe*, a vertical tube of fluorescent light about 15 feet high is backed by a parabolic reflector. You see a single vertical bar rather than a point of light. Because of the characteristics of their rays, light pipes are very effective in hazy conditions.

Aeronautical lights are sometimes the first lights you see when approaching a coast. Although they are not intended for marine navigation and are not covered by the *Notice*

Both glass and plastic lenses are used in lights and buoys. Glass lenses are larger, heavier, and generally older. In many cases, the glass lenses are antiques that end up in museums when lights are modernized. Modern lenses are made of molded acrylic plastic. Glass or plastic, all are Fresnel lenses based on a principle discovered by French physicist Augustin Fresnel (fray-nel). *In a Fresnel lens, excess glass is removed from a simple convex magnifying lens. The result is far lighter and more suitable for aids to navigation and allows virtually any lens shape to be almost flat in cross section.*

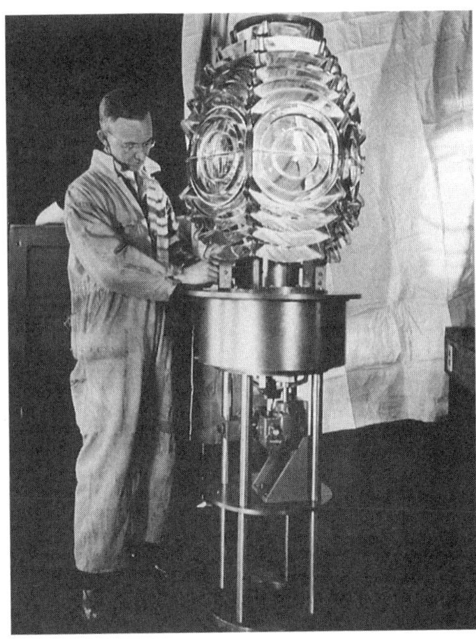

Figure 2-12. *The lens of a light or buoy concentrates the light rays into a narrow beam in the focal plane of the mariner. This Fresnel lens, which is from a lighthouse, rotates (note the motor below the base), rather than turning on and off, to make it appear to flash. (Official U.S. Coast Guard photograph)*

to Mariners, they are valuable aids to marine navigation. They most often flash a white and green pattern (abbreviated on charts as "Alt. WG") and generally are charted if they are near the coast and useful at sea.

Bridge lights indicate the presence and status of over-water bridges that you must either pass under or signal to open. Red, green, and white lights are used in various combinations to delineate bridges and the channels under them. The charts and Coast Pilots contain explanations of the lighting of each bridge.

Every light, whether on a buoy or in a lighthouse, has a *lens* to focus the light in a horizontal direction, a *lamp changer* that automatically replaces burned-out bulbs, a

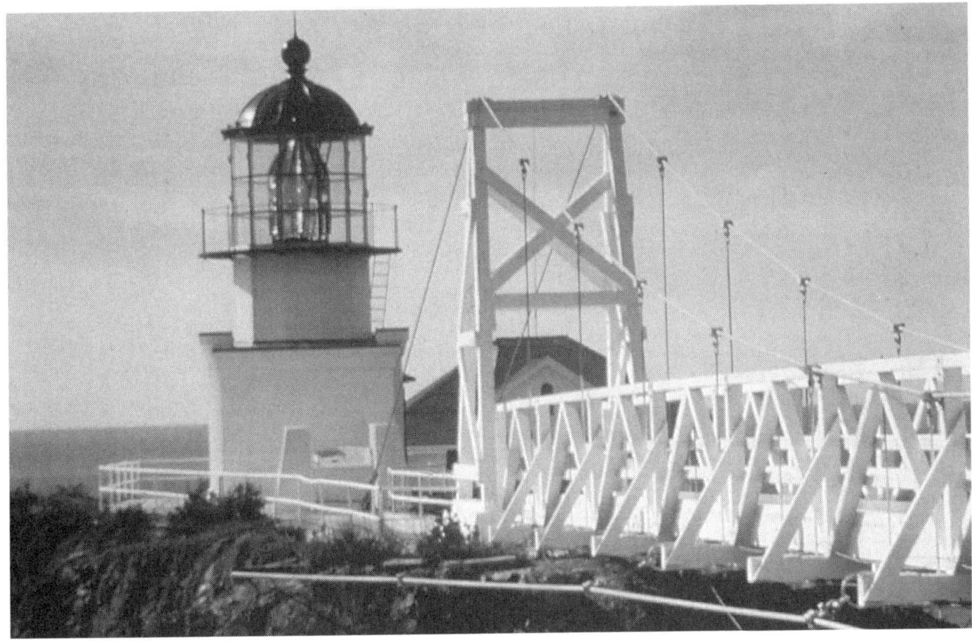

Figure 2-13. *The Fresnel lens pictured in Figure 2-12 might be placed in a lighthouse such as this one. (Official U.S. Coast Guard photograph)*

flasher that regulates the pattern, and an electrical *power supply*. The power supply may be batteries (in the case of buoys and isolated minor lights) or regular shore power.

Lights

Light Characteristics The navigator is most interested in the range, color, and characteristic of a light, although sometimes its physical description is valuable if its identity in daylight is in question. Together, these features distinguish each light from others in the area.

Every light exhibits a *characteristic,* or pattern of flashing, that distinguishes it from other nearby lights. The dark period of a light's pattern is known as its *eclipse*. The *period* of a light is measured from any point in its cycle to the same point in the next cycle. The following standard characteristics are used throughout the world:

- A ***fixed light*** (chart abbreviation: "F") is on constantly. There are no periods of eclipse. These are mostly used for range lights.
- A ***flashing light*** (chart abbreviation: "Fl") is off more than it is on. That is, its period of eclipse is longer than its period of light.
- An ***occulting light*** (chart abbreviation: "Oc") is on more than it's off. That is, its period of eclipse is less than its period of light.
- An ***isophase light*** (chart abbreviation: "Iso") is on and off an equal amount of

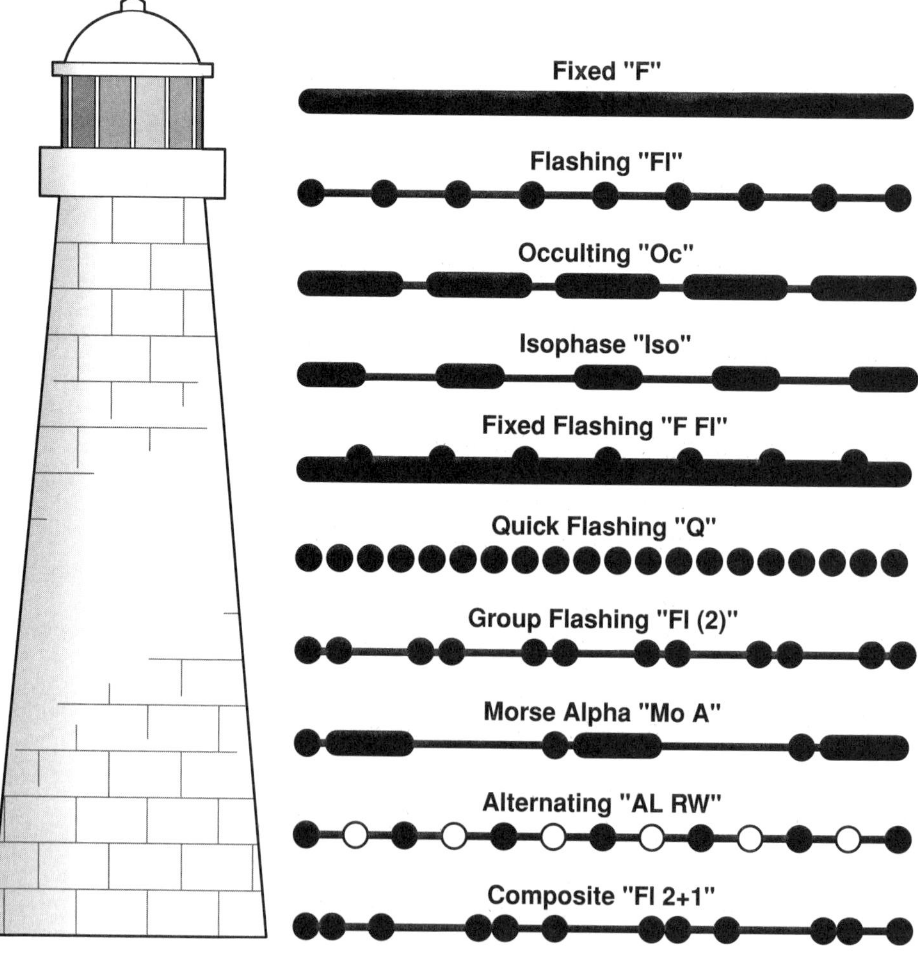

Figure 2-14. *This diagram shows some common light characteristics. Some of these same characteristics—ones that are off more than on—are also used on buoy lights. The light's color is also an important part of its characteristic.*

time. Its periods of light and eclipse are the same.

• A *fixed flashing light* (chart abbreviation: "F Fl") is on all the time and periodically flashes even brighter.

• A *quick flashing light* (chart abbreviation: "Q") is a flashing light which, as its name implies, has a much shorter period than a flashing light. While flashing lights usually have periods of two or more seconds, quick flashing lights flash about once per second. Very quick flashing lights flash about twice per second. Interrupted quick flashing lights are quick lights with regular and prolonged eclipses.

• A *group flashing light* (sample chart abbreviation: "Fl (2)") flashes in groups of two or more flashes together, followed by an eclipse. The number of flashes in a group is the number in parentheses.

• *Morse lights* (chart abbreviation: "Mo A,") flash the characteristic of a single Morse code letter. Morse letter Alpha (A, *dot-dash*) is commonly found on sea buoys. Morse Uniform (U, *dot-dot-dash*) is often seen on oil structures.

• *Alternating lights* (sample chart abbreviation: "Al RW") flash alternately in two different colors. The usual colors are white combined with either red or green. White-green lights are usually associated with airports and, although intended primarily for air navigation, are excellent aids for mariners.

A characteristic may be formed into a *composite* by including elements of two different characteristics, such as a double flash followed by a short eclipse and then a single flash (the composite characteristic would be abbreviated "Fl (2+1).")

Many of these characteristics are used on buoys as well as on beacons and lighthouses, but because buoys run on battery power, their light characteristics are chosen so that minimal power is needed.

A light normally shows the same color all around the horizon, but may have an *obscured sector* caused by natural features or a *colored sector* to indicate a special navigational feature. Sectors are shown on charts with a labeled dotted line and noted in light lists. (See Figure 2-15.)

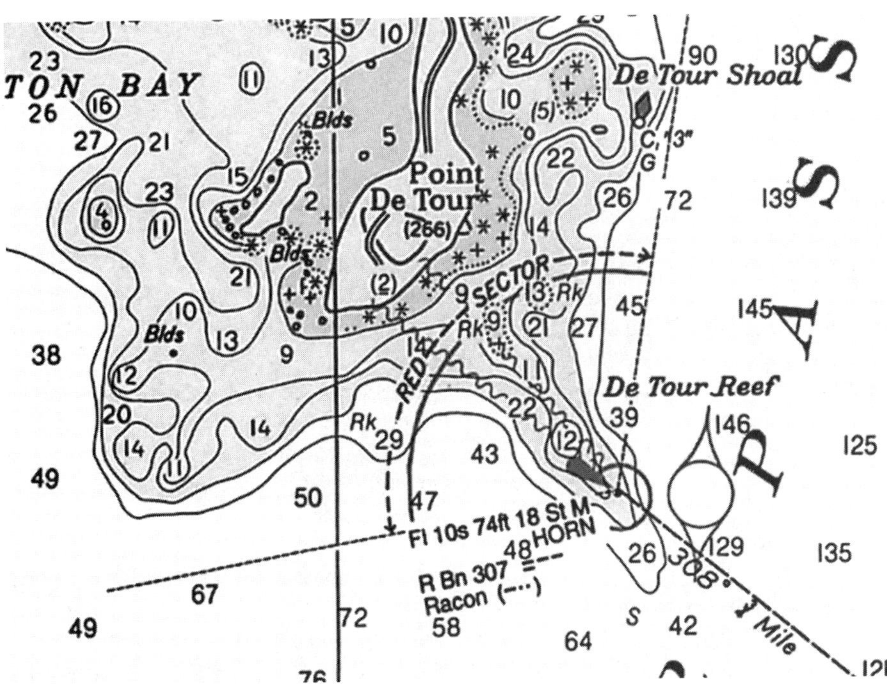

Figure 2-15. *Light sectors are used to indicate special features such as shoal areas or places where the light may be obscured. A red sector usually means danger in that area. Note the shoal water in the red sector of this light.*

Colored sectors are formed by placing colored panes of glass or plastic inside the lens. The light in that sector will show the same pattern, but will have a different color. A certain sector of a light may be intentionally obscured by placing an opaque plate inside the lens. Sectors are very carefully adjusted so that the colored area is precisely delineated. A light may have more than one sector and may be any width. A red sector is usually used to indicate danger areas such as shoals, rocks, or underwater obstructions; a green sector may indicate safe water. Obscured sectors are often caused by geographic features near the light. A look at the chart will reveal what is being singled out for attention.

Sectors are included in the light list where exact bearings are given for each sector border. These bearings are expressed in degrees true *as seen from a vessel.* This could confuse navigators because the bearing written in the light list is 180° from that drawn on the chart. However, this is logical because you view the light from the vessel, not from the light.

The exact bearings of the sector borders in the light list can sometimes be used for a rough compass check or line of position. Figure 2-14 shows a typical sector light and its light list description.

Visibility of Lights Many factors affect the *visibility* of a light, but none is more important than the atmosphere through which the light travels. Lights may be seen either much farther than expected or not at all, depending on atmospheric conditions. Although the visual acuity of the observer is also a factor, there is no way to account for it in calculating the distance at which a light can be seen. Weather is the most common atmospheric factor in limiting light ranges. Fog, rain, sleet, snow, haze, or other weather phenomena can substantially reduce a light's range, sometimes to near zero. This factor determines a light's *meteorological range.*

Light travels in straight lines (for purposes of this discussion, with apologies to Albert Einstein). A light ray from an aid to navigation travels outward tangent to the earth, touches the horizon, and then continues straight out into space. (Actually, it is bent, or refracted, slightly by the atmosphere. This refraction is incorporated in the formula used to figure the range.) The point of tangency is its horizon distance and is the point beyond which an observer at the sea surface (with zero *height of eye*) loses sight of the light. Beyond that point, the light is below the horizon. This determines a light's *geographic range,* which depends on the height of the light.

The range of a light is also affected by its own candlepower, which determines its *nominal range.* If a light has a geographic range (horizon distance) of 40 nautical miles, but only a small, low-power bulb, it can't be seen by the human eye at its full geographic range.

Because the observer's height of eye is bound to be greater than zero, lights may be seen at distances greater than their geographic range. This potential is limited, however, for small-craft sailors.

From the deck of most small craft, most lights will not be visible much beyond 20 nautical miles, regardless of their candlepower, because they will be below the horizon. The height of eye is not great enough. Even when you can't see the light at its point source, you may be able to see its *loom*—that is, its reflecting on the underside of clouds—clearly enough to get a bearing on it. This is particularly true of aeronautical lights, which project their light in an upward-slanting beam that reflects off low-lying clouds.

It is easy to gauge height of eye by adding your own height to the distance of the deck above the water, which should be measured if there is any doubt. On sailboats, the height-of-eye difference between the bow or amidships, or to weather or to leeward when heeled, can be several feet. This factor is also important in celestial navigation.

You can increase your height of eye by climbing to the cabintop or up the mast or rigging, enabling you to see a light that is below the horizon when viewed from the deck. To get a compass bearing on such a light without a hand-bearing compass, take note of a star directly over the light, return immediately to the cockpit compass and take a bearing on the star. This bearing can be plotted as an LOP from the light.

To calculate the precise *range* from a light, all three limiting factors must be considered: geographic range, luminous range, and atmospheric visibility. To help in this, use the *Luminous Range Diagram* in the front of each volume of the light list. However, most small-craft navigators find it quicker and easier to use experience and common sense, along with the tables and/or calculations in this section.

Certain special atmospheric conditions can play tricks on the navigator. The brightest light may seem distant in dense fog or in a snowstorm, even if the light is a few hundred yards away. Conversely, on a very clear night, even a weak light may be seen well beyond its expected range. Therefore, it is impossible to judge the distance to a light based on its apparent brightness.

Remember that a light may be temporarily extinguished because of severe weather or other causes. Failure to see a light when expected may be cause for concern and, if possible, you should obtain a fix by another method to clarify the situation. Extinguished lights should be reported immediately to the Coast Guard.

A light may also exhibit an unexpected characteristic or color, particularly at long ranges. For example, a white light may appear yellow in a hazy atmosphere. Green sometimes appears white at long ranges. Or, the pattern of a lighted buoy may be distorted by ocean wave action.

Different colored lights with equal candlepower have different ranges. White light is the most visible, followed by amber (yellow), green, and then red. At extreme ranges, only one color of an alternating light may be visible; an alternating white-and-green flashing light (Al WG), for example, may initially be seen as flashing white (Fl W), with the green appearing only when you are closer.

Determining Distance to a Light

Although you can't determine distance to a light by its intensity, you can obtain a rough distance by noting when it first comes into view and your exact height of eye when it's first seen. Alternately standing up and crouching down to make a light appear and disappear over the horizon is called *bobbing a light,* and is a neat way to find its exact point of visibility, from which its distance can be roughly calculated.

Your *horizon distance* plus the light's horizon distance (geographic range) equals the distance to the light when first seen. To find your horizon distance, refer to the Geographic Range Table on page 34, entering it with your height of eye. To find the light's horizon distance, enter its height as listed in the light list. Do not use the range listed on the chart or in the light list because they assume a standard height of eye of 15 feet, which is too high for many small craft.

To find the distance to a light by "bobbing," determine your exact height of eye when you first see the light by alternately standing and crouching to make the light appear and disappear. Enter the Geographic Range Table on page 34 with the exact height of eye and find the horizon distance. Next, find the height of the light from the chart or light list. Enter the table again with that height and find the light's horizon distance. (Note: Entries are every foot to 25 feet of height, then every 5 feet to 100 feet of height.)

The sum of these distances is the approximate distance from the observer to the light. The accuracy of this method depends on the accuracy of the height-of-eye of the measurement.

Example:

Observer's height of eye: 7 ft.

Observer's horizon distance: 3.1 NM

Height of light: 77 ft.

Light's horizon distance: 10.3 NM

Distance to light when it's first seen on horizon: 13.4 NM

To find values in between those given, use rough interpolation, or round to the nearest value.

If a calculator is handy, the formula is as follows:
Distance to horizon = 1.17 × square root of height (of eye or light) in feet.

Horizon distance tables are also printed in each volume of the light list and in *Pub. 9, The American Practical Navigator.*

Geographic Range Table

Height of eye or light (ft.)	Distance to horizon (nm)
1	1.2
2	1.7
3	2.0
4	2.3
5	2.6
6	2.9
7	3.1
8	3.3
9	3.5
10	3.7
11	3.9
12	4.1
13	4.2
14	4.4
15	4.5
16	4.7
17	4.8
18	5.0
19	5.1
20	5.2
21	5.4
22	5.5
23	5.6
24	5.7
25	5.9
30	6.4
35	6.9
40	7.4
45	7.8
50	8.3
55	8.7
60	9.1
65	9.4
70	9.8
75	10.1
80	10.5
85	10.8
90	11.1
95	11.4
100	11.7

Using Light Lists

When giving light ranges, both the National Imagery and Mapping Agency (NIMA) and Coast Guard light lists assume a height of eye of 15 feet. If the navigator's height of eye is close to that standard 15 feet, it is acceptable—except when you're calculating a precise distance as described on pages 246–247—to use the range given in the light list or on the chart, with a small allowance for the difference.

The range listed in the light list tells you how far you can expect to see the light in average conditions. Coastal navigators can use this information to choose routes that pass within the geographic range of coastal lights. Bearings to these lights will provide useful lines of position.

Buoys

Because *buoys* float, certain limitations are imposed on their use, for both their custodians and navigators. They are placed where fixed aids would be difficult to build and maintain, in order to warn mariners of dangers and indicate safe channels.

A wide variety of buoy shapes and sizes meets the needs of the location and the mariner. Type and characteristics are determined by the Coast Guard in accordance with its design for the system of aids in the area. Five general types of buoys are in use:

- ***Lateral buoys*** mark the sides of channels.
- ***Isolated Danger buoys*** mark isolated dangers.
- ***Safe Water buoys*** mark the middle of channels.
- ***Special buoys*** mark unusual features or areas.
- ***Information/regulatory buoys*** mark officially regulated areas.

The *International Association of Lighthouse Authorities (IALA) Buoyage System* is the international standard for all aids to navigation. IALA Region B comprises North and South America, Korea, Japan, and the Philippines. All other countries are in Region A. All aids to navigation in the U.S., in Region B, conform in most details to this international system. A buoy may be lighted or unlighted and it may or may not have a sound signal.

Sound Signals

Sound signals are especially useful in fog and at night. The sound can indicate the direction to the aid and can distinguish it from other aids nearby. A chart must be consulted to ensure that the aid is not approached from its dangerous side.

To hear sound signals when motoring in thick fog, shut down the engine(s) and listen carefully. A sailing vessel can luff up or bear off to reduce a noisy bow wave. The foredeck is often the best place to listen for sound signals.

Each type of *sound signal* makes a distinctive noise. Common signals are the *bell, gong, whistle, siren,* and *horn*. The chart label for these signals is written in all capital letters ("BELL," "GONG"). The horn and siren depend on electrical power; the other types are activated by the motion of the sea. Horns and sirens are most common at shore installations where constant electrical power is available, but can be on large buoys as well.

Sound signals have serious limitations as aids to navigation. You often cannot determine from a sound signal the direction of, or distance to, the aid, because atmospheric conditions may cause sound to reflect or attenuate (be shielded) in certain locations. Uncertainty also results from the fact that upwind signals can be heard at far greater distances than downwind signals.

Buoys with only bells or gongs and no lights have shallow, cone-shaped hulls that rock easily in the sea, increasing the amount of noise they make. Lighted buoys, conversely, have deep counterweights to keep them upright so their lights stay in your field of view.

Buoy Colors

Buoys are colored according to the IALA system, which specifies that red and green are used for lateral marks, and yellow for special purpose marks. Other types of marks have either red-and-white vertical stripes or black-yellow or black-red horizontal bands. In IALA Region B, red buoys are placed to starboard and green buoys to port as seen from a vessel approaching land from seaward, entering a harbor from the sea, going upstream in a river, or going with the flood tide. This is the basis for the phrase "Red Right Returning."

A buoy may also have a letter or number *designation* painted on its side. Often the outermost buoy in a channel is a safe-water mark with a letter designation corresponding to the nearby harbor. The Chesapeake Bay entrance buoy, for example, is designated "CB." Progressing up the channel into a harbor, buoys are numbered, with even numbers to starboard and odd numbers to port.

Figure 2-16. *This buoy, Lighted Horn Buoy "PR" at Pollock Rip Channel in Massachusetts, has a horn placed just below the light. (Official U.S. Coast Guard photograph)*

Figure 2-17. *Buoys can be in the shape of a can, cone (also known as "nun," shown here), sphere, pillar, or spar. Ordinarily, only the pillar buoys are lighted. In the U.S. (IALA Region B) cans are always green and odd-numbered; nuns are always red and even-numbered. Spherical and spar buoys can be any color and designation. Spar buoys are rarely used in the U.S., while spherical buoys are mostly used to mark construction. (Official U.S. Coast Guard photograph)*

Buoys are made in five shapes: *can, cone, sphere, pillar,* and *spar.* With cans, cones, and sphere buoys, shape indicates the correct side on which to pass. Pillar and spar buoys make no such distinction by virtue of their shapes, but their paint color, number of letter designation, and light color may indicate the side on which to pass them. In the U.S., the cone-shaped buoy is often called a "nun."

Some buoys are equipped with *topmarks,* which are distinctive shapes placed at their tops that indicate their purpose. Topmarks can often be seen before other characteristics such as color and designation are evident.

A lighted buoy has a battery-pack stored inside the hull, a lamp-changer to change bulbs as they burn out, a flasher to control the characteristic, and a lens to focus the light in the mariner's field of view. These elements are also found in a shore-based light.

A buoy only sits upright in a quiet sea. When the sea is not calm, the buoy rocks and heaves, which causes the focal plane of the

Figure 2-18. *Can buoys are cylindrical shaped and, if numbered, have odd numbers (in the U.S.). In addition to indicating the limits of a channel, a buoy can also reveal currents. With a little practice, you can estimate the current with fair accuracy. Here, the current is about 2 knots. (Official U.S. Coast Guard photograph)*

Figure 2-19. *Some buoys have topmarks, distinctive shapes that indicate their purpose. In this case, the red-ball topmark indicates that the buoy marks safe water and can be passed on either side, which is also indicated by the red-and-white stripes on the buoy. (Official U.S. Coast Guard photograph)*

Figure 2-20. *A light on a pillar buoy is placed on a tower so it can be seen at a good distance. Sound signals may also be mounted in the tower. A counterweight keeps the hull upright and a heavy chain and sinker keep it on-station. Three different types of pillar buoys are shown here undergoing refurbishment at a Coast Guard base. (Official U.S. Coast Guard photograph)*

light to swing in and out of your field of view, disrupting the characteristic flash. So, in rough weather, observe a lighted buoy's flashing characteristic carefully before deciding on which side to pass, especially when nearby aids might be mistaken for it.

Differences Between Buoys and Lights

The largest buoys in the U.S. are designated *large navigational buoys (LNBs).* About 40 feet in diameter, LNBs were developed to replace *lightships,* which were far more expensive to maintain. Usually moored well offshore at the entrance to a major port, an LNB is disk-shaped with a central pillar to support a light and sound signal. A *mooring,* consisting of a chain and a large cement or steel *sinker,* keeps the buoy on station. Smaller, disk-shaped buoys, about 20 feet in diameter, are used in less exposed locations.

The next largest buoys are the more common *pillars,* with cylindrical hulls, counterweights to keep them upright, a tower or pillar to support a light and sound signal, and moorings to keep them from drifting from their stations. Pillar buoys range in diameter from five to nine feet.

Figure 2-21. *Concrete or steel sinkers anchor a buoy in one spot. This small concrete sinker is suitable for a small harbor buoy. The largest sinkers weigh more than six tons. The chain attached to the sinker is shackled to the buoy at its other end. (Official U.S. Coast Guard photograph)*

Can and *cone-shaped* buoys, which are smaller than the lighted and sound-equipped buoys, are placed in sheltered waters.

A buoy is usually moored with a chain that's about two to three times longer than the water depth. So, in 40 feet of water, a buoy will have 80 to 120 feet of chain between itself and its sinker. This scope allows wind and current to move the buoy around in an area known as a *watch circle.* Even though the moorings are heavily built, a buoy may break away in a storm or be rammed loose from its mooring.

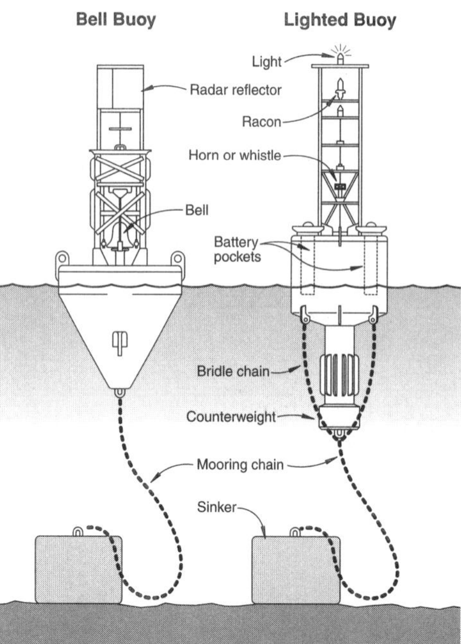

Figure 2-22. *This diagram shows the parts of a 9 × 36 buoy (nine feet in diameter and 36 feet tall) designed for open-water locations, and an unlighted bell buoy designed for inshore locations. The lighted buoy has a deep counterweight to keep the light upright, while the sound buoy has a shallow hull that rings the bell when it rocks in the sea. A buoy's sinker is placed in the charted position and the buoy swings around it in its watch circle. (Based on diagram provided by the U.S. Coast Guard)*

For this reason, rely on bearings on buoys only when their positions are exactly where expected and they are the only available method of fixing your position. This is rarely the case, however, for when buoys are present, land is usually not far away. Because the positions of buoys are not continuously monitored, you should use them in conjunction with other position-fixing methods. Relying totally on buoys for navigation is dangerous.

Figure 2-23. *Buoys are maintained by the U.S. Coast Guard. In this view, a recently refurbished buoy is being reset in its charted position, where it will likely serve the navigator without further attention for perhaps a year or more. (Official U.S. Coast Guard photograph)*

Indeed, the buoy symbol itself indicates that its position is inexact. Although the position of a light is marked on charts with a *light dot* and *flare symbol,* the position of a buoy is indicated by a *position circle,* which represents the watch circle and reminds the mariner that the position is variable. Any buoy that appears to be off-station or lacking its proper characteristic should be reported immediately to the Coast Guard.

A buoy is sometimes placed to indicate a temporary danger or moved about when conditions are changing. A buoy marking a growing shoal, for example, will be placed at the end of the ever-changing shoal and not necessarily where the chart indicates. In any case, the chart may well be two or three years old and discrepancies between charted and real positions may exist. When in doubt, consult the *Local Notice to Mariners* (see Chapter 1 for more information on the *Notice to Mariners*) and treat the buoys with caution.

Wreck buoys mark shipwrecks that pose a danger to navigation. Because of the difficulty and danger in placing a buoy sinker directly on a wreck, it is usually placed to its channelward or seaward side. A large wreck may have a buoy at each end. The exact placement will be given in the *Local Notice to Mariners,* often with details of any salvage activities and other particulars. The wreck will be charted in its exact position, and the position of the buoys will be offset according to the scale of the chart. Particular caution is advised around wrecks, as both wreck and buoy are subject to movement caused by strong currents and storms.

Beacons

Beacons are fixed aids to navigation placed on shore or on pilings in shallow water. They vary in design and size from tall lighthouses to single-pile daymarks.

An unlighted beacon, which is called a *daybeacon,* may have a colored and numbered *dayboard* for identification. Daybeacons are prevalent in protected waters such as the *Atlantic Intracoastal Waterway*.

Miscellaneous Systems

The United States has introduced variations to the standard IALA B system to handle special features of certain waters. For instance, the *Atlantic Intracoastal Waterway (ICW) Marking System* uses the same color scheme as in other U.S. waters, but adds a yellow marking to ICW aids. Yellow triangles indicate ICW starboard-hand aids, while yellow squares show ICW port-hand aids. Yellow bands indicate an ICW aid with no lateral significance. Some ICW aids have both ICW and IALA significance.

The *Uniform State Waterway Marking System (USWMS)* is used in state waters that lie entirely within a single state and have no access to the sea. In this system, buoys are usually placed in pairs on opposite sides of a channel—red to starboard going upstream and green to port. You should pass a white buoy with a red top to the south or west; pass a white buoy with a green top to the north or east. A vertical red-and-white striped buoy marks a shoal or obstruction extending to the shore.

Buoys or marks that convey regulatory information have orange bands on white backgrounds, with geometric shapes indicating the type of regulation. A diamond shape indicates danger; a diamond with a cross indicates that no vessels are allowed in the area; a circle indicates such operating restrictions as speed limits; and a rectangle contains specific written directions or information.

Certain individuals, companies, or organizations can place *private aids to navigation* in U.S. waters. If placed in federal waters, they are subject to Coast Guard approval and, in general, must follow the U.S. lateral system. You may encounter a variety of temporary aids—lights, construction buoys, dredging marks, and others—that are not charted because they are temporary. Use caution when encountering an uncharted aid. The *Local Notice to Mariners* or a call to the Coast Guard may ease your concern.

All aids to navigation are protected by federal laws that prohibit mooring to them or in any way harming them. The laws require you to report accidents involving aids to the Coast Guard.

Chapter Three

The Compass

A COMPASS IS A practical instrument and a symbol of direction with romantic aspects. We speak of one's "moral compass," or of an "internal compass" that guides behavior in the way the marine compass guides the navigator. The compass was developed to meet the mariner's need for a directional reference when out of sight of land. It's possible to sail virtually anywhere without a compass. The Polynesians sailed the entire Pacific Ocean without compass or paper charts by using the sun, moon, and stars for directional reference. However, a compass provides a mathematical reference to direction—day and night in all weather—that is more accurate and more dependable than the heavens.

There are magnetic, gyroscopic, and digital compasses. In this chapter, you will examine the common magnetic compass, familiar to every boatowner and perhaps the most important piece of navigation gear. You'll find out what makes it work, the sources of its errors, and how to correct those errors so you can steer accurate courses and take precise bearings.

Although some accounts credit Marco Polo with introducing the marine compass to the West after his epic trip to China in the thirteenth century, we are certain that the Norsemen used one in the eleventh century. Also, regular trade from northern Europe to the Mediterranean existed well before that, indicating a western origin. Perhaps compasses were developed in different places at about the same time.

Development of the Compass

The *magnetic compass* has developed continually over at least nine centuries, with major advances from time to time. The earliest compasses reportedly appeared when people noticed that a lodestone, or naturally occurring magnetic rock, sought the north-south axis of the earth when it was free to spin, as when floating on a piece of cork or wood, as shown in Figure 3-1.

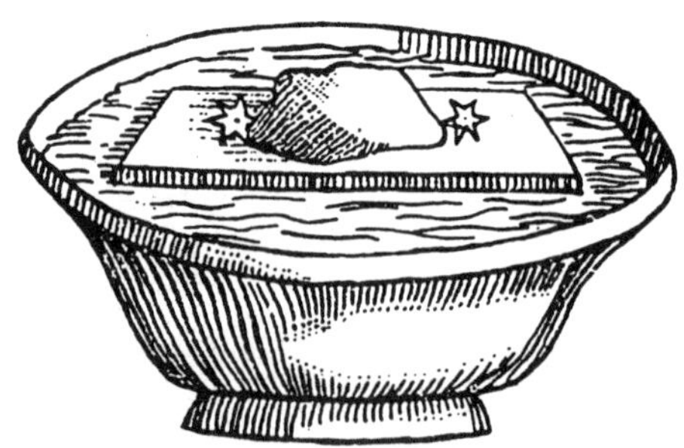

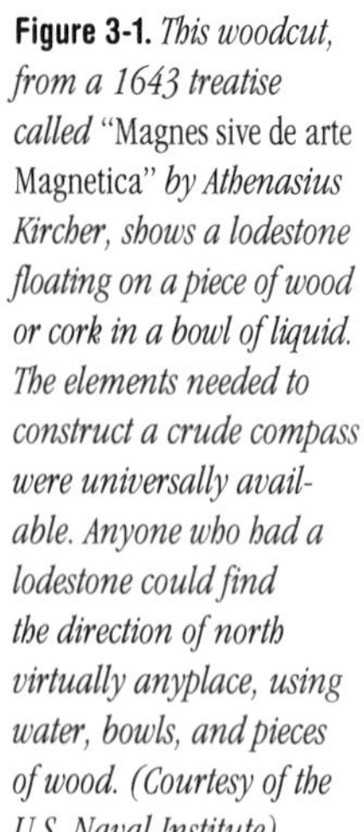

Figure 3-1. *This woodcut, from a 1643 treatise called* "Magnes sive de arte Magnetica" *by Athenasius Kircher, shows a lodestone floating on a piece of wood or cork in a bowl of liquid. The elements needed to construct a crude compass were universally available. Anyone who had a lodestone could find the direction of north virtually anyplace, using water, bowls, and pieces of wood. (Courtesy of the U.S. Naval Institute)*

In its simplest form, a compass is a magnetic needle stuck through a cork that is floating on water. Thirteenth-century writers describe a "floating needle" with a "lubber line" to show the centerline of the vessel, and an attached device for taking bearings of distant objects.

A breakthrough in compass development came in the 1870s when Lord Kelvin developed a reliable *dry-card compass* mounted in a *binnacle* to protect it from the elements. This was the standard until the liquid-filled compass was developed in the early 1900s.

Figure 3-2. *An indirect-reading compass is read on the opposite side of the card from the observer. The card remains pointing to north as the boat turns. These compasses are usually placed in the open, in front of the helm, and can be used to take bearings. (Photo courtesy of Ritchie Navigation)*

The Modern Compass

Today's nautical compass is extremely reliable and relatively inexpensive. It has a *card* with printed numbers corresponding to degrees and (usually) letters corresponding to the *cardinal* and perhaps the *intercardinal* directions (N, E, S, and W, and NE, SE, SW, and NW). The card is encased in a *bowl* filled with liquid and balanced on a single center pivot. The liquid, usually a mixture of alcohol and water, dampens and stabilizes the motions of the card in rough weather.

A rubber *diaphragm* exposed to the air allows for expansion and contraction of the liquid due to temperature changes. Without the diaphragm, the bowl could burst. When fluid leaks out, usually due to a hole in the diaphragm, a bubble will form in the top of the compass. This bubble should be removed as soon as possible. A *lubber's line* drawn on the compass bowl or housing indicates the centerline of the vessel and is the reference point for steering.

On an *indirect-reading, or flat-card, compass,* bearings are taken and courses steered by reading side of the card opposite from the observer. This is logical and intuitive because, as the boat turns, the card remains pointing in the same direction and objects can be sighted directly across the card for bearings. In steering courses with the indirect-reading compass, you "follow the compass," steering to the right when the desired course mark moves to the right, and left when it moves left. (See Figure 3-2.)

A *direct-reading* compass, another type, has the directions and bearings on the near edge of the card. This type of compass may be confusing to use, especially for the novice, and takes some getting used to. The direct-reading compass shown in Figure 3-3 is usually installed in vertical bulkheads where the opposite side of the card cannot easily be seen.

Some compasses are cleverly designed to be read in both ways, as shown in Figure 3-4. Usually bulkhead-mounted, they are difficult to use in taking bearings.

Depending on its level of sophistication, the modern nautical compass has two or more *compensating magnets* that are used to remove errors caused by nearby magnetic influences. The simplest compensating magnets are located in pairs inside the base below the compass card and are adjusted by

Figure 3-3. *A direct-reading compass is read from the side nearest the observer. For most people, the indirect-reading type is the easiest to use. (Photo courtesy of Ritchie Navigation)*

turning small screws. The adjusting screw in the fore-and-aft direction corrects errors on east-west headings; the screw in the athwartships direction corrects errors on north-south headings.

More sophisticated compasses are mounted in a freestanding *binnacle,* inside of which are a number of compensating magnets mounted in racks in both fore-and-aft and athwartships directions. These compasses may also be equipped with a large vertical bar of iron called a *Flinders bar* and with a pair of soft-iron spheres called *quadrantal spheres* mounted on brackets beside the compass bowl. These devices, placed equidistant from the compass, neutralize certain components of magnetic force inherent in steel boats and ships, and are rarely seen on other types of vessels.

However, small boats made of steel should have a compass with quadrantal spheres as shown in Figure 3-5. These spheres are adjusted by moving them closer to or farther from the compass card along their brackets and securing them when the compass error is least. This is a job best left to a professional compass adjuster, at least the first time.

Because the inherent magnetism of the steel in a boat can change over time, you should check the compass annually, including examining the spheres to see if they've acquired magnetism. Such a check is easy to do: Simply rotate the spheres in place 180° without changing their distance from the compass. Any change in compass heading indicates that the spheres have acquired magnetism and must be *annealed* by heating them to a dull red and then allowing them to cool slowly. This process will remove their acquired magnetism, after which they can be reinstalled and the compass readjusted.

The most modern small-craft compass is an electronic *digital compass,* as shown in Figure 3-6, which gives a digital readout instead of a traditional analog readout on a compass card. Digitizing the data allows the instrument to internally calculate and correct

Figure 3-4. *This combination compass can be read as a direct- or indirect-reading type. It also has an inclinometer to measure the heeling angle of the vessel. Heeling can affect the reading of the compass because it changes the location of nearby magnetic influences relative to the earth's magnetic field. (Photo courtesy of Ritchie Navigation)*

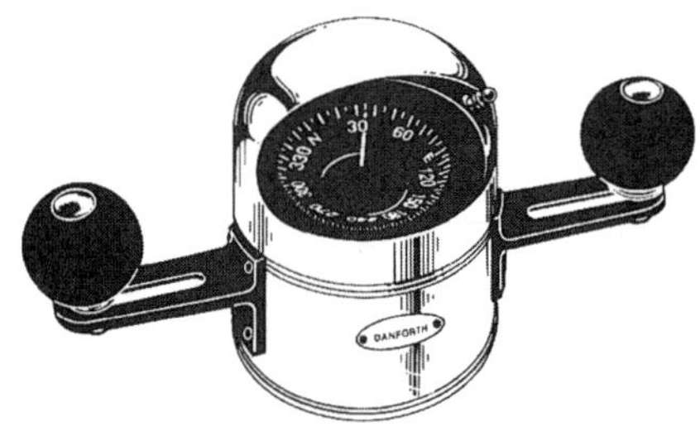

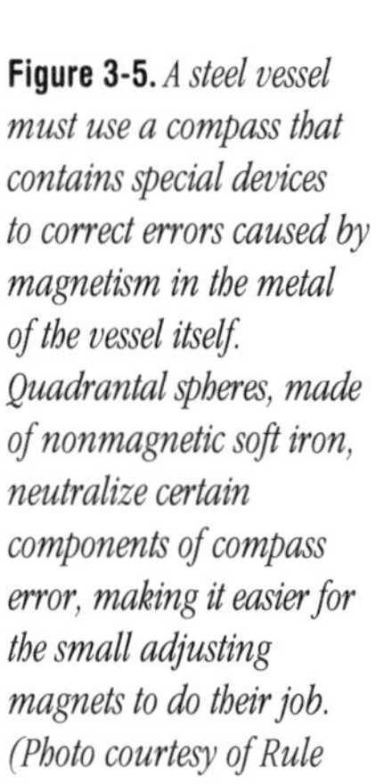

Figure 3-5. *A steel vessel must use a compass that contains special devices to correct errors caused by magnetism in the metal of the vessel itself. Quadrantal spheres, made of nonmagnetic soft iron, neutralize certain components of compass error, making it easier for the small adjusting magnets to do their job. (Photo courtesy of Rule Industries, Inc.)*

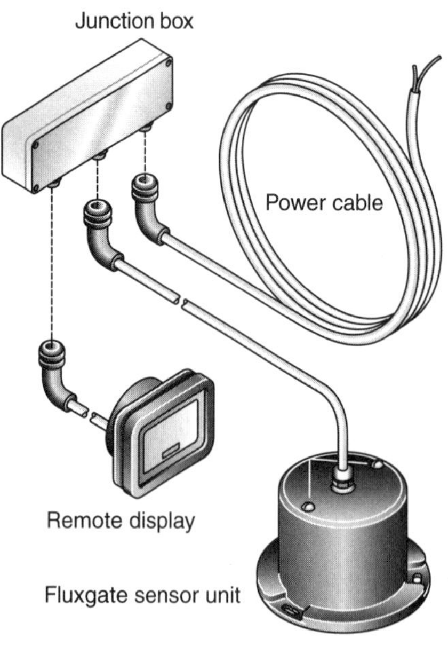

Figure 3-6. *A digital compass converts its internal magnetic compass readings into digital data that can then be corrected mathematically before being displayed. The result is a compass reading corrected for deviation—the effect of onboard magnetic influences on the compass.*

errors, eliminating the usual compensation process. Compensation, which is done internally and mathematically by computer algorithms, is accomplished simply by turning the boat through 360° one or more times. The computer mathematically determines the shape of the error curve (usually close to a sine wave) and brings the readings as close to actual magnetic as possible, in effect flattening the sine wave to near-zero error.

It is also possible, in some designs, to remotely mount the compass sensor where magnetic influences and motion are the least, to minimize the initial error, placing the digital readout at a convenient location near the helm station.

Makers of the most advanced digital compasses feature continuous automatic compensation and guarantee accuracy to one-half a degree. Electronic compasses are excellent for steering and course-keeping because of their accuracy and stability in rough weather. They require a steady source of power, however, and therefore cannot replace the standard magnetic compass in a power failure. Also, because of their physical configuration, they may not be suitable for taking bearings—which is unfortunate because they nearly or totally eliminate deviation as a source of error in visual compass bearings.

Gyrocompasses, which are used on large commercial and naval vessels, are too expensive for the average small-boat owner. They work on the principle of the *gyroscope,* a rapidly spinning wheel that tends to remain stable and senses changes in motion. A ship's gyroscope, powered by a small motor, senses changes in the direction of the vessel and converts mechanical changes into electrical signals that can be routed throughout the ship to *repeaters,* which look and act just like compasses.

Gyrocompasses are not subject to the errors associated with magnetic compasses, but they require a continuous source of power. Their errors are quite constant and small—typically a degree or less.

Compass Error Sources—Variation

Compasses are subject to two types of error: *variation* and *deviation.* For each type, there are two components: amount and direction.

Variation is the difference, measured in degrees, between true north and magnetic north. *Deviation* is the difference, again in degrees, between magnetic north and compass north. When you know the amount and direction of each type of error, you can make corrections to deduce *true north,* which is needed to navigate.

Variation exists because the magnetic north pole and the geographic north pole are in different places and because the earth's magnetic field is not uniform. (See Figure 3-7.) The *geographic north pole* is, of course, the northerly axis of the earth's rotation. The *magnetic north pole* is several hundred miles south of the geographic pole in northern Canada.

There are lines of 0° variation in different locations throughout the world where no variation correction is needed. You are far more likely, however, to be located where there is an angular difference between magnetic and geographic north. This difference varies between 0° and 20° or more for locations in the continental U.S., with the line of 0° variation passing roughly through Chicago and Tampa Bay, Florida. The farther you go east or west from this line, the greater the variation, reaching 20° or more in the states of Washington and Maine. Variations in Alaska and Labrador are as much as 30°, and reach still higher amounts in high polar latitudes.

Because the earth is not a uniformly magnetic body, the lines of equal variation, called *isogonic lines,* don't form a consistent pattern. Thus, you can't compute variation for a location; you must observe it.

Fortunately, isogonic lines worldwide have been accurately mapped, as shown in Figure 3-8. In fact, navigators once thought that longitude could be determined by measuring

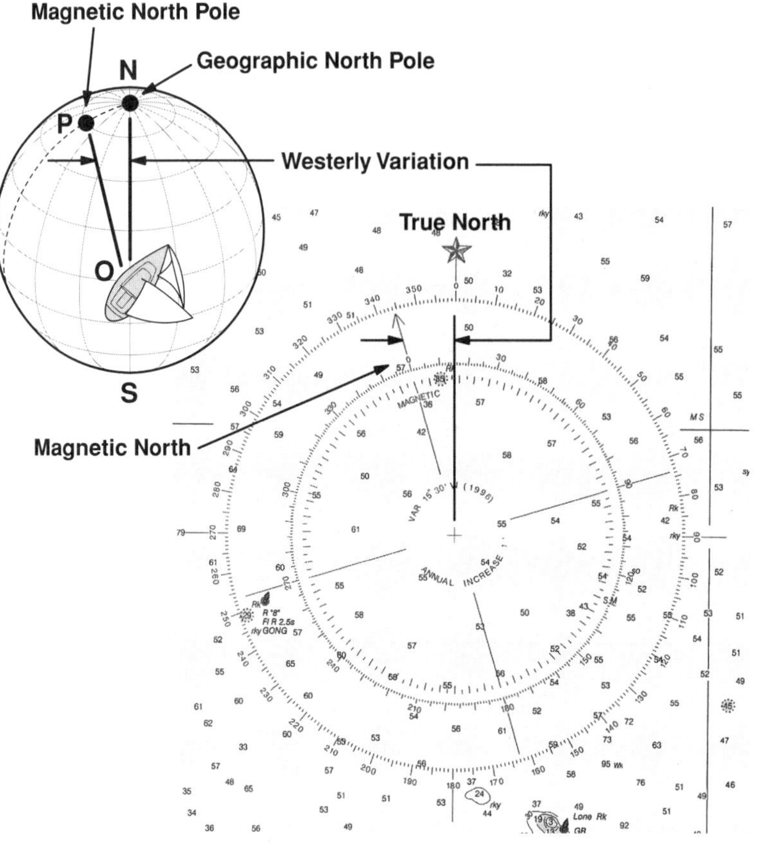

Figure 3-7. *Variation is the angular difference, measured in degrees, between the geographic and magnetic poles, modified by irregularities in the earth's magnetic field. In this figure, it is the angle NOP, formed by lines from the north geographic pole and the north magnetic pole to the observer. Anywhere on meridian segment PS (due south of the poles) the variation is 0°, while on meridian segment PN (between the two poles) it is 180° because the north magnetic pole is south of the north geographic pole. Due to inconsistencies in the earth's magnetic field, the line of zero variation is not actually straight. Variation is shown on charts, and is plotted on pilot charts, as isogonic (equal variation) lines.*

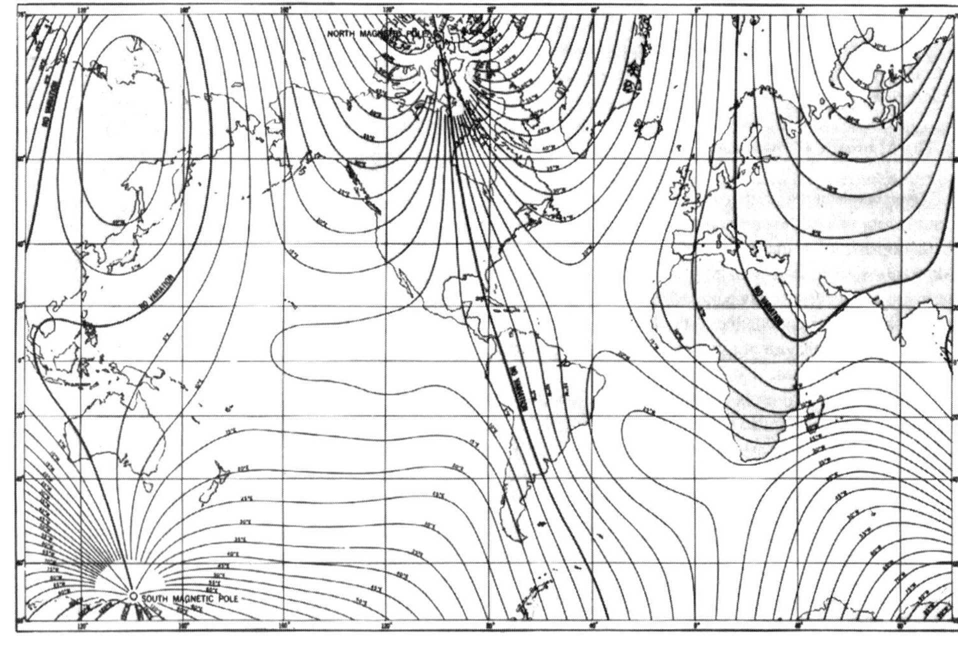

Figure 3-8. *Lines of equal magnetic variation are called isogonic lines, as shown on this world chart. Note the line of 0° variation, where no variation correction to the compass is necessary. It may still be necessary to correct for deviation. (Diagram by NIMA)*

variation—but the method proved inaccurate because of variation's non-uniform nature.

Most nautical charts show the amount of variation for the local area in the center of each compass rose. (See Chapter 1, "Basic Navigational Concepts," for further explanation of compass roses.) Some small-scale charts (showing large areas) show the isogonic lines themselves. By examining the chart, you can determine the amount of variation to apply when correcting or uncorrecting the compass (a process that is detailed in the last section of this chapter).

Variation not only changes from place to place, it also changes slowly over time in the same place because the magnetic poles migrate slowly. Although the variation in your harbor may be 5°W today, it is likely increasing or decreasing according to the changes in the earth's magnetism. These changes are small—on the order of a few minutes of angle each year—so you rarely include them in your corrections. The annual rate of change is given in the center of the compass rose, in parentheses after the variation. When a chart is more than a few years old, you may have to apply the annual change to the variation correction, but this is rarely necessary.

Variation is either east (E) or west (W). East of the line of 0° variation, the error is west; and west of that line, the error is east. This direction is indicated on the chart and is vitally important in correcting the compass.

Compass Error—Deviation

Deviation, the second source of compass error, is the result of magnetic influences aboard the vessel. On a boat with no such influences, the compass points unerringly to magnetic north. The average boat, however, carries many objects with magnetic properties—radio and stereo speakers, a steel or iron engine block, energized electrical wires, alternators, and generators, to name a few—that draw the magnetic compass away from magnetic north. Portable items such as tools and flashlights can also cause errors. Furthermore, the influence of these objects varies with the heading of the vessel because their direction from the compass changes as the vessel turns.

For this reason, the amount and direction of deviation changes with changes in the direction of the vessel. When you construct a graph of the deviation for a vessel by measuring the deviation on a number of different headings, the error will typically describe a sine wave about the 0° axis, as shown in Figure 3-9. That is, the error will be 0° when the vessel is headed north, will increase to a maximum of several degrees on an easterly heading, will decrease to 0° on a southerly heading, and will increase again to several degrees on a westerly heading—but in the opposite direction to the easterly error—and return to 0° at north.

If all of the error is in one direction (E or W), but varies according to the usual sine-wave pattern (that is, if the entire curve is above or below the 0° axis), this indicates a bias error, which is usually easy to correct. Inconsistencies in the sine-wave pattern itself are more difficult to compensate for.

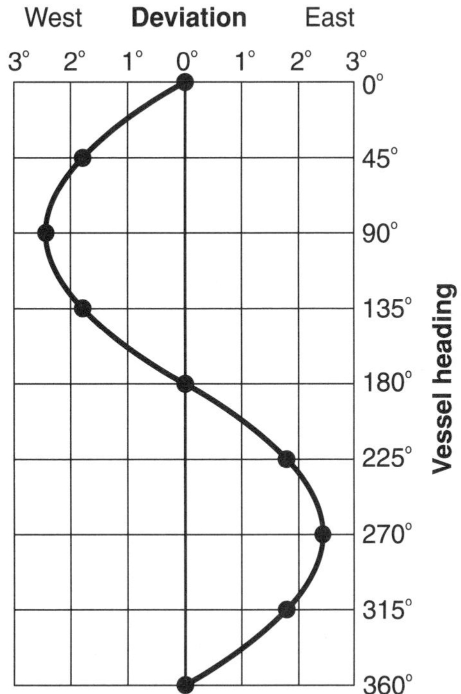

Figure 3-9. *Deviation theoretically occurs in the form of a sine wave about the 0° axis. It may be all in one direction, east or west, and may not be the same magnitude on either side of the 0° axis.*

Compass Error—Dip

The earth's magnetic force field is horizontal to the earth's surface at the *magnetic equator* and vertical at the *magnetic poles*. At any point in between, magnetic force is some combination of horizontal and vertical forces. The horizontal component is stronger the closer you are to the magnetic equator and the vertical component is stronger closer to the magnetic poles.

The horizontal component provides the useful force driving the magnetic compass, which is why magnetic compasses are inaccurate near the poles where they can't settle on a heading.

Some magnetic compasses have internal settings that compensate for slight irregularities in the force field in the areas of the world where the compass will principally be used. One setting applies for all installations in most of the northern hemisphere. South of the equator, a number of settings are necessary due to the peculiarities there of the earth's magnetic field.

In most cases, horizontal-dip compensation is a minor correction and a compass that is adjusted for the northern hemisphere is adequate for worldwide use. Total error from dip, except in polar areas, should be no more than a degree or so.

Compass Compensation

Compass compensation corrects deviation as much as possible and makes the compass easier to use. It is seldom possible to eliminate all deviation, but a good compass, well compensated, should have errors no more than 2° or 3° E and W, with the 0° line about in the middle of the sine wave. It is possible to do better than this, with errors of a degree or so—in such cases, the error can usually be ignored.

The process of compensation consists of maneuvering the vessel on a series of courses chosen with reference to a true direction. Variation is applied to convert the true direction to a magnetic direction. With that done, any difference between magnetic and compass direction can be attributed to deviation.

A professional *compass adjuster* usually uses the sun as a reference to true direction by computing its *azimuth* (direction in degrees from north). The adjuster makes a graph of azimuth changes for the duration of the adjustment process and refers to this graph to keep the reference to true north accurate.

The adjuster uses a *pelorus*—in essence, an adjustable compass card with a tall pin in the center—to measure the sun's azimuth. The pelorus may be equipped with a rotating ring on which two sight vanes are mounted (see Figure 3-10). When the instrument is properly aligned with the centerline of the boat, the pin casts a shadow that is related to the proper azimuth of the sun. An adjuster using this method can only work on sunny days. No sun, no reference to true north.

The pelorus was named for the man who served as navigator and pilot for Carthaginian leader Hannibal (247–183 B.C.). After crossing the Pyrenees and the Alps and fighting the Romans for some 15 years, Hannibal was forced to return to Carthage in 203 B.C. to defend it against Roman attacks. Pelorus successfully navigated Hannibal's forces across the Mediterranean Sea from Italy to Carthage.

An adjuster takes about an hour to compensate a small-craft compass. The job takes a lot less time and the results are more accurate when the person at the helm steers a steady course—usually a northerly course first, then around to south, then back to north, then east and west. On each cardinal course, the adjuster carefully turns one of the compensating magnets in the base of the compass bowl with a nonmagnetic screwdriver to eliminate all or part of the error noted between magnetic and compass directions.

A quick check of the intercardinal points (NE, SE, SW, and NW) provides enough information to make up a *deviation card* for a vessel. The card is a record of the deviation noted at the time of compensation that will be used when correcting the compass for navigation.

Deviation cards for large ships often list more points than those for small craft. Large ships may also carry a graph of the deviation so the exact deviation on any heading can be easily seen. Large ships, however, can often steer with an accuracy of 1°, or even ½° in good conditions, something a small craft can't do.

A compass should be rechecked when any equipment having a magnetic field is added to or removed from a vessel.

One of the biggest offenders in throwing the compass out of adjustment is a dinghy motor, which is often mounted on the stern pulpit during offshore passages. Also beware of audio speakers—for stereos, radios, and tape players—that are placed near the compass.

Figure 3-10. *A pelorus, named after Hannibal's navigator, is used by a compass adjuster to find true north. The adjuster precomputes azimuths of the sun for the time of the adjustment.*

You can easily check compass adjustment during normal operation by using any natural or man-made range to provide the needed reference to true direction. Look for ranges formed by any two charted objects. For this purpose, all objects that are charted are accurate enough to work, except those labeled "PA," which indicates "position approximate." Lights, towers, stacks, steeples, cupolas, tanks, and other objects can be lined up to serve as ranges. Tangents to distant points of land and charted mountain peaks are among the natural features that can be used for ranges.

Simply steer on the range and note the compass heading. Measure on the chart, or look up in the light list, the true direction of the range and correct for variation. This is what the compass *would* read if there were no deviation.

When deviation is present, the compass reading will differ from the magnetic bearing of the range. If the reading matches the amount of deviation listed on the deviation card or graph, deviation is unchanged and the compass need not be recompensated.

Adjusting the Small-Craft Compass

Although large ships and commercial vessels employ the services of a professional compass adjuster, with a little care and planning you can do the job well on your own boat.

To adjust the compass, you need two or more ranges that you can accurately measure on a chart and steer. Ideally, you should select a range at each cardinal point of the compass (N, S, E, and W). You may need to use just one range for north and south headings and another for east and west.

Although steering "over the shoulder" on reverse ranges is difficult, you can still get good results with teamwork between the persons observing and steering.

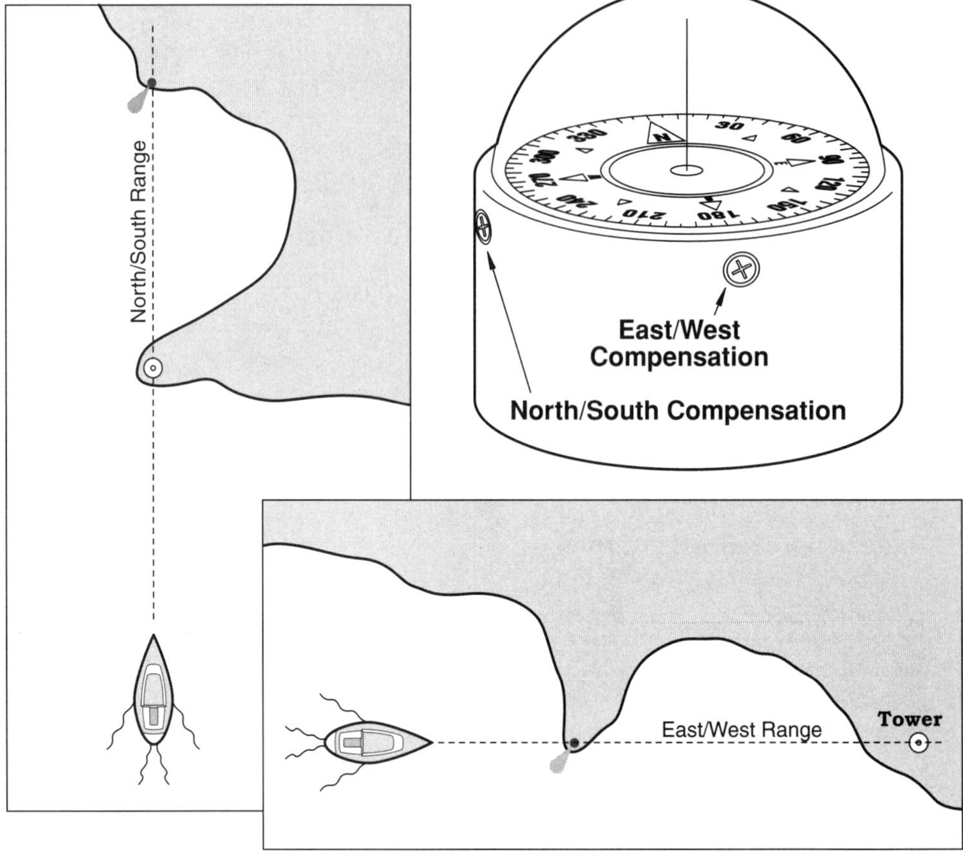

Figure 3-11. *Adjusting a small-craft compass requires selecting a range at each cardinal point of the compass (N, S, E, and W), or at least one N–S range and one E–W range and turning the compensation screws on your compass with something nonmagnetic, such as a plastic screwdriver.*

Before getting under way for compass adjustment, stow everything on the vessel in its proper place for sea. All tools and other iron or steel equipment should be stowed as far away as conveniently possible from the compass. (Note: Stainless steel, because of its molecular structure, is nonmagnetic, and may be placed near the compass if necessary.) As a general rule, anything that has its own magnetic field should not be placed within two feet of the compass. This list includes speakers (including those in radios), wiper motors, fans (including those inside electronic gear), tachometers, steering motors, and autopilots. All electronic gear normally activated while under way should be turned on during compensation because electrical fields can affect the compass. You may need two deviation tables if the effect on the compass of the radar, engine, or other equipment changes when they are energized. The changes in the radar's effect can be checked by running the ranges both with the radar on and off and comparing deviations.

Be sure that the lubber line is exactly in line with the centerline of the vessel. Compasses mounted off a vessel's centerline must be checked using carefully established reference points forward on the deck *the same distance from the vessel's centerline as the compass itself.*

All ranges used in compensation should be drawn accurately on the chart and the magnetic bearings calculated and written for each. Each should be within a few degrees of a cardinal compass point. You should also identify intercardinal ranges; these will be used to check the adjustment and fill out the deviation card.

The next step is to get under way at moderate speed and steer on the easterly range, observing the difference between the com-

North-south errors are adjusted with the athwartships adjusting screw; east-west errors, with the fore-and-aft screw. (See Figure 3-11.) A plastic screwdriver (supplied with many compasses) is available from electronics shops, but you can make a magnetically neutral screwdriver with any nonmagnetic material—even a small piece of hardwood. When turning the magnets, remember where they were at the outset, and turn them in increments of 1/4 or 1/8 of a turn. You can always turn them to their former position, and the compass will be no worse off than before. Corrections of 5° to 10° are commonly needed in newly installed compasses. Corrections of 15° or more are usually beyond the compensating capability of internal magnets and require supplementation by externally mounted magnets, with the internal magnets used for fine-tuning. This is best left to a professional adjuster.

pass heading and the charted magnetic bearing of the range (true bearing corrected for variation). Slowly turn the fore-and-aft adjusting screw with a nonmetallic screwdriver to remove all deviation error on this heading. Next, turn the vessel 180° and steady on the westerly course, using the reverse of the previous range or one ahead of you. Note the error and then turn the same adjusting screw to remove one-half of the error. Turn 180° again, back to the easterly course, and again remove one-half of the error. Return again to the opposite course and check the error. It should now be at its minimum possible for east-west headings. Record the error on each heading.

Next, steer on the north-south range(s) and follow the same steps, using the athwartships adjusting screw. Record the error on these headings.

If possible, check the error on intercardinal points (NE, SE, SW, and NW), using charted ranges. Note the error on each point and record it.

After you remove all possible error, make a graph or table that shows the error on the various headings. In constructing a graph you can fair in or curve the line gently from point to point, so that you can see at a glance the deviation on any heading—even those not steered on or checked. If you use a table you can interpolate between points to estimate missing numbers. A good interval between points on a small-craft deviation table is 30°.

Once the compass is adjusted, check it frequently by steering on known ranges and carefully looking for error. You can often readily do this during normal operation such as when transiting an entrance channel inbound and outbound. The compass should certainly be checked before any long voyage.

Correcting and Uncorrecting the Compass

You must correct and uncorrect the compass to be able to take accurate bearings and to steer accurate courses. Charts are drawn on the Mercator projection with a latitude-longitude grid referenced to true north. A bearing taken from a vessel's magnetic compass will differ from this by the net amount of any variation and deviation. To plot true bearings, both factors must be accounted for.

It is perfectly acceptable to plot magnetic bearings using the magnetic compass readings given on the inner circle of a compass rose, as shown in Figure 3-12. This eliminates the need to correct for variation, but deviation still must be accounted for.

The best way to sort out compass-correction problems is to set up a small table with the following columns: compass, deviation, magnetic, variation, true, or C, D, M, V, T. Use the mnemonic *Can Dead Men Vote Twice?* to help you.

Remember that a compass error has an amount and a direction. The direction will be either east or west depending on whether the compass needle points to the east or west of where it should. A simple rule to determine whether an error is east or west is *Com-*

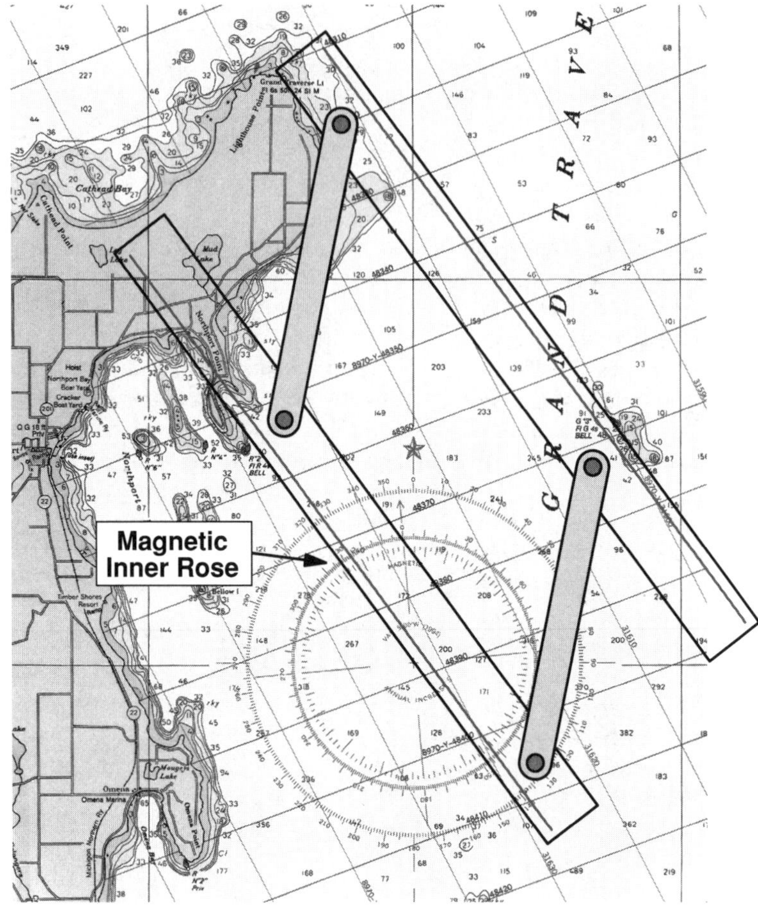

Figure 3-12. *Compass roses have true bearings on the outer ring and magnetic bearings on the inner ring. Magnetic bearings taken for fixes can be plotted directly on the chart using the inner ring. The modern compass rose is a plain representation of the ancient rose, a fanciful and artistic work that probably led to its name.*

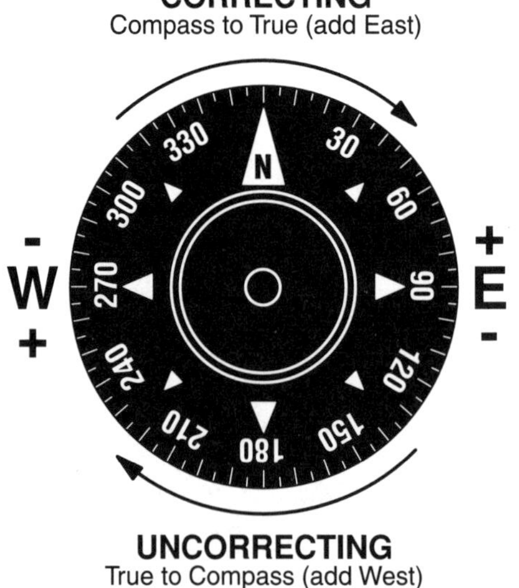

Figure 3-13. *The navigator always knows three of the five elements of a compass problem: variation from the chart, deviation from the deviation card, and compass, true or magnetic bearing. From these, the remaining two can always be determined. The rule is* "correcting add east," *which reminds us that we must add easterly errors and subtract westerly ones when correcting, and do the opposite when uncorrecting.*

pass Least, Error East; Compass Best, Error West. That is, if the compass bearing is less than the true or magnetic, the error is easterly. If the compass bearing is more, the error is westerly.

In these problems, there are always three knowns and two unknowns. You know (1) variation (from the chart's compass rose); (2) deviation (from the vessel's heading and the deviation table or card); and (3) the compass or true direction. From these, you can always determine the unknown directions. If you want to convert a compass direction to true for the purpose of plotting a bearing for a position fix, then the compass is being *corrected.* If, on the other hand, you start with a true bearing taken from the chart and want to convert it to a compass bearing, the compass is being *uncorrected.*

CORRECTING

	Compass		Deviation		Magnetic		Variation		True
Easterly Variation --------►	90°	+	2°E	=	092°	+	8°E	=	100°
Westerly Variation --------►	90°	+	2°E	=	092°	-	8°W	=	084°

UNCORRECTING

	True		Variation		Magnetic		Deviation		Compass
Easterly Variation -------►	110°	-	8°E	=	102°	-	2°E	=	100°
Westerly Variation -------►	110°	+	15°W	=	125°	-	2°E	=	122°

Figure 3-14. *In this example of correcting a compass bearing, the compass bearing is 090°, the deviation is 2° E, and the variation 8° E. Adding the deviation ("correcting add east") to compass bearing yields the magnetic bearing, and adding variation to this yields the true bearing. The magnetic bearing can be plotted directly on the chart using the magnetic (inner) compass rose.*

The table in Figure 3-14 works for both types of problems.

With this table, use the rule: *Correcting Add East*. That is, when correcting the compass, add easterly errors and subtract westerly ones. When uncorrecting, do the opposite.

If you want to convert a bearing of an object taken with your magnetic compass to a true bearing to plot on the chart, fill in the table with the compass bearing, the variation, and the deviation—the three "knowns." Applying the deviation error to the compass bearing yields the magnetic bearing; applying variation to the just-found magnetic bearing yields the true bearing. (See Figure 3-14.)

When uncorrecting, do the opposite. If you want to convert a true bearing from the chart to a compass bearing to steer by, simply fill in the true bearing, the variation, and the deviation, apply the corrections, and you have an "uncorrected" bearing to steer. The mnemonics *True Virgins Make Dull Companions* or *TeleVision Makes Dull Children* can help you remember the steps.

If you apply the algebraic sum of both variation and deviation (in this case, (+) 8° E + (+) 2° E = 10° E), the conversion can be done in a single operation. Note that variation and deviation can partially or fully cancel each other out. For example, if deviation is 3° E in an area where the variation is 3° W, the correction is zero [(+) 3° E + (–) 3° W = 0°], and the compass actually reads true on that heading.

Also note that, within a local area, variation doesn't change appreciably. When you get into the habit of applying the same variation in a local area, solving the compass-correcting problems becomes easier.

Deviation is another matter. Because it changes with the heading of your vessel, the correction will be different with each course, which is why we try to minimize deviation by compensating the compass. It is much easier to add or subtract 1 or 2 degrees than

Figure 3-15. *Use the mnemonic* Can Dead Men Vote Twice? *to help you sort out compass-correction problems.*

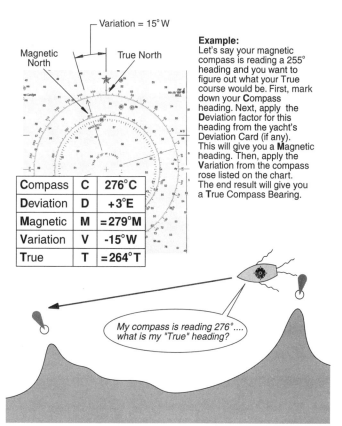

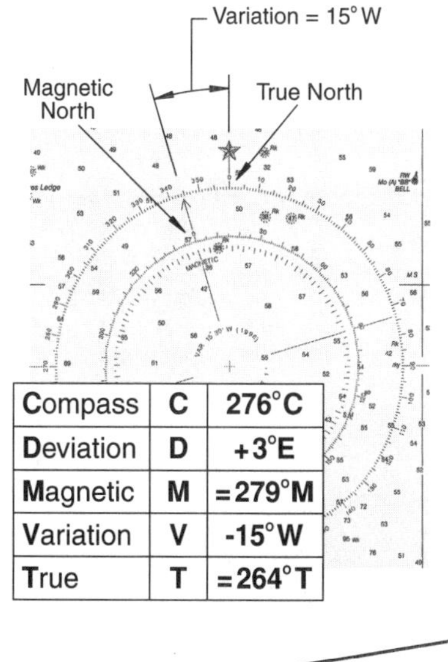

Variation = 15° W
Magnetic North
True North
Compass | C | 276°C
Deviation | D | +3°E
Magnetic | M | =279°M
Variation | V | -15°W
True | T | =264°T

Example:
Let's say your magnetic compass is reading a 255° heading and you want to figure out what your True course would be. First, mark down your **C**ompass heading. Next, apply the **D**eviation factor for this heading from the yacht's Deviation Card (if any). This will give you a **M**agnetic heading. Then, apply the **V**ariation from the compass rose listed on the chart. The end result will give you a **T**rue Compass Bearing.

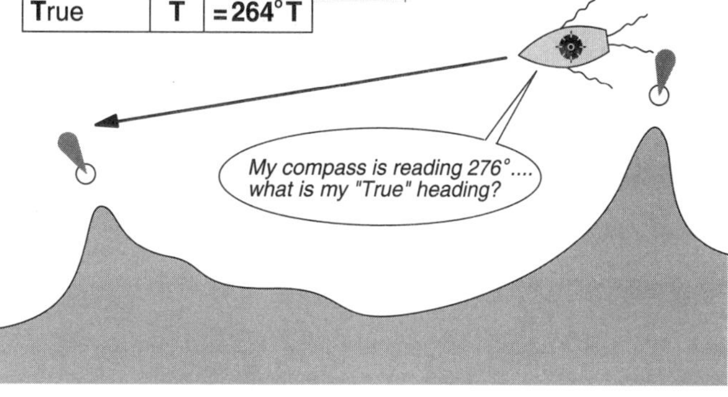

My compass is reading 276°.... what is my "True" heading?

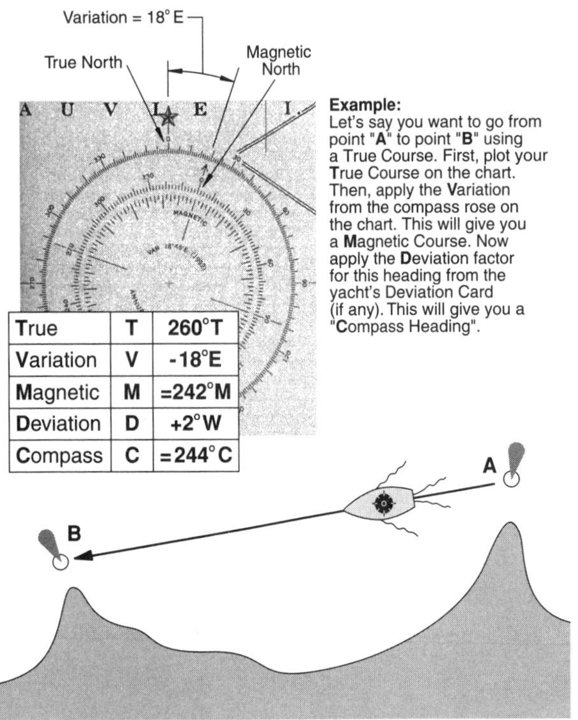

Variation = 18° E
True North
Magnetic North
Example:
Let's say you want to go from point "A" to point "B" using a True Course. First, plot your True Course on the chart. Then, apply the Variation from the compass rose on the chart. This will give you a Magnetic Course. Now apply the Deviation factor for this heading from the yacht's Deviation Card (if any). This will give you a "Compass Heading".
True T 260°T
Variation V -18°E
Magnetic M =242°M
Deviation D +2°W
Compass C =244°C
A
B

Figure 3-16. *Use the mnemonics* True Virgins Make Dull Companions *or* TeleVision Makes Dull Children *to figure a compass heading from a true course.*

10 or 15 each time we do a compass problem. And, with luck, deviation can be reduced to only a degree or less, at which point it can often be ignored, allowing the plotting of bearings directly from the compass to the chart using the magnetic compass rose.

Many small-craft navigators free themselves from the use of an awkwardly placed fixed compass and use a hand-bearing compass for taking bearings. Figures 3-17 and 3-18 show two different styles of hand-bearing compasses. Their advantage lies in their portability, freedom (in most locations on the boat) from effects of deviation, and ease of use.

No matter which type of compass you choose, the accuracy of your results will depend to a great extent on its quality. The compass is the primary navigational tool. Try not to make *any* compromises regarding its quality and suitability. You can get professional advice about compasses from yacht designers, experienced navigators, and from compass manufacturers. Don't make any decisions about buying a compass until you have thoroughly studied the types available and assessed the accuracy required for navigation in your area.

Figure 3-17. *This small puck-style hand-bearing compass can be easily worn around your neck on a lanyard, which makes it handy not only for taking bearings but for checking on the progress of competitors during racing. (Courtesy of Celestaire)*

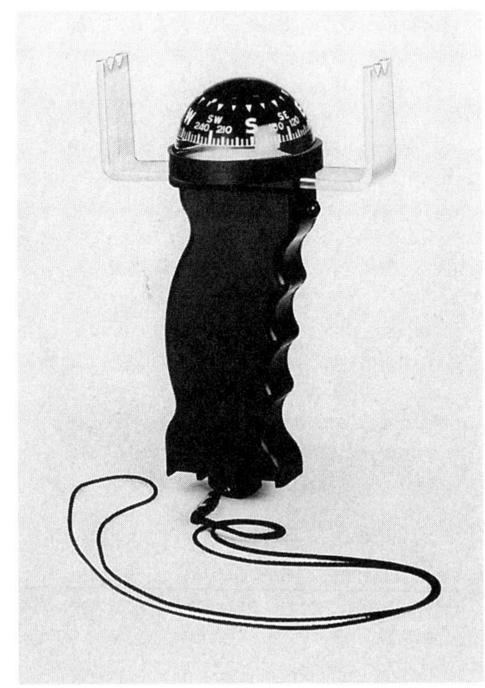

Figure 3-18. *This model of a hand-bearing compass has an optional light for use at night. It also floats and has a neck lanyard. (Courtesy of Celestaire)*

CHAPTER FOUR

Tides

THE GRAVITATIONAL ATTRACTION OF the moon and sun, along with the centrifugal force caused by the off-center revolution of the earth-moon system, causes the rise and fall of the sea, called *tides*. The sea, being free to flow across the surface of the earth, responds to these forces. The moon contributes most of this force, but the sun's contribution—which is about 46 percent of the moon's—makes it a significant factor as well.

This chapter examines the forces that create tides and their effect on navigation. You will learn how to predict tides and use them to advantage instead of fighting them.

The General Nature of Tides

Tides can either help or hurt the mariner. A high tide may allow access to a harbor or cruising area that is not accessible at low tide, as shown in Figure 4-1. The currents caused by tidal flows can increase or decrease a vessel's speed over the ground, resulting in much faster or slower passages than planned. For example, if a boat makes six knots, an adverse current of only two knots will reduce the boat's speed over the ground by one-third. The lost speed can cause missed schedules, delays in a passage, or the possibility of getting caught out after dark in a strange and busy harbor. In fact, such currents can exceed the cruising speed of many small craft, thereby preventing passage altogether.

The vertical rise and fall of water is called the *tide;* the horizontal movement of water caused by tidal flow is called *tidal current.* To keep straight these two often confused and misused terms, it helps to remember that tides rise and fall, and currents *flood* and *ebb.*

As a navigator, you will want to know the time and height of any tides, as well as the direction and speed of the tidal current. These numbers are found in tables that we will examine later in this chapter. Know the potential impact of tides and tidal current on any voyage you plan, however long or short. A trip can be timed to work with the current instead of against it.

That said, predicting water levels and currents can be a tricky business. The rise and

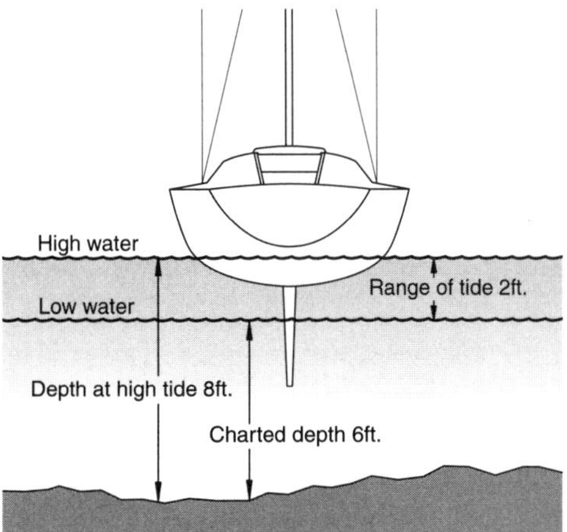

Figure 4-1. *Low tide levels may prevent certain vessels from entering a harbor or using an anchorage, or allow entry only at certain times. A tide of only a foot or two may be as important to the small-boat navigator as to the captain of a supertanker.*

fall of the tide is superimposed on changes in water level caused by other factors such as winds, freshets, and seiches. Strong winds can flush water to the leeward side of a shallow bay and alter water depths by several feet. A *freshet* is a sudden rise in water level due to heavy rain or snowmelt upstream; a *seiche* is a very sudden rise and fall in water level (occurring within a few minutes), probably caused by atmospheric pressure changes, though the event is not well understood.

We know that the earth attracts the moon with its gravity—otherwise, the moon would not stay in orbit around the earth. We also know that the moon attracts the earth, even though its attraction is one-sixth as great because it's about one-sixth the mass of the earth. It must be true, then, that in some small way the earth is revolving around the moon. In fact, the earth and the moon revolve together around a common point known as the earth-moon *barycenter*. The barycenter is located inside the earth, about 74/100 of the distance from the center of the earth to its surface. The sun-earth-moon system also has a barycenter, which is far inside the surface of the sun and of no consequence to the tides on earth. (See Figure 4-2.)

This revolution around a point that is not at the center of the earth causes the earth to wobble slightly as it moves in its orbit around the sun. Though we don't see the wobble, we do see the result of it—the centrifugal force imparted by the off-center rotation causes the tides on the side of the earth opposite the moon.

If the moon's gravitational attractive force were the only force responsible for tides, there would be a high tide on the side of the earth facing the moon, but not on the opposite side. But, of course, there is a high tide on the opposite side (caused by centrifugal force) and, just as we would expect, it is not as high as the tide on the moon's side.

If the whole earth were covered with water, the theoretical tides would measure about 1 meter. You will learn later in this chapter why tides of 30 or more feet are common in many areas.

Specific Tidal Causes

You can understand tides without engaging in complex mathematical exercises by starting with some basic terms and assumptions. One by one, this chapter examines all of the factors that cause tides, with each effect superimposed on the previous ones.

First, it is important to understand the orbits of the moon and earth. The moon orbits the earth once every 24 hours and 50 minutes, which is why it rises almost an hour later each night. The point directly beneath the moon is called the *sublunar point,* and the point exactly opposite on the earth is the *antipode*. To simplify things, assume that the moon is the only cause of tides (which it isn't), and that it's always over the equator (which it isn't). In this scenario, a high tide would occur when the moon is overhead and again when it is on the opposite side of the earth from us, 12 hours and 25 minutes later. In between high tides, there would be low tides, also 12 hours and 25 minutes apart.

The moon, however, is not the only body that causes tides. The sun's effect is 46 per-

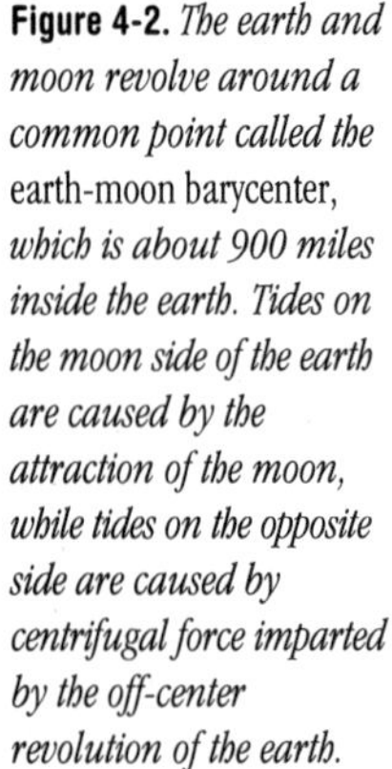

Figure 4-2. *The earth and moon revolve around a common point called the* earth-moon barycenter, *which is about 900 miles inside the earth. Tides on the moon side of the earth are caused by the attraction of the moon, while tides on the opposite side are caused by centrifugal force imparted by the off-center revolution of the earth.*

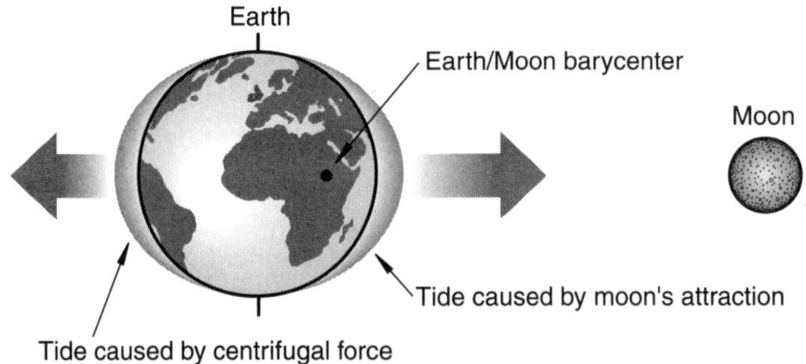

cent of the moon's, and the earth orbits the sun every 24 hours—not every 24 hours and 50 minutes. Imagine, for a moment, that the earth had no moon and that the sun caused all tides. Further, assume that the sun was always over the earth's equator. (If that were true, we would have no change of seasons on earth.) A high tide would occur every 12 hours, with the one on the sunny side of the earth slightly higher than the one on the opposite, or dark, side. In between, there would be a low tide every 12 hours. All tides would be at the same time every day: high at noon, low at sunset, high at midnight, low at dawn.

In the real world, though, the sun and moon are out of phase with each other by that 50 minute difference in the orbit of the moon and the rotational period of the earth. When the sun and moon form a nearly straight line with the earth, their effects are added together; when they are at right angles to the earth, the moon's effects are decreased by the sun's. This complicates tidal predictions, but wait—it gets even more complicated.

Both scenarios assume that the sun and moon were always over the equator. They aren't. Each moves north and south of the equator by an amount that changes continuously over time. This distance from the equator is called declination. The moon's declination ranges from about 23°N to 23°S (as shown in Figure 4-3). The tides tend to follow this declination change, moving with the moon as it slowly travels north and south in the sky, causing slight changes in tidal heights and current strengths. This movement also affects the earth-moon barycenter, which in turn affects tides at the antipodes.

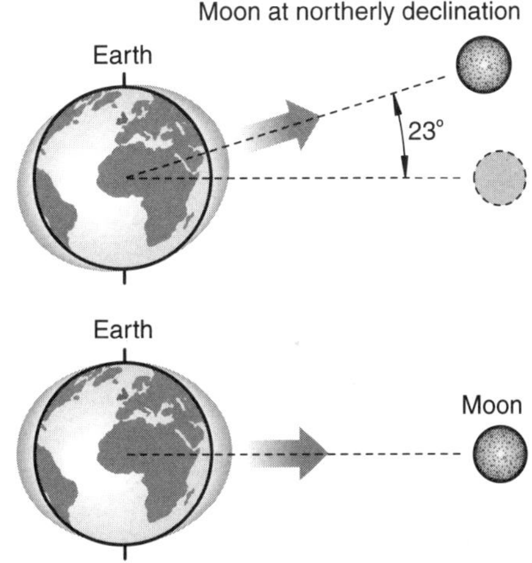

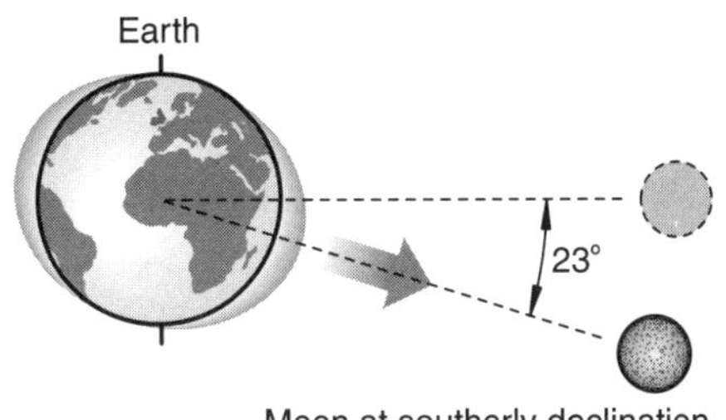

Figure 4-3. *Tidal bulges follow the movement of the moon north and south of the equator. The barycenter is also affected by these changes in the moon's declination, causing the tides at the antipode to react as well.*

The sun's changing declination not only causes seasonal climactic changes, it also adds or subtracts from the moon's tidal effects. As the sun changes declination, moving north and south of the equator, the tides caused by its gravitational attraction tend to follow it. (See Figure 4-4.)

Features of Tides

The effects on tide of the factors discussed above are both real and visible. When the

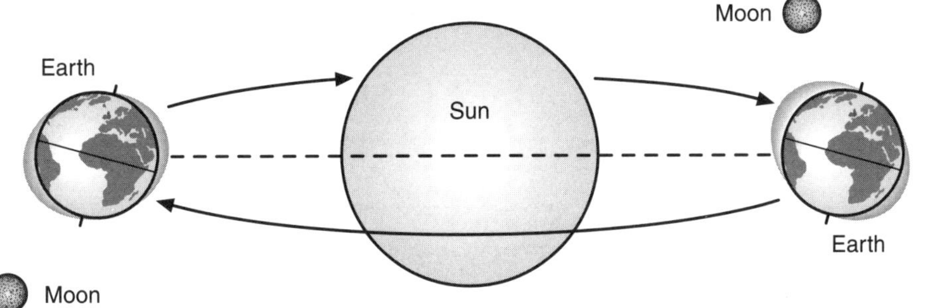

Figure 4-4. *The sun changes declination because the earth's axis is tilted, thereby giving us not only changes in seasons, but also seasonal variations in the tides, which are combined with the effects of the moon's changes in declination.*

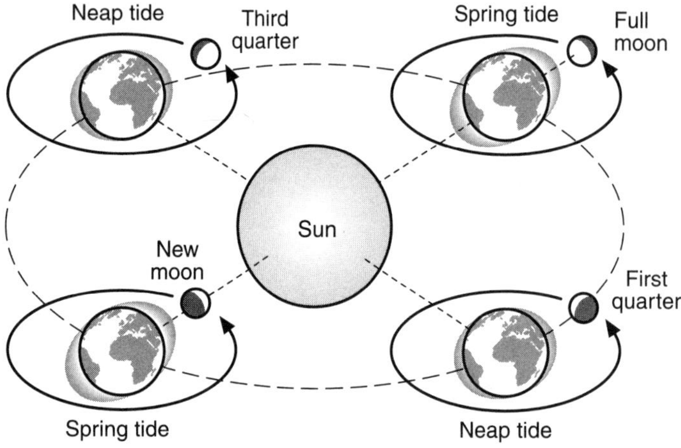

Figure 4-5. *When the moon and sun are in alignment their effects are additive. Such alignment occurs during new and full moons and causes* spring tides. *When they are at a 90° angle with the earth their effects are subtractive. This occurs during first and last quarter moons and causes* neap tides.

moon is full or new, you can expect to see higher and lower tides than normal—these tides are called spring tides. At these times, the earth, moon, and sun are in line (a condition known as *syzygy*) and their effects are additive. During first quarter and last quarter moons, when the earth and moon form a 90° angle with the earth, you can expect more moderate tides. These tides are called *neap tides*. (See Figure 4-5.)

The difference between high and low tide at any place is called the *range of the tide*. The incoming tide is the *flood,* and the outgoing tide is the *ebb*. At high and low tide, the water stops rising or falling for a period of time known as the *stand of the tide*.

Tide does not rise and fall at a constant rate. From low water, the tide rises slowly at first, increasing in rate until about three hours after low water. The rate of rise then slows until high water is reached. The ebb tide follows the same pattern. The following table shows the change in the tidal rate during one-half of a cycle. Rising and falling cycles are theoretically the same, but local geographic or environmental factors may modify them.

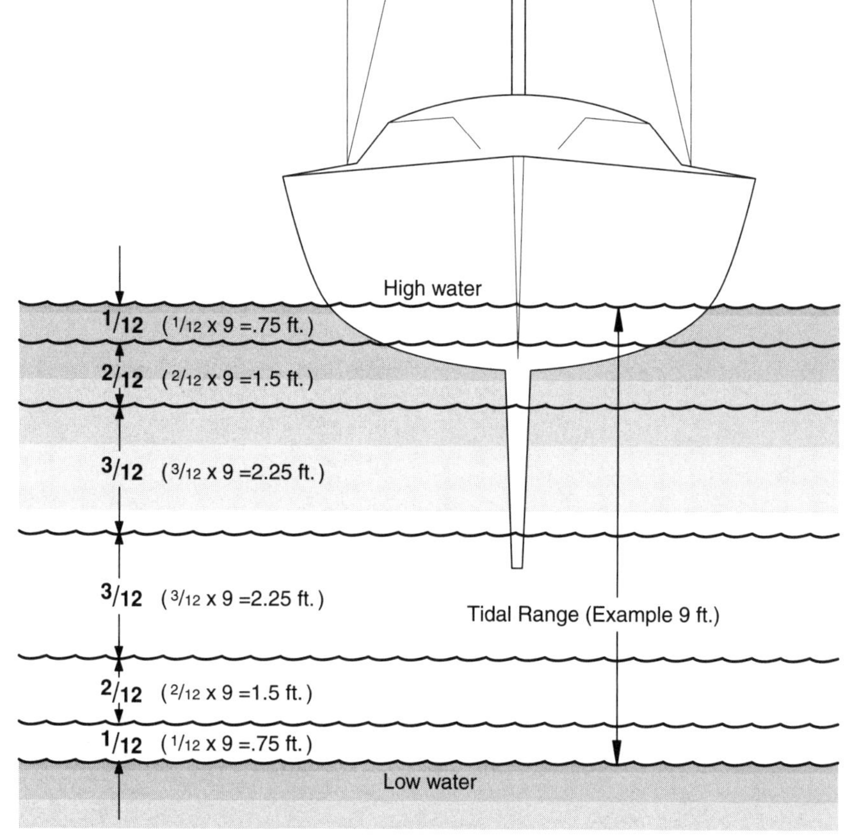

Figure 4-6. *A semidiurnal tide features two high waters each day of about equal height, and two low waters, also about equal. The rule of twelfths states that the tide will fall (or rise) a predictable amount of its range every hour: one-twelfth the first hour, two-twelfths the second hour, three-twelfths the third; then it will taper off (or increase) in mirror image for the final three hours.*

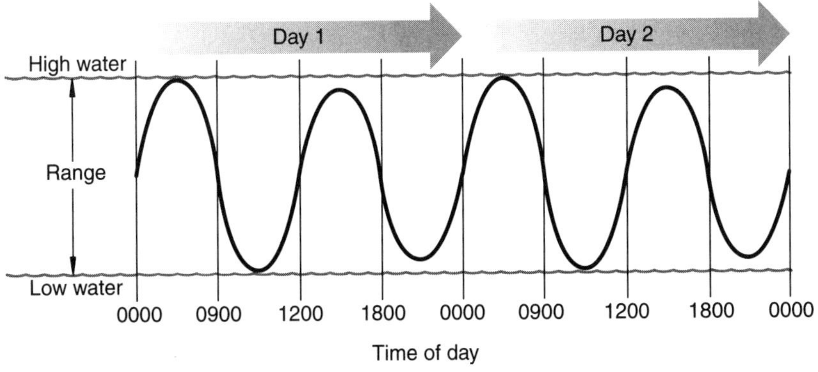

Figure 4-7. *A* semidiurnal tide *normally has two highs and two lows during a calendar day. Note that one of the highs and lows each day is a little greater than the other; this is the moon-caused tide. The lower tide is the centrifugal-force-caused tide on the side of the earth opposite the moon.*

Rate of Tidal Rise and Fall

Hours After High or Low Water	Amount of Change as Fraction of Total Range
one	1/12
two	2/12
three	3/12
four	3/12
five	2/12
six	1/12

From this table, it is easy to compute the height of tide at any time if you know the time of high or low water and the amount of rise or fall.

Types of Tides

Water, when confined to a space and in motion, has a natural period of oscillation that depends on the shape and dimensions of the space. For example, water in a small bowl will oscillate with a shorter period than water in a larger one. Ocean basins act like giant bowls; each has its own period of oscillation. Furthermore, each sea, bay, sound, and strait modifies the characteristics of the larger ocean basin of which it is a part. Thus, virtually every place on earth has a tidal pattern that is unlike any other. In fact, tides in locations only a few miles apart may differ radically in both time and range.

Some basins have sizes and shapes that are more responsive to the moon's forces; others respond more to the sun's forces; some respond equally to both. Tides are classified according to their oscillatory period as *semidiurnal, diurnal,* or *mixed.*

- In a ***semidiurnal tide*** there are two high and two low waters daily. Differences between successive highs and lows are relatively small, although the range of the tide may be large. Tides on the eastern seaboard of North America are of this type. (See Figure 4-7.)
- In a ***diurnal tide*** there is only one high and one low water each day, as shown in Figure 4-8. Tides along the northern Gulf of Mexico are of this type.
- A ***mixed tide*** has both diurnal and semidiurnal characteristics. Usually it alternates between both types, with a period in between combining the two, as depicted in Figure 4-9.

Some special tides are caused by unusual geographic configurations that accentuate movement of water. In certain areas the flood tide races inland in a wave called a tidal bore. Tidal bores several feet high are common in

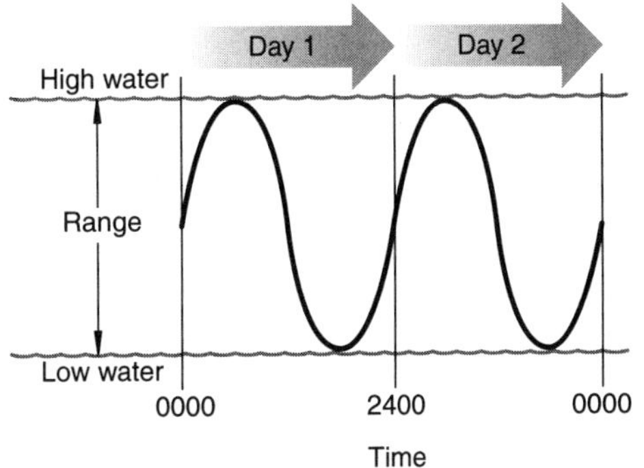

Figure 4.8. *A* diurnal tide *has only one high and one low water each day. In the U.S., diurnal tides are found along the northern shore of the Gulf of Mexico.*

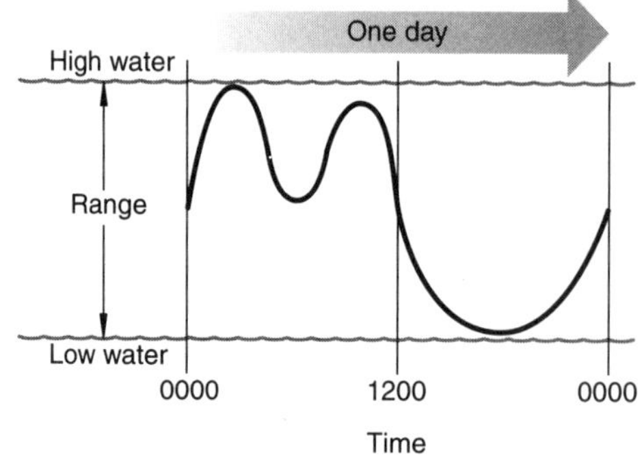

Figure 4-9. *A* mixed tide *has one high and one low daily, except on certain days of the month when it has two of each. In between there is a combination of the two types. Seattle, Washington, has a mixed tide, often characterized by a double high and a single low tide in one day.*

the Petitcodiac River in the Bay of Fundy (Figure 4-10), the mouth of the Amazon River, Turnagain Arm in Alaska (Figure 4-11), and the Tsientang Kaing in China.

Other places experience the unusual *double-high water* (Southampton, England) or a *double-low water* (Hoek van Holland) where tide reaches its normal high (or low point) and recedes only slightly before rising or falling again. These events are all a result of the peculiar characteristics of the basins in which they occur.

Tidal Datums

A *datum* is a reference point, from which we measure other points. A *tidal datum* is a vertical datum that is used to measure soundings (depths of water) and heights of objects. Every chart identifies the tidal datum that indicates the reference points used to measure the depths and heights on that particular chart.

Soundings are based on an average low tide, so even at low tide, there will be at least as much water as indicated on the chart. At a higher tide level, of course, there will be even more water. Conversely, heights of fixed objects, such as bridges and overhead cables, are referenced to an average high tide, so you

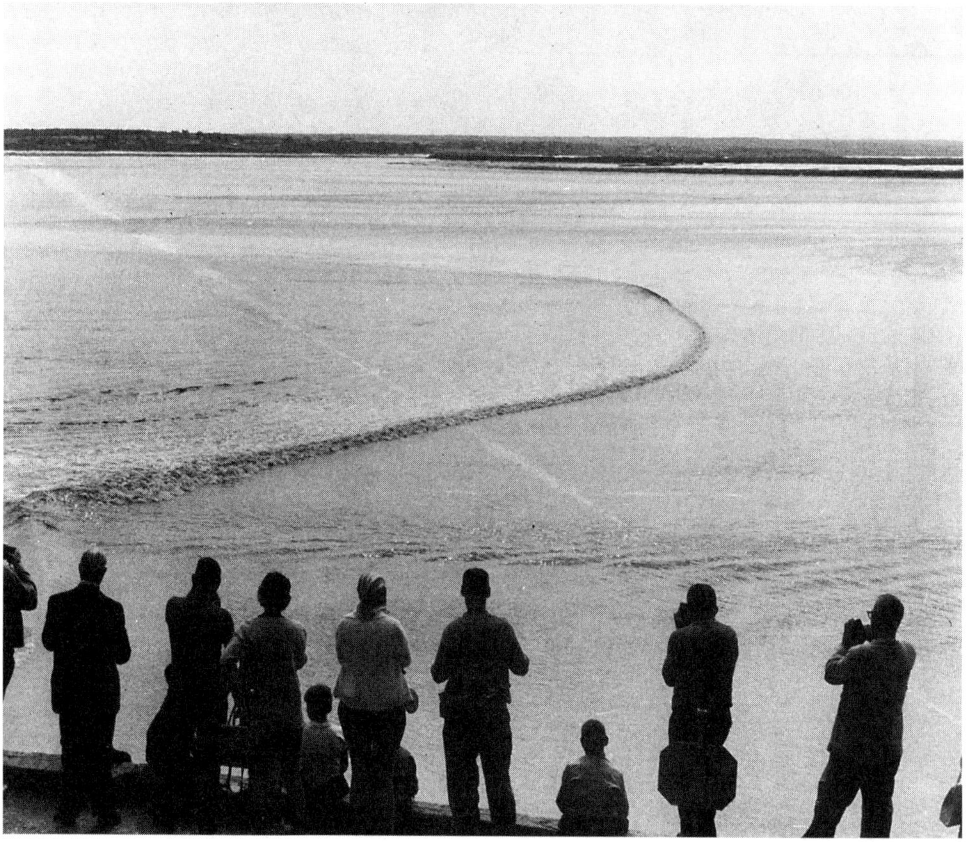

Figure 4-10. *The* tidal bore *in the Bay of Fundy is a tourist attraction that draws thousands of people each year. (NOAA photograph)*

Figure 4-11. *This* tidal bore *in Turnagain Arm, Alaska, is dangerous to small craft. If you must meet a tidal bore at all, do so head-on at slow speed. Using the* Tide Tables *will help avoid them. (Photograph courtesy of NOAA)*

can be assured that there is at least as much clearance as stated on the chart. At a lower tide level, of course, there will be even more clearance.

The different kinds of averages used for datums are given below.

For low tides:

Mean low water—The average of all low tides at a given place. About half of the low tides are below this point; about half are above.

Mean low water springs—The average of all spring low tides. Because spring tides are lower than others, this is a lower, and therefore safer, datum for the mariner.

Mean lower low water—The average of the lower of the two low waters each day (the one caused by gravitational, not centrifugal, force).

Mean lower low water springs—The average of all the lower of the two low waters occurring on the spring tides. This is the lowest datum in common use.

For high tides:

Mean high water—The average of all high tides at a given place. About half of the high tides are below this point; about half are above.

Mean high water springs—The average of all spring high tides.

Mean higher high water—The average of the higher of the two high waters each day (the one caused by gravitational, not centrifugal, force).

Mean higher high water springs—The average of all the higher of the two high waters occurring on the spring tides. This is the highest datum in common use.

There may be little relationship between the range of tide and the resulting tidal current. A large range doesn't necessarily indicate

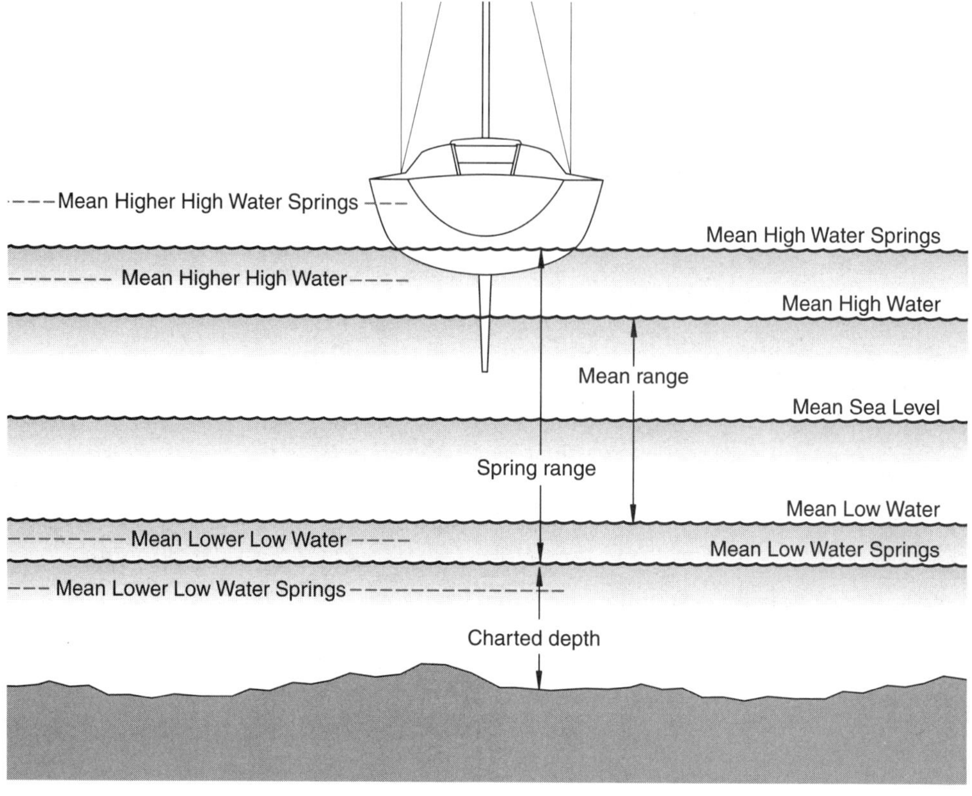

Figure 4-12. *The* range of tide *is the distance between high and low waters. Mean sea level is the average of all tides, high and low. Chart sounding datum is often Mean Low Water Springs, which is the average of all low waters at the time of spring tides. Very few tides are below this level.*

a strong current, nor does a small range a weak one. Some very strong tidal currents are found in areas with little range, and vice versa. You should be aware of the tidal range so you can arrange mooring lines and allow for adequate scope for your anchor rode. With a low range of tide—a couple of feet—it is relatively easy to moor to a wharf or pier. But with a high range—10 feet or more—it may be difficult to moor in unless floating docks are provided or the lines tended continuously during the tidal cycle.

Predicting Tides

Tide computations take account of all the variables in the orbital cycles of the earth, moon, and sun. The moon and sun appear in the same relative positions in the sky only once every 18.6 years. This phenomenon, the *Metonic Cycle,* is named after Meton, the fifth-century B.C. Athenian astronomer who discovered it.

To account for all the variables that can occur during the Metonic Cycle, tides are predicted from observations made during a selected 19-year period called the *National Tidal Datum Epoch*. The current epoch runs from 1960 to 1978. Though a new epoch is introduced every 20 years or so, tide predictions are little affected by the changeover. Modifications in the formulas used for predictions are due mostly to the availability of better data, not to changes in the forces affecting tides.

Tide predictions were once computed by large, complicated mechanical machines, as shown in Figure 4-13, but in 1966 predictions were computerized. Today, a relatively simple program can run tidal predictions on a home computer.

In the United States, although the *tide predictions* are calculated by the National Ocean Service of NOAA, the actual books—*Tide Tables*—are published by private companies and are available through marine suppliers.

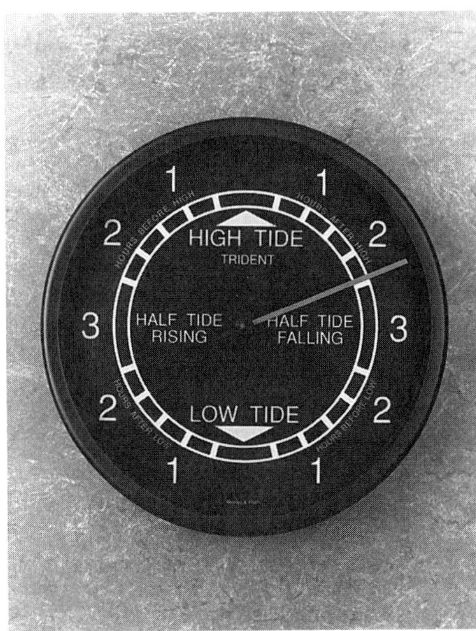

Figure 4-13 (left). *This intricate tide-predicting machine was used by NOAA and its predecessor agencies to predict tides for more than 50 years. It has been replaced by a computer program. The gears, pulleys, and wheels drive the dials and styluses on the near end of the device that draw graphs of tides. (NOAA photograph)*

Figure 4-14 (right). *A tide clock is designed to move with the moon's orbital cycle and indicates the state of normal semidiurnal tides. (Photograph courtesy Weems and Plath)*

To find the tide at a given place you must first ascertain if that place is a *reference* or a *subordinate station*. (A book that listed the tides for every single location would be massive.) Tides are listed in full for the reference stations only. For subordinate stations, only the differences from the time at the reference station are listed. To find the predicted tides for a reference station, all you have to do is look up that station. To find the tides at a subordinate station, first look up the time difference for the subordinate station and add or subtract it from the time given at the reference station. To calculate times at locations between subordinate stations, you'll have to interpolate. A rough mental interpolation is almost always adequate.

Many computer software programs are now available, as are dedicated tidal computers or *tide clocks*. These programs are generally very convenient to use and give not only the times of high and low, but also the level at any given time, which otherwise must be done by calculation using the tables. Most tide prediction programs also graph the tidal information so that the tide at any time can be quickly seen.

Because the tide tables are computed for an average low water and not the lowest water ever, it follows that a few tides will be below the chosen average. These are listed as *negative tides* and their values must be subtracted from the charted depths to find the depth of water available.

A tide clock is an ordinary clock that is set to the moon's orbital cycle instead of the earth's rotational cycle. Of course, it is not useful in areas with mixed or diurnal tides.

Tidal Currents

The horizontal movement of water is called *current*, and that part of the current caused by tidal forces is called *tidal current*. Other currents are caused by river flows, global wind patterns, or local weather; tidal currents are superimposed on these.

Tidal currents may be *bidirectional* (back and forth) or *rotary*. A bidirectional current flows in alternate directions—one way on the flood and the opposite way on the ebb. Such currents are common in narrow harbors, rivers, straits, and estuaries. A rotary current is usually found in open bays and sounds with wide entrances to the ocean; it flows continuously and gradually changes direction.

Like tides, tidal currents may be semidiurnal, diurnal, or mixed, but they are most often semidiurnal. The strength of tidal currents is often inversely related to the range of tide. Thus, in Maine, where tidal ranges are large, currents are often weak; in Nantucket Sound, where tide ranges are relatively small, currents are strong.

In shallow estuaries, tidal current is usually strongest in the deepest water. If a man-made channel is cut through a shallow area, the strongest current will be found in it. A skillful navigator will know this and may choose to stay out of a channel in an adverse current or in it during a favorable one. Also, the current usually turns first near the shore of an estuary and up to an hour later in the middle.

Tidal current may not be consistent from the top to the bottom of the water. The flood tide may begin flowing into a bay along the sea bottom before the ebb current has subsided at the surface. Flood current may also underride a surface current caused by river runoff or freshet. Large ships that take up much of the water column in shallow areas may feel this effect, but it is seldom noticed on small craft.

Tidal currents are predictable and their strengths and directions are listed in *Tidal Current Tables* that are available from marine suppliers. The format, fully explained in each volume, is similar to the one used for the *Tide Tables*. Instead of heights, though, the strength and direction of tidal currents are given for different locations. As with tidal heights, many events—droughts, floods, freshets, and meteorological conditions—can dramatically affect tidal currents. The predictions in the tables are for average conditions and it is up to you to apply corrections for these conditions based on your experience and common sense.

Current diagrams are graphical representations of the current in certain major harbors of the United States. *Tidal Current Charts* are simplified charts of certain busy harbors that use *current arrows* to show the direction of the current for different locations and times. Diagrams and charts are both important to small craft operating in waters with strong tidal flow. The timing of tidal currents are not related to the rise and fall in a universal pattern. For example, the tide may begin its vertical rise in a river mouth while the current continues to ebb. Also, tidal effects may be felt far upstream in rivers, well beyond the reach of salt water. Today, research is being conducted that may eventually add a real-time component to tide and current predictions from on-site water level and meteorological observations.

Chapter Five

Dead Reckoning

DEAD RECKONING IS ONE of the oldest skills used in navigation and is still the most fundamental one. When you plot a dead reckoning (DR) position you're using a technique familiar to Captains Cook, Columbus, Magellan, and thousands of others who navigated before recorded history. Even the equipment has changed very little over the centuries.

This chapter explores the purposes and importance of dead reckoning and the procedures used to properly perform this vital navigational function.

Purposes of Dead Reckoning

Dead reckoning is used to predict future positions and times of arrival by projecting courses and speeds into the future. Use of dead reckoning can also predict the expected times of sighting navigation lights and making landfalls, in determining a current's set and drift, and in celestial observations for determining times of sunrise and sunset.

For example, using dead reckoning you can estimate the time of arrival at a port and determine the tides there at that time. To determine the set and drift of a current, compare your projected position—based only on your course and speed without taking the current into account—with your actual position based on a fix.

When you sail in fine conditions and with local knowledge, you don't always have to keep a navigational plot. "Eyeball" navigation is safe for a day sail in a well-known area. In that case, you are keeping track of your progress in your head. It is when venturing away from familiar waters that you need to use the formal procedures of dead reckoning.

The best place to practice dead reckoning is in a familiar area. Running successful exercises there will improve your plotting and fix-taking skills and build confidence in your ability to navigate in other places.

Maintaining the DR Plot

The *dead reckoning (DR) plot* is an essential element of every form of navigation, from the simplest to the most sophisticated. Even advanced electronic chart systems use computer algorithms to provide dead reckoning positions when electronic navigational inputs fail. And you can tell from a single glance at DR plot whether it was done by an experienced navigator or a novice.

Dead reckoning is not a single event or activity—it is an ongoing process. You should maintain the DR plot continuously, correctly, neatly, and accurately, particularly when more than one person depends on the plot and when conditions are less than ideal.

The use of standard terminology and symbols ensures that all navigators use the same language at sea. U.S. maritime colleges, academies, and schools teach essentially the same procedures and terminology to their students,

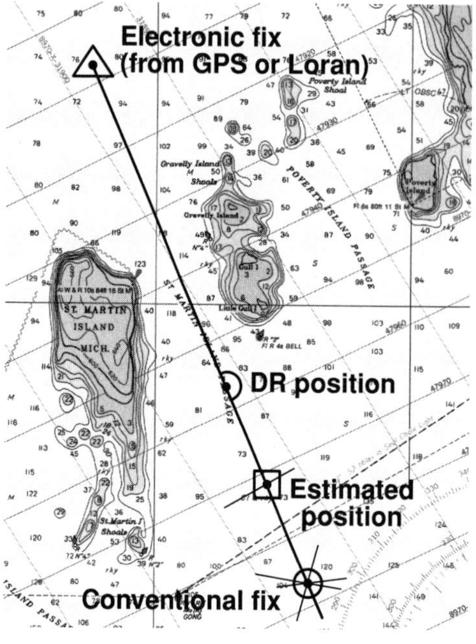

Figure 5-1. *Symbols used to mark position on a chart.*

ensuring that our Coast Guard, Navy, and merchant marine officers can readily understand the navigational practices of their colleagues. Because mariners move continually from place to place and often serve changing crews, it is important that they use standardized procedures. This book, too, presents standard terms and procedures so that you, the small-craft navigator, can use the language of mariners everywhere.

Draw the DR plot with a #2 pencil directly on the appropriate chart. Measure directions either with the *compass rose* or from latitude and longitude lines with a *protractor,* and transfer them to other parts of the chart with parallel rules or a rolling plotter. Measure distances by using the chart's latitude scale on each side border or, if available, the *distance scale* in the chart's margin. Remember that one minute of latitude equals one nautical mile, or 2,000 yards.

On small-scale charts (showing a large area) measure distances directly to the side of the area in question because the latitude scale increases as the latitude itself increases. On Mercator and similar projections, a mile measured near the bottom of the chart is shorter than a mile measured near the top. The amount of difference is significant only on small-scale charts.

To see how this works, take a small-scale chart (1:250,000 or smaller) and measure the length of a minute of latitude at the bottom of the chart with dividers. Transfer this distance to a minute near the top of the chart, and observe the difference, as shown in Figure 5-2. The smaller the scale, the greater the difference. (A glance at Chapter 1, Figure 1-1, will illustrate this concept as well.)

To accurately measure distance extending from top to bottom of a chart, use a latitude mark midway between top and bottom. For distances extending from side to side, of course, use the latitude scale directly to the side of the measured length. You can use the distance scales that are sometimes provided in chart margins, but you can make more accurate measurements using the latitude scale nearest to the area in question because the scales in chart borders are averages for the whole chart.

On large-scale charts, such as harbor charts, the yards or meters scale along the chart border may be easier to use than the latitude scale, especially for short distances and when using radar ranges that are usually provided in yards. When the scale is large, differences between top and bottom measurements are negligible.

Choosing the DR/Fix Interval

The DR plot shows the intended path and speed of the vessel. The navigator draws a desired *course line* on the chart and establishes DR positions along it. When a fix is obtained, the navigator compares that position with the DR position and makes corrections as necessary to update the plot and keep the vessel safely on its intended path.

You should choose the interval between DRs and fixes with a view to the proximity and nature of the dangers nearby, and prevailing wind and weather conditions. The rule of thumb is to choose an interval so that there are always at least two fixes between the vessel and the nearest danger. That way, you have at least two chances to catch a navigational blunder before disaster occurs.

Military navigators, who have lots of help on the bridge, take three-line fixes with considerable frequency—as often as every three minutes in harbors. Small-craft navigators may safely choose to take fixes less often, but only if they are confident of their situation. If there is any doubt about your vessel's position in relation to nearby dangers, or if strong currents make DR positions especially uncertain, use more frequent DRs and fixes, just like the "pros" do. Let common sense prevail.

In harbor areas and close to land with many dangers nearby, a fix interval of as little as six minutes or less is not too often. In coastal navigation, intervals of 15 minutes or perhaps half an hour or an hour might be sufficient. In ocean navigation, intervals of several hours to a full day are perfectly safe. It is your proximity to dangers that determines the fix interval.

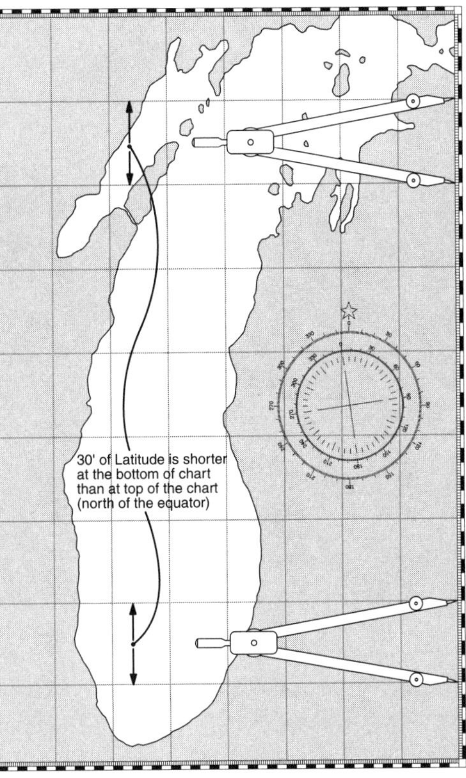

30' of Latitude is shorter at the bottom of chart than at top of the chart (north of the equator)

Figure 5-2. *In this figure the distances measured between the divider points are actually the same, though the spread of the dividers is different. On any Mercator chart, a minute of latitude (at point A) measured near the top of the chart (the bottom of the chart in southern latitudes) is longer than a minute at the bottom (at point B). This is because of the expansion of latitude lines in direct proportion to the expansion of longitude lines, which must become parallel if rhumb lines are to be straight lines. A distance near the top of the chart should be measured with the latitude scale near the top, and one at the bottom measured near the bottom. You can only use the longitude scale to measure distance when you are on the equator!*

Speed-Time-Distance Problems

Day-to-day navigation is concerned with the relationships between speed, time, and distance. Typically, you know two of the three and must find the third. For example, assuming you know your boat's speed and the distance to port, how long will it take to get there? Or, knowing the distance traveled between two points and the time it took, what was your boat's speed?

You can solve these problems by using a simple formula: Distance = Speed × Time. Though you can calculate each problem mathematically, most navigators use a nautical slide rule or speed-time-distance calculator. (See Figure 5-3.) A nautical slide rule is a square piece of plastic on which two rotating plastic disks are mounted. Windows in the outer circle allow you to view the alignment of the inner circles with each other. When you rotate the circles to the two knowns, the answer is visible.

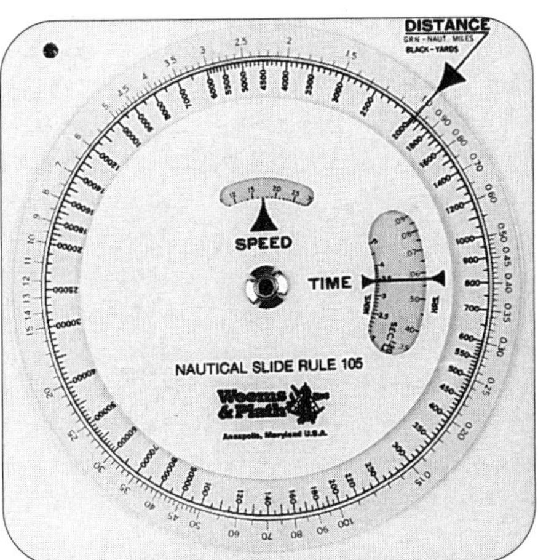

Figure 5-3. *A nautical slide rule is used to quickly figure speed-time-distance problems. You can also use the logarithmic calculator found on some charts or the nomogram found on a maneuvering board. (Photograph courtesy Weems and Plath)*

Because of the units we use to measure speed and time, it is convenient in these problems to base your calculations on three- or six-minute intervals, or intervals of time divisible by three or six so that you can use the *three-minute rule* or the *six-minute rule.*

The three-minute rule states that the number of hundreds of yards your vessel travels in three minutes equals its speed in knots. Mathematically, it is: Yards traveled in 3 minutes ÷ 100 = a vessel's speed in knots.

This rule is based on the fact that there are 60 minutes in one hour and 2,000 yards in one nautical mile. A vessel traveling at one knot (one nautical mile in one hour) goes 2,000 yards in 60 minutes, 1,000 yards in 30 minutes, and therefore 100 yards in three minutes. At two knots, the vessel would go 200 yards in three minutes. So if you travel 650 yards in three minutes, your speed is 6.5 knots. To find the speed, measure the number of hundreds of yards the vessel has traveled in three minutes. That's all there is to it.

The six-minute rule states that the number of tenths of miles your vessel travels in six minutes equals the vessel's speed in knots, or: Miles traveled in six minutes × 10 = vessel's speed in knots.

This rule is based on the fact that there are ten intervals of six minutes in an hour. A vessel going one knot (one nautical mile in one hour), is going ten-tenths of a mile in one hour, or one-tenth of a mile every six minutes. A vessel going five knots is going 50-tenths of a mile in one hour (50 ÷ 10 = 5). To find the speed, measure the number of tenths of miles traveled in six minutes. That's it.

You can use these most easily by choosing DR or fix intervals of three or six minutes, or multiples of them. Here's how this works: Suppose you are plotting a fix that is six minutes after the last one. The distance between fixes is 0.75 miles. Your speed, then, is 7.5 knots, found by simply moving the decimal point one place to the right.

To use multiples of these rules, simply divide the answer by the original multiplier. For example, you could measure the distance traveled in 30 minutes, convert that to hundreds of yards, and divide by 10 (the number of three's in 30), or convert to tenths of miles and divide by five (the number of sixes in 30).

Where the interval is short, you must plot the fixes very accurately. A one-minute timing error in a 30-minute interval is relatively small, but at a three-minute interval it's a much higher percentage. When computing speeds based on fixes at short intervals, it's best to average several together.

Actually, the three-minute interval is mostly used by fast-moving naval vessels that have large crews to take bearings, plot them, and figure courses and speeds. For slower-moving craft, the six-minute interval is fine. Of course, if six minutes is too long, you should either decrease the fix interval or slow down.

Labeling the DR Plot

Many naval conventions are based on strong logic. The symbols and practices used in a navigational plot adhere to one such convention. To make it easy for others to interpret your navigational plot at a glance, always follow the standard format (shown in Figure 5-4), using the following conventions:

- Draw the course line in the direction of the chosen course, and write and speak it in three-digit numbers to avoid misunderstandings. For example, you should write a course of 355° true as "C-355°T" and speak it as "three-five-five-degrees-true." A course of 005°M should be written as "C-005°M" (not "5°M") and spoken as "zero-zero-five-degrees-magnetic."
- Label the course above the line with a capital "C," and include either "T" or "M" to denote true or magnetic (for example, "C-180°T" or "C-005°M").
- Below the line, write the speed of the vessel, or the distance along that course, or both (for example, "S-7" and/or "D-5.2NM").
- Label a fix with two or more lines of position (LOPs) with the time it was taken (not the time it was plotted) written horizontally (for example, 0810 FIX).
- Always write the time in four digits, using the 24 hour clock, without punctuation (for example, "1900," not "7:00 P.M.").
- Mark a DR position with a semicircle and with the time, written diagonally.
- A fix position is marked with a small circle and with the time written horizontally.

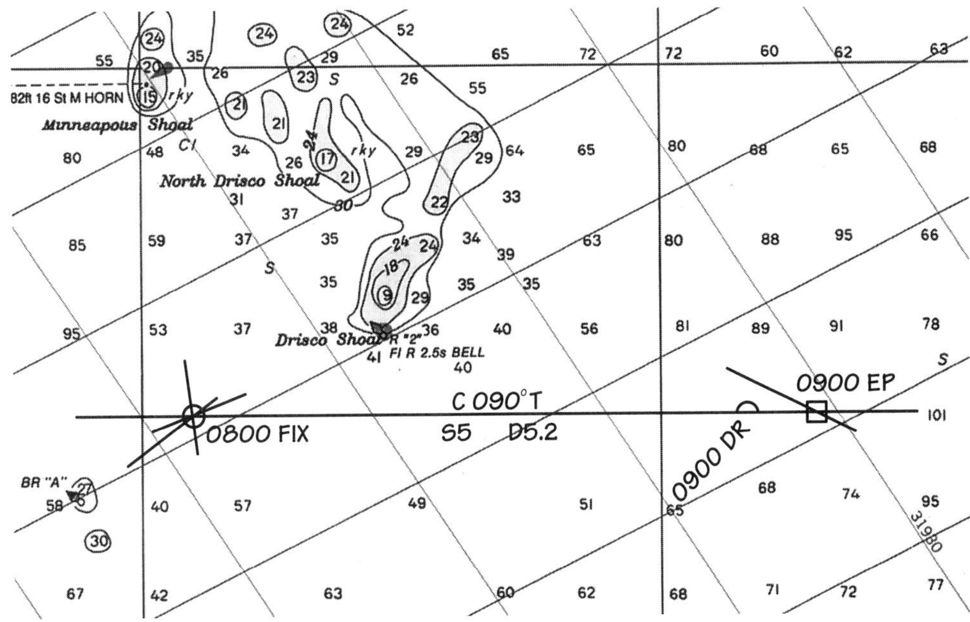

Figure 5-4. *Courses are labeled above the line; speed or distance are labeled below. Fixes are labeled horizontally; DRs are labeled diagonally. Fix positions are shown with a small circle, DR positions with a small semicircle, and EPs with a small square. Fixes derived electronically are shown with a small triangle and labeled to show the type of fix, such as "GPS Fix," "L Fix" (for loran), or "Radar Fix."*

- Mark an estimated position with a small square and the time.
- Generally plot a DR position at least every hour on the hour, except when far offshore.
- After every fix and from every estimated position, draw a new DR track from the newly established position.
- Alter the DR track with every change of course or speed.

The details of fixes are discussed in Chapter 6, "Piloting."

Fix Expansion

At times you may not be able to obtain a fix or even a single line of position for several hours or even several days. During these times, the DR plot provides the only way of knowing your position. When sailing offshore without electronic navigation gear and with overcast skies, you may have to rely on the DR plot for up to 150 to 200 miles or more. It's especially important then to plot very accurately and to assemble as much information as possible about currents, storms, and the like.

As your DR becomes older, a greater degree of uncertainty creeps into the plot. You anticipate this fact by using a method called *fix expansion*. The trick is to estimate all possible sources of error and assume the worst—that they are all operating in the same direction, with none canceling another.

Suppose that your vessel is making 8 knots, and for every hour you estimate a total possible error of ½ mile. Include in your estimate amounts for current, compass error, steering error, and leeway. At the end of one hour you can reasonably expect to be anywhere in an error circle of ½-mile radius from the DR position. At the end of two hours, the circle has a one-mile radius; after three hours, it is 1½ miles.

Two lines drawn from the previous fix tangent to the error circle encompass all possible positions of the vessel during the run, provided all sources of error have been accounted for. If there are no dangers in the area bounded by these lines, the vessel should not encounter navigational hazards. (See Figure 5-5.)

At each new fix, the DR is reset to the fix position, and a new fix expansion begins. Suppose a navigator finds that a fix can be obtained only by crossing a depth curve with a radiobeacon signal, and that the total possible error in the resulting fix is 2 miles. This

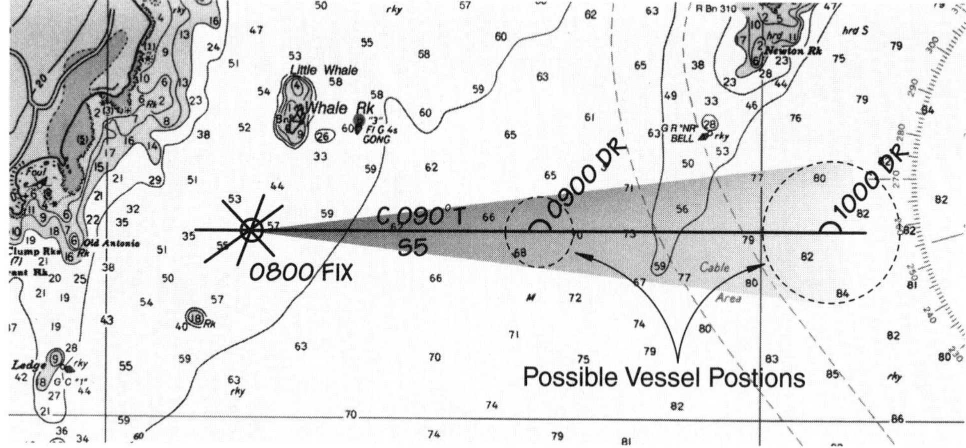

Figure 5-5. *Fix expansion is used to ensure that all unknown sources of error are accounted for. Any danger lying within the cone of possible positions is a definite navigational hazard.*

means that the fix position, instead of being a point, should really be a circle with a radius equal to the total of all possible sources of error. If the navigator estimates a possible position error of 2 miles, then the error circle is 4 miles in diameter at the fix position, and expands even farther beyond that. Any time there is uncertainty in the fix, the amount of uncertainty should be quantified and figured right from the fix.

As a newcomer to this concept, you may want to actually plot a few fix expansions until you are thoroughly familiar with it. After that, unless you encounter dangers, keep a mental fix expansion plot. You should always be able to answer the question, "What is the maximum possible error in my position right now?"

The Estimated Position

Many forces act on your boat moving through the water that cause it to stray off your intended track. Current, leeway, steering error, and compass error are the major factors that affect the course and speed of your vessel over the ground. Your focus should be on your course and speed over the ground, not through the water.

Strictly speaking, dead reckoning takes into account only the boat's course and speed through the water. When other factors are known, they can be applied to the DR and yield an *estimated position (EP)*. You'll not likely be able to quantify with precision each of the errors that apply in a given situation, so you try to calculate a reasonable estimate of the total direction and speed of all the errors combined. Because current is usually the major contributor to error, it is common practice to lump all errors under this heading. The direction of the current is called the *set* and its speed is called the *drift*. Strong beam winds may cause significant leeway, which make it necessary to add extra allowance to the current. Over time, you will develop a feel for the amount of this allowance in different conditions for different boats. You can gauge set and drift by comparing a DR position with a fix at the same time, as shown in Figure 5-6.

The 0900 DR in Figure 5-6 shows where a boat would be at 0900, absent all sources of error. The 0900 fix shows where the boat actually is. In this case, current has pushed the boat to the southeast. The bearing of the line between the DR and the fix defines the set, and the distance—converted to speed—defines the drift.

To stay on your intended path, you must allow for set and drift by steering a course that compensates for current. Suppose the set and drift are 150° at one knot. To offset its effect, steer to a point 330° from the 0900 DR; that is, to a point offset from the 0900 DR in a direction opposite to the known error and at a distance equal to the error, as shown in Figure 5-7.

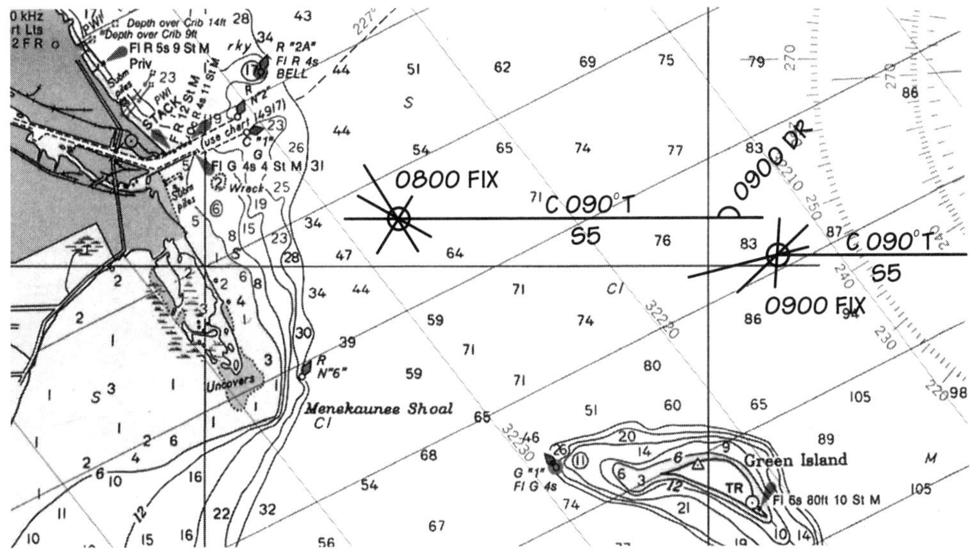

Figure 5-6. *Note how the DR plot is reset to the fix position at 0900. This indicates a current with set to the southeast and drift equal to the distance from the 0900 DR position to the fix position. (The time interval here is one hour. If another interval were used, the drift value would have to be adjusted accordingly.)*

Compensating for set and drift from the outset can save a lot of extra sailing later on. Skill in estimating set and drift comes from experience or "seaman's eye," as well as from practice in examining charts and the tide and tidal current tables.

Because the DR interval in this example is one hour, you can easily figure the drift in knots. But if the DR interval were, say, 38 minutes, then you would have to use the speed-time-distance formula to determine the rate.

If you did not compensate for current and instead steered directly for the 0900 DR position, the current would move the boat right down the line toward the 0900 EP. An EP is a DR position updated with set and drift. Two or more lines of position (LOPs) determine a fix. When only one LOP is available you can cross that with the DR track and eliminate some of the guesswork inherent in the pure DR. It's better to use this information than to ignore it. If, in the scenario depicted in Figure 5-6, you obtained only a single LOP at 0900, you would plot the result as shown in Figure 5-8.

Large-ship navigators sometimes use a graphic device called a *maneuvering board* to figure out set and drift problems. Although

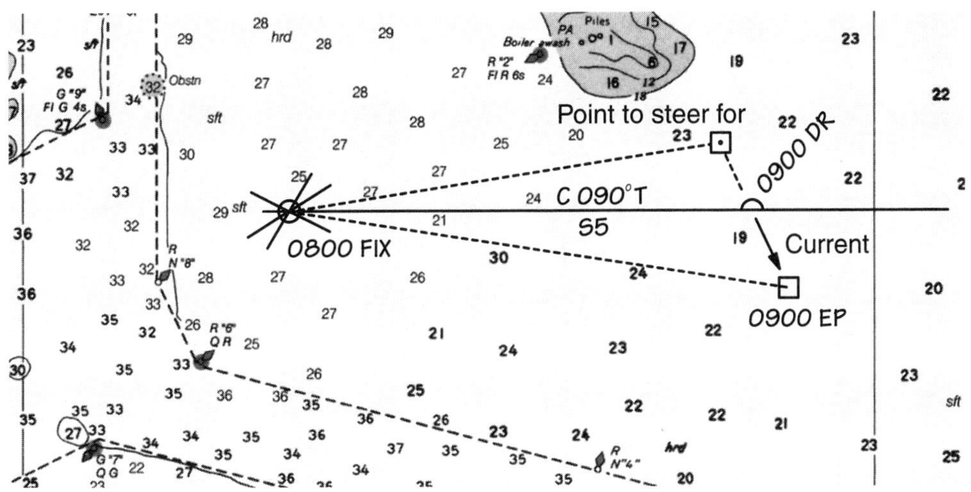

Figure 5-7. *In this case, we want to make good a course of 090° from our 0800 fix. The current, represented by the vector from our 0900 DR to the 0900 EP, will carry us to that EP if we don't compensate for it. We draw in the current vector in the opposite direction and steer for its end point, knowing that if we have judged the current correctly we will end up at our 0900 DR. Notice that the correction vector for a current is equal to, but opposite in direction from, the current's true effect.*

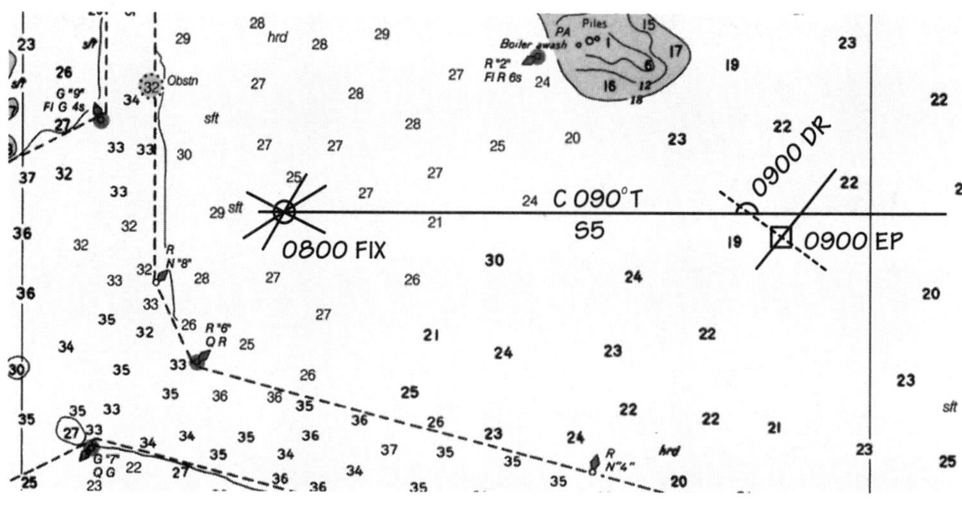

Figure 5-8. *An estimated position modifies the DR position based on set and drift or a single LOP crossed with the DR track. The EP is at the intersection of the new LOP and a vertical line from the DR. The result is not a fix, but is better than a DR position that is based only on course and speed through the water. Use an EP with caution until you can get a fix.*

A current vector *represents not only direction but distance, too. The distance—shown by the length of the line, is derived from the current's speed and elapsed time.*

Figure 5-9. *Plotting the course to steer and measure in order to reach a future DR, considering a drift of 2 knots.*

EXAMPLE:

1) From a known fix "0800" mark Track and the next DR "0900".

2) Draw a vector line from the 0900 DR in opposite direction as the set and equal in length (in this case one hour) of the DR interval.

3) Measure out 6 miles with your dividers from the latitude scale on your chart. Place the end of the dividers on the end of the vector line and scribe a line across the track line. This is the course to steer to compensate for set and drift. Also calculate any variation or deviation if necessary.

Boat Speed = 6 knots
Current
Set=180°
Drift= 2 knots

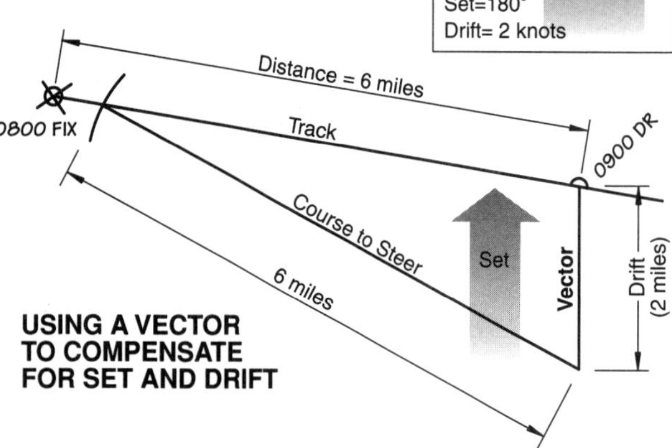

the maneuvering board might be useful in small-craft navigation, it is not really necessary. You can work most current problems directly on a chart.

First, plot a future DR position from a known fix. From that future DR, plot a line, or vector, opposite to the direction of the current with a length equal to the current's effect during the DR interval. (If the DR interval is one hour and the drift is two knots, a two-mile line is needed. If the DR interval is 15 minutes, then a ½-mile line is needed. Why? Because 15 minutes is one-quarter of an hour and one-quarter of two is one-half.) Then, simply draw a line from the fix to the end of that vector. The direction of this line indicates the course to steer. Be sure to apply any compass corrections to this direction before relaying it to the helm.

Other navigators can tell if you're a good navigator by looking at your DR plot. For reasons of safety and pride, a good navigator follows the rules of good "DR-ing" and is neat, meticulous, and orderly.

The Sailings

The sailings are, in some respects, analogous to dead reckoning, but in the sailings you determine the course and distance from one known point to another without reference to a chart. When the latitude and longitude of two different places are known, the distance and direction between them can be determined by mathematics alone. You can also use the sailings to calculate the courses to follow a great circle route that can save you miles and time compared with a rhumb line course.

The common problems of the sailings are easily solved in a few seconds using a navigational calculator or computer program. Simply enter the values requested in the program and the solution appears. The applicable algorithms are quite simple to program and all navigational calculators and programs have them. They are based on simple mathematical principles that have been known for thousands of years. All navigators, not just beginners, should use a navigational or scientific calculator to solve these problems. The mathematical solutions presented here are meant to convey an understanding of the sailings problems and provide a backup method of working out solutions should a calculator fail. To do the math, you need an understanding of basic trigonometry. (For more detail on this subject, see *The American Practical Navigator.)*

In modern navigation practice, these problems arise only during transoceanic voyages in high latitudes. For these trips, a foolproof graphic solution can be done right on a chart, as discussed below.

The sailings problems that confront the modern navigator most frequently are plane sailing and great-circle sailing. First, some definitions are in order:

- ***Plane sailing*** is used for relatively short distances (a few hundred miles) where it is acceptable to treat the earth's surface as flat.
- ***Traverse sailing*** combines several plane sailings to provide a series of courses for a somewhat longer passage.
- ***Midlatitude sailing*** uses the middle (average) or mean latitude when computing courses between places of different latitudes.
- ***Mercator sailing*** is a form of plane sailing adapted for use with the Mercator projections.
- ***Great-circle sailing*** transforms great circles into a series of rhumb lines.
- ***Composite sailing*** modifies great-circle sailing with rhumb line sailing to limit the maximum latitude.

To determine the distance and direction between two known points using plane sailing, you form an imaginary triangle with the following sides, points, and angles:

1. Side *"l"* with a length equal to the difference in latitude between the two points.
2. Side "p" with a length equal to the difference in longitude between the two points— called departure.
3. Side "D" equal to the distance between the two points, which is one of your unknowns.
4. The angle "C" between the departure point and the destination point.
5. Point P1, the departure point.
6. Point P2, the destination.

Graphically, you have:

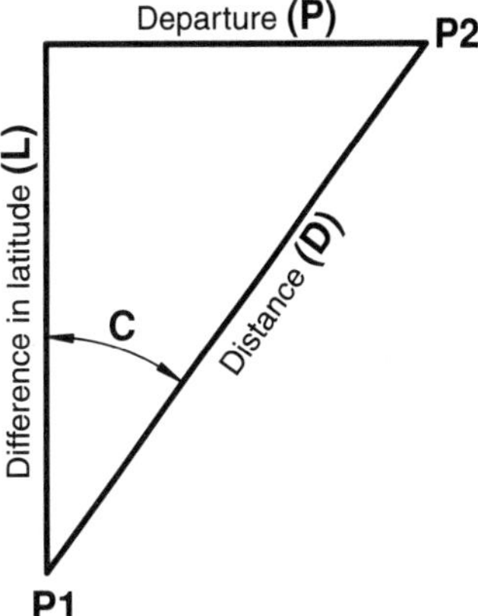

Figure 5-10. *The plane-sailing triangle is a right triangle formed by the departure point, the destination point, and the latitude and longitude lines that intersect in a right angle. The earth is assumed to be flat.*

With these plane-sailing formulas, you commonly solve two problems. In the first, you know distance sailed and determine difference in latitude and departure. The second is the opposite: You know difference of latitude and departure (difference of longitude) and determine course and distance. In doing these problems, it is a good idea to label *"l"* as

N(orth) or S(outh) and label "p" as E(ast) or W(est) to simplify finding the course. You can determine these labels by inspection, noting whether one point is lesser or greater in latitude or longitude than the other.

You can solve these mathematical problems by using logarithms or tables. Use of the tables, called traverse tables, *is not covered in this book because the tables needed to cover all possible solutions are too numerous. In any case, by using a simple calculator that does trigonometry rather than tables, you can solve these problems more accurately and in less time. In practice, solving these plane-sailing problems is more important to a professional mariner who's worried about fuel cost and exact ETA than to the average small-boat navigator who will simply plot the course and distance on a small-scale chart and measure it.*

For example, when you want to find where you will be after sailing 188 miles (D) on course 005°T (C), use these formulas: $l = D \cos C$; $p = D \sin C$.

The logarithm of 188 is 2.27416 and the logarithmic cosine of 5° is 9.99834.

D	188	log 2.27416	log 2.27416
C	005°	l cos 9.99834	l sin 8.94030
(1)	187.3'N	log 2.27250	
(2)	p 16.4 mi. E		log 1.21446

Difference of latitude is 3° 07N and departure is 16.4 miles E.

For the next example, suppose you want to get to a point 136 miles north and 203 miles west of where you are. What course do you steer and how far will you sail?

Use formulas: $\tan C = p/l$, $D = l \sec C$.

Graphically, you can do these solutions on a universal plotting sheet. Using the direction on the sheet for the midlatitude of the trip,

p	203W	log 2.30750	
l	136N	log (–) 2.13354	log (–) 2.13354
C	N56°W	l tan 0.17396	l sec 0.25447
(1)D	244 mi.		log 2.38801
(2)C	303.8		

Course is 304° (360°-56°) and distance is 244.8 miles.

set up the plotting sheet so that both extremes of latitude and longitude are included. Plot the two main points and measure the course and distance between them. (See Chapter 16 for a complete explanation of plotting sheets.)

Great-Circle Sailing

One requirement confronted in planning a transoceanic voyage is to determine the shorter great-circle route instead of the rhumb line course to your destination. A review of some definitions reveals the importance of this task.

A *great circle* is the intersection of the surface of a sphere and a plane passing through its center. A portion of a great circle is, by definition, the shortest distance between two points along the surface of the sphere. Every meridian is a great circle, so when sailing due north or due south, you are sailing a great-circle route already and don't have to convert rhumb lines to great circles. The same is true when you are sailing along the equator. It, too, is a great circle.

You need to solve great-circle sailing problems when you sail east or west for long distances in high latitudes, for there the lines of longitude converge, the distortion of the Mercator projection is pronounced, and the difference between a great circle and a rhumb line distance is substantial. To sail a pure great-circle route, you would have to continually change course during the voyage because a great-circle track meets each meridian at a different angle.

Figure 5-12 shows the difference between the same course plotted on both Mercator and gnomonic projection charts. A special property of the gnomonic projection is that it shows great circles as straight lines. Gnomonic charts are often called *great-circle charts*. They provide a graphic solution to the great-circle problem. Simply draw the course as a straight line on the gnomonic chart and mark its intersection with meridians at every five degrees or so. Then pick off the latitude and longitude of these points with dividers and plot them on a Mercator chart. Straight lines drawn between these points on the Mercator chart will approximate the great-circle course.

Recall that the Mercator chart distorts the true globe by eliminating the convergence of the meridians and expanding latitudes by an equivalent amount. That's why rhumb lines on Mercator charts are shorter than great circles, although the opposite is true on the real surface of the earth.

As with plane-sailing problems, you should use a navigational calculator or computer program to solve these problems—the solutions will be faster and more accurate. The best of these programs can calculate the waypoints at every five degrees of longitude, or four degrees, or whatever interval you choose. Keep in mind that the other easy way for you to find the rhumb line approximations of great-circle courses is to use a gnomonic chart as discussed above. A series of these charts is available for all areas of the oceans. If you must stay below a certain latitude to avoid icebergs or high-latitude storm areas, first plot the great circle completely and then, at its intersection with the limiting latitude, draw a rhumb line along that latitude, eliminating the curve above it.

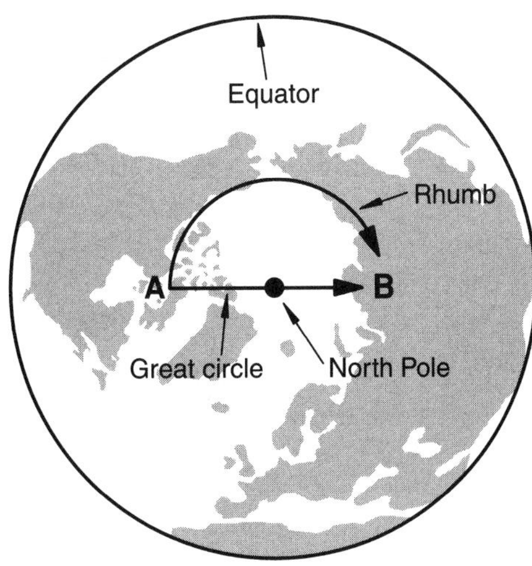

Figure 5-11. *The most dramatic example of the great-circle versus rhumb line difference is in courses which travel over the north or south pole. In the figure the rhumb line course from A to B is the half-circle along the parallel of latitude, while the great-circle course is the much shorter straight line directly across the pole. Note that at the pole the course changes from 000° to 180°. Similarly, every great-circle course not along the equator or a meridian will change continually.*

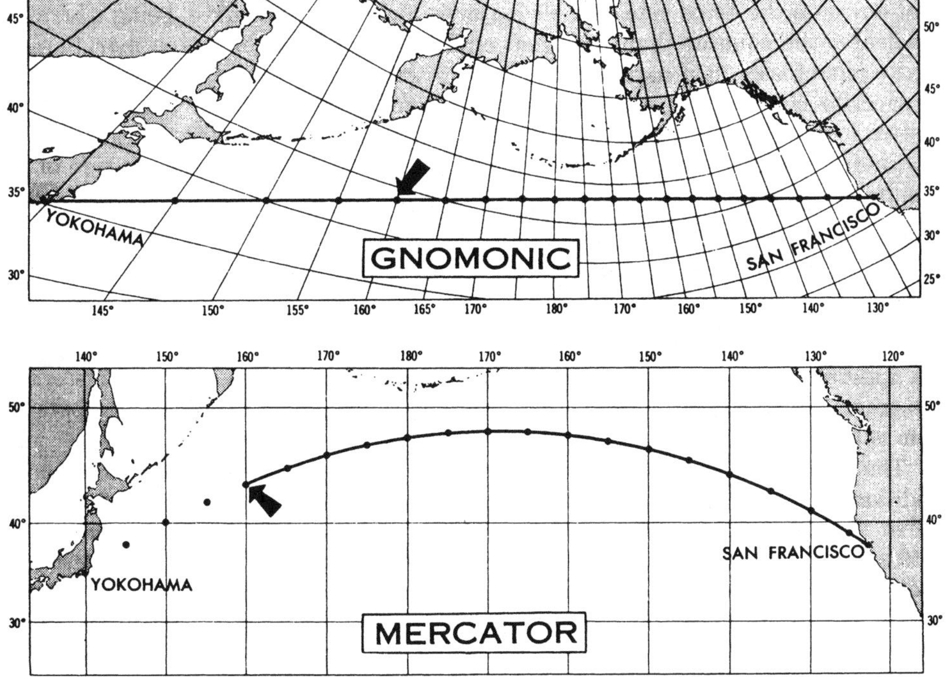

Figure 5-12. *The great-circle distance between San Francisco and Yokohama is considerably less than the rhumb line distance. A gnomonic projection is used to draw great circles as straight lines and points of latitude and longitude can be picked off and transferred to a Mercator chart or plotting sheet. Your vessel will sail a number of short legs, each slightly different in course, to approximate the great circle.*

If you're a traditionalist and familiar with celestial navigations (see Chapters 12 through 17), you can use *Pub. 229, Sight Reduction Tables for Marine Navigation* to solve these problems. Because all declinations are found on every page of *Pub. 229* and the declination becomes the destination latitude in great-circle problems, the volume of *Pub. 229* that contains the departure latitude will also contain all possible solutions.

In using these tables to solve a great-circle problem rather than a celestial sight, your entering arguments are as follows:

- Latitude becomes the latitude of departure point.
- Declination becomes the latitude of destination.
- LHA is the difference of longitude.

Just as in sight reduction, you must determine whether both latitudes have the same or contrary name. Also, if the tabular values correspond to a celestial body above the celestial horizon, the distance is 90° minus the altitude; if the body is below the celestial horizon, the distance is the altitude plus 90°, and the initial great-circle course angle is the supplement of the tabulated azimuth angle. You must give the azimuth angle a prefix of N or S and a suffix of E or W as necessary. In addition, you must interpolate unless the entering values are whole degrees.

For an example, assume that you want to find the great-circle initial course and distance in going from 32°S 116°E to 30°S 31°E. Enter *Pub. 229, Volume 3* with 32°S (latitude same name), LHA 85°, and declination 30°. If this were a celestial body it would be above the horizon, so the distance is 90° minus the altitude (90° – 19°12.4' = 70°47.6'). Converted to distance, this is 4,248 miles. The azimuth, 66.0, becomes S66W when the direction is added, and the course is therefore 246° (180° + 66° = 246°).

A corresponding body below the horizon would be indicated by the fact that the C/S line had been crossed. As in most celestial problems, it helps to visualize the problem and draw a diagram, if necessary, to establish the directional relationships of departure point and destination. It also helps to recognize and reject unreasonable answers.

To use *Pub. 229* to find waypoints along the great-circle track and the courses between them, you must use a latitude and initial course angle that are in whole degrees. Enter the proper table with the departure latitude (same name), the initial great-circle course as LHA, and 90 minus the distance to the first point as the declination. The latitude of the point on the great-circle track becomes the tabulated altitude, and the difference of longitude becomes the azimuth angle. If the C/S line must be crossed, the latitude is across the equator from the departure point, and the azimuth angle is the supplement of the difference of longitude.

To find the vertex, inspect the table until you find the maximum tabulated altitude. At this point the azimuth angle is the difference of longitude between the vertex and point of departure.

At any point, you can depart from the great-circle track to clear islands, shoals, peninsulas, or other obstructions. You can resume the original track when well clear, or you can compute a new great circle.

CHAPTER SIX

Piloting

PILOTING IS THE MOST commonly used navigation skill of the small-boat navigator and is the basis for all other navigation skills. The techniques you use in piloting are directly applicable to using GPS, Loran-C, and even celestial navigation. In piloting, you use a compass, depthsounder, charts, plotting tools, estimates of leeway and current, and visual aids to ensure safe navigation along coasts, in approaching harbors, and within harbors.

Today, with GPS and Loran-C performing many piloting functions, including calculating speeds between fixes and figuring courses and distances from point-to-point, modern piloting has been improved as well as complicated. For the beginning navigator, these devices are almost irresistible and it is easy to rely on them exclusively. It is also dangerous. When they fail—and they will—and you aren't prepared to pilot the old-fashioned way, a disaster could be in the making.

It is essential that you learn and practice good piloting skills. You can often safely omit certain routine procedures when piloting, but your decisions to do so should be made from thorough knowledge and understanding of the situation, not from ignorance.

You should practice your piloting skills during fine weather in your local waters to prepare for the time when you're navigating in a strange harbor in adverse conditions. Sooner or later, you should master all of the piloting skills discussed here. The best time to do so is long before they are necessary to save your boat and your life.

Preparing for Piloting

Piloting begins before the voyage, with preparation, research, and review. First, make sure that you have all the necessary charts and publications on board. Instruments should be ready, pencils sharpened, erasers handy, and the chart(s) for the first part of the voyage on the chart table.

The tools for piloting, some of which are illustrated in Figure 6-1, are

#2 pencils and a soft gum eraser

Dividers (for measuring distances)

Draftsman's compass (for striking arcs)

Parallel rules, roller straight-edge, or protractor/plotter (for measuring and plotting chart bearings)

Time-Speed-Distance calculator

Hand-bearing compass (for taking bearings)—optional

The first task is to review the chart you will be using, noting the scale, units of depth, notes, cautions, and any dangers near your intended route. Also, make sure that the chart is corrected from the *Local Notice to Mariners*

Figure 6-1. *A set of navigational tools is usually the novice's first purchase and an experienced navigator's pride. Dividers, parallel rules, speed-time-distance calculator, protractor, and a few sharp #2 pencils are the basic tools a navigator needs for the first and every voyage. You can buy them singly or in a kit as shown here. (Photograph courtesy Weems and Plath)*

(see Chapter 1, "Basic Navigational Concepts"). Note, and perhaps highlight, any important aids to navigation and mark the bearings of any ranges (if they are not already marked).

Next, review the depths along your intended course and note any hazards. Many professional navigators use a highlighter to mark the depth curve delineating waters shallower than their vessel's draft. Many small-craft navigators highlight the 10-foot depth contour that appears on most harbor and approach charts. Doing so will readily show the area in which you can safely navigate when you're in shallow bays and sounds where the navigable water comprises a small fraction of the total. Be sure to also note or mark isolated shoals, rocks, and obstructions.

As navigator, you must also review tide and weather information using tide tables, NOAA weather broadcasts, and local news among other resources. In most harbor cities you'll find a daily newspaper that lists tides, marine weather, times of sunrise and sunset, ship arrivals and departures, and other useful marine information. You don't have to prepare precise estimates of tidal currents when you're boating in areas where the current is weak; you can infer them from tidal height information. In areas where tidal currents are very strong, however, such as Hell Gate in New York's East River, it is essential that you study the tidal current tables and diagrams and plan carefully.

Finally, begin your chart work. Lay out your initial course(s) from a convenient point of departure, such as the last channel buoy or the pierhead, and label it properly as explained in Chapter 5, "Dead Reckoning." This trackline is the intended path of your vessel and should cover the first few hours of travel. Choose a path that is well clear of dangers and that takes advantage of available aids to navigation. Plot DR positions along your intended track at intervals based on your speed and the proximity of hazards. Be prepared to convert true or magnetic bearings to compass (as explained in Chapter 3, "The Compass").

Get underway only when you are fully prepared to navigate safely.

Course, Heading, and Track

The path of a vessel is referred to by several terms: *track* (or *trackline*), *track made good, heading,* and *course.* The *track* or *trackline* is the *intended* path of your vessel over the ground. Your actual path over the ground may be very different when you don't compensate for current, wind, and other forces that tend to set you off track. The *track made good* is a straight line between a point of departure and an actual arrival point. Your vessel need not have been right on that line at all times. A vessel's *heading* is the direction that she is pointed at any given moment. The *course* is the direction that you're trying to steer. Unavoidably, your heading wanders back and forth across the course. (See Figure 6-2.)

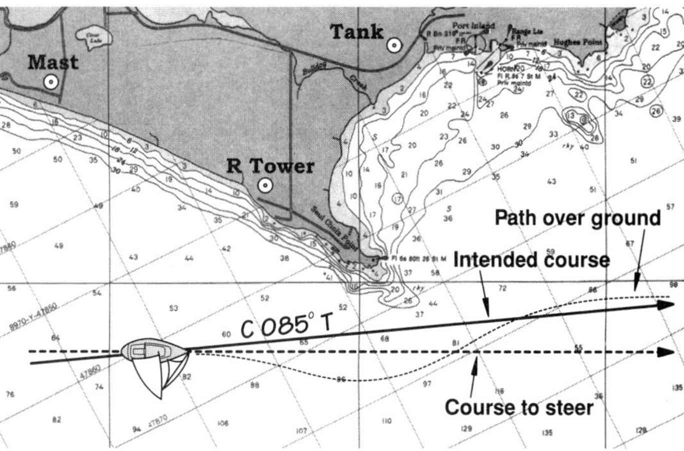

Note: Charts shown in Chapter 6 are fictitious. Masts, Towers, Tanks, Buoys and Lighthouses have been inserted into these charts for example only.

Figure 6-2. Course *is the direction that the boat should be steered to keep it on a track or trackline drawn on the chart.* Heading *is the direction in which the boat is pointed at any given time. The* path over the ground *is the actual route of the vessel over the earth.* Track made good *is the straight line direction and distance between departure and arrival points.*

Taking and Plotting Fixes

Piloting is a continual process of plotting a DR track, taking and plotting fixes, comparing each fix with the DR for that time, determining set and drift, and adjusting the course to correct for observed set and drift so your actual path will be as close as possible to your intended path. When you've made the right adjustments, your next fix will be located right at the corresponding DR position. When you've plotted a new fix, you extend the DR into the future from it and repeat the process. In fact, piloting is a constant effort to make the fixes plot on top of the DRs. They seldom do, exactly, but the goal is to keep the fixes close enough to the DR positions so your vessel never strays far from your trackline, thus straying into unsafe water.

An essential element of piloting is the *line of position (LOP)*—a line on which a vessel is located at a particular time. When you obtain two LOPs at the same time, your vessel must be located at their intersection. This constitutes a *fix*. However, LOPs are error prone—if you use only two for a fix you won't be able to determine its accuracy. By using three or more LOPs you can refine the fix and gauge its accuracy.

Lines of position can be obtained several ways, and the clever navigator uses all of them, each in its appropriate time and place, to obtain reliable fixes. Some LOPs are inherently more accurate and reliable than others; some are easily measured, and some take considerable skill.

Compass Bearings

The most common type of LOP is based on a *compass bearing*. The magnetic compass bearing to any charted object, when properly plotted on a chart, indicates the line on which the vessel was located when the bearing was taken. You can take bearings with a boat's *steering compass,* which will give reasonably accurate bearings if it has been compensated for deviation and you've made the necessary corrections (see Chapter 3, "The Compass"). (A gyrocompass is more accurate, but it's expensive and rarely available to the small-craft navigator.)

You can take very accurate compass bearings within a few degrees of dead ahead by

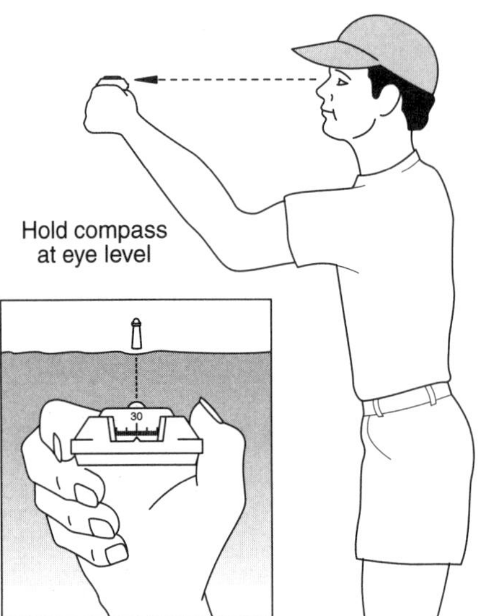

Figure 6-3. *A hand-bearing compass is great for taking compass bearings for fixes. Although it must be corrected for variation—unless the magnetic compass rose is used—it usually doesn't have to be corrected for deviation because it can be used at a location on the boat away from sources of deviation.*

steering directly toward an object and reading the compass. With an object abeam or astern, however, you'll have to crouch down so the compass card is at eye level between you and the object and carefully observe its bearing on the compass card. With practice, and in good weather and calm seas, accuracy within 2° is possible using this method.

Alternatively, you can use a *hand-bearing compass*. There are several modestly priced models on the market. You hold the small portable compass up to your eye and sight across or through an eyepiece. With practice, you'll be able to take bearings with an accuracy up to 1°. (See Figure 6-3.) Hand-bearing compasses, though, are not compensated for deviation and may have unknown and unknowable deviation errors. However, you can usually take bearings from a position well away from possible sources of deviation and thereby eliminate this source of error.

Natural or man-made *ranges* provide another type of LOP and a particularly accurate one. A range is formed by a pair of objects that line up with each other. It provides an LOP without requiring a compass measurement of its direction.

Almost any charted object can be used for bearings and ranges. Water towers, stacks, radio towers, buildings, spires, cupolas, chimneys, masts, monuments, hill- and mountaintops, among others, are charted expressly for mariners' use. Any time you see two of these objects come in line, a perfect LOP is available. You don't have to take a bearing when they are lined up. You simply place a straightedge along the line between the objects on the chart, draw a short extension of that line segment across your DR track, and jot down the time. (See Figure 6-4.)

A charted object whose position is known with precision is usually shown with a *position circle (accurate)* symbol—a small circle

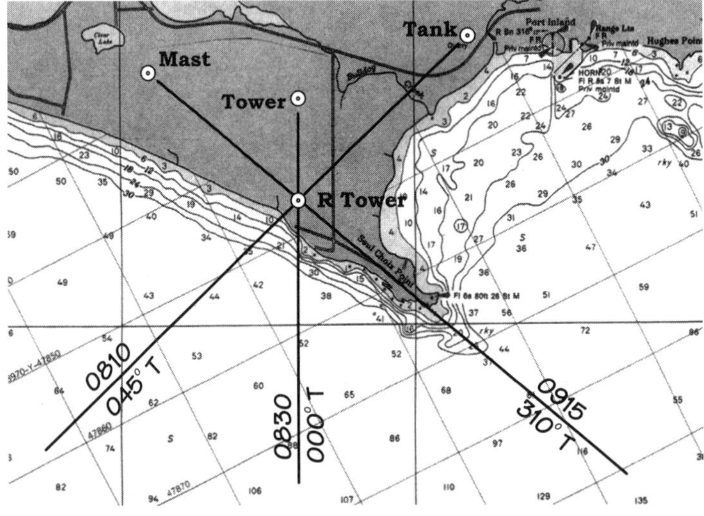

Figure 6-4. *Perfect lines of position (LOPs) can be obtained from any two charted objects in line. Simply note the exact time when they line up and draw a short line segment in the approximate position of the vessel that is an extension of the line between the two objects. Be sure to label the LOP with the time it was taken. Neither compass bearings nor compass correction is necessary.*

with a dot in the middle. An object whose position is not known exactly is not usually charted. If it is charted, though, its symbol is a *position circle (approximate)*—a small circle with no dot.

To conveniently determine set, drift, and course corrections, it's best to take a round of compass bearings at time intervals that make easier the arithmetic of the time-distance-speed problem. Bearings should be taken in this order: First, take beam bearings at the exact time you want the fix because they change most rapidly as your vessel moves. Then take bow and stern bearings. Their timing is less important because they aren't changing as rapidly.

Of course, ranges become available at odd times—rarely exactly when you want them—but they should be plotted whenever necessary. You should not feel bound to take fixes at the time of each DR plot if the situation doesn't call for them, although it's often convenient to get fixes at times corresponding to your DR positions. You should resolve any doubt about your boat's position by getting a fix right away, regardless of time.

Using Radar for LOPs

Radar's greatest contribution to navigation is in measuring the distance to objects; that is, establishing a *radar range*. The LOP resulting from this measurement is an arc of a circle that's centered on the target, passing through the vessel, whose radius is equal to the measured range. Two ranges yield a fix, as seen in Figure 6-5.

Don't confuse terrestrial ranges—beacons, lights, or other objects in line—with radar ranges. A *radar range* is a distance to a single object whose LOP is an arc of a circle.

Radar measures ranges to objects more accurately than it measures bearings. Nevertheless, you can use radar to get a two-LOP fix from a single object by observing its range and bearing. A radar bearing crossed with a range to the same object is sometimes the only type of fix available. (See Figure 6-6.)

Radar's view of the world is different from our own because it uses radio waves—not

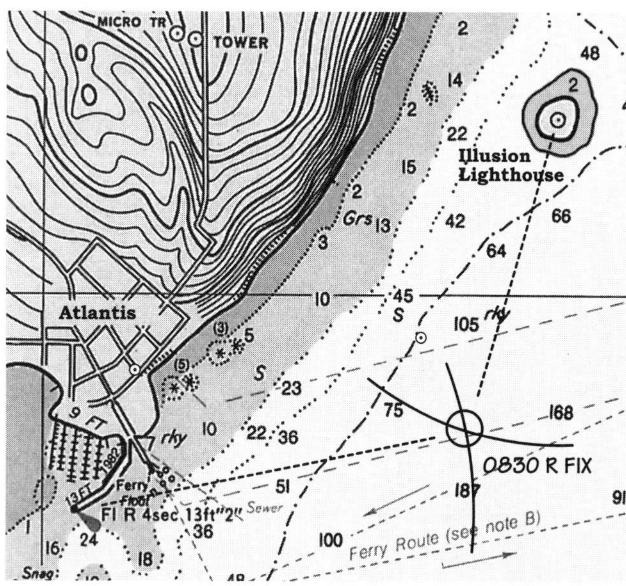

Figure 6-5. *This shows a radar fix taken on a point of land (point A) and an angle in a breakwater (point B). Radar can measure ranges very accurately, but make sure that the radar is "seeing" exactly what is charted. Label the fix with the time.*

Figure 6-6. *A radar range and a simultaneous bearing to a single object can form a useful fix. A third bearing or range would make it better.*

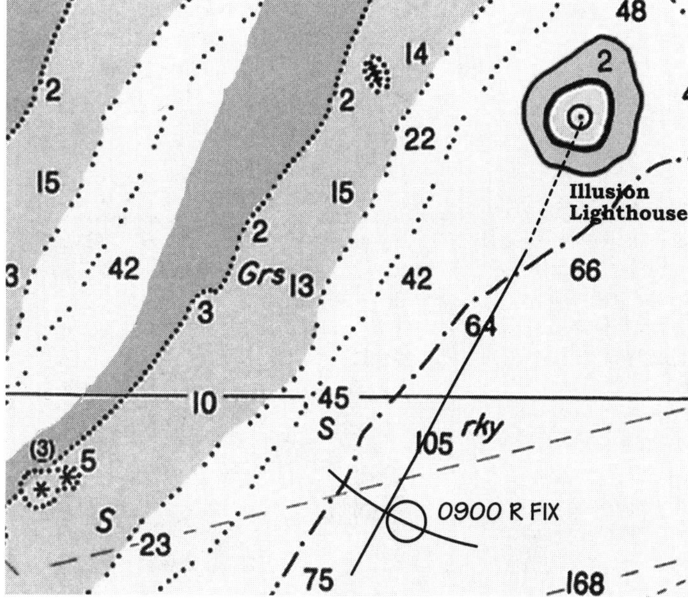

light rays—to "see" objects. Therefore, a navigator must be very careful when selecting objects and points to take ranges on and must be sure to choose items that the radar can detect well. (See Chapter 10, "Radar Navigation," for a full discussion of radar's strengths and weaknesses in navigation.)

Depth Curves as LOPs

An often overlooked source of a good LOP is the *depth curve*. A *depthsounder* is one of the most basic pieces of navigation equipment, but it is often used only in harbors or close-in coastal waters. However, in areas of gradually sloping bottom contours, you can use it farther offshore as well. In Figure 6-6 a depth curve passes near the fix position and can be used as an LOP to further confirm the radar fix.

One reason why so few navigators use depthsounders to get LOPs is the time and trouble it takes. First, you must measure the water depth with the sounder. Then you must add to that measurement the depth of the sounder's transducer below the water's surface. Finally, to relate the observed depth to charted depths you must account for the effect of tide (assuming tide is a factor) and, to do so, must figure the exact height of the tide at the time of the measurement.

For example, if the measurement is 25 feet, and the sounder's transducer is four feet below the water's surface, the water depth is 29 feet. To relate this to charted depths you must add the height of the tide, if any, above your chart's low-water datum at that time.

Since U.S. tide tables and charts use the same datums, you can calculate the tidal heights quite easily using the tide tables. The rise of the tide is not linear. That is, it does not occur at the same rate during its rise and during its fall. For accuracy, then, it should be figured in advance and plotted or noted for later use. (This is part of the preparation for piloting that introduced this chapter.)

You can cross a *depth-curve LOP* with any other type of LOP for a fix, but do so carefully because not all areas are suitable for this technique. The bottom should slope gently and uniformly or be uniformly flat except for well-defined and separated shoals or deeps. You can sometimes identify these features just by watching the depthsounder as your boat passes over them. In Figure 6-7 a depthsounder indicates that the vessel has just passed over a shoal which, if charted, serves as a good navigation aid.

Information from depthsounders can be integrated electronically with other navigational data such as speed, course, water temperature, and the like.

Along shores with uniformly sloping sea bottoms and without distinctive navigational aids or features, or in foggy weather, it's sometimes possible to safely navigate by following a depth curve along the shore. You should head inshore when the sounding increases and offshore when it decreases in order to stay on the same curve.

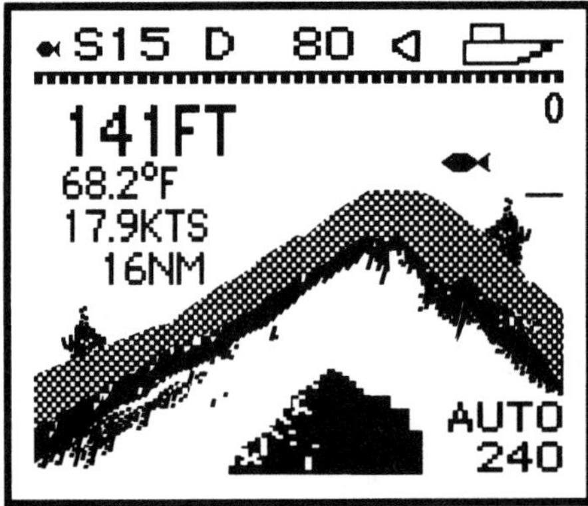

Figure 6-7. *A depthsounder shows depth below the transducer, not below the surface, and so does not give total water depth. It is a good source of LOPs if the sea bottom configuration is appropriate. Digital depthsounders integrated with other electronics can display other information such as course and speed. (Photograph courtesy Raytheon)*

Running Fixes

In addition to taking a radar range and bearing, there is another way to get a fix from a single object, but it's a fix of a different type. Suppose, for example, that you are sailing along a stretch of coast where only one light is visible. If you take a bearing on the light at a certain time, you'll get an LOP for that time (and, when crossed with the vessel's DR track, you'll get an EP for that time, too). If you then advance that LOP along the DR track to a later time when you take a second bearing to the same light and plot another

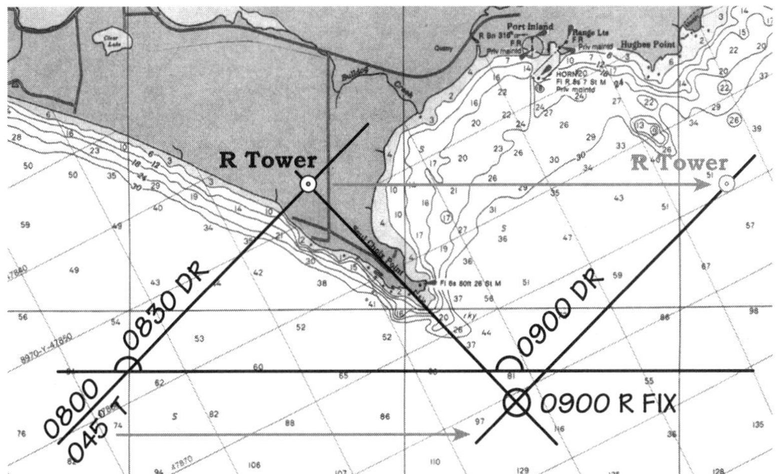

Figure 6-8. *In a running fix, you advance an earlier LOP for the course and distance run during the time between taking two bearings to the same object. You can either advance the LOP itself or advance the object and replot the LOP from the new position. The result is the same. A running fix is labeled with the time and "R FIX."*

LOP, the intersection of the advanced (first) LOP and the new (second) LOP comprises a *running fix*. Running fixes are not as accurate as regular two- or three-LOP fixes, but they are better than an EP. (See Figure 6-8.)

The trick in getting a useful running fix is to advance the earlier LOP for the exact course and distance run between the times of the two bearings. There are two ways to do this. The first is to advance the earlier LOP itself for the course and distance run. The second is to advance the object the bearing was taken from for the course and distance run and replot the fix from that position. If you know set and drift you should figure that information in as well.

The accuracy of a running fix, of course, depends on the accuracy of the course and speed used in the DR projection during the time between taking the two bearings. In areas of strong unknown currents, running fixes are quite inaccurate and can lead to false confidence. Though it is comforting to see lines intersecting on a chart indicating your boat's position, you must not rely on them when they are based on questionable data or assumptions. Remember, and review if necessary, the concept of *fix expansion* explained in Chapter 5, "Dead Reckoning."

Using a single object, it's possible to use certain geometric relationships to establish an approximate position. The approach is similar to that used in a running fix.

Imagine that you are cruising along a coast on a course of 090°, and that you want to find your distance off the land to the north—on your port side. When you pass any charted object on shore (for example, a lighthouse, spire, tank, tower), note the time—let's say 1200 hours—when it bears 045°. (This measurement can be either magnetic or true direction.) Also note your speed—let's say it's six knots—and be careful not to change course or speed for the next few minutes. When the object bears 000° (directly abeam), note the time again—now it's 1215. At a speed of six knots you've gone 1.5 miles while the bearing to the object has changed 45°. (See Figure 6-9.) Your course

Figure 6-9. *A bearing of any object when it is exactly 45° off the course, and another when it is exactly abeam, will yield an easy running fix. In this case, the vessel's distance from the radio tower at B must be equal to the distance traveled between A and C, because line AC equals line BC. The running fix at point C is subject to error based on incorrect estimates of course and speed between A and C.*

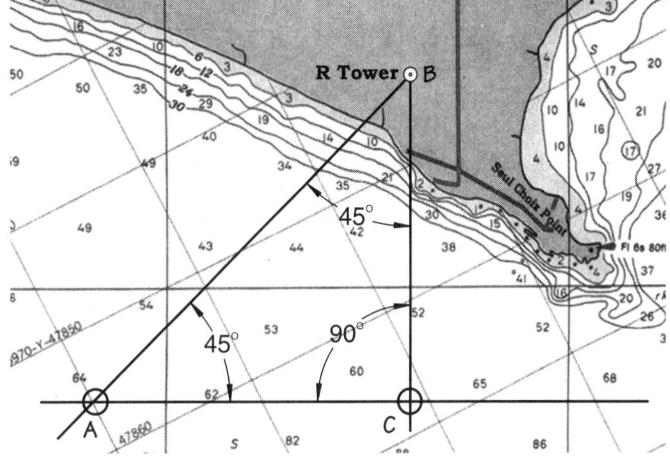

When cotangents of any two bearings to a single object differ by exactly one (unity), the distance run between the bearings will equal the distance off the object when it is abeam. The following table includes pairs of bearings whose cotangents differ by one. Using this table you can predict how far offshore you will be from a given point long before arriving there. All these types of problems assume that you are holding a steady course and speed between the times of bearings taken and that no correction is necessary for current or wind.

As an example, if a boat sails five miles between the time when an object bears 26½° and 45°, it will be five miles off the object when it is abeam. Of course, using plane trigonometry it is possible to solve any triangle to find the distance off but, as in most navigation, a little foresight will save a lot of calculations.

To achieve precision using this table you must be able to take bearings to ½° accuracy. Expensive gyrocompasses on large ships can do this, but compasses on small craft can't. Therefore, all calculations using this method should be considered approximate.

Pairs of Bearings Whose Cotangents Differ by One

20	29¾
21	31¾
22	34
23	36¼
24	38¾
25	41
26	43½
26½	45
27	46
28	48½
29	51
30	53¾
31	56¼
32	59
33	61½
34	64¼
35	66¾
36	69¼
37	71¾
38	74¼
39	76¾
40	79
41	81¼
42	83½
43	85¾
44	88
45	90

Remember that no allowance is made for set and drift in this solution, and that the distance off must be measured from the object itself and not the shore in front of it.

line, the line of the first bearing, and the line of the second bearing form an isosceles right triangle. The two legs of this triangle that form the right angle must be equal in length. You are, therefore, 1.5 miles from the object when it's abeam. Note that the angle has doubled from 045° relative to 090° relative. This particular version of this technique is called *bow and beam bearings.*

You can use the geometric relationships in other triangles in the same way. Any time the relative bearing to an object doubles, an isosceles triangle is formed, and the distance run between the times of the bearings equals a fraction of the distance off the object when it is abeam. This technique is called *doubling the angle on the bow* and can help you stay the required distance offshore.

Here are some of the rule-of-thumb fractions that mariners frequently use:

- ***Seven-tenths rule:*** The distance to an object directly abeam equals 7⁄10 of the distance traveled while the bearing changes from 22½° to 45° relative or from 135° to 157½° relative.
- ***Seven-eighths rule:*** The distance to an object equals 7⁄8 of the distance traveled while the bearing changes from 30° to 60° relative or from 129° to 150° relative.
- ***Seven-thirds rule:*** The distance to an object on the beam equals 7⁄3 of the dis-

tance traveled while the bearing changes from 22½° to 26½° relative, from 67½° to 90° relative, from 90° to 112½° relative, or from 153½° to 157½° relative. (This, of course, is not a case of "doubling the angle on the bow.")

Note: In these rules, as in all these problems, set and drift are not accounted for.

An ideal way to become familiar with these procedures is to use them in conjunction with the waypoint navigation capabilities of the Loran-C or GPS receiver. By setting a waypoint a certain distance off a point and plotting your vessel's course along the trackline using these distance off techniques, you can see how well they work and be ready for the day when the Loran-C or GPS break down.

Relative bearings are measured with reference to the vessel's bow, with 000° at the bow, 090° on the starboard beam, 180° directly astern, and 270° on the port beam. To convert magnetic steering or hand-bearing compass bearings to relative bearings, add or subtract your vessel's course as necessary.

For a quick approximation of distance off, use the following rule: The distance off an object is approximately equal to the time in minutes it takes for the bearing to change the same amount as the value of the speed. For example, if you're steaming at 10 knots and observe that a bearing change of 10° takes six minutes, your vessel is about six miles off.

Electronics in Piloting

The use of electronics in navigation has exploded in recent years due to new systems, lower costs, and more reliable equipment. Using this equipment in piloting is prudent and safe and often results in good fixes, accurate assessments of set and drift, and close attention to courses. But beware—although electronic devices are extremely reliable, they are not foolproof.

Global Positioning System (GPS), Loran-C, and radar are the main electronic navigation devises available to the small-craft navigator. GPS and Loran-C units that include computers capable of giving latitude and longitude coordinates are extremely useful for piloting. (Both systems are discussed in detail in Chapter 8, "Satellite Navigation," and Chapter 9, "Loran-C.") Although radar is extremely useful for navigation, it only gives LOPs and cannot compute a latitude/longitude position. Its use is discussed in Chapter 10, "Radar Navigation."

It is all too easy to simply plug in the coordinates of waypoints into your GPS or Loran-C set and steer from one waypoint to the next without referring to a chart. Don't do that. At regular intervals you should plot the latitude/longitude coordinates from the Loran-C or GPS on a chart. Also, at each waypoint you should plot the electronic position to verify the accuracy of the device and its readout.

To plot the coordinates, simply write down the latitude and longitude given by the system and use dividers, triangles, parallel rules, or a draftsman's compass to find the exact position on the chart that they represent. It's also a good idea to take a couple of visual bearings or radar ranges, if possible, for confirmation. In 1995, a large cruise ship went aground at full speed because the watch officer failed to confirm the erroneous GPS plot with other LOPs.

Loran-C is sometimes used in its *Time Difference (TD)* mode instead of the latitude/longitude mode because it is more accurate. When used in this mode, Loran-C provides LOPs that are segments of curved lines that represent the time differences between the receipt of radio signals from various stations, rather than a lat/long position. A Loran-C LOP can be crossed with any other LOP to get a fix. (See Chapter 9, "Loran-C Navigation," for additional instructions.)

Increasingly, boaters are using automatic pilots to steer small craft. Autopilots are valuable aids to navigation because they increase steering accuracy, relieve the tedium of sitting at a helm, and allow the navigator to perform other useful tasks such as monitoring traffic and taking visual fixes. Typical autopilot readouts are course ordered, speed, waypoint being steered on, and distance to that waypoint. (See Figure 6-10.)

Waypoint Navigation

Because Loran-C and GPS sets contain sophisticated computers, it's easy for manufacturers to program them to do a variety of tasks besides simply show a vessel's position. One of their most helpful tricks is to remember *waypoints*.

A waypoint is a point on the earth, expressed in latitude and longitude, Loran-C TDs, or some other measure, through which you intend to pass at some time. Most Loran-C and GPS systems can calculate the distance and bearing from any waypoint to any other. This means that, instead of drawing a course from one point to another on a chart and measuring it, you can enter the waypoints into the set and let it do the work. Distance and bearing to the next waypoint are displayed, as well as information on the relationship of the vessel to the trackline (right or left). Although using electronics to calculate waypoints may seem easier than doing it by hand on a chart, it only takes a single data entry error to produce a course far from that intended. Consequently, you should check all courses and distances between points on the chart before using waypoint readouts and carefully monitor your progress the first time they are used. Once you verify them by actual use, you have confidence in repeated uses.

Figure 6-10. *An autopilot can increase the accuracy of a boat's course, save a navigator's energy, and allow more time for close monitoring of the navigational situation. It can also lead to potentially dangerous dependence and complacency. Digital autopilots integrated with other navigation systems such as Loran-C or GPS indicate course, speed, waypoint number, distance to the waypoint, cross-track error, and perhaps other information. (Photograph courtesy Raytheon)*

The word "safe" in navigation is relative. No system is totally free of error, and electronic navigation systems, like any other, should be continually and carefully watched to make sure they are providing information that is consistent with other observations and calculations.

Accuracy Factors

Most fixes using three or more LOPs result not in a perfect intersection of lines but in a so-called *cocked hat,* as shown in Figure 6-12. When all of the LOPs are error-free, they must intersect at a single point. When there is some error in at least one of the

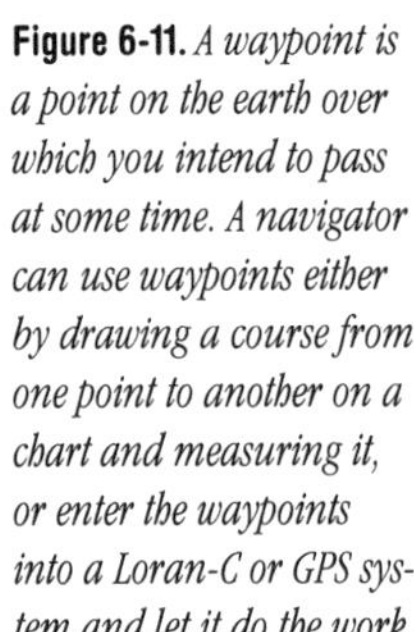

Figure 6-11. *A waypoint is a point on the earth over which you intend to pass at some time. A navigator can use waypoints either by drawing a course from one point to another on a chart and measuring it, or enter the waypoints into a Loran-C or GPS system and let it do the work.*

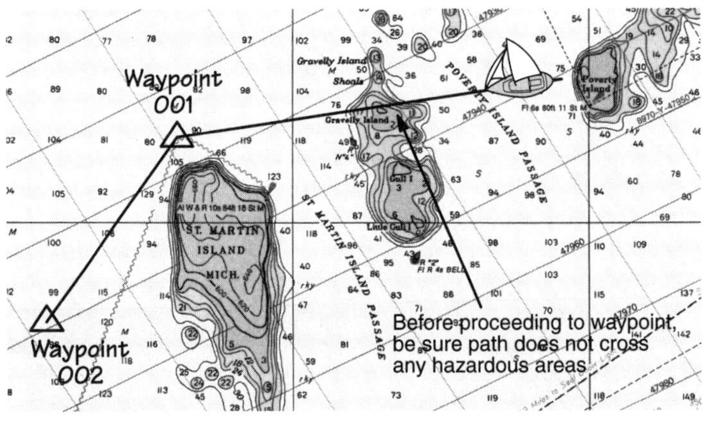

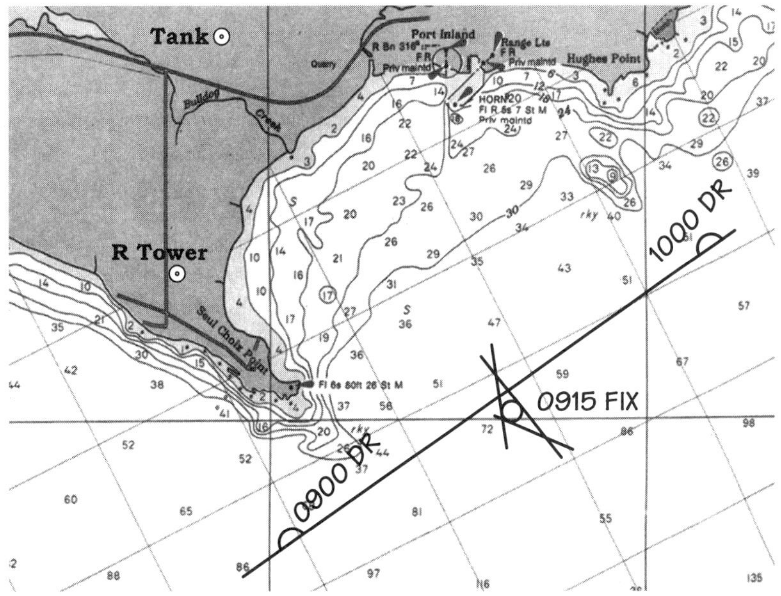

Figure 6-12. *This shows a typical "cocked hat" resulting from various errors in three LOPs. In this case, you would place the fix at the center of the triangle—but regard it with caution because each LOP represents a band of position and it's possible that your vessel is outside the triangle.*

Figure 6-13. *Given that every LOP has some error, a fix position might reasonably be anywhere within a polygon that encompasses all errors from each LOP. The larger the error, the larger is this polygon of possible positions. Though we label the intersection of the LOPs as a fix, the real position could be anywhere within this figure. Good judgement—"sea sense"—helps to refine the position beyond what is mathematically possible.*

LOPS they intersect in the triangular cocked hat pattern. It is likely—in fact, it is nearly certain—that there is some error in all LOPs. So, most of your plotted fixes will look like cocked hats.

Fix accuracy depends on the accuracy of all of the LOPs that comprise it. When taking a bearing you might make an error in the observation, in the compass correction for deviation and variation, in plotting the bearing on the chart, and so on. If there were a 0.5° error in the same direction in each of these factors, an LOP might be in error by 2° or more. Even when you don't know the errors, you can take them into account.

You can consider that an LOP is a *band of position* instead of a line of position. You might be exactly on the line, but it is also possible that you are somewhere within a band that encompasses all possible errors. Intersecting bands of position result in polygons that contain all possible positions. This is why it is so important to take more than two bearings whenever possible. Each additional bearing decreases the size of the polygon of possible positions, and refines the fix to its smallest possible area. (See Figure 6-13.)

Another factor that affects fix accuracy is the angle of intersection of the LOPs. For two LOPs, an angle of 90° is best, because it provides the smallest possible polygon. For three LOPs, angles of 60° between each one are best, again because they provide the smallest possible polygon.

You might sense which LOPs are the best in any given fix when taking the bearings. If you are uncertain about the accuracy of an LOP, take the bearing again or, even better, take a bearing to another object in about the

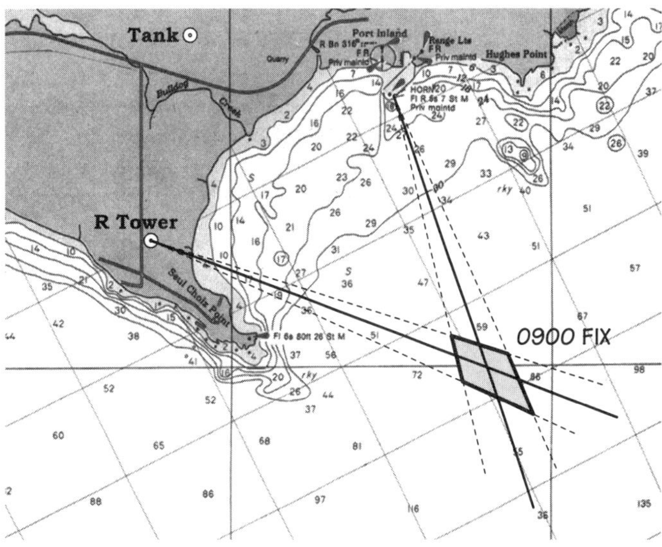

same or opposite direction. This will either confirm or belie the doubtful LOP.

The grounding and loss of ships and boats due to navigational errors are nearly always due to the navigator's failure to follow proper procedures. The most common errors are

Failure to obtain or evaluate soundings

Misidentifying aids to navigation

Failure to use available navigation aids

Failure to correct charts

Failure to compensate the compass

Failure to apply deviation

Failure to apply variation

Failure to check the compass regularly

Failure to keep a DR plot

Ignoring new information

Faulty evaluation of information

Poor judgment, often in the form of unwarranted optimism

Ignoring charts and publications

Poor organization of navigational responsibilities

Failure to plan ahead

Failure to have or use backup systems

Sophisticated computer navigation systems are able to refine a position using several sources of positioning inputs and the potential errors in each. A technique called *Kalman filtering* uses complex statistical analysis to average out all errors and give the most probable position.

A far more sophisticated process takes place in a navigator's brain—each LOP is analyzed and plotted, proper weight is given to each, and the final fix is plotted using common sense and experience. Unlike a computer, a navigator can learn from mistakes. Remember, too, that no checklist can cover all eventualities and that common sense and "sea sense" are important tools—which come only with experience.

Turn, Danger, and Anchor Bearings

Preplotted bearings are useful in a number of ways. For example, when plotting a course change you'll need to turn at some point. If the point is not near an aid to navigation, such as a buoy or light, you'll have to find a more distant reference for the point where the turn should begin. From that reference you can draw a turn bearing.

As shown in Figure 6-14, a turn bearing passes through the point of the turn. Choose the distant object so it comes as close as possible to a right angle with your existing course. Draw the bearing on the chart, label it with the degrees (magnetic or true), and convert it to a compass bearing for the course you're on going into the turn. As you pass the object its bearing will slowly change. When it reaches the turn bearing, turn to the new course.

Danger bearings are similar to turn bearings, but serve to warn you about rocks, shoals, or other obstructions. To establish a danger bearing, draw a line on the chart tangent to the danger area and to a distant object. Measure the bearing, correct for the compass, and label it. When the bearing to the distant object is on the "wrong" side of the safe bearing, the vessel is standing into danger. Mark a danger bearing line with "feathers" on the dangerous side, as shown in Figure 6-14.

You can also draw *anchor bearings*—similar to turn bearings—to indicate where you should anchor. An ideal anchor bearing is approximately at a right angle to your approach course. Be flexible, though, because you might not know your course until you reach the anchorage and assess the wind and weather conditions there. Anchor bearings are routinely used by large ships, but they can be useful for small craft in large harbors and roadsteads or where the anchor position must be especially accurate.

Once anchored, take bearings on several objects and record them to check for dragging. Bearings on your beam give you the

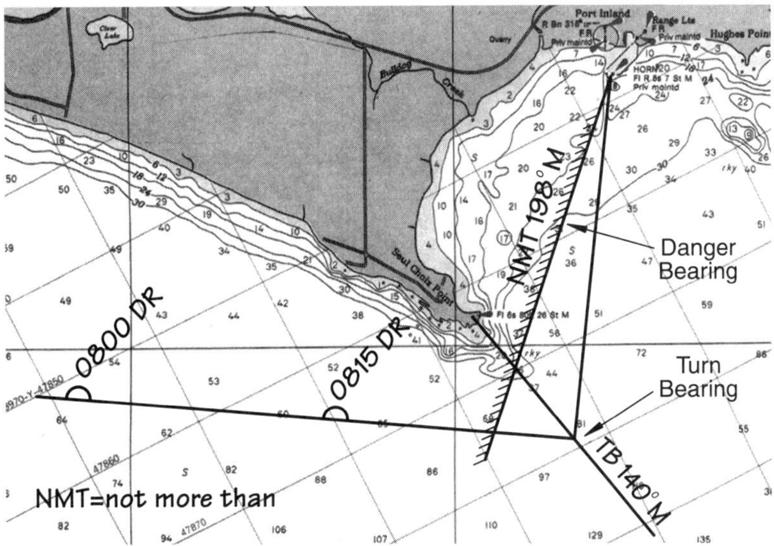

Figure 6-14. *Turn bearings can provide a reference point when turning to a new course. Large ships must plan far ahead because a turn for them can take several minutes. Small craft, which turn much faster, can make the turn at the minute the bearing is reached. Danger bearings can serve as a warning that the vessel is on the dangerous side of a line drawn from a charted object tangent to a hazardous area. Danger bearings are hatched on the dangerous side and labeled "NMT-XXX" (no more than) or "NLT-XXX" (no less than) a certain measured bearing.*

clearest indication of dragging, but you should take bearings on objects around the compass so that one or two useful bearings are available if a wind or current shift swings your boat around.

Navigation During Anchoring

A navigator's responsibilities in anchoring begin well before the anchor splashes down. Choosing a good place to anchor is the first task. *Coast Pilots, Sailing Directions,* cruising guides, charts, and local knowledge, if available, can inform you about good spots. Look for an anchorage that's free of obstructions, sheltered from adverse weather and sea conditions, deep enough to float the boat during low tides (but not too deep for the ground tackle), and a bottom composition that's good for holding the anchor without fouling or dragging.

Because you want to make your final approach into the wind or current (whichever has the greater effect on your boat), the wind or current direction will determine your final course. (With good boat-handling skills, though, it is possible to anchor downwind or down-current.) To reach the anchorage area, draw your DR trackline right to it. Preselect several charted objects so you can take bearings and plot your final fix.

In selecting a spot to lower an anchor on a large ship, the navigator must allow for the ship's length, which may be up to one fifth mile long, and lower the anchor when the ship's bow—not the pilothouse—is over the anchoring point. As the navigator on a small craft, anchoring in a tight harbor, you have to make a similar allowance for the length of the anchor rode when choosing the exact spot to lower the anchor.

After your anchor is down and holding and your boat has settled to the wind and current, take a final round of bearings and record them—it's very easy to forget the bearings

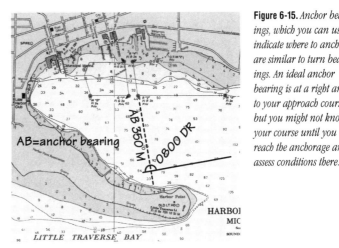

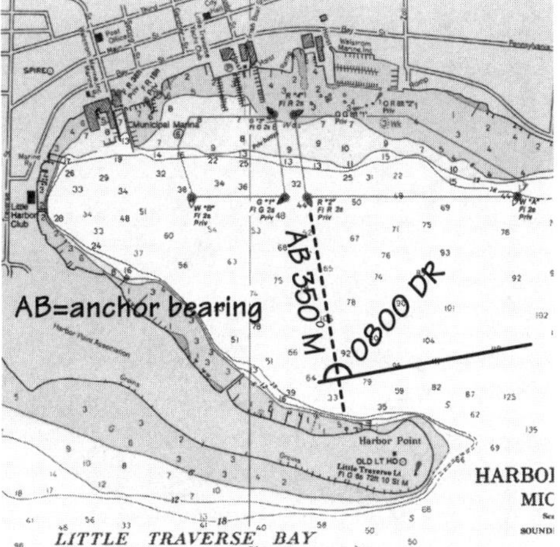

Figure 6-15. *Anchor bearings, which you can use to indicate where to anchor, are similar to turn bearings. An ideal anchor bearing is at a right angle to your approach course, but you might not know your course until you reach the anchorage and assess conditions there.*

and without them, it's impossible to tell if your anchor has dragged. Many electronic navigation systems, including loran and GPS, have *"anchor watch"* features that let you set an anchoring point. When your vessel drifts off that point, an alarm sounds.

Depthsounders often have "shallow water" alarms that are useful in large harbors, but they're subject to error. In a small anchorage your boat could well end up in serious difficulty before you could respond to such an alarm.

The Piloting Routine

Piloting is not an event. Rather, it is a circular process consisting of a series of steps that follow each other logically and lead in an endless loop until piloting is no longer appropriate for the navigational situation. In order, these steps are:

1. On a chart, draw the vessel's intended track from a known point, choose a DR interval, and plot and label DR positions.
2. Take bearings on charted objects at intervals based on the navigational situation.
3. Correct the compass bearings, plot the bearings on the chart, and label the fix.
4. Compare the fix with the corresponding DR position to determine set and drift.
5. Reset the track from the new fix and draw in the new trackline to the next DR position.
6. To compensate for set and drift, adjust the course so that your boat will likely arrive at the next DR position.
7. Repeat the process, beginning with step #2.
8. Use every available opportunity to check your position with natural and manmade ranges.

In addition to getting fixes at regular intervals, it's a good idea to plot a new fix with every change of course or speed because the factors that affect your path over the ground will have changed.

Practical Considerations in Piloting

If you followed every step in this process of piloting you'd be a busy navigator, indeed. Even so, these steps are followed religiously aboard naval vessels, with a *piloting team* consisting of as many as 10 or 15 people. When professional navigators learn their trade as cadets, instructors insist on absolute adherence to proper procedures for hours on end. Doing so builds good habits, skills, and confidence. For your training purposes, as well, follow all proper piloting procedures. You can later selectively disregard them when you've gained the experience needed to make good judgments. Practice in well-known waters in good weather, so that you can depend on your navigation skills when they're really needed. When the weather turns bad, the sea begins to rise, fog closes in, and night falls, the hours of practice and drilling in fine weather will pay off.

PART 2

ELECTRONIC NAVIGATION

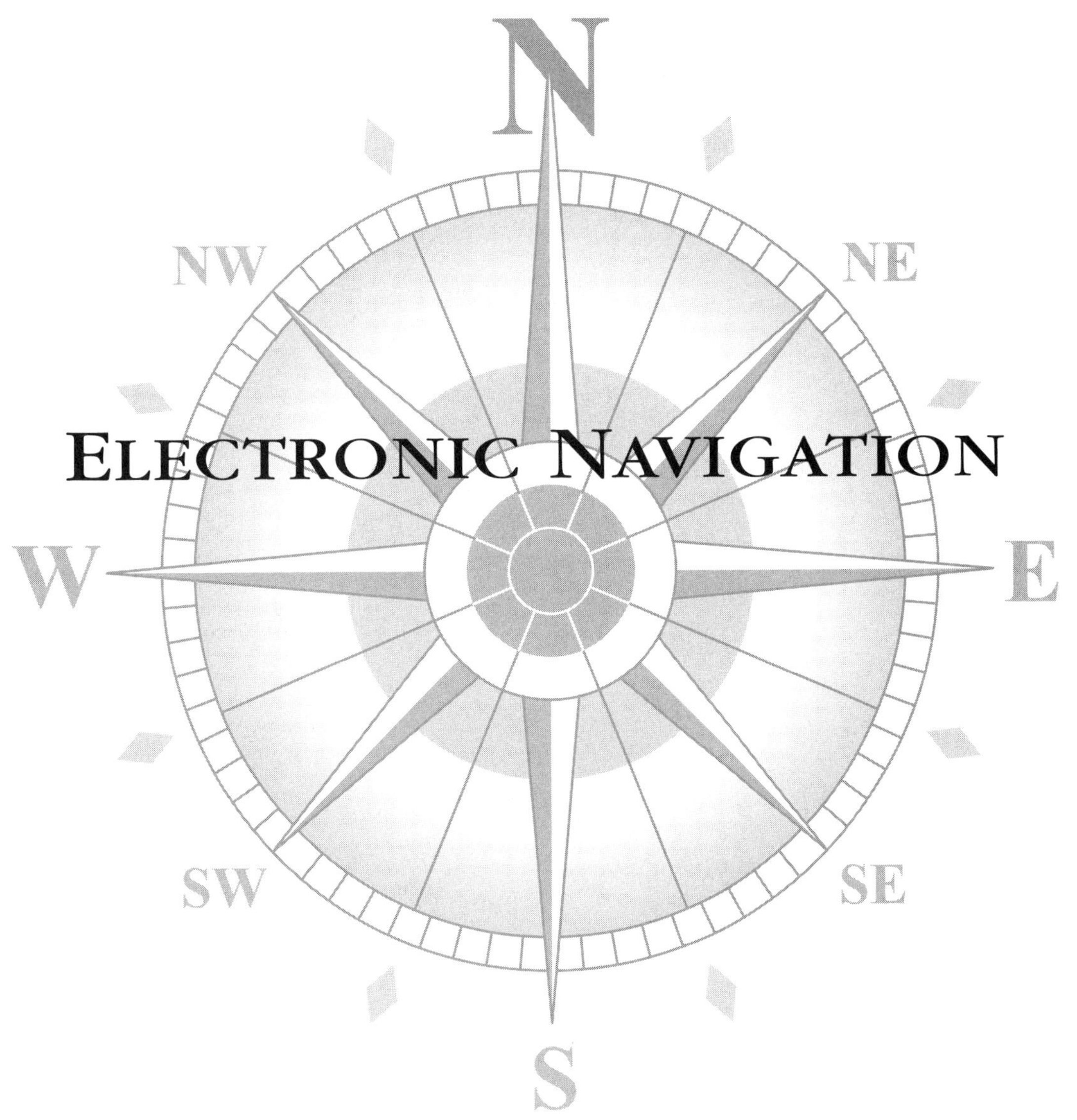

CHAPTER SEVEN

Radio Waves in Navigation

NAVIGATORS HAVE USED *RADIO waves* since very shortly after their discovery more than a century ago. In 1887 Heinrich Hertz validated the brilliant but untested theories of James Maxwell by producing the first *electromagnetic waves*. Guglielmo Marconi transmitted the first radio message in 1895; by 1901 he could send *wireless* signals some 2,000 miles. Ashore, the telegraph had already been established to provide long-distance communications, but it was at sea that the wireless came into its own, making it possible to communicate with ships hundreds of miles from land.

Radio waves have two primary uses at sea—navigation and communication. This book deals with the navigation function. The most modern satellite navigation systems use radio signals to establish position. Some systems use several signals on different frequencies to determine a position or single line of position. Although systems vary in type and number of frequencies and signals, all use radio waves that are basically identical, differing only in strength, frequency, and wavelength.

The radio energy spectrum is very broad, encompassing frequencies ranging from far below the range of human hearing to cosmic rays—from 20 cycles-per-second to 48,000 million, million, million cycles-per-second—and wavelengths ranging from 15,000,000 meters down to .0000000000062 centimeters.

Radio waves differ in other characteristics as well and are affected by forces in nature that enhance or diminish their effectiveness. Navigators should understand their characteristics so they can appreciate their limitations and capabilities. Some background knowledge is essential if you want to use electronic navigation systems intelligently.

The Source of Radio Energy

Electrical energy is the flow of *electrons* along a *conductor*. In *direct current,* electrons flow continuously in the same direction, while in *alternating current* they flow back-and-forth with no net change in position. When electrons flow in a wire, their energy heats the wire (to a degree related to the wire's ability to conduct the electrons) and forms an electromagnetic field around the wire, radiating out into space. The orientation of this field depends on the polarity—positive or negative—of the current's source.

If the current is suddenly stopped, the electromagnetic field collapses back into the wire, taking a finite amount of time to do so. If the current's polarity reverses, a field of opposite polarity develops around the wire. However, when the polarity of the field is changed so rapidly that the previous field doesn't collapse before another of opposite polarity develops, each new field forces the previous one out into space. The energy thus produced is known as *electromagnetic waves,* or radio waves.

Terminology of Radio Waves

Radio waves behave much like waves in water. They start from some zero point, build to a crest, decrease down past the zero point to a trough, and build again to zero. The *amplitude* of a radio wave is its height; the *length* of the wave determines its *frequency*. The frequency is measured in *cycles-per-second* and expressed in the term *Hertz,* named for the German physicist who first described the phenomenon. A frequency of 1,000 cycles-per-second is called one kilohertz (kHz); 1,000,000 cycles-per-second is known as a megahertz (mHz). Two radio wave systems are *in phase* if they have the same frequency and *out of phase* if their frequencies differ. (Some types of navigation systems use this important characteristic.)

The *frequency range* of radio waves is 10 kilohertz to 300,000 megahertz. Above the radio spectrum are infrared light, visible light, ultraviolet light, X-rays, and various forms of cosmic radiation.

Behavior of Radio Waves

The magnetic and electrical fields produced by radio waves are always oriented 90° to each other. Radio waves can be either horizontally or vertically polarized. All waves near the earth are vertically polarized because the earth is a conductor and quickly absorbs horizontally polarized radiation. Radio waves that strike the earth at an angle are not absorbed, but are reflected back out into space at the same angle they struck.

When a radio wave strikes the earth and is reflected, a phase shift occurs because a small part of the energy is absorbed by the earth. If a wave travels directly to a receiver and also reaches the receiver after reflecting off the earth, these signals will be slightly out of phase with each other, resulting in *wave interference.* The longer path of the reflected signal also contributes to wave interference. If the two signals are 180° different in phase and have equal amplitude, they will cancel each other out.

Systems are designed to minimize wave interference, using radio frequencies that reduce interference to the point where it is not a factor.

Radio waves share many characteristics with waves on the water—phase differences, wave interference, and reflecting properties. You will see many of these same terms used in Chapter 21 ("Oceanography").

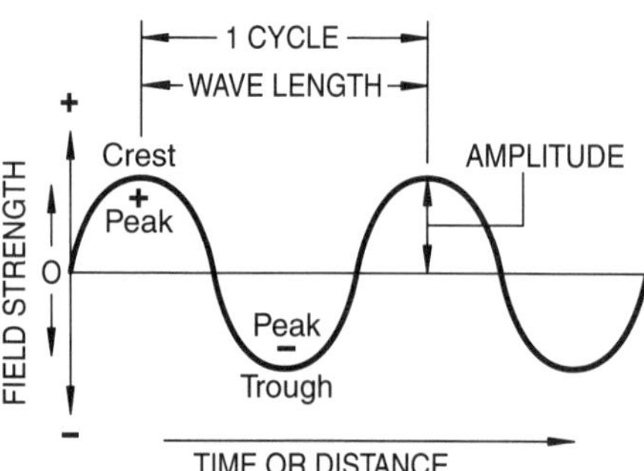

Figure 7-1. *Radio waves resemble water waves, but have their own terminology. The wave's height is called its* amplitude, *its length from crest to crest the* wavelength, *and the number of cycles per second over time or distance its* frequency.

Surfaces vary in the extent to which they reflect radio waves. Certain frequencies are reflected by precipitation and clouds, others by radiation belts high above the earth, others by solid objects. Even air masses can serve as reflecting surfaces. Radar uses these properties to detect weather phenomena—rain, snow, and thunderstorms—and the results are visible on television weather reports.

Refraction is the bending of radio waves as they pass through such atmospheric changes as sharp temperature or humidity gradients. Normal atmospheric refraction along the surface of the earth increases the range of certain radio waves by about 15 percent and accounts for radar's ability to "see" over the horizon.

A *duct* is an area in the atmosphere that allows radio waves to pass relatively unimpeded, thereby greatly increasing their range. A duct along the surface of the earth can enable radio waves to travel phenomenal distances and is usually associated with infrequent weather phenomena such as temperature inversions.

The Ionosphere and Its Effects

A normal atom is electronically neutral, but when it loses one or more of its electrons it loses its neutrality. It is then called an *ion*. During the day, sunlight—consisting of electromagnetic radiation—strikes atoms in the upper reaches of the earth's atmosphere and causes certain atoms to lose electrons, forming ion layers. In the lower reaches of the atmosphere these ions recombine with other atoms to become electrically neutral again, so the ion layers don't extend down close to the earth.

For an ion to form, the force that is acting to detach an atom's electrons must be stronger than the force holding them near the nucleus. Types of atoms differ in their reaction to radiation, and types of radiation have different effects. As a result, various reactions occur to atoms in the presence of radiation.

Two upper atmosphere ion layers, known as *F layers,* are caused by the effect of the sun on single, free, oxygen molecules. The *F1 layer* is about 90 miles above the earth and the *F2 layer* is about 125 miles above. At night, in the absence of the sun's radiation, these two layers combine in a single F layer. Below these altitudes, the radiation causing this type of ionization is absorbed. (See Figure 7-2.)

Below the F layer is the *E layer,* caused by the effect of certain frequencies of the sun's radiation on large numbers of oxygen molecules. This layer does not fluctuate as the F layer does, but instead is constant at an altitude of about 60 miles. At night the E layer is much weaker.

Below the E layer is the *D layer,* caused by the sun's effect on ozone in the atmosphere. At an altitude of about 45 miles, this layer is where most of the absorption of certain frequencies of radio waves and the reflection of others occurs.

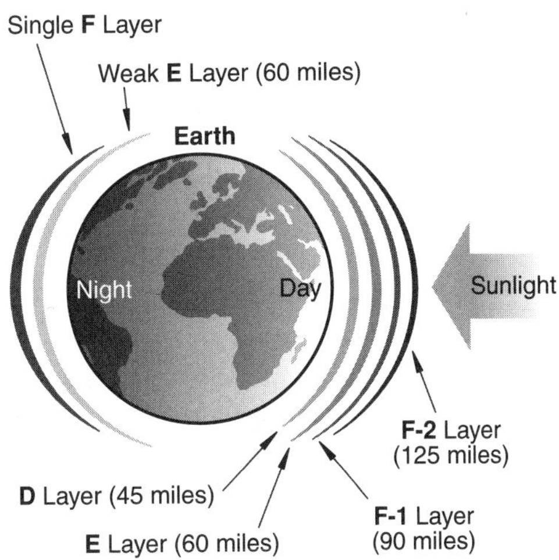

Figure 7-2. *Radiation from the sun reacts atomically with molecules in the earth's upper atmosphere to produce layers of ionospheric particles that may interfere with or enhance some radio signals. This drawing, not to scale, shows the ionospheric belts.*

Skywaves and Groundwaves

A radio wave may travel directly along the earth from transmitter to receiver, in which case it is called a *groundwave*. It may also refract off one or more of the ionospheric layers back to the earth as a *skywave*. In fact, under some conditions, a wave can travel from its source to refract off a layer of ionization, be refracted back to the ground, be refracted upward again to a layer of ionization, and then finally reach a receiver on the second refraction (See Figure 7-3.) This is a *two-hop* refraction. *One-* or *two-hop* refractions can

Figure 7-3. *Radio waves may travel in a number of different paths from source to receiver. If the wave enters the ionospheric layer at a nearly right angle, it will not be refracted enough to bend back toward the earth, but will travel out into space. One-hop E, one-hop F, and two-hop F refractions are the most common and can redirect a radio signal to carry more than 1,400 miles from its source.*

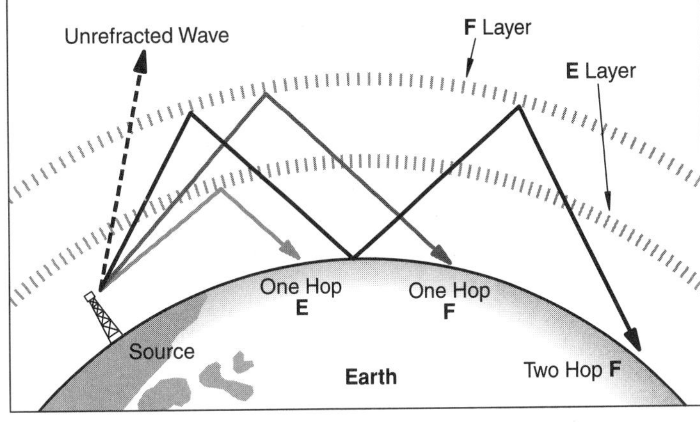

be caused by any of the ionospheric layers, depending on the frequencies of the waves and the refracting qualities of the layers.

The different distances traveled by groundwaves and skywaves may cause phase differences at the receiver. The resulting fading and distortion of the signal may vary over time because the ionospheric layers are not constant in width, altitude, or density. Imagine the earth rotating on its axis. On the side nearest the sun are the various layers of ionization caused by the sun's radiation; on the opposite side they are weak or nonexistent. Between these areas, near sunrise and sunset, where the layers are alternately forming and dissipating as the earth spins beneath, there is a region of very disturbed and fluctuating ionization that may cause severe distortion of radio signals. This phenomenon is evident on any AM radio receiver around sunset and sunrise.

Refraction is the bending of waves, while reflection is the bouncing off. Radio waves are refracted in ionospheric layers because they enter the layer and are gradually turned away again, rather than bounce off its edge.

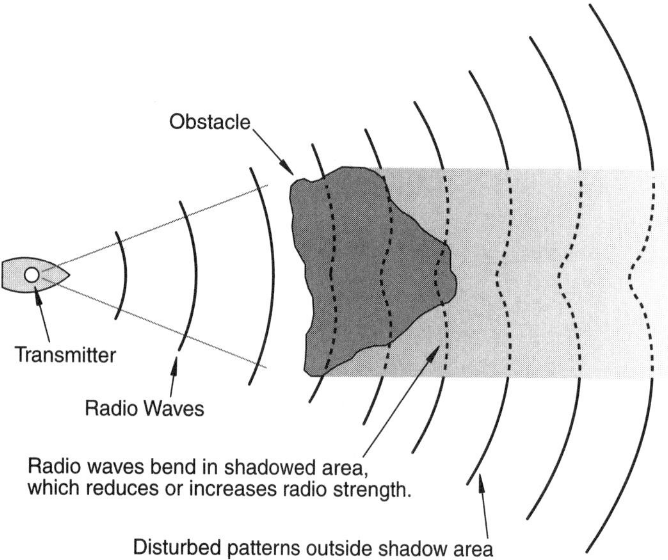

Figure 7-4. *When radio waves encounter an obstacle, such as this island, the waves bend around it. Any receiver behind the obstacle could receive a disturbed or weakened radio signal.*

Adverse Effects on Radio Waves

Diffraction is the bending of radio waves around a solid object such as an island, which may cause phase differences and consequent weakening or strengthening of the signal near the edge of the object.

As radio waves travel, they gradually lose some of their strength in a process called *attenuation*. The denser the medium the waves travel through, the greater this effect. The earth causes some attenuation because its density bends the waves downward, sapping some energy as the waves travel along. Attenuation is less if the surface over which the waves travel is a good conductor. Because the sea—with its salt water—is a better conductor than land, attenuation is greater over land. This has very important effects on radionavigation systems.

Interference is the reception of unwanted signals that conflict with the desired ones. *Noise* is caused by unintentional interference; *jamming* is deliberate interference cause by signals that intentionally conflict with desired ones. Noise can come from natural or manmade sources. Electrical storms, static electricity, and background cosmic radiation can cause natural noise, which tends to be very broad in frequency. Natural noise diminishes only above about 30 megahertz.

Any radio wave source, including nearby electronic equipment, electrical devices such as motors and generators, and static electricity can cause manmade noise. You can see its effects on a television set while a kitchen appliance is running.

Range of Radio Waves

The *range* of radio waves is determined by the outgoing signal strength, the frequency, atmospheric conditions, route of travel, noise level at the chosen frequency, and the sensitivity of the receiver. In general, low-frequency waves travel greater distances than high-frequency ones. Designers of electronic communications and navigation gear take advantage of the characteristics of different frequencies in designing systems.

It's good that the higher frequencies cannot be heard for great distances, because there are millions of sources of high frequency radio waves in the world and you would hear a cacophony if you received them all.

The geographic range of specific radio frequencies is discussed below.

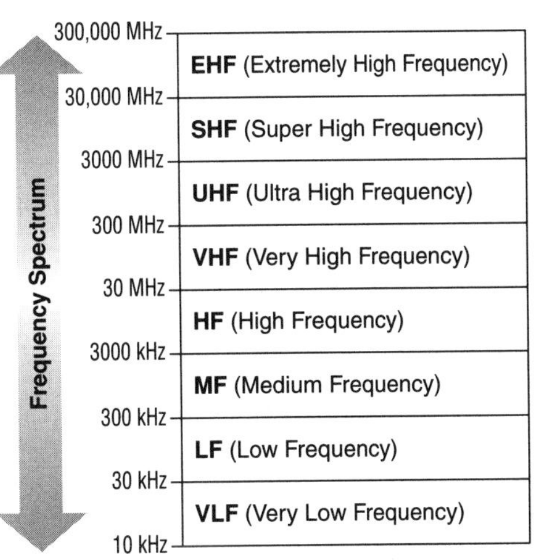

Figure 7-5. *Just as varying colors comprise the spectrum of visual light, several bands of radio frequencies comprise the radio frequency spectrum, from* Very Low Frequency *(10–30 kHz), radio signals of which can circle the globe below the surface of the sea, to* Extremely High Frequency *(30,000–300,000 MHz), whose short wavelengths virtually eliminate wave interference, diffraction, and fading.*

The RF Spectrum

For convenience, the band of electromagnetic radiation encompassing the *radio frequency (RF) spectrum* is divided into several broad categories; each interacts differently with the atmosphere. (See Figure 7-5.) These are:

Very Low Frequency **(VLF, 10 to 30 kHz)**—These signals travel below the lowest ionospheric layer, which guides them around the curvature of the earth. Their ranges are extremely long, even globe circling, and electrical storms have little effect on them. VLF signals can travel below the surface of the sea, and so are valuable for submarine communications, though the data transmission rate is slow and large antennae are needed to generate the long wavelength signals.

Low Frequency **(LF, 30 to 300 kHz)**—In this band, range is reduced by attenuation, but antennae are more efficient. LF signals are most stable in groundwave form, making this band suitable for radio direction finding, loran signals, and transmission of time signals.

Medium Frequency **(MF, 300 to 3,000 kHz)**—This band is characterized by dependable groundwaves, but a greatly reduced groundwave range. Signals are also strongly affected by the ionospheric layers, forming skywaves that allow a low power signal travel thousands of miles. This is the band of commercial AM radio stations and the ionspheric confusion is responsible for periodic loss of signals at sunrise and sunset. Skywaves lengthen reception of nighttime signals to great distances.

High Frequency **(HF, 3 to 30 MHz)**—The groundwave in this band has a very limited range, but long ranges are possible with skywaves. Frequencies of 10 to 30 mHz produce effective skywaves during the day, and 8 to 10 mHz frequencies produce them at night. This band is used for ship-to-ship and ship-to-shore communication over long distances.

Very High Frequency **(VHF, 30 to 300 MHz)**—In this band, the direct band is most useful, and skywaves are almost nonexistent. Range is normally limited to line-of-sight distances, with a little added for refraction. There is little atmospheric noise, and directional antennae can be used to increase signal strength. This band contains the entire VHF marine radio spectrum, as well as many other short-range communication systems and VHF television signals.

Ultra High Frequency **(UHF, 300 to 3,000 MHz)**—There are no effective skywaves in this band because the waves pass through the ionospheric layers and go into space. The groundwave, however, can extend beyond the visible horizon due to refraction. This band is little affected by fading and atmospheric noise, and directional antennae can beam strong signals with low-power outputs. This band is used for marine radio communications and for television signals.

Super High Frequency **(SHF, 3,000 to 30,000 MHz)**—This is the so-called microwave band. Skywaves and atmospheric noise are absent, and directional antennae can focus signals precisely. The microwave towers that dot high points of our landscape, with their dish antennae pointing in various directions, are evidence of the usefulness of this band for communications. Rain, clouds, and dust can be reflected at the upper part of this band, making it effective for radar.

Extremely High Frequency **(EHF, 30,000 to 300,000 MHz)**—The short wavelengths in this band almost nullify completely the effects of wave interference, diffraction, and fading, and produce no skywaves. Atmospheric effects are pronounced, however.

The Federal Communications Commission regulates the entire *RF spectrum* in the United States, and international agreements help to organize its use. The allocation of frequencies minimizes interference among stations and users, and bands for unauthorized use are separated from the authorized ones to further prevent interference. Within the bands authorized for use, stations—such as marine radio stations—are given the discretion to pick from among several frequencies the one most effective for their use.

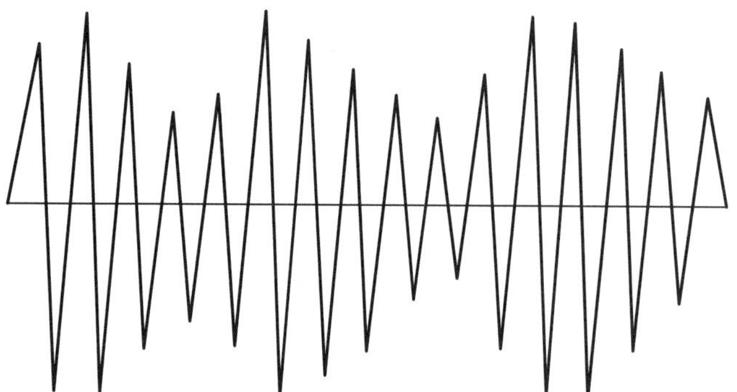

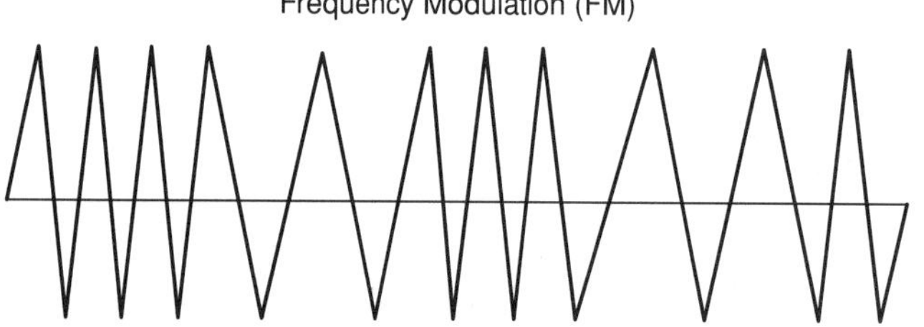

Figure 7-6. *Amplitude modulation (AM) is variation of the amplitude or wave height of the radio signal. Frequency Modulation (FM) is the variation of the frequency or wave length. These variations allow information in the form of music, voice, or navigation data to be superimposed on the basic radio wave.*

Signal Types

A radio wave of constant amplitude and frequency produces a continuous, unwavering "tone." To transmit useful information, this tone must be modified or *modulated* in some way.

In *amplitude modulation (AM)* the wave's amplitude, or "wave height," is modified. (See Figure 7-6.) An AM radio station, for example, transmits sounds of different frequencies and tones with variations in amplitude. Although AM radio operates in a frequency band that carries long range, it is subject to atmospheric noise and skywave interference. You hear their effects when listening to commercial AM radio stations during a thunderstorm that is accompanied by lightning.

In *frequency modulation (FM)* the wave's frequency, or "wave length," is modified. This type of signal is also used for radio communications, as well as in the audio portion of television signals, but it has shorter range than AM transmissions because of the frequencies used. On the other hand, this type of signal and its associated frequency band are little affected by atmospheric interference or skywaves. This is why lightning has little effect on FM radio signals.

Transmitters and Receivers

A *radio transmitter* consists of a *power source* to supply electricity, an *oscillator* to convert electrical energy into radio waves, a *frequency controller* and *modulator* to superimpose information on the basic wave pattern, an *amplifier* to increase the power of the signal, and a grounded *antenna* to radiate the signal out into space.

A *radio receiver* consists of an *antenna* to sense the passing waves of radio energy, a *demodulator* to convert the modulated basic wave pattern into usable form, and a *speaker* or other device to present the information to the user.

Both transmitter and receiver antennae are very carefully designed for optimum performance at a particular frequency. Therefore, an antenna for one type of radio may be totally unsuitable for a different type.

Receivers vary in quality according to the following properties:

Sensitivity—the ability to distinguish between a signal and background noise

Selectivity—the ability to select useful signals from others nearby

Range—the range of frequencies they can detect

Stability—the ability to stay tuned to the desired signal

Fidelity—the ability to reproduce precisely the transmitted signal

These characteristics are somewhat interrelated and some are mutually exclusive. In general, more expensive radios have better operating characteristics than cheaper ones. You should not skimp on the quality of navigation or communications gear on which your life may someday depend.

Both transmitter and receiver can be combined in a single unit called a *transceiver*. A marine VHF radio is a transceiver because it both sends and receives signals. A Loran-C or GPS navigation unit is a receiver only; it's incapable of transmitting a signal.

National Radionavigation Policy

In the United States, the *Federal Radionavigation Plan (FRP)* regulates radionavigation systems. The Plan is a biennial document prepared jointly by the Departments of Defense and Transportation, with input from many user groups and other federal and state agencies. It contains a detailed discussion of each type of navigation system and a summary of the patterns of present and future use, and it sets dates for implementing new systems and discontinuing old ones.

The *National Command Authority,* a military organization, can order a suspension of all radio navigation systems in a national emergency, thereby denying adversaries the use of our systems against us. The military would continue to use its secure version of the GPS, but this, too, could be suspended if it were compromised.

The marine radio navigation systems covered by the FRP include radiobeacons, Loran-C, Omega, GPS, and Transit. The plans for these systems are summarized below.

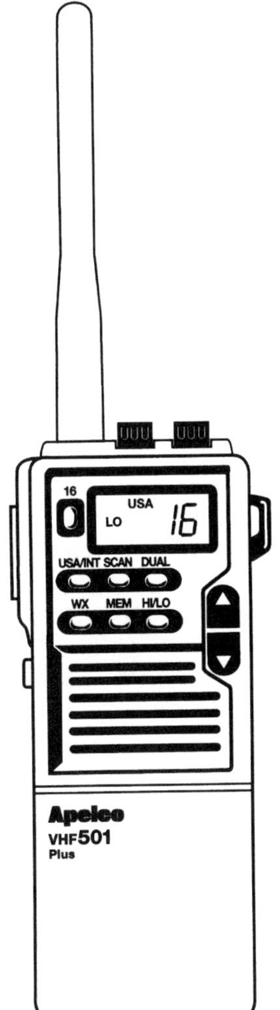

Figure 7-7. *A handheld VHF transceiver is used for short-range communications. (Courtesy Raytheon Electronics)*

Radiobeacons—The U.S. system of radiobeacons, a standard method of navigation for a generation of boaters, will be phased out as more accurate systems replace it. Most radiobeacons may be dismantled by the year 2000, though this plan is subject to review. Some radiobeacon stations will be converted to transmit differential GPS signals and thus remain in operation, though in another form.

Loran-C—Though the military need for Loran-C ended in 1994, the system still has a large civilian community of users, including hundreds of thousands of boaters and many thousand fliers. The military has dropped funding for overseas stations and some U.S. stations (such as the Hawaiian chain). Some of the foreign stations continue to operate with foreign government funding. The 1994 FRP (the latest available) commits funds for Loran-C until at least the year 2015. This policy, like most others in the FRP, is subject to review.

Omega—This worldwide system, of limited accuracy and very seldom used by small craft, is used today mainly to track meteorological balloons. It is scheduled for demise in 2005.

Transit—With the introduction of GPS, this military and commercial marine satellite system ended operation officially in December 1996.

GPS—The Global Positioning System is the satellite navigation system that will be relied upon well into the next century. Operated by the U.S. Air Force, it provides a precise positioning signal for military use and a slightly less accurate signal for civilian use. A modification of GPS, called differential GPS, provides civilians with extremely accurate positioning in many coastal areas, seaports, and harbors.

The criteria for developing or discontinuing a radio navigation system are comprehensive and require extensive study, deliberation, and user input. Life-cycle costs, impacts on users, suitability, international agreements, and other factors are evaluated before decisions are made—and many decisions are not final.

Radiobeacons

The next several chapters deal with the use of satellites, loran, and radar in navigation. Before moving on to those subjects, a brief explanation of the old radiobeacon system is given here.

The simplest type of radio navigation system consists of a radio receiver with an antenna that only receives a clear signal when oriented in a certain direction relative to the transmitting station. The United States and many other countries still maintain a few *marine radiobeacons*. This system has been largely superseded throughout the world by Loran-C, Decca (a European radio navigation system similar to Loran-C), GPS, and other systems.

To use a radiobeacon, first align the receiver to the vessel's fore-and-aft line. Next, obtain a bearing by carefully listening for a point called the *null,* or zero signal point, found by turning the receiver's *directional antenna*. This bearing indicates the direction of the transmitting station, the relative bearing of which can be read on a scale; when converted into a true or magnetic bearing, the result is LOP from the station.

Radiobeacon bearings are inaccurate and short range. On the plus side, the receivers are inexpensive, reliable, and easy to use. But, because of the reliability and far greater accuracy and range of Loran-C and GPS, the U.S. is discontinuing its radiobeacon stations. The only stations remaining are very short range (10 miles or so) and are useful only as a local homing device. You'll have little use for a radiobeacon receiver unless an active station is conveniently located in waters you frequently transit.

CHAPTER EIGHT

Satellite Navigation

SATELLITE NAVIGATION BEGAN WITH the launch of the first successful earth-orbiting satellite, Sputnik I, in 1957. Sputnik I was intended only to prove Soviet superiority in advanced technology, but it sparked an important idea in the United States.

The satellite carried a small radio transmitter that emitted a simple beeping tone. Two scientists at Johns Hopkins Applied Physics Laboratory tracked the beeps, recorded them, and soon noticed that there was a distinct and predictable *Doppler shift* in the tone as the satellite passed overhead.

Doppler shift occurs when a steady tone moves past a stationary observer. As the tone approaches the observer, its frequency is slightly elevated due to its forward speed. As it goes away, the frequency of the tone is lower. Sirens, train whistles, and car horns often illustrate this change.

The scientists reasoned that, since the Doppler shift depended on the orbital characteristics of the satellite, they should be able to define a satellite's orbit from their observation of the Doppler shift. They soon proved that their reasoning was valid.

Another scientist, noting this work, reasoned in reverse: If you could determine a satellite's orbit from observations of Doppler shift from a fixed position on earth, then by knowing an orbit and observing a particular Doppler shift, you should be able to determine your position on earth.

This reasoning was the basis for the first *satellite navigation system,* known as Transit, which became operational in prototype form in 1960. This system used radio frequencies little affected by weather and so provided global positioning regardless of meteorological conditions. The 10 Transit satellites are in polar orbits and circle the earth once every 106 minutes at an altitude of about 600 miles.

Although Transit is a very accurate system, providing fixes of 0.1 mile accuracy, it had some limitations. First, due to the relatively low number of satellites, fixes were not available for periods of up to an hour or more. Second, the receivers were too expensive for the majority of potential users. It was primarily a military (chiefly Navy) system, and a very successful one, but not widely used by civilians. It was discontinued in 1996 when the Global Positioning System became operational.

Development of the Global Positioning System (GPS)

Development of the *Global Positioning System (GPS),* begun in 1973, has gone through several phases leading to the current system. Along the way, much new technology has been developed, and GPS is revolutionizing the practice of navigation. GPS fulfills the dream of mariners for millennia: worldwide, continuous, accurate, all-weather, reliable positioning. It is reliable, that is, as long as electrical power is uninterrupted.

The *GPS satellite constellation* consists of 24 satellites (as shown in Figure 8-1), 14 more than Transit's. The satellites are in six different orbital planes, each plane angled at 55° to the equator. Twenty-one of the satellites are in active use; the other three are kept in orbit as spares in case of failure. GPS satellites are launched from Vandenberg Air Force Base in California (see Figure 8-2) and placed in orbits 20,200 kilometers high (about 10,900 miles); they orbit the earth about once every 12 hours. Each satellite weighs about 1,900 pounds and, with the solar panels extended, is 17 feet across, as seen in Figure 8-3. The satellites are not all exactly alike; the newer ones incorporate updated technology and future replacements are sure to have even more modern equipment. But, to the user, they all act exactly the same. Each is expected to last about seven years.

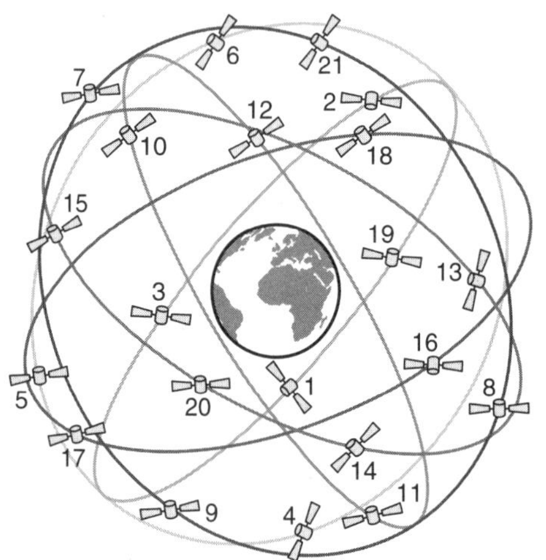

Figure 8-1. *The GPS satellite constellation consists of 24 satellites (21 operational and three in-orbit spares) in six orbital planes. At least four satellites are visible to a receiver at all times. (Signals require a direct line of sight.) At least half of the satellites are always below your horizon. (Photograph courtesy of USAF)*

Like the earlier Transit satellites, each GPS satellite is watched very closely by ground *monitoring stations* that are located in Hawaii, Kwajalein, Diego Garcia, and on Ascension Island. A *Master Control Station* is located in Colorado Springs, and new data are injected into each satellite's memory frequently from this site. These data contain updated information on the orbit of the satellite, which varies slightly over time, that enables the satellite to transmit very accurate position information in return.

Figure 8-2. *An Air Force rocket is ready to launch a GPS satellite into orbit from Vandenberg Air Force Base in California. From this launch site the rocket can place the satellite in the desired orbit and remain over the ocean during the critical first stages of launch. (Photograph courtesy of USAF)*

The GPS Fix

The lines of position (LOPs) described in Chapter 6 ("Piloting") are based on measurements of distance or direction from a fixed object whose position you know. In piloting, all objects from which you get LOPs are on the surface of the earth, which we assume to be a plane surface. Also in piloting, you fix your position at the intersection of either straight LOPs based on bearings, or circles of position based on radar ranges. GPS, a range-based system, uses the same principle, but in three dimensions—it uses *spheres of position*.

Again in piloting, when a vessel is a certain distance from a point on earth, such as a lighthouse, it is on a *circle* whose radius is equal to the range to the lighthouse. So, too, when a vessel is a certain distance from a satellite in space, it is on the surface of a *sphere* whose radius is equal to the range to the satellite. Just as the intersection of two cir-

Figure 8-3. *A GPS satellite, weighing slightly under a ton, undergoes checkout prior to launch. The solar panels are folded during launch and deployed once the satellite has reached its desired orbit. (Photograph courtesy of USAF)*

cles of position defines two points, the intersection of two spheres defines a circle. (Think of a child blowing bubbles. When a double bubble appears, the two bubbles meet in a circle.)

You can't determine your position with a circle alone—you need a third sphere. The intersection of the previously defined circle with another sphere gives two points, only one of which is on the surface of the earth. That is your position. Actually, you could use the earth itself as one of the spheres, but it is easy for a receiver to process additional satellite signals, so all commonly used receivers do so. This three-dimensional procedure also determines altitude, which was a military requirement in designing the system and removes the earth's irregular surface from the computation.

In fact, a GPS receiver uses a fourth satellite to satisfy its critical need for precise timing. You need extremely accurate timing of signals to determine the range to an orbiting object that is traveling thousands of miles per hour. GPS range measurements are based on the simple equation: distance = speed × time. The speed of the radio signal equals the speed of light—or, 186,000 miles per second (in a vacuum). So it takes only a few hundredths of a second for the signal to travel from the satellite to your position. A nonatomic clock does not provide a sufficiently accurate measurement on which to calculate the radius of your sphere of position.

Each satellite has four accurate *atomic clocks* aboard that are able to divide time into nanoseconds—a nanosecond is one-billionth of a second. If a GPS receiver had such a clock, it could get a fix from just three satellites. It would also cost you a few hundred thousand dollars, be too heavy to carry around, and need a steady supply of electricity. To keep the cost down, GPS receivers instead have inexpensive (and less accurate) clocks and use some very clever computer programming to correct them.

To correct receiver clock error, the computer program in the receiver uses the following logic: "If there were no receiver clock error this would be a perfect fix, forming a pinpoint where the four spheres intersect. I'll test for error with the trial-and-error method.

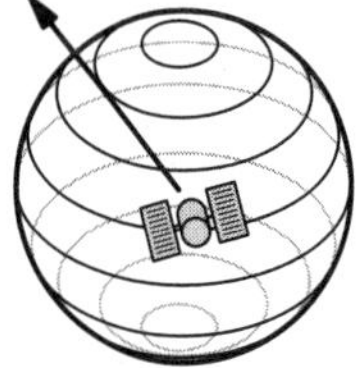
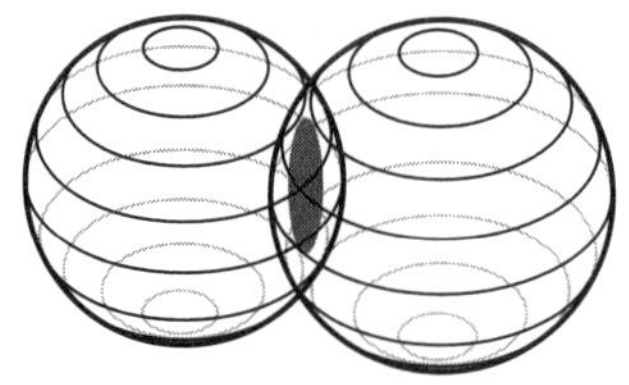
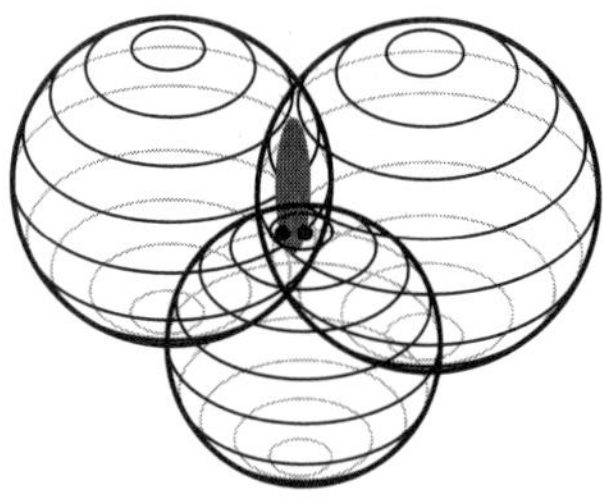

Figure 8-4. *Two spheres of position define a circle (spheres 1 and 2). That circle and a third sphere (3) define two points (at arrows), only one of which is on the earth's surface.*

I'll add a few nanoseconds to the receiver clock reading and see if that brings the fix closer to or farther from a pinpoint. If farther, I'll subtract a few nanoseconds instead, and try again. If closer, I'll add a couple more nanoseconds. I'll keep at this until I get it perfect." When, after a few microseconds, the fix is the best it can be, the receiver displays that position. Then the receiver begins its cycle again, receiving satellite signals, processing them, and displaying a fix directly or sending it to an electronic chart, automatic pilot, or other equipment.

Precise and Standard Positioning Services

The military invented and funds the GPS system, and considers it to be a valuable asset to the defense of the United States. It fears, of course, that hostile nations could use our GPS system to accurately aim weapons against our own forces, here or abroad.

To prevent that from happening, GPS has two positioning services of differing accuracy. The more accurate one, called the *Precise Positioning Service (PPS),* is available only to authorized military users and to certain contractors and U.S. allies. The less accurate one, the *Standard Positioning Service (SPS),* is available to anyone in the world with a GPS receiver. The military can further degrade the SPS signal during wartime so that it is virtually useless. This degrading process is known as *Selective Availability (SA);* it degrades the timing part of the signal, thereby introducing an error in the resulting fix.

U.S. military can also encode the signals to safeguard our receivers from false signals sent by a foreign power.

PPS provides an accuracy of 16 meters; SPS accuracy is about 100 meters. This means that about 95 percent of all fixes should fall within these distances of the receiver's true position. These accuracies apply to determinations of altitude as well as to the coordinates of a surface fix, so they are important to aeronautical navigation.

Figure 8-5. *Both satellite and receiver generate the same signal at the same time. The signal from the satellite takes time to travel to the receiver. Knowing this time and the rate of travel (speed of light), the receiver can calculate the distance to the satellite. Since the satellites' positions are known, the receiver's position can be triangulated from three or more signals.*

Pseudorandom Code

One of the many clever inventions in the GPS system is the *pseudorandom code.* The code is not really random; it just looks random because it is so long and complicated. It consists of a long string of "0's" and "1's" in no particular pattern, but in a known sequence—that is, the pattern itself is meaningless, but repetitive. (See Figure 8-5.) The pseudorandom code accomplishes two things.

First, it allows the receiver to figure out the time difference between the sending and receipt of the satellite signal. It does this by comparing the identical codes generated by the receiver and the satellite, matching them up, and figuring out the time it took for the signal to reach the receiver, assuming that they were generated at exactly the same time.

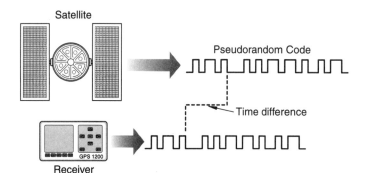

Second, the pseudorandom code allows the satellite to transmit a signal that is weaker than the background radio noise in the earth's atmosphere. This procedure enables the satellite to preserve power and allows your GPS antenna to be very small—so you don't have to carry around a large satellite dish and try to aim it at each of four satellites to get a fix.

The receiver distills the signal from the background noise by comparing the peaks and valleys of the pseudorandom code with the peaks and valleys of the background noise, and finding the place in the noise string where they match most closely. This distilled signal is then accepted as the received signal.

GPS Errors

Certain errors are inherent in any navigation system, and GPS, though fantastically accurate, is not an exception to this rule. Several sources of error can occur in the GPS fix.

One is *Geometric Dilution of Position (GDOP),* a function of the geometry of the satellite constellation at the time of the fix. (See Figure 8-6.) We can't adjust the satellites' orbits once they are in space, and the orbits are neither perfectly round nor perfectly spaced. It is theoretically possible for the four satellites that you want to use for a fix to be all directly overhead at the same time. The resulting fix would be useless, though, because the spheres of position would be tangent to each other at your position. Therefore, fix accuracy is partially dependent on the spacing of the satellites. For the best fix, one satellite would be directly overhead and the other three spaced 120° from each other around the horizon. Normally, you'll find a configuration between these extremes.

Another source of error is caused by the layers of radiation in the ionosphere. These radiation belts affect the timing signal from the satellite, causing a slight delay in its reception. Light and radio waves travel 186,000 miles per second only in a vacuum. The waves are slowed down by the earth's layers of radiation—which follow the sun around the earth—thereby causing some inaccuracy in fixes; more when the sun is high and less at night.

The GPS system corrects this *ionospheric time delay error* in two ways. The first uses two different frequencies to transmit the timing signal. The radiation affects each frequency differently and the system uses this difference to determine the delay error. Only military users have the capability to receive the second signal. The second method of correcting for ionospheric time delay uses a computer model instead of actual measurements. This method is not as accurate, but it does not require a second signal. SPS receivers use this technique and suffer some loss in accuracy compared with PPS.

A third source of error is *multipath reflection error* that occurs when the satellite signal bounces off a nearby object before reaching your receiver. The reflected signal, however, is usually not as sharp or well defined as the undeflected signal and is received later due to its longer route of travel. A receiver's antenna system can be designed to reject signals that it thinks are reflections. Doing so minimizes multipath reflection error that according to calculations should be no greater than 20 feet.

The remaining sources of error are caused by satellite clock instability, atmospheric distortion of the signals, quality of the signals,

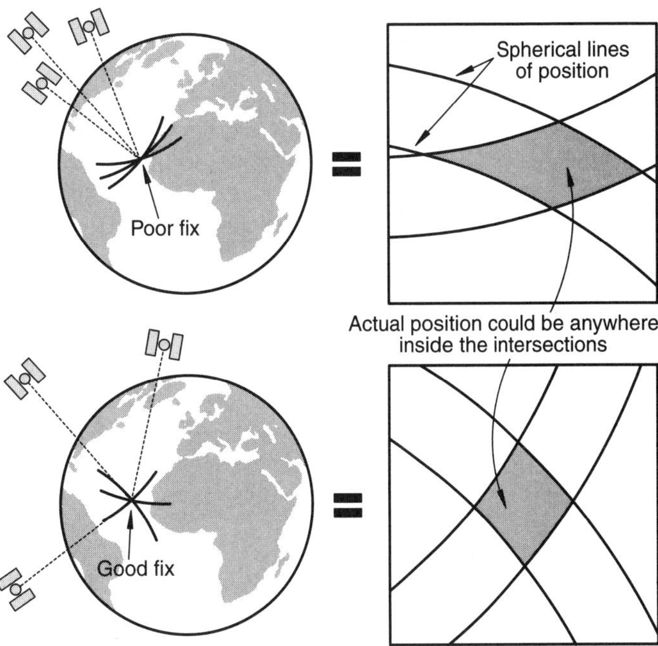

Figure 8-6. *Geometric Dilution of Position (GDOP) is one source of error in the GPS fix. GDOP results from the inevitably imperfect orbits and spacing, relative to the receiver, of the four GPS satellites from which the navigator gets fixes at any one time.*

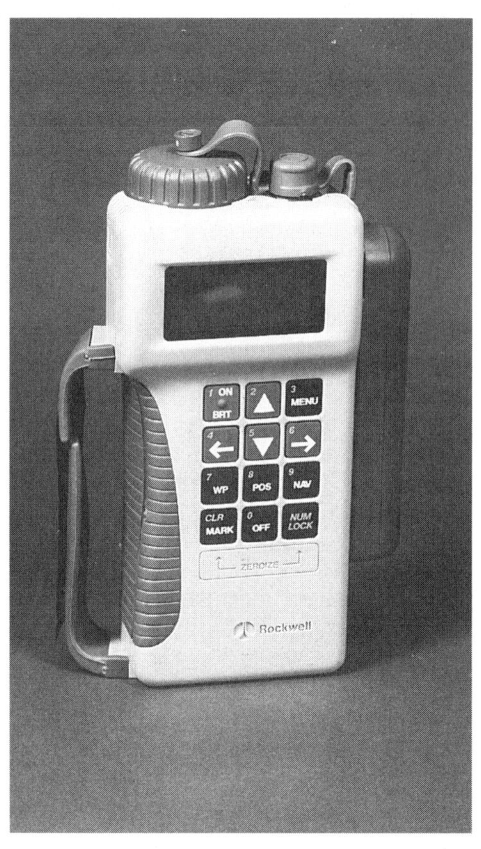

Figure 8-7. *The military version of a handheld GPS is more rugged and expensive than civilian versions. External connections to allow data communications are provided. The GPS receiver antenna is contained in the rotatable housing on the right side. (Photograph courtesy of USAF and Rockwell)*

instability of the satellites' orbits, and limits in your receiver's ability to process the timing signals. All of these errors are lumped together and called *User Equivalent Range Error (UERE)*. This error is random and uncorrectable. Fortunately, it is also very small—on the order of a few feet at most.

Receiver Design

GPS receivers are designed to get four separate timing measurements for a fix. The simplest receiver has only one channel and receives the signals from four satellites in turn. It then processes them and provides a fix before beginning the cycle again. This type of receiver may not provide positions every second as needed by electronic charts, but is performs most other navigation functions well enough.

More complex multichannel receivers have four or more separate channels and are able to process data from four or more satellites at once. The process takes only a few microseconds and provides fixes every second or so. Further, the more sophisticated models can track 12 or more satellites simul-

Figure 8-8. *A variety of GPS receivers and antenna options are available to the military navigator; some are stand-alone units and some are designed to be integrated with other equipment. (Photograph courtesy of USAF)*

taneously and use the four that provide the lowest possible Geometric Dilution of Position (GDOP). Military GPS receivers and better quality civilian units contain this feature. (See Figures 8-7 and 8-8.)

In weighing features and expense, you can compromise and choose a receiver with two or three channels. In these units, one channel measures a signal while the other(s) lock on to the next satellite. When the first channel is again clear, it searches for the next satellite in the sequence, and so on.

Periodically, each satellite sends a *system data message* of about 30 seconds' duration, causing a short delay in processing by receivers that share channels. For small-craft navigation, this is not a problem.

Each brand of GPS receiver uses one of three types of presentations, or "user interfaces." A small LCD screen shows numerical data (as in Figure 8-9), or graphical data presented as heading and track (Figure 8-10), or as lanes and cross-track error (Figure 8-11). A panel of buttons controls the function and presentation of information.

Several manufacturers integrate a GPS receiver with a loran receiver. Most of these integrated units operate in an either/or mode; the receiver presents either a Loran-C or a GPS fix. The more sophisticated ones integrate a position from both systems at once and combine them in a single fix more accurate than either system could provide sepa-

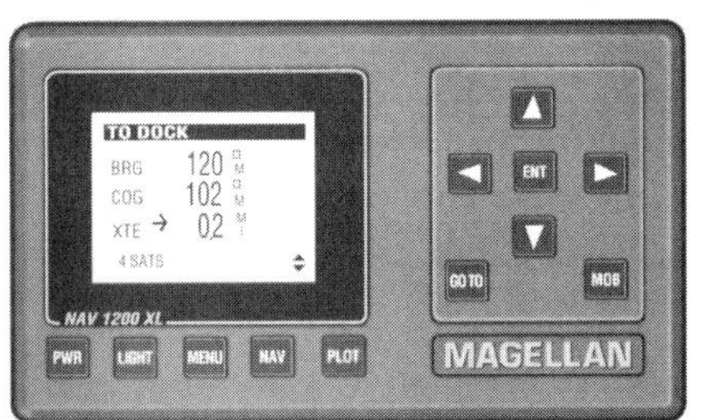

Figure 8-9. *GPS can present information numerically. In this instance the course to the dock is 120°, the course over the ground is 102°, and the cross-track error is 0.2 miles to the right. Four satellites are in use. (Courtesy Magellan Systems Corp.)*

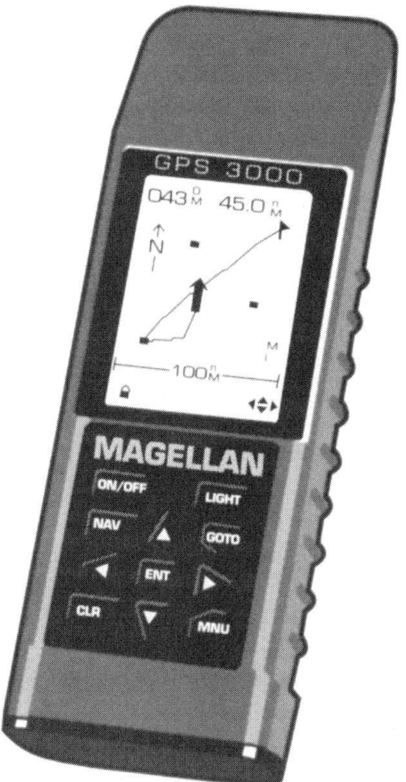

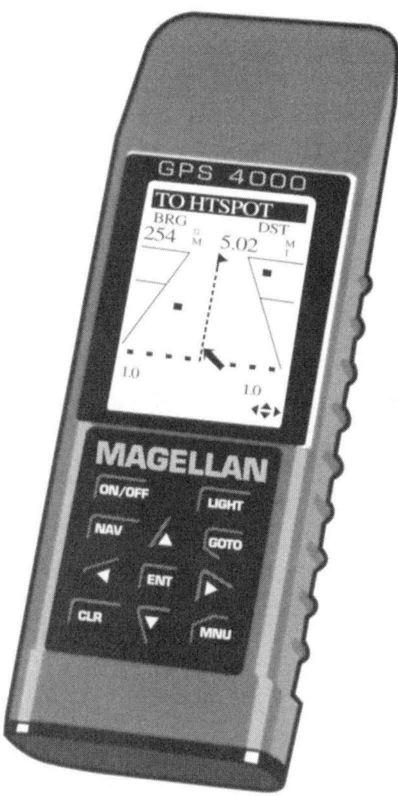

Figure 8-10. *GPS can present course and track-line information. Here the desired course is 043° and the distance to the waypoint is 45 nautical miles. (Courtesy Magellan Systems Corp.)*

Figure 8-11. *GPS can give latitude/longitude readouts or show lanes along which to steer. The receiver in this figure shows a "lane" leading to the next waypoint. The vessel's progress along the track is shown, and cross-track error is easily seen. (Courtesy Magellan Systems Corp.)*

rately. They use a complicated mathematical process called Kalman filtering, which takes account of all the LOPs from both systems.

Differential GPS

Even SPS, the civilian part of GPS, provides astounding accuracy. It is global, continuous, and more than accurate enough for the ocean and coastal phases of navigation. But what about harbor navigation?

Most dredged waterways and harbor channels are only one to two hundred meters wide. The 100-meter accuracy of SPS is not accurate enough to keep a vessel in a channel. Authorized users of PPS signals can use GPS for harbor navigation. Because these signals are not available to civilian users, another system has been invented, called *Differential GPS (DGPS).*

Here's how DGPS works. DGPS stations are placed at accurately surveyed locations—usually at Coast Guard radiobeacon stations. The stations receive satellite-timing signals just like your receiver. These signals carry information about the exact position of the satellite. The station compares the time the signal should take to travel from that position to the time it actually took. The result is broadcast on another frequency to vessels as a correction to the original satellite signal (see Figure 8-12).

To receive and process these signals, both receiver and antenna must be tuned to the frequency used to transmit correction signals, and the GPS receiver must be able to apply the corrections to the uncorrected satellite readings. In this process your receiver corrects for several types of errors—selective availability, ionospheric delay, and some parts of the catchall UERE.

The result is a fix at least as accurate as the PPS fix; that is, about a few feet. You might think it silly to purposely degrade the GPS signal for civilian use and then invent a system to correct it again, but there's a logical reason for doing this. First, DGPS correction signals have a short range of about 100 to 200 miles so a hostile power cannot use them globally. Second, they can be turned off at the flip of a switch, denying their accuracy to an enemy even in the local area.

DGPS stations are already operating in most areas of the U.S. and are planned for the entire U.S. coast. In addition, many foreign countries are establishing DGPS stations in their own waters. DGPS offers harbor navigation capability to all vessels with the proper receiver. The price of receivers is well within the range of the serious small-craft navigator.

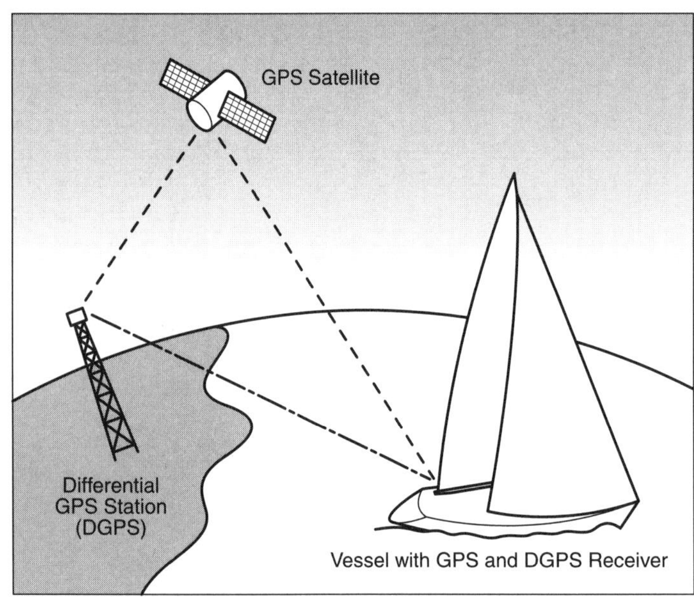

Figure 8-12. *In Differential GPS (DGPS), a receiver at a fixed location receives the GPS signal, calculates the error in it, and rebroadcasts a separate correction signal to all other receivers nearby, greatly improving GPS accuracy. To use this subsystem, you must have a Differential GPS receiver and antenna in addition to a regular GPS satellite receiver and antenna.*

GPS Receiver Operation

GPS receivers come in several types: permanently installed units, portable handheld units, "black-box" devices that only relay data to other systems, and circuit board units installed inside other systems.

An impressive amount of technology is built into even the single-channel, battery-powered, handheld GPS receiver. In a few microseconds they are able to perform calculations that would take a human several minutes to several hours, and they have multiple capabilities.

All commonly available GPS receivers indicate distance and direction from one waypoint to another. Even the least expensive accommodate 99 or more waypoints and one to 20 or more reversible routes (sequences of waypoints), as well as the ability to track up to eight satellites at a time. They also display speed—computed from previous fixes and updated at each new one—and cross-track error, either graphically or numerically. The units weigh just a few ounces and can operate continuously for several hours. Battery-saver features extend this time considerably, at the sacrifice of continuous fixes. Some models also indicate satellite geometry and signal strength and display tracks that graphically indicate direction to the next waypoint.

More sophisticated GPS units display simple charts and incorporate user-selectable alarms for cross-track error, anchor watch, and other functions. Many units, even inexpensive ones, also are "differential-ready," needing only a cable hookup to a separate differential GPS receiver to display a differential GPS fix that's accurate to just a few feet.

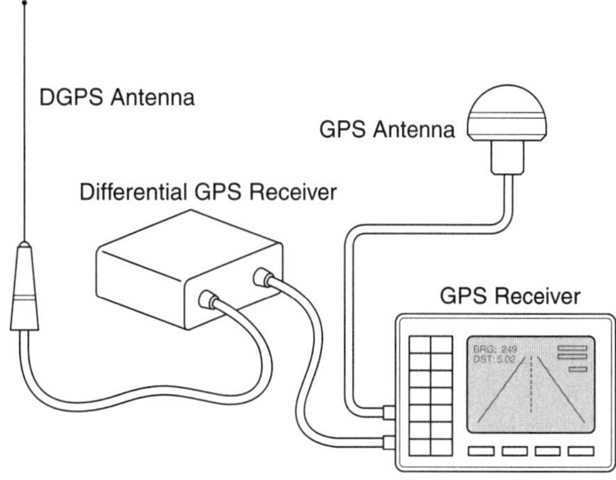

Figure 8-13. *A typical DGPS receiver system.*

The Future of GPS

According to the U.S. government's Federal Radionavigation Plan, GPS will be our primary electronic navigation system for the foreseeable future. It has superseded the Transit system and eventually will replace Loran-C. Even before the first satellite was in orbit, dozens of companies and government agencies were actively investigating its possible uses. As a result, uses were found in mapping and surveying; vehicle, vessel, aircraft, and animal tracking; air and ground navigation; and hundreds of other uses in addition to marine navigation. The discovery of uses has only begun.

CHAPTER NINE

Loran-C Navigation

DEVELOPED DURING THE 1970S as a replacement for Loran-A, and fully operational by 1980, *Loran-C* is an extremely accurate, inexpensive, reliable, and easy-to-use electronic navigation system. About one-half million people use the system today, most of them in the marine field, but many in aeronautical and terrestrial navigation. This chapter explains the easily understood scientific principle on which Loran-C is based.

Figure 9-1. *Loran-C signals are transmitted from tall towers spaced several hundred miles apart. The network of interlaced radio signals forms a pattern that a Loran-C receiver uses to determine lines of position (LOPs).*

Loran-C stations provide coverage over the continental U.S. and its surrounding waters, across the northern North Atlantic Ocean to Europe, throughout the Mediterranean Sea, in the central Pacific Ocean, and in Japan. Loran-C is an excellent navigational system for small-craft users out to about 1,000 miles at sea. Begun as a military system, Loran-C quickly became popular in the civilian community due to its reliability, utility, and low cost.

Loran signals are broadcast from tall radio towers which themselves make good visual aids to navigation. (See Figure 9-1.)

Development of Loran-C

The Loran (LOng Range Aid to Navigation) system grew out of technology developed in World War II. Needing a navigation system to reliably direct bombers flying from bases in Britain to and from targets in German-occupied Europe, the Allies came up with a predecessor system called *Gee* that used Loran principles. Gee was reliable at ranges up to about 350 to 400 miles and, though the signal was often jammed over western Europe, pilots could rely on it to find their bases once back in British skies.

Further developments in Gee led to *Loran-A,* the first operational long-range marine radio navigation system. However, Loran-A was difficult to use, often affected by skywaves (especially at long ranges), and expensive. It took five to ten (or more) minutes to get each fix, required trained operators, and wasn't very accurate.

Loran-B was an experimental military-use system that was never fully developed.

Loran-C incorporated all that was known about propagation of radio waves over long distances and about receiver design. It is better aligned to its users' needs than its predecessors. Today, Loran-C answers most of the needs of the small-craft navigator very well. Its main limitation is that it is necessarily a regional system without worldwide coverage.

How Loran-C Works

Imagine that you are standing in the middle of a football field, right on the 50-yard line. At precisely the same instant, two people, each standing under a goalpost at opposite ends of the field, blast a horn. You will hear the horns at exactly the same time because you are equal distance from both.

Now suppose you move to one of the 40-yard lines and the two people—still standing under the goalposts—sound their horns again. This time, you'll hear the closer sound first and the other a bit later after a small *time delay*. Why? Because the sound from the farther end zone travels farther. This will hold true even when you move along the 40-yard line out to and beyond the sidelines. In fact, anywhere within the range of your hearing both sounds you'll be able to determine some-thing important about your position relative to them, based on the time of receiving the sounds.

The closer you move to one end of the field or the other, the sooner you will hear the sound from that end. By carefully measuring the difference in the time of receipt—the *time delay (TD)*—of each sound, you can determine how much closer you are to one sound than to the other. This difference determines an LOP.

The LOPs resulting from this type of ranging are hyperbolas, which is why we sometimes refer to these type of navigation systems as hyperbolic systems. A hyperbola is the locus (or position) of all points equidistant, or a defined ratio of distance, from both a point and a line. A hyperbolic curve is defined by a constant difference in distance from two known points.

In the Loran-C system, the two points are two radio transmitters—they correspond to the people with the horns standing under the goalposts. (See Figure 9-2.) One is the *master station* and the other the *secondary station*. The perpendicular line that is equidistant between them—the 50-yard line—is the *centerline*. The line joining them is called the

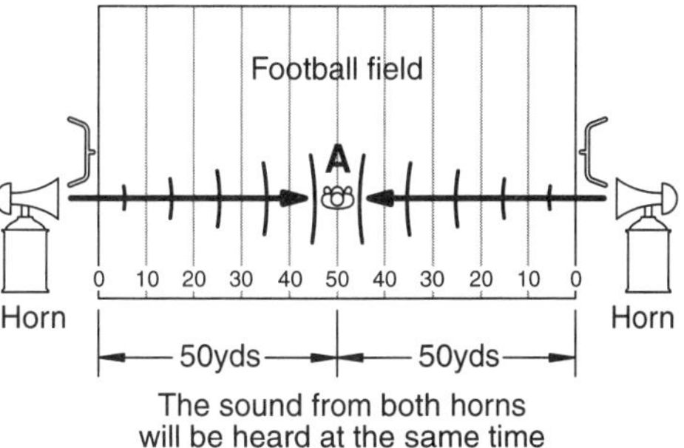

Figure 9-2. *When two sounds are generated at exactly the same time from both ends of a field, an observer in the middle of the field (point A) hears them at exactly the same time. If the observer moves closer to one end of the field (point B), the sound from that end will be heard first. The observer can determine a line on the field that includes his or her location by observing the time difference between the receipt of both sounds.*

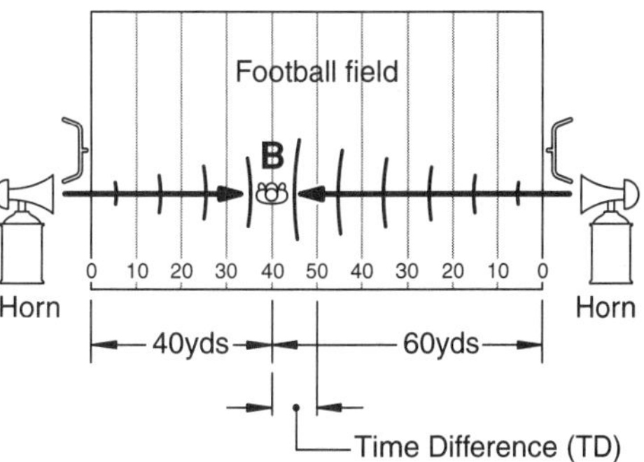

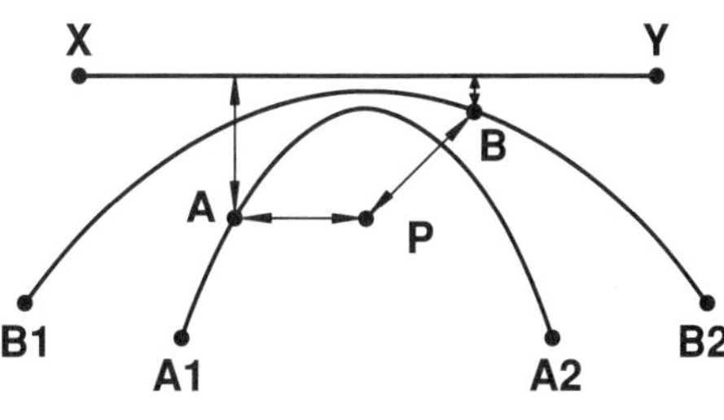

Figure 9-3. *Hyperbolic lines are defined as the locus of all points equidistant or at a certain ratio of distance from both a point and a line. In this figure, we see that point "A" is equidistant from point "P" and line XY. In fact, all points on line A1–A2 are equidistant from point "P" and line XY.*

Similarly, all points on line B1-B2 are three times as far from point "P" as from line XY—a ratio of 3 to 1. A similar family of lines exists on the opposite side of line XY about another point. These two points represent a pair of Loran-C stations hundreds of miles apart. One LOP is available from any two stations.

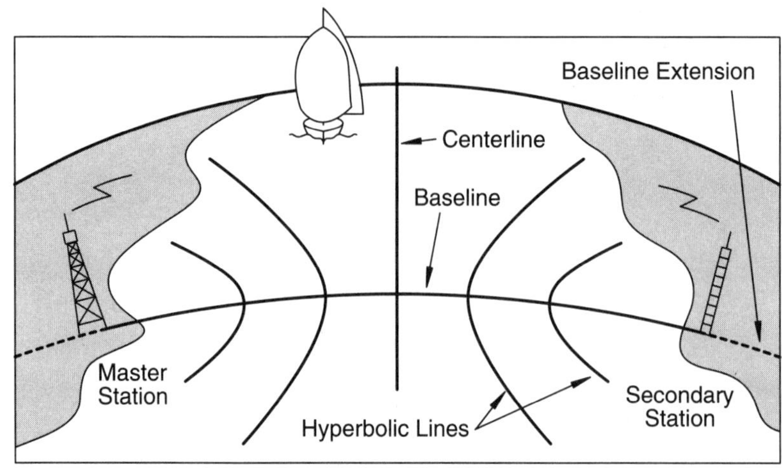

Figure 9-4. *In the Loran-C system, LOPs are hyperbolic lines resulting from the difference in time of receipt of two radio signals. One is sent by the master station; the other by the secondary station. Two stations give you one LOP. For additional LOPs, you need other stations, so one master station may have two or more secondary stations, or serve as master on one frequency and secondary on another.*

baseline, which continues past each station as the *baseline extension*. Instead of sound signals, Loran-C uses radio signals, which travel at the speed of light. And, instead of being 100 yards apart, Loran-C stations are hundreds of miles apart and their signals travel over hundreds of thousands of square miles of ocean.

Stations are arranged in three different configurations: the triad, the star, or the wye, as shown in Figure 9-5. Geographical considerations may impose some variation on these placements, but the basic shape determines the coverage and accuracy of the Loran-C signals.

The stations are grouped in *chains* that transmit families of Loran-C signals. A single master and two secondary stations give two LOPs and a fix. Figures 9-6, 9-7, and 9-8 show how a single master station and two secondaries provide two sets of hyperbolic lines that give two LOPs anywhere within the coverage area.

The Loran-C Signal

The *Loran-C signal* consists of pulses of radio energy at a frequency of 100 kHz. (See page 95 to review the characteristics of this band.) The master signal consists of nine pulses; the secondary signals, sent a few microseconds later, consist of eight pulses. Secondary stations are given the designation letters W, X, Y, and Z. Each group of signals is sent in a precisely determined sequence: the master signal is first, followed by the first secondary (W), followed by X, Y, and Z in order.

The elapsed time of a complete cycle determines the *group repetition interval,* or *GRI,* of the group. For the northeastern U.S. chain, this

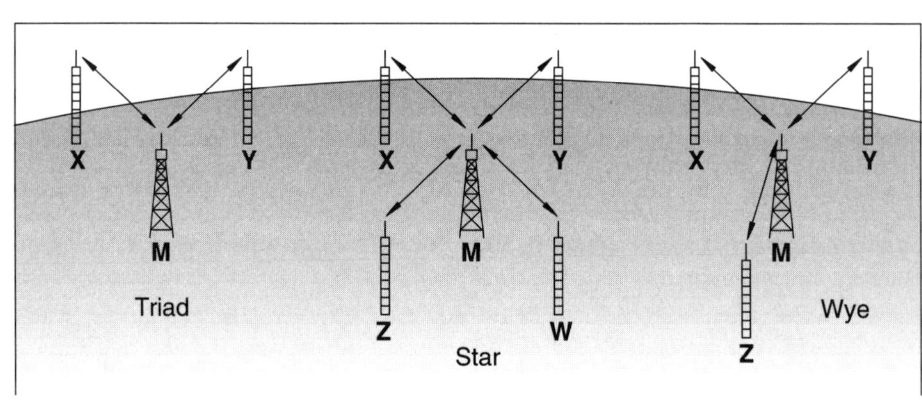

Figure 9-5. *Loran-C stations are placed in three configurations: the triad, the star, and the wye. The placement of the stations in relation to your vessel affects the range and accuracy of the Loran-C fix.*

interval is 99,600 microseconds—and the chain is known as the "9960 chain." Other chains have different GRIs. Each GRI is chosen so the series of signals propagates throughout its region before the next series begins.

A station may be the master station for one chain and serve as a secondary station for another—Dana, Indiana, as noted in Figure 9-9, is an example. At the end of this chapter is a series of maps that shows the locations and station configurations of all U.S. Loran-C stations.

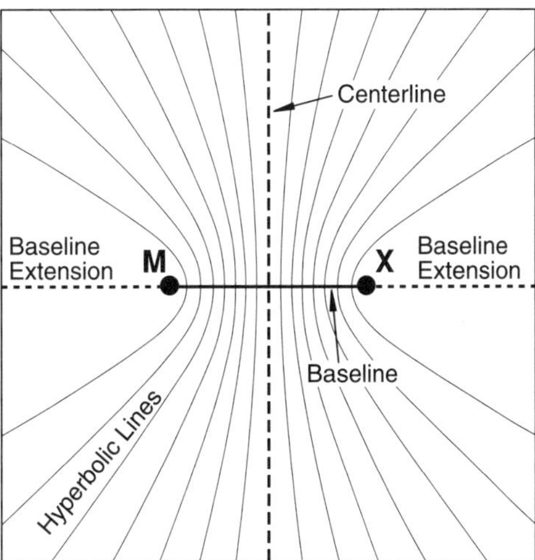

Figure 9-6. *A single Loran-C master station at "M" and a single secondary at "X" yield one set of hyperbolic LOPs. Centerline, baseline, and baseline extensions are shown. Numbers represent time differences in microseconds between receipt of the signals from each station.*

Corrections to the Loran-C Signal

Several factors influence the propagation of the Loran-C signal that would, if uncompensated, induce errors in the system and reduce accuracy.

Because radio energy travels a little slower than the speed of light in the earth's atmosphere, a correction is made to the received signal. This correction—called the *Primary Phase Factor (PF)*—is programmed into the system and is not apparent to you.

Another correction is needed because radio energy travels a little slower over land than over water. This correction—called the *Secondary Phase Factor (SF)*—is also automatically incorporated into the system and is transparent to you.

Yet another correction deals with the varying rate of travel of radio signals when they pass alternately over water and land and also with seasonal variations in weather, snow cover, and other such factors that affect radio signals. It is important to understand this correction, which is called the *Additional Secondary Phase Factor (ASF).*

ASF corrections are derived in two ways. One is through mathematical calculations based on average conditions. These corrections are less accurate than the second method, which consists of measuring the actual Loran-C readings in a given place and comparing them with theoretical values.

Manufacturers of Loran-C receivers use ASF corrections, which are published by the Coast Guard, to write computer algorithms

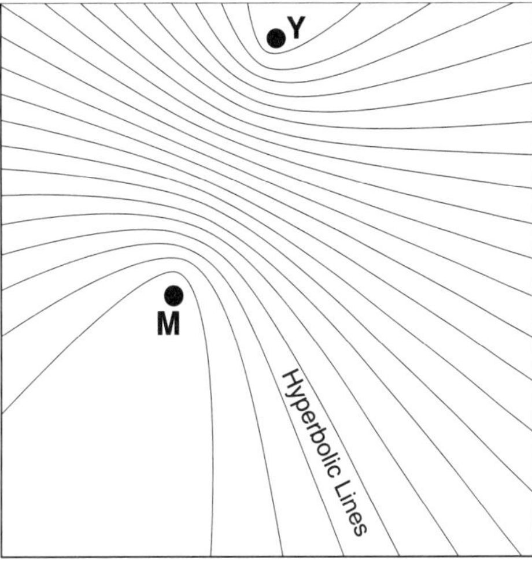

Figure 9-7. *A master station at "M" and another single secondary at "Y" yield a second set of hyperbolic LOPs. In this view, the centerline, baseline, and baseline extensions are omitted.*

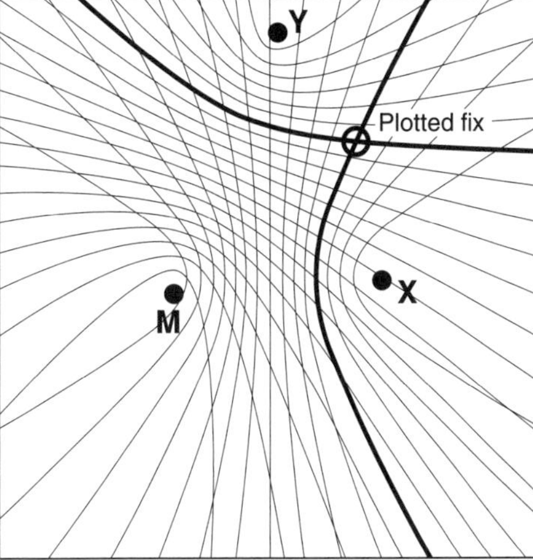

Figure 9-8. *In this figure the two station pairs of Figure 9-6 and Figure 9-7 have been combined. The intersection of any two hyperbolic LOPs determines a fix.*

Figure 9-9. *The Loran station at Dana, Indiana, is the master station for the Great Lakes chain (GRI 8970) and the Zulu secondary station for the Northeast U.S. chain (GRI 9960).*

that convert Loran-C time delays, or TDs, to latitude and longitude readings. There are several sources of error in these readings.

The first source of error varies with the manufacturer's practices in the ongoing process of comparing actual versus theoretical TDs. Whether the manufacturer uses newer values or older, less accurate ones make a difference. The second source of potential error lies in the way the manufacturer writes the computer programs that convert TDs to lat/long coordinates. Some computer programs provide more accuracy than others.

For these reasons, the Loran-C TD readings are more accurate than the lat/long coordinates. Therefore, when you need high accuracy, such as when you approach a channel in thick weather, always use the TDs and plot the fix using the Loran-C TD lines on the chart. It's also a good idea to compare TD and lat/long readings in good weather in known locations to determine the amount of ASF error. This will build your confidence in the receiver and your ability to use it.

Finally, because TD-to-lat/long conversions are prone to error, your Loran-C receiver will guide you back more accurately to a previously observed TD than to a lat/long. Therefore, you should use TDs for waypoints, preferably using readings that you made previously at the waypoints. This practice makes full use of Loran-C's potential accuracy because it deals with real values in real locations. When you enter waypoints using TDs that are not based on previous readings at the waypoints, you should use them with some caution.

The Loran-C Fix

The Loran-C fix is formed at the intersection of two or more hyperbolic Loran-C LOPs based on the time of receipt of radio signals from Loran-C transmitters.

Because the curved hyperbolic LOPs from two different station pairs can intersect in any angle from 90° down to tangency at 0°, it's important to choose signals that give you good intersecting angles. In Loran-C, as in piloting, two lines that intersect at 90°, or close to it, provide the best accuracy, as do three lines that intersect in 60° angles. The pattern of Loran-C LOPs available to you depends on the placement of the station pairs in relation to your position; it can vary from ideal to virtually useless. Using the TDs rather than lat/long to plot a Loran-C fix enables you to see the intersection angles of the LOPs and to determine which ones will give a more accurate fix.

Good Loran-C receivers have internal software programs that do this analysis automatically, but they are dependent on the skill of the programmers and other factors that are discussed later in this chapter.

Fix ambiguity results when Loran-C TDs cross at two places. You encounter this occasionally because LOPs are curved and can cross one another more than once. When this occurs, one of the intersections is many miles away from your position, and your receiver, knowing that your vessel could not have traveled fast enough to get to the distant intersection, picks the one nearby and discards the other.

Gradient is another factor that affects the accuracy of your Loran-C fix. Accuracy varies with the spacing, or gradient, of TDs. Gradient varies with distance from the baseline. Those near the baseline are very close together; those far from it are far apart.

In Figure 9-6 you'll note that the distance between TDs in the vicinity of the centerline/baseline intersection (directly between the two stations) is much closer than in the area of the baseline extensions. The most accurate fixes are taken from readings near the baseline; accuracy is less everywhere else. Readings from the area of the baseline extensions are virtually useless. (See Figure 9-11.)

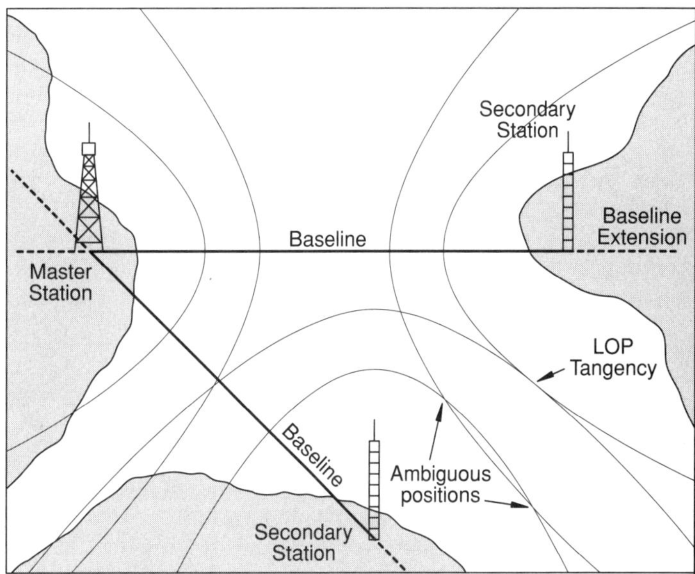

Figure 9-10. *This figure shows the fix ambiguity that can result when Loran-C LOPs cross at two different places. It is also clear from this figure that the relative position of the receiver in the chain is an important factor in fix accuracy; two LOPs nearly tangent to each other give a very poor fix.*

Loran-C Receiver Operation

To operate most Loran-C receivers you simply turn them on. Although what goes on inside the set is anything but simple, the basics can be readily understood.

As soon as you turn on the power to the Loran-C receiver, the unit begins a short warm-up period, during which time it checks out its internal circuits. It then begins to scan for the Loran-C signals in the area, using the GRI you specified. When it finds a signal the receiver monitors the master and secondary signals and determines the time difference (TD) between them. This TD is either displayed to the navigator or sent through further circuits that apply the ASF corrections to get a lat/long position.

You must allow the receiver to settle for a few minutes before using its readings. If the initial position is not exactly at the known location of the vessel, some error exists in the fix, and this should be noted as to amount and direction.

If the receiver cannot distinguish the signal from the background noise that is always present in the atmosphere, it will not be able to compute a TD. Most modern receivers have a function that displays the *SNR—Signal to Noise Ratio*. Low SNRs may result in improper TDs or none at all. SNRs are usually displayed on the panel in a numbered or lettered scale. If you have a choice of several station pairs, choose those with the highest SNRs, provided they yield good crossing angles.

When a station pair loses its synchronization, thereby causing erroneous TDs, sensors immediately alert the station watchstander who sets either the master or the secondary station (depending on which is in error) to a

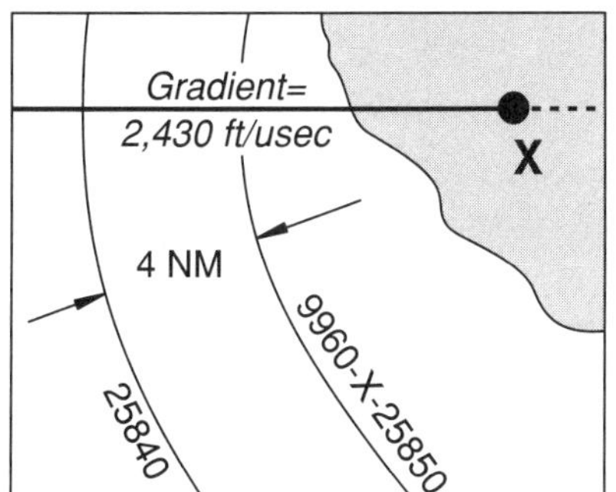

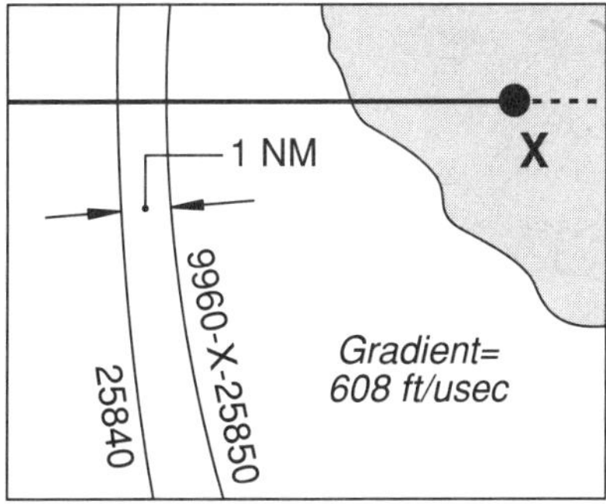

Figure 9-11. *The distance between the 25840 and 25850 TDs (which represent the difference in microseconds between the receipt of signals) for Loran-C rate 9960 X-ray may be less than a mile or more than four miles. A one-microsecond error in the reading can result in a position error of as little as 608 feet or as much as 2,430 feet, depending on the position of the receiver in the system.*

mode known as *blink*. In this mode, the display for that station will blink on-and-off, indicating to you that there is an error in the TD and that you should not use it. In most areas, you can switch to another station pair because three, four, or even five suitable station pairs are often available.

When the master is the station in error, several station pairs may be affected, rendering them all unusable. In this case, in areas of overlapping GRIs you can switch to another GRI and continue, taking care to determine that the new readings are reasonable and agree with previous fixes. If another GRI is not available you should use the last plotted Loran-C position as the starting point for a new DR plot and continue using other methods such as visual fixes, GPS, or celestial navigation.

Sometimes you see a Loran-C receiver *jump* quickly from one position to another—but you know that it's impossible for your vessel to change position that rapidly. A jump occurs when a receiver, which tracks station pairs automatically, resets to a new secondary station. As the geometry of the fix changes while you pass through the area covered by a station pair, your receiver picks out the strongest signals and those that give the best fix geometry. When your receiver locks onto a better pair, the position that is based on the new pair may differ from the last—and may be more accurate—causing the apparent jump in position.

A jump can also occur when your receiver *resets* to a new chain. If your home harbor is in an ambiguous area where jumping is a problem, you can lock your receiver onto a GRI and set of station pairs that you select rather than remain in automatic selection mode. Doing so will eliminate jumping, but might cost some accuracy.

At the outer limits of the Loran-C system range, a receiver will sometimes shift to the wrong cycle, usually in 10 microsecond intervals. This will be evident if you plot the TDs and they intersect in a large triangle. Turning the receiver off for a few seconds and on again will often correct this problem by prompting the unit to reset to the correct cycle. Some receivers allow you to "step" to the correct cycle, which you should do if you can figure out what correction is necessary.

In U.S. coastal waters you do not reach the system's outer limits because the chains overlap each other and a new chain or secondary is always available. A few hundred miles at sea, at the limits of Loran-C coverage, you should probably switch to the sextant or GPS.

The following list represents some of the messages common to modern digital Loran-C receivers. You should read your owner's manual thoroughly before navigating with your Loran-C set.

Display	Meaning
Accuracy	Accuracy of displayed position may be poor
Ambiguity	Ambiguous position
No Solution	Receiver is unable to establish a fix
SNR	The signal-to-noise ratio of one or more pairs is poor
Cycle Select	Receiver may be tracking incorrect cycle
Blink	System error, no fix possible on this rate
Battery	Low battery power
Power Failure	Primary power to the receiver interrupted or low
Memory Battery	Internal battery low, memory contents may be lost
ASF	ASFs are being used for lat/long conversion
MAG	Directional readouts are in magnetic instead of true
Manual Offset	User-noted ASFs are being used for lat/long conversion

Plotting the Loran-C Fix

You can safely use a Loran-C position in the lat/long mode where exact accuracy is not critical—such as offshore, coastwise, and in wide bays and sounds. In this mode, you can plot the geographic coordinates of the fix directly on the chart.

When you need the best Loran-C accuracy, you'll have to plot the TDs on a special *Loran-C chart,* which has the TDs for the area overprinted on the basic navigational information. These charts have the legend "Loran-C Overprinted" under the chart number.

Here are some important points about Loran-C charts:

- TDs are not shown over land
- TDs are not depicted on large-scale charts
- Not all rates available in a given area may be shown
- TD intervals may be inconsistent due to large changes in gradient
- ASF corrections are included in the plotted TDs except on very small-scale charts
- Rates are color-coded for easy identification

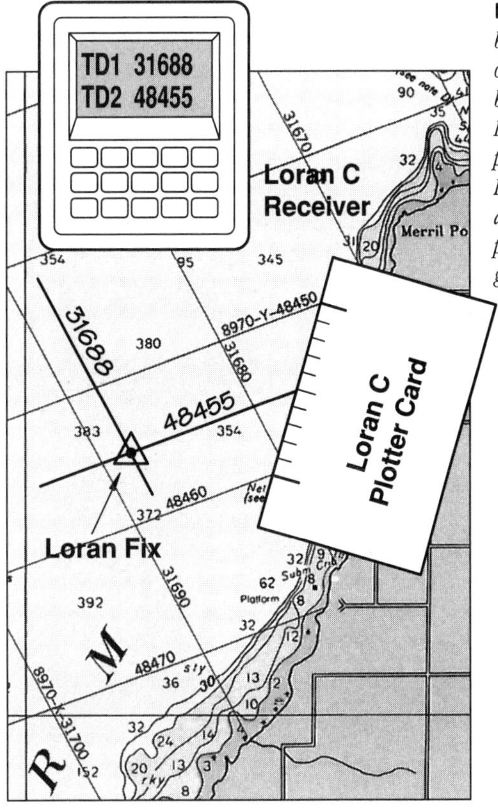

Figure 9-12. *TDs that fall between the ones plotted on the chart can be plotted by eye, by using the Loran-C linear interpolator printed on every Loran-C chart, or by a separate Loran-C plotter—a card that is graduated along its edges.*

A glance at a Loran-C chart will show that the overprinted TD lines are, in fact, curved hyperbolic lines, drawn at such convenient intervals as two, five, ten or more microseconds, chosen so that the lines are spaced about an inch apart. Each line has printed along its length the number of microseconds it represents, such as 31680, 31690, etc.

Refer to Figure 9-12 and note that a TD reading of 31690 on the Loran-C receiver would correspond to the 31690 TD line on the chart. Any other TD (or other LOP, such as a sounding) that crosses this line will yield a fix. If the reading were 31688, a TD not printed on the chart, you'd plot the LOP eight-tenths of the distance from the charted 31680 TD to the 31690 TD. It's usually easy and accurate enough to estimate by eye the correct distance between the two lines that are shown and to draw the LOP accordingly.

To help you plot readings with values that are between two charted lines, every Loran-C chart has a *Loran Linear Interpolator.* (See Figure 9-13.) To use it, first determine by inspection the interval between the charted TDs. Suppose it's ten microseconds. To plot a reading that differs from the charted TDs by, say, 8.7 microseconds, use your dividers to measure the space between two charted lines in the vicinity of your vessel's position. Without changing the spread of the dividers, move them to the interpolator. Starting from the right end, and keeping one point on the bottom or zero line, move them along the line until the other divider point touches a "10" line, a line marked with some multiple of 10. In this example, the first line touched by the right end of the dividers is the line marked "100." Without moving the "0" point of the dividers from the bottom line of the interpolator, close the dividers until the upper point is on the "8.7" line. The dividers now are spaced 8.7-tenths of the distance between the charted TDs. Move the dividers back to the

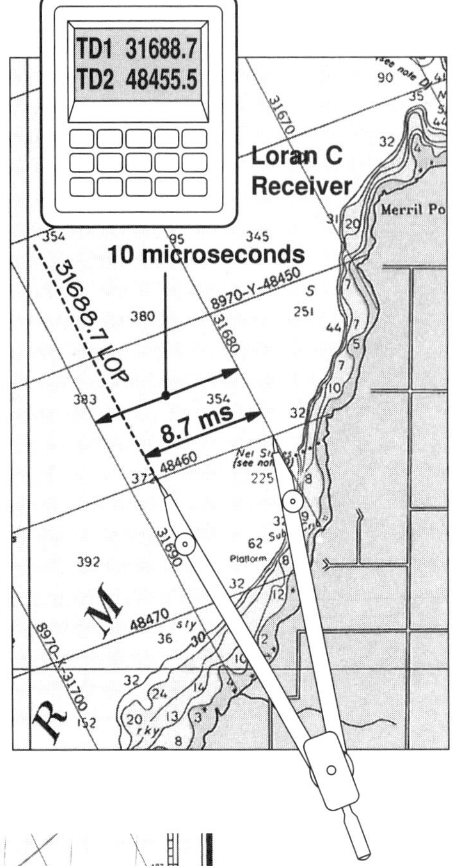

Figure 9-13. *With the Loran linear interpolator and a pair of dividers, you can more accurately measure and mark on a Loran-C chart any TDs displayed on Loran-C receivers.*

Figure 9-14. *In this example, the navigator uses the Loran linear interpolator to find the line 8.7 microseconds away from TD 31680, since this particular chart gives a printed TD for only every 10th microsecond.*

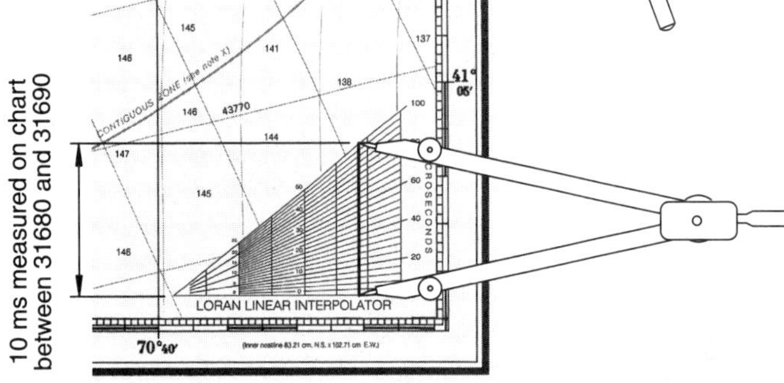

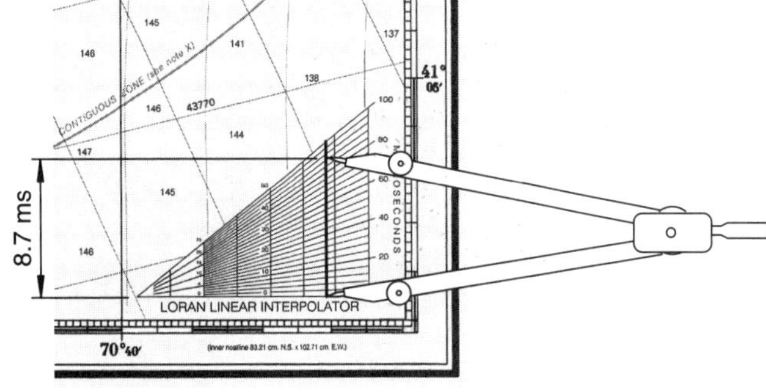

vicinity of the expected fix, mark the 8.7-tenths distance from the lesser TD, as in Figure 9-14, and draw your LOP parallel to the adjacent charted TDs.

Loran-C interpolators are also available in a card format. They look much like business cards but have graduations printed along their edges. You place a card so that the end graduation marks—"0," "5," "10," or any other interval—are aligned with the chosen TDs and you can plot any convenient fractional distance between them. (See Figure 9-12.)

Again, unless you need near-perfect accuracy, you can, with practice, get acceptable results by eyeballing the intermediate TDs and plotting them without using the interpolator.

The Future of Loran-C

The advent of GPS has made Loran-C users very nervous. When the military requirement for Loran-C ended in 1994, the Coast Guard began transferring its stations on foreign soil to the host countries and closed down the Hawaiian chain entirely, leaving only the continental U.S. under Coast Guard operation. However, the Coast Guard recognizes that the U.S. Loran-C user community is large and diverse. Many navigators are reluctant to switch to GPS and buy a new receiver, so long as Loran-C meets their needs. Of course, they may have to switch if funding for Loran-C is dropped from the Coast Guard budget.

Political considerations, not defense policy, will determine Loran-C's future. Although the 1994 FRP states an intention to fund Loran-C through the year 2015, this time frame could, at any time, be shortened or, less likely, lengthened.

Knowing about the coming demise of Loran-C, should you replace it now with GPS? Your answer might depend on how you use it. If you use Loran-C to augment piloting in cruising from place to place, you could reasonably conclude that its continued use is prudent and cost-effective. (But wouldn't it be nice to have a GPS for a backup?)

However, if you use Loran-C mostly in the TD mode as an accurate system for finding your favorite fishing holes, wrecks, or other precise locations, you should consider converting to differential GPS and then visit each site to observe firsthand its GPS coordinates on your set. This will ensure that you can find those locations with precision on future visits. You could simply convert Loran-C TDs into lat/long coordinates and enter them into the GPS receiver, but this would not be accurate enough to enable you to find that special fishing hole that you had used your Loran-C waypoints to find. For a thorough discussion of the accuracies of various types of systems, see Chapter 17.

U.S. Loran-C Chains

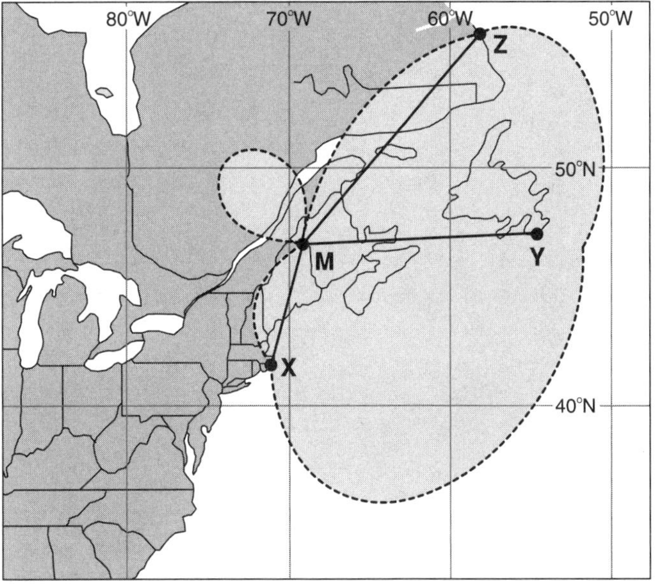

Figure 9-15. *Canadian East Coast Chain, GRI 5930*
Transmitters:
Master—Caribou, ME
X—Nantucket, MA
Y—Cape Race, Canada
Z—Fox Harbor, Canada

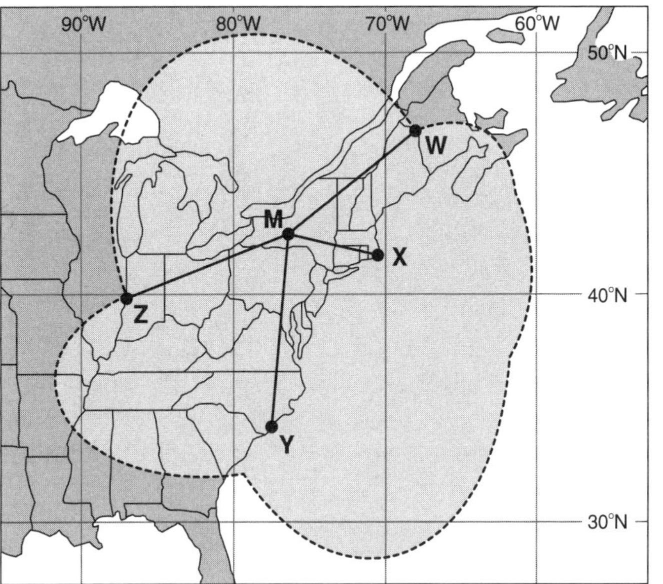

Figure 9-16. *Northeast U.S. Chain, GRI 9960*
Transmitters:
Master—Seneca, NY
W—Caribou, ME
X—Nantucket, MA
Y—Carolina Beach, NC
Z—Dana, IN

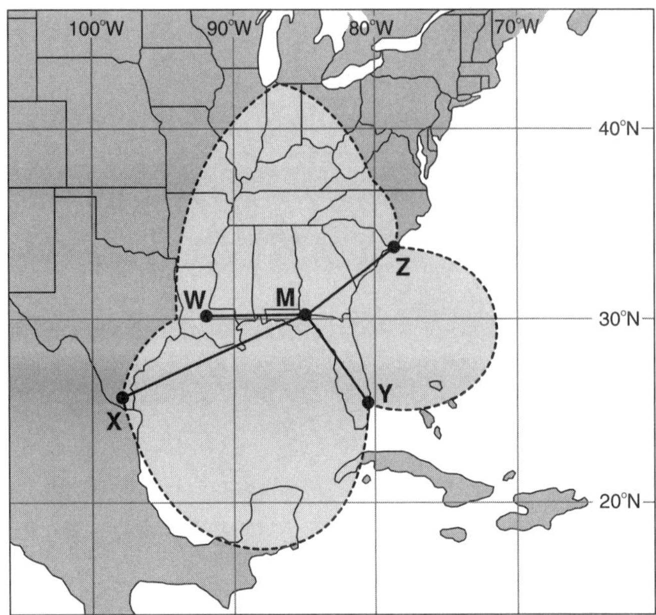

Figure 9-17. *Southeast U.S. Chain, GRI 7980 Transmitters: Master—Malone, FL W—Grangeville, LA X—Raymondville, TX Y—Jupiter, FL Z—Carolina Beach, NC*

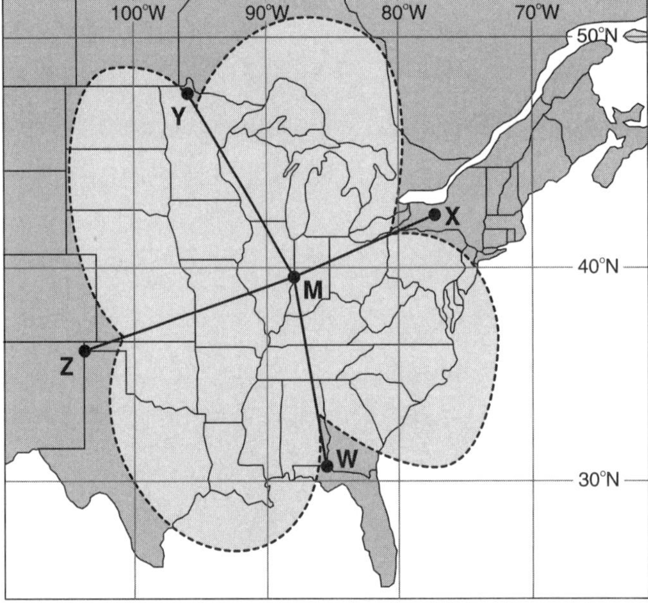

Figure 9-18. *Great Lakes Chain, GRI 8970 Transmitters: Master—Dana, IN W—Malone, FL X—Seneca, NY Y—Baudette, MN Z—Boise City, OK*

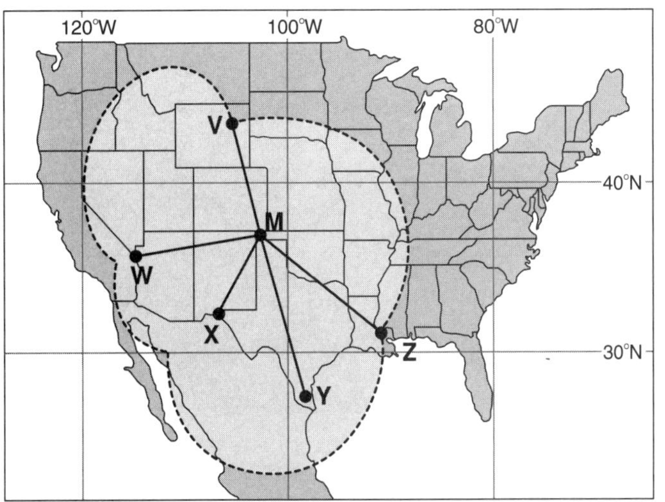

Figure 9-19. *South-Central U.S. GRI Chain, 9610 Transmitters: Master—Boise City, OK V—Gillette, WY W—Searchlight, NV X—Las Cruces, NM Y—Raymondville, TX Z—Grangeville, LA*

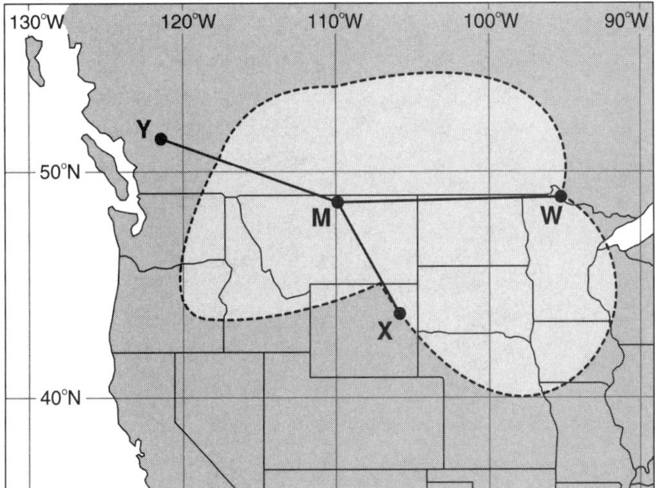

Figure 9-20. *North Central U.S. GRI Chain, 8290 Transmitters: Master—Havre, MT W—Baudette, MN X—Gillette, WY Y—Williams Lake, Canada*

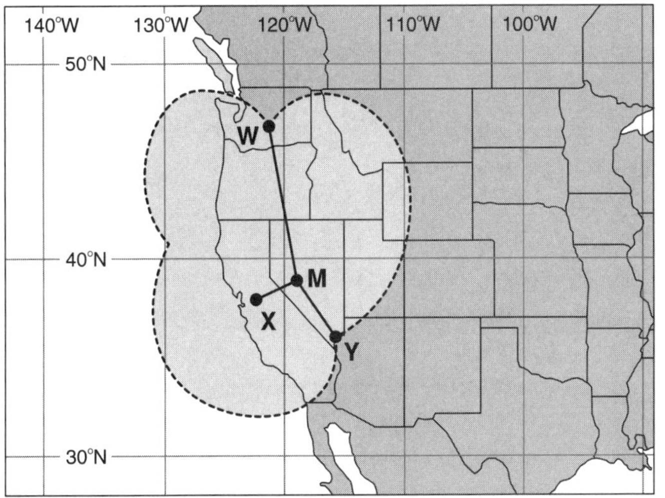

Figure 9-21. *U.S. West Coast Chain, GRI 9940 Transmitters: Master—Fallon, NV W—George, WA X—Middletown, CA Y—Searchlight, NV*

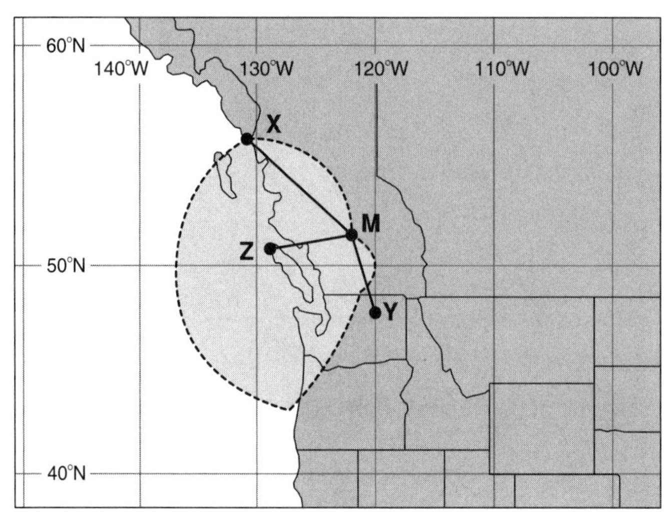

Figure 9-22. *Canadian West Coast Chain, GRI 5990 Transmitters: Master—Williams Lake, Canada X—Shoal Cove, AK Y—George, WY Z—Port Hardy, Canada*

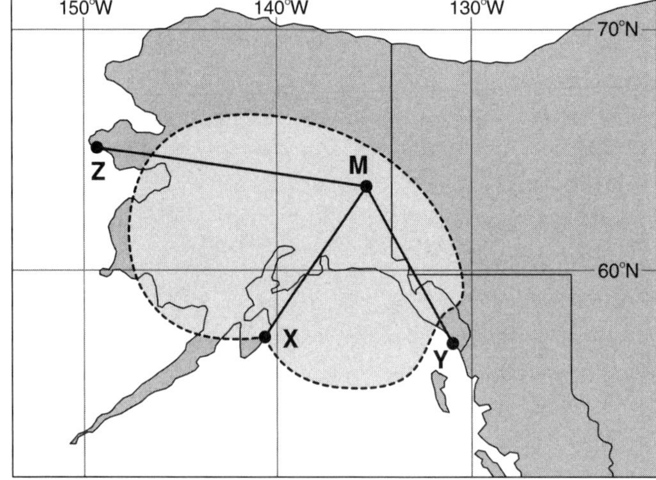

Figure 9-23. *Gulf of Alaska Chain GRI 7960 Transmitters: Master—Tok, AK X—Kodiak, AK Y—Shoal Cove, AK Z—Port Clarence, Canada*

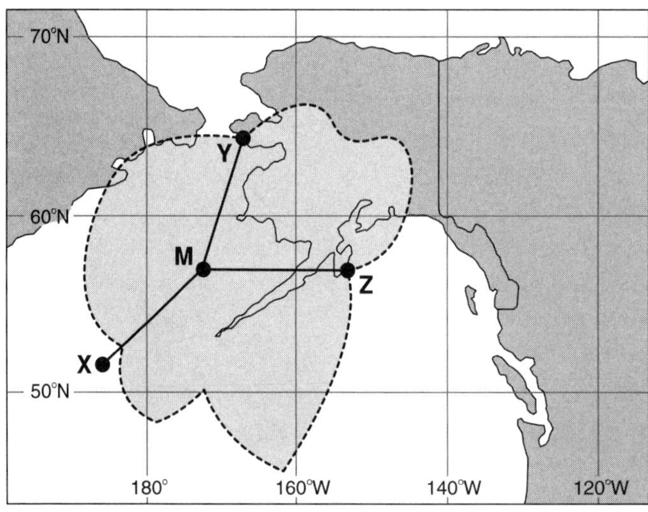

Figure 9-24. *North Pacific Chain, GRI 9990 Transmitters: Master—St. Paul, AK X—Attu, AK Y—Port Clarence, AK Z—Kodiak, AK*

CHAPTER TEN

Radar Navigation

IN 1922 TWO SCIENTISTS working at the U.S. Naval Aircraft Radio Laboratory, almost in the shadow of the Washington Monument in Washington, D.C., were testing a radio device by transmitting signals across the Potomac River. They noted that passing ships affected the signals and realized that instruments could detect their passage even when they could not be seen by the naked eye. Their observation lay dormant until 1934, when serious investigations led to the development of one of the most useful navigational and safety tools man has ever developed—*radar.*

The word "radar" is derived from *RAdio Detection And Ranging*. The USS *Leary* tested the first primitive marine radar in 1937. Though radar technology developed rapidly during the war years independently by Axis and Allied powers, the British discovery of the *magnetron,* a device that generates radar's signals, was a key breakthrough. The British shared the technology with the U.S. in 1940. By the end of the war, radar was in full military operation and ready for commercial use.

The first important use of radar was made by the British during the Battle of Britain in World War II. Radar detected incoming German bombers and allowed the limited British forces to efficiently use scarce defenses, which contributed significantly to their winning the Battle of Britain. Later, radar was employed in both ships and aircraft for navigation, targeting, weather forecasting, and collision avoidance.

You may have a mental image of radar operators hunched over large hooded scopes, fiddling with dozens of little dials. Modern radars, however, use new technology that enables operators to see the screens easily in daylight and to control them with a few buttons. They are not only far easier to use than older models, but are also more reliable and less expensive.

The Role of Radar

Radar performs two vital functions at sea. First, it is a tool for *collision avoidance*—detecting other vessels and maneuvering to prevent collisions with them. It fills this role not only in bad weather but also when weather conditions are perfect, because it provides a piece of information that is available from no other source—exact range and bearing to another vessel, from which you can compute its actual course and speed.

Second, radar provides LOPs in the form of ranges from fixed objects that you can use with any other available LOP to fix your position. In foggy weather, your radar might be the only source of LOPs. You can also use it to detect severe weather such as thunderstorms or squalls, although marine radar is not designed specifically to do this.

This chapter examines the role of radar as a navigational tool. However, if your boat is equipped with radar, remember to use all of its capabilities.

How Radar Works

Radar sends out a radio signal at the speed of light, measures the time it takes the signal to travel to an object and return, and then solves the speed-time-distance problem to find the distance to the object. (Speed is known and time is measured; in the computation, one-half of the total distance is used because the signal went out and back.) Radars have directional antennas, so they can also detect the bearing to an object, although not accurately, for reasons explained later.

A radar set cycles through a sequence of several steps. In the first step it sends out a pulse of radio energy from the transmitter part of its circuitry. As soon as this pulse leaves, an electronic switch disconnects the antenna from the transmitter and connects it to the receiver. It is now ready to sense the return echo (if there is one). After an interval a little longer than the time required for the pulse to travel to its extreme range and return, the switch resets to the transmitter and another signal is sent out. The only possible signal that it can receive, then, is the one it sent in the same cycle. This prevents ambiguity in the range calculation.

Radar transmits pulses of radio energy that have a pulse length (also called pulse duration) and *pulse repetition rate (PRR)*. The PRR is as high as 1,000 times per second.

The pulses also have a shape (illustrated in Figure 10-1) that is determined by the type of antenna used and the characteristics of the radio wave itself. Note that the radio wave is oriented in a certain direction, but there is no clear definition of its limits to the side or vertically. As it sweeps past an object, the power of the signal gradually increases from zero to a maximum, then decreases to zero again. Because radar does not sharply define the edge of an object, its ability to determine bearings is limited—an extremely important consideration in navigation that is discussed more fully later in this chapter.

A radar pulse interacts with the surface of the sea. Radar energy travels both in a direct line to a target and in an indirect line that reflects off the sea surface. The indirect signal, which travels a slightly longer distance, may interfere with or enhance the direct signal, depending on whether it is in phase with the direct signal. (See Figure 10-2.)

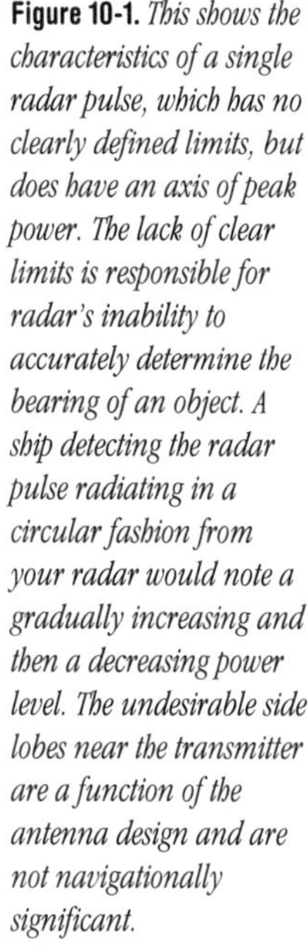

Figure 10-1. *This shows the characteristics of a single radar pulse, which has no clearly defined limits, but does have an axis of peak power. The lack of clear limits is responsible for radar's inability to accurately determine the bearing of an object. A ship detecting the radar pulse radiating in a circular fashion from your radar would note a gradually increasing and then a decreasing power level. The undesirable side lobes near the transmitter are a function of the antenna design and are not navigationally significant.*

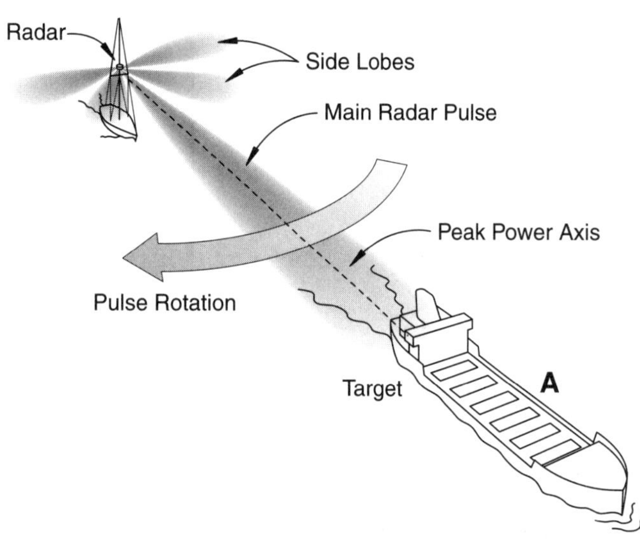

The Radar Display

There are two types of radar display. The first, called a *plan position indicator (PPI)*, was developed in the 1940s and is still used today on older sets. The PPI consists of a television-type glass tube with a round—instead of rectangular—face that is coated on the inside with phosphorescent paint. The radar's outgoing signals appear as a rotating line radiating from the center of the scope, which represents your vessel's position. Any return echoes are developed along this radial line and illuminate the phosphors on the inside surface of the tube. These continue to glow as the trace continues around the scope. They gradually fade as the trace passes by again, when they are re-illuminated, usually in a slightly different position.

A computer monitor generates the second type of display that presents the same kind of picture as the PPI. The image is a computer-generated picture of a PPI scope in a format known as a *raster* image. (For a more in-depth discussion of raster format, see page 131.) The computer can manipulate the display in ways that a PPI can't. For example, it can offset the center of the display to another place on the monitor, color the images according to the strength of the return signal, or display a track of a target across the screen. It can also combine radar with other navigational information, as discussed in Chapter 11, "Electronic Charts." (See Figure 10-3.)

The raster image is drawn on a rectangular computer monitor—not on a circular cathode ray tube. Rather than a circular sweep, a linear scan of horizontal lines generates the image, just as in a television set. The screen consists of hundreds of lines, each consisting of hundreds of *picture elements,* or *pixels*. The scan begins at the top left corner of the screen and continues across the screen, jumping to the next line and the next, until the entire screen has been covered. The best raster radars use a screen update rate of 60 complete scans per second. At a rate of 30 scans per second or less, the screen develops a noticeable "flicker." Large commercial-grade raster radar screens have more than one million pixels and update at the 60 scans per second rate, which requires a tremendous amount of computer power.

The number of pixels per unit of area affects screen resolution and the sharpness of the image and is measured in terms of *dot pitch*—the size of a pixel in millimeters. The best resolution is found in screens with a dot pitch of 0.28 or less.

Manufacturers can lower computer power and save costs by reducing the scan rate, but some choose to save by using an *interlaced display*. In this presentation, every other line of pixels is illuminated on one pass and the rest on the next pass. Although this technique reduces computer processing by one half, it can make the radar image "jitter" when any misalignment occurs between the scans. A *non-interlaced display* is more desirable—and more expensive.

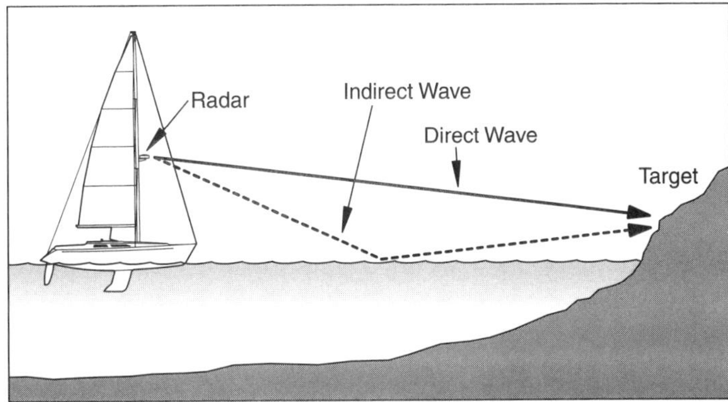

Figure 10-2. *Radar waves may take more than one path to a target. The indirect wave may interfere with or enhance the direct wave, or have no effect at all.*

A radar screen on a small craft is oriented so 000° relative—the vessel's heading—is at the top of the scope, rather than magnetic or true north. This orientation presents the information in the directional view that most operators like to see. If the vessel has a digital magnetic or gyroscopic compass, the radar can be oriented to "north up" mode by sending the compass data to the radar in digital form.

Radar Controls in Navigational Use

The more expensive radar units have more functions than cheaper ones, but all have the following basic controls:

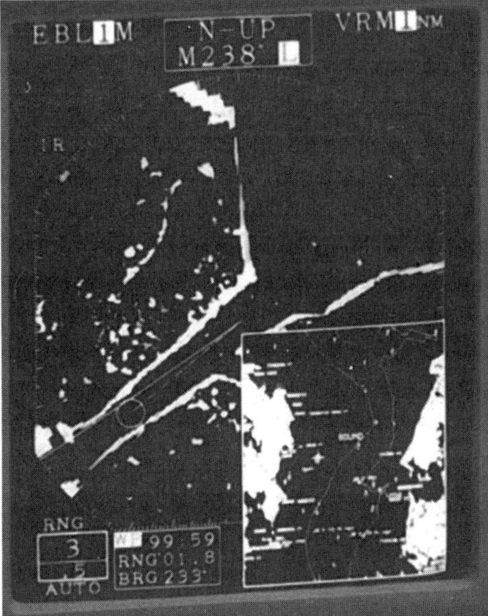

Figure 10-3. *As shown here, raster radar displays can integrate other information with the radar display, such as an electronic chart image or a depth sounder trace. In the most sophisticated systems, the radar and electronic chart are combined into one display. (Photograph courtesy of Raytheon Electronics)*

The *brightness* or *intensity control* regulates the amount of light that remains after the trace passes. You should adjust it while the gain control is at the lowest setting and set so that the trace fades away quickly after the trace passes, leaving no residual light.

Set the *gain control* so there is a very slight amount of "clutter" around the center of the scope; doing so will ensure that the radar is able to sense the smallest targets. Set the gain while you are using one of the longer-range scales, though you may need to make slight adjustments when you shift to shorter ranges.

Use the *clutter control,* but sparingly, to counteract any signals returned from precipitation. Turn the clutter control down only when needed because, in so doing, you may reduce receiver sensitivity to the point that small, poorly reflecting targets may disappear, particularly at long ranges.

The *range control* sets the maximum range at which targets can be displayed on the screen. If you select a range of four miles, the radius from the center of the scope to the edge is four miles. A target at five miles would then be off the scope and remain undisplayed unless you select a greater range. For navigation purposes, choose the lowest range setting possible that allows you to see the targets selected for fixes. At other times, you should select one of the longer ranges so you can "see" other vessels at the earliest possible time.

Fixed *range markers* are a series of concentric circles at selected distances from the center. They allow a quick estimate of the range to all visible targets, and are not adjustable.

The *variable range marker (VRM)* is adjustable; you can set it at any desired range out to the maximum range setting. The VRM appears as a circle around the center of the scope at the selected range. A numerical digital or analog readout shows the exact range to which the VRM is set.

The *heading flash* indicates the exact heading of the vessel. In vessels without gyroscopic input to the radar (this includes all small craft), all targets appear in *relative bearing*. Adjust the heading flash so that it is barely visible—then you will not lose small targets in its shadow.

A *bearing cursor* or *electronic bearing line (EBL)* measures the bearing of targets. It's a single line radiating out from the scope's center at a constant selectable bearing.

All radar sets have these controls. Some radar installations have still more complex functions and controls—and are more expensive. Commercial units, for example, commonly have a function called Automated Radar Plotting Aid (ARPA) that can track other vessels automatically. Even though your set may lack such advanced features, you can take full advantage of those it has by getting to know it thoroughly.

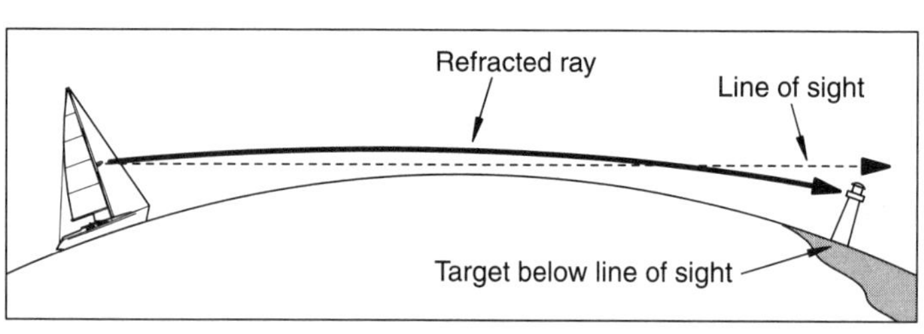

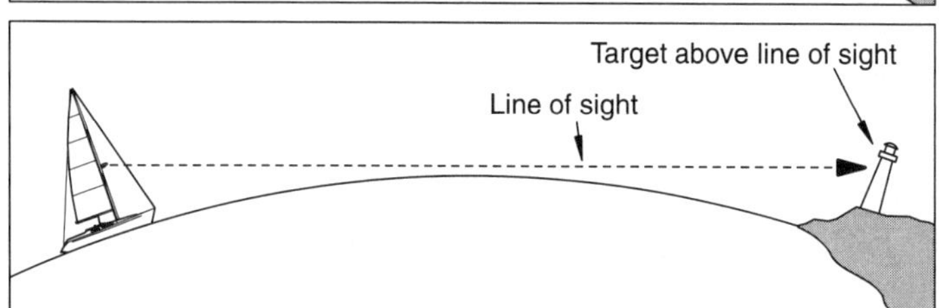

Figure 10-4. *Radar can "see" over the horizon slightly because radar waves are bent toward the earth by the density gradient of the earth's atmosphere in a process called refraction. In this figure the straight line of sight between a vessel and a target passes above the land, but radar may be able to detect it.*

Interpreting Radar Images

To properly interpret the radar images on your screen, you should understand a number of factors that affect them, some of which have already been noted.

Diffraction causes radar waves to bend around objects, enabling radar to "see" behind them to some extent. Low-frequency radar energy is subject to greater diffraction than higher frequency energy, and thus has greater ability to bend around objects.

Attenuation is the scattering and absorption of radar energy as it passes through the atmosphere. It is greater at higher frequencies and shorter wavelengths.

Refraction is the bending of radar waves as they travel through the atmosphere. Normally the waves are bent slightly toward the earth, thereby increasing the range at which objects can be detected.

The distance to the radar horizon is equal to 1.22 times the square root of the antenna's height. But that horizon distance is not the maximum range at which you can detect an object because the height of the target, as well as refraction, extends the range, just as it would in a visual sighting. (See Figure 10-4.)

At times, *super-refraction* (greater than normal downward bending) or *sub-refraction* (bending upward instead of downward) may occur. Unusual atmospheric phenomena such as temperature inversions cause these conditions. Super-refraction greatly increases radar's range; subrefraction decreases it. In very unusual conditions, ducting of the radar waves between two layers of air may cause them to travel outward many times their normal range. These conditions similarly affect light waves—so when you see mirages or other strange atmospheric distortions, use your radar with caution at long ranges.

Radar is limited in its ability to distinguish between objects on the same bearing by its *resolution in range,* which determines the point at which two objects, one in front of the other, become one blip on the radar screen. Resolution in range is primarily a function of pulse length, with the minimum theoretical resolution in range equal to one-half the length of one pulse. Another reason to be cautious in interpreting two images on the same bearing is the shadow that the nearer object might cast on the farther one. A very small object can hide at a considerable distance behind a very large one.

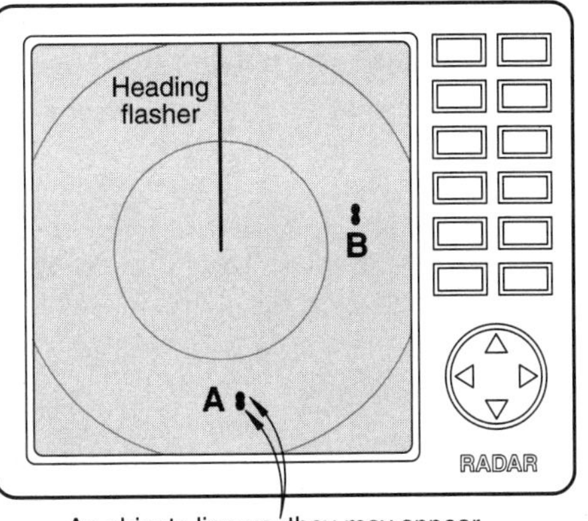

Figure 10-5. *A radar's ability to differentiate between objects that are close together determines its resolution in range (point A) or in bearing (point B). At some point, two targets moving closer together merge into one echo. Your own vessel is always at the origin of the trace, but may be offset from the center of the screen in some units.*

A radar's ability to distinguish between two objects at the same range, but close together, is called its *resolution in bearing*. As two objects at the same distance from a radar move closer together, at some point they merge into one blip on the screen. (See Figure 10-5.) This is a function of beam width and is related to practical limits in the design of the radar's rotating antenna.

You should be cautious also in interpreting images at distances beyond your radar's hori-

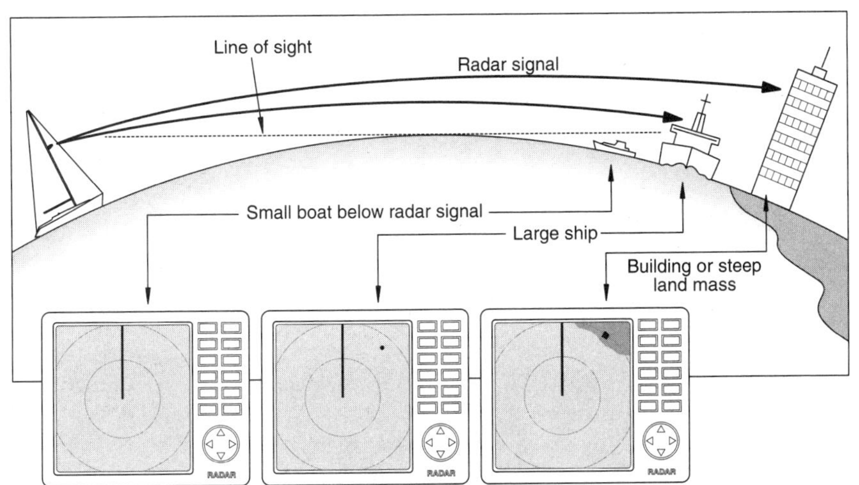

Figure 10-6. *The height of a target affects the range at which radar can detect it. Discounting the effects of refraction, an object can be seen by radar if it projects above the radar's horizon. The radar can detect any part of an object except that part which lies below the radar horizon. The radar horizon in miles equals 1.22 times the square root of the height of the antenna.*

zon distance. A large target will appear as a large blip only if it is fully above the radar horizon. If it is partially below the radar horizon, it may appear as a small blip depending on its aspect; if fully below, it will not appear at all. (See Figure 10-6.)

A target's *reflecting quality* and *aspect* also affect the image you see on the radar screen. Reflecting quality varies with a target's density. A target composed of more dense material has a higher reflecting quality. Rocks, steel, and other dense objects reflect radar waves well and generate strong echoes. Trees, grasses, and other less dense materials generate weaker echoes, or none at all—in which case they're invisible to radar.

When taking a radar range to a shoreline for a fix, you should know the type of shore you're observing to interpret the radar echoes accurately. Charts show a shoreline's location at mean low water. When the water is above that level, you can't see that shoreline either by eye or by radar. In addition, radar might not detect a shoreline that presents a low aspect. If a shore is low and nearly flat, or if extensive mud flats lie seaward of it, the radar may actually show not the shoreline but some line well beyond it, such as a bluff or a range of hills well inland, as depicted in Figure 10-7. Failure to account for this phenomenon has caused groundings to unwary skippers who thought they were much farther offshore than they actually were.

Figure 10-7. *A low, gently sloping beach may not be detected by radar, but it is likely that any high land behind it will—which may cause the radar to show a false picture of the shoreline. The dangerous result is that the vessel is much closer to shore than the radar indicates. In this figure, the radar return from the shoreline is not strong enough to generate an echo, while the returns from the cliff and lighthouse are very strong.*

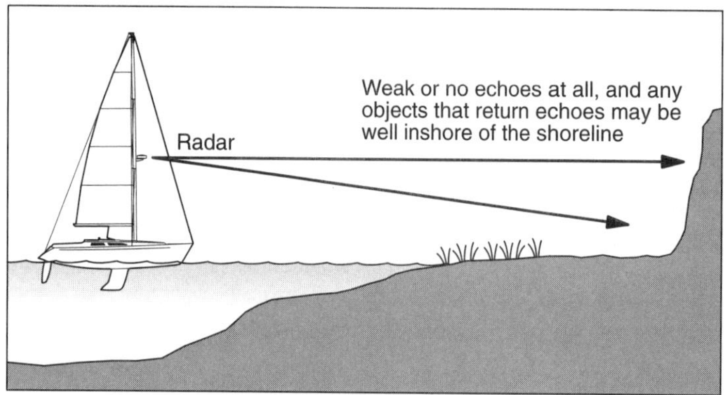

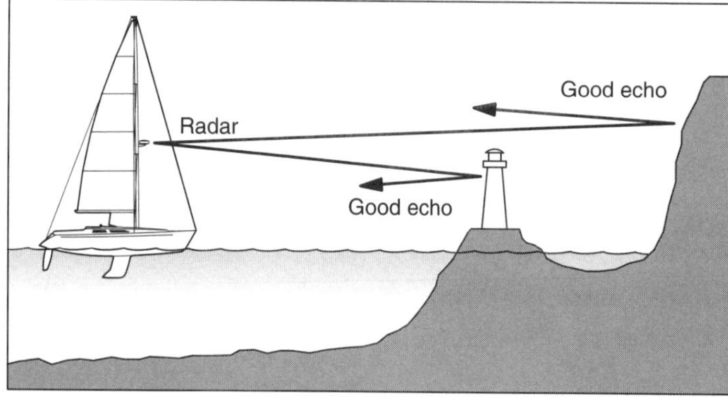

Any low-lying coast should be considered a poor radar target until proven otherwise. The *Coast Pilots* are invaluable in determining the reflecting quality of coasts, often specifically pointing out radar-conspicuous places and areas that are poor targets. In general, mud flats, sand spits, and some types of swamps are difficult to detect on radar, while rocky coasts and high bluffs provide a strong echo.

Ships, boats, and other water craft reflect radar waves according to their type of construction material. Steel and aluminum are very good reflectors; wood and fiberglass are relatively poor reflectors. On the principle of "see and be seen," many small wood and fiberglass boats carry radar reflectors high in their rigging so that other vessels' radar can more easily detect them.

The aspect of a target vessel also determines how it is perceived by the radar. For best reflectivity, a surface should be perpendicular to the radar wave. A rough or angular surface also reflects well. Most ships have plenty of surfaces that reflect radar waves very well. But even a ship can be "seen" better when it's sideways rather than bow-on to the radar observing it. At long ranges this dimension of aspect can be important.

Unwanted Echoes

Certain physical forces can affect radar waves in ways that cause presentations either of false positions of real objects or false objects. These can cause a lot of consternation if you do not recognize them.

A *false echo* occurs most often when there is another tall object, such as a mast, close to the radar antenna. In that case, the return echo can travel back to the radar via two paths: one straight to the antenna and the other reflecting off the nearby mast. Then the radar plots two objects—the real one correctly, and the false echo at the same range as the real one but on the bearing of the mast. (See Figure 10-8.)

On a two-masted sailboat, the radar antenna is usually mounted on the mizzen mast to keep the cable run short and prevent fouling the jib—but doing so places the mainmast in the direct line of the heading, and you lose some signal strength in this direction. In fog or haze you can vary your course by 10° or so every few minutes so that targets ahead are not completely hidden behind the mainmast.

You may encounter a peculiar problem when approaching an overhead power cable. A radar echo reflecting off the cable will show as a single target on a steady bearing with decreasing range, prompting you to change course to avoid collision. If you did change course the target would appear to confound you by remaining on a steady bearing and decreasing range. The reason for this is that the echo reflects from whatever part of the cable that is perpendicular to the vessel. If you don't realize what's going on, you can suffer a lot of needless anxiety. Because of their construction, bridges do not cause this false radar picture—they can be seen in their full length.

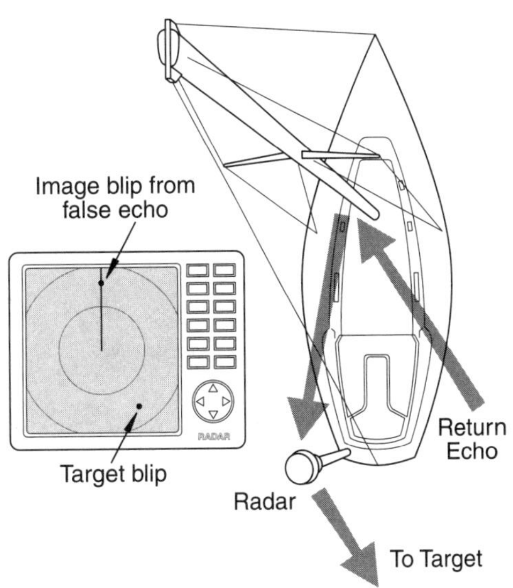

Figure 10-8. *A false echo may appear if there is an obstruction near the radar antenna that reflects the return echo. In this case, the radar on a sailboat with the antenna aft may see a real target in the correct direction and a false echo from the direction of the reflecting mainmast.*

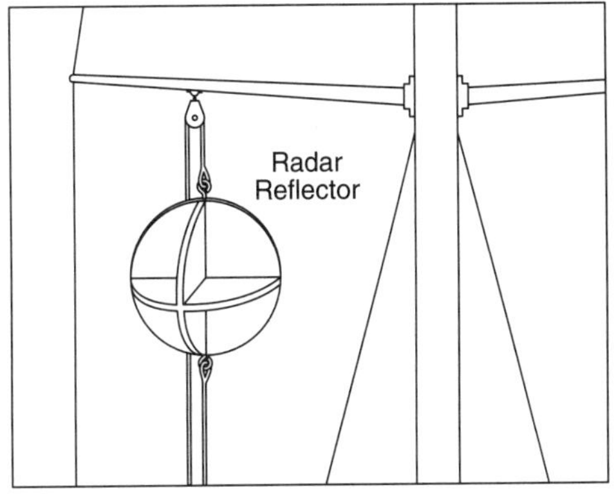

Figure 10-9. *A radar reflector consists of metal plates placed at angles that reflect radar waves back in the direction from which they came. Almost all large buoys have radar reflectors, and many small craft carry them to be more visible to other vessels' radars.*

Radar Aids to Navigation

Several devices have been developed to enhance radar's use in navigation. The first is a passive device that most boaters know about, the *radar reflector,* shown in Figure 10-9. The reflector consists of three metal plates placed at right angles to each other so they reflect any incoming radio waves back to their source.

Radar reflectors are built into the structure of all large buoys and are placed on other aids to navigation, such as beacons, where the Coast Guard considers their placement important. In examining charts you can assume that all lighted buoys have radar reflectors; other aids equipped with reflectors may have "RA REF" printed alongside them on charts. On a radar scope, the radar reflector causes a single strong blip to appear.

A simple radar reflector cannot enable you to positively identify an aid to navigation. For that, the device must emit some identifying electronic signal. When it does, it's a *radar beacon.*

There are two types of radar beacons. One is a *racon,* an electronic device that emits a coded signal in the frequency range of marine radars when it detects incoming radar waves. On your radar scope, a racon appears as a set of dashes originating at the point of the racon. (See Figure 10-10.)

The *ramark* is the other type of active radar emitter. It continually sends out a peri-

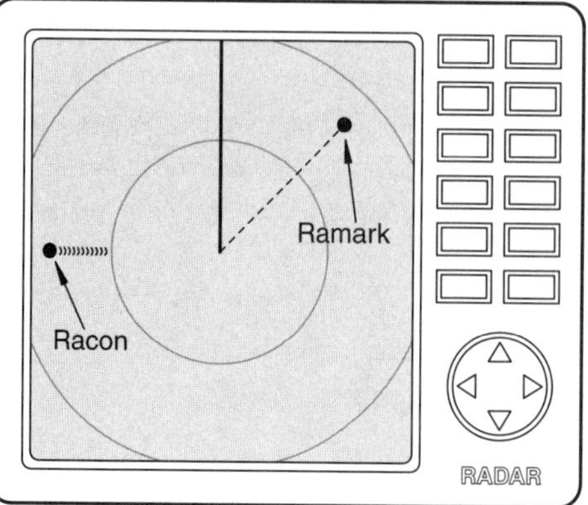

Figure 10-10. *Radar beacons are devices that enhance a radar's effectiveness by returning a separate signal in the radar frequency range. Here, the radar screen shows a* racon *signal and a* ramark *signal. A racon transmits only when it senses an incoming radar wave; a ramark transmits continually.*

odic radar frequency signal (unlike the racon, which sends its signal only when it detects a vessel's radar pulse). A ramark signal appears on the scope as a dotted or dashed line radiating outward from the center of the scope on the bearing of the ramark. (See Figure 10-10.) The periodic nature of the ramark signal ensures that other targets are not hidden in the radial lines it makes. Because of their continuous power requirements, ramarks are mostly used on fixed aids within reach of a power cable.

Radar use in Piloting

Radar is extremely valuable in piloting because it can provide precise lines of position (LOPs) in virtually any weather. However, you should take its limitations into account when deciding how to use it for plotting fixes (see Chapter 6, "Piloting").

Remember that radar computes the range to an object by a mathematical formula based on the speed of the radar signal. This determination is not affected by the shape of the signal. On the other hand, the sizeable width of the beam of radio energy makes its measurement of bearings imprecise.

When possible, you should use LOPs based on the more accurate radar ranges rather than on the less accurate radar bearings. A radar range of 8,000 yards on a strong target should not be off by more than 100 yards or so. A bearing to the same target, by contrast, could be in error by 2 or 3 degrees.

You should take ranges from clearly defined objects such as offshore lighthouses, prominent points of land, bold coastlines, and rocky or cement breakwaters. Where possible, avoid using low spits of land, swampy or grassy areas, and imprecise features such as low-lying beaches and mud flats.

When the only way to get a fix is by a radar range and bearing to a single object, use the bearing with caution. Further, try to verify all radar fixes using fewer than three LOPs with a depth reading or an LOP from another source to be sure your vessel is in safe water. If the depth reading does not agree with charted depths in the area of a single range-bearing radar fix, treat your position as unknown and stop or head offshore until the ambiguity is resolved.

Modern digital radars can be integrated with electronic charts because they use the same display technology. This allows the radar screen to be used for the radar presentation, electronic chart display, or both, depending on the capabilities of the units. So far, only the more advanced (and expensive) systems integrate the radar picture and the electronic chart into one seamless display.

Use of radar with or without its electronic chart feature does not free you from learning to navigate using traditional methods, from putting those methods to use during normal cruising to keep your skills current, or from taking and plotting fixes in the traditional way as a check or backup to electronic devices.

Modern radars are smaller, lighter, less expensive, easier to use, and more dependable than ever before. For the boater who can afford one, a radar is a valuable and safety-enhancing navigational tool. This book addresses radar's use as a navigational tool only. For instruction in its use in avoiding collision with other vessels, see *Pub. 1310, Radar Navigation Manual,* published by the National Imagery and Mapping Agency (NIMA) or one of several privately produced texts available from marine suppliers.

CHAPTER ELEVEN

Electronic Charts

FOR ALL THE CENTURIES since the development of charts, mariners have dreamed of being able to plot their position on a chart regardless of weather, time of day, visibility, or any other conditions. This dream is realized with the *electronic chart (EC),* which shows the actual geographic position of a vessel on a digital image of a chart, updated as often as every second. It uses position inputs from GPS and Loran-C that are more accurate than any previously available and, with the right equipment, can locate a vessel within a few meters of its true position. The electronic chart and its accompanying GPS and Loran-C inputs comprise what is here called the electronic chart system.

This new technology raises some complex issues regarding the role of the navigator and essentially redefines the job. No longer is the navigator's role centered on finding the position of the vessel; that's done by the electronic chart system. Now the navigator must be a system operator, monitor, data entry clerk, and administrator (and probably financial officer). The electronic chart system doesn't make the navigator's role easier, except to remove some routine tasks.

You should understand some important legal and safety issues associated with electronic charts before using this marvelous but sometimes misused new technology. The danger, of course, is complacency—reliance on this fallible system without using traditional skills to monitor its performance. Electronics will always fail at some point, and the sea has a way of prompting that failure at the least opportune moment. Though the gear may fail, sea sense, traditional skills, and experience will not.

A major maritime accident was caused by the failure of navigation personnel to monitor an electronic chart, proving (again!) that reliance on a single aid to navigation is dangerous. A cruise ship, the Royal Majesty, *using a GPS receiver to drive an autopilot, ran aground at full speed on a shoal off the coast of Massachusetts. The problem began when the GPS antenna became disconnected from its receiver, which then reverted to a dead reckoning mode without warning the navigator. The ship was driven off course by wind and tide. The watch officers failed to use any other method to confirm their position, and the DR plotted only course and speed through the water, not over the ground. The ship was 17 miles off course when she grounded.*

The Function of an Electronic Chart

A small-craft navigator has two main responsibilities at sea: navigating the vessel and avoiding collision with other vessels.

The navigation part of the job has three main parts:

1. Taking fixes and plotting them on the appropriate chart.
2. Evaluating that position in relation to the chosen track, navigational dangers, and other factors that may influence the voyage.
3. Choosing courses and speeds that will avoid dangers and bring the vessel safely to her destination.

The function of the electronic chart is to relieve the navigator of the first of these jobs, but that relief comes again with an important caveat: Nothing can relieve the navigator's responsibility to see that the electronic chart (or any other system) is functioning properly, doing its job, and operating at full performance.

When operating properly, an electronic chart system displays a vessel's position on a chart with far greater accuracy and consistency than any person ever could; it gives fixes every second that are accurate to a few dozen meters or less. Your job of making sure that the system is properly displaying positions takes far less time than getting LOPs and plotting fixes yourself, and leaves you with more time for other important functions such as collision avoidance, weather monitoring, communications, route planning, sail tending, and engine monitoring.

Detailed studies by the U.S. Coast Guard and other organizations show that the time spent on navigation as a percentage of total workload drops significantly with the use of electronic chart systems, while time spent on other necessary functions increases.

In addition to navigation, an electronic chart system can also compute and display a variety of vessel performance information on its screen, as shown in Figure 11-1.

Definitions

The *electronic chart (EC)* is actually a blend of several different technologies, each with important capabilities and limitations. The EC is a computerized device that displays nautical

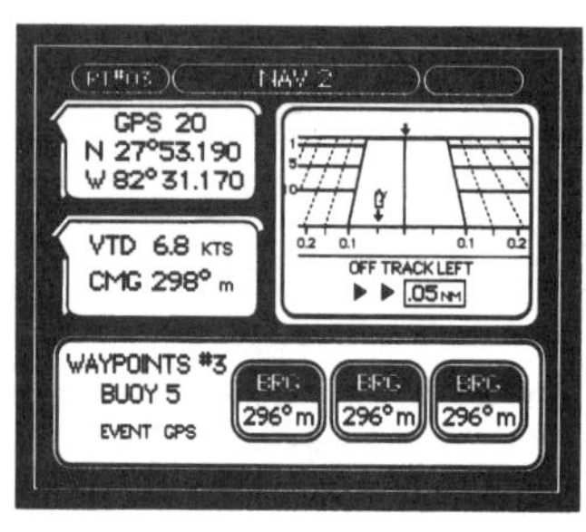

A

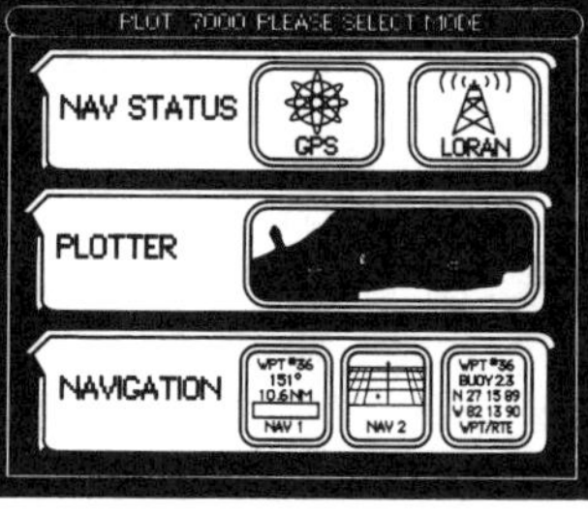

B

SELECT WAYPOINT TO EDIT
#35 TAMPA LIGHT EVENT LORAN
N 27° 11 347 ROUTES
W 82° 51 267 #3 #4
#36 TAMPA BUOY EVENT GPS
N 27° 12 781' ROUTES
W 82° 49 305' #1 #2 #7 #9
185° 36.7 m
#37 HARBOR
N 27° 13 249' ROUTES
W 82° 51 205' #1
SCROLL
ENTER

C

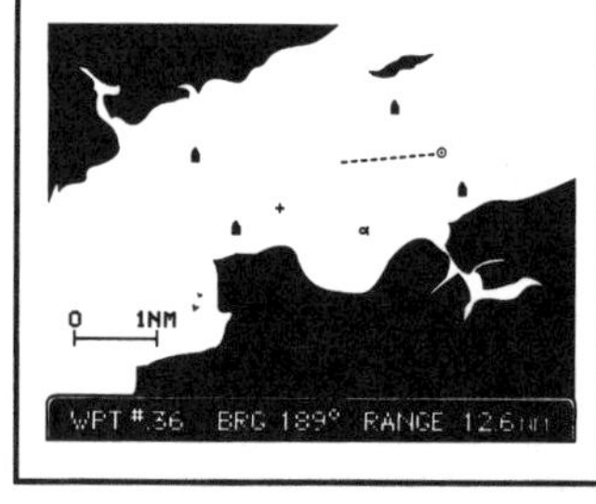

D

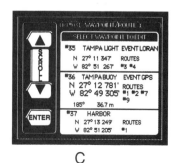

Figure 11-1. *An electronic chart can display a variety of vessel performance data in addition to its charted position. View A shows a graphic steering indicator with course and speed information from GPS. View B shows the main menu for this system that sets its modes of operation. View C shows a waypoint list. Waypoints are stored in groups, called* routes, *that lie on tracks between major destinations. View D shows a navigation screen, with a simplified "chart." The vessel's position is indicated by a circle and speed vector is indicated by a dashed line. (Courtesy of Raytheon Electronics)*

charts that have been "digitized," or converted to a format a computer can read. Two broad types of electronic chart systems are available.

Digitizing is a process that converts text or graphic information into a format that a computer can use. Why use a computer to display an image of a chart rather than the paper chart itself? Because no other technology can conveniently integrate the inputs of other positioning systems such as GPS and Loran C with a nautical chart to display an updated position once per second in any weather, at any time of day, anywhere in the world. As if by magic, electronic charts can accept this information. In addition, a radar picture can be integrated with the chart, giving a complete view of the vessel's tactical situation as well.

One type is properly and officially called an *Electronic Chart Display and Information System (ECDIS),* so designated by the International Maritime Organization (an arm of the United Nations). The ECDIS is the only system recognized under international law as an acceptable replacement for paper charts. This is an important legal point.

International law requires that a paper chart be in use at all times, unless an IMO-approved ECDIS is aboard and in use. Should an accident occur, the authorities will determine if one of these was in use at the time. An IMO-approved ECDIS costs more than most small craft themselves and so is unavailable to the average boater. Therefore, the small-craft navigator is obliged practically and legally to use paper charts for the foreseeable future.

An ECDIS uses an *Electronic Nautical Chart (ENC)* that is a subject of the *Electronic Chart Database (ECDB),* which is maintained by a national hydrographic office such as the National Ocean Service in the United States.

Many small-craft operators can afford to use the second type of electronic chart system—the so-called electronic chart. It is a functional, but not legal, equivalent of a paper chart. It typically has far fewer capabilities than the ECDIS model, but even with a reduced capacity it's light-years ahead of existing alternatives.

The reasons that small-craft ECs do not meet IMO standards are varied. One is that most inexpensive ECs don't have such functions as automatic data logging, radar integration, gyrocompass input, and other capabilities required by law. Also, most of these ECs don't have the capability to use the national hydrographic databases. (Many countries have yet to create them, anyway.) Instead, they use digital charts created by private companies that don't necessarily meet IMO standards.

The EC Display

The data presented on the computer screen by an electronic chart system can take one of two fundamental forms—*raster data* or *vector data*. The form used has important effects on the use of the system. You should understand the capabilities and limitations of each.

Raster data are usually collected from paper charts by *scanning,* a process in which a standard paper chart is laid out on a flat surface or rolled over a drum while an electronic pickup device, or *scanner,* moves back and forth over it line by line, hundreds or thousands of times. As the scanner moves over the surface of the chart, it records the colors it sees through a tiny opening and transcribes these colors into digital codes for later re-creation on the electronic chart screen.

This process records the entire chart image as a single-layer, continuous, computerized file of data, without regard to the type of point, line, or area portrayed. The result is a digital "picture" of a chart, with no attributes or characteristics attached to the features. Computer-literate people call this image a *bitmap;* it isn't capable of distinguishing among different types of data because the image consists of colors alone. The computer lights up the pixels on the screen without regard to what is being portrayed. To the computer, features have no identity—they are just collections of data points. (See Figure 11-2.)

Vector data are digitized by a much slower process in which each type of feature is placed in a separate file and accorded a specific set of characteristics. There are files for shorelines, types of aids to navigation, cultural features, transportation systems, dangers, and many other features. All the files together make up the entire chart. The cartographer can view each file separately and can correct, analyze, and manipulate them. The screen displays buoys as recognizable buoys, shoreline as shoreline, and so on. Further, the cartographer can add information to each feature via separate files—historical information, for example.

As you might infer from this description, raster chart data are relatively easy to digitize, but are "dumb," or without attribution, and take up a lot of space on whatever data storage medium is used for their distribution. Also, with raster data, all of the data must be displayed all of the time because they are not separated into different files—they are a huge collection of dots. If you zoom in or out on the image, all the data are compressed or expanded by the zoom factor, which may make it unreadable at small scales and unnecessarily large at large scales. (There are a few computer tricks to partially solve this problem.)

Figure 11-2. *Raster chart data are displayed in one layer. Although the data may be displayed in color, the information can't be edited selectively because it's in one file. Raster charts show all the data all the time; the operator can't selectively remove data to clean up the display. They also show imperfections in the original chart from which it was scanned. (Courtesy of Maptech)*

Vector data, by contrast, are difficult to digitize because they are put into separate layers according to the data type. However, vector data are "smart," containing information about each type of feature. It also takes up far less file space and thus, more vector charts can be put onto a specific storage medium, such as a CD-ROM, than can raster charts.

Because vector data are in different files that may be displayed at will, the user may deselect certain types of information that he or she doesn't want to view. Vector data can also be selectively *generalized* according to scale with the same process cartographers use in creating paper charts. Small-scale charts show less detailed data, although the density of data that's displayed remains about the same as in larger-scale charts. Vector data can also be more easily made into a seamless database because they are not limited by the borders of a single chart.

These two basic data structures have led to the development of two types of ECs for the small craft—those using vector charts and those using raster charts. Charts in each format are made by various companies. Each EC system manufacturer has chosen which type of data to use and whether to develop an in-house database of charts or use those developed by others. Several companies have already developed worldwide digital chart databases that are used by major EC hardware manufacturers.

Although the IMO standard calls for vector charts, some national hydrographic authorities—including the U.S. National Ocean Service and the British Admiralty—issue raster chart data for those who wish to use this very detailed data from current chart editions and are willing to accept its limitations.

Screen Types

Two types of screens are most commonly used to display the electronic chart: the *Liquid Crystal Display (LCD)* and the *Cathode Ray Tube (CRT)*. The LCD is less desirable for viewing because it generally has less resolution and fewer color options. Many are monochrome; that is, a single color on a black background. Because most charts rely partly on color to make distinctions among features, it's hard to think of these monochromatic devices as "charts" in the usual sense. In fact, many of these units are called "plotters." On the other hand, LCD units draw very little power and are very compact, making them ideal for sailboats and other vessels with limited space and electrical power. They are also easier to read in bright sunlight. (See Figure 11-3.)

The CRT presents a much higher quality picture due to its greater resolution, and is able to use color to great advantage. It is, however, larger, heavier, and requires more computer and electrical power than the LCD type. The raster-based CRT systems display a chart in all the colors of the original chart from which the data were collected; the vector ECs use color to separate and define different layers of data. The CRT is the same device as the one used in a television set or computer monitor.

The position of the vessel is superimposed on the EC display of a chart and is marked by crosshairs, the outline of a boat, or some other easily identifiable symbol. The position of this symbol is determined by the Loran-C or GPS receiver. Only the more sophisticated ECs are capable of using both Loran-C and GPS inputs at the same time because integration of two fixes requires additional computer processing. Most units allow you to select the positioning system you want, although many small craft have only one system aboard. Use of both is desirable, of course, because one can backup the other in the event of failure.

The display includes *event markers* that can save selected points such as fishing spots and rocks for later use. Most also have a *man overboard* button that marks a spot instantly so you can return to the exact location to recover someone lost overboard.

An EC may also provide a way of entering notice to mariners or other data by means of a marker and a text line, as shown in Figure 11-4. This feature allows the traditional (paper) *Notice to Mariners* data to be entered on the

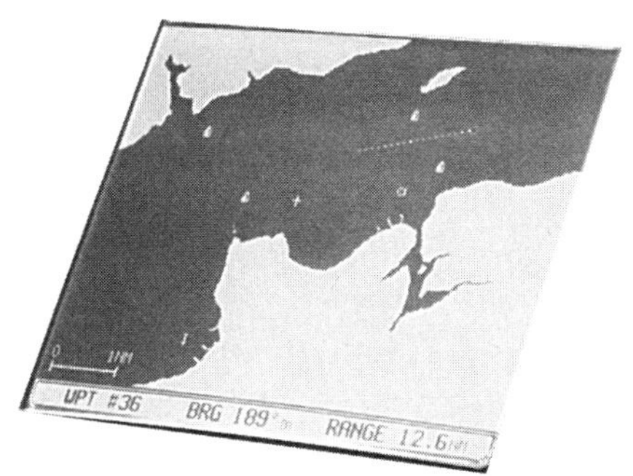

Figure 11-3. *Electronic charts with liquid crystal display (LCD) screens can be small, lightweight, and use less power than the cathode ray tube (CRT). Therefore, they are generally more suitable for sailboats. If your vessel has abundant electrical power, you might want to use the CRT type for its better resolution and color. (Photograph courtesy of Raytheon Electronics)*

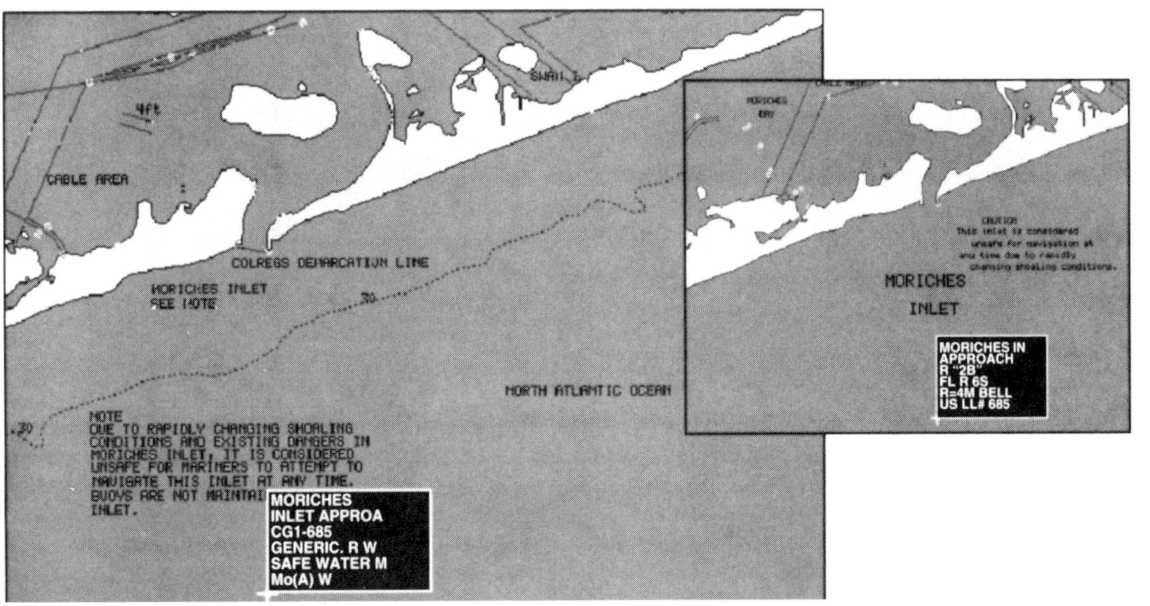

Figure 11-4. *This correction to an electronic chart indicates that Moriches Inlet Approach Buoy, a red-and-white safe-water buoy flashing characteristic Morse letter Alpha, was added or changed by First Coast Guard District* Local Notice to Mariners *number 685, in the position of the crosshairs in the lower left corner. (Courtesy of C-Map USA)*

chart. Some EC systems allow the operator to change the data presentation by manipulating the files, though this is not allowed by an ECDIS.

ECDIS and EC Capabilities

Every electronic chart system, regardless of the data type, has these features:

A *central processing unit (CPU)*—the computer that runs the software.

A screen that displays the chart.

Positioning inputs from such systems as GPS and Loran-C.

Software to display the vessel's position on the chart.

Software to do navigational calculations, store waypoints, and other tasks.

A *user interface* to program the system, change parameters, and extract information.

An ECDIS—a sophisticated system that serves as the legal and functional equivalent of a paper chart—is extremely complex (and expensive). Although the ECs used by small-craft navigators lack some of the advanced capabilities and features of an ECDIS, an EC can be equipped with a number of state-of-the-art features. Following are some of the features required by an ECDIS that should be in an EC:

1. Visible and audible alarms should sound when
    - Cross-track limits are exceeded
    - Position deviates from the programmed route
    - Chart data are displayed at larger scale than the base chart
    - Positioning system fails
    - Vessel crosses a safety contour
    - Any vital part of the system fails
2. The system should be able to calculate
    - Distance and bearing from a point to any other
    - Great-circle and rhumb-line distances between two points
    - Lat/long of a point, given a bearing and range from a known point
    - Datum transformations (converting coordinates from one horizontal datum to another)
3. If the chart data are in vector format, they should be divided into the following or similar classes:
    - Hydrography
    - Aids to navigation
    - Obstructions to navigation
    - Limits (channels, anchorages, etc.)
    - Port facilities
    - Inland waterways
    - Cultural landmarks
    - Earth cover
    - Topographic relief
    - Land cover
    - Environment
    - Data quality

The EC should allow you to deselect certain types of less important data such as topography and cultural features. It should not allow you to deselect shoreline, aids to navigation, depth information, dangers and obstructions, and other vital navigational information.

If the data are in raster format they should have been digitized using the latest charts, corrected up to the date of production.

Most electronic charts use commonly accepted conventions and standards in dealing with measurements. Position is usually given in degrees, minutes, and tenths of minutes, based on WGS '84 datum. (This works well because one minute of latitude equals one nautical mile, although some people prefer degrees, minutes, and seconds.) Depths are usually given in meters and tenths, but feet and fathoms will sometimes be used until all charts are converted to the metric system. Heights are given in meters (preferred) or in feet. Distances are given in nautical miles and tenths or in meters for short distances (less than a mile or so). Speeds are in knots and tenths.

Chart Data Storage Media

The digitized chart data must either be built into the system or be transferred to it before navigation with an EC begins, using any of several types of *computer data storage*. If the data are built in, it is safe to say that the resulting "chart" provides a very simple presentation suitable only for offshore or perhaps coastal navigation—it's more properly called a plotter, not really an electronic chart in the full sense. A data ase large enough to provide adequate coverage of more than one or two ports is far too large to fit in a small-craft EC system.

For electronic chart data storage and transfer, floppy disks and CD-ROMs can be used, but these are very fragile and generally unsuitable for sea duty aboard small boats because they are easily damaged by water, rough handling, heat, sunlight, stray magnetic fields, and other factors. Most ECs use a solid-state storage device in the form of a programmable computer chip contained in a plastic housing. This type of computer chip is known as a *Read-Only Memory (ROM)* chip, or *Erasable Programmable Read-Only Memory (EPROM)* chip. The erasable chips can be sent back to the factory to be reprogrammed when they become outdated. You discard the ROM chips when new ones become available. ROM and EPROM chips have no moving parts and a secure plastic cartridge protects them from the elements. Figure 11-5 shows one type of chart cartridge in common use.

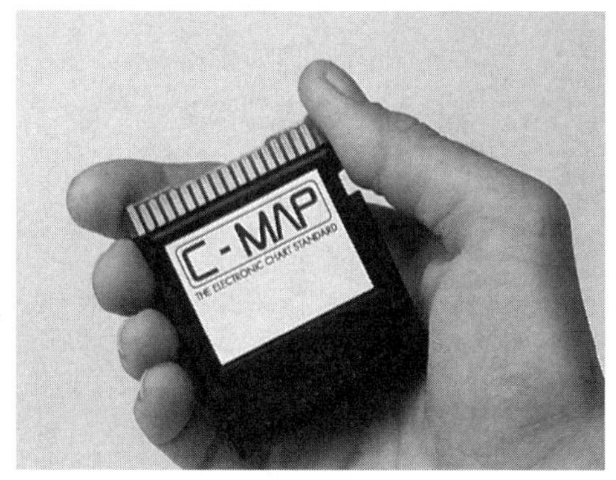

Figure 11-5. *This chart cartridge contains a number of charts in vector format for display on an electronic chart system. In general, the companies that make EC systems do not make in-house charts. Instead, they incorporate one of several types available from other companies that specialize in digital cartography. (Courtesy of C-Map USA)*

Data Formats

The International Maritime Organization has set a standard format that hydrographic offices throughout the world use to transfer electronic chart data among themselves. This standard is known as *DX-90 (Data eXchange standard of 1990)*. It allows each country to digitize its own waters, but requires each to do so in a way that enables other countries to read the data, so it forms a worldwide database.

Because the official U.S. electronic chart data are intended for military use, the United States has chosen a different standard. The National Imagery and Mapping Agency (NIMA) provides digitized chart data in the U.S. to a standard known as *Vector Product Format (VPF)*. VPF is compatible not only with the U.S. Navy's electronic chart system (which itself is part of a larger system), but also with other products made by NIMA for Defense Department agencies and branches of the armed forces.

NIMA makes charts for the U.S. military of areas outside of the U.S. Charts of U.S. waters are compiled by the National Ocean Service, which at this writing has no vector digitizing program to support users other than the military. That's the reason no official U.S. government-digitized chart data are being produced for the commercial market. The void is filled by commercial vendors of electronic charts and chart data.

NOS produces digitized chart data in raster format that it distributes on CD-ROM via its network of chart sales agents. These data are extremely detailed, but have the limitations inherent in raster data—a one-layer, nonselectable data structure that does not comply with ECDIS standards.

The advantage of compatible-format data structures is that you can use different types of equipment for more than one purpose. See Figure 11-6, which shows different equipment with integrated displays.

Correcting the Electronic Chart

Just like paper charts, electronic charts begin to become outdated the moment they are created and require correction throughout their life. However, the process of correcting a digital chart is far more complicated than cor-

Figure 11-6. *In this system, the radar on the right is being used primarily for the electronic chart display, while the radar display itself is in the small window in the lower right of the same screen. Meanwhile, on the left, another chart is temporarily displayed on the color depthsounder readout instead of the water depth and bottom profile. The unit in the center controls the electronic chart system's displays. (Courtesy of Raytheon Electronics)*

recting a paper one. The basic information must be transferred to the mariner in the correct format for his or her particular computerized electronic chart system.

You can correct a paper chart in pen and ink using data transmitted in text form via mail, radio, or facsimile; a digital chart can be corrected only by adding compatible files to the data structure. These must be transmitted by mailing computer data storage devices such as floppy disks or EPROMs, or by sending computer files via radio transmissions. Such transmissions of digital chart corrections could use satellite communications channels or high seas radio broadcasts. The effectiveness of these methods has already been tested and demonstrated. Unfortunately, they are expensive, require a lot of sophisticated hardware, and are not available to the average boater.

The advance of computer data storage technology has presented nautical chart makers and users with another possibility. Because computer data storage is cheap, you can now replace an entire digital chart as easily as you can correct one. Instead of transferring a few corrections to a user, a manufacturer can now send an entirely new chart—and several are doing just that.

The problem for ships at sea is that present costs of transmitting data via radio or satellite are too high to justify the transmission of entire charts. So, files of corrections to just a small fraction of the chart database are sent instead. This keeps transmissions short and charges low.

Most small-craft navigators will receive electronic chart corrections in the mail or from a dealer. They will not receive them weekly as they now receive the *Notice to Mariners*, but will more likely receive them every several weeks or even every six months to a year. That timing is one of the reasons you should not rely solely on an EC. And, in the event of a navigational accident, you must be able to show that a corrected paper chart was in use at the time and that sole reliance on the electronic chart was not the cause of the accident.

To apply common sense to the problem of updating electronic charts, you should know how your own EC system displays and uses data. Is it a raster- or vector-data type? Is it correctable? If yes, how are corrections made? If no, can you place a marker or warning at the sight of a correction to alert you of a change?

It's always wise to expect the unexpected at sea, especially when you're using charts, whether electronic or paper, not updated for some weeks or months. The older they are, the more likely it is that they will be deficient in some respect. No matter what kind of chart you use, you should be alert to changes in channel depths, shoal areas, aids to navigation, port facilities, and the like.

Finally, it is unwise to rely solely on a single navigation system, even though it has been serving you reliably. Sooner or later it will fail, and that failure can cause a disaster unless you systematically and continually check and validate its output.

Navigating with Electronic Charts

In using electronic charts you monitor the system's automatic progression through the steps you use in piloting. The steps listed below are nearly the same as those listed in Chapter 6, "Piloting," but are adapted for EC use. Combine these steps with a complete familiarity with your EC system. Know how to enter, select, and zoom in and out on charts, how to set waypoints, store routes, calculate courses and distances, and perform other functions. Since a waypoint is like a DR position, use the waypoint functions of an EC system to start the navigation process.

1. Before getting underway, enter a starting point as waypoint 1 and scan the charts across the area to be sailed, selecting waypoints so that the trackline between them will clear any dangers.
2. Once underway, monitor the vessel's progress along the chosen tracklines by viewing the screen display for short periods at frequent intervals (see sidebar).
3. When your vessel's path over the ground does not match the chosen trackline, correct the course to bring it back.
4. Anticipate the effects of set and drift in future courses and compensate for them.
5. Be especially careful not to put complete trust in a waypoint until you have used it at least once and proved it to be safe and accurately charted.

If you don't apply a correction for set and drift along your intended path, but only steer for the waypoint, your path over the ground may look like the one shown in Figure 11-7, in which the actual path over the ground curves continually. Such a path may take the vessel into dangerous water. By continually monitoring your progress along the trackline, you can readily see the effects of set and drift and make early adjustments.

At least one maritime disaster has demonstrated that it is not enough to simply watch the electronic chart and monitor the vessel's course across it. The best way to check on the

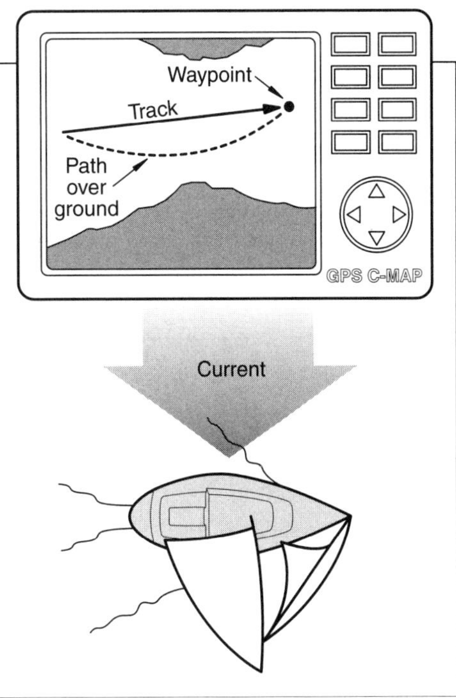

Figure 11-7. *Continually steering for the waypoint instead of correcting for set and drift all along the course may lead to an indirect, curved path over the ground—which may take the vessel into dangerous water and will surely increase distance traveled.*

You can easily be entranced by an EC display and focus too much attention on it, particularly in thick weather. As the navigator of a small craft you usually don't have a designated lookout (as does the captain of a ship) and must rely on your own eyes and ears. Your EC display can't see or hear and so will not warn you of other vessels on a collision course, obstructions floating in the water, or many other types of dangers. Your primary focus should be on the sea, not on any electronic device.

EC's reliability is to plot a fix now and then on a paper chart. Soundings can provide a rough confirmation of position very quickly. If both Loran-C and GPS systems are on board, positions from one should be checked against the other periodically.

In familiar waters where you're making frequent course changes and have plenty of close-by navigational aids to help keep track of your position, you may suspend the process of plotting fixes on paper charts and carefully "eyeball" your position with respect to the trackline, dangers, and waypoints. If the weather deteriorates, however, be sure to plot a fix to verify that the system is performing as it should before visibility is lost.

Conclusion

The electronic chart can make navigation safer by reducing the time spent on taking fixes and increasing the time spent on other tasks related to navigation safety. It can't prevent navigational accidents. Like any other newly developed technology, you should not use it until you thoroughly understand it, and even then you should continually verify the information it provides.

Electronic charts are still in their infancy and are evolving. In the years to come they will become cheaper, more dependable, easier to use, and they will incorporate additional features that the market demands. In particular, you can look forward to brighter and higher-resolution displays, more and cheaper color displays, and better data storage.

Electronic charts do, indeed, seem like magical devices, but they are not the failproof answer to navigators' prayers. The sea is too unforgiving to allow that.

PART 3

CELESTIAL NAVIGATION

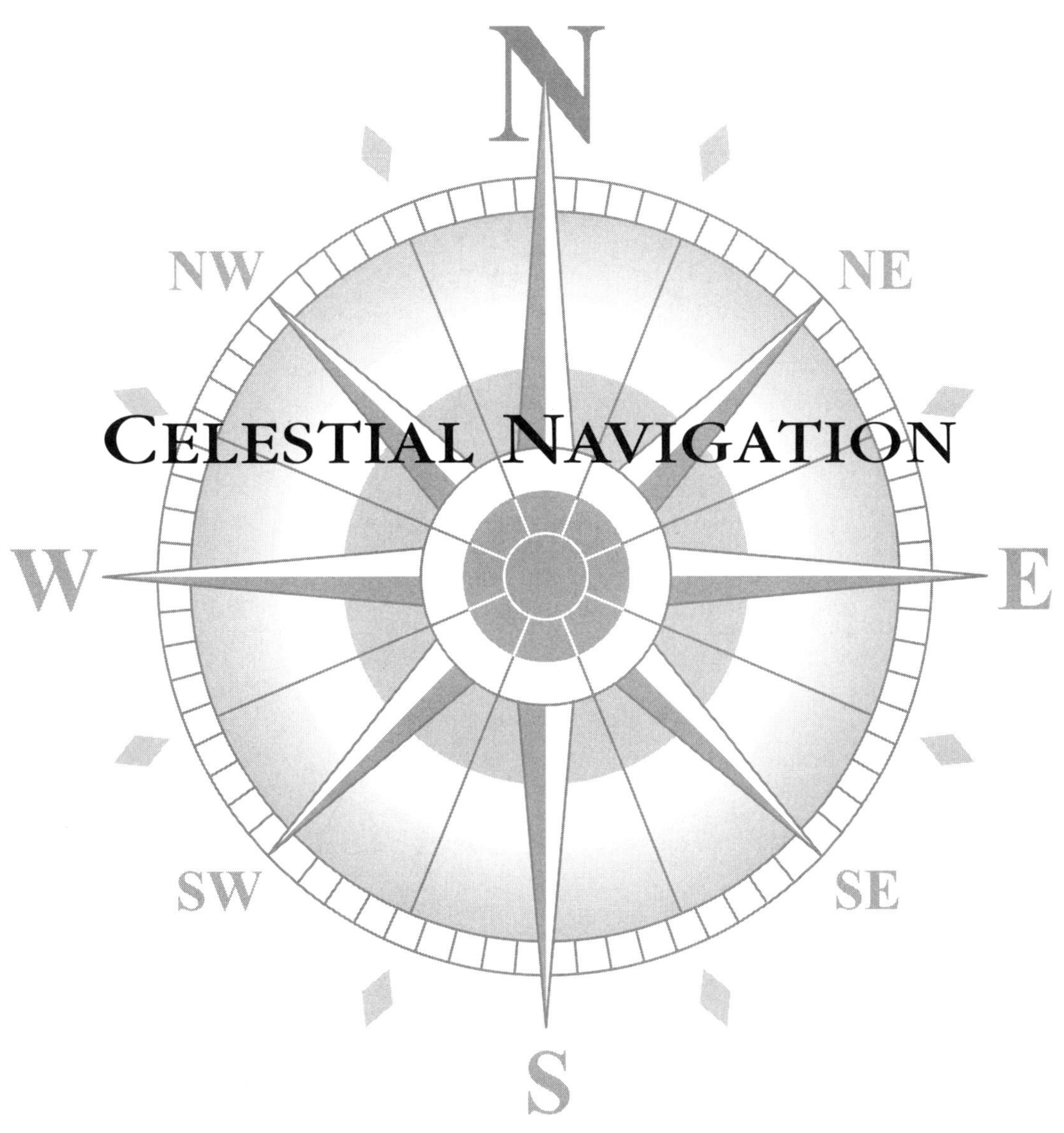

CHAPTER TWELVE

Navigational Astronomy

YOU WILL NEED AN elementary understanding of certain astronomical facts and scientific concepts to understand celestial navigation and its limitations. This is not "rocket science" and there is little mathematics involved in this discussion—just simple definitions and information that underlie celestial navigation. Further, you don't need to be able to identify by memory a lot of stars by their locations in the constellations. You will become familiar with them in due course as you use them.

In celestial navigation you use the sun, moon, planets, and stars to determine your position on the surface of the earth by creating a triangle and solving for its unknown parts using high school trigonometry. Fortunately, you don't have to do the trigonometry because tables and computers are available that reduce your mathematical calculations to addition and subtraction. How to solve the triangle is the subject of succeeding chapters. This chapter is concerned with the celestial bodies themselves.

The Concept of Celestial Navigation

It's easy to grasp a basic understanding of how heavenly bodies help to find your position. If the earth were not spinning and heavenly bodies did not change their positions over the earth—that is, if they did not appear to move across the sky each day or night—there would be directly below each body a single point on the earth, from which the body would appear directly overhead, or at an altitude of exactly 90°. This point could be called the *geographic position ("GP")* of that body and it would never move.

It would then be a simple matter to find your distance to the GP. You could simply measure the altitude of the body, subtract that number from 90°, and use the number of degrees, minutes, and seconds thus measured as the distance. That would give you a line of position (LOP) consisting of a huge circle on the earth representing all points where that same altitude could be measured, with a radius equal to the distance from you to the GP. The intersection of two such LOPs would constitute a fix.

In the real world, the GP of the star Polaris (the North Star) is always less than 2° from the North Pole. Therefore, if you measure the altitude of Polaris, the result represents your latitude, within that 2° of error. (In this case you don't subtract the altitude from 90° because the GP of Polaris is at latitude 90°N, so the reading equals latitude directly.) Columbus used Polaris in this way to find his latitude. With a few refinements, we do so today, as well.

Another ancient celestial navigation technique that's still in use involves the sun, which passes over your meridian each day at noon.

If you know the distance between the sun's GP and the equator (that is, its declination) when the sun crosses your meridian, and measure the sun's altitude at that time, you can calculate your latitude using a two-step process of addition and subtraction. (Columbus knew how to do this, too.)

Now think back to the fictitious nonmoving stars, with which this discussion started, and put them in motion across the heavens to accord with reality. They move at a rate determined by the rotation of the earth and their GPs race across the surface of the earth below them, circling the earth every 24 hours, moving 15° (degrees) per hour, 15' (minutes) per minute. (At the equator, that's 15 miles per minute, or about 900 miles per hour.) Because they are moving you have to freeze them in time when you measure their altitudes. Accurate time is thus essential to finding an LOP based on the altitude of a star. Using almanacs you can find the GPs of almost 200 stars, plus the four brightest planets, plus the moon and sun, at any time you choose. And from these GPs and measurements of altitude you can find LOPs and use them for a celestial fix.

The *navigational triangle* is basic to the solution of every sight. In two-dimensional *plane geometry,* a triangle's interior angles always equal 180°. (For celestial navigation purposes, we ignore the fact that the earth is not a perfect sphere, though this is one of several sources of error in celestial fixes.)

A *spherical triangle* is formed by the arcs of three great circles on a sphere. The three vertices of the navigational triangle are the *pole* nearest the observer (P), the observer's

The navigational triangle adds some complication to the simple process discussed earlier. Its use is necessary, though, because the scale of a chart showing enough area to plot both the observer's position and the GP of a celestial body would be too small to accurately plot a position. To reduce the scale of the plot, you have to assume a position, solve the triangle for that position, and then see how far and in which direction your assumption is in error.

assumed position (AP), and the *geographic position (GP)* of the body. When you connect these three points with lines, two of them are parts of longitude lines that end at the pole, and the other connects the body's GP and the assumed position. (See Figure 12-1.)

Only two of the three angles of the navigational triangle are needed for celestial sight calculations. The angle at the pole is called the *meridian angle,* designated with "t"; the angle at the observer is the *azimuth angle.* The angle at the GP of the body is called the *parallactic angle* and is not normally used in sight reduction.

Later chapters explain how to use the navigational triangle. Before dealing with that, though, it helps to understand how our solar system and galaxy are structured.

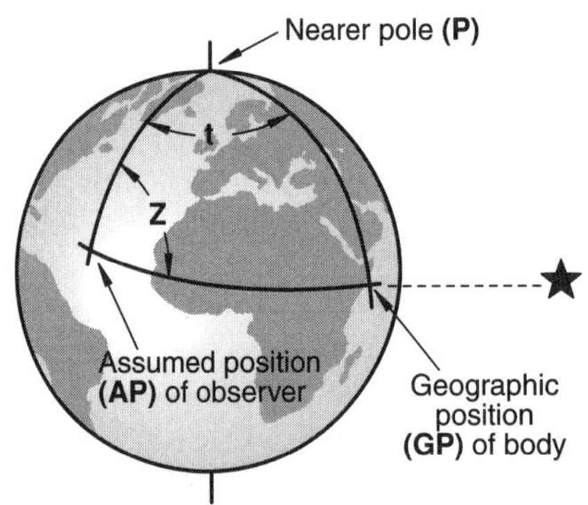

Figure 12-1. *The navigational triangle consists of three points: the nearer pole, the assumed position of the observer, and the GP of the body. Angles used in celestial navigation are the meridian angle "t" and the azimuth angle "Z."*

Astronomical Units of Measure

Because of the vast distances in outer space, our traditional earth-based units of measure do not serve very well. Astronomers use much larger units. Consider, for example, that if the earth were represented by a ball one inch in diameter, the moon would be a ball one-quarter inch in diameter 30 inches away; the sun would be a one-foot-diameter ball one-fifth mile away; and the planet Pluto would be a ball only one-half inch in diameter about seven miles away. The nearest star would be about 48,000 miles away. When you apply these relationships to their true proportions in space, you can see that "miles" as a unit of measure don't work very well.

One of the units used to measure distances in space is the *astronomical unit (AU),* the mean or average distance from the earth to the sun—92,960,000 miles. This unit of measure is useful for distances within our own solar system, but it is still too small for interstellar use, so astronomers also use the familiar *light-year,* the distance light travels in one year at a speed of 186,000 miles per second—that is, almost six trillion miles.

The nearest star, Alpha Centauri, is 4.3 light-years away from earth. Only a few other stars are less than 100 light-years away, and the nearest galaxy is more than 150,000 light-years distant. Astronomers have found galaxies as far as several billion light-years away.

The brightness of celestial bodies is measured in terms of *magnitude,* which places stars into one of six categories of brightness, with the 20 brightest stars called first magnitude. The original visual-based system has been supplanted by a mathematically based one, in which a first-magnitude star is 100 times brighter than a sixth-magnitude one. Each of the six magnitudes is about 2.5 times brighter than the preceding one.

A trained observer can distinguish a magnitude difference of about one-tenth (0.1), so magnitudes are usually calculated and listed in almanacs at intervals of one-tenth. Since a first-magnitude star is not necessarily the brightest star in the sky, and since a higher magnitude number means a star is less bright, it is possible to have *negative magnitudes* for very bright bodies. This slightly confusing concept allows the magnitude scale to be used for measuring the brightness of objects brighter than 1.0 by using negative numbers.

The brightest star in the sky is Sirius, commonly called the Dog Star, with a magnitude of –1.6. Canopus, the only other negative-magnitude star, is –0.9. Venus, the brightest celestial object other than the sun or moon, has a magnitude at its maximum brightness of –4.4. Mars, Jupiter, and Saturn also have negative magnitudes at portions of their cycles. The moon has a magnitude of –12.6, and the sun is about –26.7.

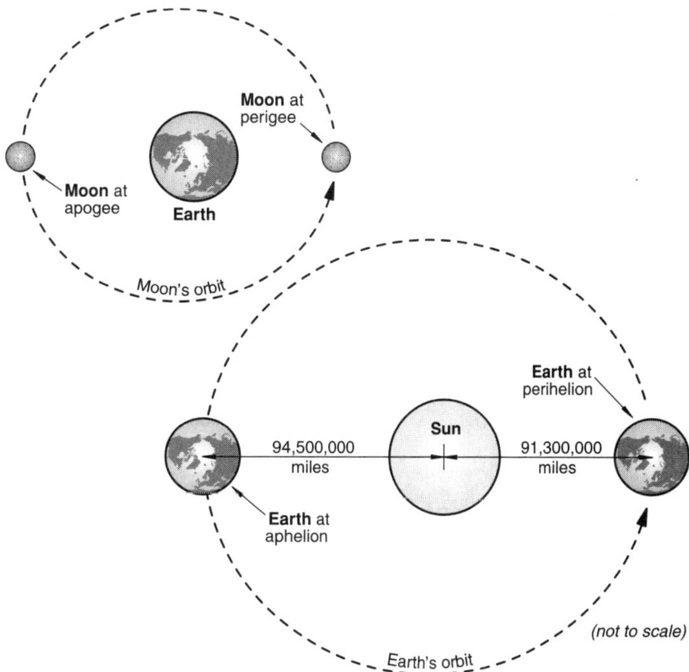

Figure 12-2. *The point where an orbiting planet is closest to its sun is its* perihelion. *The point where it is farthest is called its* aphelion. *A moon's orbit has similar points, called* perigee *and* apogee. *Earth's perihelion distance is about 91.3 million miles from the sun, its aphelion distance about 94.5 million. Because the sun is closer at perihelion, it appears slightly larger, and this affects celestial observations.*

Motions of Celestial Bodies

Everything in space is moving, and all motion is relative. The galaxies are spinning through space, stars within the galaxies are moving, and planets are revolving around the stars.

Within each solar system, including our own, each planet orbits around its sun once in a *planetary year.* Orbits are not circular—they are elliptical, or oval-shaped. The point where an orbiting planet is closest to its sun is called its *perihelion.* (See Figure 12-2.) The farthest point is called its *aphelion.* A moon's orbit has similar points, called *perigee* and *apogee.*

At perihelion, the earth is about 91,300,000 miles from the sun. At aphelion, it's about 94,500,000 miles. The sun appears slightly larger at perihelion because it is 3,200,000 miles closer. This apparent change in the sun's size affects celestial observations, requiring a correction, which will be discussed later.

Several types of bodies orbit our sun—among them are planets, comets, and asteroids—but only the planets are useful in navigation. In fact, only four of the nine planets are navigationally significant: Venus, Mars,

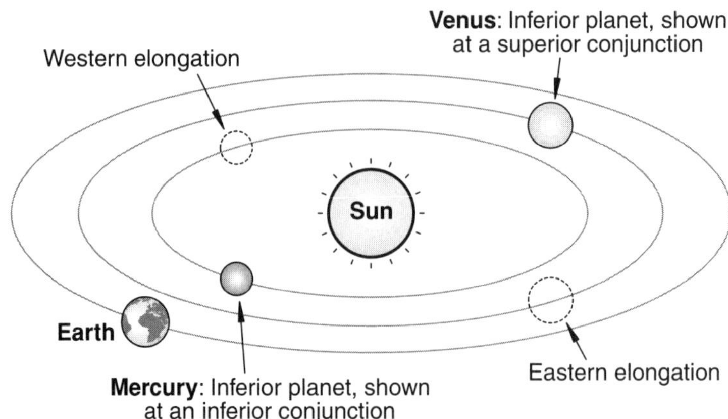

Figure 12-3. *Mercury and Venus are called* inferior planets *because their orbits are between the earth and the sun. When they are visible, you'll see them near the sun around sunrise or sunset. During a phase called* inferior conjunction, *they pass across the face of the sun, and during* superior conjunction, *they disappear behind the sun. At its most visible, Venus is the brightest object in the sky other than the sun and moon.*

Jupiter, and Saturn. The rest are too dim to be seen easily or at all with the unaided eye.

You can usually distinguish a planet from a star by its light, which does not ordinarily twinkle. The twinkling of a star is due to disturbances of the light rays as they pass through denser and denser layers of the earth's atmosphere on the way to our eye. Planets, because they are much closer to us, have a wider beam of light reflected from our own sun that is affected less by the atmosphere than a star's light.

All the planets except Pluto orbit in approximately the same plane, known as the *plane of the ecliptic,* which is discussed later in this chapter.

The Navigational Planets

Mercury and Venus are known as *inferior planets* because their orbits are between the earth and the sun. For this reason, you always see them in the vicinity of the sun around sunrise or sunset. Both planets appear to move from one side of the sun to the other, alternately appearing to pass in front of and behind the sun. Only when they are well away from the sun, at what is called *eastern elongation* or *western elongation,* can you see them. (See Figure 12-3.) Astronomers can observe them passing across the face of the sun during a phase called *inferior conjunction* and disappearing behind it during *superior conjunction.*

Venus, the only inferior navigational planet, separates by up to 47° from the sun; its magnitude of −4.4 is ideal for celestial navigation purposes. Except for the sun and the moon, Venus is clearly the brightest object in the sky at its most visible point. Under some conditions, you can even see it in the daytime. Further, you can see Venus for up to 263 days in

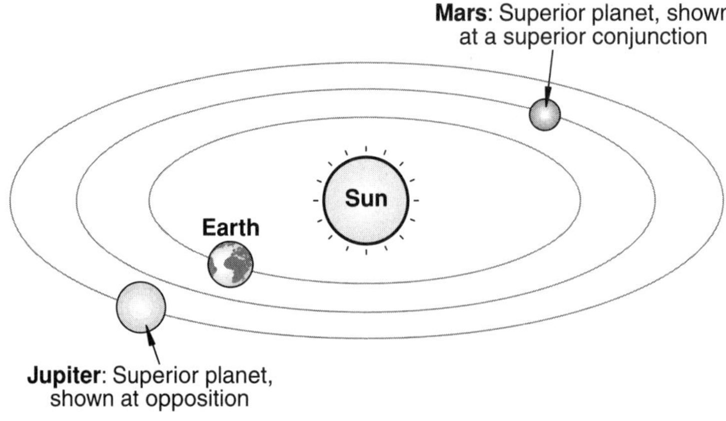

Figure 12-4. *Planets with orbits outside earth's are called* superior planets. *During* superior conjunction, *they disappear behind the sun. They are most visible when they appear to be farthest from the sun, at* opposition.

succession; it disappears in inferior conjunction for only eight days and in superior conjunction for 50 days.

Planets with orbits outside the earth's orbit are known as *superior planets*. (See Figure 12-4.) Their orbits are not confined to the neighborhood of the sun as seen from the earth, so you might find them anywhere in the sky during their orbital cycles. Though they might pass behind the sun in superior conjunction, they can't pass between the earth and the sun because their orbits are outside the earth's. Instead they appear to move farther and farther from the sun until they are at *opposition*.

Near conjunction, the superior planets' light is lost in the glare of the sun and you can't see them. Near opposition, you see them appear to rise when the sun sets and set when the sun rises because they are opposite to the sun in the sky as seen from the earth.

When observed from the earth, superior planets usually appear to travel in what is called *direct motion,* moving nightly against the backdrop of stars. Near opposition, however, they appear to slow down and then stop, reverse motion, again slow to a stop, and then resume direct motion. This reversal is called *retrograde motion* and is caused by the earth's moving faster in its orbit than the superior planets (because it's closer to the sun) and passing the planet in its orbit around the sun.

The orbital period of a superior planet is known as its *synodic period*. (See Figure 12-5.) It appears the brightest when at opposition, when it is closest to the earth and reflecting maximum sunlight.

Mars, the superior planet closest to earth, is normally between about −1.0 and −2.0 in magnitude, but can be as bright as −2.8. Its synodic period is about 780 earth days. Near conjunction it is lost in the sun for about 120 days.

Jupiter, the largest planet, is usually brighter than Mars, with a magnitude of −2.0 or more. Its synodic period is about 400 days and it disappears for about 32 days at conjunction. Four of its 16 moons are visible with good binoculars.

Saturn has a synodic period of about 380 days and disappears for about 25 days at conjunction. Its magnitude is about +0.8 to −0.2. None of its 18 moons is visible without a telescope, but its rings make it appear slightly oblong when seen through binoculars.

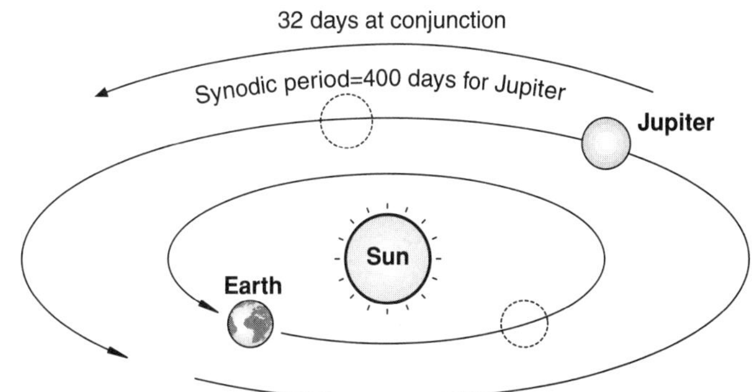

Figure 12-5. *The orbital period of a superior planet, such as Jupiter, is called its* synodic period.

The Moon

The moon revolves around the earth once every 27⅓ days, in a period known as a *sidereal month*. When viewed in relation to the sun, the moon's synodic period is 29.53 days. The difference is due to the fact that the moon's apparent motion around the earth is slower than the sun's, and so it drops back—eastward—12.2° per day. That is, tomorrow night at midnight the moon will be 12.2° east of where it is tonight at midnight.

When the moon is in conjunction with the sun (a new moon), you can't see it because it's lost in the sun's glare and reflects its light away from the earth. As it moves out of conjunction, however, you see it as a thin crescent in the west just after sunset. Each succeeding day as it waxes, the moon appears to be larger and to rise later, until at opposition, it is full. At this point, because it is opposite the sun, you see its full diameter lighted by the sun. You also see it high in the sky at midnight, while the sun is shining on the opposite side of the earth.

After the time of full moon, the moon gradually *wanes,* appearing to shrink smaller and smaller until finally it is just a thin crescent, seen in the morning sky. Then it disappears in the sun's glare again. (See Figure 12-6.)

You can often see the faint image of the

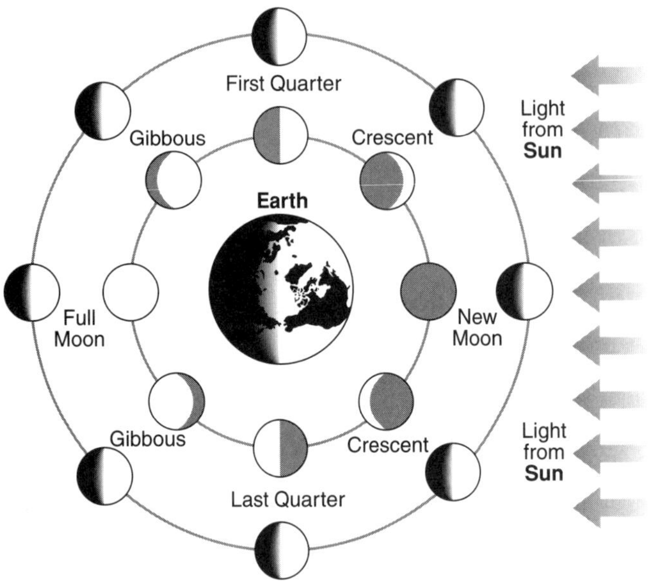

Figure 12-6. *The moon's phases are shown here, with the outer image indicating the moon's shadow and the inner ring showing the moon's appearance from the earth. (Not to scale.)*

unlighted portion of the moon during its first and last quarters because the portion of the moon that's unlighted by the sun reflects a faint amount of light from the earth.

Stars

Out of the billions of known stars, you can see only some 6,000 by your unaided eye. Half of these are below the horizon at any one time and a few hundred more are too close to the horizon to be seen clearly, leaving perhaps 2,500 stars visible on a clear night. Fortunately, in navigation, you use only a few stars. You need no more than five or six for a good fix, and 20 or 30 commonly used stars make up the navigator's entire inventory.

Stars are contained within *galaxies,* or huge groups of stars and clouds of gases. Between the galaxies is the nothingness of millions of light-years of intergalactic space. The solar system and visible stars are a part of the *Milky Way galaxy,* named for the color it imparts to a wide band of the night sky. The Milky Way is more than 100,000 light-years in diameter. When you look toward the constellation of Sagittarius you're seeing the center of the Milky Way, some 30,000 light-years distant. Only a few other galaxies are visible to the naked eye, including the Great Galaxy in the constellation of Andromeda in the northern hemisphere and the Large and Small Magellanic Clouds in the southern hemisphere.

The Ecliptic

The ecliptic is the path that the sun appears to take across the heavens, as observed from earth. The ecliptic is inclined to the celestial equator—an extension of the earth's equator projected out into the heavens—at an angle of 23° 26'. This apparent inclination of the sun's path from the celestial equator is caused by an inclination of the same amount of the earth's axis from its plane of orbit around the sun.

In its orbit around the sun, the earth is at perihelion in early January every year and at aphelion six months later. (See Figure 12-2.)

When you record the point on earth directly below the sun at the same time each day for an entire year, the points form an *analemma*—a figure-eight shape—on the earth's surface. It's a figure eight because the earth's orbit is not elliptical and doesn't revolve around the sun at a constant speed. Pulled by the sun's gravity, it "falls" toward the sun more rapidly approaching perihelion, then recedes more slowly toward aphelion. This movement causes a slight delay or advance in the sun's apparent daily position on the earth.

The northernmost point on the analemma in the northern hemisphere (at the top of the figure-eight) is the point of the *summer solstice.* (See Figure 12-7.) "Solstice" means "sun standing still" and occurs when the sun reaches its highest *declination,* or highest northerly latitude—on or about June 21 each year.

From this starting time of summer in the northern hemisphere, the sun appears lower in the sky each day. It reaches the equator on the *autumnal equinox,* on or about September 23 each year when days are equal in length everywhere on earth.

The sun continues its journey south, reaching the *winter solstice* on or about December 22. At this point, days in the northern hemisphere are shorter than those in the southern hemisphere, and the South Pole is in continuous light.

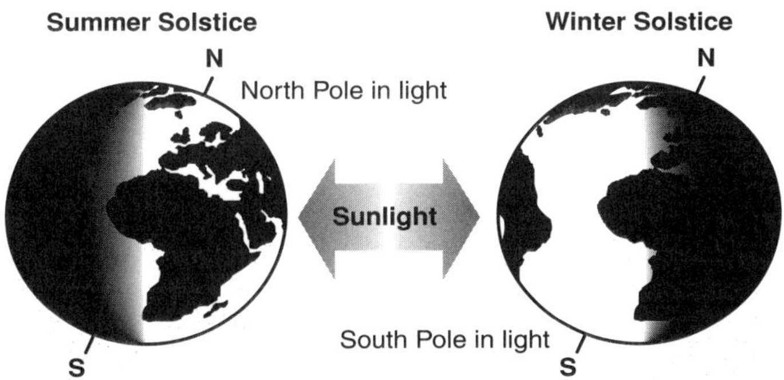

Figure 12-7. *The day of the year that the sun reaches its highest northerly latitude is called the* summer solstice, *on or about June 21 each year. The sun then begins its journey southward, a bit more every day, reaching the* winter solstice *on or about December 22.*

After the winter solstice, the sun starts northward again, reaching the equator at the *vernal equinox,* giving the earth equal days again. From this point it continues toward the next summer solstice before repeating the cycle.

It is no coincidence that the *tropic of Cancer* and the *tropic of Capricorn* (which are the latitudes on the earth directly beneath the sun during the days of the summer and winter solstices, respectively) are 23° 26' north and south of the equator—because that is the angle of tilt of the earth's axis. Everywhere between these two latitudes, the sun is exactly overhead at noon at some time during the year. Because of that same angle of tilt, the Arctic and Antarctic circles are 23° 26' from their respective poles. (See Figure 12-8.)

The tropic of Cancer and the tropic of Capricorn were named about 2,000 years ago for the constellations that the sun entered during the solstices at that time. Today, the sun enters a different constellation in the zodiac at the solstices because of a phenomenon called *precession of the equinoxes*—a very slow rotation of the axis of the earth, much like the wobble of a spinning top. Precession of the equinoxes has moved the zodiac, as seen from earth, about one full constellation out of the positions that ancient astrologers observed. It is also slowly moving the celestial North Pole closer to Polaris, which it will pass in the year 2102. In about the year 1400, at the beginning of the Age of Discovery, Vega served as the North Star.

Precession of the equinoxes contradicts astrology based on the zodiac because the constellations are not in the same positions

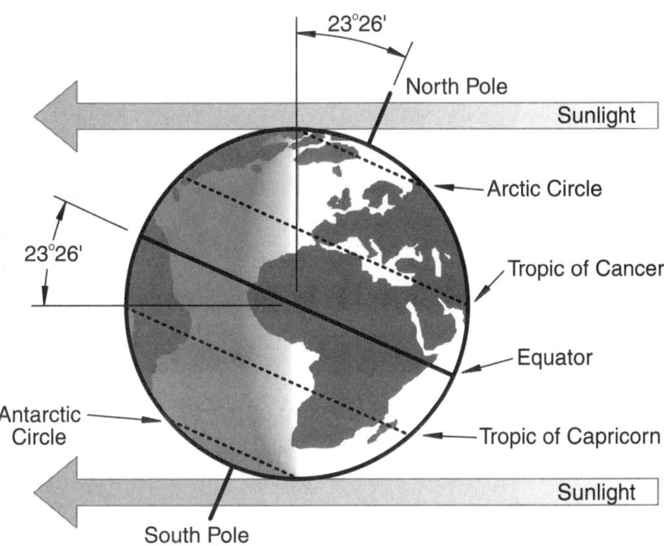

Figure 12-8. *This shows the earth at the northern hemisphere's* summer solstice. *The seasons occur because the earth's axis is tilted 23° 26' from the plane of its orbit. The* tropics of Cancer *and* Capricorn *are defined by the points where the sun's rays are directly overhead at noon on the solstices. The Arctic and Antarctic Circles are the points where the sun's rays are exactly tangent to the earth at the solstices. Six months later the sun will be on the opposite side at the* winter solstice.

The zodiac is a band of the sky about 16° wide along the plane of the ecliptic and is divided into 12 sections of 30° each (30° × 12 = 360°). More than 2,000 years ago, names and symbols were assigned to each section based on a constellation within it. However, precession of the equinoxes has caused the whole zodiac to shift about 30° since then and now the First Point of Aries—a key reference point in celestial navigation—is actually in the constellation Pisces. It is still called Aries, though, for the sake of convention.

today as they were when the astrological symbols were introduced.

First Point of Aries

The *First Point of Aries* is a single, imaginary point in the sky that navigators use as a reference point to locate the stars when obtaining a celestial line of position. This is possible because the stars all have the same period of revolution and never change positions relative to each other, while the sun, moon, and planets (the other bodies used in celestial navigation) each have a different period of revolution. As a result, each changes its relative position over time—and needs a separate entry in almanacs that give the positions of celestial bodies.

Because all the stars maintain a constant angular relationship with one another, the almanacs give the positions of the single reference point—the First Point of Aries, or simply "Aries"—and you locate all the stars from that point.

Eclipses

If the moon's orbit were in the plane of the ecliptic (the same plane as the earth's orbit of the sun), the moon would pass alternately between the earth and the sun and then through the earth's shadow on every cycle, causing an *eclipse* each time. But the moon's orbit is inclined to the ecliptic at an angle of about 5°, causing it to pass above or beneath the sun on nearly every orbit.

When the moon crosses the ecliptic, it is said to be at a *node*. When the moon intersects the ecliptic just where the sun is located, an eclipse will be seen on the earth. If the moon passes into the earth's shadow, it will disappear for a time in a *lunar eclipse*. (See Figure 12-9.) If the moon passes between the earth and the sun, it will cast a shadow a few miles wide on the earth, blocking out the sun in a *solar eclipse*. A *total eclipse* will be seen by observers located anywhere within this shadow; for many miles out to each side, the sun will be only partly obscured in a *partial eclipse*.

Because the diameters of the sun and the moon appear about the same to an observer on earth, rays of the sun project out from behind the moon during a solar eclipse. Note that the type of eclipse takes its name from the body that is obscured, as shown in Figure 12-9.

When the moon is near its *apogee* (the farthest point in its orbit from the earth), it appears slightly smaller than when it is at *perigee*. (See Figure 12-2.) For this reason, in

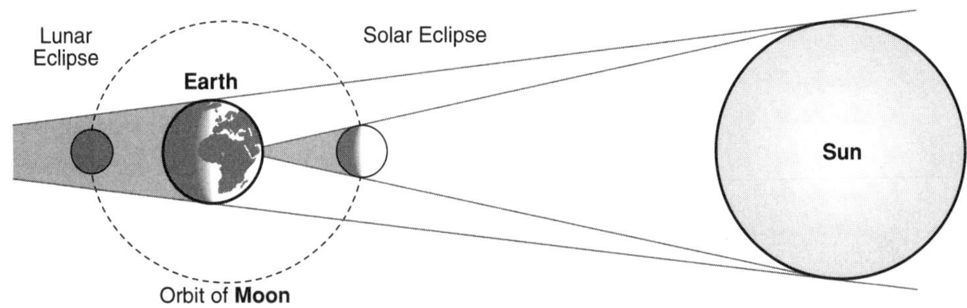

Figure 12-9. *A lunar eclipse occurs when the moon passes into the earth's shadow. A solar eclipse occurs when the moon casts its shadow on the earth, obscuring the sun. The eclipse takes its name from the body which is hidden.*

an eclipse at apogee—called an *annular eclipse*—the moon's entire shadow does not quite reach the earth, leaving a thin ring of the sun visible around its edge. Annular eclipses occur slightly more often than total eclipses. The duration of an eclipse depends on the moon's position as it crosses the sun, the relative orbital speeds of the moon, sun, and earth, and the apparent diameters. The longest possible solar eclipse lasts about seven minutes.

Because the moon crosses the ecliptic at least twice each year, there are always at least two solar eclipses each year—and there may be as many as five, depending on the relative orbital positions of the bodies. There may be as many as three lunar eclipses in a year, but occasionally there are none. Lunar eclipses are more commonly seen because they are visible over a far larger area of the earth than are solar eclipses.

The moon, the sun, and the earth are in alignment twice each year at the nodes, as the moon crosses the ecliptic. The *eclipse year* is 346.6 days long, causing *regression of the nodes,* the apparent eastward movement of the nodes across the sky. They are in the same relative position in the sky at the same exact day and time about every 18 years, which causes the eclipses to occur in distinct patterns repeated every 18 years, with minor variations due to eccentricities of the bodies' orbits. (See Chapter 4's discusion on the metonic cycle.)

Coordinates

Since Ptolemy introduced the practice in the second century A.D., we have divided circles into 360 degrees (°), each degree into 60 minutes ('), and each minute into 60 seconds ("). You can also divide a sphere into 360° in any plane and, because the earth is nearly a sphere, you can use the same measures to mark positions on its surface.

A *great circle* is the intersection of a sphere's surface and a plane passing through its center. The equator is the great circle around the earth equidistant from both poles. Latitude is a measure north or south of the equator from the equator along a great circle in a plane perpendicular to the equator. If the equator is 0° of latitude, then the poles are 90°, or one quarter of the circumference of the earth from it. Because it is measured both north and south from the equator, you need to express latitude in terms not only of the number of degrees, minutes, and seconds from the equator, but also as north or south. A position that is 35° north of the equator is at 35° north latitude (35°N).

The earth is not a perfect sphere and the distance from its center to its surface is not the same. For this reason, cartographers must account for the difference in length between a mile measured at a place on the earth's surface closer to the center of the earth, and a mile at a place farther away. The mile measured at the closer point will be shorter. Navigators don't notice this difference because it's small, but cartographers do.

Unlike latitude, longitude has no astronomical or geographical beginning point. Over the centuries, many different locations have been used as the point of zero longitude but Greenwich, England, was adopted as the point of 0° longitude—largely because the British ruled the seas when modern navigation science spread worldwide. You measure longitude both east and west from this point, again in degrees, minutes, and seconds. East and west longitudes increase with distance from Greenwich until you reach 180°—the longitude exactly opposite Greenwich. This is known as the *International Date Line* and is the point where each new day begins.

Thus, to define the location of any place on the earth, you use latitude (N or S) and longitude (E or W). Most small-craft navigators operate continually in the same quadrant. All of North America, for example, is in the northern and western hemispheres (the northwest one quarter of the globe), so all latitudes there are N and all longitudes are W. For this reason, small-craft navigators usually give little thought to N, S, E, or W designations, although they come into significant play in celestial navigation.

One minute (1⁄60 of a degree) of latitude equals one nautical mile. (One nautical mile equals 1.15 statute miles, or 6,076 feet.) You increasingly see degrees, minutes, and tenths of minutes used instead of degrees, minutes, and seconds, particularly in electronic equipment. For example, 3.75 minutes of latitude equals 3.75 (or three and three quarters) miles. Therefore, you can always use the latitude scale to measure distance. The same distance in minutes and seconds would be three minutes and 45 seconds (45" being three fourths of 60").

One degree of latitude equals 60 nautical miles, but only on a perfectly spherical earth. Because the earth is slightly flattened at the poles, a degree of latitude varies from 59.7' nautical miles at the equator to about 60.3 nautical miles at the poles.

Figure 12-10. *The 2102-D Star Finder is used in conjunction with the* Nautical *and* Air Almanacs *to find the approximate positions of stars for a celestial fix. It is also a valuable backyard star-gazing tool. (Courtesy of C Plath, No. American Division)*

Star Identification

A professional navigator may take justifiable pride in knowing the names and locations of 40 or 50 stars. The beginning navigator, however, needs to know only 10 or 15 of the stars most commonly used in celestial navigation, even by experienced navigators.

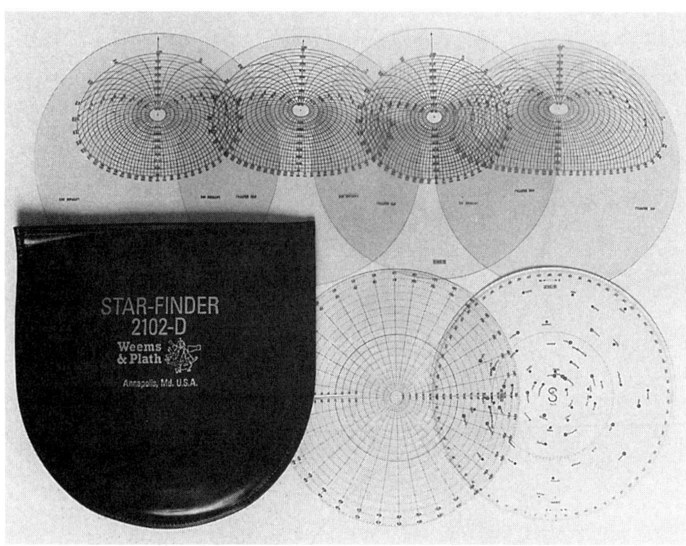

The navigational stars are easily found by recognizing the constellations in which they are located. The star charts, Figures 12-12, 12-13, 12-14, and 12-15 on pages 152–155, show these constellations. In using them, remember that the stars cross the sky every night just like the sun and moon, rising in the east and setting in the west. Each chart shows an area of sky about 90° apart from the next. Locate the North and South Poles on each chart just in from the top and bottom margins. Look at the sky toward the north and locate Ursa Major (the "Big Dipper"), whose outer two stars point toward the Pole Star. Once you recognize the Pole Star, choose the chart you need for that time of night by properly orienting the Big Dipper and Polaris. (In the southern hemisphere, look to the south and locate the Southern Cross, whose vertical axis points to the South Pole.) After placing the east and west marks in the right direction, you are able to recognize all of the named stars.

Polaris is a particularly useful star in navigation because it is very close to the celestial North Pole and can be used for an easy latitude observation. Other stars will yield lines of position (LOPs) consisting of huge circles on the earth, of which only a tiny fraction are plotted. (See Chapter 16, "Sight Reduction," for more on this subject.)

All of the navigational stars and planets are listed in the following chart, Figure 12-11 (facing page). The Bayer's name designates stars by a Greek letter and the star's constellation.

The *Nautical* and *Air Almanacs* contain star charts along with directions for their use; each also contains a *planet diagram* that shows the availability of planets for celestial observations at any time.

Star finders are useful devices for locating stars, particularly when clouds or other phenomena make constellations unrecognizable. The most common is the *No. 2102-D Star Finder,* which consists of an opaque plastic base and ten clear plastic overlays with stars as shown in Figure 12-10. One side of the base is used for north and the other for south latitudes. Nine overlays each cover ten degrees of latitude (colored blue) and the tenth (colored

(continued)

APPENDIX J

NAVIGATIONAL STARS AND THE PLANETS

Name	Pronunciation	Bayer name	Origin of name	Meaning of name	Distance*
Acamar	ā'kȧ·mär	θ Eridani	Arabic	another form of Achernar	120
Achernar	ā'kēr·när	α Eridani	Arabic	end of the river (Eridanus)	72
Acrux	ā'krŭks	α Crucis	Modern	coined from Bayer name	220
Adhara	ȧ·dā'rȧ	ε Canis Majoris	Arabic	the virgin(s)	350
Aldebaran	ăl dĕb'ȧ·răn	α Tauri	Arabic	follower (of the Pleiades)	64
Alioth	ăl'ĭ·ŏth	ε Ursa Majoris	Arabic	another form of Capella	49
Alkaid	ăl·kād'	η Ursa Majoris	Arabic	leader of the daughters of the bier	190
Al Na'ir	ăl·när'	α Gruis	Arabic	bright one (of the fish's tail)	90
Alnilam	ăl'nĭ·lăm	ε Orionis	Arabic	string of pearls	410
Alphard	ăl'färd	α Hydrae	Arabic	solitary star of the serpent	200
Alphecca	ăl·fĕk'ȧ	α Corona Borealis	Arabic	feeble one (in the crown)	76
Alpheratz	ăl·fē'răts	α Andromeda	Arabic	the horse's navel	120
Altair	ăl·tär'	α Aquilae	Arabic	flying eagle or vulture	16
Ankaa	ăn'kä	α Phoenicis	Arabic	coined name	93
Antares	ăn·tā'rēz	α Scorpii	Greek	rival of Mars (in color)	250
Arcturus	ärk·tū'rŭs	α Bootis	Greek	the bear's guard	37
Atria	ăt'rĭ·ȧ	α Trianguli Australis	Modern	coined from Bayer name	130
Avior	ā'vĭ·ôr	ε Carinae	Modern	coined name	350
Bellatrix	bĕ·lā'trĭks.	γ Orionis	Latin	female warrior	250
Betelgeuse	bĕt'ĕl·jūz	α Orionis	Arabic	the arm pit (of Orion)	300
Canopus	kȧ·nō'pŭs	α Carinae	Greek	city of ancient Egypt	230
Capella	kȧ·pĕl'ȧ	α Aurigae	Latin	little she-goat	46
Deneb	dĕn'ĕb	α Cygni	Arabic	tail of the hen	600
Denebola	dĕ·nĕb'ō·lȧ	β Leonis	Arabic	tail of the lion	42
Diphda	dĭf'dȧ	β Ceti	Arabic	the second frog (Fomalhaut was once the first)	57
Dubhe	dŭb'ĕ	α Ursa Majoris	Arabic	the bear's back	100
Elnath	ĕl'năth	β Tauri	Arabic	one butting with horns	130
Eltanin	ĕl·tā'nĭn	γ Draconis	Arabic	head of the dragon	150
Enif	ĕn'ĭf	ε Pegasi	Arabic	nose of the horse	250
Fomalhaut	fō'măl·ôt	α Piscis Austrini	Arabic	mouth of the southern fish	23
Gacrux	gă'krŭks	γ Crucis	Modern	coined from Bayer name	72
Gienah	jē'nȧ	γ Corvi	Arabic	right wing of the raven	136
Hadar	hă'där	β Centauri	Modern	leg of the centaur	200
Hamal	hăm'ăl	α Arietis	Arabic	full-grown lamb	76
Kaus Australis	kôs ôs·trā'lĭs	ε Sagittarii	Ar., L.	southern part of the bow	163
Kochab	kō'kăb	β Ursa Minoris	Arabic	shortened form of "north star" (named when it was that, c. 1500 BC–AD 300)	100
Markab	mär'kăb	α Pegasi	Arabic	saddle (of Pegasus)	100
Menkar	mĕn'kär	α Ceti	Arabic	nose (of the whale)	1,100
Menkent	mĕn'kĕnt	θ Centauri	Modern	shoulder of the centaur	55
Miaplacidus	mī'ȧ·plăs'ĭ·dŭs	β Carinae	Ar., L.	quiet or still waters	86
Mirfak	mĭr'făk	α Persei	Arabic	elbow of the Pleiades	130
Nunki	nŭn'kē	σ Sagittarii	Bab.	constellation of the holy city (Eridu)	150
Peacock	pē'kŏk	α Pavonis	Modern	coined from English name of constellation	250
Polaris	pō·lā'rĭs	α Ursa Minoris	Latin	the pole (star)	450
Pollux	pŏl'ŭks	β Geminorum	Latin	Zeus' other twin son (Castor, α Geminorum, is first twin)	33
Procyon	prō'sĭ·ŏn	α Canis Minoris	Greek	before the dog (rising before the dog star, Sirius)	11
Rasalhague	răs'ăl·hā'gwē	α Ophiuchi	Arabic	head of the serpent charmer	67
Regulus	rĕg'ū·lŭs	α Leonis	Latin	the prince	67
Rigel	rī'jĕl	β Orionis	Arabic	foot (left foot of Orion)	500
Rigil Kentaurus	rī'jĭl kĕn·tô'rŭs	α Centauri	Arabic	foot of the centaur	4.3
Sabik	sā'bĭk	η Ophiuchi	Arabic	second winner or conqueror	69
Schedar	shĕd'ĕr	α Cassiopeiae	Arabic	the breast (of Cassiopeia)	360
Shaula	shō'lȧ	λ Scorpii	Arabic	cocked-up part of the scorpion's tail	200
Sirius	sĭr'ĭ·ŭs	α Canis Majoris	Greek	the scorching one (popularly, the dog star)	8.6
Spica	spī'kȧ	α Virginis	Latin	the ear of corn	155
Suhail	sōō·hāl'	λ Velorum	Arabic	shortened form of Al Suhail, one Arabic name for Canopus	200
Vega	vē'gȧ	α Lyrae	Arabic	the falling eagle or vulture	27
Zubenelgenubi	zōō·bĕn'ĕl·jĕ·nū'bē	α Librae	Arabic	southern claw (of the scorpion)	66

PLANETS

Name	Pronunciation	Origin of name	Meaning of name
Mercury	mûr'kū·rĭ	Latin	god of commerce and gain
Venus	vē'nŭs	Latin	goddess of love
Earth	ûrth	Mid. Eng.	—
Mars	märz	Latin	god of war
Jupiter	jōō'pĭ·tēr	Latin	god of the heavens, identified with the Greek Zeus, chief of the Olympian gods
Saturn	săt'ērn	Latin	god of seed-sowing
Uranus	ū'rȧ·nŭs	Greek	the personification of heaven
Neptune	nĕp'tūn	Latin	god of the sea
Pluto	plōō'tō	Greek	god of the lower world (Hades)

Guide to pronunciations:
fāte, ădd, finȧl, lȧst, ȧbound, ärm; bē, ĕnd, camĕl, readẽr; īce, bĭt, anĭmal; ōver, pōetic, hŏt, lôrd, mōōn; tūbe, ūnite, tŭb, circŭs, ûrn

*Distances in light-years. One light-year equals approximately 63,300 AU, or 5,880,000,000,000 miles. Authorities differ on distances of the stars; the values given are representative.

Figure 12-11. *This chart lists the names of commonly used navigational stars and planets, their pronunciation, their Bayer's name (a naming convention using Greek letters and constellation names), the origins of their names, their meanings (usually related to their constellations), and their distances in light-years from earth.*

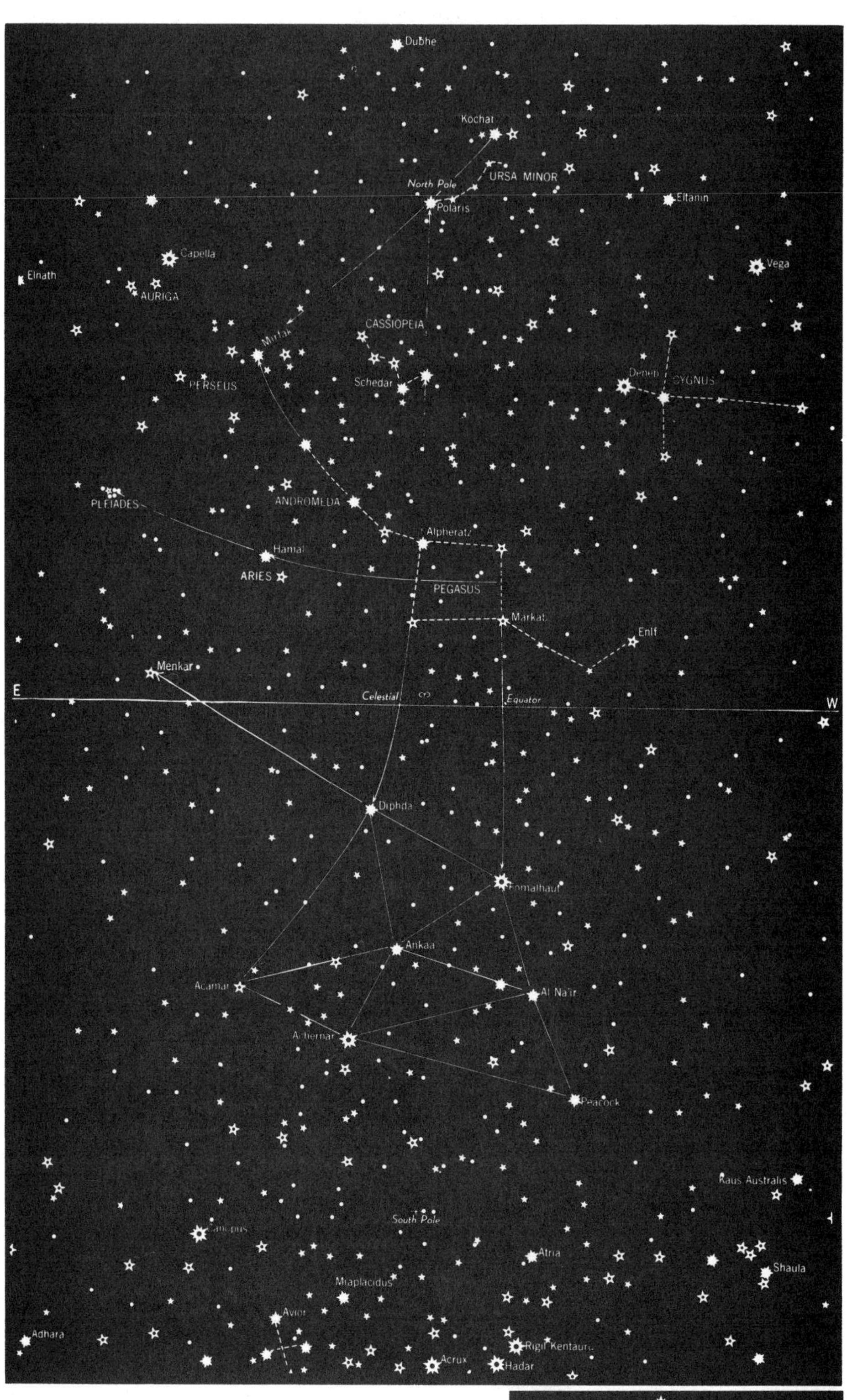

Figure 12-12. *Stars in the vicinity of Pegasus.*

Figure 12-13. *Stars in the vicinity of Orion.*

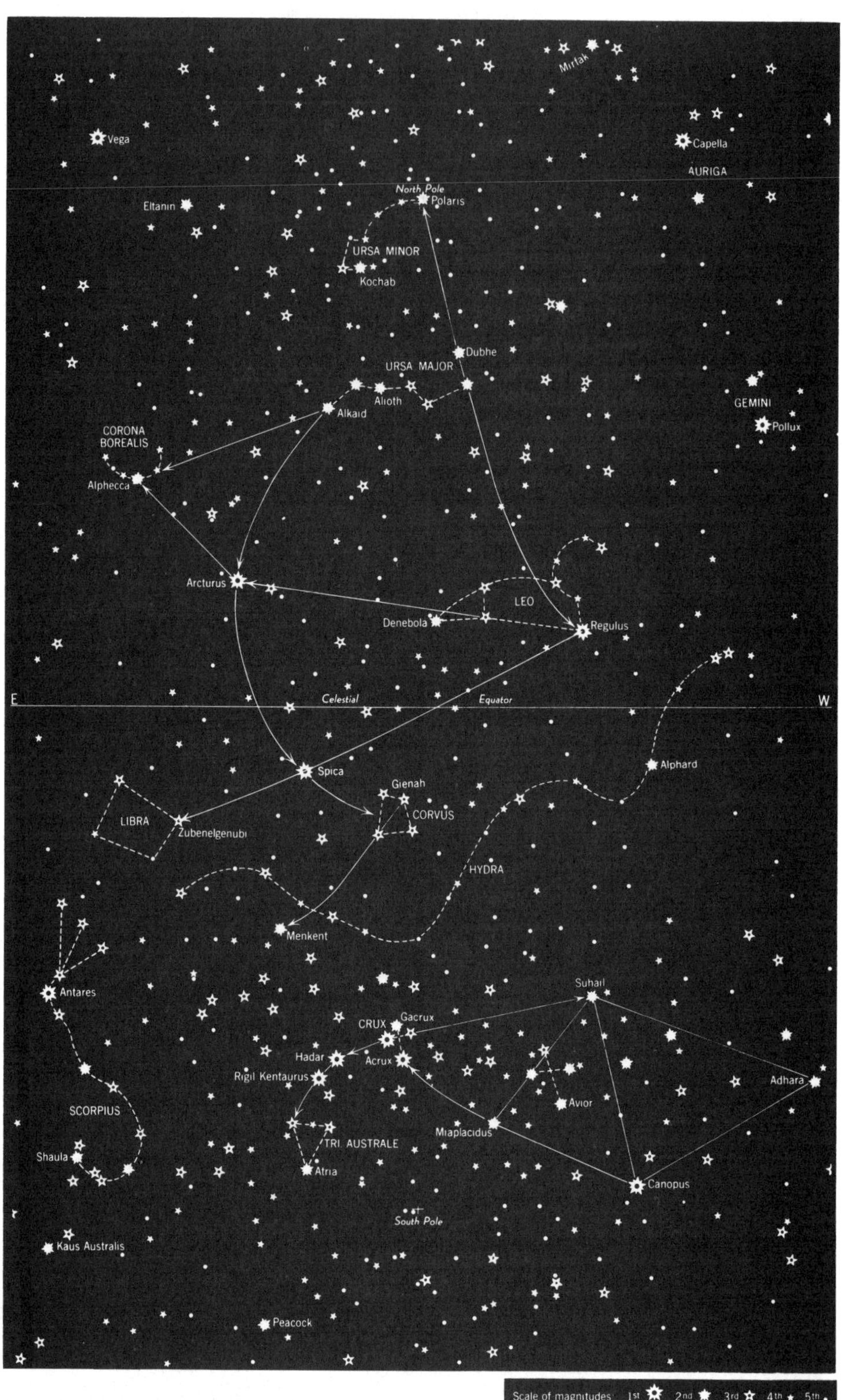

Figure 12-14. *Stars in the vicinity of Ursa Major.*

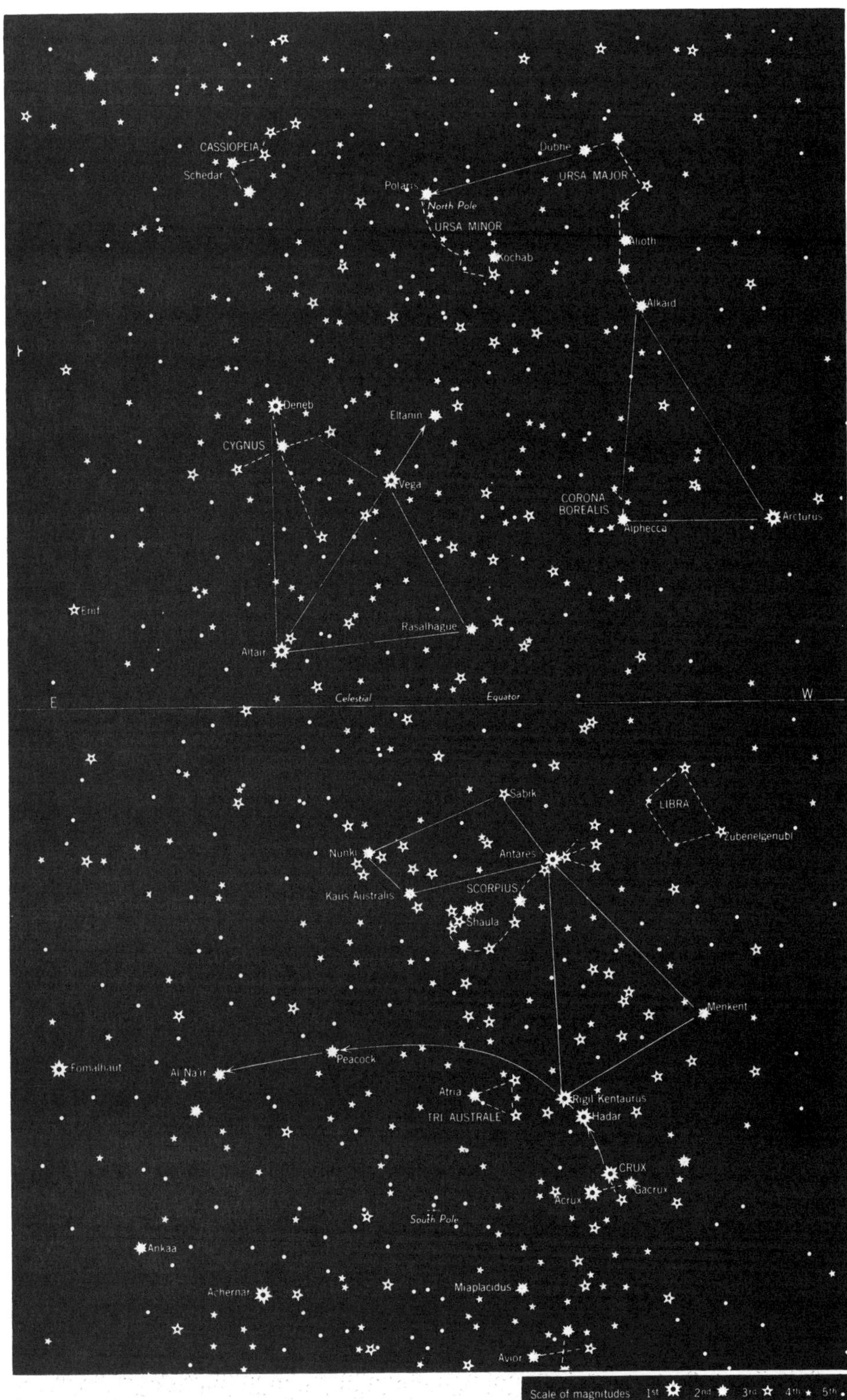

Figure 12-15. *Stars in the vicinity of Cygnus.*

Star Software

An extremely helpful star identification software program is available from Microprojects, 296 Spring Garden Avenue, North York, Ontario, Canada, M2N3H3 (e-mail address: mpj@magiv.ca).

red to distinguish it from the others) shows meridian angle and declination. Complete directions are provided with each kit.

You need to use an almanac in conjunction with the star finder because you must orient it to your location on earth. When you've oriented the overlay on the base, you can clearly see your zenith, all the navigational stars, and the portion of the sky visible from your location.

Several other more technical methods of star identification are available using the sight reduction tables. You can leave these to the professionals; they are fully explained in *The American Practical Navigator.*

Navigational calculators, both handheld and personal computer-based, can help you identify a star when you enter your location and the height and direction, called azimuth, of the star you see. These calculators are very useful in partly cloudy situations when you see only fleeting glimpses of the sky. You don't even have to identify a star before you measure its altitude to get an LOP; your computer can identify the star even as it calculates the LOP.

CHAPTER THIRTEEN

The Sextant

THE SEXTANT IS SPECIFICALLY made for navigational use to measure angles or the amount of arc between objects. It uses a system of mirrors to bring the indirect (reflected) line of sight to one object in alignment with the direct sighting of another. You read the angular distance between them from a semicircular scale.

A sextant is so named because it subtends an arc of 60°, or one-sixth of a circle. Due to a sextant's geometry you can use it to measure angles up to twice its arc, or 120°. Earlier devices similar to the sextant but subtending one-eighth of a circle were called *octants,* which were able to measure arcs of up to 90°. Octants gradually became obsolete because there are times when a measurement of more than 90° is necessary. Today, all such devices are called sextants even though some professional models read angles of 140° or more.

While reading this chapter it will be helpful to have a sextant in hand so you can inspect the various parts and see how they work.

History

Even before the time of Christ, travelers knew that the heavens held the key to navigation on earth. The *astrolabe* (from Greek words meaning "star" and "to take") was invented in about the third-century B.C. for use in astronomical observatories. Arabs had developed a portable version by the year 700 A.D. By the thirteenth century, the astrolabe was used at sea, for navigators by then knew that they could determine their latitude by measuring the altitude—height above the horizon—of the North Star. More than seven hundred years later, navigators still use this celestial navigation technique.

The astrolabe used a plumb line instead of the horizon for a reference to the horizontal plane. However, this was cumbersome and sometimes required three persons to take a sight. In rough weather, large acceleration errors were unavoidable. (See Figure 13-1.)

After the astrolabe, the *cross-staff* came into use. It consisted of a straight piece of wood—

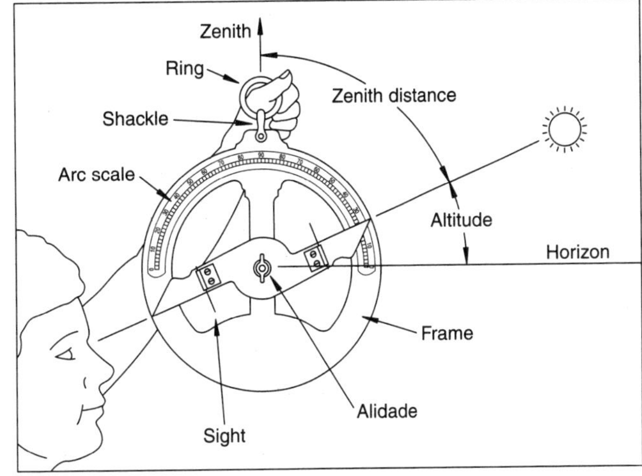

Figure 13-1. *The astrolabe was a simple device that allowed navigators to measure altitudes of heavenly bodies, but was difficult to use at sea because of a ship's motion. The device was suspended to establish a vertical reference and the altitude of a body was measured along the rotating arm.*

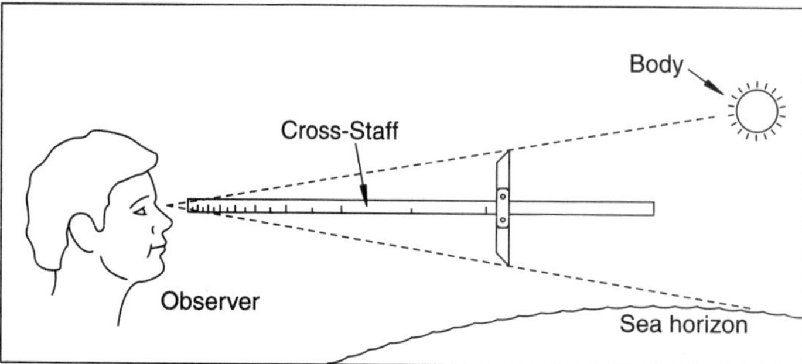

Figure 13-2. *The cross-staff was the first device to use the horizon as a reference to measure altitudes. Though crude, it was effective for the type of navigation practiced at the time and was used until the seventeenth century. The horizontal bar was graduated with angular measurement in degrees.*

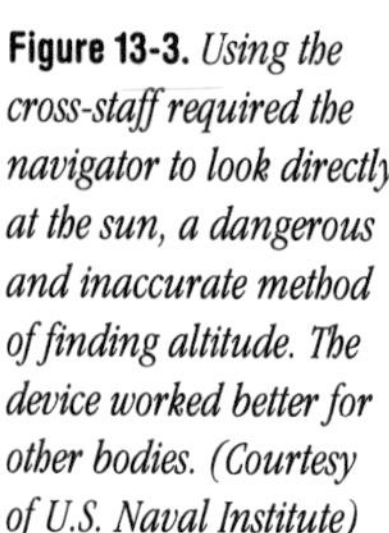

Figure 13-3. *Using the cross-staff required the navigator to look directly at the sun, a dangerous and inaccurate method of finding altitude. The device worked better for other bodies. (Courtesy of U.S. Naval Institute)*

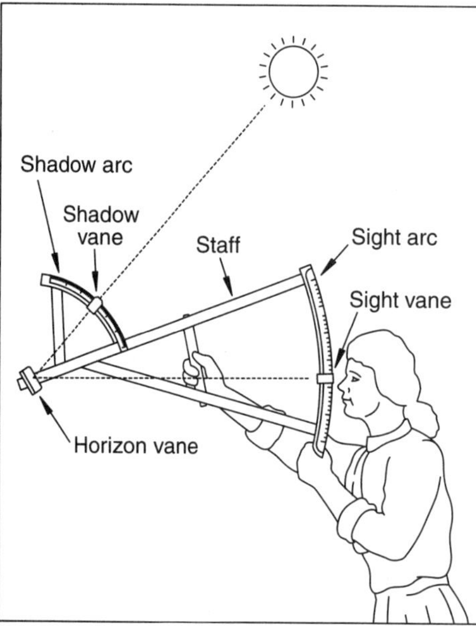

Figure 13-4. *The back-staff was developed so navigators didn't have to look directly at the sun, as was necessary with the earlier cross-staff. Mirrors, which could be smoked to shade the sun's rays, sent a reflected image of the body to the observer's eye. This development foreshadowed the modern sextant. (Courtesy of U.S. Naval Institute)*

a staff—along which a crosspiece of wood could slide while maintaining a right angle to it. The navigator sighted along the staff and adjusted the crosspiece until one end of it was on the observed body and the other on the horizon. Because the sun was the body most commonly observed, longtime navigators inevitably suffered a considerable amount of eye damage. (See Figures 13-2 and 13-3.)

The *back-staff* was invented in 1590 to counter the cross-staff's harmful effects. Using this device, the navigator faced away from the sun and used the shadow cast by the device to measure the angle between the body and the horizon, as shown in Figure 13-4. Later, mirrors were added so that bodies too dim to make shadows—the moon, planets, and stars—could be observed.

Sir Isaac Newton developed the principle of the modern sextant in 1700 and sent a design to Edmond Halley (discoverer of Halley's Comet), then Britain's Astronomer Royal. Halley never built one, but by 1730 Englishman John Hadley and American Thomas Godfrey had built two different versions. Both instruments were successfully tested at sea, but tradition-bound mariners continued to use the obsolete back-staff for another generation.

To improve measurement accuracy, Paul Vernier modified the sextant by attaching a second and smaller section of graduated arc that moved along the primary arc. The vernier principle is used today on every sextant in the world.

Two other developments transformed the sextant into the device we know today. One is the *endless tangent screw;* the other the *micrometer drum*. Together, they permit both gross and fine adjustments so that sights can be taken both quickly and accurately. So, the so-called modern sextant is nearly 300 years old. Modern materials and manufacturing technology, however, now make it far more accurate than early models.

Principle of the Sextant

The sextant relies on the simple physical principle that a ray of light reflects off a surface at the same angle it strikes the surface. That is, the angle of incidence equals the angle of reflection. (See Figure 13-5.)

In a sextant, the light from a star or other body reflects off one mirror, called the *index mirror* because it is attached to a part called the *index arm* and rotates with it. The light then reflects off a second mirror, the *horizon glass*, where it combines with the image of the horizon before traveling to the observer's eye. You adjust the index mirror so that the body and the horizon are in exact coincidence. You read the precise angle of the index arm on the arc of the sextant when coincidence occurs and use that angle to obtain a line of position. (See Figure 13-6.)

Definitions

All sextants have the same basic parts, although some options are available that produce variations. The micrometer drum sextant—the most commonly used type—is described here. You can identify each part in Figure 13-7.

The body of the sextant to which other pieces are attached is called the *frame*. Better quality (and more expensive) sextant frames are made of brass or aluminum, but plastic frames are suitable for practice, backup, or emergency use. The frame consists of two straight sides and an arc between them, called the *limb*. Engraved or inlaid along the limb are the graduations of arc that you read when measuring an angle.

The *index arm* is a movable bar that pivots about the center of the circle that the limb is on. It is made of the same material as the frame so that it will expand and contract at the same rate as the frame when temperature changes occur. At the end of the index arm is the *tangent screw*, which engages teeth on the outer edge of the limb. A release allows you to disengage the tangent

You can minimize errors due to changes in temperature and achieve precision in sights by using a metal-framed sextant—a good choice if you'll be using your sextant extensively. With a good metal-framed sextant you can consistently get fixes with accuracies of less than two miles; even one-mile accuracy is attainable with experience. With plastic-framed instruments you often can't get closer than three to five miles; their accuracy varies with temperature due to their relatively high coefficient of expansion.

The one-to-two-mile accuracy of celestial navigation does not compare favorably with GPS's 100-meter accuracy. But you use celestial navigation offshore, nearly always out of sight of land, where you don't need 100-meter accuracy; two-mile accuracy is good enough in the middle of the ocean.

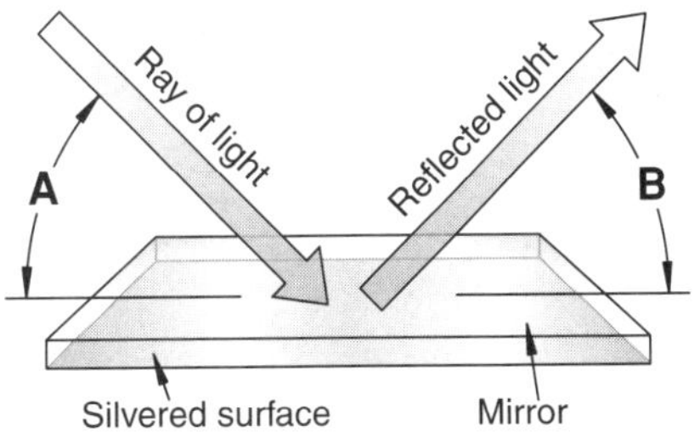

Figure 13-5. *The sextant relies on the principle that a ray of light striking a mirror will reflect from it at the same angle it struck: angle of incidence = angle of reflection; angle A = angle B. Although the glass causes a slight internal refraction, or bending, of the light ray, the equation is still true because incoming refraction equals outgoing refraction.*

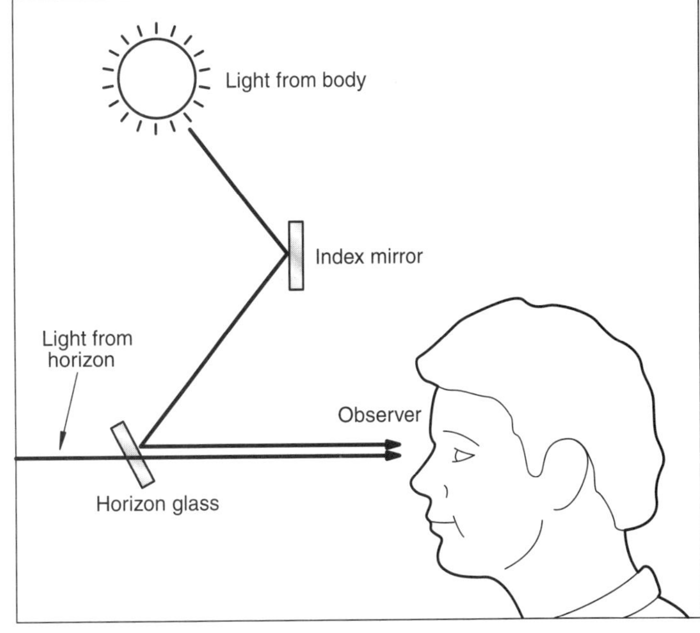

Figure 13-6. *The sextant brings light from a celestial body and from the horizon into convergence at the eye of the observer. Because of the sextant's geometry, it can measure angles twice as large as its arc. A sextant with an arc of 60° can measure an angle of 120°, which is sometimes very useful.*

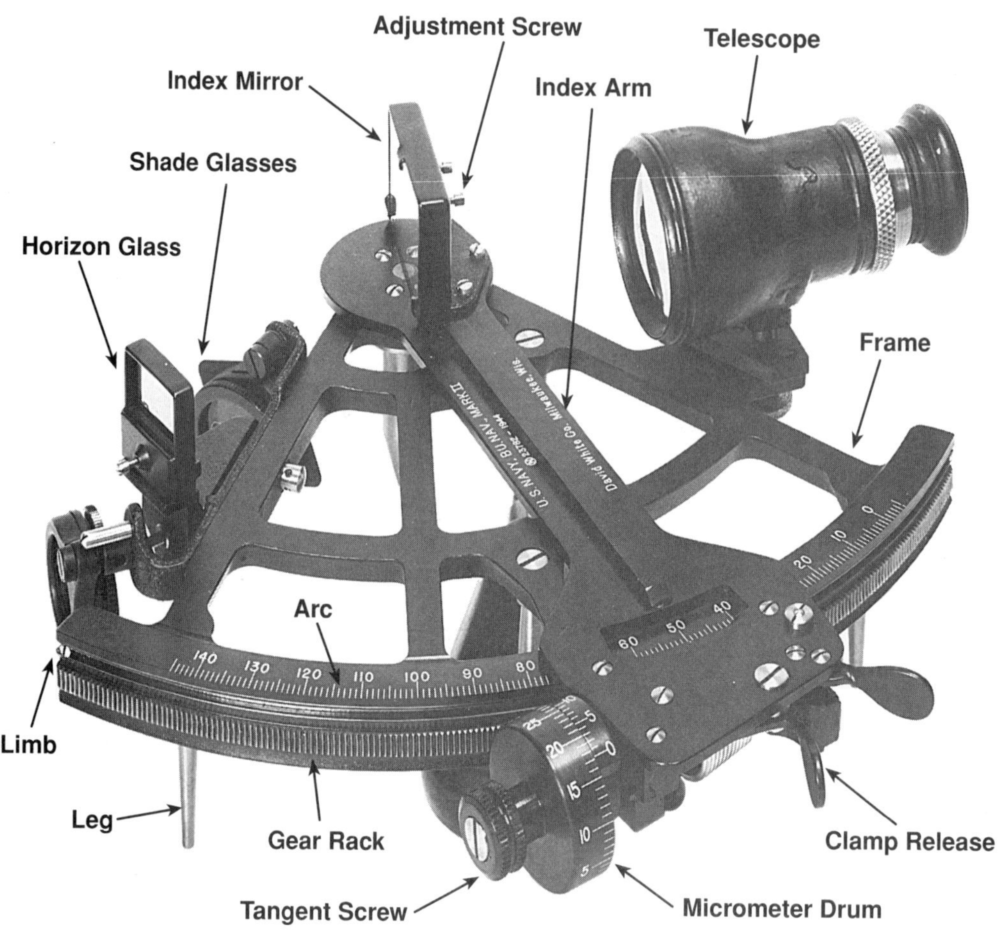

Figure 13-7. *The modern sextant is a precise navigational instrument. It consists of a frame, an index arm, index and horizon mirrors, a tangent screw, and a graduated limb for reading measured angles. A small low-powered telescope helps to sight lesser-magnitude stars and planets. (Photograph courtesy of NOAA)*

screw from the limb and rapidly move it to the approximate position you desire. Then you can make fine adjustments with the tangent screw.

Mounted perpendicular to the tangent screw is the *micrometer drum,* which rotates the tangent screw when turned. Facing the drum is the *vernier scale,* which allows you to read arcs to an accuracy of one-tenth (0.1) minute.

The sextant has two mirrors. The *index mirror* is mounted over the pivot point of the index arm, perpendicular to the frame. This mirror first catches the image of the body you're observing. The other mirror—the *horizon glass*—is actually only half of a mirror; half is clear glass. The half nearer the frame is silvered so that it reflects the image of the observed body into your eye. (See Figure 13-8.) You see the horizon alongside this image through the clear half of the glass. On better-quality instruments you can adjust these two mirrors so they are precisely parallel when the sextant reads 0° 00.0'.

A new kind of mirror, called a *whole horizon mirror,* allows you to view both the body and the horizon across the entire face of the horizon glass. Specially coated optics allow light from the horizon to travel through the mirror simultaneously with light reflected from the body. The whole horizon mirror is difficult to use in low-light situations because it doesn't transmit as much light as the silvered mirror and clear glass combination. However, you can locate a body more easily and measure its altitude more precisely with a whole horizon mirror.

Also mounted on the frame are *shade glasses* of various densities that you can rotate into the field of view of both the body and the horizon. These permit you to look directly at the sun or the bright horizon below it.

A *telescope* is an optional and very useful addition to a sextant. Mounted precisely parallel to the frame, it magnifies the image three to four times for more accurate viewing. A small battery-powered *light* may also be fitted to the frame so that angles can be read in poor light. The batteries are in a recess in the handle.

You might still come across an older type of sextant, called a *vernier sextant,* though these have largely been replaced by the micrometer drum type. These sextants use a vernier scale directly along the graduated arc, instead of a micrometer drum, for fine adjustment. The vernier scales are difficult to read and require a magnifying glass to see the tiny graduations of arc.

All sextants are built to be held in your right hand, with the handle attached to one side of the frame; when not in use, the instrument rests on three legs. Finally, a case—possibly padded and including hold-down clips—protects the sextant from physical damage, water, and salt spray.

Various adjustments can be made in the more expensive sextants. The beginning celestial navigator should leave these to a professional instrument shop or experienced mariner who is familiar with them.

Taking Sights

You develop certain techniques in taking sextant sights only with experience. Written descriptions and study can't substitute for experience. However, some suggestions can help the beginning celestial navigator to obtain fast and accurate readings.

The best advice for the beginner is to practice, practice, and practice some more. Often, the most difficult part of celestial navigation on small craft is obtaining good sights when seas are rough. You can, though, develop techniques to keep your balance and stability in such conditions that will greatly improve the accuracy of your sights.

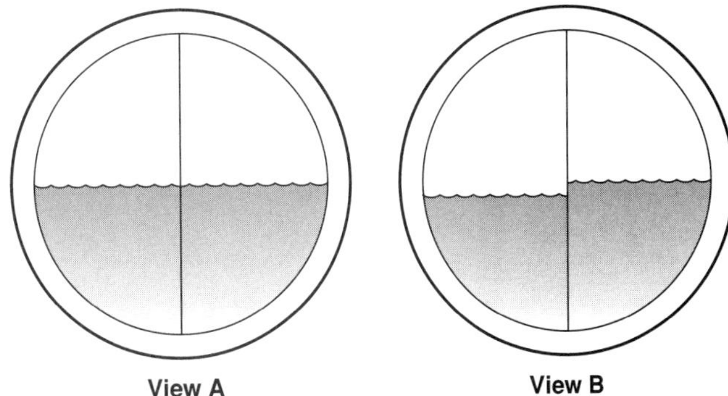

Figure 13-8. *A sextant set at 0° 00.0' that has no index error will show the horizon as in View A. In View B, the sextant is set at 0° 00.0' and an index error is present. This error should be recorded and used to correct all measured altitudes.*

Before taking a sight you should check the *index error*. This is especially important when using a plastic sextant. To do this, set the sextant to 0° 00.0' and measure the "altitude" of the horizon by carefully aligning its direct image with its reflected image. (See Figure 13-8.) Read the measured altitude. If it is not 0° 00.0', there is an index error that is caused by lack of parallelism between the index and horizon mirrors. Record this error; you must apply it to all sights taken at that time. If the sextant reading is more than 0° 00.0', the error is "on the arc" and must be subtracted from all measured altitudes. If the reading is minus, or "off the arc," the error must be added.

Sun and Moon Sights

Small-craft navigators rely heavily on sun and moon sights because they are available for a much longer period during the day. Star and planet sights must be taken at dusk and dawn when both these bodies and the horizon are clearly visible, but you can shoot the sun and moon at any time of the day when you can see them.

You'll need to use the darkest shade glasses for sun sights so you can view the sun without damaging your eyes. A set of shades is in line with the image mirror and darkens the direct image of the sun. Another set, the horizon shades, dim the glare of the sun on the water.

Select and rotate into position the darkest shade glass available. If it's too dark, you can shift to a lighter shade, but you will not have

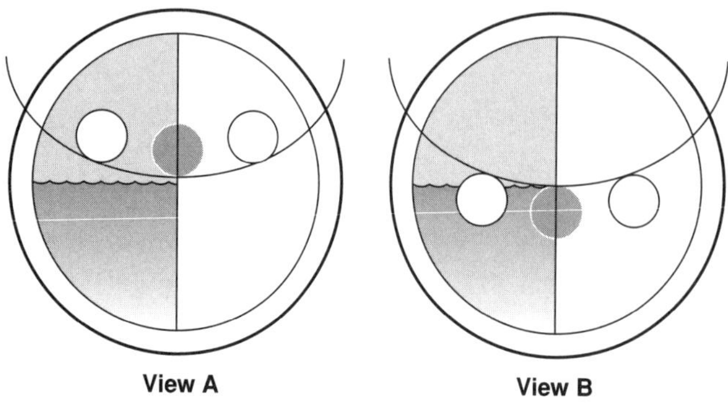

Figure 13-9. *At the instant of a sun or moon observation, the body should be exactly tangent to the horizon, either by the lower limb (View A) or upper limb (View B). You should rock the sextant slightly to establish the exact vertical; doing so will cause the image to describe a small arc. Take the reading when the bottom of the arc is tangent to the horizon. You may find it easier and more accurate to preset the sextant at a nice round number and let the sun or moon move to that altitude instead of "chasing" it.*

risked eye discomfort or damage that can result from starting with a lighter shade.

Next, hold the sextant vertically and look through the eyepiece at the horizon directly below the sun or moon. While viewing the horizon, squeeze the tangent screw release and rotate the index arm outward until you can see the image of the body. Note about how high the body is in the sky. If it's about midway between the horizon and the zenith, you'll find the sun at a setting of about 45°—or about one third of the way along the arc.

Then, release the clamp so that the tangent screw is engaged and turn the screw until the body is very close to the horizon. Now, *rock the sextant* slightly from side to side and observe that the body moves in a small arc. You may have to turn slightly to prevent the body from disappearing out of the field of view, but this ensures that your sextant is perfectly vertical when you make the observation.

Take the reading when the body is exactly at the bottom of the arc made by rocking the sextant. The most common mistake is bringing the image down too far. Look for the exact point of tangency of either the upper edge of the body, called its *upper limb,* or the corresponding *lower limb.* (Later, you'll have to apply corrections for this factor and several others.) Due to the moon's phases, you most often use the upper limb.

Some navigators prefer to set the sextant to a convenient reading (such as the next whole degree), let the body move to the horizon, and then note the exact time. This can make sight reduction easier. A little experimenting with both techniques will determine which method works best for you.

It is difficult to get an accurate moon sight at night because the horizon is usually too indistinct.

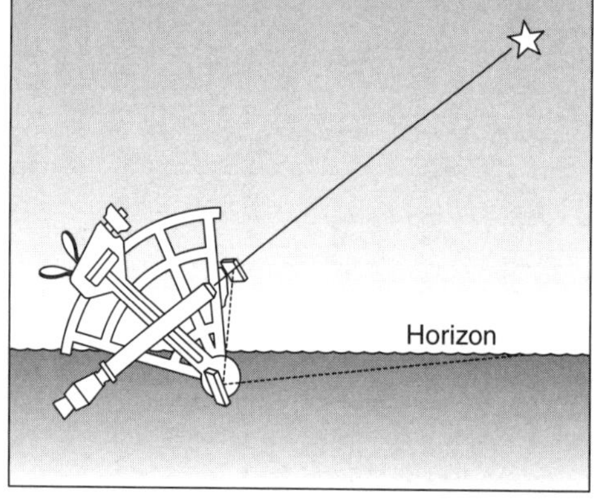

Figure 13-10. *To quickly find a star or planet, invert the sextant and view the body through the telescope while rotating the index arm until the horizon appears. Then, with the proper angle found, invert the sextant again and sight the body in the usual way.*

Star and Planet Sights

It's relatively easy to acquire the sun and moon because of their size and brightness; stars and planets, particularly those of lesser magnitude, can be difficult to see through sextant mirrors and can be frustrating. Three techniques can make the process easier.

First, set your sextant at 0° 00.0' and sight directly at the star. Keeping the image of the star in the mirrored part of the glass, slowly swing the index arm outward while rotating the sextant downward until the horizon appears. This technique works best for the brightest stars and planets. If you lose the body before the horizon is sighted, you must start again.

In the second technique you direct the line of sight at the body while holding the sextant upside down. Then rotate the index arm until you sight the horizon, invert the sextant, and take the sight as usual. (See Figure 13-10.)

The third method requires you to determine in advance the approximate altitude and azimuth of a body, using a star finder or computer program. When you set the sextant at the computed altitude and face in the direction of the computed azimuth, you should be able to find the body with little searching.

Sights of the sun and moon require you to bring the upper or lower limb to the horizon; you measure stars and planets at their centers, as in Figure 13-11. Because they have no discernible diameter, you measure to the center of the point of light. As with sun and moon sights, you should rock the sextant slightly to establish perpendicularity. The technique of setting the sextant and letting the body move to the horizon does not work as well with stars and planets as it does with the sun and moon.

Professional navigators have developed a number of techniques over the years that make taking sights more efficient and quick. A few of these are summarized below.

- When using a star finder or computer to predict the locations of stars before taking sights, get the locations of at least six or eight stars in case some are obscured by clouds when you take the round of sights.
- Try to use stars between altitudes of 30° and 70°. These will likely yield more accurate altitudes. Similarly, try to shoot stars with a good spread of azimuths. Be aware of the crossing angles of the LOPs.
- For morning sights, shoot the dimmest stars first because they will be the first to disappear with increasing daylight. In the evening, shoot the brightest stars first because they will be the first to appear in the early twilight, while the horizon is still sharp. Then, if you still need more sights, shoot the dimmer stars as they become visible in the increasing darkness.

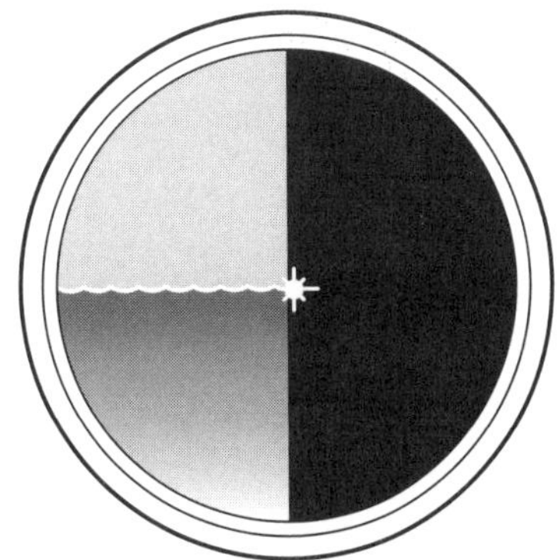

Figure 13-11. *At the instant of a planet or star observation, the body should be bisected by the horizon. Stars have no visible dimension, though the phases of the planet Venus can be seen through telescopes.*

Reading the Sextant

There are three steps to reading the micrometer drum sextant.

1. Read the degrees from the index arm, on which there is a small arrow pointing to the graduations on the arc. The next lowest whole degree is the correct reading.
2. Read the minutes from the vernier scale next to the drum. The zero point on the vernier shows the correct reading and, as before, the next lower whole number is the correct one.
3. Read tenths of minutes by noting which line on the vernier scale most closely aligns with the scale on the drum.

See Figure 13-12 for an example of a sextant reading. In addition, refer to Figure 13-7, where the sextant reading on the micrometer drum is 17.3 minutes. (Degrees are not visible in this photograph.)

You have to be careful reading the sextant "off the arc" when the index error is negative. In this case, you add the numbers algebraically. For example, an off the arc reading of –1°, +56', +0.3' translates into an error of –3.7'. Remember that the scale is backwards when you read off the arc.

With a good marine sextant you can potentially measure altitudes to the nearest 0.1' of arc. A measurement error of 0.1' would result in an LOP error of only some 200 yards. Why, then, is an accuracy of a mile considered acceptable? Because the sextants are more capable than the observers, who are the

Figure 13-12. *This illustration shows a micrometer drum sextant set at 50° 17.3'. The arrow on the index arm is between 50° and 51°. The zero mark on the vernier is between 17' and 18', and the 0.3' mark on the vernier scale is perfectly aligned with one of the marks on the drum. (The angle of view makes it appear to be set at 49°.)*

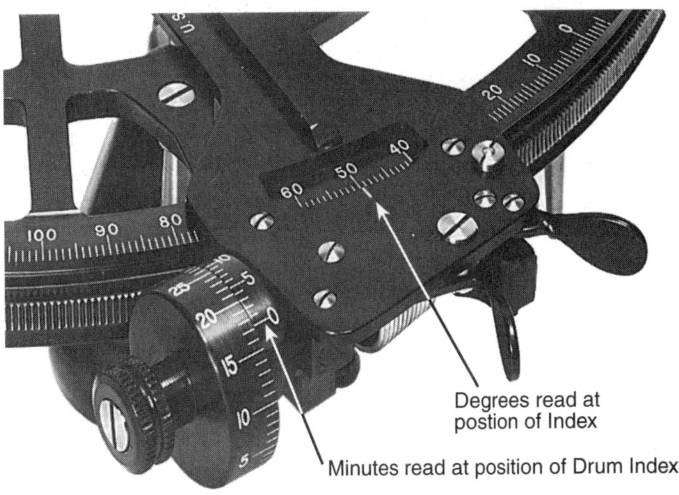

principal sources of errors in sights. U.S. Navy studies show that technique is an important determinant of celestial fix accuracy. Accuracy is poor among beginners and improves slowly, reaching journeyman levels only after several hundred sights, and peak professional levels after a thousand or more.

Don't let these findings discourage you. Few worthwhile skills are mastered right away. You don't have to be a professional to enjoy an activity, as millions of golfers, tennis players, and other sportspeople will attest. And your need for accuracy in locations far offshore will not likely exceed your beginning capability. By applying yourself, you can become competent with a sextant in one season.

Your first fix is likely to disappoint you. If Loran-C, GPS, or visual LOPs are available, you can easily assess the error of your fix and try to find its causes. Although the error may be due to factors outside your control, some types of human errors are common. They are listed below.

Improper rocking of the sextant

Poor discernment of the point of tangency

Using a false horizon

Improper reading of the index error

Poor adjustment of the sextant

Errors in computation

Using the wrong height of eye

You can take steps to reduce the errors inherent in sights. Instead of taking a single observation for the sun and moon, take several over a period of, say, half an hour, and plot the results on a graph. Graphing several sights of the same body will allow you to average the errors and estimate a reading for any point of time covered by the graph, even if no sight was taken at that point.

Nonadjustable Errors

If you use a high-quality sextant, you'll be able to make adjustments that reduce some types of errors; others are built in to the instrument. If you are inexperienced, leave the correction of some types of adjustable errors to professional instrument repair technicians. Amateur navigators risk damaging expensive instruments by attempting some adjustments. You can't make many adjustments on inexpensive sextants, so you must simply accept and compensate for them as much as possible. Of course, you must accept unadjustable errors regardless of the quality of the instrument.

In general, the amount of built-in sextant error is inversely proportional to the price of the instrument. And, with good care, you can minimize errors due to misalignment and warping.

The *nonadjustable errors*—those you must accept as part of the makeup of your instrument—are usually measured by the manufacturer, summarized as *instrument error,* and noted in writing in an error table inside the case.

One of these is called *prismatic error* (sometimes called *shade error*) and is due to a lack of parallelism between the shade glasses and the mirrors. If the shades and mirrors are not exactly parallel, light rays will be refracted, thereby altering the geometry of the sextant and causing inaccurate readings. (Shade error does not occur in eyepiece covers or shades that fit over the telescopic lens because the light from both image and horizon passes together to the eye.) You can check shade error by putting each shade glass in turn into the field of view and measuring an altitude with and without each one. Record the error of each if it is significant (more than a couple of tenths of a minute) and then measure and record the error of each combination. (You can combine these errors with the index error during the sight reduction process.)

Graduation error is another nonadjustable error. It is caused by inaccurate calibration or cutting of the teeth in the arc, micrometer drum, or vernier. There is no practical way to check error in the teeth, but you can see vernier error when the first and last marks on the vernier scale do not exactly line up with proper graduations on the drum. When you align the zero mark on the vernier with any mark on the drum, the ten mark on the vernier should align perfectly with another mark on the drum, so that ten vernier marks equal nine drum marks.

A third nonadjustable error is *centering error*, which results when the index arm does not pivot exactly about the center of the arc. There is no way you can detect this error.

Adjustable Errors

You can eliminate *adjustable errors* by carefully loosening and tightening the adjusting screws on the backs of the mirrors. If you tighten any screw be careful to first loosen a corresponding one—otherwise, the mirror may break. Adjustable errors must be removed in the following order: perpendicularity error, side error, collimation error, and index error.

Perpendicularity error is caused by lack of perpendicularity between the frame and the index mirror. You can detect this by setting the index arm at about 35° and placing the instrument on its legs on a flat surface. By sighting along the index arm from the top of the sextant you can see the arc and its continuation reflected in the index mirror. If they are not in perfect alignment, the index mirror is not perpendicular to the frame. You make necessary adjustments with screws on the back of the mirror. Again, loosen one before tightening the other.

Side error is caused by lack of perpendicularity between the frame and the horizon glass. You detect side error can by setting the index arm at zero, sighting a star or planet (not the moon or sun), and moving the tangent screw so the image moves up and down. If the moving image does not pass directly through the stationary image, side error is present.

Another way of noting side error is to sight the horizon and observe a continuous line between the real horizon and the reflected image. Rock the sextant slightly from side to side. If the reflected image moves above or below the real image, side error is present. If the horizon remains a straight line, no side error is present. You adjust side error with two screws on the back of the horizon mirror. As with the index mirror, you must loosen one screw before tightening the other.

Collimation error is present when the telescope is not exactly parallel with the frame. You can check it by placing the sextant on a flat table in a small room. Sight along the frame and mark the opposite wall exactly level with the plane of the frame. Next, measure the distance from the frame to the center of the telescope and make another mark on the wall that distance above the frame mark. The mark should then appear in the center of the field of view of the telescope. You can correct collimation error by adjusting the collar of the telescope.

Index error is usually caused by lack of parallelism between the index mirror and horizon glass when the sextant reads 0°00.0'. You can check it by setting the sextant at 0°00.0' and sighting the horizon. If the reflected image and direct image are not in perfect alignment, index error is present. You can correct index error by adjusting the index and horizon mirrors so that the horizon is in alignment at 0°00.0'.

You don't need to correct index error if you measure it and apply a correction to each measured altitude—a procedure you may prefer to the tedious process of adjustment. In any case, you may not be able to remove all error due to the construction of the instrument.

Selecting a Small-Craft Sextant

The average small-craft navigator doesn't need a high-quality sextant that costs anywhere from several hundred to several thousand dollars. In fact, if you don't venture out of sight of land for more than a few hours at a time, you'll have trouble justifying the expense or learning time involved in buying any sextant. A very high-quality sextant costs as much as a decent Loran-C and GPS together. You might better spend the money on backup electronics such as secondary GPS and/or Loran-C receivers, a handheld, portable GPS receiver, or emergency power systems.

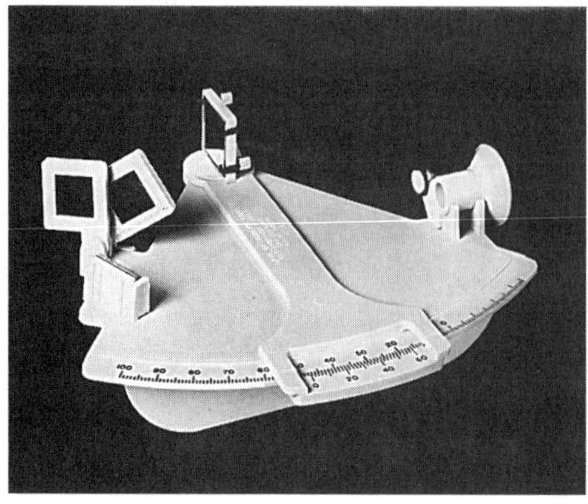

Figure 13-13. *This inexpensive plastic sextant is suitable for beginners or as a backup instrument. Notice the lack of a micrometer drum, which severely restricts its accuracy. (Courtesy of Davis Instruments)*

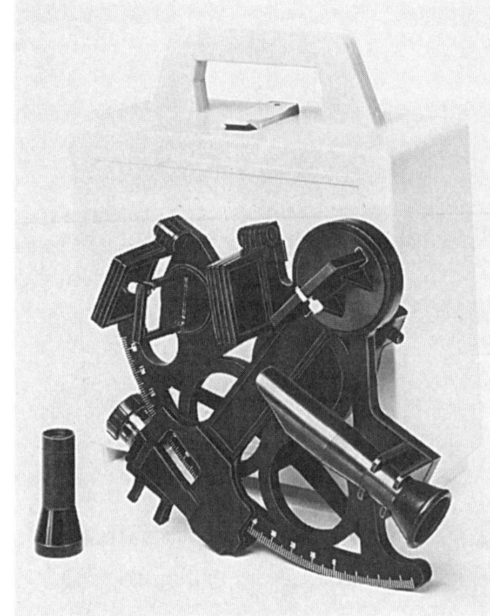

Figure 13-14. *This inexpensive plastic sextant has most of the features of a much more expensive metal model and is suitable for practice and as a backup. It lacks, however, the consistent accuracy of a metal sextant and many adjustments for common sextant errors cannot be made easily or at all. Unlike the sextant shown in Figure 13-13, this model has a micrometer drum for better accuracy in reading altitudes. (Courtesy of Davis Instruments)*

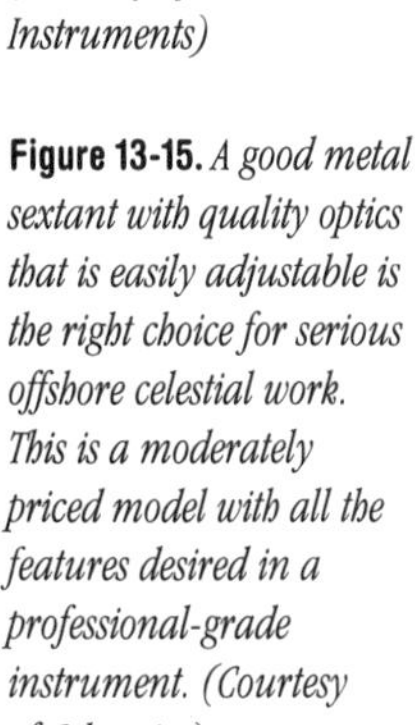

Figure 13-15. *A good metal sextant with quality optics that is easily adjustable is the right choice for serious offshore celestial work. This is a moderately priced model with all the features desired in a professional-grade instrument. (Courtesy of Celestaire)*

You should decide what role a sextant will play in your day-to-day offshore navigation. If celestial is to be your primary navigational method, then investing in a quality sextant is clearly justified; in fact, it is mandatory. However, if celestial is to be a backup or emergency method, then you should consider buying a lesser-quality sextant like one of the plastic varieties. Figures 13-13, 13-14, and 13-15 show increasing level of quality in sextant construction.

Whichever sextant you choose, accuracy will depend as much on your technique as on the instrument's quality. The key to successful celestial navigation is to become intimately familiar with the process through practice, practice, and more practice of the art.

Shop for a high-quality new sextant at reputable dealers. They will make commitments to maintaining and servicing the instrument, as well as provide advice on its care and handling. You should buy a good used sextant from a dealer experienced in used navigational equipment; if you are unable to do so, take the sextant to a marine instrument technician for examination before purchasing it.

The problems with used sextants are usually related to poor care. Bent frames, scratched lenses, worn teeth, broken mirrors, and loose fittings are common problems; the cost of their repair might approach the cost of the instrument itself. A professional technician will explain what must be done to bring a used sextant into serviceable condition.

Do not put to sea expecting to use a sextant without practicing techniques of observation and sight reduction beforehand. Practice when the use of the sextant is not necessary. As you practice, check on the accuracy of your celestial positions with GPS, Loran-C, or piloting fixes.

Artificial Horizons

You can practice celestial navigation at home if you follow a few simple procedures. Because it's unlikely that a sea horizon will be available, you'll need to find an *artificial horizon*.

Over the years, different kinds of artificial

horizons have been used at sea and ashore. At sea, an artificial horizon may be used when the natural horizon is obscured by fog or darkness, thereby allowing you to take a sight any time a body is visible. Most seagoing artificial horizon devices rely on some sort of bubble in a liquid-filled glass dome. Other types have used gyroscopes or pendulums. However, due to the motion of a vessel in a seaway, most of these give a very poor indication of the true horizontal plane.

Professional bubble horizon sextants have been used for many years in long-range aircraft navigation. Such sextants are expensive and quite inaccurate at sea. Their inaccuracy increases with sea state, and for most small craft they are quite useless due to the motion.

When you use an artificial horizon at sea, you normally have to take several sights of the same body to get a single LOP. Averaging the readings of the sights improves accuracy. This practice discourages most small-craft navigators from using artificial horizons.

On the other hand, an artificial horizon is valuable for the boater who wants to practice at home or anyplace on land where a sea horizon is not visible. You can make an artificial horizon, or liquid mirror, with a pan or tray, a little water, and some used motor oil. Place the tray on a level surface, cover the bottom with water, and float a layer of used motor oil (or blackstrap molasses) on the water. The combination creates a perfectly level mirror that will reflect the sun and moon well enough to take practice sights. Various manufactured models are also available. You may have to shelter an artificial horizon device from the wind.

Don't try to use liquid mirrors for star sights because they are too dim and difficult to see. You can use any reflective surface that can be made perfectly level as an artificial horizon. A plain mirror works best for practice with stars. See the sidebar for the author's recommendation.

Taking sights with an artificial horizon device is a little different from taking sights at sea. With sextant in hand, stand so the artificial horizon reflects the image of the body to be viewed. Bring the direct image that's reflected in the artificial horizon into view through the telescope and rotate the index arm until you also see the body in the double-reflected view of the sextant. For stars and planets, bring both images into coincidence. For the lower limb of the moon or sun, bring the bottom of the double-reflected sextant image tangent to the top of the artificial horizon image. When the two images are brought into direct coincidence, you are sighting the center of the body.

After taking the observation, record the measured altitude, apply the index correction, and divide the answer by two (because the measurement was not to the horizon but to a point below it equal to the body's altitude above it).

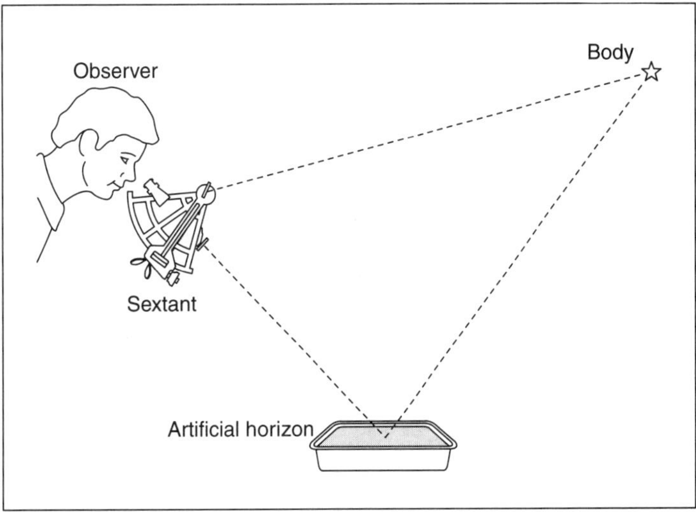

Figure 13-16. *You can make an artificial horizon for backyard practice by floating used motor oil in a pan of water. You observe the body both directly and reflected in the liquid. One-half of the measured altitude is used for calculations.*

The author uses a thick glass mirror mounted on a plywood base, aligned in the horizontal plane by three thumbscrews that he adjusts as indicated by two bubble levels placed on the glass. This device is portable, suitably accurate for practice sights, and works well with stars, planets, and sun/moon observations.

The Secret of Celestial Navigation

Celestial navigation is an enjoyable and rewarding hobby, as well as a practical and inexpensive method of offshore navigation. The secret to celestial success is simply practice. It is the only method that frees you from reliance on electricity, electronic devices, and the constant fear that an electronic failure will destroy your ability to find your position at sea.

Remember, you should have a good quality sextant if celestial is your primary means of offshore navigation. A lesser-quality sextant may serve as a backup or for practice. In either case, you should practice until you can get a good LOP every time.

CHAPTER FOURTEEN

Time

WITHOUT TIME, CELESTIAL NAVIGATORS could not determine lines of position other than latitudes. You can find latitude without reference to the time by observing a celestial body as it passes over your own meridian. You don't need a watch to determine that point, because the body passes your meridian when it's at its highest point in the sky. You can also use Polaris, which is always within a degree or so of the North Pole. Navigators have been able to measure latitude for thousands of years because its measurement is not time-dependent. Longitude, on the other hand, cannot be accurately determined celestially without using time as a reference.

The circumference of the earth is about 21,600 nautical miles. Because the earth completes a rotation once every 24 hours, the sun and all other bodies appear to move rapidly across meridians of longitude, at a rate of 360° per day or 15° per hour. At the earth's equator this translates into a rate of about 900 miles per hour, 15 miles per minute, or one-quarter mile every second. So, if you want to find longitude using a fast-moving heavenly body, you have to know its position in time very accurately. Every second of time error causes a one-quarter mile error in longitude at the equator.

In the absence of accurate time-keeping instruments, navigators centuries ago tried to use other methods of determining longitude involving the moons of Jupiter, the angle between earth's moon and various other bodies, and lines of magnetic variation. None of these was satisfactory.

Different Kinds of Time

Time is measured in several ways using different frames of reference. When you stand in one place and measure the time it takes for a star to move from directly overhead on one day to the same place on the following day, the elapsed time is very close to 24 hours. When you do the same for the sun, the elapsed time is about four minutes longer.

Because the earth rotates on its axis while it also revolves around the sun and moves through space to a different position than the day before, the sun appears to be a little farther east each day when viewed against the background of stars. The day that is reckoned according to the stars is called the *sidereal day;* the day measured with respect to the sun is called the *apparent solar day,* as shown in Figure 14-1.

The apparent solar day has three sources of inconsistency. First, because the earth's orbit is not exactly circular but elliptical, the speed of the earth in its revolution around the sun is not constant. This causes variation in the approximate four-minute time difference between the sidereal and apparent solar day. Second, time is measured with respect to movement along

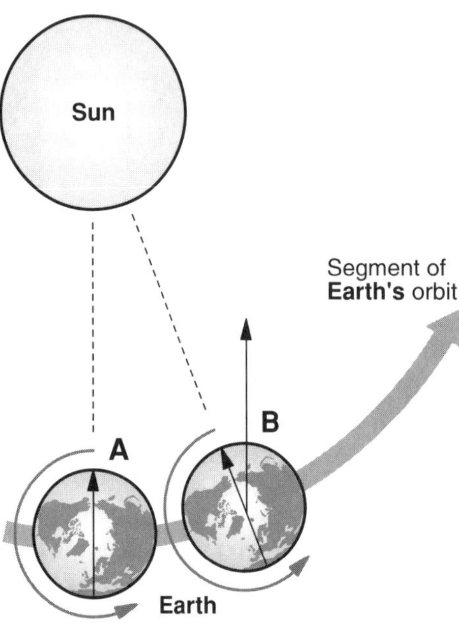

Figure 14-1. *The apparent solar day is about four minutes longer than the sidereal (star-referenced) day because, as the earth rotates, it also moves along in its orbit, causing the apparent position of the sun to change and the apparent solar day to be slightly longer. An observer at point "A" noting the sun overhead would see that, 24 hours later, it would not be overhead until it had moved to point "B," taking about four minutes longer to do so.*

Day	SUN			MOON			
	Eqn. of Time 00 h	Eqn. of Time 12 h	Mer. Pass.	Mer. Pass. Upper	Mer. Pass. Lower	Age	Phase
	m s	m s	h m	h m	h m	d	
15	00 17	00 24	12 00	17 04	04 39	06	◐
16	00 30	00 37	12 01	17 53	05 28	07•	
17	00 43	00 49	12 01	18 43	06 18	08	

Figure 14-2. *Equation of time listing in the* Nautical Almanac *for June 16, 1994. The equation of time represents the difference between the movements of the apparent (real) and mean (average) suns.*

the celestial equator; the sun travels along the ecliptic, which is inclined to the equator at an angle of 23° 27'. Third, the earth does not rotate on its axis at a constant rate.

To remove these sources of variation in time, navigators keep time with reference to a fictitious sun called the *mean sun,* which moves eastward along the celestial equator at the average speed of the real sun along the ecliptic. This evens out the inconsistencies and allows you to maintain an accurate and constant rate of time. The mean sun travels along the celestial equator at a constant rate of 15° per hour.

The apparent (real) sun gives us *apparent solar time.* The mean (fictitious) sun gives us *mean solar time,* or *mean time,* which is sometimes ahead of and sometimes behind apparent solar time. The difference is called the *equation of time* and never exceeds about 16 minutes. You use the equation of time chiefly to compute the time of meridian passage of the sun for latitude observations.

The equation of time defines the difference in time that the mean sun and the apparent sun cross your meridian. The sun you see passes over your meridian at *local apparent noon (LAN).*

You need to determine LAN to obtain a meridian altitude sight of the sun for a latitude line. The equation of time is listed in the *Nautical Almanac* on the right-hand daily pages. The sign of the equation of time is positive if the time of the sun's meridian passage is before 1200 and negative if it is later. Thus, apparent time equals mean time minus the equation of time.

Here is an example: Determine LAN for a latitude observation on June 16, 1994. In the lower right corner of the page is listed the "Eqn of Time" for June 15, 16, and 17 (excerpted in Figure 14-2). Looking across the row for June 16 we see "Mer. Pass." listed as occurring at 1201. Now look to the next column to the left, under the "12h" (because you want the value for noon, not midnight). The value is "37s," or 37 seconds. Since the 1201 time indicates that meridian passage occurs after 1200, we add the 37 seconds to 1200 and get 12:00:37 for the time of LAN. This will be true on June 16 no matter where on the earth you are. As you'll see, it is not usually necessary to know LAN this accurately.

Time and Arc

In some celestial work, you'll need to convert time to arc and vice versa. As we have seen, they are related because the mean sun moves across celestial meridians at an angular rate of 15° per hour, or 360° every 24 hours. Thus, we can refer to positions on earth with reference to both arc and time. This is a useful and necessary concept.

If each 15° of arc represents one hour of time, then 1° must equal $\frac{1}{15}$ of an hour, or four minutes. Similarly, if 1° of arc equals four minutes of time, then one second of arc must equal $\frac{1}{60}$ of four minutes, or 15 seconds of time. The following table summarizes the relationships between time and arc:

Time	Arc
24 hours	360 degrees
60 minutes	15 degrees
4 minutes	60 minutes
60 seconds	15 minutes
4 seconds	1 minute
1 second	0.25 minute/15 sec.

The arithmetic uses the following rules: To convert time to arc:

1. Multiply the hours of time by 15 to obtain degrees of arc.
2. Divide the minutes of time by four to obtain degrees of arc, and multiply the remainder by 15 to obtain minutes of arc.
3. Divide the seconds of time by four to obtain minutes of arc, and multiply the remainder by 15 to obtain seconds of arc.
4. Add the resulting hours, minutes, and seconds.

Example: Convert 14 hours 21 minutes 39 seconds of time to units of arc.

1. 14 hr × 15 = 210°
2. 21 min ÷ 4 = 5° 15' (remainder 1 × 15 = 15 minutes)
3. 39 sec ÷ 4 = 9' 45" (remainder 3 × 15 = 45 seconds)
4. Sum = 215° 24' 45"

To convert arc to time, do the opposite, as follows:

1. Divide degrees of arc by 15 to obtain hours of time, and multiply the remainder by four to obtain minutes of time (or multiply tenths and hundredths of hours by 60 to obtain minutes of time).
2. Divide minutes of arc by 15 to obtain minutes of time, and multiply the remainder by four to obtain seconds of time.
3. Divide seconds of arc by 15 to obtain seconds of time.
4. Add the resulting hours, minutes, and seconds.

Example: Convert 215° 24' 45" of arc to time units.

1. 215° ÷ 15 = 14 hrs. 20 mins. (remainder 5 × 4 = 20)
2. 24' ÷ 15 = 01 min. 36 secs. (remainder 9 × 4 = 36)
3. 45" ÷ 15 = 03 secs.
4. Sum = 14 hrs. 21 mins. 39 secs.

There are two other methods of converting arc to time. The first is to use a navigational calculator or computer program. The second is to use tables provided in the *Nautical Almanac*. Either option obviates the foregoing calculations. Use Figure 14-3, the arc-to-time conversion table from the *Nautical Almanac,* to solve the previous examples, and you'll sec how easy it is.

Time and Longitude

Think of a stationary celestial reference point over a place on the earth. In one hour the earth will have rotated until that position is 15° away. Note that any difference in longitude between two places can also be expressed as a measure of the time it took to separate them by rotation of the earth. Time is later at places east of us, and earlier at places west of us. That difference in time (expressed in units of time) is equal to the difference in longitude (expressed in units of arc).

The time directly opposite anyone's position on earth is exactly 12 hours different. When you travel around the world you gain or lose 24 hours. To keep the correct date, the *international date line* was established approximately on the 180° line of longitude in the central Pacific Ocean—set there so that the change of date affects the fewest people. (Imagine the confusion if the date line were drawn through the middle of the United States!)

Whenever you cross the international date line, you must change the date. Traveling eastward, time gets later and later; as you cross the date line you change the date to a day earlier to compensate. Therefore, when crossing the date line toward the east you subtract a day; toward the west you add a day. The date immediately to the west of the line is always one day later than on the east side.

Figure 14-3. *You can convert arc to time and vice versa by computation or by using tables in the* Nautical Almanac, *shown here. You can also use a computer program or navigational calculator.*

CONVERSION OF ARC TO TIME

0°–59°		60°–119°		120°–179°		180°–239°		240°–299°		300°–359°			0′·00	0′·25	0′·50	0′·75
°	h m	°	h m	°	h m	°	h m	°	h m	°	h m	′	m s	m s	m s	m s
0	0 00	60	4 00	120	8 00	180	12 00	240	16 00	300	20 00	0	0 00	0 01	0 02	0 03
1	0 04	61	4 04	121	8 04	181	12 04	241	16 04	301	20 04	1	0 04	0 05	0 06	0 07
2	0 08	62	4 08	122	8 08	182	12 08	242	16 08	302	20 08	2	0 08	0 09	0 10	0 11
3	0 12	63	4 12	123	8 12	183	12 12	243	16 12	303	20 12	3	0 12	0 13	0 14	0 15
4	0 16	64	4 16	124	8 16	184	12 16	244	16 16	304	20 16	4	0 16	0 17	0 18	0 19
5	0 20	65	4 20	125	8 20	185	12 20	245	16 20	305	20 20	5	0 20	0 21	0 22	0 23
6	0 24	66	4 24	126	8 24	186	12 24	246	16 24	306	20 24	6	0 24	0 25	0 26	0 27
7	0 28	67	4 28	127	8 28	187	12 28	247	16 28	307	20 28	7	0 28	0 29	0 30	0 31
8	0 32	68	4 32	128	8 32	188	12 32	248	16 32	308	20 32	8	0 32	0 33	0 34	0 35
9	0 36	69	4 36	129	8 36	189	12 36	249	16 36	309	20 36	9	0 36	0 37	0 38	0 39
10	0 40	70	4 40	130	8 40	190	12 40	250	16 40	310	20 40	10	0 40	0 41	0 42	0 43
11	0 44	71	4 44	131	8 44	191	12 44	251	16 44	311	20 44	11	0 44	0 45	0 46	0 47
12	0 48	72	4 48	132	8 48	192	12 48	252	16 48	312	20 48	12	0 48	0 49	0 50	0 51
13	0 52	73	4 52	133	8 52	193	12 52	253	16 52	313	20 52	13	0 52	0 53	0 54	0 55
14	0 56	74	4 56	134	8 56	194	12 56	254	16 56	314	20 56	14	0 56	0 57	0 58	0 59
15	1 00	75	5 00	135	9 00	195	13 00	255	17 00	315	21 00	15	1 00	1 01	1 02	1 03
16	1 04	76	5 04	136	9 04	196	13 04	256	17 04	316	21 04	16	1 04	1 05	1 06	1 07
17	1 08	77	5 08	137	9 08	197	13 08	257	17 08	317	21 08	17	1 08	1 09	1 10	1 11
18	1 12	78	5 12	138	9 12	198	13 12	258	17 12	318	21 12	18	1 12	1 13	1 14	1 15
19	1 16	79	5 16	139	9 16	199	13 16	259	17 16	319	21 16	19	1 16	1 17	1 18	1 19
20	1 20	80	5 20	140	9 20	200	13 20	260	17 20	320	21 20	20	1 20	1 21	1 22	1 23
21	1 24	81	5 24	141	9 24	201	13 24	261	17 24	321	21 24	21	1 24	1 25	1 26	1 27
22	1 28	82	5 28	142	9 28	202	13 28	262	17 28	322	21 28	22	1 28	1 29	1 30	1 31
23	1 32	83	5 32	143	9 32	203	13 32	263	17 32	323	21 32	23	1 32	1 33	1 34	1 35
24	1 36	84	5 36	144	9 36	204	13 36	264	17 36	324	21 36	24	1 36	1 37	1 38	1 39
25	1 40	85	5 40	145	9 40	205	13 40	265	17 40	325	21 40	25	1 40	1 41	1 42	1 43
26	1 44	86	5 44	146	9 44	206	13 44	266	17 44	326	21 44	26	1 44	1 45	1 46	1 47
27	1 48	87	5 48	147	9 48	207	13 48	267	17 48	327	21 48	27	1 48	1 49	1 50	1 51
28	1 52	88	5 52	148	9 52	208	13 52	268	17 52	328	21 52	28	1 52	1 53	1 54	1 55
29	1 56	89	5 56	149	9 56	209	13 56	269	17 56	329	21 56	29	1 56	1 57	1 58	1 59
30	2 00	90	6 00	150	10 00	210	14 00	270	18 00	330	22 00	30	2 00	2 01	2 02	2 03
31	2 04	91	6 04	151	10 04	211	14 04	271	18 04	331	22 04	31	2 04	2 05	2 06	2 07
32	2 08	92	6 08	152	10 08	212	14 08	272	18 08	332	22 08	32	2 08	2 09	2 10	2 11
33	2 12	93	6 12	153	10 12	213	14 12	273	18 12	333	22 12	33	2 12	2 13	2 14	2 15
34	2 16	94	6 16	154	10 16	214	14 16	274	18 16	334	22 16	34	2 16	2 17	2 18	2 19
35	2 20	95	6 20	155	10 20	215	14 20	275	18 20	335	22 20	35	2 20	2 21	2 22	2 23
36	2 24	96	6 24	156	10 24	216	14 24	276	18 24	336	22 24	36	2 24	2 25	2 26	2 27
37	2 28	97	6 28	157	10 28	217	14 28	277	18 28	337	22 28	37	2 28	2 29	2 30	2 31
38	2 32	98	6 32	158	10 32	218	14 32	278	18 32	338	22 32	38	2 32	2 33	2 34	2 35
39	2 36	99	6 36	159	10 36	219	14 36	279	18 36	339	22 36	39	2 36	2 37	2 38	2 39
40	2 40	100	6 40	160	10 40	220	14 40	280	18 40	340	22 40	40	2 40	2 41	2 42	2 43
41	2 44	101	6 44	161	10 44	221	14 44	281	18 44	341	22 44	41	2 44	2 45	2 46	2 47
42	2 48	102	6 48	162	10 48	222	14 48	282	18 48	342	22 48	42	2 48	2 49	2 50	2 51
43	2 52	103	6 52	163	10 52	223	14 52	283	18 52	343	22 52	43	2 52	2 53	2 54	2 55
44	2 56	104	6 56	164	10 56	224	14 56	284	18 56	344	22 56	44	2 56	2 57	2 58	2 59
45	3 00	105	7 00	165	11 00	225	15 00	285	19 00	345	23 00	45	3 00	3 01	3 02	3 03
46	3 04	106	7 04	166	11 04	226	15 04	286	19 04	346	23 04	46	3 04	3 05	3 06	3 07
47	3 08	107	7 08	167	11 08	227	15 08	287	19 08	347	23 08	47	3 08	3 09	3 10	3 11
48	3 12	108	7 12	168	11 12	228	15 12	288	19 12	348	23 12	48	3 12	3 13	3 14	3 15
49	3 16	109	7 16	169	11 16	229	15 16	289	19 16	349	23 16	49	3 16	3 17	3 18	3 19
50	3 20	110	7 20	170	11 20	230	15 20	290	19 20	350	23 20	50	3 20	3 21	3 22	3 23
51	3 24	111	7 24	171	11 24	231	15 24	291	19 24	351	23 24	51	3 24	3 25	3 26	3 27
52	3 28	112	7 28	172	11 28	232	15 28	292	19 28	352	23 28	52	3 28	3 29	3 30	3 31
53	3 32	113	7 32	173	11 32	233	15 32	293	19 32	353	23 32	53	3 32	3 33	3 34	3 35
54	3 36	114	7 36	174	11 36	234	15 36	294	19 36	354	23 36	54	3 36	3 37	3 38	3 39
55	3 40	115	7 40	175	11 40	235	15 40	295	19 40	355	23 40	55	3 40	3 41	3 42	3 43
56	3 44	116	7 44	176	11 44	236	15 44	296	19 44	356	23 44	56	3 44	3 45	3 46	3 47
57	3 48	117	7 48	177	11 48	237	15 48	297	19 48	357	23 48	57	3 48	3 49	3 50	3 51
58	3 52	118	7 52	178	11 52	238	15 52	298	19 52	358	23 52	58	3 52	3 53	3 54	3 55
59	3 56	119	7 56	179	11 56	239	15 56	299	19 56	359	23 56	59	3 56	3 57	3 58	3 59

The above table is for converting expressions in arc to their equivalent in time; its main use in this Almanac is for the conversion of longitude for application to L.M.T. (*added* if *west*, *subtracted* if *east*) to give G.M.T. or vice versa, particularly in the case of sunrise, sunset, etc.

On December 30, 1899, the ship Warrimoo *was en route from Vancouver, British Columbia, to Australia. Her clever and seasoned skipper, Captain John D. S. Phillips, was advised that at about midnight the ship would be crossing the intersection of the international date line and the equator. Captain Phillips changed course and speed to ensure that at exactly midnight the ship would lie at that precise point. So it happened. At 0000 hours the ship's bow was in the southern hemisphere at the height of summer and the stern was in the northern hemisphere winter. At the bow it was January 1, 1900; at the stern it was still December 30, 1899. The* Warrimoo *thus lay in two different days, two different months, two different seasons, two different years, and two different centuries. The passengers were disappointed, though, because a full day was added and New Year's Eve, December 31, 1899, never occurred for them—but they probably celebrated anyway!*

The easiest way to avoid problems with time when working celestial observations is to use *Greenwich Mean Time (GMT)* as your reference time and keep your chronometer or comparing watch set to GMT. Then, it's not necessary to convert local time to GMT for celestial observations.

Zone Time and Local Mean Time

For navigational purposes, it would be confusing to use the normal 12-hour time scale with "A.M." and "P.M." designations. Instead, 24-hour time, or "military time," is used, in which all times after 12:00 noon are expressed as 12 plus the number of hours after 12:00 noon, up to 2400 (or 0000) hours. You get used to military time with a little practice. One o'clock A.M. is 0100 (said "oh-one-hundred"). One o'clock P.M. is 1300 (said "thirteen-hundred"), two o'clock P.M. is 1400, and so on.

For convenience in human affairs, the world is divided into 24 time zones of 15° each. (See Figure 14-4.) With some variations due to local custom, convenience, and geography, each time zone is bordered by the meridians at the 15° intervals and is centered on the meridian midway between them. Each zone is designated with a letter and a number. The letters run eastward from A east of Greenwich, England, to M at the international date line (180° longitude), and then start again westward from N west of Greenwich through Y at the date line. The Greenwich zone itself is designated Z (or Zulu) time.

The numbers of each zone represent the difference in hours between the local zone and Greenwich (Zulu) time. They are positive to the west of Greenwich and negative to the east. These numbers are given a positive or negative sign to indicate what you must do to the local time to convert to Greenwich time. For example, the U.S. east coast is in the R (Romeo) or +5 time zone (except during daylight savings time when it is +4). To convert any time on the east coast to Greenwich time, add five hours. If the result is more than 24, add one day. Noon in the +5 time zone is 1200 + 5 = 1700 hours Zulu (Greenwich) time. The time of 2200 hours (10 P.M.) on the east coast is 0300 on the next day at Greenwich.

Local Mean Time is time reckoned with reference to your local meridian. Unless you are exactly on the central meridian of the time zone, your LMT will be later or earlier than your zone time depending on whether you are east or west of the central meridian of your zone.

You can calculate LMT to determine in advance the exact time of twilight for taking morning and evening star sights. As you'll see, other techniques are available.

Keeping Time at Sea

The kind of timepiece you choose depends on the role celestial navigation will play in your offshore navigation and on the length of passages you plan. If you plan to use celes-

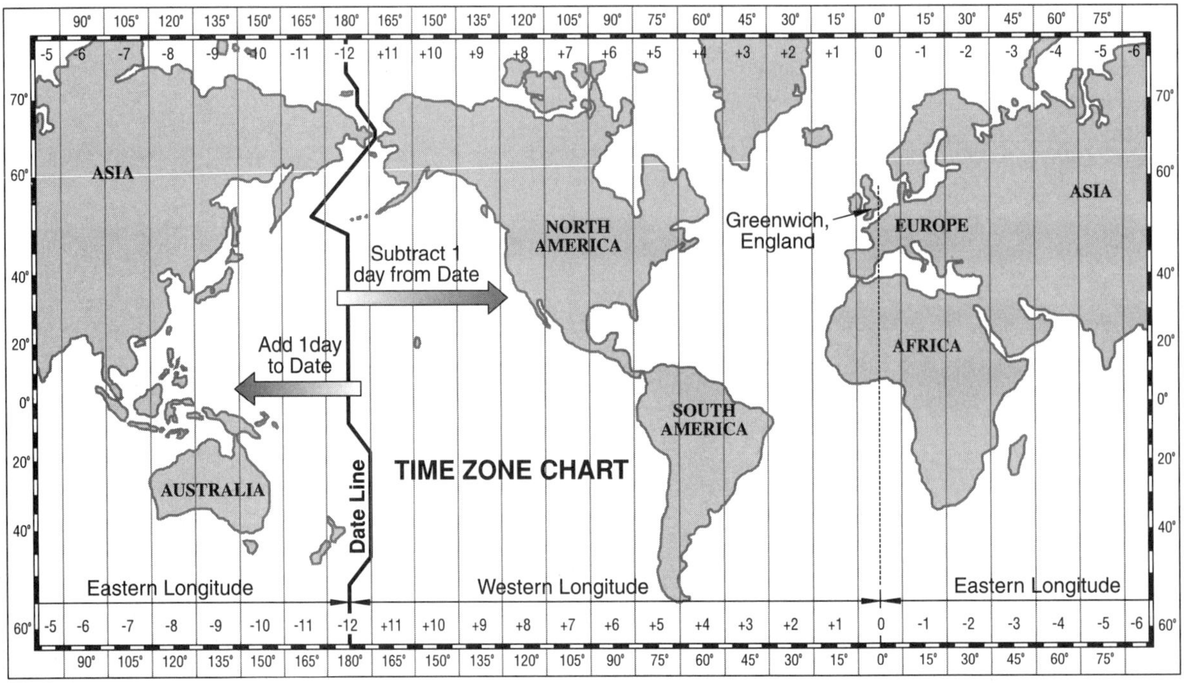

Figure 14-4. *The Time Zone Chart of the World shows the times kept in locations around the world and indicates the central meridian of each zone.*

tial only as a backup or emergency method, then you need not keep precise navigational time on your vessel; you can obtain it when needed over the radio. And, for reasonably short passages, you can use any watch with a known error and known rate of change.

A *chronometer,* which is a very precise type of clock, is the choice of navigators who want a source of accurate time that doesn't rely on radio time checks. Remember that you need to know time to the nearest second to obtain a precise line of position from a celestial body (other than a latitude line).

In the days before radio, time signals were sent to ships in major harbors with a time ball, *a large black sphere mounted on a pole atop a tower or high building near the harbor. Just before noon each day, the ball was raised to the peak of the pole. At the stroke of noon it was dropped to the bottom of the pole and all the navigators in the harbor could set their clocks or note their errors. Today, each December 31 at midnight, a ball in Times Square, New York City, drops to signify the exact start of the new year.*

Figure 14-5. *The modern quartz crystal chronometer is dependable, stable, and ideal for use by serious celestial navigators. You should also have a means of receiving time ticks if celestial is your primary navigation method.*

There are two basic types of chronometers: the older spring-wound and the modern crystal-controlled style. The spring-wound models are not suitable for use on small craft because they require a stable environment for best accuracy and a good deal more care and maintenance than the crystal ones. A good crystal-controlled chronometer (such as depicted in Figure 14-5) costs no more than the spring-wound type, is more accurate, more dependable, and more stable at sea, especially aboard small craft.

If celestial is to be your primary offshore navigational tool, you should have a chronometer intended for seagoing use. For crystal-controlled types, carry spare batteries and know how to charge them. Mount the chronometer permanently in a dry, safe place, set it several days before sailing, and determine its rate of change by daily reference to time signals.

Navigators use radio *time signals* to periodically check their chronometers and to set a comparing watch that they use to time fixes. Also, you can call the U.S. Naval Observatory time service at (202)762-1401 for the time kept on the observatory's master clock.

Radio time signals accurate to within 0.001 second are broadcast by the National Institute of Standards and Technology (NIST) on high seas frequencies of 2.5, 5, 10, 15, and 20 megahertz. These voice broadcasts are available worldwide around the clock. Other countries broadcast various types of time signal broadcasts on different frequencies; these are summarized in *Pub. 117, Radio Navigational Aids,* published by the National Imagery and Mapping Agency (NIMA).

Many amateur celestial navigators use good quality quartz crystal watches to time sights. These should be checked regularly with a time tick. A separate stopwatch or a wristwatch with a stopwatch function is useful because it can be started on a radio or telephone time tick and the elapsed time added to the stated time. A quality quartz crystal watch can serve as your primary timepiece as long as you establish its rate and check it regularly.

In 1714, in response to a navigational disaster that sent a squadron of ships and more than 2,000 sailors to the bottom of the sea, the British government established the Board of Longitude to sponsor new methods to find longitude at sea. A number of different methods were tried, but it soon became clear that the solution lay in accurate measurement of time.

The Board offered a reward for any device that could find the longitude after a voyage of six weeks. The reward was to be 10,000 pounds for an accuracy within 1° of longitude, 15,000 pounds within 40 minutes, and 20,000 pounds within 30 minutes.

John Harrison, a carpenter's son born in 1693, was a clockmaker. By 1728 he had completed plans for his chronometer, and by 1735 he had a working model. After a qualifying sea voyage, it produced an error of only three minutes of longitude—far better than required to win the award. But the Board hesitated, made a small partial payment, and demanded additional models. It took Harrison until 1761 to develop his fourth model, which passed the Board's test handily—it had less than two minutes of time error after a voyage of five months on two different ships.

Harrison again applied for the reward and was again refused. The Board agreed that Harrison's clock exceeded their standards, but insisted on building one of its own from his plans and demanded that he turn over all four models and all plans to the Board. By this time Harrison was 80 years old. Finally, in 1773 the King intervened and Harrison was paid. Just three years later, he died on his birthday, March 24, 1776.

CHAPTER FIFTEEN

The Almanacs

TO FIND YOUR POSITION on earth relative to a heavenly body, you have to know exactly where the body is. An *almanac* gives you the positions in the sky (and thus the position on the earth directly below it, known as the geographic position or GP) of stars, planets, the sun, and the moon at any time of the year.

Once you know the position of a body and measure its altitude in the sky from your position, you use sight reduction tables, a calculator, or a computer to find the unknowns in a huge triangle on the surface of the earth whose sides connect your position, the body's *geographic position (GP),* and a pole (N or S). In this process, you determine your distance from the body's GP, which is the radius of a giant circle called a circle of *equal altitude.* This circle is a line of position (LOP).

Types of Almanacs

There are several types of almanacs: the *Astronomical Almanac* used by astronomers; the *Air Almanac* used by aircraft and many marine navigators; and the *Nautical Almanac* used almost exclusively for marine navigation. This book examines the latter because it's intended especially for surface navigation.

The *Astronomical Almanac* is much more precise than the other two, but you need to go through a more elaborate process to use it for marine navigation. In any case, your attempt to get a more accurate celestial fix using the *Astronomical Almanac*'s more precise data would likely be confounded by a variety of errors not related to almanacs. No fix can be more accurate than its least accurate factor.

Many marine navigators prefer to use the *Air Almanac* in conjunction with *Pub. 249, Sight Reduction Tables for Air Navigation.* It's slightly easier to use, but slightly less accurate than the *Nautical Almanac.* Use of the *Air Almanac* was even more common before the modern *Pub. 229, Sight Reduction Tables for Marine Navigation* was introduced in the early 1970s as a companion to the *Nautical Almanac.*

The former tables for marine navigation (known as *Pub. 214,* that had accompanied the *Nautical Almanac*) required a more tedious process than the easier *Air Almanac,* prompting the use of the latter by many marine navigators. Its reduced accuracy was an acceptable trade-off. However, the current *Pub. 229* is easier to use than the former *Pub. 214* and is more accurate than the *Air Almanac,* making it the best choice for modern celestial work.

The *Nautical Almanac* is produced jointly by the *U.S. Naval Observatory* and the *Royal Greenwich Observatory.* For many years, almanacs were produced and sold by the government through sales agents. Now, however, the government produces almanacs only for its own use and contracts out the production and distribution of almanacs for private use. The government and private versions are identical in format and data, except that the private editions may contain advertising and other types of additional data.

Another type, the *computerized almanac,* provides data about the locations of bodies—and much more. Just as almanacs have been computerized, so has the entire celestial solution. Both publicly and privately produced computerized almanacs include not only the positions of bodies, but also calculate your position, among other things, when you make the required entries.

One type of computer almanac—the *Interactive Computer Ephemeris (ICE)*—is in the form of a software program that you can run on your personal computer. This publicly produced almanac from the U.S. Naval Observatory contains not only the usual data on positions of celestial bodies, but also pre-computes altitudes and azimuths of stars for sight planning, performs complete sight reduction with inputs of time, DR position, and altitude of a body, and computes the following: times of twilight for star sights; great-circle and rhumb line routes; and compass error from celestial sights. It also plots the fix on the screen and analyzes the LOPs for accuracy. The ICE is in DOS format.

A second type of computerized almanac is a battery-powered hand-held calculator that's programmed with almanac data and routines to do most of the functions of the Naval Observatory's ICE program. These are better suited for use on small craft because they don't require a separate computer. Several types are available and their prices are reasonable.

THE
NAUTICAL ALMANAC
FOR THE YEAR
1997

PUB. NO. 229
VOL. 4

SIGHT REDUCTION TABLES
FOR
MARINE NAVIGATION
LATITUDES 45°–60°, Inclusive

DEFENSE MAPPING AGENCY
HYDROGRAPHIC/TOPOGRAPHIC CENTER

Figure 15-1. *The* Nautical Almanac *is used in conjunction with* Pub. 229, Sight Reduction Tables for Marine Navigation, *to solve celestial navigation problems.*

Choosing a Method of Sight Reduction

Before buying an almanac you must choose a method of sight reduction. Although this book focuses on the *Nautical Almanac* and *Pub. 229,* you can easily shift to the *Air Almanac* and *Pub. 249* solution if you desire. Once you master *Pub. 229* you won't have any difficulty understanding the format of the *Air Almanac.*

This author recommends that the beginning navigator use a hand-held navigational calculator for sight reduction until the general process is understood and then learn the solution by tables. This recommendation is bound to upset traditionalists who insist on solving every sight the old-fashioned way—and who reason, with some justification, that reliance

Figure 15-2. *A navigational calculator contains almanac data and computer programs to solve celestial and many other types of navigation problems. (Courtesy of Celesticomp and Celestaire)*

on a battery-powered computer device will foster dependence on it and court disaster when it fails.

However, navigational calculators are the nearest thing to foolproof that can be found in navigation today; they are reliable, long-lasting, and certainly hold up in marine use if cared for properly—and they are no more subject to damage at sea than your sextant. Using a calculator removes nearly all of the tedium and mathematics from the solution by eliminating cumbersome tables and long computations that are difficult on a small boat at sea, provides a more accurate LOP, and drastically reduces the elapsed time from sight to fix. With a calculator you're more likely to use celestial navigation and build confidence and skill. In short, navigational calculators make celestial an easy method of position-finding, rather than a chore.

Although you can prudently use a navigational calculator regularly for sights, you also need to know how to use the almanac and sight reduction tables (or the relevant trigonometric formulas) should your calculator fail. Regular practice in this, with a calculator as a check, is essential.

Format of the Nautical Almanac

Nautical Almanac data, produced by the U.S. Naval Observatory in cooperation with the British Admiralty, is commercially available from chart-sales agents and boating stores worldwide. Most of the pages are taken up with tabulations of the coordinates of bodies used in navigation, given to the nearest 0.1' of arc. Each set of facing pages contains data for three days.

Greenwich hour angle (GHA), sidereal hour angle (SHA), and declination are the principal coordinates used to define the locations of bodies on the celestial sphere. The GHA is the angular measurement of a body west of the prime meridian. SHA is the angular measurement (of a star) west of the arbitrary celestial reference point, Aries. Declination corresponds to latitude. You will learn how to use these coordinates in the next chapter.

The left-hand page contains GHA and declination data for Aries, Venus, Mars, Jupiter, and Saturn, plus the sidereal hour angle (SHA) of the 57 commonly used navigational stars. The magnitude of each planet is given at the head of its column. The right-hand page contains GHA and declination data for the sun and moon, plus tables to compute sunrise, sunset, moonrise, moonset, and the equation of time.

Following the tabulations of GHA, there are examples and explanations of the different solutions that are possible with the almanac data. That section is followed by a *time-zone table* that lists the difference in time between Greenwich and many other places in the world. Next are star charts to aid in locating stars, and a complete listing of the SHA and declination of 173 stars, including those listed on the daily pages.

The *Polaris tables* follow next and give the corrections that you apply to Polaris sights to obtain a latitude line. Then there is a section that contains directions and examples for the solution of different sights using both calculator and concise sight reduction tables in the almanac. (These tables use a different sight reduction method than *Pub. 229*.)

156 1996 AUGUST 7, 8, 9 (WED., THURS., FRI.)

UT (GMT)	ARIES	VENUS −4.4		MARS +1.5		JUPITER −2.6		SATURN +0.7		STARS		
d h	G.H.A.	G.H.A.	Dec.	G.H.A.	Dec.	G.H.A.	Dec.	G.H.A.	Dec.	Name	S.H.A.	Dec.
	° ′	° ′	° ′	° ′	° ′	° ′	° ′	° ′	° ′		° ′	° ′
7 00	315 47.7	226 01.4	N19 22.1	216 51.7	N23 43.9	35 59.9	S23 16.2	308 17.9	N 0 31.9	Acamar	315 28.1	S40 18.9
01	330 50.1	241 01.6	22.3	231 52.4	43.8	51 02.6	16.3	323 20.4	31.9	Achernar	335 36.1	S57 15.0
02	345 52.6	256 01.9	22.4	246 53.0	43.7	66 05.2	16.3	338 22.9	31.8	Acrux	173 23.9	S63 05.0
03	0 55.1	271 02.1	· · 22.6	261 53.7	· · 43.7	81 07.9	· · 16.3	353 25.5	· · 31.8	Adhara	255 22.9	S28 58.0
04	15 57.5	286 02.4	22.8	276 54.4	43.6	96 10.6	16.3	8 28.0	31.8	Aldebaran	291 04.2	N16 30.0
05	31 00.0	301 02.6	22.9	291 55.0	43.5	111 13.3	16.3	23 30.5	31.7			
06	46 02.5	316 02.9	N19 23.1	306 55.7	N23 43.4	126 16.0	S23 16.4	38 33.1	N 0 31.7	Alioth	166 32.2	N55 59.0
W 07	61 04.9	331 03.1	23.2	321 56.3	43.4	141 18.7	16.4	53 35.6	31.6	Alkaid	153 09.1	N49 20.2
E 08	76 07.4	346 03.3	23.4	336 57.0	43.3	156 21.4	16.4	68 38.1	31.6	Al Na'ir	27 59.3	S46 58.4
D 09	91 09.8	1 03.6	· · 23.5	351 57.7	· · 43.2	171 24.0	· · 16.4	83 40.7	· · 31.6	Alnilam	275 59.5	S 1 12.3
N 10	106 12.3	16 03.8	23.7	6 58.3	43.1	186 26.7	16.4	98 43.2	31.5	Alphard	218 08.9	S 8 38.7
E 11	121 14.8	31 04.1	23.8	21 59.0	43.1	201 29.4	16.5	113 45.8	31.5			
S 12	136 17.2	46 04.3	N19 24.0	36 59.6	N23 43.0	216 32.1	S23 16.5	128 48.3	N 0 31.4	Alphecca	126 21.8	N26 43.9
D 13	151 19.7	61 04.5	24.1	52 00.3	42.9	231 34.8	16.5	143 50.8	31.4	Alpheratz	357 56.4	N29 04.3
A 14	166 22.2	76 04.8	24.3	67 00.9	42.8	246 37.5	16.5	158 53.4	31.4	Altair	62 20.3	N 8 51.8
Y 15	181 24.6	91 05.0	· · 24.4	82 01.6	· · 42.8	261 40.1	· · 16.5	173 55.9	· · 31.3	Ankaa	353 28.0	S42 19.2
16	196 27.1	106 05.2	24.6	97 02.3	42.7	276 42.8	16.5	188 58.4	31.3	Antares	112 41.8	S26 25.4
17	211 29.6	121 05.4	24.7	112 02.9	42.6	291 45.5	16.6	204 01.0	31.2			
18	226 32.0	136 05.7	N19 24.9	127 03.6	N23 42.5	306 48.2	S23 16.6	219 03.5	N 0 31.2	Arcturus	146 07.4	N19 12.3
19	241 34.5	151 05.9	25.0	142 04.2	42.4	321 50.9	16.6	234 06.0	31.1	Atria	107 54.7	S69 01.4
20	256 37.0	166 06.1	25.2	157 04.9	42.4	336 53.5	16.6	249 08.6	31.1	Avior	234 23.8	S59 30.0
21	271 39.4	181 06.3	· · 25.3	172 05.6	· · 42.3	351 56.2	· · 16.6	264 11.1	· · 31.1	Bellatrix	278 45.9	N 6 20.7
22	286 41.9	196 06.6	25.5	187 06.2	42.2	6 58.9	16.7	279 13.6	31.0	Betelgeuse	271 15.3	N 7 24.3
23	301 44.3	211 06.8	25.6	202 06.9	42.1	22 01.6	16.7	294 16.2	31.0			
8 00	316 46.8	226 07.0	N19 25.8	217 07.5	N23 42.0	37 04.3	S23 16.7	309 18.7	N 0 30.9	Canopus	264 02.2	S52 41.6
01	331 49.3	241 07.2	25.9	232 08.2	42.0	52 06.9	16.7	324 21.2	30.9	Capella	280 53.6	N45 59.4
02	346 51.7	256 07.4	26.1	247 08.9	41.9	67 09.6	16.7	339 23.8	30.8	Deneb	49 39.7	N45 16.3
03	1 54.2	271 07.7	· · 26.2	262 09.5	· · 41.8	82 12.3	· · 16.8	354 26.3	· · 30.8	Denebola	182 46.9	N14 35.6
04	16 56.7	286 07.9	26.4	277 10.2	41.7	97 15.0	16.8	9 28.9	30.8	Diphda	349 08.5	S18 00.1
05	31 59.1	301 08.1	26.5	292 10.8	41.6	112 17.7	16.8	24 31.4	30.7			
06	47 01.6	316 08.3	N19 26.6	307 11.5	N23 41.5	127 20.3	S23 16.8	39 33.9	N 0 30.7	Dubhe	194 08.0	N61 46.3
07	62 04.1	331 08.5	26.8	322 12.2	41.5	142 23.0	16.8	54 36.5	30.6	Elnath	278 29.0	N28 36.1
T 08	77 06.5	346 08.7	26.9	337 12.8	41.4	157 25.7	16.8	69 39.0	30.6	Eltanin	90 51.7	N51 29.7
H 09	92 09.0	1 08.9	· · 27.1	352 13.5	· · 41.3	172 28.4	· · 16.9	84 41.5	· · 30.6	Enif	33 59.3	N 9 51.8
U 10	107 11.4	16 09.1	27.2	7 14.1	41.2	187 31.0	16.9	99 44.1	30.5	Fomalhaut	15 37.7	S29 38.2
R 11	122 13.9	31 09.3	27.4	22 14.8	41.1	202 33.7	16.9	114 46.6	30.5			
S 12	137 16.4	46 09.5	N19 27.5	37 15.5	N23 41.0	217 36.4	S23 16.9	129 49.2	N 0 30.4	Gacrux	172 15.4	S57 05.8
D 13	152 18.8	61 09.7	27.6	52 16.1	41.0	232 39.1	16.9	144 51.7	30.4	Gienah	176 05.6	S17 31.4
A 14	167 21.3	76 09.9	27.8	67 16.8	40.9	247 41.8	16.9	159 54.2	30.3	Hadar	149 06.1	S60 21.6
Y 15	182 23.8	91 10.1	· · 27.9	82 17.5	· · 40.8	262 44.4	· · 17.0	174 56.8	· · 30.3	Hamal	328 15.1	N23 26.7
16	197 26.2	106 10.3	28.1	97 18.1	40.7	277 47.1	17.0	189 59.3	30.2	Kaus Aust.	84 00.4	S34 23.1
17	212 28.7	121 10.5	28.2	112 18.8	40.6	292 49.8	17.0	205 01.8	30.2			
18	227 31.2	136 10.7	N19 28.3	127 19.4	N23 40.5	307 52.5	S23 17.0	220 04.4	N 0 30.2	Kochab	137 19.7	N74 10.6
19	242 33.6	151 10.9	28.5	142 20.1	40.4	322 55.1	17.0	235 06.9	30.1	Markab	13 50.7	N15 11.3
20	257 36.1	166 11.1	28.6	157 20.8	40.4	337 57.8	17.1	250 09.5	30.1	Menkar	314 28.4	N 4 04.6
21	272 38.6	181 11.3	· · 28.8	172 21.4	· · 40.3	353 00.5	· · 17.1	265 12.0	· · 30.0	Menkent	148 22.7	S36 21.3
22	287 41.0	196 11.5	28.9	187 22.1	40.2	8 03.2	17.1	280 14.5	30.0	Miaplacidus	221 43.1	S69 42.3
23	302 43.5	211 11.7	29.0	202 22.8	40.1	23 05.8	17.1	295 17.1	29.9			
9 00	317 45.9	226 11.9	N19 29.2	217 23.4	N23 40.0	38 08.5	S23 17.1	310 19.6	N 0 29.9	Mirfak	308 58.7	N49 50.7
01	332 48.4	241 12.1	29.3	232 24.1	39.9	53 11.2	17.1	325 22.2	29.9	Nunki	76 13.8	S26 17.9
02	347 50.9	256 12.2	29.4	247 24.8	39.8	68 13.8	17.2	340 24.7	29.8	Peacock	53 38.7	S56 44.6
03	2 53.3	271 12.4	· · 29.6	262 25.4	· · 39.7	83 16.5	· · 17.2	355 27.2	· · 29.8	Pollux	243 43.7	N28 02.0
04	17 55.8	286 12.6	29.7	277 26.1	39.6	98 19.2	17.2	10 29.8	29.7	Procyon	245 13.4	N 5 14.0
05	32 58.3	301 12.8	29.8	292 26.7	39.5	113 21.9	17.2	25 32.3	29.7			
06	48 00.7	316 13.0	N19 30.0	307 27.4	N23 39.5	128 24.5	S23 17.2	40 34.9	N 0 29.6	Rasalhague	96 18.1	N12 34.0
07	63 03.2	331 13.1	30.1	322 28.1	39.4	143 27.2	17.3	55 37.4	29.6	Regulus	207 57.4	N11 59.1
08	78 05.7	346 13.3	30.2	337 28.7	39.3	158 29.9	17.3	70 39.9	29.5	Rigel	281 24.5	S 8 12.3
F 09	93 08.1	1 13.5	· · 30.4	352 29.4	· · 39.2	173 32.5	· · 17.3	85 42.5	· · 29.5	Rigil Kent.	140 09.1	S60 49.4
R 10	108 10.6	16 13.7	30.5	7 30.1	39.1	188 35.2	17.3	100 45.0	29.5	Sabik	102 27.0	S15 43.1
I 11	123 13.1	31 13.9	30.6	22 30.7	39.0	203 37.9	17.3	115 47.6	29.4			
D 12	138 15.5	46 14.0	N19 30.8	37 31.4	N23 38.9	218 40.5	S23 17.3	130 50.1	N 0 29.4	Schedar	349 54.7	N56 31.0
A 13	153 18.0	61 14.2	30.9	52 32.1	38.8	233 43.2	17.4	145 52.6	29.3	Shaula	96 39.0	S37 06.0
Y 14	168 20.4	76 14.4	31.0	67 32.7	38.7	248 45.9	17.4	160 55.2	29.3	Sirius	258 45.2	S16 42.7
15	183 22.9	91 14.5	· · 31.2	82 33.4	· · 38.6	263 48.6	· · 17.4	175 57.7	· · 29.2	Spica	158 44.8	S11 08.6
16	198 25.4	106 14.7	31.3	97 34.1	38.5	278 51.2	17.4	191 00.3	29.2	Suhail	223 02.2	S43 25.2
17	213 27.8	121 14.9	31.4	112 34.7	38.4	293 53.9	17.4	206 02.8	29.1			
18	228 30.3	136 15.0	N19 31.6	127 35.4	N23 38.3	308 56.6	S23 17.4	221 05.4	N 0 29.1	Vega	80 47.2	N38 47.2
19	243 32.8	151 15.2	31.7	142 36.1	38.2	323 59.2	17.5	236 07.9	29.1	Zuben'ubi	137 19.6	S16 01.6
20	258 35.2	166 15.4	31.8	157 36.7	38.2	339 01.9	17.5	251 10.4	29.0		S.H.A.	Mer. Pass.
21	273 37.7	181 15.5	· · 31.9	172 37.4	· · 38.1	354 04.6	· · 17.5	266 13.0	· · 29.0		° ′	h m
22	288 40.2	196 15.7	32.1	187 38.1	38.0	9 07.2	17.5	281 15.5	28.9	Venus	269 20.2	8 55
23	303 42.6	211 15.8	32.2	202 38.7	37.9	24 09.9	17.5	296 18.1	28.9	Mars	260 20.7	9 31
	h m									Jupiter	80 17.5	21 28
Mer. Pass.	2 52.4	*v* 0.2	*d* 0.1	*v* 0.7	*d* 0.1	*v* 2.7	*d* 0.0	*v* 2.5	*d* 0.0	Saturn	352 31.9	3 22

Figure 15-3. *The left-hand daily pages of the* Nautical Almanac *contain GHA and declination data for stars and planets, and the appropriate corrections, for a period of three days. The stars listed are the 57 most commonly used navigational stars.*

Figure 15-4. *The right-hand daily pages of the* Nautical Almanac *contain GHA and declination data for the sun and moon, plus twilight, sunset, moonset, and other data for solving sun and moon sights.*

1996 AUGUST 7, 8, 9 (WED., THURS., FRI.) 157

UT (GMT)	SUN G.H.A.	SUN Dec.	MOON G.H.A.	v	MOON Dec.	d	H.P.
d h	° ′	° ′	° ′	′	° ′	′	′
7 00	178 33.8	N16 24.1	263 24.4	11.5	N15 16.6	5.6	55.9
01	193 33.8	23.4	277 54.9	11.4	15 22.2	5.6	55.9
02	208 33.9	22.7	292 25.3	11.4	15 27.8	5.4	55.8
03	223 34.0	. . 22.0	306 55.7	11.5	15 33.2	5.4	55.8
04	238 34.1	21.3	321 26.2	11.5	15 38.6	5.3	55.8
05	253 34.1	20.6	335 56.7	11.4	15 43.9	5.2	55.7
06	268 34.2	N16 19.9	350 27.1	11.5	N15 49.1	5.2	55.7
W 07	283 34.3	19.2	4 57.6	11.5	15 54.3	5.0	55.7
E 08	298 34.4	18.5	19 28.1	11.4	15 59.3	5.0	55.6
D 09	313 34.4	. . 17.8	33 58.5	11.5	16 04.3	4.9	55.6
N 10	328 34.5	17.1	48 29.0	11.5	16 09.2	4.8	55.6
E 11	343 34.6	16.4	62 59.5	11.5	16 14.0	4.7	55.6
S 12	358 34.7	N16 15.7	77 30.0	11.5	N16 18.7	4.7	55.5
D 13	13 34.8	15.0	92 00.5	11.5	16 23.4	4.5	55.5
A 14	28 34.8	14.3	106 31.0	11.5	16 27.9	4.5	55.5
Y 15	43 34.9	. . 13.6	121 01.5	11.5	16 32.4	4.4	55.5
16	58 35.0	12.9	135 32.0	11.5	16 36.8	4.3	55.4
17	73 35.1	12.2	150 02.5	11.5	16 41.1	4.2	55.4
18	88 35.2	N16 11.5	164 33.0	11.5	N16 45.3	4.1	55.4
19	103 35.2	10.8	179 03.5	11.6	16 49.4	4.0	55.4
20	118 35.3	10.0	193 34.1	11.5	16 53.4	4.0	55.3
21	133 35.4	. . 09.3	208 04.6	11.5	16 57.4	3.8	55.3
22	148 35.5	08.6	222 35.1	11.6	17 01.2	3.8	55.3
23	163 35.6	07.9	237 05.7	11.5	17 05.0	3.7	55.3
8 00	178 35.6	N16 07.2	251 36.2	11.6	N17 08.7	3.6	55.2
01	193 35.7	06.5	266 06.8	11.6	17 12.3	3.6	55.2
02	208 35.8	05.8	280 37.4	11.5	17 15.9	3.4	55.2
03	223 35.9	. . 05.1	295 07.9	11.6	17 19.3	3.3	55.2
04	238 36.0	04.4	309 38.5	11.6	17 22.6	3.3	55.1
05	253 36.1	03.6	324 09.1	11.6	17 25.9	3.2	55.1
06	268 36.1	N16 02.9	338 39.7	11.6	N17 29.1	3.1	55.1
07	283 36.2	02.2	353 10.3	11.6	17 32.2	3.0	55.1
T 08	298 36.3	01.5	7 40.9	11.6	17 35.2	2.9	55.0
H 09	313 36.4	. . 00.8	22 11.5	11.6	17 38.1	2.8	55.0
U 10	328 36.5	16 00.1	36 42.1	11.6	17 40.9	2.7	55.0
R 11	343 36.6	15 59.4	51 12.7	11.6	17 43.6	2.7	55.0
S 12	358 36.6	N15 58.6	65 43.3	11.6	N17 46.3	2.6	55.0
D 13	13 36.7	57.9	80 13.9	11.7	17 48.9	2.4	54.9
A 14	28 36.8	57.2	94 44.6	11.6	17 51.3	2.4	54.9
Y 15	43 36.9	. . 56.5	109 15.2	11.7	17 53.7	2.3	54.9
16	58 37.0	55.8	123 45.9	11.7	17 56.0	2.2	54.9
17	73 37.1	55.1	138 16.6	11.6	17 58.2	2.2	54.8
18	88 37.1	N15 54.3	152 47.2	11.7	N18 00.4	2.0	54.8
19	103 37.2	53.6	167 17.9	11.7	18 02.4	2.0	54.8
20	118 37.3	52.9	181 48.6	11.7	18 04.4	1.8	54.8
21	133 37.4	. . 52.2	196 19.3	11.7	18 06.2	1.8	54.8
22	148 37.5	51.5	210 50.0	11.7	18 08.0	1.7	54.8
23	163 37.6	50.7	225 20.7	11.7	18 09.7	1.6	54.7
9 00	178 37.7	N15 50.0	239 51.4	11.8	N18 11.3	1.5	54.7
01	193 37.8	49.3	254 22.2	11.7	18 12.8	1.4	54.7
02	208 37.8	48.6	268 52.9	11.8	18 14.2	1.4	54.7
03	223 37.9	. . 47.9	283 23.7	11.7	18 15.6	1.2	54.7
04	238 38.0	47.1	297 54.4	11.8	18 16.8	1.2	54.6
05	253 38.1	46.4	312 25.2	11.8	18 18.0	1.1	54.6
06	268 38.2	N15 45.7	326 56.0	11.8	N18 19.1	1.0	54.6
07	283 38.3	45.0	341 26.8	11.8	18 20.1	0.9	54.6
08	298 38.4	44.2	355 57.6	11.8	18 21.0	0.8	54.6
F 09	313 38.5	. . 43.5	10 28.4	11.9	18 21.8	0.7	54.6
R 10	328 38.6	42.8	24 59.3	11.8	18 22.5	0.6	54.5
I 11	343 38.6	42.1	39 30.1	11.9	18 23.1	0.6	54.5
D 12	358 38.7	N15 41.3	54 01.0	11.8	N18 23.7	0.5	54.5
A 13	13 38.8	40.6	68 31.8	11.9	18 24.2	0.3	54.5
Y 14	28 38.9	39.9	83 02.7	11.9	18 24.5	0.3	54.5
15	43 39.0	. . 39.2	97 33.6	11.9	18 24.8	0.2	54.5
16	58 39.1	38.4	112 04.5	11.9	18 25.0	0.2	54.4
17	73 39.2	37.7	126 35.4	12.0	18 25.2	0.0	54.4
18	88 39.3	N15 37.0	141 06.4	11.9	N18 25.2	0.1	54.4
19	103 39.4	36.2	155 37.3	12.0	18 25.1	0.1	54.4
20	118 39.5	35.5	170 08.3	12.0	18 25.0	0.2	54.4
21	133 39.6	. . 34.8	184 39.3	12.0	18 24.8	0.3	54.4
22	148 39.7	34.1	199 10.3	12.0	18 24.5	0.4	54.4
23	163 39.7	33.3	213 41.3	12.0	18 24.1	0.5	54.4
	S.D. 15.8	*d* 0.7	S.D. 15.1		15.0		14.9

Lat.	Twilight Naut.	Twilight Civil	Sunrise	Moonrise 7	8	9	10
°	h m	h m	h m	h m	h m	h m	h m
N 72	////	////	01 27	20 33	20 05	▭	22 08
N 70	////	////	02 18	21 23	21 43	22 22	23 27
68	////	////	02 50	21 54	22 22	23 06	24 05
66	////	01 40	03 13	22 18	22 50	23 34	24 32
64	////	02 17	03 31	22 36	23 11	23 56	24 52
62	////	02 43	03 45	22 51	23 28	24 14	00 14
60	01 30	03 02	03 58	23 04	23 42	24 28	00 28
N 58	02 04	03 18	04 08	23 15	23 54	24 41	00 41
56	02 27	03 32	04 18	23 25	24 05	00 05	00 52
54	02 46	03 43	04 26	23 33	24 14	00 14	01 01
52	03 01	03 53	04 33	23 41	24 23	00 23	01 09
50	03 14	04 02	04 40	23 48	24 30	00 30	01 17
45	03 40	04 21	04 54	24 02	00 02	00 46	01 33
N 40	03 59	04 35	05 05	24 15	00 15	00 59	01 46
35	04 15	04 47	05 15	24 25	00 25	01 10	01 58
30	04 27	04 58	05 23	24 34	00 34	01 20	02 08
20	04 47	05 15	05 38	00 04	00 50	01 37	02 24
N 10	05 03	05 28	05 50	00 16	01 04	01 51	02 39
0	05 16	05 41	06 02	00 28	01 17	02 05	02 53
S 10	05 27	05 52	06 14	00 39	01 29	02 19	03 07
20	05 37	06 03	06 26	00 52	01 43	02 34	03 22
30	05 46	06 15	06 40	01 06	01 59	02 51	03 39
35	05 51	06 21	06 48	01 14	02 09	03 00	03 49
40	05 56	06 28	06 57	01 23	02 19	03 12	04 00
45	06 01	06 36	07 07	01 34	02 32	03 25	04 13
S 50	06 07	06 46	07 20	01 48	02 47	03 41	04 30
52	06 09	06 50	07 26	01 54	02 54	03 49	04 37
54	06 12	06 54	07 32	02 01	03 02	03 57	04 46
56	06 15	06 59	07 40	02 08	03 11	04 07	04 55
58	06 18	07 05	07 48	02 17	03 21	04 18	05 06
S 60	06 21	07 11	07 57	02 27	03 33	04 30	05 18

Lat.	Sunset	Twilight Civil	Twilight Naut.	Moonset 7	8	9	10
°	h m	h m	h m	h m	h m	h m	h m
N 72	22 35	////	////	17 27	19 37	▭	20 53
N 70	21 48	////	////	16 38	17 59	18 59	19 34
68	21 18	23 37	////	16 07	17 20	18 16	18 56
66	20 56	22 25	////	15 44	16 52	17 47	18 29
64	20 38	21 50	////	15 26	16 31	17 25	18 08
62	20 24	21 25	23 40	15 11	16 14	17 08	17 51
60	20 12	21 06	22 36	14 59	16 00	16 53	17 37
N 58	20 01	20 51	22 04	14 48	15 48	16 41	17 25
56	19 52	20 38	21 41	14 39	15 38	16 30	17 15
54	19 44	20 26	21 23	14 30	15 29	16 21	17 06
52	19 37	20 16	21 08	14 23	15 21	16 12	16 58
50	19 31	20 08	20 55	14 16	15 13	16 05	16 50
45	19 17	19 49	20 30	14 02	14 58	15 49	16 35
N 40	19 05	19 35	20 11	13 50	14 45	15 35	16 22
35	18 56	19 23	19 56	13 40	14 34	15 24	16 11
30	18 47	19 13	19 43	13 32	14 24	15 14	16 01
20	18 33	18 56	19 23	13 17	14 08	14 57	15 44
N 10	18 21	18 42	19 08	13 04	13 53	14 42	15 30
0	18 09	18 30	18 55	12 51	13 40	14 28	15 16
S 10	17 58	18 19	18 45	12 39	13 27	14 14	15 03
20	17 45	18 08	18 35	12 26	13 12	14 00	14 48
30	17 32	17 57	18 25	12 11	12 56	13 42	14 31
35	17 24	17 50	18 20	12 02	12 46	13 33	14 21
40	17 15	17 43	18 15	11 52	12 35	13 21	14 10
45	17 04	17 35	18 10	11 41	12 22	13 08	13 57
S 50	16 52	17 26	18 05	11 27	12 07	12 51	13 41
52	16 46	17 22	18 02	11 20	11 59	12 44	13 33
54	16 39	17 18	18 00	11 13	11 51	12 35	13 25
56	16 32	17 13	17 57	11 05	11 42	12 26	13 16
58	16 24	17 07	17 54	10 56	11 32	12 15	13 05
S 60	16 15	17 01	17 51	10 46	11 20	12 02	12 53

Day	SUN Eqn. of Time 00 h	SUN Eqn. of Time 12 h	SUN Mer. Pass.	MOON Mer. Pass. Upper	MOON Mer. Pass. Lower	Age	Phase
	m s	m s	h m	h m	h m	d	
7	05 45	05 41	12 06	06 39	19 04	23	◐
8	05 38	05 34	12 06	07 28	19 53	24	
9	05 30	05 25	12 05	08 17	20 41	25	

Following the Polaris tables and the almanac sight reduction tables are a one-page *arc-to-time conversion table* and a long table, printed on tinted paper for easy identification, called *Increments and Corrections*. You use the latter to determine the minutes and seconds of GHA; the daily pages have only hourly data.

Following the Increments and Corrections table are tables for interpolating the rising and setting of bodies and star indices.

Tables for *sextant altitude corrections* for sights of the sun, stars, and planets, and a *dip (height of eye) correction table,* are located inside the front cover, along with tables for sights taken during extremes of temperature or barometric pressure. Inside the back cover are another dip table and sextant altitude correction tables for the moon.

Using the Nautical Almanac

Enter the almanac with the name of the body and the time of the sight to find the GHA of the body and then determine its *Local Hour Angle (LHA)*. Remember that the GHA of the body is its angular distance from Greenwich, and the LHA is its angular distance from your position. Use this formula to determine LHA:

LHA = GHA + E longitude

LHA = GHA − W longitude

In the case of observations of the sun, moon, and planets, start by looking up the GHA of the body for the hour you observed it (you'll add the minutes and seconds later). In the case of a star observation you need to find the GHA of Aries first, and then get the GHA of the star. Recall that stars stay in the same positions relative to each other, so their positions can be given with reference to a single point—the first point of Aries, or simply, "Aries." To save space, the *Almanac* gives the GHA of Aries, which changes continuously over time, and the constant angular distance between Aries and your star; that is, the star's sidereal hour angle (SHA). The SHA is given in a separate table on each daily page. To find the GHA of a star, first find the GHA of Aries and then add the SHA of the star. If the answer is more than 360°, subtract 360°. Then find the LHA as before.

At this point also extract the declination, listed beside the GHA.

To add the minutes and seconds, look in the Increments and Corrections table (the yellow-tinted pages) for the proper minute of your observation and follow down the column to the proper second. Record the corrections for minutes and seconds of time, along with the *v* and *d* corrections taken from the proper column. The *v* correction enables you to make an adjustment for the difference between the actual change in GHA in one hour and the tabulated change; the *d* correction accounts for the change in declination in one hour.

Assume that the *v* correction is positive unless a minus sign precedes it, which only occurs with the planet Venus. There is no *v* correction for the sun.

The *d* correction is positive if the declination is increasing and negative if it is decreasing. You can see how its changing by inspecting the adjoining declination figures.

Here are some examples of finding the GHA and declination of various bodies. You'll use these findings in the next chapter where you'll actually work out some sights.

Finding GHA and Declination of the Sun

Enter the daily pages for the day of the sight with the whole hour of the sighting time in GMT and record the listed GHA and declination from the table. Also record the *d* correction from the bottom of the same column.

Next, enter the increments and corrections pages with the minutes and seconds of the sight. From the page indicating the proper number of minutes, move down to the seconds row and extract the value from the Sun-Planets column. Add this number to the value from the daily pages. This is the GHA of the sun.

Finally, record the value of the *d* correction for the same time and apply the value of the declination from the daily page, using the proper negative or positive sign. This is the declination of the sun.

The correction table for the GHA of the sun is based on the sun's average rate of change in

Figure 15-5. *The inside front cover of the* Nautical Almanac *contains altitude correction tables for the sun, stars, and planets, plus a height-of-eye (dip) correction tables. Notice that these tables are for altitudes of 10° to 90°. Corrections for altitudes less than 10° are found on page A3, the inside facing page.*

THE

NAUTICAL ALMANAC

FOR THE YEAR

1997

A2 ALTITUDE CORRECTION TABLES 10°-90°—SUN, STARS, PLANETS

OCT.—MAR. SUN			APR.—SEPT.			STARS AND PLANETS	
App. Alt.	Lower Limb	Upper Limb	App. Alt.	Lower Limb	Upper Limb	App Alt.	Corrn
° ′	′	′	° ′	′	′	° ′	′
9 34			9 39			9 56	
	+10.8	−21.5		+10.6	−21.2		−5.3
9 45			9 51			10 08	
	+10.9	−21.4		+10.7	−21.1		−5.2
9 56			10 03			10 20	
	+11.0	−21.3		+10.8	−21.0		−5.1
10 08			10 15			10 33	
	+11.1	−21.2		+10.9	−20.9		−5.0
10 21			10 27			10 46	
	+11.2	−21.1		+11.0	−20.8		−4.9
10 34			10 40			11 00	
	+11.3	−21.0		+11.1	−20.7		−4.8
10 47			10 54			11 14	
	+11.4	−20.9		+11.2	−20.6		−4.7
11 01			11 08			11 29	
	+11.5	−20.8		+11.3	−20.5		−4.6
11 15			11 23			11 45	
	+11.6	−20.7		+11.4	−20.4		−4.5
11 30			11 38			12 01	
	+11.7	−20.6		+11.5	−20.3		−4.4
11 46			11 54			12 18	
	+11.8	−20.5		+11.6	−20.2		−4.3
12 02			12 10			12 35	
	+11.9	−20.4		+11.7	−20.1		−4.2
12 19			12 28			12 54	
	+12.0	−20.3		+11.8	−20.0		−4.1
12 37			12 46			13 13	
	+12.1	−20.2		+11.9	−19.9		−4.0
12 55			13 05			13 33	
	+12.2	−20.1		+12.0	−19.8		−3.9
13 14			13 24			13 54	
	+12.3	−20.0		+12.1	−19.7		−3.8
13 35			13 45			14 16	
	+12.4	−19.9		+12.2	−19.6		−3.7
13 56			14 07			14 40	
	+12.5	−19.8		+12.3	−19.5		−3.6
14 18			14 30			15 04	
	+12.6	−19.7		+12.4	−19.4		−3.5
14 42			14 54			15 30	
	+12.7	−19.6		+12.5	−19.3		−3.4
15 06			15 19			15 57	
	+12.8	−19.5		+12.6	−19.2		−3.3
15 32			15 46			16 26	
	+12.9	−19.4		+12.7	−19.1		−3.2
15 59			16 14			16 56	
	+13.0	−19.3		+12.8	−19.0		−3.1
16 28			16 44			17 28	
	+13.1	−19.2		+12.9	−18.9		−3.0
16 59			17 15			18 02	
	+13.2	−19.1		+13.0	−18.8		−2.9
17 32			17 48			18 38	
	+13.3	−19.0		+13.1	−18.7		−2.8
18 06			18 24			19 17	
	+13.4	−18.9		+13.2	−18.6		−2.7
18 42			19 01			19 58	
	+13.5	−18.8		+13.3	−18.5		−2.6
19 21			19 42			20 42	
	+13.6	−18.7		+13.4	−18.4		−2.5
20 03			20 25			21 28	
	+13.7	−18.6		+13.5	−18.3		−2.4
20 48			21 11			22 19	
	+13.8	−18.5		+13.6	−18.2		−2.3
21 35			22 00			23 13	
	+13.9	−18.4		+13.7	−18.1		−2.2
22 26			22 54			24 11	
	+14.0	−18.3		+13.8	−18.0		−2.1
23 22			23 51			25 14	
	+14.1	−18.2		+13.9	−17.9		−2.0
24 21			24 53			26 22	
	+14.2	−18.1		+14.0	−17.8		−1.9
25 26			26 00			27 36	
	+14.3	−18.0		+14.1	−17.7		−1.8
26 36			27 13			28 56	
	+14.4	−17.9		+14.2	−17.6		−1.7
27 52			28 33			30 24	
	+14.5	−17.8		+14.3	−17.5		−1.6
29 15			30 00			32 00	
	+14.6	−17.7		+14.4	−17.4		−1.5
30 46			31 35			33 45	
	+14.7	−17.6		+14.5	−17.3		−1.4
32 26			33 20			35 40	
	+14.8	−17.5		+14.6	−17.2		−1.3
34 17			35 17			37 48	
	+14.9	−17.4		+14.7	−17.1		−1.2
36 20			37 26			40 08	
	+15.0	−17.3		+14.8	−17.0		−1.1
38 36			39 50			42 44	
	+15.1	−17.2		+14.9	−16.9		−1.0
41 08			42 31			45 36	
	+15.2	−17.1		+15.0	−16.8		−0.9
43 59			45 31			48 47	
	+15.3	−17.0		+15.1	−16.7		−0.8
47 10			48 55			52 18	
	+15.4	−16.9		+15.2	−16.6		−0.7
50 46			52 44			56 11	
	+15.5	−16.8		+15.3	−16.5		−0.6
54 49			57 02			60 28	
	+15.6	−16.7		+15.4	−16.4		−0.5
59 23			61 51			65 08	
	+15.7	−16.6		+15.5	−16.3		−0.4
64 30			67 17			70 11	
	+15.8	−16.5		+15.6	−16.2		−0.3
70 12			73 16			75 34	
	+15.9	−16.4		+15.7	−16.1		−0.2
76 26			79 43			81 13	
	+16.0	−16.3		+15.8	−16.0		−0.1
83 05			86 32			87 03	
	+16.1	−16.2		+15.9	−15.9		0.0
90 00			90 00			90 00	

STARS AND PLANETS — App. Alt. / Additional Corrn

1997

VENUS

Jan. 1–Sept. 26	
°	′
0	
	+0.1
60	

Sept. 27–Nov. 16	
°	′
0	
	+0.2
41	
	+0.1
76	

Nov. 17–Dec. 10	
°	′
0	
	+0.3
34	
	+0.2
60	
	+0.1
80	

Dec. 11–Dec. 25	
°	′
0	
	+0.4
29	
	+0.3
51	
	+0.2
68	
	+0.1
83	

Dec. 26–Dec. 31	
°	′
0	
	+0.5
26	
	+0.4
46	
	+0.3
60	
	+0.2
73	
	+0.1
84	

MARS

Jan. 1–Jan. 20 May 25–Dec. 31	
°	′
0	
	+0.1
60	

Jan. 21–May 24	
°	′
0	
	+0.2
41	
	+0.1
76	

DIP

Ht. of Eye	Corrn	Ht. of Eye
m	′	ft.
2.4		8.0
	−2.8	
2.6		8.6
	−2.9	
2.8		9.2
	−3.0	
3.0		9.8
	−3.1	
3.2		10.5
	−3.2	
3.4		11.2
	−3.3	
3.6		11.9
	−3.4	
3.8		12.6
	−3.5	
4.0		13.3
	−3.6	
4.3		14.1
	−3.7	
4.5		14.9
	−3.8	
4.7		15.7
	−3.9	
5.0		16.5
	−4.0	
5.2		17.4
	−4.1	
5.5		18.3
	−4.2	
5.8		19.1
	−4.3	
6.1		20.1
	−4.4	
6.3		21.0
	−4.5	
6.6		22.0
	−4.6	
6.9		22.9
	−4.7	
7.2		23.9
	−4.8	
7.5		24.9
	−4.9	
7.9		26.0
	−5.0	
8.2		27.1
	−5.1	
8.5		28.1
	−5.2	
8.8		29.2
	−5.3	
9.2		30.4
	−5.4	
9.5		31.5
	−5.5	
9.9		32.7
	−5.6	
10.3		33.9
	−5.7	
10.6		35.1
	−5.8	
11.0		36.3
	−5.9	
11.4		37.6
	−6.0	
11.8		38.9
	−6.1	
12.2		40.1
	−6.2	
12.6		41.5
	−6.3	
13.0		42.8
	−6.4	
13.4		44.2
	−6.5	
13.8		45.5
	−6.6	
14.2		46.9
	−6.7	
14.7		48.4
	−6.8	
15.1		49.8
	−6.9	
15.5		51.3
	−7.0	
16.0		52.8
	−7.1	
16.5		54.3
	−7.2	
16.9		55.8
	−7.3	
17.4		57.4
	−7.4	
17.9		58.9
	−7.5	
18.4		60.5
	−7.6	
18.8		62.1
	−7.7	
19.3		63.8
	−7.8	
19.8		65.4
	−7.9	
20.4		67.1
	−8.0	
20.9		68.8
	−8.1	
21.4		70.5

Ht. of Eye	Corrn
m	′
1.0	− 1.8
1.5	− 2.2
2.0	− 2.5
2.5	− 2.8
3.0	− 3.0
See table ←	
m	′
20	− 7.9
22	− 8.3
24	− 8.6
26	− 9.0
28	− 9.3
30	− 9.6
32	− 10.0
34	− 10.3
36	− 10.6
38	− 10.8
40	− 11.1
42	− 11.4
44	− 11.7
46	− 11.9
48	− 12.2
ft.	′
2	− 1.4
4	− 1.9
6	− 2.4
8	− 2.7
10	− 3.1
See table ←	
ft.	′
70	− 8.1
75	− 8.4
80	− 8.7
85	− 8.9
90	− 9.2
95	− 9.5
100	− 9.7
105	− 9.9
110	− 10.2
115	− 10.4
120	− 10.6
125	− 10.8
130	− 11.1
135	− 11.3
140	− 11.5
145	− 11.7
150	− 11.9
155	− 12.1

App. Alt. = Apparent altitude = Sextant altitude corrected for index error and dip.

longitude of 15° per hour, the average yearly rate of change. The tabulated values reflect slight variations in the rate as discussed in Chapter 12, "Celestial Navigation." The rate is usually slightly slower or faster than 15° per hour, and the tables account for this difference. The value of *d* is for the middle of the three days shown—the average of the three. This use of averages introduces minor but unremovable errors in the celestial fix.

Finding GHA and Declination of the Moon

For the GHA of the moon, enter the daily pages with the whole hour of the observation in GMT and record the values of the GHA and declination, plus the *v* and *d* corrections. Determine by inspection if the *d* correction is plus or minus.

Next, turn to the increments and corrections table and find the page corresponding to the proper number of minutes, follow down to the seconds row, and read across to find the GHA increment in the moon column. Record this along with the *v* and *d* corrections. Add the GHA increments to the GHA from the daily pages and apply the *v* correction. This is the GHA of the moon.

Finally, apply the *d* correction to the declination from the daily pages (again, give it the proper sign—positive if declination is increasing and negative if decreasing). This is the declination of the moon.

The minimum rate at which the moon increases in GHA is 14° 19.0' per hour. (It's different from the sun's rate.) The *v* correction for the moon adjusts for its slightly higher rate at times, so it's always positive. The *d* correction adjusts for the change in declination for each minute.

Finding GHA and Declination of a Planet

Enter the proper daily page with the whole hour of GMT and record the value of GHA and declination. Also record the *v* and *d* corrections from the bottom of the column. Then, enter the increments and corrections table for the correct minute, find the row for the correct second, and record the value of the GHA increment, the *v* correction, and the *d* correction.

Next, add the GHA increment to the value from the daily pages and apply the *v* correction. This is the GHA of the planet. Apply the *d* correction with the proper sign to the declination from the daily page. This is the declination of the planet.

The *v* correction for planets is based on the mean rate of change in GHA for the sun (the same as the planets) for the middle hour of the middle day of the three shown. The value for the other hours and days will not differ enough to cause a significant error in the LOP. The *d* correction also represents the amount of change for the middle hour of the middle day of the three.

There is only one case where the *v* correction is negative. The planet Venus, because its orbit is between the earth and the sun, sometimes appears to move backward in the sky when viewed against the other stars. This phenomenon, *retrograde motion,* sometimes causes the *v* correction to be negative.

Finding GHA and Declination of a Star

If the GHA and declination of each navigational star were given in the tables, the tables would be several times their present size and many more volumes would be needed. Rather than list separately the GHA and declination of each star, the *Almanac* lists the values for Aries and gives the relationship of all the stars to this single point—which is where the sun crosses the celestial equator at the vernal (spring) equinox. Therefore, the *Almanac* lists the GHA of Aries, and the sidereal hour angle (SHA), and the declination for each star in a separate column alongside.

To find the GHA of a star, enter the daily pages with the whole hour of GMT and record the GHA of Aries for the proper time. From the column to the right of the planets, record the SHA and declination of the chosen star.

Next, enter the increments and corrections pages and record the correction for the minutes and seconds of GMT from the Aries column. Add this to the value for the hours of GMT from the daily pages. This is the GHA of Aries.

Now add the SHA of the star to the GHA of Aries and subtract 360° if the result is greater than 360°. This is the GHA of the star. The declination of the star is the same as listed in the daily pages.

Rising, Setting, and Twilight

The *Nautical Almanac* lists the times to the nearest minute of sunrise, sunset, moonrise, moonset, and twilight at various latitudes between 72°N and 60°S. A body with visible diameter, such as the sun or moon, has risen when its upper limb reaches the horizon and has set when its upper limb disappears below it.

Because of differences in the motions of the sun and moon, times of sunrise and sunset are listed only for the middle of the three days on each daily page; times for moonrise and moonset are given for each day. The times are given in LMT; if you are on the zone meridian, this is also zone time (ZT). If you're not on the zone meridian, the actual time will be earlier if you are east of it and later if west. The time will differ by one minute of time for each 15' of longitude.

Therefore, to figure out the exact time of the event at your longitude you must determine approximately how far east or west you are of the zone meridian, divide that distance into units of 15 minutes of arc, and adjust the time of the event by that amount. You can do this either by calculation or with the arc-to-time conversion table in the *Almanac*.

Professional ship navigators, with a great many other responsibilities than navigating, often precompute the times of sunrise and sunset for each day of a passage, based on future DR positions. When they're on a tight schedule it helps them to plan sight times with some precision so they'll know in advance when to head to the bridge for sights. Large ships steaming at 15 or 20 knots sometimes experience rapid changes in their longitude, which affects the LMT and even the zone time of the event.

Small craft not only move more slowly, but their navigators are also much more in tune with the sea—they can easily gauge when sunset or sunrise will occur by simply watching the sky. Although small-craft navigators have little need to precalculate times of sunrise, sunset, moonrise, and moonset, they often have reason to calculate the times of the sun's meridian passage for a noon latitude line. You can easily do this by noting the "Mer. Pass." time listed in the bottom corner of the proper right-hand daily pages. Remember, this is LMT, which differs from zone time by the angular difference in longitude expressed in units of time.

When you're sailing rapidly east or west, the time of meridian passage changes some, so you might want to precalculate its time based on your DR plot. With a change of 15' of longitude, the time changes by one minute.

Almanacs can be rather daunting to look at for the first time, but they're easy to use once you understand their format. When you have a basic knowledge of astronomy and understand what the numbers in an almanac represent, you see that the presentation of data is logical. The best way to become familiar with an almanac is to use it for actual navigational calculations, as explained in the next chapter.

CHAPTER SIXTEEN

Sight Reduction

TO REVIEW THE PROCESS of sight reduction, some of the basic celestial concepts outlined in Chapter 12, "Celestial Navigation," are repeated here.

When you observe a body that is exactly overhead, its altitude is 90° and its geographic position (GP) is the same as your position. If the body is not directly overhead, but only slightly off, you are somewhere on a small circle whose radius is equal to the distance from your position to the GP of the body. This circle is called the *circle of equal altitude* and represents all points on the earth at which the altitude of that body is the same. This circle grows in radius as the body becomes lower and lower in the sky until the body is on the horizon, when its radius equals the circumference of the earth.

There is a direct mathematical relationship, then, between the altitude of a celestial body and your distance from its GP. The higher it is in the sky, the closer you are to its GP; the lower it is, the farther away you are. After measuring a body's altitude with a sextant and finding its GP from the almanac, you can compute your distance from the GP.

The geographic position (GP) of a body, technically speaking, is the point of intersection of the surface of the earth and a line from the center of the body to the center of the earth. In plain English, it is the point on the earth directly under the body, where the body's altitude is 90°. (See Figure 16-1.)

The Process of Sight Reduction

The term *"sight reduction"* refers to the process of computing your distance from the GP. The line of position obtained from a celestial sight will be a giant circle—*the circle of equal altitude*—with the geographic position (GP) of the body at the center, and the radius equal to your distance from it. You could plot on a chart a small portion of this line of position.

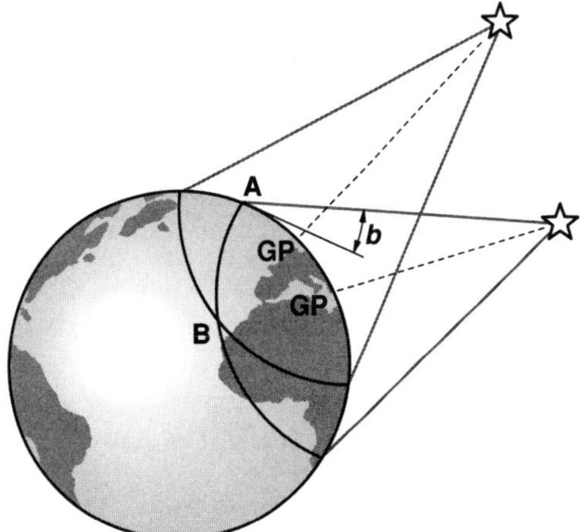

Figure 16-1. *When you observe a body directly overhead, its altitude is 90°. At point "A" the altitude of the body is angle b between the horizon and the body. The distance to the GP is the radius of a* circle of equal altitude, *which represents all points on earth where the altitude of the body is the same. One circle of equal altitude is an LOP. Two or more give a fix, as at point "B."*

However, the scale of a chart showing enough area to contain both the GP of the body and your position would normally be too small to plot your position accurately.

To get around this problem in sight reduction, you assume that you know your position and compare the distance from the body's GP to this assumed position with your actual distance from it, based on your observation of the body's altitude. The difference between these two distances is small enough to plot accurately.

To compute the distance between your assumed position and the GP, you form a triangle that joins the GP of the body, the nearer pole (N or S), and an assumed position close to your own. Knowing these three points on the surface of the spherical earth, you can use spherical trigonometry to solve for the length of the side between your assumed position and the GP. Don't be scared. Sight reduction tables or a navigational calculator make the solution easy. A scientific calculator works as well. All of the calculations you need to make in celestial navigation can be done by addition and subtraction. The only tricky part is working with degrees, minutes, and seconds, and with minutes and tenths, instead of decimal numbers.

The very clever sight reduction process was discovered in 1874 by a French naval commander named Adolph Laurent Anatole Marcq de Blond de St. Hilaire. (Fortunately, we just call him Marcq St. Hilaire today.) He realized that if he assumed he were at a position near his own, but not necessarily exactly coincident, he could calculate the altitude at which the body would be observed from that assumed position. He could then locate his actual position by finding the difference between his calculated altitude and his observed altitude—a figure known as the altitude intercept. *This Marcq St. Hilaire or altitude intercept method is the sight reduction method used today throughout the world.*

In locating points on the earth, *latitude* is measured north and south of the equator and *longitude* is measured east or west of Greenwich, England. On the celestial sphere, declination substitutes for latitude and is still measured north and south. However, the equivalent of longitude, the *Greenwich Hour Angle (GHA),* is measured all the way around the earth in one direction, starting west from Greenwich through 360°.

Because the key to celestial navigation lies in determining the distance between you and the GP of a heavenly body, it's important to locate a body's longitude (GHA) in relation to yours. The *Local Hour Angle (LHA)* does this. LHA is the angular distance between the body's GHA and your assumed position, measured westward from you. See Figure 16-7 for an example.

Steps in Sight Reduction

You use six steps to reduce a sight after you have taken a sextant altitude:

1. Correct the errors in the *sextant altitude (hs)* to obtain *observed altitude (ho).*
2. Find the GHA and declination of the body (its GP) from an almanac.
3. Select an *assumed position (AP)* and find its *Local Hour Angle (LHA)* or angular distance to the GP.
4. Compute the *altitude (hc)* and *azimuth (direction)* from the AP, using sight reduction tables.
5. Compare *hc* and *ho.*
6. Plot the LOP.

The GP of the body is usually many hundreds or even thousands of miles from the observer. If you tried to lay off such long distances on a chart that contains both you and the GP, you'd inevitably make unacceptably large errors because of the chart's small scale. By going through the steps listed above, you can use a chart or plotting sheet that represents the portion of the earth in your vicinity, covering a hundred miles or so. The scale of this chart or plotting sheet is small enough to cover the distance between your assumed position and your actual (observed) position, but is large enough to plot these accurately.

Because the radius of the circle of equal altitude is so large, the tiny portion of it near your position is very nearly a straight line and you drew it straight rather than in an arc.

Selecting the Assumed Position (AP)

The values needed to enter the sight reduction tables are the latitude of your AP, the declination of the body, and the LHA—the difference in longitude between your AP and the body's GP. The tables are set up so that you must enter with whole numbers of LHA and latitude; otherwise, the tables would have to be even longer than they already are (six volumes). Declination doesn't have to be a whole number. To obtain whole numbers for entry to the tables you need to select AP coordinates as follows:

1. For the latitude of your AP, select the whole degree of latitude nearest your DR position.
2. When you're in west longitude, select an AP longitude that is nearest to you that has the same number of minutes and seconds as the GHA of the body. In east longitude, select the nearest longitude with a number of minutes and seconds that, when added to the minutes and seconds of GHA, adds to 60—one whole degree.
3. In west longitude, subtract the assumed longitude from GHA, adding 360° to GHA if necessary. In east longitude add the two, subtracting 360° if necessary. This will give you the LHA in the whole degrees that you need.

The Sight Reduction Tables

Pub. 229, Sight Reduction Tables for Marine Navigation, are published by the National Imagery and Mapping Agency (NIMA) and consist of six volumes, each covering 15 degrees of latitude (0° to 15°, 15° to 30°, 30° to 45°, etc.). In each volume, half of the latitudes are found in the first half of the book and the rest in the last half. Arguments of LHA are listed in each upper and lower outside corner, and a dividing line across the page separates entries of latitude and declination that are the same (both north or both south) from those that are contrary (one north and the other south).

If the latitude and declination are the same, all points of the navigational triangle are in the same hemisphere; if they are contrary, the navigational triangle crosses the equator and the solution is different.

A *navigational triangle* is formed by three points—the nearer pole, the assumed position (AP) of the observer, and the geographic position (GP) of the body. The solution of the triangle is the same whether the GP is east or west of the AP and whether the nearer pole is north or south of the observer. Thus, four triangles can be solved by the same set of numbers—which accounts for the listing of four LHAs on each set of pages.

To use *Pub. 229,* first find the half of the book that contains entries for your latitude as listed in the columns across the top of the page. Then look for the proper LHA page, go down the proper latitude column on that page to the declination row, and note the three numbers there: the *hc,* the *d* correction, and the azimuth angle (Z). You need these three numbers to complete the sight reduction process, so enter them on a sight reduction form like the one given on page 189 (on this form, lines 31, 32, and 36, respectively).

Comparing Computed and Observed Altitudes

The difference between the altitude you compute using the assumed position *(hc)* and the altitude you actually measured *(ho)*—the *altitude intercept (a)*—is translated into the difference in the lengths of the radii of the circles

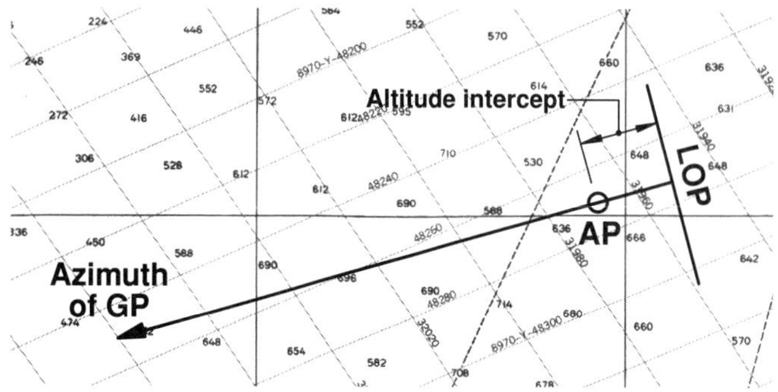

Figure 16-2. *Sight reduction answers this question: By how much and in what direction does the altitude at the assumed position differ from the altitude measured at your actual position? To compute the altitude at your assumed position, you solve the spherical triangle and then compare the computed and observed altitudes to find the* altitude intercept, *which is the difference between the two altitudes.*

of equal altitude for *hc* and *ho*. (See Figure 16-2.) The greater the altitude, the smaller the resulting circle of equal altitude. Therefore, the position associated with the greater altitude has the shorter radius. To plot the LOP you need to find the difference between *ho* and *hc* and note which is greater.

You also need to find the direction, or *azimuth*, of the GP, abbreviated as *Zn*. Find Zn according to the following rule: In north latitude, if LHA is greater than 180°, Zn = Z; that is, the azimuth you draw on the plotting sheet is the same as the Z number taken from *Pub. 229*. If LHA is less than 180°, Zn = 360 – Z.

Because the values in sight reduction tables are arranged to be used for four triangles, each a mirror image of another, vertically and horizontally, you can't always directly pick out the direction to the body. The value given in the tables, Z, could refer to differing directions. Sometimes you need to perform an arithmetic step to convert Z to the azimuth (Zn) that you use.

Next, you need to determine whether to draw Zn toward or away from the GP. That depends on whether your actual position (based on *ho*) is closer to or farther from the GP than your assumed position (corresponding to *ho*). Navigators use the mnemonic "HoMoTo" (spoken "hoe, mow, toe") to remind them that if *ho* is more than *hc*, they draw the line toward the GP. Conversely, if *hc* is greater than *ho*, they draw the line away from the GP.

To draw the LOP, plot the assumed position by its latitude and longitude, draw a line toward or away from that point (as indicated by the Ho-Mo-To rule) in the direction of Zn, and draw a line perpendicular to this line at the distance of the altitude intercept. This perpendicular line represents a very small part of the circle of equal altitude and is the LOP for that sight.

You won't be able to take all the sights at exactly the same time, of course. The difference in time for each sight depends on how long it takes you to locate the next body in the sky, find it in the index mirror of the sextant, and accurately measure its altitude. The procedure for correcting for different times is to plot all the LOPs and advance them along the DR track to the time of the last one. For most fast-moving large ships, this can be a significant correction; for small sailboats, it can be ignored if the sights are all taken within a few minutes. With experience, your judgment can guide you to decide when to make this correction.

The Sight Reduction Form

Several *sight reduction forms* are available commercially. Many of the forms developed for the professional navigator are more complex than necessary for the small-craft operator. The form presented here is suitable for all common types of sights taken aboard small craft. It can be used for three sights. It isn't as simple as some, but it's good for all types of sights. It may be copied at will.

You make different corrections and apply different rules to each type of sight—sun, star, planet, or moon. These are summarized in the explanations below. When you complete the form for each type of sight, you'll normally have numerous blanks where no entries are required. Use the sample sights below as examples of how to reduce each type.

Explanation of the Form

Section I of the Sight Reduction Form has two parts. The first corrects the sextant altitude (*hs*) to obtain apparent altitude (*ha*), and the

Sight Reduction Form

Section I:

1. Body ______ ______ ______
2. Index Correction ______ ______ ______
3. Dip correction (height of eye) ______ ______ ______
4. Sum ______ ______ ______
5. Sextant Altitude *(hs)* ______ ______ ______
6. Apparent Altitude *(ha)* ______ ______ ______
7. Altitude Correction ______ ______ ______
8. Mars/Venus Correction ______ ______ ______
9. Additional Correction ______ ______ ______
10. Horizontal Parallax Correction ______ ______ ______
11. Moon Upper Limb Correction ______ ______ ______
12. Correction to Apparent Altitude ______ ______ ______
13. Observed Altitude *(ho)* ______ ______ ______

Section II:

14. Date ______ ______ ______
15. DR Latitude ______ ______ ______
16. DR Longitude ______ ______ ______
17. Time of Sight (corrected) ______ ______ ______
18. Zone Description ______ ______ ______
19. GMT (Date ______) Time ______ ______ ______

Section III:

20. GHA (*v* corr'n. factor ______) ______ ______ ______
21. GHA increment ______ ______ ______
22. SHA (or *v* correction) ______ ______ ______
23. GHA ______ ______ ______
24. + or −360° ______ ______ ______
25. Assumed Longitude ______ ______ ______
26. LHA ______ ______ ______
27. Declination (*d* corr'n. factor ______) ______ ______ ______
28. *d* correction ______ ______ ______
29. Declination ______ ______ ______
30. Assumed Latitude ______ ______ ______

Section IV:

31. Tabulated hc/*d* (factor ______) ______ ______ ______
32. Declination Increment ______ ______ ______
33. Computed Altitude *(hc)* ______ ______ ______
34. Observed Altitude *(ho)* ______ ______ ______
35. Altitude Intercept (Toward/Away) ______ ______ ______
36. Azimuth Angle (Z) ______ ______ ______
37. Azimuth ______ ______ ______

second corrects apparent altitude to obtain the observed altitude *(ho)*, which you'll later compare with the computed altitude *(hc)* to get the altitude intercept.

1. ***Body:*** Enter the name of the body.
2. ***Index Correction:*** Enter the sextant's index correction. (See Chapter 13.)
3. ***Dip (height of eye):*** Enter correction from table inside front cover of *Nautical Almanac*.
4. ***Sum:*** Add the dip and index corrections together algebraically. Watch + and – signs!
5. ***Sextant Altitude*** **(hs)**: Enter the sextant altitude.
6. ***Apparent Altitude*** **(ha)**: Apply the line 4 correction to line 5. Watch signs!
7. ***Altitude Correction:*** Sun, planet, and star altitude corrections are inside the front cover of the *Almanac;* moon corrections are inside the back cover.
8. ***Mars/Venus Correction:*** These very small corrections are inside the front cover of the *Almanac*.
9. ***Additional Correction:*** Under nonstandard atmospheric conditions, enter the correction from Table A4 in the front of the *Almanac*.
10. ***Horizontal Parallax Correction:*** Unique to the moon sight, you find this correction by noting the HP correction factor on the right-hand daily pages and applying the corresponding correction to the upper or lower limb that's on the inside back cover of the *Almanac*.
11. ***Moon Upper Limb Correction:*** Enter –30' only if the sight was the upper limb of the moon.
12. ***Total Correction to*** **ha*:*** Algebraically sum all the corrections (lines 7–11).
13. ***Observed Altitude*** **(ho)**: Apply line 12 correction to line 6 and enter result. Watch signs!

Section II reckons the GMT time and date of the sight. (See Chapter 14, "Time.") When you set your chronometer or comparing watch to GMT, you don't have to convert from zone time. In that case, enter the GMT of the sight on line 19 and go on.)

14. ***Date:*** Enter the date of the sight at your location.
15. ***DR Latitude:*** Enter the DR latitude at the time of the sight.
16. ***DR Longitude:*** Enter the DR longitude at the time of the sight.
17. ***Time of Sight (corrected):*** Enter the zone time of the sight, corrected for any error in the comparing watch.
18. ***Zone Description:*** Enter the zone description at your location.
19. ***GMT (Date_______) GMT Time:*** Apply zone description to line 17. Watch dates!

Section III determines the Local Hour Angle (LHA) and declination of the body—two of three arguments you need to enter the sight reduction tables. (You already have the third, assumed latitude.)

20. ***GHA*** v ***corr'n (_________):*** Enter the almanac daily pages with the date and hour of GMT and record the tabulated GHA. Enter the *v* correction factor (if any) in the parentheses.
21. ***GHA increment:*** Enter the increments and corrections (yellow) pages of the almanac with the minutes of GMT and record the additional correction. This accounts for minutes after the whole hour value of GHA found in line 20.
22. ***SHA (or*** v ***corr'n):*** For a star sight, enter the SHA found on the left-hand daily pages. For planets or the moon, record the correction corresponding to the *v* correction factor from line 20 (found on the same half of the page as for line 21).
23. ***GHA:*** Add lines 20, 21, and 22. A star's GHA is the sum of the tabulated GHA of Aries, the GHA increment, and the SHA. The sun's GHA is the sum of the tabulated GHA and the GHA increment. The GHA of the moon or a planet is the sum of the tabulated GHA, the GHA increment, and the *v* correction.

24. *+ or −360°:* If the LHA will be more than 360 or negative, add or subtract 360.
25. ***Assumed Longitude:*** In west longitude, enter the minutes of longitude equal to the minutes of GHA. In east longitude, enter 60' minus the minutes of GHA. Then enter the whole degree of longitude closest to the DR longitude. It will be the same as, or one degree more or less than, the DR longitude.
26. ***LHA:*** In west longitude, subtract line 25 from line 24 or vice versa. In east longitude, add them. The result will be a whole number of degrees and used to enter the sight reduction tables.
27. ***Tabulated Declination/*d *corr'n (___):*** Record the tabulated declination from the daily pages and the *d* correction factor. You'll use it to determine the change in declination from the whole hour. Watch the signs—the *d* correction factor is positive if declination is increasing and negative if it is decreasing.
28. d ***correction:*** Enter the *d* correction found in the increments and corrections section of the almanac for the proper minutes of GMT.
29. ***Declination:*** Algebraically add lines 27 and 28. Watch signs!
30. ***Assumed Latitude:*** Enter the latitude nearest the DR latitude. Label it "same" if both latitude and declination are north or south. Label it "contrary" if one is north and the other south.

Section IV determines the azimuth and computed altitude *(hc)* using the sight reduction tables, then determines the altitude intercept. You use the altitude intercept and azimuth to plot the LOP.

31. ***Tabulated*** hc: Enter the sight reduction tables with the whole degree of LHA, go to the column for the proper assumed latitude, and go down the column to the whole degree of declination. Record the value for *hc*.
32. ***Declination Inc. (d______):*** From the same column as for line 31 (right next to the tabulated *hc*), record the *d* correction factor. Divide the minutes and tenths of declination by 60 and multiply the result by this factor. Enter the result here. This accounts for minutes and tenths of declination. (Alternative method: Use interpolation tables inside the front and back covers of *Pub. 229.*)
33. ***Computed Altitude*** (hc): Apply the *d* correction to the tabulated *hc*. Watch signs. This is the altitude you would have measured if you were at the AP at the time of the sight.
34. ***Observed Altitude*** (ho): Enter the value from line 13. This is the altitude you actually measured.
35. ***Altitude Intercept (T/A):*** This is the difference between lines 33 and 34—the difference between the circles of equal altitude for the AP and your real position. Remember "HoMoTo" and record whether the direction is toward or away from the GP.
36. ***Azimuth Angle (Z):*** Record from the same place in the sight reduction tables as for line 31.
37. ***Azimuth (Zn):*** In north latitude, if LHA is greater than 180, Zn = Z. If LHA is less than 180, Zn = 360 − Z. In south latitude, if LHA is greater than 180, Zn = 180 − Z. If LHA is less than 180, Zn = 180 + Z.

Example of Sight Reduction for a Star

Here's how to use the form to solve a star sight. Suppose you obtain a sight of Kochab on May 16, 1995, at 20 07 43. Sextant altitude is 47° 19.1'. Height of eye is 10 feet and the index error is −2.1'. The DR latitude is 39° 00.0'N and DR longitude is 157° 08.0'W. Figures 16-3 and 16-4 show the almanac and sight reduction table pages for this sight.

To reduce the sight, start filling in the form, like this:

Sight Reduction Form

Section I:

1. Body	*Kochab*
2. Index Correction	*+2.1′ (given; error is negative, so the correction is positive)*
3. Dip Correction (height of eye)	*-3.1′ (from inside front of almanac; see Figure 16-3)*
4. Sum	*-1.0′*
5. Sextant Altitude *(hs)*	*47°19.1′ (given)*
6. Apparent Altitude *(ha)*	*47°18.1′*
7. Altitude Correction	*-0.9′ (inside front cover of almanac; Figure 16-3)*
8. Mars/Venus Correction	*not applicable (inside front cover of almanac)*
9. Additional Correction	*not applicable (atmospheric corr'n; page A4 in almanac)*
10. Horizontal Parallax Correction	*not applicable (for moon, inside back cover of almanac)*
11. Moon Upper Limb Correction	*not applicable (for moon; always -30.0′)*
12. Correction to Apparent Altitude	*-0.9′ (sum of lines 7—11)*
13. Observed Altitude *(ho)*	*47°17.2′ (line 6 minus line 12)*

Section II:

14. Date	*16 May 1995 (given)*
15. DR Latitude	*39°N (given)*
16. DR Longitude	*157°08.0′W (given)*
17. Time of Sight (corrected)	*20 07 43 (given)*
18. Zone Description	*+10 (from time zone chart or computation; Chapter 14)*
19. GMT (Date *May 17*) Time	*06 07 43 (It is morning the next day in Greenwich.)*

Section III:

20. GHA (*v* corr'n. factor *n/a*)	*324°28.4′ (Aries, from daily page of almanac; Figure 16-4)*
21. GHA increment	*1° 56.1′ (increments and corrections section; Figure 16-5)*
22. SHA (or *v* correction)	*137° 18.5′ (from daily page of almanac; Figure 16-4)*
23. GHA	*463°43.0′ (-360° = 103°43′, sum of lines 20, 21, 22)*
24. + or –360°	*(not applicable in this case)*
25. Assumed Longitude	*156° 43.0′ (nearest whole degree, plus minutes from GHA)*
26. LHA	*307° (line 23 minus line 25)*
27. Declination (*d* corr'n. factor *n/a*)	*N 74° 10.6′ (from almanac daily pages; Figure 16-4)*
28. *d* correction	*(not applicable in this case)*
29. Declination	*N 74° 10.6′ (line 27 + line 28)*
30. Assumed Latitude	*N 39° (same) (nearest whole degree of latitude)*

Section IV:

31. Tabulated hc/*d* (factor *-24.8*)	*47°12.6′ (from sight reduction tables; Figure 16-6)*
32. Declination Increment	*-4.4′ (10.6′ / 60 x -24.8 = -4.4)*
33. Computed Altitude *(hc)*	*47° 08.2′ (line 31 minus line 32)*
34. Observed Altitude *(ho)*	*47° 17.2′ (from line 13)*
35. Altitude Intercept (Toward/Away)	*9.0′ Toward (line 34 minus line 33, "Ho-Mo-To")*
36. Azimuth Angle (Z)	*18.9° (from sight reduction tables; Figure 16-6)*
37. Azimuth (Zn)	*19° (round off to nearest whole degree)*

A2 ALTITUDE CORRECTION TABLES 10°-90°—SUN, STARS, PLANETS

Figure 16-3. *This page from the inside front cover of the* Nautical Almanac *shows the height of eye (dip) correction and the altitude correction for the Kochab sight reduction.*

SUN

OCT.—MAR. App. Alt.	Lower Limb	Upper Limb	APR.—SEPT. App. Alt.	Lower Limb	Upper Limb
° ′	′	′	° ′	′	′
9 34	+10·8	−21·5	9 39	+10·6	−21·2
9 45	+10·9	−21·4	9 51	+10·7	−21·1
9 56	+11·0	−21·3	10 03	+10·8	−21·0
10 08	+11·1	−21·2	10 15	+10·9	−20·9
10 21	+11·2	−21·1	10 27	+11·0	−20·8
10 34	+11·3	−21·0	10 40	+11·1	−20·7
10 47	+11·4	−20·9	10 54	+11·2	−20·6
11 01	+11·5	−20·8	11 08	+11·3	−20·5
11 15	+11·6	−20·7	11 23	+11·4	−20·4
11 30	+11·7	−20·6	11 38	+11·5	−20·3
11 46	+11·8	−20·5	11 54	+11·6	−20·2
12 02	+11·9	−20·4	12 10	+11·7	−20·1
12 19	+12·0	−20·3	12 28	+11·8	−20·0
12 37	+12·1	−20·2	12 46	+11·9	−19·9
12 55	+12·2	−20·1	13 05	+12·0	−19·8
13 14	+12·3	−20·0	13 24	+12·1	−19·7
13 35	+12·4	−19·9	13 45	+12·2	−19·6
13 56	+12·5	−19·8	14 07	+12·3	−19·5
14 18	+12·6	−19·7	14 30	+12·4	−19·4
14 42	+12·7	−19·6	14 54	+12·5	−19·3
15 06	+12·8	−19·5	15 19	+12·6	−19·2
15 32	+12·9	−19·4	15 46	+12·7	−19·1
15 59	+13·0	−19·3	16 14	+12·8	−19·0
16 28	+13·1	−19·2	16 44	+12·9	−18·9
16 59	+13·2	−19·1	17 15	+13·0	−18·8
17 32	+13·3	−19·0	17 48	+13·1	−18·7
18 06	+13·4	−18·9	18 24	+13·2	−18·6
18 42	+13·5	−18·8	19 01	+13·3	−18·5
19 21	+13·6	−18·7	19 42	+13·4	−18·4
20 03	+13·7	−18·6	20 25	+13·5	−18·3
20 48	+13·8	−18·5	21 11	+13·6	−18·2
21 35	+13·9	−18·4	22 00	+13·7	−18·1
22 26	+14·0	−18·3	22 54	+13·8	−18·0
23 22	+14·1	−18·2	23 51	+13·9	−17·9
24 21	+14·2	−18·1	24 53	+14·0	−17·8
25 26	+14·3	−18·0	26 00	+14·1	−17·7
26 36	+14·4	−17·9	27 13	+14·2	−17·6
27 52	+14·5	−17·8	28 33	+14·3	−17·5
29 15	+14·6	−17·7	30 00	+14·4	−17·4
30 46	+14·7	−17·6	31 35	+14·5	−17·3
32 26	+14·8	−17·5	33 20	+14·6	−17·2
34 17	+14·9	−17·4	35 17	+14·7	−17·1
36 20	+15·0	−17·3	37 26	+14·8	−17·0
38 36	+15·1	−17·2	39 50	+14·9	−16·9
41 08	+15·2	−17·1	42 31	+15·0	−16·8
43 59	+15·3	−17·0	45 31	+15·1	−16·7
47 10	+15·4	−16·9	48 55	+15·2	−16·6
50 46	+15·5	−16·8	52 44	+15·3	−16·5
54 49	+15·6	−16·7	57 02	+15·4	−16·4
59 23	+15·7	−16·6	61 51	+15·5	−16·3
64 30	+15·8	−16·5	67 17	+15·6	−16·2
70 12	+15·9	−16·4	73 16	+15·7	−16·1
76 26	+16·0	−16·3	79 43	+15·8	−16·0
83 05	+16·1	−16·2	86 32	+15·9	−15·9
90 00			90 00		

STARS AND PLANETS

App. Alt.	Corrⁿ
° ′	′
9 56	−5·3
10 08	−5·2
10 20	−5·1
10 33	−5·0
10 46	−4·9
11 00	−4·8
11 14	−4·7
11 29	−4·6
11 45	−4·5
12 01	−4·4
12 18	−4·3
12 35	−4·2
12 54	−4·1
13 13	−4·0
13 33	−3·9
13 54	−3·8
14 16	−3·7
14 40	−3·6
15 04	−3·5
15 30	−3·4
15 57	−3·3
16 26	−3·2
16 56	−3·1
17 28	−3·0
18 02	−2·9
18 38	−2·8
19 17	−2·7
19 58	−2·6
20 42	−2·5
21 28	−2·4
22 19	−2·3
23 13	−2·2
24 11	−2·1
25 14	−2·0
26 22	−1·9
27 36	−1·8
28 56	−1·7
30 24	−1·6
32 00	−1·5
33 45	−1·4
35 40	−1·3
37 48	−1·2
40 08	−1·1
42 44	−1·0
45 36	−0·9
48 47	−0·8
52 18	−0·7
56 11	−0·6
60 28	−0·5
65 08	−0·4
70 11	−0·3
75 34	−0·2
81 13	−0·1
87 03	0·0
90 00	

App. Alt. — Additional Corrⁿ

1995

VENUS

Jan. 1–Jan. 2

°	′
0	+0·3
34	+0·2
60	+0·1
80	

Jan. 3–Feb. 23

°	′
0	+0·2
41	+0·1
76	

Feb. 24–Dec. 31

°	′
0	+0·1
60	

MARS

Jan. 1–Apr. 10

°	′
0	+0·2
41	+0·1
76	

Apr. 11–Dec. 31

°	′
0	+0·1
60	

DIP

Ht. of Eye (m)	Corrⁿ (′)	Ht. of Eye (ft.)
2·4	−2·8	8·0
2·6	−2·9	8·6
2·8	−3·0	9·2
3·0	−3·1	9·8
3·2	−3·2	10·5
3·4	−3·3	11·2
3·6	−3·4	11·9
3·8	−3·5	12·6
4·0	−3·6	13·3
4·3	−3·7	14·1
4·5	−3·8	14·9
4·7	−3·9	15·7
5·0	−4·0	16·5
5·2	−4·1	17·4
5·5	−4·2	18·3
5·8	−4·3	19·1
6·1	−4·4	20·1
6·3	−4·5	21·0
6·6	−4·6	22·0
6·9	−4·7	22·9
7·2	−4·8	23·9
7·5	−4·9	24·9
7·9	−5·0	26·0
8·2	−5·1	27·1
8·5	−5·2	28·1
8·8	−5·3	29·2
9·2	−5·4	30·4
9·5	−5·5	31·5
9·9	−5·6	32·7
10·3	−5·7	33·9
10·6	−5·8	35·1
11·0	−5·9	36·3
11·4	−6·0	37·6
11·8	−6·1	38·9
12·2	−6·2	40·1
12·6	−6·3	41·5
13·0	−6·4	42·8
13·4	−6·5	44·2
13·8	−6·6	45·5
14·2	−6·7	46·9
14·7	−6·8	48·4
15·1	−6·9	49·8
15·5	−7·0	51·3
16·0	−7·1	52·8
16·5	−7·2	54·3
16·9	−7·3	55·8
17·4	−7·4	57·4
17·9	−7·5	58·9
18·4	−7·6	60·5
18·8	−7·7	62·1
19·3	−7·8	63·8
19·8	−7·9	65·4
20·4	−8·0	67·1
20·9	−8·1	68·8
21·4		70·5

Ht. of Eye	Corrⁿ
m	′
1·0	− 1·8
1·5	− 2·2
2·0	− 2·5
2·5	− 2·8
3·0	− 3·0
See table ←	
m	′
20	− 7·9
22	− 8·3
24	− 8·6
26	− 9·0
28	− 9·3
30	− 9·6
32	− 10·0
34	− 10·3
36	− 10·6
38	− 10·8
40	− 11·1
42	− 11·4
44	− 11·7
46	− 11·9
48	− 12·2
ft.	′
2	− 1·4
4	− 1·9
6	− 2·4
8	− 2·7
10	− 3·1
See table ←	
ft.	′
70	− 8·1
75	− 8·4
80	− 8·7
85	− 8·9
90	− 9·2
95	− 9·5
100	− 9·7
105	− 9·9
110	− 10·2
115	− 10·4
120	− 10·6
125	− 10·8
130	− 11·1
135	− 11·3
140	− 11·5
145	− 11·7
150	− 11·9
155	− 12·1

App. Alt. = Apparent altitude = Sextant altitude corrected for index error and dip.
For daylight observations of Venus, see page 260.

Figure 16-4. *This is the almanac daily page for the Kochab sight. You take the GHA of Aries from the "Aries" column and the star's SHA and declination from the "Stars" column.*

100

1995 MAY 16, 17, 18 (TUES., WED., THURS.)

UT (GMT) d h	ARIES G.H.A. ° ′	VENUS −3.9 G.H.A. ° ′	VENUS Dec. ° ′	MARS +0.7 G.H.A. ° ′	MARS Dec. ° ′	JUPITER −2.5 G.H.A. ° ′	JUPITER Dec. ° ′	SATURN +1.3 G.H.A. ° ′	SATURN Dec. ° ′
16 00	233 14.4	205 51.6	N 9 30.5	84 34.3	N14 31.2	342 02.6	S21 28.7	239 13.9	S 4 40.8
01	248 16.9	220 51.2	31.6	99 35.8	30.8	357 05.3	28.7	254 16.2	40.7
02	263 19.4	235 50.8	32.7	114 37.3	30.3	12 08.1	28.7	269 18.5	40.6
03	278 21.8	250 50.4	· · 33.8	129 38.8	· · 29.9	27 10.9	· · 28.6	284 20.7	· · 40.6
04	293 24.3	265 50.0	34.9	144 40.3	29.5	42 13.7	28.6	299 23.0	40.5
05	308 26.8	280 49.6	36.0	159 41.7	29.1	57 16.4	28.5	314 25.3	40.4
06	323 29.2	295 49.2	N 9 37.1	174 43.2	N14 28.7	72 19.2	S21 28.5	329 27.6	S 4 40.4
07	338 31.7	310 48.8	38.2	189 44.7	28.3	87 22.0	28.5	344 29.9	40.3
T 08	353 34.2	325 48.4	39.2	204 46.2	27.9	102 24.7	28.4	359 32.1	40.2
U 09	8 36.6	340 48.0	· · 40.3	219 47.7	· · 27.5	117 27.5	· · 28.4	14 34.4	· · 40.2
E 10	23 39.1	355 47.6	41.4	234 49.2	27.1	132 30.3	28.4	29 36.7	40.1
S 11	38 41.5	10 47.1	42.5	249 50.6	26.6	147 33.1	28.3	44 39.0	40.0
D 12	53 44.0	25 46.7	N 9 43.6	264 52.1	N14 26.2	162 35.8	S21 28.3	59 41.3	S 4 40.0
A 13	68 46.5	40 46.3	44.7	279 53.6	25.8	177 38.6	28.3	74 43.6	39.9
Y 14	83 48.9	55 45.9	45.8	294 55.1	25.4	192 41.4	28.2	89 45.8	39.8
15	98 51.4	70 45.5	· · 46.9	309 56.6	· · 25.0	207 44.2	· · 28.2	104 48.1	· · 39.8
16	113 53.9	85 45.1	47.9	324 58.0	24.6	222 46.9	28.2	119 50.4	39.7
17	128 56.3	100 44.7	49.0	339 59.5	24.2	237 49.7	28.1	134 52.7	39.6
18	143 58.8	115 44.3	N 9 50.1	355 01.0	N14 23.8	252 52.5	S21 28.1	149 55.0	S 4 39.6
19	159 01.3	130 43.9	51.2	10 02.5	23.3	267 55.3	28.1	164 57.3	39.5
20	174 03.7	145 43.5	52.3	25 03.9	22.9	282 58.0	28.0	179 59.5	39.4
21	189 06.2	160 43.1	· · 53.4	40 05.4	· · 22.5	298 00.8	· · 28.0	195 01.8	· · 39.4
22	204 08.7	175 42.7	54.5	55 06.9	22.1	313 03.6	28.0	210 04.1	39.3
23	219 11.1	190 42.3	55.5	70 08.4	21.7	328 06.3	27.9	225 06.4	39.2
17 00	234 13.6	205 41.9	N 9 56.6	85 09.8	N14 21.3	343 09.1	S21 27.9	240 08.7	S 4 39.1
01	249 16.0	220 41.5	57.7	100 11.3	20.9	358 11.9	27.8	255 11.0	39.1
02	264 18.5	235 41.1	58.8	115 12.8	20.5	13 14.7	27.8	270 13.2	39.0
03	279 21.0	250 40.7	9 59.9	130 14.3	· · 20.0	28 17.4	· · 27.8	285 15.5	· · 38.9
04	294 23.4	265 40.3	10 01.0	145 15.7	19.6	43 20.2	27.7	300 17.8	38.9
05	~~309 25.9~~	280 39.8	02.0	160 17.2	19.2	58 23.0	27.7	315 20.1	38.8
06	324 28.4	295 39.4	N10 03.1	175 18.7	N14 18.8	73 25.8	S21 27.7	330 22.4	S 4 38.7
W 07	~~339 30.8~~	310 39.0	04.2	190 20.2	18.4	88 28.6	27.6	345 24.7	38.7
E 08	354 33.3	325 38.6	05.3	205 21.6	18.0	103 31.3	27.6	0 26.9	38.6
D 09	9 35.8	340 38.2	· · 06.4	220 23.1	· · 17.5	118 34.1	· · 27.6	15 29.2	· · 38.5
N 10	24 38.2	355 37.8	07.4	235 24.6	17.1	133 36.9	27.5	30 31.5	38.5
E 11	39 40.7	10 37.4	08.5	250 26.0	16.7	148 39.7	27.5	45 33.8	38.4
S 12	54 43.1	25 37.0	N10 09.6	265 27.5	N14 16.3	163 42.4	S21 27.5	60 36.1	S 4 38.3
D 13	69 45.6	40 36.6	10.7	280 29.0	15.9	178 45.2	27.4	75 38.4	38.3
A 14	84 48.1	55 36.2	11.8	295 30.5	15.5	193 48.0	27.4	90 40.7	38.2
Y 15	99 50.5	70 35.7	· · 12.8	310 31.9	· · 15.0	208 50.8	· · 27.4	105 42.9	· · 38.1
16	114 53.0	85 35.3	13.9	325 33.4	14.6	223 53.5	27.3	120 45.2	38.1
17	129 55.5	100 34.9	15.0	340 34.9	14.2	238 56.3	27.3	135 47.5	38.0
18	144 57.9	115 34.5	N10 16.1	355 36.3	N14 13.8	253 59.1	S21 27.2	150 49.8	S 4 37.9
19	160 00.4	130 34.1	17.2	10 37.8	13.4	269 01.9	27.2	165 52.1	37.9
20	175 02.9	145 33.7	18.2	25 39.3	13.0	284 04.6	27.2	180 54.4	37.8
21	190 05.3	160 33.3	· · 19.3	40 40.7	· · 12.5	299 07.4	· · 27.1	195 56.7	· · 37.7
22	205 07.8	175 32.8	20.4	55 42.2	12.1	314 10.2	27.1	210 58.9	37.7
23	220 10.3	190 32.4	21.5	70 43.7	11.7	329 13.0	27.1	226 01.2	37.6
18 00	235 12.7	205 32.0	N10 22.5	85 45.1	N14 11.3	344 15.8	S21 27.0	241 03.5	S 4 37.5
01	250 15.2	220 31.6	23.6	100 46.6	10.9	359 18.5	27.0	256 05.8	37.5
02	265 17.6	235 31.2	24.7	115 48.1	10.5	14 21.3	27.0	271 08.1	37.4
03	280 20.1	250 30.8	· · 25.8	130 49.5	· · 10.0	29 24.1	· · 26.9	286 10.4	· · 37.3
04	295 22.6	265 30.4	26.8	145 51.0	09.6	44 26.9	26.9	301 12.7	37.3
05	310 25.0	280 29.9	27.9	160 52.5	09.2	59 29.6	26.9	316 15.0	37.2
06	325 27.5	295 29.5	N10 29.0	175 53.9	N14 08.8	74 32.4	S21 26.8	331 17.2	S 4 37.1
07	340 30.0	310 29.1	30.0	190 55.4	08.4	89 35.2	26.8	346 19.5	37.1
T 08	355 32.4	325 28.7	31.1	205 56.9	07.9	104 38.0	26.8	1 21.8	37.0
H 09	10 34.9	340 28.3	· · 32.2	220 58.3	· · 07.5	119 40.8	· · 26.7	16 24.1	· · 36.9
U 10	25 37.4	355 27.9	33.3	235 59.8	07.1	134 43.5	26.7	31 26.4	36.9
R 11	40 39.8	10 27.4	34.3	251 01.2	06.7	149 46.3	26.6	46 28.7	36.8
S 12	55 42.3	25 27.0	N10 35.4	266 02.7	N14 06.3	164 49.1	S21 26.6	61 31.0	S 4 36.8
D 13	70 44.8	40 26.6	36.5	281 04.2	05.8	179 51.9	26.6	76 33.3	36.7
A 14	85 47.2	55 26.2	37.5	296 05.6	05.4	194 54.7	26.5	91 35.6	36.6
Y 15	100 49.7	70 25.8	· · 38.6	311 07.1	· · 05.0	209 57.4	· · 26.5	106 37.8	· · 36.6
16	115 52.1	85 25.3	39.7	326 08.6	04.6	225 00.2	26.5	121 40.1	36.5
17	130 54.6	100 24.9	40.7	341 10.0	04.2	240 03.0	26.4	136 42.4	36.4
18	145 57.1	115 24.5	N10 41.8	356 11.5	N14 03.7	255 05.8	S21 26.4	151 44.7	S 4 36.4
19	160 59.5	130 24.1	42.9	11 12.9	03.3	270 08.6	26.4	166 47.0	36.3
20	176 02.0	145 23.6	44.0	26 14.4	02.9	285 11.3	26.3	181 49.3	36.2
21	191 04.5	160 23.2	· · 45.0	41 15.9	· · 02.5	300 14.1	· · 26.3	196 51.6	· · 36.2
22	206 06.9	175 22.8	46.1	56 17.3	02.0	315 16.9	26.2	211 53.9	36.1
23	221 09.4	190 22.4	47.2	71 18.8	01.6	330 19.7	26.2	226 56.2	36.0
Mer. Pass.	h m 8 21.7	v −0.4	d 1.1	v 1.5	d 0.4	v 2.8	d 0.0	v 2.3	d 0.1

STARS

Name	S.H.A. ° ′	Dec. ° ′
Acamar	315 29.1	S40 19.4
Achernar	335 37.4	S57 15.5
Acrux	173 24.0	S63 04.7
Adhara	255 23.5	S28 58.3
Aldebaran	291 05.3	N16 29.9
Alioth	166 32.3	N55 59.2
Alkaid	153 09.2	N49 20.3
Al Na'ir	28 00.8	S46 58.7
Alnilam	276 00.5	S 1 12.5
Alphard	218 09.5	S 8 38.6
Alphecca	126 22.2	N26 43.8
Alpheratz	357 57.8	N29 03.8
Altair	62 21.3	N 8 51.4
Ankaa	353 29.4	S42 19.7
Antares	112 42.6	S26 25.3
Arcturus	146 07.8	N19 12.4
Atria	107 56.1	S69 01.0
Avior	234 23.8	S59 30.1
Bellatrix	278 46.9	N 6 20.6
Betelgeuse	271 16.3	N 7 24.2
Canopus	264 02.6	S52 41.9
Capella	280 55.0	N45 59.5
Deneb	49 40.6	N45 15.7
Denebola	182 47.4	N14 35.8
Diphda	349 09.8	S18 00.7
Dubhe	194 08.2	N61 46.7
Elnath	278 30.2	N28 36.1
Eltanin	90 52.0	N51 29.3
Enif	34 00.5	N 9 51.2
Fomalhaut	15 39.1	S29 38.6
Gacrux	172 15.6	S57 05.5
Gienah	176 06.1	S17 31.2
Hadar	149 06.6	S60 21.2
Hamal	328 16.4	N23 26.3
Kaus Aust.	84 01.5	S34 23.0
Kochab	137 18.5	N74 10.6
~~Markab~~	~~13 52.0~~	~~N15 10.8~~
Menkar	314 29.6	N 4 04.2
Menkent	148 23.3	S36 21.0
Miaplacidus	221 42.6	S69 42.4
Mirfak	309 00.4	N49 50.6
Nunki	76 14.9	S26 18.0
Peacock	53 40.4	S56 44.7
Pollux	243 44.6	N28 02.2
Procyon	245 14.1	N 5 14.0
Rasalhague	96 18.8	N12 33.8
Regulus	207 58.0	N11 59.3
Rigel	281 25.5	S 8 12.6
Rigil Kent.	140 09.6	S60 49.0
Sabik	102 27.8	S15 43.1
Schedar	349 56.4	N56 30.5
Shaula	96 40.0	S37 05.9
Sirius	258 45.9	S16 42.8
Spica	158 45.3	S11 08.4
Suhail	223 02.5	S43 25.2
Vega	80 47.8	N38 46.7
Zuben'ubi	137 20.2	S16 01.4

	S.H.A. ° ′	Mer. Pass. h m
Venus	331 28.3	10 17
Mars	210 56.3	18 18
Jupiter	108 55.5	1 07
Saturn	5 55.1	7 58

INCREMENTS AND CORRECTIONS

6ᵐ

6ᵐ	SUN PLANETS	ARIES	MOON	v or d	Corrⁿ	v or d	Corrⁿ	v or d	Corrⁿ
s	° ′	° ′	° ′	′	′	′	′	′	′
00	1 30·0	1 30·2	1 25·9	0·0	0·0	6·0	0·7	12·0	1·3
01	1 30·3	1 30·5	1 26·1	0·1	0·0	6·1	0·7	12·1	1·3
02	1 30·5	1 30·7	1 26·4	0·2	0·0	6·2	0·7	12·2	1·3
03	1 30·8	1 31·0	1 26·6	0·3	0·0	6·3	0·7	12·3	1·3
04	1 31·0	1 31·2	1 26·9	0·4	0·0	6·4	0·7	12·4	1·3
05	1 31·3	1 31·5	1 27·1	0·5	0·1	6·5	0·7	12·5	1·4
06	1 31·5	1 31·8	1 27·3	0·6	0·1	6·6	0·7	12·6	1·4
07	1 31·8	1 32·0	1 27·6	0·7	0·1	6·7	0·7	12·7	1·4
08	1 32·0	1 32·3	1 27·8	0·8	0·1	6·8	0·7	12·8	1·4
09	1 32·3	1 32·5	1 28·0	0·9	0·1	6·9	0·7	12·9	1·4
10	1 32·5	1 32·8	1 28·3	1·0	0·1	7·0	0·8	13·0	1·4
11	1 32·8	1 33·0	1 28·5	1·1	0·1	7·1	0·8	13·1	1·4
12	1 33·0	1 33·3	1 28·8	1·2	0·1	7·2	0·8	13·2	1·4
13	1 33·3	1 33·5	1 29·0	1·3	0·1	7·3	0·8	13·3	1·4
14	1 33·5	1 33·8	1 29·2	1·4	0·2	7·4	0·8	13·4	1·5
15	1 33·8	1 34·0	1 29·5	1·5	0·2	7·5	0·8	13·5	1·5
16	1 34·0	1 34·3	1 29·7	1·6	0·2	7·6	0·8	13·6	1·5
17	1 34·3	1 34·5	1 30·0	1·7	0·2	7·7	0·8	13·7	1·5
18	1 34·5	1 34·8	1 30·2	1·8	0·2	7·8	0·8	13·8	1·5
19	1 34·8	1 35·0	1 30·4	1·9	0·2	7·9	0·9	13·9	1·5
20	1 35·0	1 35·3	1 30·7	2·0	0·2	8·0	0·9	14·0	1·5
21	1 35·3	1 35·5	1 30·9	2·1	0·2	8·1	0·9	14·1	1·5
22	1 35·5	1 35·8	1 31·1	2·2	0·2	8·2	0·9	14·2	1·5
23	1 35·8	1 36·0	1 31·4	2·3	0·2	8·3	0·9	14·3	1·5
24	1 36·0	1 36·3	1 31·6	2·4	0·3	8·4	0·9	14·4	1·6
25	1 36·3	1 36·5	1 31·9	2·5	0·3	8·5	0·9	14·5	1·6
26	1 36·5	1 36·8	1 32·1	2·6	0·3	8·6	0·9	14·6	1·6
27	1 36·8	1 37·0	1 32·3	2·7	0·3	8·7	0·9	14·7	1·6
28	1 37·0	1 37·3	1 32·6	2·8	0·3	8·8	1·0	14·8	1·6
29	1 37·3	1 37·5	1 32·8	2·9	0·3	8·9	1·0	14·9	1·6
30	1 37·5	1 37·8	1 33·1	3·0	0·3	9·0	1·0	15·0	1·6
31	1 37·8	1 38·0	1 33·3	3·1	0·3	9·1	1·0	15·1	1·6
32	1 38·0	1 38·3	1 33·5	3·2	0·3	9·2	1·0	15·2	1·6
33	1 38·3	1 38·5	1 33·8	3·3	0·4	9·3	1·0	15·3	1·7
34	1 38·5	1 38·8	1 34·0	3·4	0·4	9·4	1·0	15·4	1·7
35	1 38·8	1 39·0	1 34·3	3·5	0·4	9·5	1·0	15·5	1·7
36	1 39·0	1 39·3	1 34·5	3·6	0·4	9·6	1·0	15·6	1·7
37	1 39·3	1 39·5	1 34·7	3·7	0·4	9·7	1·1	15·7	1·7
38	1 39·5	1 39·8	1 35·0	3·8	0·4	9·8	1·1	15·8	1·7
39	1 39·8	1 40·0	1 35·2	3·9	0·4	9·9	1·1	15·9	1·7
40	1 40·0	1 40·3	1 35·4	4·0	0·4	10·0	1·1	16·0	1·7
41	1 40·3	1 40·5	1 35·7	4·1	0·4	10·1	1·1	16·1	1·7
42	1 40·5	1 40·8	1 35·9	4·2	0·5	10·2	1·1	16·2	1·8
43	1 40·8	1 41·0	1 36·2	4·3	0·5	10·3	1·1	16·3	1·8
44	1 41·0	1 41·3	1 36·4	4·4	0·5	10·4	1·1	16·4	1·8
45	1 41·3	1 41·5	1 36·6	4·5	0·5	10·5	1·1	16·5	1·8
46	1 41·5	1 41·8	1 36·9	4·6	0·5	10·6	1·1	16·6	1·8
47	1 41·8	1 42·0	1 37·1	4·7	0·5	10·7	1·2	16·7	1·8
48	1 42·0	1 42·3	1 37·4	4·8	0·5	10·8	1·2	16·8	1·8
49	1 42·3	1 42·5	1 37·6	4·9	0·5	10·9	1·2	16·9	1·8
50	1 42·5	1 42·8	1 37·8	5·0	0·5	11·0	1·2	17·0	1·8
51	1 42·8	1 43·0	1 38·1	5·1	0·6	11·1	1·2	17·1	1·9
52	1 43·0	1 43·3	1 38·3	5·2	0·6	11·2	1·2	17·2	1·9
53	1 43·3	1 43·5	1 38·5	5·3	0·6	11·3	1·2	17·3	1·9
54	1 43·5	1 43·8	1 38·8	5·4	0·6	11·4	1·2	17·4	1·9
55	1 43·8	1 44·0	1 39·0	5·5	0·6	11·5	1·2	17·5	1·9
56	1 44·0	1 44·3	1 39·3	5·6	0·6	11·6	1·3	17·6	1·9
57	1 44·3	1 44·5	1 39·5	5·7	0·6	11·7	1·3	17·7	1·9
58	1 44·5	1 44·8	1 39·7	5·8	0·6	11·8	1·3	17·8	1·9
59	1 44·8	1 45·0	1 40·0	5·9	0·6	11·9	1·3	17·9	1·9
60	1 45·0	1 45·3	1 40·2	6·0	0·7	12·0	1·3	18·0	2·0

7ᵐ

7ᵐ	SUN PLANETS	ARIES	MOON	v or d	Corrⁿ	v or d	Corrⁿ	v or d	Corrⁿ
s	° ′	° ′	° ′	′	′	′	′	′	′
00	1 45·0	1 45·3	1 40·2	0·0	0·0	6·0	0·8	12·0	1·5
01	1 45·3	1 45·5	1 40·5	0·1	0·0	6·1	0·8	12·1	1·5
02	1 45·5	1 45·8	1 40·7	0·2	0·0	6·2	0·8	12·2	1·5
03	1 45·8	1 46·0	1 40·9	0·3	0·0	6·3	0·8	12·3	1·5
04	1 46·0	1 46·3	1 41·2	0·4	0·1	6·4	0·8	12·4	1·6
05	1 46·3	1 46·5	1 41·4	0·5	0·1	6·5	0·8	12·5	1·6
06	1 46·5	1 46·8	1 41·6	0·6	0·1	6·6	0·8	12·6	1·6
07	1 46·8	1 47·0	1 41·9	0·7	0·1	6·7	0·8	12·7	1·6
08	1 47·0	1 47·3	1 42·1	0·8	0·1	6·8	0·9	12·8	1·6
09	1 47·3	1 47·5	1 42·4	0·9	0·1	6·9	0·9	12·9	1·6
10	1 47·5	1 47·8	1 42·6	1·0	0·1	7·0	0·9	13·0	1·6
11	1 47·8	1 48·0	1 42·8	1·1	0·1	7·1	0·9	13·1	1·6
12	1 48·0	1 48·3	1 43·1	1·2	0·2	7·2	0·9	13·2	1·7
13	1 48·3	1 48·5	1 43·3	1·3	0·2	7·3	0·9	13·3	1·7
14	1 48·5	1 48·8	1 43·6	1·4	0·2	7·4	0·9	13·4	1·7
15	1 48·8	1 49·0	1 43·8	1·5	0·2	7·5	0·9	13·5	1·7
16	1 49·0	1 49·3	1 44·0	1·6	0·2	7·6	1·0	13·6	1·7
17	1 49·3	1 49·5	1 44·3	1·7	0·2	7·7	1·0	13·7	1·7
18	1 49·5	1 49·8	1 44·5	1·8	0·2	7·8	1·0	13·8	1·7
19	1 49·8	1 50·1	1 44·8	1·9	0·2	7·9	1·0	13·9	1·7
20	1 50·0	1 50·3	1 45·0	2·0	0·3	8·0	1·0	14·0	1·8
21	1 50·3	1 50·6	1 45·2	2·1	0·3	8·1	1·0	14·1	1·8
22	1 50·5	1 50·8	1 45·5	2·2	0·3	8·2	1·0	14·2	1·8
23	1 50·8	1 51·1	1 45·7	2·3	0·3	8·3	1·0	14·3	1·8
24	1 51·0	1 51·3	1 45·9	2·4	0·3	8·4	1·1	14·4	1·8
25	1 51·3	1 51·6	1 46·2	2·5	0·3	8·5	1·1	14·5	1·8
26	1 51·5	1 51·8	1 46·4	2·6	0·3	8·6	1·1	14·6	1·8
27	1 51·8	1 52·1	1 46·7	2·7	0·3	8·7	1·1	14·7	1·8
28	1 52·0	1 52·3	1 46·9	2·8	0·4	8·8	1·1	14·8	1·9
29	1 52·3	1 52·6	1 47·1	2·9	0·4	8·9	1·1	14·9	1·9
30	1 52·5	1 52·8	1 47·4	3·0	0·4	9·0	1·1	15·0	1·9
31	1 52·8	1 53·1	1 47·6	3·1	0·4	9·1	1·1	15·1	1·9
32	1 53·0	1 53·3	1 47·9	3·2	0·4	9·2	1·2	15·2	1·9
33	1 53·3	1 53·6	1 48·1	3·3	0·4	9·3	1·2	15·3	1·9
34	1 53·5	1 53·8	1 48·3	3·4	0·4	9·4	1·2	15·4	1·9
35	1 53·8	1 54·1	1 48·6	3·5	0·4	9·5	1·2	15·5	1·9
36	1 54·0	1 54·3	1 48·8	3·6	0·5	9·6	1·2	15·6	2·0
37	1 54·3	1 54·6	1 49·0	3·7	0·5	9·7	1·2	15·7	2·0
38	1 54·5	1 54·8	1 49·3	3·8	0·5	9·8	1·2	15·8	2·0
39	1 54·8	1 55·1	1 49·5	3·9	0·5	9·9	1·2	15·9	2·0
40	1 55·0	1 55·3	1 49·8	4·0	0·5	10·0	1·3	16·0	2·0
41	1 55·3	1 55·6	1 50·0	4·1	0·5	10·1	1·3	16·1	2·0
42	1 55·5	1 55·8	1 50·2	4·2	0·5	10·2	1·3	16·2	2·0
43	1 55·8	1 56·1	1 50·5	4·3	0·5	10·3	1·3	16·3	2·0
44	1 56·0	1 56·3	1 50·7	4·4	0·6	10·4	1·3	16·4	2·1
45	1 56·3	1 56·6	1 51·0	4·5	0·6	10·5	1·3	16·5	2·1
46	1 56·5	1 56·8	1 51·2	4·6	0·6	10·6	1·3	16·6	2·1
47	1 56·8	1 57·1	1 51·4	4·7	0·6	10·7	1·3	16·7	2·1
48	1 57·0	1 57·3	1 51·7	4·8	0·6	10·8	1·4	16·8	2·1
49	1 57·3	1 57·6	1 51·9	4·9	0·6	10·9	1·4	16·9	2·1
50	1 57·5	1 57·8	1 52·1	5·0	0·6	11·0	1·4	17·0	2·1
51	1 57·8	1 58·1	1 52·4	5·1	0·6	11·1	1·4	17·1	2·1
52	1 58·0	1 58·3	1 52·6	5·2	0·7	11·2	1·4	17·2	2·2
53	1 58·3	1 58·6	1 52·9	5·3	0·7	11·3	1·4	17·3	2·2
54	1 58·5	1 58·8	1 53·1	5·4	0·7	11·4	1·4	17·4	2·2
55	1 58·8	1 59·1	1 53·3	5·5	0·7	11·5	1·4	17·5	2·2
56	1 59·0	1 59·3	1 53·6	5·6	0·7	11·6	1·5	17·6	2·2
57	1 59·3	1 59·6	1 53·8	5·7	0·7	11·7	1·5	17·7	2·2
58	1 59·5	1 59·8	1 54·1	5·8	0·7	11·8	1·5	17·8	2·2
59	1 59·8	2 00·1	1 54·3	5·9	0·7	11·9	1·5	17·9	2·2
60	2 00·0	2 00·3	1 54·5	6·0	0·8	12·0	1·5	18·0	2·3

v

Figure 16-5. *This is the increments and corrections page for the Kochab sight. You'll find the correction for seven minutes and 43 seconds in the "Aries" column; there is no v or d correction for stars.*

Figure 16-6. *This is the page of the sight reduction tables for the Kochab sight. Enter on the page for the LHA of 307°, in the column for latitude 39°, and the row for a declination of 74°. Find the values of the* hc, *the* d *correction, and the Z. The* hc *is the computed altitude, the* d *correction provides for the minutes and tenths of declination that you add to the whole degree of 74, and the Z will be used to find the Zn, which is the line of bearing you plot from the AP.*

53°, 307° L.H.A. LATITUDE SAME NAME AS DECLINATION

N. Lat. {L.H.A. greater than 180°......Zn=Z; L.H.A. less than 180°..........Zn=360°−Z}

Dec.	38° Hc	38° d	38° Z	39° Hc	39° d	39° Z	40° Hc	40° d	40° Z	41° Hc	41° d	41° Z
°	° ′	′	°	° ′	′	°	° ′	′	°	° ′	′	°
0	28 18.6	+41.8	114.9	27 53.1	+42.6	115.4	27 27.2	+43.3	115.8	27 00.8	+44.1	116.3
1	29 00.4	41.5	114.1	28 35.7	42.3	114.6	28 10.5	43.1	115.1	27 44.9	43.8	115.5
2	29 41.9	41.2	113.2	29 18.0	42.0	113.8	28 53.6	42.7	114.3	28 28.7	43.5	114.8
3	30 23.1	40.9	112.4	30 00.0	41.7	112.9	29 36.3	42.5	113.5	29 12.2	43.3	114.0
4	31 04.0	40.5	111.6	30 41.7	41.3	112.1	30 18.8	42.2	112.7	29 55.5	42.9	113.2
5	31 44.5	+40.2	110.7	31 23.0	+41.0	111.3	31 01.0	+41.8	111.8	30 38.4	+42.7	112.4
6	32 24.7	39.8	109.8	32 04.0	40.7	110.4	31 42.8	41.6	111.0	31 21.1	42.3	111.6
7	33 04.5	39.4	108.9	32 44.7	40.3	109.5	32 24.4	41.1	110.1	32 03.4	42.0	110.7
8	33 43.9	39.0	108.0	33 25.0	40.0	108.6	33 05.5	40.8	109.3	32 45.4	41.7	109.9
9	34 22.9	38.6	107.1	34 05.0	39.5	107.8	33 46.3	40.5	108.4	33 27.1	41.3	109.0
10	35 01.5	+38.2	106.2	34 44.5	+39.1	106.8	34 26.8	+40.0	107.5	34 08.4	+40.9	108.1
11	35 39.7	37.7	105.2	35 23.6	38.7	105.9	35 06.8	39.6	106.6	34 49.3	40.6	107.3
12	36 17.4	37.3	104.3	36 02.3	38.2	105.0	35 46.4	39.2	105.7	35 29.9	40.1	106.4
13	36 54.7	36.7	103.3	36 40.5	37.8	104.0	36 25.6	38.8	104.7	36 10.0	39.7	105.4
14	37 31.4	36.3	102.3	37 18.3	37.3	103.0	37 04.4	38.2	103.8	36 49.7	39.3	104.5
15	38 07.7	+35.7	101.3	37 55.6	+36.7	102.1	37 42.6	+37.8	102.8	37 29.0	+38.7	103.6
16	38 43.4	35.2	100.3	38 32.3	36.3	101.0	38 20.4	37.3	101.8	38 07.7	38.4	102.6
17	39 18.6	34.6	99.2	39 08.6	35.7	100.0	38 57.7	36.8	100.8	38 46.1	37.8	101.6
18	39 53.2	34.0	98.2	39 44.3	35.1	99.0	39 34.5	36.2	99.8	39 23.9	37.2	100.6
19	40 27.2	33.5	97.1	40 19.4	34.6	97.9	40 10.7	35.7	98.8	40 01.1	36.8	99.6
20	41 00.7	+32.8	96.0	40 54.0	+33.9	96.8	40 46.4	+35.0	97.7	40 37.9	+36.2	98.6
21	41 33.5	32.1	94.9	41 27.9	33.3	95.7	41 21.4	34.5	96.6	41 14.1	35.5	97.5
22	42 05.6	31.4	93.7	42 01.2	32.6	94.6	41 55.9	33.8	95.5	41 49.6	35.0	96.4
23	42 37.0	30.8	92.6	42 33.8	32.0	93.5	42 29.7	33.2	94.4	42 24.6	34.3	95.3
24	43 07.8	30.0	91.4	43 05.8	31.3	92.3	43 02.9	32.4	93.3	42 58.9	33.7	94.2
25	43 37.8	+29.2	90.2	43 37.1	+30.5	91.2	43 35.3	+31.8	92.1	43 32.6	+33.0	93.1
26	44 07.0	28.5	89.0	44 07.6	29.7	90.0	44 07.1	31.0	90.9	44 05.6	32.2	91.9
27	44 35.5	27.7	87.8	44 37.3	29.0	88.8	44 38.1	30.3	89.8	44 37.8	31.6	90.7
28	45 03.2	26.8	86.5	45 06.3	28.2	87.5	45 08.4	29.4	88.5	45 09.4	30.7	89.5
29	45 30.0	26.0	85.3	45 34.5	27.3	86.3	45 37.8	28.7	87.3	45 40.1	30.0	88.3
30	45 56.0	+25.1	84.0	46 01.8	+26.4	85.0	46 06.5	+27.8	86.0	46 10.1	+29.1	87.1
31	46 21.1	24.2	82.7	46 28.2	25.6	83.7	46 34.3	26.9	84.7	46 39.2	28.3	85.8
32	46 45.3	23.2	81.3	46 53.8	24.6	82.4	47 01.2	26.0	83.4	47 07.5	27.4	84.5
33	47 08.5	22.3	80.0	47 18.4	23.7	81.0	47 27.2	25.1	82.1	47 34.9	26.5	83.2
34	47 30.8	21.3	78.6	47 42.1	22.7	79.7	47 52.3	24.1	80.8	48 01.4	25.5	81.9
35	47 52.1	+20.2	77.2	48 04.8	+21.7	78.3	48 16.4	+23.1	79.4	48 26.9	+24.5	80.5
36	48 12.3	19.3	75.8	48 26.5	20.7	76.9	48 39.5	22.1	78.0	48 51.4	23.6	79.1
37	48 31.6	18.1	74.4	48 47.2	19.6	75.5	49 01.6	21.1	76.6	49 15.0	22.5	77.7
38	48 49.7	17.1	72.9	49 06.8	18.5	74.0	49 22.7	20.0	75.2	49 37.5	21.4	76.3
39	49 06.8	15.9	71.5	49 25.3	17.4	72.6	49 42.7	18.9	73.7	49 58.9	20.4	74.8
40	49 22.7	+14.8	70.0	49 42.7	+16.2	71.1	50 01.6	+17.7	72.2	50 19.3	+19.2	73.4
41	49 37.5	13.6	68.5	49 58.9	15.1	69.6	50 19.3	16.6	70.7	50 38.5	18.1	71.9
42	49 51.1	12.5	67.0	50 14.0	14.0	68.1	50 35.9	15.4	69.2	50 56.6	16.9	70.4
43	50 03.6	11.2	65.5	50 28.0	12.7	66.6	50 51.3	14.2	67.7	51 13.5	15.7	68.9
44	50 14.8	10.1	63.9	50 40.7	11.5	65.0	51 05.5	12.9	66.2	51 29.2	14.4	67.3
45	50 24.9	+8.8	62.4	50 52.2	+10.2	63.5	51 18.4	+11.7	64.6	51 43.6	+13.2	65.7
46	50 33.7	7.5	60.8	51 02.4	9.0	61.9	51 30.1	10.5	63.0	51 56.8	11.9	64.2
47	50 41.2	6.3	59.3	51 11.4	7.7	60.3	51 40.6	9.1	61.4	52 08.7	10.6	62.6
48	50 47.5	5.0	57.7	51 19.1	6.4	58.8	51 49.7	7.9	59.8	52 19.3	9.3	61.0
49	50 52.5	3.7	56.1	51 25.5	5.1	57.2	51 57.6	6.5	58.2	52 28.6	8.0	59.3
50	50 56.2	+2.5	54.6	51 30.6	+3.8	55.6	52 04.1	+5.2	56.6	52 36.6	+6.6	57.7
51	50 58.7	+1.1	53.0	51 34.4	2.5	54.0	52 09.3	3.8	55.0	52 43.2	5.3	56.1
52	50 59.8	−0.1	51.4	51 36.9	+1.2	52.4	52 13.1	2.5	53.4	52 48.5	3.8	54.4
53	50 59.7	1.4	49.8	51 38.1	−0.2	50.7	52 15.6	+1.2	51.7	52 52.3	2.5	52.8
54	50 58.3	2.7	48.2	51 37.9	1.5	49.1	52 16.8	−0.2	50.1	52 54.8	+1.2	51.1
55	50 55.6	−4.1	46.6	51 36.4	−2.8	47.5	52 16.6	−1.6	48.5	52 56.0	−0.3	49.5
56	50 51.5	5.2	45.0	51 33.6	4.1	45.9	52 15.0	2.9	46.8	52 55.7	1.7	47.8
57	50 46.3	6.6	43.5	51 29.5	5.4	44.3	52 12.1	4.2	45.2	52 54.0	3.0	46.1
58	50 39.7	7.8	41.9	51 24.1	6.7	42.7	52 07.9	5.6	43.6	52 51.0	4.4	44.5
59	50 31.9	9.1	40.3	51 17.4	8.0	41.1	52 02.3	6.9	42.0	52 46.6	5.8	42.8
60	50 22.8	−10.3	38.8	51 09.4	−9.3	39.5	51 55.4	−8.3	40.4	52 40.8	−7.1	41.2
61	50 12.5	11.5	37.2	51 00.1	10.6	38.0	51 47.1	9.5	38.7	52 33.7	8.5	39.6
62	50 01.0	12.7	35.7	50 49.5	11.7	36.4	51 37.6	10.8	37.2	52 25.2	9.8	37.9
63	49 48.3	13.9	34.2	50 37.8	13.0	34.9	51 26.8	12.1	35.6	52 15.4	11.2	36.3
64	49 34.4	15.0	32.7	50 24.8	14.2	33.3	51 14.7	13.3	34.0	52 04.2	12.4	34.7
65	49 19.4	−16.2	31.2	50 10.6	−15.4	31.8	51 01.4	−14.6	32.5	51 51.8	−13.7	33.1
66	49 03.2	17.3	29.7	49 55.2	16.6	30.3	50 46.8	15.7	30.9	51 38.1	14.9	31.6
67	48 45.9	18.3	28.3	49 38.6	17.6	28.8	50 31.1	17.0	29.4	51 23.2	16.2	30.0
68	48 27.6	19.5	26.8	49 21.0	18.8	27.3	50 14.1	18.0	27.9	51 07.0	17.3	28.5
69	48 08.1	20.5	25.4	49 02.2	19.9	25.9	49 56.1	19.2	26.4	50 49.7	18.5	26.9
70	47 47.6	−21.5	24.0	48 42.3	−20.9	24.5	49 36.9	−20.3	24.9	50 31.2	−19.7	25.4
71	47 26.1	22.5	22.6	48 21.4	21.9	23.0	49 16.6	21.4	23.5	50 11.5	20.8	24.0
72	47 03.6	23.4	21.2	47 59.5	22.9	21.6	48 55.2	22.4	22.1	49 50.7	21.9	22.5
73	46 40.2	24.4	19.9	47 36.6	24.0	20.3	48 32.8	23.5	20.7	49 28.8	22.9	21.1
74	46 15.8	25.3	18.6	47 12.6	24.8	18.9	48 09.3	24.4	19.3	49 05.9	23.9	19.6
75	45 50.5	−26.1	17.3	46 47.8	−25.8	17.6	47 44.9	−25.3	17.9	48 42.0	−25.0	18.3
76	45 24.4	27.0	16.0	46 22.0	26.6	16.3	47 19.6	26.3	16.6	48 17.0	25.9	16.9
77	44 57.4	27.9	14.7	45 55.4	27.6	15.0	46 53.3	27.2	15.2	47 51.1	26.8	15.5
78	44 29.5	28.6	13.5	45 27.8	28.3	13.7	46 26.1	28.1	13.9	47 24.3	27.7	14.2
79	44 00.9	29.5	12.2	44 59.5	29.2	12.4	45 58.0	28.9	12.7	46 56.6	28.7	12.9
80	43 31.4	−30.1	11.0	44 30.3	−29.9	11.2	45 29.1	−29.7	11.4	46 27.9	−29.4	11.6
81	43 01.3	30.9	9.8	44 00.4	30.7	10.0	44 59.4	30.4	10.2	45 58.5	30.3	10.4
82	42 30.4	31.6	8.7	43 29.7	31.4	8.8	44 29.0	31.3	9.0	45 28.2	31.0	9.1
83	41 58.8	32.3	7.5	42 58.3	32.2	7.6	43 57.7	32.0	7.8	44 57.2	31.9	7.9
84	41 26.5	32.9	6.4	42 26.1	32.8	6.5	43 25.7	32.6	6.6	44 25.3	32.5	6.7
85	40 53.6	−33.6	5.3	41 53.3	−33.4	5.4	42 53.1	−33.4	5.5	43 52.8	−33.3	5.5
86	40 20.0	34.1	4.2	41 19.9	34.1	4.3	42 19.7	34.0	4.3	43 19.5	33.9	4.4
87	39 45.9	34.8	3.1	40 45.8	34.7	3.2	41 45.7	34.6	3.2	42 45.6	34.6	3.3
88	39 11.1	35.3	2.1	40 11.1	35.3	2.1	41 11.1	35.3	2.1	42 11.0	35.2	2.2
89	38 35.8	35.8	1.0	39 35.8	35.8	1.0	40 35.8	35.8	1.1	41 35.8	35.8	1.1
90	38 00.0	−36.4	0.0	39 00.0	−36.4	0.0	40 00.0	−36.4	0.0	41 00.0	−36.4	0.0
	38°			39°			40°			41°		

42° Hc	42° d	42° Z	43° Hc	43° d	43° Z	44° Hc	44° d	44° Z	45° Hc	45° d	45° Z	Dec.
° ′	′	°	° ′	′	°	° ′	′	°	° ′	′	°	°
26 34.0	+44.8	116.8	26 06.8	+45.4	117.2	25 39.1	+46.2	117.6	25 11.1	+46.8	118.1	0
27 18.8	44.5	116.0	26 52.2	45.3	116.5	26 25.3	45.9	116.9	25 57.9	46.6	117.4	1
28 03.3	44.3	115.3	27 37.5	45.0	115.7	27 11.2	45.7	116.2	26 44.5	46.4	116.7	2
28 47.6	44.0	114.5	28 22.5	44.7	115.0	27 56.9	45.4	115.5	27 30.9	46.1	115.9	3
29 31.6	43.7	113.7	29 07.2	44.5	114.2	28 42.3	45.3	114.7	28 17.0	45.9	115.2	4
30 15.3	+43.5	112.9	29 51.7	+44.2	113.5	29 27.6	+44.9	114.0	29 02.9	+45.7	114.5	5
30 58.8	43.1	112.1	30 35.9	43.9	112.7	30 12.5	44.7	113.2	29 48.6	45.4	113.7	6
31 41.9	42.8	111.3	31 19.8	43.7	111.9	30 57.2	44.4	112.4	30 34.0	45.2	113.0	7
32 24.7	42.5	110.5	32 03.5	43.3	111.1	31 41.6	44.1	111.6	31 19.2	44.9	112.2	8
33 07.2	42.2	109.6	32 46.8	43.0	110.2	32 25.7	43.8	110.8	32 04.1	44.6	111.4	9
33 49.4	+41.8	108.8	33 29.8	+42.6	109.4	33 09.5	+43.5	110.0	32 48.7	+44.2	110.6	10
34 31.2	41.4	107.9	34 12.4	42.3	108.6	33 53.0	43.1	109.2	33 32.9	44.0	109.8	11
35 12.6	41.1	107.0	34 54.7	41.9	107.7	34 36.1	42.8	108.4	34 16.9	43.6	109.0	12
35 53.7	40.6	106.1	35 36.6	41.6	106.8	35 18.9	42.5	107.5	35 00.5	43.3	108.2	13
36 34.3	40.2	105.2	36 18.2	41.1	105.9	36 01.4	42.0	106.6	35 43.8	42.9	107.3	14
37 14.5	+39.8	104.3	36 59.3	+40.7	105.0	36 43.4	+41.6	105.8	36 26.7	+42.6	106.5	15
37 54.3	39.3	103.4	37 40.0	40.3	104.1	37 25.0	41.2	104.9	37 09.3	42.1	105.6	16
38 33.6	38.8	102.4	38 20.3	39.8	103.2	38 06.2	40.8	103.9	37 51.4	41.7	104.7	17
39 12.4	38.3	101.4	39 00.1	39.4	102.2	38 47.0	40.3	103.0	38 33.1	41.3	103.8	18
39 50.7	37.8	100.4	39 39.5	38.8	101.2	39 27.3	39.9	102.0	39 14.4	40.9	102.8	19
40 28.5	+37.3	99.4	40 18.3	+38.3	100.2	40 07.2	+39.3	101.1	39 55.3	+40.3	101.9	20
41 05.8	36.7	98.4	40 56.6	37.8	99.2	40 46.5	38.9	100.1	40 35.6	39.9	100.9	21
41 42.5	36.1	97.3	41 34.4	37.2	98.2	41 25.4	38.3	99.1	41 15.5	39.3	99.9	22
42 18.6	35.4	96.2	42 11.6	36.6	97.1	42 03.7	37.7	98.0	41 54.8	38.8	98.9	23
42 54.0	34.9	95.1	42 48.2	36.0	96.1	42 41.4	37.1	97.0	42 33.6	38.2	97.9	24
43 28.9	+34.2	94.0	43 24.2	+35.3	95.0	43 18.5	+36.5	95.9	43 11.8	+37.7	96.8	25
44 03.1	33.5	92.9	43 59.5	34.7	93.8	43 55.0	35.9	94.8	43 49.5	37.0	95.8	26
44 36.6	32.7	91.7	44 34.2	34.0	92.7	44 30.9	35.2	93.7	44 26.5	36.4	94.7	27
45 09.3	32.1	90.5	45 08.2	33.3	91.5	45 06.1	34.5	92.6	45 02.9	35.7	93.6	28
45 41.4	31.2	89.3	45 41.5	32.5	90.4	45 40.6	33.8	91.4	45 38.6	35.0	92.4	29
46 12.6	+30.5	88.1	46 14.0	+31.8	89.2	46 14.4	+33.0	90.2	46 13.6	+34.3	91.2	30
46 43.1	29.6	86.9	46 45.8	30.9	87.9	46 47.4	32.3	89.0	46 47.9	33.5	90.0	31
47 12.7	28.7	85.6	47 16.7	30.1	86.7	47 19.7	31.4	87.7	47 21.4	32.8	88.8	32
47 41.4	27.9	84.3	47 46.8	29.3	85.4	47 51.1	30.6	86.5	47 54.2	31.9	87.6	33
48 09.3	26.9	83.0	48 16.1	28.3	84.1	48 21.7	29.7	85.2	48 26.1	31.1	86.3	34
48 36.2	+26.0	81.6	48 44.4	+27.4	82.7	48 51.4	+28.7	83.9	48 57.2	+30.1	85.0	35
49 02.2	25.0	80.2	49 11.8	26.4	81.4	49 20.1	27.9	82.5	49 27.3	29.3	83.7	36
49 27.2	23.9	78.9	49 38.2	25.4	80.0	49 48.0	26.8	81.2	49 56.6	28.3	82.3	37
49 51.1	22.9	77.4	50 03.6	24.4	78.6	50 14.8	25.9	79.8	50 24.9	27.3	81.0	38
50 14.0	21.9	76.0	50 28.0	23.3	77.2	50 40.7	24.8	78.4	50 52.2	26.2	79.6	39
50 35.9	+20.7	74.5	50 51.3	+22.2	75.7	51 05.5	+23.7	76.9	51 18.4	+25.2	78.1	40
50 56.6	19.6	73.1	51 13.5	21.1	74.2	51 29.2	22.6	75.5	51 43.6	24.1	76.7	41
51 16.2	18.4	71.6	51 34.6	19.9	72.7	51 51.8	21.4	74.0	52 07.7	23.0	75.2	42
51 34.6	17.2	70.0	51 54.5	18.7	71.2	52 13.2	20.2	72.4	52 30.7	21.7	73.7	43
51 51.8	15.9	68.5	52 13.2	17.5	69.7	52 33.4	19.0	70.9	52 52.4	20.6	72.1	44
52 07.7	+14.7	66.9	52 30.7	+16.2	68.1	52 52.4	+17.8	69.3	53 13.0	+19.3	70.6	45
52 22.4	13.4	65.3	52 46.9	14.9	66.5	53 10.2	16.5	67.7	53 32.3	18.1	69.0	46
52 35.8	12.1	63.7	53 01.8	13.7	64.9	53 26.7	15.2	66.1	53 50.4	16.7	67.4	47
52 47.9	10.8	62.1	53 15.5	12.3	63.3	53 41.9	13.8	64.5	54 07.1	15.4	65.7	48
52 58.7	9.5	60.5	53 27.8	10.9	61.7	53 55.7	12.4	62.9	54 22.5	14.0	64.1	49
53 08.2	+8.0	58.8	53 38.7	+9.5	60.0	54 08.1	+11.1	61.2	54 36.5	+12.6	62.4	50
53 16.2	6.7	57.2	53 48.2	8.2	58.3	54 19.2	9.7	59.5	54 49.1	11.2	60.7	51
53 22.9	5.3	55.5	53 56.4	6.7	56.6	54 28.9	8.2	57.8	55 00.3	9.7	59.0	52
53 28.2	3.9	53.8	54 03.1	5.3	55.0	54 37.1	6.7	56.1	55 10.0	8.3	57.3	53
53 32.1	2.5	52.2	54 08.4	3.9	53.3	54 43.8	5.3	54.4	55 18.3	6.8	55.6	54
53 34.6	+1.0	50.5	54 12.3	+2.4	51.6	54 49.1	+3.9	52.7	55 25.1	+5.2	53.8	55
53 35.6	−0.4	48.8	54 14.7	+1.0	49.8	54 53.0	2.3	50.9	55 30.3	3.8	52.1	56
53 35.2	1.7	47.1	54 15.7	−0.5	48.1	54 55.3	+0.9	49.2	55 34.1	2.2	50.3	57
53 33.5	3.2	45.4	54 15.2	2.0	46.4	54 56.2	−0.7	47.4	55 36.3	+0.7	48.5	58
53 30.3	4.7	43.8	54 13.2	3.4	44.7	54 55.5	2.1	45.7	55 37.0	−0.8	46.8	59
53 25.6	−6.0	42.1	54 09.8	−4.8	43.0	54 53.4	−3.6	44.0	55 36.2	−2.4	45.0	60
53 19.6	7.4	40.4	54 05.0	6.3	41.3	54 49.8	5.1	42.2	55 33.8	3.8	43.2	61
53 12.2	8.7	38.8	53 58.7	7.6	39.6	54 44.7	6.6	40.5	55 30.0	5.4	41.4	62
53 03.5	10.2	37.1	53 51.1	9.1	37.9	54 38.1	8.0	38.8	55 24.6	6.9	39.7	63
52 53.3	11.4	35.5	53 42.0	10.5	36.3	54 30.1	9.5	37.1	55 17.7	8.4	37.9	64
52 41.9	−12.8	33.8	53 31.5	−11.9	34.6	54 20.6	−10.8	35.4	55 09.3	−9.9	36.2	65
52 29.1	14.1	32.2	53 19.6	13.2	32.9	54 09.8	12.3	33.7	54 59.4	11.3	34.5	66
52 15.0	15.4	30.6	53 06.4	14.5	31.3	53 57.5	13.6	32.0	54 48.1	12.7	32.8	67
51 59.6	16.6	29.1	52 51.9	15.8	29.7	53 43.9	15.0	30.4	54 35.4	14.1	31.1	68
51 43.0	17.8	27.5	52 36.1	17.1	28.1	53 28.9	16.3	28.7	54 21.3	15.5	29.4	69
51 25.2	−19.0	26.0	52 19.0	−18.3	26.5	53 12.6	−17.6	27.1	54 05.8	−16.8	27.8	70
51 06.2	20.2	24.5	52 00.7	19.5	25.0	52 55.0	18.9	25.5	53 49.0	18.2	26.1	71
50 46.0	21.3	23.0	51 41.2	20.7	23.5	52 36.1	20.1	24.0	53 30.8	19.4	24.5	72
50 24.7	22.3	21.5	51 20.5	21.9	21.9	52 16.0	21.2	22.4	53 11.4	20.7	22.9	73
50 02.4	23.5	20.0	50 58.6	22.9	20.5	51 54.8	22.4	20.9	52 50.7	21.8	21.4	74
49 38.9	−24.5	18.6	50 35.7	−24.0	19.0	51 32.4	−23.6	19.4	52 28.9	−23.1	19.8	75
49 14.4	25.5	17.2	50 11.7	25.1	17.6	51 08.8	24.6	17.9	52 05.8	24.2	18.3	76
48 48.9	26.5	15.8	49 46.6	26.1	16.2	50 44.2	25.7	16.5	51 41.6	25.2	16.8	77
48 22.4	27.4	14.5	49 20.5	27.1	14.8	50 18.5	26.8	15.1	51 16.4	26.4	15.4	78
47 55.0	28.3	13.1	48 53.4	28.0	13.4	49 51.7	27.7	13.7	50 50.0	27.4	14.0	79
47 26.7	−29.2	11.8	48 25.4	−28.9	12.1	49 24.0	−28.6	12.3	50 22.6	−28.3	12.6	80
46 57.5	30.1	10.5	47 56.5	29.9	10.7	48 55.4	29.6	11.0	49 54.3	29.4	11.2	81
46 27.4	30.8	9.3	47 26.6	30.6	9.5	48 25.8	30.5	9.6	49 24.9	30.2	9.8	82
45 56.6	31.7	8.0	46 56.0	31.5	8.2	47 55.3	31.3	8.4	48 54.7	31.1	8.5	83
45 24.9	32.4	6.8	46 24.5	32.3	7.0	47 24.0	32.1	7.1	48 23.6	32.0	7.2	84
44 52.5	−33.1	5.6	45 52.2	−33.0	5.7	46 51.9	−32.9	5.8	47 51.6	−32.8	6.0	85
44 19.4	33.9	4.5	45 19.2	33.8	4.5	46 19.0	33.7	4.6	47 18.8	33.6	4.7	86
43 45.5	34.5	3.3	44 45.4	34.5	3.4	45 45.3	34.4	3.4	46 45.2	34.4	3.5	87
43 11.0	35.2	2.2	44 10.9	35.1	2.2	45 10.9	35.1	2.3	46 10.8	35.0	2.3	88
42 35.8	35.8	1.1	43 35.8	35.8	1.1	44 35.8	35.8	1.1	45 35.8	35.8	1.1	89
42 00.0	−36.4	0.0	43 00.0	−36.4	0.0	44 00.0	−36.4	0.0	45 00.0	−36.4	0.0	90
42°			43°			44°			45°			

53°, 307° L.H.A. LATITUDE SAME NAME AS DECLINATION

A *time diagram* helps you see the relationship of the Greenwich meridian and the meridian of the body to your local meridian. With it, you can visualize the steps you take to get the LHA. The time diagram for this sight looks like Figure 16-7.

The traditional time diagram, shown in Figure 16-7, is based on a view of the earth from over the South Pole instead of the North Pole. With this view, the direction to the west of your meridian is on the left, just as on a chart. The author finds this confusing while continually navigating in the northern hemisphere, where most small-craft navigation is done, and sometimes uses a north polar view instead. This allows the GP of any body with a northern declination to be actually drawn on the time diagram along with the AP, so that the navigational triangle and its angles can be seen.

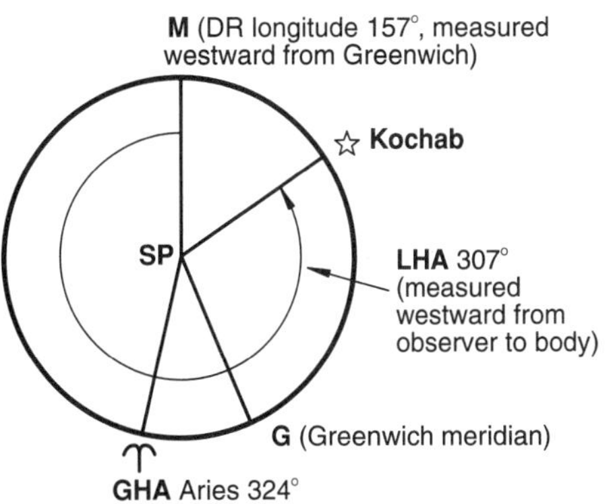

Figure 16-7. *A time diagram can help you sort out the relationships between GHA, LHA, and your assumed longitude. Imagine looking down on the earth from directly over the South Pole. Draw a line from the center to the top of the circle—it's traditionally labeled "M"—to represent your assumed longitude. Draw another line from the center to Greenwich (labeled "G"), using the angular distance between your assumed position and Greenwich—in this case, 157°—measuring counterclockwise or westward from Greenwich. Then draw another line (based on the GHA of Aries) to place Aries in relation to Greenwich. Finally, with still another line, locate the star in relation to Aries, using the star's SHA. The LHA you need to enter the sight reduction tables is the difference measured westward between your assumed longitude and the body's—in this case 307°.*

Plotting This Sight

You now have enough information to plot the LOP: the AP, the altitude intercept, the azimuth, and the direction (toward or away). Start by plotting the assumed position on a chart of the area or on a *position plotting sheet*.

To plot the Kochab sight, set up a plotting sheet for a midlatitude of 39° and mark the assumed position (AP) on the plotting sheet.

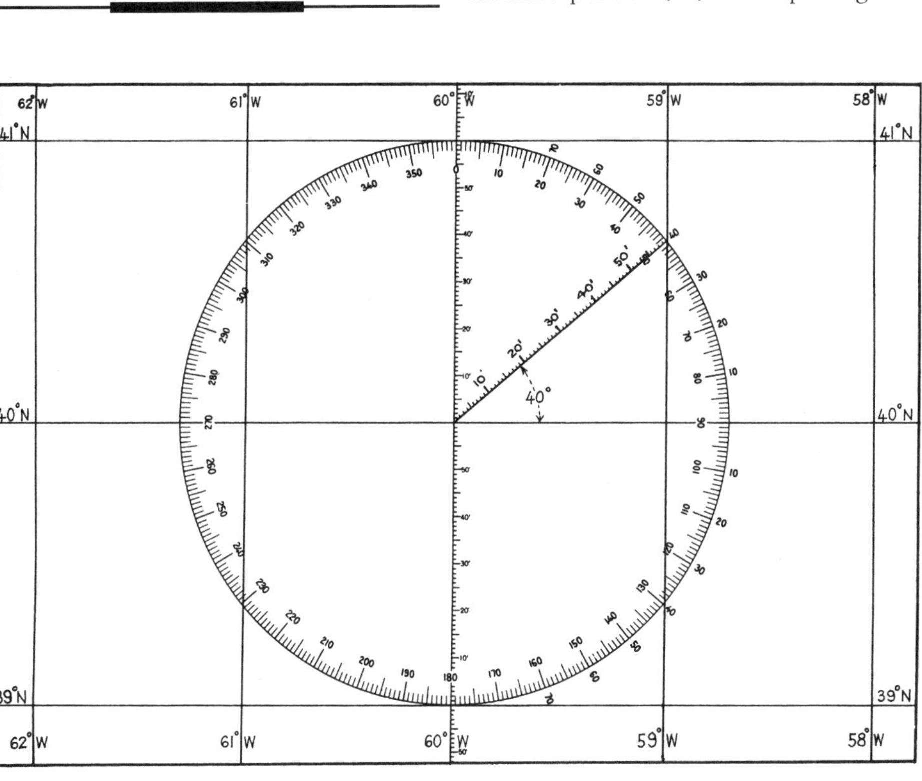

Figure 16-8. *In the open sea, the plotting sheet is used instead of a chart to plot celestial sights. You can construct a plotting sheet on any piece of plain paper. See sidebar text.*

From the AP, draw a line of bearing in the direction of the azimuth, toward or away from the body's GP, as the case may be. Next, using the latitude (vertical) scale, measure the number of minutes equal to the altitude intercept and lay out this distance along the azimuth line. At this distance, draw a line perpendicular to the azimuth. This line is a tiny portion of the circle of equal altitude at the time of the sight. Figure 16-9 shows the Kochab plot.

Example of Sight Reduction for the Sun

A *sun sight* is reduced very much like a star sight. The following example illustrates this process and introduces new corrections for *low-altitude sights* and *nonstandard atmospheric conditions*. It also includes a *v* (or *d*) correction.

The corrections for low-altitude and nonstandard atmosphere account for increased refraction under these conditions. By inspecting the tables you can see that these corrections are usually quite small, but can reach significant levels at times. Don't ignore them, even though you can safely disregard a small correction on a midocean sight. Then again, once you know what the small correction is, you might as well use it. Several small corrections all of the same sign can amount to a significant one.

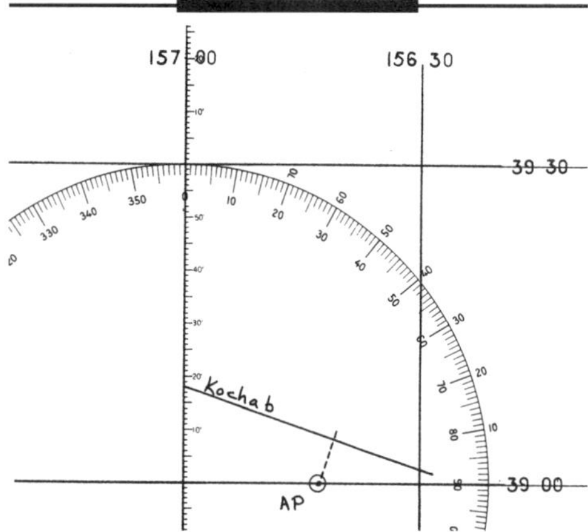

Figure 16-9. *This is the plot for the Kochab sight on a universal plotting sheet. Note that the longitude (vertical) lines intersect the circle (which has a radius equal to the latitude spacing) at the point of intersection of an angle of 39° (the assumed latitude) from the horizontal. Plot the AP, draw a line of bearing toward the GP, and mark off the altitude intercept. A perpendicular line through this point is a small part of the circle of equal altitude.*

Position plotting sheets are sold by chart dealers worldwide and come in two types. One is a simple Mercator grid on plain paper with the latitude lines labeled. The longitudes are not labeled—they must be chosen by the user. Thus, this type is specific to latitude, but can be used for any longitude.

The other type is the universal plotting sheet, which can be used for any latitude and longitude. However, you must draw the longitudes according to certain rules. To set up a universal plotting sheet, follow these steps:

1. Label the horizontal line through the center with the assumed latitude for your sight, and the parallel lines tangent to the top and bottom of the compass rose at a convenient interval, such as 1 degree or 30 minutes.

2. Note that the compass rose is graduated both inside and outside its circumference. The inside numbers are regular compass bearings; outside numbers are angles from the horizontal. Draw a vertical line (parallel to the single central vertical line) through the mark on the outside of the circle corresponding to the assumed longitude. Duplicate this line on the opposite side of the circle.

3. Graduate the latitude lines using the scale in the lower right corner of the sheet. Longitude graduations are already drawn in on the central longitude line.

You can follow the same procedure on any blank sheet of paper. Simply draw three parallel horizontal lines and label them, draw in a central longitude line, and establish other longitudes using angles from the horizontal (latitude) line.

Assume that on June 16, 1994, you take a sight of the upper limb of the sun at 05 15 23 local time, in DR position 30°N, 45°W. Your height of eye is 18 feet, the temperature is 88°, and the atmospheric pressure is 980 millibars. Sextant altitude is 3° 20.2', and there is no index correction.

The only tricky part of this sight is the atmospheric correction. For this, enter the top half of Table A-4 in the front of the almanac. Locate the proper temperature across the top and drop down vertically to the proper pressure. This puts you in zone L. Move again down zone L to the apparent altitude, where a rough interpolation gives the value +1.4'. (See Figure 16-10.)

The normal correction for altitude is next, found on the inside front cover of the almanac. (See Figure 16-11.)

You find the *v* and *d* corrections in the increments and corrections pages of the almanac for the same minutes as the GHA increments. (See Figure 16-12.)

Section I:	
1. Body	*Sun*
2. Index Correction	*none*
3. Dip Correction (height of eye)	*-4.1'*
4. Sum	*-4.1'*
5. Sextant Altitude (hs)	*3° 20.2'*
6. Apparent Altitude (ha)	*3° 16.1'*
7. Altitude Correction	*-29.4'*
8. Mars/Venus Correction	*not applicable*
9. Additional Correction	*+1.4'*
10. Horizontal Parallax Correction	*not applicable*
11. Moon Upper Limb Correction	*not applicable*
12. Correction to Apparent Altitude	*-28.0' (sum of lines 7–11)*
13. Observed Altitude *(ho)*	*2° 48.1' (line 6 minus line 12)*
Section II:	
14. Date	*16 June 1994*
15. DR Latitude	*30°N*
16. DR Longitude	*45°*
17. Time of Sight (corrected)	*05 15 23*
18. Zone Description	*+3 (from time zone chart or computation; Chapter 14)*
19. GMT (Date *June 16*) Time	*08 15 23*
Section III:	
20. GHA (*v* corr'n. factor ____)	*299° 51.3'*
21. GHA increment	*3° 50.8'*
22. SHA (or *v* correction)	*not applicable*
23. GHA	*303° 42.1' (sum of lines 20–22)*
24. + or –360°	*not applicable*
25. Assumed Longitude	*44° 42.1' (nearest whole degree, with minutes from GHA)*
26. LHA	*259° (line 23 minus line 25)*
27. Declination (*d* corr'n. factor *+0.1*)	*N 23° 20.5' (from almanac daily pages)*
28. *d* correction	*0.0*
29. Declination	*N 23° 20.5' (line 27 + line 28)*
30. Assumed Latitude	*N 30° same (nearest whole degree of latitude)*

Figure 16-10. *This is the page of the almanac used for nonstandard atmospheric conditions. It accounts for increased refraction during extremes of temperature and pressure. Under the conditions prevailing at this sun sight, an interpolated value of +1.4' should be applied to the solution.*

A4 ALTITUDE CORRECTION TABLES—ADDITIONAL CORRECTIONS

ADDITIONAL REFRACTION CORRECTIONS FOR NON-STANDARD CONDITIONS

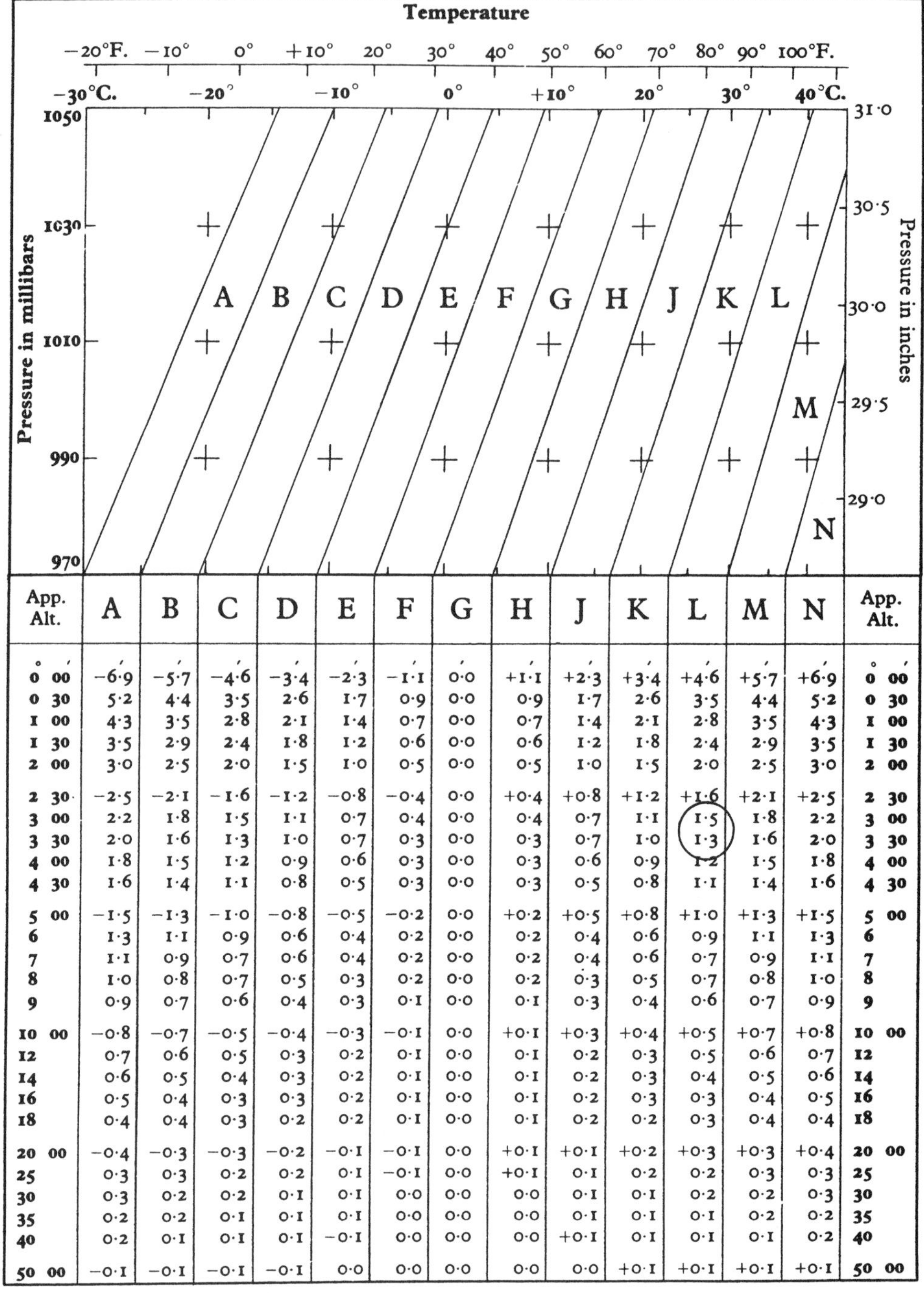

App. Alt.	A	B	C	D	E	F	G	H	J	K	L	M	N	App. Alt.
° ′	′	′	′	′	′	′	′	′	′	′	′	′	′	° ′
0 00	−6·9	−5·7	−4·6	−3·4	−2·3	−1·1	0·0	+1·1	+2·3	+3·4	+4·6	+5·7	+6·9	0 00
0 30	5·2	4·4	3·5	2·6	1·7	0·9	0·0	0·9	1·7	2·6	3·5	4·4	5·2	0 30
1 00	4·3	3·5	2·8	2·1	1·4	0·7	0·0	0·7	1·4	2·1	2·8	3·5	4·3	1 00
1 30	3·5	2·9	2·4	1·8	1·2	0·6	0·0	0·6	1·2	1·8	2·4	2·9	3·5	1 30
2 00	3·0	2·5	2·0	1·5	1·0	0·5	0·0	0·5	1·0	1·5	2·0	2·5	3·0	2 00
2 30	−2·5	−2·1	−1·6	−1·2	−0·8	−0·4	0·0	+0·4	+0·8	+1·2	+1·6	+2·1	+2·5	2 30
3 00	2·2	1·8	1·5	1·1	0·7	0·4	0·0	0·4	0·7	1·1	1·5	1·8	2·2	3 00
3 30	2·0	1·6	1·3	1·0	0·7	0·3	0·0	0·3	0·7	1·0	1·3	1·6	2·0	3 30
4 00	1·8	1·5	1·2	0·9	0·6	0·3	0·0	0·3	0·6	0·9	1·2	1·5	1·8	4 00
4 30	1·6	1·4	1·1	0·8	0·5	0·3	0·0	0·3	0·5	0·8	1·1	1·4	1·6	4 30
5 00	−1·5	−1·3	−1·0	−0·8	−0·5	−0·2	0·0	+0·2	+0·5	+0·8	+1·0	+1·3	+1·5	5 00
6	1·3	1·1	0·9	0·6	0·4	0·2	0·0	0·2	0·4	0·6	0·9	1·1	1·3	6
7	1·1	0·9	0·7	0·6	0·4	0·2	0·0	0·2	0·4	0·6	0·7	0·9	1·1	7
8	1·0	0·8	0·7	0·5	0·3	0·2	0·0	0·2	0·3	0·5	0·7	0·8	1·0	8
9	0·9	0·7	0·6	0·4	0·3	0·1	0·0	0·1	0·3	0·4	0·6	0·7	0·9	9
10 00	−0·8	−0·7	−0·5	−0·4	−0·3	−0·1	0·0	+0·1	+0·3	+0·4	+0·5	+0·7	+0·8	10 00
12	0·7	0·6	0·5	0·3	0·2	0·1	0·0	0·1	0·2	0·3	0·5	0·6	0·7	12
14	0·6	0·5	0·4	0·3	0·2	0·1	0·0	0·1	0·2	0·3	0·4	0·5	0·6	14
16	0·5	0·4	0·3	0·3	0·2	0·1	0·0	0·1	0·2	0·3	0·3	0·4	0·5	16
18	0·4	0·4	0·3	0·2	0·2	0·1	0·0	0·1	0·2	0·2	0·3	0·4	0·4	18
20 00	−0·4	−0·3	−0·3	−0·2	−0·1	−0·1	0·0	+0·1	+0·1	+0·2	+0·3	+0·3	+0·4	20 00
25	0·3	0·3	0·2	0·2	0·1	−0·1	0·0	+0·1	0·1	0·2	0·2	0·3	0·3	25
30	0·3	0·2	0·2	0·1	0·1	0·0	0·0	0·0	0·1	0·1	0·2	0·2	0·3	30
35	0·2	0·2	0·1	0·1	0·1	0·0	0·0	0·0	0·1	0·1	0·1	0·2	0·2	35
40	0·2	0·1	0·1	0·1	−0·1	0·0	0·0	0·0	+0·1	0·1	0·1	0·1	0·2	40
50 00	−0·1	−0·1	−0·1	−0·1	0·0	0·0	0·0	0·0	0·0	+0·1	+0·1	+0·1	+0·1	50 00

The graph is entered with arguments temperature and pressure to find a zone letter; using as arguments this zone letter and apparent altitude (sextant altitude corrected for dip), a correction is taken from the table. This correction is to be applied to the sextant altitude in addition to the corrections for standard conditions (for the Sun, stars and planets from page A2 and for the Moon from pages xxxiv and xxxv).

ALTITUDE CORRECTION TABLES 0°–10°—SUN, STARS, PLANETS A3

App. Alt.	SUN OCT.–MAR. Lower Limb	SUN OCT.–MAR. Upper Limb	SUN APR.–SEPT. Lower Limb	SUN APR.–SEPT. Upper Limb	STARS PLANETS
° ′	′	′	′	′	′
0 00	−18·2	−50·5	−18·4	−50·2	−34·5
03	17·5	49·8	17·8	49·6	33·8
06	16·9	49·2	17·1	48·9	33·2
09	16·3	48·6	16·5	48·3	32·6
12	15·7	48·0	15·9	47·7	32·0
15	15·1	47·4	15·3	47·1	31·4
0 18	−14·5	−46·8	−14·8	−46·6	−30·8
21	14·0	46·3	14·2	46·0	30·3
24	13·5	45·8	13·7	45·5	29·8
27	12·9	45·2	13·2	45·0	29·2
30	12·4	44·7	12·7	44·5	28·7
33	11·9	44·2	12·2	44·0	28·2
0 36	−11·5	−43·8	−11·7	−43·5	−27·8
39	11·0	43·3	11·2	43·0	27·3
42	10·5	42·8	10·8	42·6	26·8
45	10·1	42·4	10·3	42·1	26·4
48	9·6	41·9	9·9	41·7	25·9
51	9·2	41·5	9·5	41·3	25·5
0 54	− 8·8	−41·1	− 9·1	−40·9	−25·1
0 57	8·4	40·7	8·7	40·5	24·7
1 00	8·0	40·3	8·3	40·1	24·3
03	7·7	40·0	7·9	39·7	24·0
06	7·3	39·6	7·5	39·3	23·6
09	6·9	39·2	7·2	39·0	23·2
1 12	− 6·6	−38·9	− 6·8	−38·6	−22·9
15	6·2	38·5	6·5	38·3	22·5
18	5·9	38·2	6·2	38·0	22·2
21	5·6	37·9	5·8	37·6	21·9
24	5·3	37·6	5·5	37·3	21·6
27	4·9	37·2	5·2	37·0	21·2
1 30	− 4·6	−36·9	− 4·9	−36·7	−20·9
35	4·2	36·5	4·4	36·2	20·5
40	3·7	36·0	4·0	35·8	20·0
45	3·2	35·5	3·5	35·3	19·5
50	2·8	35·1	3·1	34·9	19·1
1 55	2·4	34·7	2·6	34·4	18·7
2 00	− 2·0	−34·3	− 2·2	−34·0	−18·3
05	1·6	33·9	1·8	33·6	17·9
10	1·2	33·5	1·5	33·3	17·5
15	0·9	33·2	1·1	32·9	17·2
20	0·5	32·8	0·8	32·6	16·8
25	− 0·2	32·5	0·4	32·2	16·5
2 30	+ 0·2	−32·1	− 0·1	−31·9	−16·1
35	0·5	31·8	+ 0·2	31·6	15·8
40	0·8	31·5	0·5	31·3	15·5
45	1·1	31·2	0·8	31·0	15·2
50	1·4	30·9	1·1	30·7	14·9
2 55	1·6	30·7	1·4	30·4	14·7
3 00	+ 1·9	−30·4	+ 1·7	−30·1	−14·4
05	2·2	30·1	1·9	29·9	14·1
10	2·4	29·9	2·1	29·7	13·9
15	2·6	29·7	2·4	29·4	13·7
20	2·9	29·4	2·6	29·2	13·4
25	3·1	29·2	2·9	28·9	13·2
3 30	+ 3·3	−29·0	+ 3·1	−28·7	−13·0

App. Alt.	SUN OCT.–MAR. Lower Limb	SUN OCT.–MAR. Upper Limb	SUN APR.–SEPT. Lower Limb	SUN APR.–SEPT. Upper Limb	STARS PLANETS
° ′	′	′	′	′	′
3 30	+ 3·3	−29·0	+ 3·1	−28·7	−13·0
35	3·6	28·7	3·3	28·5	12·7
40	3·8	28·5	3·5	28·3	12·5
45	4·0	28·3	3·7	28·1	12·3
50	4·2	28·1	3·9	27·9	12·1
3 55	4·4	27·9	4·1	27·7	11·9
4 00	+ 4·5	−27·8	+ 4·3	−27·5	−11·8
05	4·7	27·6	4·5	27·3	11·6
10	4·9	27·4	4·6	27·2	11·4
15	5·1	27·2	4·8	27·0	11·2
20	5·2	27·1	5·0	26·8	11·1
25	5·4	26·9	5·1	26·7	10·9
4 30	+ 5·6	−26·7	+ 5·3	−26·5	−10·7
35	5·7	26·6	5·5	26·3	10·6
40	5·9	26·4	5·6	26·2	10·4
45	6·0	26·3	5·8	26·0	10·3
50	6·2	26·1	5·9	25·9	10·1
4 55	6·3	26·0	6·0	25·8	10·0
5 00	+ 6·4	−25·9	+ 6·2	−25·6	− 9·9
05	6·6	25·7	6·3	25·5	9·7
10	6·7	25·6	6·4	25·4	9·6
15	6·8	25·5	6·6	25·2	9·5
20	6·9	25·4	6·7	25·1	9·4
25	7·1	25·2	6·8	25·0	9·2
5 30	+ 7·2	−25·1	+ 6·9	−24·9	− 9·1
35	7·3	25·0	7·0	24·8	9·0
40	7·4	24·9	7·2	24·6	8·9
45	7·5	24·8	7·3	24·5	8·8
50	7·6	24·7	7·4	24·4	8·7
5 55	7·7	24·6	7·5	24·3	8·6
6 00	+ 7·8	−24·5	+ 7·6	−24·2	− 8·5
10	8·0	24·3	7·8	24·0	8·3
20	8·2	24·1	8·0	23·8	8·1
30	8·4	23·9	8·1	23·7	7·9
40	8·6	23·7	8·3	23·5	7·7
6 50	8·7	23·6	8·5	23·3	7·6
7 00	+ 8·9	−23·4	+ 8·6	−23·2	− 7·4
10	9·1	23·2	8·8	23·0	7·2
20	9·2	23·1	9·0	22·8	7·1
30	9·3	23·0	9·1	22·7	7·0
40	9·5	22·8	9·2	22·6	6·8
7 50	9·6	22·7	9·4	22·4	6·7
8 00	+ 9·7	−22·6	+ 9·5	−22·3	− 6·6
10	9·9	22·4	9·6	22·2	6·4
20	10·0	22·3	9·7	22·1	6·3
30	10·1	22·2	9·8	22·0	6·2
40	10·2	22·1	10·0	21·8	6·1
8 50	10·3	22·0	10·1	21·7	6·0
9 00	+10·4	−21·9	+10·2	−21·6	− 5·9
10	10·5	21·8	10·3	21·5	5·8
20	10·6	21·7	10·4	21·4	5·7
30	10·7	21·6	10·5	21·3	5·6
40	10·8	21·5	10·6	21·2	5·5
9 50	10·9	21·4	10·6	21·2	5·4
10 00	+11·0	−21·3	+10·7	−21·1	− 5·3

Additional corrections for temperature and pressure are given on the following page.
For bubble sextant observations ignore dip and use the star corrections for Sun, planets, and stars.

Figure 16-11. *You find the correction for altitude for the sun inside the front cover of the almanac. There are columns for "Oct.–Mar." and "Apr.–Sept." for both upper and lower limbs. You also find star and planet altitude corrections here.*

Figure 16-12. *This figure shows how to apply* v *and* d *corrections. Enter the table with the* v *or* d *correction factor from the daily pages and find the correction in one of the three columns labelled "*v *or* d *corr'n" just to the right of the minutes entries. In this case, for a* d *factor of 0.1, the correction is 0.0'.*

14m INCREMENTS AND CORRECTIONS 15m

14m	SUN PLANETS	ARIES	MOON	v or d	Corr^{n}	v or d	Corr^{n}	v or d	Corr^{n}
s	° ′	° ′	° ′	′	′	′	′	′	′
00	3 30·0	3 30·6	3 20·4	0·0	0·0	6·0	1·5	12·0	2·9
01	3 30·3	3 30·8	3 20·7	0·1	0·0	6·1	1·5	12·1	2·9
02	3 30·5	3 31·1	3 20·9	0·2	0·0	6·2	1·5	12·2	2·9
03	3 30·8	3 31·3	3 21·1	0·3	0·1	6·3	1·5	12·3	3·0
04	3 31·0	3 31·6	3 21·4	0·4	0·1	6·4	1·5	12·4	3·0
05	3 31·3	3 31·8	3 21·6	0·5	0·1	6·5	1·6	12·5	3·0
06	3 31·5	3 32·1	3 21·9	0·6	0·1	6·6	1·6	12·6	3·0
07	3 31·8	3 32·3	3 22·1	0·7	0·2	6·7	1·6	12·7	3·1
08	3 32·0	3 32·6	3 22·3	0·8	0·2	6·8	1·6	12·8	3·1
09	3 32·3	3 32·8	3 22·6	0·9	0·2	6·9	1·7	12·9	3·1
10	3 32·5	3 33·1	3 22·8	1·0	0·2	7·0	1·7	13·0	3·1
11	3 32·8	3 33·3	3 23·1	1·1	0·3	7·1	1·7	13·1	3·2
12	3 33·0	3 33·6	3 23·3	1·2	0·3	7·2	1·7	13·2	3·2
13	3 33·3	3 33·8	3 23·5	1·3	0·3	7·3	1·8	13·3	3·2
14	3 33·5	3 34·1	3 23·8	1·4	0·3	7·4	1·8	13·4	3·2
15	3 33·8	3 34·3	3 24·0	1·5	0·4	7·5	1·8	13·5	3·3
16	3 34·0	3 34·6	3 24·3	1·6	0·4	7·6	1·8	13·6	3·3
17	3 34·3	3 34·8	3 24·5	1·7	0·4	7·7	1·9	13·7	3·3
18	3 34·5	3 35·1	3 24·7	1·8	0·4	7·8	1·9	13·8	3·3
19	3 34·8	3 35·3	3 25·0	1·9	0·5	7·9	1·9	13·9	3·4
20	3 35·0	3 35·6	3 25·2	2·0	0·5	8·0	1·9	14·0	3·4
21	3 35·3	3 35·8	3 25·4	2·1	0·5	8·1	2·0	14·1	3·4
22	3 35·5	3 36·1	3 25·7	2·2	0·5	8·2	2·0	14·2	3·4
23	3 35·8	3 36·3	3 25·9	2·3	0·6	8·3	2·0	14·3	3·5
24	3 36·0	3 36·6	3 26·2	2·4	0·6	8·4	2·0	14·4	3·5
25	3 36·3	3 36·8	3 26·4	2·5	0·6	8·5	2·1	14·5	3·5
26	3 36·5	3 37·1	3 26·6	2·6	0·6	8·6	2·1	14·6	3·5
27	3 36·8	3 37·3	3 26·9	2·7	0·7	8·7	2·1	14·7	3·6
28	3 37·0	3 37·6	3 27·1	2·8	0·7	8·8	2·1	14·8	3·6
29	3 37·3	3 37·8	3 27·4	2·9	0·7	8·9	2·2	14·9	3·6
30	3 37·5	3 38·1	3 27·6	3·0	0·7	9·0	2·2	15·0	3·6
31	3 37·8	3 38·3	3 27·8	3·1	0·7	9·1	2·2	15·1	3·6
32	3 38·0	3 38·6	3 28·1	3·2	0·8	9·2	2·2	15·2	3·7
33	3 38·3	3 38·8	3 28·3	3·3	0·8	9·3	2·2	15·3	3·7
34	3 38·5	3 39·1	3 28·5	3·4	0·8	9·4	2·3	15·4	3·7
35	3 38·8	3 39·3	3 28·8	3·5	0·8	9·5	2·3	15·5	3·7
36	3 39·0	3 39·6	3 29·0	3·6	0·9	9·6	2·3	15·6	3·8
37	3 39·3	3 39·9	3 29·3	3·7	0·9	9·7	2·3	15·7	3·8
38	3 39·5	3 40·1	3 29·5	3·8	0·9	9·8	2·4	15·8	3·8
39	3 39·8	3 40·4	3 29·7	3·9	0·9	9·9	2·4	15·9	3·8
40	3 40·0	3 40·6	3 30·0	4·0	1·0	10·0	2·4	16·0	3·9
41	3 40·3	3 40·9	3 30·2	4·1	1·0	10·1	2·4	16·1	3·9
42	3 40·5	3 41·1	3 30·5	4·2	1·0	10·2	2·5	16·2	3·9
43	3 40·8	3 41·4	3 30·7	4·3	1·0	10·3	2·5	16·3	3·9
44	3 41·0	3 41·6	3 30·9	4·4	1·1	10·4	2·5	16·4	4·0
45	3 41·3	3 41·9	3 31·2	4·5	1·1	10·5	2·5	16·5	4·0
46	3 41·5	3 42·1	3 31·4	4·6	1·1	10·6	2·6	16·6	4·0
47	3 41·8	3 42·4	3 31·6	4·7	1·1	10·7	2·6	16·7	4·0
48	3 42·0	3 42·6	3 31·9	4·8	1·2	10·8	2·6	16·8	4·1
49	3 42·3	3 42·9	3 32·1	4·9	1·2	10·9	2·6	16·9	4·1
50	3 42·5	3 43·1	3 32·4	5·0	1·2	11·0	2·7	17·0	4·1
51	3 42·8	3 43·4	3 32·6	5·1	1·2	11·1	2·7	17·1	4·1
52	3 43·0	3 43·6	3 32·8	5·2	1·3	11·2	2·7	17·2	4·2
53	3 43·3	3 43·9	3 33·1	5·3	1·3	11·3	2·7	17·3	4·2
54	3 43·5	3 44·1	3 33·3	5·4	1·3	11·4	2·8	17·4	4·2
55	3 43·8	3 44·4	3 33·6	5·5	1·3	11·5	2·8	17·5	4·2
56	3 44·0	3 44·6	3 33·8	5·6	1·4	11·6	2·8	17·6	4·3
57	3 44·3	3 44·9	3 34·0	5·7	1·4	11·7	2·8	17·7	4·3
58	3 44·5	3 45·1	3 34·3	5·8	1·4	11·8	2·9	17·8	4·3
59	3 44·8	3 45·4	3 34·5	5·9	1·4	11·9	2·9	17·9	4·3
60	3 45·0	3 45·6	3 34·8	6·0	1·5	12·0	2·9	18·0	4·4

15m	SUN PLANETS	ARIES	MOON	v or d	Corr^{n}	v or d	Corr^{n}	v or d	Corr^{n}
s	° ′	° ′	° ′	′	′	′	′	′	′
00	3 45·0	3 45·6	3 34·8	0·0	0·0	6·0	1·6	12·0	3·1
01	3 45·3	3 45·9	3 35·0	0·1	0·0	6·1	1·6	12·1	3·1
02	3 45·5	3 46·1	3 35·2	0·2	0·1	6·2	1·6	12·2	3·2
03	3 45·8	3 46·4	3 35·5	0·3	0·1	6·3	1·6	12·3	3·2
04	3 46·0	3 46·6	3 35·7	0·4	0·1	6·4	1·7	12·4	3·2
05	3 46·3	3 46·9	3 35·9	0·5	0·1	6·5	1·7	12·5	3·2
06	3 46·5	3 47·1	3 36·2	0·6	0·2	6·6	1·7	12·6	3·3
07	3 46·8	3 47·4	3 36·4	0·7	0·2	6·7	1·7	12·7	3·3
08	3 47·0	3 47·6	3 36·7	0·8	0·2	6·8	1·8	12·8	3·3
09	3 47·3	3 47·9	3 36·9	0·9	0·2	6·9	1·8	12·9	3·3
10	3 47·5	3 48·1	3 37·1	1·0	0·3	7·0	1·8	13·0	3·4
11	3 47·8	3 48·4	3 37·4	1·1	0·3	7·1	1·8	13·1	3·4
12	3 48·0	3 48·6	3 37·6	1·2	0·3	7·2	1·9	13·2	3·4
13	3 48·3	3 48·9	3 37·9	1·3	0·3	7·3	1·9	13·3	3·4
14	3 48·5	3 49·1	3 38·1	1·4	0·4	7·4	1·9	13·4	3·5
15	3 48·8	3 49·4	3 38·3	1·5	0·4	7·5	1·9	13·5	3·5
16	3 49·0	3 49·6	3 38·6	1·6	0·4	7·6	2·0	13·6	3·5
17	3 49·3	3 49·9	3 38·8	1·7	0·4	7·7	2·0	13·7	3·5
18	3 49·5	3 50·1	3 39·0	1·8	0·5	7·8	2·0	13·8	3·6
19	3 49·8	3 50·4	3 39·3	1·9	0·5	7·9	2·0	13·9	3·6
20	3 50·0	3 50·6	3 39·5	2·0	0·5	8·0	2·1	14·0	3·6
21	3 50·3	3 50·9	3 39·8	2·1	0·5	8·1	2·1	14·1	3·6
22	3 50·5	3 51·1	3 40·0	2·2	0·6	8·2	2·1	14·2	3·7
23	3 50·8	3 51·4	3 40·2	2·3	0·6	8·3	2·1	14·3	3·7
24	3 51·0	3 51·6	3 40·5	2·4	0·6	8·4	2·2	14·4	3·7
25	3 51·3	3 51·9	3 40·7	2·5	0·6	8·5	2·2	14·5	3·7
26	3 51·5	3 52·1	3 41·0	2·6	0·7	8·6	2·2	14·6	3·8
27	3 51·8	3 52·4	3 41·2	2·7	0·7	8·7	2·2	14·7	3·8
28	3 52·0	3 52·6	3 41·4	2·8	0·7	8·8	2·3	14·8	3·8
29	3 52·3	3 52·9	3 41·7	2·9	0·7	8·9	2·3	14·9	3·8
30	3 52·5	3 53·1	3 41·9	3·0	0·8	9·0	2·3	15·0	3·9
31	3 52·8	3 53·4	3 42·1	3·1	0·8	9·1	2·4	15·1	3·9
32	3 53·0	3 53·6	3 42·4	3·2	0·8	9·2	2·4	15·2	3·9
33	3 53·3	3 53·9	3 42·6	3·3	0·9	9·3	2·4	15·3	4·0
34	3 53·5	3 54·1	3 42·9	3·4	0·9	9·4	2·4	15·4	4·0
35	3 53·8	3 54·4	3 43·1	3·5	0·9	9·5	2·5	15·5	4·0
36	3 54·0	3 54·6	3 43·3	3·6	0·9	9·6	2·5	15·6	4·0
37	3 54·3	3 54·9	3 43·6	3·7	1·0	9·7	2·5	15·7	4·1
38	3 54·5	3 55·1	3 43·8	3·8	1·0	9·8	2·5	15·8	4·1
39	3 54·8	3 55·4	3 44·1	3·9	1·0	9·9	2·6	15·9	4·1
40	3 55·0	3 55·6	3 44·3	4·0	1·0	10·0	2·6	16·0	4·1
41	3 55·3	3 55·9	3 44·5	4·1	1·1	10·1	2·6	16·1	4·2
42	3 55·5	3 56·1	3 44·8	4·2	1·1	10·2	2·6	16·2	4·2
43	3 55·8	3 56·4	3 45·0	4·3	1·1	10·3	2·7	16·3	4·2
44	3 56·0	3 56·6	3 45·2	4·4	1·1	10·4	2·7	16·4	4·2
45	3 56·3	3 56·9	3 45·5	4·5	1·2	10·5	2·7	16·5	4·3
46	3 56·5	3 57·1	3 45·7	4·6	1·2	10·6	2·7	16·6	4·3
47	3 56·8	3 57·4	3 46·0	4·7	1·2	10·7	2·8	16·7	4·3
48	3 57·0	3 57·6	3 46·2	4·8	1·2	10·8	2·8	16·8	4·3
49	3 57·3	3 57·9	3 46·4	4·9	1·3	10·9	2·8	16·9	4·4
50	3 57·5	3 58·2	3 46·7	5·0	1·3	11·0	2·8	17·0	4·4
51	3 57·8	3 58·4	3 46·9	5·1	1·3	11·1	2·9	17·1	4·4
52	3 58·0	3 58·7	3 47·2	5·2	1·3	11·2	2·9	17·2	4·4
53	3 58·3	3 58·9	3 47·4	5·3	1·4	11·3	2·9	17·3	4·5
54	3 58·5	3 59·2	3 47·6	5·4	1·4	11·4	2·9	17·4	4·5
55	3 58·8	3 59·4	3 47·9	5·5	1·4	11·5	3·0	17·5	4·5
56	3 59·0	3 59·7	3 48·1	5·6	1·4	11·6	3·0	17·6	4·5
57	3 59·3	3 59·9	3 48·4	5·7	1·5	11·7	3·0	17·7	4·6
58	3 59·5	4 00·2	3 48·6	5·8	1·5	11·8	3·0	17·8	4·6
59	3 59·8	4 00·4	3 48·8	5·9	1·5	11·9	3·1	17·9	4·6
60	4 00·0	4 00·7	3 49·1	6·0	1·6	12·0	3·1	18·0	4·7

ix

LATITUDE CONTRARY NAME TO DECLINATION **L.H.A. 79°, 281°**

Dec.	30° Hc	30° d	30° Z	31° Hc	31° d	31° Z	32° Hc	32° d	32° Z	33° Hc	33° d	33° Z	34° Hc	34° d	34° Z	35° Hc	35° d	35° Z	36° Hc	36° d	36° Z	37° Hc	37° d	37° Z	Dec.
°	° ′	′	°	° ′	′	°	° ′	′	°	° ′	′	°	° ′	′	°	° ′	′	°	° ′	′	°	° ′	′	°	°
0	9 30.7	-30.5	95.6	9 24.8	-31.4	95.7	9 18.7	-32.2	95.9	9 12.5	-33.2	96.0	9 06.1	-34.0	96.2	8 59.5	-34.9	96.4	8 52.8	-35.7	96.5	8 45.9	-36.6	96.7	0
1	9 00.2	30.6	96.4	8 53.4	31.5	96.6	8 46.5	32.4	96.7	8 39.3	33.2	96.9	8 32.1	34.2	97.0	8 24.6	35.0	97.2	8 17.1	35.9	97.3	8 09.3	36.6	97.5	1
2	8 29.6	30.7	97.3	8 21.9	31.6	97.4	8 14.1	32.5	97.6	8 06.1	33.4	97.7	7 57.9	34.2	97.9	7 49.6	35.1	98.0	7 41.2	35.9	98.1	7 32.7	36.8	98.3	2
3	7 58.9	30.8	98.2	7 50.3	31.7	98.3	7 41.6	32.6	98.4	7 32.7	33.5	98.6	7 23.7	34.3	98.7	7 14.5	35.1	98.8	7 05.3	36.0	98.9	6 55.9	36.9	99.1	3
4	7 28.1	31.0	99.0	7 18.6	31.8	99.2	7 09.0	32.7	99.3	6 59.2	33.5	99.4	6 49.4	34.5	99.5	6 39.4	35.3	99.6	6 29.3	36.1	99.8	6 19.0	36.9	99.9	4
5	6 57.1	-31.0	99.9	6 46.8	-32.0	100.0	6 36.3	-32.8	100.1	6 25.7	-33.7	100.2	6 14.9	-34.5	100.3	6 04.1	-35.3	100.5	5 53.2	-36.2	100.6	5 42.1	-37.0	100.7	5
6	6 26.1	31.1	100.8	6 14.8	31.9	100.9	6 03.5	32.9	101.0	5 52.0	33.7	101.1	5 40.4	34.5	101.2	5 28.8	35.4	101.3	5 17.0	36.2	101.4	5 05.1	37.0	101.4	6
7	5 55.0	31.2	101.6	5 42.9	32.1	101.7	5 30.6	32.9	101.8	5 18.3	33.8	101.9	5 05.9	34.6	102.0	4 53.4	35.5	102.1	4 40.8	36.3	102.2	4 28.1	37.1	102.2	7
8	5 23.8	31.3	102.5	5 10.8	32.1	102.6	4 57.7	33.0	102.6	4 44.5	33.8	102.7	4 31.3	34.7	102.8	4 17.9	35.5	102.9	4 04.5	36.3	103.0	3 51.0	37.1	103.0	8
9	4 52.5	31.3	103.3	4 38.7	32.2	103.4	4 24.7	33.0	103.5	4 10.7	33.9	103.6	3 56.6	34.8	103.6	3 42.4	35.5	103.7	3 28.2	36.4	103.8	3 13.9	37.2	103.8	9
10	4 21.2	-31.4	104.2	4 06.5	-32.3	104.3	3 51.7	-33.1	104.3	3 36.8	-34.0	104.4	3 21.8	-34.7	104.4	3 06.9	-35.6	104.5	2 51.8	-36.4	104.6	2 36.7	-37.2	104.6	10
11	3 49.8	31.4	105.0	3 34.2	32.3	105.1	3 18.6	33.2	105.2	3 02.8	33.9	105.2	2 47.1	34.8	105.3	2 31.3	35.7	105.3	2 15.4	36.4	105.3	1 59.5	37.2	105.4	11
12	3 18.4	31.5	105.9	3 01.9	32.3	105.9	2 45.4	33.1	106.0	2 28.9	34.0	106.0	2 12.3	34.9	106.1	1 55.6	35.6	106.1	1 39.0	36.5	106.1	1 22.3	37.3	106.2	12
13	2 46.9	31.5	106.7	2 29.6	32.4	106.8	2 12.3	33.2	106.8	1 54.9	34.1	106.9	1 37.4	34.8	106.9	1 20.0	35.7	106.9	1 02.5	36.4	106.9	0 45.0	37.2	107.0	13
14	2 15.4	31.5	107.6	1 57.2	32.3	107.6	1 39.1	33.3	107.7	1 20.8	34.0	107.7	1 02.6	34.9	107.7	0 44.3	35.6	107.7	0 26.1	-36.5	107.7	0 07.8	-37.3	107.7	14
15	1 43.9	-31.6	108.4	1 24.9	-32.5	108.5	1 05.8	-33.2	108.5	0 46.8	-34.1	108.5	0 27.7	-34.8	108.5	0 08.7	-35.7	108.5	0 10.4	+36.5	71.5	0 29.5	+37.2	71.5	15
16	1 12.3	31.6	109.3	0 52.4	32.4	109.3	0 32.6	-33.2	109.3	0 12.7	-34.0	109.3	0 07.1	+34.9	70.7	0 27.0	+35.7	70.7	0 46.9	36.4	70.7	1 06.7	37.2	70.7	16
17	0 40.7	31.6	110.1	0 20.0	-32.4	110.2	0 00.6	+33.3	69.8	0 21.3	+34.1	69.8	0 42.0	34.9	69.9	1 02.7	35.6	69.9	1 23.3	36.4	69.9	1 43.9	37.2	69.9	17
18	0 09.1	-31.6	111.0	0 12.4	+32.4	69.0	0 33.9	33.2	69.0	0 55.4	34.0	69.0	1 16.9	34.8	69.0	1 38.3	35.6	69.1	1 59.7	36.5	69.1	2 21.1	37.2	69.1	18
19	0 22.5	+31.6	68.2	0 44.8	32.4	68.2	1 07.1	33.3	68.2	1 29.4	34.0	68.2	1 51.7	34.8	68.2	2 13.9	35.6	68.3	2 36.2	36.3	68.3	2 58.3	37.2	68.3	19
20	0 54.1	+31.6	67.3	1 17.2	+32.4	67.3	1 40.4	+33.2	67.3	2 03.4	+34.0	67.4	2 26.5	+34.8	67.4	2 49.5	+35.6	67.5	3 12.5	+36.4	67.5	3 35.5	+37.1	67.6	20
21	1 25.7	31.5	66.5	1 49.6	32.4	66.5	2 13.6	33.1	66.5	2 37.4	34.0	66.5	3 01.3	34.8	66.6	3 25.1	35.6	66.6	3 48.9	36.3	66.7	4 12.6	37.0	66.8	21
22	1 57.2	31.6	65.6	2 22.0	32.3	65.6	2 46.7	33.2	65.7	3 11.4	33.9	65.7	3 36.1	34.7	65.8	4 00.7	35.4	65.8	4 25.2	36.2	65.9	4 49.6	37.0	66.0	22
23	2 28.8	31.5	64.7	2 54.3	32.3	64.8	3 19.9	33.1	64.8	3 45.3	33.9	64.9	4 10.8	34.6	65.0	4 36.1	35.5	65.0	5 01.4	36.2	65.1	5 26.6	37.0	65.2	23
24	3 00.3	31.4	63.9	3 26.6	32.3	63.9	3 53.0	33.0	64.0	4 19.2	33.9	64.1	4 45.4	34.6	64.1	5 11.6	35.3	64.2	5 37.6	36.1	64.3	6 03.6	36.9	64.4	24
25	3 31.7	+31.4	63.0	3 58.9	+32.2	63.1	4 26.0	+33.0	63.2	4 53.1	+33.7	63.2	5 20.0	+34.6	63.3	5 46.9	+35.3	63.4	6 13.7	+36.1	63.5	6 40.5	+36.8	63.6	25
26	4 03.1	31.4	62.2	4 31.1	32.1	62.3	4 59.0	32.9	62.3	5 26.8	33.7	62.4	5 54.6	34.4	62.5	6 22.2	35.2	62.6	6 49.8	36.0	62.7	7 17.3	36.7	62.8	26
27	4 34.5	31.3	61.3	5 03.2	32.1	61.4	5 31.9	32.9	61.5	6 00.5	33.6	61.6	6 29.0	34.4	61.7	6 57.4	35.2	61.8	7 25.8	35.9	61.9	7 54.0	36.6	62.0	27
28	5 05.8	31.2	60.5	5 35.3	32.0	60.6	6 04.8	32.7	60.6	6 34.1	33.6	60.7	7 03.4	34.3	60.8	7 32.6	35.0	61.0	8 01.7	35.7	61.1	8 30.6	36.5	61.2	28
29	5 37.0	31.2	59.6	6 07.3	31.9	59.7	6 37.5	32.7	59.8	7 07.7	33.4	59.9	7 37.7	34.2	60.0	8 07.6	35.0	60.1	8 37.4	35.7	60.3	9 07.1	36.5	60.4	29
30	6 08.2	+31.0	58.8	6 39.2	+31.9	58.9	7 10.2	+32.6	59.0	7 41.1	+33.4	59.1	8 11.9	+34.1	59.2	8 42.6	+34.8	59.3	9 13.1	+35.6	59.5	9 43.6	+36.3	59.6	30
31	6 39.2	31.0	57.9	7 11.1	31.7	58.0	7 42.8	32.5	58.1	8 14.5	33.2	58.2	8 46.0	34.0	58.4	9 17.4	34.7	58.5	9 48.7	35.5	58.6	10 19.9	36.2	58.8	31
32	7 10.2	30.9	57.0	7 42.8	31.7	57.1	8 15.3	32.4	57.3	8 47.7	33.2	57.4	9 20.0	33.9	57.5	9 52.1	34.7	57.7	10 24.2	35.3	57.8	10 56.1	36.0	58.0	32
33	7 41.1	30.8	56.2	8 14.5	31.5	56.3	8 47.7	32.3	56.4	9 20.9	33.0	56.5	9 53.9	33.7	56.7	10 26.8	34.4	56.8	10 59.5	35.2	57.0	11 32.1	35.9	57.2	33
34	8 11.9	30.7	55.3	8 46.0	31.4	55.4	9 20.0	32.1	55.6	9 53.9	32.9	55.7	10 27.6	33.6	55.8	11 01.2	34.4	56.0	11 34.7	35.1	56.2	12 08.0	35.8	56.3	34
35	8 42.6	+30.5	54.4	9 17.4	+31.3	54.6	9 52.1	+32.1	54.7	10 26.8	+32.7	54.9	11 01.2	+33.5	55.0	11 35.6	+34.2	55.2	12 09.8	+34.9	55.3	12 43.8	+35.6	55.5	35
36	9 13.1	30.5	53.6	9 48.7	31.2	53.7	10 24.2	31.9	53.8	10 59.5	32.6	54.0	11 34.7	33.3	54.2	12 09.8	34.0	54.3	12 44.7	34.7	54.5	13 19.4	35.5	54.7	36
37	9 43.6	30.3	52.7	10 19.9	31.0	52.8	10 56.1	31.7	53.0	11 32.1	32.5	53.1	12 08.0	33.2	53.3	12 43.8	33.9	53.5	13 19.4	34.6	53.7	13 54.9	35.3	53.9	37
38	10 13.9	30.1	51.8	10 50.9	30.9	52.0	11 27.8	31.6	52.1	12 04.6	32.3	52.3	12 41.2	33.0	52.5	13 17.7	33.7	52.6	13 54.0	34.4	52.8	14 30.2	35.1	53.0	38
39	10 44.0	30.0	50.9	11 21.8	30.7	51.1	11 59.4	31.4	51.2	12 36.9	32.1	51.4	13 14.2	32.8	51.6	13 51.4	33.5	51.8	14 28.4	34.3	52.0	15 05.3	34.9	52.2	39
40	11 14.0	+29.9	50.1	11 52.5	+30.5	50.2	12 30.8	+31.3	50.4	13 09.0	+32.0	50.6	13 47.0	+32.7	50.7	14 24.9	+33.4	50.9	15 02.7	+34.0	51.1	15 40.2	+34.8	51.4	40
41	11 43.9	29.6	49.2	12 23.0	30.4	49.3	13 02.1	31.0	49.5	13 41.0	31.7	49.7	14 19.7	32.5	49.9	14 58.3	33.1	50.1	15 36.7	33.9	50.3	16 15.0	34.5	50.5	41
42	12 13.5	29.6	48.3	12 53.4	30.2	48.4	13 33.1	30.9	48.6	14 12.7	31.6	48.8	14 52.2	32.2	49.0	15 31.4	33.0	49.2	16 10.6	33.6	49.4	16 49.5	34.3	49.7	42
43	12 43.1	29.3	47.4	13 23.6	30.0	47.6	14 04.0	30.7	47.7	14 44.3	31.4	47.9	15 24.4	32.1	48.1	16 04.4	32.7	48.3	16 44.2	33.4	48.6	17 23.8	34.1	48.8	43
44	13 12.4	29.1	46.5	13 53.6	29.9	46.7	14 34.7	30.5	46.9	15 15.7	31.2	47.0	15 56.5	31.8	47.3	16 37.1	32.6	47.5	17 17.6	33.2	47.7	17 57.9	33.9	47.9	44
45	13 41.5	+29.0	45.6	14 23.5	+29.6	45.8	15 05.2	+30.3	46.0	15 46.9	+30.9	46.2	16 28.3	+31.7	46.4	17 09.7	+32.3	46.6	17 50.8	+33.0	46.8	18 31.8	+33.6	47.1	45
46	14 10.5	28.7	44.7	14 53.1	29.4	44.9	15 35.5	30.1	45.1	16 17.8	30.8	45.3	17 00.0	31.4	45.5	17 42.0	32.0	45.7	18 23.8	32.7	45.9	19 05.4	33.4	46.2	46
47	14 39.2	28.6	43.8	15 22.5	29.2	44.0	16 05.6	29.8	44.2	16 48.6	30.5	44.4	17 31.4	31.1	44.6	18 14.0	31.8	44.8	18 56.5	32.4	45.1	19 38.8	33.1	45.3	47
48	15 07.8	28.3	42.9	15 51.7	28.9	43.1	16 35.4	29.6	43.3	17 19.1	30.2	43.5	18 02.5	30.9	43.7	18 45.8	31.6	43.9	19 28.9	32.2	44.2	20 11.9	32.8	44.4	48
49	15 36.1	28.1	42.0	16 20.6	28.8	42.2	17 05.0	29.4	42.4	17 49.3	30.0	42.6	18 33.4	30.7	42.8	19 17.4	31.3	43.0	20 01.1	32.0	43.3	20 44.7	32.6	43.5	49
50	16 04.2	+27.8	41.0	16 49.4	+28.4	41.2	17 34.4	+29.1	41.4	18 19.3	+29.8	41.7	19 04.1	+30.3	41.9	19 48.7	+31.0	42.1	20 33.1	+31.6	42.4	21 17.3	+32.3	42.6	50
51	16 32.0	27.6	40.1	17 17.8	28.3	40.3	18 03.5	28.9	40.5	18 49.1	29.4	40.7	19 34.4	30.1	41.0	20 19.7	30.7	41.2	21 04.7	31.4	41.5	21 49.6	32.0	41.7	51
52	16 59.6	27.4	39.2	17 46.1	27.9	39.4	18 32.4	28.6	39.6	19 18.5	29.2	39.8	20 04.5	29.8	40.0	20 50.4	30.4	40.3	21 36.1	31.0	40.5	22 21.6	31.6	40.8	52
53	17 27.0	27.1	38.3	18 14.0	27.7	38.5	19 01.0	28.2	38.7	19 47.7	28.9	38.9	20 34.3	29.6	39.1	21 20.8	30.1	39.4	22 07.1	30.8	39.6	22 53.2	31.4	39.9	53
54	17 54.1	26.8	37.3	18 41.7	27.4	37.5	19 29.2	28.1	37.7	20 16.6	28.6	38.0	21 03.9	29.2	38.2	21 50.9	29.8	38.4	22 37.9	30.4	38.7	23 24.6	31.0	39.0	54
55	18 20.9	+26.6	36.4	19 09.1	+27.2	36.6	19 57.3	+27.7	36.8	20 45.2	+28.3	37.0	21 33.1	+28.9	37.3	22 20.7	+29.5	37.5	23 08.3	+30.0	37.8	23 55.6	+30.7	38.0	55
56	18 47.5	26.2	35.4	19 36.3	26.8	35.6	20 25.0	27.4	35.9	21 13.5	28.0	36.1	22 02.0	28.5	36.3	22 50.2	29.2	36.6	23 38.3	29.8	36.8	24 26.3	30.3	37.1	56
57	19 13.7	26.0	34.5	20 03.1	26.5	34.7	20 52.4	27.1	34.9	21 41.5	27.7	35.1	22 30.5	28.2	35.4	23 19.4	28.8	35.6	24 08.1	29.4	35.9	24 56.6	30.0	36.1	57
58	19 39.7	25.6	33.5	20 29.6	26.2	33.7	21 19.5	26.7	33.9	22 09.2	27.3	34.2	22 58.7	27.9	34.4	23 48.2	28.4	34.6	24 37.5	29.0	34.9	25 26.6	29.6	35.2	58
59	20 05.3	25.4	32.6	20 55.8	25.9	32.8	21 46.2	26.5	33.0	22 36.5	27.0	33.2	23 26.6	27.5	33.4	24 16.6	28.1	33.7	25 06.5	28.6	33.9	25 56.2	29.2	34.2	59
60	20 30.7	+25.0	31.6	21 21.7	+25.6	31.8	22 12.7	+26.0	32.0	23 03.5	+26.6	32.2	23 54.1	+27.2	32.5	24 44.7	+27.7	32.7	25 35.1	+28.3	33.0	26 25.4	+28.8	33.2	60
61	20 55.7	24.7	30.6	21 47.3	25.2	30.8	22 38.7	25.8	31.0	23 30.1	26.2	31.3	24 21.3	26.8	31.5	25 12.4	27.3	31.7	26 03.4	27.8	32.0	26 54.2	28.4	32.3	61
62	21 20.4	24.3	29.7	22 12.5	24.8	29.9	23 04.5	25.3	30.1	23 56.3	25.9	30.3	24 48.1	26.4	30.5	25 39.7	26.9	30.7	26 31.2	27.4	31.0	27 22.6	27.9	31.3	62
63	21 44.7	24.0	28.7	22 37.3	24.5	28.9	23 29.8	25.0	29.1	24 22.2	25.5	29.3	25 14.5	26.0	29.5	26 06.6	26.5	29.8	26 58.6	27.1	30.0	27 50.5	27.6	30.3	63
64	22 08.7	23.7	27.7	23 01.8	24.1	27.9	23 54.8	24.6	28.1	24 47.7	25.1	28.3	25 40.5	25.5	28.5	26 33.1	26.1	28.8	27 25.7	26.5	29.0	28 18.1	27.1	29.3	64
65	22 32.4	+23.2	26.7	23 25.9	+23.8	26.9	24 19.4	+24.2	27.1	25 12.8	+24.6	27.3	26 06.0	+25.2	27.5	26 59.2	+25.6	27.7	27 52.2	+26.2	28.0	28 45.2	+26.6	28.2	65
66	22 55.6	22.9	25.7	23 49.7	23.3	25.9	24 43.6	23.8	26.1	25 37.4	24.3	26.3	26 31.2	24.7	26.5	27 24.8	25.2	26.7	28 18.4	25.6	27.0	29 11.8	26.1	27.2	66
67	23 18.5	22.5	24.7	24 13.0	22.9	24.9	25 07.4	23.4	25.1	26 01.7	23.8	25.3	26 55.9	24.3	25.5	27 50.0	24.8	25.7	28 44.0	25.2	25.9	29 37.9	25.7	26.2	67
68	23 41.0	22.1	23.7	24 35.9	22.6	23.9	25 30.8	22.9	24.0	26 25.5	23.4	24.2	27 20.2	23.8	24.5	28 14.8	24.2	24.7	29 09.2	24.8	24.9	30 03.6	25.2	25.1	68
69	24 03.1	21.7	22.7	24 58.5	22.1	22.8	25 53.7	22.6	23.0	26 48.9	23.0	23.2	27 44.0	23.4	23.4	28 39.0	23.8	23.6	29 34.0	24.2	23.9	30 28.8	24.6	24.1	69
70	24 24.8	+21.3	21.6	25 20.6	+21.7	21.8	26 16.3	+22.0	22.0	27 11.9	+22.4	22.2	28 07.4	+22.9	22.4	29 02.8	+23.3	22.6	29 58.2	+23.7	22.8	30 53.4	+24.2	23.0	70
71	24 46.1	20.9	20.6	25 42.3	21.2	20.8	26 38.3	21.7	20.9	27 34.3	22.0	21.1	28 30.3	22.4	21.3	29 26.1	22.8	21.5	30 21.9	23.2	21.7	31 17.6	23.6	22.0	71
72	25 07.0	20.4	19.6	26 03.5	20.8	19.7	27 00.0	21.1	19.9	27 56.3	21.6	20.1	28 52.7	21.9	20.3	29 48.9	22.3	20.5	30 45.1	22.6	20.7	31 41.2	23.0	20.9	72
73	25 27.4	20.0	18.5	26 24.3	20.3	18.7	27 21.1	20.7	18.9	28 17.9	21.0	19.0	29 14.6	21.3	19.2	30 11.2	21.7	19.4	31 07.7	22.2	19.6	32 04.2	22.5	19.8	73
74	25 47.4	19.6	17.5	26 44.6	19.9	17.6	27 41.8	20.2	17.8	28 38.9	20.5	18.0	29 35.9	20.9	18.1	30 32.9	21.2	18.3	31 29.9	21.5	18.5	32 26.7	22.0	18.7	74
75	26 07.0	+19.1	16.4	27 04.5	+19.4	16.6	28 02.0	+19.7	16.7	28 59.4	+20.0	16.9	29 56.8	+20.3	17.1	30 54.1	+20.7	17.2	31 51.4	+21.0	17.4	32 48.7	+21.3	17.6	75
76	26 26.1	18.6	15.4	27 23.9	18.9	15.5	28 21.7	19.2	15.7	29 19.4	19.5	15.8	30 17.1	19.8	16.0	31 14.8	20.1	16.1	32 12.4	20.4	16.3	33 10.0	20.7	16.5	76
77	26 44.7	18.1	14.3	27 42.8	18.4	14.4	28 40.9	18.7	14.6	29 38.9	19.0	14.7	30 36.9	19.3	14.9	31 34.9	19.5	15.0	32 32.8	19.9	15.2	33 30.7	20.1	15.4	77
78	27 02.8	17.7	13.2	28 01.2	17.9	13.4	28 59.6	18.1	13.5	29 57.9	18.4	13.6	30 56.2	18.6	13.8	31 54.4	19.0	13.9	32 52.7	19.2	14.1	33 50.8	19.5	14.2	78
79	27 20.5	17.1	12.2	28 19.1	17.4	12.3	29 17.7	17.6	12.4	30 16.3	17.8	12.5	31 14.8	18.1	12.7	32 13.4	18.3	12.8	33 11.9	18.6	12.9	34 10.3	18.9	13.1	79
80	27 37.6	+16.7	11.1	28 36.5	+16.8	11.2	29 35.3	+17.1	11.3	30 34.1	+17.3	11.4	31 32.9	+17.6	11.5	32 31.7	+17.8	11.7	33 30.5	+17.9	11.8	34 29.2	+18.2	11.9	80
81	27 54.3	16.1	10.0	28 53.3	16.4	10.1	29 52.4	16.5	10.2	30 51.4	16.7	10.3	31 50.5	16.9	10.4	32 49.5	17.1	10.5	33 48.4	17.4	10.6	34 47.4	17.5	10.8	81
82	28 10.4	15.6	8.9	29 09.7	15.7	9.0	30 08.9	16.0	9.1	31 08.1	16.2	9.2	32 07.4	16.3	9.3	33 06.6	16.5	9.4	34 05.8	16.6	9.5	35 04.9	16.9	9.6	82
83	28 26.0	15.1	7.8	29 25.4	15.3	7.9	30 24.9	15.3	8.0	31 24.3	15.5	8.1	32 23.7	15.7	8.1	33 23.1	15.8	8.2	34 22.4	16.0	8.3	35 21.8	16.2	8.4	83
84	28 41.1	14.5	6.7	29 40.7	14.6	6.8	30 40.2	14.8	6.9	31 39.8	14.9	6.9	32 39.4	15.0	7.0	33 38.9	15.2	7.1	34 38.4	15.4	7.2	35 38.0	15.5	7.3	84
85	28 55.6	+14.0	5.6	29 55.3	+14.1	5.7	30 55.0	+14.2	5.7	31 54.7	+14.3	5.8	32 54.4	+14.4	5.8	33 54.1	+14.5	5.9	34 53.8	+14.6	6.0	35 53.5	+14.7	6.1	85
86	29 09.6	13.5	4.5	30 09.4	13.6	4.5	31 09.2	13.7	4.6	32 09.0	13.7	4.6	33 08.8	13.8	4.7	34 08.6	13.9	4.7	35 08.4	14.0	4.8	36 08.2	14.1	4.9	86
87	29 23.1	12.8	3.4	30 23.0	12.9	3.4	31 22.9	13.0	3.4	32 22.7	13.1	3.5	33 22.6	13.2	3.5	34 22.5	13.2	3.6	35 22.4	13.2	3.6	36 22.3	13.3	3.7	87
88	29 35.9	12.4	2.3	30 35.9	12.3	2.3	31 35.9	12.3	2.3	32 35.8	12.4	2.3	33 35.8	12.4	2.4	34 35.7	12.5	2.4	35 35.6	12.6	2.4	36 35.6	12.6	2.4	88
89	29 48.3	11.7	1.1	30 48.2	11.8	1.1	31 48.2	11.8	1.2	32 48.2	11.8	1.2	33 48.2	11.8	1.2	34 48.2	11.8	1.2	35 48.2	11.8	1.2	36 48.2	11.8	1.2	89
90	30 00.0	+11.2	0.0	31 00.0	+11.1	0.0	32 00.0	+11.1	0.0	33 00.0	+11.1	0.0	34 00.0	+11.1	0.0	35 00.0	+11.1	0.0	36 00.0	+11.1	0.0	37 00.0	+11.1	0.0	90
	30°			31°			32°			33°			34°			35°			36°			37°			

S. Lat. { L.H.A. greater than 180°......Zn=180°−Z; L.H.A. less than 180°............Zn=180°+Z

LATITUDE SAME NAME AS DECLINATION **L.H.A. 101°, 259°**

Figure 16-13. *This is the sight reduction table page for the sun sight example. The LHA is 259° and, in the column for 30° assumed longitude, in the row for a declination of 23°, you find the* hc, d, *and* Z *for the sun.*

Section IV:	
31. Tabulated hc/*d* (factor +31.5)	2°28.8′ (from sight reduction tables)
32. Declination Increment	+10.8′ (20.5′ / 60 x +31.5 = 10.8)
33. Computed Altitude *(hc)*	2°39.6′ (line 31 minus line 32)
34. Observed Altitude *(ho)*	2°48.1′ (from line 13)
35. Altitude Intercept (Toward/Away)	8.5′ Toward (line 34 minus line 33, "Ho-More-To")
36. Azimuth Angle (Z)	64.7° (from sight reduction tables)
37. Azimuth (Zn)	65°

From here on, you reduce the sight just like a star sight. Notice that the sun's GHA is listed directly in the daily pages; no SHA is needed, nor is there a *v* correction. Thus, GHA hours plus the increments equals the GHA of the sun.

There is a correction for the sun not used for stars—the *d* correction for declination. This accounts for the minutes of declination change after each whole hour and is found at the bottom of the sun column in the daily pages. It's positive if the sun's declination is increasing and negative if decreasing. In this case the *d* correction factor is +0.1'. The correction itself is found on the "15 minute" increments and corrections page in the right-hand columns. In this case the correction for a *d* correction factor of 0.1' is 0.0'.

With an LHA of 259°, an assumed latitude of 30° (same), and a declination of N23° 20.5', you enter the sight reduction tables. You can use either the tables for 15°–30° or 30°–45° because there is a convenient overlap at 30°. (See Figure 16-13.) Look on the page for an LHA of 259°, in the column for a latitude of 30°, and move down to the row for a declination of 23°.

The rest of the solution for this sight follows. You plot it in the same way as a star sight.

Sight Reduction Form

Section I:	
1. Body	Moon
2. Index Correction	none
3. Dip Correction (height of eye)	-4.1′
4. Sum	-4.1′
5. Sextant Altitude *(hs)*	26° 06.7′
6. Apparent Altitude *(ha)*	26° 02.6′
7. Altitude Correction	+60.5′
8. Mars/Venus Correction	not applicable
9. Additional Correction	0.0′
10. Horizontal Parallax Correction	+4.0
11. Moon Upper Limb Correction	30.0
12. Correction to Apparent Altitude	+34.5′ (sum of lines 7–11)
13. Observed Altitude *(ho)*	26° 37.1′ (line 6 minus line 12)

Example of Sight Reduction for the Moon

The moon is often used for celestial LOPs because, unlike stars and planets, it is often visible for many hours during the day. (The stars and planets are only available for sights during a few minutes of twilight in the morning and evening when it's light enough to see the horizon clearly, yet dark enough to see the bodies. Even then, clouds often interfere.) Because the moon is so close to earth, you must apply additional corrections that are not used for stars and planets.

This example includes only finding the moon's *ho,* GHA, and declination. The rest of the solution is the same as any other sight.

Assume that a navigator sights the upper limb of the moon at 10 00 00 GMT on June 16, 1994. Height of eye is 18 feet, *hs* is 26°06.7', and there is no index error. (A thoughtful navigator has carefully timed this observation at precisely 10 00 00 GMT to reduce the computations of sight reduction.)

The additional corrections to the moon sight begin with the *altitude correction for the moon,* found inside the back cover of the almanac. In the column labeled 25°–29° find entries under 26° for every 10 minutes. Interpolate between 26°00' and 26°10' to get a correction of +60.5. (See Figure 16-16.)

Next is the *horizontal parallax correction,* unique to moon sights. It accounts for the slight difference in the apparent position of the moon when it's on the horizon versus when it's at your zenith. The difference is due to the 4,000-mile radius of the earth. This correction is needed because the moon is so close to the earth. (The sun's parallax correction is so small you can ignore it, and the stars and planets have virtually none because they're essentially at infinity.)

Find this parallax correction by noting the *HP correction factor* from the daily pages in the same row as the GHA, the *v* correction factor, the declination, and the *d* correction factor. The HP factor in this case is 58.4'. Use this value to enter the HP correction table on the lower half of the inside back cover of the almanac. For an altitude *(ha)* 26°02.6', run down the "U" column (for upper limb) to the lines for 58.2' and 58.5', interpolate for the 58.4', and record the correction as +4.0'. See Figure 16-16, but note that you must obtain the HP factor first from the daily pages, as found in Figure 16-15.

The last correction is a constant –30' correction applied only to upper limb sights of the moon.

There is a hidden correction for the moon incorporated into the altitude correction called* augmentation, *which accounts for the apparent change in the moon's diameter at different altitudes. It appears bigger when it's at your zenith because you're 4,000 miles closer to it than when it is on the horizon. (See Figure 16-14.)

To find the GHA and declination of the moon (as well as the *v* correction factor, *d* correction factor, and the HP factor), enter the daily pages of the almanac for the date and time of the sight and extract the GHA for the hour of the sight, the *v* correction factor, the declination, and the *d* correction factor. (See Figure 16-15.) The *v* correction for the moon is always positive and is found on the page of increments and corrections for the proper minute of time—in this case, 00 minutes and 00 seconds. Here, note a *v* correction factor of 11.3 and a correction of 0.1'.

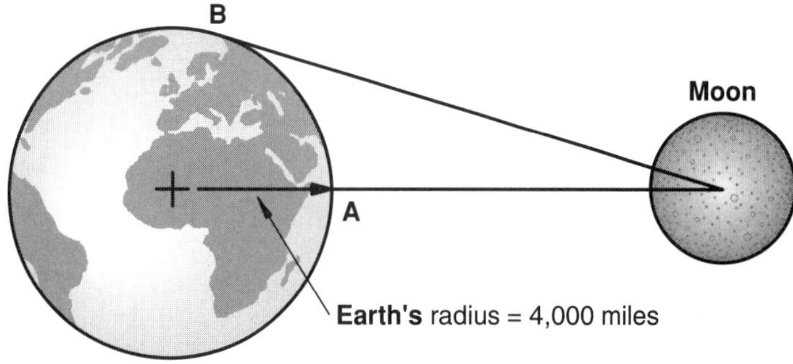

Figure 16-14. *You are about 4,000 miles closer to the moon when it is overhead (as at "A") than when it is on your horizon (as at "B"). At higher altitudes, when it's closer, it appears slightly larger. This* augmentation *is incorporated into the altitude correction for the moon. The horizontal parallax correction accounts for a slight change in position of the moon against the backdrop of the sky when you view it from different positions on earth. This difference (greatly exaggerated) is shown in the angle between A and B.*

Section III:

20. GHA (*v* corr'n. factor 11.3)	245°45.1'
21. GHA increment	0°00.0'
22. SHA (or *v* correction)	0.1'
23. GHA	245°45.2'

The declination of the moon is found in the same way as other bodies. From the daily pages extract the declination for the whole hour and the *d* factor. From the increments and corrections pages find the *d* correction, apply it to the whole hour declination value—the result is declination. In this case the *d* factor is 12.1 and the correction +0.1. Again, the *d* correction is positive if the moon's declination (not the *d* factor itself) is increasing and negative if it is decreasing. (See Figure 16-17.)

27. Declination (*d* corr'n. factor +12.1)	S00° 13.7'
28. *d* correction	+0.1
29. Declination	S00° 13.8'

After this you can determine the LHA and assumed latitude in the normal way and use the sight reduction tables to find the LOP, just as you do for other sights.

Figure 16-15. *The almanac daily page for the moon sight gives the GHA of the moon, the v and d factors, the declination, and the HP (horizontal parallax correction). This correction is necessary because the moon is relatively close to the earth when compared with other bodies, and the earth's 4,000-mile radius affects the angular height of the moon above the horizon—its altitude.*

1994 JUNE 15, 16, 17 (WED., THURS., FRI.)

UT (GMT)		SUN		MOON				
		G.H.A.	Dec.	G.H.A.	v	Dec.	d	H.P.
d	h	° ′	° ′	° ′	′	° ′	′	′
15	00	179 55.6	N23 17.2	112 24.4	11.8	N 6 28.5	11.4	57.6
	01	194 55.5	17.4	126 55.2	11.8	6 17.1	11.3	57.6
	02	209 55.4	17.5	141 26.0	11.8	6 05.8	11.4	57.6
	03	224 55.2	. . 17.6	155 56.8	11.7	5 54.4	11.4	57.7
	04	239 55.1	17.7	170 27.5	11.8	5 43.0	11.5	57.7
	05	254 55.0	17.8	184 58.3	11.8	5 31.5	11.5	57.7
	06	269 54.8	N23 17.9	199 29.1	11.7	N 5 20.0	11.6	57.7
W	07	284 54.7	18.0	213 59.8	11.8	5 08.4	11.5	57.8
E	08	299 54.6	18.1	228 30.6	11.7	4 56.9	11.7	57.8
D	09	314 54.4	. . 18.2	243 01.3	11.8	4 45.2	11.6	57.8
N	10	329 54.3	18.3	257 32.1	11.7	4 33.6	11.7	57.8
E	11	344 54.2	18.5	272 02.8	11.7	4 21.9	11.7	57.9
S	12	359 54.0	N23 18.6	286 33.5	11.7	N 4 10.2	11.8	57.9
D	13	14 53.9	18.7	301 04.2	11.7	3 58.4	11.7	57.9
A	14	29 53.8	18.8	315 34.9	11.7	3 46.7	11.8	57.9
Y	15	44 53.6	. . 18.9	330 05.6	11.7	3 34.9	11.9	58.0
	16	59 53.5	19.0	344 36.3	11.6	3 23.0	11.8	58.0
	17	74 53.4	19.1	359 06.9	11.6	3 11.2	11.9	58.0
	18	89 53.2	N23 19.2	13 37.5	11.7	N 2 59.3	11.9	58.0
	19	104 53.1	19.3	28 08.2	11.6	2 47.4	12.0	58.1
	20	119 53.0	19.4	42 38.8	11.6	2 35.4	11.9	58.1
	21	134 52.8	. . 19.5	57 09.4	11.5	2 23.5	12.0	58.1
	22	149 52.7	19.6	71 39.9	11.6	2 11.5	12.0	58.1
	23	164 52.6	19.7	86 10.5	11.5	1 59.5	12.0	58.2
16	00	179 52.4	N23 19.8	100 41.0	11.5	N 1 47.5	12.1	58.2
	01	194 52.3	19.9	115 11.5	11.5	1 35.4	12.0	58.2
	02	209 52.2	20.0	129 42.0	11.5	1 23.4	12.1	58.2
	03	224 52.0	. . 20.1	144 12.5	11.5	1 11.3	12.1	58.3
	04	239 51.9	20.1	158 43.0	11.4	0 59.2	12.1	58.3
	05	254 51.7	20.2	173 13.4	11.4	0 47.1	12.1	58.3
	06	269 51.6	N23 20.3	187 43.8	11.4	N 0 35.0	12.2	58.3
	07	284 51.5	20.4	202 14.2	11.3	0 22.8	12.1	58.4
T	08	299 51.3	20.5	216 44.5	11.3	N 0 10.7	12.2	58.4
H	09	314 51.2	. . 20.6	231 14.8	11.3	S 0 01.5	12.2	58.4
U	10	329 51.1	20.7	245 45.1	11.3	0 13.7	12.1	58.4
R	11	344 50.9	20.8	260 15.4	11.2	0 25.8	12.2	58.5
S	12	359 50.8	N23 20.9	274 45.6	11.3	S 0 38.0	12.2	58.5
D	13	14 50.7	21.0	289 15.9	11.1	0 50.2	12.2	58.5
A	14	29 50.5	21.1	303 46.0	11.2	1 02.4	12.2	58.5
Y	15	44 50.4	. . 21.1	318 16.2	11.1	1 14.6	12.2	58.6
	16	59 50.3	21.2	332 46.3	11.1	1 26.8	12.3	58.6
	17	74 50.1	21.3	347 16.4	11.0	1 39.1	12.2	58.6
	18	89 50.0	N23 21.4	1 46.4	11.0	S 1 51.3	12.2	58.6
	19	104 49.9	21.5	16 16.4	11.0	2 03.5	12.2	58.7
	20	119 49.7	21.6	30 46.4	10.9	2 15.7	12.2	58.7
	21	134 49.6	. . 21.6	45 16.3	10.9	2 27.9	12.2	58.7
	22	149 49.5	21.7	59 46.2	10.9	2 40.1	12.2	58.7
	23	164 49.3	21.8	74 16.1	10.8	2 52.3	12.2	58.8
17	00	179 49.2	N23 21.9	88 45.9	10.8	S 3 04.5	12.2	58.8
	01	194 49.1	22.0	103 15.7	10.7	3 16.7	12.2	58.8
	02	209 48.9	22.0	117 45.4	10.7	3 28.9	12.2	58.8
	03	224 48.8	. . 22.1	132 15.1	10.7	3 41.1	12.2	58.9
	04	239 48.6	22.2	146 44.8	10.6	3 53.3	12.1	58.9
	05	254 48.5	22.3	161 14.4	10.6	4 05.4	12.2	58.9
	06	269 48.4	N23 22.3	175 44.0	10.5	S 4 17.6	12.1	58.9
	07	284 48.2	22.4	190 13.5	10.5	4 29.7	12.1	59.0
	08	299 48.1	22.5	204 43.0	10.4	4 41.8	12.1	59.0
F	09	314 48.0	. . 22.6	219 12.4	10.4	4 53.9	12.1	59.0
R	10	329 47.8	22.6	233 41.8	10.3	5 06.0	12.1	59.0
I	11	344 47.7	22.7	248 11.1	10.3	5 18.1	12.1	59.1
D	12	359 47.6	N23 22.8	262 40.4	10.2	S 5 30.2	12.0	59.1
A	13	14 47.4	22.9	277 09.6	10.2	5 42.2	12.0	59.1
Y	14	29 47.3	22.9	291 38.8	10.1	5 54.2	12.0	59.1
	15	44 47.2	. . 23.0	306 07.9	10.1	6 06.2	11.9	59.2
	16	59 47.0	23.1	320 37.0	10.0	6 18.1	12.0	59.2
	17	74 46.9	23.1	335 06.0	10.0	6 30.1	11.9	59.2
	18	89 46.8	N23 23.2	349 35.0	9.9	S 6 42.0	11.9	59.2
	19	104 46.6	23.3	4 03.9	9.9	6 53.9	11.8	59.3
	20	119 46.5	23.3	18 32.8	9.8	7 05.7	11.8	59.3
	21	134 46.3	. . 23.4	33 01.6	9.7	7 17.5	11.8	59.3
	22	149 46.2	23.5	47 30.3	9.7	7 29.3	11.8	59.3
	23	164 46.1	23.5	61 59.0	9.6	7 41.1	11.7	59.4
		S.D. 15.8	d 0.1	S.D.	15.8	15.9		16.1

Lat.	Twilight Naut.	Twilight Civil	Sunrise	Moonrise 15	Moonrise 16	Moonrise 17	Moonrise 18
°	h m	h m	h m	h m	h m	h m	h m
N 72	▭	▭	▭	09 54	11 50	13 49	15 56
N 70	▭	▭	▭	10 01	11 49	13 40	15 36
68	▭	▭	▭	10 06	11 48	13 33	15 21
66	▭	▭	▭	10 11	11 47	13 26	15 09
64	////	////	01 33	10 14	11 47	13 21	14 59
62	////	////	02 10	10 18	11 46	13 17	14 50
60	////	00 52	02 36	10 20	11 46	13 13	14 43
N 58	////	01 41	02 56	10 23	11 45	13 10	14 37
56	////	02 11	03 13	10 25	11 45	13 07	14 31
54	00 48	02 33	03 27	10 27	11 45	13 04	14 26
52	01 33	02 51	03 39	10 29	11 44	13 02	14 21
50	02 00	03 06	03 50	10 30	11 44	13 00	14 17
45	02 46	03 35	04 13	10 34	11 44	12 55	14 08
N 40	03 16	03 58	04 31	10 37	11 43	12 51	14 01
35	03 39	04 16	04 46	10 39	11 43	12 48	13 54
30	03 58	04 31	04 59	10 42	11 42	12 45	13 49
20	04 27	04 56	05 20	10 45	11 42	12 40	13 39
N 10	04 49	05 16	05 39	10 49	11 41	12 35	13 31
0	05 08	05 34	05 57	10 52	11 41	12 31	13 23
S 10	05 25	05 51	06 14	10 55	11 40	12 27	13 16
20	05 41	06 09	06 33	10 59	11 40	12 23	13 07
30	05 58	06 28	06 54	11 03	11 40	12 18	12 58
35	06 06	06 38	07 06	11 05	11 39	12 15	12 53
40	06 16	06 50	07 20	11 07	11 39	12 12	12 47
45	06 26	07 03	07 37	11 10	11 39	12 08	12 40
S 50	06 38	07 19	07 58	11 14	11 38	12 04	12 32
52	06 43	07 27	08 08	11 15	11 38	12 02	12 28
54	06 49	07 35	08 19	11 17	11 38	12 00	12 24
56	06 55	07 44	08 31	11 19	11 38	11 58	12 19
58	07 02	07 54	08 46	11 21	11 38	11 55	12 14
S 60	07 09	08 06	09 03	11 24	11 37	11 52	12 09

Lat.	Sunset	Twilight Civil	Twilight Naut.	Moonset 15	Moonset 16	Moonset 17	Moonset 18
°	h m	h m	h m	h m	h m	h m	h m
N 72	▭	▭	▭	23 38	23 25	23 12	22 54
N 70	▭	▭	▭	23 35	23 29	23 23	23 16
68	▭	▭	▭	23 34	23 33	23 32	23 32
66	▭	▭	▭	23 32	23 36	23 40	23 46
64	22 29	////	////	23 31	23 38	23 47	23 57
62	21 52	////	////	23 29	23 40	23 52	24 07
60	21 26	23 10	////	23 28	23 42	23 57	24 15
N 58	21 05	22 21	////	23 27	23 44	24 02	00 02
56	20 49	21 51	////	23 26	23 45	24 06	00 06
54	20 34	21 29	23 15	23 26	23 47	24 09	00 09
52	20 22	21 11	22 29	23 25	23 48	24 13	00 13
50	20 11	20 56	22 01	23 24	23 49	24 15	00 15
45	19 49	20 26	21 16	23 23	23 52	24 22	00 22
N 40	19 31	20 04	20 45	23 22	23 54	24 27	00 27
35	19 16	19 45	20 22	23 21	23 55	24 32	00 32
30	19 03	19 30	20 04	23 20	23 57	24 36	00 36
20	18 41	19 05	19 35	23 18	24 00	00 00	00 43
N 10	18 22	18 45	19 12	23 17	24 02	00 02	00 50
0	18 04	18 27	18 53	23 15	24 05	00 05	00 55
S 10	17 47	18 10	18 36	23 14	24 07	00 07	01 01
20	17 28	17 52	18 20	23 12	24 09	00 09	01 08
30	17 07	17 34	18 03	23 10	24 12	00 12	01 15
35	16 55	17 23	17 55	23 09	24 13	00 13	01 19
40	16 41	17 11	17 45	23 08	24 15	00 15	01 24
45	16 24	16 58	17 35	23 07	24 17	00 17	01 29
S 50	16 03	16 42	17 23	23 05	24 20	00 20	01 36
52	15 53	16 34	17 18	23 04	24 21	00 21	01 39
54	15 42	16 26	17 12	23 04	24 22	00 22	01 42
56	15 30	16 17	17 06	23 03	24 23	00 23	01 46
58	15 15	16 07	16 59	23 02	24 25	00 25	01 50
S 60	14 58	15 55	16 52	23 00	24 27	00 27	01 55

Day	SUN Eqn. of Time 00h	SUN Eqn. of Time 12h	SUN Mer. Pass.	MOON Mer. Pass. Upper	MOON Mer. Pass. Lower	Age	Phase
	m s	m s	h m	h m	h m	d	
15	00 17	00 24	12 00	17 04	04 39	06	
16	00 30	00 37	12 01	17 53	05 28	07	◐
17	00 43	00 49	12 01	18 43	06 18	08	

Figure 2007. Right hand daily page of the *Nautical Almanac* for June 16, 1994.

ALTITUDE CORRECTION TABLES 0°–35°—MOON

App. Alt.	0°–4° Corr^n	5°–9° Corr^n	10°–14° Corr^n	15°–19° Corr^n	20°–24° Corr^n	25°–29° Corr^n	30°–34° Corr^n	App. Alt.
′	° ′	° ′	° ′	° ′	° ′	° ′	° ′	′
00	0 33.8	5 58.2	10 62.1	15 62.8	20 62.2	25 60.8	30 58.9	00
10	35.9	58.5	62.2	62.8	62.1	60.8	58.8	10
20	37.8	58.7	62.2	62.8	62.1	60.7	58.8	20
30	39.6	58.9	62.3	62.8	62.1	60.7	58.7	30
40	41.2	59.1	62.3	62.8	62.0	60.6	58.6	40
50	42.6	59.3	62.4	62.7	62.0	60.6	58.5	50
00	1 44.0	6 59.5	11 62.4	16 62.7	21 62.0	26 60.5	31 58.5	00
10	45.2	59.7	62.4	62.7	61.9	60.4	58.4	10
20	46.3	59.9	62.5	62.7	61.9	60.4	58.3	20
30	47.3	60.0	62.5	62.7	61.9	60.3	58.2	30
40	48.3	60.2	62.5	62.7	61.8	60.3	58.2	40
50	49.2	60.3	62.6	62.7	61.8	60.2	58.1	50
00	2 50.0	7 60.5	12 62.6	17 62.7	22 61.7	27 60.1	32 58.0	00
10	50.8	60.6	62.6	62.6	61.7	60.1	57.9	10
20	51.4	60.7	62.6	62.6	61.6	60.0	57.8	20
30	52.1	60.9	62.7	62.6	61.6	59.9	57.8	30
40	52.7	61.0	62.7	62.6	61.5	59.9	57.7	40
50	53.3	61.1	62.7	62.6	61.5	59.8	57.6	50
00	3 53.8	8 61.2	13 62.7	18 62.5	23 61.5	28 59.7	33 57.5	00
10	54.3	61.3	62.7	62.5	61.4	59.7	57.4	10
20	54.8	61.4	62.7	62.5	61.4	59.6	57.4	20
30	55.2	61.5	62.8	62.5	61.3	59.6	57.3	30
40	55.6	61.6	62.8	62.4	61.3	59.5	57.2	40
50	56.0	61.6	62.8	62.4	61.2	59.4	57.1	50
00	4 56.4	9 61.7	14 62.8	19 62.4	24 61.2	29 59.3	34 57.0	00
10	56.7	61.8	62.8	62.3	61.1	59.3	56.9	10
20	57.1	61.9	62.8	62.3	61.1	59.2	56.9	20
30	57.4	61.9	62.8	62.3	61.0	59.1	56.8	30
40	57.7	62.0	62.8	62.2	60.9	59.1	56.7	40
50	57.9	62.1	62.8	62.2	60.9	59.0	56.6	50

H.P.	L	U	L	U	L	U	L	U	L	U	L	U	L	U	H.P.
′	′	′	′	′	′	′	′	′	′	′	′	′	′	′	′
54.0	0.3	0.9	0.3	0.9	0.4	1.0	0.5	1.1	0.6	1.2	0.7	1.3	0.9	1.5	54.0
54.3	0.7	1.1	0.7	1.2	0.7	1.2	0.8	1.3	0.9	1.4	1.1	1.5	1.2	1.7	54.3
54.6	1.1	1.4	1.1	1.4	1.1	1.4	1.2	1.5	1.3	1.6	1.4	1.7	1.5	1.8	54.6
54.9	1.4	1.6	1.5	1.6	1.5	1.6	1.6	1.7	1.6	1.8	1.8	1.9	1.9	2.0	54.9
55.2	1.8	1.8	1.8	1.8	1.9	1.9	1.9	1.9	2.0	2.0	2.1	2.1	2.2	2.2	55.2
55.5	2.2	2.0	2.2	2.0	2.3	2.1	2.3	2.1	2.4	2.2	2.4	2.3	2.5	2.4	55.5
55.8	2.6	2.2	2.6	2.2	2.6	2.3	2.7	2.3	2.7	2.4	2.8	2.4	2.9	2.5	55.8
56.1	3.0	2.4	3.0	2.5	3.0	2.5	3.0	2.5	3.1	2.6	3.1	2.6	3.2	2.7	56.1
56.4	3.4	2.7	3.4	2.7	3.4	2.7	3.4	2.7	3.4	2.8	3.5	2.8	3.5	2.9	56.4
56.7	3.7	2.9	3.7	2.9	3.8	2.9	3.8	2.9	3.8	3.0	3.8	3.0	3.9	3.0	56.7
57.0	4.1	3.1	4.1	3.1	4.1	3.1	4.1	3.1	4.2	3.1	4.2	3.2	4.2	3.2	57.0
57.3	4.5	3.3	4.5	3.3	4.5	3.3	4.5	3.3	4.5	3.3	4.5	3.4	4.6	3.4	57.3
57.6	4.9	3.5	4.9	3.5	4.9	3.5	4.9	3.5	4.9	3.5	4.9	3.5	4.9	3.6	57.6
57.9	5.3	3.8	5.3	3.8	5.2	3.8	5.2	3.7	5.2	3.7	5.2	3.7	5.2	3.7	57.9
58.2	5.6	4.0	5.6	4.0	5.6	4.0	5.6	4.0	5.6	3.9	5.6	3.9	5.6	3.9	58.2
58.5	6.0	4.2	6.0	4.2	6.0	4.2	6.0	4.2	6.0	4.1	5.9	4.1	5.9	4.1	58.5
58.8	6.4	4.4	6.4	4.4	6.4	4.4	6.3	4.4	6.3	4.3	6.3	4.3	6.2	4.2	58.8
59.1	6.8	4.6	6.8	4.6	6.7	4.6	6.7	4.6	6.7	4.5	6.6	4.5	6.6	4.4	59.1
59.4	7.2	4.8	7.1	4.8	7.1	4.8	7.1	4.8	7.0	4.7	7.0	4.7	6.9	4.6	59.4
59.7	7.5	5.1	7.5	5.0	7.5	5.0	7.5	5.0	7.4	4.9	7.3	4.8	7.2	4.7	59.7
60.0	7.9	5.3	7.9	5.3	7.9	5.2	7.8	5.2	7.8	5.1	7.7	5.0	7.6	4.9	60.0
60.3	8.3	5.5	8.3	5.5	8.2	5.4	8.2	5.4	8.1	5.3	8.0	5.2	7.9	5.1	60.3
60.6	8.7	5.7	8.7	5.7	8.6	5.7	8.6	5.6	8.5	5.5	8.4	5.4	8.2	5.3	60.6
60.9	9.1	5.9	9.0	5.9	9.0	5.9	8.9	5.8	8.8	5.7	8.7	5.6	8.6	5.4	60.9
61.2	9.5	6.2	9.4	6.1	9.4	6.1	9.3	6.0	9.2	5.9	9.1	5.8	8.9	5.6	61.2
61.5	9.8	6.4	9.8	6.3	9.7	6.3	9.7	6.2	9.5	6.1	9.4	5.9	9.2	5.8	61.5

DIP

Ht. of Eye	Corr^n	Ht. of Eye	Ht. of Eye	Corr^n	Ht. of Eye
m		ft.	m		ft.
2.4		8.0	9.5		31.5
	−2.8			−5.5	
2.6		8.6	9.9		32.7
	−2.9			−5.6	
2.8		9.2	10.3		33.9
	−3.0			−5.7	
3.0		9.8	10.6		35.1
	−3.1			−5.8	
3.2		10.5	11.0		36.3
	−3.2			−5.9	
3.4		11.2	11.4		37.6
	−3.3			−6.0	
3.6		11.9	11.8		38.9
	−3.4			−6.1	
3.8		12.6	12.2		40.1
	−3.5			−6.2	
4.0		13.3	12.6		41.5
	−3.6			−6.3	
4.3		14.1	13.0		42.8
	−3.7			−6.4	
4.5		14.9	13.4		44.2
	−3.8			−6.5	
4.7		15.7	13.8		45.5
	−3.9			−6.6	
5.0		16.5	14.2		46.9
	−4.0			−6.7	
5.2		17.4	14.7		48.4
	−4.1			−6.8	
5.5		18.3	15.1		49.8
	−4.2			−6.9	
5.8		19.1	15.5		51.3
	−4.3			−7.0	
6.1		20.1	16.0		52.8
	−4.4			−7.1	
6.3		21.0	16.5		54.3
	−4.5			−7.2	
6.6		22.0	16.9		55.8
	−4.6			−7.3	
6.9		22.9	17.4		57.4
	−4.7			−7.4	
7.2		23.9	17.9		58.9
	−4.8			−7.5	
7.5		24.9	18.4		60.5
	−4.9			−7.6	
7.9		26.0	18.8		62.1
	−5.0			−7.7	
8.2		27.1	19.3		63.8
	−5.1			−7.8	
8.5		28.1	19.8		65.4
	−5.2			−7.9	
8.8		29.2	20.4		67.1
	−5.3			−8.0	
9.2		30.4	20.9		68.8
	−5.4			−8.1	
9.5		31.5	21.4		70.5

MOON CORRECTION TABLE

The correction is in two parts; the first correction is taken from the upper part of the table with argument apparent altitude, and the second from the lower part, with argument H.P., in the same column as that from which the first correction was taken. Separate corrections are given in the lower part for lower (L) and upper (U) limbs. All corrections are to be **added** to apparent altitude, *but 30′ is to be subtracted from the altitude of the upper limb.*

For corrections for pressure and temperature see page A4.

For bubble sextant observations ignore dip, take the mean of upper and lower limb corrections and subtract 15′ from the altitude.

App. Alt. = Apparent altitude = Sextant altitude corrected for index error and dip.

xxxiv

Figure 16-16. *This page from inside the back cover of the almanac shows the altitude corrections for a moon sight. You need to use the HP correction factor from the daily pages to enter the lower half of the page. These corrections are positive. When you observe the moon's upper limb, subtract 30.0′.*

Figure 16-17. *The* v *and* d *corrections for the moon sight are found in the increments and corrections pages of the almanac—in this case, for 00 minutes 00 seconds.*

INCREMENTS AND CORRECTIONS

0m

0m	SUN PLANETS	ARIES	MOON	v or d	Corrn	v or d	Corrn	v or d	Corrn
s	° ′	° ′	° ′	′	′	′	′	′	′
00	0 00·0	0 00·0	0 00·0	0·0	0·0	6·0	0·1	12·0	0·1
01	0 00·3	0 00·3	0 00·2	0·1	0·0	6·1	0·1	12·1	0·1
02	0 00·5	0 00·5	0 00·5	0·2	0·0	6·2	0·1	12·2	0·1
03	0 00·8	0 00·8	0 00·7	0·3	0·0	6·3	0·1	12·3	0·1
04	0 01·0	0 01·0	0 01·0	0·4	0·0	6·4	0·1	12·4	0·1
05	0 01·3	0 01·3	0 01·2	0·5	0·0	6·5	0·1	12·5	0·1
06	0 01·5	0 01·5	0 01·4	0·6	0·0	6·6	0·1	12·6	0·1
07	0 01·8	0 01·8	0 01·7	0·7	0·0	6·7	0·1	12·7	0·1
08	0 02·0	0 02·0	0 01·9	0·8	0·0	6·8	0·1	12·8	0·1
09	0 02·3	0 02·3	0 02·1	0·9	0·0	6·9	0·1	12·9	0·1
10	0 02·5	0 02·5	0 02·4	1·0	0·0	7·0	0·1	13·0	0·1
11	0 02·8	0 02·8	0 02·6	1·1	0·0	7·1	0·1	13·1	0·1
12	0 03·0	0 03·0	0 02·9	1·2	0·0	7·2	0·1	13·2	0·1
13	0 03·3	0 03·3	0 03·1	1·3	0·0	7·3	0·1	13·3	0·1
14	0 03·5	0 03·5	0 03·3	1·4	0·0	7·4	0·1	13·4	0·1
15	0 03·8	0 03·8	0 03·6	1·5	0·0	7·5	0·1	13·5	0·1
16	0 04·0	0 04·0	0 03·8	1·6	0·0	7·6	0·1	13·6	0·1
17	0 04·3	0 04·3	0 04·1	1·7	0·0	7·7	0·1	13·7	0·1
18	0 04·5	0 04·5	0 04·3	1·8	0·0	7·8	0·1	13·8	0·1
19	0 04·8	0 04·8	0 04·5	1·9	0·0	7·9	0·1	13·9	0·1
20	0 05·0	0 05·0	0 04·8	2·0	0·0	8·0	0·1	14·0	0·1
21	0 05·3	0 05·3	0 05·0	2·1	0·0	8·1	0·1	14·1	0·1
22	0 05·5	0 05·5	0 05·2	2·2	0·0	8·2	0·1	14·2	0·1
23	0 05·8	0 05·8	0 05·5	2·3	0·0	8·3	0·1	14·3	0·1
24	0 06·0	0 06·0	0 05·7	2·4	0·0	8·4	0·1	14·4	0·1
25	0 06·3	0 06·3	0 06·0	2·5	0·0	8·5	0·1	14·5	0·1
26	0 06·5	0 06·5	0 06·2	2·6	0·0	8·6	0·1	14·6	0·1
27	0 06·8	0 06·8	0 06·4	2·7	0·0	8·7	0·1	14·7	0·1
28	0 07·0	0 07·0	0 06·7	2·8	0·0	8·8	0·1	14·8	0·1
29	0 07·3	0 07·3	0 06·9	2·9	0·0	8·9	0·1	14·9	0·1
30	0 07·5	0 07·5	0 07·2	3·0	0·0	9·0	0·1	15·0	0·1
31	0 07·8	0 07·8	0 07·4	3·1	0·0	9·1	0·1	15·1	0·1
32	0 08·0	0 08·0	0 07·6	3·2	0·0	9·2	0·1	15·2	0·1
33	0 08·3	0 08·3	0 07·9	3·3	0·0	9·3	0·1	15·3	0·1
34	0 08·5	0 08·5	0 08·1	3·4	0·0	9·4	0·1	15·4	0·1
35	0 08·8	0 08·8	0 08·4	3·5	0·0	9·5	0·1	15·5	0·1
36	0 09·0	0 09·0	0 08·6	3·6	0·0	9·6	0·1	15·6	0·1
37	0 09·3	0 09·3	0 08·8	3·7	0·0	9·7	0·1	15·7	0·1
38	0 09·5	0 09·5	0 09·1	3·8	0·0	9·8	0·1	15·8	0·1
39	0 09·8	0 09·8	0 09·3	3·9	0·0	9·9	0·1	15·9	0·1
40	0 10·0	0 10·0	0 09·5	4·0	0·0	10·0	0·1	16·0	0·1
41	0 10·3	0 10·3	0 09·8	4·1	0·0	10·1	0·1	16·1	0·1
42	0 10·5	0 10·5	0 10·0	4·2	0·0	10·2	0·1	16·2	0·1
43	0 10·8	0 10·8	0 10·3	4·3	0·0	10·3	0·1	16·3	0·1
44	0 11·0	0 11·0	0 10·5	4·4	0·0	10·4	0·1	16·4	0·1
45	0 11·3	0 11·3	0 10·7	4·5	0·0	10·5	0·1	16·5	0·1
46	0 11·5	0 11·5	0 11·0	4·6	0·0	10·6	0·1	16·6	0·1
47	0 11·8	0 11·8	0 11·2	4·7	0·0	10·7	0·1	16·7	0·1
48	0 12·0	0 12·0	0 11·5	4·8	0·0	10·8	0·1	16·8	0·1
49	0 12·3	0 12·3	0 11·7	4·9	0·0	10·9	0·1	16·9	0·1
50	0 12·5	0 12·5	0 11·9	5·0	0·0	11·0	0·1	17·0	0·1
51	0 12·8	0 12·8	0 12·2	5·1	0·0	11·1	0·1	17·1	0·1
52	0 13·0	0 13·0	0 12·4	5·2	0·0	11·2	0·1	17·2	0·1
53	0 13·3	0 13·3	0 12·6	5·3	0·0	11·3	0·1	17·3	0·1
54	0 13·5	0 13·5	0 12·9	5·4	0·0	11·4	0·1	17·4	0·1
55	0 13·8	0 13·8	0 13·1	5·5	0·0	11·5	0·1	17·5	0·1
56	0 14·0	0 14·0	0 13·4	5·6	0·0	11·6	0·1	17·6	0·1
57	0 14·3	0 14·3	0 13·6	5·7	0·0	11·7	0·1	17·7	0·1
58	0 14·5	0 14·5	0 13·8	5·8	0·0	11·8	0·1	17·8	0·1
59	0 14·8	0 14·8	0 14·1	5·9	0·0	11·9	0·1	17·9	0·1
60	0 15·0	0 15·0	0 14·3	6·0	0·1	12·0	0·1	18·0	0·2

1m

1m	SUN PLANETS	ARIES	MOON	v or d	Corrn	v or d	Corrn	v or d	Corrn
s	° ′	° ′	° ′	′	′	′	′	′	′
00	0 15·0	0 15·0	0 14·3	0·0	0·0	6·0	0·2	12·0	0·3
01	0 15·3	0 15·3	0 14·6	0·1	0·0	6·1	0·2	12·1	0·3
02	0 15·5	0 15·5	0 14·8	0·2	0·0	6·2	0·2	12·2	0·3
03	0 15·8	0 15·8	0 15·0	0·3	0·0	6·3	0·2	12·3	0·3
04	0 16·0	0 16·0	0 15·3	0·4	0·0	6·4	0·2	12·4	0·3
05	0 16·3	0 16·3	0 15·5	0·5	0·0	6·5	0·2	12·5	0·3
06	0 16·5	0 16·5	0 15·7	0·6	0·0	6·6	0·2	12·6	0·3
07	0 16·8	0 16·8	0 16·0	0·7	0·0	6·7	0·2	12·7	0·3
08	0 17·0	0 17·0	0 16·2	0·8	0·0	6·8	0·2	12·8	0·3
09	0 17·3	0 17·3	0 16·5	0·9	0·0	6·9	0·2	12·9	0·3
10	0 17·5	0 17·5	0 16·7	1·0	0·0	7·0	0·2	13·0	0·3
11	0 17·8	0 17·8	0 16·9	1·1	0·0	7·1	0·2	13·1	0·3
12	0 18·0	0 18·0	0 17·2	1·2	0·0	7·2	0·2	13·2	0·3
13	0 18·3	0 18·3	0 17·4	1·3	0·0	7·3	0·2	13·3	0·3
14	0 18·5	0 18·6	0 17·7	1·4	0·0	7·4	0·2	13·4	0·3
15	0 18·8	0 18·8	0 17·9	1·5	0·0	7·5	0·2	13·5	0·3
16	0 19·0	0 19·1	0 18·1	1·6	0·0	7·6	0·2	13·6	0·3
17	0 19·3	0 19·3	0 18·4	1·7	0·0	7·7	0·2	13·7	0·3
18	0 19·5	0 19·6	0 18·6	1·8	0·0	7·8	0·2	13·8	0·3
19	0 19·8	0 19·8	0 18·9	1·9	0·0	7·9	0·2	13·9	0·3
20	0 20·0	0 20·1	0 19·1	2·0	0·1	8·0	0·2	14·0	0·4
21	0 20·3	0 20·3	0 19·3	2·1	0·1	8·1	0·2	14·1	0·4
22	0 20·5	0 20·6	0 19·6	2·2	0·1	8·2	0·2	14·2	0·4
23	0 20·8	0 20·8	0 19·8	2·3	0·1	8·3	0·2	14·3	0·4
24	0 21·0	0 21·1	0 20·0	2·4	0·1	8·4	0·2	14·4	0·4
25	0 21·3	0 21·3	0 20·3	2·5	0·1	8·5	0·2	14·5	0·4
26	0 21·5	0 21·6	0 20·5	2·6	0·1	8·6	0·2	14·6	0·4
27	0 21·8	0 21·8	0 20·8	2·7	0·1	8·7	0·2	14·7	0·4
28	0 22·0	0 22·1	0 21·0	2·8	0·1	8·8	0·2	14·8	0·4
29	0 22·3	0 22·3	0 21·2	2·9	0·1	8·9	0·2	14·9	0·4
30	0 22·5	0 22·6	0 21·5	3·0	0·1	9·0	0·2	15·0	0·4
31	0 22·8	0 22·8	0 21·7	3·1	0·1	9·1	0·2	15·1	0·4
32	0 23·0	0 23·1	0 22·0	3·2	0·1	9·2	0·2	15·2	0·4
33	0 23·3	0 23·3	0 22·2	3·3	0·1	9·3	0·2	15·3	0·4
34	0 23·5	0 23·6	0 22·4	3·4	0·1	9·4	0·2	15·4	0·4
35	0 23·8	0 23·8	0 22·7	3·5	0·1	9·5	0·2	15·5	0·4
36	0 24·0	0 24·1	0 22·9	3·6	0·1	9·6	0·2	15·6	0·4
37	0 24·3	0 24·3	0 23·1	3·7	0·1	9·7	0·2	15·7	0·4
38	0 24·5	0 24·6	0 23·4	3·8	0·1	9·8	0·2	15·8	0·4
39	0 24·8	0 24·8	0 23·6	3·9	0·1	9·9	0·2	15·9	0·4
40	0 25·0	0 25·1	0 23·9	4·0	0·1	10·0	0·3	16·0	0·4
41	0 25·3	0 25·3	0 24·1	4·1	0·1	10·1	0·3	16·1	0·4
42	0 25·5	0 25·6	0 24·3	4·2	0·1	10·2	0·3	16·2	0·4
43	0 25·8	0 25·8	0 24·6	4·3	0·1	10·3	0·3	16·3	0·4
44	0 26·0	0 26·1	0 24·8	4·4	0·1	10·4	0·3	16·4	0·4
45	0 26·3	0 26·3	0 25·1	4·5	0·1	10·5	0·3	16·5	0·4
46	0 26·5	0 26·6	0 25·3	4·6	0·1	10·6	0·3	16·6	0·4
47	0 26·8	0 26·8	0 25·5	4·7	0·1	10·7	0·3	16·7	0·4
48	0 27·0	0 27·1	0 25·8	4·8	0·1	10·8	0·3	16·8	0·4
49	0 27·3	0 27·3	0 26·0	4·9	0·1	10·9	0·3	16·9	0·4
50	0 27·5	0 27·6	0 26·2	5·0	0·1	11·0	0·3	17·0	0·4
51	0 27·8	0 27·8	0 26·5	5·1	0·1	11·1	0·3	17·1	0·4
52	0 28·0	0 28·1	0 26·7	5·2	0·1	11·2	0·3	17·2	0·4
53	0 28·3	0 28·3	0 27·0	5·3	0·1	11·3	0·3	17·3	0·4
54	0 28·5	0 28·6	0 27·2	5·4	0·1	11·4	0·3	17·4	0·4
55	0 28·8	0 28·8	0 27·4	5·5	0·1	11·5	0·3	17·5	0·4
56	0 29·0	0 29·1	0 27·7	5·6	0·1	11·6	0·3	17·6	0·4
57	0 29·3	0 29·3	0 27·9	5·7	0·1	11·7	0·3	17·7	0·4
58	0 29·5	0 29·6	0 28·2	5·8	0·1	11·8	0·3	17·8	0·4
59	0 29·8	0 29·8	0 28·4	5·9	0·1	11·9	0·3	17·9	0·4
60	0 30·0	0 30·1	0 28·6	6·0	0·2	12·0	0·3	18·0	0·5

Example of Sight Reduction for a Planet

Mars, Venus, Jupiter, and Saturn are the *four navigational planets*. The only difference between planet sights and sun or star sights is the need for some additional corrections for planets. These are the altitude correction, an additional correction for Mars and Venus, and the *v* correction applied to *ha*. The sign of the *v* correction is indicated in the daily pages with the *v* correction factor, which is found at the bottom of each column of planet entries.

Here's how a *planet sight* is reduced. Again, the full sight reduction is not included here—only the steps to get *ho*, GHA, and declination. The rest of the solution is the same as for other bodies.

Let's say you take a sight of Mars on July 27, 1995, at 09 45 20 GMT, and observe a sextant altitude of 33° 20.5'. Your height of eye is 18 feet, and the index correction is +0.2.

Section I:	
1. Body	*Mars*
2. Index Correction	*+0.2'*
3. Dip Correction (height of eye)	*-4.1'*
4. Sum	*-3.9'*
5. Sextant Altitude *(hs)*	*33° 20.5'*
6. Apparent Altitude *(ha)*	*33° 16.6'*
7. Altitude Correction	*-1.5'*
8. Mars/Venus Correction	*+0.1*
9. Additional Correction	*not applicable*
10. Horizontal Parallax Correction	*not applicable*
11. Moon Upper Limb Correction	*not applicable*
12. Correction to Apparent Altitude	*-1.4'*
13. Observed Altitude *(ho)*	*33° 16.3'*

The altitude correction table for stars and planets is entered with apparent altitude *(ha)*, which is the sextant altitude *(hs)* corrected for dip and index error. (Remember that index error and index correction are the same value, but the signs are opposite.) (See Figure 16-18.)

Next, enter the daily pages with *ho* and extract the tabulated GHA and *v* correction factor, the declination, and *d* correction factor, before going to the increments and corrections pages for the minutes and seconds (45' 20") of GMT and the *v* and *d* corrections. (See Figures 16-19 and 16-20.) Thus:

20. GHA (*v* corr'n. factor *1.1*)	*256° 10.6'*
21. GHA increment	*11° 20.0'*
22. SHA (or *v* correction)	*0.8'*
23. GHA	*267° 31.4'*
27. Declination (*d* corr'n. factor *+0.6*)	*S 01° 06.1'*
28. *d* correction	*+0.5*
29. Declination	*S 01° 06.6'*

Again, the sign of the *d* correction is determined by the trend of the declination (not the trend of the *d* correction factor) and the *v* correction is always positive. From this point you work out the sight just like a sun sight.

The Final Result

These four typical examples of sight reduction—star, sun, moon, and planet—are intended to introduce you to the subject. They cover all of the common situations in sight reduction. Some special cases that you work differently are the subject of the next chapter.

You can take special satisfaction in seeing the LOPs intersect in the celestial fix you get from working out a round of sights and plotting them on a plotting sheet or chart.

Figure 16-18. *The corrections for the Mars sight shown here consist of the dip correction, the altitude correction, and the additional Mars correction. Only Mars and Venus have this additional correction; Saturn and Jupiter do not.*

A2 ALTITUDE CORRECTION TABLES 10°-90°—SUN, STARS, PLANETS

SUN

OCT.—MAR. App. Alt.	Lower Limb	Upper Limb	APR.—SEPT. App. Alt.	Lower Limb	Upper Limb
° ′	′	′	° ′	′	′
9 34	+10·8	−21·5	9 39	+10·6	−21·2
9 45	+10·9	−21·4	9 51	+10·7	−21·1
9 56	+11·0	−21·3	10 03	+10·8	−21·0
10 08	+11·1	−21·2	10 15	+10·9	−20·9
10 21	+11·2	−21·1	10 27	+11·0	−20·8
10 34	+11·3	−21·0	10 40	+11·1	−20·7
10 47	+11·4	−20·9	10 54	+11·2	−20·6
11 01	+11·5	−20·8	11 08	+11·3	−20·5
11 15	+11·6	−20·7	11 23	+11·4	−20·4
11 30	+11·7	−20·6	11 38	+11·5	−20·3
11 46	+11·8	−20·5	11 54	+11·6	−20·2
12 02	+11·9	−20·4	12 10	+11·7	−20·1
12 19	+12·0	−20·3	12 28	+11·8	−20·0
12 37	+12·1	−20·2	12 46	+11·9	−19·9
12 55	+12·2	−20·1	13 05	+12·0	−19·8
13 14	+12·3	−20·0	13 24	+12·1	−19·7
13 35	+12·4	−19·9	13 45	+12·2	−19·6
13 56	+12·5	−19·8	14 07	+12·3	−19·5
14 18	+12·6	−19·7	14 30	+12·4	−19·4
14 42	+12·7	−19·6	14 54	+12·5	−19·3
15 06	+12·8	−19·5	15 19	+12·6	−19·2
15 32	+12·9	−19·4	15 46	+12·7	−19·1
15 59	+13·0	−19·3	16 14	+12·8	−19·0
16 28	+13·1	−19·2	16 44	+12·9	−18·9
16 59	+13·2	−19·1	17 15	+13·0	−18·8
17 32	+13·3	−19·0	17 48	+13·1	−18·7
18 06	+13·4	−18·9	18 24	+13·2	−18·6
18 42	+13·5	−18·8	19 01	+13·3	−18·5
19 21	+13·6	−18·7	19 42	+13·4	−18·4
20 03	+13·7	−18·6	20 25	+13·5	−18·3
20 48	+13·8	−18·5	21 11	+13·6	−18·2
21 35	+13·9	−18·4	22 00	+13·7	−18·1
22 26	+14·0	−18·3	22 54	+13·8	−18·0
23 22	+14·1	−18·2	23 51	+13·9	−17·9
24 21	+14·2	−18·1	24 53	+14·0	−17·8
25 26	+14·3	−18·0	26 00	+14·1	−17·7
26 36	+14·4	−17·9	27 13	+14·2	−17·6
27 52	+14·5	−17·8	28 33	+14·3	−17·5
29 15	+14·6	−17·7	30 00	+14·4	−17·4
30 46	+14·7	−17·6	31 35	+14·5	−17·3
32 26	+14·8	−17·5	33 20	+14·6	−17·2
34 17	+14·9	−17·4	35 17	+14·7	−17·1
36 20	+15·0	−17·3	37 26	+14·8	−17·0
38 36	+15·1	−17·2	39 50	+14·9	−16·9
41 08	+15·2	−17·1	42 31	+15·0	−16·8
43 59	+15·3	−17·0	45 31	+15·1	−16·7
47 10	+15·4	−16·9	48 55	+15·2	−16·6
50 46	+15·5	−16·8	52 44	+15·3	−16·5
54 49	+15·6	−16·7	57 02	+15·4	−16·4
59 23	+15·7	−16·6	61 51	+15·5	−16·3
64 30	+15·8	−16·5	67 17	+15·6	−16·2
70 12	+15·9	−16·4	73 16	+15·7	−16·1
76 26	+16·0	−16·3	79 43	+15·8	−16·0
83 05	+16·1	−16·2	86 32	+15·9	−15·9
90 00			90 00		

STARS AND PLANETS

App. Alt.	Corr^n
° ′	′
9 56	−5·3
10 08	−5·2
10 20	−5·1
10 33	−5·0
10 46	−4·9
11 00	−4·8
11 14	−4·7
11 29	−4·6
11 45	−4·5
12 01	−4·4
12 18	−4·3
12 35	−4·2
12 54	−4·1
13 13	−4·0
13 33	−3·9
13 54	−3·8
14 16	−3·7
14 40	−3·6
15 04	−3·5
15 30	−3·4
15 57	−3·3
16 26	−3·2
16 56	−3·1
17 28	−3·0
18 02	−2·9
18 38	−2·8
19 17	−2·7
19 58	−2·6
20 42	−2·5
21 28	−2·4
22 19	−2·3
23 13	−2·2
24 11	−2·1
25 14	−2·0
26 22	−1·9
27 36	−1·8
28 56	−1·7
30 24	−1·6
32 00	−1·5
33 45	−1·4
35 40	−1·3
37 48	−1·2
40 08	−1·1
42 44	−1·0
45 36	−0·9
48 47	−0·8
52 18	−0·7
56 11	−0·6
60 28	−0·5
65 08	−0·4
70 11	−0·3
75 34	−0·2
81 13	−0·1
87 03	0·0
90 00	

App. Alt. — Additional Corr^n

1995

VENUS

Jan. 1–Jan. 2	
°	′
0	+0·3
34	+0·2
60	+0·1
80	

Jan. 3–Feb. 23	
°	′
0	+0·2
41	+0·1
76	

Feb. 24–Dec. 31	
°	′
0	+0·1
60	

MARS

Jan. 1–Apr. 10	
°	′
0	+0·2
41	+0·1
76	

Apr. 11–Dec. 31	
°	′
0	+0·1
60	

DIP

Ht. of Eye (m)	Corr^n	Ht. of Eye (ft.)
m	′	ft.
2·4	−2·8	8·0
2·6	−2·9	8·6
2·8	−3·0	9·2
3·0	−3·1	9·8
3·2	−3·2	10·5
3·4	−3·3	11·2
3·6	−3·4	11·9
3·8	−3·5	12·6
4·0	−3·6	13·3
4·3	−3·7	14·1
4·5	−3·8	14·9
4·7	−3·9	15·7
5·0	−4·0	16·5
5·2	−4·1	17·4
5·5	−4·2	18·3
5·8	−4·3	19·1
6·1	−4·4	20·1
6·3	−4·5	21·0
6·6	−4·6	22·0
6·9	−4·7	22·9
7·2	−4·8	23·9
7·5	−4·9	24·9
7·9	−5·0	26·0
8·2	−5·1	27·1
8·5	−5·2	28·1
8·8	−5·3	29·2
9·2	−5·4	30·4
9·5	−5·5	31·5
9·9	−5·6	32·7
10·3	−5·7	33·9
10·6	−5·8	35·1
11·0	−5·9	36·3
11·4	−6·0	37·6
11·8	−6·1	38·9
12·2	−6·2	40·1
12·6	−6·3	41·5
13·0	−6·4	42·8
13·4	−6·5	44·2
13·8	−6·6	45·5
14·2	−6·7	46·9
14·7	−6·8	48·4
15·1	−6·9	49·8
15·5	−7·0	51·3
16·0	−7·1	52·8
16·5	−7·2	54·3
16·9	−7·3	55·8
17·4	−7·4	57·4
17·9	−7·5	58·9
18·4	−7·6	60·5
18·8	−7·7	62·1
19·3	−7·8	63·8
19·8	−7·9	65·4
20·4	−8·0	67·1
20·9	−8·1	68·8
21·4		70·5

Ht. of Eye	Corr^n
m	′
1·0	− 1·8
1·5	− 2·2
2·0	− 2·5
2·5	− 2·8
3·0	− 3·0
See table ←	
m	′
20	− 7·9
22	− 8·3
24	− 8·6
26	− 9·0
28	− 9·3
30	− 9·6
32	−10·0
34	−10·3
36	−10·6
38	−10·8
40	−11·1
42	−11·4
44	−11·7
46	−11·9
48	−12·2
ft.	′
2	− 1·4
4	− 1·9
6	− 2·4
8	− 2·7
10	− 3·1
See table ←	
ft.	′
70	− 8·1
75	− 8·4
80	− 8·7
85	− 8·9
90	− 9·2
95	− 9·5
100	− 9·7
105	− 9·9
110	−10·2
115	−10·4
120	−10·6
125	−10·8
130	−11·1
135	−11·3
140	−11·5
145	−11·7
150	−11·9
155	−12·1

App. Alt. = Apparent altitude = Sextant altitude corrected for index error and dip.

For daylight observations of Venus, see page 260.

148

1995 JULY 27, 28, 29 (THURS., FRI., SAT.)

UT (GMT)	ARIES	VENUS −3.9		MARS +1.3		JUPITER −2.3		SATURN +1.0		STARS		
d h	G.H.A. ° ′	G.H.A. ° ′	Dec. ° ′	G.H.A. ° ′	Dec. ° ′	G.H.A. ° ′	Dec. ° ′	G.H.A. ° ′	Dec. ° ′	Name	S.H.A. ° ′	Dec. ° ′
27 00	304 12.4	185 23.5	N21 31.7	121 00.7	S 1 00.4	60 23.8	S20 36.7	308 27.9	S 4 15.6	Acamar	315 28.7	S40 19.1
01	319 14.9	200 22.7	31.2	136 01.8	01.0	75 26.3	36.7	323 30.4	15.7	Achernar	335 36.7	S57 15.2
02	334 17.3	215 21.9	30.7	151 02.9	01.7	90 28.8	36.7	338 33.0	15.7	Acrux	173 24.6	S63 04.8
03	349 19.8	230 21.1	· · 30.2	166 04.0	· · 02.3	105 31.3	· · 36.7	353 35.5	· · 15.8	Adhara	255 23.4	S28 58.0
04	4 22.3	245 20.4	29.7	181 05.1	02.9	120 33.8	36.7	8 38.1	15.8	Aldebaran	291 05.0	N16 29.9
05	19 24.7	260 19.6	29.2	196 06.2	03.6	135 36.4	36.7	23 40.6	15.8			
06	34 27.2	275 18.8	N21 28.7	211 07.3	S 1 04.2	150 38.9	S20 36.7	38 43.1	S 4 15.9	Alioth	166 32.7	N55 59.3
07	49 29.7	290 18.0	28.2	226 08.4	04.8	165 41.4	36.7	53 45.7	15.9	Alkaid	153 09.6	N49 20.4
T 08	64 32.1	305 17.2	27.7	241 09.5	05.4	180 43.9	36.7	68 48.2	16.0	Al Na'ir	28 00.2	S46 58.7
H 09	79 34.6	320 16.4	· · 27.1	256 10.6	· · 06.1	195 46.4	· · 36.7	83 50.7	· · 16.0	Alnilam	276 00.3	S 1 12.3
U 10	94 37.1	335 15.6	26.6	271 11.7	06.7	210 48.9	36.7	98 53.3	16.1	Alphard	218 09.6	S 8 38.4
R 11	109 39.5	350 14.8	26.1	286 12.8	07.3	225 51.5	36.7	113 55.8	16.1			
S 12	124 42.0	5 14.0	N21 25.6	301 13.9	S 1 08.0	240 54.0	S20 36.7	128 58.4	S 4 16.1	Alphecca	126 22.3	N26 44.0
D 13	139 44.4	20 13.2	25.1	316 15.0	08.6	255 56.5	36.7	144 00.9	16.2	Alpheratz	357 57.2	N29 04.0
A 14	154 46.9	35 12.4	24.5	331 16.1	09.2	270 59.0	36.7	159 03.4	16.2	Altair	62 21.0	N 8 51.6
Y 15	169 49.4	50 11.6	· · 24.0	346 17.2	· · 09.8	286 01.5	· · 36.7	174 06.0	· · 16.3	Ankaa	353 28.8	S42 19.5
16	184 51.8	65 10.8	23.5	1 18.3	10.5	301 04.0	36.7	189 08.5	16.3	Antares	112 42.5	S26 25.3
17	199 54.3	80 10.0	23.0	16 19.4	11.1	316 06.6	36.7	204 11.1	16.4			
18	214 56.8	95 09.2	N21 22.5	31 20.6	S 1 11.7	331 09.1	S20 36.7	219 13.6	S 4 16.4	Arcturus	146 08.0	N19 12.5
19	229 59.2	110 08.4	21.9	46 21.7	12.4	346 11.6	36.7	234 16.1	16.4	Atria	107 56.1	S69 01.3
20	245 01.7	125 07.7	21.4	61 22.8	13.0	1 14.1	36.7	249 18.7	16.5	Avior	234 24.1	S59 29.8
21	260 04.2	140 06.9	· · 20.9	76 23.9	· · 13.6	16 16.6	· · 36.7	264 21.2	· · 16.5	Bellatrix	278 46.7	N 6 20.7
22	275 06.6	155 06.1	20.3	91 25.0	14.2	31 19.1	36.7	279 23.8	16.6	Betelgeuse	271 16.1	N 7 24.3
23	290 09.1	170 05.3	19.8	106 26.1	14.9	46 21.6	36.7	294 26.3	16.6			
28 00	305 11.6	185 04.5	N21 19.3	121 27.2	S 1 15.5	61 24.1	S20 36.7	309 28.8	S 4 16.7	Canopus	264 02.6	S52 41.6
01	320 14.0	200 03.7	18.8	136 28.3	16.1	76 26.7	36.7	324 31.4	16.7	Capella	280 54.7	N45 59.4
02	335 16.5	215 02.9	18.2	151 29.4	16.8	91 29.2	36.7	339 33.9	16.8	Deneb	49 40.1	N45 16.0
03	350 18.9	230 02.1	· · 17.7	166 30.5	· · 17.4	106 31.7	· · 36.7	354 36.5	· · 16.8	Denebola	182 47.6	N14 35.9
04	5 21.4	245 01.3	17.1	181 31.6	18.0	121 34.2	36.7	9 39.0	16.8	Diphda	349 09.2	S18 00.4
05	20 23.9	260 00.6	16.6	196 32.7	18.6	136 36.7	36.7	24 41.5	16.9			
06	35 26.3	274 59.8	N21 16.1	211 33.8	S 1 19.3	151 39.2	S20 36.7	39 44.1	S 4 16.9	Dubhe	194 08.7	N61 46.6
07	50 28.8	289 59.0	15.5	226 34.9	19.9	166 41.7	36.7	54 46.6	17.0	Elnath	278 29.9	N28 36.1
08	65 31.3	304 58.2	15.0	241 36.0	20.5	181 44.2	36.7	69 49.2	17.0	Eltanin	90 51.9	N51 29.7
F 09	80 33.7	319 57.4	· · 14.5	256 37.1	· · 21.2	196 46.7	· · 36.7	84 51.7	· · 17.1	Enif	34 00.0	N 9 51.5
R 10	95 36.2	334 56.6	13.9	271 38.2	21.8	211 49.2	36.7	99 54.3	17.1	Fomalhaut	15 38.5	S29 38.5
I 11	110 38.7	349 55.8	13.4	286 39.3	22.4	226 51.8	36.7	114 56.8	17.2			
D 12	125 41.1	4 55.1	N21 12.8	301 40.4	S 1 23.0	241 54.3	S20 36.7	129 59.3	S 4 17.2	Gacrux	172 16.1	S57 05.6
A 13	140 43.6	19 54.3	12.3	316 41.5	23.7	256 56.8	36.7	145 01.9	17.2	Gienah	176 06.3	S17 31.1
Y 14	155 46.1	34 53.5	11.7	331 42.6	24.3	271 59.3	36.7	160 04.4	17.3	Hadar	149 07.0	S60 21.3
15	170 48.5	49 52.7	· · 11.2	346 43.6	· · 24.9	287 01.8	· · 36.7	175 07.0	· · 17.3	Hamal	328 15.9	N23 26.4
16	185 51.0	64 51.9	10.6	1 44.7	25.6	302 04.3	36.7	190 09.5	17.4	Kaus Aust.	84 01.3	S34 23.1
17	200 53.4	79 51.1	10.1	16 45.8	26.2	317 06.8	36.7	205 12.1	17.4			
18	215 55.9	94 50.4	N21 09.5	31 46.9	S 1 26.8	332 09.3	S20 36.7	220 14.6	S 4 17.5	Kochab	137 19.4	N74 10.8
19	230 58.4	109 49.6	09.0	46 48.0	27.5	347 11.8	36.7	235 17.1	17.5	Markab	13 51.5	N15 11.0
20	246 00.8	124 48.8	08.4	61 49.1	28.1	2 14.3	36.7	250 19.7	17.6	Menkar	314 29.2	N 4 04.4
21	261 03.3	139 48.0	· · 07.9	76 50.2	· · 28.7	17 16.8	· · 36.7	265 22.2	· · 17.6	Menkent	148 23.4	S36 21.0
22	276 05.8	154 47.2	07.3	91 51.3	29.3	32 19.3	36.7	280 24.8	17.6	Miaplacidus	221 43.3	S69 42.1
23	291 08.2	169 46.4	06.8	106 52.4	30.0	47 21.8	36.7	295 27.3	17.7			
29 00	306 10.7	184 45.7	N21 06.2	121 53.5	S 1 30.6	62 24.3	S20 36.8	310 29.9	S 4 17.7	Mirfak	308 59.8	N49 50.5
01	321 13.2	199 44.9	05.7	136 54.6	31.2	77 26.8	36.8	325 32.4	17.8	Nunki	76 14.6	S26 18.0
02	336 15.6	214 44.1	05.1	151 55.7	31.9	92 29.3	36.8	340 34.9	17.8	Peacock	53 39.8	S56 44.8
03	351 18.1	229 43.3	· · 04.5	166 56.8	· · 32.5	107 31.8	· · 36.8	355 37.5	· · 17.9	Pollux	243 44.5	N28 02.1
04	6 20.5	244 42.5	04.0	181 57.9	33.1	122 34.3	36.8	10 40.0	17.9	Procyon	245 14.1	N 5 14.1
05	21 23.0	259 41.8	03.4	196 59.0	33.8	137 36.8	36.8	25 42.6	18.0			
06	36 25.5	274 41.0	N21 02.9	212 00.1	S 1 34.4	152 39.3	S20 36.8	40 45.1	S 4 18.0	Rasalhague	96 18.7	N12 34.0
07	51 27.9	289 40.2	02.3	227 01.2	35.0	167 41.8	36.8	55 47.7	18.1	Regulus	207 58.1	N11 59.3
S 08	66 30.4	304 39.4	01.7	242 02.3	35.6	182 44.4	36.8	70 50.2	18.1	Rigel	281 25.2	S 8 12.4
A 09	81 32.9	319 38.7	· · 01.2	257 03.4	· · 36.3	197 46.9	· · 36.8	85 52.8	· · 18.1	Rigil Kent.	140 10.0	S60 49.2
T 10	96 35.3	334 37.9	00.6	272 04.5	36.9	212 49.4	36.8	100 55.3	18.2	Sabik	102 27.7	S15 43.1
U 11	111 37.8	349 37.1	21 00.0	287 05.6	37.5	227 51.9	36.8	115 57.9	18.2			
R 12	126 40.3	4 36.3	N20 59.4	302 06.7	S 1 38.2	242 54.4	S20 36.8	131 00.4	S 4 18.3	Schedar	349 55.6	N56 30.6
D 13	141 42.7	19 35.6	58.9	317 07.8	38.8	257 56.9	36.8	146 02.9	18.3	Shaula	96 39.8	S37 06.0
A 14	156 45.2	34 34.8	58.3	332 08.9	39.4	272 59.4	36.8	161 05.5	18.4	Sirius	258 45.9	S16 42.6
Y 15	171 47.7	49 34.0	· · 57.7	347 10.0	· · 40.1	288 01.8	· · 36.8	176 08.0	· · 18.4	Spica	158 45.5	S11 08.3
16	186 50.1	64 33.2	57.2	2 11.0	40.7	303 04.3	36.8	191 10.6	18.5	Suhail	223 02.7	S43 25.0
17	201 52.6	79 32.5	56.6	17 12.1	41.3	318 06.8	36.8	206 13.1	18.5			
18	216 55.0	94 31.7	N20 56.0	32 13.2	S 1 42.0	333 09.3	S20 36.8	221 15.7	S 4 18.6	Vega	80 47.7	N38 47.1
19	231 57.5	109 30.9	55.4	47 14.3	42.6	348 11.8	36.8	236 18.2	18.6	Zuben'ubi	137 20.3	S16 01.4
20	247 00.0	124 30.1	54.9	62 15.4	43.2	3 14.3	36.8	251 20.8	18.6		S.H.A.	Mer. Pass.
21	262 02.4	139 29.4	· · 54.3	77 16.5	· · 43.8	18 16.8	· · 36.8	266 23.3	· · 18.7		° ′	h m
22	277 04.9	154 28.6	53.7	92 17.6	44.5	33 19.3	36.8	281 25.9	18.7	Venus	239 52.9	11 40
23	292 07.4	169 27.8	53.1	107 18.7	45.1	48 21.8	36.8	296 28.4	18.8	Mars	176 15.6	15 53
										Jupiter	116 12.6	19 51
Mer. Pass.	h m 3 38.6	v −0.8	d 0.5	v 1.1	d 0.6	v 2.5	d 0.0	v 2.5	d 0.0	Saturn	4 17.3	3 22

Figure 16-19. *The GHA and declination of Mars for this sight are found in the daily pages for July 27, 1995. Also note the* v *and* d *corrections found at the bottom of the Mars column. The actual corrections corresponding to these values are given in the increments and corrections pages just as for any other sight.*

Figure 16-20. *The increments and corrections page for the Mars sight shows the* v *and* d *corrections. It is entered with the minutes and seconds of GMT.*

44^m INCREMENTS AND CORRECTIONS 45^m

44^m	SUN PLANETS	ARIES	MOON	v or d	Corr^n	v or d	Corr^n	v or d	Corr^n
s	° ′	° ′	° ′	′	′	′	′	′	′
00	11 00·0	11 01·8	10 29·9	0·0	0·0	6·0	4·5	12·0	8·9
01	11 00·3	11 02·1	10 30·2	0·1	0·1	6·1	4·5	12·1	9·0
02	11 00·5	11 02·3	10 30·4	0·2	0·1	6·2	4·6	12·2	9·0
03	11 00·8	11 02·6	10 30·6	0·3	0·2	6·3	4·7	12·3	9·1
04	11 01·0	11 02·8	10 30·9	0·4	0·3	6·4	4·7	12·4	9·2
05	11 01·3	11 03·1	10 31·1	0·5	0·4	6·5	4·8	12·5	9·3
06	11 01·5	11 03·3	10 31·4	0·6	0·4	6·6	4·9	12·6	9·3
07	11 01·8	11 03·6	10 31·6	0·7	0·5	6·7	5·0	12·7	9·4
08	11 02·0	11 03·8	10 31·8	0·8	0·6	6·8	5·0	12·8	9·5
09	11 02·3	11 04·1	10 32·1	0·9	•0·7	6·9	5·1	12·9	9·6
10	11 02·5	11 04·3	10 32·3	1·0	0·7	7·0	5·2	13·0	9·6
11	11 02·8	11 04·6	10 32·6	1·1	0·8	7·1	5·3	13·1	9·7
12	11 03·0	11 04·8	10 32·8	1·2	0·9	7·2	5·3	13·2	9·8
13	11 03·3	11 05·1	10 33·0	1·3	1·0	7·3	5·4	13·3	9·9
14	11 03·5	11 05·3	10 33·3	1·4	1·0	7·4	5·5	13·4	9·9
15	11 03·8	11 05·6	10 33·5	1·5	1·1	7·5	5·6	13·5	10·0
16	11 04·0	11 05·8	10 33·8	1·6	1·2	7·6	5·6	13·6	10·1
17	11 04·3	11 06·1	10 34·0	1·7	1·3	7·7	5·7	13·7	10·2
18	11 04·5	11 06·3	10 34·2	1·8	1·3	7·8	5·8	13·8	10·2
19	11 04·8	11 06·6	10 34·5	1·9	1·4	7·9	5·9	13·9	10·3
20	11 05·0	11 06·8	10 34·7	2·0	1·5	8·0	5·9	14·0	10·4
21	11 05·3	11 07·1	10 34·9	2·1	1·6	8·1	6·0	14·1	10·5
22	11 05·5	11 07·3	10 35·2	2·2	1·6	8·2	6·1	14·2	10·5
23	11 05·8	11 07·6	10 35·4	2·3	1·7	8·3	6·2	14·3	10·6
24	11 06·0	11 07·8	10 35·7	2·4	1·8	8·4	6·2	14·4	10·7
25	11 06·3	11 08·1	10 35·9	2·5	1·9	8·5	6·3	14·5	10·8
26	11 06·5	11 08·3	10 36·1	2·6	1·9	8·6	6·4	14·6	10·8
27	11 06·8	11 08·6	10 36·4	2·7	2·0	8·7	6·5	14·7	10·9
28	11 07·0	11 08·8	10 36·6	2·8	2·1	8·8	6·5	14·8	11·0
29	11 07·3	11 09·1	10 36·9	2·9	2·2	8·9	6·6	14·9	11·1
30	11 07·5	11 09·3	10 37·1	3·0	2·2	9·0	6·7	15·0	11·1
31	11 07·8	11 09·6	10 37·3	3·1	2·3	9·1	6·7	15·1	11·2
32	11 08·0	11 09·8	10 37·6	3·2	2·4	9·2	6·8	15·2	11·3
33	11 08·3	11 10·1	10 37·8	3·3	2·4	9·3	6·9	15·3	11·3
34	11 08·5	11 10·3	10 38·0	3·4	2·5	9·4	7·0	15·4	11·4
35	11 08·8	11 10·6	10 38·3	3·5	2·6	9·5	7·0	15·5	11·5
36	11 09·0	11 10·8	10 38·5	3·6	2·7	9·6	7·1	15·6	11·6
37	11 09·3	11 11·1	10 38·8	3·7	2·7	9·7	7·2	15·7	11·6
38	11 09·5	11 11·3	10 39·0	3·8	2·8	9·8	7·3	15·8	11·7
39	11 09·8	11 11·6	10 39·2	3·9	2·9	9·9	7·3	15·9	11·8
40	11 10·0	11 11·8	10 39·5	4·0	3·0	10·0	7·4	16·0	11·9
41	11 10·3	11 12·1	10 39·7	4·1	3·0	10·1	7·5	16·1	11·9
42	11 10·5	11 12·3	10 40·0	4·2	3·1	10·2	7·6	16·2	12·0
43	11 10·8	11 12·6	10 40·2	4·3	3·2	10·3	7·6	16·3	12·1
44	11 11·0	11 12·8	10 40·4	4·4	3·3	10·4	7·7	16·4	12·2
45	11 11·3	11 13·1	10 40·7	4·5	3·3	10·5	7·8	16·5	12·2
46	11 11·5	11 13·3	10 40·9	4·6	3·4	10·6	7·9	16·6	12·3
47	11 11·8	11 13·6	10 41·1	4·7	3·5	10·7	7·9	16·7	12·4
48	11 12·0	11 13·8	10 41·4	4·8	3·6	10·8	8·0	16·8	12·5
49	11 12·3	11 14·1	10 41·6	4·9	3·6	10·9	8·1	16·9	12·5
50	11 12·5	11 14·3	10 41·9	5·0	3·7	11·0	8·2	17·0	12·6
51	11 12·8	11 14·6	10 42·1	5·1	3·8	11·1	8·2	17·1	12·7
52	11 13·0	11 14·8	10 42·3	5·2	3·9	11·2	8·3	17·2	12·8
53	11 13·3	11 15·1	10 42·6	5·3	3·9	11·3	8·4	17·3	12·8
54	11 13·5	11 15·3	10 42·8	5·4	4·0	11·4	8·5	17·4	12·9
55	11 13·8	11 15·6	10 43·1	5·5	4·1	11·5	8·5	17·5	13·0
56	11 14·0	11 15·8	10 43·3	5·6	4·2	11·6	8·6	17·6	13·1
57	11 14·3	11 16·1	10 43·5	5·7	4·2	11·7	8·7	17·7	13·1
58	11 14·5	11 16·3	10 43·8	5·8	4·3	11·8	8·8	17·8	13·2
59	11 14·8	11 16·6	10 44·0	5·9	4·4	11·9	8·8	17·9	13·3
60	11 15·0	11 16·8	10 44·3	6·0	4·5	12·0	8·9	18·0	13·4

45^m	SUN PLANETS	ARIES	MOON	v or d	Corr^n	v or d	Corr^n	v or d	Corr^n
s	° ′	° ′	° ′	′	′	′	′	′	′
00	11 15·0	11 16·8	10 44·3	0·0	0·0	6·0	4·6	12·0	9·1
01	11 15·3	11 17·1	10 44·5	0·1	0·1	6·1	4·6	12·1	9·2
02	11 15·5	11 17·3	10 44·7	0·2	0·2	6·2	4·7	12·2	9·3
03	11 15·8	11 17·6	10 45·0	0·3	0·2	6·3	4·8	12·3	9·3
04	11 16·0	11 17·9	10 45·2	0·4	0·3	6·4	4·9	12·4	9·4
05	11 16·3	11 18·1	10 45·4	0·5	0·4	6·5	4·9	12·5	9·5
06	11 16·5	11 18·4	10 45·7	0·6	0·5	6·6	5·0	12·6	9·6
07	11 16·8	11 18·6	10 45·9	0·7	0·5	6·7	5·1	12·7	9·6
08	11 17·0	11 18·9	10 46·2	0·8	0·6	6·8	5·2	12·8	9·7
09	11 17·3	11 19·1	10 46·4	0·9	0·7	6·9	5·2	12·9	9·8
10	11 17·5	11 19·4	10 46·6	1·0	0·8	7·0	5·3	13·0	9·9
11	11 17·8	11 19·6	10 46·9	1·1	0·8	7·1	5·4	13·1	9·9
12	11 18·0	11 19·9	10 47·1	1·2	0·9	7·2	5·5	13·2	10·0
13	11 18·3	11 20·1	10 47·4	1·3	1·0	7·3	5·5	13·3	10·1
14	11 18·5	11 20·4	10 47·6	1·4	1·1	7·4	5·6	13·4	10·2
15	11 18·8	11 20·6	10 47·8	1·5	1·1	7·5	5·7	13·5	10·2
16	11 19·0	11 20·9	10 48·1	1·6	1·2	7·6	5·8	13·6	10·3
17	11 19·3	11 21·1	10 48·3	1·7	1·3	7·7	5·8	13·7	10·4
18	11 19·5	11 21·4	10 48·5	1·8	1·4	7·8	5·9	13·8	10·5
19	11 19·8	11 21·6	10 48·8	1·9	1·4	7·9	6·0	13·9	10·5
20	11 20·0	11 21·9	10 49·0	2·0	1·5	8·0	6·1	14·0	10·6
21	11 20·3	11 22·1	10 49·3	2·1	1·6	8·1	6·1	14·1	10·7
22	11 20·5	11 22·4	10 49·5	2·2	1·7	8·2	6·2	14·2	10·8
23	11 20·8	11 22·6	10 49·7	2·3	1·7	8·3	6·3	14·3	10·8
24	11 21·0	11 22·9	10 50·0	2·4	1·8	8·4	6·4	14·4	10·9
25	11 21·3	11 23·1	10 50·2	2·5	1·9	8·5	6·4	14·5	11·0
26	11 21·5	11 23·4	10 50·5	2·6	2·0	8·6	6·5	14·6	11·1
27	11 21·8	11 23·6	10 50·7	2·7	2·0	8·7	6·6	14·7	11·1
28	11 22·0	11 23·9	10 50·9	2·8	2·1	8·8	6·7	14·8	11·2
29	11 22·3	11 24·1	10 51·2	2·9	2·2	8·9	6·7	14·9	11·3
30	11 22·5	11 24·4	10 51·4	3·0	2·3	9·0	6·8	15·0	11·4
31	11 22·8	11 24·6	10 51·6	3·1	2·4	9·1	6·9	15·1	11·5
32	11 23·0	11 24·9	10 51·9	3·2	2·4	9·2	7·0	15·2	11·5
33	11 23·3	11 25·1	10 52·1	3·3	2·5	9·3	7·1	15·3	11·6
34	11 23·5	11 25·4	10 52·4	3·4	2·6	9·4	7·1	15·4	11·7
35	11 23·8	11 25·6	10 52·6	3·5	2·7	9·5	7·2	15·5	11·8
36	11 24·0	11 25·9	10 52·8	3·6	2·7	9·6	7·3	15·6	11·8
37	11 24·3	11 26·1	10 53·1	3·7	2·8	9·7	7·4	15·7	11·9
38	11 24·5	11 26·4	10 53·3	3·8	2·9	9·8	7·4	15·8	12·0
39	11 24·8	11 26·6	10 53·6	3·9	3·0	9·9	7·5	15·9	12·1
40	11 25·0	11 26·9	10 53·8	4·0	3·0	10·0	7·6	16·0	12·1
41	11 25·3	11 27·1	10 54·0	4·1	3·1	10·1	7·7	16·1	12·2
42	11 25·5	11 27·4	10 54·3	4·2	3·2	10·2	7·7	16·2	12·3
43	11 25·8	11 27·6	10 54·5	4·3	3·3	10·3	7·8	16·3	12·4
44	11 26·0	11 27·9	10 54·7	4·4	3·3	10·4	7·9	16·4	12·4
45	11 26·3	11 28·1	10 55·0	4·5	3·4	10·5	8·0	16·5	12·5
46	11 26·5	11 28·4	10 55·2	4·6	3·5	10·6	8·0	16·6	12·6
47	11 26·8	11 28·6	10 55·5	4·7	3·6	10·7	8·1	16·7	12·7
48	11 27·0	11 28·9	10 55·7	4·8	3·6	10·8	8·2	16·8	12·7
49	11 27·3	11 29·1	10 55·9	4·9	3·7	10·9	8·3	16·9	12·8
50	11 27·5	11 29·4	10 56·2	5·0	3·8	11·0	8·3	17·0	12·9
51	11 27·8	11 29·6	10 56·4	5·1	3·9	11·1	8·4	17·1	13·0
52	11 28·0	11 29·9	10 56·7	5·2	3·9	11·2	8·5	17·2	13·0
53	11 28·3	11 30·1	10 56·9	5·3	4·0	11·3	8·6	17·3	13·1
54	11 28·5	11 30·4	10 57·1	5·4	4·1	11·4	8·6	17·4	13·2
55	11 28·8	11 30·6	10 57·4	5·5	4·2	11·5	8·7	17·5	13·3
56	11 29·0	11 30·9	10 57·6	5·6	4·2	11·6	8·8	17·6	13·3
57	11 29·3	11 31·1	10 57·9	5·7	4·3	11·7	8·9	17·7	13·4
58	11 29·5	11 31·4	10 58·1	5·8	4·4	11·8	8·9	17·8	13·5
59	11 29·8	11 31·6	10 58·3	5·9	4·5	11·9	9·0	17·9	13·6
60	11 30·0	11 31·9	10 58·6	6·0	4·6	12·0	9·1	18·0	13·7

xxiv

CHAPTER SEVENTEEN

Practical Techniques in Celestial Navigation

WHEN CELESTIAL NAVIGATION IS the primary—or only—means of offshore navigation, the navigator falls into a daily *navigational routine* consisting of:

1. Morning twilight stars.
2. Midmorning sun line.
3. Meridian passage of the sun (at noon).
4. Afternoon sun line.
5. Evening twilight stars.

This routine can be radically altered by weather conditions. Small-craft and large-ship routines, although similar in concept, can be quite different in execution. A small-craft navigator, who must contend with a number of influences that the ship navigator never faces, can use a number of special techniques and methods to make celestial life easier.

Ship Versus Small-Craft Celestial Navigation

Professional navigators aboard large vessels have many other responsibilities than navigating and their duties are often far removed from the sea. These include completing customs forms and other paperwork, tending to personnel issues, maintaining the ship's mechanical gear, overseeing supplies, and countless other shipkeeping chores. Such navigators view the sea from a pilothouse as much as 100 feet above the waves, in the comfort of a heated or often air-conditioned bridge. Their lives, though bound by the sea, are not as close to it as the small-craft mariner.

Aboard a small craft at sea, the situation is much different. Not only are you physically much closer to the sea—as little as a few inches and at most a few feet—you are mentally closer to the sea, the weather, and all the details of sea life. Therefore, it's much easier to be intimately connected with the sea and sky in a boat than in a ship. This closeness has a bearing on the navigation routine.

The navigator of a ship, before going to bed for the night, will often calculate the time of morning twilight and sunrise and set an alarm to be awake for morning star sights. The small-craft navigator, on the other hand, will probably just tell the person with the morning watch to give a wakeup call when the first rays of dawn appear in the eastern sky. Or, the navigator may take the morning watch.

The ship navigator might precompute a few stars for a fix, knowing that the ship will maintain a constant course and speed, that it is a stable platform for sight-taking, and that only clouds or fog would prevent getting good altitudes of the chosen bodies. The small-craft navigator, by contrast, might decide not to precompute stars knowing that course and speed will likely change in shifting winds. On sailing craft, the sails themselves may impede the taking of sights unless the skipper can be convinced to change course for a few minutes. (Often, the skipper is also the navigator.)

When the ship navigator goes out to the bridge wing for a round of sights, sextant and comparing watch in hand, he or she knows that even in rough seas the deck will be a relatively stable working surface. Not so for the small-boat navigator, who is likely to be taking sights from less than 10 feet above seas, which themselves are sometimes 10 or more feet high. This makes it difficult to compute height of eye (dip) and get a clear, smooth horizon. It's also difficult to find a stable position, shield the sextant from spray, hold on to some part of the vessel, and time the sight so that the observed horizon is not the nearest wave top. A considerable amount of art and technique make up this process.

The old sailor's phrase about "one hand for the ship and one for yourself" doesn't leave enough hands for the sextant and a comparing watch aboard a small craft at sea. It's difficult enough just to hang on, let alone have a steady hand for the sight. Salt spray can quickly obscure lenses, mirrors, and shade glasses, so a shipmate may have to shield the sextant from spray in very rough weather.

In heavy seas, the best advice is to try to take the sight from near the top of a wave and add half the wave height to the height of eye. This will give the best horizon and lessen the chance of measuring the altitude of a body based on a nearby swell or wave top.

At morning twilight, be on deck at least 15 minutes before the first sight so your night vision is at its best and you have time to locate several navigational stars. Start the round of sights with the eastern and dimmest stars because they will be the first to disappear in the increasing light. Save the brightest stars for last. In the evening, do the opposite—shoot the brightest stars first, as soon as they appear. Then you'll still have a bright horizon. Save the dimmest stars for later when they become visible.

The large-ship navigator always takes sights from the bridge wing; the small-craft navigator often has to move from the cockpit, then to the weather rail, and then to the bow pulpit to get a round of sights. On sailboats you may have to note a separate height of eye for each sight. There can be as much as 10 feet or more difference in height from the lee rail to the weather shrouds, which can significantly affect the accuracy of the fix if you don't account for it.

While using the sextant, it's important to be in rhythm with the sea (usually not a problem after a day or two out), and equally important to have a good grip on a firm piece of the vessel—backstay, shroud, forestay, mast, whatever works. You should attach the sextant to your wrist or neck with a lanyard and, especially in rough weather, you should be attached to the boat with a lanyard from a sturdy safety harness.

It's also a good idea to have someone else hold the watch and record the times and altitudes for each sight. On most boats, whoever's steering is usually available for this task. Call out a "standby" and then "mark" at the exact time you take the sight. Then read the sextant altitude so your partner can record it next to the time. A small flashlight is handy for this task; some sextants have optional battery-operated lights to help when taking readings in the dark.

Special Techniques in Celestial

Two special techniques for obtaining a celestial LOP don't require time or sight reduction tables. Not surprisingly, these methods, *meridian altitude* and *Polaris sights,* have been known for two-thousand years or more. The LOPs are latitude lines because the bodies observed are directly north or south of the observer.

Meridian Altitudes

Any time a body crosses your meridian you can obtain a latitude without using sight reduction tables. You can also obtain an approximate longitude, but its accuracy will not likely be good unless you spend some time and effort on the process. One-mile accuracy in latitude and five- to seven-mile accuracy in longitude is within reach. Such a sight is called a *meridian altitude* for the obvious reason that you are measuring a body's altitude as it crosses your meridian.

The principle of the meridian altitude sight is simple. If you observe a body with a GP at the North or South Pole, your latitude would equal the altitude of that body. This is the case of a Polaris sight, discussed later in this chapter. When any body is directly north (like Polaris) or south of you, you can still use it to get latitude if you know its declination—how far it is from the equator and, therefore, from a Pole—even though its GP is not on a Pole.

You usually use the sun for meridian altitude sights, because it's so easily observed. The example given here is for a sun observation, but the process is the same for any celestial body. The sun always crosses your meridian at noon—more particularly, at *Local Apparent Noon (LAN).*

You find the declination of the sun from the *Nautical Almanac* for any time. It's easy to translate the sun's meridian altitude and its declination into your latitude. All you need do is follow some rules regarding when to add and subtract. It will also help you predict the time of meridian passage, thereby preventing you from wasting a lot of time waiting with the sextant. Here's an example:

At 1056 on May 16, 1995, a boat is in DR position 40°04.3'N, 157°18.5'W, on course 200°, making 10 knots. Height of eye is 10 feet and the index error is −2.1. The navigator wants to get a noon latitude line from the sun's lower limb and observes actual LAN at 12 23 30 zone time.

Finding the Time of LAN of the Sun

The first step is to predict exactly when LAN will occur. For this you refer to the *Nautical Almanac* daily page. (See Figure 17-1.) In the lower right corner you find that *meridian passage* of the sun (abbreviated "Mer. Pass.") is at 1156. This means that the sun will cross your meridian at 1156 (instead of 1200). However, unless you are directly on the central meridian of your time zone, meridian passage will be earlier or later than the listed time by the amount of difference in your longitude from the central meridian.

Using a chart or plotting sheet, you can determine that your DR longitude at 1156 will be 157°23.7'W. Then identify the central meridian of your zone. In this case it's 150°W. Next, refer to the conversion of arc-to-time tables in the almanac, found at the beginning of the increments and corrections (yellow) pages. (You can do arc-to-time and time-to-arc conversions with formulas discussed in Chapter 14, "Time," although most people find the tables much more convenient or use navigational calculators or computer programs.)

In this case, the difference in longitude between your zone's central meridian and your DR longitude is 7°23' (157°23' − 150°00'). From the arc-to-time conversion tables, the corresponding time for this amount of longitude is 29 minutes and 32 seconds. (The time for 7° of longitude is 28 minutes, and the time for 23' of longitude is 1 minute 32 seconds. 28m00s + 1m32s = 29m32s. See Figure 17-2.).

Because we are west of the central meridian, you add this time to the tabulated time of meridian passage from the almanac. Thus, meridian passage at your DR longitude will occur at 12:25:32 (11h 56m 00s + 29m 32s = 12h 25m 32s) zone time.

This *first estimate of LAN* would be the time of meridian passage in your DR longitude if your vessel were not moving. Normally, this estimate is good enough for practical use if you're on deck with the sextant a few minutes early to adjust shade glasses and get ready for the actual observation. It serves well enough at the speeds of most cruising craft.

However, navigators on high-speed vessels need to do a second estimate to account for the fact that the first one does not account for vessel movement between the time of the listed meridian passage and the time of observed meridian passage. In this example you are making 10 knots on a course of 200° and to be precise need to account for this movement. You do that by making a *second estimate of LAN,* based on your DR position using the time of the first estimate rather than the almanac's time of meridian passage that you used to get the

(continued)

Figure 17-1. *The time of meridian passage of the sun is listed on each daily page of the almanac in the lower right corner of the right-hand page.*

1995 MAY 16, 17, 18 (TUES., WED., THURS.) 101

Day	UT (GMT) h	SUN G.H.A. ° ′	SUN Dec. ° ′	MOON G.H.A. ° ′	v ′	MOON Dec. ° ′	d ′	H.P. ′
16	00	180 55.1	N18 56.3	343 37.0	3.3	S19 02.9	2.4	61.2
	01	195 55.0	56.9	357 59.3	3.4	19 05.3	2.2	61.2
	02	210 55.0	57.5	12 21.7	3.4	19 07.5	2.1	61.2
	03	225 55.0	.. 58.0	26 44.1	3.3	19 09.6	1.9	61.2
	04	240 55.0	58.6	41 06.4	3.4	19 11.5	1.8	61.2
	05	255 55.0	59.2	55 28.8	3.3	19 13.3	1.6	61.2
	06	270 55.0	N18 59.8	69 51.1	3.4	S19 14.9	1.5	61.2
	07	285 55.0	19 00.4	84 13.5	3.3	19 16.4	1.3	61.2
T	08	300 55.0	01.0	98 35.8	3.4	19 17.7	1.2	61.2
U	09	315 55.0	.. 01.5	112 58.2	3.4	19 18.9	1.1	61.2
E	10	330 55.0	02.1	127 20.6	3.3	19 20.0	0.9	61.1
S	11	345 55.0	02.7	141 42.9	3.4	19 20.9	0.7	61.1
D	12	0 54.9	N19 03.3	156 05.3	3.4	S19 21.6	0.7	61.1
A	13	15 54.9	03.9	170 27.7	3.4	19 22.3	0.4	61.1
Y	14	30 54.9	04.4	184 50.1	3.4	19 22.7	0.3	61.1
	15	45 54.9	.. 05.0	199 12.5	3.5	19 23.0	0.2	61.1
	16	60 54.9	05.6	213 35.0	3.4	19 23.2	0.0	61.1
	17	75 54.9	06.2	227 57.4	3.5	19 23.2	0.1	61.1
	18	90 54.9	N19 06.7	242 19.9	3.5	S19 23.1	0.2	61.0
	19	105 54.9	07.3	256 42.4	3.5	19 22.9	0.5	61.0
	20	120 54.9	07.9	271 04.9	3.5	19 22.4	0.5	61.0
	21	135 54.8	.. ~~08.5~~	285 27.4	3.6	19 21.9	0.7	61.0
	22	150 54.8	09.0	299 50.0	3.6	19 21.2	0.8	61.0
	23	165 54.8	~~09.6~~	314 12.6	3.7	19 20.4	1.0	61.0
17	00	180 54.8	N19 10.2	328 35.3	3.6	S19 19.4	1.2	61.0
	01	195 54.8	10.8	342 57.9	3.7	19 18.2	1.2	60.9
	02	210 54.8	11.3	357 20.6	3.8	19 17.0	1.5	60.9
	03	225 54.8	.. 11.9	11 43.4	3.7	19 15.5	1.5	60.9
	04	240 54.8	12.5	26 06.1	3.9	19 14.0	1.7	60.9
	05	255 54.7	13.0	40 29.0	3.8	19 12.3	1.8	60.9
	06	270 54.7	N19 13.6	54 51.8	3.9	S19 10.5	2.0	60.8
W	07	285 54.7	14.2	69 14.7	4.0	19 08.5	2.1	60.8
E	08	300 54.7	14.7	83 37.7	4.0	19 06.4	2.3	60.8
D	09	315 54.7	.. 15.3	98 00.7	4.0	19 04.1	2.4	60.8
N	10	330 54.7	15.9	112 23.7	4.1	19 01.7	2.5	60.8
E	11	345 54.6	16.5	126 46.8	4.2	18 59.2	2.7	60.7
S	12	0 54.6	N19 17.0	141 10.0	4.2	S18 56.5	2.8	60.7
D	13	15 54.6	17.6	155 33.2	4.2	18 53.7	2.9	60.7
A	14	30 54.6	18.1	169 56.4	4.3	18 50.8	3.1	60.7
Y	15	45 54.6	.. 18.7	184 19.7	4.4	18 47.7	3.2	60.6
	16	60 54.6	19.3	198 43.1	4.4	18 44.5	3.3	60.6
	17	75 54.5	19.8	213 06.5	4.5	18 41.2	3.5	60.6
	18	90 54.5	N19 20.4	227 30.0	4.6	S18 37.7	3.6	60.6
	19	105 54.5	21.0	241 53.6	4.6	18 34.1	3.7	60.5
	20	120 54.5	21.5	256 17.2	4.7	18 30.4	3.9	60.5
	21	135 54.5	.. 22.1	270 40.9	4.7	18 26.5	4.0	60.5
	22	150 54.5	22.6	285 04.6	4.8	18 22.5	4.1	60.5
	23	165 54.4	23.2	299 28.4	4.9	18 18.4	4.2	60.4
18	00	180 54.4	N19 23.8	313 52.3	4.9	S18 14.2	4.4	60.4
	01	195 54.4	24.3	328 16.2	5.0	18 09.8	4.4	60.4
	02	210 54.4	24.9	342 40.2	5.1	18 05.4	4.6	60.4
	03	225 54.4	.. 25.4	357 04.3	5.2	18 00.8	4.8	60.3
	04	240 54.3	26.0	11 28.5	5.2	17 56.0	4.8	60.3
	05	255 54.3	26.6	25 52.7	5.3	17 51.2	5.0	60.3
	06	270 54.3	N19 27.1	40 17.0	5.4	S17 46.2	5.1	60.3
	07	285 54.3	27.7	54 41.4	5.4	17 41.1	5.1	60.2
T	08	300 54.3	28.2	69 05.8	5.6	17 36.0	5.4	60.2
H	09	315 54.2	.. 28.8	83 30.4	5.6	17 30.6	5.4	60.2
U	10	330 54.2	29.3	97 55.0	5.7	17 25.2	5.5	60.1
R	11	345 54.2	29.9	112 19.7	5.7	17 19.7	5.7	60.1
S	12	0 54.2	N19 30.4	126 44.4	5.9	S17 14.0	5.7	60.1
D	13	15 54.2	31.0	141 09.3	5.9	17 08.3	5.9	60.0
A	14	30 54.1	31.5	155 34.2	6.0	17 02.4	6.0	60.0
Y	15	45 54.1	.. 32.1	169 59.2	6.1	16 56.4	6.1	60.0
	16	60 54.1	32.6	184 24.3	6.1	16 50.3	6.2	60.0
	17	75 54.1	33.2	198 49.4	6.3	16 44.1	6.3	59.9
	18	90 54.0	N19 33.7	213 14.7	6.3	S16 37.8	6.4	59.9
	19	105 54.0	34.3	227 40.0	6.4	16 31.4	6.5	59.9
	20	120 54.0	34.8	242 05.4	6.5	16 24.9	6.6	59.8
	21	135 54.0	.. 35.4	256 30.9	6.6	16 18.3	6.7	59.8
	22	150 53.9	35.9	270 56.5	6.7	16 11.6	6.8	59.8
	23	165 53.9	36.5	285 22.2	6.7	16 04.8	6.9	59.7
		S.D. 15.8	*d* 0.6	S.D.		16.7	16.5	16.4

Lat. °	Twilight Naut. h m	Twilight Civil h m	Sunrise h m	Moonrise 16 h m	Moonrise 17 h m	Moonrise 18 h m	Moonrise 19 h m
N 72	▭	▭	▭	■	■	■	02 10
N 70	▭	▭	▭	25 14	01 14	01 29	01 31
68	////	////	01 38	24 11	00 11	00 47	01 04
66	////	////	02 16	23 36	24 18	00 18	00 43
64	////	00 57	02 42	23 10	23 57	24 27	00 27
62	////	01 45	03 03	22 50	23 39	24 13	00 13
60	////	02 14	03 19	22 34	23 24	24 01	00 01
N 58	00 51	02 36	03 33	22 20	23 12	23 51	24 21
56	01 35	02 54	03 45	22 08	23 01	23 42	24 14
54	02 02	03 09	03 55	21 58	22 52	23 34	24 08
52	02 23	03 21	04 04	21 48	22 43	23 27	24 02
50	02 39	03 32	04 12	21 40	22 35	23 21	23 58
45	03 11	03 55	04 29	21 22	22 19	23 07	23 47
N 40	03 35	04 13	04 43	21 08	22 06	22 55	23 38
35	03 53	04 27	04 55	20 56	21 54	22 45	23 30
30	04 08	04 40	05 06	20 45	21 44	22 37	23 24
20	04 32	05 00	05 23	20 27	21 27	22 22	23 12
N 10	04 50	05 16	05 39	20 11	21 12	22 09	23 02
0	05 05	05 31	05 53	19 56	20 58	21 57	22 52
S 10	05 19	05 45	06 07	19 41	20 44	21 45	22 42
20	05 32	05 58	06 22	19 26	20 29	21 31	22 32
30	05 44	06 13	06 39	19 07	20 12	21 17	22 20
35	05 51	06 21	06 48	18 57	20 02	21 08	22 13
40	05 58	06 30	07 00	18 45	19 50	20 58	22 06
45	06 05	06 41	07 13	18 31	19 37	20 46	21 57
S 50	06 13	06 53	07 29	18 13	19 20	20 32	21 46
52	06 17	06 58	07 36	18 05	19 12	20 25	21 40
54	06 21	07 04	07 44	17 56	19 04	20 18	21 35
56	06 25	07 11	07 54	17 46	18 54	20 10	21 29
58	06 29	07 18	08 04	17 34	18 43	20 01	21 21
S 60	06 34	07 26	08 16	17 21	18 30	19 50	21 13

Lat. °	Sunset h m	Twilight Civil h m	Twilight Naut. h m	Moonset 16 h m	Moonset 17 h m	Moonset 18 h m	Moonset 19 h m
N 72	▭	▭	▭	■	■	■	06 25
N 70	▭	▭	▭	02 14	03 11	05 03	07 02
68	22 19	////	////	03 12	04 14	05 45	07 28
66	21 40	////	////	03 46	04 49	06 13	07 48
64	21 13	23 04	////	04 11	05 14	06 34	08 04
62	20 52	22 12	////	04 31	05 34	06 52	08 17
60	20 35	21 41	////	04 47	05 50	07 06	08 28
N 58	20 21	21 18	23 09	05 01	06 04	07 18	08 38
56	20 09	21 00	22 22	05 13	06 16	07 28	08 46
54	19 59	20 45	21 53	05 23	06 26	07 38	08 54
52	19 50	20 33	21 32	05 32	06 35	07 46	09 01
50	19 41	20 21	21 15	05 40	06 43	07 53	09 07
45	19 24	19 58	20 43	05 58	07 01	08 09	09 20
N 40	19 10	19 41	20 19	06 12	07 15	08 22	09 30
35	18 58	19 26	20 00	06 24	07 27	08 33	09 39
30	18 47	19 14	19 45	06 35	07 38	08 42	09 47
20	18 30	18 53	19 21	06 53	07 56	08 59	10 01
N 10	18 14	18 37	19 03	07 09	08 11	09 13	10 13
0	18 00	18 22	18 47	07 23	08 26	09 26	10 24
S 10	17 46	18 08	18 34	07 38	08 40	09 40	10 35
20	17 31	17 54	18 21	07 54	08 56	09 54	10 46
30	17 14	17 39	18 08	08 12	09 14	10 10	10 59
35	17 04	17 31	18 02	08 22	09 24	10 19	11 07
40	16 53	17 22	17 55	08 34	09 36	10 29	11 16
45	16 40	17 12	17 47	08 49	09 50	10 42	11 26
S 50	16 24	16 59	17 39	09 06	10 06	10 57	11 38
52	16 16	16 54	17 35	09 14	10 14	11 04	11 43
54	16 08	16 48	17 32	09 23	10 23	11 11	11 50
56	15 58	16 41	17 27	09 33	10 33	11 20	11 56
58	15 48	16 34	17 23	09 45	10 44	11 30	12 04
S 60	15 36	16 26	17 18	09 58	10 57	11 41	12 13

Day	SUN Eqn. of Time 00^h m s	SUN Eqn. of Time 12^h m s	SUN Mer. Pass. h m	MOON Mer. Pass. Upper h m	MOON Mer. Pass. Lower h m	Age d	Phase
16	03 40	03 40	11 56	01 08	13 40	17	◑
17	03 39	03 39	~~11 56~~	02 11	14 42	18	
18	03 38	03 37	11 56	03 12	15 42	19	

CONVERSION OF ARC TO TIME

0°–59°		60°–119°		120°–179°		180°–239°		240°–299°		300°–359°			0′·00	0′·25	0′·50	0′·75
°	h m	°	h m	°	h m	°	h m	°	h m	°	h m	′	m s	m s	m s	m s
0	0 00	60	4 00	120	8 00	180	12 00	240	16 00	300	20 00	0	0 00	0 01	0 02	0 03
1	0 04	61	4 04	121	8 04	181	12 04	241	16 04	301	20 04	1	0 04	0 05	0 06	0 07
2	0 08	62	4 08	122	8 08	182	12 08	242	16 08	302	20 08	2	0 08	0 09	0 10	0 11
3	0 12	63	4 12	123	8 12	183	12 12	243	16 12	303	20 12	3	0 12	0 13	0 14	0 15
4	0 16	64	4 16	124	8 16	184	12 16	244	16 16	304	20 16	4	0 16	0 17	0 18	0 19
5	0 20	65	4 20	125	8 20	185	12 20	245	16 20	305	20 20	5	0 20	0 21	0 22	0 23
6	0 24	66	4 24	126	8 24	186	12 24	246	16 24	306	20 24	6	0 24	0 25	0 26	0 27
7	0 28	67	4 28	127	8 28	187	12 28	247	16 28	307	20 28	7	0 28	0 29	0 30	0 31
8	0 32	68	4 32	128	8 32	188	12 32	248	16 32	308	20 32	8	0 32	0 33	0 34	0 35
9	0 36	69	4 36	129	8 36	189	12 36	249	16 36	309	20 36	9	0 36	0 37	0 38	0 39
10	0 40	70	4 40	130	8 40	190	12 40	250	16 40	310	20 40	10	0 40	0 41	0 42	0 43
11	0 44	71	4 44	131	8 44	191	12 44	251	16 44	311	20 44	11	0 44	0 45	0 46	0 47
12	0 48	72	4 48	132	8 48	192	12 48	252	16 48	312	20 48	12	0 48	0 49	0 50	0 51
13	0 52	73	4 52	133	8 52	193	12 52	253	16 52	313	20 52	13	0 52	0 53	0 54	0 55
14	0 56	74	4 56	134	8 56	194	12 56	254	16 56	314	20 56	14	0 56	0 57	0 58	0 59
15	1 00	75	5 00	135	9 00	195	13 00	255	17 00	315	21 00	15	1 00	1 01	1 02	1 03
16	1 04	76	5 04	136	9 04	196	13 04	256	17 04	316	21 04	16	1 04	1 05	1 06	1 07
17	1 08	77	5 08	137	9 08	197	13 08	257	17 08	317	21 08	17	1 08	1 09	1 10	1 11
18	1 12	78	5 12	138	9 12	198	13 12	258	17 12	318	21 12	18	1 12	1 13	1 14	1 15
19	1 16	79	5 16	139	9 16	199	13 16	259	17 16	319	21 16	19	1 16	1 17	1 18	1 19
20	1 20	80	5 20	140	9 20	200	13 20	260	17 20	320	21 20	20	1 20	1 21	1 22	1 23
21	1 24	81	5 24	141	9 24	201	13 24	261	17 24	321	21 24	21	1 24	1 25	1 26	1 27
22	1 28	82	5 28	142	9 28	202	13 28	262	17 28	322	21 28	22	1 28	1 29	1 30	1 31
23	1 32	83	5 32	143	9 32	203	13 32	263	17 32	323	21 32	23	1 32	1 33	1 34	1 35
24	1 36	84	5 36	144	9 36	204	13 36	264	17 36	324	21 36	24	1 36	1 37	1 38	1 39
25	1 40	85	5 40	145	9 40	205	13 40	265	17 40	325	21 40	25	1 40	1 41	1 42	1 43
26	1 44	86	5 44	146	9 44	206	13 44	266	17 44	326	21 44	26	1 44	1 45	1 46	1 47
27	1 48	87	5 48	147	9 48	207	13 48	267	17 48	327	21 48	27	1 48	1 49	1 50	1 51
28	1 52	88	5 52	148	9 52	208	13 52	268	17 52	328	21 52	28	1 52	1 53	1 54	1 55
29	1 56	89	5 56	149	9 56	209	13 56	269	17 56	329	21 56	29	1 56	1 57	1 58	1 59
30	2 00	90	6 00	150	10 00	210	14 00	270	18 00	330	22 00	30	2 00	2 01	2 02	2 03
31	2 04	91	6 04	151	10 04	211	14 04	271	18 04	331	22 04	31	2 04	2 05	2 06	2 07
32	2 08	92	6 08	152	10 08	212	14 08	272	18 08	332	22 08	32	2 08	2 09	2 10	2 11
33	2 12	93	6 12	153	10 12	213	14 12	273	18 12	333	22 12	33	2 12	2 13	2 14	2 15
34	2 16	94	6 16	154	10 16	214	14 16	274	18 16	334	22 16	34	2 16	2 17	2 18	2 19
35	2 20	95	6 20	155	10 20	215	14 20	275	18 20	335	22 20	35	2 20	2 21	2 22	2 23
36	2 24	96	6 24	156	10 24	216	14 24	276	18 24	336	22 24	36	2 24	2 25	2 26	2 27
37	2 28	97	6 28	157	10 28	217	14 28	277	18 28	337	22 28	37	2 28	2 29	2 30	2 31
38	2 32	98	6 32	158	10 32	218	14 32	278	18 32	338	22 32	38	2 32	2 33	2 34	2 35
39	2 36	99	6 36	159	10 36	219	14 36	279	18 36	339	22 36	39	2 36	2 37	2 38	2 39
40	2 40	100	6 40	160	10 40	220	14 40	280	18 40	340	22 40	40	2 40	2 41	2 42	2 43
41	2 44	101	6 44	161	10 44	221	14 44	281	18 44	341	22 44	41	2 44	2 45	2 46	2 47
42	2 48	102	6 48	162	10 48	222	14 48	282	18 48	342	22 48	42	2 48	2 49	2 50	2 51
43	2 52	103	6 52	163	10 52	223	14 52	283	18 52	343	22 52	43	2 52	2 53	2 54	2 55
44	2 56	104	6 56	164	10 56	224	14 56	284	18 56	344	22 56	44	2 56	2 57	2 58	2 59
45	3 00	105	7 00	165	11 00	225	15 00	285	19 00	345	23 00	45	3 00	3 01	3 02	3 03
46	3 04	106	7 04	166	11 04	226	15 04	286	19 04	346	23 04	46	3 04	3 05	3 06	3 07
47	3 08	107	7 08	167	11 08	227	15 08	287	19 08	347	23 08	47	3 08	3 09	3 10	3 11
48	3 12	108	7 12	168	11 12	228	15 12	288	19 12	348	23 12	48	3 12	3 13	3 14	3 15
49	3 16	109	7 16	169	11 16	229	15 16	289	19 16	349	23 16	49	3 16	3 17	3 18	3 19
50	3 20	110	7 20	170	11 20	230	15 20	290	19 20	350	23 20	50	3 20	3 21	3 22	3 23
51	3 24	111	7 24	171	11 24	231	15 24	291	19 24	351	23 24	51	3 24	3 25	3 26	3 27
52	3 28	112	7 28	172	11 28	232	15 28	292	19 28	352	23 28	52	3 28	3 29	3 30	3 31
53	3 32	113	7 32	173	11 32	233	15 32	293	19 32	353	23 32	53	3 32	3 33	3 34	3 35
54	3 36	114	7 36	174	11 36	234	15 36	294	19 36	354	23 36	54	3 36	3 37	3 38	3 39
55	3 40	115	7 40	175	11 40	235	15 40	295	19 40	355	23 40	55	3 40	3 41	3 42	3 43
56	3 44	116	7 44	176	11 44	236	15 44	296	19 44	356	23 44	56	3 44	3 45	3 46	3 47
57	3 48	117	7 48	177	11 48	237	15 48	297	19 48	357	23 48	57	3 48	3 49	3 50	3 51
58	3 52	118	7 52	178	11 52	238	15 52	298	19 52	358	23 52	58	3 52	3 53	3 54	3 55
59	3 56	119	7 56	179	11 56	239	15 56	299	19 56	359	23 56	59	3 56	3 57	3 58	3 59

The above table is for converting expressions in arc to their equivalent in time; its main use in this Almanac is for the conversion of longitude for application to L.M.T. (*added* if *west*, *subtracted* if *east*) to give G.M.T. or vice versa, particularly in the case of sunrise, sunset, etc.

Figure 17-2. *The arc-to-time conversion tables are found in the front of the increments and corrections pages of the* Nautical Almanac. *The conversion for 7° 23′ is shown here.*

first estimate. Here, your DR position for the time of 12h 25m 32s is 157°25.2'W. Again, find the difference in longitude between this position and the central meridian and apply it to the time of meridian passage.

In this case the difference in longitude is now 7°25.2' and the corresponding arc-to-time conversion from the table in the almanac gives a time of 12h 25m 41s (7° of arc is 28m of time; 25.2' of arc is 1m 41s of time; 29m 41s + 11h 56m = 12h 25m 41s). The difference in time between the first and second estimates (only nine seconds) indicates that a second estimate is not necessary at small-craft speeds.

Finding Latitude

When you know exactly when LAN will occur you can be sure not to miss it. In fact, you can set up everything beforehand so you can have the solution right after you take the sight.

In this example, the navigator actually observes LAN at 12h 23m 30s because it occurs at the precise instant when the sun reaches its highest altitude. This is not the same time computed for LAN, but the computed time was only an estimate.

So, be guided by your observation rather than your prediction. To find your latitude you need to know the declination of the sun at that time, which is found in the *Nautical Almanac* just as for other sights.

Because your zone description is +10, the GMT of LAN was 22h 23m 30s. On the daily page the tabulated declination for 2200 hours on 16 May is 19°09.0'N and the *d* correction (for *d* of 0.6, from the increments and corrections page for 23m) is +0.2'. Therefore, the declination is 19°09.2'N.

Next, find the zenith distance of the sun, which is 90° minus the observed altitude. If you are north of the GP of the sun, you label the zenith distance "N"; if south of the GP, label it "S."

If both GP and zenith distance are N, you add them to find latitude. If the zenith distance and the declination are opposite—one north and one south—you subtract the two and the latitude takes the direction (N or S) of the

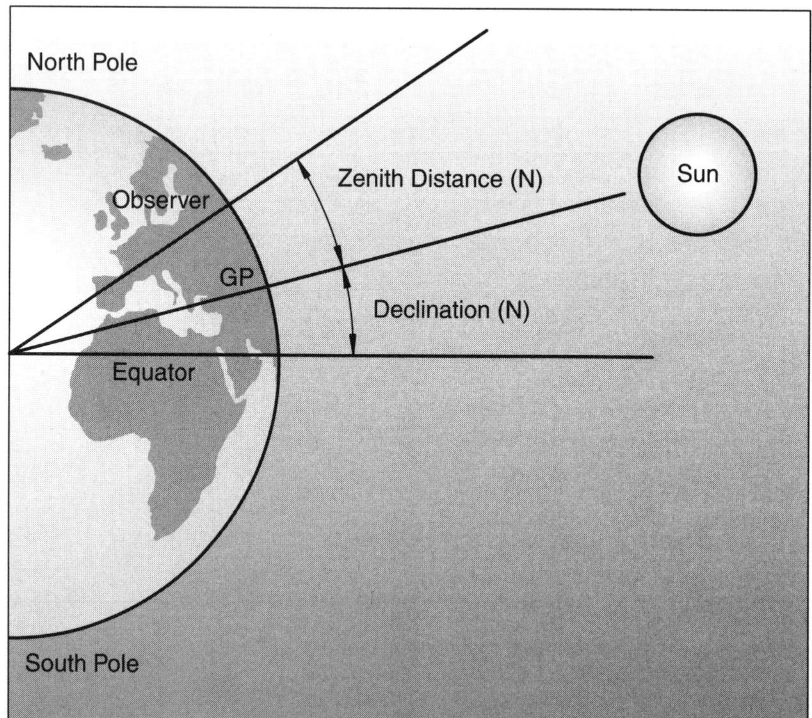

Figure 17-3. *When both the observer's zenith distance and the sun's declination are north, the latitude is the sum of them, and is north as well.*

larger. (See Figures 17-3, 17-4, and 17-5.)

In this case the *hs* is 69° 16.0', the index correction is +2.1', and the dip is −3.1', giving an *ha* of 69° 15.0'. The altitude correction for the lower limb at this altitude is +15.6; therefore, *ho* is 69° 30.6'.

To find zenith distance, subtract *ho* from 90° and get 20° 29.4'N (you are north of the sun's GP). This zenith distance, added to the declination (according to the rule above), gives a latitude of 39° 38.6'N.

Here is the whole solution in order.

Date	16 May 1995
DR lat. at ZT 1156	39° 55.0'N
DR long. at ZT 1156	157° 23.0'W
Central Meridian	150 W
Diff. in long. (arc)	7° 23.0'
Diff. in long. (time)	29m 32s
LMT Mer. Pass.	11h 56m
Estimated Mer. Pass.	12h 25m 32s
Actual ZT Mer. Pass.	12h 23m 30s
Zone Description	+10
GMT Mer. Pass.	22h 23m 30s
GMT date	16 May 1995
Tab. declination (d/+.6)	N 19° 09.0'
***d* correction**	+0.2'
Declination	N 19° 09.2'
Sextant altitude *(hs)*	69° 16.0'
Index correction	+2.1'
Dip	-3.1'
Apparent altitude *(ha)*	69° 15.0'
Altitude correction	15.6'
Observed altitude *(ho)*	69° 30.6'
(Subtract *ho* from) 90°	89° 60.0'
ho	69° 30.6'
Zenith Distance	N20° 29.4'
Declination	N 19° 09.2'
Latitude	N39° 38.6'

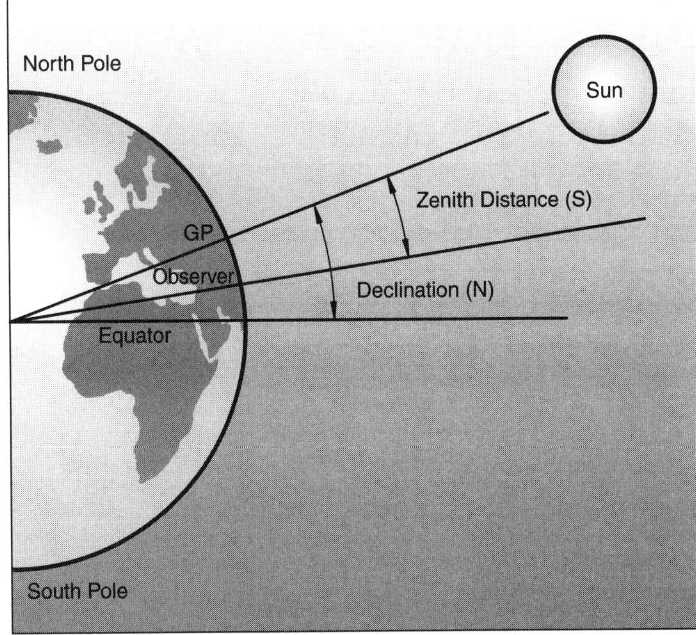

Figure 17-4. *When the zenith distance is south and the declination is north, latitude is the difference between the two and is in the direction of the larger.*

Figure 17-5. *When the zenith distance is north and the declination south, latitude is the difference between the two and is in the direction of the larger.*

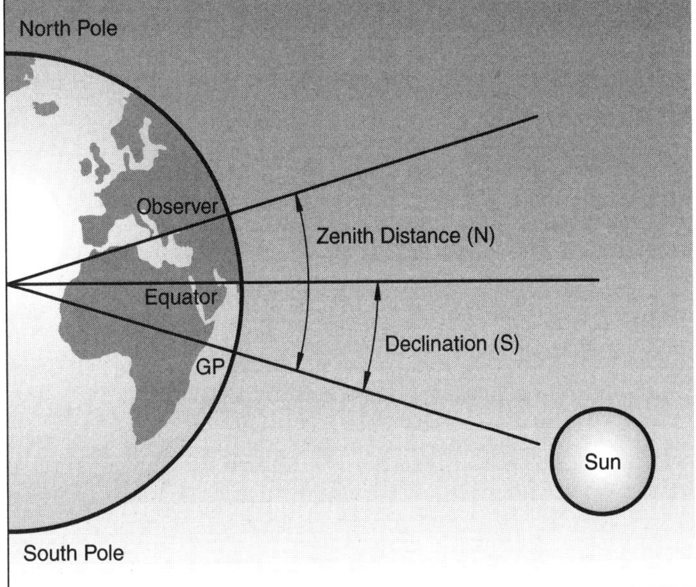

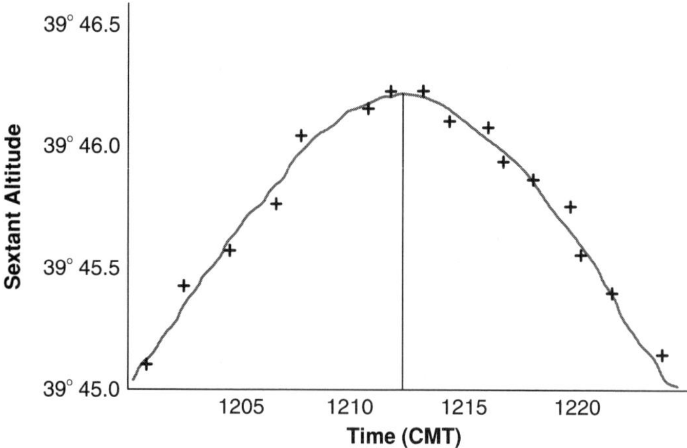

Figure 17-6. *To find longitude from a meridian altitude sight, take a number of sights before and after LAN and plot them on a graph. Then, fair in the curve and drop a perpendicular from the highest point. Where this line intersects the time axis is the time of LAN. Note that it is possible to find this time even though no sight was taken at that exact moment.*

Longitude by LAN

If you determine the time at which a body crosses your meridian and find the longitude (GHA) of the body at that time, then you know your longitude. The key is to know the time very accurately.

It's possible to find longitude within a few miles from a meridian altitude sight. Because the sun appears to move over the earth at 15° of longitude every hour—900 miles per hour at the equator—you must measure the time of meridian passage with extreme care. Fortunately, there is a way to do so even without knowing in advance the exact time of LAN.

First, compute an estimated LAN time as previously explained and be on deck with the sextant about 15 minutes beforehand. Begin taking and recording sights—about one every two minutes—as the sun approaches its highest point. As it slows its ascent in approaching LAN, increase the frequency of sights to one every minute or so. Finally, the sun will seem to hang in the sky for a few seconds before beginning to slowly decrease in altitude. Take a few more sights as the sun heads down, stopping observations about 15 minutes after LAN.

With 10 to 20 sun sights all clustered around LAN, it is a simple matter to set up a graph and fair in a curve of actual altitudes. The graph should look somewhat like the one depicted in Figure 17-6. Note that many of the sights do not plot exactly on the curve due to slight errors in the sight-taking process. These small errors are unavoidable and normal, but fairing in the curve averages them all out and provides a much truer representation of the real movement of the body.

Though this solution is time-consuming, and it takes some trouble to set up and graph, it has some advantages: It doesn't require sight reduction tables, it doesn't require time, and it averages a number of different sights to reduce errors.

Once the curve is faired in, it's a simple matter to drop a perpendicular from the highest point of the curve to the time axis and find the GHA of the body for that time just as for any other sight. In the western hemisphere the GHA is the longitude. In the eastern hemisphere, subtract from 360° and label it "E" to obtain longitude. To gauge how much it might be in error, add and subtract a few seconds from the time of LAN and look in the increments and corrections table, noting the change in longitude in relation to the change in time.

Once you've noted the possible error in longitude, you can convert the longitude error into nautical miles using the latitude scale on your chart or plotting sheet.

Another way to find longitude by LAN is to set the sextant to a value and observe the sun at this altitude when it is both approaching and receding from LAN. You should do this for at least three different values. Note the times of each pair of values, find the midtimes of each pair, then average them to determine the time of LAN.

This method is best suited for use on large ships where a stable platform is available. Due to the motion of small craft, you may have difficulty taking a sight this way except in calm weather. However, this process is a little less time consuming than the graph method.

Latitude by Polaris

Sailors have long known that the North Star, Ursa Minor, is within about a degree of the true North Pole and rotates around it in a small circle. It is convenient that most navigation has been—and still is—practiced in the northern hemisphere where Polaris can be seen, for there is no comparable star in the southern sky.

The latitude of any place is equal to the altitude of a body located over the geographic pole. Therefore, Polaris's altitude above the horizon equals the approximate latitude of the observer, and the errors caused by its slight rotation and other factors can easily be corrected. (See Figure 17-7.)

Because Polaris orbits the North Pole in a small circle, its altitude is only equal to your latitude when it's at the two points in its circular orbit. At all other times you need to apply a correction to the observed altitude. These corrections are related to the rotation of the earth on its axis and, like other stars are referenced to the GHA of Aries.

Here is an example of a Polaris sight with all corrections applied:

At 23 18 56 GMT on April 21, 1994, you sight Polaris at an observed altitude *(ho)* of 49°31.6'. The DR latitude is 50°23.8'N, and DR longitude is 37°14.0'W. What is your latitude? (Note that in this example *ho* is given; *hs* and *ha* have already been determined and corrected.)

The following equation sums up all the factors in a Polaris sight:

Latitude = *ho* – 1° + a0 + a1 + a2.

That is, the observer's latitude equals the observed altitude minus 1° plus the three corrections for Polaris. You subtract one degree (–1°) because all the tabulated Polaris corrections are listed as positive (for convenience) to prevent mixing up the signs when computing the latitude. After you add the listed values, subtract the 1°.

The Polaris tables are in the middle of the *Nautical Almanac* after the daily pages and a short explanation of the book. Enter the tables with the following:

- The LHA of Aries for the time of the sight
- The DR latitude
- The month of the year

You find the GHA of Aries in the daily pages as for any other star sight; you already know the DR latitude and month. Enter the first section (known as the "a0" section) of the tables with the LHA of Aries (in this case, 162°03.5'), moving down the column headed "160°–169°" to the row for "2°" representing 162°. You find a correction of 1°25.4'. Interpolation is necessary in this section. In this example, the difference in the correction between 162° and 163° is the difference between 25.4' and 26.1', or 0.7'. You don't need an additional correction for 162°03.5'.

Next, continue down the same column into the next (a1) section until you come to the row for your latitude of 50°, finding a correction of 0.6'.

Continue down the same column into the next (a2) section for the month where the correction for April is 0.9'. Note that the amount of change in these last two sections is not very large and no interpolation is necessary. Simply choose the nearest value. Figure 17-8 shows these corrections taken from the tables.

The next step is to add all the corrections—a0, a1, and a2—and subtract the 1°

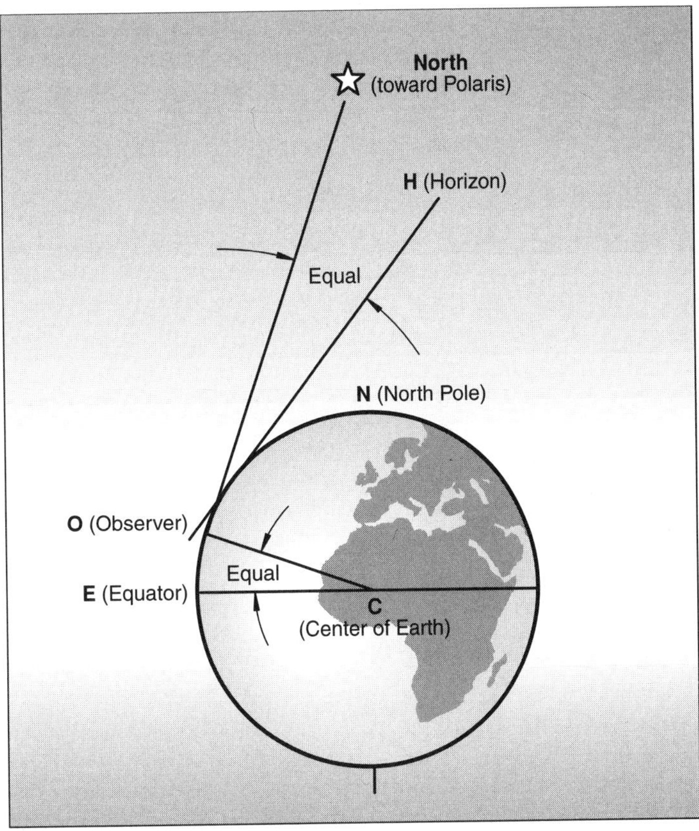

Figure 17-7. *This illustrates the principle of the Polaris sight, in which the observed altitude of Polaris above the observer's horizon equals the observer's latitude. There are some small corrections that account for the fact that Polaris actually rotates in a small circle about the Pole.*

Figure 17-8. *The* Nautical Almanac*'s Polaris tables have four sections and are entered with the LHA of Aries, the latitude, and the month. Three different corrections are added together and 1° 00.0' is subtracted from the result. This value, added to the observed altitude, is the latitude. The azimuth of Polaris is not normally determined by small craft.*

POLARIS (POLE STAR) TABLES, 1994

FOR DETERMINING LATITUDE FROM SEXTANT ALTITUDE AND FOR AZIMUTH

LHA ARIES	120°–129°	130°–139°	140°–149°	150°–159°	160°–169°	170°–179°	180°–189°	190°–199°	200°–209°	210°–219°	220°–229°	230°–239°
	a_0	a_0	a_0	a_0	a_0	a_0	a_0	a_0	a_0	a_0	a_0	a_0
°	° '	° '	° '	° '	° '	° '	° '	° '	° '	° '	° '	° '
0	0 53·9	1 01·8	1 09·7	1 17·2	1 24·1	1 30·3	1 35·5	1 39·6	1 42·5	1 44·1	1 44·3	1 43·2
1	54·7	02·6	10·4	17·9	24·8	30·9	36·0	40·0	42·7	44·2	44·3	43·0
2	55·5	03·4	11·2	18·6	25·4	31·4	36·4	40·3	42·9	44·3	44·2	42·8
3	56·3	04·2	12·0	19·3	26·1	32·0	36·9	40·6	43·1	44·3	44·1	42·6
4	57·1	05·0	12·7	20·0	26·7	32·5	37·3	40·9	43·3	44·4	44·0	42·4
5	0 57·8	1 05·8	1 13·5	1 20·7	1 27·3	1 33·0	1 37·7	1 41·2	1 43·5	1 44·4	1 43·9	1 42·1
6	58·6	06·6	14·2	21·4	27·9	33·5	38·1	41·5	43·6	44·4	43·8	41·9
7	0 59·4	07·3	15·0	22·1	28·5	34·1	38·5	41·8	43·8	44·4	43·7	41·6
8	1 00·2	08·1	15·7	22·8	29·1	34·6	38·9	42·0	43·9	44·4	43·5	41·3
9	01·0	08·9	16·4	23·5	29·7	35·0	39·3	42·3	44·0	44·4	43·4	41·0
10	1 01·8	1 09·7	1 17·2	1 24·1	1 30·3	1 35·5	1 39·6	1 42·5	1 44·1	1 44·3	1 43·2	1 40·7
Lat.	a_1	a_1	a_1	a_1	a_1	a_1	a_1	a_1	a_1	a_1	a_1	a_1
°	'	'	'	'	'	'	'	'	'	'	'	'
0	0·2	0·2	0·3	0·3	0·4	0·4	0·5	0·6	0·6	0·6	0·6	0·6
10	·3	·3	·3	·4	·4	·5	·5	·6	·6	·6	·6	·6
20	·3	·4	·4	·4	·4	·5	·5	·6	·6	·6	·6	·6
30	·4	·4	·4	·5	·5	·5	·5	·6	·6	·6	·6	·6
40	0·5	0·5	0·5	0·5	0·5	0·6	0·6	0·6	0·6	0·6	0·6	0·6
45	·5	·5	·5	·6	·6	·6	·6	·6	·6	·6	·6	·6
50	·6	·6	·6	·6	·6	·6	·6	·6	·6	·6	·6	·6
55	·7	·7	·7	·7	·6	·6	·6	·6	·6	·6	·6	·6
60	·8	·8	·7	·7	·7	·7	·6	·6	·6	·6	·6	·6
62	0·8	0·8	0·8	0·8	0·7	0·7	0·7	0·6	0·6	0·6	0·6	0·6
64	·9	·9	·8	·8	·8	·7	·7	·6	·6	·6	·6	·6
66	0·9	0·9	·9	·8	·8	·7	·7	·6	·6	·6	·6	·6
68	1·0	1·0	0·9	0·9	0·8	0·8	0·7	0·7	0·6	0·6	0·6	0·6
Month	a_2	a_2	a_2	a_2	a_2	a_2	a_2	a_2	a_2	a_2	a_2	a_2
	'	'	'	'	'	'	'	'	'	'	'	'
Jan.	0·6	0·6	0·6	0·5	0·5	0·5	0·4	0·4	0·4	0·4	0·4	0·4
Feb.	·8	·8	·7	·7	·6	·6	·5	·5	·4	·4	·4	·3
Mar.	0·9	0·9	0·9	·8	·8	·7	·6	·6	·5	·5	·4	·4
Apr.	1·0	1·0	1·0	0·9	0·9	0·8	0·8	0·7	0·7	0·6	0·5	0·5
May	0·9	1·0	1·0	1·0	1·0	0·9	·9	·9	·8	·8	·7	·6
June	·8	0·9	0·9	0·9	0·9	1·0	·9	·9	·9	·9	·8	·8
July	0·7	0·7	0·8	0·8	0·8	0·9	0·9	0·9	0·9	0·9	0·9	0·9
Aug.	·5	·5	·6	·6	·7	·7	·8	·8	·8	·9	·9	·9
Sept.	·3	·4	·4	·5	·5	·6	·6	·7	·7	·7	·8	·8
Oct.	0·3	0·3	0·3	0·3	0·3	0·4	0·4	0·5	0·5	0·6	0·6	0·7
Nov.	·2	·2	·2	·2	·2	·2	·2	·3	·3	·4	·5	·5
Dec.	0·3	0·2	0·2	0·2	0·1	0·1	0·1	0·2	0·2	0·2	0·3	0·4

Lat.	AZIMUTH											
°	°	°	°	°	°	°	°	°	°	°	°	°
0	359·2	359·2	359·3	359·3	359·4	359·5	359·6	359·7	359·8	0·0	0·1	0·2
20	359·2	359·2	359·2	359·3	359·4	359·5	359·6	359·7	359·8	0·0	0·1	0·3
40	359·0	359·0	359·1	359·1	359·2	359·3	359·5	359·6	359·8	0·0	0·1	0·3
50	358·8	358·8	358·9	359·0	359·1	359·2	359·4	359·6	359·8	0·0	0·2	0·4
55	358·7	358·7	358·7	358·8	359·0	359·1	359·3	359·5	359·7	0·0	0·2	0·4
60	358·5	358·5	358·6	358·7	358·8	359·0	359·2	359·5	359·7	0·0	0·2	0·5
65	358·2	358·2	358·3	358·4	358·6	358·8	359·1	359·4	359·6	359·9	0·3	0·6

constant. Add the result to the observed altitude *(ho)*, and the result is the latitude. Here is the whole solution:

GHA *(2300 hours)*	*194° 32.7′*
Increment *(18 56)*	*4° 44.8′*
GHA *Aries*	*199° 17.5′*
DR long (–W,+E)	*37° 14.0′*
LHA	*162° 3.5′*
a0 correction *(162° 03.5′)*	*+1° 25.4′*
a1 correction *(lat. 50°N)*	*+0.6′*
a2 correction *(April)*	*+0.9′*
Sum of corrections	*1° 26.9′*
Subtract 1° (constant)	*+26.9′*
Observed altitude ***(ho)***	*49° 31.6′*
Latitude	*49° 58.5′*

The last section of the Polaris tables gives the azimuth, a value that may be useful as a compass check for large ships able to take accurate bearings at the altitudes where Polaris is commonly observed. However, most small craft don't have this capability.

As with other types of sights, prepared forms are available for the Polaris sight. Once you understand the process, though, even a novice celestial navigator can do these simple computations without referring to forms.

Sources of Error in Celestial Fixes

Beginning celestial navigators are often frustrated with their first few fixes. At that point, many novices become disillusioned and give up. There's a reason for this—and there's also a very effective solution.

The chief reason for frustration is the tedious—and sometimes impossible—process required to isolate the many potential errors in a fix. Was the error in sextant observation? Was the time wrong? Were the data taken from the proper column in the tables? Were all the additions and subtractions correct? Were the signs all applied correctly? How about *v* and *d* corrections? The problem, of course, is that any errors made early on are compounded throughout the process and making more than one error introduces two variables, which geometrically increases the difficulty of finding them.

Most novice celestial navigators make two general types of errors: One is improper use and correcting of the sextant and the other is improper procedures in the sight reduction process. The latter is the greater source of problems.

The first step in finding out why a sight did not work out is to isolate the error to one of these two. Sextant errors can't usually be corrected. The only remedy is to take another sight, which is often impossible because twilight lasts only a few minutes—and by the time you've found the error, it's too late, and you may have to wait for the next opportunity. Only the moon and sun are available for extended periods.

You find errors in calculation by careful inspection, making sure all the rules were followed and none forgotten, and checking the mathematics, and reworking. Mathematical errors are usually due to improper application of signs (plus/minus), forgetting a correction that should be applied, and looking in the wrong column of the almanac or tables.

Minimizing Errors in Celestial Navigation

You can't completely eliminate errors in any navigation system, but you can take several steps to minimize them, especially in celestial navigation. A navigational calculator or computer program is extremely helpful to avoid making errors in mathematics, in using the tables, and in sight reduction. They allow the beginner to concentrate on becoming proficient with the sextant and foster a sense of accomplishment and progress.

To use a navigational calculator or computer program, simply read the instructions, get a time tick, and take a sight. Enter the DR position, time of the sight, the sextant altitude, index correction, and height of eye into the program at the appropriate times and places, and watch it find the azimuth and intercept. Then enter data for the next sight, and the next, and so on. The program will compute the LOPs and the fix position in a few seconds. It will not make mathematical errors; it either works or it doesn't.

You can take a couple of star sights, or 10, or 20, and a planet or two—as many as you're willing to enter data for—and obtain a calculator or computer fix in less than five minutes. By contrast, it takes professional mariners about 10 to 20 minutes to make the calculations by hand . Amateurs may take an hour or more for the same calculations and still more time to find and fix any errors.

A well-designed computer sight reduction program looks much like a sight reduction form; you type in the values and use the "tab" or "return" key to change fields. Figures 17-9 and 17-10 illustrate examples of a sight reduction program working the same star and sun sights presented on page 191 in Chapter 16. Entries that must be typed in are in squares, but some of them, such as time, may be automatically entered from other data in the program. Compare these values with those obtained in the sights worked out in Chapter 16.

Research by the U.S. Navy has shown that the accuracy of the positions obtained celestially is directly related to the number of sights the individual navigator has taken, reduced, and plotted.

By all means use a calculator or computer while learning to take sights. Later, when you've mastered the sextant, you can work out the sights using the tables and/or formulas and know that any errors are not likely in the sextant observation because you've learned to make it skillfully. And, you can check your tabular solution by entering the same sight into the program with a few keystrokes.

Using a calculator or computer can lead to dependency on it—something you should avoid. But it's better to develop the skill of taking sights, even if the calculations are automated, than not to use a sextant at all because the whole process is too daunting. Mas-

Calculators can often yield more accurate results than almanacs and sight reduction tables because they don't use simplifying assumptions or rounded off values. To illustrate this, the values for the Kochab star sight using tables in the example on page 191 in Chapter 16 can be compared with the calculator values:

	Calculator	Tables
ho	47° 17.2'	47° 17.2'
GHA Aries	326° 24.4'	326° 24.5'
SHA Kochab	137° 18.5'	137° 18.5'
LHA	306° 34.9'	307°
Declination	N 74° 10.6'	N 74° 10.6'
Intercept	14.1 Toward	9.0 Toward
Zn	18.7°	18.9°

Note the small differences in GHA, LHA, and Zn. You can be quite sure that the calculated values are more accurate. A calculator or computer does not need the LHA or latitude to be an even number, but instead can do the calculations with exact figures. For an assumed position, it can use your DR position, which is likely much closer to your real position. This results in a better approximation of the circle of equal altitude. Note that, since the assumed position is different, the intercepts are quite different, as in this case.

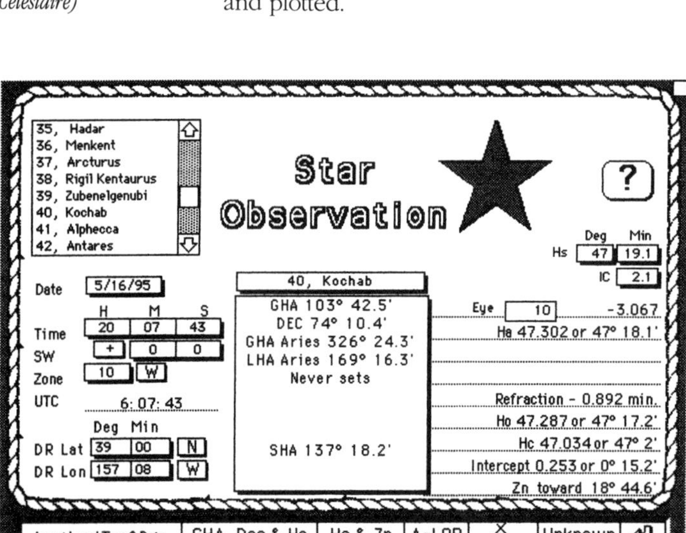

Figure 17-9. *A navigational computer program presents a sight reduction form in which one enters the appropriate values. Most sight reduction programs also calculate a lat./long. position and display the plot on the screen as it would look if plotted by hand on a plotting sheet. This allows you to select the lines on which to base the fix. This sight is the same star sight used as an example in Chapter 16. (Courtesy of MacNavigator and Celestaire)*

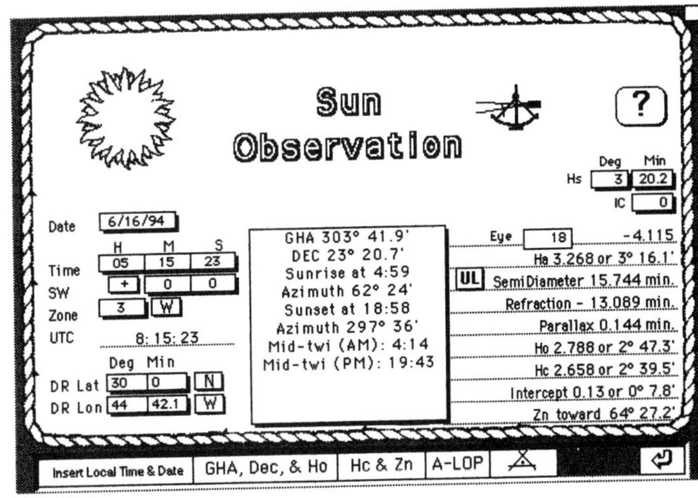

Figure 17-10. *This sun sight, solved by a computer program, is the same as presented in Chapter 16. Note the slight difference in values. The computer-generated ones are invariably more accurate. A top-quality sextant, careful observations, and computed solutions (instead of using tables) can provide celestial fix accuracies of 1 mile or less. (Courtesy of Mac-Navigator and Celestaire)*

ter the sextant first, then work on the almanac and tables.

When a power failure renders the GPS and Loran-C receivers useless and you drop the calculator in the bilge or the batteries give out, the sextant, almanac, and tables will get you home. Just don't drop the sextant, too.

Mathematical Formulas in Navigation

It is perfectly acceptable and proper to use calculators in celestial or any other type of navigation. Calculators, like computers, can make navigation easier, quicker, more accurate, and more enjoyable. The pros use them all the time. Their use, however, doesn't relieve you of the need to understand how to use the almanac and tables for sight reduction, piloting, and other tasks.

People who are proficient with pocket calculators used in their work or hobbies can easily use them for navigation when they know the applicable formulas. This section lists the formulas used in piloting and celestial navigation, as well as in weather and oceanography.

Not the least of a calculator's many advantages for navigation is increased accuracy. For instance, when you're using tables, which themselves contain rounded values, you must often interpolate between two values. A direct calculation gives a more accurate result in the same way that computer programs do. In celestial, you can use any assumed position (because the values do not have to be whole numbers) and get a more accurate calculation and a better plot of the sight.

Some mechanical calculators provide slide-rule type solutions to navigational problems. For example, the Globe-Hilsenrath Azimuth computer provides a true azimuth to commonly used bodies with inputs of latitude, declination, and hour angle. With similar inputs, you can also use it for great-circle sailing to provide an initial course.

Another such device is the celestial slide rule, a circular slide rule that has values for GHA, SHA, LHA, meridian angle *(t),* and observer's meridian. With any two known inputs, the other values are displayed. (See Figure 17-11.)

Piloting Calculations

- The hull speed of a boat = 1.34 × the square root of the waterline length. The value of 1.34 applies to an average vessel and varies with vessel shape.
- Over a one nautical mile course the speed of a vessel in knots = 3,600 divided by the elapsed time in seconds.
- Distance traveled (in nautical miles) = speed (in knots) × the time (in minutes) divided by 60.
- Distance to the radar horizon (in nautical miles) = 1.22 × square root of antenna height (in feet).

Celestial Navigation Calculations

- Distance to the horizon (dip) in nautical miles = 0.97 × square root of the height of eye (in feet). The 0.97 figure includes a factor for refraction under standard conditions.
- The computed altitude *(hc)* can be found with the following formula:

  $\sin h = \sin L \sin d + \cos L \cos d \cos LHA$.

  In this formula, h is computed altitude, *d* is declination, L is latitude, and LHA is local hour angle. If latitude and declination have a contrary name, declination has a negative sign.

- Azimuth angle (Z) can be calculated from the following formula:

  tan Z = sin LHA / cos L tan d – sin L cos LHA.

  If latitude and declination have opposite names, declination is negative. If LHA is greater than 180°, it is negative. Zn is found by the usual rule (see Chapter 16, "Sight Reduction").

Note that the formula for the maximum wave speed and the maximum hull speed of a boat are the same. This is no coincidence. As a boat moves through the water it creates waves. When nearing its hull speed (or maximum immersed speed) the length of the wave it creates is equal to the length of the boat's waterline. It can't go faster without climbing up the back side of the wave in front and beginning to plane.

Oceanographic Calculations

- The maximum theoretical length of a wave = 1.5 × square root of the fetch in nautical miles.
- The maximum theoretical height of a wave = 0.026 × wind speed (in knots) squared.
- The maximum theoretical wave speed is 3.03 × wave period (in seconds).
- The maximum theoretical wave speed is 1.34 × square root of the wave length (in feet).

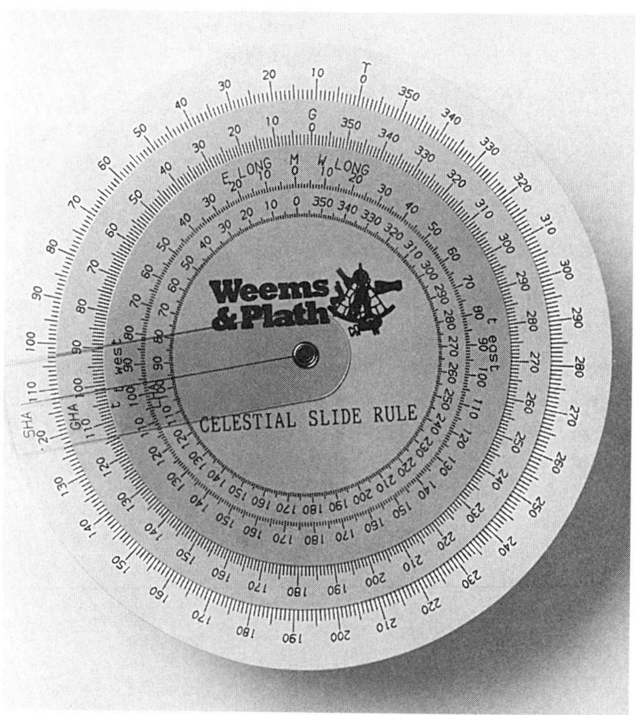

Figure 17-11. *The Celestial Slide Rule has values for GHA, SHA, LHA, meridian angle (t), and observer's meridian. If any two of these values are known and set as inputs, the others are displayed. (Courtesy Weems and Plath)*

PART 4

NAVIGATION SAFETY

CHAPTER EIGHTEEN

Navigation Rules and Regulations

UNTIL THIS CENTURY, THERE were very few regulations regarding navigation. Of course, there have always been political or practical reasons for avoiding certain areas, but otherwise a boat or ship was free to go wherever it wished without restrictions. Recently, however, many rules and regulations have been adopted that restrict movement—and a lot more.

The present network of navigational regulations covers subjects such as maritime safety, nautical rules of the road, port and harbor operations, environmental rules, and many other issues that affect the boater. This chapter discusses some of the more important navigational regulations you will encounter. It is not intended as a complete summary of all navigational rules; for that, you should refer to several other publications. For example, the *Navigation Rules* (officially known as U.S. Coast Guard *COMDTINST M16672.2B*), though summarized here, should be studied as part of your general nautical education.

The Navigation Rules

The *Navigation Rules* govern the behavior of vessels during meeting, crossing, and maneuvering situations, and specify certain lights and signals to be used at night and in other periods of low visibility. They are the most important of the rules affecting small craft because ignorance of them could result in disaster.

There are actually two sets of navigation rules: the *International Regulations for the Prevention of Collisions at Sea,* 1972 (known as the '72 COLREGS), and the *Inland Navigation Rules,* which became effective in 1981.

The dividing line between the two sets of rules is the *COLREGS Demarcation Line* (see Figure 18-1), established by the U.S. Coast Guard and shown as a purple dashed line on all official navigation charts. Inland Rules apply on the landward side of these lines and

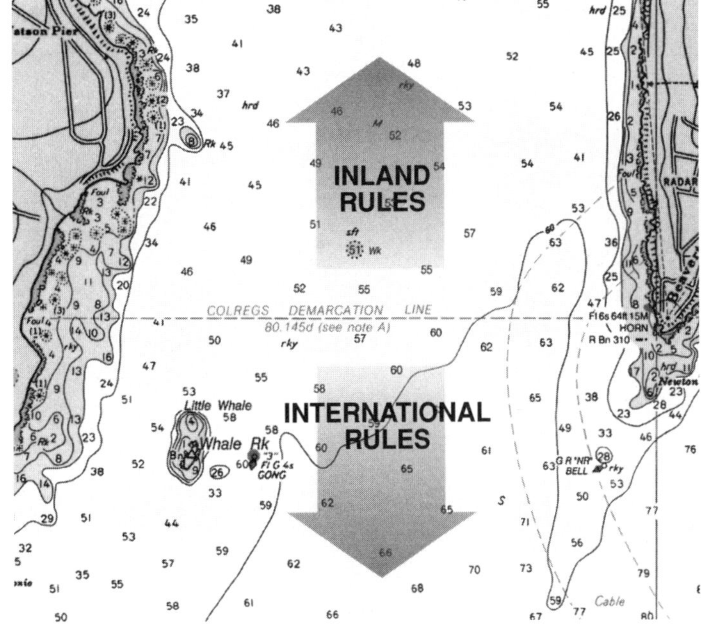

Figure 18-1. *COLREGS Demarcation Lines are indicated on charts with purple dashed lines and labeled. They generally run between major headlands or prominent aids to navigation and mark the change from International to Inland Navigation Rules.*

International Rules to seaward. The lines generally run directly between prominent points of land, landmarks, or aids to navigation that border the approaches to bays, sounds, harbors, and rivers.

Navigation rules are codified in federal law and published in *Title 33* of the United States Code. It's important for boaters to know that the rules apply to all vessels, regardless of size. It's also vital to realize that in certain cases a commercial vessel has the right-of-way over a small craft, regardless of any other considerations.

Content of the Rules

Both Inland and International Rules are intentionally very similar. Part A defines the vessels and parties to whom the rules apply. The rules of the road apply just as much to a small craft and its skipper as to a supertanker or aircraft carrier and their captains. This section also discusses the responsibility of the operator of a vessel under various conditions and defines certain terms used in the rules.

Part B, Subpart I, Steering and Sailing Rules, concerns the conduct of vessels regardless of visibility. This section specifies the following:

Requirements for proper lookouts.

Safe speed under different conditions.

What to do when risk of collision is present.

Actions to take to avoid collision.

The conduct of vessels in narrow channels.

The use of Traffic Separation Schemes and Vessel Traffic Services.

Part B, Subpart II, Conduct of Vessels in Sight of One Another, specifies the actions required by vessels in view of one another in the following situations:

Conduct of sailing vessels

Overtaking

Meeting head-on

Crossing

Actions by give-way vessels

Actions by stand-on vessels

Responsibilities between vessels

Part B, Subpart III, lists special rules for the conduct of vessels in restricted visibility.

Part C specifies the lights and shapes that vessels must show when visibility is restricted and when engaged in certain activities. These sections concern the visibility (range) of lights and the lights and shapes required for the following:

Powered vessels underway

Towing and pushing

Sailing and rowing vessels

Fishing vessels

Vessels not under control

Pilot vessels

Anchored and aground vessels

Seaplanes

Consult the *Navigation Rules* for directions about the specific size and placement of these shapes.

A "shape" ***in the context of the rules of the road is a ball, cone, diamond, or cylinder that is raised aloft to indicate certain activities. The regulations for the size and construction of these shapes are contained in annexes to the rules. Normally, pleasure craft do not engage in the activities that require shapes to be shown—fishing, towing, dredging, mine clearing, buoy tending, and the like. There are, however, exceptions:***

1. A vessel proceeding under sail and ***power in daylight must show a black conical shape, point downwards.***

2. An anchored vessel must exhibit a black spherical shape.

Although it's not necessary for you to memorize the meaning of all the shapes, you should have a copy of the *Navigation Rules* aboard for reference.

Various sound signals that are used to warn others, to attract attention, to indicate intentions, or to signal distress are the subject of Part D.

The rest of the rules include certain exceptions; some technical details of lights, shapes and sound signals; a list of the lines of demarcation between Inland and International Rules (also shown on charts); and other technical matters usually not affecting small craft.

A copy of the *Navigation Rules* should not only be aboard every vessel that is used for more than very short trips, but also read and studied. The rules are too important to be ignored.

Traffic Separation Schemes

Traffic in the major ports and harbors of the world has increased dramatically and ships carry increasingly large and more dangerous cargoes. At the same time, increasing population in shoreline areas has made the consequences of a marine accident more serious than ever.

To help mariners maneuver in busy harbors, avoid collisions and groundings, and ensure the safety of vessels and cargoes, many major ports have established *Traffic Separation Schemes (TSs)*. These delineate, through a variety of chart symbols and operating rules, different routes that commercial vessels should follow to maintain separation from each other and to ensure safe navigation among large numbers of vessels.

The *International Maritime Organization (IMO),* an official body of the Untied Nations, reviews and approves traffic separation schemes. It doesn't require or prohibit them, except in international waters, nor does it interfere with the establishment of TSSs that are wholly within the territorial waters of any nation—that is, the IMO has no legal power to require a TSSs inside territorial waters, but will approve one. Therefore, TSSs are either *IMO-approved* or *non-IMO-approved*. Only IMO-approved TSSs are shown on U.S. charts, and only in foreign waters will the boater encounter non-IMO-approved schemes.

Traffic Separation Schemes establish several rules that large vessels should follow. Notice the word "should." No vessel is required to use a TSS, but if a ship's navigator chooses not to use one that is available and subsequently is involved in a maritime accident, fault would almost certainly be assigned to that person. Nothing in the TSS rules supersedes the *Navigation Rules*.

The best advice for the small-craft navigator is to stay well away from TSS waters, if possible, leaving them for the large ships. If you must cross or use a TSS zone, you must follow certain rules to ensure safety. These are the subject of Rule 10 of the *Navigation Rules*.

A TSS consists of *traffic lanes, traffic separation lines, traffic separation zones,* and, in some cases *traffic circles*. Here are some of the rules that small craft should follow regarding TSSs:

- Vessels less than 20 meters in length, sailing vessels, and vessels engaged in fishing are not allowed to impede the passage of a vessel using a traffic lane.
- Vessels crossing a traffic lane must do so at a right angle or as close to one as possible.
- Vessels joining a traffic lane should do so at as shallow an angle as possible, and must proceed in the correct direction for that lane.
- Vessels not using a TSS should stay well clear of it.

Some TSSs have incorporated an *Inshore Traffic Zone* intended for the safe passage of small craft. You should take advantage of these zones, where you'll likely not encounter large commercial craft.

TSSs are charted using purple shaded areas, symbols, and lines, as shown in Figure 18-2. Open-outlined arrows show the recommended direction of traffic.

Buoys are often associated with the end points and turning points of TSSs. The direction of traffic flow is indicated with arrows, and limits with purple dashed lines.

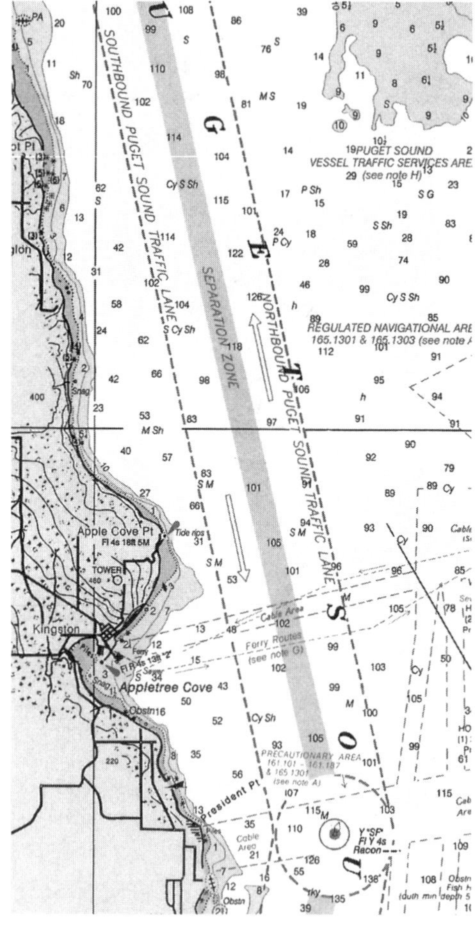

Figure 18-2. *A Traffic Separation Scheme (TSS) is shown on a chart with purple shaded areas and lines. It is meant for commercial traffic; most small craft should stay well clear unless they must enter or cross one.*

Where there is room, as in wide bays and sounds, traffic lanes are separated with *separation zones* that delineate an area within which traffic should not navigate. These are shown as purple shaded areas on charts. In narrow straits and rivers where there is not room for a zone, traffic may be separated with a *separation line,* shown with a purple dashed line. Natural features such as islands are sometimes used as separation areas as well.

Recommended Routes and Tracks

Recommended routes indicate one- or two-way paths to be followed by vessels through areas where navigation is difficult or dangerous due to numerous hazards or required course changes. Along two-way routes, vessels meeting head-to-head should pass according to the navigation rules. Recommended routes are shown with black dashed lines, with open-outlined arrows indicating the direction of travel, as shown in Figure 18-3.

A *recommended tracks* is a course line or set of lines drawn through particularly intricate passageways or around dangerous shoals or islands. It shows the best passage with black dashed lines, often not straight but winding in many directions. Simple arrowheads along the track indicate the recommended direction of travel at various points. (See Figure 18-4.)

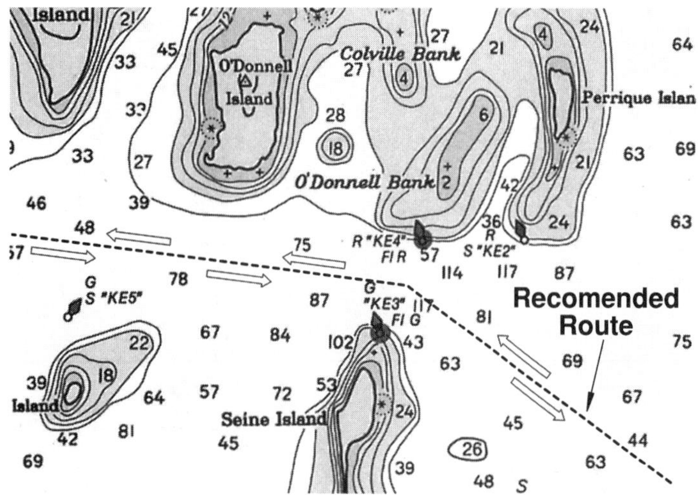

Figure 18-3. *Recommended routes indicate the preferred passage through restricted or dangerous waters. Arrows show the direction of traffic, which may be two- or one-way.*

Areas to Be Avoided

An *Area to Be Avoided* is an area officially designated by the IMO to be environmentally sensitive, valuable as a marine resource, or particularly dangerous for navigation due to numerous hazards. Specific rules apply to each area that largely concern the passage of ships carrying oil or other dangerous cargo or prohibit certain types of ships from entering a navigationally dangerous area.

An Area To Be Avoided (Figure 18-5) is shown on charts with a purple "T-dashed" or composite line—the same symbol used to depict other types of regulated areas. The specific regulations concerning these areas are found in the *Coast Pilots* (for U.S. waters) or the *Sailing Directions* (for foreign waters).

In most cases, small craft can navigate within Areas to Be Avoided without restriction because these areas are intended to limit the passage of large ships carrying dangerous cargoes. However, it's always best to check the *Coast Pilots* and *Local Notice to Mariners* for specific instructions.

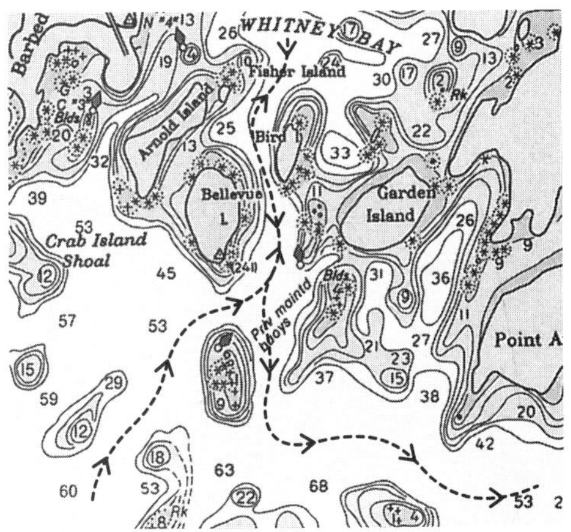

Figure 18-4. *Recommended Tracks indicate the preferred route through an area of islands or shoals where navigation can be intricate. Arrowheads along the lines indicate direction of traffic.*

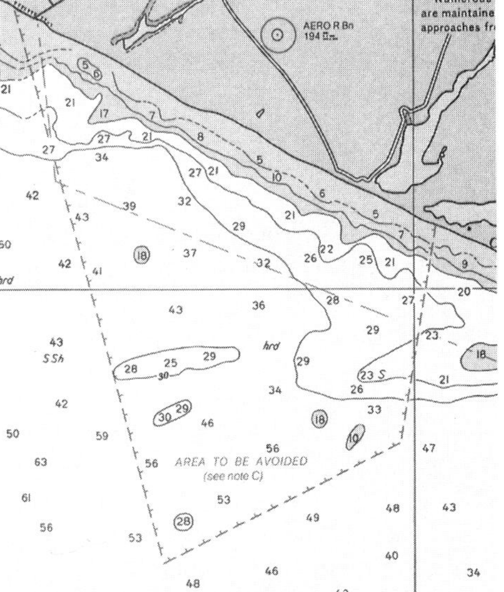

Figure 18-5. *An Area to Be Avoided is designated by the same "T-dashed" lines used for other regulated areas. You should consult the* Coast Pilot *(or, in foreign waters, the* Sailing Directions*) for specific instructions about entering these areas.*

Vessel Traffic Services (VTSs)

A Vessel Traffic Service (VTS) is a set of communications gear, monitoring equipment, and rules designed to increase the safety of shipping and boating in crowded waters, enhance navigation safety in inclement weather, and increase the capacity of a waterway.

There are two types of VTSs—*nonsurveilled* and *surveilled,* referring to whether radar surveillance is included. The nonsurveilled system consists of a network of FM radio transceivers (transmitter-receivers), charted *calling-in points,* and 24-hour monitoring. In the U.S. the monitoring authority is usually the U.S. Coast Guard, although in some areas private companies run VTS systems with Coast Guard approval and cooperation. Vessel must follow a set of navigation and communications instructions when using the VTS. The VTS authority specifies a radio frequency to monitor continuously. In most cases these apply to large ships, but in certain waterways and canals all vessels, regardless of size, must follow them. These rules are summarized in the *Coast Pilots*. Whether small craft must use the VTS depends on the regulations established by the VTS authority. Some VTSs require all vessels to use the system, while others exempt small craft on local trips. Figure 18-6 shows calling-in point symbols.

Surveilled VTSs are like nonsurveilled services, with the addition of one or more land-based radars, as well as closed-circuit television, all connected to a central operations station where technicians monitor vessel operations 24 hours a day by watching the radar and television pictures.

The VTS operators are able to identify and track individual vessels much like an air-traffic controller. A key element of both surveilled and nonsurveilled systems is the ability of the monitoring authority to advise participating vessels of the actions and intentions of other vessels in their vicinity. The emphasis in this role is on the word "advise." No VTS has the legal or physical ability to control any vessel's movements. The operator of the vessel is responsible for all decisions regarding the actions of the vessel; the VTS operator only advises the vessel operator of the actions and intentions of other vessels. Because the VTS operators can see all vessels in the area at a glance, they are able to advise vessels of the actions and intentions of other vessels to avoid misunderstandings.

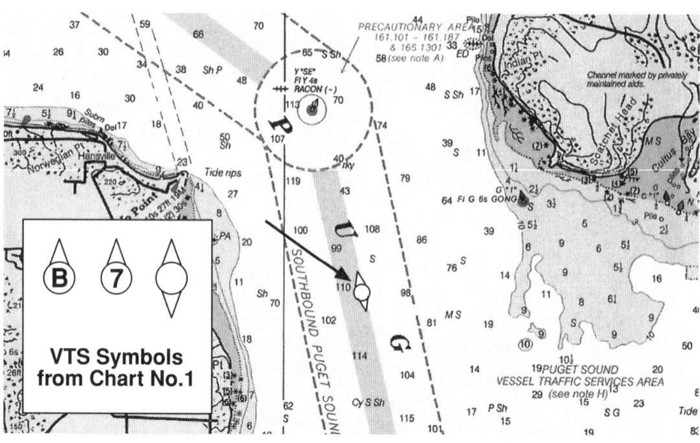

Figure 18-6. *A Calling-In Point Symbol indicates a place where vessels using the VTS system must call the controlling authority. The controller will ask for the vessel name, size, course, speed, destination, and perhaps other information. The symbol is a purple circle with an arrowhead that indicates when a vessel must call the VTS authority. The requirement applies only to a vessel traveling in the direction of the arrow. There may be a letter or number designation in the center of the circle.*

VTSs are often associated with Traffic Separation Schemes, since both systems tend to be established in busy commercial harbors and waterways.

Although most small craft are exempt from VTSs, they may use them if they wish. For the most part, a yacht or other small craft should use a VTS only in special situations. Such use might be advised in the case of a particularly large yacht, in foul or foggy weather, or perhaps at night. In these cases, it could be prudent to participate in the system and follow the recommendations of the VTS operator.

When you decide to use the VTS it's important to maintain the courses and speeds reported to the operator and to abide by all other rules. When using the system you're sharing a system used by professional harbor pilots and ship masters from around the world.

Regulated Waterways and Areas

Local authorities may establish navigation regulations in virtually any area ranging from mild restrictions on vessel movement to complete prohibition of entry. In U.S. waters the most restricted operating areas are those around military installations, where unauthorized craft are often prohibited. Such areas are noted in the *Coast Pilots*, and large signs are placed on the shore near the areas. On charts such areas are shown with the "restricted area" symbol, the T-dashed line.

In certain cases, such as along the Intracoastal Waterway in the vicinity of Camp Lejeune, North Carolina, the normally open waterway may be closed for periods of several hours to a day or more for military exercises. In other places, firing areas along seacoasts may be closed during training exercises. These normally have outer limits of a mile or more at sea and passage around them is possible even during exercises.

In certain locations navigation may periodically be restricted even far at sea, as is the case during missile launches from Cape Canaveral, Florida, or Vandenberg Air Force Base in California. These launches may fail and, in the case of space shuttle launches, the external fuel tanks are designed to drop off when empty and fall into the sea to be recovered. For these reasons, authorities are quite strict about vessel traffic in the vicinity of missile operations.

Small-craft operations may be suspended or restricted as well for other reasons such as regattas and parades, hazardous operations by harbor authorities, dredging or salvage work, and construction.

Waterways wholly within state boundaries are subject to regulations of the state. For example, the New York State Canal System, which includes the modern-day Erie Canal, has a complete body of navigation and communications regulations for boats (see Figure 18-7). Many municipal harbor authorities have established regulations on anchoring, mooring, and other vessel operations—such regulations are available at local marine stores or directly from the organizations that established them.

Large commercial waterways such as the Panama Canal are controlled by regional or government authorities. In some cases these are multinational in nature, as in the case of the St. Lawrence Seaway Development Corporation, which is jointly owned by the United States and Canada. The navigation regulations established for these waters primarily apply to the passage of large ships.

Small craft often use these commercial waterways and are sometimes subject to rules that seem unreasonable when viewed from the

Figure 18-7. *The New York State Canal System has a complete set of navigation rules, though Inland Navigation Rules of the U.S. Coast Guard also apply. Each port, harbor, or waterway authority may establish its own rules.*

deck of a boat. For example, a licensed pilot and line handlers may be required even on a very small boat, special radio frequencies may be needed, and the possession of specified mooring and anchoring gear may be required before passage is granted. Monetary charges may also be levied for unnecessary services rendered. The authority usually assumes no responsibility for damage to small craft in locks and waterways.

Chapter Nineteen

Navigation Safety

"SOS, SOS, SOS." This universally recognized distress signal has echoed across the seas since the dawn of wireless telegraphy. International regulations concerning the use of a radio at sea for maritime safety followed directly the sinking of the *Titanic* in 1912 and have saved countless sailors over the years.

The "SOS" Morse code message and its newer voice cousin, "MAYDAY," are rapidly becoming obsolete due to the introduction of a far more advanced system designed to automate messages, use advanced digital terrestrial and satellite communications systems, accurately speed rescue forces to the scene of a disaster, and more efficiently save lives and property at sea.

This system is called the *Global Maritime Distress and Safety System (GMDSS)* and is the most significant development in maritime safety since the earliest days of high seas radio and the *Titanic* disaster. It automates ship-to-ship, ship-to-shore, and shore-to-ship communications and changes the communications and distress equipment and procedures that vessel must use.

Though the GMDSS equipment requirements are intended for commercial ships, they are important to small-craft operators, for GMDSS aids all mariners with a combination of high technology and inexpensive gear. It offers a much higher degree of safety for both the offshore and near-shore boater than the previous high-seas radio system.

This chapter presents an overview of the system with an emphasis on the parts that contribute to the safety of small craft. When you know the requirements for ships, you'll see how your safety will be enhanced by using appropriate elements of the system. Other safety communications technologies are also discussed.

Global Maritime Distress and Safety System (GMDSS)

Prior to the introduction of GMDSS, the requirements for carriage of shipboard radio communications gear were based on the size of the vessel. GMDSS requirements apply to all commercial ships more than 300 gross tons or carrying 12 or more passengers for hire and are based on the area in which such vessels operate, regardless of size. Most small craft, of course, do not meet these minimum requirements. For safety reasons, however, maritime authorities encourage small craft to use GMDSS anyway.

You should become familiar with some of the new technologies incorporated in GMDSS:

- ***Digital Selective Calling (DSC)*** is a VHF, MF, and/or HF radio system that uses encoded radio signals to send messages to selected vessels, while excluding others.

- *INMARSAT* is the *International Maritime Satellite Corporation,* a consortium of communications companies that own and manage a maritime satellite communications system.
- *NAVTEX* is a maritime radio teletype system that sends printed messages to vessels within its range (about 500 miles from land).
- ***An Emergency Position-Indicating Radiobeacon* (EPIRB)** is a battery-powered radio capable of sending a continuous distress signal to satellites or to aircraft.
- ***A Search and Rescue Transponder* (SART)** sends out signals in the 9 giga-Hertz radar frequency band when activated by another radar, causing a series of distinct blips to appear on a searcher's radar set.

GMDSS divides the sea into four *Sea Areas* with somewhat indistinct boundaries determined by the range of the radio gear required. Figure 19-1 shows these areas.

- ***Sea Area A1*** extends from the coast to about 20 miles offshore, which is within range of Very High Frequency (VHF) radio stations that have Digital Selective Calling (DSC) capability.
- ***Sea Area A2*** extends from the outer limit of Area A1 to about 100 miles offshore, within the range of medium frequency (MF) DSC radio stations.
- ***Sea Area A3*** extends from the outer limit of Area A2 across all seas between about 70°N latitude and 70°S latitude. This is within the communications footprint of the INMARSAT communications satellites, through which maritime safety information is sent. (See Figure 19-2.)
- ***Sea Area A4*** includes all areas not in areas A1–A3, essentially the polar regions that aren't accessible to INMARSAT communications satellites.

All ships required to comply with GMDSS must have the following equipment:

- VHF radio with channels 6, 13, 16, and 70, with continuous DSC watch on channel 70

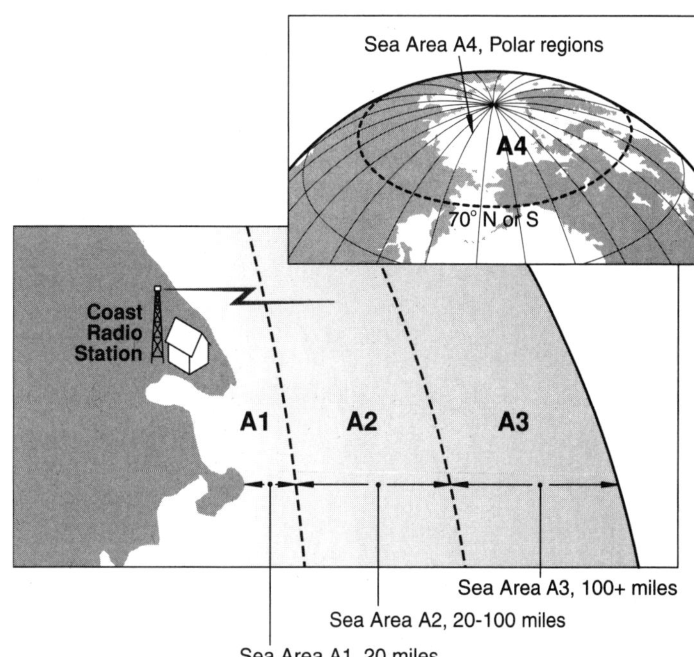

Figure 19-1. *The Global Maritime Distress and Safety System (GMDSS) determines the navigation safety equipment needed for a vessel's area of operation. Sea Areas A1 through A4 encompass all waters, but most small craft operate in Areas A1 and A2.*

- Search-and-Rescue transponders
- NAVTEX receiver
- Emergency Position-Indicating Radiobeacon (EPIRB)
- Handheld VHF radio transceivers
- High seas radio with channel 2182 (until 1999)

In Sea Area A1, vessels complying with GMDSS requirements must have:

- VHF radio
- DSC-based or satellite-based free-floating EPIRB
- Ability to make a distress call via DSC using VHF, MF, or HF radio, manual EPIRB, or satellite communications

In Sea Areas A1 and A2, complying vessels need:

- MF radiotelephone (voice) on 2182 kHz and DSC on 2187.5 kHz
- Continuous DSC watch on 2187.5 kHz
- MF radio in the 1605–4000 kHz band or satellite communications
- Ability to make a distress call via DSC using HF radio, manual EPIRB, or satellite communications

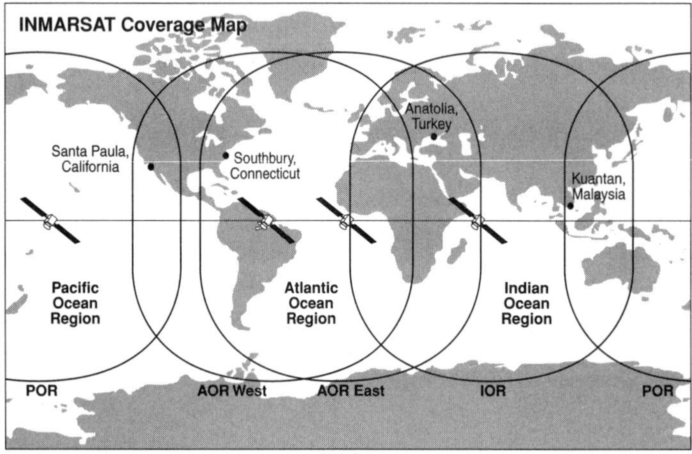

Figure 19-2. *The SafetyNet system can send Maritime Safety Information (MSI) or other messages to specific groups of vessels according to their needs, excluding others. It uses the INMARSAT communications satellites, which provide worldwide coverage everywhere except polar regions. Most small craft can't afford the expense, space, or power requirements of a satellite terminal, but MSI is disseminated in other ways as well. (Based on map provided by COMSAT Mobile Communications)*

Sea Areas A3 and A4 add requirements that are beyond the capability and budget of most small-craft owners, including satellite communications gear and/or high seas radio transmitters. However, nothing precludes the use of A1 or A2 gear in areas A3 and A4.

Maritime Safety Information

Maritime safety information (MSI) comprises information that is necessary for safe navigation as determined by worldwide government navigational authorities. It is a specific category of information defined by law and international communications policy. It consists of:

Navigational warnings

Meteorological warnings

Ice reports

Search and rescue information

Marine weather forecasts

Messages concerning electronic navigation systems (GPS, loran)

MSI is disseminated by national hydrographic offices, national weather services, national or regional search and rescue organizations, and the International Ice Patrol. MSI messages take precedence on communications channels because of their importance to safety.

SafetyNet

SafetyNet is a system that transmits MSI through INMARSAT's satellite communications network. Figure 19-3 shows this network's setup. It is part of INMARSAT's *Enhanced Group Call (EGC)* system, which allows information providers to send messages to particular vessels, particular types of vessels, vessels in certain areas, or all vessels. This targets all vessels that need the information and relieves those that don't of the bother of receiving it.

This is a vast improvement over the old high seas radio where every call was broadcast "in the open" and heard by all ships. Only one frequency could be used at a time since any other call on that same frequency would interfere.

SafetyNet messages can only be sent by a registered information provider, which ordinarily is some government organization. Unlike HF radio, which uses Morse code or voice to transmit information, SafetyNet messages are printed in English. SafetyNet is intended for vessels outside the coverage area of NAVTEX.

NAVTEX

The *NAVTEX* system is designed to provide MSI to inshore areas where costly satellite communications are not necessary. It uses a type of radio transmission known as narrowband direct printing, sometimes called *Simplex Teleprinter Over Radio (SITOR)*. NAVTEX uses a frequency of 518 kHz, providing coverage to about 200 miles from the coast, although there is wide variation in this range depending on the time of day or night and atmospheric conditions. NAVTEX messages are printed from the receiver; there is no voice capability.

A network of coastal radio stations sends NAVTEX messages according to a schedule that minimizes interference between adjacent stations. The messages consist of MSI and other traffic.

A unique capability of the NAVTEX system is its ability not only to selectively send information only to those who require it, but also only to those who have not yet received it, or who desire only certain types of information. This is made possible by a "header" in the beginning of the message that automatically alerts receivers and allows them to receive the message or not according to parameters set by the user. Certain types of information, such as distress messages, cannot be ignored.

The user can set the NAVTEX receiver to receive only MSI and distress traffic, for example, and to receive each message only once. This is important because most messages are broadcast a number of times over a period of several hours or days. The receiver, once having received a message containing a certain header, prints it and subsequently ignores additional messages containing that header. This minimizes printing while ensuring that necessary traffic is received. Any new messages concerning MSI or maritime distress will have a new header and also be printed once, as specified by the user.

The NAVTEX receiver (Figure 19-4) is a small unit with an internal printer and a relatively small receive-only antenna.

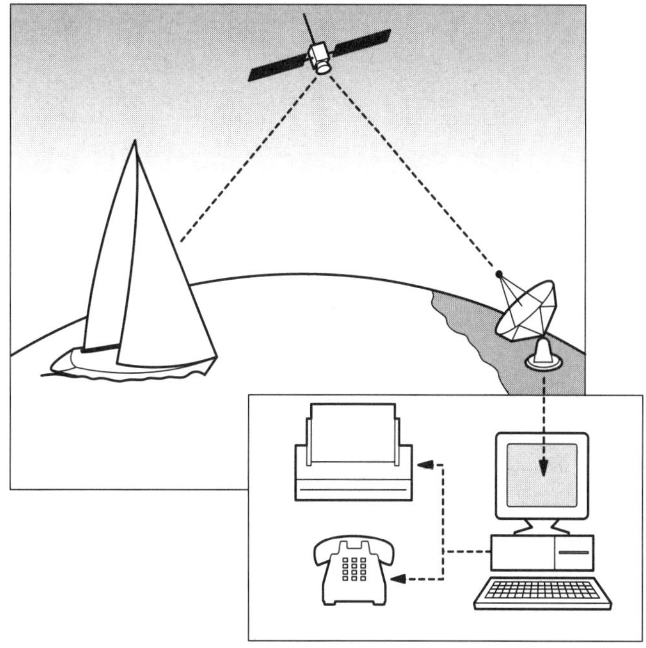

Figure 19-3. *The INMARSAT system consists of a satellite terminal aboard the boat, an orbiting satellite, and a land-based receiver that routes calls from the boat into the terrestrial telephone network. This system is appropriate only for the larger and wide-ranging small craft. (Based on map provided by COMSAT Mobile Communications)*

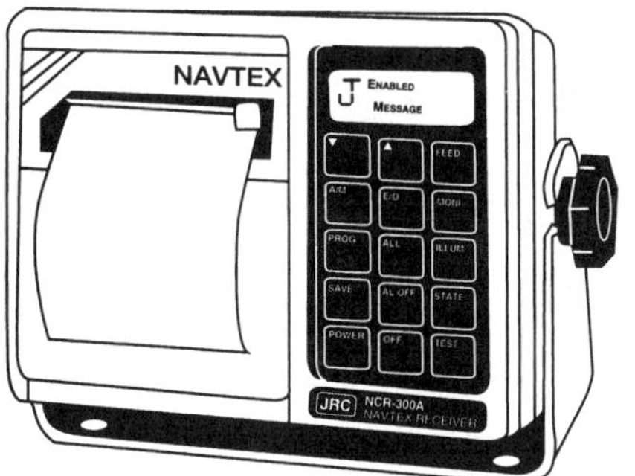

Figure 19-4. *The NAVTEX receiver automatically picks up and prints MSI broadcasts from coastal radio stations. You can program it to reject certain unimportant information, but not important information. It won't receive a given message more than once. (Courtesy Raytheon Electronics)*

Emergency Position-Indicating Radiobeacons (EPIRBs)

The *Emergency Position-Indicating Radiobeacon (EPIRB)* is probably the most useful safety device the offshore and coastal navigator can have. When activated it sends a distinct radio signal that both satellites and aircraft can receive and relay to rescue forces, which can then home in on the device. EPIRBs can be either manually or automatically activated and can even indicate what type of vessel is in trouble, allowing rescuers to arrive with appropriate gear.

There are two major types of EPIRBs, distinguished by the frequencies they use. The older and less useful, designated Class A, B, C, or S, transmits a simple noncoded signal on 121.5 and 243 MHz. This signal can be heard by passing aircraft, by ships monitoring these frequencies, and by satellites in line of sight. Signal quality is relatively poor and weak, and false alarms are so frequent that rescue forces must confirm the emergency through other means before deploying. The location accuracy is about 10 to 20 miles, and delays of one to three hours are usually incurred before rescue forces determine a final search position. Figures 19-5 and 19-6 show Class A and B EPIRBs.

The newer type of EPIRB, known as a Category I or II, transmits a coded signal on 121.5 and 406 MHz that is detectable by satellites

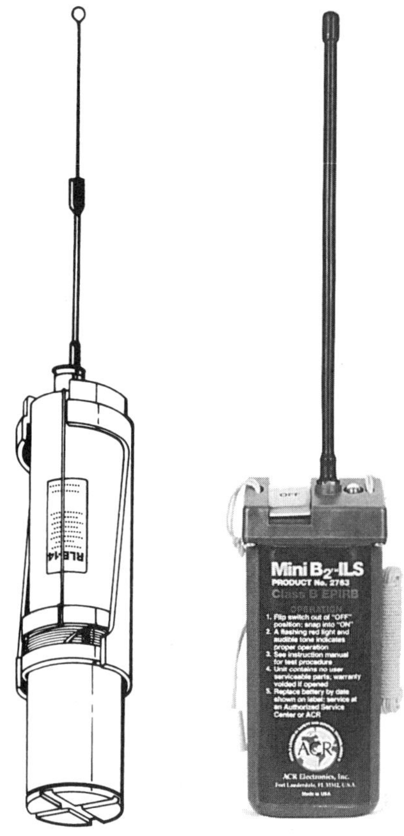

Figure 19-5. *The Class A EPIRB transmits signals on 121.5 and 243 megahertz that can be detected by orbiting satellites and aircraft. However, it has limitations in its detection abilities and the accuracy of the sender's position.It is free-floating and activates automatically. (Courtesy ACR Electronics Inc.)*

Figure 19-6. *The Class B EPIRB is a manually-activated unit with the same limitations as the Class A type. (Courtesy ACR Electronics Inc.)*

anywhere in the world with no range limitation. Satellites that are out of range of an earth receiving station retain the distress signal information and transmit it when an earth station is next in range. Signal quality is very good and false alarms are rare because each EPIRB unit is registered to a particular craft and sends out a particular signal—all of which allows rescuers to identify the vessel in distress, verify via telephone to the registered address the possibility of a distress, and to know what type of craft is in trouble and what emergency gear it has aboard or might need. The telephone call can often reveal the number and names of persons on board. The satellite is able to locate the position of the transmitting EPIRB within about three miles on the first receipt of the signal and relay this position to authorities. Rescue forces are often underway within a few minutes.

Some EPIRBs are manually activated by a switch; others are a "float-free" type that automatically activate upon separation from a sinking craft.

The following table summarizes EPIRB types and capabilities.

Type	Freq. (MHz)	Description	Detected by:
Class A	121.5/243	Float-free auto-activating	Satellites* and aircraft
Class B	121.5/243	Manually activated	Satellites* and aircraft
Class C	VHF ch 15,16	Manually activated	Marine radio receivers
Class S	121.5/243	Floating version of B	Satellites* and aircraft
Category I	121.5/406	Float-free auto-activating	Satellites and aircraft
Category II	121.5/406	Manually activated	Satellites and aircraft

** Satellite coverage is limited.*

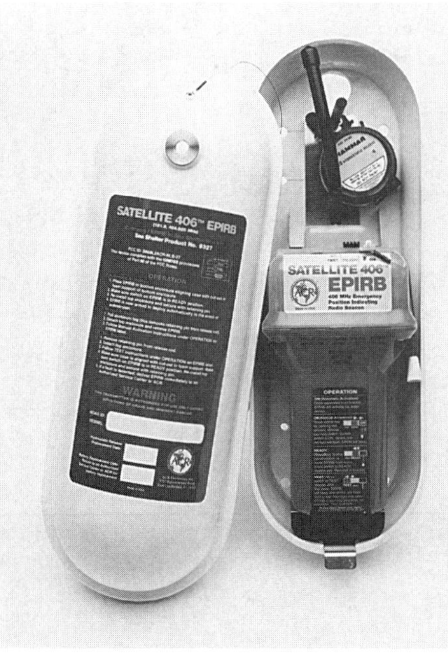

Figure 19-7. *The Category I and II EPIRBs broadcast on 406 megahertz using a coded signal that identifies the vessel in distress and locates its position much more quickly and accurately than the older Class A, B, C, and S units. (Courtesy ACR Electronics Inc.)*

As you can see, the newer Category I and II EPIRBs are much better than the older types. They provide more accurate location,

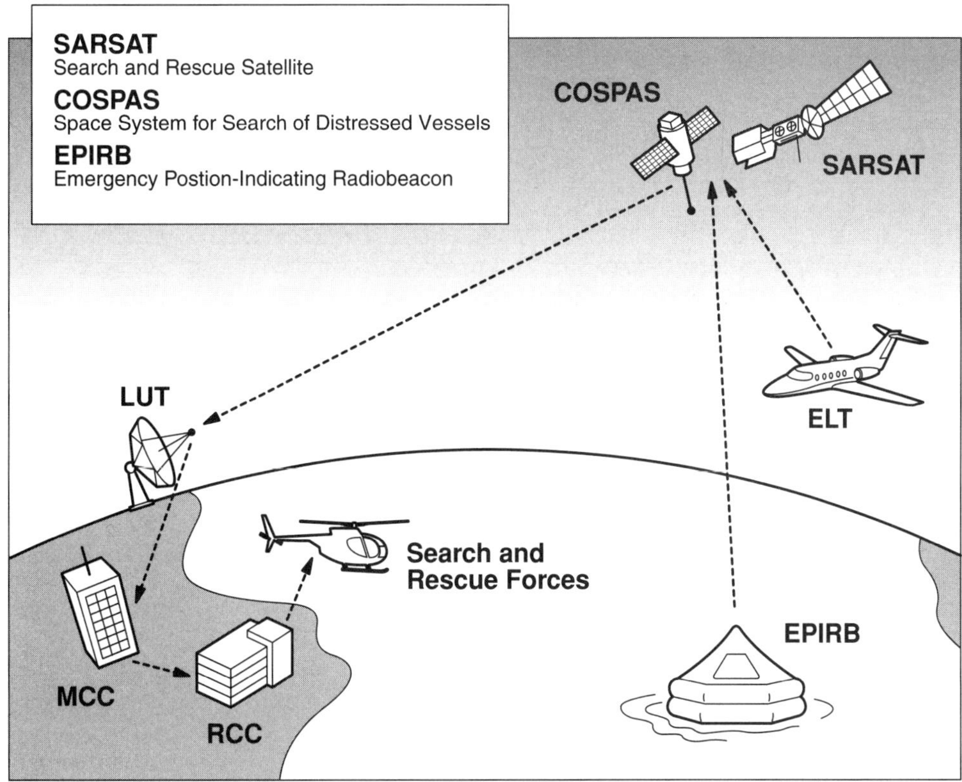

Figure 19-8. *The signal from an EPIRB is picked up by a passing satellite of the COSPAS/SARSAT system and relayed to an earth station that transmits the information to rescue forces. An emergency locator transmitter (ELT) is the aircraft equivalent of the EPIRB. MCC is mission control center; LUT is local user terminal; RCC is rescue coordination center.*

faster response, stronger signals, and a much greater possibility of detection. In addition, they are fitted with strobe lights to aid rescuers in the final stages of their search.

The registry of Category I and II EPIRBs is kept by the National Oceanic and Atmospheric Administration and is accessible continuously and worldwide so that SAR forces anywhere can obtain information upon receipt of a 406 MHz EPIRB signal.

The satellites that receive EPIRB signals and retransmit them to earth stations are part of the *COSPAS-SARSAT* system, a combined project of Russia, the U.S., Canada, and France. COSPAS is a Russian acronym for Space System for Search of Distressed Vessels; SARSAT stands for Search and Rescue Satellite. Many other countries participate in the system, helping to receive and relay information and deploying rescue forces. (See Figure 19-8.)

Because COPAS-SARSAT satellites are at relatively low altitudes and in near-polar orbits, they provide worldwide coverage. The relay of a message received by a satellite not in immediate contact with an earth station is delayed until an earth station is in range, but at the first opportunity, usually within a few minutes, the message is relayed to the earth and retransmitted to search and rescue agencies. The position of the distress can be calculated using complex computations of the Doppler shift accompanying the passage of the satellite over the transmitting EPIRB.

In addition, the 406 MHz EPIRBs transmit a coded signal that identifies the vessel in distress. The vessel registry quickly determines the type of craft, its ownership, and the names and telephone numbers of contacts ashore to verify the type of vessel and the names of persons aboard.

Another type of EPIRB is being deployed that transmits a signal through INMARSAT communication satellites. The connection with shore-based agencies is instantaneous, but no position information is available unless a GPS or other position sensor is connected to the system.

VHF Radio Safety Procedures

Though GMDSS has supplanted HF radio for most distress and safety traffic, the short-range VHF radio (see Figure 19-9) remains a vital part of the navigation safety picture for the boater. All small craft that venture out for more than a few hours should have a VHF radio. In an emergency close to shore or other boats, use your VHF radio to talk directly with rescue forces, including operators of boats and aircraft on the scene. An EPIRB is the last resort, to be used only when other distress communications are not available.

Figure 19-9. *The VHF radio is the primary safety communications unit for the small boater because it allows direct voice contact with rescue forces. An EPIRB should be activated only when VHF communications are not possible. (Courtesy Raytheon Electronics)*

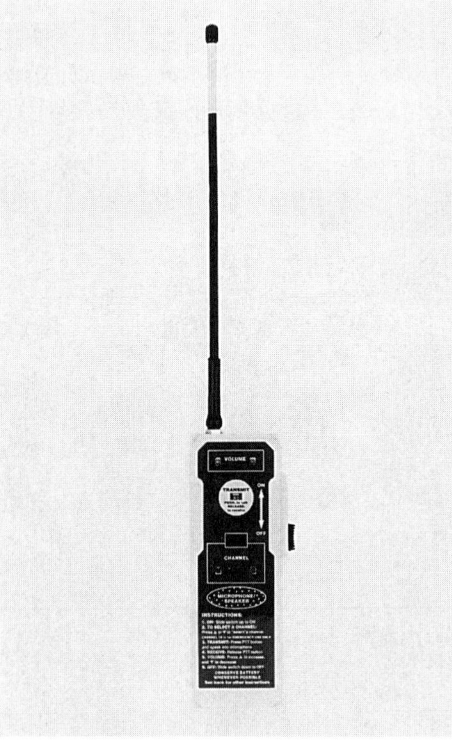

Figure 19-10. *Portable VHF radios can be carried from the vessel if necessary, allowing continued communication with rescue forces even when the regular VHF radio becomes unusable. (Courtesy ACR Electronics Inc.)*

Portable VHF radios can be carried to life rafts, if necessary, so communication with rescue forces is possible even when your boat's installed VHF radio is unusable. (See Figure 19-10.)

At one time, VHF radios and their operators needed a license to operate, but licensing requirements have been dropped for certain boats less than 66 feet long not engaged in commercial activity. You must follow proper procedures, however, when using a VHF radio, especially in distress situations.

You should monitor channel 16 on your VHF radio at all times when underway—it is the calling channel where you'll hear notification of navigational warnings, severe weather warnings, distress and emergency calls, and many routine calls. When you've established communications on channel 16, you must switch to another "working" channel to engage in conversation, except in emergencies.

A vessel can make two types of voice-radio distress calls. One is used in situations where life or property is threatened or in jeopardy and does not imply immediate danger. The signal is the spoken word "PAN," pronounced "pahn," said clearly three times, followed by the vessel's identity, location, and a brief description of the nature of the problem. The second type of distress call does imply immediate danger. The signal is the spoken word "MAYDAY," again said three times.

Follow a few simple rules for VHF radio use to keep the channels clear, the messages short and understandable, and the system operating efficiently.

- Listen before transmitting to be sure the channel is clear.
- Call on channel 16 and switch to a working channel for conversation.
- Don't engage in unnecessary or inappropriate talk.
- Use the lowest possible transmitting power setting.

VHF channels are assigned for certain uses to separate radio traffic into categories and minimize interference. The channel assignments are:

Channel	Use
16	Distress, safety, and calling
9	NE U.S. alternate calling
6	Ship-to-ship safety, search and rescue
22A	Coast Guard
24–28, 84–88	Marine Operator
70	Digital Selective Calling (DSC)
WX1–WX7	Weather reports
7A, 8, 10, 18A 79A, 80A	Commercial vessel working
9, 68, 69, 71, 72, 78A	Recreational vessel working
20, 65A, 66A, 73, 74	Port operations
13	Navigation messages (1-watt power limit)

Other channels are reserved for international use.

- Identify the vessel calling at the beginning and end of each call.

Some additional procedures can ensure that all necessary information is transmitted and understood:

- Keep the microphone two to six inches from your mouth—no closer.
- Speak clearly and distinctly.
- First say the name of the station you're calling and its call sign, then say "This is…" and identify your vessel. Wait at least one minute for a response before repeating.
- As the calling vessel, name a working channel.
- Do not call the Coast Guard for radio checks.
- End all calls by saying, "This is (name of vessel and call sign if it has one), out."

The proper procedure for a distress call is as follows:

- Listen on channel 16 to be sure it is clear.
- Say the word "PAN" or "MAYDAY" (whichever is appropriate) three times.
- Identify the vessel and call sign (if any).
- Repeat after 20 seconds.

When a distress call is answered, switch to a working channel. (It's OK to stay on channel 16 for distress traffic if necessary.) If the station answering is a Coast Guard unit, it will suggest a working channel and continue to monitor channel 16 in case the working channel fails.

Rescue authorities will want to know the following information about the vessel in distress so they can respond properly:

- Vessel's name, radio call sign (if any), and registration number.
- Nature of the distress: fire, sinking, grounding, personal injury, etc.
- Exact location of the distress.
- Description of the vessel: type, length, color, etc.
- Number of persons aboard, ages, sexes.
- Type of gear aboard to deal with the emergency.

If there is no response to a MAYDAY call after a few minutes, it's safe to assume the signal is not being transmitted or received. Only then should you activate an EPIRB.

Miscellaneous Emergency Signals

The radio and EPIRB are not the only ways to signal distress. In addition to traditional methods such as signal flares, smoke, or an upside-down U.S. flag, you can use a new technology, the cellular telephone, for distress calls. Dial "911" and ask to be connected to the Coast Guard. The range of cellular telephones can be as much as 50 miles—it depends on the line-of-sight distance to the nearest shore antenna.

Many vessels far offshore use a high frequency (HF) radio when out of VHF range. Known as single-sideband (SSB) because of the special type of radio wave they generate, these radios provide voice communications over a range of several hundred miles or more.

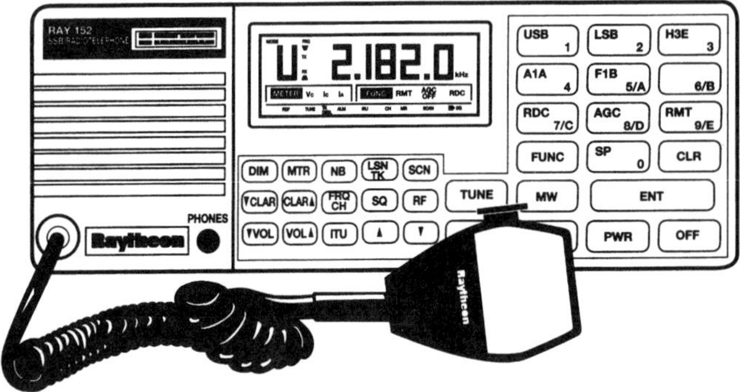

Figure 19-11. *The single-sideband radio is used by some vessels when out of VHF radio range. The distress and calling frequency is 2182 kilohertz. SSB radio frequencies are sometimes adversely affected by atmospheric conditions. (Courtesy Raytheon Electronics)*

The HF band international calling and distress frequency is 2182 kilohertz. As with VHF radio use, you should try first to make distress calls on your SSB radio and activate your EPIRB only if this fails. (See Figure 19-11.) Unlike VHF radio, SSB-HF radios can be adversely affected by atmospheric conditions.

Emergency Navigation

A navigational emergency on a small craft usually consists of the loss of one or more of the systems the navigator has come to trust for finding position. However, one navigator's dire emergency is another's minor inconvenience. It's an inconvenience when you're equipped with emergency gear and know how to use it. In an emergency, as in all navigation, the most important tool is your brain.

Even if an emergency has been precipitated by a dramatic physical disaster such as being pitchpoled, rolled, or severely flooded, it's not necessary to activate an EPIRB if you can stabilize the conditions and get the boat underway again using a jury-rigged engine or sails. If an EPIRB is set off, survivors will probably be rescued by helicopter and the vessel abandoned, unless it is close enough to the coast for a tow. If the crew is safely aboard and immediate rescue is not necessary, then you can confront the problem of navigating to a safe harbor.

In a severe navigational emergency, all electronics are lost due to generator failure, lightning strike, flooding of the engine/generator spaces and batteries, fire, or some other electrical failure. The sextant, compass, and other so-called "essential" navigation tools might be damaged beyond repair.

Many boats have been hit by lightning, which, using the boat as a conductor, usually fries every piece of electrical gear aboard—Loran-C, GPS, radio, stereo, lights—everything. (Some boats have grounding wires led to metal plates to route lightning directly to the water, but electricity is like a 500-pound gorilla on a small craft—it goes where it wants to.)

What to Do If . . .

The first thing to do in an offshore emergency is to plot your best-known position and log courses and speeds so you can plot a good DR track. With that, you can proceed to navigate with emergency gear. On a small boat, you should store a suite of emergency navigation equipment in a double-waterproof container, such as two large Ziploc bags, one inside the other (and don't forget to toss in a pack of silica gel to absorb moisture). It might include:

- A spare, handheld GPS receiver
- Plenty of spare batteries
- An inexpensive scientific calculator
- Plotting gear
- Universal plotting sheets
- Plastic sextant
- Pencils and a notebook
- Protractor
- Dividers
- Flashlight
- Portable AM-FM radio
- Hand-bearing compass
- Spare almanac
- Sight reduction tables, if celestial navigation might be necessary.

In short, nearly everything needed for everyday navigation should be available in some form for emergency navigation. An excellent book on this subject, *Emergency Navigation,* by David Burch, should be in every serious offshore sailor's emergency navigation kit.

If a handheld GPS is available, continue navigating as before, but monitor battery use carefully and turn the unit off as much as possible to save power. Manufacturers' claims about battery life are uniformly optimistic. Figure on good, strong performance for about half of the advertised lifetime to retain a margin for error. Far out at sea, it's less, not more, important to know your exact position. Save battery power for approaching the coast and making a harbor—don't waste it getting a lot of pinpoint fixes a hundred miles out.

If you lose your GPS receiver, a working Loran-C can provide an excellent backup when you're in Loran-C territory. (Though some electronics manufacturers sell combined GPS/Loran-C receivers, it might be more prudent to have two separate units connected to two different electrical circuits.)

If you lose all electronics, you must revert to more traditional navigation. With a spare plastic or makeshift sextant and an almanac, observing a meridian passage of the sun can give you both latitude and longitude with enough accuracy to make a landfall in most areas. Even if you don't know the sun's declination with precision, you should have a rough idea of what it is and know whether it is increasing or decreasing. Similarly, you can determine your latitude from Polaris and use the ancient technique of latitude sailing to make harbor.

Of course, you can't find longitude without a timepiece, but if you've been doing celestial sights using your wristwatch as a comparing watch, you should have a good idea of its error and rate of change. If you keep a daily record during the voyage you'll have a timepiece reliable enough for emergency work—unless your wristwatch is broken.

If a sextant isn't available, you can jury rig a makeshift one from a course plotter or protractor. (See Figure 19-12.) Hang a weighted string from the center point and sight along the long edge toward the body. When it is in line, pinch the string along the arc and read the resulting altitude. (There is no dip correction with this method, but a refraction correction should be applied. Use the almanac or refer to the simplified refraction table in the sidebar.) In this way you should be easy to find you latitude to within five to 10 miles each time the sun crosses your meridian.

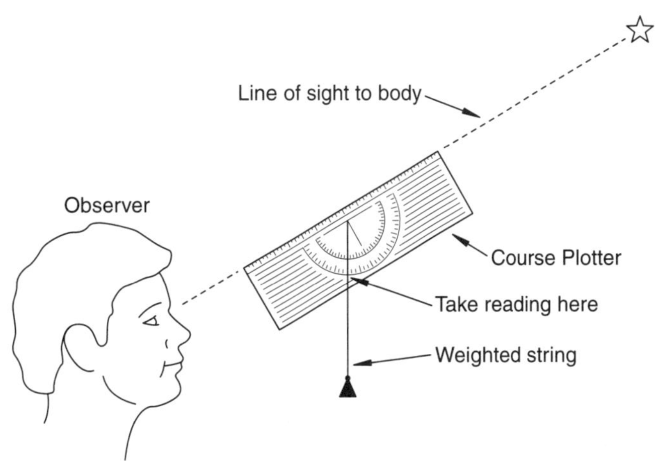

Figure 19-12. *An emergency sextant can be made from a protractor or course plotter and a weighted piece of string.*

(You can find longitude as well, using the graphing technique described in Chapter 17.)

If the compass is disabled, you can sail within 10° or 20° of your desired course using only the sun and Polaris. Obviously, you'll observe the bearing of the sun most accurately in the morning and evening, but in between those times you can use ocean swells, steady winds, distant cloud patterns, and other references to roughly determine direction. Polaris is always within 2° of true north, so in clear night weather you can use it to steer within 10° of your desired heading.

In thick weather, when you have no celestial reference, winds may provide a directional reference. For example, in the trade wind belts, winds are within 20° of their prevailing direction more than 80 percent of the time. In January the northeast trades in the Lesser Antilles are due east 56 percent of the time, 15 percent NE and 15 percent SE. You should have no trouble using them to determine which way is east.

In the region of the prevailing westerlies, winds ahead of a cold front are warm, moist, and generally from the southwest. After frontal passage, they are cool or cold, dry, and from west to northwest.

The best source of this type of data is the pilot chart, which should also be a part of your emergency navigation kit, not only for its usefulness in knowing patterns of weather, wind, and current, but also for its use as a plotting chart for offshore sailing. Though its

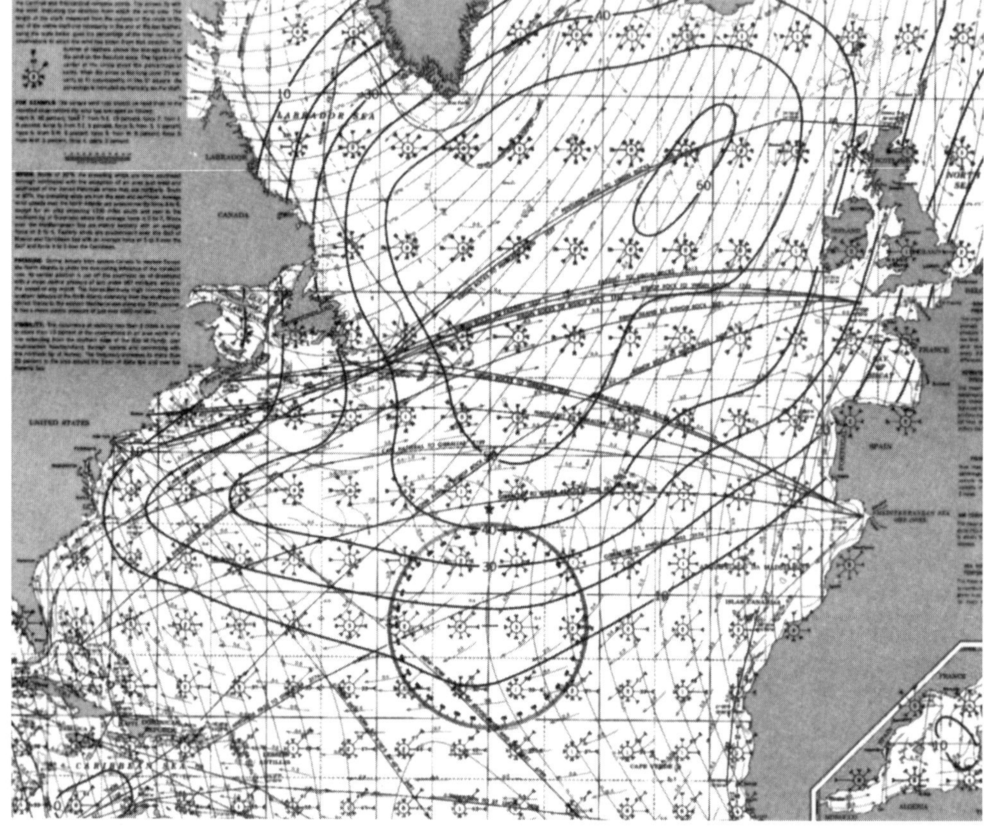

Figure 19-13. *This portion of the Defense Mapping Agency's pilot chart for the North Atlantic in the month of June includes shorthand notations for currents, wind speeds and frequencies, ice sightings, and more.*

scale is small, you can use it for open ocean plotting and it has a wealth of other information of particular value whether or not your navigation gear is disabled. (See Figure 19-13.)

Finding Latitude

Polaris is particularly useful in emergency navigation both for steering and position-finding. You can get fairly accurate latitude lines from it even with a makeshift sextant, but you must use care to get the best accuracy. Remember that Polaris describes a small circle about the true celestial pole. When it is directly above or below the celestial pole, its direction is true north and the altitude correction is greatest. This occurs when the trailing star of the Big Dipper or Cassiopeia is directly above or below Polaris. At this point, you should apply a correction of 1° to the sextant reading—added if Polaris is below the pole and subtracted if above it.

Conversely, when Polaris is directly east or west of the celestial pole, you make no altitude correction and the true direction is about 2° east or west of the pole. This occurs when the line connecting the trailing stars of the Big Dipper and Cassiopeia runs east-west. In between these times you can use rough interpolation.

Once you know your latitude you can find the declination of any body by observing it at meridian passage, using the graph method for best accuracy, just as for a sun latitude/longitude observation. (See Chapter 17.)

Finding Distance Off

Remember that distance to the horizon in miles is equal to 1.15 times the square root of your height of eye in feet. You should know the height of eye from various places on your vessel from piloting, celestial navigation, or both. You can find the distance off an object

Refraction can be accounted for in emergency celestial navigation. The following refraction table can supply the values.

Altitude	5°	6°	7°	8°	10°	12°	15°	21°	33°	63°	90°
Ref. Corr.	9'	8'	7'	6'	5'	4'	3'	2'	1'	0'	

These values are actually accurate enough for everyday use, but those in the *Nautical Almanac* are even more accurate. Even more roughly speaking, refraction is 34' for a body at the horizon, 6' from 5° to 18°, and zero above 18°. These are good enough values for use in emergencies.

Information in last year's *Nautical Almanac* for the sun, stars, and Aries is accurate enough for use this year in an emergency, so instead of disposing of it, put it in your emergency navigation kit.

Lacking an almanac, you can roughly approximate the sun's declination by the following rule: Count the days from the present date to the nearest solstice (June 21 or December 22). Divide this number by the number of days from that date to the equinox (March 21 or September 23) that occurs between it and the solstice. Multiply the result by 90°. Enter the following table with that number and extract the factor. This factor times 23.45° equals the declination.

Angle	0°	18°	31°	41°	49°	56°	63°	69°	75°	81°	87°	90°
Factor	1.0	0.9	0.8	0.7	0.6	0.5	0.4	0.3	0.2	0.1	0.0	

This table can also serve as a simplified traverse table, in which you can find the change of latitude in minutes by entering the table with the course angle and multiplying the distance run by the factor. To find departure, enter with the complement of the course angle. To convert departure to difference of longitude, enter with the midlatitude and divide the departure by the factor.

If an almanac is available, the declination of any body observed in your zenith—directly overhead—equals your latitude. Lying flat on deck and suspending a weighted string as a plumb bob above your head can help you

of known height from this formula. It's the same formula used to find the distance to a object of known height in piloting.

You can make a simple cross-staff from available materials and use the relationship between its length and span to find the distance off an object of known height or width. The ratio of the span of the crosspiece to its distance from your eye is the same as the ratio of the height (or width) of the object to its distance from you.

For example, suppose you use a makeshift cross-staff to observe an island that is 1.5 miles wide. (See Figure 19-14.) The span of the crosspiece is 18 inches and both ends of the island are in line with its ends at a distance of 31 inches from the eye. Then:

$18/31 = 1.5/D$, $D = 1.5 \times 31/18$, $D = 2.6$.

The island is 2.6 miles away.

The crosspiece can be any length, but the units on each side of the ratio must be the same, inches to inches vs. miles to miles, etc.

Another method is to hold a thin object, such as a pencil, vertically at arm's length. Sight with one eye and align the object with a distinct point on shore. Quickly close that eye and sight with the other. Estimate the actual distance the object has moved against the background. The distance off is 10 times that amount. (Practice this around the harbor; the 10:1 ratio may vary with the individual. It works because, for the average person, the distance of the outstretched arm is about 10 times the distance between the pupils.)

Other physical relationships are useful for quick reference, even in everyday piloting.

Figure 19-14. *The distance off an object of known height or length can be found with a simple cross-staff. In this example, when both ends of the crosspiece are lined up with the ends of the island, the ratio of the crosspiece length to its distance from the eye is the same as the length of the object to its distance off.*

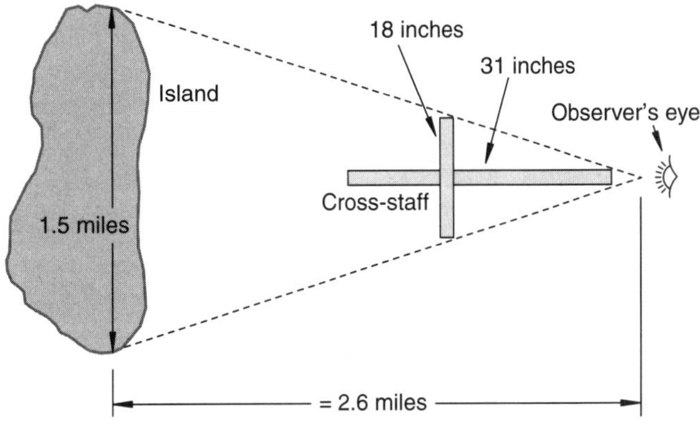

For example, one finger held at arm's length covers about 2° of arc, measured horizontally or vertically. Two fingers cover 4°. Three fingers cover 6° and give rise to the *three-finger rule:* An object that is three fingers high is about 10 times as far away as it is high. That is, a lighthouse 100 feet high just covered by three fingers is about 1,000 feet away. At six fingers it's at a distance five times its height and at a finger and a half it's 20 times the distance (all approximate).

Finding Speed

To determine speed if your knotmeter or speed log is disabled, use the following formula:

$$\textbf{Speed} = \frac{60(\text{sec./min.}) \times 60(\text{min./hr.}) \times \text{length of the boat}}{6{,}000(\text{ft./mile}) \times \text{seconds of time to pass a chip}}$$

To use this formula, take a disposable chip or piece of paper (or tie a string to a floating object so you can use it again) and toss it in the water at the bow. Then walk aft with it to determine the time it takes in seconds to reach the stern. Use the number of seconds in the above formula and solve the equation. The estimate of speed will be accurate to within about 0.1 knot. You can pre-solve the formula by making marks on the deck of your vessel 16 feet 8 inches apart. With this interval, 10 seconds = 1 knot, 5 seconds = 2 knots, etc. (To prove this, use 16.67 in the formula above for "length of boat" and set up a table using various times.)

CHAPTER TWENTY

Marine Weather

by Richard Hubbard and Michael Carr

WEATHER IS THE SUM of the conditions of the earth's atmosphere at a given time and place. It is made up of a number of different elements, all of which have some bearing on navigation. We describe the weather using physical factors such as temperature, pressure, winds, clouds, humidity, precipitation, visibility, etc. The state of the weather often determines the type of navigation that must be used, and in some cases whether navigation can proceed at all.

Weather on the earth is driven by the sun's heat, which, due to the varying density, shape, size, altitude, and color of the earth's surface, affects the earth unevenly, causing areas of hot and cold air to flow toward each other in a continuous attempt at reaching an equilibrium temperature. This flow of air brings winds that are seasonal, regional, or local in nature.

Certain combinations of conditions cause the formation of violent atmospheric phenomena such as waterspouts, tornadoes, storms, and hurricanes. While in previous centuries oceanic winds and weather were central to seafaring, modern power-driven oceangoing vessels rely less on winds. Still, even the largest ships must have accurate weather information to avoid storms and complete a voyage without damage, and at the lowest cost—and oceanic weather is the most important factor in most voyage planning.

A coastwise small-craft operator needs a sound grasp of weather principles to fully understand local weather forecasts. Conditions that may inconvenience a ship may be downright dangerous to a boat, and it is vital for navigation safety that the boater understand the conditions he or she will be sailing in. Ocean voyagers should have a more complete understanding of worldwide weather and climatic patterns for a safe and efficient trip.

The Atmosphere

The earth's *atmosphere* is a mixture of gases that, like all gases, is light, compressible, fluid, and elastic. Its weight at sea level, where it is densest, is about 1.22 ounces per cubic foot. (An equal amount of water weighs about 62 pounds.) The atmosphere's density decreases as altitude increases because of the decreased weight of air above; its pressure decreases as well.

More than three-quarters of the mass of air is concentrated in the lowest seven miles of the atmosphere, which is called the *troposphere;* this is the region where almost all

If the earth were the size of a basketball, the atmosphere would be thinner than a piece of paper.

weather occurs. At the upper edge of the troposphere is the *tropopause,* a transition zone separating the troposphere from the *stratosphere.* The tropopause is generally about 5 miles high near the poles and 10 miles high at the equator (because cold air is denser than warm air).

Above the tropopause is the stratosphere, ending about 30 miles high in the *stratopause.* Next is the *mesosphere,* from 30 to 50 miles, ending in the *mesopause,* which marks the transition to the *thermosphere,* at an altitude of 50 to 300 miles. Above the thermosphere is the void of space. Figure 20-1 shows these layers and the temperature regimes that define them.

Since the characteristics of the atmosphere vary widely, meteorologists have established a *standard atmosphere* against which to compare variations. The standard atmosphere is defined as having a sea level pressure of 1013.25 millibars (29.92 inches, 1013.25 hectopascals, 760 mm of mercury) at a temperature of 15°C (59°F). Temperature decreases with altitude at a rate of 2°C (3.6°F) per thousand feet, known as the standard lapse rate, to an altitude of 11 kilometers (36,089 feet), and is then constant at minus 56.5°C (−69.7°F).

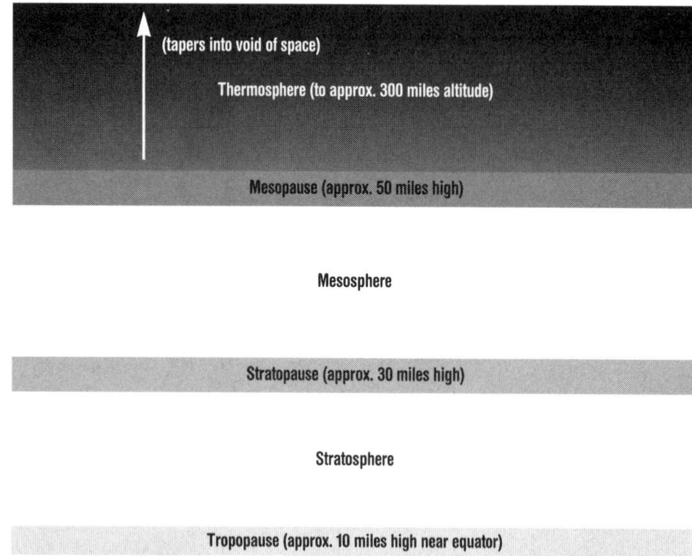

Figure 20-1. *The atmosphere surrounds the earth in layers, distinct by their temperature. The temperature decreases from the surface to the tropopause, then increases again until the stratopause, decreases to the mesopause, and slowly increases through the thermosphere. At thermospheric altitudes air is extremely thin, tapering into the void of space.*

Much of the weather on the earth's surface in temperate regions (30°N and S to 60°N and S) is controlled by a strong current of air called the *jet stream,* which acts as a steering force on weather systems at the surface. There are actually two jet streams. One, the *sub-tropical jet (STJ),* is found at altitudes near 20,000 feet at about latitude 30°N and S. The other, the *polar frontal jet (PFJ),* is found at an altitude near 15,000 ft near 60°N and S. Both jets flow from west to east, following a north-south oriented, snake-like path. Jet stream flow is so important to weather analysis and prediction that each day weather services worldwide map its flow at the 500-mb level and make this available, along with a variety of other charts, via weather facsimile broadcasts and internet services. Jet stream winds have been measured at 291 knots, reflecting both a high energy level and lack of friction.

The location of jet stream winds can often be deduced from satellite imagery, by noting movement of upper altitude cirrus clouds. Strongest jet stream flow is usually found along the poleward edge of a well-defined band of cirrus clouds, or along the poleward boundary of a line of transverse-banded cirrus.

General Circulation of the Atmosphere

When energy from the sun strikes the earth, about 29 percent is reflected back into space, 19 percent is absorbed by the atmosphere itself, and the remaining 52 percent reaches the earth's surface to be absorbed by land and water. The sun's rays pass through the atmosphere and warm the earth directly; the earth then radiates a portion of this energy in a longer wavelength, thus warming the atmosphere. It's worth remembering that water is thermally stable, absorbing and holding heat without substantial changes in temperature, whereas land is thermally unstable, absorbing and releasing heat quickly and with sharper changes of temperature. Weather patterns and systems over water tend, therefore, to be more predictable and stable.

Incoming and outgoing radiation must balance or the earth will become steadily warmer or cooler. There have been wide variations in heat energy balance over the earth's history, with various geologic eras of tropical and glacial climate. There are also energy cycles apparently related to sunspots or other solar phenomena, as well as regional and local variations.

Rays of the sun that strike the earth perpendicularly impart more energy per unit area than rays striking obliquely, as can be seen in Figure 20-2. Therefore, the equator receives more heat than polar regions. Studies confirm that at the equator more heat is received than is re-radiated away, and at the poles more is lost than is gained. If there were not some means of transferring heat from the equator to the poles, the equatorial regions would become hotter and hotter, and the poles ever colder. This transfer of heat is accomplished through movement of air (wind) and water (ocean currents).

If the earth did not rotate on its axis and had a uniform surface (either all land or all water), the air near the equator would heat and rise, creating an area of geographical low pressure, which would be filled by a flow of colder air from higher latitudes. In fact, three rotating bands of air, called Hadley cells, surround the earth and work together to move hot air away from the equator and cold air toward it. This circulation model is shown in Figure 20-3.

This *theoretical circulation,* however, is modified by the earth's rotation and the irregular disposition of water and landmasses over the earth's surface, of which some 70 percent is water. In addition, the earth's axis of rotation is tilted to its plane of orbit, causing annual regional variations in insolation. These factors have noticeable effects on the theoretical circulation. Instead of the simple circulation of the theoretical model, we have a complex and dynamic process, which largely accounts for our difficulty in making accurate long-term weather forecasts.

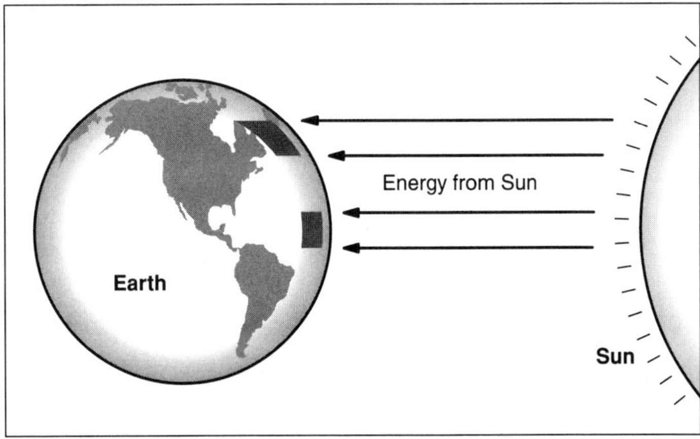

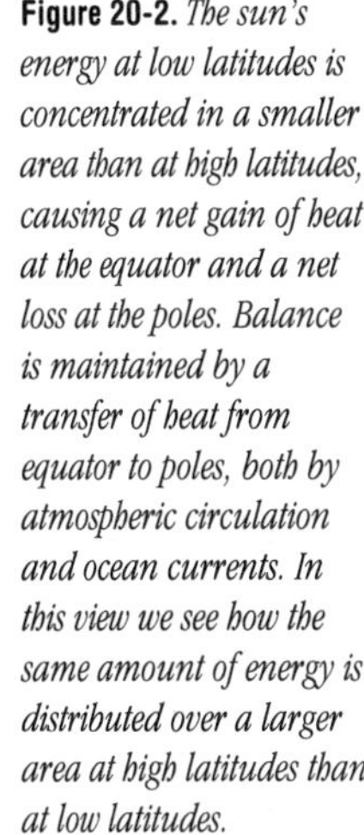

Figure 20-2. *The sun's energy at low latitudes is concentrated in a smaller area than at high latitudes, causing a net gain of heat at the equator and a net loss at the poles. Balance is maintained by a transfer of heat from equator to poles, both by atmospheric circulation and ocean currents. In this view we see how the same amount of energy is distributed over a larger area at high latitudes than at low latitudes.*

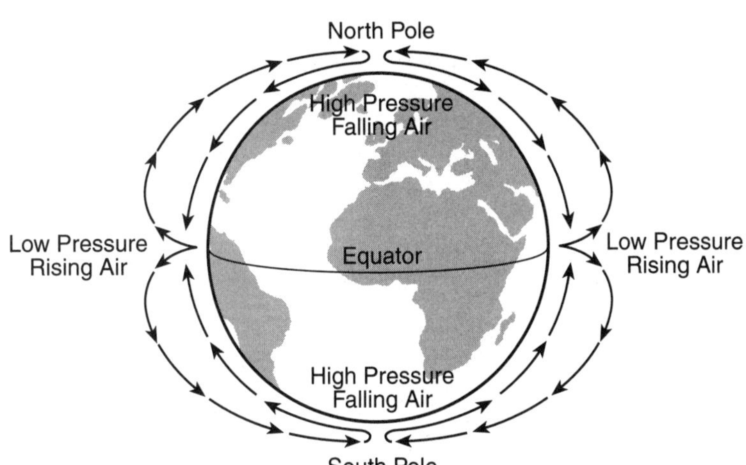

Figure 20-3. *In a theoretical model of earth's atmospheric circulation, the sun's energy would create warm, rising air and low pressures at the equator, causing a surface flow of cooler air from northern regions, and a high-altitude flow of warm air to replace it. Low pressures would form at the equator and highs at the poles. This is what actually happens, modified by a number of factors.*

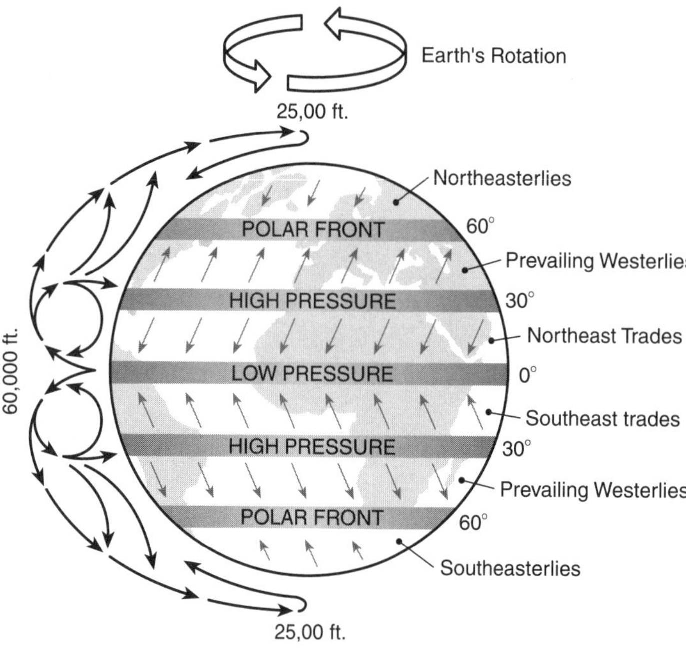

Figure 20-4. *The earth is divided into bands of prevailing winds, separated by areas of variable winds. These patterns are modifications of the theoretical circulation caused by the earth's rotation and the unequal distribution of land and water. Sailors today use these patterns for ocean voyages just as they have for centuries.*

Regional Circulation of the Atmosphere

Even given the variations, certain general rules of atmospheric circulation hold true, and knowledge of them can help us understand local weather patterns. For example, as the theoretical model predicts, atmospheric heating causes a more or less permanent area of low pressure about 15° of latitude wide on either side of the equator. Air is warmed and rises over this region, then flows north and south toward the polar regions. As this air rises away from the warm earth, it cools, and some of this cooled air descends back to earth in the region of 30° latitude north and south, forming an area of high pressure. Once reaching the earth's surface the air divides, with some moving north and some south. In the northern hemisphere this results in the northeasterly trade winds and the prevailing southwesterlies of temperate latitudes.

Not all the air that rises from the equatorial region descends at 30°N and 30°S. Some continues toward the poles, descending on arctic and antarctic regions, where high-pressure areas form. This cold, dense, polar air flows back toward the equator in a region of *prevailing easterlies,* northeast in the arctic and southeast in the antarctic.

Since air flows naturally from high to low pressure areas, the rising equatorial air is replaced by a constant surface flow from higher latitudes in the form of the *northeast* and *southeast trade winds.*

It's the earth's rotation that causes the easterly and westerly components of the prevailing winds, which would otherwise flow directly toward the equator. The earth rotates

---

The Coriolis force is the angular force that deflects matter moving across the surface of a spinning body. Imagine two points on the same meridian: one is at the equator and one is at 45° of latitude. They both complete a full rotation on the earth's surface every 24 hours, yet clearly, the point on the equator must travel farther to do so because the earth's circumference is larger there. Thus, objects on the equator have a higher speed of rotation than objects at higher latitudes, just as the center of a carousel spins more slowly than its perimeter. Now imagine a parcel of air (or water) moving northward from the equator. As it enters a region that rotates more slowly, its higher west-to-east velocity, imparted to it at the equator, will cause it to curve to the right.

Finally, imagine a parcel of air or water traveling equatorward from the north pole. It has little west-to-east velocity to begin with, so as it reaches faster-spinning lower-latitude regions, the earth will seem to rotate from beneath it, and it will once again curve to the right.

Another way to observe the Coriolis force is to put a marble in the center of a spinning phonograph record. It will trace a curved path to the outer edge as the record revolves beneath it. The Coriolis force on the earth is complicated by its spherical, not circular, surface, but the principle is the same.

---

underneath the moving air, imparting a motion to the right in the northern hemisphere and the left in the southern hemisphere. This motion, called the *Coriolis force,* also has important effects on the formation and movement of storms. Figure 20-4 shows the prevailing wind patterns of the earth.

Associated with the major prevailing circulation are various areas of more or less permanent high and low pressure. Permanent lows are roughly spaced—as might be expected—along the equator, while permanent highs lie over ocean areas at about 30°N and 30°S. These areas have a major influence on weather system development and movement in their respective regions. Figures 20-5 and 20-6 show the prevailing surface winds of the world, as well as areas of permanent high and low pressure for January–February and for July–August. Note the differences, caused by seasonal changes in the sun's declination.

Major Wind Patterns

The *general circulation* of the atmosphere creates certain persistent weather phenomena that sailors have noted for centuries. The bane of the world-traveling sailor is a region called the *doldrums,* aligned roughly along the equator and extending a few degrees either side of it. This is an area of rising warm air, heated by the sun and full of moisture evaporated from the warm tropical sea. The air cools as it rises, lowering the amount of moisture it can hold, releasing it in scattered thunderstorms. Between thunderstorms, the air is hot and sultry, winds are light and variable, and clouds are common. Because of the difficulty of sailing in light and variable winds punctuated with violent but short-lived storms, the doldrums have a deservedly poor reputation among sailors.

Lying next to the doldrums both north and south are belts of *trade winds,* which serve to replace the air that has risen out of the doldrums. Theoretically these winds would blow directly toward the equator, but because of the earth's rotation they are deflected to the right in the northern hemisphere and the left

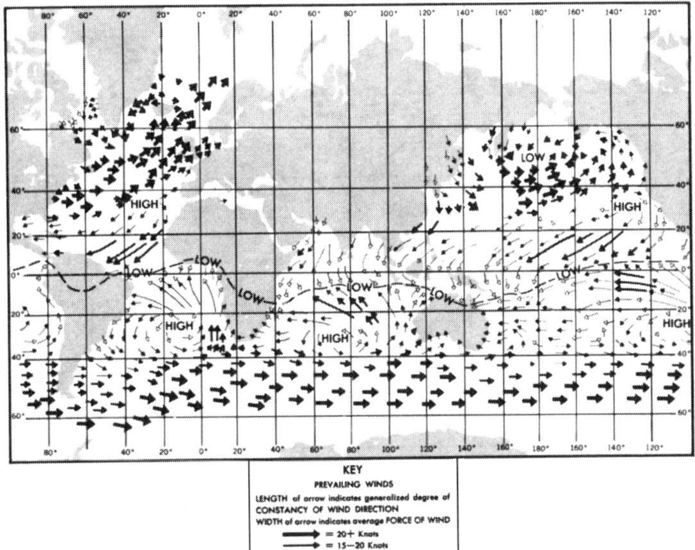

Figure 20-5. *Surface winds in January and February for the world. Note the semi-permanent lows along the equator, the highs at 30°N and 30°S, and the westerlies in the mid-latitudes, interrupted in the northern hemisphere by continents. The key explains the wind arrows.*

Figure 20-6. *Surface winds in July and August. Compare this figure to 20-5 and note the great persistence of the westerlies in the southern ocean between 40°S and 60°S, and the reversing monsoon in the Indian Ocean, which sailors have used for millennia.*

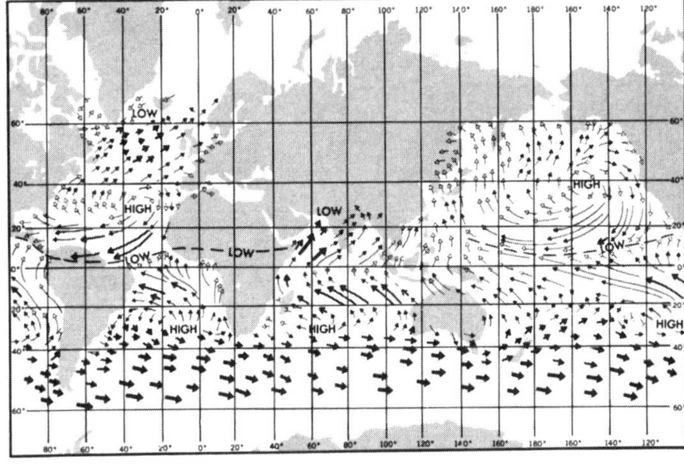

Sailors voyaging in the doldrums sometimes steer toward, not away from, thunderstorms as a means of collecting fresh water, washing down decks and persons, and finding wind. These isolated storms are seldom dangerous and pass quickly.

in the southern, resulting in the northeast and southeast trade winds. These winds blow persistently for days or weeks at a time, though they may be disrupted occasionally, and in certain areas and times may be little noticed when overcome by other factors. This is the area where tropical storms develop—hurricanes and typhoons. As the sun moves north and south in declination during the year, the trade winds move with it, such that in the northern hemisphere summer the southeast trades actually cross the equator.

The *horse latitudes* lie just poleward of the trade winds at about 30°N and S, and mark an area of descending air, replacing air that the trade winds have sent toward the equatorial low. Supposedly the region is named for the horses sailors threw overboard to save water as they lay becalmed, for this is a region of light and variable winds, generally calm seas, and relatively high atmospheric pressure. As with other regions, the horse latitudes vary in latitude with the changing annual declination of the sun.

Poleward from the horse latitudes are the *prevailing westerlies,* deflected as are the trade winds by the rotation of the earth. In this region there are marked differences between the northern and southern hemispheres, for in the north lie the major continental land masses—North America, Asia, most of Africa, and parts of South America. These areas disrupt the theoretical flow in a variety of ways. Deserts heat air masses; mountain ranges cause moving air masses to rise and release moisture; vast forests, plains, steppes, inland seas, and other regions induce regional changes in the normal westerly airflow. By contrast, the southern hemisphere in the region of the westerlies is largely free of continents, allowing the winds to sweep almost unaffected around the earth. This region, known as the *roaring forties* (referring to the latitude of 40°S) was the area sought by globe-circling sailing ships in the last century. West winds in this region can be periodically distorted by regional storms, which are themselves pushed ever eastward by the constant westerly flow.

Because cold air is denser than warm air, the air at the poles tends to flow southward from polar high pressure areas, deflected westward by the earth's rotation into the arctic *northeasterlies* in the north and the *southeasterlies* in the south. These winds meet the westerlies in a belt known as the *polar front,* where the relatively warmer westerlies rise over the south-flowing cold, dense polar air, releasing moisture in clouds and precipitation. Geophysically, the arctic and antarctic are opposites—the arctic being an ocean surrounded by land and the antarctic a landmass surrounded by ocean. Because of this, arctic winds are relatively weak and variable, modified by the relative thermal stability of the oceanic water underneath. The antarctic landmass, in contrast, causes intense cooling of the overlying air, which flows strongly northward off the high plateau, causing some of the strongest surface winds on earth.

Landmasses tend to lose and gain heat energy much faster than the oceans, which often moderate the rapid temperature and pressure swings. Even large lakes such as the Great Lakes can have this moderating effect, particularly on downwind areas.

If a landmass bounded by a large body of water is heated by the sun, overlying air will become warm and rise, to be replaced by an inflow from the sea. The most striking example of this phenomenon is the Asian *monsoon,* which in the northern summer draws Indian Ocean air strongly onto southern Asia, and in winter reverses to become a flow of cool terrestrial air out to sea. The dependable monsoon has been a driving force in the Indian Ocean sailing trade for over 3,000 years.

Air Masses

Uneven heating and cooling of the earth's surface results in uneven heating of the overlying air. This happens both on a local scale involving just a few acres, on a larger regional scale, and on a continental scale.

Local heating causes rising pockets of air called *updrafts,* much sought after by soaring pilots who use them to stay aloft in their sailplanes. Regional heating causes thunderstorms to form as warm moist air rises into the upper reaches of the troposphere, releasing moisture and large amounts of energy, often accompanied by violent weather.

Continental-scale heating of air forms huge blocks of air having uniform temperature, pressure, and humidity, called *air masses*. These air masses create the endless variety of weather in the temperate regions.

Air masses are classified according to whether they were formed over land or water as continental (c) or maritime (m), and are further classified according to the region of their formation, of which four are generally used:

- *Equatorial (E)*—the region around the equator
- *Tropical (T)*—the region of the trade winds
- *Polar (P)*—the high temperate and lower polar regions
- *Arctic/Antarctic (A)*—the true polar regions of permanent ice cover

These abbreviations are used by meteorologists to identify the type of air in an air mass, and from this the general characteristics of an air mass can be inferred. For example, an air mass designated "cP" (continental polar) would consist of cold, dense, dry, stable air, bringing clear skies, winds from poleward, and stable weather conditions. Conversely, an air mass designated "mT" would be warm, moist, and unstable, very likely with clouds and thunderstorms. (Equatorial air masses are always maritime.)

A tropical or polar air mass might be further labeled according to its temperature relative to the region over which it moves. Thus an "mT" air mass may be warmer (w) or cooler (k), and be designated "mTw" or "mTk."

An air mass that is cooler than the underlying surface can be expected to warm as it passes, resulting in currents of rising air and unstable conditions. An air mass that is warmer than the underlying surface can be expected to cool at its lower levels, sinking to the surface in a stable condition.

Winds of the World

Here are the world's major local and regional winds:

abroholos, *n.* A squall frequent from May through August between Cabo de Sao Tome and Cabo Frio on the coast of Brazil.

Bali wind. A strong east wind at the eastern end of Java.

barat, *n.* A heavy northwest squall in Manado Bay on the north coast of the island of Celebes, prevalent from December to February.

barber, *n.* A strong wind carrying damp snow or sleet and spray that freezes upon contact with objects, especially the beard and hair.

bayamo, *n.* A violent blast of wind, accompanied by vivid lightning, blowing from the land on the south coast of Cuba, especially near the Bight of Bayamo.

bentu de soli. An east wind on the coast of Sardinia.

bora, *n.* A cold, northerly wind blowing from the Hungarian basin into the Adriatic Sea.

borasco, *n.* A thunderstorm or violent squall, especially in the Mediterranean.

brave west winds. The strong, often stormy, winds from the west-northwest and northwest which blow at all seasons

---

(continued)

of the year between latitudes 40°S and 60°S.

brisa, briza, *n.* 1. A northeast wind which blows on the coast of South America or an east wind which blows on Puerto Rico during the trade wind season. 2. The northeast monsoon in the Philippines.

brisote, *n.* The northeast trade wind when it is blowing stronger than usual on Cuba.

brubu, *n.* A name for a squall in the East Indies.

bull's eye squall. A squall forming in fair weather, characteristic of the ocean off the coast of South Africa. It is named for the peculiar appearance of the small isolated cloud marking the top of the invisible vortex of the storm.

cape doctor. The strong southeast wind which blows on the South African coast. Also called *doctor.*

caver, kaver, *n.* A gentle breeze in the Hebrides.

chubasco, *n.* A very violent wind and rain squall attended by thunder and vivid lightning often encountered during the rainy season along the west coast of Central America.

churada, *n.* A severe rain squall in the Mariana Islands during the northeast monsoon. They occur from November to April or May, especially from January through March.

cierzo, *n.* See *mistral.*

collada, *n.* A strong wind (35 to 50 miles per hour or stronger) blowing from the north or northwest in the northern part of the Gulf of California and from the northeast in the southern part of the Gulf of California.

cordonazo, *n.* The "Lash of St. Francis." Name applied locally to southerly hurricane winds along the west coast of Mexico. The cordonazo is associated with tropical cyclones in the southeastern North Pacific Ocean. These storms may occur from May to November, but ordinarily affect the coastal areas most severely near or after the Feast of St. Francis, October 4.

coromell, n. A night land breeze prevailing from November to May at La Paz, near the southern extremity of the Gulf of California.

doctor, *n.* 1. A cooling sea breeze in the Tropics. 2. See *harmattan.* 3. The strong southeast wind which blows on the south African coast. Usually called *cape doctor.*

elephanta, *n.* A strong southerly or southeasterly wind which blows on the Malabar coast of India during the months of September and October and marks the end of the southwest monsoon.

etesian, *n.* A refreshing northerly summer wind of the Mediterranean, especially over the Aegean Sea.

gregale, *n.* A strong northeast wind of the central Mediterranean.

harmattan, *n.* The dry, dusty trade wind blowing off the Sahara Desert across the Gulf of Guinea and the Cape Verde Islands. Sometimes called the *doctor,* because of its supposed healthful properties.

kona storm. A storm over the Hawaiian Islands, characterized by strong southerly or southwesterly winds and heavy rains.

knik wind. A strong southeast wind in the vicinity of Palmer, Alaska, most frequent in the winter.

leste, *n.* A hot, dry, easterly wind of the Madeira and Canary Islands.

levanter, *n.* A strong easterly wind of the Mediterranean, especially in the Strait of Gibraltar, attended by cloudy, foggy, and sometimes rainy weather especially in winter.

levantera, *n.* A persistent east wind of the Adriatic, usually accompanied by cloudy weather.

levanto, *n.* A hot southeasterly wind which blows over the Canary Islands.

leveche, *n.* A warm wind in Spain, either a foehn or a hot southerly wind in advance of a low pressure area moving from the Sahara Desert. Called a *sirocco* in other parts of the Mediterranean area.

maestro, *n.* A northwesterly wind with fine weather which blows, especially in summer, in the Adriatic. It is most frequent on the western shore. This wind is also found on the coasts of Corsica and Sardinia.

Matanuska wind. A strong, gusty, northeast wind which occasionally occurs during the winter in the vicinity of Palmer, Alaska.

mistral, *n.* A cold, dry wind blowing from the north over the northwest coast of the Mediterranean Sea, particularly over the Gulf of Lions. Also called *cierzo.*

nashi, n'aschi, *n.* A northeast wind which occurs in winter on the Iranian coast of the Persian Gulf, especially near the entrance to the gulf, and also on the Makran coast. It is probably associated with an outflow from the central Asiatic anticyclone which extends over the high land of Iran. It is similar in character but less severe than the *bora.*

norte, *n.* A strong cold northeasterly wind which blows in Mexico and on the shores of the Gulf of Mexico. It results from an outbreak of cold air from the north. It is the Mexican extension of a norther.

northeaster, nor'easter, *n.* A northeast wind, particularly a strong wind or gale associated with cold rainy weather. In the U.S., nor'easters generally occur on the north side of late-season low pressure systems which pass off the Atlantic seaboard, bringing onshore gales to the region north of the low. Combined with high tides, they can be very destructive.

norther, *n.* A northerly wind. In the southern United States, especially in Texas (Texas norther) in the Gulf of Mexico, in the Gulf of Panama away from the coast, and in central America (the norte), the norther is a strong cold wind from the northeast to northwest. It occurs between November and April, freshening during the afternoon and decreasing at night. It is a cold air outbreak associated with the southward movement of a cold anticyclone. It is usually preceded by a warm and cloudy or rainy spell with southerly winds. The norther comes as a rushing blast and brings a sudden drop of temperature of as much as 25°F in 1 hour or 50°F in 3 hours in winter. The California norther is a strong, very dry, dusty, northerly wind which blows in late spring, summer and early fall in the valley of California or on the west coast when pressure is high over the mountains to the north. It lasts from 1 to 4 days. The dryness is due to adiabatic warming during descent. In summer it is very hot. The Portuguese norther is the beginning of the trade wind west of Portugal. The term is used for a strong north wind on the coast of Chile which blows occasionally in summer. In southeast Australia, a hot dry wind from the desert is called a norther.

papagayo, *n.* A violet northeasterly fall wind on the Pacific coast of Nicaragua and Guatemala. It consists of the cold air mass of a norte which has overridden the mountains of Central America. See also *tehuantepecer.*

shamal, *n.* A northwesterly wind blowing over Iraq and the Persian Gulf, in summer, often strong during the day, but decreasing during the night.

sharki, *n.* A southeasterly wind which sometimes blows in the Persian Gulf.

sirocco, n. A warm wind of the Mediterranean area, either a foehn or a hot southerly wind in advance of a low pressure area moving from the Sahara or Arabian deserts. Called *leveche* in Spain.

southeaster, sou'easter, *n.* A southeasterly wind, particularly a strong wind or gale.

(continued)

southwester, sou'wester, *n.* A southwest wind, particularly a strong wind or gale.

squamish, *n.* A strong and often violent wind occurring in many of the fjords of British Columbia. Squamishes occur in those fjords oriented in a northeast-southwest or east-west direction where cold polar air can be funneled westward. They are notable in Jervis, Toba, and Bute inlets and in Dean Channel and Portland Canal. Squamishes lose their strength when free of the confining fjords and are not noticeable 15 to 20 miles offshore.

Suestado, *n.* A storm with southeast gales, caused by intense cyclonic activity off the coasts of Argentina and Uruguay, which affects the southern part of the coast of Brazil in the winter.

sumatra, *n.* A squall with violent thunder, lightning, and rain, which blows at night in the Malacca Straits, especially during the southwest monsoon. It is intensified by strong mountain breezes.

tehuantepecer, *n.* A violent squally wind from north or north-northeast in the Gulf of Tehuantepec (south of southern Mexico) in winter. It originates in the Gulf of Mexico as a norther which crosses the isthmus and blows through the gap between the Mexican and Guatemalan mountains. It may be felt up to 100 miles out to sea. See also *papagayo.*

tramontana, *n.* A northeasterly or northerly wind occurring in winter off the west coast of Italy. It is a fresh wind of the fine weather mistral type.

vardar, *n.* A cold fall wind blowing from the northwest down the Vardar valley in Greece to the Gulf of Salonica. It occurs when atmospheric pressure over eastern Europe is higher than over the Aegean Sea, as is often the case in winter. Also called *vardarac.*

vardarac, *n.* See *vardar.*

whirly, *n.* A small violent storm, a few yards to 100 yards or more in diameter, frequent in Antarctica near the time of the equinoxes.

white squall. A sudden, strong gust of wind coming up without warning, noted by whitecaps or white, broken water; usually seen in whirlwind form in clear weather in the tropics.

williwaw, *n.* A sudden blast of wind descending from a mountainous coast to the sea, especially in the vicinity of either the Strait of Magellan or the Aleutian Islands.

Fronts

Air masses move from place to place across the earth, pushed by prevailing winds, steered by jet streams, and twisted by the Coriolis effect. There is often a line or zone of separation between a moving air mass and the air it is replacing, known as a *front* or *frontal zone*. In some cases the zone may be hundreds of miles wide, resulting in a gradual change in conditions as the front passes. Often, however, when the front is narrow, the change is dramatic and results in line squalls and thunderstorms accompanied by a dramatic and sudden wind shift and the immediate inflow of cooler air.

A *front* is the leading edge of an advancing air mass. It can be warm or cold, and signifies a change in the weather, which may be gradual or dramatic, depending on the degree of difference between the advancing air mass and the one it is replacing. Cold fronts tend to move faster than warm fronts due to several factors: a cold front has a more vertical front edge, which concentrates energy and reduces friction caused by contact with land. Also, a cold front displaces air by wedging underneath, as constrasted with a warm front which rides up and over air it encounters.

A front is not a rigidly defined line, but rather a transition zone. Winds associated with the pressure differential between the two masses cause a great deal of mixing in the atmosphere, which prevents the formation of rigidly defined boundaries. Nevertheless, for convenience, meteorologists speak of the *frontal surface* as if it were a well-defined, two-dimensional area. On the ground, the change that occurs as a cold air mass displaces a warm one usually takes several hours, although much more sudden changes are sometimes observed.

Most frontal activity occurs between a cold air mass and a warm air mass, with the leading edge of the cold, dense air mass wedging its way underneath the lighter warm air mass. The frontal surface is not vertical in extent, but slopes very gently, at angles of 1:50 to 1:250 in cross section. (Slope refers to the amount of rise in the frontal boundary per horizontal distance. That is, a slope of 1:100 means that for one hundred miles of distance there will be one mile of vertical rise in the frontal boundary.)

Because air masses will differ in temperature, humidity, pressure, and dew point, one can expect the weather to change as a front passes.

Most strong weather systems are generated along the polar front, which normally exists between 40° and 60° latititude, depending on season and local conditions, in a process known as *frontogenesis*. Strong weather systems develop when there is a relatively large difference between polar and temperate airmasses.

In a typical scenario for the northern U.S., a mass of cPk air moves southeastward over the North American continent out of Canada, preceded by a cold front. South of this cold front is a northward moving warm front, usually the leading edge of an advancing warm air mass drawn up from the Gulf of Mexico.

An area of low pressure will normally form when a cold and warm front meet under an upper level jet stream trough. Under these conditions, warm air is uplifted by the intrusion of sinking cold air, which draws in warm, moist air from southern regions. Winds circulate around this area of uplifting, but instead of moving directly toward the center of low pressure, are curved by the Coriolis force. As warm, unstable air rises it releases moisture, forming clouds and rain along the warm frontal zone.

A cold air mass gradually overtakes the warm air being drawn northward around the low's center. Since cold air is denser than warm air, it forces itself beneath the warm air, causing the warm air to rise. This warm air, rapidly forced aloft and cooled, releases its moisture in thunderstorms and rain showers. As a low pressure deepens, the isobars become increasingly tighter and circular, and winds increase.

As a low moves eastward, its center becomes more clearly defined, with the advancing cold air mass steadily overtaking the slower warm air ahead of it. Eventually the cold front catches up to the warm front, resulting in an *occluded* or stationary front. A low continues to move generally eastward with the cold front, further overriding the warm front. Eventually the low pressure center moves into the northern reaches of the North Atlantic Ocean and dissipates.

The eight scenarios in Figure 20-7 each contain two views representing progressive 12-hour phases of a typical Northern Hemi-

---

Isobars *are lines of equal atmospheric pressure, a standard feature of weather maps that help define the limits and strength of lows and highs. Air flows toward low pressure areas and away from highs, but is deflected due to the Coriolis force and friction with the earth's surface to such an extent that the resultant winds tend to flow parallel to isobars, albeit angled inward around lows and outward around highs. Isobars are invaluable in depicting weather phenomena and predicting weather for a particular area. Wind speed is proportional to the* pressure gradient *as indicated by isobar spacing. Crowded isobars indicate a strong gradient, while widely separated isobars reveal a gentle pressure gradient. A geostrophic wind scale is used to calculate wind speed from isobar spacing in the event wind speed is not indicated. When isobars curve back upon themselves to form closed circles, a high or low pressure area has formed.*

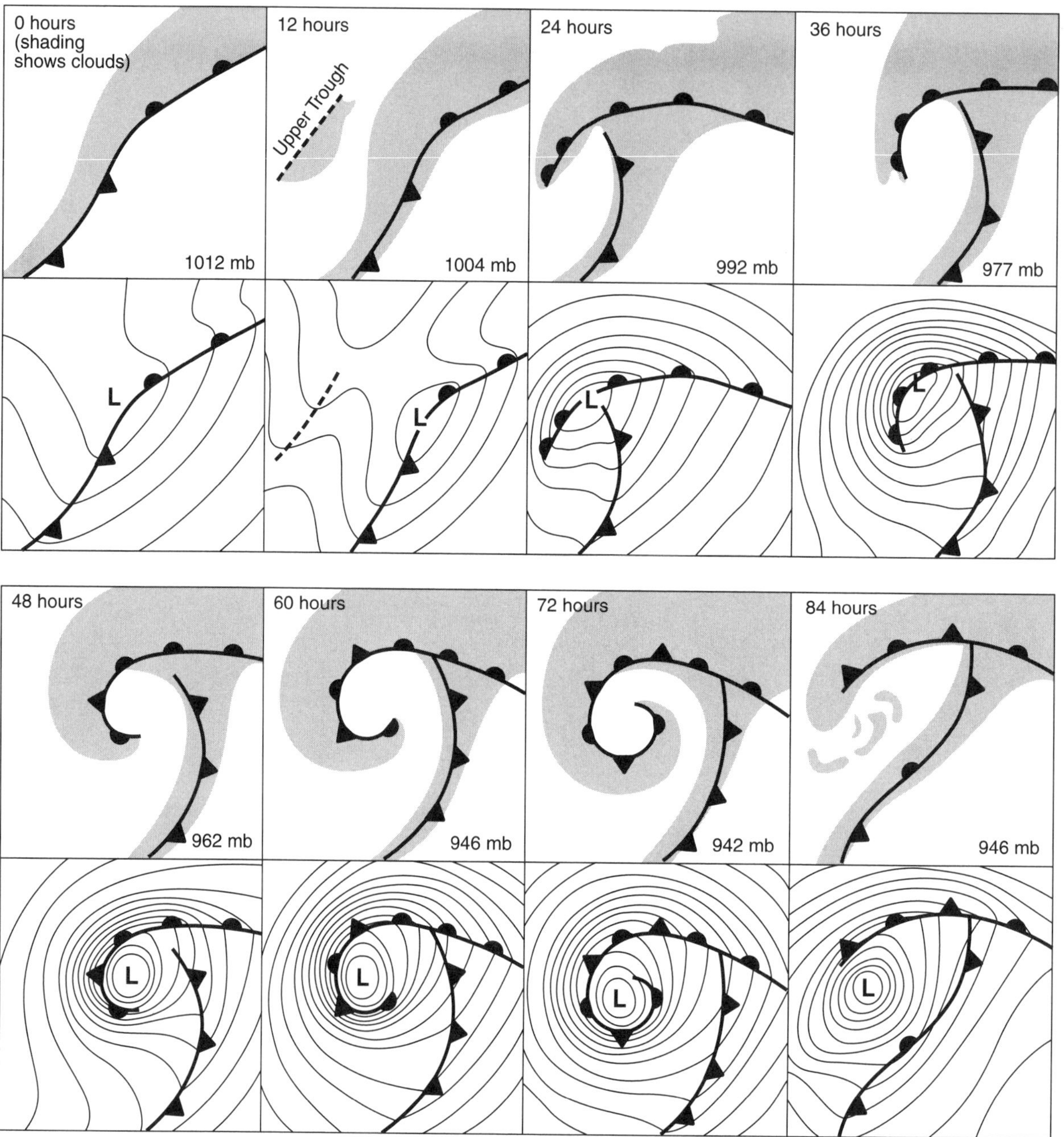

Figure 20-7. *Twelve-hour phases of a typical Northern Hemisphere Atlantic Low. A low begins as a wave in the isobars, with cold air advancing on warm air. As more and more isobars close around the low, winds increase. At maturity an area of warm air is secluded behind the cold front. This squally area will gradually weaken and dissipate. (Courtesy Michael Carr/Ocean Strategies, Inc.; redrawn by Kim Downing)*

sphere Atlantic Low. In the two views, the top shows cloud coverage and surface front locations and the bottom shows surface pressure and front locations. Using the surface fronts as a common feature in each pair, a navigator can correlate cloud cover, wind direction, wind speed, and the intensity of the low. A good navigator should be able to identify and describe each of these features.

A characteristic sequence of cloud types accompanies the passage of a front. (This sequence assumes a low's center passes poleward of an observer.) At first, wispy cirrus clouds appear in the west, moving eastward over the observer. These cirrus clouds gradually become cirrostratus as they thicken. Next come altostratus and altocumulus, followed by nimbostratus. Each type is lower and thicker than the last. The arrival of nimbostratus brings steady rain.

Winds in this scenario begin with light southerly or southeasterly breezes, increasing and becoming south to southwesterly as a cold front approaches and clouds lower. As a front passes, winds shift, sometimes very rapidly, into the northwest; skies clear and cold, dry air replaces the warm, moist air.

If an observer is poleward of a low (the low passing south of the observer in the northern hemisphere), the sequence of events is different. At first the warm front causes low clouds and showers, with winds light and variable. As the low center approaches, winds increase, becoming easterly. Clouds thicken and rain increases. As the low passes directly south of the observer, winds are strongly east to northeasterly and rain is steady. This is the classic winter "nor'easter" experienced along the northern Atlantic coast of North America. As a low passes, clouds gradually rise and periods of sunshine lead to gradually clearing skies as high pressure builds in behind the dissipating low. (See Figure 20-8.)

This process of advancing cold and warm fronts takes place in a succession in the temperate regions of both northern and southern

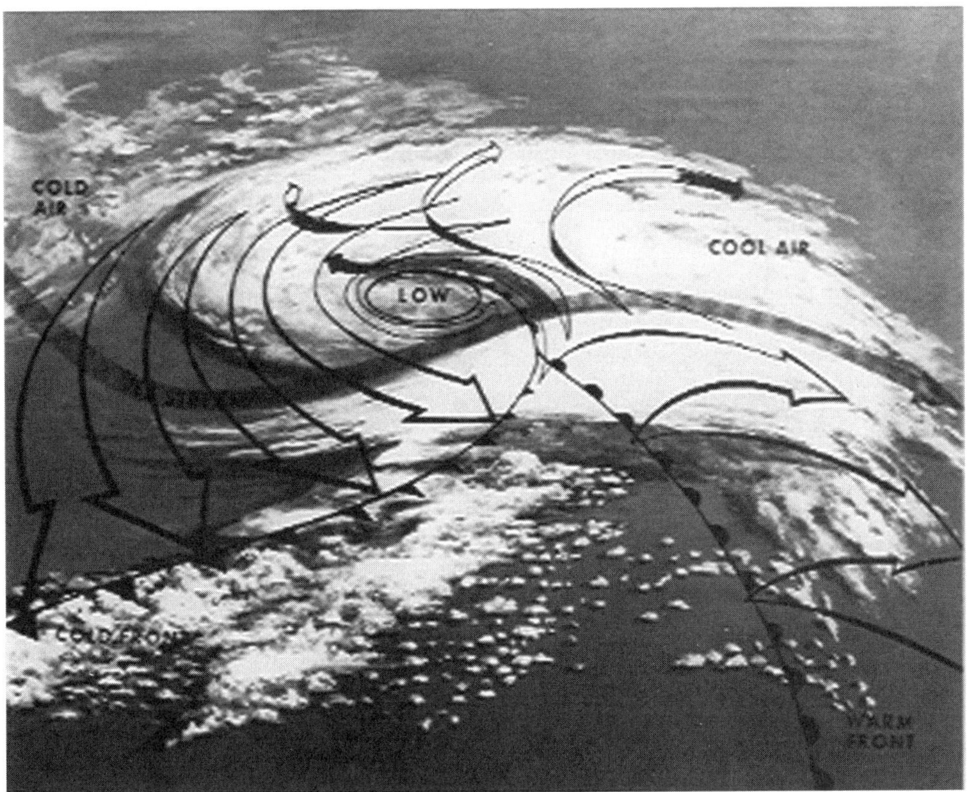

Figure 20-8. *A typical low pressure system in the northern hemisphere is preceded by a warm front and accompanied by rain and when conditions are right, by thunderstorms, hail, and tornadoes. Cold, stable air flows in behind the cold front, and the whole system is driven eastward by high-altitude jet stream winds. (Courtesy NOAA/NWS)*

hemispheres, with storm tracks moving equatorward in winter and poleward in summer, following the jet stream motion, which in turn is affected by the Sun's declination.

Cyclonic Storms

Low pressure areas tend to draw in air from adjacent higher pressure areas, just as air from high pressure areas tends to flow toward lows. These winds are deflected by the Coriolis force and become circular in nature, clockwise around highs and counterclockwise around lows in the northern hemisphere. (In the southern hemisphere these directions are reversed.) From this relationship it is possible to locate a low's center using *Buys Ballots Law,* also known as the *baric wind law.* This law states that if an observer in the northern hemisphere faces directly into the wind created by a low pressure system, the low's center will bear from 090° to 135° relative; that is, it is to the right and slightly behind the observer (directions are reversed for the southern hemisphere).

The circular nature of a storm associated with a low pressure area, with winds spiraling in toward the low center, defines it as a *cyclonic storm* or *cyclone.* Winds spiraling outward from a high pressure area define it as an *anticyclone.* Cyclones in tropical areas may strengthen dramatically to become *hurricanes* or *typhoons,* different names for the same meterological phenomenon. Cyclones in temperate regions are often called *extratropical cyclones* to distinguish them from their more violent tropical cousins.

Thunderstorms, Squalls, and Squall Lines

Thunderstorms are local storms, but are often associated with larger frontal systems. They are caused by the rapid rising of warm, moist air into the upper reaches of the atmosphere. When this rising air cools, it no longer can hold as much moisture, and water vapor condenses on microscopic particles in the atmosphere and falls as rain. Raindrops often encounter an updraft as they fall, in which case they are carried upward into freezing temperatures where they become ice. This may occur one or more times, adding a layer of ice each time until finally the frozen drop falls as a hailstone.

The upper reaches of a thunderstorm are often in temperatures of –40°C (–40°F), and at altitudes of 40,000 feet and greater. Slush and snow particles are often encountered at this altitude, but these will usually melt into rain before reaching the earth's surface. In some desert thunderstorms, rain may evaporate before reaching the earth.

Thunderstorms not associated with cold fronts are most common in the late afternoon of summer days, when the sun has heated the ground all day, which in turn radiates heat to the air above. This heated air rises and cools, causing condensation and precipitation. Figure 20-9a depicts a mature thunderstorm with associated rain.

Winds in thunderstorms can be violent and sudden, but are usually of short duration, perhaps only a few minutes. Usually the first wind felt from a nearby thunderstorm is a cool or cold outflow of air from the storm's base. This is the product of a *downdraft* of dense, cold air from the upper reaches of the storm, which has fallen to earth and fanned out from the storm's center. Since a thunderstorm is not cyclonic in nature, predicting wind direction in its vicinity is difficult; air moves out in all directions as it makes contact with the ground upon descending.

A well-found vessel need not fear a thunderstorm (except for the possibility of lightning strikes). Winds seldom last long enough to raise a sea, though gusts can be strong and are credited with knockdowns of sailboats that have kept on large amounts of sail. However, thunderstorms preceding frontal systems are a signal that the front will be arriving soon.

Precautions should be taken at the approach of squally weather, including shortening sail, securing hatches and portholes, stowing loose gear, and in general readying the vessel as if for a more lengthy storm. It may be necessary to slow the boat or change course during the worst of the squall to lessen its effects.

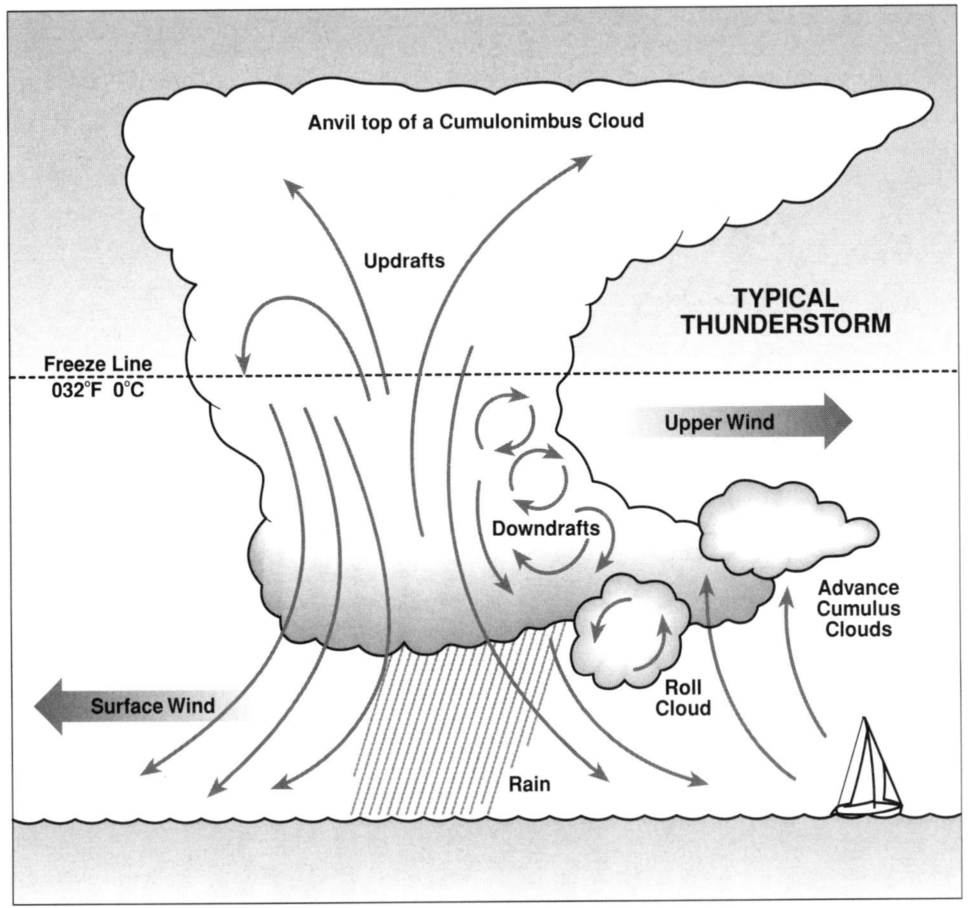

Figure 20-9a. *A thunderstorm begins with warm, moist air rising and cooling below its dew point, at which point the water vapor condenses. As the concentration of condensed water droplets increases, rain begins to fall. (See Figure 20-9b) Continuing stronger updrafts lift the warm air to great heights, and may lift water droplets repeatedly into below-freezing regions, forming hail. A thunderstorm may pose a threat to an unprepared small boat, but not to a well-found vessel. This storm is a young one which may become much larger and more dangerous as it matures. See Figure 20-15.*

A *squall* is an intense, localized wind, which may or may not be associated with a larger weather system. It is usually fast-moving and dramatic, beginning with strong winds and low, fast-moving clouds, and usually including rain, which may be torrential for brief periods.

When several squally areas develop along an advancing cold front, they may merge to form a *squall line,* sometimes preceded by a *roll cloud,* which resembles a long string of rolled-up cotton, as seen in Figure 20-10. Squall lines may precede a cold front by a hundred miles or more. Blasts of cold air associated with squall lines are downdrafts that have cooled in the upper atmosphere and released moisture as rain.

Navigationally, a squall is not usually a problem at sea (though it may be a safety hazard), although it is likely to disrupt a DR track, particularly for sailing vessels, which may have to tack, change course, or shorten sail. Inshore or in coastal waters, one should pay particular attention to the vessel's position when a squall approaches, as visibility may lessen for a while. In coastwise navigation, plot a good fix just before visibility is reduced, and maintain steady courses and speeds, if possible, to keep an accurate DR track. It's best to keep an accurate and precise log of courses and speeds if forced to divert from the DR track, so the vessel's position can later be accurately updated.

Local Winds

In addition to winds created by the general circulation of the atmosphere (such as trade winds) and those associated with moving high

Figure 20-9b. *A rain-shaft—rain hurled to earth by explosive downdrafts called microbursts—grows from convection in storms. (Courtesy NOAA/NWS)*

Figure 20-10. *A squall line is often preceded by a roll cloud and accompanied by rapid wind shifts and strong gusts. It may precede a cold front by 100 miles or more, or may occur at the frontal boundary. For the navigator, this is the time to get a good fix on the chart and prepare for bad weather. (Courtesy NOAA/NWS)*

A particularly dangerous type of storm often occurs in the autumn and spring off the northern U.S. Atlantic coast. Referred to by meteorologists as a *rapidly intensifying low,* this type of storm (formerly known as a *meteorological bomb*) is precipitated by a cold, early-winter (or late-winter) arctic air mass moving across the middle U.S. and then offshore over the Gulf Stream. When cold, dry air meets warm, moist air over the Gulf Stream rapid uplifting occurs, causing an area of low pressure to form. This disturbance rapidly deepens and intensifies if an upper level trough exists in the jet stream and these upper level winds are blowing at 105 knots or greater. Here is what happens: Strong upper-level jet stream winds pull out the rising warm air as it is pushed aloft by the invading cold surface air. When the jet stream winds are moving at speeds of 105 knots or greater, they tend to pull out air aloft faster than it can flow in on the surface. This causes a rapid drop in surface pressure and a dramatic increase in cyclonic winds, with steep, confused seas. Hence the name "rapidly intensifying low."

The seas are made more dangerous by the Gulf Stream current itself, particularly on the northwestern side of the low, where winds from the northeast blow directly into the northeasterly-flowing Gulf Stream. Wind against current always causes steep seas, and in the ocean, the effect is pronounced. High, steep, and breaking, these seas have caused the foundering of many well-found ships and are deadly for small craft. Because of its association with the northern edge or wall of the Gulf Stream, the phenomenon is often called the *North Wall Effect.*

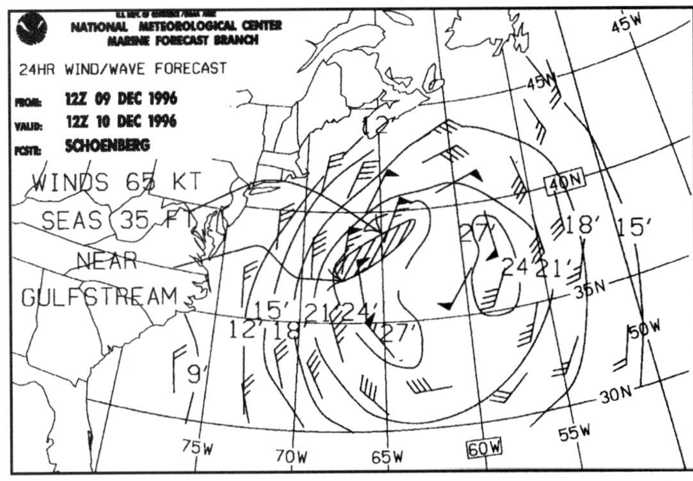

Figure 20-11. *A 24-hour wind and wave forecast from the National Meteorological Center showing the North Wall Effect: winds at 65 knots, seas 35 feet.*

and low pressure areas (such as cyclones), various winds of local origin are common. These winds often reinforce or deflect larger wind systems.

The most common of the local winds are the *sea breeze* and the *land breeze,* a kind of mini-monsoon. Along many coastlines of the world, particularly in the doldrums and subtropics, the land becomes warmer than the adjacent sea as the sun rises high in the sky each day. By late morning, this causes the air over the land to heat up and begin to rise, to be replaced by a flow of cool air from the ocean. As the sun descends in late afternoon, the land and sea become more equal in temperature, and the sea breeze dies away. At night the opposite occurs. The land cools more rapidly than the sea, causing the air above it to become more dense and flow toward the sea. This land breeze dies away toward dawn. Land and sea breezes seldom extend more than a very few miles either landward or seaward from the coast.

Some winds are caused entirely by local topography. In some areas winds commonly blow up the slopes of rising mountains, and are called *anabolic winds.* The opposite, called a *katabatic wind,* flows down a slope. There are two types of katabatic winds, known as *foehn* winds and *fall winds.*

The foehn wind is the result of air masses crossing mountain barriers. As the air rises

Figure 20-12. *A waterspout is the same thing as a tornado, occurring over water instead of land. However, it is not usually as severe as a tornado. Notice the bands of wind spiraling in toward the center of this waterspout, seen on the sea surface, and the central core of the spout itself. (NOAA photo by Dr. Joseph A. Golden, 1969)*

Any gas cools as it expands and warms as it contracts. (This is why ice forms around the nozzle of a tank of compressed gas as it is released, and diver's air tanks become hot when filled). Air, though a mixture of gases, acts like a single gas in this respect; it cools as it expands and warms as it contracts. In the case of foehn winds, the cool dry air flowing down the leeward side of a mountain range is compressed by its change in altitude from higher to lower, which raises the pressure of air pressing down from above. It does not tend to rise as warm air usually does because it is cooler and more stable than the air it replaces.

over the mountains, moisture condenses out as precipitation on the windward side. Crossing the mountains and continuing down the other side, the now-dry air is warmed by compression as it flows downhill.

Foehn winds may occur at any time and may last for a few hours or several days. Only one area in North America has a foehn wind that affects boaters—the *Santa Ana* wind of southern California, which can reach gale force.

A *fall wind* results when cold air is temporarily trapped behind a mountain range. It can then spill over the top or through a pass and blow downslope toward the sea, sometimes reaching gale force.

A *waterspout* is a small tornado that occurs at sea. Though most waterspouts are formed and dissipate entirely at sea, on rare occasions a land-formed tornado passes out over the water. Waterspouts should always be considered dangerous to small craft (though small ones may not be) and should be avoided, but are not generally as large or violent as tornadoes on land. (See Figure 20-12.)

Weather Observations

To understand weather at sea, one must know something of the measurements used to quantify weather and the terms used to describe it. Temperature, pressure, humidity, cloud type, and other factors are the physical properties of weather. Each has a different standard of measurement and method of interpretation.

Air temperature is a measure of the amount of heat energy of air. There are several temperature scales in use. The *Fahrenheit scale* is based on pure water freezing at 32° and boiling at 212°. On the *centigrade* or *Celsius scale,* water freezes at 0° and boils at 100°. On the Celsius-based *Kelvin scale* 0° is –273.16° Celsius, called *absolute zero,* and represents the complete absence of heat or kinetic energy (that is, no molecular motion). Weather professionals often use the Celsius scale for scientific work, though most American forecasters use the Fahrenheit scale.

Atmospheric pressure is measured by a *barometer,* of which there are two principal kinds—the *mercury* and the *aneroid.* In the mercury barometer, a tube filled with mercury is inverted into a bowl of mercury. The pressure of the air will support a column of mercury about 30 inches high. The aneroid (meaning "no air") barometer consists of a thin metal cell containing a partial vacuum. Changes in atmospheric pressure cause the cell to expand or contract slightly, and levers amplify this motion so it can be read on a dial.

The unit of measure of atmospheric pressure is the *millibar,* representing a pressure of 1,000 dynes per square centimeter. (A *dyne* is the force required to accelerate a mass of one gram at a rate of one centimeter per second per second.) *Inches* and *millimeters* of mercury are also used to measure pressure, but are not usually used by weather professionals except for public consumption.

A *barograph* is a recording barometer, offering a graphic representation of pressure changes over time. (See Figure 20-13.). While useful and interesting on small craft, they are delicate and require continuous maintenance.

Barometers are sensitive instruments; they are subject to a number of errors due to gravity, temperature, height, and mechanical differences. While it is best to have a barometer professionally adjusted before proceeding to

Figure 20-13. *A barograph is a recording barometer, which records barometer readings for a week. While very useful aboard small craft for weather prediction, it is delicate and requires weekly maintenance which consists of winding the clock, fitting new paper, and inking the stylus. (Courtesy Weems and Plath)*

sea, what is really relevant is the change in pressure over time and not the absolute reading. Small-craft navigators can usually get a current reading from the nearest Coast Guard station or airport, which will be accurate enough if you're not more than a few miles away. Current barometer readings are a part of nearly every broadcast weather report and forecast.

Humidity is a measure of the amount of moisture (water vapor, the gaseous form of water) contained in the air. Air can contain in evaporated form a certain amount of water vapor based on its temperature, warmer air being able to hold more than cold. Therefore the amount of water vapor in air can be measured in absolute terms or in relative terms—relative to the temperature.

Relative humidity is a measure of the water vapor in the air expressed as a percentage of the amount the air can hold at a given temperature. It is relative humidity that determines the likelihood of precipitation, fog, and other weather phenomena affecting navigation. As air temperature decreases, relative humidity increases because the air is able to hold less water vapor at the reduced temperature. When the relative humidity reaches 100 percent, any further cooling of the air will force it to release moisture. At the sea surface this will cause fog, and at altitude it will cause clouds.

Humidity is measured with a hygrometer, of which the most common type is the psychrometer. This consists of two standard thermometers, one of which has its bulb surrounded by a small piece of muslin fabric. When this fabric is wetted and well ventilated, the thermometers register two different readings, known as the dry bulb and wet bulb temperatures. These figures are used to enter tables to determine the relative humidity and dew point. These calculations are of little use to the small-craft operator, being of little value for forecasting without a great deal more information.

Wind has two components—speed and direction. Wind speed is measured with an *anemometer* and direction is expressed as the direction from which the wind is blowing. A moving vessel experiences an *apparent wind* that is modified from the true wind by its own

Since air cools at a certain rate as it rises, known as the standard lapse rate—2°C or 3.6°F per thousand feet—it is possible to calculate the base altitude of clouds by knowing the relative humidity of the air mass they form in. The altitude at which the air reaches saturation is where clouds will begin to form. In order to condense, there must be something on which to condense, since water vapor cannot condense onto nothing. At the surface we see this as dew on cool objects, or "sweat" on the surface of a cold drink glass. In the atmosphere, clouds condense onto minute particles of dust. If there are insufficient particles in the air, it may become supersaturated.

speed and its course relative to the wind. If a vessel heads directly into a 15-knot breeze at a speed of ten knots, the apparent wind will be 25 knots at 000° relative bearing. If the vessel then heads in the opposite direction, the wind will be 5 knots from 180° relative. A vessel heading other than directly into or away from the wind will experience some modification of wind speed and direction according to its motion relative to the wind. The apparent wind will always be forward of the true wind due to the vessel's own speed.

While professional mariners often use a graphic device called a *maneuvering board* to calculate the true wind, boaters need only feel the wind or look at the surface of the water and across the compass to find wind speed and direction accurately enough for most purposes.

The *Beaufort wind scale* was developed by Admiral Sir Francis Beaufort in 1806 in order to standardize the observations of British sea captains. Slightly modified over the years, it has become the standard by which all mariners measure and express wind speed at sea.

The Beaufort scale is listed below, and color views of the sea at different Beaufort numbers can be seen in the color plate section beginning after page 276 of this book.

Beaufort Number	Wind Speed (knots)	Sea State
0	0	Sea like a mirror
1	1–3	Ripples like scales, no crests
2	4–6	Small wavelets, crests glassy and do not break
3	7–10	Large wavelets, crests break, whitecaps begin
4	11–16	Small waves, numerous whitecaps
5	17–21	Moderate and longer waves; whitecaps and spray
6	22–27	Larger waves, numerous whitecaps, much spray
7	28–33	Sea heaps up, waves break, foam blows in streaks
8	34–40	Moderate waves of greater length, foam blows in long streaks
9	41–47	High waves, rolling sea, dense streaks of foam, spray reduces visibility
10	48–55	Very high waves, overhanging crests, sea white with foam, visibility reduced
11	56–63	Exceptionally high waves, sea covered with foam, visibility poor
12	64+	Waves tremendous, air filled with spray, sea white with foam, visibility nil

These photographs, provided courtesy of Environment Canada, were taken aboard the Canadian vessels *Vancouver* and *Quadra* on Ocean Station PAPA between 1976 and 1981. They represent steady-state sea conditions for many hours.

Clouds

Clouds are formed by the condensation of water vapor in the air around microscopic particles, and are reliable indicators of atmospheric conditions. They are classified, based on altitude, into three principal families:

- ***High:*** above 20,000 feet and usually composed of ice crystals
- ***Middle:*** 6,500 to 20,000 feet and composed primarily of water droplets
- ***Low:*** less than 6,500 feet

There are ten principal types of clouds, designated with variations of descriptive Latin words:

- ***Cirrus***—"lock of hair"
- ***Cumulus***—"a pile or heap"
- ***Stratus***—"to flatten or cover with a layer"
- ***Alto***—"high"
- ***Nimbus***—"rainy cloud"

High-Level Clouds

The high clouds types are cirrus, cirrocumulus, and cirrostratus. *Cirrus* clouds are composed of ice crystals and are the highest clouds seen. They resemble cotton balls pulled apart, wispy white and veil-like, often making long streaks across the sky called "mare's tails." Though cirrus are generally known as fair-weather clouds, they are often the precursors of storms a day or more in the future. Because of their altitude—up to 50,000 feet—cirrus clouds are often illuminated by the sun's light before sunrise and after sunset; observed from the earth's surface, they contribute to colorful sunrises and sunsets.

Cirrocumulus clouds are, as the name implies, accumulations of cirrus clouds, seen as flakes or waves high in the sky. These, too, are ice-crystal clouds, and sometimes appear as waves of varying thicknesses; sometimes they resemble the scales of a fish and are known as a "mackerel sky." Like cirrus, cirrocumulus are fair-weather clouds, but often precede bad weather.

Cirrostratus are cirrus clouds composed of ice crystals in a thin layer, ranging in thickness from almost unseen to a tangled web of varying thicknesses. These are the clouds which form halos around the sun and moon.

Mid-Level Clouds

The mid-level cloud types are altocumulus and altostratus. *Altocumulus* clouds are mid-level, vertically developed clouds seen as ball-like patches resembling scattered or loosely grouped cotton balls. Sometimes they are seen as long parallel rolls of thick cloud interspersed with patches of clear sky, but more commonly are uneven masses sometimes mistaken for stratocumulus. Altocumulus may signal a change to unsettled weather, indicated by their vertical development. A peculiar type is the altocumulus lenticularis (Figure 20-14), which appears like a lens over high hills and mountains.

Altostratus cloud appears as a gray sheet or veil, causing the sun or moon to appear with a *corona* (a bright ring around the circumference) when seen through it. (If a halo is seen instead of a corona, the cloud is cirrostratus.) If these clouds become lower and thicker or if ragged clouds form below them, rain is likely.

Low-Level Clouds

Low clouds are one of five types—stratocumulus, stratus, nimbostratus, cumulus, or cumulonimbus. Stratocumulus clouds appear as soft, low, gray masses moving with the wind. Forming largely during the day, they vary in altitude according to local conditions and are usually followed by clear night skies.

Stratus clouds form a low, uniform layer, with the cloud base often only a few hundred feet high. It may be thin and veil-like or thick and dark, and may be the source of mist or drizzle. Stratus clouds may be shredded by strong local winds into a specialized cloud type called *fractostratus*.

Nimbostratus clouds are the typical rain clouds, consisting of a low-level, shapeless gray layer from which rain or snow may fall steadily or intermittently. The base of the layer may be in a single even layer or may appear somewhat ragged, depending on local conditions.

Cumulus clouds have distinctive vertical development and a flat base. They are formed from vertically rising surface air from which the moisture has condensed, indicating unstable conditions. Cumulus that grow vertically a few hundred feet during the day and dissipate at nightfall are often called "fair weather cumulus." Occasionally, however, very unstable air may cause a cumulus cloud to develop vertically for thousands of feet, transforming into a cumulonimbus and becoming a thunderstorm. They may also merge with altocumulus if conditions are right.

Figure 20-14. Altocumulus lenticularis *clouds are formed when moist air is forced over the top of mountains high enough to force condensation. (Courtesy NOAA/NWS)*

The *cumulonimbus* cloud is one of the most dramatic cloud types, for this is the thunderstorm cloud, with a very dark, flat base and towering billows of white, reaching altitudes of some 50,000 feet. In its upper reaches, the cloud top is composed of ice crystals, which may blow away in fast, high altitude air currents to assume the familiar anvil shape of a mature thunderhead. This subtype is called cumulonimbus capilatus. (See Figure 20-15.)

Cumulonimbus clouds are the result of rapidly rising moist air, and may be isolated or associated with larger weather systems such as cold fronts or tropical cyclones. The chief dangers to small craft associated with cumulonimbus are from sudden strong winds and lightning, combined with the possibility of waterspouts and hail.

A peculiar species of cumulus known as *cumulo-mammatus* consists of dramatic appendages hanging from the underside of stratocumulus, as seen in Figure 20-16.

Sometimes wave clouds are formed by the passage of air into and out of a certain layer of the atmosphere in a wave-like fashion, condensing only at a certain level and forming parallel lines of clouds as in Figure 20-17.

Visibility

Fog and *haze* are the chief impediments to visibility at sea, although *smog* may be a problem downwind from large metropolitan areas. Fog is nothing more than a cloud at the earth's surface. It is very difficult to determine the amount of visibility at sea in the absence of distant objects of known size to serve as a reference. Ashore, a device called a *transmissometer* is sometimes used to measure visibility with beams of light.

While it is possible to predict fog as a general phenomenon in a local or regional area, it is not possible to predict the amount or thickness of fog in any given location. There are too many variables. Fog will be likely to

Figure 20-15. *A mature thunderstorm is known as a* cumulonimbus capilatus *cloud, which is distinguished by the "anvil" at the top, formed when the upper reaches of the cloud are swept away by high-altitude winds. The cloud at this altitude is formed of ice crystals. (Courtesy NOAA/NWS)*

Figure 20-16. Cumulo-mammatus *clouds are often associated with severe weather—tornadoes, hail, and high winds. The navigator should expect the worst if these clouds are seen overhead. (Courtesy NOAA/NWS)*

Figure 20-17. *Wave clouds are formed by the passage of air in waves, in and out of a layer of the atmosphere which causes condensation of the water vapor. (Courtesy NOAA/NWS)*

form when warm, moist air moves over colder water, for the air will cool and its moisture condense at the sea surface. This is known as *advection fog*. At some distance above the surface, the water's cooling effect will diminish to the point where condensation does not occur. This point is usually a few feet to a few hundred feet above the sea surface. (See Figure 20-18.)

Advection fogs are common along the northern Atlantic and Pacific coasts of North America, where cool ocean currents are found close offshore.

When very cold air moves over warm water, *frost smoke* (sometimes called *sea smoke*) forms, seen as a mist rising slowly from the water. Except in polar regions, this very seldom presents a visibility problem for small craft.

Radiation fog forms when moist air overlies land which cools at night, losing heat energy by radiation into space. As the land cools, so does the air above it, and if the dew point is reached, fog will form. Radiation fogs are often only a few feet thick, and dissipate when the rising sun warms the earth. Radiation fog may flow down slopes and out across the water, but seldom reaches more than a few miles offshore.

Haze is an aggregation of microscopic dust, smoke, and/or salt particles in the atmosphere sufficient to restrict visibility. It can be thick enough at times to affect visual navigation, but seldom reduces visibility to less than four or five miles.

Smog is a combination of smoke, atmospheric pollution, and perhaps fog, and is rarely a problem for sailors more than a few miles from the source, usually a large urban/industrial area.

In restricted visibility, it's vital to:

- maintain an accurate DR plot.
- exploit every opportunity for a visual fix in order to confirm electronic positions.
- follow navigation rules relating to lookouts, sound signals, and reduced speed.
- Consult the U.S. Coast Guard's *Navigation Rules* for specific information on sailing in restricted visibility.

Figure 20-18. *Advection fog is formed when moist air flows over a cold surface and its water vapor condenses. It may be a few feet or a few hundred feet high. One can easily see from this photograph how a small craft can be hidden from the view of a large ship in fog. A radar reflector would be a good idea in this situation. (Courtesy NOAA/NWS)*

Weather Routing

The navigator's first reference in planning a passage with the weather in mind is one of the *Pilot Charts* issued by NIMA. *Pilot Charts* are small scale atlases of climatic data for each major ocean basin, showing average winds, oceanic currents, temperature, pressure, and a variety of other climatic data. A close inspection of the pilot chart for one's cruising area will yield a great deal of information on what conditions can be expected along the chosen route. They are also excellent for tracking tropical storms, and show great-circle routes and distances, isogonic lines, and visibility data.

Due to advanced techniques in computers and communications and great strides in weather forecasting science, it is now possible to determine the optimum track for a vessel to follow based on weather and the desired conditions for the voyage. It is even possible to specify certain conditions and allow a computer to generate a route which will meet them.

For example, a vessel using *weather routing* might request a route from New York to St. Thomas that will not encounter winds greater than 35 knots or seas greater than 10

Every vessel has certain performance characteristics—maximum speeds given certain sea and wind conditions. These are an important part of the calculation of an optimum route. In general, a powered vessel will make its maximum speed in gentle following seas, while a sailing vessel will do best reaching. At some point of increasing wind speed and wave height, the speed curve will turn downward—speed will decrease—as increasing rudder angles needed to stay on course begin to slow the vessel, and high waves produce more and more drag.

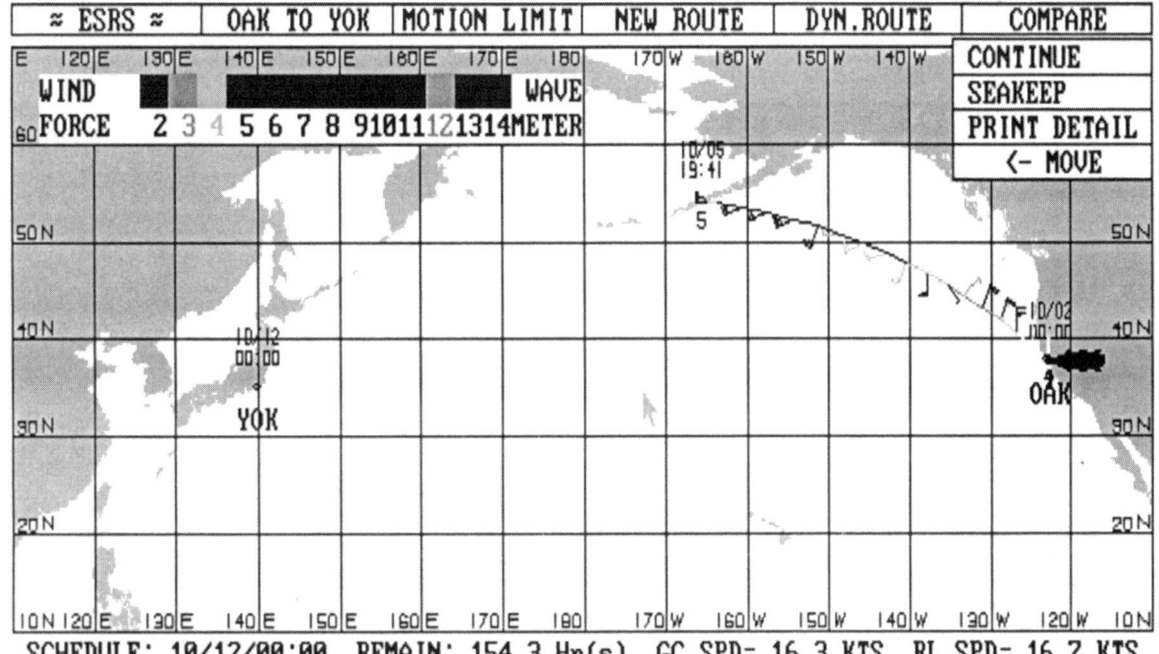

Figure 20-19. *This printout from a computer monitor shows what a weather routing plot looks like for a voyage from California to Japan. The vessel's great circle track is marked with wind arrows to indicate expected winds. The track can be altered at any time to adjust to changes in the ship's capabilities or schedule. The actual computer picture is in color. Small-craft navigators would not use this service unless they were considering an ocean voyage of some length. (Courtesy Ocean Strategies, Inc.)*

feet. The requesting vessel's speed and handling characteristics are entered into the computer and integrated with computer-generated weather forecasts to determine a route which meets those conditions if it is possible to do so. As the weather picture changes, the computer can adjust the route and relay changes to the vessel as it proceeds.

Alternatively, processed weather data can be relayed to the vessel at sea and entered into its own computer, which will analyze the data on board and determine an optimum route. The advantage of this system is that an infinite number of scenarios can be envisioned and processed on board, with the results instantly displayed with recommended courses and speeds on a color monitor.

This service is used mostly by large commercial and military ships to optimize fuel usage and minimize cargo damage, but can be a valuable service to ocean-voyaging small craft as well.

Here are sources for additional information on weather routing and weather routing programs:

1. *OCEAN: Weather Routing Software, Lunamar Inc.* 419 Barclay Rd.
Rosemont PA 19010, phone 610-525-8899.

2. *KIWITECH Marine Solutions Inc.,*
136 Beaumont St., Westhaven,
PO Box 5909, Wellesley St. Aukland NZ,
phone 64-9-307-0819, fax 64-9-307-6685,
e-mail jbilgerkiwitech.co.nz

3. *Global Meteorological Technologies, Inc.* 21808-86A Ave., Langley, BC,
Canada V3A 8G6, phone 604 882 0587,
fax 604 882 0596, e-mail gmt@infoserve.net

Sources of Weather Data

Only the most serious and dedicated offshore cruiser or racer has the need or the resources to use a vessel routing service. However, there are a number of free sources of weather information for small craft in coastal waters.

The most readily available of these are the National Weather Service's VHF broadcasts, available 24 hours a day in almost every part of the U.S. Covering local areas, these broadcasts are tailored to the small craft operator, and the range restriction of VHF radio transmissions limits their use to coastal areas where most small craft operate. All marine-band VHF radios have weather channels installed, and vessels without VHF radio aboard can purchase inexpensive receive-only radios pre-tuned to the weather radio frequencies. The voice broadcasts describe current conditions as well as weather fronts, air masses, and systems affecting the forecast area. Forecast areas are defined areas of coastal waters, as shown in Figure 20-20. These forecasts are an extremely useful and valuable part of even a short voyage, and mandatory for extended trips.

A second method of obtaining weather data is through use of a *weather facsimile* broadcast. This system requires the use of a dedicated radio facsimile receiver or the connection of a standard MF/HF radio set to a facsimile machine. The former method is by far the easiest, although the receivers are only able to receive weather facsimile transmissions, and cannot transmit. The weather facsimile radio, while yielding excellent regional weather maps, does not include forecasts, which must be made by the navigator once the map has been received and the vessel's position plotted on it. (See Figures 20-21, 20-22, and 20-23.)

Figure 20-20. *Each Weather Service Forecast Office (WSFO) issues forecasts for a certain coastal or offshore area.*

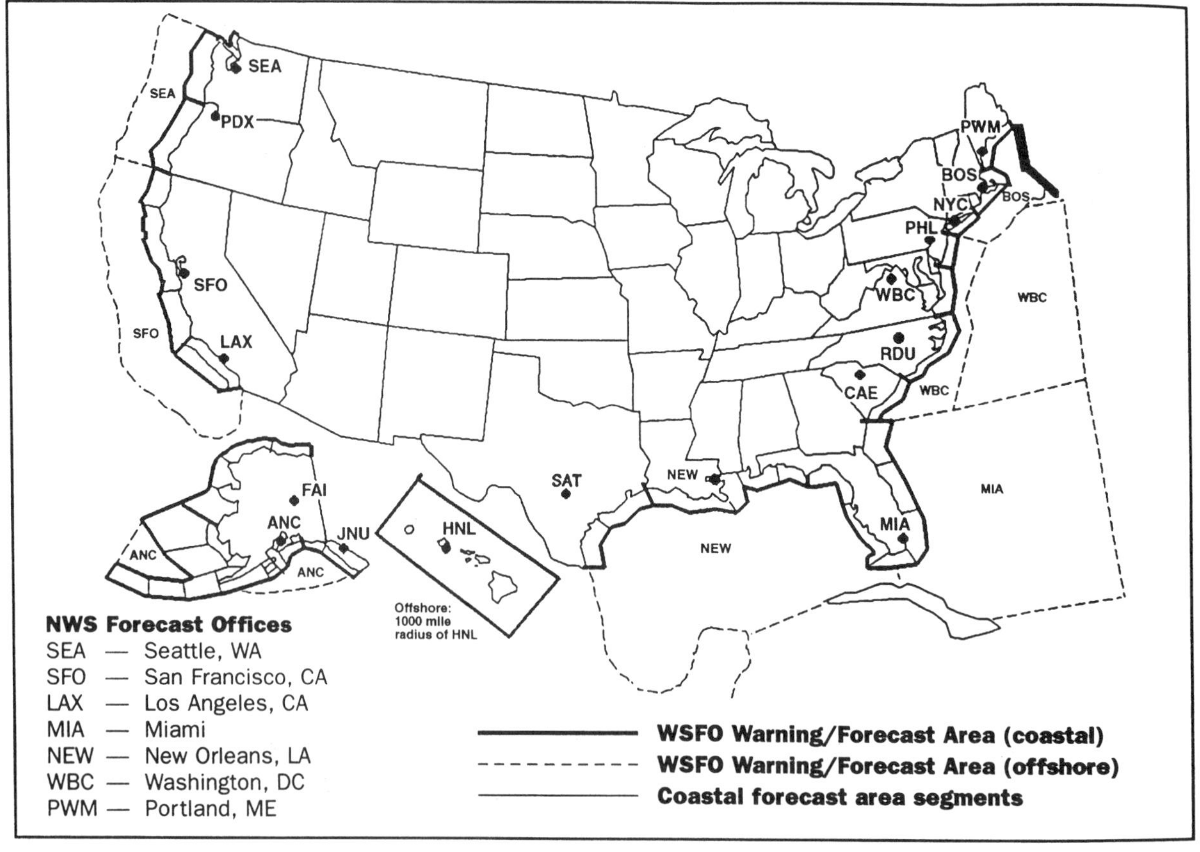

Low Cloud Types

Plate 1. *Cumulus with little vertical extent*

Plate 2. *Cumulus with moderate vertical extent*

Low Cloud Types

Plate 3. *Cumulonimbus with no anvil*

Plate 4. *Stratocumulus from spreading cumulus*

Low Cloud Types

Plate 5. *Stratocumulus not from spreading cumulus*

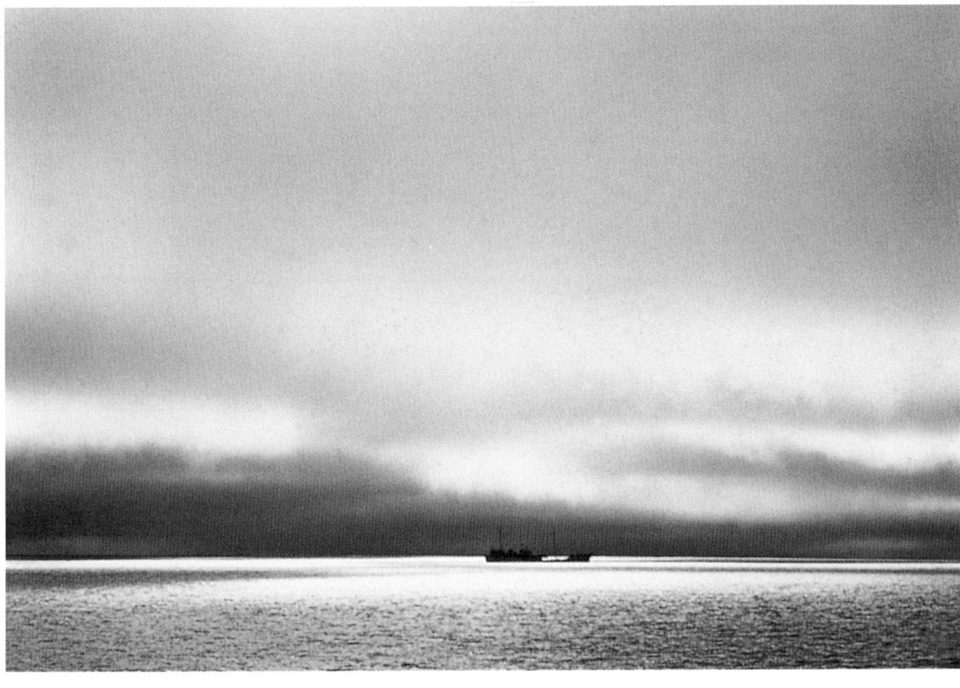

Plate 6. *Stratus in sheet or layer*

Low Cloud Types

Plate 7. *Stratus fractus/cumulus fractus of bad weather*

Plate 8. *Cumulus and stratocumulus at different levels*

Plate 9. *Cumulonimbus*

Medium Cloud Types

Plate 10. *Altostratus, translucent, sun or moon visible*

Plate 11. *Altostratus, opaque, sun or moon hidden*

Medium Cloud Types

Plate 12. *Altocumulus, semi-transparent*

Plate 13. *Altocumulus, semi-transparent, multi-level*

Medium Cloud Types

Plate 14. *Altocumulus in layers*

Plate 15. *Altocumulus from spreading cumulus*

Medium Cloud Types

Plate 16. *Altocumulus, layered, with alto- or nimbostratus*

Plate 17. *Altocumulus with tower-like sproutings*

Plate 18. *Altocumulus with broken sheets at different levels*

High Cloud Types

Plate 19. *Cirrus filaments, strands or hooks, not expanding*

Plate 20. *Dense cirrus in patches*

High Cloud Types

Plate 21. *Cirrus, anvil remaining from cumulonimbus*

Plate 22. *Cirrus hooks or filaments, increasing*

High Cloud Types

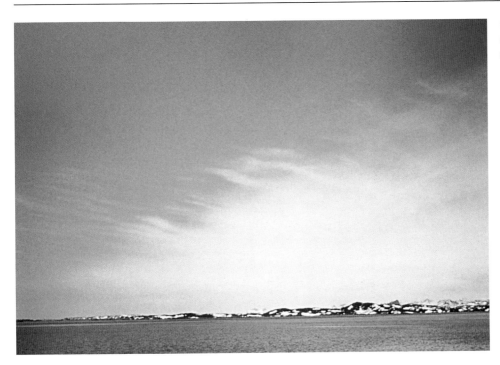

Plate 23. *Cirrostratus with bands, increasing, veil below 45 degress*

Plate 24. *Cirrostratus with bands, increasing, veil above 45 degress*

High Cloud Types

Plate 25. *Cirrostratus covering whole sky*

Plate 26. *Cirrostratus, not increasing, not covering whole sky*

Plate 27. *Cirrocumulus alone and with cirrostratus*

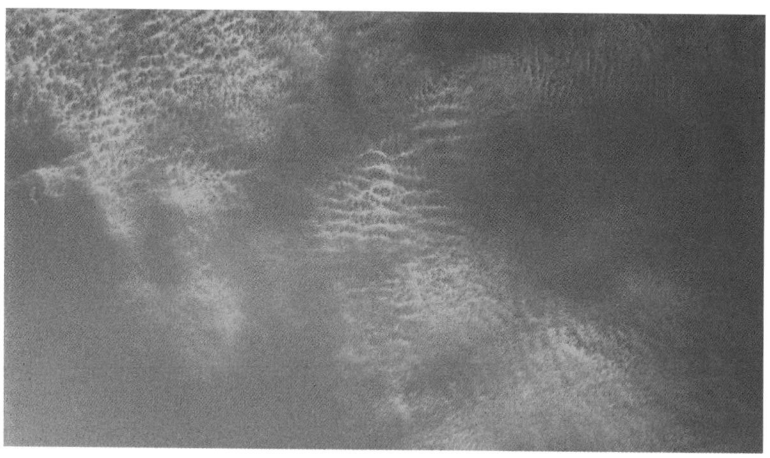

Sea States

Beaufort Number 0.

Wind: *0*
Sea state: *Sea like a mirror*

Beaufort Number 1.

Wind: *1–3*
Sea state: *Ripples like scales, no crests*

Beaufort Number 2.

Wind: *4–6*
Sea state: *Small wavelets, crests glassy and do not break*

Sea States

Beaufort Number 3.

Wind: *7–10*
Sea state: *Large wavelets, crests break, whitecaps begin*

Beaufort Number 4.

Wind: *11–16*
Sea state: *Small waves, numerous whitecaps*

Beaufort Number 5.

Wind: *17–21*
Sea state: *Moderate and longer waves; whitecaps and spray*

Sea States

Beaufort Number 6.

Wind: *22–27*
Sea state: *Larger waves, numerous whitecaps, much spray*

Beaufort Number 7.

Wind: *28–33*
Sea state: *Sea heaps up, waves break, foam blows in streaks*

Beaufort Number 8.

Wind: *34–40*
Sea state: *Moderate waves of greater length, foam blows in long streaks*

Sea States

Beaufort Number 9.

Wind: *41–47*
Sea state: *High waves, rolling sea, dense streaks of foam, spray reduces visibility*

Beaufort Number 10.

Wind: *48–55*
Sea state: *Very high waves, overhanging crests, sea white with foam, visibility reduced*

Beaufort Number 11.

Wind: *56–63*
Sea state: *Exceptionally high waves, sea covered with foam, visibility poor* *(see page 294, Chapter 20 for sea state in 90 knots)*

Weather facsimile broadcasts are made by several different government organizations and by private weather services. Some broadcasts are continuous and send several different types of weather maps in a repeating sequence. Listed below are some U.S. and Canadian government facsimile broadcasts intended for civilian use. All times are GMT.

Station	Location	Schedule	Frequency (kHz)
NAM	Cutler, ME	Continuous	3357, 8080, 10865
		0900–2100	15959
		1200–2100	20015
NPM	Pearl Harbor, HA	0600–1600	4855, 6453
		1600–0600	21735
	Adak, AK	Continuous	8494
	Stockton, CA	Continuous	6453, 9090
CFI	Halifax, NS	Continuous	122.5, 4271, 6496.4, 10536, 13510
CKN	Esquimalt, BC	Continuous	4266.1, 6454.1, 12751.1

Figure 20-21. *The dedicated weather facsimile machine is both receiver and printer, able to receive and print out radio-broadcast weather maps from a variety of sources. This is an extremely useful way for the long-distance navigator to obtain weather information. (Courtesy Raytheon Electronics)*

In addition to weather maps for the major ocean areas of the world, weather facsimile broadcasts often transmit specialized charts for particular use, such as detailed Gulf Stream charts and ice charts of the North Atlantic. Unlike voice weather broadcasts, radiofacsimile weather maps can be retained and compared over time, helping the navigator to plan routes to minimize storms and make the most of good conditions.

Another method of receiving weather information is through the *Internet,* and a good source is the National Weather Service at "http://www.nws.noaa.gov." Some television stations and various governmental organizations maintain home pages through which surface weather maps, forecasts and summaries, Doppler radar pictures, tropical storm tracks, and much other data can be viewed and downloaded. A good Internet search program will quickly locate these sources and others that are sure to be developed as technology advances.

A computer can be used at sea to obtain weather maps, and can do a lot of other navigational tasks as well—celestial sights, sailings, electronic charting, etc. The Internet has a number of weather-related sites, and the major Internet services offer marine and aviation weather as text files, maps, and satellite photographs, all easily available for downloading and printing. In fact, the same information broadcast by any of the NWS weather stations can be downloaded at any time. It is also possible to receive satellite photographs directly from the satellites. Accessing the Internet for weather informa-

If it is possible to make telephone calls at sea through a satellite, then it must also be possible to access the Internet at sea, and so it is. But the gear required is beyond the financial reach of all but owners of the largest and most expensive small craft, and more suitable for commercial vessels. A yacht which can afford a satellite terminal and computer to use at-sea Internet for weather information can also afford to sign up with a weather routing service and let the professionals choose the optimum track.

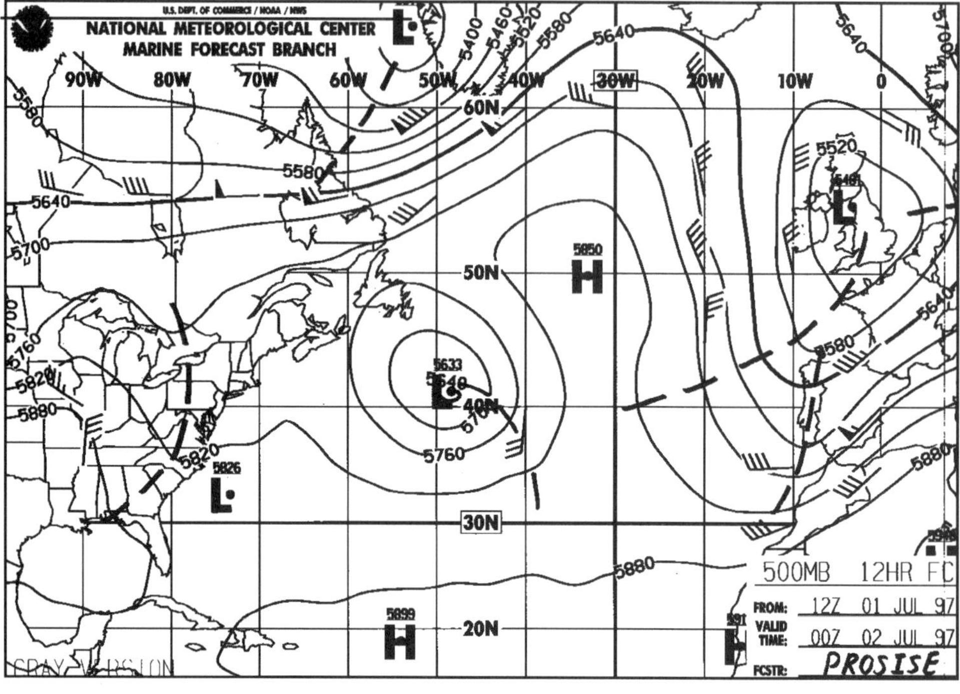

Figure 20-22. *The 12-hour forecast positions of weather features of the North Atlantic Ocean at the 500-mb pressure level. Such upper-level maps of weather features are valuable tools in predicting surface conditions. (Courtesy Ocean Strategies, Inc.)*

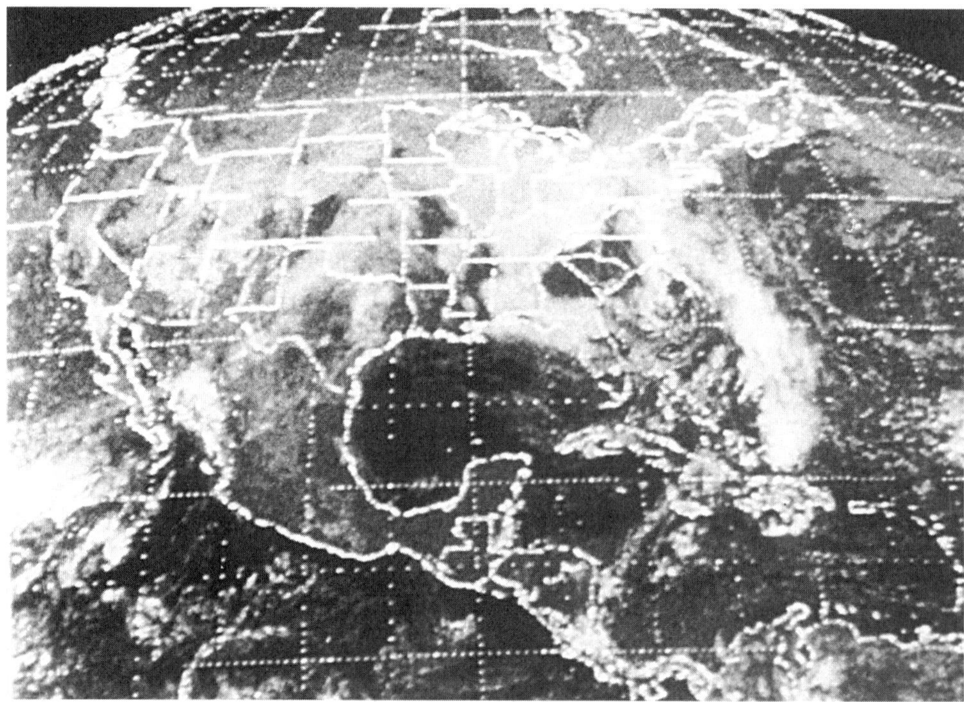

Figure 20-23. *This photograph of North and Central America was obtained from an orbiting weather satellite and rebroadcast in facsimile format for mariners' use. Satellite photographs are useful in depicting clouds and the storms with which they are associated, but standard weather maps are more useful for forecasting. (Courtesy Ocean Strategies, Inc.)*

tion can add a great deal of weather knowledge to the navigator of a coastwise vessel. However, to receive weather maps at sea the computer must have a modem and satellite communications, out of the picture for most small craft at the time of this writing.

Interpreting Weather Maps

Weather maps are complex documents containing a huge amount of information for those who know how to read them. The information is coded in a number of specialized symbols and abbreviations. The pattern of lines, letters, and numbers on the map holds the secret of the weather forecast.

A number of different types of weather maps are available, including:

- ***Surface analysis***—Shows the current weather picture at the earth's surface.
- ***Prognoses: 24, 48, and 96 hour***—Show the expected conditions in the future.
- ***Wind wave***—Shows the wind-driven (not swell) waves in a region of the ocean.
- ***500-mb***—Shows conditions at the 500 millibar level in the upper atmosphere.

Weather *fronts* are shown with one of several line types. A *cold front* is shown by a line studded with points indicating the direction of movement of the air mass. A *warm front* is shown by a line studded with semicircles, again in the direction of movement. An *occluded front* has alternating points and semicircles. A *stationary front* has both warm front semicircles and cold front points, but on opposite sides of the line. (See Figure 20-24.)

A number of abbreviations are used on weather maps. Listed below are some of the most common ones.

NWS—National Weather Service

NMC—National Meteorological Center

FNOC—Fleet Numerical Oceanography Center

GOES—Geostationary Earth Orbiting Satellite

WX—weather

SFC—surface

H—high pressure area

L—low pressure area

Prog—prognosis

Isobars on weather maps are labeled with the last two digits of the pressure expressed in millibars. Thus "1016 mb" of pressure would be "16." Some weather maps do not show the actual fronts, which can be inferred from the pattern of isobars.

Isobars are lines connecting points of equal atmospheric pressure, often seen encircling high and low pressure areas. Because winds tend to blow from highs toward lows, they would blow across the isobars were it not for Coriolis force, which causes them to blow more nearly along them. The amount of deflection varies with altitude, with high-altitude winds more nearly in line with the isobars.

Winds on weather maps are indicated with arrows, but instead of an arrowhead on the end, a small circle or point is often used. The direction of the arrow indicates the direction the wind is blowing, and the "feathers" on the arrow show the strength. Each full-length feather represents 10 knots of wind, and half-feathers indicate 5 knots. Refer to Figure 20-24.

For a portfolio of weather maps and their interpretations, see Figures 20-25 through 20-33B.

Predicting Local Weather

Given the information about how air masses move, how fronts form, and the conditions that might be encountered in various locations relative to highs and lows, the navigator should be able to predict the local weather with some confidence even in the absence of professional forecasts.

The important things to note are:

- What is the atmospheric pressure, and is it rising or falling?
- What are the direction and strength of the wind?

- What is the air temperature? Humidity?
- Are these different from yesterday? An hour ago?
- What clouds are visible?

Once these facts are known, listen to the local weather broadcast and try to imagine your own position in relation to the known weather systems in the region, correlating the observations of local weather.

For example, suppose the local NOAA weather station reports a cold front approaching. If winds are southwest and warm, with a falling barometer, expect the low center to pass north of your position as the winds veer to the northwest. If winds are southeasterly,

(continued)

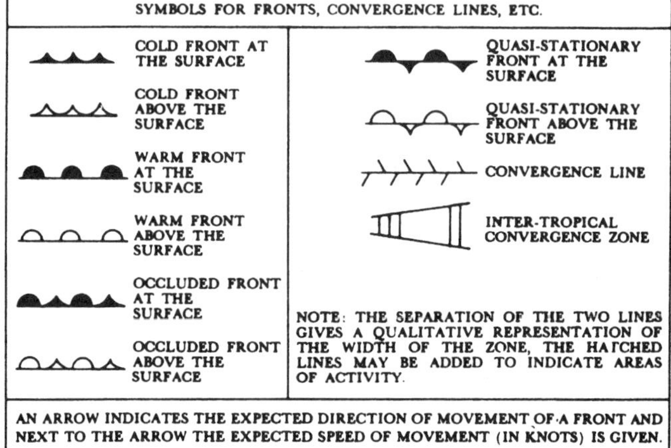

Figure 20-24. *This chart shows symbols used on weather maps, including the wind arrows. (Courtesy NOAA/NWS)*

SYMBOLS FOR SIGNIFICANT WEATHER	SYMBOLS FOR TYPES OF AIR MASSES
THUNDERSTORM	cA ARCTIC, CONTINENTAL
TROPICAL REVOLVING STORM (HURRICANE/TYPHOON, ETC.)	mA ARCTIC, MARITIME
SEVERE LINE SQUALL	cP POLAR, CONTINENTAL
HAIL	mP POLAR, MARITIME
WIDESPREAD SANDSTORM OR DUSTSTORM	cT TROPICAL, CONTINENTAL
FREEZING RAIN	mT TROPICAL, MARITIME
● RAIN	E EQUATORIAL
✱ SNOW	S SUPERIOR
	THE ABOVE SYMBOLS MAY BE FOLLOWED BY A SMALL LETTER "k" OR "w". THESE LETTERS INDICATE THE FOLLOWING:
	k THE AIR MASS IS COLDER THAN THE SURFACE OVER WHICH IT IS PASSING.
	w THE AIR MASS IS WARMER THAN THE SURFACE OVER WHICH IT IS PASSING.

OTHER SYMBOLS AND CONVENTIONS

	BOUNDARY OF AREAS OF SIGNIFICANT WEATHER

ABBREVIATIONS

CLD	—CLOUD	LYR	—LAYER OR LAYERED
FRQ	—FREQUENT	OCNL	—OCCASIONAL OR OCCASIONALLY
GRADU	—GRADUAL OR GRADUALLY	SCT	—SCATTERED

HIGH- AND LOW-PRESSURE CENTERS ARE REPRESENTED BY H AND L RESPECTIVELY, THE POSITION AT THE SURFACE OF THE POINT OF HIGHEST OR LOWEST PRESSURE BEING INDICATED BY + FOLLOWED BY THE VALUE OF THE MSL PRESSURE IN MILLIBARS. AN ARROW INDICATES THE EXPECTED DIRECTION OF MOVEMENT OF THE PRESSURE CENTER AND THE EXPECTED SPEED OF MOVEMENT (IN KNOTS). THE VALUE OF EACH ISOBAR (LINE OF EQUAL ATMOSPHERIC PRESSURE) IS LABELED.

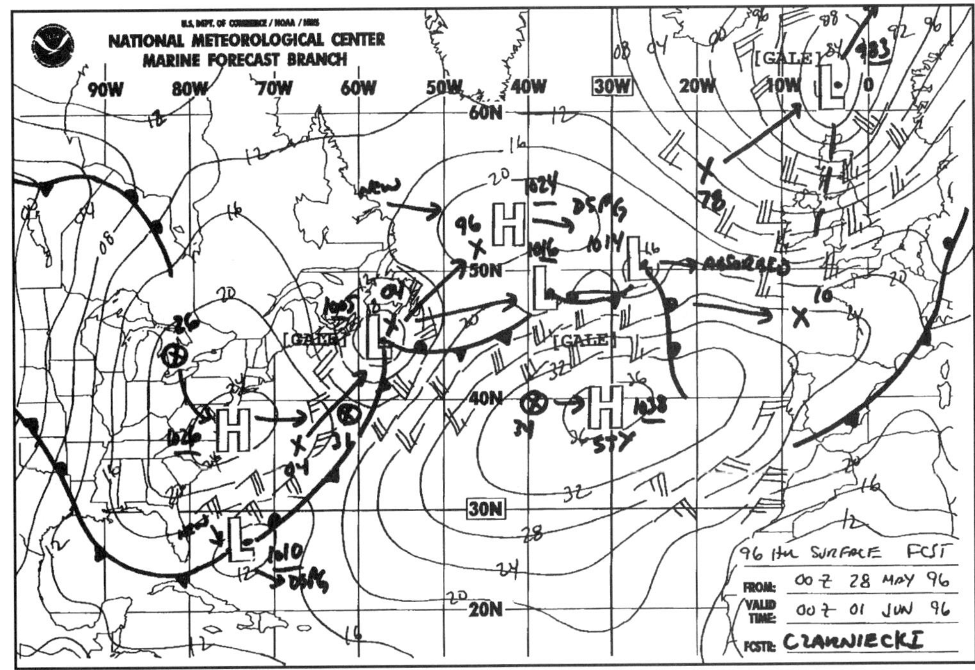

Figure 20-25. *A typical May forecast for the North Atlantic Ocean. Note the position of lows and highs, and their associated fronts.*

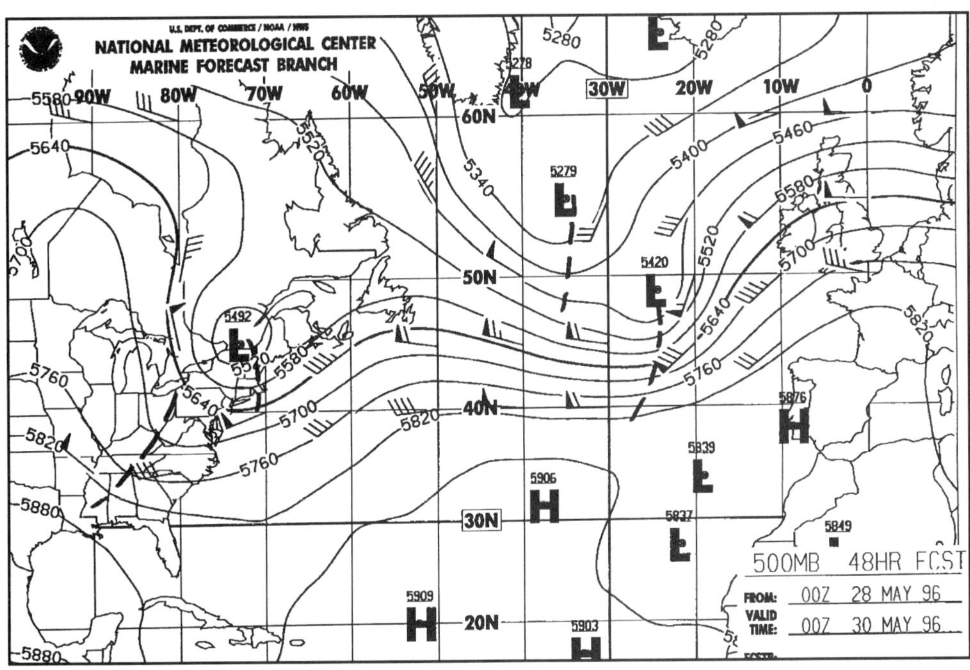

Figure 20-26. *An upper-level (500 mb) chart of the North Atlantic. The 500-mb chart is critical for forecasting surface weather.*

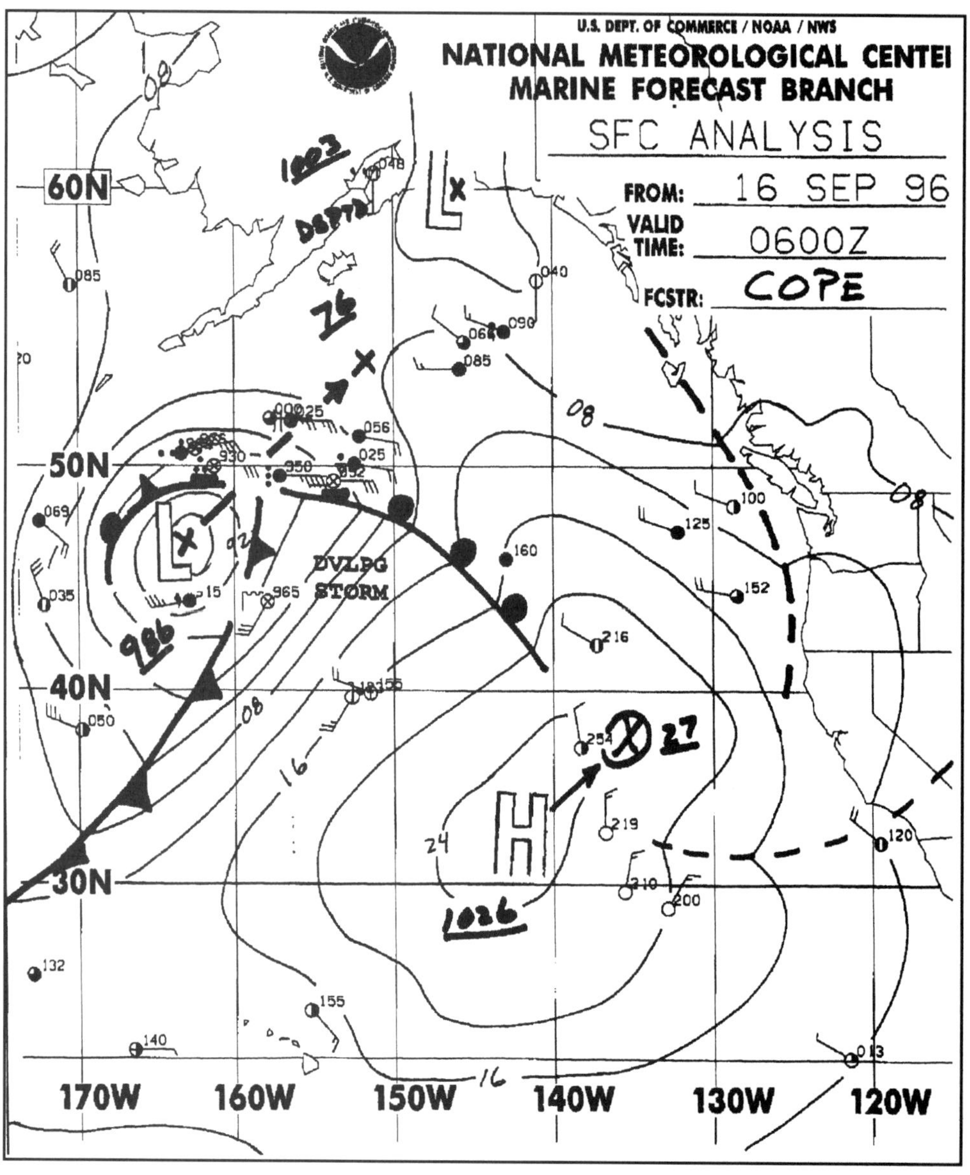

Figure 20-27. *A developing storm in the northeast Pacific Ocean. Note the wind arrows and the classic cold front/warm front configuration.*

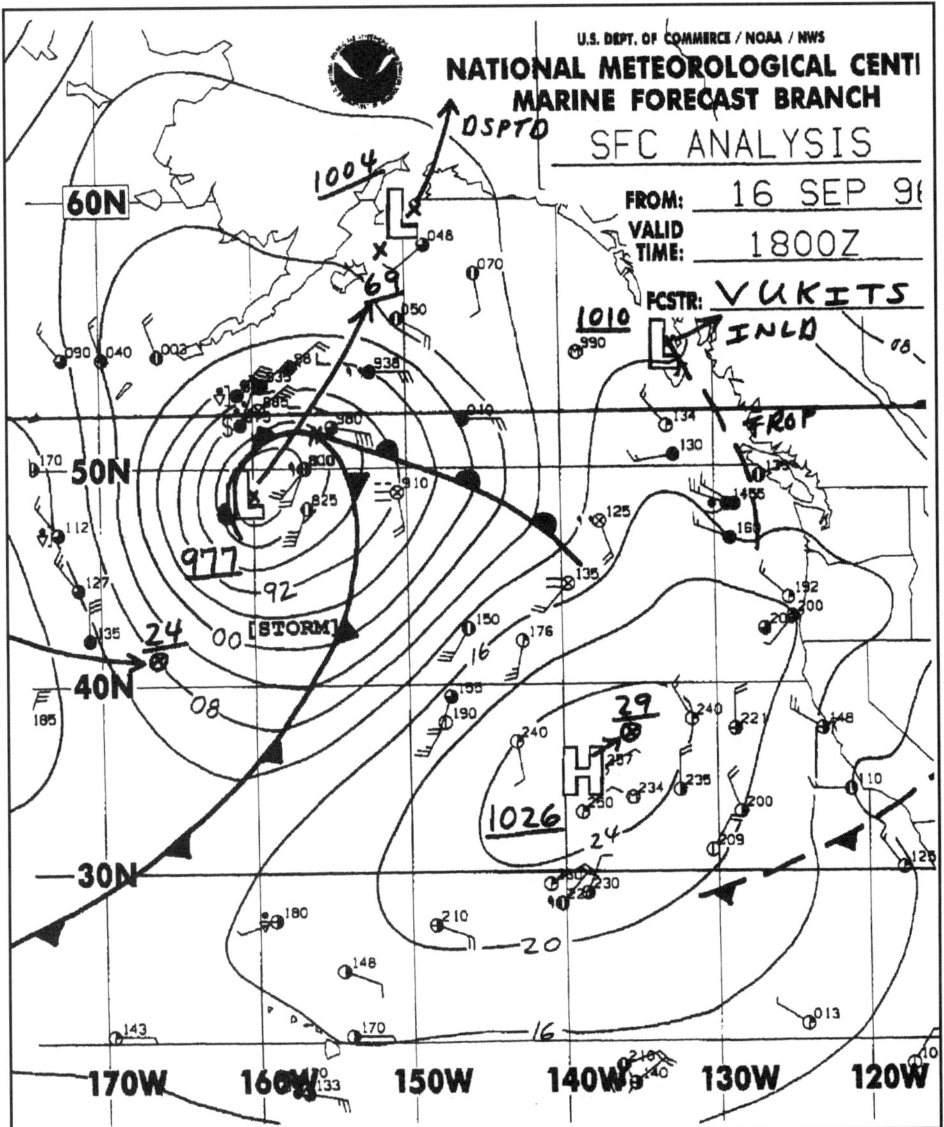

Figure 20-28. *The Pacific storm shown in Figure 20-27, 12 hours later. It has taken on the typical "comma" shape of a mature storm.*

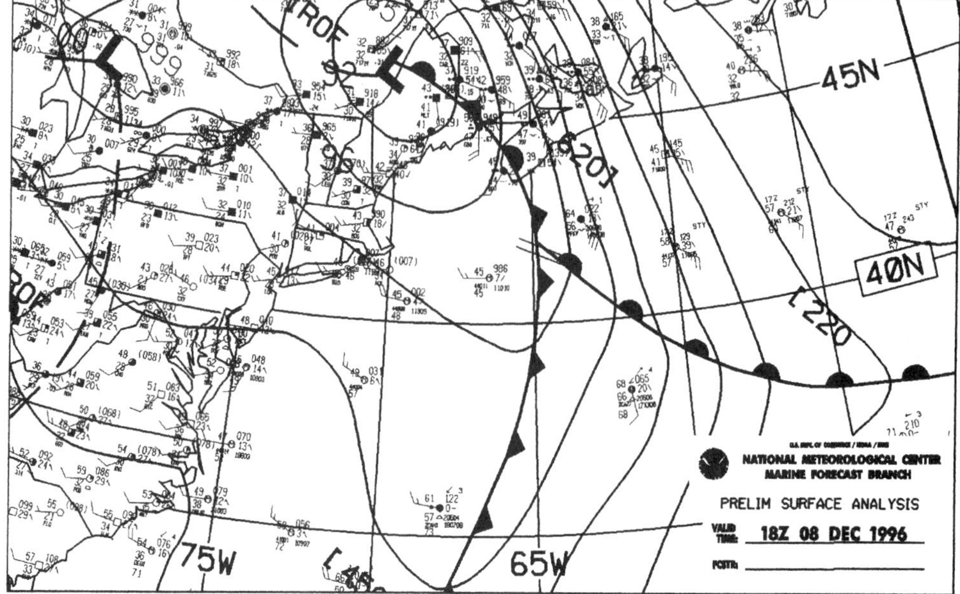

Figure 20-29. *An occluded front southeast of a low over Maine. A secondary low is likely to develop at the intersection of cold, warm, and occluded fronts, called the "triple point."*

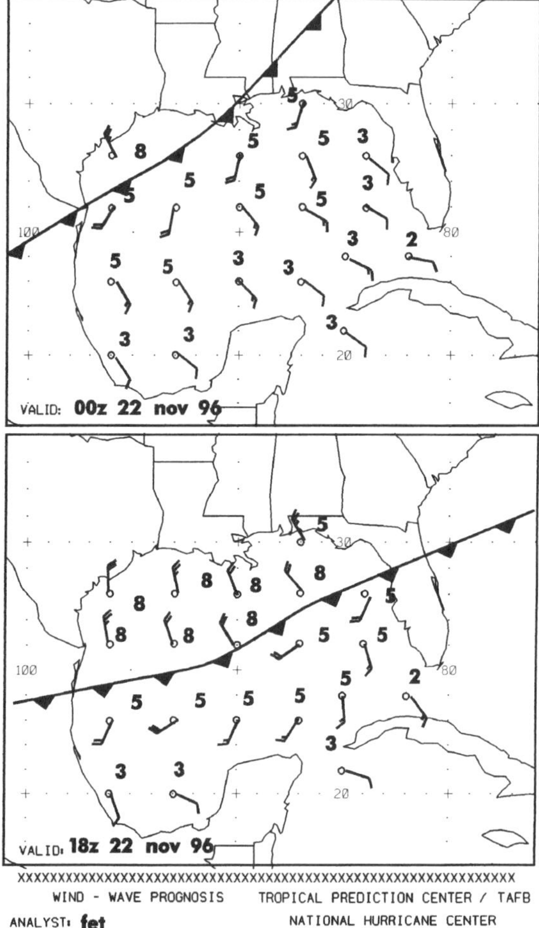

Figure 20-30. *This wind/wave prognosis shows a cold front advancing south over the Gulf of Mexico. Note the wind shift line and corresponding wave heights.*

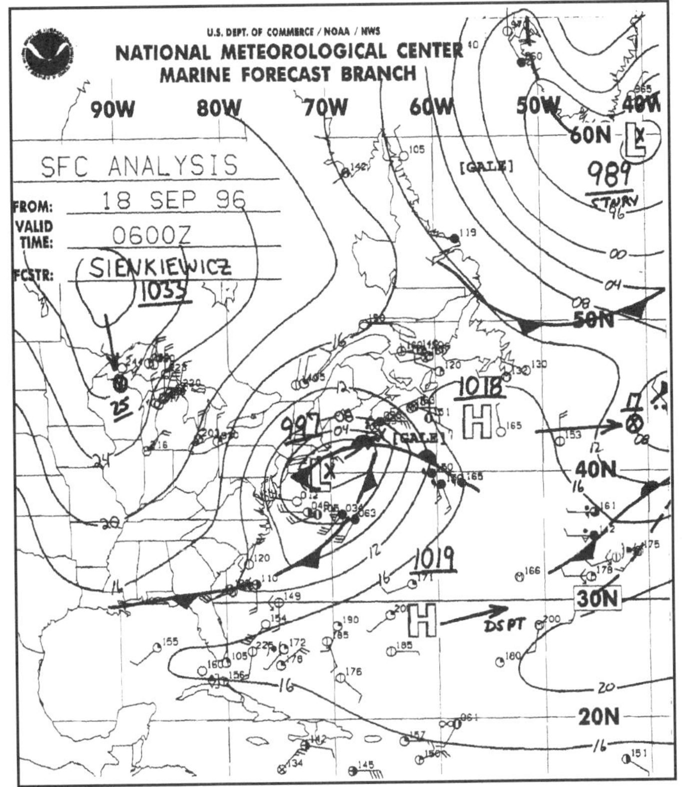

Figure 20-31a. *This classic low system is causing northeasterly gales in New England (see Figure 20-31b).*

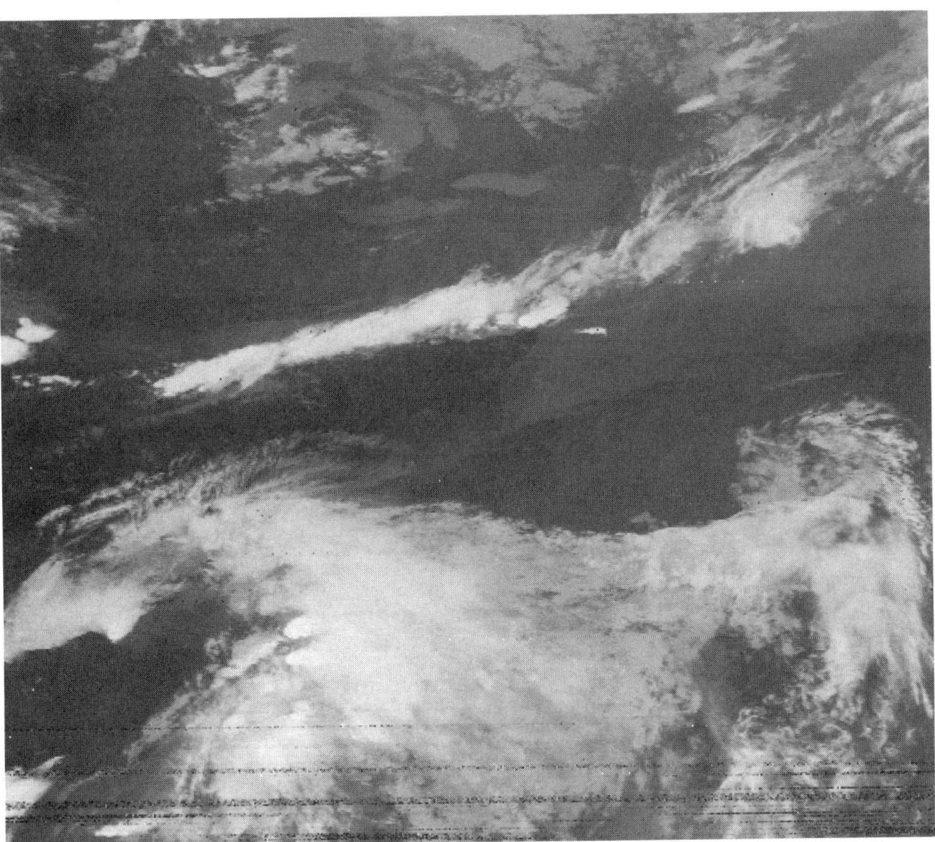

Figure 20-31b. *This satellite image shows the view from space of the storm in Figure 20-31a.*

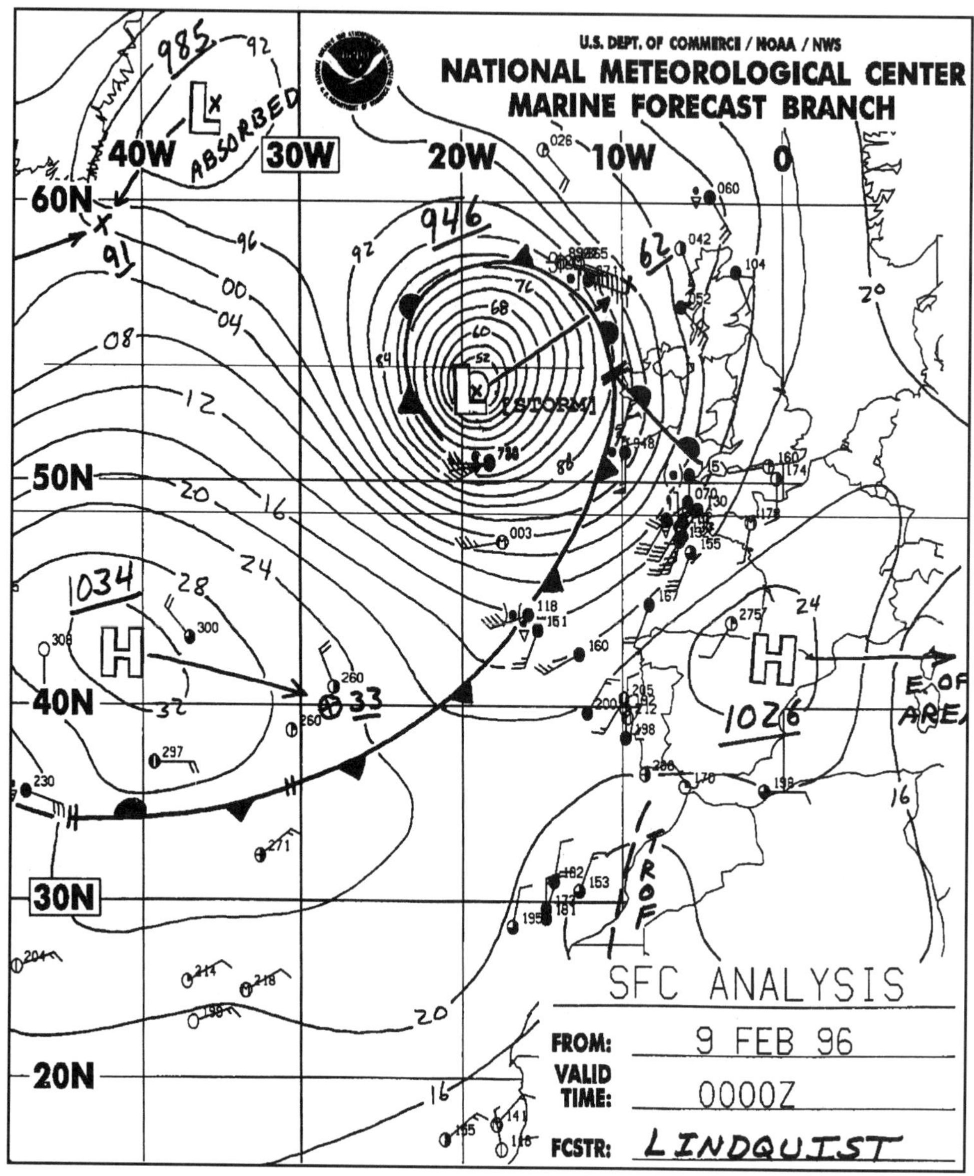

Figure 20-32. *A very intense storm sweeping toward the British Isles. Note the strength and direction of the wind arrows.*

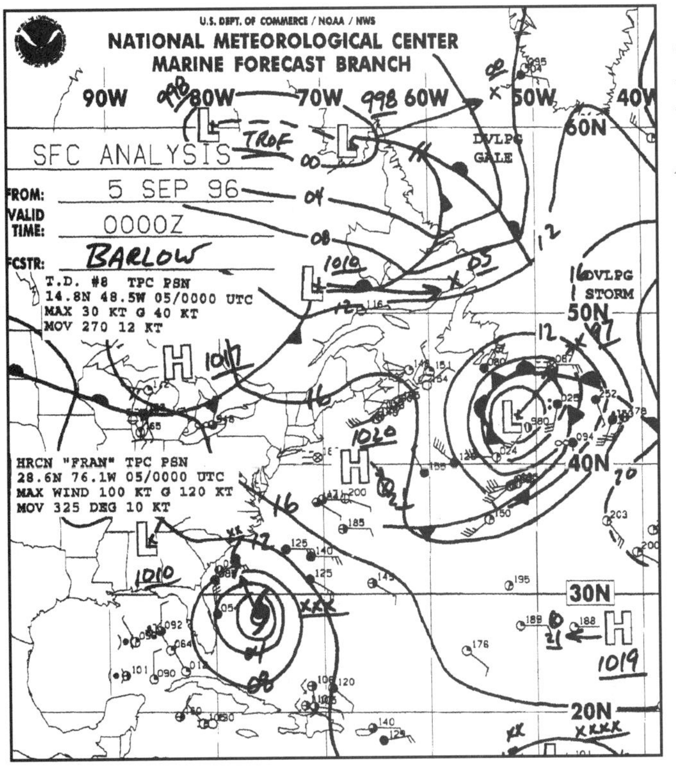

Figure 20-33a. *A surface analysis showing Hurricane Fran off the Florida coast (see Figure 20-33b). A young low-pressure center sits over Quebec, and a more mature storm over the central North Atlantic.*

Figure 20-33b. *A satellite image of Hurricane Fran, as shown in Figure 20-33a. Note the central eye and typical spiral cloud patterns.*

backing to northeasterly, with lowering clouds and rain, the low will pass to the south and a "nor'easter" is in store.

The following table will help:

WIND	BAROMETER	FORECAST
SW to NW	30.1 to 30.2, steady	Fair for 1–2 days
SW to NW	30.1 to 30.2, rising rapidly	Fair, rain in 1–2 days
SW to NW	30.2 and above	Continued fair
SW to NW	30.2 and above, falling	Fair, rising temperatures for 1–2 days
S to SE	30.1 to 30.2, falling slowly	Rain within 24 hours
S to SE	30.1 to 30.2, falling rapidly	Increasing wind, rain in 12–24 hours
SE to NE	30.1 to 30.2, falling slowly	Rain in 12–18 hours
SE to NE	30.1 to 30.2, falling rapidly	Increasing wind, rain within 12 hours
E to NE	30.1 and above, falling slowly	Summer: light winds, no rain for 2 days Winter: Rain within 24 hours
E to NE	30.1 and above, falling fast	Summer: Rain likely within 12 hours Winter: Rain or snow, windy
SE to NE	30.0 and below, falling slowly	Rain continuing 1–2 days
SE to NE	30.0 and below, falling rapidly	Winter: Rain, high winds, clearing and colder
S to SW	30.0 or below, rising slowly	Clearing, fair for several days
S to E	29.8 or below, falling rapidly	Storm imminent, then clearing and colder
E to N	29.8 or below, falling rapidly	Summer: NE gale and heavy rain Winter: Heavy snow and cold
backing to W	29.8 or below, rising rapidly	Clearing and colder

Old sayings about the weather are usually based on facts, and often are quite accurate. Some common weather rhymes and their explanations follow:

"Beware the bolts from north or west;
the bolts from south or east be best."

Weather travels from west to east. Thus, in the northern hemisphere, lightning north or west of an observer is likely approaching, while lightning in the south or east has passed or will likely pass clear.

"Rainbow to windward, foul fall the day.
Rainbow to leeward, rain runs away."

This is true on the same principle as the former rhyme.

"If woolly fleece decks the heavenly way,
be sure no rain will mar the day,"
or
"If fleecy white clouds cover the heavenly way,
no rain should mar your plans this day."

The term "woolly fleece" refers to fair weather cumulus clouds, indicating stable air.

"Mountains in the morning:
Fountains in the evening."

Towering cumulus indicates moist, unstable air, often developing into thunderstorms.

"When a halo rings the moon or sun,
rain approaches on the run."

A halo around the moon or sun is followed by rain 65% of the time.

"Long foretold, long last.
Short notice, soon past."

Long-duration storms are preceded by ample clues: falling barometer, increasing clouds, wind shifts, etc. Squalls approach with little warning.

"Seagull, seagull, get out on the sand.
We'll never have good weather
with thee on the land."

This rhyme observes that seagulls sometimes appear well inshore during storms.

"When the glass falls low, look out for a blow,"
or

"When the wind backs and the glass falls,
be on your guard for gales and squalls."

A falling barometer indicates the approach of a low pressure system, often with stormy conditions.

"Red sky at night,
sailor's delight.
Red sky in the morning,
sailor take warning."

This most well-known of weather rhymes refers to a "red sky" being seen when clouds are on the opposite horizon from the rising or setting sun. A red sky in the evening indicates clouds to the east, therefore passed by. A red sky in the morning indicates clouds to the west, and therefore approaching.

"When the wind's before the rain,
let your tops'ls draw again.
When the rain's before the wind,
tops'l sheets and halyards mind."

This rhyme refers to the fact that large storm systems usually cause gentle winds well away from their worst rain, while local squalls can contain dangerous winds preceded by rain.

"Mackerel sky and mares' tails
make lofty ships carry low sails."

The "mackerel sky and mares' tails" of this rhyme refer to cirrus clouds, which often signal the approach of a storm system, though it is usually a day or more away.

"Sound traveling far and wide
a stormy day will betide."

Temperature inversions and low clouds often cause sounds to travel farther than normal, and indicate stormy weather as well.

"Frost or dew in the morning light
shows no rain before the night."

Frost or dew indicates cool air at the earth's surface, and a stable air mass.

"First rise after low portends a stronger blow."

The greatest pressure gradient, and therefore the strongest winds, are often found on the west or trailing side of a low center or frontal system.

While each of these rhymes is based on facts and on generations of observations, none of them can be considered a rule by which weather will behave. Conditions must be observed, studied, and interpreted for accurate weather prediction. The best meteorologists will admit that even with supercomputers, weather forecasting is still a combination of art and science.

Unusual Atmospheric Effects

The ocean of air above us is dynamic and unstable. Changes in density, temperature, and content alter the way light rays travel through it and are perceived by humans. Unusual, dangerous, and even violent effects are sometimes encountered at sea.

Under standard atmospheric conditions, light rays bend slightly, or *refract,* as they pass through the air. When conditions are abnormal, light rays are refracted more or less. This may cause distortion, displacement, magnification, inversion, or multiplication of distant objects in a phenomenon known as a *mirage.*

Temperature inversions, which result when the air temperature increases with height instead of decreasing, cause abnormally high rates of refraction and *superior mirages.* This may result in distant objects appearing above the horizon, or *looming,* when under normal conditions they would be below it. The same conditions can cause *towering*—the vertical stretching of an object, or *stooping*—the apparent squashing of an object, making it look flatter than normal. An object may appear inverted or in double image, with an inverted image just above the real one. Temperature inversions can occur when warm dry air lies over very cold water.

Reverse refraction, the bending of light rays away from the surface of the earth, can cause *sinking,* the lower-than-normal appearance of an object. When an object appears to be floating above the horizon, an inverted image may appear beneath it, called an *inferior mirage.* Inferior mirages, less common than superior ones, are most likely when the surface is much warmer than the overlying air.

Pure sunlight is composed of all colors, with wavelengths between 0.000038 and 0.000076 centimeters. As it passes into the atmosphere from the sun, the shorter wavelength blue and violet rays are scattered more than the red and yellow rays at the longer end of the color spectrum, causing the sky to appear blue. As the sun sets in late afternoon, light rays must pass through much more atmosphere on their oblique path to an observer than when the sun is high. This filters out the blue end of the spectrum and causes the sun to appear more yellow or red, and its light shining on clouds causes reddish sunsets.

A rainbow forms when sunlight enters water droplets, reflects off their back surfaces, and is split into its component colors upon exiting the fronts of the droplets en route to the observer. Rainbows always occur 180° opposite the direction of the sun, and the radius of the arc of the primary rainbow is 42°. *Secondary* and *tertiary rainbows* may be seen in unusual circumstances, with arcs always larger than the primary. The colors are red, orange, yellow, green, blue, and violet, with red on the outside. In a secondary rainbow the colors are reversed, with red on the inside.

Rainbows may be seen any time sunlight is shining on rain, with the observer between the sun and rain. On very rare occasions, a *moonbow* may be observed, formed by the same process as a rainbow but with moonlight. A *fogbow* is sometimes observed as a white arc of 39° radius in a fogbank.

A *halo* around the sun or moon, usually seen with either a 22° or 46° radius, is caused by light reflected off ice crystals in the upper atmosphere. It may have a trace of rainbow colors, with reds to the inside and blues to the outside.

Sometimes a reflected image of the sun is seen at 22° or 46° from the sun at the same altitude. This is a *parhelion,* sometimes called a *mock sun* or *sun dog*. The same effect with the moon is a *paraselene, mock moon,* or *moon dog*.

A *parhelic circle,* caused by the reflection of sunlight off the vertical faces of ice crystals, is a line through the sun parallel to the horizon. The moon may have a *paraselenic circle*.

Don't confuse parhelion—the mock sun— with perihelion—the point in a planet's orbit closest to the sun.

When the sun is near the horizon, a *sun pillar* may form. This is a vertical glow of light passing through the sun and extending above and below it. A *moon pillar* may also be seen, but more rarely.

When a sun pillar and a parhelic circle are both formed together, a *sun cross* results, seen as a glowing cross with the sun at the center.

A glow of light around the sun or moon and closer to it than the effects described above is a *corona,* caused by the refraction of light through altostratus clouds. Coronas can be distinguished from halos by their smaller radii and the fact that if color is evident, the order is reversed from the halo, with reds of a corona on the outside of the arc, and blues to the inside.

The *green flash* can sometimes be observed at sunset and sunrise in tropical waters. For it to occur, there must be a sharp horizon, clear atmosphere, a temperature inversion, and a dedicated observer, for the flash usually lasts only one to two seconds. It happens because the sun's rays are refracted at different rates by a temperature inversion in the atmosphere. Refraction is greatest at the horizon, where the difference between the violet and red ends of the spectrum represents about ten seconds of arc. The sun changes altitude by this amount in only 0.7 seconds. Light rays near the red end of the spectrum are refracted least, and are the first to set and last to rise. Light rays toward the violet end of the spectrum are more easily bent and scattered by the atmosphere (which is why the sky is blue), and are not seen separately. In the middle of the spectrum is the color green, which may be the only color separately visible as the sun momentarily glows green just as it sets. The red and orange colors have set already, and the blues are dispersed, leaving green alone visible.

The green flash occurs on land, but is more often observed at sea because the conditions that cause it are more common there. It is also more common than supposed, observable at as many as 50 percent of sunsets and sunrises under ideal conditions. Observations of green flash up to ten seconds long have been reported, and green flashes of the planets Venus and Jupiter have been observed through telescopes. The length of the flash appears to be a function of the index of refraction of the atmosphere, which depends on the prevailing conditions.

Atmospheric Electrical Phenomena

A number of different atmospheric conditions produce electrical discharges. Poorly understood interactions between air masses and clouds cause a buildup of electrical potential between different parts of the atmosphere, which may be released in various ways.

Lightning, the most common electrical phenomenon, is the discharge of electrical current through the air. It occurs when storm clouds build up an electrical charge relative to each other or to the earth below. A single stroke of lightning begins with a leader stroke, which connects points of opposite polarity with dozens to hundreds of separate segments, following the line of least electrical resistance. Immediately the main stroke follows, but in the opposite direction. This is the visible lightning flash, which ionizes air molecules and causes them to emit visible radiation.

Thunder can be heard as distant as 15 miles, but usually doesn't carry that far; five to ten miles is more likely. It is caused by the compression or shock wave of the ionized air of a lightning stroke. Since the lightning's flash travels at the speed of light and the thunder at the speed of sound, the distance to a lightning stroke can be calculated by the following formula: Distance to stroke (in miles) = seconds between observing flash and hearing thunder divided by 5.5.

Heat lightning is a term used to denote lightning flashes for which thunder cannot be heard. It may be cloud-to-cloud or cloud-to-ground lightning. (All lightning produces sound waves, as do all trees that fall in a forest. Whether or not it can be heard by a listener is another matter.) The term heat lightning refers to the weather conditions that so often produce thunderstorms: hot summer days and moist air.

Saint Elmo's fire is a glow of ionized air emanating from pointed objects when the buildup of electrical energy is sufficient. The tips of a vessel's masts and yards, as well as lightning rods, steeples, and even human fingers and hair may glow with a surreal light. This may well be the first stage of a leader stroke.

Saint Elmo (also known as Erasmus) was a Christian martyr of the early 4th century. He was once honored as the patron saint of sailors, and Saint Elmo's fire was taken as a sign the ship had come under his protection.

The *aurora* is a colored, luminous glow occurring in northern and southern polar skies during periods of intense solar activity. It often appears as rapidly moving vertical shafts of light in diffused pastel colors, but may also appear as a general glow with little movement. The *aurora borealis* occurs in the northern hemisphere, and the *aurora australis* in the southern hemisphere. Both are most common in the *auroral zones* between 64° and 70° of geomagnetic latitude, although sometimes they can be seen closer to the equator, in latitudes of 45° or less.

Hurricanes and Typhoons

Christopher Columbus, on his second voyage to the New World, unknowingly sailed his fleet into the path of a hurricane, and was fortunate that none of his ships was lost. On his

Geomagnetic latitude is based on the magnetic, not geographic, poles. Since the north geomagnetic pole is actually in northern Canada, northern lights are often visible in the northern U.S., especially in winter when the air is often very clear and the nights are long. Auroral activity is closely tied to the 11-year sunspot cycle, as well as to the 27-day period of the sun's synodical rotation.

fourth and final voyage he noted the same conditions that had preceded the earlier storm, and immediately directed his ships to a safe harbor. Another commander who did not read the clues to the approaching hurricane lost most of his ships and over 500 men.

Tropical cyclones, the larger family to which the hurricane belongs, are the most damaging weather phenomena in the world. One storm in 1970 killed 300,000 people in Bangladesh. In the U.S. alone they have done untold billions of dollars in damage.

In other parts of the world a hurricane is known as a *typhoon* (North Pacific), a *baguio* (Philippines), a *willy-willy* (Australia), or simply a cyclone. The eastern South Pacific Ocean and the South Atlantic Ocean have never been known to experience a tropical cyclone. The word "typhoon" is an Anglicized version of the Cantonese word "tai fung," similar also to the Mandarin Chinese "tafeng."

Figure 20-34. *This WP3D Orion aircraft is fitted with an extensive suite of radar and other electronic gear for measuring the critical characteristics of hurricanes. It will fly through the eye several times during one mission, recording weather measurements—temperature, pressure, etc.—continuously. These measurements help to predict the storm's effects and where it will go. (Courtesy NOAA/NWS)*

Hurricane and Typhoon Generation Tropical cyclones affecting North America are generated in about latitude 10°N in the Atlantic Ocean between Africa and the northern edge of South America, and in the North Pacific just off the Central American coast. From there they move generally westward, eventually curving northward and then eastward as they dissipate.

Hurricane generation seems to depend on several poorly understood factors, among them the general humidity of west Africa, above-normal ocean surface temperatures, and high-altitude wind patterns.

Within these areas, as within other areas where tropical cyclones are born, a cyclone begins as a generalized disturbance in the atmosphere, comprising an area 100 to 300 miles in extent. There is no organized development at this stage, nor are there closed isobars, but if it lasts more than 24 hours, it is classified as a *tropical disturbance* and a close watch begins. This area is sometimes called an *easterly wave,* and atmospheric pressure may drop about 5 millibars. This is significant—normal pressure variations in these latitudes do not usually exceed 3 millibars—and the area will be closely monitored.

The next stage of development occurs with increased convection or vertical movement of air, when closed isobars begin to form and a rotary motion begins at the surface. The storm, now classified as a *tropical depression,* begins slowly moving westward, picking up heat energy and moisture from the sea and increasing in forward speed. Wind speed is a maximum of 33 knots at this stage. At this point, hurricane hunter aircraft (Figure 20-34) of the U.S. Air Force and/or NOAA are alerted.

Moving westward, the storm increases in rotary circulation, clockwise in the southern hemisphere and counter-clockwise in the northern hemisphere, picking up more energy from the warm sea and more forward speed. The low pressure area in the center deepens, causing wind speeds to increase to 34 to 63 knots. It is now classified as a *tropical storm,* and hurricane hunters take off to assess the storm.

Still moving westward, the storm continues to intensify, the low deepening, the wind increasing, and its forward motion more pronounced. When the winds reach 64 knots circulating around a central low pressure area, a *hurricane* has formed.

In the North Atlantic, hurricanes are most likely to form south of latitude 35°N between the months of June and November, with the greatest incidence in August, September, and October. A mid-season storm may last up to twelve days, and an early or late-season storm about six to eight days. An average of about 10 tropical storms are born each year, of which perhaps six become full-fledged hurricanes. The most intense hurricanes contain winds over 200 knots.

In the Eastern North Pacific, the typhoon season is from June through October, but as in the Atlantic, a storm can form in any month. About 15 tropical storms form per year, of which an average of six reach typhoon strength. Most Eastern North Pacific depressions form in the months of August and September and are slightly smaller in size than their Atlantic cousins. Because their natural paths take them mostly over open ocean, they are less destructive than Atlantic hurricanes, but when they do strike land (in Mexico or the Hawaiian Islands), their power is just as great.

The Western North Pacific has its share of typhoons, which form in about longitude 140°E and move westward, threatening western Pacific islands. South of the equator, a few tropical cyclones form between 40°E and 180°, and move in a southerly arc.

The mechanism by which tropical cyclones are formed is not fully understood, but it seems to depend on several different forces working in conjunction. The first is the release of large amounts of heat energy from the condensation of water vapor in a defined area. Since heat is needed to evaporate water, an equal amount of heat must be released when it condenses, and this heat contributes to the convective or vertical motion of the air.

It has been shown that a temperature rise of 1–3°C occurs at altitudes of about 20,000 to 40,000 feet above a developing tropical disturbance, but it is not known whether this is a direct cause of intensification or a symptom of some other process we do not yet understand.

Concurrently, there seems to be a necessity for high-altitude winds to carry away rising air in an upper-level anticyclone, before it sinks back to earth far from the disturbance. This intensifies the low pressure area. At the same time, the Coriolis force imparts a spin to the air rushing into the low, while trade winds begin to move the system westward.

The center of a typhoon or hurricane is a vortex around which winds spiral inward in circular motion. The exact center is called the *eye,* one of the most curious and awesome phenomena in nature. Averaging about 15 miles across, the eye is eerily quiet, almost windless, and completely surrounded by towering cumulus and cumulonimbus clouds. Clear sky may be visible at the top, but often cirrus clouds cover this area. The eye may be only six or eight miles across or as much as thirty miles. In general, the larger the eye the less intense the storm. (See Figure 20-35.)

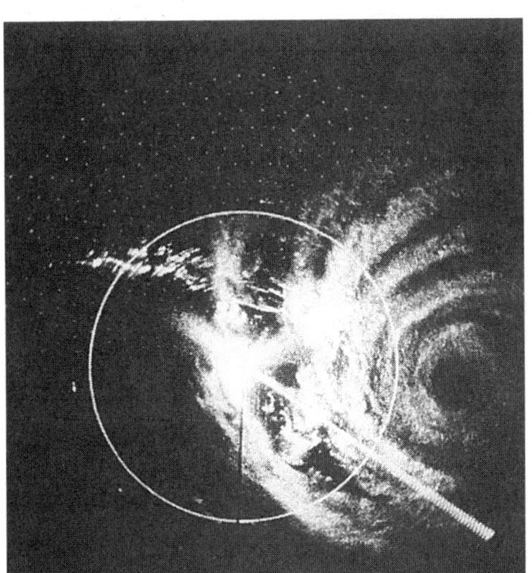

Figure 20-35. *While marine radar is not designed to pick up weather, certain storms are so severe that it is possible to see their characteristics on the screen. Weather radar uses different frequencies than marine radars, which give a better picture of the storm. This view is of the eye of a hurricane, clearly visible at the bottom of the picture, along with the feeder bands which spiral in toward it.* *(Courtesy NOAA/NWS)*

Passage of a Tropical Storm

The first sign of a tropical storm visible to the naked eye is the formation of cirrus clouds, gradually thickening and lowering, with squalls developing. The barometer begins to fall. As the clouds lower, the winds increase to as much as 40 knots, and rain is punctuated by intense squalls. A dark wall of cumulonimbus, called the *bar,* signals the approach of gale-force winds and the main mass of the storm. The eye may still be up to 200 miles away. As it approaches over the next few hours, winds increase to storm and then to hurricane force, seas become dangerously high, and a series of intense squall lines pass, each accompanied by rain blown horizontally in the wind. The sea is white with foam, as shown in Figure 20-36.

The passage of the eye directly overhead is a never-forgotten experience. As the edge of the eye approaches, winds diminish rapidly, the torrential rains stop, clouds thin and then may move away. In a well-developed eye, one can actually see the cyclonic circulation of the surrounding clouds. As the opposite side of the eye approaches, the sky grows dark and winds increase within minutes to hurricane force from the opposite direction. Torrential rains begin again, blown horizontally by the wind.

The tracks of hurricanes and typhoons move westward approximately along the 10° to 15° latitude line, for as much as 50 or more degrees of longitude. Gradually the storm curves poleward and may begin to be influenced by temperate weather patterns. The storm may continue west-northwestward (in the northern hemisphere) and dissipate over land or ocean, or it may continue to curve northerly, then northeasterly. A particularly intense storm may reach latitudes of 50°, but most deteriorate to gales before then. (See Figure 20-37.)

As it approaches temperate latitudes, the storm may be steered by weather fronts or by high and low pressure areas, and may in its final stages join up with an extratropical low moving eastward. They are much slower to dissipate over water than over land, for land robs them of their oceanic heat source and tends to retard the winds. Landfall usually signals the rapid dissolution of the tropical storm to less than hurricane force winds, and storm damage is primarily caused by flooding resulting from drenching rains.

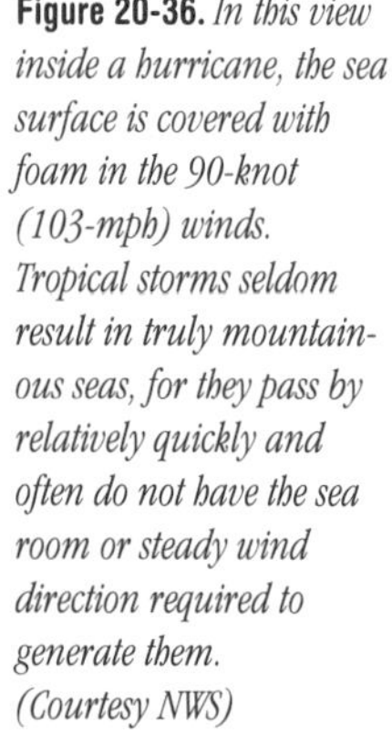

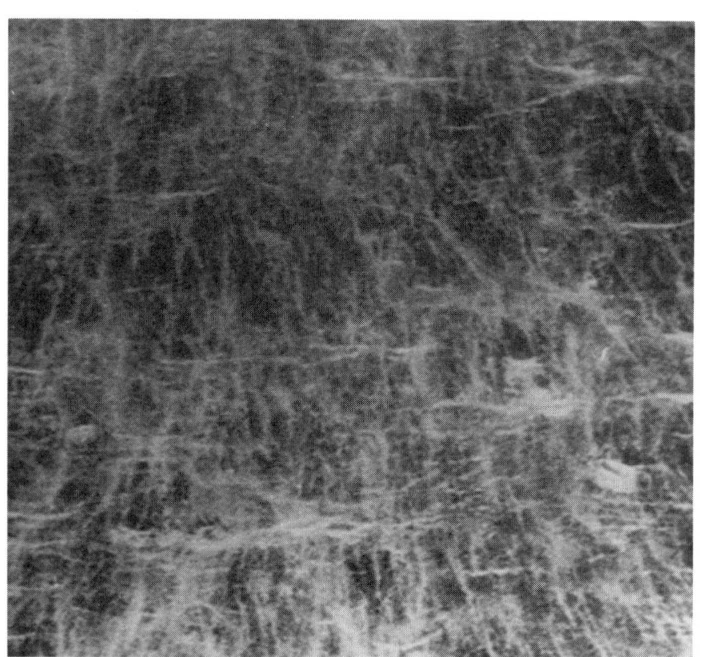

Figure 20-36. *In this view inside a hurricane, the sea surface is covered with foam in the 90-knot (103-mph) winds. Tropical storms seldom result in truly mountainous seas, for they pass by relatively quickly and often do not have the sea room or steady wind direction required to generate them. (Courtesy NWS)*

Avoiding Tropical Cyclones

The most important tool for avoiding tropical cyclones is information. Where is the storm? What direction is it traveling? How long until it is closest to your position? This information is readily available from a number of sources, including marine weather radio broadcasts, radiofacsimile transmissions, television, radio, and newspapers.

With the good weather information available today from so many sources, there is little reason for any boater to be caught unaware by a tropical storm. Storms are often reported on public news broadcasts as tropical disturbances at least a week before hitting any land. The only sure method of avoiding one is to stay out of the areas where they are encountered during the times of year when they occur. However, given the wide variation in their paths and the huge areas they affect,

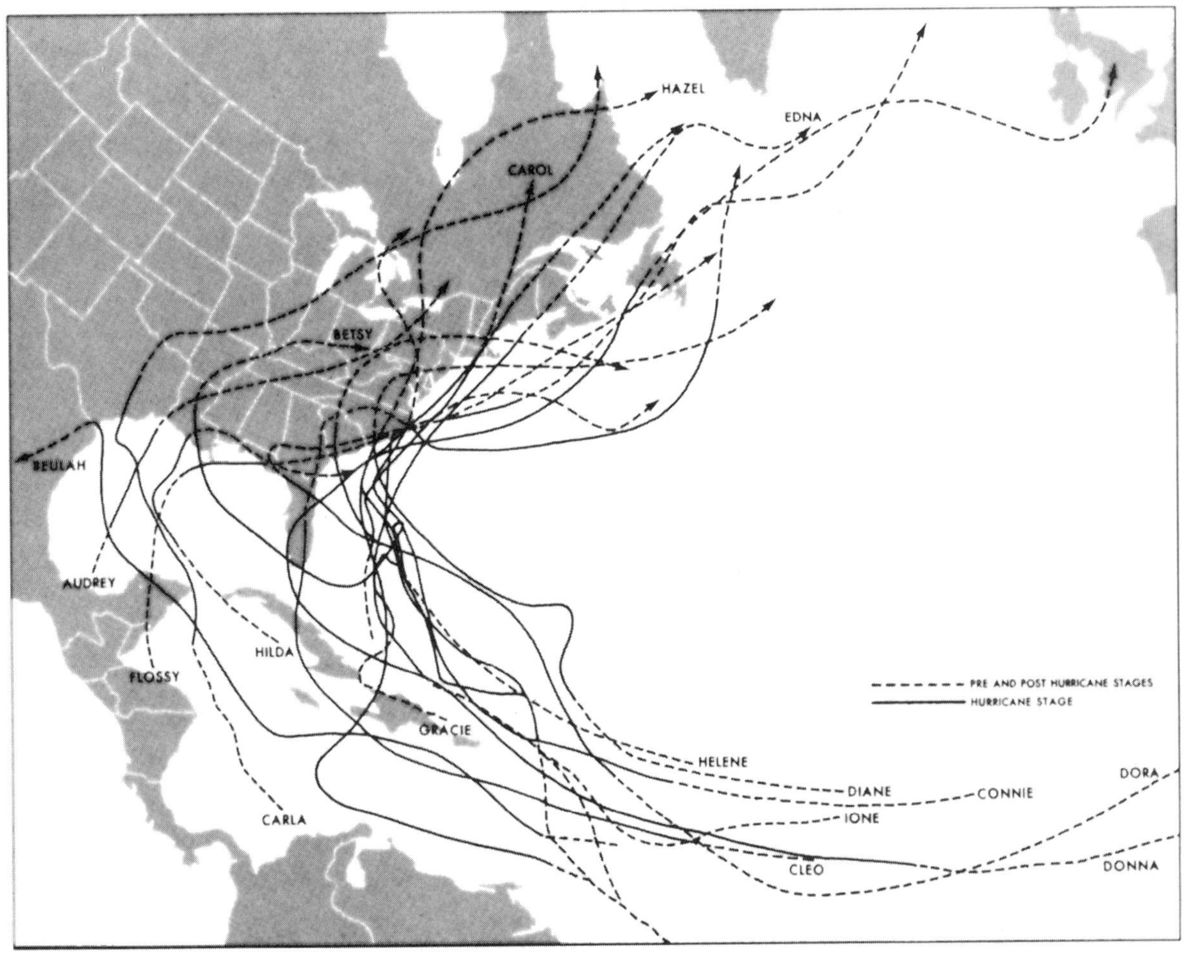

Figure 20-37. *The tracks of hurricanes vary, but those that affect the U.S. generally follow a track westward toward the southeast coast, curving northwest and then north and northeast as they dissipate. Occasionally, though, they stall, circle, and move off in an unanticipated direction, as did Hurricane Betsy in this case. Note how quickly they dissipate over land. (Courtesy NOAA/NWS)*

this is surely unreasonable. Armed with an understanding of the general patterns of tropical storm movement, the boater can make rational decisions regarding risk.

Atlantic hurricanes, born in subtropical waters between Africa and South America, travel generally westward for a few days, then curve to the northwest. On average, the farther east a storm is born, the more likely it is that it will begin this northwest movement early enough to miss the U.S. completely, and continue its poleward journey north, then northeast, to die out in the North Atlantic. The low system may continue northeasterly as a gale at less than hurricane strength to strike Europe, or may be absorbed into another mid-latitude low. The Caribbean islands are at risk from any storm forming to their east, but not from those to the west.

Storms born farther west than about 60°W often make their northwesterly turn too late to miss the U.S. mainland and the western Caribbean island groups, and can take one of several general routes. The eye of the storm may pass through the Bahamas and up the east coast of the U.S. close offshore, passing just off Cape Hatteras or striking it directly because of its exposed position. By this time the storm usually has an easterly component to its direction, and will continue northeast into the open Atlantic. Sometimes, however, influenced by a more or less permanent high pressure system called the Bermuda High, the storm will continue a more northerly course and come ashore in New England, or be driven into the southeast coast of the U.S.

If the storm passes 75°W without significant northern direction, it will usually enter the Gulf of Mexico after ravaging the western Caribbean islands. From the southern Gulf of Mexico, it may continue west-northwest to strike the Yucatan Peninsula or even farther south and dissipate in the interior of Mexico. With a more northerly motion, the storm will cross the open waters of the Gulf of Mexico and strike the southern tier of U.S. states. Western Cuba or the Yucatan area are often devastated along the way. After crossing the Gulf coast of the U.S., the storm rapidly diminishes into a typical if intense low pressure system, and steered by temperate-zone high and low pressure systems, moves northward and finally eastward across the U.S., passing into the Atlantic.

Rarely, a hurricane may pass into the eastern Gulf of Mexico, cross Florida or southern Georgia, and reemerge into the Atlantic. They have also been known to cease forward motion, drift aimlessly for hours or days, then suddenly speed off in an unexpected direction. These are the ones that drive hurricane forecasters and civil emergency planners crazy.

Atlantic hurricanes may form as far west as 80°W. Though dangerous, these storms rarely reach the destructive power or intensity of ones born in more easterly regions, for they lack the time required to become fully developed. Figure 20-38 is a hurricane tracking chart for Atlantic storms.

Pacific typhoons that affect U.S. waters are born in the region of 10°N and 90°–100°W. Many of these curve northwest, north, and then east, striking the western coast of Mexico. Rarely, they may continue as far as the northern coast of Baja California before striking land. Many more, born in the same region, pass well offshore into the open Pacific. Infrequently, one of these storms will move far to the west to threaten the Hawaiian Islands.

The path of the storm in relation to the observer controls the direction and strength of the winds experienced. If one is directly in the path of the storm and facing the eye, winds will be from the left side and slightly behind as they spiral in towards the center. They will increase in strength as the eye approaches, always from the left. As the eye passes, winds decrease within minutes to variable at about 15 knots or less. When the opposite wall of the eye passes, winds suddenly increase from the opposite direction. It only takes about 15 to 30 minutes for the eye of an average storm to pass a given point.

It is possible to roughly compute the time a storm will take to pass over a given point. For example, if hurricane-force winds extend 150 nautical miles in all directions from the center, and the eye is moving at 40 knots, the storm will take about 7.5 hours to pass over ($150 \times 2/40 = 7.5$). Remember, though, that gale-force winds may extend much farther from the center, and can be just as dangerous because of lightning, tornadoes, rain, and hail.

Tornadoes are often associated with tropical storms, but are more commonly found in Atlantic hurricanes than in typhoons of the Pacific, and usually occur along the leading or forward edge of the storm. Though dangerous, they are usually less severe than tornadoes of temperate regions.

If one is to the right of the storm's path and facing the direction in which the storm is moving, winds will be from the right side, and will gradually move clockwise as the storm center passes to the observer's left. Eventually they will be from the left and behind as they subside.

If one is to the left of the storm's path and facing the direction in which the storm is moving, winds ahead of the storm will be from ahead, gradually moving counterclockwise and slightly behind as they diminish.

These two scenarios point out an important fact about hurricanes and typhoons related to their forward speed. If a storm has winds of 100 knots and is moving at 20 knots, and one is on the right side of the

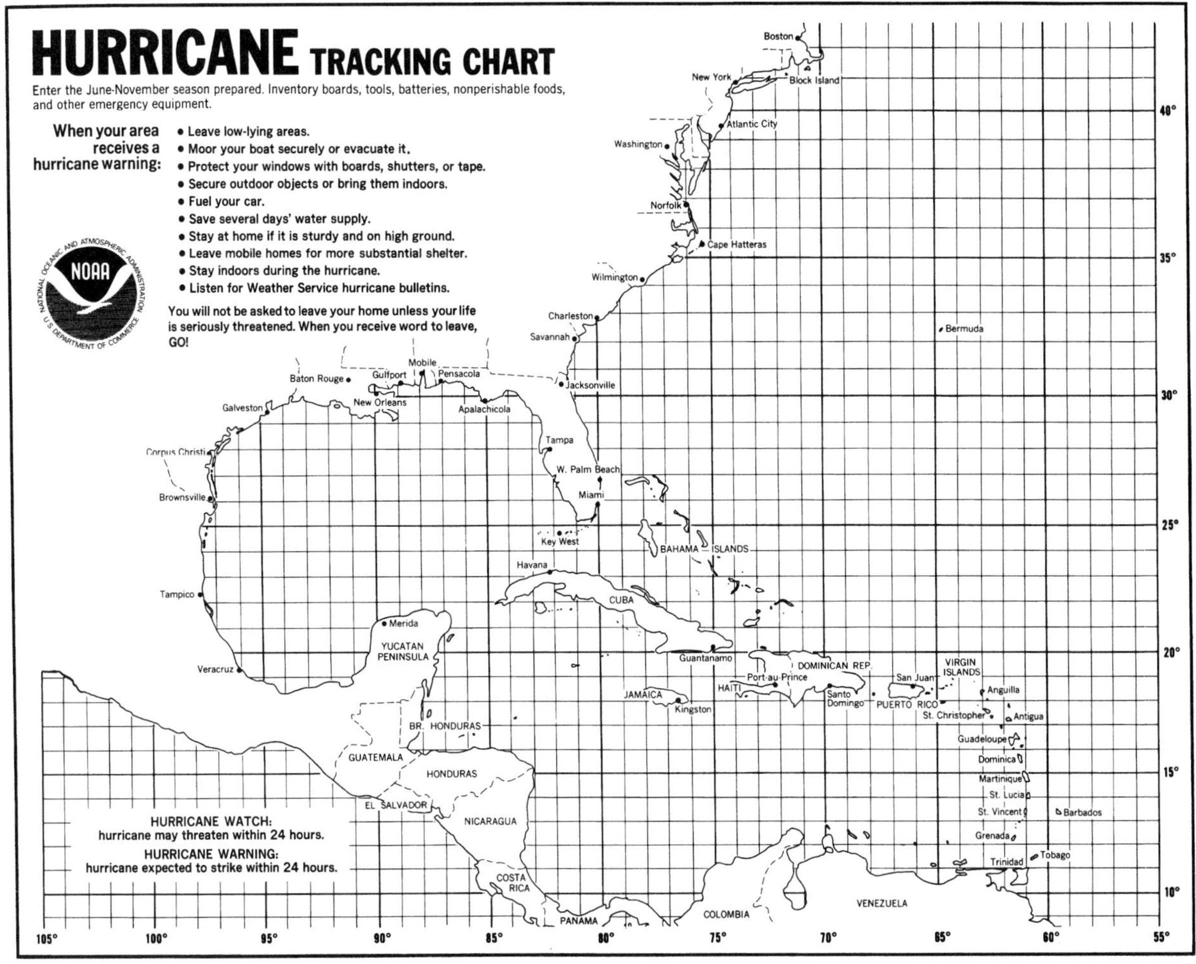
HURRICANE TRACKING CHART
Enter the June-November season prepared. Inventory boards, tools, batteries, nonperishable foods, and other emergency equipment.
When your area receives a hurricane warning:
• Leave low-lying areas.
• Moor your boat securely or evacuate it.
• Protect your windows with boards, shutters, or tape.
• Secure outdoor objects or bring them indoors.
• Fuel your car.
• Save several days' water supply.
• Stay at home if it is sturdy and on high ground.
• Leave mobile homes for more substantial shelter.
• Stay indoors during the hurricane.
• Listen for Weather Service hurricane bulletins.
You will not be asked to leave your home unless your life is seriously threatened. When you receive word to leave, GO!
NOAA
NATIONAL OCEANIC AND ATMOSPHERIC ADMINISTRATION
U.S. DEPARTMENT OF COMMERCE
HURRICANE WATCH:
hurricane may threaten within 24 hours.
HURRICANE WARNING:
hurricane expected to strike within 24 hours.
Boston
New York
Block Island
Atlantic City
Washington
Norfolk
Cape Hatteras
Wilmington
Charleston
Savannah
Bermuda
Mobile
Baton Rouge
Gulfport
Pensacola
Jacksonville
New Orleans
Galveston
Apalachicola
Tampa
Corpus Christi
W. Palm Beach
Miami
Brownsville
Key West
BAHAMA ISLANDS
Havana
Tampico
CUBA
Merida
YUCATAN PENINSULA
Veracruz
Guantanamo
DOMINICAN REP.
VIRGIN ISLANDS
Port-au-Prince
San Juan
HAITI
JAMAICA
Kingston
Santo Domingo
PUERTO RICO
Anguilla
St. Christopher
Antigua
BR. HONDURAS
Guadeloupe
GUATEMALA
Dominica
HONDURAS
Martinique
St. Lucia
EL SALVADOR
St. Vincent
Barbados
NICARAGUA
Grenada
Tobago
Trinidad
COSTA RICA
VENEZUELA
PANAMA
COLOMBIA
40°
35°
30°
25°
20°
15°
10°
105°
100°
95°
90°
85°
80°
75°
70°
65°
60°
55°

Figure 20-38. *A hurricane tracking chart can be used to track a storm's progress and help to decide when to take shelter. Marine forecasts are very good sources of hurricane information because they always give the altitude and longitude coordinates of the storm in addition to other data. (Courtesy NOAA/NWS)*

eye's forward path, one will experience winds of 120 knots. The storm's forward speed is added to the circular motion of the winds on the right. On the left side of the eye's path, where forward speed is subtracted, winds of only 80 knots will be felt. Thus the right side of a cyclone (facing in its direction of travel) is known as the *dangerous semi-circle* and the left side the *less dangerous* or *navigable semi-circle.*

For a vessel at sea, at least as dangerous as the wind speed in the dangerous semicircle is the fact that the winds tend to blow the vessel into the path of the storm and toward the center. The opposite effect is seen in the navigable semi-circle, where the effect is to blow the vessel away from the center. (See Figure 20-39.)

Buys Ballot's Law can be used to estimate the direction of the storm's center. This rule states that in the northern hemisphere an observer facing the wind has the storm center to the right side. In the southern hemisphere, the center is to the left side. Because winds do not follow the isobars exactly but angle inward toward the eye, the center will be slightly aft of abeam to the right (or left). This effect is more pronounced at the outer edges of the storm and less so toward the center, where winds tend to follow the isobars more closely.

From these facts, an observer at sea should be able to locate the direction of the center of a tropical cyclone, determine which semi-circle he or she is in, and take steps to avoid it or to minimize exposure and damage. The following rules will help, and should be understood in reference to Figure 20-39.

In the northern hemisphere:

- In the right or dangerous semi-circle, steer with the wind on the starboard bow and make best speed. If necessary, heave to on starboard tack with the bow to the seas.
- In the left or navigable semi-circle, steer with the wind on the starboard quarter (135° relative) and make best speed.
- Directly in the path of the storm, bring the wind to 160° relative until well within the navigable semi-circle, then proceed as above.
- Behind the center of the storm, make best speed directly away from the center. In the southern hemisphere, directions are reversed, with winds and relative directions to the port side.

Minimizing Damage

It is an odd fact that tropical cyclones do not generally cause seas as large as are found in temperate-zone extra-tropical cyclones, because they rarely last long enough or have the fetch available to cause truly mountainous seas. Their danger lies in the seas' steepness and confused nature, caused by the existence of winds from all directions in a relatively small area. Any vessel venturing into hurricane or typhoon areas should have a detailed heavy-weather plan and the best communications, safety, and survival gear possible (see Chapter 19, "Navigation Safety").

Coastwise, the best advice is to run for the most secure shelter available, be sure the vessel is secured well with ample scope in the mooring lines for storm tides, and find safety ashore. Do not stay aboard. The main danger is storm surge combined with high waves, chafing lines, and other vessels breaking loose and ramming one's own boat.

If time and circumstances permit, it may be well to haul the vessel out of the water and

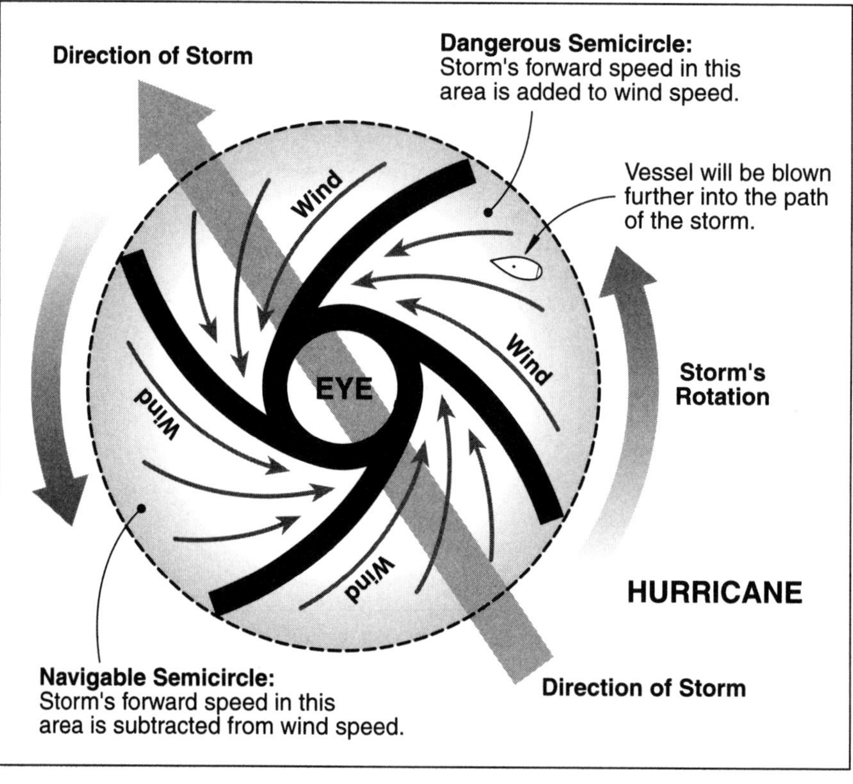
Direction of Storm
Dangerous Semicircle:
Storm's forward speed in this area is added to wind speed.
Vessel will be blown further into the path of the storm.
Wind
Wind
EYE
Wind
Wind
Storm's Rotation
HURRICANE
Navigable Semicircle:
Storm's forward speed in this area is subtracted from wind speed.
Direction of Storm

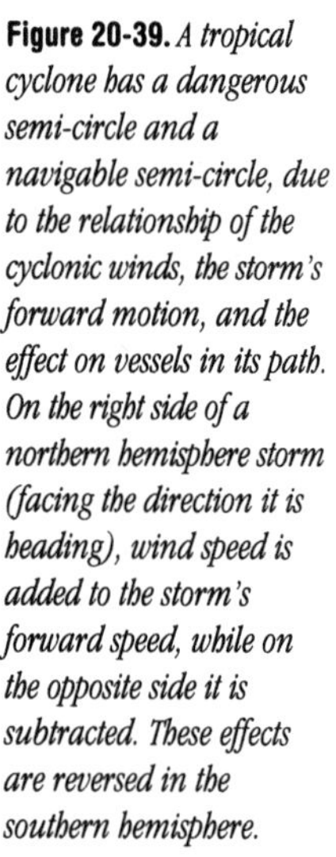
Figure 20-39. *A tropical cyclone has a dangerous semi-circle and a navigable semi-circle, due to the relationship of the cyclonic winds, the storm's forward motion, and the effect on vessels in its path. On the right side of a northern hemisphere storm (facing the direction it is heading), wind speed is added to the storm's forward speed, while on the opposite side it is subtracted. These effects are reversed in the southern hemisphere.*

Figure 20-40. *Several oceangoing ships were beached by Hurricane Camille in 1969. This was the result of* storm surge, *an abnormal rise in water level due to decreased atmospheric pressure and onshore wind, combined with high tide. (Courtesy NOAA/NWS)*

Figure 20-41. *Hundreds of small craft were lost or damaged by Hurricane Camille. Storm surge carried many ashore and left them high and dry. Those were the lucky ones. (Courtesy NOAA/NWS)*

secure it ashore. Filling the bilge with water may help to stabilize it once it is well chocked. If the mooring or shelter is in a river basin, expect severe flooding from rain water in addition to that caused directly by the storm. Regardless of the mooring arrangements, personal safety should be sought well ashore in an approved and secure storm shelter.

After the storm has passed, the navigator should be aware that severe damage to the aids to navigation system will likely have occurred. Buoys and lights will be washed away, power supplies cut off, and structures damaged. Unless movement is necessary, it is best to wait a few days for the Coast Guard to restore at least a minimum level of service to the system. The *Local Notice to Mariners*, NAVTEX, and voice VHF radio will keep one informed of the recovery efforts.

Storm surge *is a rise in the local water level caused by extreme winds and extreme low pressure. Though the intense low pressure of a tropical cyclone theoretically raises the water level as much as four feet, winds blowing onshore can raise water levels an additional 10 or more feet. When this occurs coincidentally with a high tide, severe flooding can result. A vessel moored to pilings with inadequate scope of lines will be dragged under, or the lines will chafe through and the boat be left at the mercy of the storm. While some people describe storm surge as a "wall of water," it is actually a general, slow rise in water level similar to a tide and often in conjunction with it.*

Some tropical storm rainfall records:

- *A total of 73.62 inches of rain fell during 24 hours at Reunion Island during a cyclone in 1952.*
- *Hurricane Camille caused 30 inches of rain to fall in eight hours in Virginia in 1969.*
- *During a Philippine typhoon in 1911, 46 inches of rain fell in 24 hours.*

Figure 20-42. *Low pressure causes the water level to rise. A one-inch drop in the mercury barometer can raise water level more than 13 inches. This is one elemnet of the storm surge.*

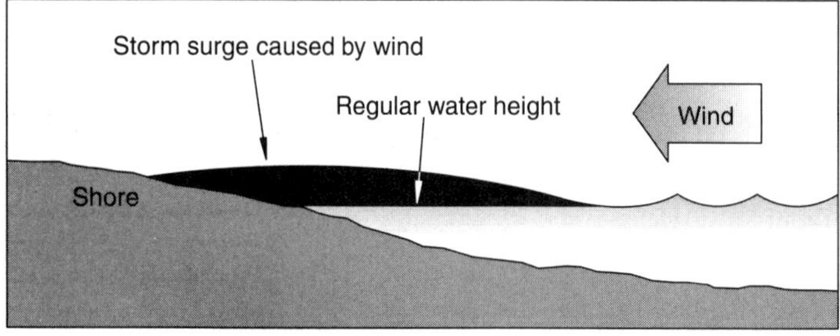

CHAPTER TWENTY-ONE

Oceanography

THE OCEANS COVER MORE than 70 percent of the earth's surface, divided as follows: the Pacific about 32 percent; the Atlantic about 16 percent; the Indian about 14 percent; and the rest about 8 percent. The Pacific Ocean alone covers more of the earth than all the land area combined.

The oceans have a profound effect on the earth's climate through a number of still poorly understood chemical, physical, and geothermal processes. We know much more about the surface of the moon than about the sea floor a few miles off our own coasts.

Understanding the applications of oceanography to navigation can help to round out your understanding of navigation practices and alert you to important safety considerations as well. For example, a 20-knot southeast wind in the Gulf Stream at the Florida Straits makes for a great sail and a good passage, while a north wind of equal strength in the same area generates dangerously rough seas. This chapter explores this and other practical aspects of oceanography that are useful to small-craft navigators.

Salinity

Salinity is the measure of how much dissolved solids (salt and a variety of other compounds) are in water. It is expressed in grams per kilogram, or parts per thousand (ppt), which is the same ratio. The salinity of average seawater is about 35 ppt. Salinity varies from about 32 to 40 ppt according to local geography. Seawater near a river might be diluted to considerably less than the average; warm tropical seas such as the Red Sea might have considerably higher salinity. Salinity in landlocked seas such as the Dead Sea and Great Salt Lake is several times higher than the average value for oceans.

Salinity used to be measured by a laborious chemical process before the discovery that it can be measured quite accurately, if indirectly, simply by measuring the water's *conductivity*—its ability to conduct electricity. A measurement of conductivity determines the ratio of dissolved solids to pure water that is almost exactly the same as the salinity ratio.

Oceanic salinity is often measured by a machine called an *STD* sensor, seen in Figure 21-1, which records salinity, temperature, and depth as it is lowered into the sea from a research ship. Many such readings from different areas in all seasons give scientists a picture of the chemical and physiological nature of the ocean.

Temperature

Ocean temperature varies both horizontally and vertically. Maximum temperatures of about 32°C occur in the Persian Gulf in summer, while minimums of −2°C are found in polar waters.

Figure 21-1. *An STD sensor is recovered after being lowered into the sea, recording salinity, temperature, and depth as it descends. Many such readings over a period of years in many different locations help scientists discover facts about the ocean. (Photograph courtesy NOAA)*

Dissolved solids such as salts retard the freezing of water as it cools, resulting in a lowering of the freezing point. A good example is an old-fashioned ice cream freezer, where adding salt to crushed ice produces salt water that reaches temperatures well below water's normal freezing point of 0°C.

Normally, temperature decreases with increased depth, except in some polar waters. In normal seas the surface layers usually mix thoroughly, resulting in nearly uniform conditions of temperature and salinity down to a certain depth, below which the temperature rapidly declines. This uniform surface layer may be a few or hundreds of meters deep, depending on ocean currents, time of year, weather, and convective overturning. In shallow seas, there may be enough mixing so that the water is uniform right to the bottom.

The boundary layer between the uniform surface mixture and the cooler water below is called a *thermocline*. Below about 400 meters, the temperature is always below 15°C. Thermoclines are extremely important to submarine operations, but have no practical effect on surface navigation of small craft.

Sea temperatures in relation to depths are measured with an instrument called a bathythermograph (from the Greek words for "depth," "temperature," and "picture"), which is dropped into the sea on a cable and winched back to the surface. During its descent, continuous temperature readings are recorded on glass plates by a stylus, to be read later by an oceanographer.

Pressure

Pressure in the ocean is often measured in units of decibars—ten decibars equal one bar. This is the same basic unit as the millibar—1,000 to each bar—used to measure air pressure. The decibar is a convenient unit because the pressure of one meter of water nearly equals one decibar, making the pressure in decibars roughly equal to the depth in meters.

Because water is only slightly compressible, pressure increases with depth at a practically linear rate. Seawater pressure seldom concerns small-craft navigators, but is important for divers and submarine operations.

Density

Density, the measure of mass per unit of volume, is measured internationally in kilograms per cubic meter. In the open ocean, seawater weighs about 1,021 kilograms per cubic meter at the surface and, because of its slight compressibility, about 1,070 kilograms per cubic meter at 10,000 meters depth. Oceanographers often omit the "thousands" in referring to density, so they state 1,021 kilograms per cubic meter as "21."

Surface water density is more variable than the density of deeper waters because vertical

Seawater density does not significantly affect small craft but, in certain situations, can affect submarines and surface ships. For example, an oceangoing ship entering fresh water sinks several inches in the transition from denser salt water to less-dense fresh water. This can require off loading of cargo to meet inland water draft restrictions on a ship loaded to full draft in salt water.

mixing, rain, and river runoff add less dense fresh water, heat, or melting ice. The deep ocean areas have a nearly uniform bottom layer of dense, cold water.

Other Properties of Seawater

Compressibility is a measure of the ability of the molecules of a substance to be forced closer together. Seawater is only slightly compressible but, interestingly, its compressibility is inversely proportional to its temperature—cold water is more compressible than warm water. It's a good thing that seawater is compressible, even if only slightly; if it weren't, the surface of the sea would be about 90 feet higher than it is now and ice would form from the bottom up.

Viscosity is a measure of resistance to flow. Salt water is slightly more viscous than fresh water and cold water is more viscous than warm.

Specific heat is a measure of the amount of heat required to raise the temperature of a given volume of a substance by a certain amount, usually stated in terms of joules per kilogram per degree centigrade. The ocean is a giant heat sink, able to store immense quantities of heat energy while rising little in temperature. Its specific heat is much greater than that of land, which accounts for the more rapid changes in temperature over land than over the sea. On land, all heat is lost or gained from a thin surface layer. In an ocean, vertical mixing distributes the heat throughout a much deeper mass.

Water transmits *sound* much faster than air, as you might expect of a much denser and practically incompressible medium. The speed of sound in seawater is related to temperature, salinity, and pressure, and varies from about 1,490 to 1,510 meters per second.

Transparency of seawater depends on the amount of suspended solids that scatter the light and on the amount of light energy converted into other forms of energy—chiefly heat—as it passes through. When light enters water, the red end of the spectrum is filtered out first and the blues and violets are the last to go as the water deepens. Water color in the open sea also varies with the kinds of materials suspended in it—phytoplankton, sediment, and the like—and the characteristics of the light reaching it.

The Sea Floor

From the coastline of most continents, the sea slopes gradually and slowly down to a depth of about 130 meters, then begins to fall away more rapidly to much greater depths. This shallow coastal area, which extends out hundreds of miles in some areas, is the *continental shelf.* The widest continental shelf lies off the Siberian Arctic. The same feature surrounding an island or group of islands is called an *island shelf.* A continental shelf is not nec-

Boaters who venture onto Bahamian or other reef-encircled shallow banks quickly become proficient in reading the depth of water by its color. (See Figure 21-2.) The deeper the color, the deeper the water, except over certain types of coral formations or vegetation. In general, light green indicates very shallow water and dark green indicates a shallow grass bottom or deeper water, depending on the shade. Brown patches usually signal coral heads; deep blues indicate deep water. Reading depths from the water's color is best done with the sun high and behind you.

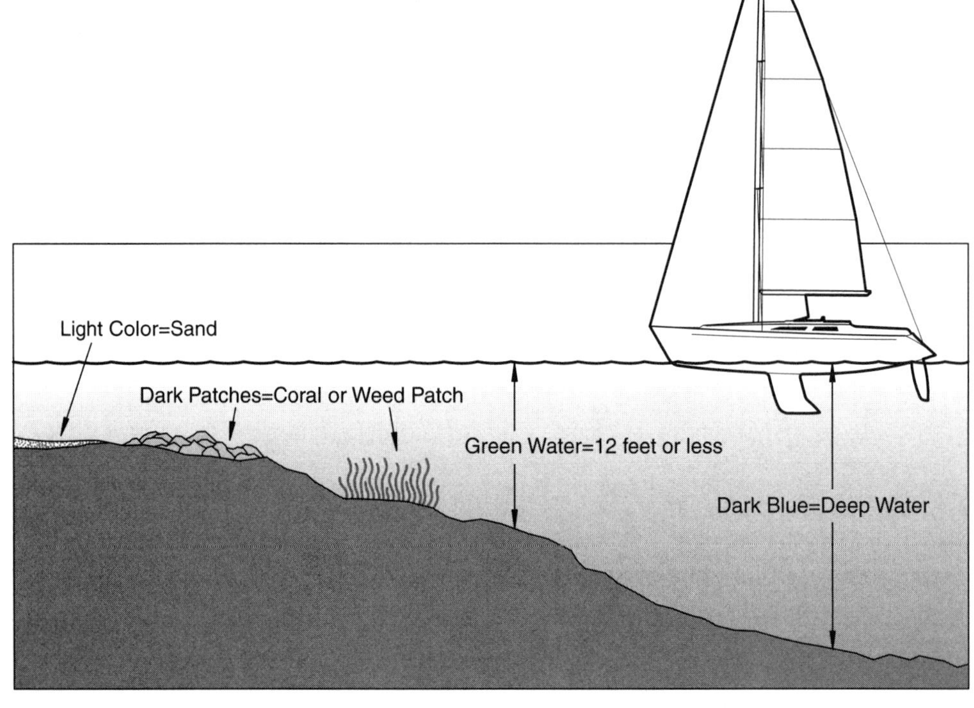

Figure 21-2. *Best done with the sun high and behind you, reading the depth of water by its color can prevent running aground. Generally, the deeper the color, the deeper the water, except over some types of coral or vegetation.*

essarily uniform; it often has hills, ridges, and valleys—some of which are as large as the Grand Canyon.

The *continental shelf* falls away in the continental slope, a 2° to 4° incline that leads to the deep sea floor. The sea floor underlying most of the ocean is made up of vast flat areas called *plains* surrounded by sills forming *basins*. *Fracture zones* are located along lines that mark divisions in the earth's crustal plates; isolated peaks called *seamounts* dot other areas.

The average water depth in the oceans is 3,795 meters. In contrast, the average land height of land is only 840 meters. The greatest known depth—11,524 meters—is in the Mariana Trench in the Pacific. (Mount Everest is 8,840 meters high and would disappear under almost 2,700 meters of water if placed in the Mariana Trench.) The sea floor is generally covered with sediment deposited over millennia by erosion of land, volcanic ash, and the remains of marine life.

Ocean Currents

Ocean currents are classified by the primary factors that generate them. The friction of the wind on the surface of the water produces *wind-driven currents*. *Thermohaline* currents are caused by differences in heat content and density between different areas. Some currents are permanent, others are seasonal, and still others respond to other cycles.

Once generated, currents are influenced by many factors including differences in density, underwater topography, weather, other currents, and the Coriolis force.

The Coriolis force deflects ocean currents toward the right in the northern hemisphere and to the left in the southern hemisphere. Its effect extends through the so-called *Ekman layer*, which varies in depth from 10 to 200 meters. The general circulation of ocean currents is driven by this *Ekman transport* and is west-flowing in the subtropics and east-flowing in the temperate zones—all of which sets up a rotary motion in each ocean basin, with the most persistent and strongest currents at the western edge. These are often called *stream currents* or *streams* like the Gulf Stream—the most notable, but not the only, example. In other areas of the rotary circulation, the less well-defined currents are called drift currents. Figure 21-3 shows the world's principal ocean currents.

Viewed in vertical cross section, the currents in the Ekman layer form a spiral, with currents at the surface deflected 15° to 45° from the wind direction (to the right in the northern hemisphere and to the left in the southern hemisphere). Subsurface currents are deflected increasingly with depth until, at the deepest part of the Ekman layer, the current flows opposite to the wind direction. The deeper currents also have less velocity than the surface currents. This phenomenon, called the *Ekman spiral,* is due entirely to Coriolis force.

Forces such as tides and density-based water movement modify the ocean current pattern. However, in general, constant trade winds generate west-flowing north and south *equatorial currents,* with an eastward *equatorial countercurrent* between them. Poleward of the equatorial currents are the midbasin vortices of rotary circulation, with northerly currents to the west and southerlies to the east. Completing the rotary pattern are east-flowing temperate zone currents driven by the prevailing westerlies, impelled at their western origins by strong stream currents like the Gulf Stream and Kuroshio Current.

In the southern hemisphere constant strong westerlies relentlessly drive the *west wind drift* current that circles the earth. In the

Figure 21-3. *The principal currents of the world form a clockwise-revolving pattern in each major ocean basin that follows the prevailing winds, but is deflected to the right (northern nemisphere) or left (southern hemisphere) by Coriolis force.*

STREAM DRIFT CHART OF THE WORLD

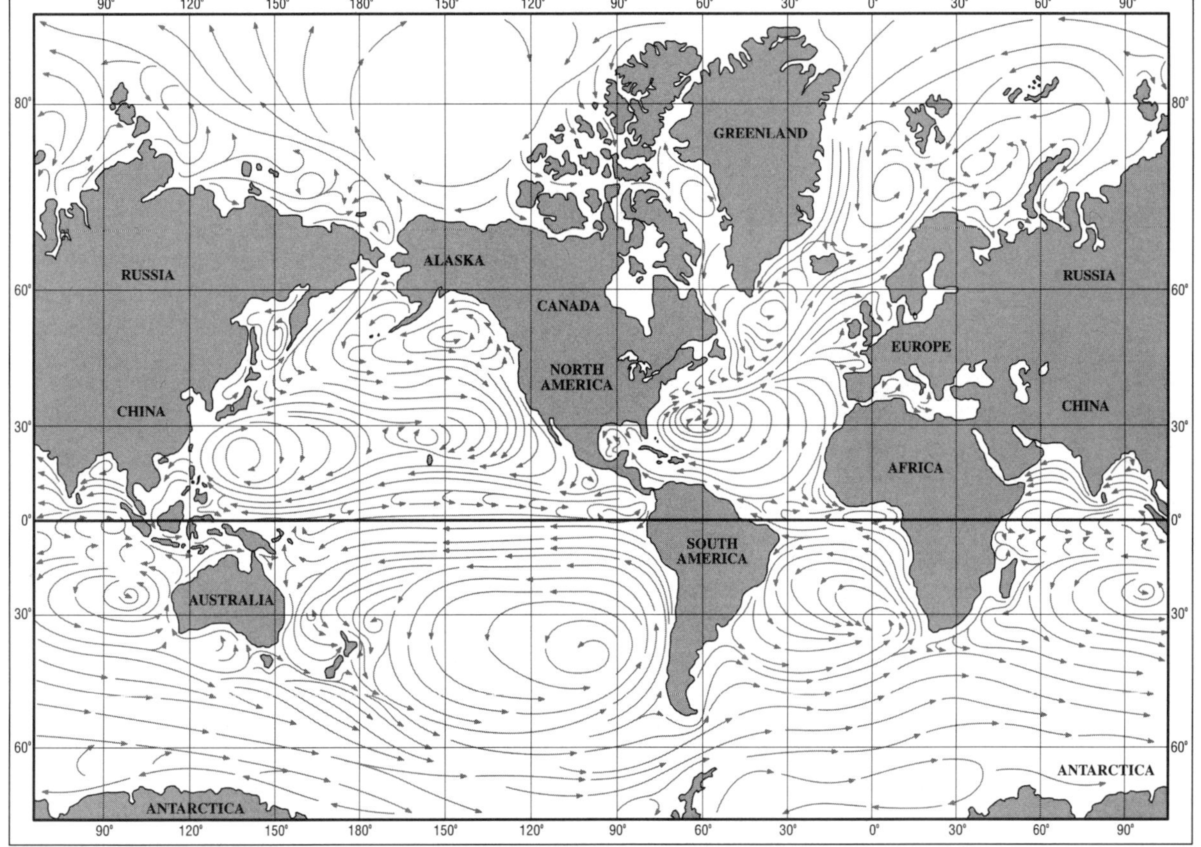

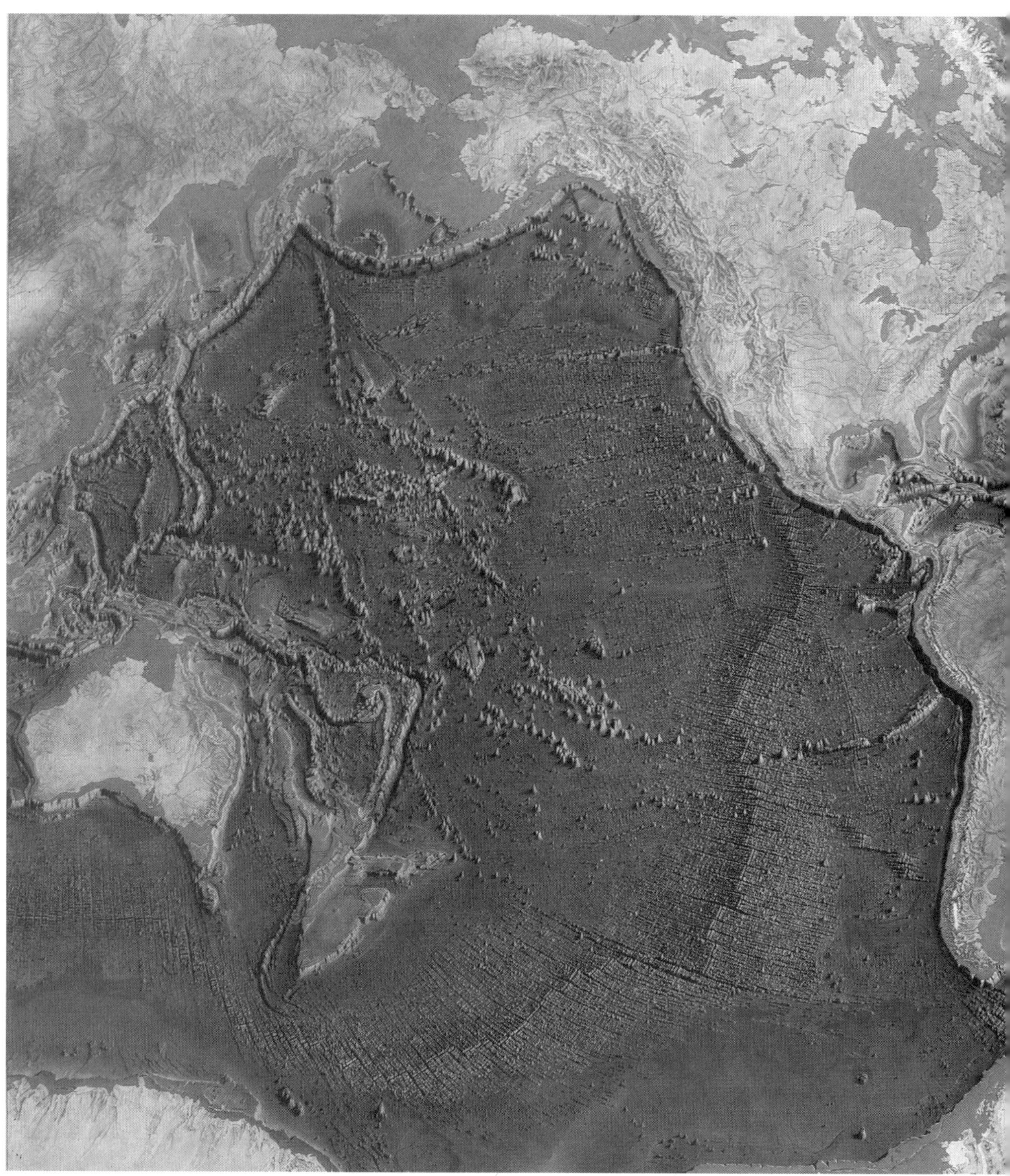

Figure 21-4. *The sea floor has a complex, rugged, and dynamic geography. The Pacific Ocean is rimmed almost completely by deep trenches and steep canyons. It is also geologically active, with much volcanic and earthquake activity. Ridges are created as crustal plates move apart, allowing partially molten material to rise from the earth's interior; trenches are formed when two plates meet, and one overrides the other. The Mid-Atlantic Ridge is a*

major feature of the Atlantic sea floor. It indicates an area of spreading that is slowly pushing the Western and Eastern hemispheres apart. Sea floor mountains, often volcanic in origin, may become islands; others lurk below the surface as sea mounts, *sometimes inducing abnormally steep seas in the waters above. (World Ocean Floor: Bruce E. Heezen and Marie Tharp, 1977.)*

northern hemisphere, where landmasses break the flow, cold Arctic Ocean currents spill down the eastern shores of both North America and Asia, meeting the warm stream currents along the coastlines in midcontinent. The boundaries between cold and warm waters are areas with high incidence of fog formed when air, moistened and warmed by the tropical stream currents, blows over the much colder arctic waters.

Principal Currents Affecting North America

In the Atlantic Ocean, the North Equatorial current flows beneath the trade winds from the Cape Verde Islands westward at a steady rate of about 0.7 knot. Its counterpart on the opposite side of the equator is the South Equatorial current, which starts off the Gulf of Guinea near Africa and then crosses the Atlantic south of the equator before being split by the continent of South America. The southern branch becomes the Brazil current, flowing south along the South American coast to meet the Falkland Current. The northerly branch travels northwest along the South American coast, joins with the North Equatorial current, and enters the Caribbean Sea around the Windward Islands. Between these two currents is the weak, easterly flowing North Equatorial countercurrent.

The combined equatorial currents entering the Caribbean Sea must exit somewhere, and they do so entirely through the narrow Yucatan Channel between Cuba and Mexico. (Weak loop currents are formed in both the Caribbean Sea and Gulf of Mexico.) Still confined, this exiting water forms the Florida current and breaks out of the tropical region through the Florida Strait between Cuba and the Florida Keys. It then flows between the Bahamas and the Florida east coast—as the familiar Gulf Stream—and continues northward off the eastern U.S. coast.

The Gulf Stream meets the Labrador current flowing south out of the Davis Strait. Some of this cold water flows as far south as Cape Hatteras. Southeast of Labrador, the Gulf Stream becomes the North Atlantic current, which continues northeast to wash the shores of northern Europe with its warm waters—without which the European climate would be brutally cold.

Part of the North Atlantic current turns southward to form the Canary current off the coast of Africa, which joins the North Equatorial current in the trade wind belt, completing a circuit of the North Atlantic.

An offshoot of the North Atlantic current turns northward as the Irminger current, which warms Iceland. A branch of the Irminger current flows back southwestward and turns up the western shore of Greenland into the Davis Strait, there known as the West Greenland current. This current carries icebergs calved in this region northward until they are caught by the southward flowing Labrador current and carried along the Labrador coast where they endanger shipping in the North Atlantic.

In the Pacific Ocean, as in the Atlantic, both North and South Equatorial currents flow westward, while between them the equatorial countercurrent returns water back to the east. The North Equatorial current turns northward along the Philippine Islands and becomes the warm Kuroshio current, Japan's "Gulf Stream."

The Oyashio current, augmented by the Siberian coast's Kamchatka current—the Pacific's counterpart to the Atlantic's Labrador current—flows from the Bering Sea southwestward along the Siberian coast to the latitude of central Japan before turning eastward and mixing with the warm Kuroshio current.

Just as in the North Atlantic, this warm, tropical water continues across the Pacific Ocean to wash the shores of North America—but not before mixing with the colder Subarctic current and becoming the North Pacific current. This current splits along the Pacific coast of North America, flowing northward as the Alaska current and southward as the California current. In winter a weak, warm, inshore current called the Davidson current flows northward along the Pacific coastline.

The California current flows southward along the Baja California coast before turning west to help form the North Equatorial current, thus completing the circuit of the North Pacific Ocean.

These large oceanic current patterns are important to small craft for two reasons. First, they influence the climate and weather regimes of the coastal areas where most small craft operate. They are directly responsible for conditions that cause fog, thunderstorms, and other significant weather. Second, they affect the navigation on small craft far more than on large and powerful ships in two ways. One, the relative affect of strong current on slower small craft is greater than on faster ships. And, when a strong current and wind are opposing each other, the result is often steep and dangerous seas—as anyone who has crossed the Gulf Stream in a Norther knows.

The series of *Pilot Chart Atlases* produced by NIMA provide the best detailed summary of oceanic currents. They show directional current arrows and current strength to the nearest tenth of a knot for each 5° block of ocean for every month of the year. Wind roses and much other information are superimposed. The *North Atlantic Atlas* also features large-scale Caribbean and northern North Atlantic data.

Unusual Current Effects

Ring currents are formed when meanders of the Gulf Stream become pinched off from the ongoing flow and continue their rotary motion independent of the Gulf Stream. They drift away from the Gulf Stream's axis, usually spinning eastward and curving southward. These eddies measure 50 to 150 miles across and are particularly important to vessels sailing between Bermuda and the northeastern U.S. coast. Weekly charts of these currents, derived from heat-sensing satellites, are available from NOAA.

Ocean currents have profound effects on the climates of adjacent land areas. As already mentioned, the Gulf Stream, which continues across the Atlantic from North America as the North Atlantic current, bathes northern Europe in its relatively warm water, thereby giving western Europe, which is at the same latitude as Labrador, a climate similar to lands at latitudes some 1,000 miles farther south. Reykjavik, Iceland, warmed by the Irminger current, has a higher average temperature than New York City. The California current cools the coasts of southern California and Baja California to a nearly ideal average climate at a latitude the same as the northern Sahara Desert, while the warm Davidson current moderates the climate of the Pacific Northwest.

Currents also contribute to the air's water vapor content which, in turn, influences the amount of precipitation. Air pressure is also affected by currents: cool currents cause a rise in pressure; warm currents result in a pressure drop.

Deep beneath the surface currents, poorly understood *countercurrents* often flow in direct opposition to the surface current. These are sometimes very cold currents, returning cold dense polar waters towards the equator from whence they came. This current pattern, like the pattern of air circulation, balances the earth's heat energy distribution.

For some undiscovered reason, the strong Pacific trade winds sometimes falter when a large area of relatively low air pressure usually found over the western Pacific shifts far to the east. The westward flowing surface currents also weaken as the winds that drive them slack off, causing a severe weakening of cold, nutrient-rich upwelling currents along the coast of South America—which shuts down the fisheries of this region—and affecting weather patterns as far away as the United States. This phenomenon, known as *El Niño* in South America, is related in a complex way to an interchange of pressure systems between the Pacific and Indian Oceans known as the Southern Oscillation. Scientists now refer to *El Niño* as *ENSO*—an acronym for *El Niño-Southern Oscillation*. Recent ENSO events have occurred in 1983–84 and 1991. In these episodes both the Indian and African monsoons failed, bringing disastrous droughts to Indonesia, Australia, and Africa. Forest fires raged on three continents. Flood destroyed large areas of South America, and strong storms swept ashore in North America, ranging all the way across the continent. Tahiti, normally not in the path of tropical cyclones, was struck by six in one year. The 1991 ENSO event lasted into the spring of 1994 and was held responsible for flooding in the American midwest and for Europe's worst winter in a generation.

Ocean Waves

Waves concern navigators more than any other ocean phenomenon. They reduce their speed, change course, alter voyage plans, and miss deadlines because of waves. High waves may be dangerous to small craft; very high waves can damage, swamp, or break apart and sink the largest ships. When you understand the forces that create waves, you can better avoid their potentially devastating effects.

Waves are formed by the effect of wind on the surface of the sea (except for tsunamis, which are generated by geophysical processes). When wind blows over a smooth water surface at a speed of less than two knots, small ripples form—which dissipate the moment the wind dies. A wind stronger than two knots forms *gravity waves,* which have enough energy to persist after the wind dies. As wind increases, wave height and the energy imparted to the wave also increase, to the point where severe storms can generate wave systems that extend hundreds of miles from their origin. Waves that are generated by local and immediate winds are called *sea waves* or *sea*. Waves that are far from their generating wind are known as *swells*. As swells move away from their generating wind, they gradually lose height and the length and period increase; that is, the swells become lower and longer. Often in the open ocean one or more systems of swells and locally produced waves come from different directions and join to produce a very confused sea state.

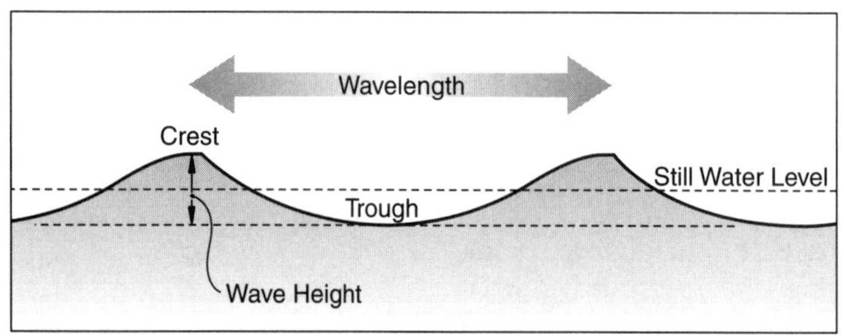

Figure 21-5. Wavelength *is the distance between successive wave crests;* height *is the vertical distance from trough to crest; and* period *is the time it takes one wavelength to pass a point.*

Anatomy of a Wave

Each wave has a *crest* and a *trough*. The horizontal distance between crests is the *wavelength* and the vertical distance from trough to crest is the *height*. The height is measured from the deepest part of the trough, not from the calm water level. A wave's *period* is the time it takes for two successive crests (or troughs) to pass a point. (See Figure 21-5.)

Waves generated by the same storm system can have different periods based on variations of the storm. As they move away from the storm area the larger waves move out ahead of the smaller ones, and the waves sort themselves into sets of several similar-sized waves.

The period of a wave system is one half that of an individual wave, for each leading wave in a set dissipates and is overtaken by the succeeding wave, which then becomes the leading wave and itself dissipates, in endless succession. The period of the system as a whole is known as its *group velocity*.

Wave height depends on several factors, including wind speed, *fetch* (the horizontal distance of open water over which the wind blows), the amount of time the wind blows, and the depth of the water. The largest waves are formed over long fetches by strong winds blowing for long periods of time. It's no accident that the largest accurately measured wave was encountered in the South Pacific Ocean in the band of the Roaring Forties, where winds and waves sweep almost unimpeded completely around the earth.

Wave length, period, and height are closely related. Figure 21-6 summarizes these relationships.

Color photographs of wave heights found in various wind conditions appear following page 276. These pictures, contributed by Environment Canada, were taken aboard two Canadian ocean station ships—*Vancouver* and *Quadra*—at 50°N 145°W and show steady-state sea conditions over as many hours as possible for each Beaufort state. (No photograph is available for Beaufort Force 12.)

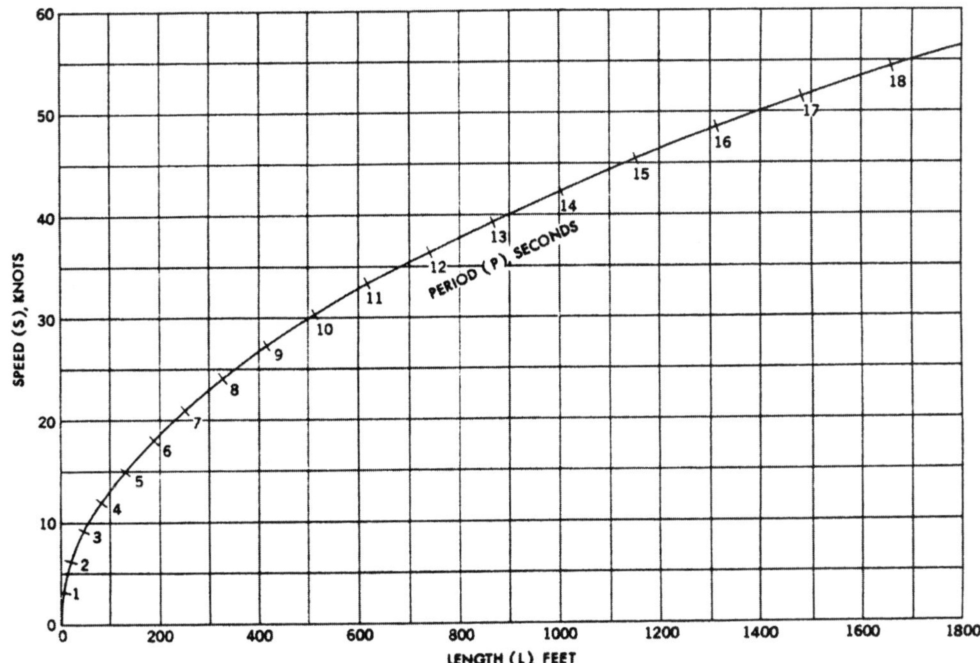

Figure 21-6. *This table shows the relationship between wave period, length, and speed. A wave's characteristics are determined by the fetch and the length of time the wind has been blowing.*

The largest accurately measured wave was 112 feet high, measured in the Roaring Forties by triangulation from the deck of the USS* Ramapo *in 1933. Waves in the Roaring Forties often reach 30 to 40 feet in height, as do North Atlantic and North Pacific waves in severe storms. Waves of 50 feet are less common but are still reported with regularity. And, there are numerous reports of waves measuring 70 to 80 feet.

Table 21-1 shows the relationship between wave height, wind duration and speed, and fetch.

Most observers tend to overstate the height of waves. However, navigators are less interested in the average than in the highest waves, because these affect decisions about course and speed. For this reason, weather forecasters sometimes use a concept called *significant wave height* to indicate wave conditions. Significant wave height is the average of the highest one third of the waves in a system. In some conditions, the highest waves may be almost twice this height.

A particle at the top of a wave moves only slightly forward as the wave passes; vertical motion is much greater. The particle follows an orbital path, moving forward with the rising front of the wave, backward with the falling back side of the wave, and ending up in a position only very slightly ahead of its original location. (See Figure 21-7.)

Groups of waves with different heights, wavelengths, and periods can combine in an infinite number of ways. The height of a wave at any point is equal to the combined height of all the waves occurring at that place and time. A crest and a trough can cancel each other out; two crests can combine into a wave much higher than each separate wave. Systems of swells that reach a coastal area from storms far at sea can radically alter local wave patterns.

Rogue waves form when two or more wave trains unite to produce a single huge wave, or even a series of them. Theoretically, when a wave of 30 feet from one swell system combines with a wave of 30 feet from another, a 60-foot wave will form. Combina-

Beaufort force of wind.	Theoretical maximum wave height (ft) unlimited duration and fetch.	Duration of winds (hours), with unlimited fetch, to produce percent of maximum wave height indicated.			Fetch (nautical miles), with unlimited duration of blow, to produce percent of maximum wave height indicated.		
		50%	75%	90%	50%	75%	90%
3	2	1.5	5	8	3	13	25
5	8	3.5	8	12	10	30	60
7	20	5.5	12	21	22	75	150
9	40	7.0	16	25	55	150	280
11	70	9.0	19	32	85	200	450

Table 21-1. *Duration of wnds and length of fetches required for various wind forces.*

tion with a third swell system can add still more height. Though these waves appear random in nature and are often referred to as *freak waves,* they are, of course, strictly obeying the laws of physics.

Waves and Current Interactions

Currents can have a dramatic effect on waves. A current flowing in the same direction as a wave increases the wavelength and decreases the height; an opposing current decreases wavelength and increases height. (See Figure 21-8.) This latter effect is especially important because even a slight opposing current in high sea conditions can make an otherwise routine passage uncomfortable or even dangerous.

You should try to avoid areas known for strong currents when winds opposing the current are forecast, regardless of whether you're traveling across water as narrow as a small river or as large as the Gulf Stream. Shallow bays, sounds, and estuaries with strong tidal flow are places where wind opposing current may cause difficulty. Areas with strong offshore currents such as the Gulf Stream can be more dangerous because they involve longer passages in open water.

Particularly dangerous in the Gulf Stream is a "norther"—a winter cold front that dips down across the southern U.S. and crosses the Gulf Stream on its way to the Atlantic Ocean. The southwesterly winds that precede the front blow with the current and build up seas in the Stream that are then directly opposed by northerly winds that accompany passage of the front. The change in wind direction can occur within a few minutes and the long southwesterly seas quickly become steep and breaking in the strongly opposing northerly winds.

In some areas where tidal or river currents are strong, current opposing the wind can form *standing waves.* These waves, while moving

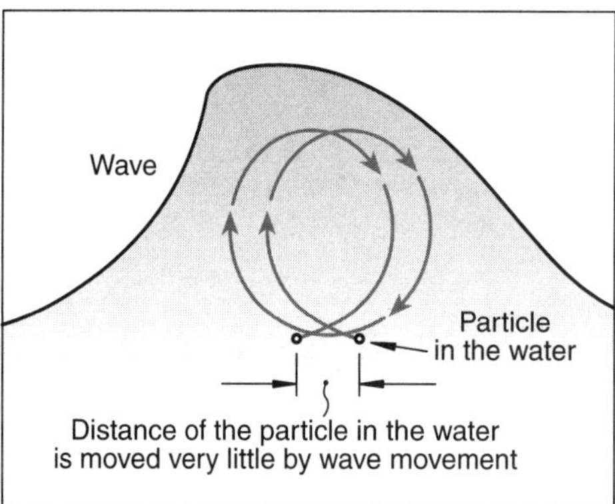

Figure 21-7. *Though waves move relentlessly forward, the water in them moves forward only slightly. This figure shows the orbital motion of a particle of water in a wave. The forward motion shown in this drawing is exaggerated.*

Waves have tremendous energy. A single wave only 4 feet high with a 10 second period expends 35,000 horsepower over a mile of beach when it breaks. Experiments have not shown that heat energy is generated by breakers. Attempts to use breakers to generate electricity have been made, but none was commercially successful.

against the current, have a speed nearly equal to it, and thus move not at all or very little over the ground. They "stand" in one place.

Tsunamis

A *tsunami* is an ocean wave or system of waves generated by a geophysical process such as volcanic eruption, earthquake, or landslide occurring on land or under the sea. Tsunamis are commonly called *tidal waves* but have no relationship to the tides. They can be extremely destructive.

Tsunami waves travel at tremendous speeds and have exceedingly long wave-

The word tsunami *is derived from the Japanese term meaning "harbor wave." A tsunami is an extreme example of a surge. Rather than crashing ashore, it usually just brings a sudden rise in seawater level that causes rapid and severe seawater flooding in coastal areas. Much of the destruction is actually caused by the water rushing back to the sea when the water recedes. These surges can be dramatic. When Krakatoa volcano in the Sunda Strait blew up on August 27, 1833, the water rose 36 meters 30 miles away and destroyed 295 coastal villages; 36,000 people were killed. Fifty miles away, a gunboat was carried 1.9 miles inland and left stranded. The explosion was distinctly heard 3,000 miles away.*

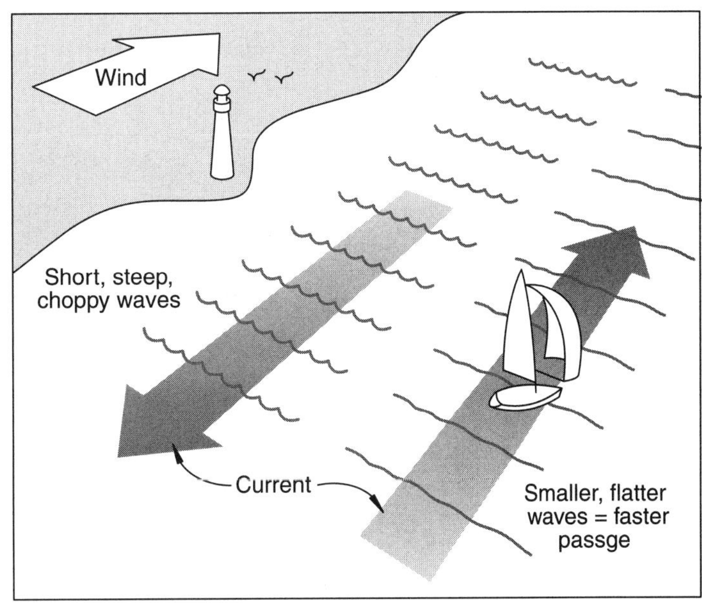

Figure 21-8. *Waves are formed by the effect of wind on the surface of the sea. Currents can dramatically affect waves. A current flowing in the opposite direction of the wind makes for short, steep, choppy waves. A current flowing in the same direction makes for smaller, flatter, longer waves—and faster passages.*

On April 1, 1946, an undersea earthquake near the Aleutian Islands generated a tsunami in the North Pacific Ocean. Nearby Scotch Cap Lighthouse, rising 57 feet above the sea, was completely washed away—along with its crew. Traveling at a speed of 490 miles per hour, the wave system reached the Hawaiian Islands in four and a half hours, lifting the water more than 50 feet to wash inshore as far as 1,000 feet. One hundred and seventy-three people drowned. The last remnants of the wave were felt in Australia a few hours later—6,700 miles away from the earthquake's epicenter.

Since then, a warning system has been set up in the Pacific Ocean that alerts authorities within minutes if a seismic event occurs. Wave heights and travel times to various islands and coasts are computed and civilian warnings sent out.

Tsunamis occur in the Hawaiian Islands only once every 20 years on average.

Figure 21-9. *A tsunami striking the shore in Kalihiwai Bay, Hawaii, then retreating. (Photographs by Rev. S.N. McCain Jr., courtesy NOAA)*

lengths and very low heights until they reach shallow waters. Wavelength can be as long as 100 miles, height only 2 or 3 feet, and speed up to 400 knots. Because tsunami waves are long and low, you usually don't even feel their presence at sea. Their effects are much more pronounced and potentially dangerous near a coast or in shallow water.

When a tsunami wave system reaches shallow water, it increases in height, the period becomes radically shorter, and it surges inland along the coast, usually washing away all in its path. A rapid receding of the water from the shore often precedes the wave front and provides a clue that a tsunami is due to strike within a few minutes or even seconds.

The height and destructive power of a tsunami depend on distance from the source, the topography of the sea floor over which it has passed, the angle at which it strikes the coast, the reflection or refraction of the wave by islands or undersea features, the shape of the coastline that it hits, and the steepness of the sea bottom at the point of impact.

A curious phenomenon, probably related to a tsunami caused by an undetected seismic event, has been reported by several merchant vessels and at least one government research vessel. In this event, some sort of shock wave, perhaps generated by an undersea earthquake or volcanic event directly under a vessel, suddenly shakes the vessel and makes a noise as if the vessel had suddenly run aground. There is no explanation.

Storm Tides and Seiches

Storm tides, sometimes called *storm surges,* are the most destructive force in tropical cyclones—they are responsible for up to three-quarters of the damage and loss of life. Caused by the force of wind on the surface of the sea and by drastic lowering of atmospheric pressure associated with severe weather, storm tides can raise the water level as much as 20 feet or more.

Most of the surge is attributable to hurricane- or typhoon-strength winds blowing against the water's surface and piling the

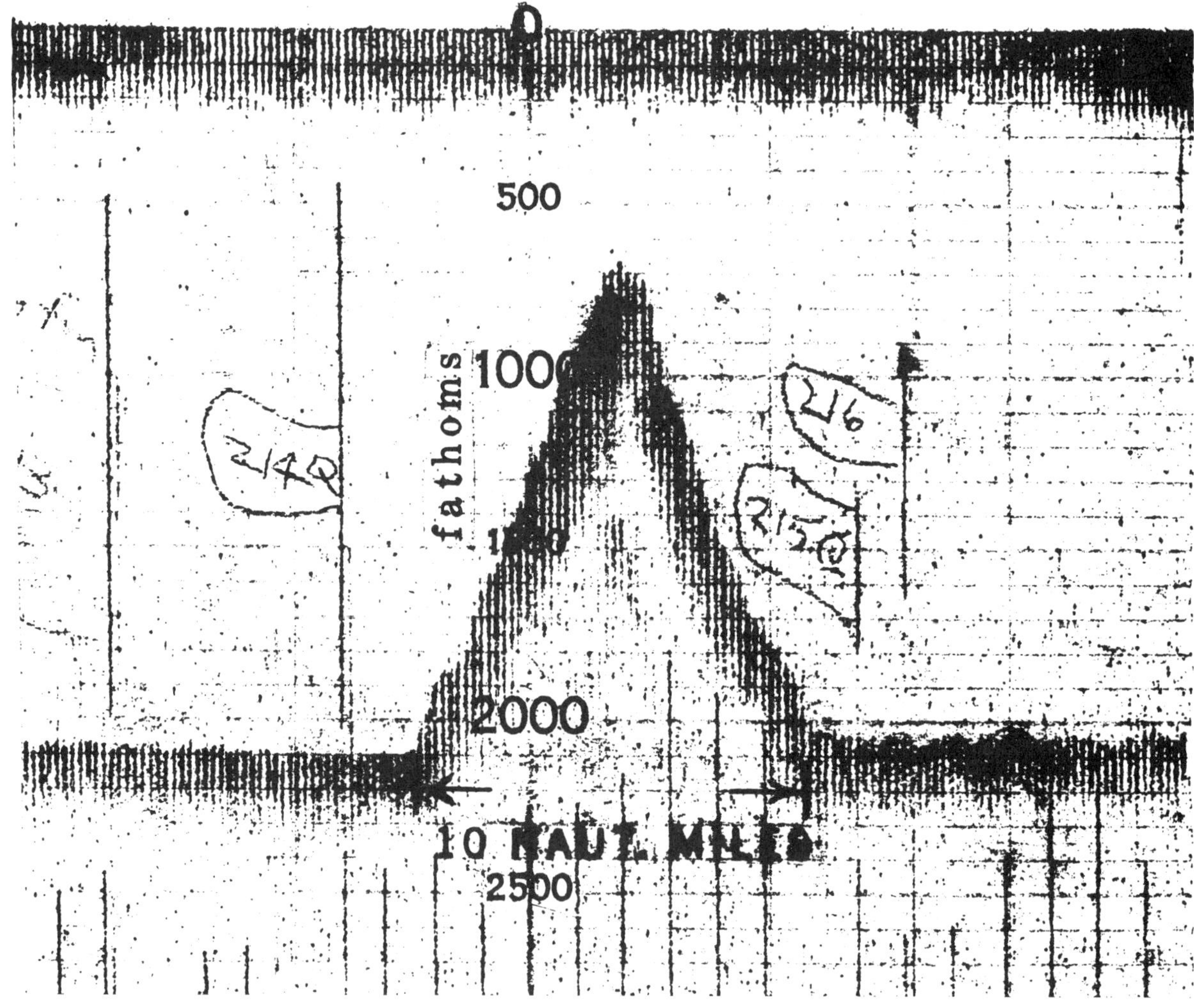

Figure 21-10. *In this image of an undersea volcano as seen by a ship's recording echo sounder, the vertical scale is exaggerated. The volcano is actually ten miles across and over one mile high. Such a feature may be classified as a* seamount, *which makes a good navigation reference point when you sail right over its top and note the depth change. (Photograph courtesy NOAA)*

water up against a coastline. The dramatic lowering of pressure also contributes by causing the sea surface to rise 13.6 inches with each inch of mercury drop in pressure.

Added to these effects is flooding caused by torrential rains associated with tropical storms that reach amounts far exceeding the capacity of drainage systems. The situation may be worsened further when a high tide coincides with the period of greatest wind, rain, and pressure drop.

When all these forces that tend to raise water levels converge—high tide, high onshore winds, lowered pressure, and heavy rains—the result can range from severe flooding to complete inundation of low coastal areas.

A *seiche* is a wave with a theoretical wavelength equal to one-half of the basin in which it occurs. The result is a rapid lowering of the water level on one side of the basin—usually a large lake—and the rapid rise on the other side. Experts believe the cause is a rapid change in atmospheric pressure. A seiche is preceded, as is a tidal wave, by a dramatic receding of the water from shore, followed by an onrushing wave that sweeps well onshore.

Effects of Waves on Boats

A boat moving through the water can be helped or hindered by waves. Generally, waves slow vessels heading into them and

On a stormy day with an intense low pressure system over Lake Michigan, a seiche occurred at Ludington, Michigan, on July 2, 1956. It began with water receding out to about 30 feet from shore, quickly followed by a surging breaker that swept inland more than 100 feet, washing away lifeguard towers and inundating the harbor's outer breakwater. Fortunately, the popular beach and breakwater had been vacated during passage of a severe line squall about an hour earlier and no one was injured.

help those heading away, but only slightly and only up to a point.

Every vessel has a natural period of both pitch and roll. If a boat is in a wave system that moves the vessel in pitch or roll at its natural rate, the motion may become severe even in moderate waves. The remedy is to change course or speed slightly so the boat's natural periods are out of synchronization with the waves. Most sailboats are more stable and comfortable in waves than power vessels because their deep, heavy keels and the press of wind in their sails keeps them out of synch.

A boat moves around three axes: pitch, roll, *and* yaw. *It pitches about an athwartships and horizontal axis that's usually located well aft; a pitching vessel's bow rises and falls. The roll axis is lengthwise along the vessel's centerline; a rolling vessel rolls from side to side. The yaw axis is vertical through the centerline; a yawing vessel's bow moves back and forth from right to left. You may experience all three motions at once, but usually pitching and/or rolling predominate.* Heaving *is the vertical lifting and falling of a boat in large waves. (It may also describe the behavior of the crew on such a vessel.)*

Large ships are subject to *hogging* and *sagging,* which occur in very large seas when the wavelength roughly equals the vessel's length. (See Figure 21-11.) In hogging, the middle of the ship is supported by a single large wave while the ends extend out over the trough of the sea. In sagging, the opposite is true—the ends are supported by waves while the middle is in the trough. Both can be dangerous for some large cargo ships that may simply break in two under repeated stress from hogging and sagging. Many ships have been lost without a trace in this manner, and a few survivors are alive to testify to the suddenness of the disaster. Hogging and sagging are not a problem for small craft, which may actually ride rather comfortably over large swells, provided that the waves are not too steep.

Pounding occurs when a vessel heading into heavy seas rises off one wave and falls heavily into the next, resulting in a shuddering and vibration of the entire hull. Unless it has been built to withstand it, a vessel can pound itself apart under these conditions. The remedy is to slow down and/or change course so that you don't encounter the waves so directly.

Because waves tend to be refracted toward shoal areas, they can become quite rough in areas of convergence as they enter shallow

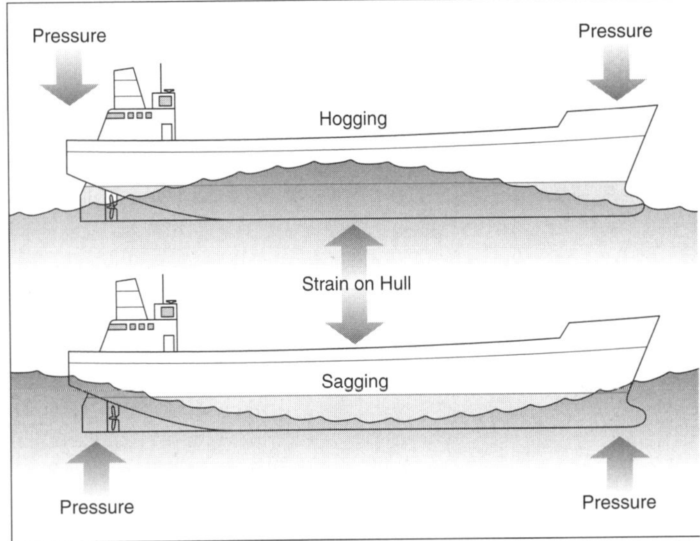

Figure 21-11. Hogging *and* sagging *occur when a ship encounters a wave system with wavelengths about the same as its own length. The stresses can break a ship in half. Small craft ride up and over these large waves, but can have a difficult time with smaller ones.*

water. Large ocean waves can become dangerously high in the approaches to a river or estuary, particularly if a sandbar lies off the mouth. The effect is greatly enhanced by a strong ebb tide. This problem is common on the coast of Washington and Oregon, but is also encountered to some extent in many other areas.

Even in fine weather, an ebbing tide and an onshore wind can make for a dangerous passage through an inlet. Waves that look innocent offshore become higher, shorter, and steeper when they encounter an outrushing tidal current. The reason is that wave energy becomes more concentrated when encountering the opposing current. When the water is so shallow that waves are further affected by the sea floor, the breaking is even worse. With a very strong current, the waves may even become standing waves whose forward speed is just equal to the opposing current's speed.

In these conditions, breaking waves tend to be the plunging type because their front faces fall forward over the wave base that is being swept seaward by the current. Navigation in such conditions ranges from tricky to dangerous, depending on the seaworthiness and power of the vessel, the speed of the waves, and the sea conditions. You should try to stay in the deepest water possible to minimize the effect of the sea floor on the waves. Skillful boat handling is essential as well.

When heading downwind, if the waves are running faster than the vessel can travel, it's best to use enough speed to maintain good steerageway, but not so much that the vessel begins to surf because then it's much more likely to broach. You might have to work the engine throttle actively to keep the proper speed and helm control while letting the waves pass in succession under your boat. Patience is the key.

If your boat can travel at the speed of the fastest waves, pick two longer waves and adjust your speed so you stay between them, but slightly closer to the one ahead. By doing this you can safely and quickly ride the back of a wave right through the dangerous zone. Periodically, each wave will be overridden by succeeding waves of the train, but your boat should be able to ride ahead to the next one with little problem.

Sailing into these types of waves, instead of with them, can cause severe pounding even at slow speeds. Your best choice might be to wait for the tide to change or for the wind and seas to drop. If you must run an inlet or channel into the waves and with the current, again it's best to try to stay in the deepest water and find a balance between progress and pounding that maximizes the former and minimizes of the latter. Most boats experience less pounding when heading directly into the waves.

Breakers and Surf

A wave is formed with energy imparted to water by wind. The energy of a wave, once acquired, gradually dissipates when the wind force is removed. Another wave-dissipating factor is shallow water and, ultimately, a coastline. Reefs, sandbars, and other offshore obstructions also play a part in dissipating wave energy.

As a wave enters shallow water, its bottom portion is met by the rising sea floor, reducing the vertical dimension of the wave and redirecting its energy into a shorter period and increased height. The bottom of the wave is also slowed by the friction of the sea bottom. When the upper portion of the wave becomes too high and fast for the slower, lower portion, the water tumbles forward in a *breaker.*

Breakers are one of three classes: A *spilling breaker* breaks only along the top of the crest over a long distance. A *plunging breaker* breaks along most of its entire height, dissipating its energy in a single crash. A *surging breaker* simply races up onto a beach with little or no foam or fuss, only a rapid onrush of water. A wave begins to be affected by the bottom when the water depth equals about one half the wavelength and breaks when water depth is about 1.3 times the height. The type of breaker that occurs in any location depends on the type of seafloor and near-shore sea conditions. Spilling and surging breakers are shown in Figures 21-12 and 21-13, respectively.

Figure 21-12. Spilling breakers *break only along their top edges for a long distance. They usually occur when large waves meet the coast along very gently sloping beaches, but you also see them in the open ocean during storms. (Photograph courtesy NOAA)*

Figure 21-13. *A* plunging breaker *breaks for most of its entire height all at once, concentrating its energy in a single crash. This type occurs mostly along steeply shoaling beaches. (Photograph courtesy NOAA)*

Waves are bent or refracted by shallow water. Waves approaching a beach at an oblique angle tend to bend so that they are parallel to the shore when they meet the beach.

Waves approaching a point are refracted toward the point and converge in a small area; waves approaching a bay are refracted in a way that stretches them out along the coast and leaves relatively calm water in the middle of the bay. (See Figures 21-14 and 21-15.)

On long straight beaches a current is formed along the shore that moves in the direction of the waves. This current can carry tremendous amounts of beach sand, causing beach erosion and channel shoaling at the openings of harbors and bays. These changes can occur over a matter of hours, and a single storm can radically alter or obliterate an entrance channel. Such an effect is not limited to ocean openings, but can occur in estuaries, large bays, lakes, and sounds.

The development of *sandbars* along shorelines varies with the average height of the waves that strike an area. These bars form parallel to the beach to heights about one-quarter the depth of water. As many as three or four separate bars may form, each parallel to the shore and each in progressively deeper water. Small craft navigating along sandy beaches should stay well offshore to avoid them.

When waves rush up a beach, they transport water ashore. The return of this water to

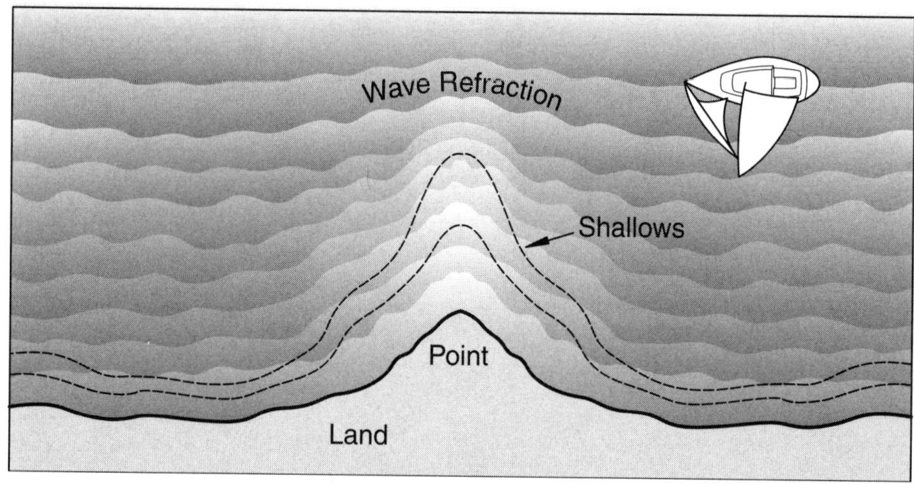

Figure 21-14. *Wave refraction occurs when a wave is slowed by shallow water, which causes each wave to meet the beach at a right angle. Convergence of waves toward shoal areas can cause rough seas to form on the point of a shoal.*

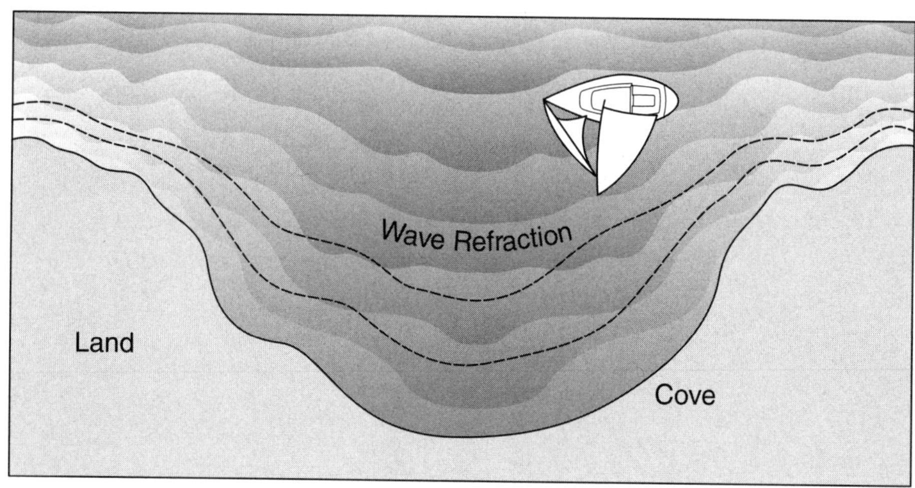

Figure 21-15. *Divergence of waves toward shoal areas adjacent to a bay dissipates the wave energy over a large area, creating relatively calm conditions in the center of the bay.*

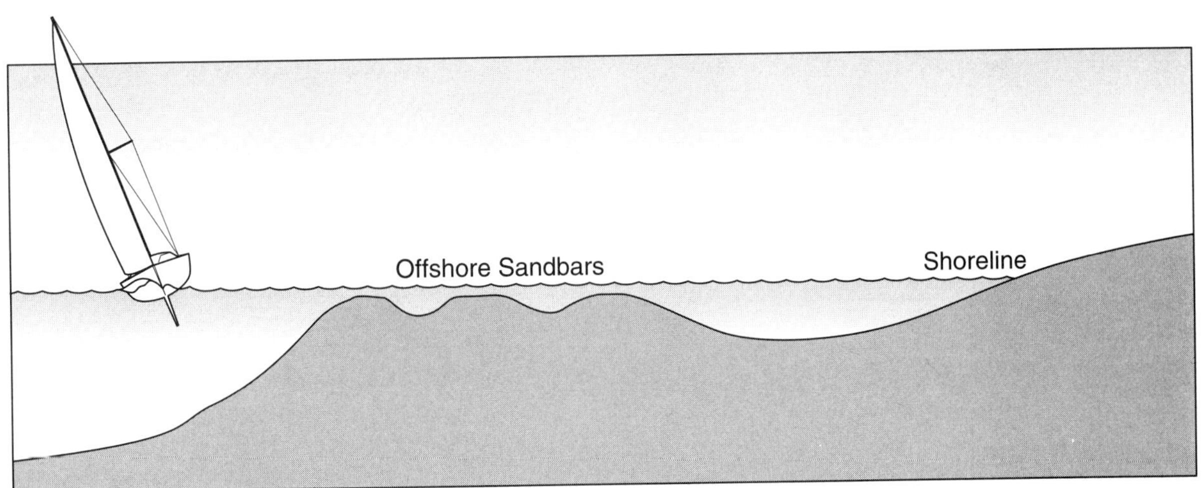

Figure 21-16. *Wave action on sandy coasts can cause the formation of sandbars offshore, a hazard for coasting craft venturing too close inshore.*

the sea is called the *backwash,* which tends to undercut the next incoming wave and cause it to break. When this current flows back out to sea in a single layer below the incoming waves, an *undertow* is formed, which can be dangerous to swimmers if it's strong.

During heavy weather, when the volume of water rushing inshore piles up behind the first sandbar, it flows parallel to the shore in a *longshore current* until it reaches a weak point in the bar, where it breaks through and rushes back out to sea in a *rip current.* Also very dangerous to swimmers, rip currents change location over time as longshore currents sweep sandbars from place to place.

Conclusion

Waves usually have a greater impact on small craft than on large vessels. You should understand the effects of waves and their causes and plan your voyages to minimize their effects.

This book doesn't address all the steps that you should take aboard a small craft to avoid heavy seas or to deal with them if they should occur. Using pilot charts, weather maps, radio broadcasts, and weather facsimile machines, combined with knowledge of weather and oceanography, can help you avoid them, if possible, or reduce their potentially damaging effects.

APPENDIX

Tables

Table 1. Conversion Table for Meters, Feet, and Fathoms—The number of feet and fathoms corresponding to a given number of meters, and vice versa, can be taken directly from this table to any value of the entering argument from 1 to 120. The entering value can be multiplied by any power of 10, including negative powers, if the corresponding values of the other units are multiplied by the same power. Thus, 420 meters are equivalent to 1,378.0 feet, and 11.2 fathoms are equivalent to 20.483 meters.

The table was computed by means of the relationships:

1 meter = 39.370079 inches
1 foot = 12 inches
1 fathom = 6 feet

Table 2. Conversion Table for Nautical and Statute Miles—This table gives the number of statute miles corresponding to any whole number of nautical miles from 1 to 100, and the number of nautical miles corresponding to any whole number of statute miles within the same range. The entering value can be multiplied by any power of 10, including negative powers, if the corresponding value of the other unit is multiplied by the same power. Thus, 2,700 nautical miles are equivalent to 3,107.1 statute miles, and 0.3 statute mile is equivalent to 0.2607 nautical mile.

The table was computed using the conversion factors:

1 nautical mile = 1.15077945 statute miles
1 statute mile = 0.86897624 nautical mile.

Table 3. Speed Table for Measured Mile—To find the speed of a vessel on a measured nautical mile in a given number of minutes and seconds of time, enter this table at the top or bottom with the number of minutes, and at either side with the number of seconds. The number taken from the table is speed in knots.

This table was computed by means of the formula:

$$S = \frac{3600}{T}$$

in which D is distance in nautical miles, S is speed in knots, and T is elapsed time in minutes.

Table 4. Speed, Time, and Distance Table—To find the distance steamed at any given speed between 0.5 and 40 knots in any given number of minutes from 1 to 60, enter this table at the top with the speed, and at the left with the number of minutes. The number taken from the table is the distance in nautical miles. If hours are substituted for minutes, the tabulated distance should be multiplied by 60; if seconds are substituted for minutes, the tabulated distance should be divided by 60.

The table was computed by means of the formula:

$$D = \frac{ST}{60}$$

in which D is distance in nautical miles, S is speed in knots, and T is elapsed time in minutes.

Table 5. Distance of the Horizon—This table gives the distance in nautical and statute miles of the visible sea horizon for various heights of eye in feet and meters. The actual distance varies somewhat as refraction changes. However, the error is generally less than that introduced by nonstandard atmospheric conditions. Also the formula used contains an approximation that introduces a small error at the greatest heights tabulated.

The table was computed using the formula:

$$D = \sqrt{\frac{2r_o\, h_f}{6076.1\ \beta_o}}$$

in which D is the distance to the horizon in nautical miles; r_o is the mean radius of the earth, 3,440.1 nautical miles; h_f is the height of eye in feet; and β_o (0.8279) accounts for terrestrial refraction.

This formula simplifies to: D (nm) $= 1.169\sqrt{h_f}$

(statute miles) $= 1.346\sqrt{h_f}$

Table 6. Geographic Range—This table gives the geographic range or the maximum distance at which the curvature of the earth permits a light to be seen from a particular height of eye without regard to the luminous intensity of the light. The geographic range depends upon the height of both the light and the eye of the observer.

The table was computed using the formula:

$$D = \sqrt{1.17H} + \sqrt{1.17h}$$

in which D is the geographic range in nautical miles, H is the height in feet of the light above sea level, and h is the height in feet of the eye of the observer above sea level.

Table 7. Time Zones, Descriptions, and Suffixes—The zone description and the single letter of the alphabet designating a time zone and sometimes used as a suffix to zone time for all time zones are given in this table.

Table 8. Conversion Table for Thermometer Scales—Enter this table with temperature Fahrenheit, F; Celsius (centigrade), C; or Kelvin, K; and take out the corresponding readings on the other two temperature scales.

On the Fahrenheit scale, the freezing temperature of pure water at standard sea level pressure is 32°, and the boiling point under the same conditions is 212°. The corresponding temperatures are 0° and 100° on the Celsius scale and 273.15° and 373.15°, respectively, on the Kelvin scale. The value of (-) 273.15° C for absolute zero, the starting point of the Kelvin scale, is the value recognized officially by the National Institute of Standards and Technology (NIST).

The formulas are:

$$C = 5/9\,(F - 32°) = K - 273.15$$

$$F = 9/5\,(C + 32°) = 9/5\,K - 459.67$$

$$K = 5/9\,(F + 459.67°) = C + 273.15°$$

Table 9. Conversion Table for Millibars, Inches of Mercury, and Millimeters of Mercury—The reading of a barometer in inches or millimeters of mercury corresponding to a given reading in millibars can be found directly from this table.

The formula for the pressure in millibars is:

$$P = \frac{BmDg}{1000}$$

in which P is the atmospheric pressure in millibars, B_m is the height of the column of mercury in millimeters, D is the density of mercury = 13.5951 grams per cubic centimeter, and g is the standard value of gravity = 980.665 dynes. Substituting numerical values:

$$P = 1.33322B_m$$

$$B_m = \frac{P}{1.33322} = 0.750064P$$

Since on millimeter = 0.03937 inches

$$B_i = \frac{0.0393P}{1.33322} = 0.0295300P$$

in which B_i is the height of the column of mercury in inches.

TABLE 1

Conversion Table for Meters, Feet, and Fathoms

Meters	Feet	Fathoms	Meters	Feet	Fathoms	Feet	Meters	Feet	Meters	Fathoms	Meters	Fathoms	Meters
1	3.28	0.55	61	200.13	33.36	1	0.30	61	18.59	1	1.83	61	111.56
2	6.56	1.09	62	203.41	33.90	2	0.61	62	18.90	2	3.66	62	113.39
3	9.84	1.64	63	206.69	34.45	3	0.91	63	19.20	3	5.49	63	115.21
4	13.12	2.19	64	209.97	35.00	4	1.22	64	19.51	4	7.32	64	117.04
5	16.40	2.73	65	213.25	35.54	5	1.52	65	19.81	5	9.14	65	118.87
6	19.69	3.28	66	216.54	36.09	6	1.83	66	20.12	6	10.97	66	120.70
7	22.97	3.83	67	219.82	36.64	7	2.13	67	20.42	7	12.80	67	122.53
8	26.25	4.37	68	223.10	37.18	8	2.44	68	20.73	8	14.63	68	124.36
9	29.53	4.92	69	226.38	37.73	9	2.74	69	21.03	9	16.46	69	126.19
10	32.81	5.47	70	229.66	38.28	10	3.05	70	21.34	10	18.29	70	128.02
11	36.09	6.01	71	232.94	38.82	11	3.35	71	21.64	11	20.12	71	129.84
12	39.37	6.56	72	236.22	39.37	12	3.66	72	21.95	12	21.95	72	131.67
13	42.65	7.11	73	239.50	39.92	13	3.96	73	22.25	13	23.77	73	133.50
14	45.93	7.66	74	242.78	40.46	14	4.27	74	22.56	14	25.60	74	135.33
15	49.21	8.20	75	246.06	41.01	15	4.57	75	22.86	15	27.43	75	137.16
16	52.49	8.75	76	249.34	41.56	16	4.88	76	23.16	16	29.26	76	138.99
17	55.77	9.30	77	252.62	42.10	17	5.18	77	23.47	17	31.09	77	140.82
18	59.06	9.84	78	255.91	42.65	18	5.49	78	23.77	18	32.92	78	142.65
19	62.34	10.39	79	259.19	43.20	19	5.79	79	24.08	19	34.75	79	144.48
20	65.62	10.94	80	262.47	43.74	20	6.10	80	24.38	20	36.58	80	146.30
21	68.90	11.48	81	265.75	44.29	21	6.40	81	24.69	21	38.40	81	148.13
22	72.18	12.03	82	269.03	44.84	22	6.71	82	24.99	22	40.23	82	149.96
23	75.46	12.58	83	272.31	45.38	23	7.01	83	25.30	23	42.06	83	151.79
24	78.74	13.12	84	275.59	45.93	24	7.32	84	25.60	24	43.89	84	153.62
25	82.02	13.67	85	278.87	46.48	25	7.62	85	25.91	25	45.72	85	155.45
26	85.30	14.22	86	282.15	47.03	26	7.92	86	26.21	26	47.55	86	157.28
27	88.58	14.76	87	285.43	47.57	27	8.23	87	26.52	27	49.38	87	159.11
28	91.86	15.31	88	288.71	48.12	28	8.53	88	26.82	28	51.21	88	160.93
29	95.14	15.86	89	291.99	48.67	29	8.84	89	27.13	29	53.04	89	162.76
30	98.43	16.40	90	295.28	49.21	30	9.14	90	27.43	30	54.86	90	164.59
31	101.71	16.95	91	298.56	49.76	31	9.45	91	27.74	31	56.69	91	166.42
32	104.99	17.50	92	301.84	50.31	32	9.75	92	28.04	32	58.52	92	168.25
33	108.27	18.04	93	305.12	50.85	33	10.06	93	28.35	33	60.35	93	170.08
34	111.55	18.59	94	308.40	51.40	34	10.36	94	28.65	34	62.18	94	171.91
35	114.83	19.14	95	311.68	51.95	35	10.67	95	28.96	35	64.01	95	173.74
36	118.11	19.69	96	314.96	52.49	36	10.97	96	29.26	36	65.84	96	175.56
37	121.39	20.23	97	318.24	53.04	37	11.28	97	29.57	37	67.67	97	177.39
38	124.67	20.78	98	321.52	53.59	38	11.58	98	29.87	38	69.49	98	179.22
39	127.95	21.33	99	324.80	54.13	39	11.89	99	30.18	39	71.32	99	181.05
40	131.23	21.87	100	328.08	54.68	40	12.19	100	30.48	40	73.15	100	182.88
41	134.51	22.42	101	331.36	55.23	41	12.50	101	30.78	41	74.98	101	184.71
42	137.80	22.97	102	334.65	55.77	42	12.80	102	31.09	42	76.81	102	186.54
43	141.08	23.51	103	337.93	56.32	43	13.11	103	31.39	43	78.64	103	188.37
44	144.36	24.06	104	341.21	56.87	44	13.41	104	31.70	44	80.47	104	190.20
45	147.64	24.61	105	344.49	57.41	45	13.72	105	32.00	45	82.30	105	192.02
46	150.92	25.15	106	347.77	57.96	46	14.02	106	32.31	46	84.12	106	193.85
47	154.20	25.70	107	351.05	58.51	47	14.33	107	32.61	47	85.95	107	195.68
48	157.48	26.25	108	354.33	59.06	48	14.63	108	32.92	48	87.78	108	197.51
49	160.76	26.79	109	357.61	59.60	49	14.94	109	33.22	49	89.61	109	199.34
50	164.04	27.34	110	360.89	60.15	50	15.24	110	33.53	50	91.44	110	201.17
51	167.32	27.89	111	364.17	60.70	51	15.54	111	33.83	51	93.27	111	203.00
52	170.60	28.43	112	367.45	61.24	52	15.85	112	34.14	52	95.10	112	204.83
53	173.88	28.98	113	370.73	61.79	53	16.15	113	34.44	53	96.93	113	206.65
54	177.17	29.53	114	374.02	62.34	54	16.46	114	34.75	54	98.76	114	208.48
55	180.45	30.07	115	377.30	62.88	55	16.76	115	35.05	55	100.58	115	210.31
56	183.73	30.62	116	380.58	63.43	56	17.07	116	35.36	56	102.41	116	212.14
57	187.01	31.17	117	383.86	63.98	57	17.37	117	35.66	57	104.24	117	213.97
58	190.29	31.71	118	387.14	64.52	58	17.68	118	35.97	58	106.07	118	215.80
59	193.57	32.26	119	390.42	65.07	59	17.98	119	36.27	59	107.90	119	217.63
60	196.85	32.81	120	393.70	65.62	60	18.29	120	36.58	60	109.73	120	219.46

TABLE 2

Conversion Table for Nautical and Statute Miles

1 nautical mile = 6,076.11548 . . . feet | 1 statute mile = 5,280 feet

Nautical miles to statute miles				Statute miles to nautical miles			
Nautical miles	Statute miles	Nautical miles	Statute miles	Statute miles	Nautical miles	Statute miles	Nautical miles
1	1.151	51	58.690	1	0.869	51	44.318
2	2.302	52	59.841	2	1.738	52	45.187
3	3.452	53	60.991	3	2.607	53	46.056
4	4.603	54	62.142	4	3.476	54	46.925
5	5.754	55	63.293	5	4.345	55	47.794
6	6.905	56	64.444	6	5.214	56	48.663
7	8.055	57	65.594	7	6.083	57	49.532
8	9.206	58	66.745	8	6.952	58	50.401
9	10.357	59	67.896	9	7.821	59	51.270
10	11.508	60	69.047	10	8.690	60	52.139
11	12.659	61	70.198	11	9.559	61	53.008
12	13.809	62	71.348	12	10.428	62	53.877
13	14.960	63	72.499	13	11.297	63	54.746
14	16.111	64	73.650	14	12.166	64	55.614
15	17.262	65	74.801	15	13.035	65	56.483
16	18.412	66	75.951	16	13.904	66	57.352
17	19.563	67	77.102	17	14.773	67	58.221
18	20.714	68	78.253	18	15.642	68	59.090
19	21.865	69	79.404	19	16.511	69	59.959
20	23.016	70	80.555	20	17.380	70	60.828
21	24.166	71	81.705	21	18.249	71	61.697
22	25.317	72	82.856	22	19.117	72	62.566
23	26.468	73	84.007	23	19.986	73	63.435
24	27.619	74	85.158	24	20.855	74	64.304
25	28.769	75	86.308	25	21.724	75	65.173
26	29.920	76	87.459	26	22.593	76	66.042
27	31.071	77	88.610	27	23.462	77	66.911
28	32.222	78	89.761	28	24.331	78	67.780
29	33.373	79	90.912	29	25.200	79	68.649
30	34.523	80	92.062	30	26.069	80	69.518
31	35.674	81	93.213	31	26.938	81	70.387
32	36.825	82	94.364	32	27.807	82	71.256
33	37.976	83	95.515	33	28.676	83	72.125
34	39.127	84	96.665	34	29.545	84	72.994
35	40.277	85	97.816	35	30.414	85	73.863
36	41.428	86	98.967	36	31.283	86	74.732
37	42.579	87	100.118	37	32.152	87	75.601
38	43.730	88	101.269	38	33.021	88	76.470
39	44.880	89	102.419	39	33.890	89	77.339
40	46.031	90	103.570	40	34.759	90	78.208
41	47.182	91	104.721	41	35.628	91	79.077
42	48.333	92	105.872	42	36.497	92	79.946
43	49.484	93	107.022	43	37.366	93	80.815
44	50.634	94	108.173	44	38.235	94	81.684
45	51.785	95	109.324	45	39.104	95	82.553
46	52.936	96	110.475	46	39.973	96	83.422
47	54.087	97	111.626	47	40.842	97	84.291
48	55.237	98	112.776	48	41.711	98	85.160
49	56.388	99	113.927	49	42.580	99	86.029
50	57.539	100	115.078	50	43.449	100	86.898

TABLE 3

Speed Table for Measured Mile

Sec.	Minutes: 1	2	3	4	5	6	7	8	9	10	11	12	Sec.
	Knots	*Knots*	*Knots*	*Knots*	*Knots*	*Knots*	*Knots*	*Knots*	*Knots*	*Knots*	*Knots*	*Knots*	
0	60.000	30.000	20.000	15.000	12.000	10.000	8.571	7.500	6.667	6.000	5.455	5.000	0
1	59.016	29.752	19.890	14.938	11.960	9.972	8.551	7.484	6.654	5.990	5.446	4.993	1
2	58.065	29.508	19.780	14.876	11.921	9.945	8.531	7.469	6.642	5.980	5.438	4.986	2
3	57.143	29.268	19.672	14.815	11.881	9.917	8.511	7.453	6.630	5.970	5.430	4.979	3
4	56.250	29.032	19.565	14.754	11.842	9.890	8.491	7.438	6.618	5.960	5.422	4.972	4
5	55.385	28.800	19.459	14.694	11.803	9.863	8.471	7.423	6.606	5.950	5.414	4.966	5
6	54.545	28.571	19.355	14.634	11.765	9.836	8.451	7.407	6.593	5.941	5.405	4.959	6
7	53.731	28.346	19.251	14.575	11.726	9.809	8.431	7.392	6.581	5.931	5.397	4.952	7
8	52.941	28.125	19.149	14.516	11.688	9.783	8.411	7.377	6.569	5.921	5.389	4.945	8
9	52.174	27.907	19.048	14.458	11.650	9.756	8.392	7.362	6.557	5.911	5.381	4.938	9
10	51.429	27.692	18.947	14.400	11.613	9.730	8.372	7.347	6.545	5.902	5.373	4.932	10
11	50.704	27.481	18.848	14.343	11.576	9.704	8.353	7.332	6.534	5.892	5.365	4.925	11
12	50.000	27.273	18.750	14.286	11.538	9.677	8.333	7.317	6.522	5.882	5.357	4.918	12
13	49.315	27.068	18.653	14.229	11.502	9.651	8.314	7.302	6.510	5.873	5.349	4.911	13
14	48.649	26.866	18.557	14.173	11.465	9.626	8.295	7.287	6.498	5.863	5.341	4.905	14
15	48.000	26.667	18.462	14.118	11.429	9.600	8.276	7.273	6.486	5.854	5.333	4.898	15
16	47.368	26.471	18.367	14.062	11.392	9.574	8.257	7.258	6.475	5.844	5.325	4.891	16
17	46.753	26.277	18.274	14.008	11.356	9.549	8.238	7.243	6.463	5.835	5.318	4.885	17
18	46.154	26.087	18.182	13.953	11.321	9.524	8.219	7.229	6.452	5.825	5.310	4.878	18
19	45.570	25.899	18.090	13.900	11.285	9.499	8.200	7.214	6.440	5.816	5.302	4.871	19
20	45.000	25.714	18.000	13.846	11.250	9.474	8.182	7.200	6.429	5.806	5.294	4.865	20
21	44.444	25.532	17.910	13.793	11.215	9.449	8.163	7.186	6.417	5.797	5.286	4.858	21
22	43.902	25.352	17.822	13.740	11.180	9.424	8.145	7.171	6.406	5.788	5.279	4.852	22
23	43.373	25.175	17.734	13.688	11.146	9.399	8.126	7.157	6.394	5.778	5.271	4.845	23
24	42.857	25.000	17.647	13.636	11.111	9.375	8.108	7.143	6.383	5.769	5.263	4.839	24
25	42.353	24.828	17.561	13.585	11.077	9.351	8.090	7.129	6.372	5.760	5.255	4.832	25
26	41.860	24.658	17.476	13.534	11.043	9.326	8.072	7.115	6.360	5.751	5.248	4.826	26
27	41.379	24.490	17.391	13.483	11.009	9.302	8.054	7.101	6.349	5.742	5.240	4.819	27
28	40.909	24.324	17.308	13.433	10.976	9.278	8.036	7.087	6.338	5.732	5.233	4.813	28
29	40.449	24.161	17.225	13.383	10.942	9.254	8.018	7.073	6.327	5.723	5.225	4.806	29
30	40.000	24.000	17.143	13.333	10.909	9.231	8.000	7.059	6.316	5.714	5.217	4.800	30
31	39.560	23.841	17.062	13.284	10.876	9.207	7.982	7.045	6.305	5.705	5.210	4.794	31
32	39.130	23.684	16.981	13.235	10.843	9.184	7.965	7.031	6.294	5.696	5.202	4.787	32
33	38.710	23.529	16.901	13.187	10.811	9.160	7.947	7.018	6.283	5.687	5.195	4.781	33
34	38.298	23.377	16.822	13.139	10.778	9.137	7.930	7.004	6.272	5.678	5.187	4.775	34
35	37.895	23.226	16.744	13.091	10.746	9.114	7.912	6.990	6.261	5.669	5.180	4.768	35
36	37.500	23.077	16.667	13.043	10.714	9.091	7.895	6.977	6.250	5.660	5.172	4.762	36
37	37.113	22.930	16.590	12.996	10.682	9.068	7.877	6.963	6.239	5.651	5.165	4.756	37
38	36.735	22.785	16.514	12.950	10.651	9.045	7.860	6.950	6.228	5.643	5.158	4.749	38
39	36.364	22.642	16.438	12.903	10.619	9.023	7.843	6.936	6.218	5.634	5.150	4.743	39
40	36.000	22.500	16.364	12.857	10.588	9.000	7.826	6.923	6.207	5.625	5.143	4.737	40
41	35.644	22.360	16.290	12.811	10.557	8.978	7.809	6.910	6.196	5.616	5.136	4.731	41
42	35.294	22.222	16.216	12.766	10.526	8.955	7.792	6.897	6.186	5.607	5.128	4.724	42
43	34.951	22.086	16.143	12.721	10.496	8.933	7.775	6.883	6.175	5.599	5.121	4.718	43
44	34.615	21.951	16.071	12.676	10.465	8.911	7.759	6.870	6.164	5.590	5.114	4.712	44
45	34.286	21.818	16.000	12.632	10.435	8.889	7.742	6.857	6.154	5.581	5.106	4.706	45
46	33.962	21.687	15.929	12.587	10.405	8.867	7.725	6.844	6.143	5.573	5.099	4.700	46
47	33.645	21.557	15.859	12.544	10.375	8.845	7.709	6.831	6.133	5.564	5.092	4.694	47
48	33.333	21.429	15.789	12.500	10.345	8.824	7.692	6.818	6.122	5.556	5.085	4.688	48
49	33.028	21.302	15.721	12.457	10.315	8.802	7.676	6.805	6.112	5.547	5.078	4.681	49
50	32.727	21.176	15.652	12.414	10.286	8.780	7.660	6.792	6.102	5.538	5.070	4.675	50
51	32.432	21.053	15.584	12.371	10.256	8.759	7.643	6.780	6.091	5.530	5.063	4.669	51
52	32.143	20.930	15.517	12.329	10.227	8.738	7.627	6.767	6.081	5.521	5.056	4.663	52
53	31.858	20.809	15.451	12.287	10.198	8.717	7.611	6.754	6.071	5.513	5.049	4.657	53
54	31.579	20.690	15.385	12.245	10.169	8.696	7.595	6.742	6.061	5.505	5.042	4.651	54
55	31.304	20.571	15.319	12.203	10.141	8.675	7.579	6.729	6.050	5.496	5.035	4.645	55
56	31.034	20.455	15.254	12.162	10.112	8.654	7.563	6.716	6.040	5.488	5.028	4.639	56
57	30.769	20.339	15.190	12.121	10.084	8.633	7.547	6.704	6.030	5.479	5.021	4.633	57
58	30.508	20.225	15.126	12.081	10.056	8.612	7.531	6.691	6.020	5.471	5.014	4.627	58
59	30.252	20.112	15.063	12.040	10.028	8.592	7.516	6.679	6.010	5.463	5.007	4.621	59
60	30.000	20.000	15.000	12.000	10.000	8.571	7.500	6.667	6.000	5.455	5.000	4.615	60
Sec.	1	2	3	4	5	6	7	8	9	10	11	12	Sec.

TABLE 4

Speed, Time, and Distance

Minutes	0.5	1.0	1.5	2.0	2.5	3.0	3.5	4.0	4.5	5.0	5.5	6.0	6.5	7.0	7.5	8.0	Minutes
	Miles	*Miles*	*Miles*	*Miles*	*Miles*	*Miles*	*Miles*	*Miles*	*Miles*	*Miles*	*Miles*	*Miles*	*Miles*	*Miles*	*Miles*	*Miles*	
1	0.0	0.0	0.0	0.0	0.0	0.0	0.1	0.1	0.1	0.1	0.1	0.1	0.1	0.1	0.1	0.1	1
2	0.0	0.0	0.0	0.1	0.1	0.1	0.1	0.1	0.2	0.2	0.2	0.2	0.2	0.2	0.2	0.3	2
3	0.0	0.0	0.1	0.1	0.1	0.2	0.2	0.2	0.2	0.2	0.3	0.3	0.3	0.4	0.4	0.4	3
4	0.0	0.1	0.1	0.1	0.2	0.2	0.2	0.3	0.3	0.3	0.4	0.4	0.4	0.5	0.5	0.5	4
5	0.0	0.1	0.1	0.2	0.2	0.2	0.3	0.3	0.4	0.4	0.5	0.5	0.5	0.6	0.6	0.7	5
6	0.0	0.1	0.2	0.2	0.2	0.3	0.4	0.4	0.4	0.5	0.6	0.6	0.6	0.7	0.8	0.8	6
7	0.1	0.1	0.2	0.2	0.3	0.4	0.4	0.5	0.5	0.6	0.6	0.7	0.8	0.8	0.9	0.9	7
8	0.1	0.1	0.2	0.3	0.3	0.4	0.5	0.5	0.6	0.7	0.7	0.8	0.9	0.9	1.0	1.1	8
9	0.1	0.2	0.2	0.3	0.4	0.4	0.5	0.6	0.7	0.8	0.8	0.9	1.0	1.0	1.1	1.2	9
10	0.1	0.2	0.2	0.3	0.4	0.5	0.6	0.7	0.8	0.8	0.9	1.0	1.1	1.2	1.2	1.3	10
11	0.1	0.2	0.3	0.4	0.5	0.6	0.6	0.7	0.8	0.9	1.0	1.1	1.2	1.3	1.4	1.5	11
12	0.1	0.2	0.3	0.4	0.5	0.6	0.7	0.8	0.9	1.0	1.1	1.2	1.3	1.4	1.5	1.6	12
13	0.1	0.2	0.3	0.4	0.5	0.6	0.8	0.9	1.0	1.1	1.2	1.3	1.4	1.5	1.6	1.7	13
14	0.1	0.2	0.4	0.5	0.6	0.7	0.8	0.9	1.0	1.2	1.3	1.4	1.5	1.6	1.8	1.9	14
15	0.1	0.2	0.4	0.5	0.6	0.8	0.9	1.0	1.1	1.2	1.4	1.5	1.6	1.8	1.9	2.0	15
16	0.1	0.3	0.4	0.5	0.7	0.8	0.9	1.1	1.2	1.3	1.5	1.6	1.7	1.9	2.0	2.1	16
17	0.1	0.3	0.4	0.6	0.7	0.8	1.0	1.1	1.3	1.4	1.6	1.7	1.8	2.0	2.1	2.3	17
18	0.2	0.3	0.4	0.6	0.8	0.9	1.0	1.2	1.4	1.5	1.6	1.8	2.0	2.1	2.2	2.4	18
19	0.2	0.3	0.5	0.6	0.8	1.0	1.1	1.3	1.4	1.6	1.7	1.9	2.1	2.2	2.4	2.5	19
20	0.2	0.3	0.5	0.7	0.8	1.0	1.2	1.3	1.5	1.7	1.8	2.0	2.2	2.3	2.5	2.7	20
21	0.2	0.4	0.5	0.7	0.9	1.0	1.2	1.4	1.6	1.8	1.9	2.1	2.3	2.4	2.6	2.8	21
22	0.2	0.4	0.6	0.7	0.9	1.1	1.3	1.5	1.6	1.8	2.0	2.2	2.4	2.6	2.8	2.9	22
23	0.2	0.4	0.6	0.8	1.0	1.2	1.3	1.5	1.7	1.9	2.1	2.3	2.5	2.7	2.9	3.1	23
24	0.2	0.4	0.6	0.8	1.0	1.2	1.4	1.6	1.8	2.0	2.2	2.4	2.6	2.8	3.0	3.2	24
25	0.2	0.4	0.6	0.8	1.0	1.2	1.5	1.7	1.9	2.1	2.3	2.5	2.7	2.9	3.1	3.3	25
26	0.2	0.4	0.6	0.9	1.1	1.3	1.5	1.7	2.0	2.2	2.4	2.6	2.8	3.0	3.2	3.5	26
27	0.2	0.4	0.7	0.9	1.1	1.4	1.6	1.8	2.0	2.2	2.5	2.7	2.9	3.2	3.4	3.6	27
28	0.2	0.5	0.7	0.9	1.2	1.4	1.6	1.9	2.1	2.3	2.6	2.8	3.0	3.3	3.5	3.7	28
29	0.2	0.5	0.7	1.0	1.2	1.4	1.7	1.9	2.2	2.4	2.7	2.9	3.1	3.4	3.6	3.9	29
30	0.2	0.5	0.8	1.0	1.2	1.5	1.8	2.0	2.2	2.5	2.8	3.0	3.2	3.5	3.8	4.0	30
31	0.3	0.5	0.8	1.0	1.3	1.6	1.8	2.1	2.3	2.6	2.8	3.1	3.4	3.6	3.9	4.1	31
32	0.3	0.5	0.8	1.1	1.3	1.6	1.9	2.1	2.4	2.7	2.9	3.2	3.5	3.7	4.0	4.3	32
33	0.3	0.6	0.8	1.1	1.4	1.6	1.9	2.2	2.5	2.8	3.0	3.3	3.6	3.8	4.1	4.4	33
34	0.3	0.6	0.8	1.1	1.4	1.7	2.0	2.3	2.6	2.8	3.1	3.4	3.7	4.0	4.2	4.5	34
35	0.3	0.6	0.9	1.2	1.5	1.8	2.0	2.3	2.6	2.9	3.2	3.5	3.8	4.1	4.4	4.7	35
36	0.3	0.6	0.9	1.2	1.5	1.8	2.1	2.4	2.7	3.0	3.3	3.6	3.9	4.2	4.5	4.8	36
37	0.3	0.6	0.9	1.2	1.5	1.8	2.2	2.5	2.8	3.1	3.4	3.7	4.0	4.3	4.6	4.9	37
38	0.3	0.6	1.0	1.3	1.6	1.9	2.2	2.5	2.8	3.2	3.5	3.8	4.1	4.4	4.8	5.1	38
39	0.3	0.6	1.0	1.3	1.6	2.0	2.3	2.6	2.9	3.2	3.6	3.9	4.2	4.6	4.9	5.2	39
40	0.3	0.7	1.0	1.3	1.7	2.0	2.3	2.7	3.0	3.3	3.7	4.0	4.3	4.7	5.0	5.3	40
41	0.3	0.7	1.0	1.4	1.7	2.0	2.4	2.7	3.1	3.4	3.8	4.1	4.4	4.8	5.1	5.5	41
42	0.4	0.7	1.0	1.4	1.8	2.1	2.4	2.8	3.2	3.5	3.8	4.2	4.6	4.9	5.2	5.6	42
43	0.4	0.7	1.1	1.4	1.8	2.2	2.5	2.9	3.2	3.6	3.9	4.3	4.7	5.0	5.4	5.7	43
44	0.4	0.7	1.1	1.5	1.8	2.2	2.6	2.9	3.3	3.7	4.0	4.4	4.8	5.1	5.5	5.9	44
45	0.4	0.8	1.1	1.5	1.9	2.2	2.6	3.0	3.4	3.8	4.1	4.5	4.9	5.2	5.6	6.0	45
46	0.4	0.8	1.2	1.5	1.9	2.3	2.7	3.1	3.4	3.8	4.2	4.6	5.0	5.4	5.8	6.1	46
47	0.4	0.8	1.2	1.6	2.0	2.4	2.7	3.1	3.5	3.9	4.3	4.7	5.1	5.5	5.9	6.3	47
48	0.4	0.8	1.2	1.6	2.0	2.4	2.8	3.2	3.6	4.0	4.4	4.8	5.2	5.6	6.0	6.4	48
49	0.4	0.8	1.2	1.6	2.0	2.4	2.9	3.3	3.7	4.1	4.5	4.9	5.3	5.7	6.1	6.5	49
50	0.4	0.8	1.2	1.7	2.1	2.5	2.9	3.3	3.8	4.2	4.6	5.0	5.4	5.8	6.2	6.7	50
51	0.4	0.8	1.3	1.7	2.1	2.6	3.0	3.4	3.8	4.2	4.7	5.1	5.5	6.0	6.4	6.8	51
52	0.4	0.9	1.3	1.7	2.2	2.6	3.0	3.5	3.9	4.3	4.8	5.2	5.6	6.1	6.5	6.9	52
53	0.4	0.9	1.3	1.8	2.2	2.6	3.1	3.5	4.0	4.4	4.9	5.3	5.7	6.2	6.6	7.1	53
54	0.4	0.9	1.4	1.8	2.2	2.7	3.2	3.6	4.0	4.5	5.0	5.4	5.8	6.3	6.8	7.2	54
55	0.5	0.9	1.4	1.8	2.3	2.8	3.2	3.7	4.1	4.6	5.0	5.5	6.0	6.4	6.9	7.3	55
56	0.5	0.9	1.4	1.9	2.3	2.8	3.3	3.7	4.2	4.7	5.1	5.6	6.1	6.5	7.0	7.5	56
57	0.5	1.0	1.4	1.9	2.4	2.8	3.3	3.8	4.3	4.8	5.2	5.7	6.2	6.6	7.1	7.6	57
58	0.5	1.0	1.4	1.9	2.4	2.9	3.4	3.9	4.4	4.8	5.3	5.8	6.3	6.8	7.2	7.7	58
59	0.5	1.0	1.5	2.0	2.5	3.0	3.4	3.9	4.4	4.9	5.4	5.9	6.4	6.9	7.4	7.9	59
60	0.5	1.0	1.5	2.0	2.5	3.0	3.5	4.0	4.5	5.0	5.5	6.0	6.5	7.0	7.5	8.0	60

Speed in knots

TABLE 4

Speed, Time, and Distance

Minutes	8.5	9.0	9.5	10.0	10.5	11.0	11.5	12.0	12.5	13.0	13.5	14.0	14.5	15.0	15.5	16.0	Minutes
	Miles	*Miles*	*Miles*	*Miles*	*Miles*	*Miles*	*Miles*	*Miles*	*Miles*	*Miles*	*Miles*	*Miles*	*Miles*	*Miles*	*Miles*	*Miles*	
1	0.1	0.2	0.2	0.2	0.2	0.2	0.2	0.2	0.2	0.2	0.2	0.2	0.2	0.2	0.3	0.3	1
2	0.3	0.3	0.3	0.3	0.4	0.4	0.4	0.4	0.4	0.4	0.4	0.5	0.5	0.5	0.5	0.5	2
3	0.4	0.4	0.5	0.5	0.5	0.6	0.6	0.6	0.6	0.6	0.7	0.7	0.7	0.8	0.8	0.8	3
4	0.6	0.6	0.6	0.7	0.7	0.7	0.8	0.8	0.8	0.9	0.9	0.9	1.0	1.0	1.0	1.1	4
5	0.7	0.8	0.8	0.8	0.9	0.9	1.0	1.0	1.0	1.1	1.1	1.2	1.2	1.2	1.3	1.3	5
6	0.8	0.9	1.0	1.0	1.0	1.1	1.2	1.2	1.2	1.3	1.4	1.4	1.4	1.5	1.6	1.6	6
7	1.0	1.0	1.1	1.2	1.2	1.3	1.3	1.4	1.5	1.5	1.6	1.6	1.7	1.8	1.8	1.9	7
8	1.1	1.2	1.3	1.3	1.4	1.5	1.5	1.6	1.7	1.7	1.8	1.9	1.9	2.0	2.1	2.1	8
9	1.3	1.4	1.4	1.5	1.6	1.6	1.7	1.8	1.9	2.0	2.0	2.1	2.2	2.2	2.3	2.4	9
10	1.4	1.5	1.6	1.7	1.8	1.8	1.9	2.0	2.1	2.2	2.2	2.3	2.4	2.5	2.6	2.7	10
11	1.6	1.6	1.7	1.8	1.9	2.0	2.1	2.2	2.3	2.4	2.5	2.6	2.7	2.8	2.8	2.9	11
12	1.7	1.8	1.9	2.0	2.1	2.2	2.3	2.4	2.5	2.6	2.7	2.8	2.9	3.0	3.1	3.2	12
13	1.8	2.0	2.1	2.2	2.3	2.4	2.5	2.6	2.7	2.8	2.9	3.0	3.1	3.2	3.4	3.5	13
14	2.0	2.1	2.2	2.3	2.4	2.6	2.7	2.8	2.9	3.0	3.2	3.3	3.4	3.5	3.6	3.7	14
15	2.1	2.2	2.4	2.5	2.6	2.8	2.9	3.0	3.1	3.2	3.4	3.5	3.6	3.8	3.9	4.0	15
16	2.3	2.4	2.5	2.7	2.8	2.9	3.1	3.2	3.3	3.5	3.6	3.7	3.9	4.0	4.1	4.3	16
17	2.4	2.6	2.7	2.8	3.0	3.1	3.3	3.4	3.5	3.7	3.8	4.0	4.1	4.2	4.4	4.5	17
18	2.6	2.7	2.8	3.0	3.2	3.3	3.4	3.6	3.8	3.9	4.0	4.2	4.4	4.5	4.6	4.8	18
19	2.7	2.8	3.0	3.2	3.3	3.5	3.6	3.8	4.0	4.1	4.3	4.4	4.6	4.8	4.9	5.1	19
20	2.8	3.0	3.2	3.3	3.5	3.7	3.8	4.0	4.2	4.3	4.5	4.7	4.8	5.0	5.2	5.3	20
21	3.0	3.2	3.3	3.5	3.7	3.8	4.0	4.2	4.4	4.6	4.7	4.9	5.1	5.2	5.4	5.6	21
22	3.1	3.3	3.5	3.7	3.8	4.0	4.2	4.4	4.6	4.8	5.0	5.1	5.3	5.5	5.7	5.9	22
23	3.3	3.4	3.6	3.8	4.0	4.2	4.4	4.6	4.8	5.0	5.2	5.4	5.6	5.8	5.9	6.1	23
24	3.4	3.6	3.8	4.0	4.2	4.4	4.6	4.8	5.0	5.2	5.4	5.6	5.8	6.0	6.2	6.4	24
25	3.5	3.8	4.0	4.2	4.4	4.6	4.8	5.0	5.2	5.4	5.6	5.8	6.0	6.2	6.5	6.7	25
26	3.7	3.9	4.1	4.3	4.6	4.8	5.0	5.2	5.4	5.6	5.8	6.1	6.3	6.5	6.7	6.9	26
27	3.8	4.0	4.3	4.5	4.7	5.0	5.2	5.4	5.6	5.8	6.1	6.3	6.5	6.8	7.0	7.2	27
28	4.0	4.2	4.4	4.7	4.9	5.1	5.4	5.6	5.8	6.1	6.3	6.5	6.8	7.0	7.2	7.5	28
29	4.1	4.4	4.6	4.8	5.1	5.3	5.6	5.8	6.0	6.3	6.5	6.8	7.0	7.2	7.5	7.7	29
30	4.2	4.5	4.8	5.0	5.2	5.5	5.8	6.0	6.2	6.5	6.8	7.0	7.2	7.5	7.8	8.0	30
31	4.4	4.6	4.9	5.2	5.4	5.7	5.9	6.2	6.5	6.7	7.0	7.2	7.5	7.8	8.0	8.3	31
32	4.5	4.8	5.1	5.3	5.6	5.9	6.1	6.4	6.7	6.9	7.2	7.5	7.7	8.0	8.3	8.5	32
33	4.7	5.0	5.2	5.5	5.8	6.0	6.3	6.6	6.9	7.2	7.4	7.7	8.0	8.2	8.5	8.8	33
34	4.8	5.1	5.4	5.7	6.0	6.2	6.5	6.8	7.1	7.4	7.6	7.9	8.2	8.5	8.8	9.1	34
35	5.0	5.2	5.5	5.8	6.1	6.4	6.7	7.0	7.3	7.6	7.9	8.2	8.5	8.8	9.0	9.3	35
36	5.1	5.4	5.7	6.0	6.3	6.6	6.9	7.2	7.5	7.8	8.1	8.4	8.7	9.0	9.3	9.6	36
37	5.2	5.6	5.9	6.2	6.5	6.8	7.1	7.4	7.7	8.0	8.3	8.6	8.9	9.2	9.6	9.9	37
38	5.4	5.7	6.0	6.3	6.6	7.0	7.3	7.6	7.9	8.2	8.6	8.9	9.2	9.5	9.8	10.1	38
39	5.5	5.8	6.2	6.5	6.8	7.2	7.5	7.8	8.1	8.4	8.8	9.1	9.4	9.8	10.1	10.4	39
40	5.7	6.0	6.3	6.7	7.0	7.3	7.7	8.0	8.3	8.7	9.0	9.3	9.7	10.0	10.3	10.7	40
41	5.8	6.2	6.5	6.8	7.2	7.5	7.9	8.2	8.5	8.9	9.2	9.6	9.9	10.2	10.6	10.9	41
42	6.0	6.3	6.6	7.0	7.4	7.7	8.0	8.4	8.8	9.1	9.4	9.8	10.2	10.5	10.8	11.2	42
43	6.1	6.4	6.8	7.2	7.5	7.9	8.2	8.6	9.0	9.3	9.7	10.0	10.4	10.8	11.1	11.5	43
44	6.2	6.6	7.0	7.3	7.7	8.1	8.4	8.8	9.2	9.5	9.9	10.3	10.6	11.0	11.4	11.7	44
45	6.4	6.8	7.1	7.5	7.9	8.2	8.6	9.0	9.4	9.8	10.1	10.5	10.9	11.2	11.6	12.0	45
46	6.5	6.9	7.3	7.7	8.0	8.4	8.8	9.2	9.6	10.0	10.4	10.7	11.1	11.5	11.9	12.3	46
47	6.7	7.0	7.4	7.8	8.2	8.6	9.0	9.4	9.8	10.2	10.6	11.0	11.4	11.8	12.1	12.5	47
48	6.8	7.2	7.6	8.0	8.4	8.8	9.2	9.6	10.0	10.4	10.8	11.2	11.6	12.0	12.4	12.8	48
49	6.9	7.4	7.8	8.2	8.6	9.0	9.4	9.8	10.2	10.6	11.0	11.4	11.8	12.2	12.7	13.1	49
50	7.1	7.5	7.9	8.3	8.8	9.2	9.6	10.0	10.4	10.8	11.2	11.7	12.1	12.5	12.9	13.3	50
51	7.2	7.6	8.1	8.5	8.9	9.4	9.8	10.2	10.6	11.0	11.5	11.9	12.3	12.8	13.2	13.6	51
52	7.4	7.8	8.2	8.7	9.1	9.5	10.0	10.4	10.8	11.3	11.7	12.1	12.6	13.0	13.4	13.9	52
53	7.5	8.0	8.4	8.8	9.3	9.7	10.2	10.6	11.0	11.5	11.9	12.4	12.8	13.2	13.7	14.1	53
54	7.6	8.1	8.6	9.0	9.4	9.9	10.4	10.8	11.2	11.7	12.2	12.6	13.0	13.5	14.0	14.4	54
55	7.8	8.2	8.7	9.2	9.6	10.1	10.5	11.0	11.5	11.9	12.4	12.8	13.3	13.8	14.2	14.7	55
56	7.9	8.4	8.9	9.3	9.8	10.3	10.7	11.2	11.7	12.1	12.6	13.1	13.5	14.0	14.5	14.9	56
57	8.1	8.6	9.0	9.5	10.0	10.4	10.9	11.4	11.9	12.4	12.8	13.3	13.8	14.2	14.7	15.2	57
58	8.2	8.7	9.2	9.7	10.2	10.6	11.1	11.6	12.1	12.6	13.0	13.5	14.0	14.5	15.0	15.5	58
59	8.4	8.8	9.3	9.8	10.3	10.8	11.3	11.8	12.3	12.8	13.3	13.8	14.3	14.8	15.2	15.7	59
60	8.5	9.0	9.5	10.0	10.5	11.0	11.5	12.0	12.5	13.0	13.5	14.0	14.5	15.0	15.5	16.0	60

Speed in knots

TABLE 4

Speed, Time, and Distance

Minutes	16.5	17.0	17.5	18.0	18.5	19.0	19.5	20.0	20.5	21.0	21.5	22.0	22.5	23.0	23.5	24.0	Minutes
	Miles	*Miles*	*Miles*	*Miles*	*Miles*	*Miles*	*Miles*	*Miles*	*Miles*	*Miles*	*Miles*	*Miles*	*Miles*	*Miles*	*Miles*	*Miles*	
1	0.3	0.3	0.3	0.3	0.3	0.3	0.3	0.3	0.3	0.4	0.4	0.4	0.4	0.4	0.4	0.4	1
2	0.6	0.6	0.6	0.6	0.6	0.6	0.6	0.7	0.7	0.7	0.7	0.7	0.8	0.8	0.8	0.8	2
3	0.8	0.8	0.9	0.9	0.9	1.0	1.0	1.0	1.0	1.0	1.1	1.1	1.1	1.2	1.2	1.2	3
4	1.1	1.1	1.2	1.2	1.2	1.3	1.3	1.3	1.4	1.4	1.4	1.5	1.5	1.5	1.6	1.6	4
5	1.4	1.4	1.5	1.5	1.5	1.6	1.6	1.7	1.7	1.8	1.8	1.8	1.9	1.9	2.0	2.0	5
6	1.6	1.7	1.8	1.8	1.8	1.9	2.0	2.0	2.0	2.1	2.2	2.2	2.2	2.3	2.4	2.4	6
7	1.9	2.0	2.0	2.1	2.2	2.2	2.3	2.3	2.4	2.4	2.5	2.6	2.6	2.7	2.7	2.8	7
8	2.2	2.3	2.3	2.4	2.5	2.5	2.6	2.7	2.7	2.8	2.9	2.9	3.0	3.1	3.1	3.2	8
9	2.5	2.6	2.6	2.7	2.8	2.8	2.9	3.0	3.1	3.2	3.2	3.3	3.4	3.4	3.5	3.6	9
10	2.8	2.8	2.9	3.0	3.1	3.2	3.2	3.3	3.4	3.5	3.6	3.7	3.8	3.8	3.9	4.0	10
11	3.0	3.1	3.2	3.3	3.4	3.5	3.6	3.7	3.8	3.8	3.9	4.0	4.1	4.2	4.3	4.4	11
12	3.3	3.4	3.5	3.6	3.7	3.8	3.9	4.0	4.1	4.2	4.3	4.4	4.5	4.6	4.7	4.8	12
13	3.6	3.7	3.8	3.9	4.0	4.1	4.2	4.3	4.4	4.6	4.7	4.8	4.9	5.0	5.1	5.2	13
14	3.8	4.0	4.1	4.2	4.3	4.4	4.6	4.7	4.8	4.9	5.0	5.1	5.2	5.4	5.5	5.6	14
15	4.1	4.2	4.4	4.5	4.6	4.8	4.9	5.0	5.1	5.2	5.4	5.5	5.6	5.8	5.9	6.0	15
16	4.4	4.5	4.7	4.8	4.9	5.1	5.2	5.3	5.5	5.6	5.7	5.9	6.0	6.1	6.3	6.4	16
17	4.7	4.8	5.0	5.1	5.2	5.4	5.5	5.7	5.8	6.0	6.1	6.2	6.4	6.5	6.7	6.8	17
18	5.0	5.1	5.2	5.4	5.6	5.7	5.8	6.0	6.2	6.3	6.4	6.6	6.8	6.9	7.0	7.2	18
19	5.2	5.4	5.5	5.7	5.9	6.0	6.2	6.3	6.5	6.6	6.8	7.0	7.1	7.3	7.4	7.6	19
20	5.5	5.7	5.8	6.0	6.2	6.3	6.5	6.7	6.8	7.0	7.2	7.3	7.5	7.7	7.8	8.0	20
21	5.8	6.0	6.1	6.3	6.5	6.6	6.8	7.0	7.2	7.4	7.5	7.7	7.9	8.0	8.2	8.4	21
22	6.0	6.2	6.4	6.6	6.8	7.0	7.2	7.3	7.5	7.7	7.9	8.1	8.2	8.4	8.6	8.8	22
23	6.3	6.5	6.7	6.9	7.1	7.3	7.5	7.7	7.9	8.0	8.2	8.4	8.6	8.8	9.0	9.2	23
24	6.6	6.8	7.0	7.2	7.4	7.6	7.8	8.0	8.2	8.4	8.6	8.8	9.0	9.2	9.4	9.6	24
25	6.9	7.1	7.3	7.5	7.7	7.9	8.1	8.3	8.5	8.8	9.0	9.2	9.4	9.6	9.8	10.0	25
26	7.2	7.4	7.6	7.8	8.0	8.2	8.4	8.7	8.9	9.1	9.3	9.5	9.8	10.0	10.2	10.4	26
27	7.4	7.6	7.9	8.1	8.3	8.6	8.8	9.0	9.2	9.4	9.7	9.9	10.1	10.4	10.6	10.8	27
28	7.7	7.9	8.2	8.4	8.6	8.9	9.1	9.3	9.6	9.8	10.0	10.3	10.5	10.7	11.0	11.2	28
29	8.0	8.2	8.5	8.7	8.9	9.2	9.4	9.7	9.9	10.2	10.4	10.6	10.9	11.1	11.4	11.6	29
30	8.2	8.5	8.8	9.0	9.2	9.5	9.8	10.0	10.2	10.5	10.8	11.0	11.2	11.5	11.8	12.0	30
31	8.5	8.8	9.0	9.3	9.6	9.8	10.1	10.3	10.6	10.8	11.1	11.4	11.6	11.9	12.1	12.4	31
32	8.8	9.1	9.3	9.6	9.9	10.1	10.4	10.7	10.9	11.2	11.5	11.7	12.0	12.3	12.5	12.8	32
33	9.1	9.4	9.6	9.9	10.2	10.4	10.7	11.0	11.3	11.6	11.8	12.1	12.4	12.6	12.9	13.2	33
34	9.4	9.6	9.9	10.2	10.5	10.8	11.0	11.3	11.6	11.9	12.2	12.5	12.8	13.0	13.3	13.6	34
35	9.6	9.9	10.2	10.5	10.8	11.1	11.4	11.7	12.0	12.2	12.5	12.8	13.1	13.4	13.7	14.0	35
36	9.9	10.2	10.5	10.8	11.1	11.4	11.7	12.0	12.3	12.6	12.9	13.2	13.5	13.8	14.1	14.4	36
37	10.2	10.5	10.8	11.1	11.4	11.7	12.0	12.3	12.6	13.0	13.3	13.6	13.9	14.2	14.5	14.8	37
38	10.4	10.8	11.1	11.4	11.7	12.0	12.4	12.7	13.0	13.3	13.6	13.9	14.2	14.6	14.9	15.2	38
39	10.7	11.0	11.4	11.7	12.0	12.4	12.7	13.0	13.3	13.6	14.0	14.3	14.6	15.0	15.3	15.6	39
40	11.0	11.3	11.7	12.0	12.3	12.7	13.0	13.3	13.7	14.0	14.3	14.7	15.0	15.3	15.7	16.0	40
41	11.3	11.6	12.0	12.3	12.6	13.0	13.3	13.7	14.0	14.4	14.7	15.0	15.4	15.7	16.1	16.4	41
42	11.6	11.9	12.2	12.6	13.0	13.3	13.6	14.0	14.4	14.7	15.0	15.4	15.8	16.1	16.4	16.8	42
43	11.8	12.2	12.5	12.9	13.3	13.6	14.0	14.3	14.7	15.0	15.4	15.8	16.1	16.5	16.8	17.2	43
44	12.1	12.5	12.8	13.2	13.6	13.9	14.3	14.7	15.0	15.4	15.8	16.1	16.5	16.9	17.2	17.6	44
45	12.4	12.8	13.1	13.5	13.9	14.2	14.6	15.0	15.4	15.8	16.1	16.5	16.9	17.2	17.6	18.0	45
46	12.6	13.0	13.4	13.8	14.2	14.6	15.0	15.3	15.7	16.1	16.5	16.9	17.2	17.6	18.0	18.4	46
47	12.9	13.3	13.7	14.1	14.5	14.9	15.3	15.7	16.1	16.4	16.8	17.2	17.6	18.0	18.4	18.8	47
48	13.2	13.6	14.0	14.4	14.8	15.2	15.6	16.0	16.4	16.8	17.2	17.6	18.0	18.4	18.8	19.2	48
49	13.5	13.9	14.3	14.7	15.1	15.5	15.9	16.3	16.7	17.2	17.6	18.0	18.4	18.8	19.2	19.6	49
50	13.8	14.2	14.6	15.0	15.4	15.8	16.2	16.7	17.1	17.5	17.9	18.3	18.8	19.2	19.6	20.0	50
51	14.0	14.4	14.9	15.3	15.7	16.2	16.6	17.0	17.4	17.8	18.3	18.7	19.1	19.6	20.0	20.4	51
52	14.3	14.7	15.2	15.6	16.0	16.5	16.9	17.3	17.8	18.2	18.6	19.1	19.5	19.9	20.4	20.8	52
53	14.6	15.0	15.5	15.9	16.3	16.8	17.2	17.7	18.1	18.6	19.0	19.4	19.9	20.3	20.8	21.2	53
54	14.8	15.3	15.8	16.2	16.6	17.1	17.6	18.0	18.4	18.9	19.4	19.8	20.2	20.7	21.2	21.6	54
55	15.1	15.6	16.0	16.5	17.0	17.4	17.9	18.3	18.8	19.2	19.7	20.2	20.6	21.1	21.5	22.0	55
56	15.4	15.9	16.3	16.8	17.3	17.7	18.2	18.7	19.1	19.6	20.1	20.5	21.0	21.5	21.9	22.4	56
57	15.7	16.2	16.6	17.1	17.6	18.0	18.5	19.0	19.5	20.0	20.4	20.9	21.4	21.8	22.3	22.8	57
58	16.0	16.4	16.9	17.4	17.9	18.4	18.8	19.3	19.8	20.3	20.8	21.3	21.8	22.2	22.7	23.2	58
59	16.2	16.7	17.2	17.7	18.2	18.7	19.2	19.7	20.2	20.6	21.1	21.6	22.1	22.6	23.1	23.6	59
60	16.5	17.0	17.5	18.0	18.5	19.0	19.5	20.0	20.5	21.0	21.5	22.0	22.5	23.0	23.5	24.0	60

Speed in knots

TABLE 4

Speed, Time, and Distance

Minutes	24.5	25.0	25.5	26.0	26.5	27.0	27.5	28.0	28.5	29.0	29.5	30.0	30.5	31.0	31.5	32.0	Minutes
	Miles	*Miles*	*Miles*	*Miles*	*Miles*	*Miles*	*Miles*	*Miles*	*Miles*	*Miles*	*Miles*	*Miles*	*Miles*	*Miles*	*Miles*	*Miles*	
1	0.4	0.4	0.4	0.4	0.4	0.4	0.5	0.5	0.5	0.5	0.5	0.5	0.5	0.5	0.5	0.5	1
2	0.8	0.8	0.8	0.9	0.9	0.9	0.9	0.9	1.0	1.0	1.0	1.0	1.0	1.0	1.0	1.1	2
3	1.2	1.2	1.3	1.3	1.3	1.4	1.4	1.4	1.4	1.4	1.5	1.5	1.5	1.6	1.6	1.6	3
4	1.6	1.7	1.7	1.7	1.8	1.8	1.8	1.9	1.9	1.9	2.0	2.0	2.0	2.1	2.1	2.1	4
5	2.0	2.1	2.1	2.2	2.2	2.2	2.3	2.3	2.4	2.4	2.5	2.5	2.5	2.6	2.6	2.7	5
6	2.4	2.5	2.6	2.6	2.6	2.7	2.8	2.8	2.8	2.9	3.0	3.0	3.0	3.1	3.2	3.2	6
7	2.9	2.9	3.0	3.0	3.1	3.2	3.2	3.3	3.3	3.4	3.4	3.5	3.6	3.6	3.7	3.7	7
8	3.3	3.3	3.4	3.5	3.5	3.6	3.7	3.7	3.8	3.9	3.9	4.0	4.1	4.1	4.2	4.3	8
9	3.7	3.8	3.8	3.9	4.0	4.0	4.1	4.2	4.3	4.4	4.4	4.5	4.6	4.6	4.7	4.8	9
10	4.1	4.2	4.2	4.3	4.4	4.5	4.6	4.7	4.8	4.8	4.9	5.0	5.1	5.2	5.2	5.3	10
11	4.5	4.6	4.7	4.8	4.9	5.0	5.0	5.1	5.2	5.3	5.4	5.5	5.6	5.7	5.8	5.9	11
12	4.9	5.0	5.1	5.2	5.3	5.4	5.5	5.6	5.7	5.8	5.9	6.0	6.1	6.2	6.3	6.4	12
13	5.3	5.4	5.5	5.6	5.7	5.8	6.0	6.1	6.2	6.3	6.4	6.5	6.6	6.7	6.8	6.9	13
14	5.7	5.8	6.0	6.1	6.2	6.3	6.4	6.5	6.6	6.8	6.9	7.0	7.1	7.2	7.4	7.5	14
15	6.1	6.2	6.4	6.5	6.6	6.8	6.9	7.0	7.1	7.2	7.4	7.5	7.6	7.8	7.9	8.0	15
16	6.5	6.7	6.8	6.9	7.1	7.2	7.3	7.5	7.6	7.7	7.9	8.0	8.1	8.3	8.4	8.5	16
17	6.9	7.1	7.2	7.4	7.5	7.6	7.8	7.9	8.1	8.2	8.4	8.5	8.6	8.8	8.9	9.1	17
18	7.4	7.5	7.6	7.8	8.0	8.1	8.2	8.4	8.6	8.7	8.8	9.0	9.2	9.3	9.4	9.6	18
19	7.8	7.9	8.1	8.2	8.4	8.6	8.7	8.9	9.0	9.2	9.3	9.5	9.7	9.8	10.0	10.1	19
20	8.2	8.3	8.5	8.7	8.8	9.0	9.2	9.3	9.5	9.7	9.8	10.0	10.2	10.3	10.5	10.7	20
21	8.6	8.8	8.9	9.1	9.3	9.4	9.6	9.8	10.0	10.2	10.3	10.5	10.7	10.8	11.0	11.2	21
22	9.0	9.2	9.4	9.5	9.7	9.9	10.1	10.3	10.4	10.6	10.8	11.0	11.2	11.4	11.6	11.7	22
23	9.4	9.6	9.8	10.0	10.2	10.4	10.5	10.7	10.9	11.1	11.3	11.5	11.7	11.9	12.1	12.3	23
24	9.8	10.0	10.2	10.4	10.6	10.8	11.0	11.2	11.4	11.6	11.8	12.0	12.2	12.4	12.6	12.8	24
25	10.2	10.4	10.6	10.8	11.0	11.2	11.5	11.7	11.9	12.1	12.3	12.5	12.7	12.9	13.1	13.3	25
26	10.6	10.8	11.0	11.3	11.5	11.7	11.9	12.1	12.4	12.6	12.8	13.0	13.2	13.4	13.6	13.9	26
27	11.0	11.2	11.5	11.7	11.9	12.2	12.4	12.6	12.8	13.0	13.3	13.5	13.7	14.0	14.2	14.4	27
28	11.4	11.7	11.9	12.1	12.4	12.6	12.8	13.1	13.3	13.5	13.8	14.0	14.2	14.5	14.7	14.9	28
29	11.8	12.1	12.3	12.6	12.8	13.0	13.3	13.5	13.8	14.0	14.3	14.5	14.7	15.0	15.2	15.5	29
30	12.2	12.5	12.8	13.0	13.2	13.5	13.8	14.0	14.2	14.5	14.8	15.0	15.2	15.5	15.8	16.0	30
31	12.7	12.9	13.2	13.4	13.7	14.0	14.2	14.5	14.7	15.0	15.2	15.5	15.8	16.0	16.3	16.5	31
32	13.1	13.3	13.6	13.9	14.1	14.4	14.7	14.9	15.2	15.5	15.7	16.0	16.3	16.5	16.8	17.1	32
33	13.5	13.8	14.0	14.3	14.6	14.8	15.1	15.4	15.7	16.0	16.2	16.5	16.8	17.0	17.3	17.6	33
34	13.9	14.2	14.4	14.7	15.0	15.3	15.6	15.9	16.2	16.4	16.7	17.0	17.3	17.6	17.8	18.1	34
35	14.3	14.6	14.9	15.2	15.5	15.8	16.0	16.3	16.6	16.9	17.2	17.5	17.8	18.1	18.4	18.7	35
36	14.7	15.0	15.3	15.6	15.9	16.2	16.5	16.8	17.1	17.4	17.7	18.0	18.3	18.6	18.9	19.2	36
37	15.1	15.4	15.7	16.0	16.3	16.6	17.0	17.3	17.6	17.9	18.2	18.5	18.8	19.1	19.4	19.7	37
38	15.5	15.8	16.2	16.5	16.8	17.1	17.4	17.7	18.0	18.4	18.7	19.0	19.3	19.6	20.0	20.3	38
39	15.9	16.2	16.6	16.9	17.2	17.6	17.9	18.2	18.5	18.8	19.2	19.5	19.8	20.2	20.5	20.8	39
40	16.3	16.7	17.0	17.3	17.7	18.0	18.3	18.7	19.0	19.3	19.7	20.0	20.3	20.7	21.0	21.3	40
41	16.7	17.1	17.4	17.8	18.1	18.4	18.8	19.1	19.5	19.8	20.2	20.5	20.8	21.2	21.5	21.9	41
42	17.2	17.5	17.8	18.2	18.6	18.9	19.2	19.6	20.0	20.3	20.6	21.0	21.4	21.7	22.0	22.4	42
43	17.6	17.9	18.3	18.6	19.0	19.4	19.7	20.1	20.4	20.8	21.1	21.5	21.9	22.2	22.6	22.9	43
44	18.0	18.3	18.7	19.1	19.4	19.8	20.2	20.5	20.9	21.3	21.6	22.0	22.4	22.7	23.1	23.5	44
45	18.4	18.8	19.1	19.5	19.9	20.2	20.6	21.0	21.4	21.8	22.1	22.5	22.9	23.2	23.6	24.0	45
46	18.8	19.2	19.6	19.9	20.3	20.7	21.1	21.5	21.8	22.2	22.6	23.0	23.4	23.8	24.2	24.5	46
47	19.2	19.6	20.0	20.4	20.8	21.2	21.5	21.9	22.3	22.7	23.1	23.5	23.9	24.3	24.7	25.1	47
48	19.6	20.0	20.4	20.8	21.2	21.6	22.0	22.4	22.8	23.2	23.6	24.0	24.4	24.8	25.2	25.6	48
49	20.0	20.4	20.8	21.2	21.6	22.0	22.5	22.9	23.3	23.7	24.1	24.5	24.9	25.3	25.7	26.1	49
50	20.4	20.8	21.2	21.7	22.1	22.5	22.9	23.3	23.8	24.2	24.6	25.0	25.4	25.8	26.2	26.7	50
51	20.8	21.2	21.7	22.1	22.5	23.0	23.4	23.8	24.2	24.6	25.1	25.5	25.9	26.4	26.8	27.2	51
52	21.2	21.7	22.1	22.5	23.0	23.4	23.8	24.3	24.7	25.1	25.6	26.0	26.4	26.9	27.3	27.7	52
53	21.6	22.1	22.5	23.0	23.4	23.8	24.3	24.7	25.2	25.6	26.1	26.5	26.9	27.4	27.8	28.3	53
54	22.0	22.5	23.0	23.4	23.8	24.3	24.8	25.2	25.6	26.1	26.6	27.0	27.4	27.9	28.4	28.8	54
55	22.5	22.9	23.4	23.8	24.3	24.8	25.2	25.7	26.1	26.6	27.0	27.5	28.0	28.4	28.9	29.3	55
56	22.9	23.3	23.8	24.3	24.7	25.2	25.7	26.1	26.6	27.1	27.5	28.0	28.5	28.9	29.4	29.9	56
57	23.3	23.8	24.2	24.7	25.2	25.6	26.1	26.6	27.1	27.6	28.0	28.5	29.0	29.4	29.9	30.4	57
58	23.7	24.2	24.6	25.1	25.6	26.1	26.6	27.1	27.6	28.0	28.5	29.0	29.5	30.0	30.4	30.9	58
59	24.1	24.6	25.1	25.6	26.1	26.6	27.0	27.5	28.0	28.5	29.0	29.5	30.0	30.5	31.0	31.5	59
60	24.5	25.0	25.5	26.0	26.5	27.0	27.5	28.0	28.5	29.0	29.5	30.0	30.5	31.0	31.5	32.0	60

Speed in knots

TABLE 4

Speed, Time, and Distance

Minutes	Speed in knots																Minutes
	32.5	33.0	33.5	34.0	34.5	35.0	35.5	36.0	36.5	37.0	37.5	38.0	38.5	39.0	39.5	40.0	
	Miles	*Miles*	*Miles*	*Miles*	*Miles*	*Miles*	*Miles*	*Miles*	*Miles*	*Miles*	*Miles*	*Miles*	*Miles*	*Miles*	*Miles*	*Miles*	
1	0.5	0.6	0.6	0.6	0.6	0.6	0.6	0.6	0.6	0.6	0.6	0.6	0.6	0.6	0.7	0.7	1
2	1.1	1.1	1.1	1.1	1.2	1.2	1.2	1.2	1.2	1.2	1.2	1.3	1.3	1.3	1.3	1.3	2
3	1.6	1.6	1.7	1.7	1.7	1.8	1.8	1.8	1.8	1.8	1.9	1.9	1.9	2.0	2.0	2.0	3
4	2.2	2.2	2.2	2.3	2.3	2.3	2.4	2.4	2.4	2.5	2.5	2.5	2.6	2.6	2.6	2.7	4
5	2.7	2.8	2.8	2.8	2.9	2.9	3.0	3.0	3.0	3.1	3.1	3.2	3.2	3.2	3.3	3.3	5
6	3.2	3.3	3.4	3.4	3.4	3.5	3.6	3.6	3.6	3.7	3.8	3.8	3.8	3.9	4.0	4.0	6
7	3.8	3.8	3.9	4.0	4.0	4.1	4.1	4.2	4.3	4.3	4.4	4.4	4.5	4.6	4.6	4.7	7
8	4.3	4.4	4.5	4.5	4.6	4.7	4.7	4.8	4.9	4.9	5.0	5.1	5.1	5.2	5.3	5.3	8
9	4.9	5.0	5.0	5.1	5.2	5.2	5.3	5.4	5.5	5.6	5.6	5.7	5.8	5.8	5.9	6.0	9
10	5.4	5.5	5.6	5.7	5.8	5.8	5.9	6.0	6.1	6.2	6.2	6.3	6.4	6.5	6.6	6.7	10
11	6.0	6.0	6.1	6.2	6.3	6.4	6.5	6.6	6.7	6.8	6.9	7.0	7.1	7.2	7.2	7.3	11
12	6.5	6.6	6.7	6.8	6.9	7.0	7.1	7.2	7.3	7.4	7.5	7.6	7.7	7.8	7.9	8.0	12
13	7.0	7.2	7.3	7.4	7.5	7.6	7.7	7.8	7.9	8.0	8.1	8.2	8.3	8.4	8.6	8.7	13
14	7.6	7.7	7.8	7.9	8.0	8.2	8.3	8.4	8.5	8.6	8.8	8.9	9.0	9.1	9.2	9.3	14
15	8.1	8.2	8.4	8.5	8.6	8.8	8.9	9.0	9.1	9.2	9.4	9.5	9.6	9.8	9.9	10.0	15
16	8.7	8.8	8.9	9.1	9.2	9.3	9.5	9.6	9.7	9.9	10.0	10.1	10.3	10.4	10.5	10.7	16
17	9.2	9.4	9.5	9.6	9.8	9.9	10.1	10.2	10.3	10.5	10.6	10.8	10.9	11.0	11.2	11.3	17
18	9.8	9.9	10.0	10.2	10.4	10.5	10.6	10.8	11.0	11.1	11.2	11.4	11.6	11.7	11.8	12.0	18
19	10.3	10.4	10.6	10.8	10.9	11.1	11.2	11.4	11.6	11.7	11.9	12.0	12.2	12.4	12.5	12.7	19
20	10.8	11.0	11.2	11.3	11.5	11.7	11.8	12.0	12.2	12.3	12.5	12.7	12.8	13.0	13.2	13.3	20
21	11.4	11.6	11.7	11.9	12.1	12.2	12.4	12.6	12.8	13.0	13.1	13.3	13.5	13.6	13.8	14.0	21
22	11.9	12.1	12.3	12.5	12.6	12.8	13.0	13.2	13.4	13.6	13.8	13.9	14.1	14.3	14.5	14.7	22
23	12.5	12.6	12.8	13.0	13.2	13.4	13.6	13.8	14.0	14.2	14.4	14.6	14.8	15.0	15.1	15.3	23
24	13.0	13.2	13.4	13.6	13.8	14.0	14.2	14.4	14.6	14.8	15.0	15.2	15.4	15.6	15.8	16.0	24
25	13.5	13.8	14.0	14.2	14.4	14.6	14.8	15.0	15.2	15.4	15.6	15.8	16.0	16.2	16.5	16.7	25
26	14.1	14.3	14.5	14.7	15.0	15.2	15.4	15.6	15.8	16.0	16.2	16.5	16.7	16.9	17.1	17.3	26
27	14.6	14.8	15.1	15.3	15.5	15.8	16.0	16.2	16.4	16.6	16.9	17.1	17.3	17.6	17.8	18.0	27
28	15.2	15.4	15.6	15.9	16.1	16.3	16.6	16.8	17.0	17.3	17.5	17.7	18.0	18.2	18.4	18.7	28
29	15.7	16.0	16.2	16.4	16.7	16.9	17.2	17.4	17.6	17.9	18.1	18.4	18.6	18.8	19.1	19.3	29
30	16.2	16.5	16.8	17.0	17.2	17.5	17.8	18.0	18.2	18.5	18.8	19.0	19.2	19.5	19.8	20.0	30
31	16.8	17.0	17.3	17.6	17.8	18.1	18.3	18.6	18.9	19.1	19.4	19.6	19.9	20.2	20.4	20.7	31
32	17.3	17.6	17.9	18.1	18.4	18.7	18.9	19.2	19.5	19.7	20.0	20.3	20.5	20.8	21.1	21.3	32
33	17.9	18.2	18.4	18.7	19.0	19.2	19.5	19.8	20.1	20.4	20.6	20.9	21.2	21.4	21.7	22.0	33
34	18.4	18.7	19.0	19.3	19.6	19.8	20.1	20.4	20.7	21.0	21.2	21.5	21.8	22.1	22.4	22.7	34
35	19.0	19.2	19.5	19.8	20.1	20.4	20.7	21.0	21.3	21.6	21.9	22.2	22.5	22.8	23.0	23.3	35
36	19.5	19.8	20.1	20.4	20.7	21.0	21.3	21.6	21.9	22.2	22.5	22.8	23.1	23.4	23.7	24.0	36
37	20.0	20.4	20.7	21.0	21.3	21.6	21.9	22.2	22.5	22.8	23.1	23.4	23.7	24.0	24.4	24.7	37
38	20.6	20.9	21.2	21.5	21.8	22.2	22.5	22.8	23.1	23.4	23.8	24.1	24.4	24.7	25.0	25.3	38
39	21.1	21.4	21.8	22.1	22.4	22.8	23.1	23.4	23.7	24.0	24.4	24.7	25.0	25.4	25.7	26.0	39
40	21.7	22.0	22.3	22.7	23.0	23.3	23.7	24.0	24.3	24.7	25.0	25.3	25.7	26.0	26.3	26.7	40
41	22.2	22.6	22.9	23.2	23.6	23.9	24.3	24.6	24.9	25.3	25.6	26.0	26.3	26.6	27.0	27.3	41
42	22.8	23.1	23.4	23.8	24.2	24.5	24.8	25.2	25.6	25.9	26.2	26.6	27.0	27.3	27.6	28.0	42
43	23.3	23.6	24.0	24.4	24.7	25.1	25.4	25.8	26.2	26.5	26.9	27.2	27.6	28.0	28.3	28.7	43
44	23.8	24.2	24.6	24.9	25.3	25.7	26.0	26.4	26.8	27.1	27.5	27.9	28.2	28.6	29.0	29.3	44
45	24.4	24.8	25.1	25.5	25.9	26.2	26.6	27.0	27.4	27.8	28.1	28.5	28.9	29.2	29.6	30.0	45
46	24.9	25.3	25.7	26.1	26.4	26.8	27.2	27.6	28.0	28.4	28.8	29.1	29.5	29.9	30.3	30.7	46
47	25.5	25.8	26.2	26.6	27.0	27.4	27.8	28.2	28.6	29.0	29.4	29.8	30.2	30.6	30.9	31.3	47
48	26.0	26.4	26.8	27.2	27.6	28.0	28.4	28.8	29.2	29.6	30.0	30.4	30.8	31.2	31.6	32.0	48
49	26.5	27.0	27.4	27.8	28.2	28.6	29.0	29.4	29.8	30.2	30.6	31.0	31.4	31.8	32.3	32.7	49
50	27.1	27.5	27.9	28.3	28.8	29.2	29.6	30.0	30.4	30.8	31.2	31.7	32.1	32.5	32.9	33.3	50
51	27.6	28.0	28.5	28.9	29.3	29.8	30.2	30.6	31.0	31.4	31.9	32.3	32.7	33.2	33.6	34.0	51
52	28.2	28.6	29.0	29.5	29.9	30.3	30.8	31.2	31.6	32.1	32.5	32.9	33.4	33.8	34.2	34.7	52
53	28.7	29.2	29.6	30.0	30.5	30.9	31.4	31.8	32.2	32.7	33.1	33.6	34.0	34.4	34.9	35.3	53
54	29.2	29.7	30.2	30.6	31.0	31.5	32.0	32.4	32.8	33.3	33.8	34.2	34.6	35.1	35.6	36.0	54
55	29.8	30.2	30.7	31.2	31.6	32.1	32.5	33.0	33.5	33.9	34.4	34.8	35.3	35.8	36.2	36.7	55
56	30.3	30.8	31.3	31.7	32.2	32.7	33.1	33.6	34.1	34.5	35.0	35.5	35.9	36.4	36.9	37.3	56
57	30.9	31.4	31.8	32.3	32.8	33.2	33.7	34.2	34.7	35.2	35.6	36.1	36.6	37.0	37.5	38.0	57
58	31.4	31.9	32.4	32.9	33.4	33.8	34.3	34.8	35.3	35.8	36.2	36.7	37.2	37.7	38.2	38.7	58
59	32.0	32.4	32.9	33.4	33.9	34.4	34.9	35.4	35.9	36.4	36.9	37.4	37.9	38.4	38.8	39.3	59
60	32.5	33.0	33.5	34.0	34.5	35.0	35.5	36.0	36.5	37.0	37.5	38.0	38.5	39.0	39.5	40.0	60

TABLE 5

Distance of the Horizon

Height **Feet**	Nautical miles	Statute miles	Height *meters*	Height **Feet**	Nautical miles	Statute miles	Height *meters*
1	1.2	1.3	.30	120	12.8	14.7	36.58
2	1.7	1.9	.61	125	13.1	15.1	38.10
3	2.0	2.3	.91	130	13.3	15.4	39.62
4	2.3	2.7	1.22	135	13.6	15.6	41.15
5	2.6	3.0	1.52	140	13.8	15.9	42.67
6	2.9	3.3	1.83	145	14.1	16.2	44.20
7	3.1	3.6	2.13	150	14.3	16.5	45.72
8	3.3	3.8	2.44	160	14.8	17.0	48.77
9	3.5	4.0	2.74	170	15.3	17.6	51.82
10	3.7	4.3	3.05	180	15.7	18.1	54.86
11	3.9	4.5	3.35	190	16.1	18.6	57.91
12	4.1	4.7	3.66	200	16.5	19.0	60.96
13	4.2	4.9	3.96	210	17.0	19.5	64.01
14	4.4	5.0	4.27	220	17.4	20.0	67.06
15	4.5	5.2	4.57	230	17.7	20.4	70.10
16	4.7	5.4	4.88	240	18.1	20.9	73.15
17	4.8	5.6	5.18	250	18.5	21.3	76.20
18	5.0	5.7	5.49	260	18.9	21.7	79.25
19	5.1	5.9	5.79	270	19.2	22.1	82.30
20	5.2	6.0	6.10	280	19.6	22.5	85.34
21	5.4	6.2	6.40	290	19.9	22.9	88.39
22	5.5	6.3	6.71	300	20.3	23.3	91.44
23	5.6	6.5	7.01	310	20.6	23.7	94.49
24	5.7	6.6	7.32	320	20.9	24.1	97.54
25	5.9	6.7	7.62	330	21.3	24.5	100.58
26	6.0	6.9	7.92	340	21.6	24.8	103.63
27	6.1	7.0	8.23	350	21.9	25.2	106.68
28	6.2	7.1	8.53	360	22.2	25.5	109.73
29	6.3	7.3	8.84	370	22.5	25.9	112.78
30	6.4	7.4	9.14	380	22.8	26.2	115.82
31	6.5	7.5	9.45	390	23.1	26.6	118.87
32	6.6	7.6	9.75	400	23.4	26.9	121.92
33	6.7	7.7	10.06	410	23.7	27.3	124.97
34	6.8	7.9	10.36	420	24.0	27.6	128.02
35	6.9	8.0	10.67	430	24.3	27.9	131.06
36	7.0	8.1	10.97	440	24.5	28.2	134.11
37	7.1	8.2	11.28	450	24.8	28.6	137.16
38	7.2	8.3	11.58	460	25.1	28.9	140.21
39	7.3	8.4	11.89	470	25.4	29.2	143.26
40	7.4	8.5	12.19	480	25.6	29.5	146.30
41	7.5	8.6	12.50	490	25.9	29.8	149.35
42	7.6	8.7	12.80	500	26.2	30.1	152.40
43	7.7	8.8	13.11	510	26.4	30.4	155.45
44	7.8	8.9	13.41	520	26.7	30.7	158.50
45	7.8	9.0	13.72	530	26.9	31.0	161.54
46	7.9	9.1	14.02	540	27.2	31.3	164.59
47	8.0	9.2	14.33	550	27.4	31.6	167.64
48	8.1	9.3	14.63	560	27.7	31.9	170.69
49	8.2	9.4	14.94	570	27.9	32.1	173.74
50	8.3	9.5	15.24	580	28.2	32.4	176.78
55	8.7	10.0	16.76	590	28.4	32.7	179.83
60	9.1	10.4	18.29	600	28.7	33.0	182.88
65	9.4	10.9	19.81	620	29.1	33.5	188.98
70	9.8	11.3	21.34	640	29.5	34.1	195.07
75	10.1	11.7	22.86	660	30.1	34.6	201.17
80	10.5	12.0	24.38	680	30.5	35.1	207.26
85	10.8	12.4	25.91	700	31.0	35.6	213.36
90	11.1	12.8	27.43	720	31.4	36.1	219.46
95	11.4	13.1	28.96	740	31.8	36.6	225.55
100	11.7	13.5	30.48	760	32.3	37.1	231.65
105	12.0	13.8	32.00	780	32.7	37.6	237.74
110	12.3	14.1	33.53	800	33.1	38.1	243.84
115	12.5	14.4	35.05	820	33.5	38.6	249.94

TABLE 6

Geographic Range

Object height		Height of eye of observer in feet and meters										Object height	
Feet		7	10	13	16	20	23	26	30	33	36		Feet
	Meters	2	3	4	5	6	7	8	9	10	11	Meters	
		Miles	Miles	Miles	Miles	Miles	Miles	Miles	Miles	Miles	Miles		
0	0	3.1	3.7	4.2	4.7	5.2	5.6	6.0	6.4	6.7	7.0	0	0
3	1	5.1	5.7	6.2	6.7	7.3	7.6	8.0	8.4	8.7	9.0	1	3
7	2	6.2	6.8	7.3	7.8	8.3	8.7	9.1	9.5	9.8	10.1	2	7
10	3	6.8	7.4	7.9	8.4	8.9	9.3	9.7	10.1	10.4	10.7	3	10
13	4	7.3	7.9	8.4	8.9	9.5	9.8	10.2	10.6	10.9	11.2	4	13
16	5	7.8	8.4	8.9	9.4	9.9	10.3	10.6	11.1	11.4	11.7	5	16
20	6	8.3	8.9	9.5	9.9	10.5	10.8	11.2	11.6	12.0	12.3	6	20
23	7	8.7	9.3	9.8	10.3	10.8	11.2	11.6	12.0	12.3	12.6	7	23
26	8	9.1	9.7	10.2	10.6	11.2	11.6	11.9	12.4	12.7	13.0	8	26
30	9	9.5	10.1	10.6	11.1	11.6	12.0	12.4	12.8	13.1	13.4	9	30
33	10	9.8	10.4	10.9	11.4	12.0	12.3	12.7	13.1	13.4	13.7	10	33
36	11	10.1	10.7	11.2	11.7	12.3	12.6	13.0	13.4	13.7	14.0	11	36
39	12	10.4	11.0	11.5	12.0	12.5	12.9	13.3	13.7	14.0	14.3	12	39
43	13	10.8	11.4	11.9	12.4	12.9	13.3	13.6	14.1	14.4	14.7	13	43
46	14	11.0	11.6	12.2	12.6	13.2	13.5	13.9	14.3	14.7	15.0	14	46
49	15	11.3	11.9	12.4	12.9	13.4	13.8	14.2	14.6	14.9	15.2	15	49
52	16	11.5	12.1	12.7	13.1	13.7	14.0	14.4	14.8	15.2	15.5	16	52
56	17	11.9	12.5	13.0	13.4	14.0	14.4	14.7	15.2	15.5	15.8	17	56
59	18	12.1	12.7	13.2	13.7	14.2	14.6	15.0	15.4	15.7	16.0	18	59
62	19	12.3	12.9	13.4	13.9	14.4	14.8	15.2	15.6	15.9	16.2	19	62
66	20	12.6	13.2	13.7	14.2	14.7	15.1	15.5	15.9	16.2	16.5	20	66
72	22	13.0	13.6	14.1	14.6	15.2	15.5	15.9	16.3	16.6	16.9	22	72
79	24	13.5	14.1	14.6	15.1	15.6	16.0	16.4	16.8	17.1	17.4	24	79
85	26	13.9	14.5	15.0	15.5	16.0	16.4	16.8	17.2	17.5	17.8	26	85
92	28	14.3	14.9	15.4	15.9	16.5	16.8	17.2	17.6	17.9	18.2	28	92
98	30	14.7	15.3	15.8	16.3	16.8	17.2	17.5	18.0	18.3	18.6	30	98
115	35	15.6	16.2	16.8	17.2	17.8	18.2	18.5	19.0	19.3	19.6	35	115
131	40	16.5	17.1	17.6	18.1	18.6	19.0	19.4	19.8	20.1	20.4	40	131
148	45	17.3	17.9	18.5	18.9	19.5	19.8	20.2	20.6	21.0	21.3	45	148
164	50	18.1	18.7	19.2	19.7	20.2	20.6	20.9	21.4	21.7	22.0	50	164
180	55	18.8	19.4	19.9	20.4	20.9	21.3	21.7	22.1	22.4	22.7	55	180
197	60	19.5	20.1	20.6	21.1	21.7	22.0	22.4	22.8	23.1	23.4	60	197
213	65	20.2	20.8	21.3	21.8	22.3	22.7	23.0	23.5	23.8	24.1	65	213
230	70	20.8	21.4	22.0	22.4	23.0	23.4	23.7	24.2	24.5	24.8	70	230
246	75	21.4	22.1	22.6	23.0	23.6	24.0	24.3	24.8	25.1	25.4	75	246
262	80	22.0	22.6	23.2	23.6	24.2	24.5	24.9	25.3	25.7	26.0	80	262
279	85	22.6	23.2	23.8	24.2	24.8	25.2	25.5	26.0	26.3	26.6	85	279
295	90	23.2	23.8	24.3	24.8	25.3	25.7	26.1	26.5	26.8	27.1	90	295
312	95	23.8	24.4	24.9	25.3	25.9	26.3	26.6	27.1	27.4	27.7	95	312
328	100	24.3	24.9	25.4	25.9	26.4	26.8	27.2	27.6	27.9	28.2	100	328
361	110	25.3	25.9	26.4	26.9	27.5	27.8	28.2	28.6	29.0	29.3	110	361
394	120	26.3	26.9	27.4	27.9	28.5	28.8	29.2	29.6	29.9	30.2	120	394
427	130	27.3	27.9	28.4	28.9	29.4	29.8	30.1	30.6	30.9	31.2	130	427
459	140	28.2	28.8	29.3	29.7	30.3	30.7	31.0	31.5	31.8	32.1	140	459
492	150	29.0	29.7	30.2	30.6	31.2	31.6	31.9	32.4	32.7	33.0	150	492
525	160	29.9	30.5	31.0	31.5	32.0	32.4	32.8	33.2	33.5	33.8	160	525
558	170	30.7	31.3	31.9	32.3	32.9	33.2	33.6	34.0	34.4	34.7	170	558
591	180	31.5	32.1	32.7	33.1	33.7	34.1	34.4	34.9	35.2	35.5	180	591
623	190	32.3	32.9	33.4	33.9	34.4	34.8	35.2	35.6	35.9	36.2	190	623
656	200	33.1	33.7	34.2	34.6	35.2	35.6	35.9	36.4	36.7	37.0	200	656
722	220	34.5	35.1	35.7	36.1	36.7	37.0	37.4	37.8	38.2	38.5	220	722
787	240	35.9	36.5	37.0	37.5	38.1	38.4	38.8	39.2	39.5	39.8	240	787
853	260	37.3	37.9	38.4	38.9	39.4	39.8	40.1	40.6	40.9	41.2	260	853
919	280	38.6	39.2	39.7	40.1	40.7	41.1	41.4	41.9	42.2	42.5	280	919
984	300	39.8	40.4	40.9	41.4	41.9	42.3	42.7	43.1	43.4	43.7	300	984

TABLE 6

Geographic Range

Object height		Height of eye of observer in feet and meters										Object height	
Feet		39	43	46	49	52	56	59	62	66	69		Feet
	Meters	12	13	14	15	16	17	18	19	20	21	Meters	
		Miles	Miles	Miles	Miles	Miles	Miles	Miles	Miles	Miles	Miles		
0	0	7.3	7.7	7.9	8.2	8.4	8.8	9.0	9.2	9.5	9.7	0	0
3	1	9.3	9.7	10.0	10.2	10.5	10.8	11.0	11.2	11.5	11.7	1	3
7	2	10.4	10.8	11.0	11.3	11.5	11.9	12.1	12.3	12.6	12.8	2	7
10	3	11.0	11.4	11.6	11.9	12.1	12.5	12.7	12.9	13.2	13.4	3	10
13	4	11.5	11.9	12.2	12.4	12.7	13.0	13.2	13.4	13.7	13.9	4	13
16	5	12.0	12.4	12.6	12.9	13.1	13.4	13.7	13.9	14.2	14.4	5	16
20	6	12.5	12.9	13.2	13.4	13.7	14.0	14.2	14.4	14.7	15.0	6	20
23	7	12.9	13.3	13.5	13.8	14.0	14.4	14.6	14.8	15.1	15.3	7	23
26	8	13.3	13.6	13.9	14.2	14.4	14.7	15.0	15.2	15.5	15.7	8	26
30	9	13.7	14.1	14.3	14.6	14.8	15.2	15.4	15.6	15.9	16.1	9	30
33	10	14.0	14.4	14.7	14.9	15.2	15.5	15.7	15.9	16.2	16.4	10	33
36	11	14.3	14.7	15.0	15.2	15.5	15.8	16.0	16.2	16.5	16.7	11	36
39	12	14.6	15.0	15.2	15.5	15.7	16.1	16.3	16.5	16.8	17.0	12	39
43	13	15.0	15.3	15.6	15.9	16.1	16.4	16.7	16.9	17.2	17.4	13	43
46	14	15.2	15.6	15.9	16.1	16.4	16.7	16.9	17.1	17.4	17.7	14	46
49	15	15.5	15.9	16.1	16.4	16.6	16.9	17.2	17.4	17.7	17.9	15	49
52	16	15.7	16.1	16.4	16.6	16.9	17.2	17.4	17.6	17.9	18.2	16	52
56	17	16.1	16.4	16.7	16.9	17.2	17.5	17.7	18.0	18.3	18.5	17	56
59	18	16.3	16.7	16.9	17.2	17.4	17.7	18.0	18.2	18.5	18.7	18	59
62	19	16.5	16.9	17.1	17.4	17.6	18.0	18.2	18.4	18.7	18.9	19	62
66	20	16.8	17.2	17.4	17.7	17.9	18.3	18.5	18.7	19.0	19.2	20	66
72	22	17.2	17.6	17.9	18.1	18.4	18.7	18.9	19.1	19.4	19.6	22	72
79	24	17.7	18.1	18.3	18.6	18.8	19.2	19.4	19.6	19.9	20.1	24	79
85	26	18.1	18.5	18.7	19.0	19.2	19.5	19.8	20.0	20.3	20.5	26	85
92	28	18.5	18.9	19.2	19.4	19.7	20.0	20.2	20.4	20.7	20.9	28	92
98	30	18.9	19.3	19.5	19.8	20.0	20.3	20.6	20.8	21.1	21.3	30	98
115	35	19.9	20.2	20.5	20.7	21.0	21.3	21.5	21.8	22.1	22.3	35	115
131	40	20.7	21.1	21.3	21.6	21.8	22.1	22.4	22.6	22.9	23.1	40	131
148	45	21.5	21.9	22.2	22.4	22.7	23.0	23.2	23.4	23.7	24.0	45	148
164	50	22.3	22.7	22.9	23.2	23.4	23.7	24.0	24.2	24.5	24.7	50	164
180	55	23.0	23.4	23.6	23.9	24.1	24.5	24.7	24.9	25.2	25.4	55	180
197	60	23.7	24.1	24.4	24.6	24.9	25.2	25.4	25.6	25.9	26.1	60	197
213	65	24.4	24.7	25.0	25.3	25.5	25.8	26.1	26.3	26.6	26.8	65	213
230	70	25.1	25.4	25.7	25.9	26.2	26.5	26.7	27.0	27.2	27.5	70	230
246	75	25.7	26.0	26.3	26.5	26.8	27.1	27.3	27.6	27.9	28.1	75	246
262	80	26.2	26.6	26.9	27.1	27.4	27.7	27.9	28.2	28.4	28.7	80	262
279	85	26.8	27.2	27.5	27.7	28.0	28.3	28.5	28.8	29.0	29.3	85	279
295	90	27.4	27.8	28.0	28.3	28.5	28.9	29.1	29.3	29.6	29.8	90	295
312	95	28.0	28.3	28.6	28.9	29.1	29.4	29.7	29.9	30.2	30.4	95	312
328	100	28.5	28.9	29.1	29.4	29.6	29.9	30.2	30.4	30.7	30.9	100	328
361	110	29.5	29.9	30.2	30.4	30.7	31.0	31.2	31.4	31.7	31.9	110	361
394	120	30.5	30.9	31.2	31.4	31.7	32.0	32.2	32.4	32.7	32.9	120	394
427	130	31.5	31.8	32.1	32.4	32.6	32.9	33.2	33.4	33.7	33.9	130	427
459	140	32.4	32.7	33.0	33.3	33.5	33.8	34.1	34.3	34.6	34.8	140	459
492	150	33.3	33.6	33.9	34.1	34.4	34.7	34.9	35.2	35.5	35.7	150	492
525	160	34.1	34.5	34.7	35.0	35.2	35.6	35.8	36.0	36.3	36.5	160	525
558	170	34.9	35.3	35.6	35.8	36.1	36.4	36.6	36.9	37.1	37.4	170	558
591	180	35.7	36.1	36.4	36.6	36.9	37.2	37.4	37.7	37.9	38.2	180	591
623	190	36.5	36.9	37.1	37.4	37.6	38.0	38.2	38.4	38.7	38.9	190	623
656	200	37.3	37.6	37.9	38.2	38.4	38.7	39.0	39.2	39.5	39.7	200	656
722	220	38.7	39.1	39.4	39.6	39.9	40.2	40.4	40.7	40.9	41.2	220	722
787	240	40.1	40.5	40.8	41.0	41.3	41.6	41.8	42.0	42.3	42.5	240	787
853	260	41.5	41.8	42.1	42.4	42.6	42.9	43.2	43.4	43.7	43.9	260	853
919	280	42.8	43.1	43.4	43.7	43.9	44.2	44.5	44.7	45.0	45.2	270	919
984	300	44.0	44.4	44.6	44.9	45.1	45.5	45.7	45.9	46.2	46.4	300	984

TABLE 6

Geographic Range

Object Height		Height of eye of observer in feet and meters										Object Height	
Feet		72	75	79	82	85	89	92	95	98	115		Feet
	Meters	22	23	24	25	26	27	28	29	30	35	Meters	
		Miles	Miles	Miles	Miles	Miles	Miles	Miles	Miles	Miles	Miles		
0	0	9.9	10.2	10.4	10.6	10.8	11.0	11.2	11.4	11.6	12.5	0	**0**
3	1	12.0	12.2	12.4	12.6	12.8	13.1	13.2	13.4	13.6	14.6	1	**3**
7	2	13.0	13.3	13.5	13.7	13.9	14.1	14.3	14.5	14.7	15.6	2	**7**
10	3	13.6	13.9	14.1	14.3	14.5	14.7	14.9	15.1	15.3	16.2	3	**10**
13	4	14.1	14.4	14.6	14.8	15.0	15.3	15.4	15.6	15.8	16.8	4	**13**
16	5	14.6	14.9	15.1	15.3	15.5	15.7	15.9	16.1	16.3	17.2	5	**16**
20	6	15.2	15.4	15.6	15.8	16.0	16.3	16.5	16.6	16.8	17.8	6	**20**
23	7	15.5	15.8	16.0	16.2	16.4	16.6	16.8	17.0	17.2	18.2	7	**23**
26	8	15.9	16.2	16.4	16.6	16.8	17.0	17.2	17.4	17.5	18.5	8	**26**
30	9	16.3	16.6	16.8	17.0	17.2	17.4	17.6	17.8	18.0	19.0	9	**30**
33	10	16.6	16.9	17.1	17.3	17.5	17.8	17.9	18.1	18.3	19.3	10	**33**
36	11	16.9	17.2	17.4	17.6	17.8	18.1	18.2	18.4	18.6	19.6	11	**36**
39	12	17.2	17.5	17.7	17.9	18.1	18.3	18.5	18.7	18.9	19.9	12	**39**
43	13	17.6	17.9	18.1	18.3	18.5	18.7	18.9	19.1	19.3	20.2	13	**43**
46	14	17.9	18.1	18.3	18.5	18.7	19.0	19.2	19.3	19.5	20.5	14	**46**
49	15	18.1	18.4	18.6	18.8	19.0	19.2	19.4	19.6	19.8	20.7	15	**49**
52	16	18.4	18.6	18.8	19.0	19.2	19.5	19.7	19.8	20.0	21.0	16	**52**
56	17	18.7	19.0	19.2	19.4	19.5	19.8	20.0	20.2	20.3	21.3	17	**56**
59	18	18.9	19.2	19.4	19.6	19.8	20.0	20.2	20.4	20.6	21.5	18	**59**
62	19	19.1	19.4	19.6	19.8	20.0	20.3	20.4	20.6	20.8	21.8	19	**62**
66	20	19.4	19.7	19.9	20.1	20.3	20.5	20.7	20.9	21.1	22.1	20	**66**
72	22	19.9	20.1	20.3	20.5	20.7	21.0	21.2	21.3	21.5	22.5	22	**72**
79	24	20.3	20.6	20.8	21.0	21.2	21.4	21.6	21.8	22.0	22.9	24	**79**
85	26	20.7	21.0	21.2	21.4	21.6	21.8	22.0	22.2	22.4	23.3	26	**85**
92	28	21.2	21.4	21.6	21.8	22.0	22.3	22.4	22.6	22.8	23.8	28	**92**
98	30	21.5	21.8	22.0	22.2	22.4	22.6	22.8	23.0	23.2	24.1	30	**98**
115	35	22.5	22.7	22.9	23.1	23.3	23.6	23.8	24.0	24.1	25.1	35	**115**
131	40	23.3	23.6	23.8	24.0	24.2	24.4	24.6	24.8	25.0	25.9	40	**131**
148	45	24.2	24.4	24.6	24.8	25.0	25.3	25.5	25.6	25.8	26.8	45	**148**
164	50	24.9	25.2	25.4	25.6	25.8	26.0	26.2	26.4	26.6	27.5	50	**164**
180	55	25.6	25.9	26.1	26.3	26.5	26.7	26.9	27.1	27.3	28.2	55	**180**
197	60	26.3	26.6	26.8	27.0	27.2	27.5	27.6	27.8	28.0	29.0	60	**197**
213	65	27.0	27.3	27.5	27.7	27.9	28.1	28.3	28.5	28.7	29.6	65	**213**
230	70	27.7	27.9	28.1	28.3	28.5	28.8	29.0	29.1	29.3	30.3	70	**230**
246	75	28.3	28.6	28.7	28.9	29.1	29.4	29.6	29.8	29.9	30.9	75	**246**
262	80	28.9	29.1	29.3	29.5	29.7	30.0	30.1	30.3	30.5	31.5	80	**262**
279	85	29.5	29.7	29.9	30.1	30.3	30.6	30.8	30.9	31.1	32.1	85	**279**
295	90	30.0	30.3	30.5	30.7	30.9	31.1	31.3	31.5	31.7	32.6	90	**295**
312	95	30.6	30.9	31.1	31.3	31.4	31.7	31.9	32.1	32.2	33.2	95	**312**
328	100	31.1	31.4	31.6	31.8	32.0	32.2	32.4	32.6	32.8	33.7	100	**328**
361	110	32.2	32.4	32.6	32.8	33.0	33.3	33.5	33.6	33.8	34.8	110	**361**
394	120	33.2	33.4	33.6	33.8	34.0	34.3	34.4	34.6	34.8	35.8	120	**394**
427	130	34.1	34.4	34.6	34.8	35.0	35.2	35.4	35.6	35.8	36.7	130	**427**
459	140	35.0	35.3	35.5	35.7	35.9	36.1	36.3	36.5	36.6	37.6	140	**459**
492	150	35.9	36.2	36.4	36.5	36.7	37.0	37.2	37.4	37.5	38.5	150	**492**
525	160	36.7	37.0	37.2	37.4	37.6	37.8	38.0	38.2	38.4	39.4	160	**525**
558	170	37.6	37.8	38.0	38.2	38.4	38.7	38.9	39.0	39.2	40.2	170	**558**
591	180	38.4	38.6	38.8	39.0	39.2	39.5	39.7	39.8	40.0	41.0	180	**591**
623	190	39.1	39.4	39.6	39.8	40.0	40.2	40.4	40.6	40.8	41.8	190	**623**
656	200	39.9	40.2	40.4	40.6	40.8	41.0	41.2	41.4	41.5	42.5	200	**656**
722	220	41.4	41.6	41.8	42.0	42.2	42.5	42.7	42.8	43.0	44.0	220	**722**
787	240	42.8	43.0	43.2	43.4	43.6	43.9	44.0	44.2	44.4	45.4	240	**787**
853	260	44.1	44.4	44.6	44.8	45.0	45.2	45.4	45.6	45.8	46.7	260	**853**
919	280	45.4	45.7	45.9	46.1	46.3	46.5	46.7	46.9	47.1	48.0	280	**919**
984	300	46.6	46.9	47.1	47.3	47.5	47.7	47.9	48.1	48.3	49.2	300	**984**

TABLE 7

Time Zones. Zone Descriptions, and Suffixes

ZONE	ZD	SUFFIX	ZONE	ZD	SUFFIX
7½°W. to 7½°E.	0	Z	7½°W. to 22½°W.	+ 1	N
7½°E. to 22½°E.	− 1	A	22½°W. to 37½°W.	+ 2	O
22½°E. to 37½°E.	− 2	B	37½°W. to 52½°W.	+ 3	P
37½°E. to 52½°E.	− 3	C	52½°W. to 67½°W.	+ 4	Q
52½°E. to 67½°E.	− 4	D	67½°W. to 82½°W.	+ 5	R
67½°E. to 82½°E.	− 5	E	82½°W. to 97½°W.	+ 6	S
82½°E. to 97½°E.	− 6	F	97½°W. to 112½°W.	+ 7	T
97½°E. to 112½°E.	− 7	G	112½°W. to 127½°W.	+ 8	U
112½°E. to 127½°E.	− 8	H	127½°W. to 142½°W.	+ 9	V
127½°E. to 142½°E.	− 9	I	142½°W. to 157½°W.	+10	W
142½°E. to 157½°E.	−10	K	157½°W. to 172½°W.	+11	X
157½°E. to 172½°E.	−11	L	172½°W. to 180°	+12	Y
172½°E. to 180°	−12	M			

NOTE.—G M T is indicated by suffix Z. Standard times as kept in various places or countries are listed in *The Nautical Almanac* and *The Air Almanac.*

TABLE 8

Conversion Tables for Thermometer Scales

F = Fahrenheit, C = Celsius (centigrade), K = Kelvin

F	C	K	F	C	K	C	F	K	K	F	C
°	°	°	°	°	°	°	°	°	°	°	°
−20	−28.9	244.3	+40	+4.4	277.6	−25	−13.0	248.2	250	−9.7	−23.2
19	28.3	244.8	41	5.0	278.2	24	11.2	249.2	251	7.9	22.2
18	27.8	245.4	42	5.6	278.7	23	9.4	250.2	252	6.1	21.2
17	27.2	245.9	43	6.1	279.3	22	7.6	251.2	253	4.3	20.2
16	26.7	246.5	44	6.7	279.8	21	5.8	252.2	254	2.5	19.2
−15	−26.1	247.0	+45	+7.2	280.4	−20	−4.0	253.2	255	−0.7	−18.2
14	25.6	247.6	46	7.8	280.9	19	2.2	254.2	256	+1.1	17.2
13	25.0	248.2	47	8.3	281.5	18	−0.4	255.2	257	2.9	16.2
12	24.4	248.7	48	8.9	282.0	17	+1.4	256.2	258	4.7	15.2
11	23.9	249.3	49	9.4	282.6	16	3.2	257.2	259	6.5	14.2
−10	−23.3	249.8	+50	+10.0	283.2	−15	+5.0	258.2	260	+8.3	−13.2
9	22.8	250.4	51	10.6	283.7	14	6.8	259.2	261	10.1	12.2
8	22.2	250.9	52	11.1	284.3	13	8.6	260.2	262	11.9	11.2
7	21.7	251.5	53	11.7	284.8	12	10.4	261.2	263	13.7	10.2
6	21.1	252.0	54	12.2	285.4	11	12.2	262.2	264	15.5	9.2
−5	−20.6	252.6	+55	+12.8	285.9	−10	+14.0	263.2	265	+17.3	−8.2
4	20.0	253.2	56	13.3	286.5	9	15.8	264.2	266	19.1	7.2
3	19.4	253.7	57	13.9	287.0	8	17.6	265.2	267	20.9	6.2
2	18.9	254.3	58	14.4	287.6	7	19.4	266.2	268	22.7	5.2
−1	18.3	254.8	59	15.0	288.2	6	21.2	267.2	269	24.5	4.2
0	−17.8	255.4	+60	+15.6	288.7	−5	+23.0	268.2	270	+26.3	−3.2
+1	17.2	255.9	61	16.1	289.3	4	24.8	269.2	271	28.1	2.2
2	16.7	256.5	62	16.7	289.8	3	26.6	270.2	272	29.9	1.2
3	16.1	257.0	63	17.2	290.4	2	28.4	271.2	273	31.7	−0.2
4	15.6	257.6	64	17.8	290.9	−1	30.2	272.2	274	33.5	+0.8
+5	−15.0	258.2	+65	+18.3	291.5	0	+32.0	273.2	275	+35.3	+1.8
6	14.4	258.7	66	18.9	292.0	+1	33.8	274.2	276	37.1	2.8
7	13.9	259.3	67	19.4	292.6	2	35.6	275.2	277	38.9	3.8
8	13.3	259.8	68	20.0	293.2	3	37.4	276.2	278	40.7	4.8
9	12.8	260.4	69	20.6	293.7	4	39.2	277.2	279	42.5	5.8
+10	−12.2	260.9	+70	+21.1	294.3	+5	+41.0	278.2	280	+44.3	+6.8
11	11.7	261.5	71	21.7	294.8	6	42.8	279.2	281	46.1	7.8
12	11.1	262.0	72	22.2	295.4	7	44.6	280.2	282	47.9	8.8
13	10.6	262.6	73	22.8	295.9	8	46.4	281.2	283	49.7	9.8
14	10.0	263.2	74	23.3	296.5	9	48.2	282.2	284	51.5	10.8
+15	−9.4	263.7	+75	+23.9	297.0	+10	+50.0	283.2	285	+53.3	+11.8
16	8.9	264.3	76	24.4	297.6	11	51.8	284.2	286	55.1	12.8
17	8.3	264.8	77	25.0	298.2	12	53.6	285.2	287	56.9	13.8
18	7.8	265.4	78	25.6	298.7	13	55.4	286.2	288	58.7	14.8
19	7.2	265.9	79	26.1	299.3	14	57.2	287.2	289	60.5	15.8
+20	−6.7	266.5	+80	+26.7	299.8	+15	+59.0	288.2	290	+62.3	+16.8
21	6.1	267.0	81	27.2	300.4	16	60.8	289.2	291	64.1	17.8
22	5.6	267.6	82	27.8	300.9	17	62.6	290.2	292	65.9	18.8
23	5.0	268.2	83	28.3	301.5	18	64.4	291.2	293	67.7	19.8
24	4.4	268.7	84	28.9	302.0	19	66.2	292.2	294	69.5	20.8
+25	−3.9	269.3	+85	+29.4	302.6	+20	+68.0	293.2	295	+71.3	+21.8
26	3.3	269.8	86	30.0	303.2	21	69.8	294.2	296	73.1	22.8
27	2.8	270.4	87	30.6	303.7	22	71.6	295.2	297	74.9	23.8
28	2.2	270.9	88	31.1	304.3	23	73.4	296.2	298	76.7	24.8
29	1.7	271.5	89	31.7	304.8	24	75.2	297.2	299	78.5	25.8
+30	−1.1	272.0	+90	+32.2	305.4	+25	+77.0	298.2	300	+80.3	+26.8
31	0.6	272.6	91	32.8	305.9	26	78.8	299.2	301	82.1	27.8
32	0.0	273.2	92	33.3	306.5	27	80.6	300.2	302	83.9	28.8
33	+0.6	273.7	93	33.9	307.0	28	82.4	301.2	303	85.7	29.8
34	1.1	274.3	94	34.4	307.6	29	84.2	302.2	304	87.5	30.8
+35	+1.7	274.8	+95	+35.0	308.2	+30	+86.0	303.2	305	+89.3	+31.8
36	2.2	275.4	96	35.6	308.7	31	87.8	304.2	306	91.1	32.8
37	2.8	275.9	97	36.1	309.3	32	89.6	305.2	307	92.9	33.8
38	3.3	276.5	98	36.7	309.8	33	91.4	306.2	308	94.7	34.8
39	3.9	277.0	99	37.2	310.4	34	93.2	307.2	309	96.5	35.8
+40	+4.4	277.6	+100	+37.8	310.9	+35	+95.0	308.2	310	+98.3	+36.8

TABLE 9

Conversion Table for Millibars, Inches of Mercury, and Millimeters of Mercury

Millibars	Inches	Millimeters	Millibars	Inches	Millimeters	Millibars	Inches	Millimeters
900	26.58	675.1	960	28.35	720.1	1020	30.12	765.1
901	26.61	675.8	961	28.38	720.8	1021	30.15	765.8
902	26.64	676.6	962	28.41	721.6	1022	30.18	766.6
903	26.67	677.3	963	28.44	722.3	1023	30.21	767.3
904	26.70	678.1	964	28.47	723.1	1024	30.24	768.1
905	26.72	678.8	965	28.50	723.8	1025	30.27	768.8
906	26.75	679.6	966	28.53	724.6	1026	30.30	769.6
907	26.78	680.3	967	28.56	725.3	1027	30.33	770.3
908	26.81	681.1	968	28.58	726.1	1028	30.36	771.1
909	26.84	681.8	969	28.61	726.8	1029	30.39	771.8
910	26.87	682.6	970	28.64	727.6	1030	30.42	772.6
911	26.90	683.3	971	28.67	728.3	1031	30.45	773.3
912	26.93	684.1	972	28.70	729.1	1032	30.47	774.1
913	26.96	684.8	973	28.73	729.8	1033	30.50	774.8
914	26.99	685.6	974	28.76	730.6	1034	30.53	775.6
915	27.02	686.3	975	28.79	731.3	1035	30.56	776.3
916	27.05	687.1	976	28.82	732.1	1036	30.59	777.1
917	27.08	687.8	977	28.85	732.8	1037	30.62	777.8
918	27.11	688.6	978	28.88	733.6	1038	30.65	778.6
919	27.14	689.3	979	28.91	734.3	1039	30.68	779.3
920	27.17	690.1	980	28.94	735.1	1040	30.71	780.1
921	27.20	690.8	981	28.97	735.8	1041	30.74	780.8
922	27.23	691.6	982	29.00	736.6	1042	30.77	781.6
923	27.26	692.3	983	29.03	737.3	1043	30.80	782.3
924	27.29	693.1	984	29.06	738.1	1044	30.83	783.1
925	27.32	693.8	985	29.09	738.8	1045	30.86	783.8
926	27.34	694.6	986	29.12	739.6	1046	30.89	784.6
927	27.37	695.3	987	29.15	740.3	1047	30.92	785.3
928	27.40	696.1	988	29.18	741.1	1048	30.95	786.1
929	27.43	696.8	989	29.21	741.8	1049	30.98	786.8
930	27.46	697.6	990	29.23	742.6	1050	31.01	787.6
931	27.49	698.3	991	29.26	743.3	1051	31.04	788.3
932	27.52	699.1	992	29.29	744.1	1052	31.07	789.1
933	27.55	699.8	993	29.32	744.8	1053	31.10	789.8
934	27.58	700.6	994	29.35	745.6	1054	31.12	790.6
935	27.61	701.3	995	29.38	746.3	1055	31.15	791.3
936	27.64	702.1	996	29.41	747.1	1056	31.18	792.1
937	27.67	702.8	997	29.44	747.8	1057	31.21	792.8
938	27.70	703.6	998	29.47	748.6	1058	31.24	793.6
939	27.73	704.3	999	29.50	749.3	1059	31.27	794.3
940	27.76	705.1	1000	29.53	750.1	1060	31.30	795.1
941	27.79	705.8	1001	29.56	750.8	1061	31.33	795.8
942	27.82	706.6	1002	29.59	751.6	1062	31.36	796.6
943	27.85	707.3	1003	29.62	752.3	1063	31.39	797.3
944	27.88	708.1	1004	29.65	753.1	1064	31.42	798.1
945	27.91	708.8	1005	29.68	753.8	1065	31.45	798.8
946	27.94	709.6	1006	29.71	754.6	1066	31.48	799.6
947	27.96	710.3	1007	29.74	755.3	1067	31.51	800.3
948	27.99	711.1	1008	29.77	756.1	1068	31.54	801.1
949	28.02	711.8	1009	29.80	756.8	1069	31.57	801.8
950	28.05	712.6	1010	29.83	757.6	1070	31.60	802.6
951	28.08	713.3	1011	29.85	758.3	1071	31.63	803.3
952	28.11	714.1	1012	29.88	759.1	1072	31.66	804.1
953	28.14	714.8	1013	29.91	759.8	1073	31.69	804.8
954	28.17	715.6	1014	29.94	760.6	1074	31.72	805.6
955	28.20	716.3	1015	29.97	761.3	1075	31.74	806.3
956	28.23	717.1	1016	30.00	762.1	1076	31.77	807.1
957	28.26	717.8	1017	30.03	762.8	1077	31.80	807.8
958	28.29	718.6	1018	30.06	763.6	1078	31.83	808.6
959	28.32	719.3	1019	30.09	764.3	1079	31.86	809.3
960	28.35	720.1	1020	30.12	765.1	1080	31.89	810.1

Glossary of Marine Navigation

A

abaft, adv. In a direction farther aft in a ship than a specified reference position, such as abaft the mast.

abaft the beam. Any direction between broad on the beam and astern.

abeam, adv. In a line approximately at right angle to the ship's keel—opposite the waist or middle part of a ship.

absolute accuracy. The ability of a navigation or positioning system to define an exact location in relation to a coordinate system.

absolute zero. The theoretical temperature at which molecular motion ceases, −459.69°F or −273.16°C.

absorption. The process by which radiant energy is absorbed and converted to other forms of energy.

abyss, n. A very deep area of the ocean. The term is used to refer to a particular deep part of the ocean or to any part below 300 fathoms.

accidental error. An error of accidental nature. (Not to be confused with MISTAKE.)

accuracy, n. 1. In navigation, a measure of the difference between the position indicated by measurement and the true position. Some expressions of accuracy are defined in terms of probability. 2. A measure of how close the outcome of a series of observations or measurements approaches the true value of a desired quantity. The degree of exactness with which the true value of the quantity is determined from observations is limited by the presence of both systematic and random errors.

additional secondary phase factor correction. A correction in addition to the secondary phase factor correction for the additional time (or phase delay) for transmission of a low-frequency signal over a composite land-water path when the signal transit time is based on the free-space velocity.

admiralty. Pertaining to the body of law that governs maritime affairs.

advanced line of position. A line of position that has been moved forward along the course line to allow for the run since the line was established. The opposite is RETIRED LINE OF POSITION.

advection fog. A type of fog caused by the advection of moist air over a cold surface, and the consequent cooling of that air to below its dew point. SEA FOG is a very common advection fog that is caused by moist air in transport over a cold body of water.

aeronautical light. A luminous or lighted aid to navigation intended primarily for air navigation. Often shortened to AERO LIGHT.

aft, adv. Near, toward, or at the stern of a craft.

age of the moon. The elapsed time, usually expressed in days, since the last new moon.

agonic line. A line joining points of no magnetic variation, a special case of an isogonic line.

aground, adj. & adv. Resting or lodged on the bottom.

ahead, adv. Bearing approximately 000° relative. The term is often used loosely for DEAD AHEAD or bearing exactly 000° relative. The opposite is ASTERN.

ahull. The condition of a vessel making no way in a storm, allowing wind and sea to determine the position of the ship. Sailing vessels lying ahull lash the helm alee, and may carry storm sails.

aid, n. Short for AID TO NAVIGATION.

aid to navigation. A device or structure external to a craft, designed to assist in determination of position, to define a safe course, or to warn of dangers or obstructions. If the information is transmitted by light waves, the device is called a visual aid to navigation; if by sound waves, an audible aid to navigation; if by radio waves, a radio aid to navigation.

air almanac. A periodical publication of astronomical data designed primarily for air navigation, but often used in marine navigation.

air mass. An extensive body of air with fairly uniform (horizontal) physical properties, especially temperature and humidity. In its incipient stage the properties of the air mass are determined by the characteristics of the region in which it forms. It is a cold or warm air mass if it is colder or warmer than the surrounding air.

air-mass classification. Air masses are classified according to their source regions. Four such regions are generally recognized: (1) equatorial (E), the doldrum area between the north and south trades; (2) tropical (T), the trade wind and lower temperate regions, (3) polar (P), the higher temperate latitudes; and (4) Arctic or Antarctic (A), the north or south polar regions of ice and snow. This classification is a general indication of relative temperature, as well as latitude of origin. Air masses are further classified as maritime (m) or continental (c), depending upon whether they form over water or land. This classification is an indication of the relative moisture content of the air mass. A third classification sometimes applied to tropical and polar air masses indicates whether the air mass is warm (w) or cold (k) relative to the underlying surface. The w and k classifications are primarily indications of stability, cold air being more stable.

algorithm. A defined procedure or routine

used for solving a specific mathematical problem.

align, v., t. To place objects in line.

almanac, n. A periodical publication of ephemeral astronomical data. If information is given in a form and to a precision suitable for marine navigation, it is called a nautical almanac; if designed primarily for air navigation, it is called an air almanac.

alphanumeric. Referring to a set of computer characters consisting of alphabetic and numeric symbols.

alternating current. An electric current that continually changes in magnitude and periodically reverses polarity.

alternating fixed and flashing light. A fixed light varied at regular intervals by a single flash of greater luminous intensity, with color variations in either the fixed light or flash, or both.

alternating fixed and group flashing light. A fixed light varied at regular intervals by a group of two or more flashes of greater luminous intensity, with color variations in either the fixed light or flashes or both.

alternating flashing light. A light showing a single flash with color variations at regular intervals, the duration of light being shorter than that of darkness.

alternating group flashing light. A group flashing light that shows periodic color change.

alternating group occulting light. A group occulting light that shows periodic color change.

alternating occulting light. A light totally eclipsed at regular intervals, the duration of light always being longer than the duration of darkness, that shows periodic color change.

alternating light. A light showing different colors alternately.

altitude, n. Angular distance above the horizon; the arc of a vertical circle between the horizon and a point on the celestial sphere, measured upward from the horizon.

altitude intercept. The difference in minutes of arc between the computed and the observed altitude (corrected sextant altitude) or between precomputed and sextant altitudes. It is labeled T (toward) or A (away) as the observed (or sextant) altitude is greater or smaller than the computed (or precomputed) altitude. Also called ALTITUDE DIFFERENCE, INTERCEPT.

alto-. A prefix used in cloud classification to indicate the middle level.

altocumulus, n. Clouds within the middle level (mean height 6,500–20,000 ft.) composed of flattened globular masses, the smallest elements of the regularly arranged layers being fairly thin, with or without shading. These elements are arranged in groups, in lines, or waves, following one or two directions, and are sometimes so close together that their edges join.

altostratus, n. A sheet of gray or bluish cloud within the middle level (mean height 6,500–20,000 ft.). Sometimes the sheet is composed of a compact mass of dark, thick, gray clouds of fibrous structure; at other times the sheet is thin and through it the sun or moon can be seen dimly.

ambiguity, n. In navigation, the condition obtained when a given set of observations defines more than one point, direction, line of position, or surface of position.

American Practical Navigator. A navigational text and reference book published by the NATIONAL IMAGERY AND MAPPING AGENCY (NIMA); originally by Nathaniel Bowditch in 1802. Popularly called BOWDITCH.

amidships, adv. At, near, or toward the middle of a ship.

amplification, n. 1. An increase in signal magnitude from one point to another, or the process causing this increase. 2. Of a transducer, the scalar ratio of the signal output to the signal input.

amplifier, n. A device that enables an input signal to control power from a source independent of the signal and thus be capable of delivering an output that is greater than the input signal.

amplitude modulation. The process of changing the amplitude of a carrier wave in accordance with the variations of a modulating wave.

anabatic wind. Any wind blowing up an incline. A KATABATIC WIND blows down an incline.

analemma, n. A graduated scale of the declination of the sun and the equation of time for each day of the year located in the Torrid Zone on the terrestrial globe.

anchor, n. A device used to secure a ship to the sea floor.

anchor, v., t. To use the anchor to secure a ship to the sea floor. If more than one anchor is used the ship is moored.

anchorage buoy. A buoy that marks the limits of an anchorage, not to be confused with a MOORING BUOY.

anchor buoy. A buoy marking the position of an anchor on the bottom, usually painted green for the starboard anchor and red for the port anchor, and secured to the crown of the anchor by a buoy rope.

anchor light. A light shown from a vessel or aircraft to indicate its position when riding at anchor. Also called RIDING LIGHT.

anemometer, n. An instrument for measuring the speed of the wind. Some instruments also indicate the direction from which it is blowing.

aneroid barometer. An instrument that determines atmospheric pressure by the effect of such pressure on a thin-metal cylinder from which the air has been partly exhausted.

angle, n. The inclination to each other of two intersecting lines, measured by the arc of a circle intercepted between the two lines forming the angle, the center of the circle being the point of intersection. An acute angle is less than 90°; a right angle, 90°; an obtuse angle, more than 90° but less than 180°; a straight angle, 180°; a reflex angle, more than 180° but less than 360°; a perigon, 360°. Any angle not a multiple of 90 is an oblique angle. If the sum of two angles is 90°, they are complementary angles; if 180°, supplementary angles; if 360°, explementary angles.

angle of cut. The smaller angular difference of two bearings or lines of position.

angle of deviation. The angle through which a ray is bent by refraction.

angle of elevation. The angle in a vertical plane between the horizontal and an ascending line, as from an observer to an object. A negative angle of elevation is usually called an ANGLE OF DEPRESSION. Also called ELEVATION ANGLE.

angle of incidence. The angle between the line of motion of a ray of radiant energy and the perpendicular to a surface, at the point of impingement. This angle is numerically equal to the ANGLE OF REFLECTION.

angle of reflection. The angle between the line of motion of a ray of reflected radiant energy and the perpendicular to a surface, at the point of reflection. This angle is numerically equal to the ANGLE OF INCIDENCE.

angle of refraction. The angle between a refracted ray and the perpendicular to the refracting surface.

angular, adj. Of or pertaining to an angle or angles.

angular distance. 1. The angular difference between two directions, numerically equal to the angle between two lines extending in the given directions. 2. The arc of the great circle joining two points, expressed in angular units. 3. Distance between two points, expressed in angular units of a specified frequency.

annual, adj. Of or pertaining to a year; yearly.

annular, adj. Ring-shaped.

annular eclipse An eclipse in which a thin ring of the source of light appears around the obscuring body. Annular solar eclipses occur, but never annular lunar eclipses.

anomalistic month. The average period of revolution of the moon from perigee to perigee, a period of 27 days, 13 hours, 18 minutes, and 33.2 seconds in 1900. The secular variation does not exceed a few hundredths of a second per century.

anomalistic period. The interval between

two successive passes of a satellite through perigee. Also called PERIGEE-TO-PERIGEE PERIOD RADIAL PERIOD.

anomalistic year. The period of one revolution of the earth around the sun, from perihelion to perihelion, averaging 365 days, 6 hours, 13 minutes, 53.0 seconds in 1900, and increasing at the rate of 0.26 seconds per century.

Antarctic air. A type of air whose characteristics are developed in an Antarctic region. Antarctic air appears to be colder at the surface in all seasons, and at all levels in fall and winter, than ARCTIC AIR.

Antarctic Circle. The parallel of latitude at about 66°33'S, marking the northern limit of the south Frigid Zone. This latitude is the complement of the sun's greatest southerly declination, and marks the approximate northern limit at which the sun becomes circumpolar. The actual limit is extended somewhat by the combined effect of refraction, semidiameter of the sun, parallax, and the height of the observer's eye above the surface of the earth. A similar circle marking the southern limit of the north Frigid Zone is called ARCTIC CIRCLE or NORTH POLAR CIRCLE. Also called SOUTH POLAR CIRCLE.

Antarctic front. The semi-permanent, semi-continuous front between the Antarctic air of the Antarctic Continent and the polar air of the southern oceans; generally comparable to the arctic front of the Northern Hemisphere.

ante meridian (AM). Before noon, or the period of time between midnight (0000) and noon (1200). The period between noon and midnight is called POST MERIDIAN (PM).

antenna, n. A structure or device used to collect or radiate electromagnetic waves.

antenna coupler. A radio-frequency transformer used to connect an antenna to a transmission line or to connect a transmission line to a radio receiver.

anthelion, n. A rare kind of halo that appears as a bright spot at the same altitude as the sun and 180° from it in azimuth.

anticorona, n. A diffraction phenomenon very similar to but complementary to the corona, appearing at a point directly opposite to the sun or moon from the observer. Also called BROKEN BOW, GLORY.

anti-crepuscular rays. Extensions of crepuscular rays, converging toward a point 180° from the sun.

anticyclone, n. An approximately circular portion of the atmosphere, having relatively high atmospheric pressure and winds that blow clockwise around the center in the Northern Hemisphere and counterclockwise in the Southern Hemisphere. An anticyclone is characterized by good weather. Also called HIGH.

anticyclonic winds. The winds associated with a high pressure area and constituting part of an anticyclone.

antipode, n. Anything exactly opposite to something else. Particularly, that point on the earth 180° from a given place.

antisolar point. The point on the celestial sphere 180° from the sun.

antitrades, n., pl. The prevailing western winds that blow over and in the opposite direction to the trade winds. Also called COUNTERTRADES.

antitwilight, n. The pink or purplish zone of illumination bordering the shadow of the earth in the dark part of the sky opposite the sun after sunset or before sunrise. Also called ANTI-CREPUSCULAR ARCH.

anvil cloud. Heavy cumulus or cumulonimbus having an anvil-like upper part.

aphelion, n. That point in the elliptical orbit of a body about the sun farthest from the sun. That point nearest the sun is called PERIHELION.

apogee, n. That orbital point of a non-circular orbit farthest from the center of attraction. Opposite is PERIGEE.

apparent altitude. Sextant altitude corrected for inaccuracies in the reading (instrument, index, and personal errors) and inaccuracies in the reference level (principally dip or Coriolis/acceleration), but not for other errors. Apparent altitude is used in obtaining a more accurate refraction correction than would be obtained with an uncorrected sextant altitude. Also called RECTIFIED ALTITUDE.

apparent motion. Motion relative to a specified or implied reference point that may itself be in motion. The expression usually refers to movement of celestial bodies as observed from the earth. Usually called RELATIVE MOVEMENT when applied to the motion of one vessel relative to that of another. Also called RELATIVE MOTION.

apparent noon. Twelve o'clock apparent time, or the instant the apparent sun is over the upper branch of the meridian. Apparent noon may be either local or Greenwich depending upon the reference meridian. High noon is local apparent noon.

apparent precession. Apparent change in the direction of the axis of rotation of a spinning body, such as a gyroscope, due to rotation of the earth. As a result of gyroscopic inertia or rigidity in space, to an observer on the rotating earth a gyroscope appears to turn or precess.

apparent solar day. The duration of one rotation of the earth on its axis, with respect to the apparent sun. It is measured by successive transits of the apparent sun over the lower branch of a meridian. The length of the apparent solar day is 24 hours of apparent time and averages the length of the mean solar day, but varies somewhat from day to day.

apparent sun. The actual sun as it appears in the sky. Also called TRUE SUN.

apparent time. Time based upon the rotation of the earth relative to the apparent or true sun. This is the time shown by a sun dial. Apparent time may be designated as either local or Greenwich, as the local or Greenwich meridian is used as the reference. Also called TRUE SOLAR TIME.

apparent wind. The speed and true direction from which the wind appears to blow with reference to a moving point. Sometimes called RELATIVE WIND.

approach chart. A chart used to approach a harbor.

arc, n. 1. A part of a curved line, as of a circle. 2. The semi-circular graduated scale of an instrument for measuring angles.

arctic, adj. Of or pertaining to the arctic, or intense cold.

arctic air. A type of air that develops mostly in winter over the arctic. Arctic air is cold aloft and extends to great heights, but the surface temperatures are often higher than those of POLAR AIR. For two or three months in summer, arctic air masses are shallow and rapidly lose the characteristics as they move southward.

Arctic Circle. The parallel of latitude at about 66°33'N, marking the southern limit of the north Frigid Zone. This latitude is the complement of the sun's greatest northerly declination and marks the approximate southern limit at which the sun becomes circumpolar. The actual limit is extended somewhat by the combined effect of refraction, semidiameter of the sun, parallax, and the height of the observer's eye above the surface of the earth. A similar circle marking the northern limit of the south Frigid Zone is called ANTARCTIC CIRCLE or SOUTH POLAR CIRCLE. Also called NORTH POLAR CIRCLE.

arctic front. The semi-permanent, semi-continuous front between the deep, cold arctic air and the shallower, generally less cold polar air of northern latitudes; generally comparable to the ANTARCTIC FRONT of the Southern Hemisphere.

area feature. A topographic feature, such as sand, swamp, vegetation, etc., which extends over an area. It is represented on the published map or chart by a solid or screened color, by a prepared pattern of symbols, or by a delimiting line.

area to be avoided. A ship routing measure comprising an area, with defined limits, that should be avoided by all ships, or certain classes of ships; instituted to protect natural features or to define a particularly hazardous area for navigation.

Aries, n. 1. Vernal equinox. Also called FIRST

POINT OF ARIES. 2. The first sign of the zodiac.

articulated light. An offshore aid to navigation consisting of a pipe attached to a mooring by a pivoting or universal joint; more accurate in position than a buoy but less than a fixed light.

artificial horizon. A device for indicating the horizontal, such as a bubble, gyroscope, pendulum, or the surface of a liquid.

artificial range. A range formed by two objects such as buildings, towers, etc., not designed as aids to navigation.

ASCII. Acronym for American Standard Code for Information Interchange, a standard method of representing alphanumeric characters with numbers in a computer.

ashore, adj. & adv. On the shore; on land; aground.

aspect, n. The relative bearing of one's own ship from the target ship, measured 0° to 180° port (red) or starboard (green).

assumed latitude. The latitude at which an observer is assumed to be located for an observation or computation, as the latitude of an assumed position or the latitude used for determining the longitude of time sight. Also called CHOSEN LATITUDE.

assumed longitude. The longitude at which an observer is assumed to be located for an observation or computation, as the longitude of an assumed position or the longitude used for determining the latitude by meridian altitude. Also called CHOSEN LONGITUDE.

assumed position. A point at which a craft is assumed to be located, particularly one used as a preliminary to establishing certain navigational data, as that point on the surface of the earth for which the computed altitude is determined in the solution of a celestial observation, also called CHOSEN POSITION.

astern, adv. Bearing approximately 180° relative. The term is often used loosely for DEAD ASTERN, or bearing exactly 180° relative. The opposite is AHEAD.

asteroid, n. A minor planet, one of the many small celestial bodies revolving around the sun, most of the orbits being between those of Mars and Jupiter. Also called PLANETOID, MINOR PLANET.

astrolabe, n. An instrument that measures altitudes of celestial bodies, used for determining an accurate astronomical position, usually while ashore in survey work.

astronomical, adj. Of or pertaining to astronomy.

Astronomical Almanac. An annual publication prepared jointly by the Nautical Almanac Office, U.S. Naval Observatory, and H.M. Nautical Almanac Office, Royal Greenwich Observatory.

astronomical day. Prior to January 1, 1925, a mean solar day which began at mean noon, 12 hours later than the beginning of the calendar day of the same date. Since 1925, the astronomical day agrees with the civil day.

astronomical equator. A line connecting points having 0° astronomical latitude. Because the deflection of the vertical varies from point to point, the astronomical equator is not a plane curve. But since the verticals through all points on it are parallel, the zenith at any point on the astronomical equator lies in the plane of the celestial equator. When the astronomical equator is corrected for station error, it becomes the GEODETIC EQUATOR. Sometimes called TERRESTRIAL EQUATOR.

astronomical latitude. Angular distance between the plumb line at a station and the plane of the celestial equator. It is the latitude that results directly from observations of celestial bodies, uncorrected for deflection of the vertical, which in the United States may amount to as much as 25". Astronomical latitude applies only to positions on the earth and is reckoned from the astronomical equator (0°), north and south through 90°. Also called ASTRONOMIC LATITUDE and sometimes GEOGRAPHIC LATITUDE.

astronomical longitude. Angular distance between the plane of the celestial meridian at a station and the plane of the celestial meridian at Greenwich. It is the longitude that results directly from observations of celestial bodies, uncorrected for deflection of the vertical, the prime vertical component of which, in the United States, may amount to more than 18". Astronomical longitude applies only to positions on the earth, and is reckoned from the Greenwich meridian (0°) east and west through 180°. Also called ASTRONOMIC LONGITUDE and sometimes GEOGRAPHIC LONGITUDE.

astronomical meridian. A line connecting points having the same astronomical longitude. Because the deflection of the vertical (station error) varies from point to point, the astronomical meridian is not a plane curve. When the astronomical meridian is corrected for station error, it becomes the GEODETIC MERIDIAN. Also called TERRESTRIAL MERIDIAN and sometimes called GEOGRAPHIC MERIDIAN.

astronomical position. 1. A point on the earth whose coordinates have been determined as a result of observation of celestial bodies. The expression is usually used in connection with positions on land determined with great accuracy for survey purposes. 2. A point on the earth, defined in terms of astronomical latitude and longitude.

astronomical tide. The tide without constituents having their origin in the daily or seasonal variations in weather conditions that may occur with some degree of periodicity.

astronomical time. Time used with the astronomical day, which prior to 1925 began at noon of the civil day of same date. The hours of the day were numbered consecutively from 0 (noon) to 23 (11 AM of the following morning).

astronomical triangle. The navigational triangle either terrestrial or celestial, used in the solution of celestial observations.

astronomical twilight. The period of incomplete darkness when the center of the sun is more than 12° but not more than 18° below the celestial horizon.

astronomical unit. 1. The mean distance between the earth and the sun, approximately 92,960,000 miles. 2. The astronomical unit is often used as a unit of measurement for distances within the solar system. In the system of astronomical constants of the International Astronomical Union the adopted value for it is 1 AU = $149{,}600 \times 10^6$ meters.

astronomy, n. The science that deals with the size, constitution, motions, relative position, etc., of celestial bodies, including the earth. Astronomy of direct use to a navigator, comprising principally celestial coordinates, time, and the apparent motions of celestial bodies is called navigational or nautical astronomy.

atmosphere, n. 1. The envelope of air surrounding the earth and bound to it by gravity. 2. The gaseous envelope surrounding any celestial body, including the earth.

atmospheric absorption. The loss of power in transmission of radiant energy by dissipation in the atmosphere.

atmospheric pressure. The pressure exerted by the weight of the earth's atmosphere, about 14.7 pounds per square inch.

atmospheric refraction. Refraction resulting when a ray of radiant energy passes obliquely through the atmosphere.

atoll, n. A ring-shaped coral reef that has closely spaced islands or islets on it enclosing a central area or lagoon. The diameter may vary from less than a mile to 80 or more.

atollon, n. A large reef ring in the Maldive Islands consisting of many smaller reef rings. The word ATOLL was derived from this name.

atomic clock. A precision clock that depends for its operation upon an electrical oscillator regulated by an atomic system.

Atomic Time. Time based on transitions in an atom. International Atomic Time (TAI) is the time reference coordinate established by the Bureau International de l'Heure (BIH) on the basis of the readings of atomic clocks functioning in various establishments in accordance with the definition of the atomic second, the unit of time in the International System of Units (SI).

attenuation, n. 1. A lessening in amount, particularly the reduction of the amplitude of a wave with distance from the origin. 2. The decrease in the strength of a radar wave resulting from absorption, scattering, and reflection by the medium through which it passes (wave guide, atmosphere) and by obstructions in its path.

attitude, n. The position of a body as determined by the inclination of the axes to some other frame of reference. If not otherwise specified, this frame of reference is fixed to the earth.

audible aid to navigation. An aid to navigation that uses sound waves.

audio frequency. A frequency within the audible range, about 20 to 20,000 hertz. Also called SONIC FREQUENCY.

augmentation, n. The apparent increase in the semidiameter of a celestial body as its altitude increases, due to the reduced distance from the observer. The term is used principally in reference to the moon.

augmentation correction. A correction due to augmentation, particularly that sextant altitude correction due to the apparent increase in the semidiameter of a celestial body as its altitude increases.

aureole, n. A poorly developed corona, characterized by a bluish-white disk immediately around the luminary and a reddish-brown outer edge. An aureole, rather than a corona, is produced when the cloud responsible for this diffraction effect is composed of droplets distributed over a wide size-range.

aurora, n. A luminous phenomenon due to electrical discharges in the atmosphere, probably confined to the thin air high above the surface of the earth. It is most commonly seen in high latitudes, where it is most frequent during periods of greatest sunspot activity. If it occurs in the Northern Hemisphere, it is called aurora borealis or northern lights; and if in the Southern, aurora Australis.

aurora Australis. The aurora in the Southern Hemisphere.

aurora borealis. The aurora in the Northern Hemisphere. Also called NORTHERN LIGHTS.

auroral zone. The area of maximum auroral activity. Two such areas exist, each being a 10°-wide annulus centered at an average distance of 23° from a geomagnetic pole.

aurora polaris. A high-latitude aurora borealis.

Automated Mutual-assistance Vessel Rescue System. Operated by the United States Coast Guard, the AMVER System is a maritime mutual assistance program that aids coordination of search-and-rescue efforts in the oceans of the world, by maintaining a computerized worldwide merchant vessel plot.

automatic radar plotting aid. A computer-assisted radar data processing system that generates predicted ship vectors based on the recent plotted positions.

auto pilot, n. A device that steers a vessel unattended along a given bearing.

autumnal, adj. Pertaining to fall (autumn). The corresponding adjectives for winter, spring, and summer are hibernal, vernal, and aestival.

autumnal equinox. That point of intersection of the ecliptic and the celestial equator occupied by the sun as it changes from north to south declination, on or about September 23. Also called SEPTEMBER EQUINOX, FIRST POINT OF LIBRA. 2. The instant the sun reaches the point of zero declination when crossing the celestial equator from north to south.

azimuth, n. The horizontal direction or bearing of a celestial point from a terrestrial point, expressed as the angular distance from a reference direction. It is usually measured from 000° at the reference direction clockwise through 360°. An azimuth is often designated as true, magnetic, compass, grid, or relative as the reference direction is true, magnetic, compass, or grid north, or heading, respectively.

azimuth angle. Azimuth measured from 0° at the north or south reference direction clockwise or counterclockwise through 90° or 180°. It is labeled with the reference direction as a prefix and the direction of measurement from the reference direction as a suffix. When azimuth angle is measured through 180°, it is labeled N or S to agree with the latitude and E or W to agree with the meridian angle.

azimuth circle. A ring designed to fit snugly over a compass or compass repeater, and provided with means for observing compass bearings and azimuths. A similar ring without the means for observing azimuths of the sun is called a BEARING CIRCLE.

azimuth instrument. An instrument for measuring azimuths, particularly a device that fits over a central pivot in the glass cover of a magnetic compass.

B

back, v., i. 1. A change in wind direction in reverse of the normal pattern, or counterclockwise in the Northern Hemisphere and clockwise in the Southern Hemisphere. Change in the opposite direction is called veer. 2. To go stern first, or to operate the engines in reverse. 3. To brace the yard of a square sail so as to bring the wind on the forward side.

back azimuth. An azimuth 180° from a given azimuth.

back range. A range observed astern, particularly one used as guidance for a craft moving away from the objects forming the range.

backrush, n. The seaward return of water following the uprush onto the foreshore.

back sight. A marine sextant observation of a celestial body made by facing away from the body, measuring an angle of more than 90°.

backstaff, n. A forerunner of the sextant, consisting of a graduated arc and a single mirror.

backwash, n. Water or waves thrown back by an obstruction such as a seaward, breakwater, cliff, etc.

ball, n. 1. A spherical identifying mark. 2. A time ball.

band, n. A specific section or range of anything.

band of error. An area either side of a line of position, within which, for a stated level of probability, the true position is considered to lie.

bank, n. 1. An elevation of the sea floor typically located on a shelf, over which the depth of water is relatively shallow. Reefs or shoals, dangerous to surface navigation, may rise above the general depths of a bank. 2. A shallow area of shifting sand, gravel, mud, etc., such as a sand bank, mud bank, etc. 3. A ridge of any material such as earth, rock, snow, etc., or anything resembling such a ridge, as a fog bank or cloud bank. 4. The edge of a cut or fill. 5. The margin of a watercourse. 6. A number of similar devices connected so as to be used as a single device in common.

banner cloud. A banner-like cloud streaming off from a mountain peak in a strong wind.

bar, n. 1. A ridge or mound of sand, gravel, or other unconsolidated material below the high-water level, especially at the mouth of a river or estuary, or lying a short distance from and usually parallel to the beach, and which may obstruct navigation. 2. A unit accepted temporarily for use with the International System of Units; 1 bar is equal to 100,000 pascals.

barograph, n. A recording barometer. A highly sensitive barograph may be called a microbarograph.

barometer, n. An instrument for measuring atmospheric pressure.

barometric pressure. Atmospheric pressure as indicated by a barometer.

barometric pressure correction. A correction due to nonstandard barometric pressure, particularly the sextant altitude correction due to changes in refraction caused by difference between the actual barometric pressure and the standard barometric pressure used in the computation of the refraction table.

bar scale. A line or series of lines on a chart, subdivided and labeled with the distances represented on the chart. Also called GRAPHIC SCALE.

barycenter, n. The center of mass of a system of masses; the common point about which two or more celestial bodies revolve.

base line. 1. The reference used to position limits of the territorial sea and the contiguous zone. 2. One side of a series of connected survey triangles, the length of which is measured with prescribed accuracy and precision, and from which the lengths of the other triangle sides are obtained by computation.

baseline delay. The time interval needed for the signal from a master station of a hyperbolic radionavigation system to travel the length of the baseline, introduced as a delay between transmission of the master and slave (or secondary) signals to make it possible to distinguish between the signals and to permit measurement of time differences.

baseline extension. The extension of the baseline in both directions beyond the transmitters of a pair of radio stations operating in conjunction for determination of a line of position.

basin, n. 1. A depression of the sea floor approximately equidimensional in plan view and of variable extent. 2. An area of water surrounded by quay walls, usually created or enlarged by excavation, large enough to receive one or more ships for a specific purpose. 3. An area of land that drains into a lake or sea through a river and its tributaries. 4. A nearly land-locked area of water leading off an inlet, firth, or sound.

bathymetric chart. A topographic chart of the seabed of a body of water or a part of it. Generally, bathymetric charts show depths by contour lines and gradient tints.

bathymetry, n. The science of measuring water depths (usually in the ocean) in order to determine bottom topography.

baud. A measure of the speed of computer data transmission in bits per second.

bay, n. A recess in the shore, on an inlet of a sea or lake between two capes or headlands, that may vary greatly in size but is usually smaller than a gulf but larger than a cove.

bayou, n. A minor, sluggish waterway or estuaries creek, generally tidal or with a slow or imperceptible current, and with its course generally through lowlands or swamps, tributary to or connecting with other bodies of water. Various specific meanings have been implied in different parts of the southern United States. Sometimes called SLOUGH.

beach, n. The zone of unconsolidated material that extends landward from the low water line to the place where there is a marked change in material or physiographic form, or to the line of permanent vegetation (usually the effective limit of storm waves). A beach includes foreshore and backshore. The beach along the margin of the sea may be called SEABEACH. Also called STRAND, especially when the beach is composed of sand.

beach, v., t. & i. To intentionally run a craft ashore.

beacon, n. A fixed artificial navigation mark.

beam sea. Waves moving in a direction approximately 90° from the vessel's heading. Those moving in a direction approximately opposite to the heading are called HEAD SEA, those moving in the general direction of the heading are called FOLLOWING SEA, and those moving in a direction approximately 45° from the heading (striking the quarter) are called QUARTERING SEA.

beam tide. A tidal current setting in a direction approximately 90° from the heading of a vessel. One setting in a direction approximately 90° from the course is called a CROSS TIDE. In common usage these two expressions are usually used synonymously. One setting in a direction approximately opposite to the heading is called a HEAD TIDE. One setting in such a direction as to increase the speed of a vessel is called a FAIR TIDE.

beam wind. Wind blowing in a direction approximately 90° from the heading. One blowing in a direction approximately 90° from the course is called a CROSS WIND. In common usage these two expressions are usually used synonymously, BEAM WIND being favored by mariners, and CROSS WIND by aviators. One blowing from ahead is called a HEAD WIND. One blowing from astern is called a FOLLOWING WIND by mariners and a TAIL WIND by aviators.

bear, v., i. To be situated as to direction, as, the light bears 165°.

bearing, n. The horizontal direction of one terrestrial point from another, expressed as the angular distance from a reference direction. It is usually measured from 000° at the reference direction clockwise through 360°. The terms BEARING and AZIMUTH are sometimes used interchangeably, but in navigation the former customarily applies to terrestrial objects and the latter to the direction of a point on the celestial sphere from a point on the earth. A bearing is often designated as true, magnetic, compass, grid, or relative as the reference direction is true, magnetic, compass, or grid north, or heading, respectively.

bearing book. A log for the recording of visual bearings.

bearing circle. A ring designed to fit snugly over a compass or compass repeater, and provided with vanes for observing compass bearings. A similar ring provided with means for observing azimuths of the sun is called an AZIMUTH CIRCLE.

bearing cursor. The radial line on a radar set inscribed on a transparent disk, which can be rotated manually about an axis coincident with the center of the PPI. It is used for bearing determination. Also called MECHANICAL BEARING CURSOR.

Beaufort wind scale. A numerical scale for indicating wind speed, devised by Admiral Sir Francis Beaufort in 1805. Beaufort numbers (or forces) range from force 0 (calm) to force 12 (hurricane).

before the wind. In the direction of the wind. The expression applies particularly to a sailing vessel having the wind well aft.

bell, n. A device for producing a distinctive sound by the vibration of a hollow, cup-shaped metallic vessel that gives forth a ringing sound when struck.

bell book. The log of ordered engine speeds and directions.

bell buoy. A buoy with a skeleton tower in which a bell is fixed.

bench mark. A fixed physical object used as reference for a vertical datum. A tidal bench mark is one near a tide station to which the tide staff and tidal datums are referred. A primary tidal bench mark is the principal (or only) mark of a group of tidal bench marks to which the tide staff and tidal datums are referred. A geodetic bench mark identifies a surveyed point in the National Geodetic Vertical Network. Geodetic bench mark disks contain the inscription VERTICAL CONTROL MARK, NATIONAL GEODETIC SURVEY with other individual identifying information. Bench mark disks of either type may, on occasion, serve simultaneously to reference both tidal and geodetic datums. Numerous bench marks, both tidal and geodetic, still bear the inscription U.S. COAST & GEODETIC SURVEY.

berth, n. A place for securing a vessel.

berth, v., t. To secure a vessel at a berth.

bifurcation, n. A division into two branches.

bifurcation buoy. A buoy that indicates the place at which a channel divides into two.

bifurcation mark. A navigation mark that indicates the place at which the channel divides into two.

bight, n. 1. A long and gradual bend or recess in the coastline that forms a large open receding bay. 2. A bend in a river or mountain range. 3. An extensive crescent-shaped indentation in the ice edge.

bill, n. A narrow promontory.

binary notation. Referring to a system of numbers with a base of 2; used extensively in computers, which use electronic on-off storage devices to represent the numbers 0 and 1.

binnacle, n. The stand in which a compass is mounted. For a magnetic compass it is usually provided with means of mounting various correctors for adjustment and compensation of the compass.

binocular, n., adj. 1. An optical instrument for use with both eyes simultaneously. 2. Referring to vision with two eyes.

bioluminescence, n. The production of light by living organisms in the sea. Generally, these displays are stimulated by surface wave action, ship movement, subsurface waves, up welling, eddies, physical changes in sea water, surfs, and rip tides.

bisect, v., t. To divide into two equal parts.

bit (from binary digit). The smallest unit of information in a computer. Bits are grouped together into bytes, which represent characters or other information.

bit-map. A type of computerized display that consists of a single layer of data; individual elements cannot be manipulated.

blinking, n. A means of providing information in radionavigation systems of the pulse type by modifying the signal at its source so that the signal presentation alternately appears and disappears or shifts along the time base. In Loran, blinking is used to indicate that a station is malfunctioning.

blip, n. On a radarscope, a deflection or spot of contrasting luminescence caused by an echo, i.e., the radar signal reflected back to the antenna by an object. Also called PIP, ECHO, RETURN.

bluff, n. A headland or stretch of cliff having a broad, nearly perpendicular face.

boat, n. A small vessel. The term is often modified to indicate the means of propulsion, such as motorboat, rowboat, steamboat, or sailboat, and sometimes to indicate the intended use, such as lifeboat, fishing boat, etc.

boat compass. A small compass mounted in a box for convenient use in small craft.

boat harbor. A sheltered area in a harbor set aside for the use of boats, usually with docks, moorings, etc.

boat sheet. The work sheet used in the field for plotting details of a hydrographic survey as it progresses.

bobbing a light. Quickly lowering the height of eye and raising it again when a navigational light is first sighted to determine if the observer is at the geographic range of the light.

bollard, n. A post (usually steel or reinforced concrete) firmly secured on a wharf, quay, etc., for mooring vessels with lines.

border break. A cartographic technique used when it is required to extend cartographic detail of a map or chart beyond the neatline into the margin, eliminating the necessity of producing an additional sheet. Also called BLISTER.

bow, n. The forward part of a ship, craft, aircraft, or float.

bow and beam bearings. Successive relative bearings (right or left) of 45° and 90° taken on a fixed object to obtain a running fix. The length of the run between such bearings is equal to the distance of the craft from the object at the time the object is broad on the beam, neglecting current.

Bowditch. 1. Nathaniel Bowditch (1773–1838), American mathematician, navigator, shipmaster, and author of *American Practical Navigator*. 2. Popular title for Pub. No. 9, *American Practical Navigator*.

bow wave. 1. The wave set up by the bow of a vessel moving through the water. Also called WAVE OF DISPLACEMENT. 2. A shock wave in front of a body such as an airfoil.

breaker, n. A wave that breaks, either because it becomes unstable, usually when it reaches shallow water, or because it dashes against an obstacle. Instability is caused by an increase in wave height and a decrease in the speed of the trough of the wave in shallow water.

breakwater, n. A line of rocks, concrete, pilings, or other material that breaks the force of the sea at a particular place, forming a protected area. Often an artificial embankment built to protect the entrance to a harbor or to form an artificial harbor.

breeze, n. 1. Wind of force 2 to 6 (4–31 miles per hour or 4–27 knots) on the Beaufort wind scale. Wind of force 2 (4–7 miles per hour or 4–6 knots) is classified as a light breeze; wind of force 3 (8–12 miles per hour or 7–10 knots), a gentle breeze; wind of force 4 (13–18 miles per hour or 11–16 knots), a moderate breeze; wind of force 5 (19–24 miles per hour or 17–21 knots), a fresh breeze; and wind of force 6 (25–31 miles per hour or 22–27 knots), a strong breeze. 2. Any light wind.

Broadcast Notice to Mariners. Notices to mariners disseminated by radio broadcast, generally of immediate interest to navigators.

broad on the beam. Bearing 090° relative (broad on the starboard beam) or 270° relative (broad on the port beam). If the bearings are approximate, the expression ON THE BEAM or ABEAM should be used.

broad on the bow. Bearing 045° relative (broad on the starboard bow) or 315° relative (broad on the port bow). If the bearings are approximate, the expression ON THE BOW should be used.

broad on the quarter. Bearing 135° relative (broad on the starboard quarter) or 225° relative (broad on the port quarter). If the bearings are approximate, the expression ON THE QUARTER should be used.

bubble horizon. An artificial horizon parallel to the celestial horizon, established by means of a bubble level.

bubble sextant. A sextant with a bubble or spirit level to indicate the horizontal.

buffer. In computers, a temporary storage area used when incoming data cannot be processed as fast as it is transmitted.

building, n. A label on a nautical chart used when the entire structure is the landmark, rather than an individual feature of it. Also labeled HOUSE.

buoy, n. An unmanned floating device moored or anchored to the bottom as an aid to navigation. Buoys may be classified according to shape as spar, cylindrical or can, conical, nun, spherical, barrel, or pillar buoy.

buoyage, n. A system of buoys. One in which the buoys are assigned shape, color, and number distinction in accordance with location relative to the nearest obstruction is called a cardinal system. One in which buoys are assigned shape, color, and number distinction as a means of indicating navigable waters is called a lateral system.

buoy tender. A vessel designed for, and engaged in, servicing aids to navigation, particularly buoys.

Buys Ballot's law. Named after Dutch meteorologist C. H. D. Buys Ballot, who published it in 1857, a rule useful in locating the center of cyclones and anticyclones. It states that, facing the wind in the northern hemisphere, the center of the storm lies to the right and slightly behind the observer. Facing the wind in the southern hemisphere, it is to the left and slightly behind.

byte. Basic unit of measurement of computer' memory. A byte usually consists of 8 BITS; each ASCII character is represented by 1 byte.

C

cable, n. 1. A unit of distance equal to one-tenth of a sea mile. 2. A chain or very strong fiber or wire rope used to anchor or moor vessels or buoys. 3. A stranded conductor or an assembly of two or more electric conductors insulated from each other, but laid up together with a strong, waterproof covering.

cage, n. The upper part of the buoy built on top of the body of the buoy and used as a daymark or part thereof, usually to support a light, topmark, and/or radar reflector. Also called SUPERSTRUCTURE.

caisson, n. A watertight gate for a lock, basin, etc.

calculator. A device for mathematical computations; originally mechanical, modern ones are exclusively electronic and able to run simple programs. A navigational calculator contains ephemeral data and algorithms for the solution of navigation problems. Compare with computers, which can be used for many other applications and run complex programs.

caldera, n. A volcanic crater.

calendar day. The period from midnight to midnight. The calendar day is 24 hours of mean solar time in length and coincides with the civil day unless a time change occurs during a day.

calendar year. The year of the calendar. Common years have 365 days and leap years 366 days. Each year exactly divisible by 4 is a leap year, except century years (1800, 1900, etc.), which must be exactly divisible by 400 (2000, 2400, etc.) to be leap years. The calendar year is based on the tropical year. Also called CIVIL YEAR.

calibration error. The error in an instrument due to imperfection of calibration or maladjustment of its parts. Also called SCALE ERROR.

calibration table. A list of calibration corrections or calibrated values. A card having such a table on it is called a CALIBRATION CARD.

calm belt. 1. The doldrum sides of the trade winds, called calms of Cancer and calms of Capricorn, respectively.

canal, n. 1. An artificial waterway for navigation. 2. A long, fairly straight natural channel with steep sloping sides. 3. Any watercourse or channel. 4. A sluggish coastal stream, as used locally on the Atlantic coast of the U.S.

can buoy. An unlighted buoy of which the upper part of the body (above the waterline), or the larger part of the superstructure has the shape of a cylinder or nearly so. Also called CYLINDRICAL BUOY.

canyon, n. On the sea floor, a relatively narrow, deep depression with steep sides, the bottom of which generally has a continuous slope.

cape, n. A relatively extensive land area jutting seaward from a continent, or large island, that prominently marks a change in or interrupts notably the coastal trend.

cardinal heading. A heading in the direction of any of the cardinal points of the compass.

cardinal mark. An IALA aid to navigation intended to show the location of a danger to navigation based on its position relative to the danger. Its distinguishing features are black double-cone topmarks and black and yellow horizontal bands.

cardinal point. Any of the four principal directions; north, east, south, or west. Directions midway between cardinal points are called INTERCARDINAL POINTS.

cardinal system. A system of aids to navigation in which the shape, color, and number distinction are assigned in accordance with location relative to the nearest obstruction. The cardinal points delineate the sectors for aid location. The cardinal system is particularly applicable to a region having numerous small islands and isolated dangers. In the LATERAL SYSTEM, used in United States waters, the aids are assigned shape, color, and number distinction as a means of indicating navigable waters.

carrier, n. A radio wave having at least one characteristic that may be varied from a known reference value by modulation.

carrier frequency. 1. The frequency of the unmodulated fundamental output of a radio transmitter. 2. In a periodic carrier, the reciprocal of its period. The frequency of a periodic pulse carrier often is called PULSE REPETITION FREQUENCY.

cartographer, n. One who designs and constructs charts or maps.

cartographic feature. A natural or cultural object shown on a map or chart by a symbol or line.

cartography, n. The art and science of making charts or maps.

catenary, n. The curve formed by a uniform cable supported only at its ends. Navigators are concerned with the catenary of overhead cables, which determines clearance underneath, and the catenary of the anchor rode, which in part determines holding power and swing circle.

cathode, n. 1. The electrode through which a primary stream of electrons enters the interelectrode space. 2. The general term for a negative electrode.

cathode ray. A stream of electrons emitted from the cathode of any vacuum tube, but normally used in reference to special purpose tubes designed to provide a visual display.

cathode-ray tube (CRT). A vacuum tube in which the instantaneous position of a sharply focused electron beam, deflected by means of electrostatic or electromagnetic fields, is indicated by a spot of light produced by impact of the electrons on a fluorescent screen at the end of the tube opposite the cathode. Used in radar displays.

cay, kay, n. A low, flat, tropical or sub-tropical island of sand and coral built up on a reef lying slightly above high water. Also called KEY.

celestial, adj. Of or pertaining to the heavens.

celestial body. Any aggregation of matter in space constituting a unit for astronomical study, as the sun or moon, a planet, comet, star, nebula, etc. Also called HEAVENLY BODY.

celestial coordinates. Any set of coordinates used to define a point on the celestial sphere. The horizon, celestial equator, and the ecliptic systems of celestial coordinates are based on the celestial horizon, celestial equator, and the ecliptic, respectively, as the primary great circle.

celestial equator. The primary great circle of the celestial sphere, everywhere 90° from the celestial poles; the intersection of the extended plane of the equator and the celestial sphere. Also called EQUINOCTIAL.

celestial equator system of coordinates. A set of celestial coordinates based on the celestial equator as the primary great circle. Also called EQUINOCTIAL SYSTEM OF COORDINATES.

celestial fix. A fix established by means of two or more celestial bodies.

celestial horizon. That circle of the celestial sphere formed by the intersection of the celestial sphere and a plane through the center of the earth and perpendicular to the zenith-nadir line. Also called RATIONAL HORIZON.

celestial latitude. Angular distance north or south of the ecliptic; the arc of a circle of latitude between the ecliptic and a point on the celestial sphere, measured northward or southward from the ecliptic through 90°, and labeled N or S to indicate the direction of measurement.

celestial line of position. A line of position determined by means of a celestial body.

celestial longitude. Angular distance east of the vernal equinox, along the ecliptic; the arc of the ecliptic or the angle at the ecliptic pole between the circle of latitude of the vernal equinox at the circle of latitude of a point on the celestial sphere, measured eastward from the circle of latitude of the vernal equinox, through 360°.

celestial meridian. A great circle of the celestial sphere, through the celestial poles and the zenith. The expression usually refers to the upper branch, that half from pole to pole that passes through the zenith; the other half is called the lower branch. The celestial meridian coincides with the hour circle through the zenith and the vertical circle through the elevated pole.

celestial navigation. Navigation by celestial bodies.

celestial observation. Observation of celestial phenomena. The expression is applied in navigation principally to the measurement of the altitude of a celestial body, and sometimes to measurement of azimuth, or to both altitude azimuth.

celestial pole. Either of the two points of intersection section of the celestial sphere and the extended axis of the earth, labeled

N or S to indicate whether the north celestial pole or the south celestial pole.

celestial sphere. An imaginary sphere of infinite radius concentric with the earth, on which all celestial bodies except the earth are imagined to be projected.

celestial triangle. A spherical triangle on the celestial sphere, especially the navigational triangle.

Celsius temperature. The designation given to the temperature measured on the International Practical Temperature Scale with the zero taken as 0.01° below the triple point of water, that is, the condition when its gaseous, liquid, and solid phases can exist in equilibrium.

centering error. Error in an instrument due to inaccurate pivoting of a moving part, as the index arm of a marine sextant. Also called ECCENTRIC ERROR.

centi-. A prefix meaning one-hundredth.

centimeter, n. One-hundredth of a meter.

central processing unit (CPU). The computer chip that is the brain of a computer, which runs PROGRAMS and processes DATA; also the container in which the CPU is located, along with many other associated devices such as the power supply, disk drives, etc., distinct from the MONITOR and other peripherals.

chain, n. A group of associated stations of a radionavigation system. A Loran-C chain consists of a master station and two to four secondary stations.

change of the moon. The time of new moon.

channel, n. 1. The part of a body of water deep enough for navigation through an area otherwise not suitable. It is usually marked by a single or double line of buoys and sometimes by ranges. 2. The deepest part of a stream, bay, or strait, through which the main current flows. 3. A name given to certain large straits, such as the English Channel. 4. A hollow bed through which water may run. 5. A band of radio frequencies within which a radio station must maintain its modulated carrier frequency to prevent interference with stations on adjacent channels. Also called FREQUENCY CHANNEL.

characteristic, n. 1. The color and shape of a daymark or buoy or the color and period of a light used for identifying the aid. 2. The identifying signal transmitted by a radiobeacon. 3. That part of a logarithm (base 10) to the left of the decimal point. That part of a logarithm (base 10) to the right of the decimal point is called the MANTISSA. 4. A quality, attribute, or distinguishing property of anything.

characteristic color. The unique identifying color of a light.

characteristic frequency. A frequency that can be easily identified and measured in a given emission.

characteristic phase. Of a light, the sequence and length of light and dark periods by which a navigational light is identified, i.e., whether fixed, flashing, interrupted quick flashing, etc.

characteristics of a light. The sequence and length of light and dark periods and the color or colors by which a navigational light is identified.

chart, n. A map intended primarily for navigational use by aircraft or vessels.

chart catalog. A list or enumeration of navigational charts, sometimes with index charts indicating the extent of coverage of the various navigational charts.

chart convergence. Convergence of the meridians as shown on a chart.

charted depth. The vertical distance from the chart sounding datum to the bottom.

chartlet, n. A corrected reproduction of a small area of a nautical chart that is pasted to the chart for which it is issued. These chartlets are disseminated in *Notice to Mariners* when the corrections are too numerous or of such detail as not to be feasible in printed form. Also called BLOCK, BLOCK CORRECTION, CHART AMENDMENT PATCH.

chart scale. The ratio between a distance on a chart and the corresponding distance represented as a ratio such as 1:80,000 (natural scale) or 30 miles to an inch (numerical scale). May be called MAP SCALE when applied to any map.

chart sounding datum. The tidal datum to which soundings and drying heights on a chart are referred. It is usually taken to correspond to a low-water stage of the tide. Often shortened to CHART DATUM, especially when it is clear that reference is not being made to a horizontal datum.

chart symbol. A character, letter, or similar graphic representation used on a chart to indicate some object, characteristic, etc.

check bearing. An additional bearing, using a charted object other than those used to fix the position, observed and plotted in order to ensure that the fix is not the result of a blunder.

chip log. A historical speed-measuring device consisting of a weighted wooden quadrant (quarter of a circle) attached to a bridle in such a manner that it will float in a vertical position, and a line with equally spaced knots, usually each 47 feet, 3 inches apart. Speed is measured by casting the quadrant overboard and counting the number of knots paid out in a unit of time, usually 28 seconds.

chronograph, n. An instrument for producing a graphical record of time as shown by a clock or other device.

chronometer, n. A timepiece with a nearly constant rate, accurate enough to be used for navigation.

chronometer correction. The amount that must be added algebraically to the chronometer time to obtain the correct time. Chronometer correction is numerically equal to the chronometer error, but of opposite sign.

chronometer error. The amount by which chronometer time differs from the correct time to which it was set, usually Greenwich mean time.

chronometer rate. The amount gained or lost by a chronometer in a unit of time. It is usually expressed in seconds per 24 hours, to an accuracy of 0.1s, and labeled gaining or losing, as appropriate, when it is sometimes called DAILY RATE.

chronometer time. The hour of the day as indicated by a chronometer. Shipboard chronometers are generally set to Greenwich mean time.

circle of equal altitude. A circle on the surface of the earth, on every point of which the altitude of a given celestial body is the same at a given instant. The center of this circle is the geographical position of the body, and the great circle distance from this point to the circle is the zenith distance of the body.

circle of position. A circular line of position. The expression is most frequently used with reference to the circle of equal altitude surrounding the geographical position of a celestial body. Also called POSITION CIRCLE.

circle of uncertainty. A circle having as its center a given position and as its radius the maximum likely error of the position—a circle within which a vessel is considered to be located.

circular error probable. 1. In a circular normal distribution (the magnitudes of the two one-dimensional input errors are equal and the angle of cut is 90°), the radius of the circle containing 50 percent of the individual measurements being made, or the radius of the circle inside of which there is a 50-percent probability of being located. 2. The radius of a circle inside of which there is a 50-percent probability of being located even though the actual error figure is an ellipse. That is, it is the radius of a circle of equivalent probability when the probability is specified as 50 percent.

circumscribed halo. A halo formed by the junction of the upper and lower tangent arcs of the halo of 22°.

circumzenithal arc. A brilliant rainbow-colored arc of about a quarter of a circle with its center at the zenith and about 46° above the sun. It is produced by refraction and dispersion of the sun's light striking the top of prismatic ice crystals in the atmosphere. It usually lasts for only a few minutes.

cirriform, adj. Like cirrus; more generally, descriptive of clouds composed of small particles, mostly ice crystals, which are fairly widely dispersed, usually resulting in relative transparency and whiteness, and often producing halo phenomena not observed with other cloud forms.

cirro-. A prefix used in cloud classification to indicate the highest of three levels generally recognized.

cirrocumulus, n. A principal cloud type (cloud genus), appearing as a thin, white patch of cloud without shadows, composed of very small elements in the form of grains, ripples, etc. The elements may be merged or separate, and more or less regularly arranged; they subtend an angle of less than 1° when observed at an angle of more than 30° above the horizon. Holes or rifts often occur in a sheet of cirrocumulus.

cirrostratus, n. A principal cloud type (cloud genus), appearing as a whitish veil, usually fibrous but sometimes smooth, which may totally cover the sky, and which often produces halo phenomena, either partial or complete. Sometimes a banded aspect may appear, but the intervals between the bands are filled with thinner cloud veil.

cirrus, n. A principal cloud type (cloud genus) composed of detached cirriform elements in the form of delicate filaments or white (or mostly white) patches, or of narrow bands. These clouds have a fibrous aspect and/or a silky sheen. Many of the ice crystal particles of cirrus are sufficiently large to acquire an appreciable speed of fall; therefore, the cloud elements have a considerable vertical extent. Wind shear and variations in particle size usually cause these fibrous trails to be slanted or irregularly curved.

civil day. A mean solar day beginning at midnight.

civil noon. United States terminology from 1925 through 1952.

civil time. United States terminology from 1925 through 1952.

civil twilight. The period of incomplete darkness when the upper limb of the sun is below the visible horizon, and the center of the sun is not more than 6° below the celestial horizon.

civil year. A year of the Gregorian calendar of 365 days in common years, or 366 days in leap years.

clamp screw. A screw for holding a moving part in place, as during an observation or reading, particularly such a device used in connection with the tangent screw of a marine sextant.

clamp screw sextant. A marine sextant having a clamp screw for controlling the position of the tangent screw.

cliff, n. Land arising abruptly for a considerable distance above water or surrounding land.

climate, n. The prevalent or characteristic meteorological conditions of a place or region, in contrast with weather, the state of the atmosphere at any time.

climatology, n. 1. The study of climate. 2. An account of the climate of a particular place or region.

clinometer, n. An instrument for indicating the degree of the angle of heel, roll, or pitch of a vessel; may be of the pivot arm or bubble type, usually indicating in whole degrees.

clock, n. A timepiece not meant to be carried on the person.

clock speed. The speed with which a computer performs operations, commonly measured in megahertz.

close aboard. Very near.

closed, adj. Said of a manned aid to navigation that has been temporarily discontinued for the winter season.

closed sea. 1. A part of the ocean enclosed by headlands, within narrow straits, etc. 2. A part of the ocean within the territorial jurisdiction of a country. The opposite is OPEN SEA.

cloud, n. A hydrometeor consisting of a visible aggregate of minute water and/or ice particles in the atmosphere above the earth's surface. Cloud differs from fog only in that the latter is, by definition, in contact with the earth's surface.

cloud bank. A fairly well-defined mass of clouds observed at a distance; it covers an appreciable portion of the horizon sky but does not extend overhead.

cloudburst, n. In popular terminology, any sudden and heavy fall of rain. An unofficial criterion sometimes used specifies a rate of fall equal to or greater than 100 millimeters (3.94 inches) per hour. Also called RAIN GUSH, RAIN GUST.

cloud classification. 1. A scheme of distinguishing and grouping clouds according to their appearance and, where possible, to their process of formation. The one in general use, based on a classification system introduced by Luke Howard in 1803, is that adopted by the World Meteorological Organization and published in the International Cloud Atlas (1956). The ten cloud genera are cirrus, cirrocumulus, cirrostratus, altocumulus, altostratus, nimbostratus, stratocumulus, stratus, cumulus, and cumulonimbus. The fourteen cloud species are fibratus, uncinus, spissatus, castellanus, floccus, stratiformis, nebulous, lenticularis, fractus, humilis, mediocris, congestus, calvus, and capillatus. The nine cloud varieties are intortus, vertebratus, undulatus, radiatus, lacunosis, duplicatus, translucidus, perlucidus, and opacus. The nine supplementary features and accessory clouds are inclus, mamma, virga, praecipitatio, arcus, tuba, pileus, velum, and pannus. 2. A scheme of classifying clouds according to their usual altitudes. Three classes are distinguished: high, middle, and low. High clouds include cirrus, cirrocumulus, cirrostratus, and occasionally altostratus and the tops of cumulonimbus. The middle clouds are altocumulus, altostratus, nimbostratus, and portions of cumulus and cumulonimbus. The low clouds are stratocumulus, stratus, most cumulus and cumulonimbus bases, and sometimes nimbostratus. 3. A scheme of classifying clouds according to their particulate composition: water clouds, ice-crystal clouds, and mixed clouds.

cloud height. In weather observations, the height of the cloud base above local terrain.

cloud layer. An array of clouds, not necessarily all of the same type, whose bases are at approximately the same level. It may be either continuous or composed of detached elements.

Coast and Geodetic Survey. Mapping, charting, and surveying arm of the National Ocean Service (NOS), a component of the National Oceanic and Atmospheric Administration (NOAA).

Coast Earth Station (CES). A station that receives communications from an earth orbiting satellite for retransmission via landlines, and vice versa.

cocked hat. Error triangle formed by lines of position that do not cross at a common point.

coding delay. An arbitrary time delay in the transmission of pulse signals. In hyperbolic radionavigation systems of the pulse type, the coding delay is inserted between the transmission of the master and slave (or secondary) signals to prevent zero or small readings, and thus aid in distinguishing between master and slave (or secondary) station signals.

cold air mass. An air mass that is colder than surrounding air. The expression implies that the air mass is colder than the surface over which it is moving.

cold front. Any non-occluded front, or portion thereof, that moves so that the colder air replaces the warmer air, i.e., the leading edge of a relatively cold air mass. While some occluded fronts exhibit this characteristic, they are more properly called COLD OCCLUSIONS.

cold wave. Unseasonably low temperatures extending over a period of a day or longer, particularly during the cold season of the year.

collision bearing. A constant bearing maintained while the distance between two craft is decreasing.

collision course. A course that, if followed, will bring two craft together.

COLREGS, n. Acronym for International Regulations for Prevention of Collisions at Sea.

COLREGS Demarcation Lines. Lines delineating the waters upon which mariners must comply with the International Regulations for Preventing Collisions at Sea 1972 (72 COLREGS) and those waters upon which mariners must comply with the Navigation Rules for Harbors, Rivers, and Inland Waters (Inland Rules). The waters outside the lines are COLREGS waters. For specifics concerning COLREGS Demarcation Lines see U.S. Code of Federal Regulations, Title 33, Navigation and Navigable Waters; Part 82, COLREGS Demarcation Lines.

common year. A calendar year of 365 days. One of 366 days is called a LEAP YEAR.

communication, n. The transfer of intelligence between points. If by wire, radio, or other electromagnetic means, it may be called telecommunication; if by radio, radiocommunication.

commutation, n. A method by means of which the transmissions from a number of stations of a radionavigation system are time shared on the same frequency.

compact disk. A type of computer storage media that records data using bubbles melted into the surface of a disk. It cannot be erased and is therefore called Read Only Memory (ROM).

comparing watch. A watch used for timing observations of celestial bodies. Generally its error is determined by comparison with a chronometer, hence its name. A comparing watch normally has a large sweep second hand to facilitate reading time to the nearest second. Sometimes called HACK WATCH.

compass, adj. Of or pertaining to a compass or related to compass north.

compass, n. An instrument for indicating a horizontal reference direction relative to the earth. A magnetic compass depends for its directive force upon the attraction of the magnetism of the earth for a magnet free to turn in any horizontal direction. A compass having one or more gyroscopes as the directive element is called a gyrocompass.

compass adjustment. The process of neutralizing undesired magnetic effects on a magnetic compass. Permanent magnets and soft iron correctors are arranged about the binnacle so that their effects are about equal and opposite to the magnetic material in the craft, thus reducing the deviations and eliminating the sectors of sluggishness and unsteadiness.

compass amplitude. Amplitude relative to compass east or west.

compass azimuth. Azimuth relative to compass north.

compass bearing. Bearing relative to compass north.

compass bowl. The housing in which the compass card is mounted, usually filled with liquid.

compass card. The part of a compass on which the direction graduations are placed. It is usually in the form of a thin disk or annulus graduated in degrees, clockwise from 0° at the reference direction to 360°, and sometimes also in compass points.

compass compensation. The process of neutralizing the effects of degaussing currents on a marine magnetic compass. The process of neutralizing the magnetic effects the vessel itself exerts on a magnetic compass is properly called COMPASS ADJUSTMENT, but the expression COMPASS COMPENSATION is often used for this process, too.

compass course. Course relative to compass north.

compass dirction. Horizontal direction expressed as angular distance from compass north.

compass error. The angle by which a compass direction differs from the true direction; the algebraic sum of variation and deviation; the angle between the true meridian and the axis of the compass card, expressed in degrees east or west to indicate the direction of compass north with respect to true north.

compasses, n. An instrument for drawing circles.

compass heading. Heading relative to compass north.

compass north. The direction north as indicated by a magnetic compass; the reference direction for measurement of compass directions.

compass points. The 32 divisions of a compass, at intervals of 11¼°. Each division is further divided into quarter points. Stating in order the names of the points (and sometimes the half and quarter points) is called BOXING THE COMPASS.

compass repeater. That part of a remote-indicating compass system that repeats at a distance the indications of the master compass. One used primarily for observing bearings may be called a bearing repeater. Also called REPEATER COMPASS.

compass rose. A circle graduated in degrees, clockwise from 0° at the reference direction to 360°, and sometimes also in compass points. Compass roses are placed at convenient locations on the Mercator chart or plotting sheet to facilitate measurement of direction.

composite group flashing light A light similar to a group flashing light except that successive groups in a single period have different numbers of flashes.

composite group occulting light. A group occulting light in which the occultations are combined in successive groups of different numbers of occultations.

composite sailing. A modification of great-circle sailing used when it is desired to limit the highest latitude. The composite track consists of a great circle from the point of departure and tangent to the limiting parallel, a course line along the parallel, and a great circle tangent to the limiting parallel to the destination. Composite sailing applies only when the vertex lies between the point of departure and destination.

compound tide. A tidal constituent with a speed equal to the sum or difference of the speeds of two or more elementary constituents. Compound tides are usually the result of shallow water.

computed altitude. 1. Tabulated altitude interpolated for increments of latitude, declination, or hour angle. If no interpolation is required, the tabulated altitude and computed altitude are identical. 2. Altitude determined by computation, table, mechanical computer, or graphics, particularly such an altitude of the center of a celestial body measured as an arc on a vertical circle of the celestial sphere from the celestial horizon. Also called CALCULATED ALTITUDE.

computed azimuth. Azimuth determined by computation, table, mechanical device, or graphics for a given place and time.

computed azimuth angle. Azimuth angle determined by computation, table, mechanical device, or graphics for a given place and time.

conformal, adj. Having correct angular representation.

conformal chart. A chart using a conformal projection; also called orthomorphic chart.

conformal map projection. A map projection in which all angles around any point are correctly represented. In such a projection the scale is the same in all directions about any point. Very small shapes are correctly represented, resulting in an orthomorphic projection. The terms conformal and orthomorphic are used synonymously since neither characteristic can exist without the other.

conic chart. A chart on a conic projection.

conic chart with two standard parallels. A chart on the conic projection with two standard parallels. Also called SECANT CONIC CHART.

conic map projection. A map projection in which the surface of a sphere or spheroid, such as the earth, is conceived as projected onto a tangent or secant cone that is then developed into a plane. In a simple conic map projection the cone is tangent to the sphere or spheroid, in a conic map projection with two standard parallels the cone intersects the sphere or spheroid along two chosen parallels, and in a polyconic map projection a series of cones are tangent to the sphere or spheroid.

conic map projection with two standard parallels. A conic map projection in which the surface of a sphere or spheroid is conceived as developed on a cone that intersects the sphere or spheroid along two standard parallels, the cone being spread out to form a plane. The Lambert conformal map projection is an example.

conjunction, n. The situation of two celestial bodies having either the same celestial longitude or the same sidereal hour angle. A planet is at superior conjunction if the sun is between it and the earth, at inferior conjunction if it is between the sun and the earth. The situation of two celestial bodies having either celestial longitudes or sidereal hour angles differing by 180° is called OPPOSITION.

conn, n. Control of the maneuvering of a ship.

conn, v., t. To direct the course and speed of a vessel. The person giving orders to the helmsman (not just relaying orders) is said to have the conn or to be conning the ship.

constant error. A systematic error of unchanging magnitude and sign throughout a given series of observations. Also called BIAS ERROR.

constellation, n. A group of stars that appear close together, regardless of actual distances, particularly if the group forms a striking configuration. Among astronomers a constellation is now considered a region of the sky having precise boundaries so arranged that all of the sky is covered, without overlap.

contact, n. Any echo detected on the radarscope and not evaluated as clutter or as a false echo. Although the term contact is often used interchangeably with target, the latter term specifically indicates that the echo is from an object about which information is being sought.

contiguous zone. The band of water outside or beyond the territorial sea in which a coastal nation may exercise customs control and enforce public health and other regulations.

continental climate. The type of climate characteristic of the interior of a large land mass, the distinctive features of which are large annual and daily temperature range and dry air with few clouds, in contrast with MARINE CLIMATE.

continental rise. A gentle slope rising from oceanic depths toward the foot of a continental slope.

continental shelf. A zone adjacent to a continent that extends from the low water line to a depth at which there is usually a marked increase of slope towards oceanic depths.

Continental United States. United States territory, including the adjacent territorial waters, located within the North American continent between Canada and Mexico.

continuous quick light. A quick-flashing light (flashing 50–80 times per minute) that operates continuously with no eclipses.

continuous ultra-quick light. An ultra-quick light (flashing not less than 160 flashes per minute) with no eclipses.

continuous very quick light. A very quick light (flashing 80–160 times per minute) with no eclipses.

continuous wave. 1. Electromagnetic radiation of a constant amplitude and frequency. 2. Radio waves, the successive sinusoidal oscillations of which are identical under steady-state conditions.

contour, n. The imaginary line on the ground, all points of which are at the same elevation above or below a specified datum.

contour interval. The difference in elevation between two adjacent contours.

contour line. A line connecting points of equal elevation or equal depth. One connecting points of equal depth is usually called a depth contour, but if depth is expressed in fathoms, it may be called a fathom curve or fathom line.

controlling depth. 1. The least depth in the approach or channel to an area, such as a port or anchorage, governing the maximum draft of vessels that can enter. 2. The least depth within the limits of a channel; it restricts the safe use of the channel to drafts of less than that depth. The centerline controlling depth of a channel applies only to the channel centerline; lesser depths may exist in the remainder of the channel. The mid-channel controlling depth of a channel is the controlling depth of only the middle half of the channel.

convection, n. Circulation in a fluid of nonuniform temperature, due to the differences in density and the action of gravity. In the atmosphere, convection takes place on a large scale. It is essential to the formation of many clouds, especially those of the cumulus type. Heat is transferred by CONVECTION and also by ADVECTION, CONDUCTION, and RADIATION.

convention, n. A body of regulations adopted by the IMO that regulate one aspect of maritime affairs.

conventional direction of buoyage. 1. The general direction taken by the mariner when approaching a harbor, river, estuary, or other waterway from seaward. 2. The direction determined by the proper authority. In general it follows a clockwise direction around land masses.

convergence of meridians. The angular drawing together of the geographic meridians in passing from the equator to the poles. At the equator all meridians are mutually parallel; passing from the equator, they converge until they meet at the poles, intersecting at angles that are equal to their differences of longitude.

conversion angle. The angle between the rhumb line and the great circle between two points. Also called ARC TO CHORD CORRECTION.

conversion scale. A scale for the conversion of units of one measurement to equivalent units of another measurement.

conversion table. A table for the conversion of units of one measurement to equivalent units of another measurement.

coordinate, n. One of a set of magnitudes defining a point in space. If the point is known to be on a given line, only one coordinate is needed; if on a surface, two are required; if in space, three. Cartesian coordinates define a point relative to two intersecting lines, called AXES. Spherical coordinates define a point on a sphere or spheroid by its angular distances from a primary great circle and from a reference secondary great circle. Geographical or terrestrial coordinates define a point on the surface of the earth. Celestial coordinates define a point on the celestial sphere. The horizon, celestial equator, and the ecliptic systems of celestial coordinates are based on the celestial horizon, celestial equator, and the ecliptic, respectively, as the primary great circle.

coordinate conversion. Changing the coordinate values from one system to those of another.

Coordinated Universal Time (UTC). The time scale that is available from most broadcast time signals. It differs from International Atomic Time (TAI) by an integral number of seconds. UTC is maintained within 1 second of UT1 by the introduction of 1-second steps (leap seconds) when necessary, normally at the end of December. DUT1, an approximation to the difference UT1 minus UTC, is transmitted in code on broadcast time signals.

coral, n. The hard skeleton of certain tiny sea animals; the stony, solidified mass of a number of such skeletons.

coral head. A large mushroom- or pillar-shaped coral growth.

coral reef. A reef made up of coral, fragments of coral and other organisms, and the limestone resulting from their consolidation. Coral may constitute less than half of the reef material.

Coriolis acceleration. An acceleration of a body in motion in a relative (moving) coordinate system. The total acceleration of the body, as measured in an inertial coordinate system, may be expressed as the sum of the acceleration within the relative system, the acceleration of the relative system itself, and the Coriolis acceleration. In the case of the earth, moving with angular velocity W, a body moving relative to the earth with velocity V has the Coriolis acceleration $2\Omega \times V$. If Newton's laws are to be applied in the relative system, the Coriolis acceleration and the acceleration of the relative system must be treated as forces.

Coriolis correction. 1. A correction applied to an assumed position, celestial line of position, celestial fix, or a computed or observed altitude to allow for Coriolis acceleration. 2. In inertial navigation equipment, an acceleration correction that must be applied to measurements of acceleration with respect to a coordinate system in translation to compensate for the effect of any angular motion of the coordinate system with respect to inertial space.

Coriolis force. An inertial force acting on a body in motion, due to rotation of the earth, causing deflection to the right in the Northern Hemisphere and to the left in the Southern Hemisphere. It affects air (wind), water (current), etc. and introduces an error in bubble sextant observations made from a moving craft due to the liquid in the bubble being deflected, the effect increasing with higher latitude and greater speed of the craft.

corner reflector. A radar reflector consisting of three mutually perpendicular flat reflecting surfaces designed to return incident electromagnetic radiation toward its source. The reflector is used to render objects such as buoys and sailboats more conspicuous to radar observations.

coromell, n. A night land breeze prevailing from November to May at La Paz, near the southern extremity of the Gulf of California.

corona, n. 1. The luminous envelope surrounding the sun but visible only during a total eclipse. 2. A luminous discharge due to ionization of the air surrounding an electric conductor. 3. A set of one or more rainbow-colored rings of small radii surrounding the sun, moon, or other source of light covered by a thin cloud veil. It is caused by diffraction of the light by tiny droplets in the atmosphere, and hence the colors are in the reverse order to those of a HALO caused by refraction. 4. A circle of light occasionally formed by the apparent convergency of the beams of the aurora.

corona discharge. Luminous and often audible discharge of electricity intermediate between a spark and a point discharge.

corrected compass course. Compass course with deviation applied; magnetic course.

corrected compass heading. Compass heading with deviation applied; magnetic heading.

corrected sextant altitude. Sextant altitude corrected for index error, height of eye, parallax, refraction, etc. Also called OBSERVED ALTITUDE, TRUE ALTITUDE.

correcting, n. The process of applying corrections, particularly the process of converting compass to magnetic direction, or compass, magnetic, or gyro to true direction. The opposite is UNCORRECTING.

corrector, n. A magnet, piece of soft iron, or device used in the adjustment of a magnetic compass.

corrosion, n. The wearing or wasting away by chemical action, usually by oxidation. A distinction is usually made between CORROSION and EROSION, the latter referring to the wearing away of the earth's surface primarily by non-chemical action.

COSPAS/SARSAT. A cooperative search-and-rescue satellite system operated by the U.S. and Russia that provides worldwide coverage by sensing the signals of Emergency Position Indicating Radiobeacons (EPIRBs).

course, n. The direction in which a vessel is steered or intended to be steered, expressed as angular distance from north, usually from 000° at north, clockwise through 360°. Strictly, the term applies to direction through the water, not the direction intended to be made good over the ground. The course is often designated as true, magnetic, compass, or grid as the reference direction is true, magnetic compass, or grid north, respectively. TRACK MADE GOOD is the single resultant direction from the point of departure to point of arrival at any given time. The use of this term to indicate a single resultant direction is preferred to the use of the misnomer "course made good." A course line is a line, as drawn on a chart, extending in the direction of a course.

course board. A board located on the navigation bridge used to display the course to steer, track, drift angle, leeway angle, compass error, etc.

course line. 1. The graphic representation of a ship's course, usually with respect to true north. 2. A line of position approximately parallel to the course line (definition 1), thus providing a check as to deviating left or right of the track.

course made good. A misnomer indicating the resultant direction from a point of departure to a point of arrival at any given time.

course of advance. An expression sometimes used to indicate the direction intended to be made good over the ground. The preferred term is TRACK (definition 1). This is a misnomer in that courses are directions steered or intended to be steered through the water with respect to a reference meridian.

course over ground. The direction of the path over the ground actually followed by a vessel. The preferred term is TRACK (definition 1). It is normally a somewhat irregular line. This is a misnomer in that courses are directions steered or intended to be steered through the water with respect to a reference meridian.

course recorder. A device that makes an automatic graphic record of the headings of a vessel versus time.

crab, v., t. To drift sideways while in forward motion.

crepuscular rays. Literally, "twilight rays," alternating lighter and darker bands (rays and shadows) that appear to diverge in fanlike array from the sun's position at about twilight. This term is applied to two quite different phenomena: a. It refers to shadows cast across the purple light, a true twilight phenomenon, by cloud tops that are high enough and far enough away from the observer to intercept some of the sunlight that would ordinarily produce the purple light. b. A more common occurrence is that of shadows and rays made visible by haze in the lower atmosphere. Towering clouds produce this effect also, but they may be fairly close to the observer and the sun need not be below the horizon. The apparent divergence of crepuscular rays is merely a perspective effect. When they continue across the sky to the antisolar point, these extensions are called ANTICREPUSCULAR RAYS. Also called SHADOW BANDS.

critical table. A single entering argument table in which values of the quantity to be found are tabulated for limiting values of the entering argument. In such a table interpolation is avoided through dividing the argument into intervals so chosen that successive intervals correspond to successive values of the required quantity, called the respondent.

cross-staff, n. A forerunner of the modern sextant used for measuring altitudes of celestial bodies, consisting of a wooden rod with one or more perpendicular cross pieces free to slide along the main rod. Also called FORESTAFF, JACOB'S STAFF.

cruising radius. The distance a craft can travel at cruising speed without refueling. Also called CRUISING RANGE.

crystal, n. A crystalline substance that allows electric current to pass in only one direction.

cumuliform, adj. Like cumulus; generally descriptive of all clouds, the principal characteristic of which is vertical development in the form of rising mounds, domes, or towers. This is the contrasting form to the horizontally extended STRATIFORM types.

cumulonimbus, n. An exceptionally dense cloud of great vertical development, occurring either as an isolated cloud or one of a line or wall of clouds with separated upper portions. These clouds appear as mountains or huge towers, at least a part of the upper portions of which are usually smooth, fibrous, striated, and almost flattened. This part often spreads out in the form of an anvil or plume. Under the base of cumulonimbus, which often is very dark, there frequently exists virga, precipitation, and low, ragged clouds, either merged with it or not. Its precipitation is often heavy and always of a showery nature. The usual occurrence of lightning and thunder within or from this cloud leads to its being popularly called THUNDERCLOUD and THUNDERHEAD. The latter term usually refers to only the upper portion of the cloud.

cumulus, n. A cloud type in the form of individual, detached elements that are generally dense and possess sharp non-fibrous outlines. These elements develop vertically, appearing as rising mounds, domes, or towers, the upper parts of which often resemble a cauliflower. The sunlit parts of these clouds are mostly brilliant white; their bases are relatively dark and nearly horizontal.

cupola, n. A label on a nautical chart that indicates a small dome-shaped tower or turret rising from a building.

current, n. A horizontal movement of water. Currents may be classified as tidal and nontidal. Tidal currents are caused by gravitational interactions between the sun, moon, and earth and are a part of the same general movement of the sea that is manifested in the vertical rise and fall, called TIDE. Tidal currents are periodic with a net velocity of zero over the tidal cycle. Nontidal currents include the permanent currents in the general circulatory systems of the sea as well as temporary currents arising from more pronounced meteorological variability. The SET of a current is the direction toward which it flows; the DRIFT is its speed. In British usage, tidal current is called TIDAL STREAM, and nontidal cur-rent is called CURRENT.

current chart. A chart on which current data are graphically depicted.

current diagram. A graphic table showing the speeds of the flood and ebb currents and the times of slack and strength over a considerable stretch of the channel of a tidal waterway, the times being referred to tide or tidal current phases at some reference station.

current direction. The direction toward which a current is flowing, called the SET of the current.

current meter. An instrument for measuring the speed and direction or just speed of a current. The measurements are usually Eulerian since the meter is most often fixed or moored at a specific location.

current sailing. The process of allowing for current when predicting the track to be made good or of determining the effect of a current on the direction of motion of a vessel. The expression is better avoided, as the process is not strictly a sailing.

current station. The geographic location at which current observations are conducted. Also, the facilities used to make current observations. These may include a buoy, ground tackle, current meters, recording mechanism, and radio transmitter.

cursor, n. A device used with an instrument to provide a moveable reference. A symbol indicating the location in a file of the data entry point of a computer.

cut in. To observe and plot lines of position locating an object or craft, particularly by bearings.

cut-off, n. 1. A new and relatively short channel formed when a stream cuts through the neck of an oxbow or horseshoe bend. 2. An artificial straightening or short-cut in a channel.

cycle, n. One complete train of events or phenomena that recur sequentially. When used in connection with sound or radio the term refers to one complete wave, or to a frequency of one wave per second.

cycle match. In Loran-C, the comparison, in time difference, between corresponding carrier cycles contained in the rise times of a master and secondary station pulse. The comparison is refined to a determination of the phase difference between these two cycles.

cyclogenesis, n. A development or strengthening of cyclonic circulation in the atmosphere. The opposite is CYCLOLYSIS. The term is applied to the development of cyclonic circulation where previously it did not exist, as well as to the intensification of existing cyclonic flow. While cyclogenesis usually occurs with a deepening (a decrease in atmospheric pressure), the two terms should not be used synonymously.

cyclone, n. 1. A meteorological phenomena characterized by relatively low atmospheric pressure and winds that blow counterclockwise around the center in the Northern Hemisphere and clockwise in the Southern Hemisphere. 2. The name by which a tropical storm having winds of 34 knots or greater is known in the South Indian Ocean.

cyclonic winds. The winds associated with a low-pressure area and constituting part of a cyclone.

cylindrical chart. A chart on a cylindrical map projection.

cylindrical map projection. A map projection in which the surface of a sphere or spheroid, such as the earth, is conceived as developed on a tangent cylinder, which is then spread out to form a plane.

cylindrical surface. A surface formed by a straight line moving parallel to itself and constantly intersecting a curve. Also called a CYLINDER.

D

damping, n. 1. The reduction of energy in a mechanical or electrical system by absorption or radiation. 2. The act of reducing the amplitude of the oscillations of an oscillatory system; hindering or preventing oscillation or vibration; diminishing the sharpness of resonance of the natural frequency of a system.

dan buoy. A buoy consisting of a ballasted float carrying a staff that supports a flag or light. Dan buoys are used principally in minesweeping, and by fisherman to mark the position of deep-sea fishing lines or nets.

danger angle. The maximum (or minimum) angle between two points, as observed from a craft indicating the limit of safe approach to an off-lying danger. A horizontal danger angle is measured between points shown on the chart. A vertical danger angle is measured between the top and bottom of an object of known height.

danger area. A specified area above, below, or within which there may exist potential danger.

danger bearing. The maximum or minimum bearing of a point for safe passage of an off-lying danger. As a vessel proceeds along a coast, the bearing of a fixed point on shore, such as a lighthouse, is measured frequently. As long as the bearing does not exceed the limit of the predetermined danger bearing, the vessel is on a safe course.

danger buoy. A buoy marking an isolated danger to navigation, such as a rock, shoal, or sunken wreck.

danger line. 1. A line drawn on a chart to indicate the limits of safe navigation for a vessel of specific draft. 2. A line of small dots used to draw the navigator's attention to a danger that would not stand out clearly enough if it were represented on the chart solely by the specific symbols. This line of small dots is also used to delimit areas containing numerous dangers, through which it is unsafe to navigate.

dangerous semicircle. The half of a cyclonic storm in which the rotary and forward motions of the storm reinforce each other and the winds tend to blow a vessel into the storm track. In the Northern Hemisphere this is to the right of the storm center (when facing the direction the storm is moving) and in the Southern Hemisphere it is to the left. The opposite is the NAVIGABLE (or less dangerous) SEMICIRCLE.

danger sounding. A minimum sounding chosen for a vessel of specific draft in a given area to indicate the limit of safe navigation.

data base. A uniform, organized set of data.

data processing. Changing data from one form or format to another by application of specified routines or algorithms.

data reduction. The process of transforming raw data into more ordered data.

data smoothing. The process of fitting dispersed data points to a smooth or uniform curve or line.

date line. The line coinciding approximately with the 180th meridian, at which each calendar day first begins; the boundary between the −12 and +12 time zones. The date on each side of this line differs by 1 day, but the time is the same in these two zones. When crossing this line on a westerly course, the date must be advanced 1 day; when crossing on an easterly course, the date must be put back 1 day. Sometimes called INTERNATIONAL DATE LINE.

datum, n. Any numerical or geometrical quantity or set of such quantities that may serve as reference or base for other quantities. In navigation two types of datums are used: horizontal and vertical.

datum transformation. The systematic elimination of discrepancies between adjoining or overlapping triangulation networks from different datums by moving the origins, rotating, and stretching the networks to fit each other.

day, n. The duration of one rotation of a celestial body on its axis. It is measured by successive transits of a reference point on the celestial sphere over the meridian, and each type takes its name from the reference used. Thus, for a solar day on earth the reference is the sun; a mean solar day uses the mean sun; and an apparent solar day uses the apparent sun.

daybeacon, n. An unlighted beacon. A daybeacon is identified by its color and the color, shape, and number of its daymark. The simplest form of daybeacon consists of a single pile with a daymark affixed at or near its top.

daylight control. A photoelectric device that automatically lights and extinguishes a navigation light, usually lighting it at or about sunset and extinguishing it at or about sunrise.

daylight saving time. A variation of standard time in order to make better use of daylight. In the United States the "Uniform Time Act of 1966" (Public Law 89-387) establishes the annual advancement and retardation of standard time by 1 hour at 2 AM on the last Sunday of April and October, respectively, except in those states that have by law exempted themselves from the observance of daylight saving time.

daymark, n. 1. The daytime identifying characteristics of an aid to navigation. 2. An unlighted navigation mark. 3. The shaped signals used to identify vessels engaged in special operations during daytime, more properly known as day shapes.

dead ahead. Bearing 000° relative.

dead astern. Bearing 180° relative.

deadhead, n. 1. A block of wood used as an anchor buoy. 2. A bollard, particularly one of wood set in the ground.

deadman. Timber or other long sturdy object buried in ice or ground to which ship's mooring lines are attached.

dead reckoning. Determining the position of a vessel by adding to the last fix the ship's course and speed for a given time. The position so obtained is called a DEAD RECKONING POSITION. Comparison of the dead reckoning position with the fix for the same time indicates the sum of currents, winds, and other forces acting on the vessel during the intervening period.

dead reckoning plot. The graphic plot of the dead reckoning, suitably labeled with time, direction, and speed.

decameter, n. Ten meters.

December solstice. Winter solstice in the Northern Hemisphere.

decibel, n. A dimensionless unit used for expressing the ratio between widely different powers. It is 10 times the logarithm to the base 10 of the power ratio.

decimeter, n. One-tenth of a meter.

declination, n. 1. Angular distance north or south of the celestial equator; the arc of an hour circle between the celestial equator and a point on the celestial sphere, measured northward or southward from the celestial equator through 90°, and labeled N or S (+ or −) to indicate the direction of measurement. 2. Short for MAGNETIC DECLINATION.

definition, n. The clarity and fidelity of the detail of radar images on the radarscope. A combination of good resolution and focus is required for good definition.

degree, n. 1. A unit of circular measure equal to 1⁄360th of a circle. 2. A unit of measurement of temperature.

deka-. A prefix meaning ten (10).

demodulation, n. The process of obtaining a modulating wave from a modulated carrier. The opposite is MODULATION.

departure, n. 1. The distance between two meridians at any given parallel of latitude, expressed in linear units, usually nautical miles; the distance to the east or west made good by a craft in proceeding from one point to another. 2. The point at which reckoning of a voyage begins. It is usually established by bearings of prominent landmarks as the vessel clears a harbor and proceeds to sea. When a navigator establishes this point, he is said to take departure. Also called POINT OF DEPARTURE. 3. Act of departing or leaving. 4. The amount by which the value of a meteorological element differs from the normal value.

dependent surveillance. Position determination requiring the cooperation of the tracked craft.

depressed pole. The celestial pole below the horizon, of opposite name to the latitude. The celestial pole above the horizon is called ELEVATED POLE.

depression, n. A developing cyclonic area or low pressure area.

depth contour. A line connecting points of equal depth below the sounding datum. It may be called FATHOM CURVE or FATHOM LINE if depth is expressed in fathoms. Also called DEPTH CURVE, ISOBATH.

depth of water. The vertical distance from the surface of the water to the bottom.

derelict, n. Any property abandoned at sea, often large enough to constitute a menace to navigation; especially an abandoned vessel.

developable surface. A curved surface that can be spread out in a plane without distortion, e.g., the cone and the cylinder.

deviation, n. The angle between the magnetic meridian and the axis of a compass card, expressed in degrees east or west to indicate the direction in which the northern end of the compass card is offset from magnetic north. Deviation is caused by magnetic influences in the immediate vicinity disturbing the compass.

deviation table. A table of the deviation of a magnetic compass on various headings, magnetic or compass. Also called MAGNETIC COMPASS TABLE.

dew point. The temperature to which air must be cooled at constant pressure and constant water vapor content to reach saturation. Any further cooling usually results in the formation of dew or frost.

diaphone, n. A sound signal emitter operating on the principle of periodic release of compressed air controlled by the reciprocating motion of a piston operated by compressed air. The diaphone usually emits a powerful sound of low pitch that often concludes with a brief sound of lowered pitch called the GRUNT. The emitted signal of a TWO-TONE DIAPHONE consists of two tones of different pitch; the second tone is of lower pitch.

diaphragm horn. A sound signal emitter comprising a resonant horn excited at its throat by impulsive emissions of compressed air regulated by an elastic diaphragm.

difference of latitude. The shorter arc of any meridian between the parallels of two places, expressed in angular measure.

difference of longitude. The smaller angle at the pole or the shorter arc of a parallel between the meridians of two places, expressed in angular measure.

differential. Relating to the technology of increasing the accuracy of an electronic navigation system by monitoring the system error from a known, fixed location and transmitting corrections to vessels using the system.

diffraction, n. 1. The bending of the rays of radiant energy around the edges of an obstacle or when passing near the edges of an opening, or through a small hole or slit, resulting in the formation of a spectrum. 2. The bending of a wave as it passes an obstruction.

digit, n. A single character representing an integer.

digital. Referring to the use of discreet expressions to represent variables.

digital calculator. In navigation, a small electronic device that does arithmetical calculations by applying mathematical formulas (ALGORITHMS) to user-entered values. A navigational calculator has preloaded programs to solve navigational problems.

digital computer. An electronic device larger and more sophisticated than a calculator that can operate a variety of software programs. In navigation, computers are used to run celestial sight reduction programs, tide computing programs, electronic chart programs, and ECDIS, and for a number of other tasks in ship management.

digital navigation chart (DNC). The electronic chart data base used in the U.S. Navy's NAVSSI.

digital selective calling (DSC). A communications technique using coded digitized signals that allows transmitters and receivers to manage message traffic, accepting or rejecting messages according to certain variables.

digitize. To convert analog data to digital data.

dihedral angle. The angle between two intersecting planes.

dihedral reflector. A radar reflector consisting of two flat surfaces intersecting mutually at right angles. Incident radar waves entering the aperture so formed with a direction of incidence perpendicular to the edge, are returned parallel to their direction of incidence.

dike, n. A bank of earth or stone used to form a barrier, which restrains water outside of an area that is normally flooded.

dip, n. The vertical angle, at the eye of an observer, between the horizontal and the line of sight to the visible horizon. Altitudes of celestial bodies measured from the visible sea horizon as a reference are too great by the amount of dip. Since dip arises from and varies with the elevation of the eye of the observer above the surface of the earth, the correction for dip is sometimes called HEIGHT OF EYE CORRECTION. Dip is smaller than GEOMETRICAL DIP by the amount of terrestrial refraction. Also called DIP OF THE HORIZON.

dip, v., i. To begin to descend in altitude after reaching a maximum on or near meridian transit.

dip correction. The correction to sextant altitude due to dip of the horizon. Also called HEIGHT OF EYE CORRECTION.

direction, n. The position of one point in space relative to another without reference to the distance between them. Direction may be either three-dimensional or two-dimensional, the horizontal being the usual plane of the latter. Direction is not an angle but is often indicated in terms of its angular distance from a REFERENCE DIRECTION. Thus, a horizontal direction may be specified as compass, magnetic, true, grid, or relative.

directional antenna. An antenna designed so that the radiation pattern is largely concentrated in a single lobe.

direction light. A light illuminating a sector of very narrow angle and intended to mark a direction to be followed. A direction light bounded by other sectors of different characteristics that define its margins with small angles of uncertainty is called a SINGLE STATION RANGE LIGHT.

direction of waves or swell. The direction from which waves or swell are moving.

direction of wind. The direction from which a wind is blowing.

direct motion. The apparent motion of a planet eastward among the stars. Apparent motion westward is called RETROGRADE MOTION. The usual motion of planets is direct.

directory. A list of files in a computer.

direct wave. 1. A radio wave that travels directly from the transmitting to the receiving antenna without reflections from any object or layer of the ionosphere. The path may be curved as a result of refraction. 2. A radio wave that is propagated directly through space; it is not influenced by the ground. Also called SPACE WAVE.

discontinuity, n. A zone of the atmosphere within which there is a comparatively rapid transition of any meteorological element.

disk. A type of computer data storage that consists of a plastic or metallic disk that rotates to provide access to the stored data. Data is stored in discreet areas of the disk known as tracks and sectors.

display, n. 1. The visual presentation of radar echoes or electronic charts. 2. The equipment for the visual display.

disposal area. Area designated by the U.S. Army Corps of Engineers for depositing dredged material where existing depths indicate that the intent is not to cause sufficient shoaling to create a danger to surface navigation. Disposal areas are shown on nautical charts.

diurnal, adj. Having a period or cycle of approximately one day.

diurnal inequality. The difference in height of the two high waters or of the two low waters of each tidal day; the difference in speed between the two flood tidal currents or the two ebb tidal currents of each tidal day. The difference changes with the declination of the moon and to a lesser extent with declination of the sun.

D-layer, n. The lowest of the ionized layers in the upper atmosphere, or ionosphere. It is present only during daylight hours, and its density is proportional to the altitude of the sun. The D-layer's only significant effect upon radio waves is its tendency to absorb their energy, particularly at frequencies below 3 megahertz. High angle radiation and signals of a frequency greater than 3 megahertz may penetrate the D-layer and be refracted or reflected by the somewhat higher E-layer.

doldrums, n., pl. The equatorial belt of calms or light variable winds, lying between the two trade wind belts. Also called EQUATORIAL CALMS.

dolphin, n. A post or group of posts, used for mooring or warping a vessel. The dolphin may be in the water, on a wharf, or on the beach.

doppler effect. First described by Christian Johann Doppler in 1842, an effect observed as a frequency shift resulting from relative motion between a transmitter and receiver.

doppler radar. Any form of radar that detects radial motion of a distant object relative to a radar apparatus by means of the change of the radio frequency of the echo signal due to motion.

double ebb. An ebb tidal current having two maxima of speed separated by a lesser ebb speed.

double flood. A flood tidal current having two maxima of speed separated by a lesser flood speed.

double interpolation. Interpolation when there are two arguments or variables.

double sextant. A sextant designed to enable the observer to simultaneously measure the left and right horizontal sextant angles of the three-point problem.

double tide. A high water consisting of two maxima of nearly the same height separated by a relatively small depression, or a low water consisting of two minima separated by a relatively small elevation. Sometimes called AGGER.

doubling the angle on the bow. A method of obtaining a running fix by measuring the distance a vessel travels on a steady course while the relative bearing (right or left) of a fixed object doubles. The distance from the object at the time of the second bearing is equal to the run between bearings, neglecting drift.

draft, n. The depth to which a vessel is submerged.

draft marks. Numerals placed on the sides of a vessel, customarily at the bow and stern, to indicate the depth to which a vessel is submerged.

dragging, n. 1. The process of towing a wire or horizontally set bar below the surface, to determine the least depth in an area or to ensure that a given area is free from navigational dangers to a certain depth. 2. The process of pulling along the bottom, as in dragging anchor.

draw, v., i. 1. To be immersed to a specified draft. 2. To change relative bearing forward or aft, or to port or starboard.

dredge, n. A vessel used to dredge an area.

dredge, v., t. To remove solid matter from the bottom of a water area.

dredging area. An area where dredging vessels may be encountered dredging material for construction. Channels dredged to provide an adequate depth of water for navigation are not considered as dredging areas.

dredging buoy. A buoy marking the limit of an area where dredging is being performed.

drift, n. 1. The speed of a current. 2. The speed of the current. 3. The distance a craft is moved by current and wind. 4. Downwind or downcurrent motion of airborne or waterborne objects due to wind or current. 5. Material moved from one place and deposited in another, as sand by a river, rocks by a glacier, material washed ashore and left stranded, snow or sand piled up by wind.

drift, v., i. To move by action of wind or current without control.

drift angle. 1. The angle between the tangent to the turning circle and the centerline of the vessel during a turn. 2. The angular difference between a vessel's ground track and the water track.

drift current. A wide, slow-moving ocean current principally caused by prevailing winds.

drizzle, n. Very small, numerous, and uniformly dispersed water drops that may appear to float while following air currents. Unlike fog droplets, drizzle falls to the ground. It usually falls from low stratus clouds and is frequently accompanied by low visibility and fog.

drogue, n. A current-measuring assembly consisting of a weighted parachute and an attached surface buoy.

dry compass. A compass without a liquid-filled bowl, particularly a magnetic compass having a very light compass card. Such a magnetic compass is seldom, if ever, used in marine applications.

drying heights. Heights above chart sounding datum of those features that are periodically covered and exposed by the rise and fall of the tide.

dual-rate blanking. To provide continuous service from one Loran-C chain to the next, some stations are operated as members of two chains and radiate signals at both rates. Such a station is faced periodically with an impossible requirement to radiate two overlapping pulse groups at the same time. During the time of overlap, the subordinate signal is blanked or suppressed. Blanking is accomplished in one of two ways: priority blanking in which case one rate is always superior or alternate blanking in which case the two rates alternate in the superior and subordinate roll.

dumping ground. An area used for the disposal of dredge spoil. Although shown on nautical charts as dumping grounds in United States waters, the Federal regulations for these areas have been revoked and their use for dumping discontinued. These areas will continue to be shown on nautical charts until they are no longer considered to be a danger to navigation.

dump site. Area established by Federal regulation in which dumping of dredged and fill material and other nonbuoyant objects is allowed with the issuance of a permit. Dump sites are shown on nautical charts.

duration of flood, duration of ebb. Duration of flood is the interval of time in which a tidal current is flooding, and the duration of ebb is the interval in which it is ebbing; these intervals being reckoned from the middle of the intervening slack waters or minimum currents. Together they cover, on an average, a period of 12.42 hours for a semidiurnal tidal current or a period of 24.84 hours for a diurnal current.

duration of rise, duration of fall. Duration of rise is the interval from low water to high water, and duration of fall is the interval from high water to low water. Together they cover, on an average, a period of 12.42 hours for a semidiurnal tide or a period of 24.84 hours for a diurnal tide.

dust devil. A well-developed dust whirl, a small but vigorous whirlwind, usually of short duration, rendered visible by dust, sand, and debris picked up from the ground. Diameters of dust devils range from about 10 feet to greater than 100 feet; their average height is about 600 feet, but a few have been observed as high as several thousand feet. They have been observed to rotate anticyclonically as well as cyclonically.

dust storm, n. An unusual, frequently severe weather condition characterized by strong winds and dust-filled air over an extensive area. Prerequisite to a dust storm is a period of drought over an area of normally arable land, thus providing very fine particles of dust, which distinguish it from the much more common SANDSTORM.

Dutchman's log. A buoyant object thrown overboard to determine the speed of a vessel. Speed is determined by the time required for a known length of the vessel to pass the object.

dynamical mean sun. A fictitious sun conceived to move eastward along the ecliptic at the average rate of the apparent sun. The dynamical mean sun and the apparent sun occupy the same position when the earth is at perihelion in January.

E

earthlight, n. The faint illumination of the dark part of the moon by sunlight reflected from the earth. Also called EARTHSHINE.

easting, n. The distance a craft makes good to the east. The opposite is WESTING.

ebb, n. Tidal current moving away from land or down a tidal stream. The opposite is FLOOD.

ebb current. The movement of a tidal current away from shore or down a tidal river or estuary. The opposite is FLOOD CURRENT.

ebb strength. Phase of the ebb tidal current at the time of maximum velocity. Also, the velocity at this time. Also called STRENGTH OF EBB.

echogram, n. A graphic record of depth measurements obtained by an echo sounder.

echo ranging. The determination of distance by measuring the time interval between transmission of a radiant energy signal and the return of its echo.

echo sounder. An instrument used to determine water depth by measuring the time interval for sound waves to go from a source of sound near the surface to the bottom and back again. Also called DEPTH FINDER, ACOUSTIC DEPTH FINDER.

eclipse, n. 1. Obscuring of a source of light by the intervention of an object. When the moon passes between the earth and the sun, casting a shadow on the earth, a solar eclipse takes place within the shadow. When the moon enters the earth's shadow, a lunar eclipse occurs. When the moon enters only the penumbra of the earth's shadow, a penumbral lunar eclipse occurs. A solar eclipse is partial if the sun is partly obscured and total if the entire surface is obscured; or annular if a thin ring of the sun's surface appears around the obscuring body. A lunar eclipse can be either total or partial. 2. An interval of darkness between flashes of a navigation light.

ecliptic, n. The apparent annual path of the

sun among the stars; the intersection of the plane of the earth's orbit with the celestial sphere. This is a great circle of the celestial sphere inclined at an angle of about 23°27' to the celestial equator.

E-layer, n. From the standpoint of its effect upon radio wave propagation, the lowest useful layer of the Kennelly-Heaviside radiation region. Its average height is about 70 miles, and its density is greatest about local apparent noon. For practical purposes, the layer disappears during the hours of darkness.

electric field. That region in space that surrounds an electrically charged object and in which the forces due to this charge are detectable.

electrode, n. A terminal at which electricity passes from one medium into another. The positive electrode is called the anode; the negative electrode is called the cathode.

electromagnetic energy. All forms of radiant energy, such as radio waves, light waves, X-rays, heat waves, gamma rays, and cosmic rays.

electromagnetic field. 1. The field of influence that an electric current produces around the conductor through which it flows. 2. A rapidly moving electric field and its associated magnetic field located at right angles to both electric lines of force and to their direction of motion. 3. The magnetic field resulting from the flow of electricity.

electromagnetic log. A speed-sensing device containing an electromagnetic sensor element extended below the hull of the vessel, which produces a voltage directly proportional to speed through the water.

electromagnetic waves. Waves of associated electric and magnetic fields characterized by variations of the fields. The electric and magnetic fields are at right angles to each other and to the direction of propagation. The waves are propagated at the speed of light and are known as radio (Hertzian) waves, infrared rays, light, ultraviolet rays, X-rays, etc., depending on their frequencies.

electromagnetism, n. 1. Magnetism produced by an electric current. 2. The science dealing with the physical relations between electricity and magnetism.

electronic aid to navigation. An aid to navigation using electronic equipment. If the navigational information is transmitted by radio waves, the device may be called a RADIO AID TO NAVIGATION.

electronic bearing cursor. The bright rotatable radial line on the display of a marine radar set, used for bearing determination.

electronic chart (EC). A chart displayed on a video terminal, usually integrated with other navigational aids.

electronic chart data base (ECDB). The master electronic chart data base for the electronic navigation chart held in digital form by the hydrographic authority.

electronic chart display and information system (ECDIS). An electronic chart system that complies with IMO guidelines and is the legal equivalent of a paper chart.

electronic cursor. Short for ELECTRONIC BEARING CURSOR.

electronic navigation. Navigation by means of electronic equipment. The expression is more inclusive than RADIONAVIGATION, since it includes navigation involving any electronic device or instrument.

electronic navigation chart (ENC). The standardized electronic data base, a subset of the ECDB, issued by a hydrographic authority for use with an ECDIS.

electronics, n. The science and technology relating to the emission, flow, and effects of electrons in a vacuum or through a semiconductor such as a gas, and to systems using devices in which this action takes place.

elevated pole. The celestial pole above the horizon, agreeing in name with the latitude. The celestial pole below the horizon is called DEPRESSED POLE.

elongation, n. The angular distance of a body of the solar system from the sun; the angle at the earth between lines to the sun and another celestial body of the solar system. The greatest elongation is the maximum angular distance of an inferior planet from the sun before it starts back toward conjunction. The direction of the body east or west of the sun is usually specified, as greatest elongation east (or west).

Emergency Position Indicating Radiobeacon. A small portable radiobeacon carried by vessels and aircraft that transmits radio signals to be used by search-and-rescue authorities to locate a marine emergency.

emergency position indicating radiobeacon station. As defined by the International Telecommunication Union (ITU), a station in the mobile service whose emissions are intended to facilitate search-and-rescue operations.

emission delay. 1. A delay in the transmission of a pulse signal from a slave (or secondary) station of a hyperbolic radionavigation system, introduced as an aid in distinguishing between master and slave (or secondary) station signals. 2. In Loran-C the time interval between the master station's transmission and the secondary station's transmission in the same group repetition interval (GRI).

endless tangent screw. A tangent screw that can be moved over its entire range without resetting.

endless tangent screw sextant. A marine sextant having an endless tangent screw for controlling the position of the index arm and the vernier or micrometer drum. The index arm may be moved over the entire arc without resetting, by means of the endless tangent screw.

enhanced group call (EGC). A global automated satellite communications service capable of addressing messages to specific areas or specific groups of vessels.

envelope match. In Loran-C, the comparison, in time difference, between the leading edges of the demodulated and filtered pulses from a master and secondary station. The pulses are superimposed and matched manually or automatically.

ephemeris (pl. ephemerides), n. 1. A periodical publication tabulating the predicted positions of celestial bodies at regular intervals, such as daily, and containing other data of interest to astronomers and navigators. 2. A statement, not necessarily in a publication, presenting a correlation of time and position of celestial bodies or artificial satellites.

epoch, n. 1. A particular instant of time or a date for which values of data, which vary with time, are given. 2. A given period of time during which a series of related acts or events takes place. 3. Angular retardation of the maximum of a constituent of the observed tide behind the corresponding maximum of the same constituent of the hypothetical equilibrium. Also called PHASE LAG, TIDAL EPOCH. 4. As used in tidal datum determinations, a 19-year Metonic cycle over which tidal height observations are meaned in order to establish the various datums.

equal-area map projection. A map projection having a constant area scale. Such a projection is not conformal and is not used for navigation. Also called AUTHALIC MAP PROJECTION, EQUIVALENT MAP PROJECTION.

equal interval light. A navigation light having equal periods of light and darkness. Also called ISOPHASE LIGHT.

equation of time. The difference at any instant between apparent time and local mean time. It is a measure of the difference of the hour angles of the apparent (true) sun and the mean (fictitious) sun. The equation of time is tabulated in the *Nautical Almanac,* without sign, for 00h and 12h GMT on each day. To obtain apparent time, apply the equation of time to mean time with a positive sign when GHA sun at 00h GMT exceeds 180°, or at 12h exceeds 0°, corresponding to a meridian passage of the sun before 12h GMT; otherwise apply with a negative sign.

equator, n. The primary great circle of a sphere or spheroid, such as the earth, perpendicular to the polar axis, or a line resembling or approximating such a circle. The terrestrial equator is 90° from the earth's geographical poles, the celestial equator or equinoctial is 90° from the celestial poles. The magnetic equator or aclinic line is the line on the surface of the earth connecting all points at which the magnetic dip is zero. The geomagnetic equator is the great circle 90° from the geomagnetic poles of the earth.

equatorial bulge. The excess of the earth's equatorial diameter over the polar diameter.

equatorial chart. 1. A chart of equatorial areas. 2. A chart on an equatorial map projection.

equatorial gravity value. The mean acceleration of gravity at the equator, approximately equal to 978.03 centimeters per second per second.

equinoctial, adj. Of or pertaining to an equinox or the equinoxes.

equinoctial point. One of the two points of intersection of the ecliptic and the celestial equator. Also called EQUINOX.

equinoctial tides. Tides occurring near the times of the equinoxes, when the spring range is greater than average.

equinox, n. 1. One of the two points of intersection of the ecliptic and celestial equator, occupied by the sun when its declination is 0°. The point occupied on or about March 21, when the sun's declination changes from south to north, is called vernal equinox, March equinox, or first point of Aries; the point occupied on or about September 23, when the declination changes from north to south, is called autumnal equinox, September equinox, or first point of Libra. Also called EQUINOCTIAL POINT. 2. The instant the sun occupies one of the equinoctial points.

error, n. The difference between the value of a quantity determined by observation, measurement, or calculation and the true, correct, accepted, adopted, or standard value of that quantity. Usually, the true value of the quantity cannot be determined with exactness due to insufficient knowledge of the errors encountered in the observations. Exceptions occur (1) when the value is mathematically determinable, or (2) when the value is an adopted or standard value established by authority. In order to analyze the exactness with which the true value of a quantity has been determined from observations, errors are classified into two categories, random and systematic errors.

error of perpendicularity. That error in the reading of a marine sextant due to non-perpendicularity of the index mirror to the frame.

established direction of traffic flow. A traffic flow pattern indicating the directional movement of traffic as established within a traffic separation scheme.

establishment of the port. Average high water interval on days of the new and full moon. This interval is also sometimes called the COMMON or VULGAR ESTABLISHMENT to distinguish it from the CORRECTED ESTABLISHMENT, the latter being the mean of all high water intervals. The latter is usually 10 to 15 minutes less than the common establishment. Also called HIGH WATER FULL AND CHANGE.

estimated position. The most probable position of a craft determined from incomplete data or data of questionable accuracy. Such a position might be determined by applying a correction to the dead reckoning position, as for estimated current; by plotting a line of soundings; or by plotting lines of position of questionable accuracy.

estimated time of arrival (ETA). The predicted time of reaching a destination or waypoint.

estimated time of departure (ETD). The predicted time of leaving a place.

estuary, n. 1. An embayment of the coast in which fresh river water entering at its head mixes with the relatively saline ocean water. When tidal action is the dominant mixing agent, it is usually called TIDAL ESTUARY. 2. The lower reaches and mouth of a river emptying directly into the sea where tidal mixing takes place. Sometimes called RIVER ESTUARY. 3. A drowned river mouth due to sinking of the land near the coast.

Eulerian motion. A slight wobbling of the earth about its axis of rotation, often called polar motion, and sometimes wandering of the poles. This motion, which does not exceed 40 feet from the mean position, produces slight variation of latitude and longitude of places on the earth.

evening star. The brightest planet appearing in the western sky during evening twilight.

evening twilight. The period of time between sunset and darkness.

excess of arc. That part of a sextant arc beginning at zero and extending in the direction opposite to that part usually considered positive.

existence doubtful. Of uncertain existence. The expression is used principally on charts to indicate the possible existence of a rock, shoal, etc., the actual existence of which has not been established.

external noise. In radio reception, atmospheric radio noise and man-made noise, singly or in combination. Internal noise is produced in the receiver circuits.

extragalactic nebula. An aggregation of matter beyond our galaxy, large enough to occupy a perceptible area but which has not been resolved into individual stars.

extrapolation, n. The process of estimating the value of a quantity beyond the limits of known values by assuming that the rate or system of change between the last few known values continues.

extratropical cyclone. Any cyclonic-scale storm that is not a tropical cyclone, usually referring only to the migratory frontal cyclones of middle and high latitudes. Also called EXTRATROPICAL LOW.

extreme high water. The highest elevation reached by the sea as recorded by a tide gauge during a given period. The National Ocean Survey routinely documents monthly and yearly extreme high waters for its control stations.

extreme low water. The lowest elevation reached by the sea as recorded by a tide gauge during a given period. The National Ocean Survey routinely documents monthly and yearly extreme low water for its control stations.

extremely high frequency. Radio frequency of 30,000 to 300,000 megahertz.

eye of the storm. The center of a tropical cyclone marked by relatively light winds, confused seas, rising temperature, lowered relative humidity, and often by clear skies. The general area of lowest atmospheric pressure of a cyclone is called STORM CENTER.

eye of the wind. Directly into the wind; the point or direction from which the wind is blowing.

F

Fahrenheit temperature. Temperature based on a scale in which, under standard atmospheric pressure, water freezes at 32° and boils at 212° above zero.

fair, adj. Not stormy; good; fine; clear.

fair tide. A tidal current setting in such a direction as to increase the speed of a vessel. One setting in a direction approximately opposite to the heading is called a HEAD TIDE. One abeam is called a BEAM TIDE. One approximately 90° from the course is called a CROSS TIDE.

fairway, n. 1. The main thoroughfare of shipping in a harbor or channel. 2. The middle of a channel.

fairway buoy. A buoy marking a fairway, with safe water on either side. Its color is red and white vertical stripes. Also called MIDCHANNEL BUOY.

falling tide. The portion of the tide cycle between high water and the following low water in which the depth of water is decreasing. Sometimes the term EBB is used as an equivalent, but since ebb refers primarily to horizontal rather than vertical movement, falling tide is considered more appropriate. The opposite is RISING TIDE.

false horizon. A line resembling the VISIBLE HORIZON but above or below it.

fata morgana. A complex mirage, characterized by marked distortion, generally in the vertical. It may cause objects to appear towering, magnified, and at times even multiplied.

fathom, n. A unit of length equal to 6 feet. This unit of measure is used principally as a measure of depth of water and the length of lead lines, anchor chains, and cordage.

fathom curve, fathom line. A depth contour, with depths expressed in fathoms.

favorable current. A current flowing in such a direction as to increase the speed of a vessel over the ground. The opposite is UNFAVORABLE CURRENT.

federal project depth. The design dredging depth of a channel constructed by the U.S. Army Corps of Engineers; the project depth may or may not be the goal of maintenance dredging after completion of the channel. For this reason Federal project depth must not be confused with CONTROLLING DEPTH.

fetch, n. 1. An area of the sea surface over which seas are generated by a wind having a constant direction and speed. Also called GENERATING AREA. 2. The length of the fetch area, measured in the direction of the wind, in which the seas are generated.

fictitious sun. An imaginary sun conceived to move eastward along the celestial equator at a rate equal to the average rate of the apparent sun or to move eastward along the ecliptic at the average rate of the apparent sun.

field of view. The maximum angle of vision, particularly of an optical instrument.

filling, n. Increase in atmospheric pressure, particularly within a low. Decrease in pressure is called DEEPENING.

final great-circle course. The direction, at the destination, of the great circle through that point and the point of departure, expressed as the angular distance from a reference direction, usually north, to that part of the great circle extending beyond the destination.

first estimate–second estimate method. The process of determining the value of a variable quantity by trial and error. The expression applies particularly to the method of determining time of meridian transit (especially local apparent noon) at a moving craft.

first light. The beginning of morning nautical twilight, i.e., when the center of the morning sun is 12° below the horizon.

first quarter. The phase of the moon when it is near east quadrature, when the western half of it is visible to an observer on the earth.

firth, n. A long, narrow arm of the sea.

fish havens. Areas established by private interests, usually sport fishermen, to simulate natural reefs and wrecks that attract fish. The reefs are constructed by dumping assorted junk in areas that may be of very small extent or may stretch a considerable distance along a depth contour. Fish havens are outlined and labeled on charts. Also called FISHERY REEFS.

fishing zone. The offshore zone in which exclusive fishing rights and management are held by the coastal nation. The U.S. fishing zone, known as the fishery conservation zone, is defined under P.L. 94-265. The law states, "The inner boundary of the fishery conservation zone is a line conterminous with the seaward boundary of catch of the coastal states, and the outer boundary of such zone is a line drawn in such manner that each point on it is 200 nautical miles from the baseline from which the territorial sea is measured."

fish stakes. Poles or stakes placed in shallow water to outline fishing grounds or to catch fish.

fish trap areas. Areas established by the U.S. Army Corps of Engineers in which traps may be built and maintained according to established regulations. The fish stakes that may exist in these areas are obstructions to navigation and may be dangerous. The limits of fish trap areas and a cautionary note are usually charted.

fix, n. A position determined without reference to any former position; the common intersection of two or more lines of position obtained from simultaneous observations. Fixes obtained from electronic systems are often given as latitude/longitude coordinates determined by algorithms in the system software.

fixed. A light that is continuously on.

fixed and flashing light. A light in which a fixed light is combined with a flashing light of higher luminous intensity. The aeronautical light equivalent is called UNDULATING LIGHT.

fixed and group flashing light. A fixed light varied at regular intervals by a group of two or more flashes of greater intensity.

fixed light. A light that appears continuous and steady. The term is sometimes loosely used for a light supported on a fixed structure, as distinct from a light on a floating support.

fixed mark. A navigation mark fixed in position.

flashing light. A navigation light in which the total duration of light in a cycle is shorter than the total duration of darkness. The term is commonly used for a SINGLE-FLASHING LIGHT, a flashing light in which a flash is regularly repeated at a rate of less then 50 flashes per minute.

F-layer, n. The second principal layer of ionization in the Kennelly-Heaviside region (the E-layer is the first principal layer; the D-layer is of minor significance except for a tendency to absorb energy from radio waves in the medium frequency range). Situated about 175 miles above the earth's surface, the F-layer exists as a single layer only during the hours of darkness. It divides into two separate layers during daylight hours.

F1-layer, n. The lower of the two layers into which the F-layer divides during daylight hours. Situated about 140 miles above the earth's surface, it reaches its maximum density at noon. Since its density varies with the extent of the sun's radiation, it is subject to daily and seasonal variations. It may disappear completely at some point during the winter months.

F2-layer, n. The higher of the two layers into which the F-layer divides during daylight hours. It reaches its maximum density at noon and, over the continental U.S., varies in height from about 185 miles in winter to 250 miles in the summer. The F2-layer normally has a greater influence on radio wave propagation than the F1-layer.

FleetNET. INMARSAT broadcast service for commercial marine traffic.

flood, n. Tidal current moving toward land or up a tidal stream. The opposite is EBB. Also called FLOOD CURRENT.

flood axis. Average direction of tidal current at strength of flood.

flood current. The movement of a tidal current toward the shore or up a tidal river or estuary. In the mixed type of reversing current, the terms greater flood and lesser flood are applied respectively to the flood currents of greater and lesser speed of each day.

flotsam, n. Floating articles, particularly those that are thrown overboard to lighten a vessel in distress.

foehn, n. A warm, dry, wind blowing down the leeward slope of a mountain and across a valley floor or plain.

fog, n. A visible accumulation of tiny droplets of water, formed by condensation of water vapor in the air, with the base at the surface of the earth. It reduces visibility below 1 kilometer (0.54 nautical mile).

fog bank. A well-defined mass of fog observed at a distance, most commonly at sea.

fogbound, adj. Surrounded by fog. The term is used particularly with reference to vessels unable to proceed because of the fog.

fogbow, n. A faintly colored circular arc similar to a RAINBOW but formed on fog layers containing drops whose diameters are of the order of 100 microns or less.

fog detector. A device used to automatically determine conditions of visibility that warrant sounding a fog signal.

foot, n. Twelve inches or 30.48 centimeters. The latter value was adopted in 1959 by

Australia, Canada, New Zealand, South Africa, the United Kingdom, and the United States. 2. The bottom of a slope, grade, or declivity.

foreshore, n. That part of the shore or beach that lies between the low water mark and the upper limit of normal wave action.

forward of the beam. Any direction between broad on the beam and ahead.

foul bottom. A term used to describe the bottom of a vessel when encrusted with marine growth.

foul ground. An area unsuitable for anchoring or fishing due to rocks, boulders, coral, or other obstructions.

fracto-. A prefix used with the name of a basic cloud form to indicate a torn, ragged, and scattered appearance caused by strong winds.

freeboard, n. The vertical distance from the uppermost complete, watertight deck of a vessel to the surface of the water, usually measured amidships. Minimum permissible freeboard may be indicated by LOAD LINE MARKS.

free wave. A wave that continues to exist after the generating force has ceased to act, in contrast with a FORCED WAVE that is generated and maintained by a continuous force.

freezing rain. Rain that falls in liquid form but freezes upon impact to form a coating of ice on the ground and exposed objects.

frequency, n. The rate at which a cycle is repeated.

frequency band. 1. A specified segment of the frequency spectrum. 2. One of two or more segments of the total frequency coverage of a radio receiver or transmitter, each segment being selectable by means of a band change switch. 3. Any range of frequencies extending from a specified lower to a specified upper limit.

frequency channel. The assigned frequency band commonly referred to by number, letter, symbol, or some salient frequency within the band.

frequency modulation. Angle modulation of a sinewave carrier in which the instantaneous frequency of the modulated wave differs from the carrier frequency by an amount proportional to the instantaneous value of the modulating.

fresh breeze. Wind of force 5 (17 to 21 knots or 19 to 24 miles per hour) on the Beaufort wind scale.

freshen, v., i. To become stronger, applied particularly to wind.

fresh gale. A term once used by seamen to what is now called GALE on the Beaufort wind scale.

friction, n. Resistance to motion due to interaction between the surface of a body and anything in contact with it.

friction error. The error of an instrument reading due to friction in the moving parts of the instrument.

frigid zones. Either of the two zones between the polar circles and the poles, called the north frigid zone and the south frigid zone.

fringing reef. A reef attached directly to the shore of an island or continental landmass. Its outer margin is submerged and often consists of algal limestone, coral rock, and living coral.

front, n. The interface or transition zone between two air masses of different density. The term front is used ambiguously for: frontal zone, the three-dimensional zone or layer of large horizontal density gradient, bounded by frontal surfaces across which the horizontal density gradient is discontinuous (frontal surface usually refers specifically to the warmer side of the frontal zone); and surface front, the line of intersection of a frontal surface or frontal zone with the earth's surface or, less frequently, with a specified constant-pressure surface.

frontal, adj. Of or pertaining to a front.

frontal cyclone. In general, any cyclone associated with a front; often used synonymously with WAVE CYCLONE or with EXTRATROPICAL CYCLONE (as opposed to tropical cyclones, which are non-frontal).

front light. The closer of two range lights. It is the lowest of the lights of an established range. Also called LOW LIGHT.

frontogenesis, n. 1. The initial formation of a front or frontal zone. 2. In general, an increase in the horizontal gradient of an air mass property, principally density, and the development of the accompanying features of the wind field that characterize a front.

frontolysis, n. 1 The dissipation of a front or frontal zone. 2. In general, a decrease in the horizontal gradient of an air mass property, principally density, and the dissipation of the accompanying features of the wind field.

frost, n. 1. A deposit of interlocking ice crystals formed by direct sublimation on objects, usually those of small diameter freely exposed to the air. 2. The condition existing when the temperature of the earth's surface and earthbound objects falls below 0°C or 32°F. Temperatures below the freezing point of water are sometimes expressed as "degrees of frost."

frozen precipitation. Any form of precipitation that reaches the ground in frozen form; i.e., snow, snow pellets, snow grains, ice crystals, ice pellets, and hail.

full moon. The moon at opposition, when it appears as a round disk to an observer on the earth because the illuminated side is toward him.

funnel cloud. A cloud column or inverted cloud cone, pendant from a cloud base. This supplementary feature occurs mostly with cumulus and cumulonimbus; when it reaches the earth's surface, it constitutes a tornado or waterspout. Also called TUBA, TORNADO CLOUD.

G

G, n. An acceleration equal to the acceleration of gravity, approximately 32.2 feet per second per second at sea level.

gain, n. The ratio of output voltage, current, or power to input voltage, current, or power in electronic instruments.

galaxy, n. A vast assemblage of stars, planets, nebulae, and other bodies composing a distinct group in the universe. The sun and its family of planets is part of a galaxy commonly called the MILKY WAY.

gale, n. Wind of force 8 on the Beaufort wind scale (34 to 40 knots or 39 to 46 miles per hour) is classified as a gale. Wind of force 9 (41 to 47 knots or 47 to 54 miles per hour) is classified as a strong gale. Wind of force 7 (28 to 33 knots or 32 to 38 miles per hour) is classified as a near gale.

Gegenschein, n. A faint light area of the sky always opposite the position of the sun on the celestial sphere. It is believed to be the reflection of sunlight from particles moving beyond the earth's orbit. Also called COUNTERGLOW.

generalization. The process of selectively removing less important features of charts as scale becomes smaller, to avoid overcrowding charts.

general precession. The resultant motion of the components causing precession of the equinoxes westward along the ecliptic at the rate of about 50.3" per year, completing the cycle in about 25,800 years.

gentle breeze. Wind of force 3 (7 to 10 knots or 8 to 12 miles per hour) on the Beaufort wind scale.

geo-. A prefix meaning earth.

geocentric, adj. Relative to the earth as a center; measured from the center of the earth.

geocentric latitude. The angle at the center of the reference ellipsoid between the celestial equator and a radius vector to a point on the ellipsoid. This differs from the geographic latitude by a maximum of 11.6' of arc at Lat. 45°.

geocentric parallax. The difference in apparent direction of a celestial body from a point on the surface of the earth and from the center of the earth. This difference varies with the body's altitude and distance from the earth. Also called DIURNAL PARALLAX.

geodesy, n. The science of the determination of the size and shape of the earth.

geodetic, adj. Of or pertaining to geodesy; geodesic.

geodetic survey. A survey that takes into account the shape and size of the earth. It is applicable for large areas and long lines and is used for the precise location of basic points suitable for controlling other surveys.

geographical coordinates. Spherical coordinates defining a point on the surface of the earth, usually latitude and longitude. Also called TERRESTRIAL COORDINATES.

geographical mile. The length of 1 minute of arc of the equator, or 6,087.08 feet. This approximates the length of the nautical mile.

geographical pole. Either of the two points of intersection of the surface of the earth with its axis, where all meridians meet, labeled N or S to indicate whether the north geographical pole or the south geographical pole.

geographical position (GP). 1. The point on the earth at which a given celestial body is in the zenith at a specified time. The geographical position of the sun is also called the subsolar point, of the moon the sublunar point, and of a star the substellar or subastral point. 2. Any position on the earth defined by means of its geographical coordinates either astronomical or geodetic.

geographic number. The number assigned to an aid to navigation for identification purposes in accordance with the lateral system of numbering.

geographic parallel. A general term applying to astronomical and geodetic parallels.

geographic range. The maximum distance at which the curvature of the earth and terrestrial refraction permit an aid to navigation to be seen from a particular height of eye without regard to the luminous intensity of the light. The geographic range sometimes printed on charts or tabulated in light lists is the maximum distance at which the curvature of the earth and terrestrial refraction permit a light to be seen from a height of eye of 15 feet above the water when the elevation of the light is taken above the height datum of the largest scale chart of the locality. Therefore, this range is a nominal geographic range.

geographic sign conventions. In mapping, charting, and geodesy, the inconsistent application of algebraic sign to geographical references and the angular reference of azimuthal systems is a potential trouble area in scientific data collection. The following conventions have wide use in the standardization of scientific notation: Longitude references are positive eastward of the Greenwich meridian to 180° and negative westward of Greenwich. Latitude references are positive to the north of the equator and negative to the south. Azimuths are measured clockwise, using South as the origin and continuing to 360°. Bearings are measured clockwise, using North as the origin and continuing to 360°. Tabulated coordinates, or individual coordinates, are annotated N, S, E, W, as appropriate.

geoid, n. The equipotential surface in the gravity field of the earth; the surface to which the oceans would conform over the entire earth if free to adjust to the combined effect of the earth's mass attraction and the centrifugal force of the earth's rotation. As a result of the uneven distribution of the earth's mass, the geoidal surface is irregular. The geoid is a surface along which the gravity potential is everywhere equal (equipotential surface) and to which the direction of gravity is always perpendicular. Also called FIGURE OF THE EARTH.

geoidal height. The distance of the geoid above (positive) or below (negative) the mathematical reference ellipsoid. Also called GEOIDAL SEPARATION, GEOIDAL UNDULATION, UNDULATION OF THE GEOID.

geological oceanography. The study of the floors and margins of the oceans, including description of submarine relief features, chemical and physical composition of bottom materials, interaction of sediments and rocks with air and seawater, and action of various forms of wave energy in the submarine crust of the earth.

geomagnetic equator. The terrestrial great circle everywhere 90° from the geomagnetic poles. GEOMAGNETIC EQUATOR is not the same as the MAGNETIC EQUATOR, the line connecting all points of zero magnetic dip.

geomagnetic latitude. Angular distance from the geomagnetic equator, measured northward or southward on the geomagnetic meridian through 90° and labeled N or S to indicate the direction of measurement. GEOMAGNETIC LATITUDE should not be confused with MAGNETIC LATITUDE.

geomagnetic pole. Either of two antipodal points marking the intersection of the earth's surface with the extended axis of a bar magnet assumed to be located at the center of the earth and approximating the source of the actual magnetic field of the earth. The pole in the Northern Hemisphere (at about lat. 78°5N, long. 69°W) is designated north geomagnetic pole, and the pole in the Southern Hemisphere (at about lat. 78°S, long. 111°E) is designated south.

geomagnetism, n. Magnetic phenomena, collectively considered, exhibited by the earth and its atmosphere. Also called TERRESTRIAL MAGNETISM.

geometrical horizon. Originally, the celestial horizon; now more commonly the intersection of the celestial sphere and an infinite number of straight lines tangent to the earth's surface, and radiating from the eye of the observer. If there were no terrestrial refraction, geometrical horizons and VISIBLE HORIZONS would coincide.

geometric dilution of precision. All geometric factors that degrade the accuracy of position fixes derived from externally referenced navigation systems. Often shortened to GEOMETRIC DILUTION.

geostrophic wind. The horizontal wind velocity for which the Coriolis force exactly balances the horizontal pressure force.

geosynchronous satellite. An earth satellite whose period of rotation is equal to the period of rotation of the earth about its axis. The orbit of a geosynchronous satellite must be equatorial if the satellite is to remain fixed over a point on the earth's equator. Also called TWENTY-FOUR HOUR SATELLITE.

gibbous, adj. Bounded by convex curves. The term is used particularly in reference to the moon when it is between first quarter and full or between full and last quarter, or to other celestial bodies when they present a similar appearance.

gigahertz, n. One thousand megahertz, or one billion cycles per second.

GLONASS. A satellite navigation system operated by Russia, analogous to the U.S. Global Positioning System (GPS).

gloom, n. The condition existing when daylight is very much reduced by dense cloud or smoke accumulation above the surface, the surface visibility not being materially reduced.

gnomonic chart. A chart constructed on the gnomonic projection and often used as an adjunct for transferring a great circle to a Mercator chart. Commonly called GREAT CIRCLE CHART.

gong buoy. A buoy fitted with a group of saucer-shaped bells of different tones as an audible signal.

gradient, n. 1. A rate of rise or fall of a quantity against horizontal distance expressed as a ratio, decimal, fraction, percentage, or the tangent of the angle of inclination. 2. The rate of increase or decrease of one quantity with respect to another. 3. A term used in radionavigation to refer to the spacing between consecutive hyperbolas of a family of hyperbolas per unit time difference. If the gradient is high, a relatively small time-difference error in determining a hyperbolic line of position will result in a relatively high position error.

gradient wind. Any horizontal wind velocity tangent to the contour line of a constant pressure surface (or to the isobar of a geopotential surface) at the point in question. At such points where the wind is gradient, the Coriolis force and the centrifugal force together exactly balance the horizontal pressure force.

graduation error. Inaccuracy in the graduations of the scale of an instrument.

graticule, n. 1. The network of lines representing parallels and meridians on a map, chart, or plotting sheet. A fictitious graticule represents fictitious parallels and fictitious meridians. 2. A scale at the focal plane of an optical instrument to aid in the measurement of objects.

gravitation, n. 1. The force of attraction between two bodies. According to Newton, gravitation is directly proportional to the product of the masses of two bodies and inversely proportional to the square of the distance between them. 2. The acceleration produced by the mutual attraction of two masses, directed along the line joining their centers of mass, and of magnitude inversely proportional to the square of the distance between the two centers of mass.

gravity, n. The force of attraction of the earth, or another body, on nearby objects.

gravity data. Information concerning that acceleration that attracts bodies and is expressed as observations or in the form of gravity anomaly charts or spherical harmonics for spatial representation of the earth and other celestial bodies.

gravity wind. A wind blowing down an incline. Also called KATABATIC WIND.

great circle. The intersection of a sphere and a plane through its center. The intersection of a sphere and a plane that does not pass through its center is called a small circle. Also called ORTHODROME, ORTHODROMIC CURVE.

great-circle bearing. The initial direction of a great circle through two terrestrial points, expressed as angular distance from a reference direction. It is usually measured from 000° at the reference direction clockwise through 360°. Bearings obtained by any form of radiant energy are great-circle bearings.

great-circle chart. A chart on which a great circle appears as a straight line or approximately so, particularly a chart on the gnomonic map projection.

great-circle course. The direction of the great circle through the point of departure and the destination, expressed as the angular distance from a reference direction, usually north, to the direction of the great circle. The angle varies from point to point along the great circle. At the point of departure it is called initial great-circle course; at the destination it is called final great-circle course.

great-circle sailing. Any method of solving the various problems involving courses, distance, etc., as they are related to a great-circle track.

great-circle track. The track of a vessel following a great circle, or a great circle that it is intended that a vessel follow approximately.

great diurnal range. The difference in height between mean higher high water and mean lower low water. Often shortened to DIURNAL RANGE. The difference in height between mean lower high water and mean higher low water is called SMALL DIURNAL RANGE.

green flash. A brilliant green coloring of the upper edge of the sun as it appears at sunrise or disappears at sunset when there is a clear, distinct horizon. It is due to refraction by the atmosphere, which disperses the first (or last) spot of light into a spectrum and causes the colors to appear (or disappear) in the order of refrangibility. The green is bent more than red or yellow and hence is visible sooner at sunrise and later at sunset.

Greenwich apparent noon. Local apparent noon at the Greenwich meridian; 12 o'clock Greenwich apparent time, or the instant the apparent sun is over the upper branch of the Greenwich meridian.

Greenwich apparent time. Local apparent time at the Greenwich meridian; the arc of the celestial equator, or the angle at the celestial pole between the lower branch of the Greenwich celestial meridian and the hour circle of the apparent or true sun, measured westward from the lower branch of the Greenwich celestial meridian through 24 hours; Greenwich hour angle of the apparent or true sun, expressed in time units, plus 12 hours.

Greenwich hour angle. Angular distance west of the Greenwich celestial meridian; the arc of the celestial equator, or the angle at the celestial pole, between the upper branch of the Greenwich celestial meridian and the hour circle of a point on the celestial sphere, measured westward from the Greenwich celestial meridian through 360°; local hour angle at the Greenwich meridian.

Greenwich mean time. Local mean time at the Greenwich meridian; the arc of the celestial equator, or the angle at the celestial pole, between the lower branch of the Greenwich celestial meridian and the hour circle of the mean sun, measured westward from the lower branch of the Greenwich celestial meridian through 24 hours; Greenwich hour angle of the mean sun expressed in time units, plus 12 hours. Also called UNIVERSAL TIME, ZULU TIME.

Greenwich meridian. The meridian through Greenwich, England, serving as the reference for Greenwich time, in contrast with LOCAL MERIDIAN. It is accepted almost universally as the PRIME MERIDIAN, or the origin of measurement of longitude.

Greenwich sidereal time. Local sidereal time at the Greenwich meridian; the arc of the celestial equator, or the angle at the celestial pole, between the upper branch of the Greenwich celestial meridian and the hour circle of the vernal equinox, measured westward from the upper branch of the Greenwich celestial meridian through 24 hours; Greenwich hour angle of the vernal equinox expressed in time units.

Greenwich time. Time based upon the Greenwich meridian as reference.

grid, n. 1. A series of lines, usually straight and parallel, superimposed on a chart or plotting sheet to serve as a directional reference for navigation. 2. Two sets of mutually perpendicular lines dividing a map or chart into squares or rectangles to permit location of any point by a system of rectangular coordinates. Also called REFERENCE GRID.

groin, n. A structure (usually one of a group) extending approximately perpendicular from a shore to protect the shore from erosion by tides currents, or waves or to trap sand for making a beach.

ground swell. A long, deep swell or undulation of the ocean often caused by a long-continued gale and sometimes a seismic disturbance and felt even at a remote distance. In shallow water the swell rises to a prominent height.

ground tackle. The anchors, anchor chains, fittings, etc., used for anchoring a vessel.

groundwave. A radio wave that is propagated over the earth and is ordinarily influenced by the presence of the ground and the troposphere. Except for ionospheric and tropospheric waves, the groundwave includes all components of a radio wave.

group flashing light. A flashing light in which the flashes are combined in groups, each group having the same number of flashes, and in which the groups are repeated at regular intervals. The eclipses separating the flashes within each group are of equal duration and this duration is clearly shorter than the duration of the eclipse between two successive groups.

group occulting light. An occulting light in which the occultations are combined in groups, each group including the same number of occultations, and in which the groups are repeated at regular intervals. The intervals of light separating the occultations within each group are of equal duration, and this duration is clearly shorter than the duration of the interval of light between two successive groups.

group quick light. A quick-flashing light in which a specified group of flashes is regularly repeated.

group repetition interval. The specified time interval of a Loran-C chain for all stations of the chain to transmit their pulse groups. For each chain a minimum group repetition interval (GRI) is selected of sufficient duration to provide time for each station to transmit its pulse group and additional time between each pulse group so that signals from two or more stations cannot overlap in time anywhere within the coverage area. The GRI is normally stated in terms of tens of microseconds; i.e., the GRI having a duration of 79,900 microseconds is stated as 7900.

group repetition interval code. The group repetition interval in microseconds divided by 10.

group very-quick light. A very-quick-flashing light in which a specified group of flashes is regularly repeated.

gulf, n. A major indentation of the sea into the land, usually larger than a bay.

Gulf Coast Low Water Datum (GCLWD). Defined as mean lower low water when the type of tide is mixed and mean low water when the type of tide is diurnal. GCLWD was used as chart tidal datum from November 14, 1977, to November 28, 1980, for the coastal waters of the gulf coast of the United States.

Gulf Stream. A warm, well-defined, swift, relatively narrow ocean current that originates where the Florida Current and the Antilles Current meet north of Grand Bahama Island. It gains its impetus from the large volume of water that flows through the Straits of Florida. Near the edge of the Grand Banks of Newfoundland extensions of the Gulf Stream and the Labrador Current continue as the NORTH ATLANTIC CURRENT, which fans outward and widens in a northeastward to eastward flow across the ocean. The Florida Current, the Gulf Stream, and the North Atlantic Current together form the GULF STREAM SYSTEM. Sometimes the entire system is referred to as the Gulf Stream. The Gulf Stream forms the western and northwestern part of the general clockwise oceanic circulation of the North Atlantic Ocean.

gust, n. 1. A sudden brief increase in the speed of the wind of more transient character than a squall, and followed by a lull or slackening of the wind. 2. The violet wind or squall that accompanies a thunderstorm.

gyre, n. A closed circulatory system, larger than a whirlpool or eddy.

gyrocompass, n. A north-seeking compass having one or more gyroscopes as the directive element. Its operation depends upon four natural phenomena, namely gyroscopic inertia, gyroscopic precession, the earth's rotation, and gravity. When such a compass controls remote indicators, called GYRO REPEATER, it is called a master gyrocompass.

gyro error. The error in the reading of the gyrocompass, expressed in degrees east or west to indicate the direction in which the axis of the compass is offset from true north.

gyropilot, n. An automatic device for steering a vessel by means of control signals received from a gyrocompass. Also called AUTOPILOT.

gyro repeater. A device that displays at a different location the indications of the master gyrocompass.

gyroscope, n. A rapidly rotating mass free to move about one or both axes perpendicular to the axis of rotation and to each other. It is characterized by GYROSCOPIC INERTIA and PRECESSION. Usually shortened to GYRO. The term also refers colloquially to the GYROCOMPASS.

H

hail, n. Frozen precipitation consisting of ice balls or irregular lumps of ice of varying size, ranging from that of a raindrop to an inch or considerably more. They are composed of clear ice or of alternate layers of ice and snow, and may fall detached or frozen together into irregular lumps. Hail is usually associated with thunderstorms. A hailstone is a single unit of hail. Small hail consists of snow pellets surrounded by a very thin ice covering.

half tide. The condition or time of the tide when midway between high and low.

half-tide level. A tidal datum midway between mean high water and mean low water. Mean sea level may coincide with half-tide level, but seldom does; the variation is generally about 3 centimeters and rarely exceeds 6 centimeters. Also called MEAN TIDE LEVEL.

halo, n. Any of a group of optical phenomena caused by refraction or reflection of light by ice crystals in the atmosphere. The most common form is a ring of light of radius 22° or 46° around the sun or moon.

harbor, n. 1. A body of water providing protection for vessels and, generally, anchorage and docking facilities. 2. A haven or space of deep water so sheltered by the adjacent land as to afford a safe anchorage for ships.

harvest moon. The full moon occurring nearest the autumnal equinox.

haul, v., i. 1. A counterclockwise change in direction of the wind. 2. A shift in the direction of the wind forward. The opposite is to VEER.

haul, v., t. To change the course of a sailing vessel to bring the wind farther forward, usually used with up, such as haul up.

heading, n. The horizontal direction in which a ship actually points or heads at any instant, expressed in angular units from a reference direction, usually from 000° at the reference direction clockwise through 360°. Heading is often designated as true, magnetic, compass, or grid. Heading should not be confused with COURSE, which is the intended direction of movement through the water. At a specific instant the heading may or may not coincide with the course. The heading of a ship is also called SHIP'S HEAD.

heading angle. Heading measured from 0° at the reference direction clockwise or counterclockwise through 90° or 180°. It is labeled with the reference direction as a prefix and the direction of measurement from the reference direction as a suffix.

heading flasher. An illuminated radial line on the radar for indicating one's own ship's heading on the bearing dial. Also called HEADING MARKER.

heading line. The line extending in the direction of a heading.

head sea. A sea in which the waves move in a direction approximately opposite to the heading. The opposite is FOLLOWING SEA.

head tide. A tidal current setting in a direction approximately opposite to the heading of a vessel. One setting in such a direction as to increase the speed of a vessel is called a FAIR TIDE. One abeam is called a BEAM TIDE. One approximately 90° from the course is called a CROSS TIDE.

headway, n. Motion in a forward direction. Motion in the opposite direction is called STERNWAY.

head wind. Wind from ahead of the vessel.

heat lightning. A flash of light from an electric discharge, without thunder, believed to be the reflection by haze or clouds of a distant flash of lightning, too far away for the thunder to be audible.

heave, n. The oscillatory vertical rise and fall, due to the entire hull being lifted by the force of the sea. Also called HEAVING.

heel, n. Lateral inclination of a vessel.

heel, v., t. & i. To incline or be inclined to one side.

height, n. Vertical distance above a datum.

height of eye correction. The correction to sextant altitude due to dip of the horizon. Also called DIP CORRECTION.

height of tide. Vertical distance from the chart sounding datum to the water surface at any stage of the tide. It is positive if the water level is higher than the chart sounding datum. The vertical distance from the chart sounding datum to a high water datum is called RISE OF TIDE.

helm, n. The apparatus by which a vessel is steered; the tiller or wheel.

hertz, n. The special name for the derived unit of frequency in the International System of Units, it is one cycle per second.

Hevelian halo. A faint white halo consisting of a ring occasionally seen 90° from the sun, and probably caused by the refraction and internal reflection of the sun's light by bi-pyramidal ice crystals.

hexagon, n. A closed plane figure having six sides.

high, n. An area of high pressure. Since a high is, on a synoptic chart, always associated with anticyclonic circulation, the term is used interchangeably with ANTICYCLONE.

high clouds. Types of clouds the mean lower level of which is above 20,000 feet. The principal clouds in this group are cirrus, cirrocumulus, and cirrostratus.

higher high water. The higher of the two high waters of any tidal day.

higher lower water. The higher of the two low waters of any tidal day.

high fidelity. The ability to reproduce modulating waves at various audio frequencies without serious distortion.

high frequency. Radio frequency of 3 to 30 megahertz.

high water. The maximum height reached by a rising tide. The height may be due solely to the periodic tidal forces or it may have superimposed upon it the effects of prevailing meteorological conditions. Use of the synonymous term HIGH TIDE is discouraged.

high water inequality. The difference between the heights of the two high waters during a tidal day.

high water line. 1. The intersection of the land with the water surface at an elevation of high water. 2. The line along the shore to which the waters normally reach at high water.

high water mark. A line or mark left upon tide flats, beach, or alongshore objects indicating the elevation of the intrusion of high water. It should not be confused with the MEAN HIGH WATER LINE or MEAN HIGHER HIGH WATER LINE.

high water springs. Short for MEAN HIGH WATER SPRINGS.

high water stand. The condition at high water when there is no sensible change in the height of the water. A similar condition at low water is called LOW WATER STAND.

holding ground. The bottom ground of an anchorage. The expression is usually used with a modifying adjective to indicate the quality of the holding power of the material constituting the bottom.

hook, n. A feature resembling a hook in shape, particularly a spit or narrow cape of sand or gravel that turns landward at the outer end or a sharp bend or curve, as in a stream.

hop, n. Travel of a radio wave to the ionosphere and back to earth. The number of hops a radio signal has experienced is usually designated by the expression one-hop, two-hop, multihop, etc.

H.O. Pub. No. 214. *Tables of Computed Altitude and Azimuth*. A nine-volume set of sight reduction tables of the inspection type published between 1936 and 1946 by the U.S. Navy Hydrographic Office and reprinted from time to time until discontinued on December 31, 1973, by the successor, the Defense Mapping Agency Hydrographic/Topographic Center. These tables were superseded by Pub. No. 229, *Sight Reduction Tables for Marine Navigation*.

horizon, n. The great circle of the celestial sphere midway between the zenith and nadir, or a line resembling or approximating such a circle. A radio horizon is the line at which direct rays from a transmitting antenna become tangent to the earth's surface. A radar horizon is the radio horizon of a radar antenna.

horizon glass. The glass of a marine sextant, attached to the frame, through which the horizon is observed. The half of this glass nearer the frame is silvered to form the HORIZON MIRROR for reflecting the image of a celestial body; the other half is clear.

horizon mirror. The mirror part of the horizon glass. The expression is sometimes used somewhat loosely to refer to the horizon glass.

horizon prism. A prism that can be inserted in the optical path of an instrument, such as a bubble sextant, to permit observation of the visible horizon.

horizontal geodetic datum. The basis for computations of horizontal control surveys in which the curvature of the earth is considered.

horizontal parallax. The geocentric parallax when a body is on the horizon. The expression is usually used only in connection with the moon, for which the tabulated horizontal parallax is given for an observer on the equator. The parallax at any altitude is called PARALLAX IN ALTITUDE.

horse latitudes. The regions of calms and variable winds coinciding with the subtropical high-pressure belts on the poleward sides of the trade winds. The expression is generally applied only to the northern of these two regions in the North Atlantic Ocean or to the portion of it near Bermuda.

hour, n. 1. A 24th part of a day. 2. A specified interval.

hour angle. Angular distance west of a celestial meridian or hour circle; the arc of the celestial equator, or the angle at the celestial pole, between the upper branch of a celestial meridian or hour circle and the hour circle of a celestial body or the vernal equinox, measured westward through 360°. It is usually further designated as local, Greenwich, or sidereal as the origin of measurement is the local or Greenwich celestial meridian or the hour circle of the vernal equinox.

hour circle. On the celestial sphere, a great circle through the celestial poles. An hour circle through the zenith is called a celestial meridian. Also called CIRCLE OF DECLINATION, CIRCLE OF RIGHT ASCENSION.

humidity, n. The amount of water vapor in the air. The mass of water vapor per unit volume of air is called absolute humidity. The mass of water vapor per unit mass of moist air is called specific humidity. The ratio of the actual vapor pressure to the vapor pressure corresponding to saturation at the prevailing temperature is called relative humidity.

hunter's moon. The full moon next following the harvest moon.

hunting, n. Fluctuation about a mid-point due to instability, as oscillations of the needle of an instrument about the zero point.

hurricane, n. Wind of force 12 (64 knots and higher or 73 miles per hour and higher) on the Beaufort wind scale.

hydraulic current. A current in a channel caused by a difference in the surface level at the two ends. Such a current may be expected in a strait connecting two bodies of water in which the tides differ in time or range. The current in the East River, NY, connecting Long Island Sound and New York Harbor, is an example.

hydrographic datum. A datum used for referencing depths of water or the heights of predicted tides.

hydrographic survey. The survey of a water area, with particular reference to submarine relief, and any adjacent land.

hydrography, n. The science that deals with the measurement and description of the physical features of the oceans, seas, lakes, rivers, and their adjoining coastal areas, with particular reference to their use for navigation.

hydrology, n. The scientific study of the waters of the earth, especially with relation to the effects of precipitation and evaporation upon the occurrence and character of ground water.

hydrosphere, n. The water portion of the earth as distinguished from the solid part, called the LITHOSPHERE, and from the gaseous outer envelope, called the ATMOSPHERE.

hygrometer, n. An instrument for measuring the humidity of the air. The most common type is a psychrometer consisting of dry-bulb and wet-bulb thermometers.

hyperbola, n. An open curve with two parts, all points of which have a constant difference in distance from two fixed points called FOCI.

hyperbolic lattice. A pattern formed by two or more families of intersecting hyperbolas.

hyperbolic line of position. A line of position in the shape of a hyperbola, determined by measuring the difference in distance to two fixed points. Loran-C lines of position are an example.

hyperbolic navigation. Radionavigation based on the measurement of the time differences in the reception of signals from several pairs of synchronized transmitters. For each pair of transmitters the isochrones are substantially hyperbolic. The combination of isochrones for two or more pairs of transmitters forms a hyperbolic lattice within which position can be determined according to the measured time differences.

hypotenuse, n. The side of a plane right triangle opposite the right angle; the longest side of a plane right triangle.

I

IALA Maritime Buoyage System. A uniform system of maritime buoyage that is now implemented by most maritime nations. Within the single system there are two buoyage regions, designated as Region A and Region B, where lateral marks differ only in the colors of port and starboard hand marks. In Region A, red is to port on entering; in Region B, red is to starboard on entering. The system is a combined cardinal and lateral system, and applies to all fixed and floating marks, other than lighthouses, sector lights, leading lights and marks, lightships, and large navigational buoys.

iceberg, n. A massive piece of ice greatly varying in shape, showing more than 5 meters above the sea surface, that has broken away from a glacier, and that may be afloat or aground. Icebergs may be described as tabular, dome shaped, pinnacled, drydock, glacier or weathered, blocky, tilted blocky, or drydock icebergs. For reports to the International Ice Patrol they are described with respect to size as small, medium, or large icebergs.

improved channels. Dredged channels under the jurisdiction of the U.S. Army Corps of Engineers, and maintained to provide an assigned CONTROLLING DEPTH. Symbolized on National Ocean Survey charts by black, broken lines to represent side limits, with the controlling depth and date of the survey given together with a tabulation of more detailed information.

incineration area. An officially designated offshore area for the burning of chemical waste by specially equipped vessels. The depiction of incineration areas on charts (in conjunction with radio warnings) is necessary to ensure that passing vessels do not mistake the burning of waste for a vessel on fire.

inclination of an orbit. As defined by the International Telecommunication Union (ITU), the angle determined by the plane containing an orbit and the plane of the earth's equator.

increment, n. A change in the value of a variable. A negative increment is also called DECREMENT.

independent surveillance. Position determination by means requiring no cooperation from the craft or vehicle.

index (pl. indices or indexes), n. 1. A mark on the scale of an instrument, diagram, etc., to indicate the origin of measurement. 2. A pointer or part of an instrument that points to a value, like the needle of a gauge. 3. A list or diagram serving as a guide to a book, set of charts, etc. 4. A ratio or value used as a basis for comparison of other values.

index arm. A slender bar carrying an index, particularly the bar that pivots at the center of curvature of the arc of a marine sextant and carries the index and the vernier or micrometer.

index correction. The correction due to index error.

index error. The error in the reading of an instrument equal to the difference between the zero of the scale and the zero of the index. In a marine sextant it is due primarily to lack of parallelism of the index mirror and the horizon glass at zero reading.

index mirror. The mirror attached to the index arm of a marine sextant. The bubble or pendulum sextant counterpart is called INDEX PRISM. Also called INDEX GLASS.

index prism. A sextant prism that can be rotated to any angle corresponding to altitudes between established limits. It is the bubble or pendulum sextant counterpart of the INDEX MIRROR of a marine sextant.

Indian summer. An indefinite and irregular period of mild, calm, hazy weather often occurring in autumn or early winter, especially in the United States and Canada.

indirect echo. A radar echo caused by the electromagnetic energy being transmitted to the target by an indirect path and returned as an echo along the same path. An indirect echo may appear on the radar display when the main lobe of the radar beam is reflected off part of the structure of the ship (the stack for example) from which it is reflected to the target. Returning to one's own ship by the same indirect path, the echo appears on the PPI at the bearing of the reflecting surface. Also called FALSE ECHO.

indirect wave. A radio wave that reaches a given reception point by a path from the transmitting point other than the direct line path between the two. An example is the SKYWAVE received after reflection from one of the layers of the ionosphere.

in extremis. Condition in which either course or speed changes or both are required on the part of both ships if the ships are to avoid collision.

inferior conjunction. The conjunction of an inferior planet and the sun when the planet is between the earth and the sun.

inferior planets. The planets with orbits smaller than that of the earth; Mercury and Venus.

infinity, n. Beyond finite limits. In navigation, a source of light is regarded as at infinity if it is at such a great distance that rays from it can be considered parallel. The sun, planets, and stars can be considered at infinity without serious error.

infrared, adj. Having a frequency immediately beyond the red end of the visible spectrum; rays of longer wavelength than visible light, but shorter than radio waves.

infrasonic, adj. Having a frequency below the audible range. Frequencies above the audible range are called ULTRASONIC.

initial great-circle course. The direction, at the point of departure, of the great circle through that point and the destination, expressed as the angular distance from a reference direction, usually north, to that part of the great circle extending toward the designation. Also called INITIAL GREAT-CIRCLE DIRECTION.

Inland Rules of the Road. Officially the Inland Navigation Rules. Rules to be followed by all vessels while navigating upon certain defined inland waters of the United States.

inland sea. A body of water nearly or completely surrounded by land, especially if very large or composed of salt water. If completely surrounded by land, it is usually called a LAKE. This should not be confused with CLOSED SEA, that part of the ocean enclosed by headlands, within narrow straits, etc., or within the territorial jurisdiction of a country.

inlet, n. A narrow body of water extending into the land from a larger body of water. A long, narrow inlet with gradually decreasing depth inward is called a ria. Also called ARM, TONGUE.

inner planets. The four planets nearest the sun; Mercury, Venus, Earth, and Mars.

in phase. The condition of two or more cyclic motions that are at the same part of their cycles at the same instant. Two or more cyclic motions that are not at the same part of their cycles at the same instant are said to be OUT OF PHASE.

inshore traffic zone. A routing measure comprising a designated area between the landward boundary of a traffic separation scheme and the adjacent coast, intended for local traffic.

insolation, n. Solar radiation received; the rate of delivery of such radiation.

instability line. Any non-frontal line or band of convective activity in the atmosphere. This is the general term and includes the developing, mature, and dissipating stages. However, when the mature stage consists of a line of active thunderstorms, it is properly called SQUALL LINE; therefore, in practice, instability line often refers only to the less active phases. Instability lines are usually hundreds of miles long (not necessarily continuous), 10 to 50 miles wide, and are most often formed in the warm sectors of wave cyclones. Unlike true fronts, they are transitory in character, ordinarily developing to maximum intensity in less than 12 hours and then dissipating in about the same time. Maximum intensity is usually attained in late afternoon.

instrument correction. That correction due to instrument error.

instrument error. The inaccuracy of an instrument due to imperfections within the instrument.

insular, adj. Of or pertaining to an island or islands.

integrated navigation system. A navigation system that comprises two or more positioning systems combined in such manner as to achieve performance better than either constituent system.

intercardinal heading. A heading in the direction of any of the intercardinal points.

intercardinal point. Any of the four directions midway between the cardinal points; northeast, southeast, southwest, or northwest. Also called QUADRANTAL POINT.

interlaced. Referring to a computer monitor that displays data by scanning alternate lines instead of each line sequentially.

international call sign. An alpha-numeric symbol assigned in accordance with the provisions of the International Telecommunications Union to identify a radio station. The nationality of the radio station is identified by the first three characters; also referred to as call letters or signal letters.

international chart. One of a coordinated series of small-scale charts for planning and long range navigation. The charts are prepared and published by different Member States of the International Hydrographic Organization using the same specifications.

International Great Lakes Datum (1955). Mean water level at Pointe-au-Pere, Quebec, on the Gulf of St. Lawrence over the period 1941–1956, from which dynamic elevations throughout the Great Lakes region are measured. The term is often used to mean the entire system of dynamic elevations rather than just the referenced water level.

International Hydrographic Organization. An institution formed in 1921, consisting of representatives of maritime nations organized for the purpose of coordinating the hydrographic work of the participating governments.

International Maritime Organization (IMO). A specialized agency of the United Nations responsible for maritime safety and efficiency of navigation. The IMO provides for cooperation among governments in the field of governmental regulations and practices relating to technical matters of all kinds affecting shipping engaged in international trade: to encourage the general adoption of the highest practicable standards in matters concerning maritime safety, efficiency of navigation, and the prevention and control of marine pollution from ships, and to deal with legal matters related to the purposes set out in Article 1 of the Convention.

International Nautical Mile. A unit of length equal to 1,852 meters, exactly.

international number. The number of a navigational light, assigned in accordance with the resolution adopted at the Fifth International Hydrographic Conference in 1949 by member nations of the International Hydrographic Bureau (now the International Hydrographic Organization). This number is in italic type and under the light list number in the light list.

International System of Units. A modern form of the metric system adopted in 1960 by the General Conference of Weights and Measures (CGPM). The units of the International System of Units (SI) are divided into three classes. The first class of SI units are the base units or the seven well-defined units that by convention are regarded as dimensionally independent: the meter, the kilogram, the second, the ampere, the kelvin, the mole, and the candela. The second class of SI units are the derived units, i.e., the units that can be formed by combining base units according to the algebraic relations linking the corresponding quantities. Several of these algebraic expressions in terms of base units can be replaced by special names and symbols that can themselves be used to form other derived units. The third class of SI units are the supplementary units, those units not yet classified by the CGPM as either base units or derived units.

interpolation, n. The process of determining intermediate values between given values in accordance with some known or assumed rate or system of change. Linear interpolation assumes that changes of tabulated values are proportional to changes in entering arguments. Interpolation is designated as single, double, or triple if there are one, two, or three arguments or variables respectively. The extension of the process of interpolation beyond the limits of known value is called EXTRAPOLATION.

interrupted quick-flashing light. A quick-flashing light (50–80 flashes per minute) is interrupted at regular intervals by eclipses of long duration.

interrupted quick light. A quick light in which the sequence of flashes is interrupted by regularly repeated eclipses of constant and long duration.

interrupted very quick light. A very quick light (80–160 flashes per minute) in which the sequence of flashes is interrupted by regularly repeated eclipses of long duration.

Intracoastal Waterway. An inside protected route for small craft and small commercial vessels extending through New Jersey; from Norfolk, Virginia, to Key West, Florida; across Florida from St. Lucie Inlet to Fort Myers, Charlotte Harbor, Tampa Bay, and Tarpon Springs; and from Carabelle, Florida, to Brownsville, Texas. Some portions are in exposed waters; some portions are very limited in depth.

inversion, n. In meteorology, a departure from the usual decrease or increase with altitude of the value of an atmospheric property. This term is almost always used to refer to a temperature inversion, an atmospheric condition in which the temperature increases with increasing altitude.

ion, n. An atom or group of atoms that has become electrically charged, either positively or negatively, by the loss or gain of one or more electrons.

ionization, n. The process by which neutral atoms or groups of atoms become electrically charged either positively or negatively, by the loss or gain of electrons; or the state of a substance whose atoms or groups of atoms have become thus charged.

ionized layers. Layers of charged particles existing in the upper reaches of the atmosphere as a result of solar radiation.

ionosphere, n. 1. The region of the atmosphere extending from about 40 to 250 miles above the earth's surface, in which there is appreciable ionization. The presence of charged particles in this region profoundly affects the propagation of certain electromagnetic radiation. 2. A region composed of highly ionized layers at varying heights above the surface of the earth that may cause the return to the earth of radio waves originating below these layers.

ionospheric correction. A correction for ionospheric refraction, a major potential source of error in all satellite radionavigation systems. Navigation errors can result from the effect of refraction on the measurement of the doppler shift and from the errors in the satellite's orbit if refraction is not accurately accounted for in the satellite tracking. The refraction contribution can be eliminated by the proper mixing of the received Doppler shift from two harmonically related frequencies to yield an accurate estimate of the vacuum doppler shift. Also called REFRACTION CORRECTION.

ionospheric error. The total systematic and random error resulting from the reception of a navigation signal after ionospheric reflections. It may be due to variations in transmission paths, non-uniform height of the ionosphere, or non-uniform propagation within the ionosphere. Also called IONOSPHERIC-PATH ERROR, SKYWAVE ERROR.

ionospheric storm. An ionospheric disturbance characterized by wide variations from normal in the state of the ionosphere, such as turbulence in the F-region, absorption increase, height increase, and ionization density decreases. The effects are most marked in high magnetic latitudes and are associated with abnormal solar activity.

irradiation, n. The apparent enlargement of a bright surface against a darker background.

island, n. An area of land not a continent, surrounded by water.

islet, n. A very small and minor island.

iso-. A prefix meaning equal.

isobar, n. A line connecting points having the same atmospheric pressure reduced to a common datum, usually sea level.

isolated danger mark (or buoy). An IALA navigation aid marking a danger with clear water all around; it has a double ball topmark and is black with at least one red band. If lighted its characteristic is Fl(2).

isophase, adj. Referring to a light having a characteristic of equal intervals of light and darkness.

isthmus, n. A narrow strip of land connecting two larger portions of land. A submarine elevation joining two land areas and separating two basins or depressions by a depth less than that of the basins is called a submarine isthmus.

J

jetsam, n. Articles that sink when thrown overboard, particularly those jettisoned for the purpose of lightening a vessel in distress.

jet stream. Relatively strong winds (50 knots or greater) concentrated in a narrow stream in the atmosphere. It usually refers only to a quasihorizontal stream of maximum winds imbedded in the middle latitude westerlies and concentrated in the high troposphere.

jetty, n. A structure built out into the water to restrain or direct currents, usually to protect a river mouth or harbor entrance from silting, etc.

Julian calendar. A revision of the ancient calendar of the city of Rome, instituted in the Roman Empire by Julius Caesar in 46 B.C., that reached its final form in about 8 A.D. It consisted of a year of 365 days, with an intercalary day every fourth year. The current Gregorian calendar is the same as the Julian calendar except that October 5, 1582, of the Julian calendar became October 15, 1582, of the Gregorian calendar, and, of the centurial years, only those divisible by 400 are leap years.

junction buoy. A buoy that, when viewed from a vessel approaching from the open sea or in the same direction as the main stream of flood current, or in the direction established by appropriate authority, indicates the place at which two channels meet.

junction mark. A navigation mark that, when viewed from a vessel approaching from the open sea or in the same direction as the main stream of flood current, or in the direction established by appropriate authority, indicates the place at which two channels meet.

Jupiter, n. The navigational planet whose orbit lies between those of Mars and Saturn. Largest of the known planets.

K

katabatic wind. Any wind blowing down an incline. If the wind is warm, it is called a foehn; if cold, a fall wind. An ANABATIC WIND blows up an incline. Also called GRAVITY WIND.

kedge, v., t. To move a vessel by carrying out an anchor, letting it go, and winching the ship to the anchor.

kelp, n. 1. A family of seaweed found in cool to cold waters along rocky coasts, characterized by its extreme length. 2. Any large seaweed. 3. The ashes of seaweed.

kelvin, n. The base unit of thermodynamic temperature in the International System of Units; it is the fraction $1/273.16$ of the thermodynamic temperature of the triple point of water, which is −273.16°K.

Kelvin temperature. Temperature based upon a thermodynamic scale with its zero point at absolute zero (−273.16°C) and using Celsius degrees. Rankine temperature is based upon the Rankine scale starting at absolute zero (−459.69°F) and using Fahrenheit degrees.

kilo-. A prefix meaning one thousand.

kilobyte. One thousand bytes of information in a computer.

kilocycle, n. One thousand cycles, the term is often used as the equivalent of one thousand cycles per second.

kilogram, n. 1. The base unit of mass in the International System of Units; it is equal to the mass of the international prototype of the kilogram, which is made of platinum-iridium and kept at the International Bureau of Weights and Measures. 2. One thousand grams exactly, or 2.204623 pounds, approximately.

kilometer, n. One thousand meters; about 0.54 nautical mile, 0.62 U.S. Survey mile, or 3,281 feet.

knot, n. A unit of speed equal to 1 nautical mile per hour.

L

Lambert conformal map projection. A conformal map projection of the conic type, on which all geographic meridians are represented by straight lines that meet in a common point outside the limits of the map, and the geographic parallels are represented by a series of arcs of circles having this common point for a center. Meridians and parallels intersect at right angles, and angles on the earth are correctly represented.

land breeze. A breeze blowing from the land to the sea. It usually blows by night, when the sea is warmer than the land, and alternates with a SEA BREEZE, which blows in the opposite direction by day.

landfall, n. The first sighting of land when approached from seaward. By extension, the term is sometimes used to refer to the first contact with land by any means, as by radar.

landing, n. 1. A place where boats receive or discharge passengers, freight, etc. 2. Bringing of a vessel to a landing.

land sky. Dark streaks or patches or a grayness on the underside of extensive cloud areas, due to the absence of reflected light from bare ground. Land sky is not as dark as WATER SKY. The clouds above ice or snow covered surfaces have a white or yellowish white glare called ICE BLINK.

lapse rate. The rate of decrease of temperature in the atmosphere with height, or, sometimes, the rate of change of any meteorological element with height.

large navigational buoy (LNB). A large buoy designed to take the place of a lightship where construction of an offshore light station is not feasible. These buoys may show secondary lights from heights of about 30–40 feet above the water. In addition to the light, they may mount a radiobeacon and provide sound signals.

large scale. A scale involving a relatively small reduction in size. A large-scale chart is one covering a small area. The opposite is SMALL SCALE.

last quarter. The phase of the moon when it is near west quadrature, when the eastern half of it is visible to an observer on the earth.

lateral mark. A navigation aid intended to mark the sides of a channel or waterway.

lateral system. A system of aids to navigation in which the shape, color, and number are assigned in accordance with their location relative to navigable waters.

latitude, n. Angular distance from a primary great circle or plane. Terrestrial latitude is angular distance from the equator, measured northward or southward through 90° and labeled N or S to indicate the direction of measurement. A parallel of latitude is a circle (or approximation of a circle) of the earth, parallel to the equator, and connecting points of equal latitude, or is a circle of the celestial sphere, parallel to the ecliptic. Celestial latitude is angular distance north or south of the ecliptic.

latitude line. A line of position extending in a generally east-west direction. Sometimes called OBSERVED LATITUDE.

lattice, n. A pattern formed by two or more families of intersecting lines, such as that pattern formed by two or more families of hyperbolas representing, for example, curves of equal time difference associated with a hyperbolic radionavigation system. Sometimes the term pattern is used to indicate curves of equal time difference, with the term lattice being used to indicate its representation on the chart.

L-band. A radio-frequency band of 390 to 1,550 megahertz.

lead, n. A weight attached to a line. A sounding lead is used for determining depth of water.

leading line. On a nautical chart, a straight line, drawn through leading marks. A ship moving along such line will clear certain dangers or remain in the best channel.

lead line. A line, graduated with attached marks and fastened to a sounding lead, used for determining the depth of water when making soundings by hand. The lead line is usually used in depths of less than 25 fathoms. Also called SOUNDING LINE.

leap second. A step adjustment to Coordinated Universal Time (UTC) to maintain it within 0.95s of UT1. The 1-second adjustments, when necessary, are normally made at the end of June or December. Because of the variations in the rate of rotation of the earth, the occurrences of the leap second adjustments are not predictable in detail.

leap year. A calendar year having 366 days as opposed to the COMMON YEAR having 365 days. Each year exactly divisible by 4 is a leap year, except century years (1800, 1900, etc.), which must be exactly divisible by 400 (2000, 2400, etc.) to be leap years.

lee, adj., Referring to the downwind or sheltered side of an object.

lee, n. The sheltered area on the downwind side of an object.

lee shore. As observed from a ship, the shore toward which the wind is blowing.

lee side. The side of a craft that is away from the wind and therefore sheltered.

leeward, adj. & adv. Toward the lee or in the general direction toward which the wind is blowing. The opposite is WINDWARD.

leeway, n. The leeward motion of a vessel due to wind.

leeway angle. The angular difference between a vessel's course and the track due to the effect of wind in moving a vessel bodily to leeward.

leg, n. A part of a ship's track line that can be represented by a single course line.

legend, n. A title or explanation on a chart, diagram, illustration, etc.

lens, n. A piece of glass or transparent material with plane, convex, or concave surfaces adapted for changing the direction of light rays to enlarge or reduce the apparent size of objects.

levee, n. 1. An artificial bank confining a stream channel or limiting adjacent areas subject to flooding. 2. On the sea floor, an embankment bordering a canyon, valley, or sea channel.

light air. Wind of force 1 (1 to 3 knots or 1 to 3 miles per hour) on the Beaufort wind scale.

light attendant station. A shore unit established for the purpose of servicing minor aids to navigation within an assigned area.

light breeze. Wind of force 2 (4 to 6 knots or 4 to 7 miles per hour) on the Beaufort wind scale.

lighted beacon. A beacon exhibiting a light. Also called LIGHT-BEACON.

lighted buoy. A buoy exhibiting a light.

lightering area. An area designated for handling ship's cargo by barge or lighter.

light-float, n. A buoy having a boat-shaped body. Light-floats are usually unmanned and are used instead of smaller lighted buoys in waters where strong currents are experienced.

lighthouse, n. A distinctive structure exhibiting a major navigation light.

light list. A publication giving detailed information regarding lighted navigational aids and fog signals. In the United States, lights lists are published by the U.S. Coast Guard as USCG Light Lists and by the National Imagery and Mapping Agency as List of Lights.

light list number. The sequential number used to identify a navigational light in the light list. This may or may not be the same as the INTERNATIONAL NUMBER, which is an identifying number assigned by the International Hydrographic Organization. The international number is in italic type and is located under the light list number in the list.

light sector. As defined by bearings from seaward, the sector in which a navigational light is visible or in which it has a distinctive color different from that of adjoining sectors, or in which it is obscured.

lightship, n. A distinctively marked vessel providing aids to navigation services similar to a light station, i.e., a light of high intensity and reliability, sound signal, and radiobeacon, and moored at a station where erection of a fixed structure is not feasible. Most lightships are anchored to a very long scope of chain and, as a result, the radius of their swinging circle is considerable. The chart symbol represents the approximate location of the anchor. Also called LIGHT VESSEL.

lights in line. Two or more lights so situated that when observed in transit they define the alignment of a submarine cable, the limit of an area, an alignment for use in anchoring, etc. Not to be confused with RANGE LIGHTS, which mark a direction to be followed.

light station. A manned station providing a light usually of high intensity and reliability. It may also provide sound signal and radiobeacon services.

light-year, n. A unit of length equal to the distance light travels in 1 year, equal to about 5.88×10^{12} miles. This unit is used as a measure of stellar distances.

limb, n. 1. The graduated curved part of an instrument for measuring angles, such as the part of a marine sextant carrying the altitude scale or ARC. 2. The circular outer edge of a celestial body, usually referred to with the designation upper or lower.

linear, adj. 1. Of or pertaining to a line. 2. Having a relation such that a change in one quantity is accompanied by an exactly proportional change in a related quantity.

linear interpolation. Interpolation in which changes of tabulated values are assumed to be proportional to changes in entering arguments.

linear light. A luminous signal having perceptible length, as contrasted with a POINT LIGHT, which does not have perceptible length.

line blow. A strong wind on the equator side of an anticyclone, probably so called because there is little shifting of wind direction during the blow, as contrasted with the marked shifting that occurs with a cyclonic windstorm.

line of force. A line indicating the direction in which a force acts, as in a magnetic field.

line of position. A plotted line on which a vessel is located, determined by observation or measurement. Also called POSITION LINE.

line of sight. The straight line, between two

points, that does not follow the curvature of the earth.

line squall. A squall that occurs along a squall line.

list, n. Inclination to one side. LIST generally implies equilibrium in an inclined condition caused by uneven distribution of mass aboard the vessel itself, while HEEL implies either a continuing or momentary inclination caused by an outside force, such as the wind. The term ROLL refers to the oscillatory motion of a vessel rather than its inclined condition.

list, v., t. & i. To incline or be inclined to one side.

little brother. A secondary tropical cyclone sometimes following a more severe disturbance.

littoral, adj. & n. 1. A littoral region. 2. The marine environment influenced by a land mass. 3. Of or pertaining to a shore, especially a seashore.

load line marks. Markings stamped and painted amidships on the side of a vessel, to indicate the minimum permissible freeboard. Also called PLIMSOLL MARKS.

local apparent noon. Twelve o'clock local apparent time or the instant the apparent sun is over the upper branch of the local meridian. Local apparent noon at the Greenwich meridian is called Greenwich apparent noon. Sometimes called HIGH NOON.

local apparent time. The arc of the celestial equator, or the angle at the celestial pole, between the lower branch of the local celestial meridian and the hour circle of the apparent or true sun, measured westward from the lower branch of the local celestial meridian through 24 hours; local hour angle of the apparent or true sun, expressed in time units, plus 12 hours. Local apparent time at the Greenwich meridian is called Greenwich apparent time.

local hour angle (LHA). Angular distance west of the local celestial meridian; the arc of the celestial equator, or the angle at the celestial pole, between the upper branch of the local celestial meridian and the hour circle of a point on the celestial sphere, measured westward from the local celestial meridian through 360°. The local hour angle at longitude 0° is called Greenwich hour angle.

local knowledge. The term applied to specialized, detailed knowledge of a port, harbor, or other navigable water considered necessary for safe navigation. Local knowledge extends beyond that available in charts and publications, being more detailed, intimate, and current.

local magnetic disturbance. An anomaly of the magnetic field of the earth, extending over a relatively small area, due to local magnetic influences. Also called LOCAL ATTRACTION, MAGNETIC ANOMALY.

local mean time. The arc of the celestial equator, or the angle at the celestial pole, between the lower branch of the local celestial meridian and the hour circle of the mean sun, measured westward from the lower branch of the local celestial meridian through 24 hours; local hour angle of the mean sun, expressed in time units, plus 12 hours. Local mean time at the Greenwich meridian is called Greenwich mean time, or Universal Time.

local meridian. The meridian through any particular place of observer, serving as the reference for local time, in contrast with GREENWICH MERIDIAN.

local noon. Noon at the local meridian.

Local Notice to Mariners. A notice issued by each U.S. Coast Guard District to disseminate important information affecting navigational safety within the district. The *Local Notice* reports changes to and deficiencies in aids to navigation maintained by and under the authority of the U.S. Coast Guard. It may be obtained, free of charge, by making application to the appropriate Coast Guard District Commander.

local time. Time based upon the local meridian as reference, as contrasted with that based upon a standard meridian. Local time was in general use in the United States until 1883, when standard time was adopted. 2. Any time kept locally.

lock, n. A basin in a waterway with caissons or gates at each end by means of which vessels are passed from one water level to another.

lock, v., t. To pass through a lock, referred to as locking through.

lock on. To identify and begin to continuously track a target in one or more coordinates (e.g., range, bearing, elevation).

log, n. 1. An instrument for measuring the speed or distance or both traveled by a vessel. 2. A written record of the movements of a craft, with regard to courses, speeds, positions, and other information of interest to navigators, and of important happenings aboard the craft. The book in which the log is kept is called a LOG BOOK. Also called DECK LOG.

long-flashing light. A navigation light with a duration of flash of not less than 2 seconds.

longitude, n. Angular distance, along a primary great circle, from the adopted reference point. Terrestrial longitude is the arc of a parallel, or the angle at the pole, between the prime meridian and the meridian of a point on the earth measured eastward or westward from the prime meridian through 180°, and labeled E or W to indicate the direction of measurement.

longitude line. A line of position extending in a generally north-south direction. Sometimes called OBSERVED LONGITUDE.

long-range systems. Radionavigation systems providing positioning capability on the high seas. Loran-C is an example.

longshore current. A current paralleling the shore largely within the surf zone. It is caused by the excess water brought to the zone by the small net mass transport of wind waves. Longshore currents feed into rip currents.

loom, n. The diffused glow observed from a light below the horizon, due to atmospheric scattering of its light rays.

looming, n. 1. An apparent elevation of distant terrestrial objects by abnormal atmospheric refraction. Because of looming, objects below the horizon are sometimes visible. The opposite is SINKING. 2. The appearance indistinctly of an object during a period of low visibility.

loran, n. The general designation of a type of radionavigation system by which a hyperbolic line of position is determined through measuring the difference in the times of reception of synchronized signals from two fixed transmitters. The name loran is derived from the words long range navigation.

Loran-A, n. A long-range medium-frequency (1850–1950 kHz) radionavigation system by which a hyperbolic line of position of medium accuracy was obtained. System operation in U.S. waters was terminated on December 31, 1980.

Loran-C, n. A long-range, low-frequency (90–110 kHz) radionavigation system by which a hyperbolic line of position of high accuracy is obtained by measuring the difference in the times of arrival of signals radiated by a pair of synchronized transmitters (master station and secondary station), which are separated by several hundred miles.

Loran-C reliability diagram. One of a series of charts that depict the following data for the area covered: (1) for each station of the chain, predicted maximum usable groundwave signal limits for signal-to-noise ratios of 1:3 and 1:10, and (2) contours that indicate the regions within which positions can be fixed with repeatable accuracies of 500, 750, or 1,500 feet or better on a 95-percent probability basis.

low, n. Short for area of low pressure. Since a low is, on a synoptic chart, always associated with cyclonic circulation, the term is used interchangeably with CYCLONE.

low clouds. Types of clouds the mean level of which is between the surface and 6,500 feet. The principal clouds in this group are stratocumulus, stratus, and nimbostratus.

lower branch. The half of a meridian or celestial meridian, from pole to pole, that passes through the antipode or nadir of a place.

lower high water. The lower of the two high waters of any tidal day.

lower limb. The lower edge (closest to the horizon) of a celestial body having measurable diameter; opposite is the UPPER LIMB or the upper edge.

lower low water. The lower of the two low waters of any tidal day.

lower low water datum. An approximation of mean lower low water that has been adopted as a standard reference for a limited area and is retained for an indefinite period regardless of the fact that it may differ slightly from a better determination of mean lower low water from a subsequent series of observations. Used primarily for river and harbor engineering purposes. Columbia River lower low water datum is an example.

lower transit. Transit of the lower branch of the celestial meridian. Transit of the upper branch is called UPPER TRANSIT. Also called INFERIOR TRANSIT, LOWER CULMINATION.

low water. The minimum height reached by a falling tide. The height may be due solely to the periodic tidal forces or it may have superimposed upon it the effects of meteorological conditions.

low water datum. The dynamic elevation for each of the Great Lakes, Lake St. Clair, and the corresponding sloping surfaces of the St. Marys, St. Clair, Detroit, Niagara, and St. Lawrence Rivers to which are referred the depths shown on the navigation charts and the authorized depths for navigation improvement projects.

low water equinoctial springs. Low water spring tides near the times of the equinoxes. Expressed in terms of the harmonic constituents, it is an elevation depressed below mean sea level by an amount equal to the sum of the amplitudes of certain constituents as given in the *Tide and Current Glossary* published by the National Ocean Survey.

low water line. The intersection of the land with the water surface at an elevation of low water.

low water springs. Short for MEAN LOW WATER SPRINGS.

low water stand. The condition at low water when there is no sensible change in the height of the tide. A similar condition at high water is called HIGH WATER STAND.

lubber's line. A reference line on a compass marking the reading that coincides with the heading.

lubber's line error. The angular difference between the heading as indicated by a lubber's line, and the actual heading; the horizontal angle, at the center of an instrument, between a line through the lubber's line and one parallel to the keel.

lumen, n. The derived unit of luminous flux in the International System of Units; it is the luminous flux emitted within unit solid angle (1 steradian) by a point source having a uniform luminous intensity of 1 candela.

luminous, adj. Emitting or reflecting light.

luminous flux. The quantity characteristic of radiant flux that expresses its capacity to produce a luminous sensation, evaluated according to the values of spectral luminous efficiency. Unless otherwise indicated, the luminous flux relates to photopic vision and is connected with the radiant flux in accordance with the formula adopted in 1948 by the International Commission on Illumination. The derived unit of luminous flux in the International System of Units is the LUMEN.

luminous range diagram. A diagram used to convert the nominal range of a light to its luminous range under existing conditions.

lunar, adj. Of or pertaining to the moon.

lunar cycle. An ambiguous expression that has been applied to various cycles associated with the moon's motion, including CALLIPPIC CYCLE, METONIC CYCLE, NODE CYCLE, SYNODICAL MONTH, or LUNATION.

lunar day. 1. The duration of one rotation of the earth on its axis, with respect to the moon. Its average length is about 24 hours, 50 minutes of mean solar time. Also called TIDAL DAY. 2. The duration of one rotation of the moon on its axis, with respect to the sun.

lunar distance. The angle, at an observer on the earth, between the moon and another celestial body. This was the basis of a method formerly used to determine longitude at sea.

lunar eclipse. An eclipse of the moon. When the moon enters the shadow of the earth, it appears eclipsed to an observer on the earth. A lunar eclipse is penumbral when it enters only the penumbra of the earth's shadow, partial when part of its surface enters the umbra of the earth's shadow, and total if its entire surface is obscured by the umbra.

lunar tide. That part of the tide due solely to the tide-producing force of the moon. That part due to the tide-producing force of the sun is called SOLAR TIDE.

lunisolar effect. Gravitational effects caused by the attractions of the moon and of the sun.

M

mackerel sky. An area of sky with a formation of rounded and isolated cirrocumulus or altocumulus resembling the pattern of scales on the back of a mackerel.

magnetic annual change. The amount of secular change in the earth's magnetic field that occurs in 1 year.

magnetic annual variation. The small systematic temporal variation in the earth's magnetic field that occurs after the trend for secular change has been removed from the average monthly values.

magnetic bearing. Bearing relative to magnetic north; compass bearing corrected for deviation.

magnetic compass. A compass depending for its directive force upon the attraction of the horizontal component of the earth's magnetic field for a magnetized needle or sensing element free to turn in a horizontal direction.

magnetic course. Course relative to magnetic north; compass course corrected for deviation.

magnetic direction. Horizontal direction expressed as angular distance from magnetic north.

magnetic diurnal variation. Oscillations of the earth's magnetic field that have a periodicity of about a day and that depend to a close approximation only on local time and geographic latitude. Also called MAGNETIC DAILY VARIATION.

magnetic heading. Heading relative to magnetic north; compass heading corrected for deviation.

magnetic lines of force. Closed lines indicating by their direction the direction of magnetic influence.

magnetic meridian. A line of horizontal magnetic force of the earth. A compass needle without deviation lies in the magnetic meridian.

magnetic needle. A small, slender, magnetized bar that tends to align itself with magnetic lines of force.

magnetic north. The direction indicated by the north-seeking pole of a freely suspended magnetic needle, influenced only by the earth's magnetic field.

magnetic pole. 1. Either of the two places on the surface of the earth where the magnetic dip is 90°, that in the Northern Hemisphere being designated north magnetic pole, and that in the Southern Hemisphere being designated south magnetic pole. Also called MAGNETIC DIP POLE. 2. Either of those two points of a magnet where the magnetic force is greatest.

magnetic secular change. The gradual variation in the value of a magnetic element that occurs over a period of years.

magnetic storm. A disturbance in the earth's magnetic field, associated with abnormal solar activity, and capable of seriously affecting both radio and wire transmission.

magnetism, n. The phenomena associated

with magnetic fields and their effects upon magnetic materials, notably iron and steel. The magnetism of the earth is called terrestrial magnetism or geomagnetism.

magnetometer, n. An instrument for measuring the intensity and direction of the earth's magnetic field.

magnetron, n. An electron tube characterized by the interaction of electrons with the electric field of circuit element in crossed steady electric and magnetic fields to produce an alternating current power output. It is used to generate high power output in the ultra-high and super-high frequency bands.

magnitude, n. Relative brightness of a celestial body. The smaller (algebraically) the number indicating magnitude, the brighter the body. The expression first magnitude is often used somewhat loosely to refer to all bodies of magnitude 1.5 or brighter, including negative magnitudes.

magnitude ratio. The ratio of relative brightness of two celestial bodies differing in magnitude by 1.0. This ratio is 2.512, the fifth root of 100. A body of magnitude 1.0 is 2.512 times as bright as a body of magnitude 2.0, etc.

major light. A light of high intensity and reliability exhibited from a fixed structure or on marine site (except range lights). Major lights include primary seacoast lights and secondary lights.

maneuvering board. A polar coordinate plotting sheet devised to facilitate solution of problems involving relative movement.

manned light. A light operated and maintained by full-time resident personnel.

map, n. A representation, usually on a plane surface, of all or part of the surface of the earth, celestial sphere, or other area, showing relative size and position, according to a given projection, of the features represented. A chart that shows the distribution of meteorological conditions over an area at a given moment may be called a weather map.

map projection. A systematic drawing of lines on a plane surface to represent the parallels of latitude and the meridians of longitude of the earth or a section of the earth. A map projection may be established by analytical computation or may be constructed geometrically.

mare's tails. Long, slender, well-defined streaks of cirrus cloud that resemble horses' tails.

marigram, n. A graphic record of the rise and fall of the tide. The record is in the form of a curve, in which time is generally represented on the abscissa and the height of the tide on the ordinate.

marine climate. The type of climate characteristic of coastal areas, islands, and the oceans, the distinctive features of which are small annual and daily temperature range and high relative humidity in contrast with CONTINENTAL CLIMATE, which is characteristic of the interior of a large landmass, and the distinctive features of which are large annual and daily temperature range and dry air with few clouds.

marine light. A luminous or lighted aid to navigation intended primarily for marine navigation. One intended primarily for air navigation is called an AERONAUTICAL LIGHT.

marine radiobeacon. A radiobeacon whose service is intended primarily for the benefit of ships.

marine railway. A track, a wheeled cradle, and winching mechanism for hauling vessels out of the water so that the bottom can be exposed.

marine sanctuary. An area established under provisions of the Marine Protection, Research, and Sanctuaries Act of 1972, Public Law 92-532 (86 Stat. 1052), for the preservation and restoration of its conservation, recreational, ecological, or esthetic values. Such an area may lie in ocean waters as far seaward as the outer edge of the continental shelf, in coastal waters where the tide ebbs and flows, or in the Great Lakes and connecting waters.

marine sextant. A sextant designed primarily for marine navigation.

Maritime Safety Information (MSI). Designation of the IHO/IMO referring to navigational information of immediate importance to mariners, affecting the safety of life and/or property at sea.

mark, n. An artificial or natural object of easily recognizable shape or color, or both, situated in such a position that it may be identified on a chart. A fixed artificial navigation mark is often called a BEACON. This may be lighted or unlighted. Also called NAVIGATION MARK; SEAMARK.

mark, v., i. "Now" or "at this moment." A call used when simultaneous observations are being made, to indicate to the second person the moment a reading is to be made, as when the time of a celestial observation is to be noted; or the moment a reading is a prescribed value, as when the heading of a vessel is exactly a desired value.

marker buoy. A small, brightly painted moored float used to temporarily mark a location on the water while placing a buoy on station.

master compass. The main part of a remote-indicating compass system that determines direction for transmission to various repeaters.

master station. In a radionavigation system, the station of a chain that provides a reference by which the emissions of other (slave or secondary) stations are controlled.

masthead light. A fixed running light placed on the centerline of a vessel showing an unbroken white light over an arc of the horizon from dead ahead to 22.5° abaft the beam on either side of the vessel.

maximum thermometer. A thermometer that automatically registers the highest temperature occurring since its last setting. One that registers the lowest temperature is called a MINIMUM THERMOMETER.

mean higher high water. A tidal datum that is the average of the highest high water height of each tidal day observed over the National Tidal Datum Epoch. For stations with shorter series, simultaneous observational comparisons are made with a control tide station in order to derive the equivalent of a 19-year datum.

mean higher high water line. The intersection of the land with the water surface at the elevation of mean higher high water.

mean high water. A tidal datum, the average of all the high water heights observed over the National Tidal Datum Epoch. For stations with shorter series, simultaneous observational comparisons are made with a control tide station in order to derive the equivalent of a 19-year datum.

mean high water line. The intersection of the land with the water surface at the elevation of mean high water.

mean latitude. Half the arithmetical sum of the latitudes of two places on the same side of the equator. Mean latitude is labeled N or S to indicate whether it is north or south of the equator. The expression is occasionally used with reference to two places on opposite sides of the equator, but this usage is misleading as it lacks the significance usually associated with the expression. When the places are on opposite sides of the equator, two mean latitudes are generally used, the mean of each latitude north and south of the equator. The mean latitude is usually used in middle-latitude sailing for want of a practicable means of determining the middle latitude.

mean lower low water. A tidal datum that is the average of the lowest low water height of each tidal day observed over the National Tidal Datum Epoch. For station with shorter series, simultaneous observational comparisons are made with a control tide station in order to derive the equivalent of a 19-year datum.

mean lower low water line. The intersection of the land with the water surface at the elevation of mean lower low water.

mean low water. A tidal datum that is the average of all the low water heights observed over the National Tidal Datum Epoch. For stations with shorter series, simultaneous observational comparisons are made with a control tide station in order to derive the equivalent of a 19-year datum.

mean low water line. The intersection of the land with the water surface at the elevation of mean low water.

mean low water springs. A tidal datum that is the arithmetic mean of the low waters occurring at the time of the spring tides observed over a specific 19-year Metonic cycle (the National Tidal Datum Epoch). It is usually derived by taking an elevation depressed below the halftide level by an amount equal to one-half the spring range of tide, necessary corrections being applied to reduce the result to a mean value.

mean noon. Twelve o'clock mean time or the instant the mean sun is over the upper branch of the meridian. Mean noon may be either local or Greenwich depending upon the reference meridian. Zone, standard, daylight saving, or summer noon are also forms of mean noon, the mean sun being over the upper branch of the zone, standard, daylight saving, or summer reference meridian, respectively.

mean range of tide. The difference in height between mean high water and mean low water.

mean rise of tide. The height of mean high water above the reference or chart sounding datum.

mean sea level. A tidal datum that is the arithmetic mean of hourly water elevations observed over a specific 19-year Metonic cycle (the National Tidal Datum Epoch). Shorter series are specified in the name, e.g., monthly mean sea level and yearly mean sea level.

mean solar day. The duration of one rotation of the earth on its axis, with respect to the mean sun. The length of the mean solar day is 24 hours of mean solar time or 24 hours, 3 minutes, 56.555 seconds of mean sidereal time.

mean sun. A fictitious sun conceived to move eastward along the celestial equator at a rate that provides a uniform measure of time equal to the average apparent time. It is used as a reference for reckoning mean time, zone time, etc. Also called ASTRONOMICAL MEAN SUN.

mean time. Time based upon the rotation of the earth relative to the mean sun. Mean time may be designated as local or Greenwich as the local or Greenwich meridian as the reference. Greenwich mean time is also called UNIVERSAL TIME. Zone, standard, daylight saving, or summer time are also variations of mean time, specified meridians being used as the reference.

mean water level. The mean surface elevation as determined by averaging the heights of the water at equal intervals of time, usually hourly.

mean water level line. The line formed by the intersection of the land with the water surface at an elevation of mean water level.

measured mile. A length of 1 nautical mile, the limits of which have been accurately measured and are indicated by ranges ashore. It is used by vessels to calibrate logs, engine revolution counters, etc., and to determine speed.

megahertz, n. One million hertz or one million cycles per second.

Mercator chart. A chart on the Mercator projection. This is the chart commonly used for marine navigation. Also called EQUATORIAL CYLINDRICAL ORTHOMORPHIC CHART.

Mercator map projection. A conformal cylindrical map projection in which the surface of a sphere or spheroid, such as the earth, is developed on a cylinder tangent along the equator. Meridians appear as equally spaced vertical lines and parallels as horizontal lines drawn farther apart as the latitude increases, such that the correct relationship between latitude and longitude scales at any point is maintained. The expansion at any point is equal to the secant of the latitude of that point, with a small correction for the ellipticity of the earth. Also called EQUATORIAL CYLINDRICAL ORTHOMORPHIC MAP PROJECTION.

Mercator sailing. A method of solving the various problems involving course, distance, difference of latitude, difference of longitude, and departure by considering them in the relation in which they are plotted on a Mercator chart. It is similar to plane sailing, but uses meridional difference and difference of longitude in place of difference of latitude and departure, respectively.

meridian, n. A north-south reference line, particularly a great circle through the geographical poles of the earth. The term usually refers to the upper branch, the half, from pole to pole, that passes through a given place, the other half being called the lower branch. The prime meridian passes through longitude 0°. Sometimes designated TRUE MERIDIAN to distinguish it from magnetic meridian, compass meridian, or grid meridian, the north-south lines relative to magnetic, compass, or grid direction, respectively.

meridian altitude. The altitude of a celestial body when it is on the celestial meridian of the observer, bearing 000° or 180° true.

meridian angle. Angular distance east or west of the local celestial meridian; the arc of the celestial equator, or the angle at the celestial pole, between the upper branch of the local celestial meridian and the hour circle of a celestial body measured eastward or westward from the local celestial meridian through 180°, and labeled E or W to indicate the direction of measurement.

meridian observation. Measurement of the altitude of a celestial body on the celestial meridian of the observer, or the altitude so measured.

meridian sailing. Following a true course of 000° or 180°, sailing along a meridian.

meridian transit. The passage of a celestial body across a celestial meridian. Upper transit, the crossing of the upper branch of the celestial meridian, is understood unless lower transit, the crossing of the lower branch, is specified. Also called TRANSIT, MERIDIAN PASSAGE, CULMINATION.

meteor, n. The phenomenon occurring when a solid particle from space enters the earth's atmosphere and is heated to incandescence by friction of the air. A meteor whose brightness does not exceed that of Venus (magnitude −4) is popularly called SHOOTING STAR or FALLING STAR.

meteorite, n. 1. The solid particle that causes the phenomenon known as a METEOR. 2. The remnant of the solid particle, causing the meteor, that reaches the earth.

Meteorological Optical Range Table. A table from the International Visibility Code that gives the code number of meteorological visibility and the meteorological visibility for several weather conditions.

meteorological tide. A change in water level caused by local meteorological conditions, in contrast to an ASTRONOMICAL TIDE, caused by the attractions of the sun and moon.

meteorological visibility. The greatest distance at which a black object of suitable dimensions can be seen and recognized by day against the horizon sky, or, in the case of night observations, could be seen and recognized if the general illumination were raised to the normal daylight level. It has been established that the object may be seen and recognized if the contrast threshold is 0.05 or higher. The term may express the visibility in a single direction or the prevailing visibility in all directions.

meter, n. The base unit of length in the International System of Units, equal to 1,650,763.73 wavelengths in vacuum of the radiation corresponding to the transition between the levels 2p10 and 5p5 of the krypton-86 atom. It is equal to 39.37008 inches, approximately, or approximately one-ten-millionth of the distance from the equator to the North or South Pole.

Metonic cycle. A period of 19 years or 235 lunations, devised by Meton, an Athenian astronomer who lived in the fifth century B.C., for the purpose of obtaining a period in which new and full moon would recur on the same day of the year. Taking the Julian year of 365.25 days and the synodic month as 29.53058 days, we have the 19-year period of 6,939.75 days as compared with the 235 lunations of 6,939.69 days, a difference of only 0.06 days.

metric system. A decimal system of weights and measures based on the meter as the unit of length and the kilogram as a unit of mass.

micrometer, n. A device to provide measurement of very small angles or dimensions by an instrument such as a telescope.

micrometer drum. A cylinder carrying an auxiliary scale and sometimes a vernier, for precise measurement, as in certain type sextants.

micrometer drum sextant. A marine sextant providing a precise reading by means of a micrometer drum attached to the index arm and having an endless tangent screw for controlling the position of the index arm. The micrometer drum may include a vernier to enable a more precise reading. On a vernier sextant the vernier is directly on the arc.

microprocessor. An integrated circuit in a computer that executes machine-language instructions.

microwave, n. A very short electromagnetic wave, usually considered to be about 1 millimeter to 30 centimeters in length. While the limits are not clearly defined, it is generally considered as the wavelength of radar operation.

mid-channel mark. A navigation mark serving to indicate the middle of a channel, which can be passed on either side safely.

middle clouds. Types of clouds the mean level of which is between 6,500 and 20,000 feet. The principal clouds in this group are altocumulus and altostratus.

middle-latitude sailing. A method that combines plane sailing and parallel sailing. Plane sailing is used to find difference of latitude and departure when course and distance are known, or vice versa. Parallel sailing is used to inter-convert departure and difference of longitude.

mile, n. A unit of distance. The nautical mile, or sea mile, is used primarily in navigation. Nearly all maritime nations have adopted the International Nautical Mile of 1,852 meters proposed in 1929 by the International Hydrographic Bureau. The U.S. Departments of Defense and Commerce adopted this value on July 1, 1954. Using the yard-meter conversion factor effective July 1, 1959 (1 yard = 0.9144 meter, exactly) the International Nautical Mile is equivalent to 6,076.11549 feet, approximately. The geographical mile is the length of 1 minute of arc of the equator, or 6,087.08 feet. The U.S. Survey mile or land mile (5,280 feet in the United States) is commonly used for navigation on rivers and lakes, notably the Great Lakes of North America.

Milky Way. The galaxy of which the sun and its family of planets are a part. It appears as an irregular band of misty light across the sky. Through a telescope, it is seen to be composed of numerous individual stars.

milli-. A prefix meaning one-thousandth.

millibar, n. A unit of pressure equal to 1,000 dynes per square centimeter, or 1/1,000th of a bar. The millibar is used as a unit of measure of atmospheric pressure, a standard atmosphere being equal to 1,013.25 millibars or 29.92 inches of mercury.

millimeter, n. One-thousandth of a meter; one-tenth of a centimeter; 0.03937008 inch.

minimum thermometer. A thermometer that automatically registers the lowest temperature occurring since its last setting. One that registers the highest temperature is called a MAXIMUM THERMOMETER.

minor light. An automatic unmanned light on a fixed structure usually showing low to moderate intensity. Minor lights are established in harbors, along channels, along rivers, and in isolated locations.

minute, n. 1. The sixtieth part of a degree of arc. 2. The sixtieth part of an hour.

mirage, n. An optical phenomenon in which objects appear distorted, displaced (raised or lowered), magnified, multiplied, or inverted due to varying atmospheric refraction when a layer of air near the earth's surface differs greatly in density from surrounding air.

mist, n. An aggregate of very small water droplets suspended in the atmosphere. It produces a thin, grayish veil over the landscape. It reduces visibility to a lesser extent than fog. The relative humidity with mist is often less than 95 percent. Mist is intermediate in all respects between haze (particularly damp haze) and fog.

mixed tide. Type of tide with a large inequality in either the high and/or low water heights, with two high waters and two low waters usually occurring each tidal day. All tides are mixed, but the name is usually applied to the tides intermediate to those predominantly semidiurnal and those predominantly diurnal.

mobile offshore drilling unit (MODU). A movable drilling platform used in offshore oil exploration and production. It is kept stationary by vertically movable legs or by mooring with several anchors. After drilling for oil it may be replaced by a production platform or a submerged structure.

moderate breeze. Wind of force 4 (11 to 16 knots or 13 to 18 miles per hour) on the Beaufort wind scale.

moderate gale. A term once used by seamen for what is now called NEAR GALE on the Beaufort wind scale.

modified Lambert conformal projection. A modification of the Lambert conformal projection for use in polar regions, one of the standard parallels being at latitude 89°59'58" and the other at latitude 71° or 74°, and the parallels being expanded slightly to form complete concentric circles. Also called NEY'S MAP PROJECTION.

modulation, n. A variation of some characteristic of a radio wave, called the CARRIER WAVE in accordance with instantaneous values of another wave called the MODULATING WAVE. These variations can be amplitude, frequency, phase, or pulse.

mole, n. A structure, usually massive, on the seaward side of a harbor for its protection against current and wave action, drift ice, wind, etc. Sometimes it may be suitable for the berthing of ships.

monsoon, n. A name for seasonal winds first applied to the winds over the Arabian Sea, that blow for 6 months from the northeast (northeast monsoon) and for 6 months from the southwest (southwest monsoon). The primary cause is the much greater annual variation of temperature over large land areas compared with the neighboring ocean surfaces, causing an excess of pressure over the continents in winter and a deficit in summer, but other factors such as the relief features of the land have a considerable effect.

monsoon current. A seasonal wind-driven current occurring in the northern part of the Indian Ocean and the northwest Pacific Ocean.

monsoon fog. An advection fog occurring as a monsoon circulation transports warm moist air over a colder surface.

month, n. 1. The period of the revolution of the moon around the earth. The month is designated as sidereal, tropical, anomalistic, nodical, or synodical, according to whether the revolution is relative to the stars, the vernal equinox, the perigee, the ascending node, or the sun. 2. The calendar month, which is a rough approximation to the synodical month.

moon, n. The astronomical satellite of the earth.

moonbow, n. A rainbow formed by light from the moon. Colors in a moonbow are usually very difficult to detect. Also called LUNAR RAINBOW.

moonrise, n. The crossing of the visible horizon by the upper limb of the ascending moon.

moonset, n. The crossing of the visible horizon by the upper limb of the descending moon.

moor, v., t. To secure a vessel to land by tying to a pier, wharf or other land-based structure, or to anchor with two or more anchors.

mooring, n. 1. The act of securing a craft to the ground, a wharf, pier, quay, etc., other than anchoring with a single anchor. 2. The place where a craft may be moored. 3. Chains, bridles, anchors, etc., used in securing a craft to the ground.

mooring buoy. A buoy secured to the bottom by permanent moorings and provided with means for mooring a vessel by use of its anchor chain or mooring lines.

morning star. The brightest planet appearing in the eastern sky during morning twilight.

morning twilight. The period of time between darkness and sunrise.

Morse code light. A navigation light that flashes one or more characters in Morse code.

multipath error. Interference between radio waves that have traveled between the transmitter and the receiver by two paths of different lengths, which may cause fading or phase changes at the receiving point due to the vector addition of the signals, making it difficult to obtain accurate information.

multiple echoes. Radar echoes that may occur when a strong echo is received from another ship at close range. A second or third or more echoes may be observed on the radarscope at double, triple, or other multiples of the actual range of the radar target, resulting from the echo's being reflected by one's own ship back to the target and received once again as an echo at a multiple of the preceding range to the target. This term should not be confused with MULTIPLE-TRACE ECHO.

multiple-hop transmission. Radio wave transmission in which the waves traveling between transmitter and receiver undergo multiple reflections and refractions between the earth and ionosphere. Also called MULTIHOP TRANSMISSION.

N

nadir, n. The point on the celestial sphere vertically below the observer; 180° from the zenith.

nanosecond, n. One-billionth of a second.

National Tidal Datum Epoch. The specific 19-year cycle adopted by the National Ocean Survey as the official time segment over which tide observations are taken and reduced to obtain mean values (e.g., mean lower low water, etc.) for tidal datums. It is necessary for standardization because of apparent periodic and apparent secular trends in sea level.

National Water Level Observation Network (National Tidal Datum Control Network). A network composed of the primary control tide stations of the National Ocean Service. This network of coastal observation stations provides the basic tidal datums for coastal boundaries and chart datums of the United States.

natural frequency. The lowest resonant frequency of a body or system.

natural magnet. A magnet occurring in nature, as contrasted with an ARTIFICIAL MAGNET produced by artificial means.

natural range. A range formed by natural objects such as rocks, peaks, etc.

nautical, adj. Of or pertaining to ships, marine navigation, or seamen.

nautical almanac. 1. A periodical publication of astronomical data designed primarily for marine navigation. Such a publication designed primarily for air navigation is called an AIR ALMANAC. 2. *Nautical Almanac,* a joint annual publication of the U.S. Naval Observatory and the Nautical Almanac Office of the Royal Greenwich Observatory, listing the Greenwich hour angle and declination of various celestial bodies to a precision of 0.1' at hourly intervals; time of sunrise, sunset, moon rise, moonset; and other astronomical information useful to navigators.

nautical chart. A representation of a portion of the navigable waters of the earth and adjacent coastal areas on a specified map projection, designed specifically to meet requirements of marine navigation.

nautical mile. A unit of distance used principally in navigation. For practical consideration it is usually considered the length of 1 minute of any great circle of the earth, the meridian being the great circle most commonly used. Because of various lengths of the nautical mile in use throughout the world, due to differences in definition and the assumed size and shape of the earth, the International Hydrographic Bureau in 1929 proposed a standard length of 1,852 meters, which is known as the International Nautical Mile. This has been adopted by nearly all maritime nations. The U.S. Departments of Defense and Commerce adopted this value on July 1, 1954. With the yard-meter relationship then in use, the International Nautical Mile was equivalent to 6,076.10333 feet, approximately. Using the yard-meter conversion factor effective July 1, 1959, (1 yard = 0.1944 meter, exactly) the International Nautical Mile is equivalent to 6,076.11549 feet, approximately.

nautical twilight. The time of incomplete darkness that begins (morning) or ends (evening) when the center of the sun is 12° below the celestial horizon. The times of nautical twilight are tabulated in the *Nautical Almanac.* At the times given the horizon is generally not visible and it is too dark for marine sextant observations.

nautophone, n. A sound signal emitter comprising an electrically oscillated diaphragm. It emits a signal similar in power and tone to that of a REED HORN.

navigable semicircle (less dangerous semicircle). The half of a cyclonic storm area in which the rotary and forward motions of the storm tend to counteract each other and the winds are in such a direction as to tend to blow a vessel away from the storm track. In the Northern Hemisphere this is to the left of the storm center and in the Southern Hemisphere it is to the right. The opposite is DANGEROUS SEMICIRCLE.

navigable waters. Waters usable, with or without improvements, as routes for commerce on water.

navigation, n. The process of planning, recording, and controlling the movement of a craft or vehicle from one place to another. The word navigate is from the Latin *navigatus,* the past participle of the verb *navigere,* which is derived from the words *navis,* meaning "ship," and *agere* meaning "to move" or "to direct."

navigational aid. An instrument, device, chart, method, etc., intended to assist in the navigation of a craft. This expression is not the same as AID TO NAVIGATION, which refers to devices external to a craft such as lights and buoys.

navigational astronomy. Astronomy of direct use to a navigator, comprising principally celestial coordinates, time, and the apparent motions of celestial bodies. Also called NAUTICAL ASTRONOMY.

navigational planets. The four planets commonly used for celestial observations: Venus, Mars Jupiter, and Saturn.

navigational plot. A graphic depiction of the movements of a craft.

navigational triangle. The spherical triangle solved in computing altitude and azimuth and great circle sailing problems. The celestial triangle is formed on the celestial sphere by the great circles connecting the elevated pole, zenith of the assumed position of the observer, and a celestial body. The terrestrial triangle is formed on the earth by the great circles connecting the pole and two places on the earth; the assumed position of the observer and geographical position of the body for celestial observations, and the point of departure and destination for great circle sailing problems. The expression astronomical triangle applies to either the celestial or terrestrial triangle used for solving celestial observations.

navigation, head of. A transshipment point at the end of a waterway where loads are transferred between water carriers and land carriers; the point at which a river is no longer navigable due to rapids or falls.

navigation lights. Statutory, required lights shown by vessels during the hours between sunset and sunrise, in accordance with international agreements.

navigation satellite. An artificial satellite used in a system that determines positions based upon signals received from the satellite.

navigator, n. 1. A person who navigates or is directly responsible for the navigation of a craft. 2. A book of instructions on navigation, as the *American Practical Navigator* (Bowditch).

NAVSTAR Global Positioning System. A satellite navigation system developed by the U.S. Department of Defense. The system provides highly accurate position and velocity information in three dimensions and precise time and time interval on a global basis continuously, to an unlimited number of users. It is unaffected by weather and provides a worldwide common grid reference system.

NAVTEX. A medium-frequency radiocommunications system intended for the broadcast of navigational information up to 200 miles at sea, using narrow-band direct printing technology to print out MSI and safety messages aboard vessels, without operator monitoring.

neap rise. The height of neap high water above the elevation of reference or datum of chart.

neap tidal currents. Tidal currents of decreased speed occurring semimonthly as the result of the moon being in quadrature.

neap tides. Tides of decreased range occurring semimonthly as the result of the moon being in quadrature. The neap range of the tide is the average semidiurnal range occurring at the time of neap tides and is most conveniently computed from the harmonic constants. It is smaller than the mean range where the type of tide is either semidiurnal or mixed and is of no practical significance where the type of tide is diurnal. The average height of the high waters of the neap tides is called neap high water or high water neaps and the average height of the corresponding low waters is called neap low water or low water neaps.

near gale. Wind of force 8 (28 to 33 knots or 32 to 38 miles per hour) on the Beaufort wind scale.

nearshore current system. The current system caused by wave action in or near the surf zone. The nearshore current system consists of four parts: the shoreward mass transport of water; longshore currents; rip currents; the longshore movement of expanding heads of rip currents.

neatline, n. That border line that indicates the limit of the body of a map or chart. Also called SHEET LINE.

new moon. The moon at conjunction, when little or none of it is visible to an observer on the earth because the illuminated side is away from him. Also called CHANGE OF THE MOON.

Newton's laws of motion. Universal laws governing all motion, formulated by Isaac Newton.

night order book. A notebook in which the commanding officer of a ship writes orders with respect to courses and speeds, any special precautions concerning the speed and navigation of the ship, and all other orders for the night for the officer of the deck.

nimbostratus, n. A dark, low shapeless cloud layer (mean upper level below 6,500 ft.) usually nearly uniform; the typical rain cloud. When precipitation falls from nimbostratus, it is in the form of continuous or intermittent rain or snow, as contrasted with the showery precipitation of cumulonimbus.

nimbus, n. A characteristic rain cloud. The term is not used in the international cloud classification except as a combining term, as cumulonimbus.

no-bottom sounding. A sounding in which the bottom is not reached.

node, n. 1. One of the two points of intersection of the orbit of a planet, planetoid, or comet with the ecliptic, or of the orbit of a satellite with the plane of the orbit of its primary. That point at which the body crosses to the north side of the reference plane is called the ascending node; the other, the descending node. The line connecting the nodes is called LINE OF NODES. Also called NODAL POINT. 2. A zero point in any stationary wave system.

nomogram, n. A diagram showing, to scale, the relationship between several variables in such manner that the value of one that corresponds to known values of the others can be determined graphically. Also called NOMOGRAPH.

non-dangerous wreck. A term used to describe a wreck having more than 20 meters of water over it. This term excludes a FOUL GROUND, which is frequently covered by the remains of a wreck and is a hazard only for anchoring, taking the ground, or bottom fishing.

noon, n. The instant at which a time reference is over the upper branch of the reference meridian. Noon may be solar or sidereal as the sun or vernal equinox is over the upper branch of the reference meridian. Solar noon may be further classified as mean or apparent as the mean or apparent sun is the reference. Noon may also be classified according to the reference meridian, either the local or Greenwich meridian or, additionally in the case of mean noon, a designated zone meridian. Standard, daylight saving, or summer noon are variations of zone noon.

noon constant. A predetermined value added to a meridian or ex-meridian sextant altitude to determine the latitude.

noon sight. Measurement of the altitude of the sun at local apparent noon, or the altitude so measured.

normal distribution. A mathematical law predicting the probability that the random error of any given observation of a series of observations of a certain quantity will lie within certain bounds. The law can be derived from the following properties of random errors: (1) positive and negative errors of the same magnitude are about equal in number, (2) small errors occur more frequently than large errors, and (3) extremely large errors rarely occur. One immediate consequence of these properties is that the average or mean value of a large number of observations of a given quantity is zero.

normal tide. A non-technical term synonymous with tide, i.e., the rise and fall of the ocean due to the gravitational interactions of the sun, moon, and earth alone.

north, n. The primary reference direction relative to the earth; the direction indicated by 000° in any system other than relative. True north is the direction of the north geographical pole; magnetic north, the direction north as determined by the earth's magnetic compass; grid north, an arbitrary reference direction used with grid navigation.

North American Datum of 1983. The modern geodetic datum for North America; it is the functional equivalent of the World Geodetic System (WGS). It is based on the GRS 80 ellipsoid, which fits the size and shape of the earth more closely and has its origin at the earth's center of mass.

northeaster, nor'easter, n. A northeast wind, particularly a strong wind or gale associated with cold rainy weather. In the U.S., nor'easters generally occur on the north side of late-season low-pressure systems that pass off the Atlantic seaboard, bringing onshore gales to the region north of the low. When combined with high tides, they can be very destructive.

north geographical pole. The geographical pole in the Northern Hemisphere, at lat. 90°N.

north geomagnetic pole. The geomagnetic pole in the Northern Hemisphere. This term should not be confused with NORTH MAGNETIC POLE.

northing, n. The distance a craft makes good to the north. The opposite is SOUTHING.

north magnetic pole. The magnetic pole in the Northern Hemisphere. This term should not be confused with NORTH GEOMAGNETIC POLE.

North Pole. 1. The north geographical pole. 2. The north-seeking end of a magnet.

north temperate zone. That part of the earth between the Tropic of Cancer and the Arctic Circle.

north up, north upward. One of the three basic orientations of display of relative or true motion on a radarscope or electronic chart. In the NORTH UP orientation, the presentation is in true (gyrocompass) directions from one's own ship, north being maintained UP or at the top of the radarscope.

notch filter. An arrangement of electronic components designed to attenuate or reject a specific frequency band with a sharp cut-off at either end.

notice board. A signboard used to indicate speed restrictions, cable landings, etc.

notice to mariners. A periodic publication used by the navigator to correct charts and publications.

Notice to Mariners. A weekly publication of the Defense Mapping Agency Hydrographic/Topographic Center prepared jointly with the National Ocean Survey and the U.S. Coast Guard giving information on changes in aids to navigation, dangers to navigation, selected items from the *Local Notice to Mariners,* important new soundings, changes in channels, harbor construction, radionavigation information, new and revised charts and publications, special warnings and notices, pertinent HYDROLANT, HYDROPAC, NAVAREA IV and XII messages and corrections to charts, manuals, catalogs, sailing directions (pilots), etc. The *Notice to Mariners* should be used routinely for updating the latest editions of nautical charts and related publications.

numerical scale. A statement of that distance on the earth shown in one unit (usually an inch) on the chart, or vice versa.

nun buoy. An unlighted buoy of which the upper part of the body (above the waterline) or the larger part of the superstructure has a cone shape with vertex upwards.

O

oblique, adj. Neither perpendicular nor parallel; slanting.

oblique angle. Any angle not a multiple of 90°.

oblique chart. A chart on an oblique map projection.

oblique map projection. A map projection with an axis inclined at an oblique angle to the plane of the equator.

oblique Mercator map projection. A conformal cylindrical map projection in which points on the surface of a sphere or spheroid, such as the earth, are developed by Mercator principles on a cylinder tangent along an oblique great circle. Also called OBLIQUE CYLINDRICAL ORTHOMORPHIC MAP PROJECTION.

observed altitude. Corrected sextant altitude; angular distance of the center of a celestial body above the celestial horizon of an observer measured along a vertical circle, through 90°. Occasionally called TRUE ALTITUDE.

obstruction, n. Anything that hinders or prevents movement, particularly anything that endangers or prevents passage of a vessel or aircraft. The term is usually used to refer to an isolated danger to navigation, such as a submerged rock or reef.

obstruction buoy. A buoy used to indicate a dangerous obstruction.

obstruction light. A light indicating a radio tower or other obstruction to aircraft.

obstruction mark. A navigation mark used to indicate a dangerous obstruction.

obtuse angle. An angle greater than 90° and less than 180°.

occasional light. A light put into service only on demand.

occluded front. A composite of two fronts, formed when a cold front overtakes a warm front or stationary front. This is common in the late stages of wave-cyclone development but is not limited to occurrence within a wave-cyclone. There are three basic types of occluded front, determined by the relative coldness of the air behind the original cold front to the air ahead of the warm (or stationary) front. A cold occlusion results when the coldest air is behind the cold front. The cold front undercuts the warm front and, at the earth's surface, cold air replaces less-cold air. When the coldest air lies ahead of the warm front, a warm occlusion is formed in which case the original cold front is forced aloft at the warm-front surface. At the earth's surface, cold air is replaced by less-cold air. A third and frequent type, a neutral occlusion, results when there is no appreciable temperature difference between the cold air masses of the cold and warm fronts. In this case frontal characteristics at the earth's surface consist mainly of a pressure trough, a wind-shift line, and a band of cloudiness and precipitation. Commonly called OCCLUSION. Also called FRONTAL OCCLUSION.

occultation, n. 1. The concealment of a celestial body by another that crosses the line of view. Thus, the moon occults a star when it passes between the observer and the star. 2. The interval of darkness in the period of the light.

occulting light. A light totally eclipsed at regular intervals, with the duration of light always longer than the intervals of darkness called OCCULTATIONS. The term is commonly used for a SINGLE OCCULTING LIGHT, an occulting light exhibiting only single occultations that are repeated at regular intervals.

ocean, n. 1. The major area of salt water covering the greater part of the earth. 2. One of the major divisions of the expanse of salt water covering the earth.

ocean current. A movement of ocean water characterized by regularity, either of a cyclic nature, or as a continuous stream flowing along a definable path. Three general classes may be distinguished, by cause: (a) currents associated with horizontal pressure gradients, comprising the various types of gradient current; (b) wind-driven currents, which are those directly produced by the stress exerted by the wind upon the ocean surface; (c) currents produced by long-wave motions. The latter are principally tidal currents, but may also include currents associated with internal waves, tsunamis, and seiches. The major ocean currents are of continuous, stream-flow character and are of first-order importance in the maintenance of the earth's thermodynamic balance.

oceanographic survey. The study or examination of conditions in the ocean or any part of it, with reference to zoology, chemistry, geology, or other scientific disciplines.

oceanography, n. The study of the sea, embracing and integrating all knowledge pertaining to the sea's physical boundaries, the chemistry and physics of sea water, and marine biology. Strictly, oceanography is the description of the marine environment, whereas OCEANOLOGY is the study of the oceans.

ocean waters. For application to the provisions of the Marine Protection, Research, and Sanctuaries Act of 1972, those waters of the open sea lying seaward of the base line from which the territorial sea is measured.

octant, n. A double-reflecting instrument for measuring angles, used primarily for measuring altitude of celestial bodies. It has a range of 90°, with the graduated arc subtending 45°, or ⅛ of a circle, hence the term octant; a precursor of the sextant, whose arc subtends 60° or ⅙ of a circle.

off-center PPI display. A plan position indicator display in which the center about which the sweep rotates is offset from the center of the radarscope.

offshore light stations. Manned light stations built on exposed marine sites to replace lightships.

offshore navigation. Navigation at a distance from a coast, in contrast with COASTWISE NAVIGATION in the vicinity of a coast.

offshore wind. Wind blowing from the land toward the sea. An ONSHORE WIND blows in the opposite direction.

off soundings. Navigating beyond the 100-fathom curve. In earlier times, said of a vessel in water deeper than could be sounded with the sounding lead.

off station. Not in charted position.

omnidirectional antenna. An antenna

whose radiating or receiving properties at any instant are the same on all bearings. Also called OMNIAZIMUTHAL ANTENNA.

omnidirectional light. A light that presents the same characteristic over the whole horizon of interest to marine navigation. Also called ALL-ROUND LIGHT.

onshore wind. Wind blowing from the sea towards the land. An OFFSHORE WIND blows in the opposite direction.

on soundings. Navigating within the 100-fathom curve. In earlier times, said of a vessel in water sufficiently shallow for sounding by sounding lead.

on the beam. Bearing approximately 090° relative (on the starboard beam) or 270° relative (on the port beam). The expression is often used loosely for BROAD ON THE BEAM, or bearing exactly 090° or 270° relative. Also called ABEAM.

on the bow. Bearing approximately 045° relative (on the starboard bow) or 315° relative (on the port bow). The expression is often used loosely for BROAD ON THE BOW, or bearing exactly 045° or 315° relative.

on the quarter. Bearing approximately 135° relative (on the starboard quarter) or 225° relative (on the port quarter). The expression is often used loosely for BROAD ON THE QUARTER, or bearing exactly 135° or 225° relative.

open roadstead. A roadstead with relatively little protection from the sea.

open sea. 1. The part of the ocean not enclosed by headlands, within narrow straits, etc. 2. The part of the ocean outside the territorial jurisdiction of any country. The opposite is CLOSED SEA.

opposition, n. The situation of two celestial bodies having either celestial longitudes or sidereal hour angles differing by 180°. The term is usually used only in relation to the position of a superior planet or the moon with reference to the sun. The situation of two celestial bodies having either the same celestial longitude or the same sidereal hour angle is called conjunction.

optical path. The path followed by a ray of light through an optical system.

optical system. A series of lenses, apertures, prisms, mirrors, etc., so arranged as to perform a definite optical function.

optics, n. The science dealing with light, lenses, etc.

orbit, n. The path of a body or particle under the influence of a gravitational or other force.

orbital altitude. The mean altitude of the orbit of a satellite above the surface of the parent body.

orbital elements. Parameters that specify the position and motion of a body in orbit. The elliptical orbit of a satellite attracted by an exactly central gravitational force is specified by a set of six parameters as follows: Two parameters, the semimajor axis and eccentricity of the ellipse, establish the size and shape of the elliptical orbit. A third parameter, time of perifocal passage, enables determination of the location of the satellite in its orbit at any instant. The three remaining parameters establish the orientation of the orbit in space. These are the inclination of the orbital plane to a reference plane, the right ascension of the ascending node of the satellite, and the argument of pericenter.

orbital motion. Continuous motion in a closed path about and as a direct result of a source of gravitational attraction.

orbital path. One of the tracks on a primary body's surface traced by the subpoint of a satellite that orbits about it several times in a direction other than normal to the primary body's axis of rotation. Each track is displaced in a direction opposite and by an amount equal to the degrees of rotation between each satellite orbit and of the nodical precession of the plane of the orbit. Also called SUBTRACK.

orbital period. If the orbit is unchanging and ideal, the travel between successive passages of a satellite through the same point in its orbit. If the orbit is not ideal, the point must be specified. When the perigee is specified it is called radial or anomalistic period. When the ascending node is specified, it is called nodical period. When the same geocentric right ascension is specified, it is called sidereal period. Also called PERIOD OF SATELLITE.

orbital plane. The plane of the ellipse defined by a central force orbit.

orbital velocity. The velocity of an earth satellite or other orbiting body at any given point in its orbit.

orographic rain. Rain resulting when moist air is forced upward by a mountain range.

orthogonal, adj. Right angled, rectangular.

orthographic, adj. Of or pertaining to right angles or perpendicular lines.

orthographic chart. A chart on the orthographic map projection.

oscilloscope, n. An instrument for producing a visual representation of oscillations or changes in an electric current. The face of the cathode-ray tube used for this representation is called a SCOPE or SCREEN.

outfall, n. The discharge end of a narrow street sewer, drain, etc.

outfall buoy. A buoy marking the position where a sewer or other drain discharges.

overcast, adj. Pertaining to a sky cover of 95 percent or more.

overfalls, n. pl. Breaking waves caused by the meeting of currents or by waves moving against the current.

overhead cable effect. A radar phenomenon that may occur in the vicinity of an overhead power cable. The echo from the cable appears on the plan position indicator as a single echo, the echo being returned from that part of cable where the radar beam is at right angles to the cable.

paint, n. The bright area on the phosphorescent plan position indicator screen resulting from the brightening of the sweep by the echoes.

paint, v., t & i. To brighten the phosphorescent plan position indicator screen through the effects of the echoes on the sweep.

parabolic reflector. A reflecting surface having the cross section along the axis in the shape of a parabola. Parallel rays striking the reflector are brought to a focus at a point, or, if the source of the rays is placed at the focus, the reflected rays are parallel.

parallactic angle. That angle at the navigational triangle at the celestial body; the angle between a body's hour circle and its vertical circle. Also called POSITION ANGLE.

parallax, n. The difference in apparent direction or position of an object when viewed from different points. For bodies of the solar system, parallax is the difference in the direction of the body due to the displacement of the observer from the center of the earth and is called geocentric parallax, varying with the body's altitude and distance from the earth.

parallax correction. A correction due to parallax, particularly that sextant altitude correction due to the difference between the apparent direction from a point on the surface of the earth to celestial body and the apparent direction from the center of the earth to the same body.

parallel of latitude. 1. A circle (or approximation of a circle) on the surface of the earth, parallel to the equator, and connecting points of equal latitude. Also called a PARALLEL. 2. A circle of the celestial sphere, parallel to the ecliptic, and connecting points of equal celestial latitude. Also called CIRCLE OF LONGITUDE.

parallel rulers. An instrument for transferring a line parallel to itself. In its most common form it consists of two parallel bars or rulers connected in such manner that when one is held in place, the other may be moved, remaining parallel to its original position.

parallel sailing. A method of converting departure into difference of longitude, or vice versa, when the true course is 090° or 270°.

paranthelion, n. A phenomenon similar to a PARHELION but occurring generally at a distance of 120° (occasionally 90° or 140°) from the sun.

paraselene (pl. paraselenae), n. A form of halo consisting of an image of the moon at the same altitude as the moon and some distance from it, usually about 22°, but occasionally about 46°. Similar phenomena may occur about 90°, 120°, 140°, or 180° from the moon. A similar phenomenon in relation to the sun is called a PARHELION, SUN DOG, or MOCK SUN. Also called MOCK MOON.

paraselenic circle. A halo consisting of a faint white circle through the moon and parallel to the horizon. It is produced by reflection of moonlight from vertical faces of ice crystals. A similar circle through the sun is called a PARHELIC CIRCLE.

parhelic circle. A halo consisting of a faint white circle through the sun and parallel to the horizon. It is produced by reflection of sunlight from vertical faces of ice crystals. A similar circle through the moon is called a PARASELENIC CIRCLE. Also called MOCK SUN RING.

parhelion (pl. parhelia), n. A form of halo, consisting of an image of the sun at the same altitude as the sun and some distance from it, usually about 22°, but occasionally about 40°. A similar phenomenon occurring at a distance of 90°, 120°, or 140° from the sun is called a PARANTHELION, and if occurring at a distance of 180° from the sun, an ANTHELION. A similar phenomenon in relation to the moon is called PARASELENE, MOON DOG, or MOCK MOON. The term PARHELION should not be confused with PERIHELION, the orbital point near the sun when the sun is the center of attraction. Also called SUN DOG, MOCK SUN.

partial eclipse. An eclipse in which only part of the source of light is obscured.

passage, n. 1. A navigable channel, especially one through reefs or islands. Also called PASS. 2. A transit from one place to another; one leg of a voyage.

passing light. A low-intensity light that may be mounted on the structure of another light to enable the mariner to keep the latter light in sight when he passes out of its beam.

passive system. A term used to describe a navigation system whose operation does not require the user to transmit a signal.

pelorus, n. A dumb compass, or a compass card (called a PELORUS CARD) without a directive element, suitably mounted and provided with vanes to permit observation of relative bearings unless used in conjunction with a compass to give true or magnetic bearings.

pelorus card. The part of a pelorus on which the direction graduations are placed. It is usually in the form of a thin disk or annulus graduated in degrees, clockwise, from 0° at the reference direction to 360°.

penumbra, n. 1. That part of a shadow in which light is partly cut off by an intervening object. The penumbra surrounds the darker UMBRA in which light is completely cut off. 2. The lighter part of a sun spot, surrounding the darker UMBRA.

penumbral lunar eclipse. The eclipse of the moon when the moon passes only through the penumbra of the earth's shadow.

perigean tides. Tides of increased range occurring monthly as the result of the moon being in perigee or nearest the earth.

perigee, n. The orbital point nearest the earth when the earth is the center of attraction. The orbital point farthest from the earth is called APOGEE.

perihelion, n. That orbital point nearest the sun when the sun is the center of attraction. That point farthest from the sun is called APHELION.

perimeter, n. 1. The length of a closed plane curve or the sum of the sides of a polygon. 2. The boundary of a plane figure. Also called PERIPHERY.

period, n. 1. The interval needed to complete a cycle. 2. The interval of time between the commencement of two identical successive cycles of the characteristic of a light.

permanent current. A current that runs fairly continuously and is independent of tides and other temporary causes.

permanent echo. An echo from an object whose position relative to the radar set is fixed.

permanent light. A light used in regular service.

permanent magnetism. The magnetism acquired by hard iron, not readily magnetized by induction, but retaining a high percentage of magnetism acquired unless subjected to a demagnetizing force. The strength and polarity of this magnetism in a craft depends upon the heading, magnetic latitude, and building stresses imposed during construction.

personal error. A systematic error in the observation of a quantity due to the personal idiosyncrasies of the observer. Also called PERSONAL EQUATION.

perspective map projection. A map projection produced by the direct projection of the points of the ellipsoid (used to represent the earth) by straight lines drawn through them from some given point. The projection is usually made upon a plane tangent to the ellipsoid at the end of the diameter joining the point of projection and the center of the ellipsoid.

perspective projection. The representation of a figure on a surface, either plane or curved, by means of projecting lines emanating from a single point, which may be infinity. Also called GEOMETRIC PROJECTION.

phantom target. An indication of an object on a radar display that does not correspond to the presence of an actual object at the point indicated. Also called PHANTOM ECHO.

phase, n. The amount by which a cycle has progressed from a specified origin. For most purposes it is stated in circular measure, a complete cycle being considered 360°.

phase coding. In Loran-C, the shifting in a fixed sequence of the relative phase of the carrier cycles between certain pulses of a group. This shifting facilitates automatic synchronization in identical sequence within the group of eight pulses that are transmitted during each group repetition interval. It also minimizes the effect of unusually long skywave transmissions causing one pulse to interfere with the succeeding pulse in the group received by groundwave.

phase inequality. Variations in the tides or tidal currents due to changes in the phase of the moon. At the times of new and full moon the tide-producing forces of the moon and sun act in conjunction, causing the range of tide and speed of the tidal current to be greater than the average, the tides at these times being known as spring tides. At the time of quadrature of the moon these forces are opposed to each other, causing the neap tides with diminished range and current speed.

phases of the moon. The various appearances of the moon during different parts of the synodical month. The cycle begins with new moon or change of the moon at conjunction. The visible part of the waxing moon increases in size during the first half of the cycle until full moon appears at opposition, after which the visible part of the waning moon decreases for the remainder of the cycle. First quarter occurs when the waxing moon is at east quadrature; last quarter when the waning moon is at west quadrature. From last quarter to new and from new to first quarter the moon is crescent; from first quarter to full and from full to last quarter it is gibbous. The elapsed time, usually expressed in days, since the last new moon is called age of the moon. The full moon occurring nearest the autumnal equinox is called harvest moon; the next full moon, hunter's moon.

pierhead, n. The outer end of a pier or jetty.

pile, n. A long, heavy timber or section of steel, concrete, etc., forced into the earth to serve as a support, as for a pier, or to resist lateral pressure.

pillar buoy. A buoy composed of a tall central structure mounted on a broad flat base.

pilot, n. 1. A person who directs the movement of a vessel through pilot waters, usually a person who has demonstrated extensive knowledge of channels, aids to navigation, dangers to navigation, etc., in a particular area and is licensed in that area. 2. A book of sailing directions. For waters, the United States and its possessions, they are prepared by the National Ocean Survey and are called COAST PILOTS.

pilotage, n. 1. The services of especially qualified navigators having local knowledge who assist in the navigation of vessels in particular areas. Also called PILOTAGE SERVICE. 2. A term loosely used for piloting.

pilot chart. A chart of a major ocean area that presents in graphic form averages obtained from weather, wave, ice, and other marine data gathered over many years in meteorology and oceanography to aid the navigator in selecting the quickest and safest routes; published by the National Imagery and Mapping Agency (NIMA) from data provided by the U.S. Naval Oceanographic Office and the Environmental Data and Information Service of the National Oceanic and Atmospheric Administration.

piloting, n. Navigation involving frequent or continuous determination of position relative to observed geographical points, to a high order of accuracy; directing the movements of a vessel near a coast by means of terrestrial reference points is called coast piloting. Sometimes called PILOTAGE.

pilot rules. Regulations supplementing the Inland Rules of the Road, superseded by the adoption of the Inland Navigation Rules in 1980 (1983 on the Great Lakes).

pitch, n. 1. Oscillation of a vessel about the transverse axis due to the vessel's bow and stern being raised or lowered on passing through successive crests and troughs of waves. Also called PITCHING. 2. The distance a propeller would advance longitudinally in one revolution if there were no slip.

pixel. The smallest area of phosphors on a video terminal that can be excited to form a picture element.

plane, n. A surface without curvature, such that a straight line joining any two of its points lies wholly on the surface.

plane sailing. A method of solving the various problems involving a single course and distance, difference of latitude, and departure, in which the earth, or that part traversed, is considered as a plane surface.

planet, n. A celestial body of a solar system, in orbit around the sun or a star and shining by reflected light. The word planet is of Greek origin, meaning, literally, wanderer, applied because the planets appear to move relative to the stars.

planning chart. A chart designed for use in planning voyages or flight operations or investigating areas of marine or aviation activities.

plan position indicator. An intensity-modulated radar display in which the radial sweep rotates on the cathode-ray tube in synchronism with the rotating antenna. The display presents a maplike representation of the positions of echo-producing objects. It is generally one of two main types: RELATIVE MOTION DISPLAY or TRUE MOTION DISPLAY.

plot, n. A drawing consisting of lines and points representing certain conditions graphically, as the progress of a craft.

plot, v., t. To draw lines and points to represent certain conditions graphically, as the various lines and points on a chart or plotting sheet representing the progress of a vessel, a curve of magnetic azimuths versus time or of altitude versus time, or a graphical solution of a problem, such as a relative motion solution.

plotter, n. An instrument used for plotting straight lines and measuring angles on a chart or plotting sheet.

plotting chart. An outline chart on a specific scale and projection, usually showing a graticule and compass rose, designed to be used ancillary to a standard nautical chart, and produced either as an independent chart or part of a coordinated series.

P.M. Abbreviation for Post Meridian; after noon in zone time.

point of departure. The point from which the initial course to reach the destination begins. It is usually established by bearings of prominent landmarks as the vessel clears a harbor and proceeds to sea. When a person establishes this point, he is said to take departure. Also called the DEPARTURE.

polar, adj. Of or pertaining to a pole or the poles.

polar air. A type of air whose characteristics are developed over high latitudes, especially within the subpolar highs. Continental polar air has low surface temperature, low moisture content, and, especially in its source regions, has great stability in the lower layers. It is shallow in comparison with arctic air. Maritime polar air initially possesses similar properties to those of continental polar air, but in passing over warmer water it becomes unstable with a higher moisture content.

polar axis. 1. The straight line connecting the poles of a body. 2. A reference line for one of the spherical coordinates.

polar chart. 1. A chart of polar areas. 2. A chart on a polar projection. The projections most used for polar charts are the gnomonic, stereographic, azimuthal equidistant, transverse Mercator, and modified Lambert conformal.

polar circles. The minimum latitudes, north and south, at which the sun becomes circumpolar.

polar continental air. Air of an air mass that originates over land or frozen ocean areas in polar regions. Polar continental air is characterized by low temperature, stability, low specific humidity, and shallow vertical extent.

polar coordinates. A system of coordinates defining a point by its distance and direction from a fixed point, called the POLE. Direction is given as the angle between a reference radius vector and a radius vector to the point. If three dimensions are involved, two angles are used to locate the radius vector.

polar distance. Angular distance from a celestial pole; the arc of an hour circle between a celestial pole, usually the elevated pole, and a point on the celestial sphere, measured from the celestial pole through 180°.

polar front. The semi-permanent, semi-continuous front separating air masses of tropical and polar origin. This is the major front in terms of air mass contrast and susceptibility to cyclonic disturbance.

Polaris correction. A correction to be applied to the corrected sextant altitude of Polaris to obtain latitude. This correction for the offset of Polaris from the north celestial pole varies with the local hour angle of Aries, latitude, and date.

polar map projection. A map projection centered on a pole.

polar maritime air. An air mass that originates in the polar regions and is then modified by passing over a relatively warm ocean surface. It is characterized by moderately low temperature, moderately high surface specific humidity, and a considerable degree of vertical instability. When the air is colder than the sea surface, it is further characterized by gusts and squalls, showery precipitation, variable sky, and good visibility between showers.

polar navigation. Navigation in polar regions, where unique considerations and techniques are applied. No definite limit for these regions is recognized but polar navigation techniques are usually used from about latitude 70°N.

polar orbit. An earth satellite orbit that has an inclination of about 90° and, hence, passes over or near the earth's poles.

pole, n. 1. Either of the two points of intersection of the surface of a sphere or spheroid and its axis, labeled N or S to indicate whether the north pole or south pole. The two points of intersection of the surface of the earth with its axis are called geographical poles. The two points of intersection of the celestial sphere and the extended axis of the earth are called celestial poles. The celestial pole above the horizon is called the elevated pole, that below the horizon the depressed pole. The ecliptic poles are 90° from the ecliptic. Also, one of a pair of similar points on the surface of a sphere or spheroid, as a magnetic pole (definition 1); a geomagnetic pole; or a fictitious pole. 2. A magnetic pole (definition 2). 3. The origin of measurement of distance in polar or spherical coordinates. 4. Any point around which something centers.

polyconic, adj. Consisting of or related to many cones.

polyconic map projection. A conic map projection in which the surface of a sphere or spheroid, such as the earth, is conceived as developed on a series of tangent cones, which are then spread out to form a plane. A separate cone is used for each small zone. This projection is widely used for maps but seldom used for charts, except for survey purposes. It is not conformal.

polygon, n. A closed plane figure bounded by straight lines.

poop, n. A short enclosed structure at the stern of a vessel, extending from side to side. It is covered by the poop deck, which is surrounded by the poop rail.

pooped. To have shipped a sea or wave over the stern.

port, n. 1. A place provided with moorings and transfer facilities for loading and discharging cargo or passengers, usually located in a harbor. 2. The left side of a craft, facing forward. The opposite is STARBOARD.

port hand buoy. A buoy that is to be left to the port side when approaching from the open sea or proceeding in the direction of the main stream of flood current or in the direction established by appropriate authority.

port of call. A port visited by a ship.

position, n. A point defined by stated or implied coordinates, particularly one on the surface of the earth. A fix is a relatively accurate position determined without reference to any former position. A running fix is a position determined by crossing lines of position obtained at different times and advanced or retired to a common time. An estimated position is determined from incomplete data or data of questionable accuracy. A dead reckoning position is determined by advancing a previous position for courses and distances. A most probable position is a position judged to be most accurate when an element of doubt exists as to the true position. It may be a fix, running fix, estimated position, or dead reckoning position depending upon the information upon which it is based. An assumed position is a point at which a craft is assumed to be located. A geographical position is that point on the earth at which a given celestial body is in the zenith at a specified time, or any position defined by means of its geographical coordinates. A geodetic position is a point on the earth the coordinates of which have been determined by triangulation from an accurately known initial station, or one defined in terms of geodetic latitude and longitude. An astronomical position is a point on the earth whose coordinates have been determined as a result of observation of celestial bodies, or one defined in terms of astronomical latitude and longitude. A maritime position is the location of a seaport or other point along a coast. A relative position is one defined with reference to another position, either fixed or moving.

position approximate. Of inexact position. The expression is used principally on charts to indicate that the position of a wreck, shoal, etc., has not been accurately determined or does not remain fixed.

position circle. The chart symbol denoting the position of a buoy.

position doubtful. Of uncertain position. The expression is used principally on charts to indicate that a wreck, shoal, etc., has been reported in various positions and not definitely determined in any.

position plotting sheet. A blank chart, usually on the Mercator projection, showing only the graticule and a compass rose. The meridians are usually unlabeled by the publisher so that they can be appropriately labeled when the chart is used in any longitude. It is designed and intended for use in conjunction with the standard nautical chart.

post meridian (PM). After noon, or the period of time between noon (1200) and midnight (2400). The period between midnight and noon is called ANTE MERIDIAN.

precautionary area. A routing measure comprising an area within defined limits where ships must navigate with particular caution and within which the direction of traffic flow may be recommended.

precession, n. The change in the direction of the axis of rotation of a spinning body, as a gyroscope, when acted upon by a torque. The direction of motion of the axis is such that it causes the direction of spin of the gyroscope to tend to coincide with that of the impressed torque. The horizontal component of precession is called drift, and the vertical component is called topple.

precession of the equinoxes. The conical motion of the earth's axis about the vertical to the plane of the ecliptic, caused by the attractive force of the sun, moon, and other planets on the equatorial protuberance of the earth. The effect of the sun and moon, called lunisolar precession, is to produce a westward motion of the equinoxes along the ecliptic. The effect of other planets, called planetary precession, tends to produce a much smaller motion eastward along the ecliptic. The resultant motion, called general precession, is westward along the ecliptic at the rate of about 50.3" per year. The component of general precession along the celestial equator, called precession in right ascension, is about 46.1" per year, and the component along a celestial meridian, called precession in declination, is about 20.0" per year.

precipitation, n. 1. Any or all forms of water particles, whether liquid or solid, that fall from the atmosphere and reach the ground. It is distinguished from cloud, fog, dew, rime, frost, etc., in that it must fall; and it is distinguished from cloud and virga in that it must reach the ground. Precipitation includes drizzle, rain, snow, snow pellets, snow grains, ice crystals, ice pellets, and hail. 2. The amount usually expressed in inches of liquid water depth, of the water substance that has fallen at a given point over a specified period of time.

precision, n. A measure of how close the outcome of a series of observations or measurement cluster about some estimated value of a desired quantity. Precision should not be confused with ACCURACY. Observations may be of high precision but inaccurate due to the presence of systematic errors. For a quantity to be accurately measured, both systematic and random errors should be small. For a quantity to be known with high precision, only the random errors due to irregular effects need to be small.

predictable accuracy. The accuracy of predicting position with respect to precise space and surface coordinates.

predicted tides. The times and heights of the tide as given in the Tide Tables in advance of their occurrence.

preferred datum. A geodetic datum selected as a base for consolidation of local independent datums within a geographical area. Also called MAJOR DATUM.

pressure tendency. The character and amount of atmospheric pressure change for a 3-hour or other specified period ending at the time of observation. Also called BAROMETRIC TENDENCY.

prevailing westerlies. The prevailing westerly winds on the poleward sides of the sub-tropical high-pressure belts.

prevailing wind. The average or characteristic wind at any place.

primary seacoast light. A light established for purpose of making landfall or coastwise past from headland to headland. Also called LAND FALL LIGHT.

prime meridian. The 0° meridian of longitude, used as the origin for measurement of longitude. The meridian of Greenwich, England, is almost universally used for this purpose.

prime vertical circle. The vertical circle perpendicular to the principal vertical circle. The intersections of the prime vertical circle with the horizon define the east and west points of the horizon. Often shortened to PRIME VERTICAL. Sometimes called TRUE PRIME VERTICAL to distinguish from magnetic, compass, or grid prime vertical, defined as the vertical circle passing through the magnetic, compass, or grid east and west points of the horizon, respectively.

prismatic error. That error due to lack of parallelism of the two faces of an optical element, such as a mirror or a shade glass.

private aids to navigation. In United States waters, those aids to navigation not established and maintained by the U.S. Coast Guard. Private aids include those established by other federal agencies with prior U.S. Coast Guard approval, aids to navigation on marine structures or other works that the owners are legally obligated to establish, maintain, and operate as prescribed by the U.S. Coast Guard, and those aids that are merely desired, for one reason or another, by the individual corporation, state or local government, or other body that has established the aid with U.S. Coast Guard approval.

production platform. A term used to indicate a permanent offshore structure equipped to control the flow of oil or gas. For charting purposes, the use of the term is extended to include all permanent platforms associated with oil or gas production, e.g., field terminal, drilling, and accommodation platforms, and "booster" platforms sited at intervals along some pipelines. It does not include entirely submarine structures.

prognostic chart. A chart showing the expected pressure pattern of a given synoptic chart at a specified future time. Usually, positions of fronts are also included, and the forecast values of other meteorological elements may be superimposed.

prohibited area. 1. An area shown on nautical charts within which navigation and/or anchoring is prohibited except as authorized by appropriate authority. 2. A specified area within the land areas of a state or territorial waters adjacent thereto over which the flight of aircraft is prohibited.

projection, n. The extension of lines or planes to intersect a given surface; the transfer of a point from one surface to a corresponding position on another surface by graphical or analytical means.

propagation, n. The travel of waves of energy through or along a medium other than a specially constructed path such as an electrical circuit.

proper motion. The component of the space motion of a celestial body perpendicular to line of sight, resulting in the change of a star's apparent position relative to other stars. Proper motion is expressed in angular units.

proportional dividers. An instrument consisting in its simple form of two legs pointed at both ends and provided with an adjustable pivot, so that for any given pivot setting, the distance between one set of pointed ends always bears the same ratio to the distance between the other set. A change in the pivot changes the ratio. The dividers are used in transferring measurements between charts or other graphics not of the same scale.

protractor, n. An instrument for measuring angles on a surface; an angular scale. In its most usual form it consists of a circle or part of one (usually a semicircle) graduated in degrees.

psychrometer, n. A type of hygrometer (an instrument for determining atmospheric humidity) consisting of dry-bulb and wet-bulb thermometers. The dry-bulb thermometer indicates the temperature of the air, and the wet bulb thermometer the lowest temperature to which air can be cooled by evaporating water into it at constant pressure. With the information obtained from a psychrometer, the humidity, dew point, and vapor pressure for any atmospheric pressure can be obtained by means of appropriate tables.

Pub. 9. *American Practical Navigator.* A publication of the National Imagery and Mapping Agency (NIMA), originally by Nathaniel Bowditch (1773–1838) and first published in 1802, comprising a complete manual of navigation with tables for solution of navigational problems. Popularly called BOWDITCH.

Pub. 102. *International Code of Signals.* A publication of the National Imagery and Mapping Agency (NIMA) intended primarily for communication at sea in situations involving safety of life at sea and navigational safety, especially when language difficulties arise between ships or stations of different nationalities. The code is suitable for transmission by all means of communication, including radiotelephony, radiotelegraphy, sound, flashing light, and flags.

Pub. 117. *Radio Navigational Aids.* A publication of the National Imagery and Mapping Agency (NIMA) that contains data on radio aids to navigation services provided to mariners. Information on radio direction finder and radar stations, radio time signals, radio navigational warnings, distress signals, stations transmitting medical advice, long-range radionavigation systems, emergency procedures and communications instructions, listed in text and tabular format.

Pub. 150. *World Port Index.* A publication of the National Imagery and Mapping Agency (NIMA) listing the location, characteristics, known facilities, and available services of ports, shipping facilities, and oil terminals throughout the world. The applicable chart and Sailing Direction volume is given for each place listed. A code indicates certain types of information.

Pub. 151. *Distances Between Ports.* A publication of the National Imagery and Mapping Agency (NIMA) providing calculated distances in nautical miles over water areas between most of the seaports of the world. A similar publication for United States waters, published by the National Ocean Service, is entitled *Distances between United States Ports*.

Pub. 217. *Maneuvering Board Manual.* A publication of the National Imagery and Mapping Agency (NIMA) providing explanations and examples of various problems involved in maneuvering and in relative movement.

Pub. 221. *Loran-C Table.* A series of tables published by the National Imagery and Mapping Agency (NIMA), published primarily for manufacturers who use computers to correct Loran-C time differences to geographic coordinates. The tables also correct time differences for ASF.

Pub. 229. *Sight Reduction Tables for Marine Navigation.* A publication of the National Imagery and Mapping Agency (NIMA), in six volumes, each of which includes two 8° zones of latitude. An overlap of 1° of latitude occurs between volumes. The six volumes cover latitude bands 0°–15°, 15°–30°, 30°–45°, 45°–60°, 60°–75°, and 75°–90°. For entering arguments of integral degrees of latitude, declination, and local hour angle, altitudes and their differences are tabulated to the nearest tenth of a minute, azimuth angles to the nearest tenth of a degree. The tables are designed for precise interpolation of altitude for declination only by means of interpolation tables that facilitate linear interpolation and provide additionally for the effect of second differences. The data are applicable to the solutions of sights of all celestial bodies; there are no limiting values of altitude, latitude, hour angle, or declination.

Pub. 249. *Sight Reduction Tables for Air Navigation.* A publication of the National Imagery and Mapping Agency (NIMA), in three volumes, with Volume 1 containing tabulated altitudes and azimuths of selected stars, the entering arguments being latitude, local hour angle of the vernal equinox, and the name of the star; and Volumes 2 and 3 containing tabulated altitudes and azimuth angles of any body within the limits of the entering arguments, which are latitude, local hour angle, and declination (0°–29°) of the body.

Pub. 1310. ***Radar Navigation Manual.*** A publication of the National Imagery and Mapping Agency (NIMA) that explains the fundamentals of shipboard radar, radar operation collision avoidance, radar navigation, and radar-assisted vessel traffic systems in the U.S.

pulse-modulated radar. The type of radar generally used for shipboard navigational applications. The radio-frequency energy transmitted by a pulse-modulated radar consists of a series of equally spaced short pulses having a pulse duration of about one microsecond or less. The distance to the target is determined by measuring the transmit time of a pulse and its return to the source as a reflected echo. Also called PULSE RADAR.

pulse modulation. 1. The modulation of a carrier wave by a pulse train. In this sense, the term describes the process of generating carrier-frequency pulses. 2. The modulation of one or more characteristics of a pulse carrier. In this sense, the term describes methods of transmitting information on a pulse carrier.

pulse repetition rate. The average number pulses per unit of time.

pumping, n. Unsteadiness of the mercury in a barometer, caused by fluctuations of the air pressure produced by a gusty wind or due to the motion of a vessel.

pure tone. A sound produced by a sinusoidal acoustic oscillation. Also called PURE SOUND.

Q

Q-correction. The Polaris correction as tabulated in the *Air Almanac*.

quadrant, n. 1. A quarter of a circle; either an arc of 90° or the area bounded by such an arc and two radii. 2. A double-reflecting instrument for measuring angles used primarily for measuring altitudes of celestial bodies.

quarantine anchorage. An area where a vessel anchors while satisfying quarantine regulations.

quarantine buoy. A buoy marking the location of a quarantine anchorage. In U.S. waters a quarantine buoy is yellow.

quartering sea. Waves striking the vessel on the quarter, or relative bearings approximately 045°, 135°, 225°, and 315°.

quick-flashing light. A light flashing 50–80 flashes per minute.

R

race, n. A rapid current or a constricted channel in which such a current flows. The term is usually used only in connection with a tidal current, when it may be called a TIDE RACE.

racon, n. As defined by the International Telecommunication Union (ITU), in the maritime radionavigation service, a receiver-transmitter device that, when triggered by a surface search radar, automatically returns a distinctive signal that can appear on the display of the triggering radar, providing range, bearing, and identification information.

radar (from radio detection and ranging), n. A radio system that measures distance and usually direction by a comparison of reference signals with the radio signals reflected or retransmitted from the target whose position is to be determined.

radar beacon. A radar transmitter whose emissions enable a ship to determine its direction and frequently position relative to the transmitter using the ship's radar equipment. There are two general types of radar beacons: one type, the RACON, must be triggered by the ship's radar emissions; the other type, the RAMARK, transmits continuously and provides bearings only.

radar conspicuous object. An object that returns a strong radar echo that can be identified with a high degree of certainty.

radar fix. A fix established by means of radar.

radar horizon. The sensible horizon of a radar antenna.

radar indicator. A unit of a radar set that provides a visual indication of radar echoes received using a cathode-ray tube or video monitor. Besides the cathode-ray tube, the radar indicator is comprised of sweep and calibration circuit, and associated power supplies. Often shortened to INDICATOR.

radar range. 1. The distance of a target as measured by radar. 2. The maximum distance at which a radar is effective in detecting targets.

radar receiver. A unit of a radar set that demodulates received radar echoes, amplifies the echoes and delivers them to the radar indicator. A radar receiver differs from the usual superheterodyne communications receiver in that its sensitivity is much greater; it has a better signal noise ratio, and it is designed to pass a pulse-type signal.

radar reflector. A device arranged so that incident electromagnetic energy reflects back to its source.

radar repeater. A unit that duplicates the radar display at a location remote from the main radar indicator installation. Also called PPI REPEATER, REMOTE PPI.

radarscope, n. The cathode-ray tube or video monitor in the indicator of a radar set that displays the received echo to indicate range and bearing. Often shortened to SCOPE.

radar set. An electronic apparatus consisting of a transmitter, antenna, receiver, and indicator for sending out radio-frequency energy and receiving and displaying reflected energy so as to indicate the range and bearing of the reflecting object.

radar shadow. The area shielded from radar signals because of an intervening obstruction or absorbing medium. The shadow region appears as an area void of targets.

radial motion. Motion along a radius, or a component in such a direction, particularly the component of space motion of a celestial body in the direction of the line of sight.

radiation, n. 1. The process of emitting energy in the form of electromagnetic waves. 2. The energy radiated in definition 1 above.

radiational cooling. The cooling of the earth's surface and adjacent air, occurring mainly at night whenever the earth's surface suffers a net loss of heat due to terrestrial radiation.

radiation fog. A major type of fog, produced over land when radiational cooling reduces the temperature to or below its dew point. Radiation fog is a nighttime occurrence although it may begin to form by evening twilight and often does not dissipate until after sunrise.

radio aid to navigation. An aid to navigation transmitting information by radio waves.

radiobeacon, n. A radio transmitting station that emits a distinctive or characteristic signal so a navigator can determine the direction of the source using a radio direction finder, providing a line of position.

radiodetermination, n. As defined by the International Telecommunication Union (ITU), the determination of position using propagation properties of radio waves.

radio direction finder. A radio receiver system used for radio direction finding.

radio guard. A ship, aircraft, or radio station designated to listen for and record transmissions and to handle traffic on a designated frequency for a certain unit or units.

radio interference. Interference due to unwanted signals from other radio transmitting stations operating on the same or adjacent frequencies.

radio mast. A label on a nautical chart that indicates a pole or structure for elevating radio antennas, usually found in groups.

radionavigation, n. 1. The determination of position, or the obtaining of information relating to position, for the purposes of navigation by means of the propagation properties of radio waves. 2. As defined by the International Telecommunication Union (ITU), radiodetermination used for the purposes of navigation, including obstruction warning.

radio navigational warning. A radio-transmitted message affecting the safe navigation of vessels or aircraft.

radionavigation-satellite service. As defined by the International Telecommunication Union (ITU) a radiodetermination-satellite service used for the same purposes as the radionavigation service; in certain cases this service includes transmission or retransmission of supplementary information necessary for the operation of radionavigation systems.

radio receiver. An electronic device connected to an antenna or other receptor of radio signals that receives and processes the signals for use.

radio spectrum. The range of electromagnetic radiation useful for communication by radio (approximately 10 kilohertz to 300,000 megahertz).

radio station. A place equipped with one or more transmitters or receivers and accessory equipment for carrying on a radiocommunication service.

radio tower. A label on a nautical chart that indicates a tall pole or structure for elevating radio antennas.

radio transmitter. Equipment for generation and modulation of radio-frequency energy for the purpose of radiocommunication.

radio waves. Electromagnetic waves of frequencies lower than 3,000 gHz propagated in space without artificial guide. The practicable limits of radio frequency are approximately 10 kHz to 100 gHz. Also called HERTZIAN WAVES.

radius vector. A straight line connecting a fixed reference point or center with a second point, which may be moving. In astronomy the expression is usually used to refer to the straight line connecting a celestial body with another that revolves around it.

radome, n A dome-shaped structure used to enclose radar apparatus.

rain, n. Liquid precipitation consisting of drops of water larger than those that comprise DRIZZLE. Orographic rain results when moist air is forced upward by a mountain range.

rainbow, n. A circular arc of concentric spectrally colored bands formed by the refraction of light in drops of water. One seen in ocean spray is called a marine or sea rainbow.

rain clutter. Clutter on the radarscope that is the result of the radar signal being reflected by rain or other forms of precipitation.

rain shadow. The condition of diminished rainfall on the lee side of a mountain or mountain range, where the rainfall is noticeably less than on the windward side.

ramark (from radar marker), n. A radar beacon that continuously transmits a signal appearing as a radial line on the radar display, indicating the direction of the beacon from the ship. For identification purposes, the radial line may be formed by a series of dots or dashes. The radial line appears even if the beacon is outside the range for which the radar is set, as long as the radar receiver is within the power range of the beacon. Unlike the RACON, the ramark does not provide the range to the beacon.

random error. One of the two categories of errors of observation and measurement, the other category being systematic error. Random errors are the errors that occur when irregular, randomly occurring conditions affect the observing instrument, the observer and the environment, and the quantity being observed so that observations of the same quantity made with the same equipment and observer under the same observing conditions result in different values of the observed quantity.

range, n. 1. Two or more objects in line. Such objects are said to be in range. An observer having them in range is said to be on the range. Two beacons are frequently located for the specific purpose of forming a range to indicate a safe route or the centerline of a channel. 2. Distance in a single direction or along a great circle. 3. The extreme distance at which an object or light can be seen is called VISUAL RANGE. When the extreme distance is limited by the curvature of the earth and the heights of the object and the observer, this is called geographic range; when the range of a light is limited only by its intensity, clearness of the atmosphere, and sensitiveness of the observer's eyes, it is called luminous range. 4. The extreme distance at which a signal can be detected or used. The maximum distance at which reliable service is provided is called operating range. The spread of ranges in which there is an element of uncertainty of interpretation is called critical range. 5. The distance a vessel can travel at cruising speed without refueling is called CRUISING RADIUS. 6. The difference in extreme values of a variable quantity. 7. A series of mountains or mountain ridges is called MOUNTAIN RANGE. 8. A predetermined line along which a craft moves while certain data are recorded by instruments usually placed below the line, or the entire station at which such information is determined. 9. An area where practice firing of ordnance equipment is authorized is a firing range. 10. On the sea floor, a series of ridges or seamounts.

range, v., t. 1. To place in line. 2. To determine the distance to an object. 3. To move along or approximately parallel to something, as to range along a coast.

range daymark. 1. One of a pair of unlighted structures used to mark a definite line of bearing. 2. A daymark on a range light.

range finder. An optical instrument for measuring the distance to an object.

range lights. Two or more lights at different elevations so situated to form a range (leading line) when brought into transit. The one nearest the observer is the front light and the one farthest from the observer is the rear light. The front light is at a lower elevation than the rear light.

range marker. A visual presentation on a radar display for measuring the range or for calibrating the time base.

range of tide. The difference in height between consecutive high and low waters. The mean range is the difference in height between mean high water and mean low water. The great diurnal range or diurnal range is the difference in height between mean higher high water and mean lower low water. Where the type of tide is diurnal the mean range is the same as the diurnal range.

range ring. One of a set of equally spaced concentric rings, centered on one's own ship's position, providing a visual presentation of range on a radar display.

ranging mode. A mode of operation of a radionavigation system in which the times for the radio signals to travel from each transmitting station to the receiver are measured rather than their differences as in the HYPERBOLIC MODE. Also called RHO-RHO MODE, RANGE-RANGE MODE.

rate, n. 1. Quantity or amount per unit of something else, usually time. 2. With respect to Loran-A and Loran-C, the term rate, implying the number of pulses per unit time, is used for the character designation, and also the station pair, their signals, and the resulting hyperbolic lines of position and the tables and curves by which they are represented.

reach, n. A comparatively straight segment of a river or channel between two bends.

rear-light. The range light farthest from the observer. It is the highest of the lights of an established range. Also called HIGH LIGHT.

receiver, n. A person who or a device that receives anything, particularly a radio receiver.

receiver gain control. An operating control on a radar indicator used to increase or decrease the sensitivity of the receiver. The control regulates the intensity of the echoes displayed on the radarscope.

reciprocal bearing. A bearing differing by 180° or one measured in the opposite direction, from a given bearing.

recommended direction of traffic flow. A traffic flow pattern indicating a recommended directional movement of traffic in a routing system within which it is impractical or unnecessary to adopt an established direction of traffic flow.

recommended track. A route that has been examined to ensure that it is free of dangers and along which vessels are advised to navigate.

rectangular error. An error that results from rounding off values prior to their inclusion in a table or that results from the fact that an instrument cannot be read closer than a certain value.

rectangular projection. A cylindrical map projection with uniform spacing of the parallels. This projection is used for the star chart in the *Air Almanac*.

red sector. A sector of the circle of visibility of a navigational light in which a red light is exhibited. Such sectors are designated by their limiting bearings, as observed from a vessel. Red sectors are often located to warn of dangers.

reef, n. 1. An offshore consolidated rock hazard to navigation with a depth of 16 fathoms (or 30 meters) or less over it. 2. Sometimes used as a term for a low rocky or coral area some of which is above water.

reference datum. A general term applied to any datum, plane, or surface used as a reference or base from which other quantities can be measured.

reference ellipsoid. A theoretical figure whose dimensions closely approach the dimensions of the geoid; the exact dimensions of the ellipsoid are determined by various considerations of the section of the earth's surface of concern.

reference station. A tide or current station for which independent daily predictions are given in the Tide Tables and Tidal Current Tables, and from which corresponding predictions are obtained for subordinate stations by means of differences and ratios. Also called STANDARD STATION.

reflector, n. A reflecting surface situated behind the primary radiator, an array of primary radiators or a feed for the purpose of increasing forward and reducing backward radiation from antenna.

refraction, n. The change in direction of motion of a ray of radiant energy as it passes obliquely from one medium into another in which the speed of propagation is different. Atmospheric refraction is caused by the atmosphere and may be further designated astronomical refraction if the ray enters from outside the atmosphere or terrestrial refraction if it emanates from a point on or near the surface of the earth. Superrefraction is greater than normal and subrefraction is less than normal.

refraction correction. A correction due to refraction, particularly such a correction to a sextant altitude, due to atmospheric refraction.

refractive index. The ratio of the velocity of light in vacuum to the velocity of light in a medium. This index is equal to the ratio of the sines of the angles of incidence and refraction when a ray crosses the surface separating vacuum and medium.

relative, adj. Having relationship. In navigation the term has several specific applications: a. related to a moving point; apparent, as relative wind, relative movement; b. related to or measured from the heading, as relative bearing; c. related or proportional to a variable, as relative humidity.

relative accuracy. The accuracy with which a user can measure current position relative to that of another user of the same navigation system at the same time. Hence, a system with high relative accuracy provides good rendezvous capability for the users of the system. The correlation between the geographical coordinates and the system coordinates is not relevant.

relative bearing. Bearing relative to the heading of a vessel, expressed as the angular difference between the heading and the direction. It is usually measured from 000° at the heading clockwise through 360° but is sometimes measured from 0° at the heading either clockwise or counterclockwise through 180°, when it is designated right or left.

relative movement. Motion of one object relative to another. The expression is usually used in connection with problems involving motion of one vessel to another, the direction such motion being called DIRECTION RELATIVE MOVEMENT and the speed of the motion being called SPEED OF RELATIVE MOVEMENT or RELATIVE SPEED. Distance relative to a specified reference point, usually one in motion, is called RELATIVE DISTANCE. Usually called APPARENT MOTION applied to the change of position of a celestial body as observed from the earth. Also called RELATIVE MOTION.

relative wind. The wind with reference to a moving point. Sometimes called APPARENT WIND.

relief, n. 1. The elevations of a land surface; represented graphics by contours, hypsometric tints, spot elevations, hachures, etc. Similar representation of the ocean floor is called SUBMARINE RELIEF. 2. The removal of a buoy (formerly also referred to lightships) from station and provision of another buoy having the operating characteristics authorized for that station.

remote-indicating compass. A compass equipped with one or more indicators to repeat at a distance the readings of the master compass. The directive element and controls are called a master compass to distinguish this part of the system from the repeaters or remote indicators. Most marine gyrocompass installations are of this type. Also called REMOTE-READING COMPASS.

repeatability, n. 1. A measure of the variation in the accuracy of an instrument when identical tests are made under fixed conditions. 2. In a navigation system, the measure of the accuracy with which the system permits the user to return to a specified point as defined only in terms of the coordinates peculiar to that system.

repeatable accuracy. In a navigation system, the measure of the accuracy with which the system permits the user to return to a position as defined only in terms of the coordinates peculiar to that system. For example, the distance specified for the repeatable accuracy of a system such as Loran-C is the distance between two Loran-C positions established using the same stations and time-difference readings at different times. The correlation between the geographical coordinates and the system coordinates may or may not be known.

repeater, n. A device for repeating at a distance the indications of an instrument or device.

representative fraction. The scale of a map or chart expressed as a fraction or ratio that relates unit distance on the map to distance measured in the same unit on the ground. Also called NATURAL SCALE, FRACTIONAL SCALE.

residuals, n., pl. The remaining deviation of a magnetic compass on various headings after adjustment or compensation.

resolution, n. 1. The ability of an optical system to distinguish between individual objects; the degree of ability to make such a separation, called RESOLVING POWER, is expressed as the minimum distance between two objects that can be separated. 2. The degree of ability of a radar set to indicate separately the echoes of two targets in range, bearing, and elevation.

restricted area. 1. An area (land, sea, or air) in which there are special restrictive measures employed to prevent or minimize interference between friendly forces. 2. An area under military jurisdiction in which special security measures are employed to prevent unauthorized entry.

restricted waters. Areas that for navigational reasons such as the presence of shoals or other dangers confine the movements of shipping within narrow limits.

retire, v., t. & i. To move back, as to move a line of position back, parallel to itself, along a course line to obtain a line of position at an earlier time. The opposite is ADVANCE.

retrograde motion. The apparent motion of a planet westward among the stars. Apparent motion eastward, called DIRECT MOTION, is more common. Also called RETROGRESSION.

reversing current. A tidal current that flows alternately in approximately opposite directions with a slack water at each reversal of direction.

reversing falls. Falls that flow alternately in opposite directions in a narrow channel in the St. John River, New Brunswick, Canada, due to the large range of tide and a constriction in the river. The direction of flow is upstream or downstream according to whether it is high or low water on the outside, the falls disappearing at the half-tide level.

revolution, n. Circular motion about an axis usually external to the body. The terms REVOLUTION and ROTATION are often used interchangeably, but, with reference to the motions of a celestial body, REVOLUTION refers to the motion in an orbit or about an axis external to the body while ROTATION refers to motion about an axis within the body. Thus, the earth revolves about the sun annually and rotates about its axis daily.

revolution counter, revolution indicator. An instrument for registering the number of revolutions of a shaft, particularly a propeller shaft of a vessel. This information is useful in estimating a vessel's speed through the water.

revolution table. A table listing the number of shaft revolutions corresponding to various speeds of a vessel.

revolving storm. A cyclonic storm, or one in which the wind revolves about a central low-pressure area.

rhumb line. A line on the surface of the earth making the same oblique angle with all meridians; a loxodrome or loxodromic curve spirals toward the poles in a constant true direction. Parallels and meridians, which also maintain constant true directions, may be considered special cases of the rhumb line. A rhumb line is a straight line on a Mercator projection.

rhumb-line course. The direction of the rhumb line from the point of departure to the destination, expressed as the angular distance from a reference direction, usually north. Also called MERCATOR COURSE.

rhumb-line distance. Distance point to point along a rhumb line, usually expressed in nautical miles.

rhumb-line sailing. Any method of solving the various problems involving course, distance, difference of latitude, difference of longitude, and departure as they are related to a rhumb line.

right angle. An angle of 90°.

right ascension. Angular distance east of the vernal equinox; the arc of the celestial equator, or the angle at the celestial pole, between the hour circle of the vernal equinox and the hour circle of a point on the celestial sphere, measured eastward from the hour circle of the vernal equinox through 24 hours. Angular distance west of the vernal equinox, through 360°, is SIDEREAL HOUR ANGLE.

rip current. A narrow intense current setting seaward through the surf zone. It removes excess water brought to the zone by the small net mass transport of waves, and is fed by longshore currents. Rip currents usually occur at points, groins, jetties, etc., of irregular beaches, and at regular intervals along straight, uninterrupted beaches.

riprap. Mounds of stone maintained around light structures to protect them against ice damage and scouring action. Submerged portions present a hazard to vessels attempting to pass very close aboard.

rips, n., pl. Agitation of water caused by the meeting of currents or by a rapid current setting over an irregular bottom. Called TIDE RIPS when the tidal current is involved.

rise of tide. Vertical distance from the chart sounding datum to a higher water datum.

rising tide. A tide in which the depth of water is increasing. Sometimes the term FLOOD is used as an equivalent, but since flood refers primarily to horizontal rather than vertical movement RISING TIDE is more appropriate. The opposite is FALLING TIDE.

river buoy. A lightweight nun or can buoy especially designed to withstand strong currents.

road, n. An open anchorage affording less protection than a harbor. Some protection may be afforded by reefs, shoals, etc. Often used in the plural. Also called ROADSTEAD.

roaring forties. The area of the oceans between 40° and 50° south latitude, where strong westerly winds prevail.

rock, n. 1. An isolated rocky formation or single large stone, usually one constituting a danger to navigation. It may be always submerged, always uncovered, or alternately covered and uncovered by the tide. A pinnacle is a sharp-pointed rock rising from the bottom. 2. The naturally occurring material that forms the firm, hard, and solid masses of the ocean floor. Also, rock is a collective term for hard material generally not smaller than 256 millimeters.

rock awash. A rock that becomes exposed, or nearly so, between chart sounding datum and mean high water. In the Great Lakes, the rock awash symbol is used on charts for rocks that are awash, or nearly so, at low water datum.

roll, n. Oscillation of a craft about its longitudinal axis. Also called ROLLING.

roll, v., t. & i. To oscillate or be oscillated about the longitudinal axis.

rollers, n. Amongst the islands of the West Indies, the South Atlantic and the South Indian Ocean, swell waves that after moving into shallow water have grown to such height as to be destructive.

root mean square. The square root of the arithmetical mean of the squares of a group of numbers.

root mean square error. For the one-dimensional error distribution, this term has the same meaning as STANDARD DEVIATION or STANDARD ERROR. For the two-dimensional error distribution, this term has the same meaning as RADIAL (drms) ERROR. However, such use of the term is deprecated. Root mean square error is commonly called RMS ERROR.

rotary current. A tidal current that flows continually, with the direction of flow changing through 360° during the tidal period.

rotating light. A light with one or more beams that rotate. Sometimes called REVOLVING LIGHT.

rotation, n. Turning of a body about an axis within the body, such as the daily rotation of the earth.

round, v., t. To pass and alter direction of travel, as a vessel ROUNDS A CAPE. If the course is nearly reversed, the term DOUBLE may be used.

roundabout, n. A routing measure comprising a separation point or circular separation zone and a circular traffic lane within defined limits. Traffic within the roundabout moves in a counterclockwise direction around the separation point or zone.

round of bearings. A group of bearings observed together for plotting as a fix.

round of sights. A group of celestial observations made together for plotting a fix.

routing system. Any system of one or more defined tracks and/or traffic control measures for reducing the risk of casualties; it includes traffic separation schemes, two-way routes, recommended tracks, areas to be avoided, inshore traffic zones, roundabouts, precautionary areas, and deep water routes.

rubble, n. 1. Fragments of hard sea ice, roughly spherical and up to 5 feet in diameter, resulting from the disintegration of larger ice formations. When afloat, commonly called BRASH ICE. 2. Loose angular rock fragments.

rules of the road. The International Regulations for Prevention of Collisions at Sea, commonly called International Rules of the Road, and the Inland Navigation Rules, to be followed by all vessels while navigating upon certain inland waters of the United States. Also called RULES OF NAVIGATION.

run before the wind. To steer a course downwind, especially under sail.

run down a coast. To sail approximately parallel with the coast.

running fix. A position determined by crossing lines of position obtained at different times and advanced or retired to a common time. However in celestial navigation or when using long-range electronic aids, a position determined by crossing lines of position obtained within a few minutes is considered a FIX; the expression RUNNING FIX is applied to a position determined by advancing or retiring a line over a considerable period of time. There is no sharp dividing line between a fix and a running fix in this case.

run of the coast. The directional trend of the coast.

run-up. The rush of water up a structure on the breaking of a wave. The amount of run-up is the vertical height above the still water level that the rush of water reaches. Also called UPRUSH.

S

safety lanes. Specified sea lanes designated for use by submarines and surface ships in transit to prevent attack by friendly forces. They may be called SUBMARINE SAFETY LANES when designated for use by submarines in transit.

SafetyNET. The INMARSAT broadcast service for MARITIME SAFETY INFORMATION (MSI).

sailing, n. A method of solving the various problems involving course, distance, difference of latitude, difference of longitude, and departure. The various methods are collectively spoken of as the sailings.

sailing directions. A descriptive book for the use of mariners, containing detailed information of coastal waters, harbor facilities, etc., of an area. For waters of the United States and its possessions, they are published by the National Ocean Survey and are called UNITED STATES COAST PILOTS. Sailing directions, as well as light lists, provide the information that cannot be shown graphically on the nautical chart and that is not readily available elsewhere.

St. Elmo's fire. A luminous discharge of electricity from pointed objects such as the masts and arms of ships, lightning rods, steeples, etc., occurring when there is a considerable atmospheric difference in potential. Also called CORPOSANT, CORONA DISCHARGE.

St. Hilaire method. Establishing a line position from observation of the altitude of a celestial body by using an assumed position, the difference between the observed and computed altitudes, and the azimuth.

sallying ship. Producing rolling motion of a ship by having the crew run in unison from side to side. This is usually done to help float a ship that is aground or to assist it to make way when it is beset by ice.

sandstorm, n. A strong wind carrying sand through the air, the diameter of most of the particles ranging from 0.08 to 1.0 millimeter. In contrast to a DUST STORM, the sand particles are mostly confined to the lowest 10 feet and rarely rise more than 50 feet above the ground.

sandwave, n. A large wavelike sea-floor sediment feature in very shallow water and composed of sand. The wavelength may reach 100 meters, the amplitude is about 0.5 meter. Also called MEGARIPPLE.

Sargasso Sea. The west central region of the subtropical gyre of the North Atlantic Ocean. It is bounded by the North Atlantic, Canary, Atlantic North Equatorial, and Antilles Currents, and the Gulf Stream. It is characterized by the absence of well-marked currents and by large quantities of drifting Sargassum or gulfweed.

sargassum, n. A genus of brown algae characterized by a bushy form, a substantial holdfast when attached, and a yellowish brown, greenish yellow, or orange color. Species of the group have a large variety of forms and are widely distributed in warm seas as attached and free floating plants. Two species (S. fluitans and S. matans) make up 99 percent of the macroscopic vegetation in the Sargasso Sea.

Saros, n. A period of 223 synodic months corresponding approximately to 19 eclipse years or 18.03 Julian years, and is a cycle in which solar and lunar eclipses repeat themselves under approximately the same conditions.

satellite, n. 1. A body, natural or manmade, that orbits about another body, the primary body. The moon is a satellite of the earth, the primary body. 2. As defined by the International Telecommunication Union (ITU), a body that revolves around another body of preponderant mass and that has a motion primarily and permanently determined by the force of attraction of that other body.

scale, n. 1. A series of marks or graduations at definite intervals. A linear scale is a scale graduated at uniform intervals; a logarithmic scale is graduated in the logarithms of uniformly spaced consecutive numbers. 2. The ratio between the linear dimensions of chart, map drawing, etc., and the actual dimensions.

scarf cloud. A thin cirrus-like cloud sometimes observed above a developing cumulus.

scud, n. Shreds or small detached masses of cloud moving rapidly before the wind, often below a layer of lighter clouds.

scud, v., i. To run before a storm.

sea, n. 1. A body of salt water more or less confined by continuous land or chains of islands and forming a distinct region. 2. A body of water nearly or completely surrounded by land, especially if very large or composed of salt water. Sometimes called INLAND SEA. 3. Ocean areas in general, including major indentations in the coast line, such as gulfs. 4. Waves generated or sustained by winds within their fetch as opposed to SWELL. 5. The character of a water surface, particularly the height, length (period), and direction of travel of waves generated locally.

sea anchor. An object towed by a vessel, usually a small one, to keep the vessel end-on to a heavy sea or surf or to reduce the drift. Also called DRAG, DROGUE.

Sea Area. A defined area under the Global Maritime Distress and Safety System (GMDSS), which regulates certain safety and communication equipment necessary according to the area of the ship's operations. Sea Area A-1 is within coverage of VHF coast radio stations (25–30 miles) providing digital selective calling. Sea Area A-2 is within range of the medium-frequency coast radio stations (to approximately 300 miles). Sea Area A-3 is within the footprint of the geostationary INMARSAT communications satellites, covering the rest of the open seas except the poles. Sea Area A-4 covers the rest of the earth, chiefly the polar areas. The areas do not overlap.

seaboard, n. The region of land bordering the sea.

sea breeze. A breeze blowing from the sea to adjacent land. It usually blows by day, when the land is warmer than the sea, and alternates with a LAND BREEZE, which blows in the opposite direction by night.

sea buoy. The outermost buoy marking the entrance to a channel or harbor.

sea fog. A type of advection fog formed when air that has been lying over a warm water surface is transported over colder water, resulting in cooling of the lower layer of air below its dew point.

sea gate. 1. A gate that serves to protect a harbor tidal basin from the sea, such as one of a pair of supplementary gates at the entrance to a tidal basin exposed to the sea. 2. A movable gate that protects the main deck of a ferry from waves and sea spray.

sea kindliness. A measure of the ease of motion of a vessel in heavy seas, particularly in regard to rolling, pitching, and shipping water. It is not to be confused with seaworthiness, which implies that the vessel is able to sustain heavy rolling, pitching, etc., without structural damage or impaired stability.

sea level. Height of the surface of the sea at any time.

sea mile. An approximate mean value of the nautical mile equal to 6,080 feet; the length of a minute of arc along the meridian at latitude 48°.

seamount, n. On the sea floor, an elevation rising generally more than 1,000 meters and of limited extent across the summit.

search-and-rescue radar transponder (SART). An electronic device that transmits a homing signal on the radar frequency used by rescue ships and aircraft.

sea return. Clutter on the radarscope that is the result of the radar signal being reflected from the sea, especially near the ship. Also called SEA CLUTTER.

sea room. Space in which to maneuver without danger of grounding or colliding.

season, n. 1. One of the four principal divisions of the year: spring, summer, autumn, and winter. 2. An indefinite part of the year, such as the rainy season.

seasonal current. An ocean current that changes in speed or direction due to seasonal winds.

seaway, n. 1. A moderately rough sea. Used chiefly in the expression in a seaway. 2. The sea as a route of travel from one place to another; a shipping lane.

second, n. 1. The base unit of time in the International System of Units (SI). In 1967 the second was defined by the Thirteenth General Conference on Weights and Measures as the duration of 9,192,631,770 periods of the radiation corresponding to the transition between two hyperfine levels of the ground state of the cesium-133 atom. This value was established to agree as closely as possible with the ephemeris second. Also called ATOMIC SECOND. 2. A sixtieth part of a minute in either time or arc.

secondary, n. A small low-pressure area accompanying a large or primary one. The secondary often grows at the expense of the primary, eventually replacing it.

secondary control tide station. A tide station at which continuous observations have been made over a minimum period of 1 year but less than a 19-year Metonic cycle. The series is reduced by comparison with simultaneous observations from a primary control tide station. This station provides for a 365-day harmonic analysis including the seasonal fluctuation of sea level.

secondary light. A major light, other than a primary seacoast light, established at harbor entrances and other locations where high intensity and reliability are required.

secondary phase factor correction. A correction for additional time (or phase delay) for transmission of a low-frequency signal over an all-seawater path when the signal transit time is based on the free-space velocity. The Loran-C lattices as tabulated in tables or overprinted on the nautical chart normally include compensation for secondary phase factor.

secondary radar. 1. Radar in which the target is fitted with a transponder and in which the target retransmits automatically on the interrogating frequency or a different frequency. The response may be coded. 2. As defined by the International Telecommunication Union (ITU), a radiodetermination system based on the comparison of reference signals with radio signals retransmitted from the position to be determined.

secondary station. In a radionavigation system, the station of a chain whose emissions are made with reference to the emissions of a master station without being triggered by the emissions of such station, as in Loran-C.

second-trace echo. A radar echo received from a target after the following pulse has been transmitted. Second-trace echoes are unusual except under abnormal atmospheric conditions or conditions under which super-refraction is present, and are received from targets at actual ranges greater than the radar range scale setting. They may be recognized through changes in their position on the radarscope on changing the pulse repetition rate; their hazy, streaky, or distorted shape; and their erratic movements on plotting. Also called MULTIPLE-TRACE ECHO.

sector light. A light having sectors of different colors or the same color in specific sectors separated by dark sectors.

sector scanning. In the use of radar, the process of scanning within a sector as opposed to scanning around the horizon.

seiche, n. A stationary wave usually caused by strong winds and/or changes in barometric pressure. It is usually found in lakes and semienclosed bodies of water. It may also be found in areas of the open ocean.

semidiameter, n. Half the angle at the observer subtended by the visible disk of a celestial body. Sextant altitudes of the sun and moon should be corrected for semidiameter unless the center is observed.

semidiameter correction. A correction due to semidiameter, particularly that sextant altitude correction, when applied to the observation of the upper or lower limb of a celestial body, determines the altitude of the center of that body.

semidiurnal, adj. Having a period or cycle of approximately one-half of a day. The predominating type of tide throughout the world is semidiurnal, with two high waters and two low waters each tidal day. The tidal current is said to be semidiurnal when there are two flood and two ebb periods each tidal day.

semidiurnal current. Tidal current in which tidal day current cycle consists of two flood currents and two ebb currents, separated by slack water; or two changes in direction, 360° of a rotary current.

sensible horizon. The circle of the celestial sphere formed by the intersection of the celestial sphere and a plane through any point, such as the eye of an observer, and perpendicular to the zenith-nadir line.

separation line. A line separating the traffic lane in which ships are proceeding in opposite or nearly opposite directions, or separating a traffic lane from the adjacent inshore traffic zone.

separation zone. A defined zone that separates traffic lanes in which ships are proceeding in opposite directions, or that separates traffic lanes from the adjacent inshore traffic zone.

set, n. The direction towards which a current flows.

set, v., i. Of a celestial body, to cross the visible horizon while descending. The opposite is RISE.

set, v., t. To establish, as to set a course.

seven-eighths rule. A rule of thumb, stating that the approximate distance to an object broad on the beam equals ⅞ of the distance traveled by a craft while the relative bearing (right or left) changes from 30° to 60° or from 120° to 150°, neglecting current and wind.

seven seas. Figuratively, all the waters or oceans of the world. Applied generally to the seven oceans: Arctic, Antarctic, North Atlantic, South Atlantic, North Pacific, South Pacific, and Indian.

seven-tenths rule. A rule of thumb, stating that the approximate distance to an object broad on the beam equals 7/10 of the distance traveled by a craft while the relative bearing (right or left) changes from 22.5° to 45° or from 135° to 157.5°, neglecting current and wind.

seven-thirds rule. A rule of thumb, stating that the approximate distance to an object broad on the beam equals 7/3 of the distance traveled by a craft while the relative bearing (right or left) changes from 22.5° to 26.5°, 67.5° to 90°, 90° to 112.5°, or 153.5° to 157.5°, neglecting current and wind.

sextant, n. A double-reflecting instrument for measuring angles, primarily altitudes of celestial bodies. As originally used, the term applied only to instruments having an arc of 60°, a sixth of a circle, from which the instrument derived its name. Such an instrument had a range of 120°. In modern practice the term applies to a similar instrument, regardless of its range, very few modern instruments being sextants in the original sense. Thus, an octant, having a range of 90°; a quintant, having a range of 144°; and a quadrant, having a range of 180°, may be called sextants.

sextant adjustment. The process of checking the accuracy of a sextant and removing or reducing its error.

sextant altitude. Altitude as indicated by a sextant or similar instrument, before corrections are applied.

sextant altitude correction. Any of several

corrections applied to a sextant altitude in the process of converting it to observed altitude.

sextant error. The error in reading a sextant, due either to lack of proper adjustment or imperfection of manufacture.

shade error. The error of an optical instrument due to refraction in the shade glasses. If this effect is due to lack of parallelism of the faces it is usually called PRISMATIC ERROR.

shade glass. A darkened transparent glass that can be moved into the line of sight of an optical instrument, such as a sextant, to reduce the intensity of light reaching the eye. Also called SHADE.

shadow region. A region shielded from radar signals because of an intervening obstruction or absorbing medium. This region appears as an area void of targets on a radar display such as a plan position indicator. The phenomenon is called RADAR SHADOW.

shelf, n. A zone adjacent to a continent, or around an island, that extends from the low water line to a depth at which there is usually a marked increase of slope towards oceanic depths.

ship, n. Originally a sailing vessel with three or more masts, square-rigged on all. The term is now generally applied to any large, ocean-going vessel, except submarines, which are called boats regardless of size.

ship earth station (SES). An INMARSAT satellite system installed aboard a vessel.

shipping lane. An established route traversed by ocean shipping.

Ship Routing. A publication of the International Maritime Organization (IMO) that describes the general provisions of ships' routing, traffic separation schemes, deep water routes, and areas to be avoided, that have been adopted by IMO. All details of routing systems are promulgated through *Notices to Mariners* and *Sailing Directions* and are depicted on charts.

ship's head. Heading of a vessel.

ship simulator. A computerized system that uses video projection techniques to simulate navigational and shiphandling situations. A full-capability system includes a completely equipped ship's bridge and can duplicate almost any aspect of ship operation; partial systems focus on a particular function, such as radar collision avoidance or nighttime navigation.

ship weather routing. A procedure whereby an optimum route is developed based on the forecasts of weather and seas and the ship's characteristics for a particular transit. Within specified limits of weather and sea conditions, ship weather routing seeks maximum safety and crew comfort, minimum fuel consumption, minimum time underway, or any desired combination of these factors.

shoal, n. An offshore hazard to navigation on which there is a depth of 16 fathoms (or 30 meters) or less, composed of unconsolidated material.

shoal patches. Individual and scattered elevations of the bottom, with depths of 16 fathoms (or 30 meters) or less, but composed of any material except rock or coral.

shoal water. Shallow water; water over a shoal.

shoreface, n. The narrow zone seaward from the low tide shoreline, permanently covered by water, over which the beach sands and gravels actively oscillate with changing wave conditions.

short range systems. Radionavigation systems limited in their positioning capability to coastal regions or those systems limited to making landfall.

short sea. A sea in which the waves are short, irregular, and broken.

short wave. A radio wave shorter than those of the standard broadcast band.

shower, n. Precipitation from a convective cloud. Showers are characterized by the suddenness with which they start and stop, by the rapid changes of intensity, and usually by rapid changes in the appearance of the sky. In weather observing practice, showers are always reported in terms of the basic type of precipitation that is falling, i.e., rain showers, snow showers, sleet showers.

side error. The error in the reading of a sextant due to nonperpendicularity of horizon glass to the frame.

side lights. Running lights placed on the sides of a vessel, green to starboard and red to port, showing an unbroken light over an arc of the horizon from dead ahead to 22.5° abaft the beam.

side lobe. Any lobe of the radiation pattern of a directional antenna other than the main lobe.

sidereal, adj. Of or pertaining to the stars, though SIDEREAL generally refers to the stars and TROPICAL to the vernal equinox, sidereal time and the sidereal day are based upon position of the vernal equinox relative the meridian. The SIDEREAL YEAR is based on the stars.

sidereal hour angle. Angular distance west of the vernal equinox; the arc of the celestial equator or the angle at the celestial pole between the hour circle of the vernal equinox and the hour circle of a point on the celestial sphere, measured westward from the hour circle of the equinox through 360°. Angular distance east of the vernal equinox, through 24 hours, is RIGHT ASCENSION.

sidereal month. The average period of revolution of the moon with respect to the stars, a period of 27 days, 7 hours, 43 minutes, 11.5 seconds.

sidereal time. Time defined by the daily rotation of the earth with respect to the vernal equinox of the first point of Aries. Sidereal time is numerically measured by the hour angle of the equinox, which represents the position of the equinox in the daily rotation.

sidereal year. The period of one apparent rotation of the earth around the sun, with relation to a fixed point or a distant star devoid proper motion, being 365 days, 6 hours, 9 days, and 9.5 seconds in 1900, and increasing at a rate of 0.0001 second annually. Because of the precession of the equinoxes this is about 20 minutes longer than a tropical year.

sight, n. Observation of the altitude, and sometimes also the azimuth, of a celestial body for a line of position; or the data obtained by such observation. An observation of a celestial body made by facing 180° from the azimuth of the body is called a back sight.

sight reduction. The process of deriving from a sight the information needed for establishing a line of position.

sight reduction tables. Tables for performing sight reduction, particularly those for comparison with the observed altitude of a celestial body to determine the altitude difference for establishing a line of position. Sight Reduction Tables for Air Navigation. Sight Reduction Tables for Marine Navigation.

signal-to-noise ratio. The ratio of the magnitude of the signal to that of the noise, often expressed in decibels.

simple conic map projection. A conic map projection in which the surface of a sphere or spheroid, such as the earth, is conceived as developed on a tangent cone, which is then spread out to form a plane.

sine curve. Characteristic simple wave pattern; a curve that represents the plotted values of sines of angles, with the sine as the ordinate and the angle as the abscissa. The curve starts at 0 amplitude at the origin, increases to a maximum at 90°, decreases to 0 at 180°, increases negatively to a maximum negative amplitude at 270°, and returns to 0 at 360°, to repeat the cycle. Also called SINUSOID.

siren, n. A sound signal emitter using the periodic escape of compressed air through a rotary shutter.

skeleton tower. A tower, usually of steel and often used for navigation aids, constructed of open legs with various horizontal and diagonal bracing members.

skywave, n. A radio wave that is propagated by way of the ionosphere. Also called IONOSPHERIC WAVE.

skywave correction. The correction to be applied to the time difference reading of signals received via the ionosphere to convert it to the equivalent groundwave reading. The correction for a particular place is established on the basis of an average height of the ionosphere.

skywave transmission delay. The amount by which the time of transit from transmitter to receiver of a pulse carried by skywaves reflected once from the E-layer exceeds the time of transit of the same pulse carried by groundwaves.

slack water. The state of a tidal current when its speed is near zero, especially the moment when a reversing current changes direction and its speed is zero. The term is also applied to the entire period of low speed near the time of turning of the current when it is too weak to be of any practical importance in navigation. The relation of the time of slack water to the tidal phases varies in different localities. For standing tidal waves, slack water occurs near the times of high and low water, while for progressive tidal waves, slack water occurs midway between high and low water.

slave station. In a radionavigation system, the station of a chain whose emissions are made with reference to the emissions of a master station, its emissions being triggered by the emissions of the master station.

sleet, n. Also known as ICE PELLETS; colloquially some parts of the United States, precipitation in the form of a mixture of rain and snow.

slip, n. 1. A berthing space between two piers. Also called DOCK. 2. The difference between the distance a propeller would travel longitudinally in one revolution if operating in a solid and the distance it travels through a fluid.

small area plotting sheet. For a relatively small area, a good approximation of a Mercator position plotting sheet, constructed by the navigator by either of two methods based upon graphical solution of the secant of the latitude which approximates the expansion. A partially completed small area plotting sheet printed in advance for later rapid completion according to requirements is called UNIVERSAL PLOTTING SHEET.

small circle. The intersection of a sphere and plane that does not pass through its center.

small scale. A scale involving a relatively large reduction in size. A small-scale chart usually covers a large area. The opposite is LARGE SCALE, which covers a small area.

smog, n. Originally a natural fog contaminated by industrial pollutants, or a mixture of smoke and fog. Today, smog is a common term applied to visible air pollution with or without fog.

smoke, n. Small particles of carbon and other solid matter, resulting from incomplete combustion, suspended in the air. When it settles, it is called SOOT.

smooth sea. Sea with waves no higher than ripples or small wavelets.

snow, n. 1. Frozen precipitation consisting of translucent or white ice crystals that fall either separately or in loose clusters called snowflakes. Very fine, simple crystals, or minute branched, star-like snowflakes are called snow grains. Snow pellets are white, opaque, roundish grains that are crisp and easily compressible, and may rebound or burst when striking a hard surface. Snow is called brown, red, or yellow when it is colored by the presence of brown dust, red dust or algae, or pine or cypress pollen, respectively. 2. The speckled background on the plan position indicator or video display due to electrical noise.

solar, adj. Of or pertaining to the sun.

solar day. 1. The duration of one rotation of the earth on its axis, with respect to the sun. This may be either a mean solar day or an apparent solar day, as the reference is the mean or apparent sun, respectively. 2. The duration of one apparent rotation of the sun.

solar eclipse. An eclipse of the sun. When the moon passes between the sun and the earth, the sun appears eclipsed to an observer in the moon's shadow. A solar eclipse is partial if the sun is partly obscured; total if the entire surface is obscured, or annular if a thin ring of the sun's surface appears around the obscuring body.

solar flare. A bright eruption from the sun's chromosphere. Solar flares may appear within minutes and fade within an hour.

solar noon. Twelve o'clock solar time, or the instant the sun is over the upper branch of the reference meridian. Solar noon may be classified as mean if the mean sun is the reference, or as apparent if the apparent sun is the reference. It may be further classified according to the reference meridian, either the local or Greenwich meridian or additionally in the case of mean noon, a designated zone meridian. Standard, daylight saving, or summer noon are variations of zone noon. Local apparent noon may also be called high noon.

solar system. The sun and other celestial bodies within its gravitational influence, including planets, planetoids, satellites, comets, and meteors.

solar tide. 1. The part of the tide that is due to the tide-producing force of the sun. 2. The observed tide in areas where the solar tide is dominant. This condition provides for phase repetition at about the same time each solar day.

solar time. Time based upon the rotation of the earth relative to the sun. Solar time may be classified as mean if the mean sun is the reference; or as apparent if the apparent sun is the reference. The difference between mean and apparent time is called EQUATION OF TIME. Solar time may be further classified according to the reference meridian, either the local or Greenwich meridian or additionally in the case of mean time, a designated zone meridian. Standard and daylight saving or summer time are variations of zone time. Time may also be designated according to the timepiece, as chronometer time or watch time, the time indicated by these instruments.

solid color buoy. A buoy painted only one color above the water line.

solstice, n. 1. One of the two points of the ecliptic farthest from the celestial equator; one of the two points on the celestial sphere occupied by the sun at maximum declination. That in the Northern Hemisphere is called the summer solstice and that in the Southern Hemisphere the winter solstice. Also called SOLSTITIAL POINT. 2. That instant at which the sun reaches one of the solstices about June 21 (summer solstice) or December 22 (winter solstice).

sonar, n. A system that determines distance and/or direction of an underwater object by measuring the interval of time between transmission of an underwater sonic or ultrasonic signal and the return of its echo. The name sonar is derived from the words sound navigation and ranging.

sonic depth finder. A direct-reading instrument that determines the depth of water by measuring the time interval between the emission of a sound and the return of its echo from the bottom. A similar instrument utilizing signals above audible range is called an ULTRASONIC DEPTH FINDER. Both instruments are also called ECHO SOUNDERS.

sound, n. 1. A relatively long arm of the sea or ocean forming a channel between an island and a mainland or connecting two larger bodies of water, as a sea and the ocean, or two parts of the same body but usually wider and more extensive than a strait. 2. A vibratory disturbance in air or some other elastic medium, capable of being heard by the human ear, and generally of a frequency between about 20 and 20,000 cycles per second.

sound, v., i. To measure the depth of the water.

sound, v., t. For a whale or other large sea mammal to dive for an extended period of time.

sound buoy. A buoy equipped with a gong, bell, whistle, or horn.

sounding, n. Measured or charted depth of water, or the measurement of such depth. A minimum sounding chosen for a vessel of specific draft in a given area to indicate the limit of safe navigation is called a danger sounding.

sounding datum. Short for CHART SOUNDING DATUM.

sound signal. A sound transmitted in order to convey information.

sound signal station. An attended station whose function is to operate a sound signal.

south, n. The direction 180° from north.

southeaster, sou'easter, n. A southeasterly wind, particularly a strong wind or gale.

south geographical pole. The geographical pole in the Southern Hemisphere, at lat. 90°S.

south geomagnetic pole. The geomagnetic pole in the Southern Hemisphere. This term should not be confused with SOUTH MAGNETIC POLE.

southing, n. The distance a craft makes good to the south. The opposite is NORTHING.

south magnetic pole. The magnetic pole in the Southern Hemisphere. This term should not be confused with SOUTH GEOMAGNETIC POLE.

South Pole. 1. The south geographical pole. 2. The south-seeking end of a magnet.

south temperate zone. The part of the earth between the Tropic of Capricorn and the Antarctic Circle.

southwester, sou'wester, n. A southwest wind, particularly a strong wind or gale.

space coordinates. A three-dimensional system of Cartesian coordinates by which a point is located by three magnitudes indicating distance from three planes that intersect at a point.

spar buoy. A buoy in the shape of a spar, or tapered pole, floating nearly vertically.

special purpose buoy. A buoy used to indicate a special meaning to the mariner and having no lateral significance, such as one used to mark a quarantine or anchorage area.

spectrum (pl. spectra), n. 1. A series of images formed when a beam of radiant energy is separated into its various wavelength components. 2. The entire range of electromagnetic radiation, or any part of it used for a specific purpose, such as the radio spectrum (10 kilohertz to 300 gigahertz).

speed, n. Rate of motion. The terms SPEED and VELOCITY are often used interchangeably but SPEED is a scalar, having magnitude only while VELOCITY is a vector quantity, having both magnitude and direction. Rate of motion in a straight line is called linear speed, while change of direction per unit time is called angular velocity.

speed made good. The speed estimated by dividing the distance between the last fix and an EP by the time between the fix and the EP.

speed of advance. 1. The speed intended to be made good along the track. 2. The average speed in knots that must be maintained during a passage to arrive at a destination at an appointed time.

speed over ground. The vessel's actual speed, determined by dividing the distance between successive fixes by the time between the fixes.

sphere, n. A curved surface all points of which are equidistant from a fixed point within, called the center.

sphere of position. A spherical surface upon the surface of which a craft must be located.

spherical angle. The angle between two intersecting great circles.

spherical buoy. A buoy of which the upper part of the body (above the waterline), or the larger part of the superstructure, is spherical.

spherical triangle. A closed figure having arcs of three great circles as sides.

spherical wave. A wave with a spherical wave front.

spheroid, n. An ellipsoid; a figure resembling a sphere. Also called ELLIPSOID or ELLIPSOID OF REVOLUTION, from the fact that it can be formed by revolving an ellipse about one of its axes. If the shorter axis is used as the axis of revolution, an oblate spheroid results, and if the longer axis is used, a prolate spheroid results. The earth is approximately an oblate spheroid.

spin axis. The axis of rotation of a gyroscope.

spindle buoy. A buoy having a spindle-like shape floating nearly vertically.

spoil area. Area for the purpose of disposing dredged material, usually near dredged channels. Spoil areas are usually a hazard to navigation, and navigators should avoid crossing these areas. Spoil areas are shown on nautical charts. Also called SPOIL GROUND.

spoil ground mark. A navigation mark indicating an area used for deposition of dredge spoil.

spot elevation. A point on a map or chart where height above a specified datum is noted, usually by a dot and the height value.

spring, n. The season in the Northern Hemisphere that begins astronomically at the vernal equinox and ends at the summer solstice. In the Southern Hemisphere the limits are the autumnal equinox and the winter solstice.

spring tidal currents. Tidal currents of increased speed occurring semimonthly as the result of the moon being new or full.

spring tides. Tides of increased range occurring semimonthly as the result of the moon being new or full. The spring range of tide is the average semidiurnal range occurring at the time of spring tides and is most conveniently computed from the harmonic constants.

squall, n. A wind of considerable intensity caused by atmospheric instability. It forms and dissipates relatively quickly and is often accompanied by thunder, lightning, and precipitation, when it may be called a thundersquall. An arched squall is one relatively high in the center, tapering off on both sides. A bull's-eye squall is one formed in fair weather, characteristic of the ocean off the coast of South Africa.

squall cloud. A small eddy cloud sometimes formed below the leading edge of a thunderstorm cloud, between the upward and downward currents.

squall line. A non-frontal line or narrow band of active thunderstorms (with or without squalls); a mature instability line.

squat, n. For a vessel underway, the bodily sinkage and change of trim caused by the pressure distribution on the hull due to the relative motion of water and hull. The effect begins to increase significantly at depth-to-draft ratios less than 2.5. It increases rapidly with speed and is augmented in narrow channels.

stability, n. The state or property of resisting change or of tending to return to original conditions after being disturbed. The opposite is INSTABILITY.

stabilization of radarscope display. Orientation of the radar display to some reference direction. A radarscope display is said to be STABILIZED IN AZIMUTH when the orientation of the display is fixed to an unchanging reference (usually north). The NORTH UP orientation is an example. A radarscope display is said to be UNSTABILIZED IN AZIMUTH when the orientation of the display changes with changes in one's own ship's heading. The HEAD UP orientation is an example. A radarscope display is said to be DOUBLY STABILIZED or to have DOUBLE STABILIZATION when the basic orientation of the display is fixed to an unchanging reference (usually north) but the radarscope is rotated to keep one's own ship's heading or heading flasher up on the radarscope.

stack, n. A label on a nautical chart that indicates a tall smokestack or chimney. The term is used when the stack is more prominent as a landmark than the accompanying buildings.

stadimeter, n. An instrument for determining the distance to an object of known height by measuring the vertical angle subtended by the object. The instrument is graduated directly in distance.

stand, n. The state of the tide at high or low water when there is no sensible change in the height of the tide. The water level is stationary at high and low water for only an instant, but the change in level near these times is so slow that it is not usually perceptible. In general, the duration of the apparent stand will depend upon the range of tide, being longer for a small range than for a large range, but where there is a tendency for a double tide the stand may last for several hours, even with a large range of tide. It may be called high water stand if it occurs at the time of high water, and low water stand if it occurs at low water. Sometimes called PLATFORM TIDE.

standard atmosphere. 1. A unit accepted temporarily for use with the International System of Units; 1 standard atmosphere is equal to 101,325 pascals. 2. A hypothetical vertical distribution of atmospheric temperature, pressure, and density that is taken to be representative of the atmosphere for various purposes.

standard compass. A magnetic compass designated as the standard for a vessel. It is normally located in a favorable position with respect to magnetic influences.

standard noon. Twelve o'clock standard time, or the instant the mean sun is over the upper branch of the standard meridian. DAYLIGHT SAVING or SUMMER NOON usually occurs 1 hour later than standard noon.

standard parallel. 1. A parallel of latitude used as a control line in the computation of a map projection. 2. A parallel of latitude on a map or chart along which the scale is as stated for that map or chart.

standard time. The legally established time for a given zone. The United States and its possessions are, by law, divided into eight time zones. The limits of each time zone are defined by the Secretary of Transportation in Part 71, Title 49 of the Code of Federal Regulations.

standpipe, n. A label on a nautical chart that indicates a tall cylindrical structure in a waterworks system.

star, n. A large self-luminous celestial body.

starboard, n. The right side of a craft, facing forward. The opposite is PORT.

starboard hand buoy. A buoy to be left to the starboard side when approaching from seaward or in the general direction of buoyage, or in the direction established by the appropriate authority.

star chart. A representation, on a flat surface, of the celestial sphere or a part of it, showing the positions of the stars and sometimes other features of the celestial sphere.

star cloud. A large number of stars close together, forming a congested part of a galaxy.

star cluster. A group of stars physically close together.

star finder. A device to facilitate the identification of stars. Sometimes called a STAR IDENTIFIER.

Star Finder and Identifier (No. 2102-D). A circular star finder and identifier formerly published by the U.S. Navy Hydrographic Office and later by the U.S. Naval Oceanographic Office. It consists of a white opaque base with an azimuthal equidistant projection of most of the celestial sphere on each side, one side having the north celestial pole at the center and the other side having the south celestial pole at the center, and a series of transparent templates, at 10° intervals of latitude, each template having a family of altitude and azimuth curves.

star globe. A small globe representing the celestial sphere, on which the apparent positions of the stars are indicated. It is usually provided with graduated arcs and a suitable mount for determining the approximate altitude and azimuth of the stars, to serve as a star finder. Star globes are more commonly used by the British than by Americans. Also called CELESTIAL GLOBE.

Star Sight Reduction Tables for 42 Stars. A sight reduction table that provides for the reduction of 42 selected stars by the assumed altitude method. Of the 42 stars included in the table, 21 are above the observer's horizon at any time and are so tabulated in each column for integral values of latitude and altitude. This large number of star tabulations is particularly useful when clouds make identification difficult or obscure stars. Since the tabulations are for a given epoch, provision is made for precession and nutation corrections.

star telescope. An accessory of the marine navigational sextant designed primarily for star observations.

static, n. 1. Radio wave interference caused by natural electrical disturbances in the atmosphere, or the electromagnetic phenomena capable of causing such interference. 2. Noise heard in a radio receiver caused by electrical disturbances in the atmosphere, such as lightning, northern lights, etc.

station, n. 1. The authorized location of an aid to navigation. 2. One or more transmitters or receivers, or a combination of transmitters and receivers, including the accessory equipment necessary at one location, for carrying on a radiocommunication service.

stationary front. A front that is stationary or nearly so. A front that is moving at a speed less than about 5 knots is generally considered to be stationary. In synoptic chart analysis, a stationary front is one that has not moved appreciably from its position on the last previous synoptic chart (3 or 6 hours before). Also called QUASI-STATIONARY FRONT.

stationary orbit. An equatorial orbit in which the satellite revolves about the primary at the angular rate at which the primary rotates on its axis. From the primary, the satellite appears to be stationary over a point on the primary's equator.

stationary wave. A wave that oscillates without progressing. One-half of such a wave may be illustrated by the oscillation of the water in a pan that has been tilted. Near the axis, which is called the node or nodal line, there is no vertical rise and fall of the water. The ends of the wave are called loops and at these places the vertical rise and fall is at a maximum. The current is maximum near the node and minimum at the loops. The period of a stationary wave depends upon the length and depth of the body of water. A stationary wave may be resolved into two progressive waves of equal amplitude and equal speeds moving in opposite directions. Also called STANDING WAVE.

station buoy. An unlighted buoy established in the vicinity of a lightship or an important lighted buoy as a reference point in case the lightship or buoy should be dragged off station. Also called WATCH BUOY.

statute mile (U.S. Survey mile). A unit of distance equal to 5,280 feet. This mile is generally used on land and is sometimes called LAND MILE. It is commonly used to express navigational distances by navigators of river and lake vessels, particularly those navigating the Great Lakes.

steady bearing. A bearing line to another vessel or object that does not change over time. An approaching or closing craft is said to be on a steady bearing if the compass bearing does not change and risk of collision therefore exists.

steam fog. Fog formed when water vapor is added to air that is much colder than the source of the vapor. It may be formed when very cold air drifts across relatively warm water. At temperatures below about −20°F, ice particles or droxtals may be formed in the air producing a type of ice fog known as frost smoke.

steerage way, n. Any speed at which a ship has sufficient way to respond to rudder movements to maintain a desired course.

steering compass. A compass by which a craft is steered, generally meaning the magnetic compass at the helm.

steering repeater. A compass repeater by which a craft is steered. Sometimes loosely called a STEERING COMPASS.

stellar, adj. Of or pertaining to stars.

stereographic chart. A chart on the stereographic map projection.

stereographic map projection. A perspective, conformal, azimuthal map projection in which points on the surface of a sphere or spheroid, such as the earth, are conceived as projected by radial lines from any point on the surface to a plane tangent to the antipode of the point of projection.

Circles project as circles except for great circles through the point of tangency, which project as straight lines. The principal navigational use of the projection is for charts of the polar regions. Also called AZIMUTHAL ORTHOMORPHIC MAP PROJECTION.

stern light. A running light placed on the centerline of a vessel showing a continuous white light, from dead astern to 67.5° to either side.

sternway, n. Making way through the water in a direction opposite to the heading. Motion in the forward direction is called HEADWAY.

stooping, n. Apparent decrease in the vertical dimension of an object near the horizon, due to large inequality of atmospheric refraction in the line of sight to the top and bottom of the object. The opposite is TOWERING.

storm, n. 1. Wind of force 10 (48 to 55 knots or 55 to 63 miles per hour) on the Beaufort wind scale. 2. Any disturbed state of the atmosphere implying severe weather. In synoptic meteorology, a storm is a complete individual disturbance identified on synoptic charts as a complex of pressure, wind, clouds, precipitation, etc., or identified by such means as radar. Thus, storms range in scale from tornadoes and thunderstorms, through tropical cyclones, to widespread extra tropical cyclones. From a local and special interest viewpoint, a storm is a transient occurrence identified by its most destructive or spectacular aspect. Examples are rain storms, wind storms, hail storms, snow storms, etc. Notable special cases are blizzards, ice storms, sandstorms, and dust storms. 3. A term once used by seamen for what is now called VIOLENT STORM on the Beaufort wind scale.

storm center. The area of lowest atmospheric pressure of a cyclone. This is a more general expression than EYE OF THE STORM, which refers only to the center of a well-developed tropical cyclone, in which there is a tendency of the skies to clear.

storm surge. Increase or decrease in sea level by strong winds such as those accompanying a hurricane or other intense storm. Reduced atmospheric pressure often contributes to the decrease in height during hurricanes. It is potentially catastrophic, especially in deltaic regions with onshore winds at the time of high water and extreme wind wave heights. Also called STORM TIDE, STORM WAVE, TIDAL WAVE.

storm track. The horizontal component of the path followed or expected to be followed by a storm center.

strand, v., t. & i. To run hard aground. The term STRAND usually refers to a serious grounding, while the term GROUND refers to any grounding, however slight.

stratiform, adj. Descriptive of clouds of extensive horizontal development, as contrasted to the vertically developed CUMULIFORM types.

stratocumulus, n. A principal cloud type (cloud genus), predominantly stratiform, in the form of a gray and/or whitish layer or patch, that nearly always has dark parts and is non-fibrous (except for virga). Its elements are tessellated, rounded, roll-shaped, etc.; they may or may not be merged, and usually are arranged in orderly groups, lines or undulations, giving the appearance of a simple (or occasionally a cross-pattern) wave system.

stratosphere, n. The atmospheric shell extending upward from the tropopause to the height where the temperature begins to increase in the 20- to 25-kilometer region.

stratus, n. A low cloud (mean upper level below 6,500 ft.) in a uniform layer, resembling fog but not resting on the surface.

stream current. A relatively narrow, deep, fast-moving ocean current. The opposite is DRIFT CURRENT.

strength of current. Phase of tidal current in which the speed is a maximum; also the speed at this time.

stripes, n. In navigation terminology, stripes are vertically arranged areas of color. Horizontal areas are called bands.

strong breeze. Wind of force 6 (22 to 27 knots or 25 to 31 miles per hour) on the Beaufort wind scale.

strong gale. Wind of force 9 (41 to 47 knots or 47 to 54 miles per hour) on the Beaufort wind scale.

sub-. A prefix meaning under, less, or marginal. The opposite is SUPER-.

sublimation, n. The transition of a substance directly from the solid state to the vapor state, or vice versa, without passing through the intermediate liquid state.

sublunar point. The geographical position of the moon; the point on the earth at which the moon is in the zenith.

submarine cable. A submarine conductor or fiber-optic conduit for electric current or communications.

submerged, adj. & adv. 1. Under water. The opposite is UNCOVERED. 2. Having descended below the surface. The opposite is SURFACED.

submerged breakwater. A breakwater with its top below the still-water level. When this structure is struck by a wave, part of the wave energy is reflected seaward. The remaining energy is largely dissipated in a breaker, transmitted shoreward as a multiple crest system or as a simple wave system.

submerged production well. An oil or gas well that is a seabed installation only, i.e., the installation does not include a permanent production platform.

submerged rock. A rock covered at the chart sounding datum and considered to be potentially dangerous to navigation.

submerged screw log. A type of electric log actuated by the flow of water past a propeller.

subordinate current station. 1. A current station from which a relatively short series of observations is reduced by comparison with simultaneous observations from a control current station. 2. A station listed in the Tidal Current Tables for which predictions are to be obtained by means of differences and ratios applied to the full predictions at a reference station.

subordinate tide station. 1. A tide station from which a relatively short series of observations is reduced by comparison with simultaneous observations from a tide station with a relatively long series of observations. 2. A station listed in the Tide Tables for which predictions are to be obtained by means of differences and ratios applied to the full predictions at a reference station.

sub-refraction, n. Less-than-normal refraction, particularly as related to the atmosphere. Greater than normal refraction is called SUPER-REFRACTION.

subsidence, n. Decrease in the elevation of land without removal of surface material due to tectonic, seismic, or artificial forces.

subsidiary light. A light placed on or near the support of a main light and having a special use in navigation.

subsolar point. The geographical position of the sun; the point on the earth at which the sun is in the zenith at a specified time.

substellar point. The geographical position of a star; that point on the earth at which the star is in the zenith at a specified time. Also called SUBASTRAL POINT.

substratosphere, n. A region of indefinite lower limit just below the stratosphere.

subsurface current. An underwater current that is not present at the surface.

subtropical anticyclones. High-pressure belts that prevail on the poleward sides of the trade winds characterized by calms, light breezes, and dryness.

Summary of Corrections. A cumulative summary of corrections to charts, *Sailing Directions,* and *United States Coast Pilots* previously published in *Notice to Mariners,* published by the Defense Mapping Agency Hydrographic/Topographic Center.

summer, n. In the Northern Hemisphere summer begins astronomically at the summer solstice and ends at the autumnal equinox. In the Southern Hemisphere the limits are the winter solstice and the vernal equinox. The meteorological limits vary with the locality and the year.

summer solstice. 1. The point on the ecliptic

occupied by the sun at maximum northerly declination. Sometimes called JUNE SOLSTICE, FIRST POINT OF CANCER. 2. That instant at which the sun reaches the point of maximum northerly declination, about June 21.

Sumner line. A line of position established by the Sumner method or, loosely, any celestial line of position.

Sumner method. The establishing of a line of position from the observation of the altitude of a celestial body by assuming two latitudes (or longitudes) and calculating the longitudes (or latitudes) through which the line of position passes. The line of position is the straight line connecting these two points (extended if necessary). This method, discovered by Thomas H. Sumner, an American sea captain, is seldom used by modern navigators, an adaptation of it, called ST. HILAIRE METHOD, being favored.

sun, n. The luminous celestial body at the center of the solar system, around which the planets, asteroids, and comets revolve. Our sun is an average star in terms of size and age. The sun visible in the sky is called apparent or true sun. A fictitious sun conceived to move eastward along the celestial equator at a rate that provides a uniform measure of time equal to the average apparent time is called mean sun or astronomical mean sun; a fictitious sun conceived to move eastward along the ecliptic at the average rate of the apparent sun is called dynamical mean sun. When the sun is observable at midnight, in high latitudes, it is called midnight sun.

sun cross. A rare halo phenomenon in which horizontal and vertical shafts of light intersect at the sun. It is probably due to the simultaneous occurrence of a sun pillar and a parhelic circle.

sun line, n. A line of position determined from a sextant observation of the sun.

sun pillar. A glittering shaft of light, white or reddish, extending above and below the sun, most frequently observed at sunrise or sunset. If a parhelic circle is observed at the same time, a SUN CROSS results.

sunrise, n. The crossing of the visible horizon by the upper limb of the rising sun.

sunset, n. The crossing of the visible horizon by the upper limb of the setting sun.

sunspot, n. A dark spot on the sun's surface. These spots are apparently magnetic in character and exert a disturbing influence on radio propagation on the earth.

super-buoy. A very large buoy, generally more than 5 meters in diameter, used for navigation, offshore mooring, or data acquisition.

superior conjunction. The conjunction of an inferior planet and the sun when the sun is between the earth and the other planet.

superior planets. The planets with orbits outside that of the Earth: Mars, Jupiter, Saturn Uranus, Neptune, and Pluto.

super-refraction, n. Greater than normal refraction, particularly as related to the atmosphere. Less than normal refraction is called SUB-REFRACTION.

supersaturation, n. Beyond the usual point of saturation. As an example, if saturated air is cooled, condensation takes place only if nuclei are present. If they are not present, the air continues to hold more water than required for saturation until the temperature is increased or until a nucleus is introduced.

surf, n. The region of breaking waves near a beach or over a detached reef.

surface chart. Short for SYNOPTIC SURFACE CHART.

surface current. A current that does not extend more than about 3 meters below the surface.

surface duct. A tropospheric radio duct in which the lower boundary is the surface of the earth. Also called GROUND-BASED DUCT.

surf zone. The area between the outermost limit of breakers and the limit of wave uprush.

surge, n. The bodily motion of a vessel in a seaway forward and backward along the longitudinal axis, caused by the force of the sea acting alternately on the bow and stern.

surveillance, n. The observation of an area or space for the purpose of determining the position and movements of craft or vehicles in that area or space. Surveillance can be either dependent, independent, or pseudo-independent.

surveillance radar. A primary radar installation at a land station used to display at that station the position of vessels within its range, usually for advisory purposes.

survey, n. 1. The operation of making measurements for determining the relative positions of points on, above, or beneath the earth's surface. 2. The results of operations as in definition 1. 3. An organization for making surveys.

surveying, n. The branch of applied mathematics that teaches the art of determining accurately the area of any part of the earth's surface, the lengths and directions of bounding lines, the contour of the surface, etc., and accurately delineating the whole on a map or chart for a specified datum.

swash, n. 1. A narrow channel or sound within a sand bank or between a sand bank and the shore. 2. A bar over which the sea washes. 3. The rush of water up onto the beach following the breaking of a wave.

sweeping, n. 1. The process of towing a line or object below the surface, to determine whether an area is free from isolated submerged dangers to vessels and to determine the position of any dangers that exist, or to determine the least depth of an area. 2. The process of clearing an area or channel of mines or other dangers to navigation.

swell, n. A relatively long wind wave, or series of waves, that has traveled out of the generating area. In contrast the term SEA is applied to the waves while still in the generating area. As these waves travel away from the area in which they are formed, the shorter ones die out. The surviving waves exhibit a more regular and longer period with flatter crests. When these waves reach shoal water, they become more prominent in height and of decreased wave length and are then known as ground swell.

swell direction. The direction from which swell is moving.

swinging buoy. A buoy placed at a favorable location to assist a vessel to adjust its compass or swing ship. The bow of the vessel is made fast to one buoy and the vessel is swung by means of lines to a tug or to additional buoys. Also called COMPASS ADJUSTMENT BUOY.

swinging ship. The process of placing a vessel on various headings and comparing magnetic compass readings with the corresponding magnetic directions, to determine deviation. This usually follows compass adjustment or compass compensation, and is done to obtain information for making a deviation table.

swinging the arc. The process of rotating a sextant about the line of sight to the horizon to determine the foot of the vertical circle through a body being observed. Also called ROCKING THE SEXTANT.

synchronization error. In radionavigation, the error due to imperfect timing of two operations.

synchronous, adj. Coincident in time, phase, rate, etc.

synchronous lights. Two or more lights the characteristics of which are in synchronism.

synodical month. The average period of revolution of the moon about the earth with respect to the sun, a period of 29 days, 12 hours, 44 minutes, 2.8 seconds. This is sometimes called the MONTH OF THE PHASES, since it extends from new moon to the next new moon. Also called LUNATION.

synodic period. The interval of time between any planetary configuration of a celestial body, with respect to the sun, and the next successive same configuration of that body, as from inferior conjunction to inferior conjunction. Also called SYNODICAL PERIOD.

synoptic chart. In meteorology, any chart or map on which data and analyses are presented that describe the state of the atmosphere over a large area at a given moment of time. A synoptic surface chart is an analyzed synoptic chart of surface weather observations.

system accuracy. The expected accuracy of a navigation system expressed in drms units, not including errors that may be introduced by the user, or geodetic or cartographic errors.

systematic error. One of the two categories of errors of observation, measurement, and calculation, the other category being random error. Systematic errors are characterized by an orderly trend, and are usually predictable once the cause is known. They are divided into three classes: (1) errors resulting from changing or nonstandard natural physical conditions, sometimes called theoretical errors, (2) personal (nonaccidental) errors, and (3) instrument errors. Also called REGULAR ERROR.

system electronic navigation chart. The electronic chart data base actually accessed aboard ship for the display of electronic charts. It is developed from the ENC provided by hydrographic authorities but is specific to the shipboard system. When corrected, it is the equivalent of a paper chart.

syzygy, n. 1. A point of the orbit of a planet or satellite at which it is in conjunction or opposition. The term is used chiefly in connection with the moon at its new and full phase. 2. A west wind on the seas between New Guinea and Australia preceding the summer northwest monsoon.

T

tablemount, n. A seamount having a comparatively smooth, flat top. Also called GUYOT.

tabulated altitude. In navigational sight reduction tables, the altitude taken directly from a table for the entering arguments. After interpolation for argument increments, i.e., the difference between each entering argument and the actual value, it is called COMPUTED ALTITUDE. Also called TABULAR ALTITUDE.

tabulated azimuth. Azimuth taken directly from a table, before interpolation. After interpolation, it becomes COMPUTED AZIMUTH.

tabulated azimuth angle. Azimuth angle taken directly from a table, before interpolation. After interpolation, it becomes COMPUTED AZIMUTH ANGLE.

taffrail log. A log consisting of a rotator towed through the water by a braided log line attached to a distance-registering device usually secured at the taffrail. Also called PATENT LOG.

target, n. In navigation, an object observed on a radar screen.

target angle. The relative bearing of one's own ship from a target vessel, measured clockwise through 360°.

target tail. The display of diminishing luminance seen to follow a target on a radar display that results from afterglow and the progress of the target between successive scans of the radar. Also called TARGET TRAIL.

telltale compass. A marine magnetic compass, usually of the inverted type, frequently installed in the master's cabin for his convenience.

temperate zone. Either of the two zones between the frigid and torrid zones, called the north temperate zone and the south temperate zone.

temperature, n. Intensity or degree of heat. Fahrenheit temperature is based upon a scale in which water freezes at 32°F and boils at about 212°F; Celsius temperature upon a scale in which water freezes at 0°C and boils at 100°C. Absolute temperature is measured from absolute zero, which is zero on the Kelvin scale, −273.16° on the Celsius scale, and −459.69° on the Fahrenheit scale. Absolute temperature based upon degrees Fahrenheit is called Rankine temperature and that based upon degrees Celsius is called Kelvin temperature.

temperature inversion. An atmospheric condition in which the usual lapse rate is inverted, i.e., the temperature increases with increasing altitude.

tend, v., i. To extend in a stated direction, as an anchor cable.

terminator, n. The line separating illuminated and dark portions of a non-self-luminous body, as the moon.

terrestrial equator. The earth's equator, 90° from its geographical poles.

terrestrial latitude. Latitude on the earth; angular distance from the equator, measured northward or southward through 90° and labeled N or S to indicate the direction of measurement.

terrestrial longitude. Longitude on the earth, the arc of a parallel, or the angle at the pole, between the prime meridian and the meridian of a point on the earth, measured eastward or westward from the prime meridian through 180°, and labeled E or W to indicate the direction of measurement.

terrestrial radiation. The total infrared radiation emitted from the earth's surface.

terrestrial refraction. Atmospheric refraction of a ray of radiant energy emanating from a point on or near the surface of the earth, as contrasted with ASTRONOMICAL REFRACTION of a ray passing through the earth's atmosphere from outer space.

territorial sea. The zone off the coast of a nation immediately seaward from a base line. Sovereignty is maintained over this coastal zone by the coastal nation, subject to the right of innocent passage to the ships of all nations. The United States recognizes this zone as extending 4.8 kilometers from the base line.

thermometer, n. An instrument for measuring temperature. A maximum thermometer automatically registers the highest temperature and a minimum thermometer the lowest temperature since the last thermometer setting.

three-arm protractor. An instrument consisting of a circle graduated in degrees, to which is attached one fixed arm and two arms pivoted at the center and provided with clamps so that they can be set at any angle to the fixed arm, within the limits of the instrument. It is used for finding a ship's position when the horizontal angles between three fixed and known points are measured.

thundersquall, n. Strictly, the combined occurrence of a thunderstorm and a squall, the squall usually being associated with the downrush phenomenon typical of a well-developed thunderstorm.

thunderstorm, n. A local storm invariably produced by a cumulonimbus cloud and always accompanied by lightning and thunder, usually with strong gusts of wind, heavy rain, and sometimes with hail. It is usually of short duration. Sometimes called ELECTRICAL STORM.

tick, n. A short, audible sound or beat, as that of a clock. A time signal in the form of one or more ticks is called a TIME TICK.

tidal, adj. Of or pertaining to tides.

tidal bore. A tidal wave that propagates up a relatively shallow and sloping estuary or river in a solitary wave. The leading edge presents an abrupt rise in level, frequently with continuous breaking and often immediately followed by several large undulations. An uncommon phenomenon, the tidal bore is usually associated with very large ranges in tide as well as wedge-shaped and rapidly shoaling entrances.

tidal current. A horizontal movement of the water caused by gravitational interactions between the sun, moon, and earth. The horizontal component of the particulate motion of a tidal wave. Part of the same general movement of the sea that is manifested in the vertical rise and fall, called tide. Also called TIDAL STREAM.

tidal current charts. 1. Charts on which tidal current data are depicted graphically. 2. Tidal Current Chart, as published by the National Ocean Survey, part of a set of charts that depict, by means of arrows and figures, the direction and velocity of the tidal current for each hour of the tidal cycle. The charts, which may be used for any year, present a comprehensive view of the tidal current movement in the respective waterways as a whole and also supply a means for readily determining for any time the direction and velocity of the current at various localities throughout the water area covered.

tidal current diagrams. Monthly diagrams that are used with tidal current charts to provide a convenient method to determine the current flow on a particular day.

tidal current tables. 1. Tables that give the predicted times of slack water and the predicted times and velocities of maximum current flood and ebb for each day of the year at a number of reference stations, together with time differences and velocity ratios for obtaining predictions at subordinate stations. 2. Tidal Current Tables, published annually by the National Ocean Survey.

tidal cycle. A complete set of tidal conditions as those occurring during a tidal day, lunar month, or Metonic cycle.

tidal difference. Difference in time or height of a high or low water at a subordinate station and at a reference station for which predictions are given in the Tide Tables. The difference, when applied according to sign to the prediction at the reference station, gives the corresponding time or height for the subordinate station.

tidal wave. 1. A wave caused by the gravitational interactions between the sun, moon, and earth. Essentially, high water is the crest of a tidal wave and low water is the trough. Tide is the vertical component of the particulate motion and tidal current is the horizontal component. The observed tide and tidal current can be considered the result of the combination of several tidal waves, each of which may vary from nearly pure progressive to nearly pure standing and with differing periods, heights, phase relationships, and directions. 2. Any unusually high and destructive water level along a shore. It usually refers to either a storm surge or tsunami.

tide, n. The periodic rise and fall of water resulting from gravitational interactions between the sun, moon, and earth. The vertical component of the particulate motion of a tidal wave. Although the accompanying horizontal movement of the water is part of the same phenomenon, it is preferable to designate this motion as TIDAL CURRENT.

tide-bound, adj. Unable to proceed because of insufficient depth of water due to tidal action.

tide curve. A graphic representation of the rise and fall of the tide in which time is usually represented by the abscissa and height by the ordinate of the graph. For a normal tide the graphic representation approximates a cosine curve.

tide gauge. An instrument for measuring the rise and fall of the tide.

tidehead, n. Inland limit of water affected by a tide.

tide indicator. The part of a tide gauge that indicates the height of tide at any time. The indicator may be in the immediate vicinity of the tidal water or at some distance from it.

tideland, n. Land under water at high tide and uncovered at low tide.

tidemark, n. 1. A high-water mark left by tidal water. 2. The highest point reached by a high tide. 3. A mark placed to indicate the highest point reached by a high tide, or, occasionally, any specified state of tide.

tide notes. Notes included on nautical charts that give information on the mean range or the diurnal range of the tide, mean tide level, and extreme low water at key places on the chart.

tide race. A very rapid tidal current through a comparatively narrow channel. Also called RACE.

tide rips. Small waves formed on the surface of water by the meeting of opposing tidal currents or by a tidal current crossing an irregular bottom. Vertical oscillation, rather than progressive waves, is characteristic of tide rips.

tide rode. The condition of a ship at anchor heading into the tidal current.

tide signals. Signals showing to navigators the state or change of the tide according to a prearranged code or by direct display on a scale.

tide station. The geographic location at which tidal observations are conducted. Also, the facilities used to make tidal observations. These may include a tide house, tide gauge, tide staff, and tidal bench marks.

tide tables. Tables that give the predicted times and heights of high and low water for every day in the year for a number of reference stations, and tidal differences and ratios by which additional predictions can be obtained for subordinate stations. From these values it is possible to interpolate by a simple procedure the height of the tide at any hour of the day.

tidewater, n. Water affected by tides or sometimes that part of it that covers the tideland. The term is sometimes used broadly to designate the seaboard.

time, n. 1. The interval between two events. 2. The date or other designated mark on a time scale.

time ball. A visual time signal in the form of a ball. Before the widespread use of radio time signals, time balls were dropped, usually at local noon, from conspicuously-located masts in various ports. The accuracy of the signal was usually controlled by a telegraphic time signal from an observatory.

time diagram. A diagram in which the celestial equator appears as a circle, and celestial meridians and hour circles as radial lines; used to facilitate solution of time problems and others involving arcs of the celestial equator or angles at the pole, by indicating relations between various quantities involved.

time scale. A system of assigning dates to events. There are three fundamental scales: Ephemeris Time, time based upon the rotation of the earth, and atomic time or time obtained by counting the cycles of a signal in resonance with certain kinds of atoms. Ephemeris Time (ET), the independent variable in the gravitational theories of the solar system, is the scale used by astronomers as the tabular argument of the precise, fundamental ephemerides of the sun, moon, and planets. Universal Time (UT1), time based on the rotation of the earth, is the scale used by astronomers as the tabular argument for most other ephemerides, e.g., the *Nautical Almanac*. Although ET and UT1 differ in concept, both are determined in arrears from astronomical observations and are extrapolated into the future based on International Atomic Time (TAI). Coordinated Universal Time (UTC) is the scale disseminated by most broadcast time services; it differs from TAI by an integral number of seconds.

time sight. Originally, an observation of the altitude of a celestial body, made for the purpose of determining longitude. Now, the expression is applied primarily to the common method of reducing such an observation.

time signal. An accurate signal marking a specified time or time interval. It is used primarily for determining errors of timepieces; usually sent from an observatory by radio. As defined by the International Telecommunications Union (ITU), a radiocommunication service for the transmission of time signals of stated high precision, intended for general reception.

time tick. A time signal consisting of one or more short audible sounds or beats.

time zone. An area in all parts of which the same time is kept. In general, each zone is 15° of longitude in width with the Greenwich meridian (0° longitude) designated as the central meridian of zone 0 and the remaining zones centered on a meridian whose longitude is exactly divisible by 15. The zone boundary may vary considerably to conform to political and geographic boundaries.

tonnage. A measure of the weight, size, or capacity of a vessel. Deadweight tonnage refers to the number of tons (2,240 pounds per ton) that a vessel will carry in salt water loaded to summer marks. It may also be considered the difference between loaded and light displacement tonnage. Displacement tonnage refers to the amount of water displaced by a vessel afloat, and is thus a measure of actual weight. Gross tonnage or gross register tonnage refers to the total measured cubic volume (100 cubic feet per ton of 2,240 pounds), based on varying formulas. Net tonnage or net registered tonnage refers to the gross tonnage minus spaces generally not used for cargo, according to varying formulas. Register tonnage is the tonnage listed on the ship's registration certificate, usually gross and/or net. Cargo tonnage refers to the weight of the cargo, independent of the vessel. Merchant ships are normally referred to by their gross or deadweight tonnage, warships by their displacement tonnage.

topmark, n. One or more objects of characteristic shape and color placed on top of a beacon or buoy to aid in its identification.

topographic map. A map that presents the vertical position of features in measurable form as well as their horizontal positions.

topography, n. 1. The configuration of the surface of the earth, including its relief and the position of features on it; the earth's natural and physical features collectively. 2. The science of delineation of natural and man-made features of a place or region especially in a way to show their positions and elevations.

tornado, n. A violently rotating column of air, pendant from a cumulonimbus cloud, and nearly always observable as a funnel cloud. On a local scale, it is the most destructive of all atmospheric phenomena. Its vortex, commonly several hundreds of yards in diameter, whirls usually cyclonically with wind speeds estimated at 100 to more than 200 miles per hour. Its general direction of travel is governed by the motion of its parent cloud. Tornadoes occur on all continents, but are most common in Australia and the United States where the average number is 140 to 150 per year.

torrid zone. The region of the earth between the Tropic of Cancer and the Tropic of Capricorn. Also called the TROPICS.

total eclipse. An eclipse in which the entire source of light is obscured.

tower, n. A tall, slender structure, which may be charted with a position circle.

towing light. A yellow light having the same characteristics as a STERN LIGHT.

trace, n. The luminous line resulting from the radial movement of the points of impingement of the electron stream on the face of the cathode-ray tube of a radar indicator.

track, n. 1. The intended or desired horizontal direction of travel with respect to the earth. The track as expressed in degrees of the compass may be different from the course due to such factors as making allowance for current or sea or steering to resume the TRACK (definition 2). 2. The path of intended travel with respect to the earth as drawn on the chart. Also called INTENDED TRACK, TRACK-LINE. 3. The actual path of a vessel over the ground, such as may be determined by tracking.

track, v., t. To follow the movements of an object such as by radar or an optical system.

track chart. A chart showing recommended, required, or established tracks, and usually indicating turning points, courses, and distances. A distinction is sometimes made between a TRACK CHART and a ROUTE CHART, the latter generally showing less specific information, and sometimes only the area for some distance each side of the great circle or rhumb line connecting two terminals.

tracking, n. In the operation of automated radar plotting aids, the process of observing the sequential changes in the position of a target to establish its motion.

track made good. The single resultant direction from a point of departure to a point of arrival at any given time. The use of this term to indicate a single resultant direction is preferred to the use of the misnomer course made good.

trade winds. Relatively permanent winds on each side of the equatorial doldrums, blowing from the northeast in the Northern Hemisphere and from the southeast in the Southern Hemisphere.

traffic control signals. Visual signals placed in a harbor or waterway to indicate to shipping the movements authorized or prohibited at the time at which they are shown. Also called DOCKING SIGNALS.

traffic lane. An area of defined limits in which one-way traffic is established.

traffic separation scheme. A routing measure designed for separating opposing streams of traffic in congested areas by the establishment of traffic lanes, precautionary areas, and other measures.

training wall. A wall, bank, or jetty, often submerged, built to direct or confine the flow of a river or tidal current.

transceiver, n. A combination transmitter and receiver in a single housing, with some components being used by both parts.

transducer, n. A device that converts one type of energy to another, such as the part of a depth sounder that changes electrical energy into acoustical energy.

transit, n. 1. The passage of a celestial body across a celestial meridian, usually called MERIDIAN TRANSIT. 2. The apparent passage of a celestial body across the face of another celestial body or across any point, area, or line. 3. An instrument used by an astronomer to determine the exact instant of meridian transit of a celestial body. 4. A reversing instrument used by a surveyor for accurately measuring horizontal and vertical angles; a theodolite that can be reversed in its supports without being lifted from them.

transit, v., t. To cross. In navigation the term is generally used with reference to the passage of a celestial body over a meridian, across the face of another celestial body, or across the reticle of an optical instrument.

transition mark. A navigation mark indicating the transition between the lateral and cardinal systems of marking.

transponder, n. A component of a secondary radar system capable of accepting the interrogating signal, received from a radar set or interrogator, and in response automatically transmitting a signal that enables the transponder to be identified by the interrogating station. Also called TRANSPONDER BEACON.

transverse bar. A bar that extends approximately normal to the shoreline.

transverse map projection. A map projection with its axis in the plane of the equator.

transverse Mercator map projection. A conformal cylindrical map projection, being in principle equivalent to the regular Mercator map projection turned (transversed) 90° in azimuth. In this projection, the central meridian is represented by a straight line, corresponding to the line that represents the equator on the regular Mercator projection. Neither the geographic meridians (except the central meridian) nor the geodetic parallels (except the equator) are represented by straight lines. Also called INVERSE MERCATOR MAP PROJECTION, TRANSVERSE CYLINDRICAL ORTHOMORPHIC MAP PROJECTION, INVERSE CYLINDRICAL ORTHOMORPHIC MAP PROJECTION.

transverse wave. A wave in which the vibration is perpendicular to the direction of propagation, as in light waves. This is in contrast with a LONGITUDINAL WAVE, in which the vibration is in the direction of propagation.

traverse sailing. A method of determining the equivalent course and distance made good by a craft following a track consisting of a series of rhumb lines. The solution is usually made by means of traverse tables.

traverse table. A table giving relative values of various parts of plane right triangles, for use in solving such triangles, particularly in connection with various sailings.

triad, n. Three radionavigation stations operated as a group for the determination of positions. Also called TRIPLET.

triangulation, n. A method of surveying in which the stations are points on the ground, located on the vertices of a chain or network of triangles. The angles of the triangles are measured instrumentally, and the sides are derived by computation from selected sides called BASE LINES, the lengths of which are obtained from direction measurements on the ground.

trim, n. The relation of the draft of a vessel at the bow and stern.

triple interpolation. Interpolation when there are three arguments or variables.

tropic, adj. Of or pertaining to a tropic or the tropics.

tropic, n. Either of the two parallels of declination (north or south), approximately 23°27' from the celestial equator, reached by the sun at its maximum declination, or the corresponding parallels on the earth. The northern of these is called the TROPIC OF CANCER and the southern, the TROPIC OF CAPRICORN. The region of the earth between these two parallels is called the TORRID ZONE, or often the TROPICS.

tropical air. Warm air of an air mass originating in subtropical anticyclones, further classified as tropical continental air and tropical maritime air, as it originates over land or sea, respectively.

tropical continental air. Air of an air mass originating over a land area in low latitudes, such as the Sahara desert. Tropical continental air is characterized by high surface temperature and low specific humidity.

tropical cyclone. The general term for cyclones originating in the tropics or subtropics. These cyclones are classified by form and intensity as follows: A tropical disturbance is a discrete system of apparently organized convection generally 100 to 300 miles in diameter, having a nonfrontal migratory character, having maintained its identity for 24 hours or more. It may or may not be associated with a detectable perturbation of the wind field. It has no strong winds and no closed isobars, i.e., isobars that completely enclose the low. In successive stages of intensification, tropical cyclones are classified as tropical disturbance, tropical depression, tropical storm, and hurricane or typhoon. The tropical depression has one or more closed isobars and some rotary circulation at the surface. The highest sustained (1-minute mean) surface wind speed is 33 knots. The tropical storm has closed isobars and a distinct rotary circulation. The highest sustained (1-minute mean) surface wind speed is 34 to 63 knots. The hurricane or typhoon has closed isobars, a strong and very pronounced rotary circulation, and a sustained (1-minute mean) surface wind speed of 64 knots or higher.

tropical maritime air. Air of an air mass originating over an ocean area in low latitudes. Tropical maritime air is characterized by high surface temperature and high specific humidity.

tropic currents. Tidal currents occurring semimonthly when the effect of the moon's maximum declination is greatest. At these times the tendency of the moon to produce a diurnal inequality in the current is at a maximum.

tropic higher high water. The higher high water of tropic tides.

tropic higher high water interval. The lunitidal interval pertaining to the higher high waters at the time of the tropic tides.

tropic higher low water. The higher low water of tropic tides.

tropic high water inequality. The average difference between the two high waters of the day at the times of the tropic tides. Applicable only when the tide is semidiurnal or mixed.

tropic lower high water. The lower high water of tropic tides.

tropic lower low water. The lower low water of tropic tides.

tropic lower low water interval. The lunitidal interval pertaining to the lower low waters at the time of tropic tides.

tropic low water inequality. The average difference between the two low waters of the day at the times of the tropic tides. Applicable only when the type of tide is semidiurnal or mixed.

Tropic of Cancer. The northern parallel of declination, approximately 23°27' from the celestial equator, reached by the sun at its maximum northerly declination, or the corresponding parallel on the earth. It is named for the sign of the zodiac in which the sun reached its maximum northerly declination at the time the parallel was so named.

Tropic of Capricorn. The southern parallel of declination, approximately 23°27' from the celestial equator, reached by the sun at its maximum southerly declination, or the corresponding parallel on the earth. It is named for the sign of the zodiac in which the sun reached its maximum southerly declination at the time the parallel was so named.

tropic tides. Tides occurring semimonthly when the effect of the moon's maximum declination is greatest. At these times there is a tendency for an increase in the diurnal range. The tidal datums pertaining to the tropic tides are designated as tropic higher high water, tropic lower high water, tropic higher low water, and tropic lower low water.

tropopause, n. The boundary between the troposphere and the stratosphere.

troposphere, n. The portion of the atmosphere from the earth's surface to the tropopause, i.e., the lowest 10 to 20 kilometers of the atmosphere. It is characterized by decreasing temperature with height, appreciable vertical wind motion, appreciable water vapor content, and variable weather.

tropospheric radio duct. A quasi-horizontal layer in the troposphere between the boundaries of which radio energy of sufficiently high frequency is substantially confined and propagated with abnormally low attenuation. The duct may be formed in the lower portion of the atmosphere when there is a marked temperature inversion or a sharp decrease in water vapor with increased height.

trough, n. 1. A long depression of the sea floor, characteristically flat-bottomed and steep-sided, and normally shallower than a trench. 2. In meteorology, an elongated area of relatively low pressure. The opposite of a trough is called RIDGE. The term trough is commonly used to distinguish the above elongated area from the closed circulation of a low (or cyclone). But a large-scale trough may include one or more lows. 3. The lowest part of a wave between two crests.

true, adj. 1. Related to true north. 2. Actual, as contrasted with fictitious, such as the true sun. 3. Related to a fixed point, either on the earth or in space, such as true wind, in contrast with RELATIVE, which is related to a moving point. 4. Corrected, as in the term true altitude.

true bearing. Bearing relative to true north; compass bearing corrected for compass error.

true course. Course relative to true north.

true direction. Horizontal direction expressed as angular distance from true north.

true heading. Heading relative to true north.

true meridian. A meridian through the geographical pole.

true motion display. A type of radarscope display in which one's own ship and other moving targets move on the plan position indicator in accordance with their true courses and speeds. All fixed targets appear as stationary echoes. However, uncompensated set and drift of one's own ship may result in some movement of the echoes of stationary targets. This display is similar to a navigational (geographical) plot.

true motion radar. A radar set that provides a true motion display as opposed to the relative motion display most commonly used. The true motion radar requires one's own ship's speed input, either log or manual, in addition to one's own ship's course input.

true north. The direction of the north geographical pole; the reference direction for measurement of true directions.

true sun. The actual sun as it appears in the sky. Usually called APPARENT SUN.

true track of target. The motion of a radar target on a true motion display. When the true motion display is ground-stabilized, i.e., allowance is made for the set and drift of current, the motion displayed is called GROUND TRACK. Without such stabilization the motion displayed is called WATER TRACK.

true wind. Wind relative to a fixed point on the earth. Wind relative to a moving point is called APPARENT or RELATIVE WIND.

tsunami, n. A long-period sea wave, potentially catastrophic, produced by a submarine earthquake or volcanic eruption. It may travel unnoticed across the ocean for thousands of miles from its point of origin, building up to great heights over shoal water. Also called SEISMIC SEA WAVE, TIDAL WAVE.

turning basin. A water area, usually dredged to well-defined limits, used for turning vessels.

turning buoy. A buoy marking a turn in a channel.

turning circle. The path described by the pivot point of the vessel as it makes a turn of 360° with constant rudder and speed.

twilight, n. The period of incomplete darkness following sunset (evening twilight) or preceding sunrise (morning twilight). Twilight is designated as civil, nautical, or astronomical, as the darker limit occurs when the center of the sun is 6°, 12°, or 18° below the celestial horizon, respectively.

twinkle, v., i. To flicker randomly or vary in intensity.

two-way route. A route within defined limits in which two-way traffic is established, aimed at providing safe passage of ships through waters where navigation is difficult or dangerous.

type of tide. A classification based on characteristic forms of a tide curve. Qualitatively, when the two high waters and two low waters of each tidal day are approximately equal in height, the tide is said to be semidiurnal; when there is a relatively large diurnal inequality in the high or low waters or both, it is said to be mixed; and when there is only one high water and one low water in each tidal day, it is said to be diurnal.

typhoon, n. See under TROPICAL CYCLONE.

U

ultra-quick light. A navigation light flashing at a rate of not less than 160 flashes per minute.

umbra, n. 1. The darkest part of a shadow in which light is completely cut off by an intervening object. A lighter part surrounding the umbra, in which light is only partly cut off, is called the PENUMBRA. 2. The darker central portion of a sun spot, surrounded by the lighter PENUMBRA.

uncorrecting, n. The process of converting true to magnetic, compass, or gyro direction, or magnetic to compass direction. The opposite is CORRECTING.

uncovered, adj. & adv. Above water. The opposite is SUBMERGED.

undercurrent, n. A current below the surface, particularly one flowing in a direction or at a speed differing from the surface current.

undertow, n. Receding water below the surface of breakers on a beach.

underway, under way, adv. Not moored or anchored.

undevelopable, adj. A surface not capable of being flattened without distortion. The opposite is DEVELOPABLE.

Uniform State Waterway Marking System. An aids to navigation system developed jointly by the U.S. Coast Guard and state boating administrators to assist the small-craft operator in inland state waters marked by states. It consists of two categories of aids to navigation. One is a system of aids to navigation, generally compatible with the Federal lateral system of buoyage, to supplement the Federal system in state waters. The other is a system of regulatory markers to warn the small-craft operator of dangers or to provide general information and directions.

United States Coast Pilot. One of a series of SAILING DIRECTIONS published by the National Ocean Service, that cover a wide variety of information important to navigators of U.S. coastal and intracoastal waters, and waters of the Great Lakes. Most of this information cannot be shown graphically on the standard nautical charts and is not readily available elsewhere. This information includes navigation regulations, outstanding landmarks, channel and anchorage peculiarities, dangers, weather, ice, currents, and port facilities. Each *Coast Pilot* is corrected through the dates of *Notices to Mariners* shown on the title page and should not be used without reference to the *Notices to Mariners* issued subsequent to those dates.

Universal Time. Conceptually, time as determined from the apparent diurnal motion of a fictitious mean sun that moves uniformly along the celestial equator at the average rate of the apparent sun.

Universal Transverse Mercator (UTM) grid. A military grid system based on the transverse Mercator map projection, applied to maps of the earth's surface extending to 84°N and 80°S.

unlighted buoy. A buoy not fitted with a light, whose shape and color are the defining features; may have a sound signal.

unmanned light. A light that is operated automatically and may be maintained in service automatically for extended periods of time, but with routine visits for maintenance purposes. Also called UNWATCHED LIGHT.

unstabilized display. A radarscope display in which the orientation of the relative motion presentation is set to the ship's heading and changes with it.

upper limb. The upper edge of a celestial body, in contrast with the LOWER LIMB, the lower edge.

uprush, n. The rush of the water onto the foreshore following the breaking of a wave.

upwelling, n. The process by which water rises from a lower to a higher depth, usually as a result of divergence and offshore currents. Upwelling is most prominent where persistent wind blows parallel to a coastline so that the resultant wind-driven current sets away from the coast.

U.S. Survey foot. The foot used by the National Ocean Service in which 1 inch is equal to 2.540005 centimeters. The foot equal to 0.3048 meter, exactly, adopted by Australia, Canada, New Zealand, South Africa, the United Kingdom, and the United States in 1959 was not adopted by the National Ocean Service because of the extensive revisions that would be necessary to their charts and measurement records.

U.S. Survey mile. A unit of distance equal to 5,280 feet. This mile is generally used on land and is sometimes called LAND MILE. It is commonly used to express navigational distances by navigators of river and lake vessels, particularly those navigating the Great Lakes.

V

Van Allen Radiation Belts. Popular term for regions of high energy charged particles trapped in the earth's magnetic field. Definition of size and shape of these belts depends on selection of an arbitrary standard of radiation intensity and the predominant particle component. Belts known to exist are: a proton region centered at about 2,000 miles altitude at the geomagnetic equator; an electron region centered at about 12,000 miles altitude at the geomagnetic equator; overlapping electron and proton regions centered at about 20,000 miles altitude at the geomagnetic equator. Trapped radiation regions from artificial sources also exist. These belts were first reported by Dr. James A. Van Allen of Iowa State University.

vane, n. 1. A device to sense or indicate the direction from which the wind blows. Also called WEATHER VANE, WIND VANE. 2. A sight on an instrument used for observing bearings, as on a pelorus, azimuth circle, etc. That vane nearest the observer's eye is called near vane and that on the opposite side is called far vane. Also called SIGHTING VANE. 3. In current measurements, a device to indicate the direction toward which the current flows.

vapor pressure. The pressure exerted by the vapor of a volatile liquid. Each component of a mixed-gas vapor has its own pressure, called partial pressure.

variable range marker. An adjustable range ring on the radar display.

variable star. A star that is not of constant magnitude.

variation, n. 1. The angle between the magnetic and geographic meridians at any place, expressed in degrees and minutes east or west to indicate the direction of magnetic north from true north. The angle between magnetic and grid meridians is called GRID MAGNETIC ANGLE, GRID VARIATION, or GRIVATION. Called MAGNETIC VARIATION when a distinction is needed to prevent possible ambiguity. Also called MAGNETIC DECLINATION. 2. Change or difference from a given value.

vector, n. Any quantity, such as a force, velocity, or acceleration, that has both magnitude and direction, as opposed to a SCALAR, which has magnitude only. Such a quantity may be represented geometrically by an arrow of length proportional to its magnitude, pointing in the given direction.

vector, adj. A type of computerized display consisting of layers of differentiated data, each with discreet features. Individual data files can be independently manipulated.

vector diagram. A diagram of more than one vector drawn to the same scale and reference direction and in correct position relative to each other. A vector diagram composed of vectors representing the actual courses and speeds of two craft and the relative motion vector of either one in relation to the other may be called a SPEED TRIANGLE.

veer, v., i. 1. For the wind to change direction in a clockwise direction in the Northern Hemisphere and a counterclockwise direction in the Southern Hemisphere. Change in the opposite direction is called BACK. 2. Of the wind, to shift aft. The opposite motion is to HAUL forward.

veer, v., t. To pay or let out, as to veer anchor chain.

Venus, n. The second planet from the sun in our solar system.

vernal, adj. Pertaining to spring. The corresponding adjectives for summer, fall, and winter are aestival, autumnal, and hibernal.

vernal equinox. 1. The point of intersection of the ecliptic and the celestial equator, occupied by the sun as it changes from south to north declination, on or about March 21. Also called MARCH EQUINOX, FIRST POINT OF ARIES. 2. That instant the sun reaches the point of zero declination when crossing the celestial equator from south to north.

vernier, n. A short, auxiliary scale situated alongside the graduated scale of an instrument, by which fractional parts of the smallest division of the primary scale can be measured with greater accuracy by a factor of ten. If 10 graduations on a vernier equal 9 graduations on the micrometer drum of a sextant, when the zero on the vernier lies one-tenth of a graduation beyond zero on the micrometer drum, the first graduation beyond zero on the vernier coincides with a graduation on the micrometer drum. Likewise, when the zero on the vernier lies five-tenths of a graduation beyond zero on the micrometer drum, the fifth graduation beyond zero on the vernier coincides with a graduation on the micrometer drum.

vernier sextant. A marine sextant providing a precise reading by means of a vernier used directly with the arc, and having either a clamp screw or an endless tangent screw for controlling the position of the index arm. The micrometer drum on a micrometer drum sextant may include a vernier to enable a more precise reading.

vertical circle. A great circle of the celestial sphere through the zenith and nadir. Vertical circles are perpendicular to the horizon. The prime vertical circle or prime vertical passes through the east and west points of the horizon. The principal vertical circle passes through the north and south points of the horizon and coincides with the celestial meridian.

vertical datum. A base elevation used as a reference from which to reckon heights or depths. It is called TIDAL DATUM when defined by a certain phase of the tide. Tidal datums are local datums and should not be extended into areas that have differing topographic features without substantiating measurements. In order that they may be recovered when needed, such datums are referenced to fixed points known as bench marks.

vertical geodetic datum. Any level surface taken as a surface of reference from which to reckon elevations. Also called VERTICAL DATUM, VERTICAL CONTROL DATUM.

vertical lights. Two or more lights disposed vertically or geometrically to form a triangle, square, or other figure. If the individual lights serve different purposes, those of lesser importance are called AUXILIARY LIGHTS.

very quick flashing light. A navigation light flashing 80–160 flashes per minute.

vessel, n. Any type of craft that can be used for transportation on water.

Vessel Traffic Services. A system of regulations, communications, and monitoring facilities established to provide active position monitoring, collision avoidance services, and navigational advice for vessels in confined and busy waterways. There are two main types of VTS, surveilled and non-surveilled. Surveilled systems consist of one or more land-based radar sites that output their signals to a central location where operators monitor and to a certain extent control traffic flows. Non-surveilled systems consist of one or more calling-in points at which ships are required to report their identity, course, speed, and other data to the monitoring authority.

viaduct, n. A type of bridge that carries a roadway or railway across a ravine; distinct from an aquaduct, which carries water over a ravine.

violent storm. Wind of force 11 (56 to 63 knots or 64 to 72 miles per hour) on the Beaufort wind scale.

virga, n. Wisps or streaks of water or ice particles falling out of a cloud but evaporating before reaching the earth's surface as precipitation. Virga are frequently seen trailing from altocumulus and altostratus clouds, but also are discernible below the bases of high-level cumuliform clouds from which precipitation is falling into a dry subcloud layer. It typically exhibits a hooked form in which the streaks descend nearly vertically just under the precipitation source but appear to be almost horizontal at their lower extremities. Such curvature of virga can be produced simply by effects of strong vertical windshear, but ordinarily it results from the fact that droplet or crystal evaporation decreases the particle terminal fall velocity near the ends of the streaks. Also called FALL STREAKS, PRECIPITATION TRAILS.

visibility, n. A measure of the ability of an observer to see objects at a distance through the atmosphere. A measure of this property is expressed in units of distance. This term should not be confused with VISUAL RANGE.

visible horizon. The line where earth and sky appear to meet, and the projection of this line upon the celestial sphere. If there were no terrestrial refraction, VISIBLE and GEOMETRICAL HORIZONS would coincide. Also called APPARENT HORIZON.

visual aid to navigation. An aid to navigation that transmits information through its visible characteristics. It may be lighted or unlighted.

visual bearing. A bearing obtained by visual observation.

visual range. The maximum distance at which a given object can be seen, limited by the atmospheric transmission. The distance is such that the contrast of the object with its background is reduced by the atmosphere to the contrast threshold value for the observer. This term should not be confused with VISIBILITY.

visual range of light. The predicted range at which a light can be observed. The predicted range is the lesser of either the luminous range or the geographic range. If the luminous range is less than the geographic range, the luminous range must be taken as the limiting range. The luminous range is the maximum distance at which a light can be seen under existing visibility conditions. This luminous range takes no account of the elevation of the light, the observer's height of eye, the curvature of the earth, or interference from background lighting. The luminous range is determined from the nominal range and the existing visibility conditions, using the Luminous Range Diagram. The nominal range is the maximum distance at which a light can be seen in clear weather as defined by the International Visibility Code (meteorological visibility of 10 nautical miles). The geographic range is the maximum distance at which the curvature of the earth and terrestrial refraction permit a light to be seen from a particular height of eye without regard to the luminous intensity of the light. The geographic range sometimes printed on charts or tabulated in light lists is the maximum distance at which the curvature of the earth and refraction permit a light to be seen from a height of eye of 15 feet above the water when the elevation of the light is taken above the height datum of the largest scale chart of the locality.)

voyage, n. A trip by sea.

W

waning moon. The moon between full and new when its visible part is decreasing.

warm air mass. An air mass that is warmer than surrounding air. The expression implies that the air mass is warmer than the surface over which it is moving.

warm front. Any non-occluded front, or portion thereof, that moves in such a way that warmer air replaces colder air. While some occluded fronts exhibit this characteristic, they are more properly called WARM OCCLUSIONS.

warm sector. An area at the earth's surface bounded by the warm and cold fronts of a cyclone.

warping buoy. A buoy located so that lines to it can be used for the movement of ships.

watch, n. A small timepiece of a size convenient to be carried on the person. A hack or comparing watch is used for timing observations of celestial bodies. A stop watch can be started, stopped, and reset at will, to indicate elapsed time. A chronometer watch is a small chronometer, especially one with an enlarged watch-type movement.

watch error. The amount by which watch time differs from the correct time. It is usually expressed to an accuracy of 1 second and labeled fast (F) or slow (S) as the watch time is later or earlier, respectively, than the correct time.

watch time. The hour of the day as indicated by a watch or clock. Watches and clocks are generally set approximately to zone time. Unless a watch or clock has a 24-hour dial, watch time is usually expressed on a 12-hour cycle and labeled AM or PM.

waterline, n. The line marking the junction of water and land.

water sky. Dark streaks on the underside of low clouds, indicating the presence of water features in the vicinity of sea ice.

waterspout, n. 1. A tornado occurring over water; most common over tropical and subtropical waters. 2. A whirlwind over water comparable in intensity to a dust devil over land.

water tower. A structure erected to store water at an elevation above the surrounding terrain; often charted with a position circle and label.

wave, n. 1. An undulation or ridge on the surface of a fluid. 2. A disturbance propagated in such a manner that it may progress from point to point.

wave basin. A basin close to the inner entrance of a harbor in which the waves from the outer entrance are absorbed, thus reducing the size of the waves entering the inner harbor.

wave crest. The highest part of a wave.

wave cyclone. A cyclone that forms and moves along a front. The circulation about the cyclone center tends to produce a wavelike deformation of the front. The wave cyclone is the most frequent form of extratropical cyclone (or low). Also called WAVE DEPRESSION.

wave direction. The direction from which waves are coming.

wave height. The distance from the trough to the crest of a wave, equal to double the amplitude and measured perpendicular to the direction of advance.

wavelength, n. The distance between corresponding points in consecutive cycles in a wave train, measured in the direction of propagation at any instant.

wave period. The time interval between passage of successive wave crests at a fixed point.

wave train. A series of waves moving in the same direction.

wave trap. Breakwaters situated close within the entrance used to reduce the size of waves from sea or swell that enter a harbor before they penetrate into the harbor.

wave trough. The lowest part of a wave form between successive wave crests.

waxing moon. The moon between new and full when its visible part is increasing.

waypoint, n. A reference point on the track.

weather, adj. Pertaining to the windward side, or the side in the direction from which the wind is blowing. LEE pertains to the leeward or sheltered side.

weather, n. The state of the atmosphere as defined by various meteorological elements, such as temperature, pressure, wind speed and direction, humidity, cloudiness, precipitation, etc. This is in contrast with CLIMATE, the prevalent or characteristic meteorological conditions of a place or region.

weather map. A map depicting various features of weather for a given area.

weather shore. As observed from a vessel, the shore lying in the direction from which the wind is blowing.

weather side. The side of a ship exposed to the wind or weather.

weather vane. A device to indicate the direction from which the wind blows. Also called WIND DIRECTION INDICATOR, WIND VANE.

wellhead, n. A submarine structure projecting some distance above the seabed and capping a temporarily abandoned or suspended oil or gas well.

west, n. The direction 90° to the left or 270° to the right of north.

westerlies, n., pl. Winds blowing from the west on the poleward sides of the subtropical high-pressure belts.

westing, n. The distance a craft makes good to the west. The opposite is EASTING.

westward motion. The motion in a westerly direction of the subtrack of a satellite, including the motion due to the earth's rotation and the nodical precession of the orbital plane.

wet-bulb temperature. The lowest temperature to which air can be cooled at any given time by evaporating water into it at constant pressure, when the heat required for evaporation is supplied by the cooling of the air. This temperature is indicated by a well-ventilated wet-bulb thermometer.

wet-bulb thermometer. A thermometer having the bulb covered with a cloth, usually muslin or cambric, saturated with water.

wharf, n. A structure of open pilings covered with a deck along a shore or a bank, providing berthing for ships and possibly cargo-handling facilities. A similar facility of solid construction is called QUAY.

whirlpool, n. Water in rapid rotary motion.

whirlwind, n. A general term for a small-scale, rotating column of air. More specific terms include DUST WHIRL, DUST DEVIL, WATERSPOUT, and TORNADO.

whistle, n. A sound signal emitter comprising a resonator having an orifice of suitable shape such that when a jet of air is passed through the orifice the turbulence produces a sound.

whistle buoy. A sound buoy equipped with a whistle operated by wave action. The whistle makes a loud moaning sound as the buoy rises and falls in the sea.

whitecap, n. A crest of a wave that becomes unstable in deep water, toppling over or "breaking." The instability is caused by the too-rapid addition of energy from a strong wind. A wave that becomes unstable in shallow water is called a BREAKER.

white squall. A sudden, strong gust of wind coming up without warning, noted by whitecaps or white, broken water; usually seen in whirlwind form in clear weather in the tropics.

white water. 1. Frothy water as in whitecaps or breakers. 2. Light-colored water over a shoal.

whole gale. A term once used by seamen for what is now called STORM on the Beaufort wind scale.

williwaw, n. A sudden blast of wind descending from a mountainous coast to the sea, especially in the vicinity of either the Strait of Magellan or the Aleutian Islands.

wind. Air in horizontal motion over the earth.

wind direction. The direction from which wind blows.

wind driven current. A current created by the action of the wind.

wind indicator. A device to indicate the direction or speed of the wind.

wind rode. A ship riding at anchor is said to be wind rode when it is heading into the wind.

wind rose. A diagram showing the relative frequency and sometimes the average speed of the winds blowing from different directions in a specified region.

winds aloft. Wind speeds and directions at various levels beyond the domain of surface weather observations.

wind-shift line. In meteorology, a line or narrow zone along which there is an abrupt change of wind direction.

wind sock. A tapered fabric sleeve mounted so as to catch and swing with the wind, thus indicating the wind direction. Also called WIND CONE.

wind speed. The rate of motion of air.

windward, adj. & adv. In the general direction from which the wind blows; in the wind; on the weather side. The opposite is LEEWARD.

windward tide. A tidal current setting to windward. One setting in the opposite direction is called a LEEWARD TIDE or LEE TIDE.

wind wave. A wave generated by friction between wind and a fluid surface. Ocean waves are produced principally in this way.

winter, n. The coldest season of the year. In the Northern Hemisphere, winter begins astronomically at the winter solstice and ends at the vernal equinox. In the Southern Hemisphere, the limits are the summer solstice and the autumnal equinox. The meteorological limits vary with the locality and the year.

winter buoy. An unlighted buoy maintained in certain areas during winter months when other aids to navigation are temporarily removed or extinguished.

winter light. A light in service during the winter months when the regular light is out of service. It has lower intensity than the regular light but usually has the same characteristic.

winter marker. An unlighted buoy or small lighted buoy established as a replacement during the winter months when other aids are out of service or withdrawn.

winter solstice. The point on the ecliptic occupied by the sun at maximum southerly declination. Sometimes called DECEMBER SOLSTICE, FIRST POINT OF CAPRICORNUS.

wire drag. An apparatus for surveying rock areas where the normal sounding methods are insufficient to insure the discovery of all existing obstructions above a given depth or for determining the least depth of an area. It consists of a buoyed wire towed at the desired depth by two vessels. Often shortened to DRAG.

withdrawn, adj. Removed from service during severe ice conditions or for the winter season. Compare with the term disestablished, which means permanently removed.

World Geodetic System. A consistent set of parameters describing the size and shape of the earth, the positions of a network of points with respect to the center of mass of the earth, transformations from major geodetic datums, and the potential of the earth (usually in terms of harmonic coefficients).

World Geographic Reference System. A worldwide position reference system that may be applied to any map or chart graduated in latitude and longitude (with Greenwich as prime meridian) regardless of projection. It is a method of expressing latitude and longitude in a form suitable for rapid reporting and plotting. Commonly referred to as GEOREF.

World Meteorological Organization. A specialized agency of the United Nations that seeks to facilitate world-wide cooperation in the establishment of stations for meteorological and related geophysical observations.

Worldwide Marine Weather Broadcasts. A joint publication of the National Weather Service and the Naval Weather Service Command providing information on marine weather broadcasts in all areas of the world. In general, English language broadcasts (or foreign language broadcasts repeated in English) are included in the publication. For areas where English language broadcasts are not available foreign language transmissions are also included.

World Wide Navigational Warning Service. Established through the joint efforts of the International Hydrographic Organization (IHO) and the Intergovernmental Maritime Consultative Organization (IMCO) now called the International Maritime Organization (IMO), the World Wide Navigational Warning Service (WWNWS) is a coordinated global service for the promulgation by radio of information on hazards to navigation that might endanger international shipping. Transmissions usually occur frequently enough during day to fall within at least one normal radio watch period, and the information is repeated with varying frequency as time passes until either the danger has passed or the information on it has appeared as a notice to mariners.

wreck, n. The ruined remains of a vessel that has been rendered useless, usually by violent action by the sea and weather, on a stranded or sunken vessel. In hydrography the term is limited to a wrecked vessel, either submerged or visible, attached to or foul of the bottom or cast up on the shore. In nautical cartography wrecks are designated visible, dangerous, or non-dangerous according to whether they are above tidal datum, less than, or more than 20 meters (66 feet; 11 fathoms) below tidal datum, respectively.

wreck buoy. A buoy marking the position of a wreck. It is usually placed on the seaward or channel side of the wreck and as near to the wreck as conditions will permit. To avoid confusion in some situations, two buoys may be used to mark the wreck.

wreck mark. A navigation mark that marks the position of a wreck.

X-Y-Z

yard, n. A unit of length equal to 3 feet, 36 inches, or 0.9144 meter.

yaw, n. The oscillation of a vessel in a seaway about a vertical axis approximately through the center of gravity.

year, n. A period of one revolution of a planet around the sun. The period of one revolution of the earth with respect to the vernal equinox, averaging 365 days, 5 hours, 48 minutes, 46 seconds in 1900, is called a tropical, astronomical, equinoctial, or solar year. The period with respect to the stars, averaging 365 days, 6 hours, 9 minutes, 9.5 seconds in 1900, is called a sidereal year. The period of revolution from perihelion to perihelion, averaging 365 days, 6 hours, 13 minutes, 53.0 seconds in 1900, is an anomalistic year. The period between successive returns of the sun to a sidereal hour angle of 80° is called a fictitious or Besselian year. A civil year is the calendar year of 365 days in common years, or 366 days in leap years. A light-year is a unit of length equal to the distance light travels in 1 year, about 5.88×10^{12} miles. The term year is occasionally applied to other intervals such as an eclipse year, the interval between two successive conjunctions of the sun with the same node of the moon's orbit, a period averaging 346 days, 14 hours, 52 minutes, 50.7 seconds in 1900, or a great or Platonic year, the period of one complete cycle of the equinoxes around the ecliptic, about 25,800 years.

zenith, n. The point on the celestial sphere vertically overhead. The point 180° from the zenith is called the NADIR.

zenith distance. Angular distance from the zenith; the arc of a vertical circle between the zenith and a point on the celestial sphere, measured from the zenith through 90°, for bodies above the horizon. This is the same as COALTITUDE with reference to the celestial horizon.

zephyr, n. A warm, gentle breeze, especially one from the west.

zodiac, n. The band of the sky extending 9° either side of the ecliptic. The sun, moon, and navigational planets are always within this band, with the occasional exception of Venus. The zodiac is divided into 12 equal parts, called signs, each part being named for the principal constellation originally within it.

zone description. The number, with its sign, that must be added to or subtracted from the zone time to obtain the Greenwich mean time. The zone description is usually a whole number of hours.

zone meridian. The meridian used for reckoning zone time. This is generally the nearest meridian whose longitude is exactly divisible by 15°. The DAYLIGHT SAVING MERIDIAN is usually 15° east of the zone meridian.

zone noon. Twelve o'clock zone time, or the instant the mean sun is over the upper branch of the zone meridian. Standard noon is 12 o'clock standard time.

zone time. The local mean time of a reference or zone meridian whose time is kept throughout a designated zone. The zone meridian is usually the nearest meridian whose longitude is exactly divisible by 15°. Standard time is a variation of zone time with irregular but well-defined zone limits.

Bibliography

Aids to Navigation~Technical. COMDTINST M16500.3A, U.S. Coast Guard, 1990.

Air Almanac. U.S. Naval Observatory. Washington, DC: U.S. Government Printing Office, various editions.

American Practical Navigator. Pub. 9, U.S. Defense Mapping Agency Hydrographic/Topographic Center, 1984, 1995.

An Album of Map Projections. U.S. Geological Survey Paper 1453. Washington, DC: U.S. Government Printing Office, 1989.

Beck, Horace. *Folklore and the Sea.* Wesleyan University Press (an imprint of University Press of New England, Hanover, NH), 1973.

Brogdon, Bill. *Boat Navigation for the Rest of Us.* Camden, ME: International Marine, 1995.

Casson, Lionel. *The Ancient Mariners.* Princeton, NJ: Princeton University Press, 1991.

Hern, Jeff. *Differential GPS Explained.* Trimble Navigation, 1989.

Hern, Jeff. *GPS.* Trimble Navigation, 1989.

Light List. U.S. Coast Guard. Washington, DC: U.S. Government Printing Office, various editions.

List of Lights. U.S. Defense Mapping Agency Hydrographic/Topographic Center, various editions.

Loran-C User Handbook. COMDTPUB P16562.6, U.S. Coast Guard, 1992.

Maneuvering Board Manual. Pub. 217, U.S. Defense Mapping Agency, 1984.

Marine Electronics Quick Reference. Davis Instruments, 1994.

May, Commander W. E. *A History of Marine Navigation.* G. T. Foulis & Co. Ltd. (an imprint of Haynes Publishing Group, Newbury Park, CA), 1973.

Nautical Almanac. U.S. Naval Observatory. Washington, DC: U.S. Government Printing Office, various editions.

Nautical Chart Symbols, Abbreviations, and Terms. Chart 1, prepared jointly by U.S. Defense Mapping Agency Hydrographic/Topographic Center and U.S. Department of Commerce, 1990.

Navigation Rules, International & Inland. COMDTINST M16672.2B, U.S. Coast Guard, 1990.

Observing Handbook 1. National Weather Service, National Oceanic and Atmospheric Administration, 1995.

Radar Navigation Manual. Pub. 1310, U.S. Defense Mapping Agency Hydrographic/Topographic Center, 1994.

Radio Navigational Aids. Pub. 117, U.S. Defense Mapping Agency Hydrographic/Topographic Center, 1995.

Sailing Directions (Enroute). U.S. Defense Mapping Agency Hydrographic/Topographic Center, various editions.

Sailing Directions (Planning Guide). U.S. Defense Mapping Agency Hydrographic/Topographic Center, various editions.

Sobel, Dava. *Longitude.* New York: Walker and Co., 1995.

Sellar, Joseph. *Kindergarten of Celestial Navigation.* Los Angeles, CA: Joseph Sellar, 1974.

United States Coast Pilot. U.S. Dept. of Commerce, National Oceanic and Atmospheric Administration, National Ocean Service, various editions.

Wilford, John Noble. *The Mapmakers.* New York: Alfred A. Knopf, 1981.

Wind Waves at Sea, Breakers and Surf. Pub. 602, U.S. Naval Oceanographic Office, 1981.

Wyatt, Stanley P. *Principles of Astronomy.* Boston: Allyn and Bacon, Inc., 1971.

Index

Page references in **bold type** indicate illustrations

A

Abroholos, 255
Absolute zero, 267
Additional Secondary Phase Factor (ASF), 111
Advection fog, 273, **274**
Aeronautical lights, 28–29
Aids to navigation, 24, **25**; cardinal system, 23, **23**; definition, 23; ICW Marking System, 39; lateral system, 24, **24**; private, 39; radar, 127–28; USWMS system, 39
Air Almanac, 21, 150, 176, 177
Air masses, 255
Air temperature, 267
Alaska current, 308
Almanacs, 21, 176–84; computerized, 177; types of, 176–77. *See also specific almanacs*
Alternating current, 91
Altitude: circle of equal, 185, **185**; computed *vs* observed, 187–88, **188**; equal, 176; meridian, 214–15
Altitude corrections: for moon sights, 204, **207**; for sun sights, 181, **201**; tables, **182**
Altitude intercept, 186, 187
Altitude intercept method, 186
Alto clouds, 270
Altocumulus clouds, 270
Altocumulus lenticularis clouds, 270, **271**
Altostratus clouds, 270
AM. *See* Amplitude modulation
American Practical Navigator, The, (Pub. 9), 34, 156
Amplitude modulation (AM), 96, **96**
Anabolic winds, 265
Analemma, 146
Anchor bearings, 86, **87**
Anchor watch, 88
Anchoring: navigation during, 87–88
Anemometer, 268
Aneroid, 267
Annular eclipses, 149
Anticyclone, 262
Antipode, 54
AP. *See* Assumed position
Aphelion, 143, **143**, 146
Apogee, 148
Apparent solar day, 169, **170**
Apparent solar time, 170
Arc-to-time conversion, 170–71; tables, 171, **172**, 181, 215, **217**
Areas To Be Avoided, 232–33, **233**
Aries, First Point of, 148
ARPA. *See* Automated Radar Plotting Aid
Artificial horizons, 166–67, **167**
ASF. *See* Additional Secondary Phase Factor
Assumed position (AP), 142, 187
Astrolabe, 157, **157**
Astronomical Almanac, 176
Astronomical unit (AU), 143
Astronomy, navigational, 141–56; units of measure, 142–43
Atlantic hurricanes, 293, 295–96
Atlantic Intracoastal Waterway (ICW), 234; Marking System, 39
Atmosphere, 249–50, **250**; electrical phenomena, 291; general circulation of, 250–51, **251**, 253; nonstandard conditions, 198; regional circulation of, 252–53; standard, 250; theoretical circulation of, 251, **251**; unusual effects of, 289–91
Atomic clocks, 101
Attenuation: radar, 124; radio, 94; wave, 320, **320**
AU. *See* Astronomical unit
Augmentation, 205, **205**
Aurora, 291
Aurora australis, 291
Aurora borealis, 291
Auroral zones, 291
Automated Radar Plotting Aid (ARPA), 124
Autopilots, 83–84, **84**
Autumnal equinox, 146
Azimuth, 46, 188
Azimuth angle, 142

B

Back-staff, 158, **158**
Backwash, 321
Baguio, 292
Bali wind, 255
Band of position, 85
Bar, 294
Barat, 256
Barber, 255
Baric wind law, 262
Barograph, 267, **268**
Barometer, 267
Basins, 304
Bathythermograph, 302
Bayamo, 255
Bayer's name, 150
Beacons, 27, **27**, 38–39; buoyant, 27; daybeacons, 27, 38–39; definitions, 23–39; EPIRBs, 237, 239–40, **240**, 241–42; radiobeacons, 98
Beam bearings, 82
Bearing cursor, 124
Bearings, 86–87; anchor, 86, **87**; bow and beam, 82; danger, 86, **87**; pairs whose cotangents differ by one, 82; preplotted, 86; radiobeacon, 98; relative, 124; turn, 86, **87**
Beaufort wind scale, 269, 310, 311, **312**
Bells, 35
Bentu de soli, 255
Bermuda High, 295
Binnacle, 41, 42
Bitmaps, 131
Board of Longitude (U.K.), 175
"Bobbing a light," 33
Bora, 255
Borasco, 256
Bow and beam bearings, 82
Brave west winds, 255

Brazil current, 308
Breakers, 318–21; plunging, 318, **319**; spilling, 318, **319**
Bridge lights, 29
Brisa, 255
Brisote, 256
Briza, 255
Brubu, 256
Bull's eye squall, 256
Buoyant beacons, 27
Buoys, 24, **25**, **26**, 34–35, 37–38; can, 36, **36**; colors, 35–37; cone-shaped (nun), 36, **36**, 37; definitions, 23–39; designation, 35; information/regulatory, 34; isolated danger, 34; large navigational (LNBs), 37; lateral, 34; maintenance of, **38**; parts of, **38**; safe water, 34; shapes, 36; sound signals, 35, **35**; special, 34; topmarks, 36, **36**; types of, 34
Buys Ballot's Law, 262, 297

C

Calculations: celestial navigation, 225–26; oceanographic, 226; piloting, 225
Calculators, navigational, 156, 177–78, **178**; accuracy of, 224
California current, 308–9
Calling-in points, 233; symbols, 233, **234**
Can buoys, 36, 37
"Can Dead Men Vote Twice?" rule, 49, **51**
Canary current, 308
Cape doctor, 256
Cardinal directions, 41
Cardinal marks, 23, **23**
Cathode Ray Tube (CRT), 132, 133
Caver, 256
Celestial bodies: motions of, **143**, 143–44. *See also specific bodies, planets, stars*
Celestial navigation, **7**, 139–226; almanacs, 176–84; assumed position (AP), 142; calculations, 225–26; concept of, 141–42; geographic position (GP), 141, 142; minimizing errors, 223–25; practical techniques, 213–26; secret of, 168; sextants, 157–68; ship *vs* small-craft, 213–14; sight reduction, 177–78, 185–212; sources of error in fixes, 223; special techniques, 214
Celestial Slide Rule, 225, **226**
Celsius scale, 267
Centering error, 165
Centigrade or Celsius scale, 267
Central processing unit (CPU), 134
Chart No. 1. See Nautical Chart Symbols and Abbreviations
Charts. *See* Nautical charts
Chronometers, **174**, 174–75
Chubasco, 256
Churada, 256
Cierzo. *See* Mistral
Circle of equal altitude, 185, **185**
Circles, great, 72, **73**, 149; great-circle charts, 73; great-circle sailing, 71, 72–74, **73**
Circles, paraselenic, 290
Circles, parhelic, 290
Circles, position, 38; accurate (symbol), 78–79; approximate (symbol), 79
Circles, traffic, 231
Circles, watch, 37
Cirrocumulus clouds, 270
Cirrostratus clouds, 270
Cirrus clouds, 270
Clouds, 269–70; alto, 270; cirrus, 270; classification of, 269; cumulus, 270; high-level, 269, 270; low-level, 269, 270–71, **272**; mid-level, 269, 270, **271**; nimbus, 270; roll, 263, **264**; stratus, 270; types of, 270
Coast Pilots, 17–18, **18**, 126, 233, 234
Coastal charts, 8
Coastal navigation, 8
"Cocked hats," 84, **85**
Cold fronts, 279
Collada, 256
Collimation error, 165
Collision avoidance, 121
COLREGS. *See International Regulations for the Prevention of Collisions at Sea*
Columbus, Christopher, 291
Commercial publications, 22
Compass(es), 40–52; adjusting, 47–49, **48**; combination, 42; components of, 41; correcting and uncorrecting, 49–52, **50**, **51**; development of, 40–41; digital, **42**, 42–43; direct-reading, 41, **41**; dry-card, 41; gyrocompasses, 43; hand-bearing, 52, **52**, 78, **78**; indirect-reading or flat-card, 41, **41**; magnetic, 40, **40**; modern, 41–43; quadrantal, 42, **42**; steering, 77
Compass adjuster, 46
Compass bearings, 77–79
Compass compensation, 46–47
Compass error: deviation, 45; dip, 46; variation, 43–45
"Compass Least, Error East; Compass Best, Error West" rule, 49–50
Compass rose, 15, **17**, 49, **50**
Composite sailing, 71
Compressibility, 303
Computed altitude, 187–88
Computer chips: Erasable Programmable Read-Only Memory (EPROM), 135; Read-Only Memory (ROM), 135
Computer data storage, 135, **135**
Computer software: electronic charts (ECs), 129–38; *Interactive Computer Ephemeric (ICE)*, 21, 177; OCEAN: Weather Routing Software (Lunamar Inc.), 275; sight reduction programs, 224, **224**
Computerized almanacs, 177
Computers: CRT units, 132–33; Globe-Hilsenrath Azimuth, 225; LCD units, 132–33, **133**
Conduct of Vessels in Sight of One Another, 230
Conductivity, 301
Cone-shaped (nun) buoys, 36, **36**, 37
Conical projections, 6
Continental shelf, 303, 304
Coordinates, 149–50
Copernicus, 3
Cordonazo, 256
Coriolis force, 252, 253, 304
Coromell, 256
Corona, 270, 290
"Correcting Add East" rule, 50, 51, **51**
COSPAS/SARSAT satellite system, 241, **241**
Countercurrents, 309; equatorial, 305
Course, 77, **77**
CPU. *See* Central processing unit
Cross-staff, 157–58, **158**; finding distance off with, 247, **247**
CRT. *See* Cathode Ray Tube
Cumulo-mammatus clouds, 271, **272**
Cumulonimbus capilatus clouds, 271, **272**
Cumulonimbus clouds, 271
Cumulus clouds, 270
Current(s): affecting North America, 308–9; countercurrents, 305, 309; drift, 68; equatorial, 305; longshore, 321; ocean, 304–8, **305**; ring, 309; rip, 321; set, 68; stream, 305; tidal, 53, 61–62; wave interactions, 312–13, **313**; west wind drift, 305–6; wind-driven, 304
Current arrows/vectors, 62, 71
Current diagrams, 62
Cyclones, 262; dangerous and navigable semicircles of, 297, **298**; extratropical, 262; tropical, 292, 294–98, 298–300
Cyclonic storms, 262
Cygnus star chart, **155**
Cylindrical projection, 6, **6**

D

D layer, 93, **93**
Danger bearings, 86, **87**
Datums, 9, 58; low water, **10**; National Tidal Datum Epoch, 60; tidal, 58–60
Davidson current, 308, 309
Daybeacons, 27, 38–39
Dayboards, 39
Dead reckoning (DR), 7, **7**, 63–74; course line, 64; estimated position, 68–70, **69**, **70**; fix expansion, 67–68, **68**; position/fix interval, 64–65; purposes of, 63; speed-time-distance problems, 65–66
Dead reckoning (DR) plot: labeling, 66–67, **67**; maintaining, 63–64, **65**; standard format for, 66–67; symbols to mark position, **64**
Decca system, 98
Declination: data for stars and planets, **179**; data for sun and moon, **180**; example findings, 181–82, 183; solar, 146
Defense Mapping Agency: pilot charts, 245–46, **246**
Density, seawater, 302–3
Depth-curve LOPs, 80, **80**
Depthsounders, 80, **80**; integrated displays, 135, **136**
Deviation, 43, 45
Deviation cards, **45**, 46–47
DGPS. *See* Differential Global Positioning System
Differential Global Positioning System (DGPS), 98, 106, **106**; receiver system, 106, **107**;

stations, 106
Diffraction: radar, 124; radio, 94; wave, 320, **320**
Digital compass, **42**, 42–43
Digital Selective Calling (DSC), 236–37
Digitized charts. *See* Electronic charts
Dip (height-of-eye) correction table, 181, **182**
Direct current, 91
Direct motion, 145
Directions: magnetic, 15; true, 15
Distance off: finding, 246–48, **247**; rule for quick approximation of, 83
Distance to lights: determining, 33–34
Distances Between Ports (Pub. 151), 21
Distress calls: "MAYDAY," 242, 243; "PAN," 242, 243; SSB-HF radios, 243–44; VHF procedures, 243
Doctor, 256
Doldrums, 253
Doppler shift, 99
Dot pitch, 123
Double-high water, 58
Double-low water, 58
Doubling the angle on the bow, 82
DR. *See* Dead reckoning
Drift, 68
DSC. *See* Digital Selective Calling
Duct: radio wave, 92
DX-90 (Data eXchange standard of 1990), 135
Dyne, 267

E

E layer, 93, **93**
Earth-moon barycenter, 54, **54**
Easterlies, prevailing, 252, **252**
Easterly wave, 292
Eastern elongation, 144
Eastern North Pacific: typhoon season, 293
Ebb tide, 56
EBL. *See* Electronic bearing line
ECDB. *See* Electronic Chart Database
ECDIS. *See* Electronic Chart Display and Information System
Eclipse year, 149
Eclipses, 148–49; of light, 30; lunar, 148, **148**; solar, 148, **148**
Ecliptic, 146–48
ECs. *See* Electronic charts
EGC system. *See* Enhanced Group Call system
EHF. *See* Extremely High Frequency radio
Ekman layer, 304
Ekman spiral, 305
Ekman transport, 304
El Niño, 309
El Niño-Southern Oscillation (ENSO), 309
Electrical energy, 91
Electrical phenomena, atmospheric, 291
Electromagnetic waves, 91
Electronic bearing line (EBL), 124
Electronic Chart Database (ECDB), 131
Electronic chart display, 131–32; CRT units, 132–33; event markers, 133; integrated, 135, **136**; LCD units, 132–33, **133**; man overboard buttons, 133; raster data, 131, **132**; screen types, 132–34, **133**; vector data, 131, 132
Electronic Chart Display and Information System (ECDIS), 131, 134
Electronic charts (ECs), 129–38; capabilities, 134; corrections to, **133**, 133–34, 135–37; data formats, 135; data storage media, 135, **135**; definition of, 130–31; function of, 130, **130**; navigating with, **137**, 137–38; safety of, 129, 138; system features, 134; system requirements, 134; terminology, 130–31; types of, 131
Electronic Nautical Charts (ENCs), 131
Electronics: in navigation, 89–138; in piloting, 83–84
Elephanta, 256
Elmo, Saint, 291
Emergency navigation, 244; finding distance off, 246–48, **247**; finding latitude, 246; finding speed, 248; what to do, 244–46
Emergency Navigation (Burch), 244
Emergency navigation kit, 244, 245, 247
Emergency Position-Indicating Radiobeacons (EPIRBs), 237, 239; Category I and II, 239–40, **240**; Class A, 239, **240**; Class B, 239, **240**; COSPAS/SARSAT satellite system, 241, **241**; INMARSAT satellite, 241–42; types and capabilities, 240
Emergency sextant, 245, **245**
Emergency signals, 243–44
ENCs. *See* Electronic Nautical Charts
Endless tangent screw, 158
Enhanced Group Call (EGC) system, 238
Enroute Sailing Directions (NIMA), 18, **18**
ENSO (El Niño-Southern Oscillation), 309
EP. *See* Estimated position
EPIRBs. *See* Emergency Position-Indicating Radiobeacons
EPROM chips. *See* Erasable Programmable Read-Only Memory chips
Equal altitude, 176
Equator, magnetic, 46
Equatorial countercurrents, 305
Equatorial currents, 305
Equinoxes: precession of, 147; vernal, 147
Equipment: emergency navigation kit, 244, 245, 247; navigational tools, 75, **76**; requirements for Sea Areas A1 and A2, 237–38; tools for piloting, 75, **76**
Erasable Programmable Read-Only Memory (EPROM) chips, 135
Erasmus, 291
Eratosthenes, 3
Estimated position (EP), 68–70, **69**, **70**
Etesian, 256
Event markers, 133
Extratropical cyclones, 262
Extremely High Frequency (EHF) radio, 96

F

F layers, 93, **93**
Facsimile machines, dedicated weather, 276, **277**
Facsimile weather broadcasts, 276, 277, **278**
Fahrenheit scale, 267
Falkland current, 308
Fall winds, 265, 267
Federal Radionavigation Plan (FRP), 97–98
Fetch, 310, **312**
First Point of Aries, 148
Fixes: accuracy, 85; expansion, 67–68, **68**; interval, choosing, 64–65; running, 80–83, **81**; taking and plotting, 77
Fixes, celestial: sources of error in, 223
Fixes, GPS, 100–102
Fixes, Loran-C, **111**, 112–13, **113**; accuracy, 113, **113**; ambiguity, 112, **113**; plotting, **115**, 115–16, **116**
Flare symbol, 38
Flashers, 30
Flinders bar, 42
Flood tide, 56
Floppy Almanac, 21
FM. *See* Frequency modulation
Foehn winds, 265–67
Fog, 271; advection, 273, **274**; radiation, 273
Fogbows, 290
Fractions, rule-of-thumb, 82
Fractostratus clouds, 270
Freak waves, 312
Frequency modulation (FM), 96, **96**
Frequency of radio waves, 92; radio frequency (RF) spectrum, **95**, 95–96
Frequency range of radio waves, 92
Freshet, 54
Fresnel, Augustin Jean, 29
Fresnel lens, 29, **29**
Frisius, Gemma, 5
Front range, 28
Frontal surface, 258–59
Frontal zone, 258
Frontogenesis, 259
Fronts, 258–62; cold, 279; occluded, 259, 279, **284**; stationary, 279; warm, 279; on weather maps, 279
Frost smoke, 273
FRP. *See Federal Radionavigation Plan*

G

Galaxies, 146
GDOP. *See* Geometric Dilution of Position
Gee, 108
Generalization, 8
Geographic position (GP), 141, 142, 176; definition of, 185, **185**
Geographic range, 32
Geographic Range Table, 34
Geometric Dilution of Position (GDOP), 103, **103**
Geometry, plane, 142
GHA. *See* Greenwich Hour Angle
Global Maritime Distress and Safety System (GMDSS), 236–38; equipment requirements, 237; Sea Areas, 237, **237**
Global Meteorological Technologies, Inc., 275
Global Positioning System (GPS), 98; develop-

ment of, 99–100; differential, 98, 106, **106**, **107**; errors, 103–4; fixes, 100–102; future of, 107; integrated Loran-C receivers, 105–6; Master Control Station, 100; monitoring stations, 100; in piloting, 83; Precise Positioning Service (PPS), 102; pseudorandom code, **102**, 102–3; receiver design, **104**, 104–6, **105**; receiver operation, 106–7; safety of, 129; satellites, 100, **100**, **101**; Standard Positioning Service (SPS), 102
Globe-Hilsenrath Azimuth computer, 225
GMDSS. *See* Global Maritime Distress and Safety System
GMT. *See* Greenwich Mean Time
Godfrey, Thomas, 158
Gongs, 35
GP. *See* Geographic position
GPS. *See* Global Positioning System
Gradient, 113
Graduation error, 164–65
Graticule, 10
Gravity waves, 310
Great circles, 72, **73**, 149
Great-circle charts, 73
Great-circle sailing, 72–74, **73**; definition, 71
Green flash, 290
Greenwich Hour Angle (GHA), 178, **179**, **180**, 186; findings, 181–82, 183; for stars and planets, **179**; for sun and moon, **180**
Greenwich Mean Time (GMT), 173
Gregale, 256
GRI. *See* Group repetition interval
Groundwaves, 93–94
Group repetition interval (GRI), 110–11
Gulf Stream, 308, 309

H

Hadley, John, 158
Halley, Edmond, 158
Halos, 290
Handheld receivers: GPS, **104**, 104–5; VHF transceivers, 97, **97**
Harbor charts, 8
Harbor/harbor approach, 7
Harmattan, 256
Harrison, John, 175
Haze, 271, 273
Heading, 77
Heat, specific, 303
Heat lightning, 291
Heaving, 317
Height-of-eye (dip) correction table, 181, **182**
Hertz, 92
HF radio. *See* High Frequency radio
High Frequency (HF) radio, 95; distress calls, 243–44
High tides, 59
High water: double-high water, 58; mean, 59; mean higher, 59
High water springs: mean, 59; mean higher, 59
Hogging, 317, **317**
HoMoTo mnemonic, 188
Horizon distance, 33
Horizon distance tables, 34
Horizon glass, 159, 160
Horizon mirror, **160**
Horizontal parallax correction, 205
Horns, 35, **35**
Horse latitudes, 254
HP correction factor, 205
Hull speed, maximum, 227
Humidity, 268
Hurricane Camille, **299**, 300
Hurricane Fran, **287**
Hurricane hunter aircraft, 292, **292**
Hurricanes, 262, 291–93; dangerous and navigable semi-circles of, 297, **298**; eye, 293, **293**; generation of, 292–93; minimizing damage, 298–300; passage of, 294, **294**; tracking, 294, **295**, **297**

I

IALA. *See* International Association of Lighthouse Authorities
ICE. *See Interactive Computer Ephemeris*
ICW. *See* Atlantic Intracoastal Waterway
IMO. *See* International Marine Organization
Increments and Corrections, 181
Index arm, 159, **160**
Index error, 161, **161**, 165
Index mirror, 159, 160, **160**
Inferior conjunction, 144
Inferior mirages, 289
Inland Navigation Rules, 229
Inland water navigation, 7
INMARSAT (International Maritime Satellite Corporation), 237, **239**; coverage, 237, **238**; Enhanced Group Call (EGC) system, 238; EPIRBs, 241–42
Inshore Traffic Zone, 231
Interactive Computer Ephemeris (ICE), 21, 177
Intercardinal directions, 41
Interference, 94
International Association of Lighthouse Authorities (IALA): Buoyage System, 35; Region A, 35; Region B, 35
International Code of Signals, 21
International Date Line, 149, 172
International Ice Patrol, 238
International Marine Organization (IMO), 231
International Maritime Organization, 131, 135
International Maritime Satellite Corporation. *See* INMARSAT
International Regulations for the Prevention of Collisions at Sea (COLREGS), 229; Demarcation Lines, 229, **229**
Internet, 277
Intracoastal Waterway (ICW), 234; Marking System, 39
Ionosphere, 93; time delay error, 103
Irminger current, 308, 309
Island shelf, 303
Isobars, 259, 279
Isogonic lines, 15, 43–44, **44**

J

Jamming, 94
Jet stream, 250
Jupiter, **144**, 144

K

Kalman filtering, 86, 106
Kamchatka current, 308
Katabatic winds, 265
Kaver, 256
Kelvin scale, 267
KIWITECH Marine Solutions Inc., 275
Knik wind, 256
Kochab star sight, example, 191; calculator values, 224; plotting, 197–98, **198**; reduction, 191–97, **192**, **193–196**
Kona storm, 256
Kramer, Gerhard, 5
Kuroshio current, 308

L

Labrador current, 308
Lamp changers, 29
LAN. *See* Local apparent noon
Land breeze, 265
Large navigational buoys (LNBs), 37
"Lash of St. Francis," 256
Lateral marks, 24, **24**
Latitude, 186; finding, **218**, 218–19, **219**, 246; horse latitudes, 254; by Polaris, 220–23, **221**; solution for, 219; traverse table, 247
Latitude/longitude grid, 9–10
LCD. *See* Liquid Crystal Display
Lenses, 29
Leste, 256
Levanter, 256
Levantera, 256
Levanto, 256
Leveche, 257
LF radio. *See* Low Frequency radio
LHA. *See* Local Hour Angle
Light dot, 38
Light Lists (U.S. Coast Guard), 18–19, **19**, 34
Light pipe, 28
Light sectors, 31, **31**, 32
Lightning, 291
Lights, 30–33, 37–38; aeronautical, 28–29; alternating, 31; articulated, 27; bobbing, 33; bridge, 29; characteristics of, **30**, 30–31; classes, 24–26; composite characteristics, 31; definitions, 23–39; finding distance to, 33–34; fixed, 30; fixed flashing, 31; flashing, 30; geographic range, 32; group flashing, 31; isophase, 30–31; meteorological range, 32; minor, 26, **27**; Morse, 31; nominal range, 32; occulting, 30; period, 30; power supply, 30; primary seacoast, 24–26, **26**; quick flashing, 31; range, 28, **28**, 32; secondary, 26, **27**; sector, **30**, 32; visibility of, 32–33
Lightships, 37
Light-years, 143

Luminous Range diagram, 33
Lines of position (LOPs), 77; accuracy, 85, **85**; "cocked hats," 84, **85**; depth-curve, 80, **80**; Loran-C, 109, **110**, **111**; perfect, 78, **78**; radar, 121–22, 128; radar for, **79**, 79–80; running fixes, 80–83, **81**
Liquid Crystal Display (LCD), 132–33, **133**
Lists of Lights (NIMA), 19, **20**
LMT. *See* Local Mean Time
LNBs. *See* Large navigational buoys
Local apparent noon (LAN), 170, 215; example determination of, 170, **170**; finding time of, 215–18, **216–217**; first estimate of, 215; longitude by, 220, **220**; second estimate of, 215–18
Local Hour Angle (LHA), 186; formula for, 181
Local Mean Time (LMT), 173
Local Notice to Mariners (U.S. Coast Guard), 10–11, **11**, 13, 38; from Coast Guard district offices, 13, **14**; via fax, 14
Local weather: predicting, 279–89
Local winds, 263–67
Logarithmic tables, 72
Logarithms, 72
Long Range Aid to Navigation. *See* Loran
Longitude, 186; by LAN, 220, **220**; time and, 171–73
Longshore currents, 321
Loom, 32
Looming, 289
LOPs. *See* lines of position
Loran (LOng Range Aid to Navigation), 108
Loran Linear Interpolator, 115, **116**
Loran-A, 108–9
Loran-B, 109
Loran-C, 98, 108–20; Additional Secondary Phase Factor (ASF), 111; baseline, 110; baseline extension, 110; blink mode, 114; centerline, 109; chains, 110, **111**, **117–120**; development of, 108–9; fixes, 112–13, **113**; future of, 116–17; how it works, **109**, 109–10, **110**; integrated GPS receivers, 105–6; master stations, 109, **112**; national system, 98; in piloting, 83; plotting fixes, **115**, 115–16, **116**; Primary Phase Factor (PF), 111; radio towers, 108, **108**; receiver displays, 114; receiver operation, 113–14; Secondary Phase Factor (SF), 111; secondary stations, 109, **112**; signal, 110–11; signal corrections, 111–12; stations, 110, **110**; Time Difference (TD) mode, 83; U.S. chains, **117–120**
Loran-C chart, 115, **115**
Low Frequency (LF) radio, 95
Low tides, 59
Low water: double-low water, 58; mean, 59; mean lower, 59
Low water springs: mean, 59; mean lower, 59
Low-altitude sights: corrections for, 198, **201**
Lows, rapidly intensifying, 265
Lubber's line, 41
Lunamar Inc., 275
Lunar eclipse, 148, **148**

M

Mackerel sky, 270, 289
Maestro, 257
Magnetic compasses, 40, **40**
Magnetic deviation, 43, 45
Magnetic directions, 15
Magnetic equator, 46
Magnetic poles, 46
Magnetic variation, 15, 43–45, **44**
Magnetron, 121
Man overboard buttons, 133
Maneuvering board, 269
Maneuvering Board Manual, 21
Marcq St. Hilaire or altitude intercept method, 186
Mare's tails, 270
Mariana Trench, 304
Marine radiobeacons, 98
Marine weather, 249–300; minimizing damage, 298–300
Maritime Safety Information (MSI), 238, **238**
Mars, **144**, 145; GHA and declination of, **211**; increments and corrections for sights, **210**, **212**
Matanuska wind, 257
Mathematical formulas, 225
"MAYDAY," 242, 243
Mean high water, 59
Mean high water springs, 59
Mean higher high water, 59
Mean higher high water springs, 59
Mean low water, 59
Mean low water springs, 59
Mean lower low water, 59
Mean lower low water springs, 59
Mean solar time, 170
Mean sun, 170
Mean time, 170; Local Mean Time (LMT), 173
Medium Frequency (MF) radio, 95
Mercator, Gerhardus, 5
Mercator projection, 5–6, **6**
Mercator sailing, 71
Mercury, 144, **144**
Mercury, 267
Meridian altitude(s), 214–15
Meridian altitude sights: finding longitude from, 220, **220**
Meridian angle, 142
Meridian passage of sun, 215, **216**
Mesopause, 250
Mesophere, 250
Meteorological bomb, 265
Meteorological range, 32
Meton, 3
Metonic Cycle, 3, 60
MF. *See* Medium Frequency radio
Microbursts, **264**
Micrometer drum, 158, 160; steps to reading, 163
Midlatitude sailing, 71
Military time, 173
Milky Way galaxy, 146
Millibar, 267
Minute fractions: converting, 10
Mirages, 289
Mistral, 257
Mock moon, 290
Mock sun, 290
Moon, 145–46; GHA and declination of, 183, 205, **208**; phases of, 145, **146**
Moon dog, 290
Moon pillar, 290
Moon sights, 161–62, **162**; altitude corrections for, 204, **207**; augmentation, 205, **205**; horizontal parallax correction for, 205, **206**, **207**; reduction, **204**, 204–5, **205**, **206**
Moonbows, 290
Moorings, 37
Morse lights, 31
MSI. *See* Maritime Safety Information
Multipath reflection error, 103

N

Nashi or n'aschi, 257
National Command Authority, 97
National Imagery and Mapping Agency (NIMA), 12, 15; chart catalogues, 15; digitized chart data, 135. *See also specific publications*
National Institute of Standards and Technology (NIST), 175
National Ocean Service (NOS), 15, 135; chart catalogues, 15; digitized chart data, 135; tide predictions, 60. *See also specific publications*
National Oceanographic and Atmospheric Administration (NOAA), 15, 241; hurricane hunter aircraft, 292, **292**; tide predictions, **61**
National Tidal Datum Epoch, 60
National Weather Service: Forecast Offices, **276**; VHF broadcasts, 276; weather maps, **278**; web site, 277
Nautical Almanac, 21, 150, 176, 177, **177**; accuracy of, 247; altitude corrections for moon sight, **207**; altitude corrections for sun sight, **201**; arc-to-time conversion tables, 171, **172**, 215, **217**; corrections for Mars sight, **210**; corrections for moon sight, **208**; corrections for non-standard conditions, **200**; daily page for moon sight, **206**; daily pages, 215, **216**; equation of time, **170**; format of, 178–81, **179**, **180**, **182**, **203**; GHA and declination of Mars, **211**; GHA and declination of moon, 183; GHA and declination of planets, 183; GHA and declination of stars, 183; GHA and declination of sun, 181–82, 215; increments and corrections for Mars, **212**; increments and corrections for sun, **202**; Polaris tables, 221, **222**; rising, setting, and twilight, 184; usage, 181, **193–196**
Nautical Chart Symbols and Abbreviations (Chart No. 1), 14, 15, **16**
Nautical charts, 9–10; area features, 14, **15**; border formats, 10, **11**; *Chart No. 1*, 14; coastal, 8; datums, 9, **10**; development of,

4–5; electronic, 129–38; features, 14–15; general, 8; great-circle, 73; harbor, 8; insets or plans, 8; latitude/longitude grid, 9–10, **11**; line features, 14, **15**; Loran-C, 115, **115**; modern, 8–9; pilot charts, 245–46, **246**, 274; point features, 14, **15**; projection, 9; sailing, 8; scale, 8; tick marks, 10; *Tidal Current Charts*, 62; tidal information notes, **10**; title block, 9, **9**; U.S., 15–17
Nautical publications, 17; commercial, 22. *See also specific publications*
Nautical slide rules, 65, **65**
Navigation: during anchoring, 87–88; basic concepts, 3–22; celestial, **7**, 139–226; coastal, 8; common errors, 86; electronic, 89–138; with electronic charts, **137**, 137–38; emergency, 244; founders, 3; fundamentals of, 1–88; harbor/harbor approach, 7; historical perspectives, 4; inland water, 7; Loran-C, 108–20; mathematical formulas in, 225; ocean, 8; phases of, 7–8; radar, **7**, 121–28; radio, **7**, 91–98; rules and regulations, 229–35; satellite, 7, **7**, 99–107; short-range aids to, 23; types and uses, 8; types of, 6–8, **7**; waypoint, 84, **84**. *See also* Aids to navigation
NAVigation INFOrmation NETwork (NAVINFONET), 13–14
Navigation Rules, 21, 229–30; content of, 230–31
Navigation safety, 236–48
Navigational astronomy, 141–56
Navigational calculators, 156, 177–78, **178**; accuracy of, 224
Navigational planets. *See* Planets
Navigational routine, 213
Navigational stars. *See* Stars
Navigational tools, 75, **76**
Navigational triangle, 142, **142**, 187
Navigator job parts, 130
NAVINFONET (NAVigation INFOrmation NETwork), 13–14
NAVTEX, 237, 238–39; receiver, 239, **239**
Neap tides, 56, **56**
New York State Canal System, 234, **235**
Newton, Sir Isaac, 158
NIMA. *See* National Imagery and Mapping Agency
Nimbostratus clouds, 270
Nimbus clouds, 270
NIST. *See* National Institute of Standards and Technology
No. 2102D Star Finder, 150, **150**
NOAA. *See* National Oceanographic and Atmospheric Administration
Nodes, 148; regression of, 149
Noise, 94; Signal to Noise Ratio (SNR), 113
Nominal range, 32
Nonstandard atmospheric conditions, 198; corrections for, 198, **200**
Nor'easter, 257, 261, **261**; predicting, 288
Norte, 257
North: magnetic, 43, **44**; true, 43, **44**
North America: principal currents affecting, 308–9
North Atlantic Atlas, 309
North Atlantic current, 308
North Equatorial current, 308–9
North Pacific current, 308
North pole: geographic, 43, **44**; magnetic, 43, **44**, 46
North Wall Effect, 265, **265**
Northeast trade winds, 252, **252**
Northeaster, 257
Northeasterlies, 254
Norther, 257, 312
Northern Hemisphere Atlantic Low, 259–61, **260**
Northern lights, 292
NOS. *See* National Ocean Service
Notice to Mariners (NIMA), 10–14, **13**, 38; from Coast Guard offices, 13, **14**; *Summary of Corrections*, 13; via fax, 14; via modem, 13–14
Nun buoys, 36, **36**
NWS. *See* National Weather Service

Oblique cylindrical projection, 6
Observed altitude, 187–88
Occluded fronts, 279, **284**
OCEAN: Weather Routing Software (Lunamar Inc.), 275
Ocean currents, 304–8, **305**; affecting North America, 308–9; unusual effects, 309–10
Ocean floor, **306–307**
Ocean navigation, 8
Ocean temperature, 301–2
Ocean waves, 310
Oceanographic calculations, 226
Oceanography, 301–21
Omega system, 98
Orion star chart, **153**
Oyashio current, 308

P

Pacific typhoons, 296
"PAN," 242, 243
Panama Canal, 235
Papagayo, 257
Parallactic angle, 142
Paraselene, 290
Paraselenic circle, 290
Parhelic circle, 290
Parhelion, 290
Path over the ground, **77**
Pegasus star chart, **152**
Pelorus (compass card), 46, **47**
Pelorus (navigator), 46
Perception, 4
Perigee, **143**, 148
Perihelion, 143, **143**, 146
Perpendicularity error, 165
PF. *See* Primary Phase Factor
PFJ. *See* Polar frontal jet
Phillips, Captain John D. S., 173
Picture elements or pixels, 123
Pillar buoys, 36, 37, **37**
Pilot Chart Atlases, 309
Pilot charts, 245–46, **246**, 274
Piloting, 7, **7**, 75–88; accuracy factors, 84–86; calculations, 225; "cocked hats," 84, **85**; common errors, 86; course, heading, and track, 77, **77**; electronics in, 83–84; practical considerations in, 88; preparing for, 75–77; radar use in, 128; routine, 87; taking and plotting fixes, 77; tools for, 75, **76**
Piloting team, 88
Pilots, 17–19
Pitch, 317
Pixels, 123
Plains, 304
Plan position indicator (PPI), 122
Plane geometry, 142
Plane of the ecliptic, 144
Plane sailing, 71, **71**
Planet diagrams, 150
Planet sights, **162**, 162–63, **163**; reduction, 209, **209**, **210–212**
Planets, **144**, 144–45, 209; chart, **151**; finding GHA and declination of, 183; inferior, 144, **144**; superior, **144**, 145, **145**
Planning Guide (NIMA), 18
Plotting fixes, 77
Plotting Loran-C fixes, **115**, 115–16, **116**
Plotting sheets, 197, **197**
Plotting sights, 197–98, **198**
Plotting vessels: Automated Radar Plotting Aid (ARPA), 124
Plunging breakers, 318, **319**
Polar front, 254
Polar frontal jet (PFJ), 250
Polaris, 150; latitude by, 220–23, **221**; sights, 221, **221**; tables, 178, 221, **222**
Pole Star, 150
Poles, magnetic, 43, **44**, 46
Position circle, 38
Position circle (accurate) symbol, 78–79
Position circle (approximate) symbol, 79
Position plotting sheets, 197, **197**; setting up, 198
Pounding, 317
PPI. *See* Plan position indicator
PPS. *See* Precise Positioning Service
Precise Positioning Service (PPS), 102
Pressure, seawater, 302
Prevailing westerlies,**252**, **253**, 254
Prevailing winds, **252**, 252–53, **253**
Primary Phase Factor (PF), 111
Prismatic error, 164
Private aids to navigation, 39
Projections, 5; chart, 9; conical, 6; cylindrical, 5–6, **6**; Mercator, 5–6, **6**; oblique cylindrical, 6
PRR. *See* Pulse repetition rate
Pseudorandom code, **102**, 102–3
Ptolemy, 3
Pub. 9. See American Practical Navigator, The
Pub. 117. See Radio Navigational Aids
Pub. 150. See World Port Index
Pub. 151. See Distances Between Ports

Pub. 214, 176
Pub. 229. *See Sight Reduction Tables for Marine Navigation*
Pub. 249. *See Sight Reduction Tables for Air Navigation*
Pub. 1310. *See Radar Navigation Manual*
Publications, 19–22; commercial, 22; nautical, 17. *See also specific publications*
Pulse repetition rate (PRR), 122, **122**
Pythagoras, 3

R

Racons, 127, **128**
Radar (RAdio Detection And Ranging), 121; controls, 123–24; how it works, 122, **123**; in piloting, 128; pulse repetition rate (PRR), 122, **122**; range control, 124; resolution in bearing, 125, **125**; resolution in range, 125, **125**; role of, 121–22; target reflecting quality and aspect, 126, **126**; technology, 121; weather, **293**
Radar beacons, 127
Radar display, 122–23; brightness or intensity control, 124; clutter control, 124; echoes, 126–27; false echo, 126–27, **127**; gain control, 124; heading flash, 124; image interpretation, 124–26, **125**; integrated, 135, **136**; interlaced, 123; non-interlaced, 123; picture elements or pixels, 123; plan position indicator (PPI), 122; raster, 123, **123**
Radar navigation, 7, **7**, 121–28; aids to navigation, 127–28; LOPs, **79**, 79–80
Radar Navigation Manual (Pub. 1310), 21, 128
Radar range, 79
Radar reflectors, 127, **127**
Radiation fog, 273
Radio(s): energy source, 91–92; Extremely High Frequency (EHF), 96; High Frequency (HF), 95, 243–44; Low Frequency (LF), 95; Medium Frequency (MF), 95; single-sideband (SSB), 243–44, **244**; Super High Frequency (SHF), 96. *See also* Very High Frequency radio
RAdio Detection And Ranging. *See* Radar
Radio frequency (RF) spectrum, **95**, 95–96
Radio navigation, 7, **7**; *Federal Radionavigation Plan (FRP)*, 97–98; national policy, 97–98
Radio Navigation Aids (Pub. 117), 21, 175
Radio receivers, 97
Radio transceivers, 97
Radio transmitters, 96–97
Radio waves, 91–98; adverse effects on, 94; amplitude, 92, **92**; amplitude modulation (AM), 96, **96**; behavior of, **92**, 92–93; cycles-per-second, 92; frequency, 92; frequency modulation (FM), 96, **96**; frequency range, 92; ionosphere and, 93, **93**; phase, 92; range of, 94–95; refraction of, 92, **93**, 93–94; signal types, 96; terminology, 92
Radiobeacon bearings, 98
Radiobeacons, 98; EPIRBs, 237, 239–40, **240**, 241–42; marine, 98; national system, 98
Rainbows, 290
Rainfall, 300
Rainshafts, **264**
Ramarks, 127–28, **128**
Range(s): bearing, 78; Geographic Range Table, 34; light, 28, **28**, 32; Luminous Range Diagram, 33; radar, 79, 124; radio receiver, 97; of radio waves, 94–95; tidal, 56, **56**, **60**
Range lights, 28, **28**
Range markers, 124
Rapidly intensifying low, 265
Raster image, 123
Read-Only Memory (ROM) chips, 135
Rear range, 28
Recommended Routes, 232, **232**
Recommended Tracks, 232, **233**
Red sky, 289
Refraction: accounting for, 247; one-hop, 93, **93**; radar, **124**, 125; radio wave, 92, **93**, 93–94; reverse, 289; sub-refraction, 125; two-hop, 93, **93**; wave, 320, **320**
Refraction table, 247
Regression of the nodes, 149
Regulated waterways and areas, 234–35, **235**
Regulations, 229–35. *See also specific regulations*
Retrograde motion, 145
RF spectrum. *See* Radio frequency spectrum
Ring currents, 309
Rip currents, 321
Rising, 184
Roaring forties, 254
Rogue waves, 311
Roll, 317
Roll clouds, 263, **264**
ROM chips. *See* Read-Only Memory chips
Royal Greenwich Observatory, 176
Royal Majesty, 129
Rule of twelfths, **56**
Rule-of-thumb fractions, 82
Rules and regulations: navigation, 229–35; regarding TSSs, 231; for VHF radio use, 242–43. *See also specific rules and regulations*
Running fixes, 80–83, **81**; example, 83

S

SA. *See* Selective Availability
Safe water buoys, 34
Safety, 84, 227–321; of electronic charts, 129, 138; emergency signals, 243–44; of GPS, 129; navigation, 236–48; VHF radio procedures, 242–43
SafetyNet, 238, **238**, **239**
Sagging, 317, **317**
Sailing(s), 70–72; composite, 71; definitions, 71; great-circle, 71, 72–74, **73**; Mercator, 71; midlatitude, 71; plane, 71, **71**; traverse, 71
Sailing charts, 8
Sailing directions, 17
Sailing Directions (NIMA), 18, **18**, 233; *Enroute Sailing Directions*, 18, **18**; *Planning Guide*, 18
St. Elmo's fire, 291
St. Hilaire, Adolph Laurent Anatole Marcq de Blond de, 186
St. Lawrence Seaway Development Corporation, 235
Salinity, 301
Sandbars, 320, **321**
Santa Ana, 267
SART. *See* Search and Rescue Transponder
Satellite navigation, 7, **7**, 99–107
Satellites: COSPAS/SARSAT system, 241, **241**; GPS, 100, **100**, **101**; INMARSAT, 237, 238, **238**, **239**, 241–42; weather, **278**
Saturn, 145
Scanning, 131
Sea (waves), 310
Sea Areas, 237, **237**, **238**; equipment requirements, 237–38
Sea breeze, 265
Sea floor, 303–4
Sea sense, 5
Sea smoke, 273
Sea waves, 310
Seamounts, 304, **316**
Search and Rescue Satellite. *See* COSPAS/SARSAT
Search and Rescue Transponder (SART), 237
Seawater: color, 303, **304**; density, 302–3; pressure, 302; properties of, 303; salinity, 301; temperature, 301–2; transparency of, 303
Secondary Phase Factor (SF), 111
Sector lights, **30**, 32
Seiches, 54, 316, 317
Selective Availability (SA), 102
Set, 68
Setting, 184
Seven-eighths rule, 82
Seven-tenths rule, 82
Seven-thirds rule, 82
Sextant(s), 157–68; adjustable errors, 165; altitude corrections, 181; components of, 159, **159**, **160**; definitions, 159–61; emergency, 245, **245**; history of, 157–58; human errors, 164; index error, 161, **161**; metal or metal-framed, 159, 166, **166**; nonadjustable errors, 164–65; plastic or plastic-framed, 159, 166, **166**; principle of, 158–59, **159**; reading, **163**, 163–64; selecting, 165–66; star and planet sights, **162**, 162–63, **163**; sun and moon sights, 161–62, **162**; taking sights, 161, 163; vernier, 161
SF. *See* Secondary Phase Factor
SHA. *See* Sidereal hour angle
Shade error, 164
Shade glasses, 161
Shamal, 257
Shapes, 230
Sharki, 257
SHF. *See* Super High Frequency radio
Side error, 165
Sidereal day, 169
Sidereal hour angle (SHA), 178, **179**
Sidereal month, 145

Sight reduction, 185–212, **188**; choosing method for, 177–78; computed *vs* observed altitudes, 187–88, **188**; computer programs, 224, **224**, **225**; definition of, 185; example for moon, **204**, 204–5, **205**, **206**, **207**, **208**; example for planets, 209, **209**, **210–212**; example for star, 191–97, **192**, **193–196**; example for sun, 198–203, **199**, **200–202**, **203**, **204**; Marcq St. Hilaire or altitude intercept method, 186; process of, 185–86; selecting assumed position (AP), 187; steps in, 186–87
Sight reduction form, 188–91, **189**; computerized, 224, **224**; example for moon, 204, **204**, **205**; example for planet, 209, **209**; example for star, 191, **192**; example for sun, 199, **199**, **204**
Sight Reduction Tables for Air Navigation (Pub. 249), 21, 176, 177
Sight Reduction Tables for Marine Navigation (Pub. 229), 21, **22**, 74, 176, 177, **177**, 187
Sights: low-altitude, 198; plotting, 197–98, **198**; star and planet, **162**, 162–63, **163**; sun and moon, 161–62, **162**; taking, 161, 163
Signal to Noise Ratio (SNR), 113
Signals: emergency, 243–44; *International Code of Signals*, 21; shapes, 230; sound, 35, **35**; time, 175
Simplex Teleprinter Over Radio (SITOR), 238
Single-sideband (SSB) radios, 243–44, **244**
Sinkers, 37, **37**
Sinking, 289
Sirens, 35
Sirocco, 257
SITOR. *See* Simplex Teleprinter Over Radio
Skywaves, 93–94
Slide rules: celestial, 225, **226**; nautical, 65, **65**
Smog, 271, 273
Smoke: frost, 273; sea, 273
SNR. *See* Signal to Noise Ratio
Software. *See* Computer software
Solar eclipse, 148, **148**
Solar time: apparent, 170; mean, 170
Sou'easter, 257
Sound: speed in seawater, 303
Sound signals, 35, **35**
South Equatorial current, 308
South Pacific: typhoons, 293
South pole, magnetic, 46
Southeast trade winds, 252, **252**
Southeaster, 257
Southeasterlies, 254
Southwester, 257
Sou'wester, 257
Space System for Search of Distressed Vessels. *See* COSPAS
Spar buoys, 36
Specific heat, 303
Speed: finding, 248; formula for, 248; maximum hull speed, 227; maximum wave speed, 227; of sound in seawater, 303
Speed-time-distance calculators, 65
Sphere buoys, 36
Spheres of position, 100, **102**
Spherical triangle, 142
Spilling breakers, 318, **319**
SPS. *See* Standard Positioning Service
Squall lines, 263, **264**
Squalls, 263; bull's eye, 256
Squamish, 258
SSB radios. *See* Single-sideband radios
Standard lapse, 269
Standard Positioning Service (SPS), 102
Standing waves, 312–13
Star charts, 150, **151**, **152–155**
Star finders, **150**, 150–56
Star sights, **162**, 162–63, **163**; computerized reduction programs, 224, **224**; plotting, 197–98, **198**; reduction, 191–97, **192**, **193–196**
Stars, 146, **151**; Bayer's name, 150; finding GHA and declination of, 183; identification of, 150–56
Stationary fronts, 279
STD sensor, 301, **302**
Steering and Sailing Rules, 230
Steering compass, 77
Stooping, 289
Storm surges, **299**, 300, **300**, 315
Storm tides, 315–16
Storms: cyclonic, 262; dangerous, 265; fronts, 258–62, 279, **284**; kona, 256; thunderstorms, 262–63, **263**; tropical, 293, 294, **294**, 300. *See also specific types*
Stratosphere, 250
Stratus clouds, 270
Stream currents, 305
Streams, 305
Sublunar point, 54
Sub-refraction, 125
Sub-tropical jet (STJ), 250
Suestado, 258
Sumatra, 258
Summer solstice, 146, **147**
Sun: finding GHA and declination of, 181–82, 215; finding time of LAN of, 215–18, **216–217**; mean, 170; meridian passage of, 215, **216**
Sun cross, 290
Sun dog, 290
Sun pillar, 290
Sun sights, 161–62, **162**; altitude corrections for, 181, **201**; computerized reduction programs, 224, **225**; corrections for low-altitude, 198, **201**; reduction, 198–203, **199**, **200–202**, **203**, **204**
Super High Frequency (SHF) radio, 96
Superior conjunction, 144
Superior mirages, 289
Super-refraction, 125
Surf, 318–21
Surface winds, prevailing, 253, **253**
Surges, storm, **299**, 300, **300**, 315
Surging breakers, 318
Swell, 310
Symbols: flare, 38; to mark position, **64**; *Nautical Chart Symbols and Abbreviations (Chart No. 1)*, 14, 15, **16**; position circle (accurate), 78–79; position circle (approximate), 79; weather map, 279, **280**
Synodic period, 145, **145**
System data message, 105
Syzygy, 56

T

Tangent screw, 159, **160**
TD. *See* Time delay
TD mode. *See* Time Difference mode
Technology: radar, 121. *See also specific technologies*
Tehuantepecer, 258
Telescope, sextant, 161
"TeleVision Makes Dull Children" rule, 51, **52**
Temperature: inversions, 289; ocean, 301–2
Terminology, 290; buoys, beacons, and lights, 23–39; electronic chart, 130–31; radio waves, 92; sailings, 71; sextant, 159–61; tidal, 53, 58; weather map abbreviations, 279
Thales, 3
Thermocline, 302
Thermohaline currents, 304
Thermosphere, 250
Three-finger rule, 248
Thunder, 291
Thunderstorms, 262–63, **263**
Tidal bores, 57–58, **58**, **59**
Tidal current(s), 53, 61–62
Tidal Current Charts, 62
Tidal Current Tables, 62
Tidal datums, 58–60
Tidal information notes, **10**
Tidal range, 56, **56**, **60**
Tidal waves, 313
Tide clocks, 61, **61**
Tide tables, 21
Tide Tables, 21, 60
Tides, 53–62; causes, 54–55, **55**; definition of, 53; diurnal, 57, **57**; features of, 55–57; general nature of, **53**, 53–54; mixed, 57, **58**; neap, 56, **56**; negative, 61; predicting, 60–61, **61**; rate of rise and fall, 57; reference or subordinate stations for, 61; semidiurnal, 57, **57**; stand of, 56; storm, 315–16; types of, 57–58
Time, 169–75; arc-to-time conversion, 170–71, **172**, 215, **217**; equation of, 170, **170**; Greenwich Mean Time (GMT), 173; International Date Line, 149, 172; keeping at sea, 173–75; kinds of, 169–70; of LAN of sun, 215–18, **216–217**; Local Mean Time (LMT), 173; and longitude, 171–73; mean, 170
Time balls, 174
Time delay (TD), 109
Time diagram, 197, **197**
Time Difference (TD) mode, 83
Time signals, 175
Time Zone Chart of the World, **174**
Time zones, 173, 184
Time-zone table, 178
Title 33, 230
Tools: navigational, 75, **76**; for piloting, 75, **76**.

See also Equipment
Tornadoes, 296
Towering, 289
Track (or trackline), 77
Track made good, 77, **77**
Trade winds, 253; northeast, 252, **252**; southeast, 252, **252**
Traffic circles, 231
Traffic lanes, 231
Traffic separation lines, 231, 232
Traffic Separation Schemes (TSSs), 231–32, **232**; rules to follow regarding, 231
Traffic separation zones, 231, 232
Tramontana, 258
Transceiver, 97
Transit, 99
Transit system, 98
Transmissometer, 271
Traverse sailing, 71
Traverse tables, 72
Tropic of Cancer, 147, **147**
Tropic of Capricorn, 147, **147**
Tropical cyclones, 292; avoiding, 294–98; dangerous and navigable semi-circles of, 297, **298**; extratropical, 262; minimizing damage, 298–300
Tropical depression, 292
Tropical disturbance, 292
Tropical storms, 293; passage, 294, **294**; rainfall records, 300
Tropopause, 250
Troposphere, 250
"True Virgins Make Dull Companions" rule, 51, **52**
TSSs. *See* Traffic Separation Schemes
Tsunamis, 313–15
Turn bearings, 86, **87**
Twilight, 184
Typhoons, 262, 291–93

U

UERE. *See* User Equivalent Range Error
UHF. *See* Ultra High Frequency radio
Ultra High Frequency (UHF) radio, 95–96
Undertows, 321
Uniform State Waterway Marking System (USWMS), 39
United States: chart catalogs, 17; chart numbers, 15, **17**; charts, 15–17; Loran-C chains, **117–120**; radionavigation policy, 97–98; *Title 33*, 230
United States Air Force, 292, **292**
United States Coast Guard: aids to navigation, 24, **25**; COLREGS Demarcation Lines, 229, **229**; *COMDTINST M16672.2B*, 229; district offices, 13, **14**; *Light Lists*, 18–19, **19**; *Local Notice to Mariners*, 10–11, **11**, 13; Navigation Information Service, 14; web site, 13
Updrafts, 255
Ursa Major, 150, **154**
U.S. Naval Observatory: *Interactive Computer Ephemeric (ICE)*, 21, 177; *Nautical Almanac*, 21, 150, 176, 177, **177**; time service, 175
User Equivalent Range Error (UERE), 104
USWMS. *See* Uniform State Waterway Marking System

V

Vandenberg Air Force Base (California), 100, **100**
Vardar, 258
Vardarac. *See* Vardar
Variable range marker (VRM), 124
Variation, magnetic, 15, 43–45, **44**
Vector Product Format (VPF), 135
Venus, **144**, 144–45
Vernal equinox, 147
Vernier scale, 160
Vernier sextant, 161
Very High Frequency (VHF) radio, 95, 242, **242**; channel assignments, 243; distress calls, 243; National Weather Service broadcasts, 276, **276**; portable, 242, **242**; procedures, 243; rules for use, 242–43; safety procedures, 242–43; transceivers, 97, **97**
Very Low Frequency (VLF) radio, 95
Vessel Traffic Services (VTSs), 233–34
VHF radio. *See* Very High Frequency radio
Viscosity, 303
Visibility, 271–73; restricted, 273
VLF. *See* Very Low Frequency radio
VPF. *See* Vector Product Format
VRM. *See* Variable range marker
VTSs. *See* Vessel Traffic Services

W

Warm fronts, 279
Warrimoo, 173
Watch circle, 37
Water color, 303, **304**
Waterspouts, **266**, 267
Wave clouds, 271, **273**
Wave energy, 313
Wave refraction, 320, **320**
Wave speed, maximum, 227
Wavelength, 310, **310**
Waves: anatomy of, **310**, 310–12; current interactions, 312–13, **313**; divergence of, 320, **320**, **321**; effects on boats, 316–18; freak, 312; group velocity, 310; height, 310, **310**, 311; movement in, 311, **312**; ocean, 310; period, length, and speed, 310, **310**, **311**; standing, 312–13; tidal, 313
Waypoints, 84, **84**
Weather, 249–300; data sources, 276–79; local predictions, 279–89; minimizing damage, 298–300; observations, 267–69; unusual atmospheric effects, 289–91
Weather facsimile machines, 276, **277**
Weather maps, **278**; abbreviations, 279; 500mb, 279, **281**; interpreting, 279; portfolio, **281–287**; prognoses, 279; surface analysis, 279; symbols, 279, **280**; types of, 279
Weather radar, **293**
Weather rhymes, 288–89
Weather routing, 274–75, **275**; important considerations, 274; sources for additional information, 275
Weather Service Forecast Offices (WSFOs), 276, **276**
Weather table, 288
West Greenland current, 308
West wind drift current, 305–6
Westerlies, prevailing, **252**, **253**, 254
Western elongation, 144
Western North Pacific: typhoons, 293
WGS-84. *See* World Geodetic System 84
Whirly, 258
Whistles, 35
White squall, 258
Whole horizon mirror, 160
Williwaw, 258
Willy-willy, 292
Wind-driven currents, 304
Winds: apparent, 268–69; baric wind law, 262; Beaufort scale, 269, 310, 311, **312**; components of, 268–69; duration, 311, **312**; fetch, 310, **312**; height, 311, **312**; local, 263–67; major local and regional, 255–58; major patterns, 253–54; prevailing, **252**, 252–53, **253**; variable, **252**; on weather maps, 279. *See also specific winds*
Wind/wave weather maps, 279, **284**
Winter solstice, 146, **147**
World Geodetic System 84 (WGS-84), 9
World Port Index (Pub. 150), 21
WP3D Orion aircraft, **292**
Wreck buoys, 38
Wright, Edward, 5
WSFOs. *See* Weather Service Forecast Offices

Y

Yaw, 317

Z

Zodiac, 148
Zone time (ZT), 173, 184; Time Zone Chart of the World, **174**
ZT. *See* Zone time
Zulu (Greenwich) time, 173